4/15

2

W9-ADK-032

A History of the World

AKIRA IRIYE AND JÜRGEN OSTERHAMMEL, GENERAL EDITORS

Global Interdependence

The World after 1945

Edited by

Akira Iriye

The Belknap Press of Harvard University Press

CAMBRIDGE, MASSACHUSETTS

LONDON, ENGLAND

2014

Copyright © 2014 by the President and Fellows of Harvard College
All rights reserved
Printed in the United States of America

This volume is a joint publication of Harvard University Press and C. H. Beck Verlag.

German language edition © 2013 by C. H. Beck Verlag.

Maps by Isabelle Lewis

Book design by Dean Bornstein

Library of Congress Cataloging-in-Publication Data

Global interdependence : the world after 1945 / edited by Akira Iriye.
        pages   cm. — (A history of the world)
    Includes bibliographical references and index.
    ISBN 978-0-674-04572-9 (alk. paper)
      1. Globalization. 2. Transnationalism. 3. International relations. 4. International
economic relations. 5. World politics—1945–1989. 6. World politics—1989–
I. Iriye, Akira.
    JZ1320.G55   2014
    303.48'2—dc23   2013013579

Contents

FOUR
Global Cultures
Petra Goedde

FIVE
The Making of a Transnational World
Akira Iriye

Introduction

Akira Iriye

"A MAN without bias cannot write interesting history—if, indeed, such a man exists."[1] So wrote Bertrand Russell, the British mathematician, philosopher, and peace activist, in his memoirs. He was undoubtedly right. As historians, the contributors to this volume would agree. They all have their points of view, or "biases" as the philosopher puts it. But as the reader will discover, there is a great deal that the contributors share in common. First of all, we are committed to contributing a fresh perspective on "contemporary history," which may be defined as the history of the most recent decades, covering the years since the end of the Second World War in 1945. Second, we also share the conviction that this history—or for that matter the history of any epoch—must be understood in the global context, not just in terms of separate national or regional histories.

Third, and even more important, is our contention that this global history has many layers, which do not usually overlap but which are nevertheless connected to one another. There is the history of the world as played out by individual countries, whether separately or collectively. In post-1945 history, this history has tended to be put in the overarching framework of the Cold War, but, as the following chapters demonstrate, there were many other national and international developments that need to be brought into the picture for a fuller understanding of contemporary history. Parallel to this layer, essentially defined geopolitically, other layers developed with their own momentums. One was economic, and another was cultural, in which national units were less important variables than goods, capital, ideas, and other products and pursuits in various parts of the world. All these layers sometimes overlapped and even became merged, but each had its own story, chronology, and agendas. An altogether different layer consisted of the natural habitat that humans shared with animals, plants, water, air, and all other physical existences.

None of these layers claimed a privileged status all the time. There might be periods in which specifically national issues or international relations determined how people lived, whereas in other times vicissitudes in transnational economic or cultural forces might define the character of their existence, while the natural environment might intrude upon all human timetables with its own, often (to humans) unpredictable, ways. History is a record of all such layers of action and interaction. One is reminded of the American artist Robert Motherwell (1915–1991), who once referred to his paintings as consisting of layers of consciousness. Historians, too, try to point to the existence of multiple themes at a given moment in time in the hope that the reader would become aware of the richness of the human experience—and of the human interaction with the physical universe—without presuming that one layer or one meaning would qualify as the determinant for the way people lived.

This does not mean, however, that diverse themes are presented in these chapters—within the overall framework of global history, to be sure—without focus. What emerges from the following presentation of post–World War II history is the unprecedented degree of interactions across borders, among people and their communities, ideas, and goods, to such an extent that, whether we are talking about political, economic, social, or cultural affairs, the destinies of nations, civilizations, individuals, and the natural habitat became closely linked. In *A World Connecting*, a previous volume of our History of the World, the contributors noted how, during 1870–1945, the world became more and more transnationalized even as nations retained their powerful presence. The same trends continued after 1945. A key difference between these two eras of global transformation may be understood if we note that in the earlier period, whereas technological innovations and economic transactions brought all corners of the Earth into close contact, at the same time the world had never been so rigidly divided in other ways—between colonizer and colonized, capital and labor, the West and the non-West, "civilized" and "uncivilized," not to mention the "great powers" and weaker states. Transnationalization, in other words, took two forms, one tending toward the unity of humankind and the other toward divisiveness. In contrast, we may note that the world since 1945 has transformed itself into a series of interlocking relationships in such a way as to bridge the gap, although never entirely, between human unity and human division. Whereas earlier the engine of global transformation had been primarily modern technology and ideology that had been developed in the West, this time literally millions of individuals and groups of people have partaken of the process, in doing so breaking down many walls of separation that had existed earlier. Countries and peoples in non-Western parts of the world have been actively making history, rather than fitting into a world shaped by the West. As a result, there has grown a greater consciousness of the unity of humankind, even as men and women have become aware of their diversity. Whether, in such circumstances, humans are capable of mastering their destiny, a destiny that they now share with the natural habitat, will emerge as a central question as they face the twenty-first century.

The chapters that follow deal with these and related issues from various angles. In Chapter 1, Wilfried Loth provides an overview of international politics after the Second World War, with a main focus on Europe, combined with a careful analysis of developments in other parts of the world. The transition from the anti-Axis alliance that won the war to the emergence of the US-USSR antagonism was, at one level, a traditional geopolitical story of great-power rivalries, but, as the author explains, the Cold War entailed many other dimensions, especially as the areas of the world that had traditionally remained outside the great-power drama gained their independence and became increasingly assertive. World politics, in other words, was more than ever global in scope.

The key question in any discussion of the Cold War, of course, is why it remained "cold" and did not turn into a third world war. The chapter provides a fresh perspective on that question by not assuming that the Washington-Moscow relationship was destined from the beginning to be mutually antagonistic, but instead taking the view that a series of mishaps, misunderstandings, and miscalculations somehow led to a view of world politics in which the bipolar contest became the key ingredient. Both sides, too, found it convenient to magnify the crisis for domestic reasons. Military mobilization, political unity, economic strategy—all could be promoted in the name of national security. Still, the bipolar situation proved more capable of avoiding global war than the great powers had during the first half of the twentieth century. On the other hand, there were violent clashes locally, in Korea, Vietnam, South Asia, the Middle East, and Africa, resulting in roughly the same number of total casualties as the victims of the Second World War. Loth elaborates each conflict and provides essential information on its origins and outcomes.

While the Cold War tended from time to time to divide the world, economic forces after 1945 were moving in the opposite direction. The development of global economic interconnectedness is traced by Thomas Zeiler in Chapter 2. Zeiler stresses the role of the United States in promoting an open, interconnected system of trade, investment, and related transactions, which eventually brought about full-scale economic globalization. As the author details the story, this policy was often, but not always, tied to the US Cold War strategy aimed at enhancing the relative economic strength of US allies against the Soviet-bloc nations, and sometimes the two objectives—economic and geopolitical—did not prove compatible. Even more pertinent, the liberalization of trade practices led to the enhancement of the economic strength of Germany, Japan, and other countries that emerged as the United States' major competitors. In the absence of the Cold War, economic globalization might have proceeded along a different path, although it would still have taken place.

An important question that is pursued throughout the chapter concerns the gains and losses of what Zeiler calls the "American open-door regime." It clearly succeeded in globalizing the world economy, and it undoubtedly contributed to the prosperity of Europe and Asia. Until the end of the twentieth century, however, most countries in the Middle East and Latin America had not similarly benefited, and Africa remained underdeveloped. The situation began to change in the twenty-first century, but by then the US economy itself was in deep trouble. Here, too, to read Chapters 1 and 2 together makes one aware of the interrelationships between the geopolitical and economic layers of the world. If, as observers worldwide were beginning to assert, the "American century" was ending, was it because the world created by the military and economic power of the United States had been transformed to such an extent that the nation was no longer as primary an engine of change as earlier? Or was it because nonstrategic and noneconomic developments were greatly increasing in relevance in determining the fate of humankind?

Chapters 3 and 4 make suggestive reading in this context. In the former, John McNeill and Peter Engelke go back to the origins of the human species to trace the relationship between the Earth and its inhabitants. As they show, until recently there was some equilibrium between the two, the natural environment providing more than adequate space and resources for a myriad of activities of a slowly increasing world population. The picture changed drastically after the Second World War, however, because of the doubling and then tripling of the global population, more and more of whom moved to urban centers to live in greater comfort than their forebears. Industrialization in the meantime made use of, and eventually polluted, air and water to such an extent that people began to become sick, sometimes even to die, from breathing polluted air and drinking poisoned water. In the meantime, energy resources proved inadequate to support all such human activities, the balance breaking down for the first time in history during the oil crises of the 1970s. The search for alternative sources of energy led to the construction of nuclear power plants in North America, Europe, Asia, and eventually in all parts of the globe. Inevitably, there were crises ("meltdowns") at these plants, starting in the 1970s and involving the United States, the Soviet Union, and Japan.

This is a story that is as much a part of contemporary history as the Cold War and economic globalization are. And yet the history of the environment and of environmentalism (the movement to do something to protect the natural habitat and to develop "clean energy") has tended to be treated in isolation. This volume is one of the first attempts at juxtaposing environmental history with the history of political, economic, and cultural affairs and at demonstrating that the natural habitat is as much humankind's "home" as are nations, families, and other manmade creations.

Of those creations, cultural products hold their own place in contemporary history. As Petra Goedde details in Chapter 4, post-1945 global history cannot be fully understood unless we recognize how people and their communities were affected by, and contributed to, cultural globalization. At the same time, cultural traditions and social habits did not all disappear. Diversity and homogenization went hand in hand. Consciousness of shared ideas, tastes, and ways of life developed together with the assertion of diversity. Within this broad framework, the chapter describes in detail various phenomena such as migrations, tourism, and consumerism that brought people of distant lands closer together, in the process enriching global cultures, if not producing a single global culture.

Readers of this chapter will particularly welcome its detailed discussion of women's lives, whose stories are usually put in the framework of national histories, or else of cross-national women's rights movements. Here Goedde describes global women—that is, women in all parts of the world as simultaneous existences, sharing so many ideas and interests across borders, although they differed among themselves, just as men did, about other aspects of life. At one level, this is a story of human rights. Like other rights, the advancement of women's rights was a globally shared objective, even if its implementation differed from region to region. But it is not a history with a known, happy ending, a teleological presentation of how things got better during the nearly seven decades after the Second World War. Human rights violations continue into the twenty-first century, and intolerance of diversity remains.

Nevertheless, there is little doubt that men, women, and children today are more aware of what goes on globally than their forebears were. The growth of the sense of interdependence, of humankind's shared destiny, is one of the remarkable aspects of contemporary history. This is a theme that is taken up in Chapter 5. On the basis of what is presented in the first four chapters, the concluding chapter considers how the consciousness of transnational linkages developed, in the middle of profound changes in the political, economic, environmental, and cultural affairs of the world. It is a story of an idea, an attitude, a mind trying to make sense of what goes on around individuals, in the process of which an awareness of interconnectedness grows. It may be noted, in this connection, that such awareness has not been limited to grown men and women but has embraced the younger generation as well. How youth, however one defines its age spread, contributes to the making of history is not a focus of sustained discussion in this volume, but it is an important subject of contemporary history, and Chapters 4 and 5 allude to ways in which young people worldwide have become part of, indeed have played significant roles in, the story of transnationalism.

To be sure, not all such transnational connections and ideas equate with peace or justice, and post-1945 history shows numerous instances of incomprehension toward unfamiliar people and objects, even of hostility against those who do not share one's faith. Nevertheless, the growth of the realization that men, women, children, the spaces they inhabit, and animals, birds, fish, and plants are all interdependent beings informs this entire volume—and the other volumes of the History of the World series.

·[ONE]·

States and the Changing Equations of Power

Wilfried Loth

Introduction

THE END of the Second World War brought with it the end of the prevailing European state system, which had held sway since the emergence of a modern global society and which was characterized by rivalry and balance between the major powers of Europe. The fault lines in this system had started to appear ever since the spread of industrialization, and in particular the advances in weapons technology, began increasingly to undermine the autonomy of the former great powers. At the same time, a contributory factor was the rapid advance of the United States to the forefront of the industrialized nations. Yet this system had essentially remained in place after the upheavals of the First World War, not least because the American public believed that it could once again afford to withdraw from involvement in European affairs, and because postrevolutionary Russia initially had great difficulty in asserting itself as a leading power broker on the international stage. Nazi Germany's attempt to regain sovereignty in the classic sense by extending its hegemony succeeded only in bringing about the swift collapse of the old European order: it precipitated the corrosive effect already unleashed by economic and technological progress and at the same time forced the non-European powers to enter into a substantial and long-term involvement in Europe. Ultimately, German hegemony in Europe also threatened the continent's security, a threat that was realized all too soon due to the revolutionary dynamism with which Adolf Hitler had imbued the new German regime. Yet German dominance could be overcome only through external intervention. Those European states that had fallen victim to German aggression were no longer in a position to restore the old system of equilibrium through their own efforts.[1]

European Losses

The rapid acceleration in the decline of the old Europe was first and foremost a result of the terrible losses resulting from a global conflict waged with twentieth-century military technology. It is estimated that the Second World War was responsible for the death of 52 million people, of which 27 million alone were Soviet citizens; the Soviet Union bore the brunt of the war in Europe—though the precise figures are uncertain, the sheer magnitude of the losses is beyond dispute.[2] After the USSR, the next greatest body count was in Eastern and Southeastern Europe, with 7.5 million dead, or some 9 percent of the total population, including 4 million from the Jewish community alone. Germany (within the 1937 borders of the *Reich*) lost 5.6 million people, or 8 percent of its populace. The remaining areas of Europe, which were less badly affected by the war, accounted for another 4 million dead. All told, the losses incurred were five to six times greater than those suffered in the First World War. In addition, some 50 million people in continental Europe were made either temporarily or permanently homeless: these included combatants, POWs, victims of the Nazi "segregation policies" in Eastern Europe, Lorraine, and the South Tyrol (2.8 million); evacuees (6.2 million in Germany alone), refugees, and people driven from their homelands in areas of German ethnic settlement east of the Oder-Neisse Line and in Czechoslovakia at the end of the war (of whom 12 million made it to the four administrative zones of occupied Germany, while 2.5 million died en route), and finally refugees and deportees from the Baltic states and Poland, who were resettled in regions formerly belonging to the German Empire (2 million). There are no statistics that can quantify the personal connections and social structures that were irreparably lost in this great upheaval.

With the exception of the neutral states and Great Britain, almost all the major European cities were destroyed in the war. Damage was especially heavy in Eastern Europe, where both German and Soviet troops adopted a "scorched earth" policy during their withdrawal; in Italy, Yugoslavia, and Greece; in the Netherlands, where retreating German forces blew up embankments and dykes; in northern France, which saw bitter fighting after the Allied landings of June 1944; and finally in Germany itself, whose cities and industrial facilities became the target of massed bombing raids. In economic terms, far greater damage was caused by the destruction of Europe's transport infrastructure. By war's end, only 35 percent of the French railway network and merchant navy was serviceable, the German railway had to all intents and purposes been bombed to destruction, and the Belgian and Dutch canal systems lay in ruins. The shortage of manpower, machines, and transport links also brought about a slump in agricultural production. By 1946–1947, the output of agricultural goods throughout the whole of Europe had reached only around 75 percent of the prewar figure. An estimated 100 million people were forced to subsist on daily rations of just 1,500 calories. Hunger, cold, and a lack of all of life's basic amenities characterized the everyday lives of Europe's citizens.

There are no reliable figures available on the state of total industrial output in Europe at the end of the war. In France in 1945, production amounted to around 35 percent of 1938 output (which itself was already some 20 percent below the 1929 figure, before the onset of the Great Depression). Neutral countries, and those less badly affected by the war, did somewhat better, whereas Germany, Austria, and Greece fared far worse. Even in late 1946, the industrial output of France and the Benelux countries stood at only 89 percent of prewar figures; Eastern, Southeastern, and Southern Europe managed just 60 percent; and Germany a paltry 40 percent. Between 1938 and 1946, the per capita share of GNP in Southern and Eastern Europe had fallen from US$120 to $90, whereas in France and the Benelux countries it had slumped from $290 to $260. By contrast, Great Britain, Switzerland, and the Scandinavian countries saw a modest rise from $420 to $580. The cost of the war and its aftermath had devastated public finances and unleashed inflationary tendencies. In Germany there was seven times more money in circulation than before the war, in France prices had risen fourfold, and in Greece and Hungary the currency collapsed. Belgium and Norway avoided the same fate only by devaluing their currencies. Not only the defeated nations, therefore, but also the victors had to pay dearly for the war.[3]

Moreover, the material and political losses suffered by European nations precipitated a liberation struggle by those peoples who had been colonized by European countries during the age of imperialism. In 1941, to stop India from throwing in its lot with the Axis powers, Great Britain had had to guarantee a postwar independence settlement. Britain duly withdrew from India in 1947 and Burma in 1948, while Ceylon (Sri Lanka) had already gained independence the year before. Plus, the Commonwealth countries of Canada, South Africa, Australia, and New Zealand, whose ties to the "motherland" had loosened considerably even during the First World War, now went entirely their own way. Likewise, while vying for influence over Syria and Lebanon with the Vichy regime in 1941, the "Free French" committee under General Charles de Gaulle found itself obliged to promise these mandated regions independence, as well as having to agree to "reforms" in its other colonies. By 1944, homegrown liberation movements in Morocco and Tunisia were demanding independent status, and bloody clashes broke out in Algeria in 1945, while following the defeat of the Japanese occupation force in Indochina that same year, the Viet Minh movement unilaterally declared that the country was no longer under French rule. In the same way, Indonesian nationalists exploited the Japanese surrender there to proclaim the country's independence from its former Dutch colonial masters.

France and the Netherlands certainly tried to regain their colonial possessions by remodeling their administrations along the lines of the British Commonwealth. Equally, in Great Britain itself there was resistance, at least against the more radical independence movements. Yet these attempts to restore the old imperial order resulted only in protracted armed struggles in the colonies, which the colonial powers had little chance of winning—not least because the two principal victors of the Second World War (the United States even more so than the USSR) had firmly nailed their colors to the mast of freedom for the former colonies of Asia and Africa. Far from fulfilling their expectations of using this overseas potential as a way of reviving their economies, the European powers' renewed colonial posturing succeeded only in further weakening Europe—economically, militarily, and morally.

Shifts in the Balance of Power

European losses appeared all the more dramatic when set against the backcloth of the corresponding impetus that this same conflict gave to the United States, occasioning its breathtaking rise as both an economic and a global military power. Between 1938 and 1945, US industrial production soared as a result of the demand from combatant nations and the slump in European output to less than a third of its former capacity. By the end of the war, the United States was responsible for more than half of all the world's industrial output. Over this same period, the per capita share of GNP increased from US$550 to $1,260, four times the European average. Correspondingly, the terms of trade worsened for European economies; moreover, the liquidation of European overseas investment to finance the war and the suspension of its provision of services (notably shipping) gave rise to a deficit in Europe's overall balance of trade that by 1947 had reached the staggering sum of $7.5 billion. That same year the United States recorded a trade surplus of $10 billion.

The United States' role as creditor and supplier of war materiel played a major part in furthering its ultimate aim of finding new markets for American goods and new spheres of American influence. At the founding of the International Monetary Fund (IMF) at the Bretton Woods Conference in the summer of 1944, future members had to sign on to the principle of free convertibility of their currencies. Simultaneously, the United States rose to become the world's foremost strategic military power, both at sea and in the air. Its military superiority was underpinned by its possession of the atomic bomb, first tested at Alamogordo in the US state of New Mexico on July 16, 1945, and first deployed on August 6 and 9, 1945, against the Japanese cities of Hiroshima and Nagasaki. At least initially, no other country could counter with anything comparable. All these developments saw the United States advance to a position of dominance that for the first time in history warranted the term *superpower*. This enabled it to exert more leverage than any other power in shaping the peacetime world.

In comparison, the European states' influence was further weakened by the substantial strategic gains that the Soviet Union also secured as one of the victorious powers. Certainly, from a Russian point of view, the war did not pan out nearly so positively as it did for the United States: the 27 million Soviet citizens who perished represented some 14 percent of the prewar population. Furthermore, the entire west of the country had been devastated: American estimates put the war damage at US$35.7 billion, but a Soviet audit published in 1947 put that figure at $128 billion. Farming, which in 1941 had just begun to recover from the effects of forced collectivization, was severely disrupted by the fighting on Russian soil and foraging by German forces. Industrial development was set back by years, and Soviet control over the country was seriously undermined by the German occupation and the liberation struggle. Thus, the Soviet Union at this stage was far from being a real superpower. Even so, Josef Stalin not only managed to regain most of the regions lost by the USSR during the struggle to establish the Bolshevik regime after the First World War, he also gained control over large tracts of Eastern and Southeastern Europe, areas that in the interwar period had been a breeding ground for anti-Soviet groupings. Finally, the Red Army's advance to the Elbe-Werra Line made it the most formidable military force in Europe. All this gave the Soviet Union a strong voice in the settlement regarding what was to happen to Germany postwar.

The two principal strategic results of the war for Germany were firstly the loss of the eastern zones of settlement, which had been conquered as far back as the late Middle Ages, and secondly the demise of the "small German" (*kleindeutsch*) nation-state established by Chancellor Otto von Bismarck between 1866 and 1871. There was a large measure of disagreement among the victorious powers as to exactly *how* to prevent renewed German aggression. But they were united in their determination that the world had to be afforded a more enduring safeguard against the German threat than that implemented after the First World War. Consequently, the basic thrust of all their plans was to hinder the rebirth of an independent German nation-state along traditional lines. The unconditional German surrender, which President Franklin D. Roosevelt had set as one of his main war aims, gave the victorious powers a free hand in attaining this primary objective. The signature of the instrument of surrender on May 8 and 9, 1945, formally transferred absolute sovereignty over all former German territory and the German people to the Allied powers. De facto this spelled the end of the German Empire of 1871, even though the tensions that later arose among the Four Powers prevented it from being formally codified in international law.

The simple fact that both the United States and the USSR had wrested a large measure of executive authority over the Central European region in their capacity as occupying powers in Germany and Austria confirmed that the demise of the German nation-state also signaled the end of the old Europe. Inasmuch as it impacted on their own security, they were loath to relinquish this authority. The two European Allies also took a formal part in the occupation of Germany and Austria, but palpably played second fiddle to the United States and the Soviets. Great Britain, which in 1940–1941 had conducted a lone and desperate fight against German expansion, was now forced to watch as its parlous economic state annulled its former preeminence in diplomatic experience and consigned it to dependence on America as the leading power. The only strategy left for British foreign policy was to try to use this position to gain the greatest possible freedom for maneuver, by, on the one hand, engaging the United

States as a permanent counterweight to the USSR in European affairs, and, on the other hand, forming the smaller European states—insofar as they had not fallen under the Soviet sphere of influence—into a bloc to offset any heavy-handed American attempts to assert its dominance. But there was never any question of this balancing act allowing Britain to regain its autonomy as a major power. Rather, of necessity, British foreign policy could only contribute to stabilizing the new balance of power in Europe.

France was even less well equipped to regain its status as an independent major power, once tactical errors by its General Staff and a widespread collapse of morale had led to its capitulation in June 1940. The establishment of the French Resistance and Free French forces under de Gaulle at least spared it the ignominy of military occupation by British and American forces, as Roosevelt had originally envisaged. More importantly, the new national consensus that coalesced around these liberation forces finally allowed the country to reenter the international political arena as a serious, active player after the bitter internecine feuding of the 1930s. However, they could do little to bring about the liberation of France itself, while in economic terms as well, after years of plunder by the German occupiers, the country was obliged to turn to the United States for help. Thus, France was confronted with much the same geostrategic problems that faced Britain; the only difference was its far greater dependence on America and its even more precarious claim on an independent role in world affairs. It was only after Britain argued for a strengthening of the European component in the new order that France was belatedly granted occupying-power status in Germany and Austria. French representatives were not involved in the agreements concerning postwar Europe that emerged from the conferences at Yalta in the Crimea and at Potsdam in February and May 1945, respectively. The resultant gulf between France's formal and actual power certainly gave later French leaders greater wiggle room, but it could also on occasion lead to a counterproductive unilateralism.

The smaller states of Europe were so profoundly affected by the general loss of European influence that they found themselves excluded from any discussions on the future of Germany. Even where the settlement of other European questions was concerned, they were more spectators than active participants. Those states that had fallen into the Red Army's sphere of influence had to cleave closely to Soviet foreign policy. Two of them, Poland and Czechoslovakia, were even forced to cede ethnically disputed regions to the USSR. Meanwhile, security and economic considerations persuaded the states of Western Europe and Italy to form an alliance with the Western powers. Their only room for maneuver within this new entity lay in their ability to use European integration to water down America's dominant role in this alliance, while at the same time countering French dominance within an integrated Europe through the inclusion of Great Britain. And even those states that, thanks to a favorable marginal location and/or clever foreign policy, managed to escape the incipient division of Europe into Eastern and Western blocs, still had to suffer further constraints on their autonomy. Their security now depended entirely on how the relationship between the two major victorious powers shaped up, yet they had no appreciable way of exerting any influence in this regard.

The upshot of all this was that Europe not only forfeited its traditional leading role in world affairs, but it also lost its ability to formulate independent policies. In place of the old European balance of power there now arose a polarization between the two principal victors of the Second World War. European states, clustered around the power vacuum that was postwar Germany, were inexorably drawn into the undertow of this polarization.

Remaining Room for Maneuver

The demise of the old Europe did not mean that the two former marginal powers, which from a European perspective now loomed large as world powers, simply carved Europe up between them. Just Europe's economic potential alone, which it had sustained despite widespread destruction, was too significant. Material losses were not so severe as a cursory glance at the ruins might at first have suggested. Thus, in the industrial Ruhr region of Germany, whose coalfields were producing only 25,000 tons at the end of the war as against 400,000 in the prewar period, only some 15 to 20 percent of machinery was beyond repair. Overall, the value of German industrial plant in 1946 was greater than it had been a decade before. Indeed, the destruction of factories often proved conducive to greater efficiency, because it allowed technological innovations to be adopted more readily than would have been possible under normal conditions. And despite the fact that the flood of refugees and displaced persons created problems of provision and integration, they also provided a ready-made reserve army of often highly qualified labor that enabled wages to be kept low and investment to flourish.

Furthermore, the two major powers had a vested interest in a rapid stabilization of the old continent—the United States because it was fearful of slipping into a massive crisis of overproduction in the absence of strong European trading partners and vibrant consumer markets at the end of the war, and the Soviet Union because it feared instability lest it drive weakened states into an even greater economic dependence on the United States. In the immediate aftermath of the war, the United States therefore tried to allay the economic difficulties being experienced by European states by extending credit and supplying aid (though initially the United States greatly underestimated how much help was needed). For its part, the Soviet Union (contrary to the expectations of Western observers, and counter to what many commentators still maintain) attempted to mobilize the people of Europe—inasmuch as they were influenced by domestic communist parties—to renounce consumerism and bend all their efforts toward rapid reconstruction. Once the transport infrastructure was restored and once problems of political organization had been overcome in some measure, production would quickly get back on its feet. And European national economies did indeed experience a fairly steady upturn in the late 1940s—before the aid provided by the Marshall Plan could take effect, and largely irrespective of what political ideology was in force in the individual countries concerned.[4]

The only countries that came under the direct sway of an occupying power were those within the sphere of the Red Army. Other countries were at least able to limit their economic dependence, especially by pooling their resources and presenting a united policy front. They could also exploit the fact that it would not be in the interests of the Soviet leadership to drive them into the arms of the American allies and thereby further strengthen the US presence on the old continent. Moreover, they were well placed to take advantage of the fact that the United States was dependent upon cooperative partners who could offset the American public's abhorrence of costly political intervention (and yet who, in their inexperience, still remained receptive to European overtures).

Besides, the strategic thinking of the new leading powers was not necessarily geared toward confrontation and the creation of blocs within Europe. For sure, the two main victors arrived with opposing ideological systems: American democracy with its hope that liberal-democratic values would take root in the liberated countries, and Stalin with his claim to be at the vanguard of a revolutionary movement that would one day achieve the historically inevitable conquest of the bourgeois-capitalist order. Their fundamentally different social systems entailed diametrically opposed foreign policy strategies—in the United States the expansion of the principle of free trade and a clarion call for the dissemination of liberal ideals, and in the USSR a screening-off of all market forces and liberal values. Neither the United States nor the Soviet Union had much experience in dealing with foreign powers, and in both an ideological mindset traditionally played a prominent role in settling international problems, making communication and compromise all the more difficult to achieve.

On the other hand, there were compelling reasons for maintaining the peaceful cooperation that had ensured victory for the anti-Hitler coalition, and hence for an amicable settlement of the peacetime order. Neither the US administration nor the Soviet leadership wanted a new war. The former dreaded the prospect because, aside from the cost in both human and economic terms, the American public had been persuaded only with extreme difficulty to enter the war that had just ended and now the prevailing clamor was for swift demobilization. The Soviets were equally keen to avoid conflict because their regime had escaped collapse only by a whisker and because it would take many years of strenuous reconstruction work even to restore prewar conditions. Also, the sheer cost and destructive potential of major wars, which grew exponentially with technological advances, made it advisable to avoid them—especially now that deployment of such a devastating weapon as the A-bomb became a very real possibility. But if war was out of the question as a way of shaping US-Soviet relations, it made absolute sense to reduce the potential for conflict. This in turn argued in favor of not allowing two mutually antagonistic blocs to arise in the first place.

For all the differences in their economic and political systems, the basic commercial interests of the two main powers were in large measure complementary: while the United States, following its industrial expansion to meet war demands, needed to find new markets in order to prevent an overproduction crisis, with its attendant high unemployment and recession, the USSR needed a large influx of manufactured goods to make good war damage and to meet its citizens' expectations of a higher standard of living through the import of more consumer products. Provided that the United States would first agree to loan the USSR sufficient capital, the Soviets could meet their import requirements from American production. The opening up of Soviet markets that this entailed responded to the Americans' desire for a global multilateral system of trade; meanwhile, to make good their balance-of-trade deficit with the United States, the Soviets could give American industry access to its huge untapped raw material resources. Little wonder, then, that it was the liberal business world that urged the US administration to maintain cooperation with its Soviet allies; in the Soviet Union, economic technocrats also gave signals in the same direction.

Above all, however, both the United States and the Soviet Union displayed a fair degree of flexibility in the choice of methods they employed, while the mutual threat they posed in pursuit of their divergent security interest never became really critical. Although the United States sought to give the new political and economic world order a liberal orientation, in the interests of its own economic expansion it was still perfectly able to do business with partners that did not meet its ideal political or commercial expectations. Nor did it have any particular strategic or economic interest in Eastern Europe, the primary focus of Soviet security policy. Before the Second World War, around 2 percent of American exports were to Eastern Europe, about 3.5 percent of its imports came from there, and 5.5 percent of its foreign subsidiaries were based there. Accordingly, President Roosevelt argued in favor of letting the Soviet Union impose its own sphere of influence on Eastern Europe and extending loans to help the country reconstruct its war-ravaged territories. The theory was that this would help overcome Stalin and the Moscow politburo's abiding mistrust of Western "imperialists" and so lay the foundations of lasting cooperation.

By contrast, Stalin and the entire ruling elite of the Soviet Union remained in thrall to Marxist-Leninist ideology. This maintained that the industrialized capitalist states were all condemned to destruction and that the final victory of socialism, which had achieved its first breakthrough in the Russian October Revolution of 1917, was inevitable. And so there was no question of any lasting cooperation with the imperialist powers and their leaders, only strictly temporary tactical alliances. Yet Stalin was enough of a realist to distinguish between "reactionary" and less reactionary, "aggressive" and less aggressive groups and representatives of capitalism. At the same time, he also had a keen understanding of the true levers of power: he knew (or had learned through bitter experience) that virtually no European country was ripe for revolution, and he was well aware that the United States had emerged from the war far stronger than the war-torn Soviet Union. He also registered the American breakthrough in developing the atomic bomb as a major defeat that threatened to annul the victory his forces had just secured over Nazi Germany.

As a result, to consolidate his gains and forestall a renewed threat to the Soviet state by aggressive imperialists, Stalin sought an accommodation with the Western powers. He identified the basis for such an arrangement in the pragmatism of the British leadership and in the progressive stance of the Roosevelt administration. On this basis, the wartime alliance could be transformed into a peacetime confederation. The Commission on Matters regarding the Peace Agreements and the Postwar Order that Stalin set up in September 1943, issued a memorandum in November 1944 that recommended a clear demarcation of spheres of influence in Europe. In it, Finland, Sweden, Poland, Hungary, Czechoslovakia, Romania, the Balkan states, and Turkey were included in the "maximum Soviet sphere of influence." The Netherlands, Belgium, France, Spain, Portugal, and Greece were counted as being "unquestionably within the British sphere." In demarcating these spheres of influence, it was taken as meaning "that Britain should forge no especially close relations with the countries within our zone," nor should it maintain any military bases there. Conversely, the same rules pertained for the Soviet Union within the British zone. In a third, neutral zone, which encompassed Norway, Denmark, Germany, Austria, and Italy, it was envisaged that "both sides should cooperate on an equal footing, with regular mutual consultations."[5]

This insistence upon a Soviet security zone did not mean that Stalin wanted to introduce the Soviet system there immediately. In an extensive memorandum sent by the Soviet deputy commissar of foreign affairs Ivan Maisky to key members of the Soviet leadership on January 11, 1944, an orientation to "the broad principles of democracy in the spirit of the popular front" was recommended for *all* liberated countries, from France to Germany and Poland. The victorious powers should cooperate closely in the "democratization of administrations in postwar Europe."[6] Accordingly, even Communist Party leaders in Eastern Europe were advised that the socialist revolution and adoption of the Soviet system was not yet on the agenda: "This is not so straightforward a task as some people

Prime Minister Winston Churchill, President Franklin D. Roosevelt, and Marshal Josef Stalin at the Yalta Conference, February 1945. The "Big Three" agreed on the main lines of a common post-war order. (Library of Congress)

imagine."[7] For Germany and Austria, this meant a joint reorganization by the victorious powers. German communists were instructed to crack down on any attempts to undermine the unity of the anti-Hitler coalition and to work for "realization of the bourgeois-democratic revolution" of 1848.[8]

Accordingly, the leaders in Washington and Moscow undertook initiatives to ensure continuing cooperation between the Allies after the end of the war. Thus, a decision was taken at the Yalta Conference to divide Germany and Austria into zones of occupation and to place the capital cities of Berlin and Vienna, which both lay well inside the Soviet Zone, under joint administration by the Four Powers. At Potsdam, the "Big Three" (Stalin; Roosevelt's successor, Harry S. Truman; and the British prime minister, Winston Churchill, and then his successor, Clement Attlee) agreed to administer the occupation zones under the overall command of an Allied control commission and to charge a joint commission of foreign ministers with the task of drafting a peace treaty. It was decided that a central German government should not be created immediately, but instead that "individual central administrative authorities" should be established to look after key areas, such as the economy, finance, and transport.

In parallel with this, with the establishment of the United Nations the Big Three created an organization that made the maintenance of peace contingent upon permanent agreement among the victorious powers, thereby underlining how vital their cooperation was. The UN Charter, which was signed on June 26, 1945, in San Francisco, drew a clear distinction between permanent members of the Security Council—which included France and the United Kingdom alongside the United States, the USSR, and China—and other member countries. Permanent Security Council members were accorded the right of veto over any Security Council resolutions. Meanwhile, the General Assembly of all member states had to make do with a merely advisory capacity on measures aimed at creating a "peaceful world order."

At the end of the war, then, the future of Germany, Europe, and the new world order remained unresolved in many respects. For instance, it had still not been decided whether the demise of the Third Reich should be followed by joint rule by the victorious powers, which would then gradually be transmuted into a controlled form of autonomy, or whether Germany should be divided into two states that would be integrated into opposing eastern and western blocs. Equally, it was still uncertain how rigid these power blocs should be and whether cooperation or confrontation would set the predominant tone in relations between them. Likewise, it was unclear how far the states within the Soviet sphere of influence would lose their autonomy and be forced to fall in line with the Stalinist model. And finally it remained open whether or to what extent the rest of Europe would become either a stabilizing factor between the United States and the USSR or the object and victim of their confrontation. Decisions in all these four areas were closely bound up with one another. In this matter, the United States' strategic and economic dominance saddled it with a particularly heavy responsibility; yet much also depended on Stalin's attitude—and, albeit to a much lesser degree, on how the Western European nations themselves behaved.

1. *Postwar Upheavals*

THE FACT that the opportunities for an amicable settlement of the postwar order were largely missed, and that instead Europe found itself divided by the incipient Cold War, was initially a result of some very specific failures. For a start, the communist leadership had no idea how to behave in order to make their offers of cooperation appear remotely plausible, while Western societies found it hard to adopt the kind of farsightedness necessary for meaningful cooperation. This resulted in a second phase characterized by mutually skewed perceptions, with both sides increasingly regarding the other as aggressive, despite this not being the case. The more this misperception spread, the more there obtruded the question of security, which arises in every situation of competition between opposing powers (this was phase three of the relationship). Both sides, then, took precautions against the attack they feared the other might instigate. In turn, these precautions were construed by each as proof of the other's aggressive intentions, thereby provoking further measures—a double vicious circle with no easy chance of escape.

The Sovietization of Eastern Europe

The process of dividing Europe began with the realization by the Soviet authorities in Moscow that it would be by no means as simple as they had assumed it would be to eradicate fascism and establish a Soviet-friendly outlook among people living in the countries on the western fringes of the USSR's sphere of influence. This prompted the communists to resort, in those places where the Red Army held sway, to tried-and-tested Leninist methods: agitation among the proletariat, manipulation behind the scenes, the threat of coercion, and ultimately suppression of free speech by the police and military authorities with no constitutional checks and balances. Of course, these methods were wholly incompatible with the principles of democracy and the rule of law. In practice, then, "antifascist agitation" in the area controlled by the Red Army took on many aspects that were reminiscent of Marxist-Leninist revolution.

So, for a long time Stalin did not consider a simple seizure of power by Polish communists to be the most appropriate means of preventing Poland from taking an anti-Soviet course. Rather, up to the summer of 1944 he tried to identify potentially acquiescent and cooperative members of the Polish government in exile in London. Only when it became clear that none were to be found did he accede to pressure from Polish communists to take steps to ensure that a communist-dominated regime came to power. This was why he refused the help he could have given the noncommunist Warsaw Uprising of August 1944 against the Nazis; and when the Red Army occupied Poland in the winter of 1944–1945, resistance leaders who tried to negotiate any positions of influence for themselves were summarily arrested. It was only as a result of American pressure that at the end of June 1945 the Peasants' Party, as potentially the strongest political grouping in the country, was granted four cabinet posts in the communist-established administration, plus another one for the socialists. But when the majority of the Peasants' Party refused to join the communist- and socialist-dominated Democratic Front, the communists responded by postponing elections to a constituent assembly until January 1947, and then manipulated them to such an extent (unnecessarily, as it turned out) that the Democratic Front won 394 out of a possible 444 parliamentary seats. This left Poland's communists with a completely free hand. Admittedly, they began by adopting an "independent path to Socialism," which was designed to bring both the rural peasant masses and the Catholic Church on board in working toward a socialist state.

Yet Stalin did find the sort of cooperation he had sought in vain among the Polish government in exile among the equivalent Czechoslovakian body. State president Eduard Benes and a majority of the country's democratic forces concluded from the 1938 Munich Agreement and the shift in the continent's balance of power that they needed to win over the Soviet Union as a protector to safeguard their independence. Accordingly, at the Soviets' behest, Benes readily dropped the plan for a Polish-Czech federation, acceded to their wish to have the autonomous Carpatho-Ukraine region transferred to Soviet control, and represented the Soviet position in international affairs. So, following the country's liberation by Soviet and (to a much lesser extent) American forces, political power was vested in a National Front made up of communists, social democrats, nationalist-socialists, the Catholic People's Party, and the Slovakian Democratic Party. Although the communists were in a strong position in this grouping, the policy of root-and-branch social reorganization (including the expulsion of the Sudeten Germans) was supported by a broad consensus among the coalition partners.

In Hungary, under the aegis of the Red Army, Stalin had put in place a coalition government of communists, socialists, and the Small Country Landowners' Party that instituted social reforms in gradual stages in the country, which hitherto had been governed in quasi-authoritarian fashion by a small ruling elite and had been closely allied with Germany. However, here there was no broad basis for a Soviet-friendly line; quite the contrary, in fact—in the October 1945 elections, the communists suffered a resounding defeat, with just 17 percent of the vote (as against 57 percent for the Small Country Landowners' Party and 17.4 percent for the Socialists). The leader of the Country Landowners, Ferenc Nagy, was accepted as prime minister by the Soviets but then came under increasing pressure from his communist colleagues in the cabinet. In January 1947, several prominent members of the Small Country Landowners' Party were accused of involvement in an attempted coup and were arrested, and by the end of that same year their most important minister was barred from the cabinet. This cleared the path for a communist monopoly on power.

In Romania, the Soviet leadership initially tried to deal with the group of conspirators, comprising opposition politicians and sympathetic generals, which had toppled the Hitler-friendly regime of Ion Antonescu in August 1944. Demands by Romanian communist leaders for a greater share of power were dismissed out of hand. But fearing general unrest among the rural populace, who were decidedly anti-Bolshevist in their outlook, in February 1945 the Soviet occupiers forced King Michael to put together a communist-controlled cabinet. Opposition to the new regime was considerable, and even began to grow, but had no further means of asserting itself. In August 1945, King Michael tried in vain to bring down the new government. In January 1946, American pressure brought cabinet appointments for two representatives of opposition parties, although they never secured any real influence there. And when voters served up a resounding defeat to the communists in the elections of November 1946, the results were simply falsified. The following year brought the wholesale arrest of opposition leaders, erosion of their party funds by a currency reform, the expunging of independent elements from the Democratic Bloc, and finally the forced abdication of King Michael on December 30.

In September 1944 in Bulgaria, as Red Army troops closed in, a Patriotic Front comprising members of the Peasants' Party, communists, socialists, and officers belonging to the nonparty Zveno political and military organization, staged a coup against the ruling pro-Hitler authoritarian regime. Within the new ruling coalition, the Communist Party, here with rapidly growing mass support and protected by the presence of the Soviet army of occupation, soon came to occupy a dominant position. Encouraged by British forces' suppression of the communist partisan movement in neighboring Greece, in July 1945 acting prime minister Nikola Petkov attempted a showdown with the communists by suddenly quitting the Patriotic Front along with a substantial section of his Peasants' Party. Yet the move backfired when only a single list of approved candidates from the Front was allowed to contest the November 1945 elections, which consequently topped the poll with 88 percent of the electorate on a turnout of 85 percent. However, negotiations on taking two opposition politicians back into the government (in line with a pledge given by the Soviet authorities to the United States) foundered on the communists' refusal to grant the opposition any real influence. Following the conclusion of the peace accord on April 10, 1947, and the disbanding of the joint Allied Control Commission, whose presence had ensured the opposition at least some measure of protection, Petkov was arrested and sentenced to death, and his already crippled Peasants' Party was dissolved.

In Yugoslavia, the communist partisan movement under Josip Broz Tito had—largely through its own efforts alone—managed to assert itself against rival resistance groups and take the leading role in the struggle against the Axis powers. While Stalin urged cooperation with the bourgeois forces and the country's exiled king, Tito accorded the noncommunist elements only a subservient role in the People's Front. He pressed ahead with dispossession of the large landowners and industrialists on the Soviet model and instituted criminal proceedings against active members of former rival groupings, especially the Serbian nationalist Chetniks and the collaborationist Croatian Ustaše. Yet despite toeing a largely communist line in such matters, Tito's regime soon came into conflict with Stalin, who regarded the revolutionary zeal of his Yugoslavian comrades as too rash in many regards.

Under quite different circumstances, Soviet influence in Finland was also strictly limited. On two separate occasions—in the Winter War of 1939–1940 and again during the Soviet Karelian Offensive in the summer of 1944—the Finnish army had fought the Red Army to a standstill. Throughout the entire course of the war, the United States signaled its active interest in maintaining democratic rule in Finland, while the pronouncedly Soviet-friendly foreign policy line adopted by the Paasikivi government, which took the helm at the end of hostilities, deprived the Kremlin of any pretext to attempt renewed intervention.

Western Europe and Germany

In the countries within the American and British forces' sphere of influence—and especially in France and Italy—the communists, acting on Stalin's instructions, mobilized all available forces to engage in reconstruction, which was to take place in conjunction with the traditional elites. So, in France, the communists helped the Free French leader General Charles de Gaulle to disarm the various militias of the French Resistance; they then refused to support their socialist coalition partners' demands for the nationalization of all major industries, a planned economy, and participation in government. In Italy, the Communist Party under the leadership of Palmiro Togliatti rejected the reform plans put forward by the socialists and the Action Party formed by former resistance members in favor of cooperation with the Liberals and above all with the Christian Democrats.

Yet the US leadership failed to acknowledge the communists' contribution to restoring stability in Western Europe, choosing to focus instead on their actions in Eastern Europe, which were regarded as a breach of the agreements reached at the Yalta Conference, in which Stalin had guaranteed all liberated countries "governments commensurate with the will of the people."[9] In line with this, the considerable gains made by communist parties in the first postwar elections held in various Western European countries were seen as a harbinger of their intention to seize power throughout the region, including in Germany.

A Yugoslavian soldier at a barricade in Trieste, May 1, 1946. The "Iron Curtain from Stettin in the Baltic to Trieste in the Adriatic," denounced by Winston Churchill in his speech in Fulton, Missouri, on March 5, 1946, was strengthened during the years of bloc building. (Time & Life Pictures/ Getty Images)

Economic hardship and communist agitation were considered to be a highly explosive mix. Most European countries stood "close to the edge of the abyss and could at any time be pushed over," warned the State Department's undersecretary for economic affairs, William Clayton, in a memorandum of March 5, 1947; in Greece and France in particular, it was easy to foresee an economic collapse resulting in a communist takeover.[10]

In the course of its attempts at "containment" of Soviet expansion (a concept promoted by the American diplomat George F. Kennan from the spring of 1946 onward), the administration of Harry S. Truman deliberately targeted its economic aid at countering communist influence, and pressed socialists and Christian Democrats to exclude communists from all governmental responsibility. However, those who were already in partnership with communists in government, and who relied on their support to enact their own reform plans, initially showed little inclination to accede to the Americans' demands. But they soon came under pressure from anticommunist forces within their own countries, whose influence increased with the growing confrontation between East and West. In France, for instance, de Gaulle's convening, after leaving office, of a broad coalition of political forces to form the Rally of the French People (Rassemblement du Peuple Français; RPF) posed a right-wing challenge to the Christian Democrats; in Italy, meanwhile, tradition-minded dignitaries and the Vatican were trying to engineer a split between the Christian Democrats and the communists. Consequently, the communists' position within governments grew progressively weaker, and their followers became increasingly discontent over the policy of compliance dictated by Moscow. By the spring of 1947, the frustration of the communist rank and file, on the one hand, and the pressure exerted by anticommunists, on the other, had reached such a pitch that all governing coalitions that included communists had fragmented, beginning in Belgium on March 11, then in France on May 5, and finally in Italy on May 13.

Germany, which the victorious powers initially intended to govern in concert, felt the force of the East–West confrontation even more profoundly. Whereas Roosevelt had basically agreed with the Soviet plan for German reparations (which involved the confiscation of industrial plant and the provision of goods from continuing production to the tune of US$20 billion, half of which was to go to the Soviet Union), Truman feared that reparations of this magnitude might lead to the economic ruination of Europe. The only thing, therefore, that the Allies could agree on at Potsdam was that each of the victorious powers should for the present meet its reparations needs only through supplies from the zone that it controlled. In addition, the USSR was granted one-tenth of all dismantled industrial plant from the Western zones of occupation (the full extent of which, however, remained unspecified).

The effects of this division of the reparations spoils were all the more damaging because France, which was not represented at Potsdam, vetoed the establishment of joint control commissions in the four zones of occupations. In doing so, De Gaulle wanted to ensure that the Rhineland was hived off from any potential German Confederation, and that the industrial Ruhr region was brought under international control—both vital preconditions, as he saw it, for France's future security. But in reality, the sole effect of the absence of any suprazonal authorities was to make de-Nazification of German society in East and West a very haphazard affair. In the West, it was conducted less thoroughly, though in accordance with the necessary bases of the constitutional state, whereas in the Eastern zone it was often carried out brutally and quite arbitrarily. When, in the Soviet zone, the Social Democrats threatened to become the largest party, the occupying powers forced them to merge with the communists. The resulting new Socialist Unity Party (Sozialistische Einheitspartei Deutschlands; SED), which came into being at a congress held on April 21–22, 1946, remained restricted to the Soviet zone, thereby deepening the rift between East and West.

Moreover, this rigid Soviet pressure to merge German workers parties only served to heighten the Western powers' misgivings over Soviet intentions in Germany. The suspicion that Stalin was trying to bring the whole of the country within the Soviet sphere of influence checked their eagerness to draw up common regulations for all four occupation zones. Although plans for nationwide administrative bodies, such as the American offer of a Four-Power Security Council for the Demilitarization of Germany, or the British suggestion of a step-by-step creation of a provisional government, were seriously discussed right up to the foreign ministers' meeting in Moscow in March–April 1947, these all regularly foundered on intractable Soviet–American disagreements on the reparations question. In the spring of 1946, therefore, the British government began promoting the idea of state building inside the three Western occupation zones without Soviet involvement. Barely a year later, the US administration also formally adopted this policy. Accordingly, on January 1, 1947, the US and British zones were merged to form the Bizone. By contrast, Stalin continued to insist on pan-German objectives, while at the same time the authorities within his occupation zone continued the process of eradicating National Socialism there in ways that flew in the face of all democratic principles.

Under these circumstances, plans for a European "Third Force" between the USSR and the United States scarcely made any headway. The re-creation of an Internationale of socialist parties from East and West, a potential reservoir of pro-unification forces, foundered on the fear of the Eastern Europeans and the British Labour Party alike that its room for maneuver would be severely restricted. Likewise, attempts to forge stronger relationships between Western and Eastern European states, such as the French plan for a Franco-Czech Alliance, never got beyond the first planning stage. And, as a result of British vacillation and French insistence on a separation of the Rhineland from German sovereign territory, initiatives for a Western European confederation under joint French and British leadership led only to the watered-down Dunkirk Pact of May 4, 1947, which apart from agreeing mutual support in the event of renewed German aggression, contained no substantial provisions for cooperation.

Efforts to weld Western Europe and the United States together into a bloc to oppose Soviet expansion also met with little success at first. Winston Churchill, now the British leader of the opposition, spoke publicly in March 1946 of an Iron Curtain that had descended between East and West, and of the necessity for transatlantic solidarity. In September 1946 he urged the French and Germans to create a "kind of United States of Europe" in the West. On both occasions his comments met with more rejection than assent in Europe.

The Marshall Plan as a Turning Point

The change toward a lasting division of Europe began with the attempt by the US administration in the spring of 1947 to intensify its stabilization policies for Western Europe, including the Western areas of Germany. From an American standpoint, this attempt was necessary, because the amount of aid thus far distributed to countries outside the Soviet sphere of influence had proven too small, with the result that the European countries in question were threatening to slip back into protectionism. Yet it was also extraordinarily difficult: the US Congress showed itself unwilling to approve new credit for Europe, while the French government refused to approve the rapid reconstruction of West German industry that was essential for a lasting recovery of Europe's economy. The Truman administration overcame the reluctance of Congress by deliberately magnifying the Soviet threat. In the Truman Doctrine presented to Congress on March 12, 1947, as part of the request to furnish Greece and Turkey with more financial aid, the conflict between the Soviet Union and the United States was painted as a global struggle between a regime of "terror and repression" and "freedom"; the United States was now faced with the challenge of defending this freedom worldwide. In the meantime, Kennan (who by this stage was head of policy planning at the State Department) and US secretary of state George C. Marshall tried to overcome French resistance by bundling up the planned aid for various European countries into a multilateral Reconstruction Program, which, in opening the way for integration of the participating countries, offered France a new form of control over German resurgence. In order to sell this program—which since its presentation by the secretary of state on June 5, 1947, was known as the Marshall Plan—in Western European countries with their strong traditions of communist and socialist activism, in addition the Americans offered it to Eastern European countries, including the Soviet Union. Although it was not the main aim of the plan's instigators, this also had the advantage of holding out one further chance of reversing the division of Europe, which was already under way.

In both Western and Eastern Europe, the announcement of the Marshall Plan raised great hopes for the realization of the Third Force, and for some time Stalin vacillated between worrying that the West might form a concerted bloc if he rejected the plan, and fear that his sphere of influence in Eastern Europe might begin to loosen, or even dissolve completely, if he took part in it. He therefore set conditions for Soviet participation, in the hope that the Western European governments would rally to him. However, when they refused, he had effectively excluded himself from the program. On July 2, 1947, the Soviet foreign minister, Vyacheslav Molotov, formally rejected the alleged "plan for the subjugation of Europe" by American imperialism. The governments of Eastern Europe, which without exception had expressed an interest in taking part in the Marshall Plan, and which were all (except for Yugoslavia) still determined to take part even after the Soviet rebuff, were forced by the Kremlin to retract their acceptance. To forestall a possible Soviet intervention, Finland decided of its own accord not to participate.

To thwart the Americans' plans, during the summer of 1947 Stalin devised a two-pronged strategy that involved both mobilizing Western European opinion against the supposed subjugation, and bringing Eastern European regimes more firmly in line with the Soviet model and more firmly under Moscow's control. At the end of September, at a conference in Szklarska Poręba in Silesia, the leaders of the most significant communist parties were informed of this new direction in Soviet policy and obliged to cooperate in a Communist Information Bureau (Cominform). In a mirror image of the Truman Doctrine, the leader of the Soviet delegation, Andrei Zhdanov, defined the East–West conflict as a global life-and-death struggle between the "imperialist and antidemocratic camp" under the leadership of the United States and "anti-imperialist and anti-fascist forces" headed by the Soviet Union.

In Eastern European countries, the pressure from Moscow, combined with the ongoing crisis of reconstruction—exacerbated by the lack of any American financial aid—had the effect of eliminating any remaining freedom of maneuver for independent political forces. In Czechoslovakia, a dramatic trial of strength between the Communist Party and its democratic coalition partners ended, on February 29, 1948, in the establishment of a regime rigidly loyal to Moscow and the complete disempowerment of the noncommunists. In other Eastern European states as well, all remaining organized opposition groups were abolished, social democratic parties (following extensive purges) were merged with the communists, all labor organizations were brought under communist control, and all those suspected of having not shown unswerving loyalty to Stalin at all times were weeded out of the Communist Party elites. The restructuring of society was carried out along strictly Soviet lines, and in place of pragmatic alliances with groups that were at least partially amenable to reform, there now came police-state terror organized by a minority. Following the Soviet pattern, top priority was invariably given to the development of heavy industry, central planning methods were introduced, and the collectivization of all agriculturally worthwhile land pressed ahead, in the face of widespread opposition. Economic output was increasingly geared to the needs of Soviet reconstruction, with ties to Western markets heavily reduced. This multifaceted indirect Soviet suzerainty over Eastern Europe turned it into a closed Soviet Bloc.

In Western Europe, the leaders of communist parties gave their supporters and fellow travelers free rein to vent the discontent that had been building up since the war's end. In France and Italy in the winter of 1947–1948, there developed massive strike movements that sometimes took on the flavor of a general insurrection. Far from hampering the United States in achieving its aims in Europe, though, these helped it: faced with the spectacle of these strikes and the accompanying communist ideological offensive, the overwhelming majority of Western Europeans, who up to this point had always tended to dismiss as groundless American fears about an expansion of Soviet influence in Western Europe, now themselves became convinced that the communist parties were indeed attempting to topple the existing order in Western Europe and that the Kremlin was trying to bring the whole of the continent under its control. There now seemed no possibility of taking communists back into constitutional government. And so it was that the communists found themselves consigned to the ghetto of the "counterculture," as the political pendulum swung noticeably to the right, and reconstruction under the Marshall Plan proceeded on the basis of a broad anticommunist consensus.

Restoring the Status Quo in Western Europe

Hence, from the winter of 1947–1948 on, the Cold War became an inescapable fact of domestic politics in Western European states. In France, the socialists saw themselves forced by circumstances into taking on the role of left-wing fringe group within a coalition headed by Christian Democrats and Conservatives; as time passed, this coalition moved further and further away from the reforming spirit of the immediate postwar administrations that had emerged from the resistance movement. In the Italian elections of April 1948, the Christian Democrats, with massive American support, beat a coalition of communists and left-wing socialists; the ghettoization of the communists henceforth ensured the Christian Democrats an uncontested grip on power. In the western regions of

Germany, the Social Democratic Party (SPD) found its backing much reduced as a result of the heavy concentration of its supporters in areas now within the Soviet Zone, while Christian socialists lost their former key position within the Christian Democratic Union (CDU). Overall, the new anticommunist consensus and a growing fear of the Soviet threat helped the traditional bourgeois ruling elites, discredited either by their collaboration with the National Socialists or by their defeat in the face of Nazi expansion, rehabilitate themselves and resume their positions of power. In Great Britain, the ruling Labour Party came under increasing pressure from the Conservatives and in the elections of 1951 lost the majority it had gained in 1945.

This trend toward restoring the old order was greatly strengthened by the American pressure for rapid reconstruction and integration of European economies. Although in principle it was by no means hostile to social-democratic ideas of reform, the Truman administration nevertheless thought that it could ill afford any further experiments, given the desperate situation in Western Europe. Accordingly, it organized reconstruction under the Marshall Plan along the lines of its own successful economic-liberal template. The rebuilding of western Germany's heavy industry was no longer held back on security grounds, with the result that German business soon began to assume its leading role on the continent once more. In the fall of 1947, under massive American pressure, nationalization of the Ruhr industrial heartland—the linchpin of reforming programs sponsored by everyone from the German Christian Democrats to the French Socialists—was postponed until the establishment of an elected West German government, and so de facto killed off. In the preparations for West German currency reform, the American occupation authorities worked closely with traditional liberal powers; by favoring existing asset holders and yet not at the same time instituting a compensation scheme, the architects of West Germany's new financial structure clearly paved the way for a market economy that left the prevailing state of property ownership fundamentally unaltered. American Marshall Plan funds had to be petitioned afresh from Congress every year, and their disbursement was under the ultimate control of the American Economic Cooperation Administration (ECA); these two factors made it difficult for participating countries to undertake any long-term economic planning, because the Americans could use their position to influence certain aspects of a country's national investment policy in favor of their own conceptions of a liberal economic order.

Admittedly, the Western Europeans largely had themselves to blame for the fact that they did not manage to assert their autonomy to any great extent in the enactment of the Marshall Plan: given that it had no interest in a long-term structural dependence of European countries on the United States, but instead wanted to regain robust, independent trading partners, in the summer of 1947 the Truman administration expressly left the initiative for formulating the details of the aid package to the participating countries themselves. Only after the Europeans found themselves unable to agree on an integrated reconstruction program and even the first step toward integration of the member countries, in the form of a European Customs Union, had fallen through, did the Truman administration begin to impose its concept of an optimal reconstruction program. The French government made repeated attempts to achieve unity among the Marshall Plan countries in the interests both of European self-determination and (insofar as this was still possible) of mediation in the East–West conflict, but the British Labour government balked at committing the country to such close ties to the continent. And without British involvement, most continental Europeans, especially the Left and the Benelux countries, did not want to proceed with European integration. As a result, despite a considerable surge in support for the unification movement in 1947–1949, the policy of European union never got beyond the planning stage. The founding of the Council of Europe in 1949—which, in the eyes of continental Europeans, after exhaustive negotiations was a first step toward the creation of a federal Europe—really only signaled a further delay in concrete moves toward real integration: the British resisted all attempts to grant the Council responsibility for communal initiatives, and in so doing condemned it to irrelevance.

Western Bloc Building

While European unification stagnated and the concept of the Third Force also continued, de facto, to languish, the creation of blocs in Western Europe proceeded apace. Deeply unsettled by the prospect of Soviet encroachment into Western Europe, as early as December 1947 the British foreign secretary, Ernest

Bevin, urged his American counterpart, Marshall, to create "some Western democratic system comprising the Americans, ourselves, France, Italy, etc. and of course the Dominions," which would guarantee the Europeans in particular military protection by the United States.[11] In advance, he offered the Americans a collective defensive pact between Great Britain, France, Belgium, the Netherlands, and Luxembourg: the Treaty of Brussels signed on March 17, 1948. After the violent end to Czechoslovak democracy in February 1948, which made the specter of military aggression very real for many Western Europeans, this policy gained mass support in Western Europe. Equally, in the United States, where the government had initially been lukewarm about a military pact because it did not believe Europe was under military threat, there now arose a new willingness to support the Brussels Pact with its own commitment. On June 11, 1948, the US Senate voted in favor of a declaration that for the first time in American history committed the United States to a defensive alliance in peacetime.

The process of Western bloc building was accelerated by Stalin's frankly desperate attempts to prevent at the last moment the establishment of a West German state—a logical outcome of the integration of all three Western occupation zones into the Western European reconstruction program. After representatives from the United States and the Brussels Pact nations had reached an agreement in London at the beginning of June 1948 on the basic form the new West German state should take, Stalin took the implementation of currency reform in the Western sectors of Berlin as a pretext to sever all road and rail links between Berlin and the Western occupation zones (as of June 24). This appeared to him the only possible way to prevent the London declarations from being put into practice and to revive negotiations about a settlement that would take in the whole of Germany.

In fact, the US State Department now seriously entertained a plan for the withdrawal of troops by all sides from the four occupied zones, in the hope of thereby avoiding what threatened to become a debacle for American policy on Germany. The British and French military governors in Germany also argued in the same vein. But when, from the end of August onward, it became clear that it would be perfectly feasible to supply the populace of West Berlin by an airlift to the British and American sectors, including for the coming winter, Marshall and Truman not only resolved to stick it out—they also quite deliberately spun out negotiations over lifting the blockade. Because it provided such stark proof of the aggressiveness and cynical brutality of the Soviets, it was an excellent means of countering any remaining resistance to the idea of Western bloc building—be this in the form of the West Germans' hesitation in formally establishing a state that would manifestly deepen the rift with fellow Germans in the Soviet zone, or French misgivings about the rise of a strong new Germany on their eastern borders, or, at home, congressional resistance to a costly and enduring American military commitment to Europe. On April 4, 1949, representatives from the United States, Canada, Great Britain, France, the Benelux countries, Italy, Norway, Denmark, Iceland, and Portugal signed the North Atlantic Treaty in Washington, DC, and on May 8 the Parliamentary Council of representatives from the West German *Länder* (states) approved the Basic Law for the Federal Republic of Germany.

When Stalin realized that his land blockade of West Berlin could not prevent the founding of the Federal Republic, his only choice was to reopen the road, rail, and canal links. The blockade was lifted on May 12, 1949. Even so, he still hoped for a groundswell of popular resistance to the establishment of a West German state. He repeatedly rebuffed requests by the SED leadership to follow the West German example and form a government for the Eastern Zone; instead, the German comrades were instructed to form a National Front to fight for the "economic and political unification" of Germany.[12] Only after elections for the first federal German parliament had taken place on August 14 and all hopes had vanished that the Allied Council of Foreign Ministers would reconvene did Stalin finally agree, in September, to implement a constitution for a German Democratic Republic, which a "German People's Congress" had already adopted (with dubious legitimacy) on May 30, and which for the time being would have force only within the area covered by the Soviet occupation zone. This state was formally founded on October 7, 1949, although the elections provided for in the constitution were put back for a year. When they finally did take place, on October 15, 1950, they were conducted on the principle of a single list of candidates, with no real choice for voters. So, right from its inception the second German state lacked democratic legitimacy.

By the end of 1949, the defunct system of a balance of power in Europe had thus been replaced by two opposing blocs dominated by the two principal victors of the Second World War, which split Europe into an Eastern and a Western hemisphere. The power vacuum left behind after the collapse of the Third Reich was now filled, with the spheres of influence of the superpowers clearly demarcated and realization of their fundamental interests secured. It remained unclear whether and for how long the state of confrontation that had given rise to this division would persist, what dimensions the American and Soviet involvement in Europe would assume, and hence how lasting this split would turn out to be.

The Chinese Revolution

Unlike the downfall of the German Third Reich in Europe, the collapse of the Japanese Empire in East and Southeast Asia did not lead to a partition of the region under the auspices of the Cold War. The prime reason for this was that the liberation of the East Asian region did not come about through a coalition of Western and Soviet armed forces, but was basically carried out by US forces alone. The Soviet Union did not enter the war against Japan until right at the end, on August 7, 1945. Even though the Russian offensive against Japanese troops in Manchuria played a significant part in the Japanese High Command's decision to offer its surrender on August 10, Stalin failed to achieve anything beyond a nominal Soviet involvement in the occupation of Japan. Officially, the occupying force comprised eleven nations, but in reality 90 percent of the troops were from the United States, and their commanding officer, General Douglas MacArthur, as Supreme Allied Commander, wielded practically unlimited power.

Yet the fact that East Asia was still sucked into the undertow of the East-West conflict can be ascribed to the attraction of Leninist political models for populations in the region whose traditional modes of existence had been challenged by their encounter with Western modernity. This resulted in the growth of communist-nationalist movements that became as much of a problem for the USSR as they were for the United States.

Nowhere was this more dramatically evident than in China. Following the withdrawal of Japanese troops, who had controlled the east of the Chinese Empire from Manchuria to Canton and whom the warring parties on the Chinese side had found it impossible to dislodge through their own efforts, the Chinese civil war between the Guomindang (GMD) National Party under General Chiang Kai-shek and the communists under the new leadership of Mao Zedong broke out with renewed force. US liberation forces in the country tried to persuade the two sides to reach an accord, but the Guomindang, who had pushed forward from their power base in the southwestern province of Sichuan to disarm the great majority of the Japanese troops and take over the regions they had once occupied, were adamant in their refusal to share power with the communists. For their part, the communists, who operated from a few strongholds in the North, would agree to renounce the armed struggle only if in return they were ensured a role in a coalition government.

Nor could Stalin prevail upon the communists to fall in line with the clearly dominant administration of the Guomindang. Even though the Soviet dictator allowed communist guerrillas to establish a foothold in the rural areas of Manchuria overrun by the Red Army, he still denied the communists any substantial military or economic aid, preferring instead to form an alliance with the Chiang Kai-shek government on August 14, 1945. This agreement ensured his control over Outer Mongolia and confirmed Russian rights to use of the railroads and harbors in Manchuria. After first dismantling and transporting large sections of the industrial infrastructure set up by the Japanese in this region, as agreed upon with the US government, Soviet troops withdrew for good from Manchuria in the spring of 1946.

Truman, on the other hand, decided to support the Chiang Kai-shek government with large amounts of money and arms; he rejected any intervention by US forces in the Chinese civil war. Instead, General George C. Marshall was dispatched on December 15, 1945, as the American special envoy to China, with instructions to persuade both parties to enter into a coalition. Marshall could do little more than arrange a temporary ceasefire in January 1946. In July 1946 Chiang Kai-shek decided to launch a renewed attack on the communist strongholds in the North. With armed forces totaling 4.3 million men at his disposal, he reckoned on quickly overwhelming the numerically inferior and far less well equipped communist army of 1.2 million and finally stamping his authority—already ensured internationally—on the whole of his native country.

The two superpowers were not moved to change their positions by this resumption of hostilities. American observers were not convinced that Chiang Kai-shek's forces would be able to secure victory over the communist guerrillas; they also realized that the corrupt GMD regime was deeply unpopular and was fast losing support. Consequently, it seemed prudent to provide nothing other than economic assistance, even though its effect became more than questionable. Conversely, Stalin did not believe that the communists would prevail any time soon; he was also concerned that the Chinese civil war might drag him involuntarily into a confrontation with the United States. At first, then, he withheld any support and once more urged restraint on his Chinese comrades. The outcome of the civil war was therefore largely decided by the warring parties within the country.

Contrary to Chiang Kai-shek's expectations, the decisive action in this conflict took place in the political rather than the military arena. Rural China's populace had experienced the GMD's commanders as ruthless extorters of conscripts and levies. By contrast, the communists, in the areas they controlled, instituted an "agricultural revolution" by dispossessing rural landlords and redistributing 43 percent of land under cultivation to 60 percent of the peasantry. At the same time the GMD government also increasingly alienated city dwellers through its repressive measures against workers, its handing over of factories seized by the Japanese to greedy party functionaries, and its reactionary policies that caused galloping inflation and soon drove state employees and others on fixed incomes into penury while favorites of the regime raked in millions. By the end of 1947, then, most of the Guomindang's legitimacy had evaporated.

Over time the growing support of the populace began to make up for what the communists lacked in military firepower and supplies. From the beginning of 1948 onward, entire units of the nationalist army defected to the communist People's Liberation Army (PLA). After the communists had gained control first over rural areas in the North and then over large swaths of Central China, at the beginning of November 1948 a decisive battle was fought out at Xuzhou (the most important railroad hub in Central China). In this long engagement, which lasted until early January 1949, a key factor that turned the tables in favor of the communists was guerrilla leader Deng Xiaoping's mobilization of two million peasants from the four neighboring districts to provide logistical support for the

Communist forces parade a banner of their leaders from a truck after the fall of Shanghai, May 1949. After crossing the Yangzi River in April, Mao Zedong brought the whole of the south and west of China under his control. By the end of December, the last significant city in nationalist hands, Chengdu, had also surrendered. (Popperfoto/Getty Images)

PLA. Thereafter, all the major cities of the central region that Chiang Kai-shek's troops had garrisoned fell into communist hands with little in the way of resistance. These victories began at Tianjin and ended with the capture of Beijing on January 31, 1949.

In response to the communists' success in Central China, Chiang Kai-shek entered into ceasefire negotiations, but these proved inconclusive. In April 1949, in defiance of Stalin's strong advice against it, Mao Zedong led his troops across the Yangzi River and in a lightning campaign brought the whole of the south and west of the country under his control. The GMD forces occupying Shanghai were forced to surrender as early as May. On October 1, 1949, Mao duly proclaimed the foundation of the People's Republic of China in Beijing. Two weeks later the PLA overran Guangzhou, and by the end of December the last significant city in nationalist hands, Chengdu in Sichuan, had also surrendered. In the meantime, Chiang Kai-shek had withdrawn to the island of Taiwan (Formosa). Around half a million of his troops also decamped there.

The US government regarded the Chinese communist victory as a "bitter political defeat," in the words of a National Security Council memorandum distributed in December 1949.[13] Yet Washington perceived no threat to American security resulting from it, if only because the new regime would for the foreseeable future have its work cut out dealing with the massive social and economic problems that had bedeviled China's imperial rulers. Truman could not bring himself to recognize the communist regime in Beijing, but he also ruled out any military action to restore Chiang Kai-shek. In a speech before the National Press Club on January 12, 1950, Secretary of State Dean Acheson announced that the US defense perimeter in Asia extended from Japan to the Philippines. This clearly indicated that neither the nationalists on Taiwan nor any other regime on the East Asian mainland could now count on American military support.

Stalin was persuaded by his advisers to pledge the victorious Mao Zedong economic aid and military assistance in the event of a US attack. However, in concrete terms the formal friendship treaty between the Soviet Union and the PRC that was concluded on February 14, 1950, stated only that the territorial concessions made by Chiang Kai-shek to the USSR in 1945 would not be rescinded. In Stalin's view, the new regime in China was far from being communist, and Mao was not a reliable ally. Indeed, eleven of the twenty-four members of the new Chinese administration were not members of the Communist Party. To forcibly transform coalition-led China into a full-blown communist country, Mao required several further campaigns, most of them conducted with bloody terror. In the course of the Great Leap Forward program instituted in 1958, for instance, 15 to 46 million Chinese starved to death, and during the Great Proletarian Cultural Revolution of 1966 onward, fanatical Red Guards systematically liquidated the country's educational and administrative elite.

The Korean War

The process of turning China into a socialist country was accelerated by the Korean War. After Japan's forty-year hegemony over the Korean Peninsula was ended by defeat in August 1945, the Japanese governor lost no time in installing a Korean administrator, the left-leaning and extremely popular Yuh Woon-Hyung, in his place. From representative groups that had formed throughout the country, Yuh assembled the Committee for Preparation of Korean Independence, and the People's Republic of Korea was duly proclaimed on September 6, 1945. One of the first acts of the broadly based coalition government was to put in place a program for expropriating the landed aristocracy, nationalizing major industrial concerns, and bringing in limited social reforms. While this was happening, Soviet troops moved into northern Korea from Manchuria, while US forces landed in the south. Stalin had raised no objections when, after the dropping of the atomic bombs on Hiroshima and Nagasaki, and in contravention of agreements reached at the Yalta Conference, Truman had demanded US involvement in the occupation of Korea and proposed that the border between the occupation zones be drawn at the 38th Parallel.

While the Soviets allowed the government of the People's Republic free rein, the Americans installed a military government that relied heavily on former collaborators with the Japanese occupation regime and often forcefully rode roughshod over decisions of the People's Committees. An attempt to create a new administration for the whole of Korea was defeated by extremists from both left and right. Accordingly, in September 1947 the US government decided to entrust organization of the upcoming elections to the United Nations. But the interim Committee of the People's Republic in the northern zone, under the leadership of the communist Kim Il Sung, refused entry to the UN representatives. As a result, the elections were held only in the southern zone (in May 1948), and led to the founding of the Republic of Korea, whose jurisdiction extended solely over the American occupation zone. Because supporters of the People's Republic and moderate groups had boycotted the poll for fear that it would split the country, the conservative Syngman Rhee, a long-term exile in America, was free to secure the presidency. The North responded by holding its own elections on August 25, 1948, from which Kim Il Sung emerged as president of the Democratic People's Republic of Korea. Soviet troops withdrew by the end of 1948. The American army of occupation followed suit in the South in June 1949.

Yet neither Syngman Rhee and his constituency of property owners and former collaborators nor Kim Il Sung and the liberation movement were prepared to let the division of the country stand. Both sides rearmed and tried to get their protecting powers to support them in a "war of liberation." Rhee's pleas fell on deaf ears in Washington, but Kim Il Sung, after lengthy persuasion, finally got Stalin to listen. In mid-June 1950, the Soviet dictator gave his assent to an attack on the South by North Korean forces. Evidently Kim had convinced Stalin that war was inevitable in any case, that Syngman Rhee's regime would quickly collapse, and that the Americans would not return to rescue him.

North Korean troops crossed the 38th Parallel on June 25, 1950. As foreseen by Kim, they advanced south rapidly; by the end of July they had overrun the whole peninsula except for a narrow strip of land in the southeast around the city of Busan. However, Truman and his advisers, who by now had come to view the attack as part of a wider Soviet strategy of expansion through client states, were determined to resist. Driven not least by the weight of domestic public opinion, which still blamed the administration for letting China fall into communist hands too easily, they ordered General Douglas MacArthur, the US proconsul in Japan, to urgently deploy naval and air power to help the South Korean regime. Because the Kremlin was boycotting the UN Security Council at the time (in protest at China's seat still being occupied by the Chiang Kai-shek government), the Americans succeeded in securing a mandate from the United Nations to defend South Korea. A total of sixteen nations, including Australia, Canada, and Great Britain, took part in the military operation under MacArthur's overall command. Even so, half of the UN force was supplied by the Americans; South Korea's own troops made up another 40 percent.

MacArthur's counteroffensive began on September 15 with a seaborne landing at Inchon (the port near the capital, Seoul). Within a fortnight Seoul was recaptured, and the UN force capitalized on this success to drive the North Korean army back across the 38th Parallel. Stalin, who was still determined to avoid at all costs a direct confrontation with the United States, had already resigned himself to an American victory. "So what?" he told the Politburo in Moscow. "Let the United States of America be our neighbors in the Far East. They will come there but we shall not fight them now. We are not ready to fight."[14]

Kim Il Sung's regime was rescued by Mao Zedong. As MacArthur's forces advanced along a broad front toward the Chinese border, Mao overruled his prime minister, Zhou Enlai, and on October 13 decided to heed Stalin's call for Chinese involvement in the conflict. Mao feared that MacArthur's troops would not halt at the Yalu River. But above all he was worried that an American victory in Korea might embolden Chinese Nationalist forces to take up arms against his regime again. On November 25, then, just after the UN forces had reached the Yalu, China launched a major offensive. MacArthur's troops were driven back south once more. On December 31, Chinese and North Korean forces recrossed the 38th Parallel, and shortly afterward Seoul was in communist hands again.

MacArthur now called for an invasion of the mainland by Chinese Nationalist troops and advocated nuclear strikes against China. With imminent defeat staring him in the face, Truman came close to acceding to these demands. He decided against this course of action only after the front stabilized once more. The war thus remained confined to Korea. Following a new American offensive, which retook Seoul in March 1951, and a failed Chinese spring offensive, the conflict descended into a static war of attrition. In early April, when MacArthur tried to lobby Congress in favor of taking the war to China, Truman dismissed him for insubordination. The Truman administration was afraid that the USSR would use an expansion of US involvement in East Asia as an opportunity for further encroachment into Europe and the Persian Gulf. It took the view that a war against China was "the wrong war, at the wrong place, at the wrong time, and with the wrong enemy."[15]

But even this "limited war," as it was called thereafter in Washington, claimed many lives. Estimates of Korean dead, both soldiers and civilians, are put at some 1.3 million in the South plus 1.4 million in the North, or around 10 percent of the total population. In addition, around a million Chinese soldiers and fifty-four thousand Americans were killed. Cities and industrial installations on the peninsula were largely destroyed. Accordingly, in June 1951 the North Korean and Chinese leadership called for ceasefire negotiations to begin. These dragged on for a long time with no definite outcome, not least because Stalin advised his allies not to settle too hastily. He had a vested interest in keeping US forces tied down in Korea. Only after his death in March 1953, with his successors seeking "an acceptable path toward the soonest possible conclusion of the war in Korea,"[16] could an armistice agreement be signed at Panmunjom near the demarcation line.

The ceasefire line in part ran south of the 38th Parallel, and in part north of it. Korea was now permanently divided, with a brutal regime in the North that became increasingly Stalinist but still sought to tread a fine line between its two powerful socialist neighbors, and a South that was entirely dependent on US aid. Under the protection of American troops, Syngman Rhee continued to rule in authoritarian fashion until April 26, 1960, when the army refused to suppress a protest by students and university teachers and forced him to step down. South Korea then entered a brief phase of democracy, before a military regime under General Park Chung Hee embarked upon an extensive modernization program.

Democratizing Japan

American involvement in Japan went on longer than originally envisaged, as a result of the Korean War. The American occupation authorities began by instituting a democratization program that involved demilitarizing the country, bringing war criminals to justice, introducing an extensive land reform, and establishing a parliamentary system. In October 1946 they had the Japanese parliament enact a constitution that had been drafted by US officials and that, among other provisions, reduced the role of the emperor to a figurehead, a "symbol of the State and the unity of the people," and established a bicameral legislature. Civil and human rights were guaranteed by the constitution, and women were placed on an equal legal footing with men. Furthermore, in Article 9 of the Constitution the Japanese people agreed to "renounce war as a sovereign right of the nation and the threat or use of force as means of settling international disputes."

It was this clause above all that proved the most contentious among the Japanese populace. Yet the first postwar election, held on April 25, 1947, returned a socialist-led government that overwhelmingly backed the demilitarization plan. Shortly thereafter, definite moves became apparent in Washington to turn Japan both economically and militarily into a buffer state to contain communist expansion in the region. Accordingly, efforts to break up the cartels formed by Japan's major industrial conglomerates (*zaibatsu*) abated, the right to strike was curtailed in light of increasing union militancy, and a purge of ultranationalists was supplanted by a purge of left-leaning forces. After the outbreak of the Korean

War, Japan was granted the right to maintain a seventy-five-thousand-strong National Police Reserve, which included tanks, combat aircraft, and naval units.

The Pentagon now dropped its objection to a formal peace treaty with Japan, albeit on the condition that American strategic bases be allowed to remain on Japanese soil. In fact, under the terms of the Treaty of San Francisco, signed on September 8, 1951, the United States retained full jurisdiction over the island of Okinawa, which, along with 117 American military bases, played a vital role in the creation of a US defensive shield in the Pacific region. In a security pact concluded at the same time, Japan agreed to the stationing of US troops on Japanese sovereign territory. Mindful of public opinion, Prime Minister Yoshida Shigeru, a conservative, resisted American pressure to have the Japanese obligation to rearm written into this treaty; in response, the United States made no formal commitment to defend Japan against foreign aggression.

Nevertheless, in secret Yoshida had been obliged to promise the US negotiators that he would establish a domestic force of fifty thousand troops. However, it was March 1954 before a bill providing for the creation of a Self-Defense Force could command a majority in the Japanese parliament. This prompted calls within Japan for the government to revise the unequal security treaty of 1951. Difficult negotiations finally resulted in the revised security pact of January 21, 1960. This still accorded the United States the right to station its forces in Japan and to expand existing airbases. In return, though, the United States now pledged Japan military assistance and committed both sides to mutual consultation on defense questions. In addition Japan was granted the right to rescind the treaty unilaterally. Yet despite these concessions, the new pact was vehemently opposed by the socialists, communists, and labor unions. It was ratified against the backdrop of mass demonstrations and a general strike. The Japanese conservatives, now unified in the Liberal Democratic Party, won the ensuing November 1960 elections with a clear majority. The Left was consigned by these events to long-term opposition, a position it has occupied virtually uninterrupted ever since.

The United States also exerted pressure on Japan to reach an accommodation with other former enemies. A peace treaty was agreed to with the Chinese Nationalist regime on Taiwan as early as 1952. To ensure that the 1951 security pact was ratified by the US Congress, Yoshida expressly refused to recognize the

People's Republic of China. Deals with countries like Burma (1954), the Philippines (1956), Indonesia (1958), and South Vietnam (1959) took far longer to conclude, due to the settlement of war reparations claims. The most difficult negotiations of all were with South Korea; the legacy of bitterness left by the Japanese occupation of Korea meant that diplomatic relations between the two countries were not established until 1965, and even then amid furious protests by the Korean opposition. An agreement on the formal cessation of hostilities was signed with the Soviet Union in October 1956. Japan had demanded the return of former territory now under Russian control but in the end had to settle for a joint declaration promising the handover of Shikotan and the Habomais in the southern Kuril Islands chain to Japan.

Decolonization in Southeast Asia

The first adversary faced by the communist-nationalist liberation movement in Indochina was France, the former colonial power. When the Japanese occupiers of this region surrendered on August 14, 1945, mass demonstrations were held in the cities in favor of national independence, and local committees of the League for the Independence of Vietnam (Viet Nam Doc Lap Dong Minh Hoi, or Viet Minh for short) assumed control. On September 2, their leader, the communist Ho Chi Minh, proclaimed the Democratic Republic of Vietnam in Hanoi. However, international recognition of the new state was not forthcoming. Instead, Charles de Gaulle dispatched troops to the south of the country, which had temporarily been occupied by the British. By February 1946 de Gaulle's force was able to reestablish French military and political authority. Meanwhile, in order to be rid of the Chinese troops occupying the North, Ho Chi Minh was prepared to reach a compromise with the French: in a treaty of March 6, 1946, French troops were granted free access to the North. In return, France undertook to withdraw from Vietnam within five years. It was agreed that a plebiscite would be held on unification of the country; it was then envisaged that Vietnam would constitute a free state within the framework of an Indochinese federation, which in turn would form part of the Union Française—the entity created to replace the old French colonial system, a French equivalent of the British Commonwealth. This arrangement meant that France was de facto foreseeing a situation where the Viet Minh extended their authority over the south of the country as well, albeit with the proviso that the country as a whole would remain within the French sphere of influence.

However, this compromise did not last long. Thierry d'Argenlieu, head of the French civil administration in the South, was under no circumstances prepared to hand control of the country over to the Viet Minh. Instead, on July 1, 1946, he established in Saigon the autonomous government of Cochinchina, which in the long term was expected to rule over the North also. Because no one in Paris dared to countermand d'Argenlieu, negotiations on how to implement the compromise of March 6 soon reached an impasse. Parallel with this development, on both sides the advocates of military confrontation were gaining the upper hand. In response to attacks by the Viet Minh on French garrisons, on November 23 French forces bombarded Viet Minh positions in the port of Haiphong, killing some six thousand Vietnamese in the process. General Vo Nguyen Giap, commander in chief of a Viet Minh army that had in the interim grown to one hundred thousand men, responded on December 19 with an attack on French settlements in Hanoi.

For a long time the war was at a stalemate. Although France was able to bring most of the cities under its control, the countryside and jungle remained firmly in the hands of the elusive guerrilla army. Even the installation of the former Annamese emperor, Bao Dai, as ruler of the State of Vietnam within the French Union, failed to win hearts and minds: a large section of the Vietnamese people regarded Bao Dai as so corrupt that he actually became a liability to the former colonial power. Following Mao Zedong's victory in China, the Viet Minh also began to get weapons and logistical support from China, a fact that the French used to persuade the Americans to provide material help for their crusade against the advance of communism. The fighting came to an end only after the fall of the key French military bastion at Dien Bien Phu, 300 kilometers west of Hanoi on the border with Laos, on May 7, 1954. This devastating loss finally convinced Paris that the war was unwinnable.

However, because Stalin was concerned to keep Mao in check, and because Mao himself wanted to avoid any new confrontation with the United States, the French defeat did not amount to victory for the Viet Minh. Instead, an embittered Ho Chi Minh was forced to accept the provisional division of Vietnam along the 17th Parallel that was settled at the peace conference in Geneva, attended by delegates from the two Vietnams, alongside representatives of France, Great Britain, the United States, the Soviet Union, and China. In the armistice agreement of July 21, 1954, it was agreed that all French troops should withdraw south of this demarcation line. Two years later, free elections were planned for both parts of the country.

These elections never came about. In June 1954 the Catholic leader Ngo Dinh Diem became prime minister of the State of Vietnam and with American backing forced French troops to withdraw from the whole of the country. He then deposed Bao Dai, appointed himself head of state, and in May 1956 refused to participate in the joint elections, on the grounds that his administration had not signed the Geneva peace accords. This move effectively postponed the reunification of Vietnam indefinitely. As Ho Chi Minh consolidated his grip on power in the North, often using brutal methods to recast the country into a socialist state, Diem's corrupt and authoritarian rule in the South acted as an effective recruiting sergeant for opposition guerrilla units. In September 1960 the Vietnamese Workers' Party voted to widen the military campaign for reunification. Thus, the war in Indochina entered a second phase, which would go down in history as the Vietnam War.

Island Southeast Asia also witnessed a clash between an independence movement, which proclaimed an autonomous republic after the Japanese surrender on August 17, 1945, and a former colonial power, which after the temporary occupation by British forces resumed control over its old domain. But before Dutch troops arrived in the region in March 1946, the government of the Republic of Indonesia under Sukarno had taken over Java, Sumatra, and Madura. After repulsing the first offensives by the Dutch, however, the Republican administration was forced to reach an accommodation with the colonialists in the Linggadjati Agreement of November 15, 1946. The Netherlands agreed to recognize Republican authority over the region so long as the Republic became a constituent state of the United States of Indonesia and formed the Netherlands-Indonesian Union (with the mother country and other former Dutch colonies). This compromise did not last long, either. In July 1947, in response to alleged treaty violations by the Indonesian government, the Dutch launched a bloody police action, occupying most of the cities on Java and a large part of Sumatra.

The Indonesian government was saved only by the intervention of the United Nations. On January 17, 1948, a UN arbitration commission brokered a new settlement, the Renville Agreement, which saw Republican control reduced still further to Central Java and the highlands of Sumatra. The important rice-growing area in West Java, along with the plantations and oil resources on Sumatra, all remained in Dutch hands. Nevertheless, the Netherlands government still pressed for this rump republic to be incorporated within an Indonesian federation. Faced with Sukarno's implacable opposition, the Dutch resumed hostilities in December 1948. Following an assault on the Republican seat of government in Yogyakarta, Sukarno, his deputy Mohammad Hatta, and almost the entire administration were taken into custody.

A decisive factor in the outcome of this conflict was the fact that, unlike in Vietnam, communists did not play a prominent role in the Indonesian independence movement. After the suppression of a revolt at Maidun in East Java in September 1948, in which Indonesian communists were involved, their position had grown even weaker. This helped sway US public opinion in favor of the Indonesian nationalists, and the administration joined the Arab League and Indian subcontinent countries in calling for recognition of Indonesian independence. In the fall of 1949, a threat by Washington to the Netherlands to suspend aid under the Marshall Plan brought about a change of heart in The Hague. On November 2, 1949, the Dutch duly waived all territorial claims in Southeast Asia, with the exception of West Papua (Irian Jaya Barat). Sukarno was able to assert his authority there only in 1963, after mobilizing Indonesian forces for an armed intervention.

On the neighboring Philippines, the United States was itself the colonial power. However, it had already guaranteed the territory independence for July 1, 1946, according to a plan for step-by-step liberation, which it had begun to implement from the mid-1930s onward (albeit while retaining certain economic and military privileges). The United States therefore found itself on the side of the government when a peasants' revolt against the politically dominant major landowners broke out there shortly after independence had been declared. The Huk movement, which grew out of the People's Anti-Japanese Army, was partially supported by the communists but by no means controlled by them. Even so, America's allies on the Philippines chose to regard it as a communist threat.

US support for the regime of President Manuel Roxas was correspondingly robust. Although the Huk gained a strong following in some parts of the country, they were forced to give up military operations in May 1954. This gave the United States a free hand to strengthen its economic influence and its key military bases on the Philippines right up to the late 1980s.

On the Malay Archipelago, it was the British who returned as the colonial power after the Japanese surrender and found themselves faced with demands for independence. The liberation movement was led by the communists, but was confined to the Chinese part of the population. In suppressing the rebellion that broke out in 1948, the British high commissioner could therefore draw on loyal support from indigenous Malay army and police units. After more than half a million Chinese peasants were relocated from guerrilla-controlled regions to "new villages," the rebels were able to operate only in a restricted area along the Thai border. The British invested a great deal in the economic development of the country and withdrew peacefully in 1955 once the rival ethnic groups of Malays, Indians, and nationalist Chinese had agreed to form an electoral coalition. In doing so, the former colonial power ensured that the Federation of Malaya, which gained its independence on August 1, 1957, remained closely tied to Great Britain.

Overall, communism was successful in places where it could help poor peasants improve their wretched conditions, and where its activities were not opposed by an alliance of a local elite with the former colonial power. The Cold War drew the United States deeper into these conflicts than its anticolonial philosophy would otherwise have allowed, causing it to grow into the foremost military and economic sovereign power in the Pacific region. Yet this region never attained anything like the political cohesion of the Atlantic alliance. Countless problems associated with the internal composition of nation-states, plus the continuing antagonism between Japan and its former colonies, meant that when the United States called for a military alliance against "communist aggressors" in the spring of 1954, the only countries to rally to the cause—alongside the Commonwealth countries of Great Britain, Australia, and New Zealand—were the Philippines, Thailand, and Pakistan. As a result, the Southeast Asia Treaty Organization (SEATO), officially established on September 8, 1954, had little political significance.

The Partition of India

The process of decolonization was not restricted to those regions that had once been part of Japan's empire. In the Near and Middle East, South Asia, and Africa as well, the great European powers of Great Britain and France found themselves obliged to wind up their former empires. In Latin America also, there were growing attempts in many quarters to end the region's economic dependence on the United States. As in East and Southeast Asia, detachment from colonial hegemony was inextricably bound up with moves toward modernization and ambitious efforts to forge modern nation-states. Thus, even where these developments were not directly caught up in the East–West standoff, they were still characterized by conflict. And because the former colonial powers and the nationalist modernizers alike displayed varying degrees of shrewdness in their dealings, the outcomes were also very divergent. Many problems therefore arise in trying to reduce the process to some facile formula like the emergence of the Third World or the proliferation of nonaligned nations.

By the end of the war, the transition of India from subjugation under the British Raj into an independent nation had become an urgent and incontrovertible necessity. The arrest of sixty thousand supporters and leaders of the Congress Party for demanding immediate independence in 1942 had achieved nothing except bloody unrest in northern India. There was widespread concern as to how more than two million Indian soldiers, who had been mobilized for service in the British Indian Army, were to be kept under control. But the overriding problem was that Indian manufacturing industry, which had been developed to aid the war effort and was now turning out goods at a far lower cost, was beginning to make inroads into Great Britain's export earnings on global markets, while Britain's reliance on this mass production to prosecute the war had made India into a major creditor of the mother country. British debts to India amounted to one-fifth of the country's gross national product.

The chief problem with independence was that it was completely unclear to which bodies the administration of the various provinces and the plethora of local authorities should be handed over. The Congress Party under the leadership of Jawaharlal Nehru seemed the obvious partner for creating a centralized Indian state that would unify all of the country's diverse racial groups, castes, and religious communities. However, its authority was challenged by the Muslim League led by Muhammad Ali Jinnah, who called for the creation of a separate state for India's Islamic population—a "Land of the Pure," or in his native Urdu, Pakistan. It is conceivable that Jinnah's demand was designed only to ensure equal treatment of Muslim and Hindu states within a loose Indian confederation. But because this notion was wholly incompatible with the Congress Party's plans for a unitary state, in practice independence could be achieved only at the cost of partition.

In March 1947 the British Labour government sent Lord Louis Mountbatten to India as viceroy, with a mandate to bring about the country's independence by August of the following year. After several failed attempts to win Jinnah round to the idea of a single state, Mountbatten opted for a partition along ethnic-religious lines. This meant that Jinnah could secure neither the whole of the province of the Punjab in the northeast nor the southeast province of Bengal in its entirety for Pakistan, but only those districts that had a Muslim majority. The fertile eastern districts of the Punjab and the teeming metropolis of Calcutta (Kolkata) remained within India. In an attempt to forestall upheaval and anarchy, Mountbatten took immediate steps to institute this plan. Agreement was finally reached on June 3, 1947, and on August 15, India and Pakistan were declared independent republics.

Yet bloody clashes between Hindus and Muslims could not be avoided. As early as August 1946 in Calcutta, the Bengali prime minister, Shaheed Suhrawardy, had incited Muslims to purge the city of Hindu workers, through expulsions and murder, in the hope that it would thereby be co-opted into the Muslim state. At the point when independence was proclaimed, however, the charismatic leader (*mahatma*) of the independence movement, Mohandas Gandhi, forced Suhrawardy to spend time with him in a poor quarter of Calcutta and to beg forgiveness for the bloodbath. This action, plus a hunger strike by Gandhi lasting several days, succeeded in largely quelling the unrest in West Bengal. But violence exploded in the Punjab all the more savagely. Hundreds of thousands of Hindus and Sikhs fled to Delhi, where they threatened to take revenge on the city's Muslims. Gandhi rushed to the west to try to stem the tide of violence in Delhi as well. When the interior minister of the Indian government refused to release to the Pakistanis the share of treasury funds proportionate to their population that was owing to them, Gandhi began a new hunger strike. On January 30, 1948, the Mahatma was shot dead by a young Hindu extremist, who claimed his action was justified retribution for Gandhi's supposed high treason.

The exact number of those killed during Partition will never be known, but is estimated at somewhere between 250,000 and 1 million. No fewer than 17 million Indians fled in one direction or the other across the border. Hundreds of thousands of civil servants and railway employees were exchanged, as the manpower and plant belonging to administrative departments were punctiliously divided up. In Kashmir, which as an independent princely state was free to decide which of the two successor countries of the British Raj it would join, armed conflict broke out. When Pakistani irregulars attempted to annex the overwhelmingly Muslim state for Pakistan, the Hindu maharaja asked the Indian government for military assistance and formally declared the state an integral part of the Indian republic. It was only in January 1948 that the United Nations was able to broker a ceasefire. Since then, two-thirds of the territory has been under Indian control.

India under Nehru's stewardship persistently refused to hold the plebiscite in Kashmir that was promised under the UN agreement. In all other respects, though, it did manage to establish a remarkably stable parliamentary system based on a delicate balance of power between individual states and central government. The first nationwide elections, held between October 1951 and February 1952, secured a clear majority for the Congress Party, an outcome repeated time and again until the 1990s. This gave Nehru a mandate to set India on a course of socialist modernization, which yielded some impressive results in the development of heavy industry but made little headway against either the caste system or the country's entrenched power structures. Even so, hundreds of independent princely states were incorporated with virtually no violence into the central state, while the numerous language conflicts were defused by some clever redrawing of state boundaries.

In stark contrast, the successors to Jinnah (who died in September 1948) experienced enormous difficulties in trying to forge a unified state from the two former Muslim-majority regions of India, which lay a thousand miles (1,600 kilometers) apart. The Pakistani leadership comprised both the ruling elite in the Punjab and supporters of the Muslim League who had fled there from southern India; the unrepresented remaining western provinces and Bengal in the far east had no option but to fall in line with this clique's authoritarian directives. Only in 1956 did the constitution of a presidential Islamic Republic of Pakistan come into force. Even then elections were still postponed, not least because the ruling elite feared a Bengali majority. During his term as president (1958 to 1969), General Mohammad Ayub Khan achieved a degree of stability coupled with economic growth. But when in the spring of 1971 the West Pakistani minority tried to block the formation of an elected national assembly, the East Bengalis resolved to secede from the unitary state. The West Pakistan Army took steps to quell the secession but was forced to surrender to Indian troops, who came to the aid of the East Bengalis. On December 16, 1971, the newly independent state of Bangladesh was recognized by Pakistan.

Conflict over Palestine

In the Near and Middle East, the principal European powers found themselves facing awakening Arab nationalism, fueled by the rise of a modern middle class. The nationalist movement opposed both dependence upon the imperialist powers and the traditional elites on whom the Europeans relied to maintain order in the region. Consequently, once formal independence was granted, the European powers were largely unable to sustain any economic and military influence; not infrequently, they were ousted by internal revolts and unrest.

The growth of Arab nationalism was greatly accelerated by the conflict over Palestine, resulting from Great Britain's Balfour Declaration of November 1917, which had promised to support "the establishment in Palestine of a national home for the Jewish people." While the British government attempted to transform its League of Nations–mandated rule over the territory into a binational state for Arabs and Jews, at the end of the Second World War Jewish settlers demanded the immediate formation of their own state. From October 1945 onward, extremists reinforced these demands with a series of attacks against British targets and assassinations in Palestine. In September 1947 the British authorities announced their impending withdrawal from the mandated territory by the following summer. As in the case of India, they hoped to use the prospect of independence to bring about a resolution between the opposing parties.

But under the influence of an effective Zionist lobby, which argued for the urgent need to offer a new homeland to Jewish refugees still remaining in Europe after the Nazi genocide, on November 29, 1947, two-thirds of the UN General Assembly voted in favor of a partition plan that involved the formation of two states in Palestine. The two were to form an economic union, while Jerusalem would be placed within an international zone under UN trusteeship. That same day, fighting broke out between Jewish military units and Palestinian Arab militias, both determined to either prevent the other side from forming its own state or at least expand the boundaries of its own territory.

By the time the last British troops departed on May 14, 1948, without having formally handed the territory over to anybody, Jewish forces were already in a strong position. David Ben-Gurion, chairman of the Jewish National Council, immediately proclaimed the independent state of Israel. This was recognized straight away not only by the United States but also by the USSR, which saw the creation of a Jewish state as a good opportunity to counter the influence of its rival, Great Britain, in the Near East. Soviet arms shipments and military training helped the Jewish fighters establish a modern army and stave off the armed threat facing the fledgling state.

The Palestinian Arabs did receive some support from Arab states. However, their leaders were less concerned with expelling the Jews than they were with limiting the territorial ambitions of their neighbors. As a result, the Israeli army was able to press home its advantage and make extensive territorial gains beyond the areas originally envisaged in the UN Partition Plan. Around one million Arabs were forced out or fled, and over 350 Arab villages destroyed. The first six months of 1949 saw a succession of Arab states sue for peace, beginning with Egypt (February 24), soon followed by Lebanon (March 23), Jordan (April 3), and finally Syria (July 20). The West Bank was left under Jordanian control, and the Gaza Strip was placed under Egyptian jurisdiction. But on four-fifths of the Palestinian territory there now arose a Jewish state, which deliberately refused to integrate those Arabs who had remained. For the most part, displaced Arabs were resettled in temporary camps in neighboring states, often in appallingly squalid conditions. These camps became the breeding ground for the Palestine Liberation Organization (PLO), which in the 1960s would spark a new round of conflict over the future of Palestine.

Arab Self-Determination

Defeat by Israel prompted Arab nationalists to rise up against their traditional rulers. In Syria, which had gained independence following the departure of the last French and British troops on April 14, 1946, a military coup in March 1949 swept away the regime of the old urban elite, which was widely blamed for the debacle in Palestine. Further coups and countercoups followed, from which the Baath Socialist Party (Party of Rebirth) emerged as the country's strongest political grouping. In Jordan, also independent since early 1946, King Abdullah found it difficult to integrate East and West Jordanians and a large influx of Palestinian refugees. In July 1951 Abdullah was assassinated in Jerusalem by a Muslim extremist. His grandson Hussein, who ascended the throne in May 1953 while still a minor, had great difficulty fending off Syrian and Iraqi territorial designs on his country.

In Egypt, discontent with the collaborationist regime erupted in the first months of 1952. The country had been nominally independent since 1922, but in reality the British (in conjunction with the French) still controlled the strategic Suez Canal and maintained an extensive complex of military bases within the so-called Canal Zone. In January 1952, after British troops opened fire on the barracks of a rebellious Egyptian police unit, killing fifty policemen, rioting broke out in Cairo. Farouk gradually lost control of his country. On the night of July 23, 1952, a group of "free officers" under Gamal Abdel Nasser and Anwar Sadat seized power. Farouk was driven into exile, and a respected general, Muhammad Naguib, was installed as prime minister. Two years later Nasser had consolidated his power sufficiently to assume the role of prime minister himself. After a failed assassination attempt, the radical Muslim Brotherhood organization was banned and elections to a constituent assembly were postponed indefinitely.

Negotiations with the British authorities led to an agreement in October 1954 in which the British government undertook to withdraw its forces within twenty months. However, if the Arab states or Turkey were subject to an attack by any country other than Israel (a clear allusion to the Soviet Union), then the British retained the right, up to 1961, to return to their former bases. Through this accord, Nasser hoped to have secured British and American support for his modernization plans. But when in September 1955, fearing an attack by Israel, he signed an agreement on arms shipments with the USSR, the Western powers' reaction was instant and hostile: London and Washington immediately stopped financing construction of the Aswan High Dam, Nasser's flagship civil engineering project, which was intended both to secure Egypt's electricity supplies and to rationalize its agricultural production. In July 1956, Secretary of State John Foster Dulles publicly announced that the United States was withdrawing from the dam project for good.

Nasser countered by announcing that he intended to nationalize the Suez Canal. The revenue from ship transit fees would offset the lost British and American subvention for the Aswan High Dam project. Shareholders in the Canal Company were compensated, and on September 15, 1956, the canal began operating once more, this time under Egyptian management. Under the auspices of the United Nations, where Britain had lodged a formal complaint against the nationalization, a resolution was prepared calling for joint regulation of canal operations by the Egyptians and a conglomerate of the principal user states.

Yet the British and French government had no intention of letting this perceived humiliation stand. As far as they were concerned, Nasser's attempt to style himself as the leader of Arab nationalism threatened Britain's role in the Middle East and undermined France's position in Algeria. And so French prime minister Guy Mollet and his British counterpart, Anthony Eden, agreed to ask the Israelis to spearhead an attack on the Palestinian guerrillas and their Egyptian backers. British and French troops would then intervene in this conflict, ostensibly to separate the warring parties, but in reality in order to retake the Suez Canal Zone and depose Nasser. The Israel Defense Forces (IDF) duly launched their offensive against Egyptian positions on October 29, 1956. Britain and France, as agreed, presented their ultimatums and on October 31 started bombing cities in the Canal Zone.

But just when the two European powers were on the point of taking control of Egypt, US president Dwight D. Eisenhower brought the operation to a grinding halt. For Eisenhower, this attempt at unilateral action by Europe's colonial powers on the eve of the US presidential election was not just extremely insensitive. He was also concerned that the Soviet Union might exploit this situation to parade its credentials as the advocate of oppressed peoples everywhere. Moscow, which was just about to crush the Hungarian Uprising, threatened all parties involved in the conflict that it would deploy its "devastating weapons of mass destruction" unless a ceasefire was agreed upon forthwith. At the instigation of the United States, the UN Security Council therefore passed a resolution on November 6 calling for an immediate ceasefire and the withdrawal of all offensive forces. Eden was the first to comply, leaving Mollet and Ben-Gurion no choice but to follow suit.

This defeat saw Great Britain and France relinquish forever any meaningful role in the Near East. Nasser rose to become the leader of a pan-Arab movement whose influence was felt all across the region and that reached its high-water mark in the formal union of Egypt and Syria on January 2, 1958, in the so-called United Arab Republic. On July 14, 1958, Nasserite sympathizers in the Iraqi military deposed Faisal II, king of Iraq, and established a Baathist regime, which forced the British to withdraw. The Soviet Union, presenting itself as the protector of the nascent Arab states, supplied Egypt, Syria, and Iraq with extensive military hardware and economic aid. In November 1958, Moscow also pledged the bulk of the funds needed to complete the Aswan High Dam. The United States countered by assuming the role of the USSR's main adversary in this region as well, determined at all costs to keep Jordan and Lebanon in the anti-Egyptian camp.

Above all, however, the United States rose to become the protecting power of Israel, which had emerged from the Suez Crisis militarily strengthened but diplomatically totally isolated. Positions in the Gaza Strip from which Palestinian militants had carried out border raids against Israel were destroyed, the Egyptian sea blockade of the Gulf of Aqaba was lifted, and UN peacekeepers were installed in both locations. Yet the grudging respect for Israel's military strength among her Arab neighbors, earned by the IDF's rapid gains in October 1956, could not in itself guarantee peace in the long term. As a result, Israeli democracy became increasingly dependent on US military and economic support.

Support for Israel and for anti-Nasser groups in Lebanon and Jordan went hand in hand with an alliance with conservative-feudal forces in the major oil-producing countries in the region. After a nationalist coalition in Iran had nationalized the Anglo-Iranian Oil Company in 1951 and began to make moves to depose the shah, in August 1953 the CIA helped organize a coup d'état, which overthrew prime minister Mohammad Mosaddegh and rescued the Pahlavi dynasty. The shah collaborated with mainly American companies in exploiting his country's oil wealth; the British now had to make do with a much smaller share. Saud, king of Saudi Arabia, after an initial flirtation with Arab nationalism, also soon found himself reliant upon the United States in quelling revolutionary movements. His brother Faisal, who took over the reins of power in 1958, became the main political and ideological adversary of pan-Arabism. For many years all the profits accruing from oil production in Saudi Arabia were split evenly between the Saudi government and the United States.

Oil also played a part in Algeria, which had been a French colony since the early 1830s. But an even more significant factor here was the large number of French settlers (*pieds-noirs*) who had established themselves as landowners, thereby largely eradicating the country's traditional tribal culture. By the early 1950s, more than eight hundred thousand of Algeria's inhabitants, or around 11 percent of the population, were French. In constitutional terms, the country, which was divided into three *departments*, was an integral part of the French motherland. After their enforced withdrawal from Indochina, the French extricated themselves relatively easily from their protectorates in Tunisia and Morocco after an outbreak of bloody unrest in 1956. By contrast, in Algeria, where a radical faction of the nationalist movement, the Front de Libération Nationale (FLN), under Ahmed Ben Bella embarked on a terror campaign from November 1954 onward, the colonial power responded with unchecked violence. Shocked, the same government of Guy Mollet that had readily granted Tunisia and Morocco independence curtailed an attempt to meet Algerian Muslims' concerns through a program of social reform and equal citizens' rights in the face of furious protests by the *pieds-noirs*. The war escalated into a full-blown French troop deployment against an increasingly strong and daring guerrilla movement, with atrocities committed by both sides.

A solution to the Algerian conflict became a realistic prospect only after de Gaulle was returned to power in France in May 1958; both the terrified settlers and the impotent advocates for granting Algeria its independence hailed him as a savior. After repeated failed attempts at ending the fighting by offering concessions to the Liberation Front, in January 1961 the founder of the Fifth Republic organized a referendum, which gave him a clear mandate to begin pulling French forces out of Algeria. Against the backdrop of a failed coup by rebel generals and attacks on prominent supporters of independence (de Gaulle himself was the target of two assassination attempts), the negotiations finally led to the signing of an independence agreement at Evian on March 18, 1962. France secured oil concessions, the right to conduct nuclear tests in the Algerian Sahara, and continuing use of the naval base at Mers-el-Kébir; however, hundreds of thousands of French Algerian settlers fled the country for fear of reprisals.

Disaster in Sub-Saharan Africa

Compared with Southeast Asia and the Arab countries, the mainsprings of modern nationalism—export-driven agriculture, trade networks, and industrial growth—were still largely undeveloped in sub-Saharan Africa at the end of the Second World War. The governments in London and Paris therefore believed that the way forward lay in "development through partnership." By this, they meant modernization through exploitation of the continent's abundant raw material resources, which would at the same time help foster economic recovery in the exhausted mother countries. An integral part of this modernization would be the creation of new African elites, to whom responsibility and power would gradually devolve. But in what ultimate measure this would occur remained unclear; most of those charged with implementing this program envisaged it as a long-term process of thirty years or more.

However, this concept bore only modest fruit in countries dominated by rural societies and where European interests were limited to trade: notably in certain regions of West Africa. For example, in the Gold Coast, long held up as a model colony, the British introduced a legislative assembly as early as 1946; on January 1, 1951, they put a constitution in place that held out the prospect of limited joint governance by an elected assembly. The election winner, Kwame Nkrumah, achieved internal autonomy with a purely African cabinet in 1954, and after being reelected in 1956 won full independence. The new state of Ghana came into being on March 1, 1957; separatist movements advocating different state boundaries had to concede defeat in the face of Nkrumah's overwhelming majority in the former British colony.

The French government reacted in similar fashion to the rise in their colony of Côte d'Ivoire (Ivory Coast) of the *Rassemblement Démocratique Africain* (RDA; African Democratic Assembly) under Félix Houphouët-Boigny, a prosperous

In Ghana, Kwame Nkrumah achieved internal autonomy with a purely African cabinet in 1954 and, after being reelected in 1956, won full independence for his country. The new state was one of the rare cases where the British concept of "development through partnership" bore fruit. (© Bettmann/CORBIS)

cocoa farmer. Suppressed at first, the RDA was given free rein to campaign by the French from July 1950 onward in return for agreeing that the Ivory Coast would join a commonwealth of former colonies within the planned French Union. In January 1956, Houphouët-Boigny became a minister in the Mollet cabinet. With his assistance, the French National Assembly passed a framework law for overseas territories on July 23, 1956, which put in place national assemblies based on universal suffrage in all of France's African territories and announced increasing governmental responsibility for the executive councils elected to serve in these assemblies. Accordingly, Côte d'Ivoire became an autonomous republic within the French Community on December 4, 1958, with Houphouët-Boigny as prime minister.

But in the neighboring territory of Guinea, the concept of mutually beneficial evolution ran aground. Guinea was rich in resources, such as bauxite, gold, and diamonds, that the French were still keen to exploit. So here the French were far less prepared to make concessions, which in turn made opposition to their rule, by a working-class independence movement, all the more militant. In a French Union referendum, the movement's leader, Ahmed Sékou Touré, pushed for a No vote, which was duly delivered, and Guinea, alone among France's African colonies, achieved full independence without becoming part of the French Community, on October 2, 1958. This clean break spelled the end of all financial and other support from the mother country. The former colonial masters even took the telephones with them when they left.

What had been designed as a deterrent sanction had precisely the opposite effect, as all other executive councils now clamored for full independence. De Gaulle, who was preoccupied with the Algeria question, granted it without any regard for individual countries' level of development or the territorial configuration of the frequently fragmented colonial possessions, which took no account of economic links or ethnic differences. By September 1960, fourteen French colonial territories in Africa were transformed into formally independent states. Even Houphouët-Boigny, fearful of being sidelined by more radical forces, jumped on the full-independence bandwagon. Admittedly these countries remained heavily dependent on France in economic terms; the only difference was that French firms now had to compete with other Western countries' representatives in the exploitation of raw material resources.

In eastern and southern Africa, the stronger presence of white settlers had the effect of driving the strategy of "development through partnership" into the realms of the absurd. British settlers in Kenya, Uganda, Tanganyika, and Rhodesia put up such stubborn resistance to London's attempts to grant equal voting rights to the majority black population that the nationalist movements in these colonies, inspired by France's capitulation, also began to press for full independence. The first to achieve his goal was Julius Nyerere in Tanganyika in May 1961. In October 1962 it was Uganda's turn, with Milton Obote as prime minister, followed by Kenya (Jomo Kenyatta, December 1963), Nyasaland, henceforth known as Malawi, under Hastings Banda in May 1964, and finally Northern Rhodesia, as the Republic of Zambia, under Kenneth Kaunda in October 1964. In November 1965, Southern Rhodesia, which in 1923 had become a self-governing British crown colony run by white settlers, proclaimed its Unilateral Declaration of Independence (UDI), thereby cementing white supremacy and thwarting any chance of independence under black majority rule. Negotiations with the British government over democratization and the lifting of sanctions went on until 1980.

Yet although Britain took more seriously than France did its responsibilities for the development of the peoples it had colonized, such considerations did not figure at all for the smaller European powers. Portugal responded to liberation movements in its colonies of Angola, Mozambique, and Guinea-Bissau with military crackdowns; only after the dictatorship in Portugal was toppled in the 1974 Carnation Revolution did disengagement from the colonies become a reality. Belgium, which had combined its development of mining and the industrial sector in the Congo with a strict ban on any political activity, reacted to an outbreak of serious unrest in the capital, Leopoldville, in January 1959 by announcing the earliest possible transition to independence. This was duly granted on June 30, 1960. After Europeans left the country in droves and the administrative infrastructure collapsed, armed conflict broke out over the secession of the provinces of Katanga and Kasai, along with violent power struggles among the central government leadership. The fighting finally came to an end with the establishment of a repressive military dictatorship by General Joseph Mobutu in November 1965. In 1962, Belgium also granted Rwanda and Burundi their independence, without having first addressed the long-standing problem of deep animosity between the Hutu and Tutsi people in these territories.

Therefore, the price that had to be paid for swift decolonization was a vicious circle of economic stagnation and renewed repression. Only very rarely did self-supporting economic development get under way in the newly developed states. A far more common situation was an unholy alliance between a regional plutocracy and European concerns who continued to exercise a stranglehold over the country's commerce, mining, and manufacturing industries. With progress largely bypassing the indigenous population, then, sub-Saharan Africa degenerated into a Fourth World, lacking any long-term positive economic prospects.

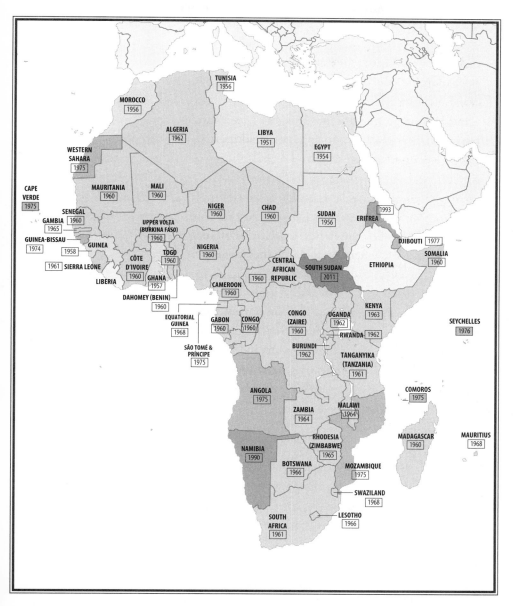

The rise of independent states in Africa, 1945–2012.

US Intervention in Latin America

Compared to Africa, the nations of Central and South America were well advanced on the road of postcolonial development. But during the first half of the twentieth century, the neighboring United States rose to become the region's principal foreign investor, bringing the States into a strategic alliance with domestic economic elites in those countries. So long as the people who found themselves disadvantaged in this scheme of things—subsistence farmers, factory workers, and other members of the lower classes—sought their salvation in corporatist regimes—say, in Mexico and Brazil, but above all in Peronist Argentina—the United States saw no reason for direct intervention. After Mexico and Brazil nationalized the oil companies, the United States merely responded by boycotting exports. And when a workers' and peasants' revolutionary movement seized power in Bolivia in 1952, the Eisenhower administration even supported the new regime with food and economic aid. Its gamble that this would strengthen moderate elements within the Bolivian government paid off.

But as soon as Latin American revolutionaries made common cause with communists, the United States adopted a hard line against them. This first occurred in Guatemala in June 1952, when President Jacobo Árbenz Guzmán, with the support of the country's small but increasingly influential Communist Party, began expropriating and redistributing uncultivated farmland. The main victim of these expropriations was the United Fruit Company, a powerful American concern that had long controlled Guatemala's whole economy through its extensive banana plantations. The condemnation by its owners of the land reforms as a Soviet bid to seize power prompted Eisenhower to order the CIA to destabilize and bring down the Árbenz regime. And so, in June 1954 the CIA launched an "invasion" by hundreds of expatriate guerrillas from neighboring Honduras; CIA aircraft bombed Guatemala City and other urban centers. The majority of army officers promptly defected from the Árbenz government; the president was forced to flee, and the new military junta that took his place drove the peasants off their newly acquired land.

The US reaction was the same when Fidel Castro came to power in Cuba in early 1959, after a bitterly fought guerrilla campaign that had lasted more than two years, and immediately instituted a land reform that threatened American sugar plantations on the island. Castro was no communist, but in the struggle to control the revolutionary regime, he came increasingly to rely on the support of the Communist Party, the only mass-membership political organization on Cuba. In February 1960 he concluded a trade agreement with the Soviet Union that was intended to break the American stranglehold over the sugar export market. In Eisenhower's eyes, this was enough to brand him as the ringleader of a revolutionary movement that threatened to engulf the whole of Latin America. The president therefore detailed the CIA to prepare an invasion on the Guatemalan model. When Castro went on to nationalize the most important US concerns on the island, Congress restricted sugar imports and placed a partial embargo on all trade with Cuba. In February 1962 this was extended to cover all imports.

The invasion plan was executed by Eisenhower's successor, John F. Kennedy, in April 1961. Unlike in Guatemala, however, the fourteen hundred Cuban exiles, armed and trained by the CIA, failed in their mission. Castro had completely reorganized the Cuban army and also took the precaution of jailing one hundred thousand political opponents. As a result, there was no popular uprising against Castro, and the hapless invaders were forced to surrender after three days. Far from toppling Castro, the Bay of Pigs fiasco only succeeded in strengthening his position. Encouraged by the example of the Cuban revolution, revolutionary activists now began guerrilla campaigns in several Latin American countries. In time these were all put down by police and military units that had been trained in counterinsurgency techniques by American security experts and that were also funded in part through US military aid programs. Even so, the threat remained, and the United States fell into disrepute for filling the vacuum left by the demise of European imperialism with its own brand of superpower hegemony.

2. *A Global Cold War*

THE superpowers' interpretation of decolonization within the broader picture of the Cold War lent further impetus to the formation of blocs in Europe. The institutions that were created in 1949 were initially only of a provisional nature. Neither the Truman administration nor the American public regarded the North Atlantic Treaty as laying the foundation for a lasting American military presence in Europe; rather, they fully expected US troops to come home immediately after the specified term of occupation was over in Germany and Austria. The constitution of the Federal Republic of Germany was quite expressly conceived as a Basic Law, which was designed to impart "a new sense of order" to affairs of state in West Germany "during a transitional period."[17] Likewise, the GDR was, in Stalin's eyes, just a first—and by no means voluntary—step on the path toward a "peace-loving, democratic Germany."[18] In the telegram of congratulation he sent to the leaders of the new state, there was no mention of socialism in Germany.

Naturally, over time these provisional arrangements began to take on an air of permanence. But just as the division of Europe threatened to become a lasting reality, resistance against the idea made itself felt in many quarters. A vehement debate arose over the formation of blocs within Europe, whose outcome became clear only in the mid-1950s.

NATO and the European Defence Community

On the American side, it was the successful testing of the first Soviet atom bomb on August 29, 1949, that triggered a change of attitude. Up to that point the Truman administration had banked on America's monopoly in nuclear weapons lasting for many years and so took the view that it could afford to scale down the nation's conventional arsenal. Strategic planning for the eventuality of a Soviet attack on Western Europe (which was considered highly unlikely) envisaged the withdrawal of US troops to the Atlantic coast, followed by a massive air offensive against the invading forces. But now there could be no fallback on nuclear superiority, while the communist victory in China also suggested that containment through economic means alone, as was being practiced in the Marshall Plan, was not enough. A memorandum (NSC-68) issued by the National Security Council on April 7, 1950—primarily the work of Secretary of State Dean Acheson and his director of policy planning, Paul Nitze—therefore urged that the communist "design for world domination" be checked by building up US military superiority. To this end, the memo argued, an effective organization for Western defense needed to be created, plus defense spending increased by a factor of four to five times the current level.[19]

Logic dictated that the creation of an effective defense organization for the West necessarily entailed deploying German troops. After all, the Federal Republic was in the most exposed position, right on the front line of the West's defenses. It was therefore inconceivable to leave it defenseless or to ignore the contribution it could make to its own security. But because rearming Germany raised the specter of a revival of aggressive German nationalism, at first there was a considerable reluctance to address this aspect of the program to upgrade Europe's defensive capability. Proponents of rearming the Federal Republic were able to go over to the offensive only after the North Korean attack on South Korea suddenly made far more plausible the scenario of East German communists launching an offensive against West Germany. On August 29, 1950, Federal Chancellor Konrad Adenauer offered to make "a contribution in the form of a German contingent in the event of an international Western European army being created."[20] Two weeks later, Acheson called on the British and the French governments not only to increase their defense budgets, but also to throw their weight behind the raising of around ten divisions of German troops. Only if these conditions were met would the US government be prepared to strengthen its own military contingent in Europe and assume overall command of the Joints Chiefs of Staff of the North Atlantic Treaty Organization (NATO).

The French government responded to this blackmail by putting forward its own suggestion of a European Defence Community. If the deployment of German troops was inevitable, then at least this force should be under the control of a joint West European High Command rather than the Federal German government. Therefore, as prime minister René Pleven explained on October 24, 1950, France proposed the creation of a European army, answerable to a European defense minister, and comprising various national contingents "on the basis of the smallest practicable unit."[21] This meant that there would be no German General Staff; instead, existing European armed forces would be involved in the new organization only as far as was necessary for the defense of Europe. The defense of European interests in overseas territories was to remain the preserve of individual countries.

Of course, such discrimination against the Germans within a Western defense community was wholly untenable within Germany, and Adenauer rejected the plan out of hand. On the contrary, he wanted to use the need for German troops as leverage to try to break the shackles of the occupation statute that the victorious Western powers had imposed on the young West German state. Likewise, the governments in Washington and London also considered the French suggestion a complete nonstarter—politically unviable and utterly absurd in military terms. Faced with the danger of US troops being withdrawn from Germany to bolster the war effort in Korea, the French government therefore agreed in principle on December 6 to the deployment of German troops within the context of NATO; at this stage, the precise form the German contribution would take was still undecided. In return, on December 18–19, at a meeting in Brussels, the ministerial council of the North Atlantic Treaty voted to create an integrated NATO force. General Dwight D. Eisenhower, the legendary supreme commander of the Allied Expeditionary Force in the Second World War, was named its first commander in chief.

Long, drawn-out negotiations finally brought agreement over the exact form of the West German contribution to NATO. In mid-1951, Acheson reached the conclusion that the idea could not be sold in France unless it was presented in terms of an integrated European solution. In return, though, the French foreign minister, Robert Schuman, would have to accept that the Germans must be accorded the same rights within the European army as all other member states. The European Defence Community (EDC) Treaty, which was signed in Paris on May 27, 1952, by representatives from France, the Federal Republic of Germany, Italy, Belgium, the Netherlands, and Luxembourg, made all resolutions contingent upon a unanimous vote by the ministerial council. The troops were to be integrated at division level, and the Federal Republic was to have its own Ministry of Defense. For the time being, at least, the Federal Republic was not made a full member of NATO, though the Federal Republic government was granted the right to call joint sessions of the EDC ministerial council and the NATO council. The Convention on Relations between the Three Powers and the Federal Republic, concluded in Bonn on May 26, 1952, also anticipated the ending of the occupation statute. At the same time, however, the Western powers retained all rights relating to "Germany as a whole" and banned Germany from manufacturing strategic arms for the foreseeable future.

The Korean War and the readiness of the Europeans to reach compromises in the interest of their own security helped steer the ambitious rearmament program embodied in the NSC-68 memorandum through Congress. It approved not only the increase in US troop numbers in Europe (from two to six divisions), plus new military aid for America's European allies, but also the development of the hydrogen bomb (subsequently tested successfully for the first time in November 1952) and the expansion of the US Army from 1.5 to 3.5 million men. From $13 billion in 1950, the US defense budget increased to over $50 billion by 1953, while the share of defense spending as a proportion of GNP rose from 5 to 13 percent. The United States thus became the overwhelmingly dominant military power within the Western alliance.

Soviet Offers

Stalin reacted to the West's move to rearm, and to the militarization of West Germany, by instituting his own rearmament program. Certainly, as long as US troops were engaged in Korea, he considered an attack by the West on Soviet positions in Europe unlikely, but he seriously entertained the possibility of such an attack in the period thereafter. Accordingly, at a planning meeting in Moscow in the second week in January 1951, Communist Party leaders and defense ministers from the Eastern European peoples' democracies were enrolled into a coordinated rearmament program, which was designed to bring their combined troop strength up to three million men by the end of 1953. Plans to develop a

Soviet hydrogen bomb were also fast-tracked; the first successful test of this weapon took place in August 1953, just ten months after the detonation of the American device.

At the same time, Stalin renewed his efforts to restart negotiations on a peace treaty with West Germany, which would at least dispel the danger of its potential military might being added to the West's arsenal. In November 1950, the Soviet government called for a new conference of the Allied Council of Foreign Ministers to be convened; in February 1951 the Kremlin began work on a draft treaty for presentation at this meeting. But Acheson refused point-blank to discuss the German question until the decision to deploy West German troops had been implemented. In response Moscow decided to go public with the basic provisions contained in the Soviet peace plan, in the hope that this would spur "public opinion to exert strong pressure on both the parliaments and governments,"[22] both in West Germany and elsewhere in the Western alliance, thereby persuading the politicians to agree to a German peace treaty after all. So, on March 10, 1952, the Kremlin published all its memoranda on this subject to Western governments. These held out to the Germans the prospect of an end to the occupation and the withdrawal of all occupying forces, albeit in return for West Germany agreeing not to enter into an alliance that clearly had hostile intent toward one of the victorious powers.[23]

However, the Soviet attempt to mobilize West German and international opinion in favor of a neutral Germany failed miserably. In their reply, the Western powers called for free elections throughout the whole of Germany with no precondition of neutrality. Stalin's reaction was to include the GDR in his rearmament program; SED general secretary Walter Ulbricht was given the green light to "proceed at full speed toward socialism." After Stalin's death on March 5, 1953, his successors tried to revive the idea of a peace treaty. Lavrentiy Beria went farther than Stalin in emphasizing that a unified Germany "would take the form of a bourgeois-democratic republic,"[24] and he instructed the SED leadership to halt their drive toward socialism. This sparked a flurry of discussion and intrigue within the SED Politburo, which culminated on June 24, 1953, in a recommendation to depose Ulbricht.

Hopes that an agreement might indeed be reached on a peace treaty with Germany were boosted by the fact that Winston Churchill, reelected as British prime minister in 1951, now believed the time was ripe for an accord with the Soviet Union. In a speech in the House of Commons on May 11, 1953, he called for an urgent summit, at which the Soviets should be given cast-iron assurance that neither Germany nor the Western powers would attack them. As he explained to his colleague Pierson Dixon, one sure signal of the West's good faith would be to create a "reunified and neutralized Germany."[25]

The June 17 Uprising

However, moves to reach an understanding on the German question, which ran counter to the general trend toward bloc building, were thwarted by two events. First, the glaring contrast between the announcement of a "new" direction in the GDR, geared toward reunification, and the leadership's insistence on raising the work norms in the country led, on June 16, to a street protest by construction workers in East Berlin, which expanded into a nationwide revolt the next day. Beria declared a state of emergency and sent in Soviet tanks to confront the protesters. The crushing of the uprising against the SED regime cost fifty-one lives—enough to inflame public opinion throughout the West and put advocates of a neutral Germany on the back foot. By mid-July, Adenauer met with no opposition among his Western allies when he suggested that, the next time a Four-Power Conference was held, there should be an a priori insistence on free elections throughout Germany and unrestricted freedom of action for any pan-German administration. There was no longer any talk of Churchill's guarantees to the Soviets.

On June 26, Beria was arrested; he was executed six months later. Yet his rivals in the Presidium of the Supreme Soviet, who wanted to preempt their own fall from grace, pursued fundamentally Beria's course on the German question and with regard to détente with the West; yet they were much more naive in their grasp of political realities in Germany than their deposed comrade, and acted far less flexibly and consistently than he had. At the beginning of July, Foreign Minister Vyacheslav Molotov resolved to stop Ulbricht from being toppled. On July 18, Ulbricht's opponents lost their majority in the SED Politburo, and eight days later the Central Committee voted for their expulsion. The party line in the GDR swung once more toward the "implementation of socialism."

When on August 15 the Soviet leadership put forward the suggestion—already mooted under Beria—of allowing a provisional all-German government to organize elections to a constituent National Assembly, there was no further mention of Beria's plan for a simultaneous withdrawal of the occupation forces. Instead it was envisaged that the administrations of the two divided states should remain in office until a new constitution for the whole of Germany had been passed. This sounded like a hedge against the eventuality that the elections might not turn out as the Soviets wished and took most of the shine off the proposal. But when the Council of Foreign Ministers of the Four Powers met in Berlin on January 25, 1954, after much diplomatic wrangling Molotov appeared more flexible, floating the idea that only small contingents of troops responsible for "control duties" would remain stationed in Germany until the peace treaty came into force.

However, this concession was not enough to mobilize significant support for the idea of a neutral Germany. Churchill's demand that the Soviets be offered security guarantees now seemed hopelessly out of step with current thinking. Rather, the representatives of the Western powers at the Berlin conference demanded that a commission for overseeing the elections be allowed to adjudicate on a majority basis and that any future pan-German government should have the right to form alliances with other states "for peaceful purposes." The intention behind this was to preserve the European Defence Community after reunification and to incorporate the GDR into its realm of jurisdiction. No one was surprised that Molotov rejected this proposal. Indeed, Western negotiating tactics were aimed precisely at ensuring that this conference would fail, thus paving the way for final ratification of the EDC Treaty.

Conversely, Molotov's proposal for a European treaty on collective security found little resonance among his Western counterparts. As long as reunification had not yet taken place, it provided that the two existing German states should both be signatories. By contrast, the United States was accorded only observer status, along with China as the final permanent member of the UN Security Council. This remained unacceptable to Western governments even when Molotov conceded that the creation of such a security pact need not entail the dissolution of NATO. The Berlin Conference ended on February 18, 1954, with no progress whatever achieved on the German question. At the end of March the

Kremlin followed up with a memorandum in which it conceded that the United States could participate on an equal footing in a European collective security system, and also proposed that the Soviet Union might become part of NATO. But these belated suggestions failed to deflect the Western powers from their determination to integrate the Federal Republic into a Western alliance.

The Failure of the EDC

Ultimately the Soviet leadership scored just one success with all their offers and initiatives: the collapse of the European Defence Community project. In particular, the notion of a European treaty on collective security raised such great hopes in France for a rapprochement between East and West—a potential way out of the invidious position of having to both sacrifice its own sovereignty and accept German rearmament—that the American government's insistence at the same time that the EDC treaty be ratified became counterproductive. As such, no parliamentary majority could be found to approve the treaty. A rapid succession of administrations in Paris kept putting off ratification and urging their allies to make further concessions that would increase the chances of the National Assembly passing the legislation; however, these pleas fell on deaf ears.

On August 30, 1954, French prime minister Pierre Mendès France finally put the treaty to the vote, without risking his own future by lobbying for a positive outcome. As expected, the treaty was resoundingly rejected. By a majority of 319 to 264, the delegates declined even to enter into discussion of the EDC pact. Adenauer and his American allies were outraged at this humiliating snub, while Moscow believed that it was finally close to the long-awaited breakthrough.

Yet the Soviets' euphoria was short-lived. Faced with the danger of a complete collapse of the Western security system, all the Western allies suddenly found themselves prepared to make concessions that they had previously avoided. Mendès France accepted without demur the Federal Republic's immediate entry into NATO. Churchill's successor, Anthony Eden, voted in favor of including West Germany and Italy in the Treaty of Brussels (the modified treaty led to the formation of the Western European Union). US secretary of state John Foster Dulles announced that he was in a position to increase the American military presence in Europe. Adenauer stressed his country's renunciation of all atomic, biological, and chemical weapons production, and also signed the Saar Statute, which recognized the Saarland's continuing economic ties to France until such time as a peace treaty was concluded. On October 23, 1954, the Western foreign ministers signed the Paris Agreements, which set out the terms for resolution of all these issues.

The Kremlin redoubled its diplomatic efforts to block Western integration of the Federal Republic, once again sending out signals that it was prepared to make concessions in all the contentious matters concerning the mechanism for a peace treaty and in the establishment of a collective security system. This charm offensive was at its most effective in March 1955, when the Soviets agreed not to make their withdrawal of their troops from Austria contingent any longer upon signature of a peace treaty with Germany. With the Austrian government making its own unilateral offer of a state of armed neutrality, it proved possible to conclude an Austrian State Treaty in no time, which was duly signed on May 15, 1955, in Vienna. Soviet troops began withdrawing from the east of the country, and the Soviet media was only too keen to emphasize that the same thing could also happen in Germany. At the beginning of June, Adenauer was invited to Moscow to inaugurate diplomatic relations, which, as the invitation expressly stated, would help "restore the unity of a German democratic state."[26]

Yet none of this made any real inroads with the majority of people in favor of an integration of the Federal Republic with the West. A general strike in protest at the Paris Agreements, called by the pro-unification, anti-bloc Paulskirche movement, never came to anything. On February 27 the Bundestag ratified the Paris Agreements by a clear majority. Exactly a month later the upper chamber of the French National Assembly also ratified them. The Agreements entered into force on May 5, 1955. Four days later, delegates from the Federal Republic government took part in a meeting of the NATO ministerial council. In November 1955 the first volunteers moved into the barracks of the newly formed Bundeswehr (federal army). Two more years would elapse before a large influx of conscripts doing compulsory military service swelled the ranks.

After all attempts to prevent the Federal Republic from being incorporated into NATO had proved fruitless, Nikita Khrushchev, the new strongman in the Soviet Presidium, steered the Kremlin's European policies increasingly toward stabilizing the SED's rule in the German Democratic Republic. When the leaders of the Eastern Bloc met in Warsaw on May 14, 1955, to conclude a Treaty of Friendship, Cooperation and Mutual Assistance, the prime minister of the GDR was also present, and the country, albeit initially only with observer status, was incorporated into the Warsaw Pact organization. Following a series of futile soundings during the July 1955 summit in Geneva, Khrushchev announced at a rally in East Berlin that "the German question cannot be solved at the cost of the interests of the German Democratic Republic" and that it was out of the question to "set aside all its many social and political achievements."[27] Two months later, on September 20, 1955, the USSR signed a treaty with the GDR on mutual relations, which proclaimed the GDR "free to decide on matters of its own internal and foreign policy," subject to the provisions of the Four-Power Agreements governing "Germany as a whole." At the start of 1956 the National People's Army (Nationale Volksarmee; NVA) was formed from units of the Barracked People's Police. Its integration into the military organization of the Warsaw Pact under Soviet overall command, decided by the committee of signatory nations on January 28, 1956, concluded the formation of a military bloc in the East.

The Spirit of Geneva

Despite the fears voiced by advocates of neutrality in both the East and the West, the completion of the bloc-building process did not result in a sudden increase in tension. Rather—given that expansion of its own sphere of influence was not on the immediate agenda of either the Western alliance or Moscow—it lent impetus to efforts to reach an accommodation on the basis of the existing status quo. A series of test explosions of H-bombs in the spring of 1954, which brought home vividly to both sides the very real danger of humankind annihilating itself, served to sharpen this pragmatic approach. Ten years after the end of the Second World War, a sense of relief on either side that its own camp had been consolidated and concern to avoid a nuclear conflict combined to create a new dialogue that transcended the frontiers of the two blocs.

This first became apparent at the Geneva Summit of July 18–23, 1955, which the Western powers agreed to hold following the signing of the Austrian State Treaty. At this meeting the Soviets put forward a disarmament plan that would entail transferring inspection of nuclear arms production, with no right of veto, to a UN agency and would impose identical upper limits on conventional arms stocks on both sides. Eisenhower, who had replaced Truman in the White House in January 1953, was not yet ready to sign on to such an ambitious plan, which ran counter to his concept of nuclear deterrence as a way of offsetting a shortfall in conventional capability. However, as a first practical step he did suggest an open-skies policy on reconnaissance overflights and a free exchange of information on military installations. Both sides agreed to continue dialogue on disarmament measures. As Khrushchev remarked, Geneva demonstrated "that there was no prewar situation in existence at that time and that our enemies were afraid of us in the same way as we were of them."[28]

The Kremlin's offer to establish diplomatic relations with the Federal Republic of Germany also helped further the goal of an understanding on the basis of the status quo. For Adenauer, this was an ambivalent offer: on the one hand, he must have been interested in opening up a direct line to Moscow, but on the other, it risked undermining his claim to speak on behalf of the Germans in the GDR as well. But the Soviet leadership's pledge to release the last ten thousand German prisoners of war who had been sentenced to hard labor in gulags, made during his visit to Moscow on September 9–13, 1955, forced his hand. Thereafter West German diplomacy sought to limit the damage caused by the Soviet Union's recognition of two German states, threatening any other states that recognized the GDR with "serious consequences," including as a last sanction the severing of diplomatic ties. Furthermore, the Federal Republic refused to maintain diplomatic relations with those Eastern Bloc countries that had already recognized the GDR. Although this so-called Hallstein Doctrine (named for Adenauer's secretary of state for foreign affairs) helped isolate the GDR internationally, it also proved a stumbling block to all attempts at healing the division of Germany.

In the context of a mutual nuclear threat, the "policy of liberation" toward Eastern Europe, which Dulles had raised during the US presidential election campaign as a counterpart to Adenauer's reunification concept, turned out to be nothing but rhetoric. When an uprising broke out in Hungary on October 23, 1956, against the country's Stalinist regime, Dulles was at pains to stress that the United States did not look upon Moscow's satellites as "potential military allies."[29] Nonetheless, the new reformist Communist prime minister, Imre Nagy, announced that Hungary would institute multiparty democracy and leave the Warsaw Pact.

Men remove a pile of smoking rubble from a street during the 1956 anticommunist uprising in Hungary. Impelled both by fear for his position and by real concern that the Eastern Bloc might begin to unravel, Nikita Khrushchev let Soviet troops crush the uprising against the country's Stalinist regime. (© Hilton-Deutsch Collection/CORBIS)

On October 31, impelled both by fear for his own position and real concern that the Eastern Bloc might begin to unravel, Khrushchev ordered Soviet troops into Hungary to crush the uprising. On November 4 they began their assault on Budapest; by November 10 they had managed to put down bitter resistance throughout the country. The Eisenhower administration confined itself to submitting resolutions protesting the Soviet action to the UN General Assembly.

·[83]·

In this way, the system of nuclear "mutually assured destruction" conspired to keep communist functionaries in power in Eastern Bloc countries and to cement the Soviet Union's dominance over its allies. No sooner had it been created than the Warsaw Pact proved itself an instrument for safeguarding this hegemony, not just against external threats, but much more so against liberation movements within its own camp. But at the very least, from the time the Hungarian Uprising was crushed, in the West the Soviet model lost much of the appeal that it had once held for the labor movement and for intellectual critics of the capitalist system. The brutal measures enacted to ensure the continuance of communist rule stood in glaring contrast to the West's success in fostering economic recovery and stabilizing popular democracies throughout Western Europe.

European Unification

The failure of the European Defence Community did not spell an end to efforts to unify Europe. These had begun long before the Cold War and were not solely aimed at strengthening the West in its conflict with the Soviet Bloc. The prime mover behind the European unification movement, which had its origins in democratic resistance (including exiled parliamentarians) during the Second World War, was ensuring peace on the continent. Another major concern was to create a larger economic region that would allow European countries to compete with the economic superpower of the United States. Together these two factors led to the conviction that only lasting cooperation and economic integration among Europeans (and the prosperity that flowed from this) would create a firmer bedrock for democracy in Europe than had been achieved after the First World War. This was especially true of Germany: only integration of the Germans into a strong European community could ensure that Germany would no longer pose a threat to its neighbors. And finally, a unified Europe might also help stave off the risk of a one-sided dependence upon either of the two main victorious powers, the United States and the USSR.

The European unification movement was a continent-wide movement. The first agreement on forming a confederation in the postwar world was signed on January 15, 1942, between the Greek and Yugoslavian governments in exile. One week later came a similar accord between the exiled governments of Poland and

Czechoslovakia. On September 5, 1944, the governments of Belgium, the Netherlands, and Luxembourg agreed to establish a customs union (Benelux), which would come into force on January 1, 1948. Once Stalin had forbidden Eastern European governments from taking part in the Marshall Plan, planning and discussion on questions of unification could be realized only in Western Europe. The decisive first step was taken by the French government when, in July 1948, it put forward the idea of a European Parliamentary Assembly, which would form "the core of a European federal organization."[30] If the establishment of a West German state was inevitable, then it should at least be brought within the control of a European community.

Yet because, right from the outset, most continental Europeans were keen to include the British within this European community, but the British were reluctant to accede to the jurisdiction of any supranational authority, the French initiative led only, in the first instance, to the creation of the Council of Europe. But the French foreign minister, Robert Schuman, was not prepared to let the matter rest there. In signaling his willingness (in the Declaration of May 9, 1950) to create the European Coal and Steel Community, which would bring these key industries of the time under a single regulating authority, he effectively forced the British there and then to decide for or against participation in a supranational Europe. As widely anticipated, the British voted against. Accordingly, the only signatories to the treaty establishing the European Coal and Steel Community (ECSC) were France, the Federal Republic of Germany, Italy, Belgium, the Netherlands, and Luxembourg. The treaty's entry into force on July 23, 1952, marked the beginning of the supranational Inner Six. A High Authority of the ECSC, which was installed in Luxembourg under the presidency of Jean Monnet, henceforth saw to it that the reconstruction and modernization of European heavy industry neither led to a new German dominance nor disadvantaged the employees who were engaged in it.

Avid supporters of the idea of an integrated Europe tried to salvage the treaty on the European Defence Community by supplementing it with a European Political Community. For the Italian prime minister, Alcide de Gasperi, the establishment of a supranational authority with the power to rule on matters of foreign policy and defense was a necessary prerequisite for the foundation of a European army; the plan also found favor with many people in France as a way of permanently dispelling any danger of Germany going it alone. In September 1952 the parliamentary assembly of the ECSC was tasked with producing a draft treaty for the creation of a Political Community. However, the project became bogged down in negotiations over the form the new government commission should take: the Netherlands would agree to participate in a Political Community only on the condition that the Inner Six formed a common market at the same time. Yet the French were opposed to this idea, because they thought their economy was not yet sufficiently competitive.

The rejection of the EDC by the French Assembly on August 30, 1954, also cut the ground from under the feet of the European Political Community (EPC), a full draft of which had been prepared in the interim. In the search for alternatives that would carry on the European project beyond the ECSC, Jean Monnet's next move was to propose that a European Atomic Energy Community be established. This would be a vital step if France and the other European nations were to keep abreast of the technological change, while also being more achievable than any economic or political union. National atomic authorities had not had a chance to develop yet, meaning that there were no existing lobbies to form a common front against the formation of another supranational authority. But the Dutch foreign minister, Johan Willem Beyen, once more raised the question of a common market, which was especially important in regard to his country's exports to Germany. Restricting integration to just a few areas of commercial activity like coal and steel or the nuclear industry seemed to him to be economically counterproductive.

Hence, real progress in achieving unity among the Inner Six could be made only by agreeing to a bilateral approach: the creation of an Atomic Energy Community and an Economic Community. The first step toward a compromise came when the Inner Six's foreign ministers passed a resolution at a conference in Messina, Sicily, in early June 1955, to appoint an expert commission to examine both proposals. Its chairman, Paul-Henri Spaak, showed great deftness of touch in putting forward a viable plan, and thereafter Adenauer and his French colleague Mollet ensured that the plan made it over several tricky negotiating hurdles. Both had to push the concept through in the face of domestic political opposition: Mollet against a majority in the French parliament, who were skeptical in particular about the idea of economic union, and Adenauer against certain sectors of the business community and his own administration. For instance, his own finance minister, Ludwig Erhard, considered a customs union with just six members to be "economic nonsense."[31]

Political interests in forging a stronger integration therefore played a more important role than pure economic considerations in achieving a breakthrough in the negotiations. The eventual outcome was the Rome Treaties of March 25, 1957. They embodied the creation of the European Economic Community (EEC), albeit in three stages over a period of twelve years (or fifteen at the outside), and the formation of the European Atomic Energy Community (EURATOM), which had no commercial or regulatory interest in the military domain. These were framework treaties, each of which laid down the bases for creating common institutions—for example, a Customs Union, a Common Agricultural Policy, and an agreement on ownership of fissile material—but they made the devolution of further political responsibilities to community level contingent on unanimous agreement by the individual participating governments. In the background, working to ensure that the treaties were ratified, was the Action Committee for the United States of Europe, in which Monnet, following the expiration of his term as president of the High Authority, gathered together important parliamentarians from all the member nations. Both treaties came into force on January 1, 1958. An independent commission of nine members, which was to manage the day-to-day business of the economic community, set to work in Brussels, at first on a provisional basis.

The readiness of France and the Federal Republic of Germany to compromise on the basis of the Rome Treaties also helped dispel a potential problem arising from the reaction of the people of the Saar region to the Paris Agreements of 1954. Contrary to the expectations of the governments in Paris and Bonn, in a referendum held on October 23, 1955, voters in the Saar region overwhelmingly rejected the idea of it becoming a joint European territory. As things stood, the only solution was to incorporate it with the Federal Republic. Yet this threatened to deprive France of the Saarland's rich coal stocks, which all French governments and the French people had taken as settled since the end of the war. In the context of the negotiations on the economic community, Adenauer agreed that coal in the Saarland's seams could continue to be mined from French territory and also promised German aid in financing the canalization of the Moselle

River, essential for the transportation of French iron ore and steel. The result was the formal accession of the Saarland to the Federal Republic on January 1, 1957. Transfer from a French to a German economic region, with the Deutschmark rather than the franc as legal tender, took place, after a transitional period, on July 6, 1959.

Great Britain did not join either the EEC or EURATOM. Instead it pushed the idea of a free trade zone involving all the member states of the Organization for European Economic Co-operation (OEEC), which had been set up to administer the Marshall Plan. By gradually abolishing the tariffs on manufactured goods between the member states, while maintaining various trade barriers with third-party states, this arrangement was designed to prevent British industry from being excluded from a liberalized Common Market among the Inner Six. However, discussions on the formation of such a zone foundered at the end of 1958 when the French demanded special protectionist provisions for the Common Market. The British government responded by assembling other OEEC members, who for various reasons also rejected membership of the EEC, into a "smaller" Free Trade Area—the European Free Trade Association (EFTA), founded on May 3, 1960. Aside from Britain, its members were Denmark, Sweden, Norway, Austria, Switzerland, and Portugal. Finland joined as an associate member in 1961.

De Gaulle and Political Europe

De Gaulle's accession to power in May 1958 shifted the balance between the Atomic Energy Community and the Economic Community. For the president of the French Fifth Republic, the maintenance of absolute independence from the American nuclear industry was more important than the research and development synergy any joint nuclear program might bring. But this meant that precisely the country that had been the main driving force behind the creation of an Atomic Energy Community now dropped out of the picture. As a result, no common market for nuclear reactors came into being, nor was it even possible to integrate the various nuclear research programs. On the other hand, the Economic Community became a reality faster than originally agreed. De Gaulle drove the modernization of France ahead full-speed and knew how to exploit the instruments of the Economic Community to this end. The favorable economic conditions in Western Europe when he took office helped him immeasurably, and the boom was lent further impetus by the progressive dismantling of economic barriers between countries. So, although negotiations on the creation of an Economic Community did not go entirely without a hitch, the upshot was that the Customs Union of the Inner Six was completed on July 1, 1968, eighteen months before the deadline stipulated in the treaty.

De Gaulle also lobbied for a political union among the Inner Six. The primary purpose of this would be to carve out autonomy after all for Europe in defense matters, thereby overcoming its foreign policy dependence on the United States. Because the USSR had, since the late 1950s, developed long-range bombers that could deliver a nuclear payload on American soil, he no longer placed any credence in the American guarantee to deploy nuclear weapons if Western Europe should be invaded by the Soviets. Thus, de Gaulle reasoned, Europe should develop its own nuclear capability. He was prepared to use the French A-bomb in the defense of Europe; but in the long term, he envisaged a scenario in which other European nations would have their own nuclear weapons, perhaps even under a joint command structure. Following the first successful testing of the French atom bomb in February 1960, on September 5 of that year he put forward to his EEC colleagues the idea of a standing committee of European heads of state, with the power to formulate common foreign and defense policies.

Adenauer was extremely interested in de Gaulle's proposal. The German chancellor was also looking for some reassurance in the event that the American guarantee was no longer valid, and he also wanted to forestall any agreement between France and the Soviet Union at the Federal Republic's expense. In contrast, Belgium and the Netherlands could see no merit in the plan: they feared French dominance in place of American protection, and in order to prevent this they wanted to bring great Britain into the Common Market. De Gaulle also showed an inclination to subordinate existing European institutions to the new ministerial committee, whose votes, at least for the time being, had to be unanimous. This threatened, then, to impose a loss of supranational organization after all, a retrograde step that many found unacceptable.

Negotiations on political union therefore turned out to be commensurately difficult. A French proposal of October 19, 1961, drafted by Christian Fouchet, a confederate of de Gaulle, (the so-called "Fouchet plan") floated the idea of revising the treaty on the European Union after three years, with the aim of unifying foreign and security policy and centralizing the existing institutions. Yet the Netherlands, Belgium, and Italy insisted that after three years, the rights of the European Parliament should be strengthened and that a system of majority voting should be introduced in the ministerial committee. When de Gaulle rejected their suggestions, in April 1962, they promptly quit the negotiating table. The French president then tried a new tack, putting forward the idea of a dual union between France and the Federal Republic. Adenauer hesitated at first but then, during a visit to Paris on January 21–22, 1963, surprised everyone by signing the Franco-German Friendship and Cooperation Treaty (Élysée Treaty). This committed both signatories to working closely together in formulating foreign and defense policy. In addition, summits were to be held at least twice a year, while the foreign and defense ministers were to meet every three months, and lower-ranking officials even more frequently. Another provision was the creation of a Franco-German Youth Office, to help put understanding between the two peoples on a long-term firm footing. The two governments agreed to "consult one another over all important questions of foreign policy before any decisions are reached" and in the defense realm to "pool ideas in order to arrive at a mutually acceptable approach."[32]

However, this went too far for most German politicians, both in the government and in the opposition. Incited to revolt by Jean Monnet, who feared that Europe was turning its back on the United States and that European institutions were being weakened, when the treaty came to be ratified in the German parliament, they added a preamble that effectively prevented it from being fully enforced. In this preamble the delegates stated their determination to uphold the close ties with the United States and to work toward as swift an integration as possible of Great Britain into the Economic Community. De Gaulle rightly interpreted this as a slap in the face. In July 1964 he made one last effort to get Adenauer's successor, Ludwig Erhard, to sign on to a common foreign and defense policy; when this failed, he viewed with extreme skepticism all German and Italian initiatives on resuming negotiations about political union.

In the absence of any realistic prospect of an independent Europe, in the years that followed de Gaulle concentrated on giving those he perceived as

Konrad Adenauer and Charles de Gaulle at a Franco-German military parade in Reims, July 8, 1962. By inviting the German chancellor to a prestigious state visit in France, the French president promoted the idea of a dual union between France and the Federal Republic. Adenauer gave in and signed the Franco-German Friendship and Cooperation Treaty of January 22, 1963. (© Bettmann/ CORBIS)

America's allies clear object lessons in his understanding of independence. Thus, in the spring of 1965, when the EEC Commission, with Walter Hallstein as president, tried to use France's interest in communal finance arrangements for the Common Agricultural Policy (CAP) as a lever to strengthen the rights of the European Parliament and hence also the Commission, the French president responded with his notorious "empty chair" policy: on June 30, 1965, his foreign minister broke off all negotiations on the funding of the CAP. He then proceeded to boycott all Community activities for the next seven months, paralyzing the Commission. His price for the return of French representatives was that the plan to go over to qualified majority voting in the Council, which was due to come into force on January 1, 1966, be dropped.

But de Gaulle had overplayed his hand. His EEC partners knew full well that France needed the Economic Community just as much as they did. And while this affair did effectively defer any increase in power for the European Parliament, it also delayed a definitive settlement on the question of CAP financing. At the end of January, de Gaulle gave up his boycott, even though his fellow EEC members had not acceded to the French demand that unanimity voting should be mandatory in the Council where vital national interests were at stake. Only on the question of the role of the Commission could de Gaulle, after more than six months' more wrangling, score a nominal victory: so that the merging of the executive functions of the three communities (and with it the development of a common energy policy) would be delayed no further, at the end of April 1967 the Federal Republic chancellor, Kurt Georg Kiesinger, agreed to restrict Hallstein's term in office as president of the joint commission of the ECSC, the EEC, and EURATOM to six months and to immediately name his successor. Hallstein was not prepared to go along with this, however, and so when the three executives were merged on July 1, 1967, Hallstein stepped down and the Belgian Jean Rey took his place.

On March 7, 1966, de Gaulle announced France's withdrawal from NATO's military organization, without having managed to advance his plan for a European alternative to Atlantic integration. France remained a member of the Atlantic Pact but withdrew its troops from NATO command and asked the Allies to quit their bases on French soil. France's NATO partners acceded to this demand, moving the organization's headquarters from Paris to Brussels. Though this allowed de Gaulle to secure the independence of the French nuclear *Force de Frappe*, it made political union among the Inner Six an even more distant prospect: France's European partners once again felt snubbed by de Gaulle's unilateral behavior and so sought an even closer understanding with the United States. At the end of 1967, the remaining NATO members officially adopted the policy of "flexible response."

British Accession to the EEC

The stakes in the discussions over the future development of the European Communities were raised in the summer of 1961, when Harold Macmillan's government set about reviewing Britain's original decision not to participate in European integration. Trade with the countries of the dynamic European Community of Six gradually became more important for the British economy than its traditional ties to the Commonwealth. At the same time, Britain was keen to avoid the threat of French or German political dominance on the continent. Accordingly, on August 9, 1961, the British government lodged a formal request to join the EEC. The Irish and Danish governments immediately followed suit, Ireland because of its close commercial ties with Great Britain, and Denmark because it had a keen interest in free access to the German market. In April 1962, Norway also asked to join, fearful that it would find itself economically isolated if the bids by the other three were successful.

By and large, these applications were warmly received by the Inner Six. Great Britain and the other applicants were welcomed with regard to both the Community's economic development and its future political strength, and their accession was viewed by the smaller member states as promising to create a counterbalance against either French or German preeminence. Yet de Gaulle and other advocates of a politically integrated Europe were concerned that any expansion of the Community before this had been achieved might risk a collapse of the whole edifice. In particular, de Gaulle believed that the goal of an independent Europe was seriously threatened by the transatlantic slant in British politics.

Under these circumstances it was to prove counterproductive for Macmillan, with an eye to appeasing the conservative establishment, to insist upon special provisions with respect to Britain's Commonwealth links and to prevaricate over the question of a joint European nuclear deterrent. Negotiations on British accession ground to a halt in August 1962. When no progress had been made after several months, de Gaulle unilaterally guillotined the discussions at a press conference on January 14, 1963. His veto brought bitter recriminations from continental supporters of British accession, but it could not be rescinded. The other countries' bids to join were also thrown out.

Four years later, though, the question of Britain joining was back on the table. The Labour prime minister, Harold Wilson, submitted a new request to join on May 11, 1967; once more the governments of Ireland, Denmark, and Norway also put in their own submissions. In view of the continuing decline of the British economy, joining the EEC was a more pressing matter for Wilson than it had been for his Conservative predecessor. From the outset he was at pains to stress that he was ready to waive any special provisions, and declared himself in favor of a politically integrated Europe. This secured him not only the unanimous support of the smaller member states, but also the support of Italy and Germany. Unlike in 1961, this time the Commission also threw its weight behind the accession bids. Another unilateral intervention by de Gaulle on November 27, 1967, served to delay the start of negotiations but ultimately could not entirely prevent them.

As long as de Gaulle opposed the start of accession negotiations, the governments of the Benelux states and Italy blocked every move to strengthen the European Communities that also benefited France: not only a new attempt to forge a Political Union, but also the development of a common energy policy and a technology policy that would help Europe make up some of the ground lost to the Americans, plus plans for monetary union, which had become all the more pressing in the face of West Germany's growing economic dominance. When EEC members began entertaining the possibility of political cooperation with Great Britain without French participation, de Gaulle finally gave in: on February 4, 1969, he informed the British ambassador, Christopher Soames, that he was ready to begin talks on reconstituting the Communities as a larger economic association.

Because Wilson preferred accession to the existing Communities to some nebulous new formulation, though, this proposal only led to a further souring of Anglo-French relations. But under de Gaulle's successor, Georges Pompidou, France finally gave the green light to commence negotiations over British accession. These duly began in July 1970, five weeks after the Conservative Edward Heath had succeeded Harold Wilson as prime minister. Heath was able to extract some concessions from Pompidou on the question of the importation of dairy goods from New Zealand and sugar from the Caribbean, which were of vital importance for producers in those countries, but he had to accept that Great Britain, in line with EEC regulations, would have to contribute a disproportionate amount to the financing of these importations. The negotiations came to an end in June 1971, and the accession treaty was signed, in conjunction with those of the other three countries, on January 22, 1972, in Brussels.

Because accession inevitably impinged upon certain vested commercial interests, objections were raised in all the candidate countries against joining on the terms that had been negotiated. So vehement was the opposition in Britain that Wilson was even prompted to call for further talks. However, on July 13, 1972, the House of Commons ratified accession, albeit by only a slim majority. By contrast, a referendum had to be called in Denmark, resulting in 63 percent in favor. In Norway the outcome was 54 percent against. And so, when the treaties on the first enlargement of the EEC entered into force on January 1, 1973, Norway was no longer present.

Consolidating the Communities

France's acquiescence in the matter of accession also paved the way for the development of Community projects that supporters of enlargement had up to that point been vetoing for tactical reasons. At the Hague Summit, the heads of state and government agreed on a final package for financing the Common Agricultural Policy from community contributions, combined with an extension of the European Parliament's powers to set budgets. In addition they also agreed for the following year, in close collaboration with the Commission, to draft a phased plan for the creation of a full economic and monetary union. Lastly, they tasked the foreign ministers with working out a proposal for "progress in the realm of political union."[33]

French reservations meant that the institutionalization of collaboration on foreign and defense policies did not go as far as German chancellor Willy Brandt deemed necessary. In line with a report prepared by an expert commission under the chairmanship of the Belgian diplomat Étienne Davignon, October 1970 saw the founding of the European Political Cooperation (EPC) system, an informal intergovernmental consultation mechanism enabling foreign ministers to meet regularly to search for a common approach to major international policy questions. The administrative basis of the foreign ministers' meetings was restricted to a Committee of the Political Directors of the foreign ministries concerned. Nevertheless, it did not take long for the governments of the Communities to develop a common policy on both the Middle East and South Africa. In the preparation and execution of the Conference on Security and Cooperation in Europe (CSCE), held in 1973–1975, they spoke with one voice and consequently were largely successful in pushing through their agenda. The Final Act of the

CSCE was signed on behalf of the European Communities by Aldo Moro, then president of the European Council.

Where monetary union was concerned, the plan of an expert commission chaired by the Luxembourg prime minister, Pierre Werner, which also reported back in October 1970, envisioned a package of measures aimed at convergence of the economic, budgetary, and monetary policies of the national governments, combined with a step-by-step development of communal institutions. This would pave the way for the introduction of a common currency within a decade. The plan was adopted by the member states' governments, with some modifications, in March 1971. However, its implementation was immediately compromised by wild fluctuations on the currency markets; thereafter, French concerns over loss of sovereignty and German fears of inflation meant that hardly any unanimous regulations on reaching agreed-upon targets were ever put in place.

Even so, in April 1972 the six European Community states, together with Great Britain, Ireland, and the Scandinavian countries, agreed to establish the European Exchange Rate Mechanism—the so-called currency snake. This provided for purchasing weak currencies and selling strong currencies in order to limit fluctuations between them, thereby creating a haven of currency stability in a sea of raging worldwide speculation. Yet even this interim step proved too ambitious: Great Britain was forced to leave the snake even before it joined the European Community, in May 1973 the Federal Republic suspended its support for weak currencies, and following the onset of the global crisis that resulted from a fourfold increase in the price of crude oil in 1973–1974, France also found itself obliged to withdraw from the snake. At this stage, a common currency seemed only a distant mirage.

In the light of the difficulties experienced in realizing both political and monetary union, Willy Brandt (as in the matter of a common currency, following the advice of Jean Monnet) argued strongly in favor of institutionalizing summits. His first success on this front was to persuade Pompidou to hold another summit following the conclusion of the negotiations on enlargement—the Paris Summit of October 1972. One year later he also secured the French president's agreement to hold regular meetings of the heads of state and government. The plan was for them to meet three times a year to resolve problems on the way to achieving European Union. But because the smaller member states feared that such a European Council might disempower the Commission and lead to a loss of supranationality, no agreement to implement this body could be reached at the Copenhagen Summit in December 1973. It was only at the Second Paris Summit in December 1974 that it was finally decided to establish the European Council. However, to try to assuage any lingering concerns about the role of the Commission, its president was now included in discussions between the heads of state and government. At the same time, it was agreed to lay the groundwork for direct elections to the European Parliament from 1978 onward.

Following the establishment of the European Council, Jean Monnet dissolved his Action Committee for the United States of Europe. He regarded it as redundant, given that crisis management and further development of the European Communities was now the responsibility of the heads of state and government: "Our committee, which had helped create and breathe life into this mechanism, now seemed to me to be less essential and less able to see through a task that, in the wake of all the treaties had now been expressly entrusted to the organs of the Communities, individual governments and the new institutions."[34] And in truth, after many disagreements and compromises, the project for European union had now, in its basic configuration and working method, taken on a form that would prove extremely durable.

The Berlin Crisis

For financial reasons, the plans that both the Western powers and the Eastern Bloc drew up at the start of the 1950s for a huge increase in conventional arms could not be realized in full. Both the American and the Soviet leadership therefore came to rely increasingly upon their nuclear deterrents: the threat to deploy atomic weapons was designed both to compensate for a shortfall in conventional arms and to enable a reduction in the costly conventional arsenal. Yet the transition to a system of nuclear deterrence also invoked the specter of total annihilation. As a result, the leaders of the two nuclear-capable superpowers found themselves obliged to engage in a constant dialogue. This was an arduous process, hampered on both sides by ideological misconceptions and lack of experience in dealing with nuclear stalemate, and it led on many occasions to a ratcheting up of tension in East–West relations.

The rapid expansion of the United States' nuclear arsenal began even under the Eisenhower administration. In 1955 the United States had a fleet of 1,309 long-range bombers that could reach Soviet territory, 698 tactical nuclear weapons for deployment in Europe, and a total of 3,008 warheads. The doctrine of massive retaliation dictated that any potential Soviet conventional offensive would be met with an extensive nuclear counterstrike against targets within the Soviet Union. As compensation for the planned scaling down of American troop numbers in Europe in 1956, the European allies asked for their own forces to be equipped with miniaturized tactical battlefield nuclear weapons. In 1957 Washington agreed to this request in principle, albeit with the proviso that the nuclear warheads would remain under American control; the Allies would only be supplied with American launch vehicles.

In an effort to counter this move, the Soviets under Khrushchev likewise began to shift from conventional to nuclear arms: from a high point of 5.7 million men in 1955, built up by Stalin in the final years of his life, by 1959 the Red Army had shrunk to around 3.6 million, while at the same time an arsenal of intermediate-range missiles that could hit targets in Europe was assembled. However, the buildup of the Soviet nuclear medium-range arsenal was a slow process, and even slower was the construction of long-range bombers and intercontinental ballistic missiles that could reach American territory. Therefore, Moscow was predisposed to view the expansion of NATO's tactical arsenal as a new advance in the arms race that it could scarcely match; moreover, it appeared all the more dangerous in that it gave the Western powers and the Federal Republic new options. Accordingly, Khrushchev gave his backing to a proposal by the Polish foreign minister, Adam Rapacki, that the two German states and Poland should become a nuclear weapons-free zone.

Because Rapacki's suggestion gained a good deal of support in the West as well, in March 1958 Khrushchev managed to persuade the Western powers to call a new summit to discuss creating a zone in Central Europe in which arms proliferation would be limited and subject to inspection. However, he miscalculated badly in his attempts to stir up public opinion in the West for this proposal and to introduce the question of a peace treaty with the two German states into the summit agenda. The Western governments were able to portray this as a sign that Khrushchev was not really serious about disarmament, giving them an excuse to drag their feet over calling the meeting. Instead, at the end of March, Adenauer got a majority of the Bundestag to vote in favor of making the Bundeswehr nuclear-capable, while on April 8, the defense ministers of the Federal Republic, France, and Italy concluded a treaty on joint production of nuclear arms.

The failure of the Rapacki Plan was all the more galling for Khrushchev because he was being pressured at the same time by Ulbricht to do something about the continuing presence of the Western allies in West Berlin, who were thwarting his attempts to secure an economic victory in the struggle between the ideological systems in the two Germanies. Every month, some ten thousand or more citizens of the GDR used the border between the sectors in Berlin as an escape route to the West. In particular, well-educated, professional people were leaving the country in droves; in the long term this threatened not only the ability of the Workers' and Peasants' State to compete with its neighbor, but also its very survival. Khrushchev responded to these developments by issuing the Berlin Ultimatum of November 27, 1958: in a memorandum to the three Western powers and the governments of the two German states, he called for Berlin to be transformed into a free city without Western troops, and for an understanding to be reached with the GDR about access to the city. In the event that regulations to this effect could not be agreed upon within six months, he announced, the USSR would conclude a separate peace treaty with the GDR.

In making this threat, Khrushchev's main aim was to force the Western powers to recognize the GDR. In turn, he hoped, recognition would make the Workers' and Peasants' State a more attractive place and stem the flow of refugees. In addition, a peace treaty would free the two Germanies from their existing military alliances. Thus, a nuclear weapons-free zone could be achieved in central Europe after all and, freed from the constraints of military confrontation, socialism could demonstrate that it offered the better model for society.

Under the pressure of Khrushchev's ultimatum, the Western powers did indeed begin to move toward recognition of the GDR. Yet the effect of this brutal Soviet threat was to put advocates of a disengagement of the world powers from Germany even further on the back foot. A meeting of the Council of Foreign Ministers held by the four victorious powers in Geneva from May 11, 1959, onward to discuss the German question and the status of Berlin quickly ground to a halt. And a summit that Khrushchev had arranged with Eisenhower while on a state visit to the United States in late September 1959 was over before it had begun: because it had become clear in the meantime that the West would make no concessions on the German question, Khrushchev took the discovery of Western spy-plane flights over the Soviet Union as a pretext to demand an apology from Eisenhower before the talks opened in Paris on May 16, 1960. When this was not forthcoming, he immediately left the French capital in a flurry of furious imprecations.

Another attempt to reach an agreement, this time with Eisenhower's successor, John F. Kennedy, foundered on the young president's determination to not let himself be intimidated. When Khrushchev and Kennedy met on June 5–6 in Vienna, the president announced without more ado that he would not "give up" Berlin under any circumstances. Khrushchev responded by reviving the long-since lapsed ultimatum, and Kennedy prepared himself and public opinion for the possibility of armed confrontation over freedom of access to Berlin. Nonetheless, in order to not completely close off any last remaining avenues of understanding, when he made his public announcement stressing his readiness to fight, Kennedy also clearly spelled out his essential non-negotiable conditions: free access to Berlin, the right of the Western powers to maintain a military and diplomatic presence there, and freedom of movement into the Western sectors.

This gave Khrushchev the opportunity to enact a measure to stem the growing flood of refugees from the GDR that was totally at variance with the objective of neutralizing West Berlin or even incorporating it into the GDR—namely, to seal off the border between the sectors by building a wall straight across the city. Ulbricht had repeatedly demanded just such a solution but had been rebuffed by Khrushchev, who thought that it ran too great a risk of sparking a war. But after Kennedy had failed to include the rights of the Allies to travel freely throughout the whole of Berlin in his list of "essentials" that he was prepared to go to war over, Khrushchev thought that a provisional cordoning off of the sector border might be a viable option. On August 1, 1961, Ulbricht got the go-ahead to build the Wall, which was put up during the night of August 13.

Kennedy's reaction was one of relief, and he signaled his readiness to discuss recognition of the GDR, so long as the freedom of West Berlin was guaranteed. In turn this enabled Khrushchev to rescind the ultimatum once more and renounce his intention of signing a separate peace treaty with the GDR by year's end, much to Ulbricht's disappointment. However, informal preliminary talks on regulating matters relating to the two Germanies and Berlin came to nothing, as Adenauer and de Gaulle once again took their stand against any form of concession.

The Cuban Missile Crisis

In this tense situation, an urgent request by Fidel Castro for aid to help him resist another American invasion tempted Khrushchev into an all-or-nothing gamble that brought the world to the brink of a third world war. The Soviet Union had no further means of strengthening Cuba's conventional arsenal or even of sending troops to fight off an invasion. And so Khrushchev hit upon the idea of supplanting conventional arms with nuclear arms in this theater as well. Stationing Soviet intermediate-range missiles on Cuba was also designed to lessen the danger of an American first strike. In the interim, US nuclear arms superiority had increased hugely: the United States now possessed seventeen times as many long-range bombers and ICBMs as the Soviet Union, giving it the capability of largely or completely wiping out the Soviet nuclear arsenal in a single massive surprise attack. Soviet intermediate-range missiles on Cuba, which could hit American cities, could not redress this situation in military terms. But their visible presence there alone might dissuade US leaders from entertaining the possibility of a preemptive strike. So, at the end of May 1962, Khrushchev steered through the Presidium of the Soviet Central Committee a resolution to station the missiles; from July onward, eighty missiles and forty warheads would be shipped to Cuba.

But what Khrushchev had failed to take into consideration was the domestic political pressure that Kennedy found himself under. Since the Bay of Pigs debacle, he had been criticized for doing too little to help liberate Cuba. Therefore, when the first rumors began to circulate about the stationing of missiles on Cuba at the beginning of September, he immediately declared publicly that he would not tolerate the presence of any offensive missiles on the island. When the news was confirmed in mid-October, he found himself obliged to back his words with action. His first inclination was to destroy the missile sites in a surprise air assault before they had a chance to become operational. But because this risked starting a full-scale conflict, he decided instead, on October 21, to put in place a naval blockade to prevent the arrival of any more Soviet missiles and warheads, and to publicly challenge Khrushchev to withdraw the missiles already on Cuba. On October 22 he went on television to tell the American people about the missile threat and to let Khrushchev and the world know what his response would be.

The Soviet leader's first reaction was to tough it out, but during the night of October 25 he ordered the Soviet freighters to stop just outside the American exclusion zone. In the Presidium, he sought authorization to withdraw the missiles on the condition that the United States would not attempt to occupy Cuba. However, an agreement on this basis initially faltered after Khrushchev, in a radio broadcast on October 27, made an additional demand that the United States dismantle the medium-range missiles that it had stationed in Turkey. Kennedy refused to agree to this extra condition for the withdrawal of missiles from Cuba, because he was afraid of losing the trust of his allies. Only when his chiefs of staff urged an attack on Cuba within forty-eight hours did he give his assent in a secret communiqué to Khrushchev, albeit with the proviso that his concession on the Turkish missiles not be made public. Khrushchev concurred, and in another radio address on the morning of October 28 (Washington time) announced the immediate dismantling of the missile sites on Cuba, with no mention of Turkey. The threat of war was thereby dispelled.

Mutual awareness of having stood on the brink of nuclear annihilation caused the leaders of the two superpowers, despite their diametrically opposed positions, to come together to try and find ways of ensuring peace. After an initial phase of continued saber rattling, blamed on the hawks on both sides, the spring and summer of 1963 brought a string of attempts at rapprochement and concrete accords. Khrushchev ceased demanding that Berlin be made a free city, thereby making the provisional division of the city into a permanent arrangement. To forestall the danger of a nuclear war breaking out over a misunderstanding, a telex line and a direct radio link were established between the two capitals (the "red telephone" hotline). The foreign ministers of Great Britain, the United States, and the USSR signed the first nuclear test-ban treaty, outlawing all aboveground testing.

A Cuban refugee in Miami watches President John F. Kennedy's television address of October 22, 1962. By announcing a naval blockade and challenging Nikita Khrushchev to withdraw the nuclear missiles already in Cuba, Kennedy compelled the Soviet leader to break off his provocative maneuver and consent to a more cooperative course to forestall the danger of a nuclear war. (© Bettmann/ CORBIS)

In June 1963 Kennedy urged the American people to "re-examine our attitude toward the Soviet Union";[35] for his part, after the signing of the Test-Ban Treaty, Khrushchev invoked a Spirit of Moscow, in the tradition of the Spirit of Geneva. In the fall Kennedy suggested another summit meeting with Khrushchev, at which the agenda would include further steps toward improving relations: cooperation in spaceflight, expansion of trade links, and reciprocal reductions in troop numbers. In addition, Khrushchev mooted further talks on banning nuclear weapons in space, nuclear-free zones, and the conclusion of a Non-Aggression Pact between NATO and the Warsaw Pact.

Even though the dialogue on détente that these initiatives opened up suffered setbacks when Kennedy was assassinated in November 1963 and Khrushchev was deposed in October 1964, it was basically unstoppable. Both sides were now all too aware that any attempts to alter the status quo could lead to a nuclear catastrophe. And so they focused their policies on securing control of their own camps and limiting the spread of nuclear weapons and reducing the chances of their deployment. Talks between the administration of President Lyndon B. Johnson and Khrushchev's successors, headed by general secretary Leonid Brezhnev and Prime Minister Alexei Kosygin, led in 1966 to an accord on the nonproliferation of nuclear weapons. After some difficult horse-trading with non-nuclear nations and those on the brink of acquiring nuclear capability, the agreement was finally signed on July 1, 1968.

The Vietnam War

The ongoing dialogue on détente was also hampered by US involvement in Vietnam. When the North Vietnamese communist government decided to widen the guerrilla war being waged by the Viet Cong against the Diem regime in the South, the Kennedy administration responded by bringing the various opposition groups together under the umbrella of the National Liberation Front (NLF) and implementing a complex "pacification program." This comprised three key elements: first, corralling the rural populace of the South into "strategic villages" that offered protection against the rebels; second, strengthening the South Vietnamese forces by equipping them with modern weapons and providing military training; and third, sending in American "military advisors," some of them within their own discrete units. This program was intended to halt infiltration from the North within eighteen months. Kennedy was well aware of the weakness of the Diem regime, but he was also worried that a communist victory in South Vietnam would encourage anti-American elements in South Korea and Japan and undermine his own credibility as the leader of the free West.

Yet the pacification missions undertaken by the American "advisors," who up to the fall of 1963 totaled some sixteen thousand, had little effect, not least because Diem's arrogant brother Ngo Dinh Nhu and his wife managed to so antagonize the country's Buddhists that they rose up against the government. When Nhu ordered army units to storm Buddhist temples in August 1963, killing or wounding many monks in the process, the Kennedy administration lent their support to a military coup. This took place on November 1, 1963; Diem and

Nhu were shot dead. There followed a quick succession of regimes in Saigon, while the NLF secured control over more of the country's rural areas.

Under President Johnson, the covert operations rapidly developed into a regular, if still undeclared, war. On February 1, 1964, South Vietnamese units began, with American support, an offensive against military positions along the northern coast. During this operation, in the night of August 2–3, a US destroyer allegedly came under fire from North Vietnamese patrol boats in the Gulf of Tonkin. Johnson responded on August 5 by ordering the first air strike against supply bases in North Vietnam, whereupon the regime in Hanoi mobilized the regular troops, who rushed to lend support to the Viet Cong in the South. Johnson's advisors now concluded that a huge increase in American troop numbers would be required, to prevent a communist victory. In March 1965, round-the-clock bombing raids began against targets in the North and in areas occupied by the Viet Cong (Operation codename "Rolling Thunder"); May saw the arrival of fresh American ground forces, whose mission was to make the decisive breakthrough in winning back areas captured by the Viet Cong.

US combat troop numbers in Vietnam increased from 40,000 in May 1965 to 275,000 in July, and 443,000 in December. By June 1966 the US Expeditionary Force numbered 542,000 men, the large majority of them conscripts. They were supported by 50,00 troops from South Korea, 11,000 from Thailand, 1,500 from the Philippines, 8,000 from Australia, and 500 from New Zealand—all driven by the fear that communist influence might spread throughout Southeast Asia. The South Vietnamese also expanded their forces to over half a million. In June 1965 the government of South Vietnam was taken over by a military junta led by Nguyen Van Thieu and Nguyen Cao Ky; however, the direction of the war was left entirely in the hands of the American general staffs. Up to the end of October 1968, the US Air Force flew 107,700 combat missions, dropping 2.5 million tons of bombs in the process—more than in the entire Second World War.

Yet for all the massive deployment of men and materiel, the United States got no closer to achieving its desired "pacification" of South Vietnam. The Viet Cong and North Vietnamese Army were outnumbered (with forces of around 230,000 guerrillas and 50,000 regular troops), but they had the advantage of fighting from the cover of the jungle regions. They built a warren of tunnels into which they could melt if pursued, and used a network of concealed supply lines (the so-called Ho Chi Minh Trail) that ran mainly through the east of Laos and Cambodia, to ensure a constant flow of men and weapons from the North. In an attempt to deny their opponents the cover afforded by the dense jungle canopy, the Americans sprayed the region from the air with a defoliant containing the highly toxic chemical dioxin. The use of Agent Orange not only destroyed an area of forest the size of the Netherlands but also afflicted countless Vietnamese with liver cancers, epilepsy, and a wide range of allergies. But this action brought no breakthrough in the conflict either. To the contrary, the brutal tactics of the American forces only increased the population's sympathies for the Viet Cong guerrillas. The bombing campaign against munitions dumps and factories in the North was offset by regular supplies from the Soviet Union and China. Mao Zedong was happy to provide this kind of limited support, not only to help weaken the Americans' position in the region, but also to ensure that the Vietnamese did not become too strong. The Soviet leadership, on the other hand, was more concerned to maintain its standing within the wider communist movement.

To bolster this reputation still further, Brezhnev and Kosygin also declined an invitation by Johnson to visit the United States and thrash out the difficult questions surrounding disarmament. In February and June 1967 they did support Johnson's peace initiatives by acting as go-betweens to convey to Ho Chi Minh the offers Johnson made during talks. But contrary to Johnson's hopes, they did not bring any special pressure to bear on the leadership in Hanoi to accept these offers. The Vietnamese communists were not prepared to bring a halt to the US bombing campaign against the North by renouncing their claims on the South, nor were they ready for peace talks with the United States. A chance encounter between Johnson and Kosygin on the fringes of a meeting of the UN General Assembly in the small town of Greensboro, New Jersey, on June 23–24, 1967, was perfectly affable but brought no concrete results.

After the Viet Cong launched a coordinated offensive against a number of towns in the South on January 31, 1968 (the Tet Offensive), American public opinion and the US military leadership began to incline to the view that the war was unwinnable. The fragmentation of the Viet Cong into various factions brought considerable losses, but Johnson now went public with his negotiating offer: on March 31, he announced that he was prepared to suspend the bombing of targets in North Vietnam if the regime in Hanoi would engage in peace talks.

Now that the North Vietnamese leadership had also had its faith in decisive victory shaken by the failure of the Tet Offensive, this time they accepted Johnson's offer. Mediated by de Gaulle, who had set himself up as early as 1965 as an opponent of US involvement in Vietnam, armistice talks got under way in Paris on May 13, 1968. The bombing campaign against North Vietnam finally ended on November 1, 1968.

The Path to Détente

All the impediments to a meaningful dialogue on détente meant that the arms race continued to escalate. The United States installed a new generation of Minuteman intercontinental ballistic missiles in silos, while also greatly enlarging its arsenal of submarine-launched missiles. These grew from a stockpile of 144 in 1962 to 416 in 1964 and 656 in 1967, while the total number of American ICBMs increased from 296 to 834 to 1,054. After the Cuban debacle, the Soviet Union also invested heavily in constructing ICBMs and nuclear-armed submarines, though progress was slower than in the United States. By 1964 the two dozen or more ICBMs that the Soviets possessed on the eve of the Cuban missile crisis had increased to some 190, and three years later stood at 500. These were supplemented from 1963 onward by around a hundred submarine-launched missiles. This expansion gave the USSR a clear second-strike capability, even though the Americans retained the upper hand in the arms race.

When, in 1964, Soviet missile experts put forward plans to create an antiballistic missile (ABM) system designed initially to shield the Greater Moscow region and the Western borders of the USSR on the Baltic from incoming missiles, US defense minister Robert McNamara immediately pressed for a treaty to outlaw the building of such systems. In his opinion they only served to escalate the arms race without offering any real protection. Accordingly, both sides should, he reasoned, settle for mutually assured destruction (MAD). Moscow agreed to engage in talks to this effect only on the condition that strategic arms limitation be discussed at the same time. Conversely, though, this proposal found no favor in Washington, because it was clearly aimed at achieving strategic parity for the Soviet Union. As a result, contacts on arms limitation remained in place without negotiations ever coming to fruition.

This slow pace of the American-Soviet dialogue allowed de Gaulle to put his own European slant on détente. His concept of détente was aimed at overcoming the existing deadlock, gradually dismantling the military blocs within Europe, and changing the totalitarian character of the Soviet empire through intensive contacts between East and West. "We must seek the resolution," he told Khrushchev in March 1960, "not by having two monolithic blocs, but rather by practicing détente, entente, and cooperation one after another on the Continent. In this way, we will create a relationship, binding ties between Europeans from the Atlantic to the Urals, bring about an atmosphere that would firstly take the virulence out of the German problems, including Berlin, then allow the Federal Republic and your republic to the East to approach one another and to unite and finally to bring the whole Germanic entity securely into a Europe of peace and progress where it can develop anew."[36]

In parallel with this, de Gaulle also widened his cooperation with the Soviet Union. A cultural exchange between the two countries in 1963 was followed by a trade agreement in October 1964, including France's extension of long-term credit to the USSR. March 1965 saw the conclusion of an agreement in which the Soviet Union adopted French technology for the inception of color television. Two months later the two countries reached an accord on cooperation in the peaceful use of atomic energy. Finally, during a prestigious state visit by de Gaulle to Moscow, agreement was reached on regular contact at the highest level, to be prepared by a standing joint commission, as well as an accord on cooperation in space travel. De Gaulle was also the first Western head of government to establish diplomatic relations with Mao Zedong's regime in China. And during a state visit to Poland in September 1967, he openly encouraged his hosts to go farther in asserting their independence from Soviet domination.

Under pressure from de Gaulle, the Federal Republic of Germany also began to move toward a policy of détente. In 1964 the Erhard government signed trade treaties with Poland, Hungary, Romania, and Bulgaria. The Berlin Senate, with Willy Brandt as the governing mayor, also signed a passage agreement with the GDR government that allowed West Berliners to visit relatives in the east of the city over the Christmas period. Similar arrangements were put in place for All Saints' Day and Christmas the following year, for Easter, Pentecost, and Christmas in 1965, and for Easter and Pentecost in 1966. Over and above this, in

November 1966 the Grand Coalition government of West Germany, in which Brandt headed up the foreign ministry, announced that it was prepared to establish diplomatic relations with Eastern European states. This signaled, for all intents and purposes, a renunciation of the Hallstein Doctrine. In late January 1967 the Federal Republic announced the beginning of diplomatic ties with Romania, which under Nicolae Ceaușescu had begun to follow a course of pronounced autonomy from Moscow. The resumption of diplomatic contacts with Yugoslavia followed in December 1967.

However, Moscow made it abundantly clear to the governments of Hungary, Bulgaria, and Czechoslovakia, which were keen to follow Romania's example, that they should not allow the GDR to become isolated. At the end of April 1967, a conference of communist parties held at Karlsbad (at which neither Romania nor Yugoslavia were represented) proclaimed that Bonn's "repudiation of its presumption of sole representation," its recognition of the "inviolability of existing borders in Europe," and the normalization of relations "between the special political entity West Berlin and the GDR" were prerequisites for normalized relations with the Federal Republic.[37] To obviate the danger of an erosion of the Warsaw Pact, which might result from the French or German attempts at rapprochement, the Soviet Union rescinded its offer of significant reductions in troop numbers in Europe, hitherto a constant feature of its disarmament proposals. At the same time, the especially embattled GDR was bolstered by treaties of friendship and mutual assistance, which its Eastern European brother states concluded at the behest of Moscow.

The limits of the European conception of détente were brought even more sharply into focus when Czechoslovakia embarked on an attempt to liberalize its regime in the spring of 1968. In the face of major economic difficulties, tensions with the Slovakian minority, and massive student protests, reformist forces came to the fore in the country's Party and state apparatus. Under the leadership of the former Slovakian Communist Party chief Alexander Dubček, an action program passed by the Czechoslovakian Communist Party promised "socialism with a human face." Many intellectuals understood this to mean self-government, as proclaimed in Yugoslavia. Economic reformers argued in favor of a significant increase in trade with the West, while foreign policy officials called for genuine sovereignty and equality in relations with the Soviet Union. The secret police were disbanded and a separation of party and state was initiated. The new interior minister, Josef Pavel, took up the struggle against KGB influence. Elements in the army loyal to Moscow were dismissed, and party authorities prepared for the abolition of "democratic centralism."

The dynamics of the Prague Spring soon mobilized defenders of the established order—chief among them Walter Ulbricht, who was having to contend with economic problems similar to those in Czechoslovakia. Other members of the old guard were Władysław Gomułka in Poland, who found himself facing student unrest, the Ukrainian party leader Petro Shelest, who saw that the nationalist undertones of the Czech movement were fast catching on in his own republic, and not least of all the top leadership of the KGB. As early as May 8, Ulbricht and Gomułka demanded military action against the counterrevolution in Czechoslovakia. At that stage Brezhnev was not prepared to go that far, but after the presence of Soviet troops remaining in Czechoslovakia after taking part in maneuvers had failed to persuade the party presidium to take action against the reformers, and the KGB had put forward fabricated "proof" of a Western plot, he decided on August 14 to give in to the urgings of those calling for intervention. Occupation forces moved into Czechoslovakia on the night of August 21. Taking part in the invasion alongside Soviet forces were Polish, Hungarian, and Bulgarian units; the GDR National People's Army provided logistical support. Dubček was not toppled immediately, but had to watch as the Soviets imposed a gradual "normalization" on the country. In April 1969, he was forced to relinquish his office to the Soviet yes-man Gustáv Husák.

Brezhnev's decision to crush the Prague Spring helped him consolidate his grip on power. Defending the privileges of the "new class" of communist functionaries (as described in a famous essay by the former Yugoslav communist leader Milovan Đilas) now took center stage in Soviet politics. A lead article in *Pravda* maintained that the "sovereignty and right of self-determination of the Socialistic states must be subordinated to the interests of the Socialistic world system."[38] The West reacted with outrage to this Brezhnev Doctrine and its brutal application. Those who, like de Gaulle, had placed great faith in the effects of the West opening up to the East found themselves bitterly disappointed.

However, the process of détente was only temporarily knocked off course by this "frustrating event" (as President Johnson called it). Shortly before the decision was taken to invade Czechoslovakia, the leadership of both superpowers had finally agreed to begin negotiations on both an ABM treaty and the limitation of strategic arms. Moscow had given in to Johnson's urging to hold a new summit, and had invited the US president to Moscow at the beginning of October. Prompted by the widespread sense of outrage at the suppression of the Prague Spring, at first Johnson was disinclined to accept this invitation straight away, and no new date could be settled on before his term of office expired in January 1969. Yet across Western capitals there was general consensus that the former policy of détente and ushering in a peaceful world order should be continued. Richard M. Nixon, elected in November 1968 as Johnson's successor in the White House, shared this view. For all his past anticommunist rhetoric, he had become enough of a realist to see the creation of a "structure of peace"[39] as the best method of containing Soviet power and avoiding the danger of nuclear catastrophe.

Soviet leaders were all the more concerned to reach an agreement with the West because tensions with the Chinese communists, which had been evident since Mao's proclamation of the Great Leap Forward in 1958, now escalated seriously at the end of the 1960s. After Beijing had made a clean ideological break with the motherland of the socialist revolution in July 1964, with the publication of a lead article entitled "On Khrushchev's Pseudo-Communism and Its Historical Lessons for the World," fierce clashes took place on the Sino-Soviet border along the Ussuri River in March 1969. These emphasized that China could no longer be co-opted to support the Soviet position in the global power struggle. Rather, the country had become a serious rival of the USSR in the struggle to gain influence in the Third World.

The Era of Détente

After the painful learning experiences of the 1960s, the prospects of achieving some substantive results in the dialogue on détente finally looked favorable. Leonid Brezhnev's decision to intervene in Czechoslovakia placed him firmly in the driving seat within the Soviet Union—a party functionary concerned with securing power, who accorded top priority to the maintenance of peace, and who regarded any success in furthering détente as an opportunity to boost his own prestige. His opposite number in the United States, Richard Nixon, who came to office in January 1969, was a pragmatically minded Republican who in discussions with his Soviet adversary needed to take less heed of ideological hard-liners and the "military-industrial complex" (which President Eisenhower had complained about) than either of his Democratic predecessors. Finally and most importantly, the election in the Federal Republic of Germany of a socialist–liberal coalition under the leadership of Willy Brandt as chancellor in October 1969 signaled the country's resolution not to stand in the way of détente any longer, but rather to use the process to make the border between the two Germanies more porous.

The Federal Republic's Eastern Treaties

At first Nixon put off the summit that Johnson had been at pains to arrange with the Soviet leadership, and also dragged his feet on beginning negotiations on strategic arms limitation. Before he started concluding any treaties, the new president first wanted to get an overview of the situation and to consolidate the Western alliance under his leadership. This delay caused Brezhnev to focus his attention in the détente dialogue far more intently on the Europeans than he had done hitherto—and in particular on the Germans. In his Budapest Appeal of March 17, 1969, he softened the hard line against the Federal Republic expressed in the Karlsbad resolutions of April 1967. Recognition of the GDR and the Oder-Neisse Line were now seen, not as prerequisites for normalization of relations, but instead as interim goals in the context of a "pan-European conference on security." And the Warsaw Pact countries no longer demanded a "peace settlement based on the existence of two German states" but instead sought just "recognition of the GDR's existence"; they also left a good deal of latitude regarding exactly what form this recognition should take.

West Germany's Grand Coalition government responded to the Budapest Appeal by proposing that negotiations on a reciprocal renunciation of force should be resumed. Coalition members disagreed, though, over how far they should go in these discussions. Accordingly, on the night of the federal elections (September 28, 1969) Brandt decided to form a coalition with the Free Democrats, who were more open to rapprochement with the East than were the Christian Democrats. A government declaration of October 28 contained the decisive concession that was essential for a compromise in the German question: "Even if two states exist in Germany," ran the key passage in the document, "they are not foreigners to one another; their relations to one another can only be of a special nature."[40] One month later, the Federal Republic signed the Nuclear Weapons Non-Proliferation Treaty, which the Christian Democrats had consistently opposed.

In the discussions between the Federal German government and the Soviets, which began in December 1969 at the Soviet Foreign Ministry, the Soviet foreign minister, Andrei Gromyko, at first insisted on unqualified legal recognition of the GDR and on explicit rejection of any possibility of reunification. But with the discreet support of KGB head Yuri Andropov, Brandt's negotiator Egon Bahr managed to push through a formulation that allowed for the possibility of recognizing the GDR while still keeping the basic question of the two Germanies open; thus, in the Moscow Treaty concluded between the Federal Republic and the USSR, and signed by Brandt and Kosygin on August 12, 1970, there was only mention of the "inviolability" of the existing borders within Europe, "including the Oder-Neisse Line, which forms the western state boundary of the People's Republic of Poland, and the border between the Federal Republic of Germany and the German Democratic Republic." At the same time, the Soviet government accepted without challenge a diplomatic note from the German foreign minister, Walter Scheel, in which the Federal Republic government announced that "this treaty does not contradict the Federal Republic of Germany's wider goal of working toward a state of peace in Europe, in which the German people might regain its unity through free self-determination."[41]

The Moscow Treaty provided the framework for the Federal Republic to enter into agreements henceforth with the GDR, Poland, and Czechoslovakia. The Poles—who would have preferred to conclude a treaty with Bonn before the Moscow signing in order to stress their independence—made the first move. The signing of the treaty between the countries on December 7, 1970, at which Brandt spontaneously knelt down in front of the memorial to the victims of the Warsaw Ghetto, was seen throughout the world as an expression of German contrition and a final renunciation of all territorial claims in the East. Discussions with the GDR turned out to be more problematic. Only when implementation

Chancellor Willy Brandt spontaneously kneels before the memorial to the victims of the Warsaw Ghetto after the signing of the treaty between Poland and the Federal Republic on December 7, 1970. His act was seen throughout the world as an expression of German contrition and a final renunciation of all territorial claims in the East. (© Bettmann/CORBIS)

of the "new Eastern policy" ran into difficulties in the Federal Republic's domestic political arena did the GDR leadership show itself willing to sign a Basic Treaty (on December 21, 1972), in which the two sides agreed to improve inter-German relations and facilitate exchanges, although the preamble made it clear that there were "different perceptions on the national question."[42] Negotiations with Czechoslovakia dragged on even longer. The main sticking point—the question of the validity of the Munich Agreement of October 1938, which had ceded the Sudetenland to the German Empire—was resolved in the treaty of December 11, 1973, in which both sides declared Munich null and void, though without touching upon the thorny question of the nationality of the Sudeten Germans.

At the same time the Moscow Treaty smoothed the way for a resolution of the Berlin problem. The Federal Republic government announced that the treaty could not enter into force until a satisfactory settlement of the Berlin issue had been reached. This prompted the Four Powers to declare themselves ready to make compromises in the Berlin negotiations, which had begun in March 1970. With the active mediation of Egon Bahr (who was not officially a participant in the discussions), the Soviet ambassador, Valentin Falin, and his American opposite number, Kenneth Rush, agreed on the formulation that although West Berlin did not form part of the Federal Republic, the "connections" between the two should be "maintained and developed." The Soviet Union expressly assumed responsibility for guaranteeing free passage between the western sectors of the city and the Federal Republic, and the Federal Republic retained the right to represent West Berliners at consular level and under certain conditions to include them in international agreements. This Berlin Accord was duly initialed by the ambassadors of the Four Powers on September 3, 1971.[43] Thereafter, at short notice, Brezhnev invited Brandt to a personal face-to-face. At the meeting in Oreanda in the Crimea in the third week of September, the Soviet leader showed much sympathy for Brandt's call for détente to be realized in concrete terms through disarmament.

US–Soviet Accords

The rapprochement between Bonn and Moscow persuaded Nixon and his security advisor, Henry Kissinger, to abandon their reservations about the Strategic Arms Limitations Talks (SALT). Preliminary discussions began in Helsinki in November 1969, and from April 1970 onward the plenary negotiations got under way in Vienna. The Americans' first priority was to prevent the Soviets from closing the gap in the stockpiles of intercontinental ballistic missiles, a process in which they had made rapid strides in the latter half of the 1960s. Therefore, their opening gambit was to suggest restricting reductions to land-based ICBMs and setting an upper limit for the number of "modern, heavy missiles" each side could deploy. Multiple-warhead missiles (MIRVs; multiple independently targetable reentry vehicles), such as those the United States had developed in the interim, would be banned only on the condition that the Soviet side agreed to mutual on-site inspections.

The Soviets did not agree to this condition, and so the SALT talks soon reached a dead end. The only progress came in May 1971 when both sides consented to conclude an agreement limiting ABM systems, so long as these were linked to an understanding about certain limitations on intercontinental missiles. But on the American side this concession was still very much bound up with the idea that the United States should maintain its strategic superiority. The Americans were prepared to allow the Soviets to develop just one ABM system; they themselves planned to set up four. At the same time, the stockpile of submarine-launched ICBMs, far smaller on the Soviet side than on the American, was to be frozen at current levels. This once again made any agreement difficult.

In February 1972, Nixon went on a state visit to China, primarily with the aim of securing Mao's support for an "honorable" US withdrawal from Vietnam. But the opening of relations with the Chinese communists, whom the Americans had shunned up until then, might also have the useful side effect of making the Soviet leadership more compliant on the question of the strategic balance of power. But once Nixon realized that this was a vain hope, he did finally assent to the principle of strategic parity with the USSR. Kissinger was now free to propose an upper limit to submarine-launched ICBMs that accorded with Soviet expansion plans. And on a quick visit to Moscow on April 21–22, 1972, he also accepted two ABM systems for each side—one to protect their command and control centers and one guarding an offensive missile installation. Accordingly, the package of measures in the first strategic arms limitation treaty (SALT I) included not only the ABM accord but also an agreement to freeze the launching facilities for ICBMs at the current (in the interim, roughly equal) level, plus a protocol on the upper limit of launching facilities aboard submarines. These agreements were limited to five years.

Nixon's planned signing of SALT I on a long-awaited presidential visit to Moscow was jeopardized at the eleventh hour by a major offensive by North Vietnamese troops that threatened to disrupt his strategy of "Vietnamizing" the war, and to which he responded by mining North Vietnam's coastal waters and resuming the bombing campaign against Hanoi and Haiphong. This gave opponents of arms limitation in Moscow an opening to argue that the general secretary could not play host to a US president who was engaged in bombing a socialist brother country. After several days of inconclusive discussions, Brezhnev managed to prevail by arguing that cancellation of the Nixon visit would jeopardize the impending ratification of the Eastern Treaties in the West German parliament. Thus, without knowing it, Brandt came to the aid of both Brezhnev and Nixon. Conversely, both Moscow and Washington brought their influence to bear in helping the Eastern Treaties get over parliamentary hurdles. And when Brandt was about to be ousted by a vote of no confidence, the GDR even ensured his survival by bribing a Christian Democrat member of parliament. Negotiations on the Basic Treaty were concluded shortly before the federal elections of November 19, 1972, which effectively became a referendum on the "new Eastern policy."

Nixon's state visit to Moscow on May 22–26, 1972, was one of the high-water marks in the politics of détente. Brezhnev immediately took the opportunity to forge a personal relationship with the American president, while Nixon showed himself thoroughly receptive to the general secretary's friendly overtures. In addition to the SALT package, the two men signed a whole raft of agreements on bilateral cooperation. Moreover, it was agreed that talks on strategic arms limitation should continue, especially with regard to technical innovations such as multiple warheads. Nixon also gave his backing to the Warsaw Pact's call for a Conference on European Security and Cooperation to take place the following year. The two leaders concurred that the question of reductions in conventional forces should be discussed at a separate conference, because it concerned only the members of the two military alliances. But above all Brezhnev and Nixon agreed to keep in regular personal touch with one another in the future, with summits between the leaders of the world's two superpowers becoming a fixed arrangement. Both men were sure that they had laid the foundations for peaceful cooperation.

By October 1972, negotiations on a US-Soviet trade deal had also been successfully concluded. This agreement guaranteed the Soviet Union "most favored nation" status, provided for trade credits, and included clauses on avoiding disruption of markets and regulating trade disputes, as well as the establishment of official trade missions in Washington and Moscow. A separate agreement regulated the mutual opening of ports and the equal distribution of cargo between US and Soviet ships. Furthermore, the US president gave the Export-Import

Bank of the United States authority to extend its credit facilities to the Soviet Union. The intention was to make American capital and American know-how readily available for the exploitation of raw materials in the USSR—which for economic representatives in the Soviet leadership was one of the key objectives of détente, scarcely less important than the goals of maintaining peace on the basis of the status quo and limiting the amount of resources squandered on the arms race.

Brezhnev's return visit to the United States took place in June 1973. After first stopping over in Washington, at the president's special request the general secretary then flew in the presidential jet to Nixon's country retreat in San Clemente, California. There, further treaties were signed, including agreements on strengthening cultural and scientific ties and on the peaceful use of nuclear energy. Brezhnev supported Nixon's suggestion that summits should henceforth be held on a yearly basis, alternating between the two countries. Finally, an accord on the prevention of nuclear war was concluded; it addressed the long-standing Soviet call for a mutual renunciation of the first use of nuclear weapons. The United States had always rejected this idea, because it effectively meant revoking the guarantee of deterrence for America's European allies. After some tough negotiations, Nixon now put his signature to a general repudiation of the use of force combined with an undertaking to consult the other side if a nuclear conflict looked likely. Aside from being a goodwill gesture, this arrangement did little more than formalize the existing consultation framework.

In parallel with the development of US-Soviet relations, America began to withdraw from Vietnam. After China halted its supply of military and other aid in the wake of Nixon's visit to Beijing, the North Vietnamese leadership were persuaded—not least by the ferocious bombing offensive in the spring 1972—to fall in with an arrangement that allowed the United States to at least maintain the semblance of a "peace with honor." It entailed American troops, who by 1972 had already been reduced to 78,000 men, to withdraw completely from the country, while the Thieu administration and the revolutionary government of the NLF would remain in place until new countrywide elections were held in South Vietnam. Thieu was opposed to this settlement, fearing that he could not hold out for long against the Viet Cong with only material aid from the United States. But after a resumption of the bombing campaign over Christmas 1972, which only succeeded in stirring up public condemnation around the world, he was forced to give in. A peace agreement on Vietnam was signed in Paris by Kissinger and Hanoi's representative, Le Duc Tho, on January 23, 1973. Five days later, the guns fell silent—albeit only temporarily.

The CSCE and MBFR Talks

Preparatory talks on the forthcoming Conference on Security and Cooperation in Europe began in Helsinki on November 22, 1972. By the start of June 1973, the thirty-five nations involved—including every European state except Albania, plus Canada and the United States—were all agreed on the agenda, which was to comprise four main points: questions of security in Europe; questions of cooperation in trade, science, and technology, as well as environmental concerns; questions of cooperation in humanitarian and other areas; and lastly, questions on the follow-up after the conference had ended. Initially for the first point, informally dubbed Basket One, there was to be worked out a catalog of principles to which the participants would commit themselves to adhere to in their relations with one another. Over and above that, pressure from the European NATO member states and some neutrals secured approval for negotiations on confidence-building measures in the military sphere. On the third point, delegates from the Federal Republic and their Western European allies managed to get onto the agenda negotiations on reunifying families, freedom of information and of travel, as well as cultural and other kinds of exchanges. The representatives of the Soviet Union and the Warsaw Pact states accepted this only very reluctantly; ultimately, though, they realized that if such matters were not discussed, no significant progress would be made on economic cooperation (Basket Two), an issue that they set great store by.

At the conference proper, which got under way on July 3 in Helsinki and was continued by diplomats thereafter in Geneva, representatives of the Western powers, mainly with the support of neutral countries, called for all joint communiqués to reflect Western principles of cooperation and peaceful change. Gromyko, who led the Soviet negotiating team and was concerned to protect the Soviet empire, was vehemently opposed to this demand, but in the end gave in every time it was raised. He did not want to be held responsible for scuttling the conference, which had always played a pivotal role in the Soviet conception of détente.

Indeed, the conference proceedings were ultimately a greater expression of a commitment to change than they were an acknowledgment of the status quo. In the basic declaration, the participants did stress the principles of territorial integrity, the inviolability of borders, and the commitment not to become involved in the internal affairs of other states. Yet at the same time they called on all states to observe "freedom and political independence" and to grant their peoples the right to self-determination, pledged to repudiate "all forms of armed intervention or threat of such action against another member state," promised to respect "human rights and basic liberties," and declared that observance of these rights was a basic prerequisite for the "furtherance of friendly relations and cooperation" between states. At the urging of the Federal Republic of Germany, a passage was even included in the basic declaration of principles granting states the right to amend their borders "through peaceful means and agreement." Basket Three contained a commitment to the "free exchange of persons, information, and opinions." And in the Document on Confidence-Building Measures, the participants undertook to announce major military exercises well in advance. Follow-up conferences would examine to what extent agreements had been observed.[44]

In the Moscow Politburo, this impressive statement of Western principles raised the question of whether the Helsinki Final Act did not in fact open the floodgates for the Western powers to interfere in the internal affairs of the Soviet empire. Nevertheless, Brezhnev still forced through its signature—because he knew that he depended upon cooperation with the West, and because he was confident he could always deal with any potential dissidents in the customary manner. From July 30 to August 1, the thirty-five heads of government and state met in the Finnish capital to put their signature to the Helsinki Final Act in a grand closing ceremony. It was subsequently published *in extenso* in all the Party and government newspapers of the Warsaw Pact. This was in line with standard practice in socialist countries, but in this instance it was also done to showcase Brezhnev's great negotiating triumph. Evidently no one in power paid any heed to the fact that it also gave citizens of Eastern Bloc states the possibility of appealing to the CSCE Final Act.

The West was far less successful in the negotiations to reduce troop numbers in Europe—for the simple reason that, unlike with the CSCE, the Western nations could not settle on a common position that had any chance of being accepted. While the Federal Republic pressed for a substantial reduction in both foreign (American and Soviet) and domestic troops as a major contribution to the creation of a peaceful order in Europe, France opposed against any scaling-down whatsoever of the American military presence. The Netherlands and Belgium did not want to be affected by troop reductions, and the United States, after showing some initial sympathy for Egon Bahr's proposal, ended up offering only minimal reductions in troop numbers. After several failed attempts to bring the matter to a vote, preliminary talks opened in Vienna on January 31, 1973, between delegations from NATO and the Warsaw Pact. By the end of July, consensus had been reached on holding a conference on mutual and balanced force reductions (MBFR), to include on the Western side the Federal Republic and the Benelux countries alongside the United States, Great Britain, and Canada as occupying powers, and on the Eastern side the GDR, Poland, and Czechoslovakia together with the Soviet Union as the occupying power. It was also agreed that there should be present observers who were not themselves directly affected by troop reductions—namely, Hungary and Romania on the Eastern side and Norway, Denmark, Italy, Greece, and Turkey on the Western side. France took no part in the conference.

The proposal that NATO brought to the conference table when the negotiations proper began in October 1973 did not put forward any percentage reductions, but instead set identical maximum troop strengths for both sides. The suggested ceiling of 700,000 men entailed a reduction of 235,000 for the Warsaw Pact but for NATO just 80,000. Likewise, the Warsaw Pact would have to withdraw nine thousand tanks, while NATO would not have to withdraw a single one. Qualitative aspects of the reductions were not discussed, nor was there any suggestion by what stages this unequal cutback on the part of the Eastern Bloc forces should proceed. In contrast, the Warsaw Pact countries called for modest reductions over three years to roughly equal strengths, with the occupation forces simply returning home, not disbanding entirely. In view of the great difference in distance of the United States and the Soviet Union from Central Europe, this was clearly to the disadvantage of the Western nations.

Because NATO showed no sign of backing down from its demand that the Warsaw Pact's superiority in numbers be drastically cut back, Brezhnev did not feel overly pressured to require his own forces to make any major cuts. His awareness of the need for substantial reductions, which he stressed repeatedly in discussions with Brandt and Bahr, clearly took a backseat to the traditional strategic dogma of maintaining the balance of power. And so the conference fizzled out in fruitless wrangling over different conceptions of parity, which effectively precluded any possibility of agreement. The Federal Republic government was not robust enough to break this vicious circle, and quickly gave up any attempt to do so. This meant that, for the time being, one absolutely key aspect of West Germany's Eastern policy remained in abeyance.

The Rocky Road to SALT II

The limits to personal diplomacy, on which Brezhnev and Nixon had staked so much, immediately became apparent in the negotiations over strategic arms. Over the course of 1974, Brezhnev lost both of his former confederates in his détente policy: Brandt stepped down in May, after realizing that the unmasking of his personal aide Günter Guillaume as a GDR spy meant political and personal ruin for him; in August, Nixon announced his departure after the House of Representatives instituted impeachment proceedings against him due to his conduct in the Watergate affair. As a result, the German détente process ran out of steam, while the remaining American advocates of the policy lacked Nixon's stature. Brezhnev, for his part, was by now beset by serious health problems that sapped his former assertiveness; in November he suffered his first stroke, from which he only partially recovered.

The erosion of his authority during his last months in office also meant that Nixon ran into great difficulties in negotiating even the question of parity in MIRVs with the Soviets. During his third meeting with Brezhnev in late June 1974—initially in Moscow and then at Brezhnev's summer dacha in Oreanda where he had received Brandt—the only accords they could come to were on subsidiary matters, such as a reduction in the permitted ABM systems from two to one for either side, a ban on underground nuclear tests with yields of more than 150 kilotons, and regulations for replacing and destroying outmoded strategic weapons. At a meeting in Vladivostok on November 23 and 24, Nixon's successor, Gerald Ford, thrashed out an agreement with Brezhnev that obliged the Soviet Union to downgrade the superiority in strategic launch vehicles that it had in the meantime attained but that at the same time gave the USSR the opportunity of gradually making up its shortfall in MIRVs. But just as the experts began working out the fine details of this settlement in January 1975, the American delegates suddenly insisted on counting the new Soviet Backfire long-range bomber into their calculations of the upper weapons limit for the Soviet side, while refusing to put the equally new American cruise missiles on the negotiating table.

In December 1974 the Soviet side found itself even less willing to accede to this unreasonable demand after the US Congress decided to make the granting of most-favored-nation status to the USSR and the extension of low-interest credit—as stipulated in the Trade Treaty of October 1972—contingent on Soviet guarantees of free emigration for Russian Jews. Brezhnev had tried to forestall just such an embargo on the Trade Treaty by tacitly increasing the USSR's emigration quotas. But after Senator Henry Jackson made free passage for Soviet Jews a condition of economic support, the general secretary saw no further possibility of saving the treaty. The treaty was rescinded, emigration dwindled, and Brezhnev was faced with the problem of having to justify the military concessions made in the Vladivostok accord with no tangible economic benefits to show for pursuing détente.

Jackson's moral crusade against the policy of détente was lent greater resonance by the American defeat in Indochina. Whereas the Paris Peace Accords had somewhat glossed over the unpalatable fact that it was a defeat, it was plain for all to see in the spring of 1975. The corrupt and demoralized Thieu regime collapsed under the onslaught of a new offensive by the North Vietnamese, who captured the capital, Saigon, on April 30, 1975. Television images of the last US helicopter to leave the city, unable to take all the supporters of the old regime who had assembled on the roof of the US Embassy, brought home dramatically to the whole world the humiliation of the mighty American military machine. A few days earlier, Phnom Penh, the capital of neighboring Cambodia, had fallen into the hands of the Khmer Rouge, exponents of a drastic form of hard-line communism, who promptly set about liquidating or resettling the country's entire urban population. In Laos, which had also been drawn in to the Vietnam War, the communists were also able to assert themselves: at the end of August, the Pathet Lao seized control of the country.

The impression that communism was on the rise everywhere was further enhanced by the collapse of the Portuguese colonial empire. In April 1974 a group of young, left-leaning military officers toppled the heir to the long-standing Salazar dictatorship, Marcello Caetano, immediately granted independence to Portugal's African colonies, and with the assistance of a rapidly growing Communist Party conducted an enforced expropriation of large landholdings in the south of the country. This Carnation Revolution raised the specter of a communist takeover in one of the oldest NATO partners in Western Europe—albeit only fleetingly, before the radicals were ousted by more moderate fellow officers in the fall of 1975. Thereafter, Cuban support for the Marxist liberation movement in Angola raised further concerns. Castro's troops were bolstered by Soviet arms shipments and logistical support—just as the CIA gave its backing to the South Africans, who intervened in Angola on the side of rival, noncommunist guerrilla groups. When the Marxist Movimento Popular de Libertação de Angola (MPLA) gained the upper hand in the Angolan civil war in February 1976, it looked like yet another Soviet victory.

After Kissinger had managed to draw Egypt into the Western camp, following its largely futile attack on Israel in October 1973, Brezhnev had no reservations in responding to a request for help from the Marxist leader of Ethiopia, Lieutenant Mengistu Haile Mariam, whose country came under attack from Somalian troops in June 1977. To underscore its military might, the Soviet Union's support was deliberately organized on a grand scale. From December 1977, Soviet airplanes ferried to Ethiopia huge amounts of weapons and tanks, fifteen hundred Soviet military advisors, and twelve thousand Cuban combat troops. With their help, Mengistu managed to drive back the Somalians by February 1978. The Moscow Politburo was quite happy to let the rest of the world construe this victory as yet more evidence of a concerted communist strategy of global expansion.

The American presidential elections of November 1976 were won, not by Henry Jackson, but by his Democratic Party colleague Jimmy Carter. Carter was a political greenhorn who was eager to continue the process of détente, but who went about it so ineptly that at first he succeeded only in making communication between the two sides more difficult. His desire to sidestep limitation and instead bring about a radical reduction in strategic arms brought a new negotiating proposal from the Pentagon, who in an attempt to reassert American dominance unpicked the carefully woven compromise reached at Vladivostok, provoking corresponding counterdemands from the Soviet military. At the same time Carter made a great show of publicly lending his support to Soviet dissidents, which not only led to the Soviet authorities persecuting them more vigorously but also made it more difficult for Brezhnev to establish a direct link with the US president.

In view of the supposed successes of the Soviet expansion strategy in Africa, Carter also allowed himself to be persuaded by his security advisor, Zbigniew Brzezinski, to play the Chinese card more demonstrably than before. In May 1978 he sent Brzezinski to Beijing to discuss the possibility of strategic cooperation and technological aid. The Chinese honored this clear display of partisanship in the Sino-Soviet border dispute by indicating their willingness to normalize relations with the United States without insisting any longer that America first abandon its support for Taiwan. In mid-December, a joint Chinese-American communiqué announced to an astonished world the establishment of diplomatic relations. On a state visit to Washington in late January 1979, Deng Xiaoping, the new strong man in the Chinese Politburo, called upon his hosts to join in an alliance against the Soviet Union.

On February 17, 1979, Chinese troops invaded North Vietnam, which had just concluded a formal pact with the USSR and was waging war against the Khmer Rouge in Cambodia. Carter, who had strongly advised Deng during his visit against such a move, now realized that he had gone too far in taking the Chinese side against the Soviet Union. On February 27 he instructed Brzezinski to tell the Soviets that he regarded the "development of good relations between our two countries" as his "*greatest* responsibility as president" and therefore viewed it as a matter of great urgency that the current tension be overcome.[45] He then intervened personally to remove the last vestiges of resistance by Brzezinski and the Pentagon to restoring the Vladivostok formula in the SALT negotiations.

The SALT II package, which was signed by Brezhnev and Carter at a summit in Vienna on June 15–18, 1979 (Brezhnev's planned visit to Washington had been waived in view of his poor state of health), provided for a rapid reduction in the number of Soviet strategic nuclear delivery vehicles to the agreed-upon common upper limit of 2,250, in return for the Americans limiting both their stockpile of missiles equipped with multiple warheads to 1,200 and the payload of cruise missiles carried by each heavy bomber. The problem of the Backfire bomber was solved by limiting their number to 275, while Soviet ICBMs were reduced by 150. This was once again an arrangement that brought no substantive reduction in nuclear arms, but at least it set limits to a potentially unrestricted arms race and could thereby serve as a basis for further agreements.

The meeting between Brezhnev and Carter was overshadowed by the poor health of the general secretary (who in the meantime, in 1977, had also assumed the office of president of the Supreme Soviet) and by the US president's clear lack of preparation. However, both men assured one another that they were keen to take the process of international détente forward. They also broke the ice in their personal relations. Carter, who at first had behaved in a very formal manner, was by the third day making toasts to "my new friend, President Brezhnev," while in private circles Brezhnev described the American president as "essentially quite a nice guy after all."[46] After both had signed the SALT II Treaty at the conclusion of negotiations, Brezhnev took the initiative to kiss Carter. The press photo of this moment became an abiding universal symbol of the Vienna Summit.

3. New Players

WHILE East and West learned the hard way how to do business with one another, new centers of power and new protagonists began to emerge in global politics. This first came about as a result either of decolonization or of the liberation of individual states from American or Soviet dominance. The process continued when, during the 1970s and 1980s, a number of Asian states made the transition to becoming modern industrialized societies. Finally, the creation of cartels among oil-exporting countries also brought shifts in the balance of power that worked against the bipolar state structure. Western industrialized states experienced some difficulty in coming to terms with these changes, giving rise to many disputes, particularly between the United States and its European allies.

The Non-Aligned Movement

The origins of the movement of nonaligned states can be traced back to 1947, when Jawaharlal Nehru, in his role as interim president even prior to Indian independence, invited Asian and Arab governments and leaders to New Delhi to attend the Asian Relations Conference. The aim of the Indian premier was to foster a sense of solidarity among the colonized peoples of the Asian continent and thereby create a more concerted front when dealing with the world's major powers. This proved a difficult task, however. The permanent organization of participating states that he called into being was largely insignificant. Common principles such as freedom of association and neutrality vis-à-vis the two superpowers were not formulated until a conference organized by Egypt's president Nasser in Cairo in 1952. A conference in the Indonesian city of Bandung in April 1955, attended by delegations from six African and twenty-three Asian countries (including, at Nehru's insistence, the People's Republic of China), then promulgated a list of further principles, including reciprocal recognition of sovereignty, noninterference in the internal affairs of other countries, the settlement of disputes by peaceful means, and cooperation. There was also a call for a ban on all nuclear weapons.

In the same year, Nehru established relations with Josip Broz Tito of Yugoslavia, who in 1948 had thwarted Stalin's attempt to have him replaced, for his insubordinate attitude, by more compliant comrades, and who ever since had been pursuing his own individual path toward socialism. This contact served to expand the hitherto somewhat nebulous sense of solidarity among African and Asian countries into a much more rigidly organized group of nonaligned states. In September 1961, representatives of twenty-five nonaligned countries met in Belgrade; those taking part included Cuba, together with a number of the newly independent African states, led by Ghana and Guinea. Nehru now tried to present the group as a champion of world peace, but without much success. Highminded resolutions calling on the great world powers to return to the negotiating table tended to gloss over Soviet transgressions such as the building of the Berlin Wall.

But the movement ran into a real crisis in October 1962 when Chinese troops occupied the unpopulated region of eastern Ladakh, vital for communications with Tibet, which lawfully belonged to India. Nehru's response was to try to draw the Soviet Union into the circle of Afro-Asiatic powers as a counterweight to China. Indonesia voiced concern at this development and Pakistan found it totally unacceptable; as a result, discussions on holding a second Bandung Conference, which Indonesia's President Sukarno had been strongly lobbying for, ended in October 1965 with an indefinite postponement of the planned meeting. However, Tito and Nasser made sure that the Non-Aligned Movement continued as an organization, by convening a second conference in Cairo in October 1964. China was not invited to these talks; instead, a whole slew of new African countries took part in proceedings.

Yet the real impetus in giving new direction to the movement, and at the same time securing its long-term future, was provided by Fidel Castro with his Solidarity Conference of the Peoples of Asia, Africa, and Latin America, held in Havana in January 1966, to which he invited representatives of eighty-two countries. This meeting emphasized for the first time the continuing economic dependence on the world's major industrialized countries of nations that had emerged from colonialism, drawing states from three separate continents into a single common-interest group. Under the influence of dependency theory, which had been formulated by Latin American social scientists, the participant nations laid aggressive demands at the door of imperialist and colonialist "exploiters." At a further conference in Algiers in October 1967, attended by seventy-seven states, these claims were enunciated more precisely: these now focused on granting tariff preferences for raw materials and commodities from developing countries, more generous development aid packages from the industrialized countries, and according developing countries special unconditional drawing rights in the International Monetary Fund. The Group of 77 thereby established itself as the economic lobby for the Third World.

The Group's international profile rose in the 1970s when the huge debt problems of many developing countries started to emerge. Summits of the nonaligned countries were by then being held on a regular cycle of every three years, and were increasingly dominated by Latin American countries. At the same time the Group of 77 increasingly began using the United Nations as a forum to air their grievances. In 1974, at the Sixth Special Session of the General Assembly, they managed to get passed a resolution calling for the creation of a "new world economic order." And at the Fourth United Nations Conference on Trade and Development (UNCTAD IV), which met in Nairobi in 1976, they obtained an agreement to implement an integrated program for commodities that, it was hoped, would provide protection from excessive fluctuations in the price of raw materials. The next two meetings of UNCTAD, in 1979 and 1983, yielded no concrete proposals, but UNCTAD VII in Geneva in 1987 saw a rapprochement between developing and developed countries, with the latter agreeing to provide targeted support for homegrown development projects.

Naturally, UNCTAD accords suffered ultimately from their lack of binding force. The Non-Aligned Movement was also weakened by political disagreements. In the late 1970s, Castro's attempt to get the nonaligned nations to form a closer relationship with the Soviet Union was vetoed by Tito. Cuba's military intervention on the side of the USSR in the conflict between Ethiopia and Somalia was heavily criticized, and Castro lost his leading role in the movement. More intensive South–South relations, such as the Cuban support for the MPLA regime in Angola or the trade links between Brazil and several African countries, were either strictly temporary or confined to individual countries. Even so, cohesion between the nonaligned nations helped counter the polarization between East and West. They also succeeded in putting the problem of underdevelopment firmly on the agenda of international politics. Their efforts ensured that this issue came to the fore again and was engaged with more seriously once the East-West conflict had drawn to a close.

Japan and the Tiger Economies

However, of far greater influence on the course of international politics was the rise of Japan and the smaller East Asian states and territories of South Korea, Taiwan, Hong Kong, and Singapore. This development had its roots in industrialization processes that began in the nineteenth century; although these were then seriously disrupted by civil wars and other regional conflicts in the first half of the twentieth century, they were not halted altogether. Shrewd, though individually quite different, development strategies and discreet support by the American or British colonial powers ensured that the growth of these territories' industrial sectors took on a dynamism that earlier industrialized societies had not experienced, and that in consequence took the Western world by surprise.

This development first became apparent in Japan. Under the protection of high tariff walls and further aided by an undervaluing of the yen—both of which were tolerated by the United States in order to maintain stability in the region during the Cold War—industrialization took off in Japan from the mid-1950s onward. More and more people moved from the countryside into the cities. Substantial investment in education and low wages promoted the growth of a number of world-beating branches of manufacturing, aided by a political organization of the market, which was geared to raising productivity. The first industries to become competitive in the international arena were textiles and the manufacture of optical instruments. These were followed in the 1960s by shipbuilding and steelmaking, and shortly thereafter by the automobile industry. The next sector to experience a boom, favored by rising wages in the interim, was electronics. Thus, as early as 1968, Japan generated a higher gross national product than the Federal Republic of Germany, and it became the world's second strongest economic power after the United States. Per capita income in the country doubled in less than a decade, while the proportion of Japanese who worked in agriculture fell from 38 percent in 1955 to just 12.6 percent in 1975.

Growth rates slowed in the 1970s, in part as a result of the fourfold increase in the price of crude during the oil crisis of late 1973, but also thanks to growing pressure to improve the standard of living. Public spending as a proportion of GNP increased from 12.7 percent in 1973 to 17.7 percent in 1980. In principle, though, growth continued unabated, because Japan flooded the world market with high-value but still relatively cheap consumer goods. Japanese manufacturing also partly benefited from a homegrown industrial know-how that outstripped foreign competition. Major investment in research and the targeted development of high-tech industries (such as computers, electronics) laid the foundation of an unprecedented export boom in the first half of the 1980s.

Japan's economic rise played a major part in securing the country's autonomy from the American occupying power. As early as 1967 the government demanded that the United States return Okinawa to Japanese sovereignty. During a 1969 visit to Washington, Prime Minister Satō Eisaku secured a US pledge to hand back the island by May 15, 1972. The American military bases would remain, but jurisdiction over the territory would be transferred to the Japanese authorities. In the renewal of the US-Japanese Security Treaty in June 1970, both sides were accorded the right to terminate this arrangement with one year's notice. When Nixon established contact with the Chinese leadership in the spring of 1972 without first consulting his Japanese allies, Tokyo decided to instigate diplomatic relations with Beijing with no further regard for American interests. During a state visit by Prime Minister Tanaka Kakuei to Beijing in September 1972, Japan announced that the peace treaty it had signed with the Chinese Nationalist regime on Taiwan in 1952 was now null and void: Japan recognized Taiwan as an integral part of the People's Republic of China.

The forging of diplomatic relations with Mao Zedong's China by Japan was followed by their intensification. When negotiations over a peace treaty with the Soviet Union foundered on the Japanese demand for return of the southern Kuril Islands, Japan promptly signed a Peace and Cooperation Treaty with the PRC on August 12, 1978, despite opposition from the Soviet Union. Though it did not put the Peace Treaty with the United States in jeopardy, through this act Japan had laid the foundation for an independent role in the four-cornered balance of power in the Pacific region.

This role was further strengthened by a dramatic rise in Japanese overseas investment. From 1975 to 1987, Japanese direct investment in foreign production facilities increased tenfold. These investments were made in part to circumvent protectionist measures in foreign markets, but also to outsource manufacturing to countries with lower wages. There was also increasing investment in foreign bonds, shares, and debt securities. As a result of the US trade deficit, by 1985 Japan had become the leading provider of credit in the global economy. In 1987, Tokyo replaced New York as the world's leading stock market. In the same year, though, it became clear that Japanese banks had incurred huge losses by speculating on investment and property in Southeast Asia. The stock markets crashed, and banks and companies recorded massive losses. Yet this end to disproportionate growth could not alter the fact that Japan had firmly established itself as a leading international power in industry and finance.

The change to an industrialized society came later in South Korea and Taiwan than in Japan, but when it did come, it was even more dynamic. In both countries, politically motivated support by the United States played a major role. A specific division of labor with Japan was also highly significant. Japanese firms invested in South Korea in order to take advantage of the lower wages there, and Taiwanese companies imported Japanese raw materials and partly finished goods for processing. In both cases, therefore, industrial growth was export-driven right from the start. High-value finished goods at competitive prices were shipped primarily to the United States—initially cheap, labor-intensive products such as textiles and toys, followed in the 1970s by heavy industrial goods like ships and construction plant, and in the 1980s by high-specification electronic appliances. Particularly with regard to the latter, South Korea developed world-beating technical know-how.

Export-oriented growth was still more dynamic in the city-territories of Hong Kong and Singapore. Here it was not so much a case of a transition from agriculture to industry, but rather from trade to manufacturing. Both cities had developed as commercial centers and military bases of the British Empire, and they now saw themselves cut adrift from their respective hinterlands: Hong Kong by Mao Zedong's communist regime, which became a closed, inward-looking

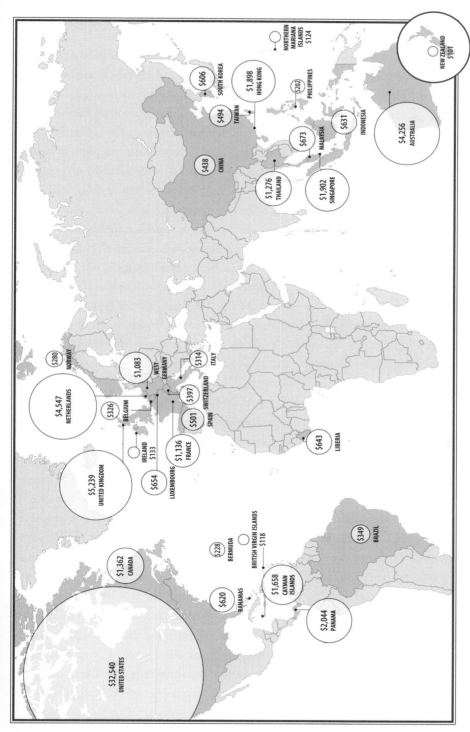

Major recipients of Japanese foreign direct investment, 1989 (in millions of US dollars).

economic entity, and Singapore by its separation from the Federation of Malaysia in 1965. In the switch to producing high-quality goods, Hong Kong benefited from the influx of well-educated Chinese refugees and Chinese capital. Singapore opted for openness to foreign investment in conjunction with state control over the development of infrastructure. Both states by necessity manufactured from the outset for the world market, in the process developing a product range very much akin to that of South Korea and Taiwan but without the heavy industrial component, which was an option only in states with more territory at their disposal. Up to the 1980s, both also became important financial centers.

In this way, the per capita income of Hong Kong and Singapore rose during the 1980s to more than twice that in South Korea and Taiwan. What made the growth of these four East Asian states so significant in terms of global politics was that by 1988 their combined output accounted for 8.1 percent of world trade. This was only slightly less than that of Japan (9.6 percent) and almost double that of all Latin American countries put together (4.2 percent). Considering that this share had been just 1.6 percent in 1963 explains why these states collectively became known in the West as "tiger economies."[47] They preferred to refer to themselves as the "four little dragons."

Politically, the growth of the East Asian states took place under more or less authoritarian regimes. In Japan the ruling Liberal Democratic Party, in fact a coalition of rival conservative groups, was able to consolidate its grip on power in an unbroken series of election victories; only after the economic collapse in the late 1980s did a coalition of opposition parties take over the reins of government for a short spell from 1993 onward. In May 1961 in South Korea, General Park Chung Hee established a military government that oscillated between repression and seeking an electoral mandate, but did not allow free and fair elections until 1987. Taiwan was ruled by the Guomindang, who had moved to the island after losing the civil war, with their leader, Chiang Kai-shek, serving as president from 1950 until his death in 1975. Only when martial law was lifted in 1987 did the democratic process begin. In Singapore, the originally socialist People's Action Party (PAP) won election after election. Its longtime leader Lee Kuan Yew, prime minister from 1959 to 1990, repeatedly turned to repressive measures from the 1970s onward to stifle any opposition. Lastly, Hong Kong remained a British Crown Colony until it was handed back to China in 1997 (the transfer was agreed to in 1984); its people were governed by a paternalistic administration that allowed them only minimal participation.

It is a matter of political debate as to whether this curtailing of democratic rights promoted the modernization process. But what is beyond dispute is that all five states were characterized by an extremely shrewd combination of entrepreneurial freedom with precise political micromanagement of the economy. However, protracted rule by a single party, or a single president, led in the case of Japan and South Korea to a high degree of corruption. It is also true to say that in all five countries the social consequences of economic modernization undermined authoritarian rule over time.

The Middle East Conflict and the Oil-Producing States

The rise of the oil-producing states started long before the world began to take notice of it. Over the course of the 1960s, the industrialized countries of Europe and Japan became increasingly dependent for their energy supplies on imported oil. At the same time, American oil imports rose by 50 percent in ten years, as US domestic oil reserves began to dwindle. Hand in hand with the increasing importance of oil reserves in the Near and Middle East in supplying the energy needs of the industrialized world—from just 7 percent at the end of the Second World War, their share of world production had grown to 38 percent by 1973[48]— came a growing sense of self-confidence within the regimes of oil-producing countries and consequently an ever-greater share in the revenue generated by extraction. In 1970 Colonel Muammar Gaddafi used the threat of nationalizing the Libyan oil industry to demand a substantial hike in prices and quotas. Because Western European states imported a quarter of their oil from Libya, Gaddafi's gambit paid off, opening the floodgates for other oil-producing countries to impose similar increases. Around the same time, the British withdrew its forces from Kuwait and the United Arab Emirates on the Persian Gulf, which together supplied more than one-third of all the oil from the Near and Middle East.

Crude oil prices skyrocketed as the Middle East conflict loomed. Driven by growing criticism from the Arab World, Egypt's president Nasser decided in the spring of 1967 to launch a new assault on Israel. The Israeli government preempted his attack by ordering, on June 5, 1967, an air strike that virtually destroyed the entire air forces of Egypt, Jordan, Syria, and Iraq on the ground. Thereafter, the ground forces of the Arab allies stood no chance. Within the space of four days, Israeli troops had occupied the Old City of Jerusalem, the West Bank, and the Sinai Peninsula as far as the Suez Canal. They heeded a UN appeal for a ceasefire only after taking control of the Golan Heights on the border with Syria on June 10. However, this lightning-fast Six-Day War brought Israel no nearer to peace. The Arab nations continued to deny the right of the State of Israel to exist, and a war of attrition set in on the country's borders.

Yet the Arab states could not endure the humiliation of the 1967 defeat for long. Nasser's successor, Anwar Sadat, found himself pressured to attack Israel once again in 1973, this time with the aim of securing a frontier that would be acceptable to both sides. With this objective in mind, Egyptian troops were to seize the zone around the Suez Canal, while Syria was to simultaneously retake the Golan Heights. These could then become bargaining chips to get Israel to the negotiating table; at the same time the oil-exporting countries, primarily Saudi Arabia, would bring pressure to bear on Western governments. Once Faisal, king of Saudi Arabia, had assured him of his support in August 1973, Sadat prepared for war.

The armies of Egypt and Syria began their offensive on October 6, 1973, on Yom Kippur, the Jewish Day of Atonement. Equipped with far better arms than in 1967, they soon achieved all their objectives. However, from October 8 onward, Israeli armored units and ground-attack aircraft began to recapture the Golan Heights. An Egyptian relief offensive in the Sinai was repulsed, and the Israelis established a bridgehead on the west bank of the Suez Canal. Now that a military stalemate had been reached, the Organization of Petroleum Exporting Countries (OPEC), meeting on October 17 in Kuwait and led by Saudi Arabia's skillful oil minister Ahmed Zaki Yamani, decided to raise oil prices by 70 percent and to progressively choke off supplies, at a rate of 5 percent per month, to countries that supported Israel. When President Nixon announced $2.2 billion in aid for Israel two days later, Faisal imposed a total oil embargo on the United States.

But the pressure resulting from these decisions now prompted the Nixon administration to throw its weight behind an early ceasefire and a lasting peace settlement. The Soviet Union had initially supported the Arab side by airlifting men and materiel, for fear that otherwise it would lose any influence over its allies. At the same time, though, it also called for a ceasefire. The Nixon administration responded in kind, airlifting vital supplies to Israel and seeking an end to the fighting. When Israel, whose forces were now advancing beyond the west bank of the Suez Canal, showed no sign of complying, Brezhnev sent a telegram to Nixon on October 24 urging the dispatch of a joint US-Soviet military contingent. If necessary, Brezhnev added, the Soviet Union would not shy away from "taking appropriate steps unilaterally."[49] This message prompted Kissinger to put US forces worldwide on red alert. He followed this up by putting pressure on Israel to fall in line, and hostilities were suspended on the night of October 26.

In order to progress swiftly from a ceasefire to a peace settlement, Kissinger now embarked on an intensive round of shuttle diplomacy between Cairo, Tel Aviv, and Damascus. By January 18, 1974, he had brokered a disengagement agreement between Egypt and Israel, under which Israeli forces would pull back to positions just forward of the passes through the Sinai and hand over control of the Suez Canal Zone to UN peacekeeping troops. The negotiations with Syria went on much longer; only at the end of May 1974, after a brief resumption in the fighting, did Syria's president, Hafez al-Assad, agree to a settlement that involved Israeli forces withdrawing from the positions they had taken in October 1973 and the creation of another UN buffer zone on the border with the Golan Heights. The oil-producing countries acknowledged Kissinger's efforts by lifting their embargo against the United States.

Yet irreconcilable demands still stood in the way of a wider peace settlement. In November 1977, Sadat, driven by Egypt's crippling debt to sue for peace, made a dramatic bid to break the deadlock in the negotiations: he announced that he would go "to the ends of the Earth" to secure peace, even to the Knesset. Israel felt duty-bound to invite him. On November 20 he told the Knesset his price for recognizing Israel and engaging in peaceful cooperation: withdrawal from the areas occupied in 1967 and the establishment of a Palestinian state on the West Bank. This initiative was widely applauded throughout the world and placed Israel under pressure to assent.

Following a series of fruitless bilateral negotiations between Israel and Egypt, at a meeting with Sadat and the Israeli prime minister, Menachem Begin, on September 6–17, 1978, President Jimmy Carter finally managed to obtain an

Israeli promise to end its military occupation of the West Bank and the Gaza Strip. He then stymied Israel's attempts to retreat from this position with trips to Cairo and Jerusalem in March 1979. On March 26, 1979, the Israel-Egyptian Peace Agreement was signed in Washington. Carter also signed as a witness. In line with this accord, Israel's forces withdrew from the Sinai in two phases by 1982; Israeli settlements in the Sinai were also abandoned. Two months after the agreement went into force, talks began on realizing Palestinian autonomy. These, though, were to be the source of new friction, this time between the Israelis and the Palestinians themselves.

At a meeting on November 4–5, 1973, the representatives of the oil-producing states passed further resolutions that resulted in a quadrupling of the oil price compared to its cost at the beginning of November. In doing so, they were carrying out the strategic role in the Middle East conflict that had been envisaged for them by Sadat's alliance strategy, by radically shifting the economic balance of power in their favor. Overall, OPEC's oil revenues increased more than threefold in 1973 alone, from US$33 billion to $108 billion—a sum that represented 13 percent of the value of all exports worldwide.[50] At a stroke, then, the OPEC states became major players on the stage of global politics—able not only to influence commercial activity but also to attract foreign workers and invest a portion of their immense profits in the industrialized countries.

The new influx of wealth into the countries of the Arabian Peninsula brought about an abrupt shift from seminomadic feudal societies to paternalistic welfare-state systems that enabled the ruling sheikhdoms to consolidate their hold on power. Their dependency on prosperous merchant families declined, while the leaders of rival tribal groups could be involved in administering the new prosperity, and the general populace, who formerly had to eke out a precarious existence, could now be pacified through generous state spending on welfare programs. As world-renowned architects set about transforming traditional royal capitals and ports into ultramodern cities, and foreign workforces assembled a state-of-the-art petrochemical industry, governments in the region instituted comprehensive educational programs and began to develop their own manufacturing industries. However, this sector's share of GNP remained modest. Also, the great majority of the newly educated indigenous population were absorbed into the rapidly growing civil service—the so-called petro-bureaucracy. In Saudi Arabia, which called the shots in the region, the royal family was also careful not to upset the religious leaders of the influential Wahhabi sects, thereby ensuring that they did not become rallying points for potential opposition to its rule.

In contrast, in Iran the new wealth was visited upon a much more advanced, complex society; but the reigning shah, Reza Pahlavi, proved much less competent in distributing it. The shah staked everything on developing a modern industrial sector at the cost of alienating the traditional middle classes; he also poured huge sums into the armed forces, used police repression to keep the country's progressive elite from gaining power, and alienated Iran's religious leaders with his attempts at modernization. When the country went into recession in 1978 as a result of failed investments, the Shi'ite spiritual leader Ayatollah Ruhollah Khomeini attracted a mass following with his tirades against the godless shah who had made common cause with the Western "devils."

The Pahlavi regime's brutal crackdown on protests only encouraged their spread. Khomeini was expelled in August 1978, but his influence continued to grow while he was in exile. From a Paris suburb he dispatched messages on cassette tapes to be replayed to the faithful in mosques and assembly rooms, and issued instructions by telephone to the leaders of various opposition groups. At the beginning of December, he used the occasion of the commemoration of the death of the Shi'ite martyr Hussein ibn Ali in AD 680 to call for a mass protest: on December 10 almost two million people joined a demonstration in Tehran against the shah's rule. Reza Pahlavi's last resort was to install a civilian government and flee the country with his family on January 16, 1979, intending to return when the situation had calmed down.

However, things did not pan out this way. Khomeini returned in triumph from exile on February 1 and immediately set up an alternative government. He managed to largely neutralize the generals, and after a single, if bloody, battle between the Imperial Guard and dissident air force units, the shah's regime stood down on February 11.

In the ensuing power struggle to establish a new political order, two events played into Khomeini's hands: the occupation of the US Embassy in Tehran by militant students on November 4, 1979, and the war with Iraq, which began with an attack by the new Iraqi leader, Saddam Hussein, on September 22, 1980. In the embassy the students uncovered documents discrediting Western-leaning

A woman, wearing a black chador and carrying a G3 machine gun, Tehran, February 12, 1979. She is participating in the occupation of Tehran University one day after the Iranian Revolution. Ayatollah Ruhollah Khomeini succeeded in mobilizing a mass following with his tirades against the godless Shah who had made common cause with the Western "devils." (Getty Images)

politicians. When the US government then sent aid to Saddam Hussein (following in the footsteps of Saudi Arabia, Kuwait, and France) to prevent the Iranian Revolution from spreading to Iraq, this only inflamed anti-American sentiment in Iran. In December 1979 a constitution was approved by referendum that invested a Supreme Religious Leader with extensive executive powers. The war against Iraq gave the theocracy the opportunity to liquidate both moderate politicians and militant terrorist opposition; conservative clerics who opposed the idea of a Supreme Leader were also sidelined.

But it was not just in Iran that rapid socioeconomic modernization resulting from contact with the West contributed to a strengthening and politicizing of Islam. Other regimes, from Libya to Pakistan, also used Islam's social cohesiveness to hold their states and societies together during major upheavals. Large sections of the populace set great store by their religious observance as a way of asserting patriarchal family structures against the modern trend toward individualism. Finally, many young students who saw themselves deprived by economic crises and rigid bureaucracies of any opportunities for advancement were drawn into becoming militant champions of fundamentalist Islam, which presently began to emerge as a political movement in its own right. The occupation of the Great Mosque in Mecca by about four hundred Islamist students in November 1979 gave a first indication of its growing significance.

The fall of the shah triggered a second hike in oil prices, with the price of a barrel of crude increasing by 1981 (taking inflation into account) to ten times its cost a decade before. However, this time the increase was not due to concerted action by the producers, but instead was caused by panic in the markets over the outcome of the Iranian Revolution and the conflict between two major producers, Iran and Iraq. The result was a further impetus to economic growth and modernization in the oil-producing countries. Concurrently, though, OPEC lost much of the power it had gained in 1973, as there came into being a complex market mechanism that caused oil prices to fall again from 1985 onward.

The Rambouillet Conference

The second rise in oil prices also had less dramatic consequences because the industrialized countries had learned in the meantime how to deal with this new challenge. At the time of the first increase, the industrialized nations of Western Europe had just completed the long reconstruction process after the Second World War, while the costs of the Vietnam War had plunged the United States into a trade deficit. The Nixon administration had reacted to this development by abandoning the pegging of the US dollar to the gold standard; eighteen months later, in the spring of 1973, strenuous efforts to revert to a system of currency parity came to nothing. The heavy burden imposed by the increased cost of oil led to across-the-board price increases and inflation; growth was slowed once more, and individual governments' attempts to crisis-manage the situation were offset by wild currency fluctuations.

Deeply concerned about the political consequences of inflation, economic stagnation, and unemployment, French president Valéry Giscard d'Estaing and German chancellor Helmut Schmidt endeavored to work out a common strategy for the industrialized countries to weather the crisis. To this end they invited the American president, Gerald Ford, and the British prime minister, Harold Wilson, to an intimate summit from November 15–18, 1975, in the Château de Rambouillet, 50 kilometers west of Paris. In acknowledgment of his country's major role in the global economy, the Japanese prime minister Miki Takeo was asked to attend. And to ward off the danger of the eurocommunists getting into government in Rome, the Italian prime minister, Aldo Moro, was also invited.

The six leaders agreed to undermine the cartel of oil-producing countries by promoting consumption: none of the oil exporters would henceforth be able to afford to artificially choke off the oil supply, but instead all of them would be tempted to increase their revenues at the expense of the competition. In addition, there was also a convergence between the French and American positions on the question of the currency markets: the participants did not agree to return to fixed exchange rates, as Giscard had demanded, but they did agree to make "every effort to restore stability" and to take steps to prevent "unsettled market conditions and unpredictable exchange-rate fluctuations."[51] An interim committee drafted appendices to this effect for the treaty governing the International Monetary Fund (IMF) in 1976. Governments were committed to exercising firm discipline in their budgetary and economic policies, and the IMF was charged with monitoring this process.

The success of the Rambouillet Conference prompted the participants to make meetings between heads of state and government a regular feature. The second meeting took place the very next year, this time with Canada present as well. The meetings of the Group of Seven (G-7) helped counter the demands resulting from the rise of the new players on the world stage. Nevertheless, the tangible results of these meetings often failed to live up to expectations: the tendency to bask in the reflected glory of the economically most powerful nations often trumped any readiness to undertake genuine coordinated action.

Toward a Second Cold War?

The loss of financial and commercial supremacy, and even more so the humiliating experience of the occupation of the US Embassy in Tehran, strengthened the trend toward a renunciation of the politics of détente in the United States. President Carter did not manage to secure the release of the fifty-two embassy staff taken hostage, either through drastic sanctions such as the seizure of Iranian capital assets in the United States or through diplomatic channels. An attempt to free the hostages through direct military action in April 1980 was a disastrous failure. In the event, it was 444 days before the imprisoned diplomats were able to leave the embassy, on January 20, 1981. For the whole of 1980, then, US impotence and the hatred of Islamic fundamentalists were the lead stories night after night on American television. In these circumstances, opposition politicians, who accused the Carter administration of wantonly sacrificing American interests in the face of Soviet supremacy, had a field day.

The image of Carter and Brezhnev embracing one another after signing the SALT II agreement in Vienna was grist to the mill of the opponents of détente, who had been lobbying strongly against the treaty for months. A Committee on the Present Danger, which included hard-liners from previous administrations, such as Eugene Rostow, Paul Nitze, and Dean Rusk, warned of the dangers of not putting up fierce opposition to Soviet rearmament, which in their view exposed the United States to the risk of a first-strike knockout blow. Others deplored the restriction in the number of multiple warheads and cruise missiles the United States was permitted to deploy, complaining that the Soviets were being allowed to keep their "heavy" ICBMs, which had no counterpart in the US nuclear arsenal. Many regarded arms control treaties in general as a waste of time, as long as the USSR violated human rights and was busy spreading its influence throughout the Third World. Senator Jackson, who had accused Carter, immediately before he left for Vienna, of pursuing a policy of appeasement, announced his intention to defeat the treaty in the Senate. Edward Rowny, representing the Joint Chiefs of Staff in the US SALT delegation, resigned in protest at the concessions the Carter administration was prepared to make.

However, the dark warnings about massive Soviet rearmament had little basis in fact. Certainly, in 1975 the Soviet Union had begun gradually to equip its intercontinental ballistic missiles with multiple warheads, and their submarine-launched missiles surpassed the number of equivalent US weapons, increasing from 459 on June 30, 1972, to 923 on September 30, 1979, as against the constant figure of 656 American submarine-launched ballistic missiles (SLBMs). Older rockets were replaced by new ones with more accurate targeting systems, while the expansion of the Soviet Navy continued. Yet given the huge numerical superiority of the American fleet, there was never even the slightest question of the Soviet Union catching up with the United States in terms of naval assets. By the mid-1970s, a single US aircraft carrier had more firepower than all vessels in the Soviet overseas fleet put together. The American MIRV program was also proceeding at a far faster pace than that of the Soviets. By the start of the 1980s the United States possessed around 9,500 individual warheads for intercontinental offensive weapons, while the USSR only had some 5,000; according to the provisions of SALT II, the United States was allowed a total of 11,500, and the Soviet Union 9,500. In addition, the American modernization program was not lagging behind the Soviets' in any way; indeed, with their cruise missiles, which were undetectable by radar, the Americans could even boast a new factor, to which the Soviets initially had no response. Moreover, defense expenditure in the Soviet Union had remained static, with some major cuts in the acquisition of new weapons systems from 1976 onward.[52]

The restrictions on modernization programs and on the number of multiple warheads per missile that were agreed upon in SALT II could not, however, entirely dispel the threat of a Soviet knockout blow against American land-based ICBMs. And the same was true of the American capacity to deliver a preemptive knockout blow, which would take out a far greater percentage of the Soviet arsenal than a Soviet first strike. And with the construction of a new generation of MX ICBMs, which could be moved between several launch sites, the United States was unilaterally acquiring a weapon that could not be neutralized in a first strike and that was also very hard to verify. These factors more than outweighed the fact that the Soviet Union was the only side with "heavy" intercontinental missiles. Furthermore, according to the SALT II stipulations, only the USSR was required to make real cuts in its nuclear missile arsenal (losing 350 missiles or bombers by January 1, 1981), whereas the United States was still able to reach targets in the Soviet Union with its cruise missiles.

More justified was Helmut Schmidt's concern that the "strategic parity" between the two superpowers, as laid down in the SALT treaties, made increasingly implausible the threat of a first strike using NATO tactical battlefield nuclear weapons or an American retaliatory strike. The new Soviet SS-20 intermediate-range missiles, which had been phased in from 1977 onward to replace their six hundred or so older SS-4s and SS-5s, were precisely designed to give the Soviets a first-strike capability against the European NATO allies. Unlike their predecessors, they were mobile and hence practically invulnerable; they also had a longer range and—with their lighter launch weight and smaller explosive force—far greater accuracy; what was more, each missile was fitted with three warheads. It was therefore not inconceivable that Soviet military chiefs might use them, in conjunction with their fast and hard-to-stop Backfire bombers, to launch a surprise attack that would largely eliminate NATO's ground troops, air force, and nuclear weapons stationed in Europe. Because the Europeans could not rely on the fact that their American allies would then really undertake a retaliatory nuclear strike against the Soviet Union, the only realistic strategy for preventing such a first strike was to give ongoing assurances of goodwill.

Even so, the second-strike capacity of the Soviet Union by no means precluded a credible threat of US retaliation in the event of a Soviet attack on the European NATO allies. Even if most of the fixed missile silos had been wiped out, the number of American missiles that would still be available to deliver an unacceptably costly retaliatory strike was larger than ever, and their selective deployment remained a real option. Plus, by upgrading from the Polaris to the Poseidon missile system, the US military had increased fivefold (from 80 to 400) the number of submarine-based warheads within range of the USSR that the NATO Chiefs of Staff could deploy, as well as more than doubling (from 80 to 164) their strike force of nuclear-armed F-111 swing-wing bombers that, flying from air bases in Great Britain, could penetrate deep into Soviet territory. Thus, in principle NATO also had the potential for a "proportionate" response to an attempted Soviet preemptive strike against Western Europe.

As a result, Brezhnev found Schmidt's concerns hard to understand. He regarded the replacement of the increasingly dilapidated and vulnerable SS-4 and SS-5 missiles as a quite normal procedure, comparable to the modernization of short-range missiles and forward-based systems that the West was then engaged in. It appeared all the more necessary because the United States had steadfastly refused to include the forward-based systems in any arms control agreement, and because France, Great Britain, and China had not only modernized but also expanded their intermediate-range arsenals. Brezhnev therefore reacted with incomprehension when Schmidt, on his very first visit to Moscow in October 1974, tried to engage with him on the problem of the Euro-strategic imbalance. And when Schmidt attempted in June 1979 to persuade him to reduce the number of SS-20s stationed in Europe, Brezhnev did not step in to countermand Defense Minister Dmitriy Ustinov's flat refusal.

Following endless arguments about the possible replacement of a part of the tactical weapons arsenal stationed in Europe with "neutron bombs" (which were meant to cause less damage to infrastructure), at a meeting on the Caribbean island of Guadeloupe in early 1979 Carter, Schmidt, Giscard, and British prime minister James Callaghan signaled their agreement in principle to stationing new intermediate-range missiles in Europe as a response to Soviet nuclear arms modernization. European defense experts advocated the deployment of 464 cruise missiles, which could get under Soviet missile defenses, and 108 Pershing II missiles, which could hit strategic targets in the Soviet Union within minutes. This decision gave NATO another first-strike option, though it did not, admittedly, obviate the threat of a theoretical preemptive strike by SS-20s. On the other hand, the new intermediate-range missiles shifted the strategic balance of power (which, in view of the discounting of the forward-based systems, the Soviets did not think existed anyway) further in favor of the West. In the Soviets' eyes, it made no difference whether American missiles targeted on the Soviet

Union were launched from the mainland United States, from its submarine fleet, or from European soil.

In view of this basic ambivalence, the plan for strategic European rearmament also ran up against serious criticism from within Western Europe itself. To allay these concerns and neutralize any resistance to the stationing of the missiles, NATO's foreign and defense ministers therefore linked their decision to go ahead with deployment, taken on December 12, 1979, with an offer to the Soviet Union to open new talks on Euro-strategic rearmament. Deployment of the new missiles was scheduled to begin in late 1983 and would only take place if the negotiations had not yielded any concrete results by then.

The Afghanistan Crisis

Yet at first neither the Soviets nor the Americans were prepared to engage in talks. On the very same day that the Double-Track Decision was taken at NATO headquarters in Brussels, the Moscow Politburo voted in favor of sending troops to Afghanistan. Radical communists under Hafizullah Amin had seized power there in April 1978 following a military coup, and immediately put in place an energetic modernization program that provoked a violent backlash from traditional Islamic forces across the country. The Kremlin tried to persuade Amin to tone down his plans and broaden his power base, but when this fell on deaf ears, the decision was made to topple the radical communists and install a more moderate leadership that would meet with more support in the country and crush any residual Islamist resistance with the aid of Soviet troops.

The decision was controversial, given the likely difficulties of winning a guerrilla war in the Afghanistan mountains and the threat to détente that would result from another Soviet intervention in a Third World country. However, Defense Minister Ustinov was in favor, presumably counting on the fact that a quick victory would put him in pole position to succeed Brezhnev. And when he and Andropov joined forces to highlight the supposed danger of an alliance between the radical communists and the Americans, Brezhnev was won over. On December 25, 1979, Soviet troops were airlifted to Kabul and to western Afghanistan, and motorized units simultaneously crossed the border; in total, an invasion force of seventy-five thousand men was mobilized. On the evening of December

27, the presidential palace in Kabul was stormed and Amin and several of his most loyal followers were shot dead. At the same time, Babrak Karmal, leader of the moderate communists, announced in a radio broadcast that, as president of the revolutionary council, he had asked the country's Soviet friends to help him overthrow Amin's brutal dictatorship.

As it turned out, the setback for détente that the Soviets were reckoning on as a result of their actions was far more serious than Moscow had anticipated. The coup in Kabul not only left Carter contemplating the complete evaporation of any chance that SALT II would be ratified. Carter also felt personally betrayed by a Soviet president who in Vienna had promised that he would deal squarely with him in the future. He therefore accepted Brzezinski's interpretation of the Afghanistan invasion as the first stage in a concerted thrust by the Soviets through Pakistan and Iran to the Indian Ocean. On January 3, 1980, he asked the US Senate to put discussions of SALT II on hold for an indefinite period; a few days later Carter announced in a television address a wide-ranging severing of cultural and commercial ties with the Soviet Union, including a halt to grain exports, an embargo on all high-tech and strategic goods, postponement of the opening of new consulates in New York and Kiev, and a package of military and economic aid to the supposedly threatened state of Pakistan. On January 20 he also called on American athletes to boycott the Olympic Games, which were due to be held in Moscow in the summer of 1980.

Carter's European allies were not prepared to go along with this demonstrative termination of the policy of détente. In the meantime they had been busy expanding economic relations and the exchange of "people, information, and opinions" with their Eastern Bloc neighbors (including buying the freedom of political detainees), and for that reason alone were not keen to abandon their long-term project of reducing tension between the blocs. They also consistently rejected economic sanctions as a response to the invasion of Afghanistan. Instead, on many occasions they leaped in to fill the vacuum left when the Americans withdrew from various cooperative ventures, with the result that total trade between Europe and the Soviet Union expanded considerably in 1980. The American call to boycott the Olympic Games was heeded only by the Federal Republic of Germany (along with China and Japan), and then only after serious

Afghan refugees in Pakistan protest against the Soviet invasion of
Afghanistan, February 5, 1980. Soviet hopes to crush Islamist resistance in the country with the aid of an invasion force of 75,000 men
were soon disappointed. (© Pascal Manoukian/Sygma/Corbis)

political disagreement at home and out of a concern not to place excessive strain
on the Western alliance.

Giscard and Schmidt also did their best to keep the East-West dialogue on
track. To this end the French president, without seeking the prior approval of his
Western allies, went to meet Brezhnev in Warsaw on May 19, while the German
chancellor traveled to Moscow on June 30, after a heated exchange with Carter.

Although the two leaders made no headway on the question of the war in Afghanistan, Schmidt did manage to persuade the Soviet leadership to begin talks on intermediate-range missiles. Carter was reluctant to join these discussions, but when Brezhnev personally intervened on August 21 to propose a start to negotiations, he found himself unable to refuse, mindful as he was both of the clear provision for talks contained in the Double-Track Decision and of the need to hold the Western alliance together. On September 25, Andrei Gromyko and the new US secretary of state, Edmund Muskie, met on the fringes of the UN General Assembly and agreed to begin preparatory talks in Geneva on October 16 on the limitation of intermediate-range weapons.

However, this breakthrough on talks threatened to evaporate once more after Carter lost the presidential election on November 4. Despite his clear change of course after the Afghanistan invasion, he failed to prevent the electorate from voting in the Republican nominee Ronald Reagan, the very epitome of a Cold War warrior and enemy of détente. In the presidential campaign, Reagan had accused both Carter and Kissinger of selling out American interests, and now, in office, he promised explicitly to put America back on top once more.

Reagan and the Peace Movement

Reagan embarked on his presidency with a relatively simplistic worldview, which he frequently aired in public. In his eyes, détente was synonymous with Western weakness, an attitude that had allowed the Soviet Union to assemble the "greatest military machine the world has ever seen" and to reap unilateral geostrategic benefits in the developing world. This was all the more alarming inasmuch as Moscow's objective was the "promotion of world revolution."[53] To this end, said Reagan, the Kremlin was prepared to commit any crime; it was behind all the unrest that broke out in the world's hot spots; and it presided, Reagan claimed in a speech in the spring of 1983, over an "evil empire."[54] To counter this, the American nation needed to regain its "strength"—in military, economic, and moral terms. America had to take the lead role in the Western world once again, while NATO as a whole had to put up a stronger front against the USSR. This would not only help secure peace but also force the Soviets to disarm: "[They] cannot vastly increase their military productivity because they've already got their people on a starvation diet."[55]

In line with this approach, the Reagan administration made no attempt to enter into the negotiations on intermediate-range missiles that had been agreed to, or to continue the wider talks on strategic weapons reductions. Instead it focused initially on making outspoken public attacks on the Soviet Union and its rearmament program. Just two weeks after taking office, Reagan approved an increase to the $200.3 billion defense budget of $32.6 billion, a hike of 16 percent. In total, between 1981 and 1985, defense expenditure grew in real terms by 51 percent.[56] Guidelines drafted by the Pentagon, which resulted in a presidential directive of May 1982 (NSDD 332), called for the capacity to wage a conventional as well as a protracted nuclear war against the Soviet Union and to maintain the upper hand throughout. In addition, the United States should be in a position to deliver "decapitating strikes" against the Soviet leadership, and to counter regional offensives by the enemy with "horizontal escalation" in other theaters of war. In addition, plans were drawn up to develop new weapons systems that the USSR could not hope to keep pace with. The Strategic Defense Initiative (SDI; or "Star Wars" program) was expressly included in this wish list.

In the face of this unyieldingly tough stance toward the Soviet enemy, European misgivings about the collapse of the détente process developed into a broad-based peace movement with a distinctly anti-American flavor, while even in the United States itself, concerns over where an unchecked policy of rearmament was leading and the huge costs involved gave rise to a protest movement. The European peace lobby was at its strongest in the Federal Republic of Germany, where most intermediate-range missiles were due to be stationed. On October 10, 1981, 250,000 people demonstrated in the federal capital, Bonn, against the Double-Track Decision; Helmut Schmidt found it increasingly difficult to prevent his party from voting against implementing the decision. In the United States, the movement principally passed resolutions calling for a freeze in nuclear weapons at the current level. In February and March 1982, corresponding freeze motions were tabled in both houses of Congress. The administration succeeded in defeating them by a slim majority, and even then only by supporting an alternative resolution requiring substantial reductions in nuclear weapons prior to any freeze.

Faced with such overwhelming internal and external pressure, the Reagan administration found itself obliged to fall in line with the German government's request, at the spring meeting of the NATO Council on May 4–5, 1981, to resume negotiations on intermediate-range missiles. A year later it also agreed to a resumption of talks on strategic arms. In both cases, though, its starting position effectively amounted to a restoration of US superiority: in the case of the medium-range missiles, a "zero solution" that left both NATO's seaborne missiles and the British and French nuclear deterrents out of the reckoning; and in the strategic domain, a reduction strictly graded according to types of weapons, which would have left the United States with three times more warheads than the Soviets. A compromise reached by the delegates at the intermediate-range weapons negotiations in Geneva in July 1982 (the so-called Walk in the Woods formula; a reduction to seventy-five SS-20s, each with three warheads, and seventy-five launch ramps, each with four cruise missiles) found no favor either in Moscow or in Washington.

The Kremlin responded to the American offensive with counterproposals designed to ratchet up public pressure on the Reagan administration. When a nationwide strike movement in Poland brought about a clear liberalization of the country's communist regime, the Soviets were at pains not to give the West another pretext to let relations worsen still further. In particular, Moscow was concerned not to drive away the Europeans as partners in détente. It therefore raised no objection to the founding, on September 17, 1980, of the independent Solidarity labor union movement under the chairmanship of the former Gdansk shipyard welder and strike leader Lech Wałęsa. As ongoing strikes and political demands began to call the whole socialist character of Poland into question, Moscow did urge the Polish leadership to impose martial law, but at the same time it ruled out a military intervention along the lines of the Prague Spring. Even when the Polish prime minister and party leader, Wojciech Jaruzelski, requested Soviet military support in early December 1981, the Politburo remained adamant that there could be no question of dispatching troops. As Yuri Andropov explained, "Even if Poland were to be ruled by Solidarity, so be it.... We have to take care of our own country and strengthen the Soviet Union."[57]

Thus, the expansion of economic cooperation and nuclear arms limitation had in the meantime become so important for the Soviet leadership that it was now prepared to effectively throw overboard the concept of solidarity with ruling socialist parties in other countries that had been enshrined in the Brezhnev Doctrine. The decision to use Polish security forces to crush the democracy movement was Jaruzelski's alone. Although he knew that there would be no Soviet intervention, he approved the introduction of martial law on December 13, 1981—evidently fearing that he would otherwise be responsible for handing victory to the counterrevolution in Poland. Solidarity was banned as an organization, and leading members of the labor union and other opposition groups were imprisoned.

The Kremlin's calculated risk in not invoking the Brezhnev Doctrine paid off. European governments were able to resist the pressure for new sanctions against the Soviet Union, which the Reagan administration wanted to implement in retaliation for Jaruzelski's coup. The idea of breaking off negotiations on intermediate-range missiles was quickly dropped after Schmidt visited Reagan at the beginning of January 1982, and the United States ultimately went it alone on economic sanctions. When these sanctions were extended in July to cover technical equipment, which European countries were planning to supply to the USSR to help construct a gas pipeline from Siberia to Europe, a serious rift arose among the Western allies. Likewise, no change occurred in the steady development of relations between the two Germanies when Schmidt was succeeded as chancellor in October 1982 by his Christian Democrat rival, Helmut Kohl. Kohl retained the liberal Hans-Dietrich Genscher as his foreign minister. In June 1983 the Bavarian prime minister, Franz-Josef Strauss, once a sworn enemy of Bonn's Eastern Treaties, even arranged extended credit on extremely favorable terms to the GDR, which saved it from impending national insolvency.

The End of Negotiations

The thaw in inter-German relations could not halt the installation of the new missiles in Europe. Erich Honecker did not wield nearly enough influence in Moscow, while the position of the Federal Republic government was too inconsistent to sway the United States. There arose within the Social Democratic Party a tendency to respond to the Reagan administration's reluctance to negotiate by refusing to rearm. However, Schmidt shied away from weakening the Western alliance in this way, and his coalition partners, the liberal Free Democrats, were also opposed to such a move. The new coalition, which Genscher had entered into partly because of the SPD majority's challenge to the Double-Track Decision, did press for compromises beyond the zero-solution, but crucially it did not make its agreement to the stationing of the new missiles contingent upon the Americans' position in the negotiations.

There was some movement in the Soviet position after the sudden death of Brezhnev on November 10, 1982. The new general secretary, Yuri Andropov, whose appointment as secretary to the Central Committee in May had effectively earmarked him as Brezhnev's successor, was able to insist upon offering more than his defense minister Ustinov was willing to concede in return for an American agreement not to station their intermediate-range missiles in Europe. In a television address on December 21, 1982, he announced that the USSR would be prepared to restrict itself to 162 missiles—the same number as the combined British and French deterrent. In the negotiations, this developed into an offer to reduce the Soviet arsenal to 122 or at most 127 missiles—in other words, the Soviet Union was prepared to forego exactly the same number of warheads as in NATO's proposed new deployment. At a stroke, Andropov had renounced his capacity to threaten a first strike against NATO installations within Europe—the only objective grounds for concern over the stationing of the SS-20s in the first place.

Yet Washington stuck rigidly to the line that stationing of the Pershing II missiles in Europe would go ahead as planned unless the Soviet intermediate-range arsenal was completely withdrawn. On March 30, 1983, Reagan indicated that he would be amenable to an interim solution whereby the United States and the Soviet Union would deploy an equal, unspecified number of warheads for their intermediate-range nuclear forces (INF). In September he clarified his position, revealing that each side should be allowed 420 warheads *globally*, and that with regard to the Soviet missiles in Asia, not all the American intermediate-range missiles needed to be stationed in Europe. This amounted to a reduction in US rearmament by about one-fourth, in return for a reduction in the number of SS-20s stationed in Europe to around fifty. The American negotiators calculated that this was all that was required for the Europeans to agree to the rearmament decision, and that they could then, after rearmament had been completed, negotiate from a position of strength.

And indeed, this proposal by the Reagan administration succeeded. Because Andropov's compromise proposals were, among other things, aimed at preventing the ongoing installation of multiple warheads on British and French missiles, from early 1983 on, French president François Mitterrand, who had succeeded Giscard in May 1981, threw his weight strongly behind implementation of the Double-Track Decision. Addressing the West German parliament on January 20, he called for solidarity in the face of the threat from Soviet intermediate-range missiles; and at the World Economic Summit at Williamsburg, Virginia, on May 30–31, he forced through a statement excluding the inclusion of nuclear weapons from "other states" from the US-Soviet talks. Helmut Kohl did not dare embrace the proposal (put forward by Paul Warnke, a former director of the US Arms Control and Disarmament Agency) for cancellation of Pershing and cruise missile deployment in exchange for the Soviets dismantling an equivalent number of warheads, and so the governing factions in Bonn settled on the explanation that the Soviet side had not shown enough willingness to negotiate. On November 22 the West German parliament approved the deployment of Pershing II missiles.

As they had threatened beforehand, the Soviets responded by breaking off the INF negotiations in Geneva, and they also walked out of the discussions on strategic arms reductions, which for propaganda purposes the Reagan administration now dubbed the Strategic Arms *Reduction* Talks (START). At the same time, the Soviets announced their countermeasures against the stationing of the Pershing and cruise missiles: they would install their own cruise missiles in the European territory of the Soviet Union and transfer tactical battlefield nuclear weapons to the GDR's and Czechoslovakia's borders with West Germany. To Andropov, further negotiations appeared utterly pointless and in some respects even counterproductive, in that they threatened to fuel vain hopes that the Reagan administration might still be persuaded to see reason and thereby to take the necessary sting out of the protest movement against the arms race.

A new round of hawkish statements from the White House raised alarm in Moscow that Reagan might actively be preparing to go to war with the Soviet Union. On March 23, 1983, two weeks after his diatribe against the "evil empire," the US president announced that he was setting up a Strategic Defense Initiative (SDI), which involved creating a defensive missile shield in space. This proposal was tantamount to revoking the whole of the deterrent system: if it succeeded, the United States would be in a position to threaten the Soviet Union with a nuclear first strike without having to worry about a retaliatory attack. The intermediate-range missiles that were now in position in Europe thus became offensive weapons that could unleash a nuclear conflict that would remain confined to Europe. Accordingly, the KGB was detailed to watch for signs of an impending US first strike and to report back the details to Moscow. In December the number of Soviet nuclear-armed submarines patrolling within range of the US seaboard was augmented, because the Soviets believed this was the only way to counter the "increased nuclear threat facing the Soviet Union."[58]

When Reagan, mindful of securing reelection, offered the Kremlin a new round of talks in January 1984, Soviet fears of an American attack in the immediate future abated. Yet because the Soviet leaders were also keen not to help reelect a president whom they regarded as extremely dangerous, they did not respond to Reagan's offer. A high-ranking delegation of Soviet scientists was granted leave to accept an invitation to travel to the United States only on the condition that they did not engage in any talks with government representatives. On May 8 the Soviet Union announced that it would not be taking part in the 1984 Summer Olympics in Los Angeles, after it became abundantly clear that the occasion would become a forum for anti-Soviet demonstrations. All the Warsaw Pact countries except Romania found themselves obliged to join the Soviet boycott; Cuba and Vietnam also took the opportunity to demonstrate their revolutionary solidarity by staying away. In August, Honecker was forced to cancel a planned visit to the Federal Republic.

This party line was formulated by a Soviet elite that, besides Gromyko and Ustinov, included Konstantin Chernenko and Mikhail Gorbachev. Andropov was effectively ruled out of all involvement in affairs of state after being laid up indefinitely by kidney failure in late November 1983; he died on February 9, 1984. In a state of disarray, the Politburo opted for Chernenko, former second secretary and confidant of Brezhnev, to succeed him as general secretary. Gorbachev, whom Andropov had wanted to promote as his right-hand man because of his drive and enthusiasm, was still not a viable choice. Although Ustinov did put Gorbachev's name forward, he encountered serious reservations from certain members of the conservative old guard. But Chernenko was already suffering from health problems, and in any event was not the most able political operator, so Gorbachev still ended up taking on some leadership responsibilities. For instance, as in the last months of Andropov's premiership, Gorbachev chaired all meetings of the Politburo.

When Reagan's reelection looked certain, the Moscow leadership began looking around once more for opportunities to do business with this archconservative president. When Reagan invited Gromyko to take part in talks on the occasion of the next UN General Assembly meeting, the Kremlin did not refuse. After this discussion, which took place on September 28, Chernenko announced that if Reagan was really serious about resuming negotiations, "the Soviet Union will not be found wanting."[59] And after Reagan had sent a personal message to Chernenko on November 7, the Politburo assented to a new round of talks on nuclear arms and weapons in space. On November 22 it was agreed that Gromyko and his American counterpart, George Shultz, would meet in Geneva in January 1985 to map out an agenda for the new negotiating round.

Moscow did not attach any great hopes to the resumption of talks. It felt that the American initiative was too vague and that the anti-Soviet rhetoric coming out of Washington was still as strident as ever. While conducting a microphone test during the US election campaign, Reagan jokingly said, "We begin bombing [the Soviet Union] in five minutes." And just before Gromyko's visit to the White House, the press got hold of a secret CIA memorandum that claimed that the Soviet empire had "entered its terminal phase" and was therefore more dangerous than ever.[60] After his encounter with Reagan, Gromyko at least did not want to rule out the possibility of reaching agreements with the president after he had been reelected. That possibility now needed to be sounded out.

Gorbachev and the End of the Cold War

Chernenko and his Politburo colleagues were well advised to respond positively to Reagan's offer of a new round of negotiations. From the summer of 1984 onward, the president of the neoconservative revolution was convinced that he had done enough to restore America's position of strength. That allowed him not only to show willingness to negotiate but also to genuinely work toward forging new agreements with the Soviet leadership. It also enabled him to adopt positions that were realistically open to negotiation. Yet some time was to elapse before all this actually came to pass. The administration was not yet prepared to enter serious discussions, as the continuing political differences and personal rivalries among its members made it hard for it to develop coherent positions.

Even the opening to negotiations proved extraordinarily difficult. The Kremlin insisted upon including space weapons in the talks. Their primary aim was to prevent their development. Conversely, Reagan's secretary of defense, Caspar Weinberger, flatly refused to discuss the SDI program. After much wrangling, the two sides finally agreed that the negotiations, which began on March 12, 1985, in Geneva, would be conducted in three groups. The first would be concerned with strategic defense and space weapons, the second with reductions in strategic offensive weapons, and the third with medium-range missiles. Any accords reached in one group would be binding only if there was agreement in the others.

Chernenko died two days before the talks began. His death did not create a major disruption, because Gorbachev had already been taking on more responsibilities as the general secretary's health declined. Nothing now stood in the way of Gorbachev's election as general secretary; his appointment was confirmed by a unanimous vote of the Politburo on March 11, 1985. Gorbachev promptly announced that there would be "more dynamism" in foreign affairs,[61] and he kept to his word. The new Soviet premier belonged to the "generation of '56"—party functionaries who had cut their teeth during Khrushchev's crusade against Stalinism, and who for all their grounding in the Marxist-Leninist worldview aspired to a "better" form of socialism. He differed fundamentally from the old guard who had elevated him to power, in that his awareness of the unpalatable realities of the Soviet empire was not clouded to the same extent by ideological certainties.

One of the convictions that he brought to his new position was his appreciation of the need for a "common security policy." The crux of this concept—which he had gleaned from the work of the UN Commission for Disarmament and International Security chaired by the Swedish premier Olof Palme—was that, in the absence of trust-building measures, no real security or disarmament was achievable. As a result, Gorbachev immediately accepted when Reagan invited him to a face-to-face meeting. In the run-up to the meeting, which took place on November 19–20 in Geneva, he offered nothing less than a 50 percent cut in the USSR's strategic offensive weapons stockpile in return for a mutual moratorium on all weapons in space. He also mooted separate negotiations on strategic arms reductions in Europe, which France and Great Britain would also be involved in. Finally, he announced that he would mothball the additional twenty-seven SS-20 missiles that the Soviet Union had deployed in response to the stationing of Pershing and cruise missiles in Western Europe.

This was a truly tempting offer for Reagan. However, under the influence of his defense secretary and his national security advisor, he was not yet ready to abandon the SDI project. The upshot was that the two sides at Geneva were only able to agree on the principle of a 50 percent cut in nuclear weapons. Yet Reagan did affirm Gorbachev's statement that "a nuclear war cannot be won and must never be waged," while also committing himself "not to seek military superiority."[62] Compared to the war paranoia that had gripped people's minds just two years before, this represented truly astonishing and encouraging progress.

Gorbachev now tried to wear down Regan's resistance to relinquishing the SDI program by pointedly ignoring a new tide of anti-Soviet rhetoric from Washington and instead offering new concessions: the complete dismantling of all Soviet and American intermediate-range missiles in Europe, the inclusion of the European territory of the USSR in the reduction of conventional troop numbers in Europe, and a freeze in the Soviet deployment of medium-range missiles in the Far East. At a hastily convened new meeting with Reagan in Reykjavik on October 11–12, 1986, he bundled these proposals into a complete package that the American side could not in all conscience reject without renouncing their commitment to common security. And this did indeed result in the signing of a new accord that pledged a halving of strategic nuclear weapons within five years, the withdrawal of all Soviet and American intermediate-range missiles from Europe (with no mention of the French and British deterrents), and restriction of medium-range missiles outside Europe to one hundred per side. In direct talks, Reagan and Gorbachev even agreed to abolish *all* nuclear weapons within ten years.

However, how much store could be set by these agreements remained open to question, after the two leaders clashed once more at the end of the conference over the question of the Strategic Defense Initiative. Reagan agreed to a continuance of the ABM Treaty for another ten years, but he still wanted to retain the freedom to install a defensive umbrella in space. When Gorbachev tried to dissuade him, Reagan broke off the conversation in some agitation. Both leaders returned deeply disappointed to their respective capitals, where they had excited much negative comment about the concessions that they had been willing to make. Because the European allies demanded that nuclear weapons should be dismantled only once absolute conventional parity had been reached on the continent, the US representatives at the Geneva talks withdrew their original suggestion that all ballistic nuclear weapons should be abolished as part of a second phase of the disarmament process.

Faced with the danger that the consensus reached in Reykjavik might ebb away, Gorbachev now pushed through another major concession: in February 1987 he persuaded the Politburo to approve an offer to the Americans to dismantle the Soviet medium-range missiles in Europe independent of any renunciation of the SDI project, and also to stand down the shorter-range missiles that had been deployed in the GDR and Czechoslovakia in response to the West's adoption of the Double-Track Decision. In isolation, this was a unilateral weakening of the Soviet position, and many of the Soviet military and diplomatic corps were deeply uneasy about making this offer. But Gorbachev was reasonably certain that a breakthrough in the question of intermediate-range missiles would also kick-start the strategic arms control process, leaving the SDI project to fall by the wayside.

And in fact Reagan was immediately prepared to implement the zero-solution where medium- and short-range missiles were concerned. This in turn set the negotiations at the highest level in motion once more, which then went from strength to strength. Although NATO strategists tried to offset the impending loss of the medium-range missiles by invoking the right to station shorter-range weapons in Europe, Gorbachev sidestepped this by suddenly offering, during a visit by George Shultz on April 13–14, to destroy all remaining So-

Ronald Reagan shakes hands with Mikhail Gorbachev in the garden of the White House on December 8, 1987. The two leaders signed a treaty on the complete abolition of intermediate-range missiles and issued a series of detailed clarifications regarding the agreement they hoped to reach to halve their offensive strategic arsenals. (Time & Life Pictures/Getty Images)

viet short-range missiles—in other words, a double-zero-solution, which was equally unwelcome to the Soviet military strategists. When the Pentagon and the European allies were slow to take up this offer, Gorbachev extended it to include the Far East as well. Reagan found this whole package so plausible that he forced it through in the face of doubters in his own camp. In Washington on December 8, 1987, Gorbachev and Reagan signed a treaty on the complete abolition of intermediate-range missiles. At the same time, they issued a series of detailed clarifications regarding the treaty they hoped to conclude on halving their offensive strategic arsenals.

Aspects of Perestroika

Parallel with his involvement in the disarmament process, Gorbachev also instituted a series of reforms that not only fundamentally changed the West's image of the Soviet system, but also profoundly altered its very nature. His first move was to provide the Soviet people with glasnost—the courage to exhibit transparency and openness and tell the truth rather than hide behind a permanent veil of ideological self-delusion. Censorship was relaxed; critical novels dealing with the darker aspects of Soviet history were published for the first time; science was freed from political interference; and functionaries were increasingly exposed to public criticism. In December 1986, the banishment of nuclear physicist Andrei Sakharov to Gorki was lifted; his banishment had been a punishment ordered by the Party leadership for his criticism in January 1980 of the decision to invade Afghanistan. By the start of 1980, almost all political dissidents had been released from prison.

The logical next step of perestroika (reconstruction), as the reform program was ambiguously dubbed, encountered a great deal of resistance. Although from 1985 to 1987 around half of all leadership positions, right down to the Party secretaries governing cities and *raions* (districts), were replaced by new blood, it still took Gorbachev several failed attempts before he was finally able, in January 1987, to propose to a plenary session of the Central Committee that in the future functionaries should be elected in a secret ballot from a plurality of candidates. This principle was enacted only after a Party conference in June 1988, and even then only in a watered-down form. Elections within the Party were still decided by a discretionary provision, while members of the Soviets were henceforth to be chosen by secret ballot. The authority of the Soviets was strengthened, but at the same time it was determined that the first secretaries had to be put forward by members for election to the chair of their respective Soviet.

Gorbachev then scored some notable successes in the matter of implementing decisions reached by the Party conference. Not only did a plethora of independent organizations of various shades now suddenly arise, along with a welter of different newspapers claiming to represent democratic values, but elections to the Congress of People's Deputies of the Soviet Union, which would form the nucleus of a new Supreme Soviet, were called for March 1989. The responsibilities and the personnel of the Central Committee departments were cut drastically, and Gorbachev's mentors Alexander Yakovlev and Vadim Medvedev took up key positions. For the elections, it was decided that 750 delegates should be appointed through social organizations, but that 1,500 should be directly elected by the people. The result was the constitution of a Congress (on May 25, 1989) that offered a genuine plurality of viewpoints, and in which the representatives of the *nomenklatura* no longer enjoyed a majority. Indeed, 15 percent of the delegates were not even members of the Communist Party.

The strengthening of self-determination within a socialist society that Gorbachev was undertaking in the Soviet Union would also be mirrored in the socialist brother-states. For him, this was an inevitable corollary to the demise of the Brezhnev Doctrine, which had implicitly already begun at the end of the Brezhnev era. Now that the foreign Communist Party leaders could no longer count on military support from the Soviet Union, they had to tailor their policies in order to maintain or win the assent of their people. Gorbachev had already spelled that out to them in a series of encounters in Moscow on the occasion of Chernenko's funeral, but many of them did not or would not grasp his meaning, even after he rammed the message home in later meetings. At the Party conference in June 1988, he therefore spoke quite candidly about the "freedom of choice" open to every people, and branded as "dangerous" any attempt to "impose upon anyone a social system, a way of life, or policies from outside by any means, let alone military force."[63] In December of that year, he reiterated this credo at the UN plenary session.

Renouncing the Brezhnev Doctrine also enabled Gorbachev to abandon conventional military superiority in Europe, which had always been a stumbling block to any substantive disarmament agreement. In May 1987 the Warsaw Pact approved the transition from the doctrine of "offensive defense" to the concept of "defensive parity." At the Washington summit, Gorbachev offered the US president asymmetric cuts in conventional weapons, and when after several months Reagan showed no signs of responding to this offer, in December 1988 Gorbachev announced a unilateral reduction of troop numbers within the Warsaw Pact, which, while only cutting its personnel by 10 percent, still substantially compromised its offensive capability. This action was a prime mover behind a new round of negotiations on conventional armed forces in Europe (CFE), which finally got under way in Vienna on March 9, 1989; there, NATO soon responded by proposing substantial cuts of its own.

Finally, Gorbachev also ordered a Soviet withdrawal from Afghanistan by February 1989. This had been a pressing concern ever since he took office: the war, which by then had dragged on for more than five years, was patently unwinnable; all the Soviet Union had to show for it was a long list of casualties, huge financial costs, and continuing damage to the country's international reputation. Yet time and again, the military claimed to be on the verge of victory. By February 1988, Gorbachev was finally able to announce that the Soviet withdrawal would begin on May 15 of that year, when a treaty between Afghanistan and Pakistan came into effect. After this accord, which was backed by Soviet and American guarantees, was signed on April 14, half of the Soviet forces left the country, with the last troops pulling out by February 1989 as announced. The Soviet-backed regime managed to stay in power for three years after the withdrawal. Consequently, the Soviet defeat appeared far less dramatic than it actually was. No fewer than fifteen thousand Soviet soldiers had been needlessly sacrificed.

The Breakup of the Eastern Bloc

Over the course of 1989 it became clear that, once given freedom of choice, the peoples of the Soviet empire had no intention of cleaving to communism—a development totally at odds with what Gorbachev and his confederates had expected, or at least hoped. In the Congress of People's Deputies of the Soviet Union, a minority group of radical reformers (led by Andrei Sakharov until his death in December 1989) demanded a switch to a multiparty system and a free-market economy and clearly spoke for a broad coalition of social groups. The parliaments of Lithuania, Latvia, and Estonia all voted in favor of national sovereignty, while nationalist-inspired unrest broke out in Georgia, Turkmenistan, Uzbekistan, and Kazakhstan.

In Poland an electoral compromise, which the Jaruzelski regime worked out with representatives of Solidarity after a new outbreak of unrest in January 1989, led to a crushing defeat for the communists: of the 35 percent of the seats in the Sejm that were open to freely elected candidates in the poll held on June 3–4, almost all were won by the opposition; meanwhile, the newly created Senate, elected with no restrictions but with far less responsibility, consisted of 99 percent opposition deputies. Of the thirty-five high-ranking government candidates on the national list, only two obtained the required majority in the first round of voting. As a result, the Communist Party chief, Mieczysław Rakowski, declared himself willing to form an all-party administration headed by a representative of Solidarity. On August 24, Lech Wałęsa's advisor Tadeusz Mazowiecki was nominated for the post of prime minister, and on September 12 his cabinet was confirmed by the Sejm.

In similar fashion, the renewal process set in train by the Hungarian Communist Party, which had already brought about János Kádár's resignation from the post of first secretary in May 1988, ended over the course of 1989 with the communists being toppled from power. After reformers under Imre Pozsgay had pushed through a draft constitution in the Central Committee in late February that pledged free elections for Hungary, the government, led by the technocrat Miklós Németh, disengaged itself from the Party leadership, with partial elections on July bringing a victory for opposition candidates. In a referendum held on November 29, radical democrats around János Kis won the day with their proposal that in the future the president should be chosen by parliament, thereby robbing the reformist communists of the prospect of at least clinging to a vestige of power by having the popular Pozsgay elected to the post directly.

Another characteristic and momentous decision was the one taken by the Hungarian government on May 12 to tear down the barbed-wire fence along the border with Austria. Subsequently, as thousands of refugees from the GDR gathered in Hungary over the summer in the hope of reaching the West, the Németh administration issued a resolution at the end of August officially permitting these GDR citizens to cross the border into Austria. From September 11 on, GDR citizens could legally use Hungary as a transit point en route to a third country. Over the following weeks, some twenty-five thousand people desperate to leave East Germany took advantage of this escape route. Thousands of others, who did not want to await the outcome of legal emigration procedures, took refuge in the West German embassies in Prague, Warsaw, and Budapest, as well as in the Permanent Mission in East Berlin. The GDR government's ban on travel to Hungary in the third week of September was met with demonstrations calling not just for free passage but also for a root-and-branch reform of the GDR.

A key moment in developments in the GDR came on the evening of October 9, when a crowd of around seventy thousand who had assembled to protest in Leipzig went unmolested by the ever-present organs of state security. In view of Gorbachev's public renunciation of violent suppression of freedom movements, the authorities in East Berlin no longer dared issue such an order. To all intents and purposes, this signaled the end of the Socialist Unity Party (SED) regime. People lost their fear; in the ensuing weeks, hundreds of thousands came out onto the street, driving events so fast that the authorities struggled to keep up. Egon Krenz, who had replaced Erich Honecker in a belated palace coup on October 17, ordered the Politburo on November 9 to enact new travel regulations that would allow GDR citizens free passage out of and back into the country. But when on the same evening the Politburo's press spokesman, Günter Schabowski, misspoke, announcing that the regulations were effective "from now," tens of thousands of East Berliners immediately stormed the border crossings in the city and were let through, despite the fact that the law had not yet come into force. On November 22 a roundtable was convened involving members of formerly banned opposition groups, and free elections were agreed upon for the spring of 1990. On December 3 the entire Politburo stepped down; three days later Krenz also resigned his post as president of the State Council.

Confronted with the spectacular fall of the Berlin Wall, the communist monopoly on power crumbled throughout the rest of the Warsaw Pact. On November 10, Gorbachev supporters in the Bulgarian Communist Party leadership deposed the long-serving Party leader and head of state, Todor Zhivkov. Following a mass demonstration on November 18, a roundtable was also assembled in Sofia to prepare for free elections. On November 28, after ten days of mounting demonstrations, representatives of the Czechoslovakian opposition agreed to the formation of a coalition government and a new democratic constitution with the country's prime minister Ladislav Adamec. On December 11 a new administration was formed with the communists in a minority, and ten days later parliament voted in the dissident leader Václav Havel as the country's new president. On December 21 the Romanian dictator, Nicolae Ceauşescu, was greeted with a chorus of derisive whistling at a mass rally in front of the presidential palace in Bucharest, and just a couple of days later he was literally driven from the palace by an enraged mob. A moderate faction of the state administration, which was no longer ideologically wedded to communism, assumed power. Ceauşescu and his wife, Elena, were arrested as they tried to flee, and on Christmas Day 1989 they were summarily executed by a firing squad.

As communist parties lost their monopoly on power, their membership slumped dramatically. Some of them split, while the mass organizations formerly associated with them went their own way. The new Czechoslovakian government immediately demanded the withdrawal of all Warsaw Pact forces. The Hungarians followed suit in January 1990. At the same time, hundreds of thousands of people demonstrated in Georgia, Ukraine, and Latvia for the national independence for their republics. In the Soviet Union itself, calls for a multiparty system became ever more pressing. For Gorbachev (but not only for him), this was a "time in which we are hardly able to think through events, and not only on the political level."[64] By the beginning of January, it was clear to him that there could be no further delay in bringing in a multiparty democracy in the USSR as well. After heated discussions in the Politburo, the plenary session of the Central Committee on February 5–7 was presented with a platform that proposed ridding the country's constitution of the clause guaranteeing the Soviet Communist Party's monopoly on power. When this was duly adopted, perestroika had in principle gone beyond the bounds of the socialist system.

Peace Settlements

Meanwhile, the demand for freedom for the people of the GDR had become a call for German reunification. Week after week, tens of thousands of GDR citizens took advantage of their newfound freedom to travel to move permanently to the Federal Republic. By the end of 1989 more than 120,000 had done so, and there was no end in sight to the tidal wave of emigration. A further ten million GDR citizens who simply visited West Germany (the vast majority of them for the first time) were forcibly struck by the huge discrepancy in the standard of living. At the same time, the scale of the economic disaster that was the GDR became apparent, along with clear evidence of how corrupt large parts of its ruling elite had been. The vision of democratic socialism in the GDR, the driving force behind many of the opposition groups, was unsustainable in these circumstances. Instead, an overwhelming majority of the population now pressed for as swift as possible a union with the Federal Republic. When Federal chancellor Helmut Kohl met Hans Modrow, prime minister of the SED-led transitional government in Dresden on December 19, he was mobbed by a frantic crowd clamoring for him to reunify Germany.

After sober reflection on the various forces that were in play, Kohl heeded these calls for reunification. Once he had nailed his colors to the mast as the champion of a reunified Germany by drafting a Ten Point Plan on the subject on November 28 (left purposely vague as to timing), on February 6 he proposed to the GDR government that it adopt West German currency within six months. New elections to the GDR's People's Chamber, which were brought forward to March 18, thereby became a plebiscite on Helmut Kohl and on swift reunification according to Article 23 of the West German Basic Law. The big winners from this election proved to be the Christian Democrat Alliance for Germany, which took 48 percent of the vote.

Gorbachev reacted angrily to the Ten Point Plan and tried to bring to bear the avowed opposition of both British prime minister Margaret Thatcher and French president François Mitterrand to German reunification. But when his diplomatic and secret services unanimously informed him that the GDR was no longer a viable entity for East Germans, he took a decisive lead. Within a close circle of the key players involved, it was agreed on January 26, 1990, that the Soviet government should seize the initiative by convening a meeting of the Inner Six—the four victorious powers and the two German states. This conference would determine the precise nature of reunification and the future international status of a reunified Germany.

Gorbachev's conference initiative was designed to prevent NATO from using German reunification as an opportunity to simply extend its sphere of influence up to the River Oder. However, he ran up against resistance from Reagan's successor, George H. W. Bush, who conversely feared that reunification might lead to Germany becoming a neutral state. Any potential support for Gorbachev's vision of a new configuration for Germany's security vanished with the victory of the Alliance for Germany. In mid-May, in quick succession, the governments of Czechoslovakia, Poland, and Hungary threw their weight behind a reunified Germany becoming a member of NATO. Mitterrand made it clear to Gorbachev that this was now a done deal. Reminded by Bush of his commitment to freedom of choice, Gorbachev conceded in talks with the US president on May 31 that Germany should decide for itself which alliance it wants to be in.[65]

To make it easier for Gorbachev to get this decision through the Politburo, Bush and Kohl passed a series of resolutions at a NATO summit on July 5–6 that accommodated Gorbachev's wish for a common security system: a new strategy that made nuclear arms "weapons of last resort" and that replaced forward defense with the deployment of mobile rapid-reaction units; reduction in conventional forces and short-range nuclear weapons, plus a strengthening of the CSCE through annual summits and creation of a secretariat, centers for election supervision and conflict avoidance, and a parliamentary caucus. Thereafter, at a meeting at the resort of Archys in the northern Caucasus, Gorbachev and Kohl hammered out the details of the GDR's absorption into the Federal Republic: a transitional phase of three to four years before the final withdrawal of all Soviet troops, during which NATO's military authority would not extend to the territory of the former GDR; financial aid to help with the withdrawal of Soviet forces and the reintegration of troops back into civilian life; and an upper limit of 370,000 men for the army of the reunified Germany. A Two Plus Four Agreement containing these provisions was signed in Moscow on September 12. In it, the Federal Republic recognized the Oder-Neisse Line as its definitive eastern frontier. Effective as of October 3, the GDR left both the Warsaw Pact and the Council for Mutual Economic Assistance (COMECON) and joined the Federal Republic of Germany.

The negotiations on conventional armed forces in Europe (CFE) had a hard time keeping pace with the collapse of the Warsaw Pact. The withdrawal of Soviet forces from Czechoslovakia, Hungary, and the GDR made it difficult to set meaningful upper limits for both alliance systems. After the conclusion of the Two Plus Four Agreement, Poland also demanded the withdrawal of Soviet troops from its soil, while Hungary indicated its interest in quitting the Warsaw Pact. Even so, by November the delegates did manage to agree on parity in weapons systems designed for offensive use. According to the CFE Treaty of November 20, 1990, NATO was required to scrap twenty-one hundred tanks by 1994, while the Soviet Union had to destroy almost twelve thousand by the same date. The treaty was signed at a summit of the heads of state and government of CSCE member states in Paris on November 19–21. In addition, the summit approved the Vienna Document of the Conference on Confidence-Building Measures and Disarmament in Europe, which greatly strengthened the two sides' commitment to exchanging information on armed forces and military activity. And finally the creation of new CSCE institutions, as agreed upon at the NATO summit in London, was confirmed.

By contrast, it took considerably longer to sign the Strategic Arms Reduction Treaty (START) and agree to a 50 percent cut in strategic arms. At first the Soviet side refused to accept that seaborne cruise missiles were not included in the agreed-upon upper limits; then the US military balked at a disarmament plan that simply reduced the number of warheads per missile. It was only at a summit in Moscow between Gorbachev and Bush on July 30–31, 1991, that START was finally signed. Later at the same summit, Bush announced the long-awaited granting of most-favored-nation trade status to the Soviet Union.

The End of the Soviet Union

The demise of the Eastern Bloc hastened the disintegration of the Soviet Union. Elections to separate parliaments in the constituent republics, which took place during 1990, resulted everywhere in nationalist majorities who demanded independence from the USSR for their republics. Presidents mimicking the new model of Soviet state president, as laid down by the Supreme Soviet, put the republics in a position to assert their political independence. The first republic to declare its secession from the Union was Lithuania, followed soon after by Estonia and Latvia. In June the Russian Federation declared itself sovereign: and although it did not leave the Union, it expressly reserved the right to do so. In July, Ukraine linked its declaration of national sovereignty with deliberations on its own currency, citizenship rights, and neutrality. Following elections in October, Georgia announced a plebiscite on its membership in the Union.

These developments were all the more dangerous for the cohesion of the Soviet Union as, at the same time, the negative consequences of the economic reforms gradually brought in since 1987 (but with no coherent plan) became clear. The transition of factories to autonomous responsibility, which had happened on a sector-by-sector basis, led to chaos and numerous bottlenecks in supply; inadequate legal safeguards and lack of experience meant that virtually no strategic investment was forthcoming. During 1990, as even basic consumer goods and staple foods became scarce and their prices skyrocketed, Gorbachev saw his initial popularity ratings plummet. Conversely, the former first secretary of the Moscow City Committee, Boris Yeltsin, was able to present himself as a dedicated people's champion. Demoted in 1987 after a halfhearted suicide attempt, in the election to the Congress of People's Deputies of the Soviet Union he had returned in triumph to the political stage. In his current capacity as president of the Supreme Soviet of the Russian Federation, he was now busily engaged in freeing Russia from the grip of Soviet organs of state. In a speech at the 28th Convention of the Soviet Communist Party on July 12, 1990, he made a very public show of resigning his party membership.

Gorbachev, whose elevation to the state presidency by the Supreme Soviet in March 1990 meant that he could now operate independently of the Politburo, at first seemed willing to share power with Yeltsin. In the summer of 1990, economic experts from both camps devised a plan that promised to deliver a transition to a market economy "in 500 days" and that envisaged transferring fiscal sovereignty, ownership of natural resources, and price-fixing responsibility to the republics. But after some initial enthusiasm, Gorbachev became convinced that its implementation would bring the breakup of the Soviet Union. This created a permanent rift between the two rivals, and Gorbachev once more fell back for support on conservative elements in the Politburo and the Party apparatus, who were outspoken in their criticism of the loss of power on all fronts. Yakovlev was sidelined, and Foreign Minister Eduard Shevardnadze, one of the key supporters of perestroika, resigned in December in protest at Gorbachev's change of direction.

When special units of the KGB shot down peaceful demonstrators in Lithuania and Latvia in January 1991, it became clear to Gorbachev that he had allied himself with forces that were planning to use a state of emergency to violently restore the old order. He rapidly changed tack, repudiating the use of violence in the Baltic states and arranging a referendum for March on the "perpetuation of the Soviet Union as a new federation of equal sovereign republics." The Baltic republics, Moldavia, Georgia, and Armenia refused to take part; the proposal was approved in the other republics by a majority of over 70 percent, but in the Russian Federation itself by only 53 percent. Bolstered by this vote, Gorbachev entered into negotiations with representatives of the nine remaining republics on a new Union treaty, which would devolve power to a large extent to the individual republics. It was due to be signed on August 20.

This was the signal for conservative forces in the Politburo, the KGB, and the military to carry out their plan to seize power by force, even if Gorbachev was not on board. In the night of August 19, Gorbachev was detained at his summer dacha in the Crimea, and a state of emergency was declared. A self-appointed "emergency committee" claimed control of the media and the state administration—but this never transpired. From the Russian Parliament building in Moscow, Yeltsin, who two months previously had been directly elected as president of the Russian Federation, called for resistance to the attempted coup. Troops and members of the secret services fought shy of carrying out their orders. The coup leaders did not dare to attack the hundreds of thousands of demonstrators who had assembled in front of the Parliament building to form a human shield around Yeltsin and the other delegates. The coup fizzled out after two days; its ringleaders were immediately arrested, along with many open sympathizers. The Communist Party was banned from all activity in Russia, and before the end of the month it had been dissolved.

Yeltsin was now the undisputed master of a de facto independent Russian Federation. Gorbachev continued as state president, but at the same time was discredited as general secretary of the Party. He now lacked any authority to prevent the republics from going their separate ways. On December 8 the presidents of the Slavic republics of Russia, Belarus, and Ukraine proclaimed the dissolution of the Soviet Union. Along with the representatives of eight other republics (Armenia, Azerbaijan, Kazakhstan, Kyrgyzstan, Moldavia, Tajikistan, Turkmenistan, and Uzbekistan), they agreed on December 21 to form a Commonwealth of Independent States (CIS) and declared that, as of the year's end, the Soviet Union would cease to exist. Gorbachev had no choice but to go on television on December 25 to announce his resignation as state president. And so this nonviolent act of self-emancipation by the peoples of the Soviet empire led not only to the demise of communism but also to the dissolution of the last multiethnic state to survive the nineteenth century.

4. *An Emerging World Order*

THE END of the East–West conflict not only enabled the states that had formerly been part of the Soviet Bloc to "return to Europe," as the new Czechoslovakian president, Václav Havel, emphatically put it. In addition, states that for various reasons had stayed neutral in the Cold War now had a chance to participate in the project for European unification. And political forces that had once had reservations about a Western European Union because of the division of Europe that it entailed now found themselves inclined to throw their weight behind stronger European democracy and self-determination. The upshot of all these developments was to lend new impetus to European unification. This process began even before the end of the Cold War, and in its openness can even be said to have contributed to the Cold War's demise. Despite inevitable crises and delays, it led to Europe's cutting a more prominent figure on the stage of world politics.

Return to Europe

The creation of the European Council in 1974 did not put European integration back on the agenda nearly as quickly as its originators had hoped. In dealing with the aftermath of the oil crisis of 1973–1974, each country initially went its own way. After a general election victory for the Labour Party in February 1974, Great Britain even began to question its membership of the Common Market once more. Harold Wilson's second government demanded subsidies for economically deprived areas of the country and a reduction in Britain's contributions to the EEC budget. The compromise that was reached was put to the vote in a nationwide referendum on June 5, 1975, and approved. The European Community established a regional fund to help stimulate growth in depressed regions in the member states, albeit with only a very modest budget to begin with. It also promoted new initiatives in the areas of industrial policy, research and development, environmental and energy concerns, and finally educational and cultural policies.

However, proposals on the further development of the Community, which were collated by the Belgian prime minister Leo Tindemans at the behest of the European Council and published at the end of 1975, were not even discussed by the heads of state and government of the nine member countries. French policy under Valéry Giscard d'Estaing continued to oppose an extension of European parliamentary powers, Helmut Schmidt blocked larger German contributions to the Community, and Harold Wilson was adamant that he could not get any more pro-European legislation past his electorate. Greece's application to join the Common Market in 1975, followed by applications by Spain and Portugal two years later, raised further major problems: the relative economic backwardness of these southern European nations, which had only recently shrugged off dictatorships, risked overburdening the Community budget, while a glut of their farm produce threatened to unsettle the fine balance of the Common Agricultural Policy.

The introduction of the European Monetary System (EMS) on March 13, 1979, marked a first milestone in overcoming this state of "Eurosclerosis" (the term was coined in the late 1970s to describe the period of stagnation in European integration). Instigated by the Commission's president, Roy Jenkins, and politically driven by Schmidt and Giscard, this system provided much greater stimulus to forming a currency union and to overcoming the stagflation crisis than had the failed currency snake of 1972; in addition to agreeing not to allow currencies to diverge from one another by more than 2.25 percent, this time the member countries committed themselves to intervene on the currency markets and take steps to consolidate their national budgets if their own currency threatened to slip to this marginal value. To ensue that this intervention was effective, 20 percent of the member states' gold and currency reserves was transferred to the European Monetary Cooperation Fund. The creation of the European Currency Unit (ECU) ensured transparency in financial transactions between the participating countries.

In this way a mechanism was created that helped countries with weak currencies such as France fight inflation, while at the same time enabling West Germany to resist pressure, arising from the weakening of the US dollar, to revaluate the Deutschmark upward. Using this mechanism, the countries of the European Community would, it was hoped, jointly return to the path of growth and disengage themselves from dependence on the dollar. Yet Great Britain did not take part. Wilson's successor, James Callaghan, did not regard membership in a common European monetary mechanism as either necessary or electorally viable. Also, as countries with particularly weak currencies, Ireland and Italy were given special dispensation for greater divergence before they were obliged to intervene.

Regarding the southern enlargement of the European Community, Greece's prime minister, Konstantínos Karamanlís, scored a notable success by refraining from calling for subvention or insisting on special dispensations for his country. In this way he managed to disengage negotiations on Greece's entry from those on Spain's and Portugal's and to bring them to a triumphant conclusion in May 1979. On January 1, 1981, Greece acceded as the tenth member state of the European Community. But following a change of government, Karamanlís's socialist successor, Andreas Papandreou, demanded an improvement in Greece's conditions for entry, and as a new member of the Council exercised his right of veto to force his partners to adopt an Integrated Mediterranean Program as a condition for Spanish and Portuguese accession—hardly an act of great solidarity on his part. This only added to the complications in the negotiations with Spain and Portugal, which were more difficult anyway, given their great rivalry in the export of farm produce and over fishing rights. The accession treaties with the countries of the Iberian Peninsula were not signed until July 1985 and entered into force on January 1, 1986.

Another reason for the protracted delay in Spanish and Portuguese accession was that the European Community risked running out of money. After guaranteed prices led to horrendous overproduction of farm produce, the cost of funding the Common Agricultural Policy (CAP) had gone through the roof. And the British Conservative prime minister Margaret Thatcher, who came to power in May 1979, insisted on a significant reduction in Britain's contributions, which she saw as an unfair, one-sided subsidy of the questionable CAP. A solution to the problem, which in the meantime distinctly soured the atmosphere between the member states, was finally reached at a summit at Fontainebleau on June 25–26, 1984: the British PM was promised a 40 percent reduction in her country's contributions after she agreed to the ceiling on the Community's own resources being raised from 1 to 1.4 percent of a notional value-added tax (VAT) levy. Agricultural overproduction (the "beef/butter mountains" and "wine lakes") was scaled down through the introduction of milk quotas (1984), the lowering of fixed prices (1986), and the expansion of farming set-aside (1986).

The Fontainebleau agreement gave Kohl and Mitterrand an opportunity to relaunch the project for greater European union. In this, they were impelled both by a shared desire to integrate the Germans into a wider Europe and by concerns over European competitiveness vis-à-vis the new competition coming from Asia, as well as a deep unease over the hawkish tone of US policy toward the Soviet Union. Under the aegis of a Draft Treaty Establishing the European Union, which the European Parliament had passed with an overwhelming majority in February 1984, at Fontainebleau they managed to get a committee established (under the chairmanship of the Irish senator James Dooge) that would make proposals on progress toward European union through reform of the existing institutions. At the same time, an ad hoc Committee on a People's Europe was also appointed, whose task was to explore ways of strengthening the role of the European Community in the everyday lives of its citizens.

A decisive move in the long-term success of this joint Franco-German initiative was the accession to the presidency of the European Commission, on January 1, 1985, of the Frenchman Jacques Delors. His particular achievement was to keep the politics of European integration firmly focused on that part of the reform agenda that was also clearly in the British interest—namely, the completion of an internal market. Even Thatcher seemed to agree that the abolition of all nontariff trade barriers within the Community was vital if Europe was to compete effectively against the United States and the growing "tiger economies" of the Far East. She also realized that her agenda of breaking down monolithic economic structures would be easier to implement by operating within the European sphere than by trying to go it alone at home.

Delors's announcement of a realistic but definite date ("the end of 1992") for the completion of the internal market put the ball firmly in the national governments' court. His drafting, on June 15, 1984, of a white paper on the subject, which carefully laid out the "300 measures" that were still necessary to remove trade barriers, allowed him to keep up the pressure. Added to the pressure of the unequivocal proclamation by the European Parliament was that from companies, financiers, and even some employees' organizations calling for the introduction of an internal market. In the face of this concerted campaign even Thatcher and the equally Euroskeptic governments in Greece and Denmark could not hold out indefinitely against the expansion of the Community through the internal market. At the meeting of the European Council in Milan on June 28–29, 1985, these countries did vote against convening a conference to revise the Community treaties; but when the majority of Council members signaled their intention to go ahead with the conference anyway, the minority did not dare to boycott it.

Of course, the expansion of the Community that resulted from the governmental conference in the form of the Single European Act (SEA)—concluded on December 3, 1985, and officially signed in February 1986—did not go equally far in all areas. All members were agreed that the internal market should come into force on January 1, 1993. But while there was a general commitment to economic and monetary union, resistance not only by the British government but also by the Germans ensured that no firm timetable was laid down for this. The EEC assumed new powers in domains like environmental protection, research, strengthening cohesion, and the encouragement of social dialogue. In foreign policy, member states committed themselves to consultation; resolutions in this realm would still have force, even if individual countries were to abstain. And because the internal market could not come into being without it, the British government also accepted an extension of majority voting within the Council. The executive powers of the Commission were strengthened; and the European Parliament was given the right to amend the drafting of bills in certain areas so long as the Council did not signal its objection through qualified majority voting.

Despite the compromise nature of this Act (a total of nine texts), when it came into force on July 1, 1987, it was a major step toward overcoming the stagnation that had hampered the integration project. The new dynamic atmosphere gave rise to the decision, in June 1989, to embark upon the first phase of monetary union by July 1, 1990. European monetary union would promote the free movement of capital and bring Great Britain and the southern European member states into the European Monetary System. Heeding the advice of his economic experts, Helmut Kohl was prepared to sign on to a single currency only if there was a general convergence of economic circumstances and a meeting of minds on economic policy. Pressed by Mitterrand at the Council of Europe on December 8–9, 1989, he agreed to an intergovernmental summit on the implementation of monetary union, albeit only—given that he first had to win a parliamentary election—in December of the following year. With this, the prospect of monetary union finally being realized moved visibly closer.

Europe after the Cold War

The European Community was comparatively well equipped to tackle the new tasks that were thrust upon it by the breakup of the Soviet empire. It was now in a position (or rather, found itself obliged to) assume responsibilities for maintaining order on the continent, which formerly had devolved to the superpowers and their blocs. One such task was to try to contain the Germans in the wake of reunification and the withdrawal of the victorious powers. The European Community also suddenly found itself saddled with joint responsibility for the success of the plan to modernize Eastern Europe. At the same time, the political barriers that had once prevented the formerly neutral EFTA countries from joining the economically successful EEC fell away. The question of Europe's independent role in global politics became all the more pressing now that the United States had become the world's sole superpower.

Of all the challenges arising from the implosion of the Eastern Bloc, the one the Community dealt with most consummately was the integration of the now much larger Germany. This was primarily down to Helmut Kohl, who, in setting the course for German reunification in 1989–1990, recognized the need to allay the fears of his European neighbors about the future role of an enlarged German state in the middle of Europe. He did this by taking rapid steps toward a much firmer integration of the Germans into the European project. This consideration played a role, for instance, in his agreeing to hold an intergovernmental conference in December 1990 to discuss monetary union. It was also indicative that in the run-up to the European Council meeting in Maastricht on December 9–10, 1991, Kohl readily accepted a timetable for the implementation of monetary union by 1997 (or 1999 at the latest) and stuck to this decision even in the face of serious misgivings in both financial circles and in wider public opinion in Germany. The Maastricht Treaty came into effect on November 1, 1993, and on January 1, 2002, the euro was introduced as the sole legal tender in the member states of the monetary union.

Even so, in forming the monetary union, the other participating countries largely had to fall in line with German requirements if a situation was to be avoided where the Deutschmark became the de facto leading currency of the European Monetary System. Thus, on the model of the Bundesbank, the European Central Bank was set up as a politically independent financial entity, while all the participating countries agreed to stick to objective convergence criteria during the transition to monetary union. In order to consolidate their budgets, they also had to commit to confining their future budget deficits to within 3 percent of GDP and to not allowing their total national debt to exceed 60 percent of GDP. Great Britain and Denmark deferred their decision on whether to join the monetary union but ultimately opted to stick with their national currencies.

In view of the new challenges, Kohl also thought it vital to go beyond the reforms that had been agreed upon in the Single European Act on matters of political cooperation and the strengthening of Community institutions. In concert with Mitterrand, he therefore made a joint call on April 18, 1990, for another intergovernmental conference to map out a treaty on political union. Kohl and Mitterrand proposed "consolidating the democratic legitimacy of the union, organizing its institutions more efficiently, achieving unity and coherence of action within the union in matters of economy, currency, and policies; and establishing and enacting a common foreign and security policy."[66]

Despite this united Franco-German front, however, this ambitious program really only became viable after large parts of the original proposal were ditched. In terms of the Community's institutions, the Maastricht Treaty had extended majority voting within the Council of Ministers and the European Parliament's right of participation; in addition, a (purely consultative) committee of the regions was established, the powers of the European Court of Justice and the European Court of Auditors strengthened, and European citizenship introduced. In the European Community Treaty (now called the Treaty on European Union), alongside the commitments to economic and monetary union, new responsibilities were now added in the spheres of education, culture, health, consumers' rights, and social policy, while existing jurisdiction in research and environmental policy was extended, and a Cohesion Fund was established to support the financing of environmental and transportation projects in regions lacking in infrastructure.

Beyond the Community agreements, in the realm of organized cooperation between governments the Common Foreign and Security Policy (CFSP) was retained, for whose operational implementation a political committee consisting of directors of the foreign ministries had been established, along with cooperation on Justice and Home Affairs. The European Communities treaties and these two areas of intergovernmental cooperation, for which the Commission only had a limited right of initiative and the Parliament only a right of consultation, were now bound together as the pillars of a European Union. As an integral part of the Union, the Western European Union was now tasked with enacting any decisions and actions "relating to matters of defense policy."[67] The trade-off for this broadening of Community activities was a greater complexity of regulations at the European level; moreover, the expansion of Parliament's rights did not keep pace with the growth in the Council's responsibilities. As a result, the question of the Community's lack of legitimacy only became more acute.

Although the Maastricht Treaty saw a rapid increase in the number of "policy declarations" issued by the Community on foreign and security policy matters, this was not matched by a corresponding growth in the capacity to take action. In October 1991, Kohl and Mitterrand therefore announced the formation of a joint Franco-German Corps—an important first step in setting aside the traditional differences in security policy between France and the Federal Republic. Belgium, Spain, and Luxembourg soon joined this initiative, leading in November 1995 to the creation of the Eurocorps, a multilateral military unit of fifty thousand troops with its headquarters in Strasbourg. And as a result of another intergovernmental conference, which was immediately agreed upon in order to plug the loopholes left by the Maastricht regulations in the European Union treaty of 1991–1992, the Amsterdam Treaty of October 2, 1997, created the office of the High Representative for the Common Foreign and Security Policy; majority voting was introduced for operational decisions; and the General Secretariat was equipped with a strategic planning and early warning unit.

The Amsterdam Treaty also brought an expansion of the European Parliament's role in the co-decision procedure and a strengthening of the powers of the president of the Commission, whose appointment was made conditional on the agreement of the Parliament. Significant elements of the ordinances governing cooperation on Justice and Home Affairs, as well as the Social Chapter of the Maastricht Treaty, were absorbed into the EU Treaty. Likewise, the Schengen Agreement, which replaced border controls within the Community with a central information system and shared responsibility for safeguarding Europe's external borders, were integrated into the legal system of the EU. The responsibilities of the joint policing authority, Europol, were extended, while further provisions were put in place relating to health, environmental, and consumer rights.

The accession of the former EFTA countries proved relatively unproblematic. Austria had submitted its application for entry as early as June 1989; Sweden followed suit in June 1991, then Finland, Switzerland, and Norway in 1992. While the Swiss application was put on ice following the defeat of a referendum in December 1992 on accession to the proposed European Economic Area (a merger of the EU and EFTA), negotiations with the other EFTA countries got under way in January 1993. The accession treaties were signed in June 1994 and entered into force on January 1, 1995. Norway, though, had fallen by the wayside: just as in the first enlargement round in 1972–1973, ratification of the accession treaty was rejected by a plebiscite. From being a Europe of twelve members, the Community now grew to fifteen.

By contrast, the accession of the countries that had until 1990 formed part of the Eastern Bloc turned out to be far more difficult. While Great Britain, Denmark, and Germany pressed, for both strategic and economic reasons, for as swift as possible an eastward expansion of the European Union, France, the Benelux countries, and the Southern European recipients of subsidies from the Cohesion Fund regarded this as at best a project for the next generation. Initially, then, the Community confined itself to promoting political and economic reforms in Central and Eastern European countries. Support was offered in the form of the 1989 PHARE (Poland and Hungary: Assistance for Restructuring Their Economies) program, credit from the European Investment Bank and the European Bank for Reconstruction and Development (founded 1991), and

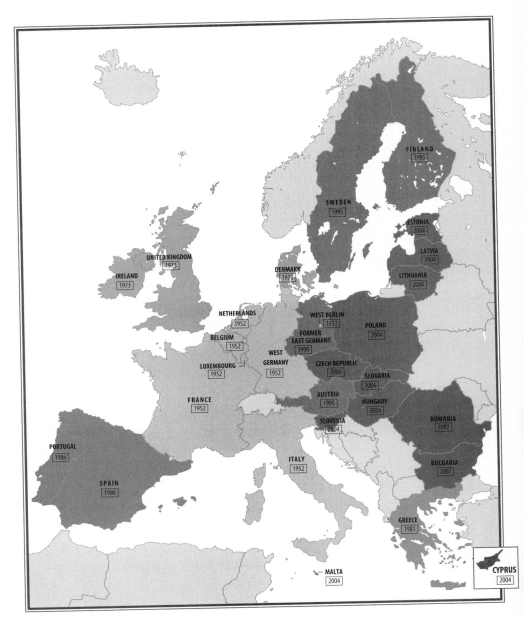

Expansion of the European Union, 1952–2012.

association agreements designed to modernize and liberalize the former socialist command economies of these countries. The first such accords were signed in October 1991 with Czechoslovakia, Poland, and Hungary, followed by Romania, Bulgaria, and Slovenia, as well as the Baltic states, in 1996.

The real prospect of accession to the Union was opened up to the countries of Central and Eastern Europe at the European Council in Copenhagen in June 1993. At their subsequent meeting in the German city of Essen in December 1994, at Helmut Kohl's instigation, the twelve Community member countries agreed to a financially cushioned "pre-accession strategy" to help the countries engage in a structured dialogue in preparation for their integration. Three years later in Luxembourg, the European Council decided to open formal negotiations with those prospective new member states that, according to a vote by the Commission, came sufficiently close to fulfilling the accession criteria. In addition to Cyprus (which had applied in 1990), these were Hungary, Poland, the Czech Republic, Estonia, and Slovenia. Preliminary talks were held with the other applicants from April 1998 on.

A Europe of Twenty-Seven Members

It was only on the threshold of the new millennium that a new sense of dynamism began to be injected into areas of action where progress had been painfully slow in the 1990s. The reasons for this were twofold: firstly, the more realistic approach to European politics evident in Britain since Tony Blair came to power in May 1997; and secondly, the learning process undergone by French president Jacques Chirac and German chancellor Gerhard Schröder.

The Commission that began work in September 1999 under the chairmanship of Romano Prodi made great strides in the negotiations with the prospective member countries, although the actual task of overseeing accession was vested in the new office of European Commissioner for Enlargement (first incumbent: Günter Verheugen). In December 1999 the European Council, meeting in Helsinki, voted to begin negotiations with Latvia, Lithuania, Slovakia, Romania, Bulgaria, and Malta. A new intergovernmental conference was scheduled for February 2000; its task was to establish, by the end of the year, the preconditions for acceptance of these new member states. At the Naples summit on

December 7–8, 2000, new rules were drawn up for the distribution of seats in the European Parliament and the weighting of votes in the Council of Ministers for a Europe of up to twenty-seven members, plus a new procedure for determining qualified majority voting. Henceforth, in the Commission, each member state would be represented by only a single commissioner. At the same time, it was agreed that the accession negotiations should be completed by the end of 2002, so that accession could take place in the spring of 2004. The citizens of the new member states would therefore be able to take part in the next elections to the European Parliament, in June 2004.

Largely thanks to Verheugen's negotiating skills, this ambitious timetable was kept to. A whole series of transitional arrangements (valid for periods ranging from three to twelve years) were agreed to by the Central and Eastern European Countries (CEECs), and a complicated compromise was worked out regarding the transfer of finance to the new member states. The accession treaty was duly signed with ten states (Poland, Hungary, the Czech Republic, Slovakia, Slovenia, Latvia, Estonia, Lithuania, Cyprus, and Malta) on April 16, 2003, in Athens. Following timely ratification in all the member states of the enlarged European Union, the Accession Treaty came into force on May 1, 2004. Bulgaria and Romania, which found it more difficult to fulfill the accession criteria, finally joined on January 1, 2007.

However, the Treaty of Nice, which was officially signed on February 26, 2001, and dealt with questions of institutional reform, set its sights much lower. Chirac and Schröder, unlike their predecessors Kohl and Mitterrand, had failed to reconcile their separate interests in the run-up to the intergovernmental conference—and so, although further extensions of the qualified majority voting system and of the Parliament's right of participation did come about, they were not part of any coherent overall plan. According to the provisions of the Treaty of Nice, fourteen separate procedures were possible before resolutions were adopted in the Council, while those involving Parliamentary participation allowed for eleven such stages. As a result, the decision-making process became even more opaque and accountability more difficult to determine.

A sizable sector of public opinion, which had been primed to expect more substantive progress by German foreign minister Joschka Fischer's public plea for a Constitution for Europe leading to the formation of a European federation, was highly critical of the Treaty of Nice. At Nice, Schröder was able to secure agreement on a further intergovernmental summit in 2004, preparations for which would this time involve the European Parliament, national parliaments, and civil society at large. Chirac was persuaded to work out a common position with the Germans prior to the conference, and Belgian prime minister Guy Verhofstadt, as president of the European Council, ensured that the Convention on the Future of Europe adopted at the Laeken meeting of the European Council on December 14–15, 2001, really did commit the EU to greater democracy and transparency.

The Convention responded to people's expectations of more concrete results by presenting, on July 20, 2003, a Draft Treaty Establishing a Constitution for Europe that represented real progress toward greater transparency and efficiency: more day-to-day decisions in the Council of Ministers and the European Parliament were to be reached by qualified majority voting; the post of European Foreign Minister was to be created; expansion of the role of the president of the European Council, a post that could no longer be held by the head of government of a member state. After making some concessions toward the special representation requirements of Poland and Spain, the heads of state and government adopted this draft treaty at a meeting in Brussels on June 18–19, 2004.

Meanwhile, the common foreign and security policy was fleshed out when Tony Blair began to warm to the idea of a credible European rapid reaction force—an idea first mooted at an informal Council meeting in the Austrian town of Pörtschach in October 1988. Following an agreement between Blair and Chirac, it was decided at the European Council meeting in Helsinki in December 1999 to set up a European reaction force of sixty thousand soldiers by 2003. At the Nice summit a year later, most of the institutions of the Western European Union (WEU) were taken over by the EU. Javier Solana, the first holder of the office of High Representative for the Common Foreign and Security Policy, also assumed the role of general secretary of the WEU. The Political Committee of the CFSP was expanded to become the Political and Security Committee (PSC), to which a Military Committee reported.

Following deep divisions over the US intervention in Iraq in 2003, the heads and states of government reached an agreement at the Brussels meeting of the European Council on December 12–13, 2003, on a common security strategy aimed at safeguarding security within Europe and its environs and an effective multilateral approach to maintaining order internationally. In adopting the Constitutional Treaty in June 2004, they undertook "progressively to improve their military capabilities" and to work toward a "common defence policy of the Union."[68] Furthermore, the replacement of the high representative by the European foreign minister, as envisaged in the treaty, opened up the prospect of an integrated European diplomatic service. There was also a provision for "structured cooperation" within the Union for member states that wanted to undertake firmer commitments toward military integration.

However, enactment of the Constitutional Treaty ran into unforeseen difficulties. In both France (in late May 2005) and the Netherlands (in early June 2005), a majority voted against its ratification. In response, German chancellor Angela Merkel and French president Nicolas Sarkozy took the initiative in amending the wording of the agreement to try to make it more acceptable to nationalist-minded voters. After a new intergovernmental conference on December 13, 2007, the European Council passed a modified treaty (the Treaty of Lisbon). Yet before it came into force on December 1, 2009, another rejection in a referendum, this time by the Irish electorate in 2008, had to be overcome by further guarantees on the question of continuing national sovereignty. The complexity of the European edifice continued, then, to be its Achilles heel.

The Limitations of the Superpower

The collapse of the Soviet Union and the discrediting of the ideology of communism that had held it together left the United States as the world's only superpower. Its economic system had proved to be superior, and thanks to faster and more efficient use of information technology, it once again secured for itself a disproportionate share of global economic growth. The political values of Western democracy, which American policy had promoted with mixed fortunes, went beyond the limitations of its erstwhile Soviet rival and, finding widespread positive resonance, persuaded many societies to commit themselves to American leadership. In the meantime the United States also opened up an unassailable lead in military technology, and with its ongoing investment in arms development, remained the world's foremost military power. In 1998 it still accounted for 35 percent of total global arms expenditure, whereas the Russian Federation's share stood at just one-tenth of this.[69] In view of this situation, it was self-evident that America should try to export the democratic model through force of arms, but its attempt to do so failed miserably, exposing the limitations of the superpower.

The technological superiority of the United States was brought home forcefully when Iraq's president, Saddam Hussein, attacked the sheikhdom of Kuwait in August 1990. Two years after the end of the devastating but inconclusive conflict with Iran, the Baghdad dictator saw the invasion of his small oil-rich neighbor as the best way to wipe out the war debts he had incurred and to silence growing discontent at home by extending his power in the Gulf region. US president George H. W. Bush decided to intervene—firstly because the Iraqi share of global oil reserves rose to 20 percent with the occupation of Kuwait, placing Saddam in a threatening position of power, and secondly because the conflict gave Bush an opportunity to consolidate America's leading role in maintaining worldwide security. The fifteen members of the UN Security Council were unanimous in their condemnation of Iraqi aggression; Gorbachev gave his blessing to sanctions and the use of military force, which began, when an ultimatum expired on January 17, 1991, with the bombing of Iraqi defensive installations.

The coalition of some thirty states that Bush had assembled against Iraq was expecting a long and bloody war. As it turned out, thanks to superior equipment and strategic planning, it took the 790,000 Allied ground troops (540,000 Americans and 250,000 troops from allied countries) under the command of General H. Norman Schwarzkopf less than one hundred hours to expel the Iraqis from Kuwait. The ground operations, which began on February 24, were halted by Bush just three days later to avoid giving the impression that the Allies were using excessive force. As a result, Saddam was able to hold on to power. But in the United States, the unqualified success of the operation instilled a new sense of self-confidence that dispelled the trauma of Vietnam and the humiliation of the Iranian hostage crisis.

US diplomacy exploited the victory in the Gulf War to kick-start the peace process in the Middle East. In October 1991, after an intense round of shuttle diplomacy, Bush's secretary of state, James Baker, succeeded in getting representatives of Israel, Syria, Jordan, and Lebanon to meet around a single conference table in Madrid. Representatives of the Palestine Liberation Organization (PLO) took part in the negotiations as nominal members of the Jordanian delegation. These discussions did not yield any immediate results. However, after Yitzhak Rabin of the Labor Party won the Israeli general election in June 1992, secret negotiations began between representatives of Israel and the PLO in a country house outside Oslo in Norway. The agreements that were hammered out there were signed on September 13, 1993, in Washington in the presence of US president Bill Clinton. Rabin and PLO chairman Yasser Arafat agreed in principle that the Israelis would hand over the Gaza Strip and the city of Jericho to Palestinian authority. A further accord, signed in September 1995 (Oslo II), confirmed the transfer of six more cities and 450 villages in the West Bank—around one-third of the territory captured by Israel during the Six-Day War in 1967—to Palestinian control.

The Oslo Accords seemed to pave the way for a two-state solution to the Middle Eastern conflict. Yet further progress down this path stalled when Rabin was assassinated by a Jewish religious extremist in November 1995 and when the right-wing Likud Party came to power in May 1996. As Israel continued to drag its feet over withdrawal from the occupied territories, the expansion of Jewish settlements within these areas put Arafat under increasing pressure. At the end of September 2000 another wave of unrest broke out in the Palestinian towns, with suicide bombings and attacks on Jewish settlers. The Israel Defense Force responded with a methodical destruction of infrastructure in the Palestinian areas and the targeted killing of Palestinian extremists. Arafat was repeatedly placed under house arrest, and his headquarters in Ramallah were largely razed to the ground in March 2002. Thereafter it became impossible to maintain any lasting cessation of violence on either side. Under pressure from more militant groups, the Palestinian leadership could not bring itself to recognize the State of Israel. Although Israel withdrew from Gaza in 2006, at the same time it still claimed large parts of the West Bank and the whole of East Jerusalem as sovereign Israeli territory.

After initial hesitation, the United States also became heavily involved in the ethnic conflict that broke out in the former Yugoslavia. The multiethnic state that had been led by Tito up to his death in May 1980 began to fragment once Party leaders like the Serbian Slobodan Milošević found that a good way of consolidating their own power base after the discrediting of communist ideology was to appeal to nationalist aspirations. In June 1991, Slovenia and Croatia seceded from the Yugoslavian Federation, followed by Bosnia and Herzegovina in October and Macedonia in November. After a brief intervention in Slovenia, the Serbian-led Federal Army withdrew; in Croatia, though, it agreed to a ceasefire (on January 2, 1992) only after it had taken control of Serbian enclaves there and driven out their Croatian inhabitants. While a UN peacekeeping force was sent in to monitor the ceasefire in Croatia, the Serbs proceeded to launch an attack on Bosnia. Bosnian Serbs under the leadership of Radovan Karadžić began "ethnically cleansing" areas under their command. From the spring of 1993, Bosnian Croats also started to conduct "cleansing" operations against Muslims.

For a long time the international community looked on helplessly as this genocide unfolded. The mandate of the UN peacekeeping force was extended to Bosnia and Herzegovina, but the force found itself unable to implement the safe zones that the Security Council had agreed upon for the various ethnic groups, instead becoming a hostage itself to Serbian forces. The Clinton administration first brokered a ceasefire between the Croats and Muslims in March 1994 before going on the offensive against the Serbian aggressors in the summer of 1995. The Americans encouraged the Croatian army to retake the areas it had lost in 1991: in late August, targeted NATO air strikes began against Serb positions in Bosnia and Herzegovina. In October, Serbia agreed to a ceasefire mediated by the Americans; a peace conference at Dayton, Ohio, led to the signing, on December 14, of a peace treaty that provided for the partition of Bosnia into a Muslim-Croatian Federation and a Serbian Republic. A sixty-thousand-strong international peacekeeping force, under NATO leadership but with Russian units also involved, was put in place to ensure its implementation.

In Kosovo, formerly an autonomous province of Serbia, a "liberation army" began to form at the beginning of 1998 among the Albanian ethnic majority population. From March onward, the Serbian paramilitary police responded with mass expulsions and massacres of civilians; before long, hundreds of thousands of Albanians had taken flight. The international community initially tried to intervene here also through negotiation. But when the Serbian government refused to sign a peace accord in March 1999, NATO reacted by bombing Serbian

A graveyard with seventy-six numbered graves in Petrovo Selo in northeast Serbia contains the remains of Albanians from Kosovo killed in 1999. The Serbian leader Slobodan Milošević responded to the formation of a "Liberation Army" among the Albanian ethnic majority with mass expulsions and massacres of civilians. (© Thorne Anderson/Corbis)

positions. At first this only provoked a further escalation of the conflict within Kosovo. Milošević backed down only when Clinton dispatched ground troops at the end of May. On June 9 an agreement was reached for the withdrawal of Serbian forces and the installation of a UN peacekeeping force. The province was placed under UN administration—officially only temporarily. Nine years later, after more unrest and the secession of Montenegro from Serbia in 2006, Kosovo finally declared independence in February 2008.

NATO's Changing Role

Its successful military intervention in Bosnia and Herzegovina and Kosovo helped NATO overcome the crisis it faced after the breakup of the Warsaw Pact. The concept of conducting peacekeeping operations beyond the bounds of the alliance—controversial to some members of the organization—had proved a viable one, and lent the alliance a new purpose. NATO also found itself increasingly prepared to identify security risks outside its normal sphere of operation and to assume responsibility for safeguarding its new European neighbors. In 1997, Poland, the Czech Republic, and Hungary were invited to join the alliance, and in March 1999 this first Eastern expansion of NATO became a reality. To allay Russian unease at this development, a joint NATO-Russian Council was convened in May 1997, which held out to the Russian Federation the prospect of "permanent consultation and cooperation."[70]

Yet the NATO-Russian Council could do nothing to mollify Russia's great annoyance at NATO's actions in Kosovo. After the government in Moscow had refused to approve the deployment of a military task force against the Serbs, NATO members decided to intervene without obtaining a UN mandate. Nevertheless, Russia did then prevail upon the Serbian-Yugoslavian regime to accept the ceasefire of June 9, 1999. A further rapprochement between Russia and the new-look NATO was catalyzed by the Islamist terror attacks on the World Trade Center and the Pentagon on September 11, 2001, in which almost three thousand people were killed. Russia and the NATO countries now found themselves confronted with a new common threat in the shape of the global terror network set up by al-Qaeda, a loose confederation of jihadists that had formed during the struggle against communist influence in Afghanistan in the 1980s. A common defense strategy was called for against this menace. In May 2002 both sides agreed to reconstitute the NATO-Russian Council as a decision-making body on security matters of common concern. Accordingly, the second round of NATO eastward expansion, decided upon in November 2002 and enacted on April 1, 2004, occurred with no damage to the relations between Russia and NATO. By now, with the accession of Estonia, Latvia, Lithuania, Bulgaria, Romania, Slovakia, and Slovenia, NATO membership stood at twenty-six countries.

At the same time, the unprecedented terror attack on the symbols of American power led to a strengthening of solidarity between the European allies and the United States. On the day after the outrage, September 12, 2001, for the first time in its history NATO invoked the clause (Article 5) in its founding charter on "collective defense." Over the following days, NATO warplanes helped patrol American airspace. Preparation for further attacks included the reorganization of national defense networks to confront the new threats, and the creation of a rapid-deployment NATO Response Force. Key NATO allies like Great Britain, Germany, and Italy took part in the campaign against the Taliban regime in Afghanistan, which was providing the main safe haven for al-Qaeda fighters. Following American air strikes on October 7, 2001, the Taliban regime was quickly toppled. A UN conference held at Hotel Petersberg in Bonn in early December established a transitional administration for Afghanistan headed by Hamid Karzai. Karzai's government would remain dependent for many years on the support of a NATO peacekeeping force.

The administration of George W. Bush did not regard the "war on terror" first and foremost as a common struggle, and was determined to call the shots on how it should be conducted. Although any international support was welcome, in the worldwide struggle for freedom and democracy the Bush administration reserved the right to act as an entirely free agent if necessary. After the fall of the Taliban regime, three more "rogue states" within an "axis of evil," as Bush put it, came within the sights of US foreign-policy makers—North Korea, Iran, and Iraq. Under the pretext that Saddam Hussein was trying to develop weapons of mass destruction that he would put at the disposal of terrorist groups, Bush's first objective was to bring about regime change in Iraq. Despite the fact that a UN weapons inspection team found no evidence that Iraq had stockpiled or was developing such weapons, a US-led coalition invaded Iraq on March 20, 2003. By April 9, Baghdad was in American hands, and on May 1 Bush declared an end to major combat operations in Iraq.

The so-called Coalition of the Willing that backed the United States in this conflict comprised NATO allies like Great Britain, Italy, Spain, and Poland, but also included Australia. In contrast, French president Jacques Chirac and German chancellor Gerhard Schröder aligned themselves with Russian premier Vladimir Putin in categorically opposing an intervention that violated the tenets of international law. Their position was vindicated when no weapons of mass destruction, nor any connections between the Saddam regime and al-Qaeda, came to light; instead, the brutal conduct of some elements of the US military only acted as a recruiting sergeant for terrorism. It proved impossible to install a stable government in the country after the fall of Saddam, and for many years the occupying forces had to contend with a violent insurrection staged primarily by Shi'ite militias. In the summer of 2008 it was estimated that anywhere from 150,000 to one million Iraqis were killed in the conflict. The United States suffered 4,000 dead and 10,000 severely injured troops.

Bush's attempt to exploit the worldwide fear of vulnerability to Islamist terrorism in order to establish a unilateral hegemony of the American superpower succeeded only in sowing division. The international reputation of the United States suffered greatly, not least after it became known that American soldiers had tortured Iraqi prisoners and that terror suspects from a wide variety of backgrounds were being incarcerated indefinitely, with no recourse to the due process of law, in a special camp at the US military base at Guantánamo Bay on Cuba. During Bush's second term in office (2004–2008), the administration's loss of standing also began to be felt at home. Offensive operations against North Korea or Iran were now out of the question, even though the latter option became a recurrent point of friction with America's European allies. Bush's successor, Barack Obama, came to office in January 2009 with a program to withdraw US forces from Iraq. He also worked out a plan with the allies to bring the peacekeeping operation in Afghanistan to a close.

The loss of America's international standing went hand in hand with a strengthening of the European position within NATO. This became evident when Georgia's president Mikheil Saakashvili attacked the disputed Russian-leaning territories of Abkhazia and South Ossetia in August 2008 to try to force NATO's hand in accepting his country's application to join. When the Russian government responded by ordering its forces to invade Georgia, it was Nicolas Sarkozy, president of the European Council at the time, and not the US president, who brokered a ceasefire. On August 15 he oversaw the signing of an accord between Saakashvili and Russia's new president, Dmitri Medvedev, that involved the withdrawal of Russian troops and the return of Georgian forces to their barracks. The autonomy of the two disputed regions was now beyond dispute. At the same time, Georgian membership in NATO, which had already been turned down on several occasions, disappeared from the organization's agenda. Ukraine's application was also shelved.

This strengthening of Europe's influence within the alliance brought about a thoroughgoing reevaluation of NATO by the Americans. From the debacle of Bush's missionary war on terror the new US administration drew the lesson that protection against terror attacks and the security of supply channels could best be achieved by bringing America's European allies on board, body and soul. In the course of the speech he delivered in Berlin on July 24, 2008, during his election campaign, Obama made a point of appealing for European support, and in doing so found himself pushing at an open door. The Europe-wide criticism of Bush's unilateral crusade ultimately resulted not in greater anti-Americanism but in a greater willingness to take on international responsibilities.

This became clear when, in the spring of 2011, an armed uprising began against the Libyan dictator Muammar Gaddafi. French president Nicolas Sarkozy immediately called for military intervention in support of the rebels. He gained the backing of British prime minister David Cameron, but failed to win over German chancellor Angela Merkel. Following a resolution of the UN Security Council on March 11 to the effect that the rebel forces should be supported with air strikes against Gaddafi's military and the country's infrastructure, primarily French and British squadrons were mobilized to carry out this task; the United States confined itself to lending technical support through the NATO control and command structure. These measures resulted in the overthrow of Gaddafi's regime by August of that year and the establishment of a National Transitional Council in the capital, Tripoli.

The uprising against Gaddafi was part of a larger wave of protest and revolution against authoritarian regimes throughout the Arab world; beginning in Tunisia, this wave swept through several countries in North Africa and the Near East. In Tunisia itself, reformers succeeded in ousting President Zine el-Abidine Ben Ali as early as January 14, 2011, while in Egypt the long-serving president Hosni Mubarak stood down on February 11. In Yemen, following months of demonstrations and armed clashes, President Ali Abdullah Saleh signed an agreement in November 2011 that pledged to hand over power to Vice President Abd Hadi. In Morocco, Algeria, and Jordan, the protests led to changes of government and constitutional reforms; in Bahrain and Saudi Arabia, however, the reform movement was brutally suppressed. Meanwhile, in Syria a civil war developed from the Assad regime's crackdown on opposition forces; by the beginning of 2013 the conflict had claimed more than seventy thousand lives. The Arab Spring prompted new demands for Europe to develop an integrated Mediterranean strategy.

The Rise of China

This tendency toward increasing US-European cooperation and developing a common front against threats emanating from Asia reflected a growing interdependence of economic spheres. With reciprocal trade and investments to the tune of almost 4 billion euros in 2007, the economies of the United States and the European Union, which each generated around 13 billion euros and together accounted for nearly one-half of all world trade, were more closely intertwined than ever before. At the same time, China rose to become the second most significant trading partner of the United States (after Canada), so underlining the vital importance of the Asian market for the US economy. Indeed, the volume of goods traded between the United States and Asia was greater than that between the United States and Europe, even though the level of investment lagged far behind.

China's rise to become an "anchor country" of global significance[71] was the result of a long process that began after Mao's death. Deng Xiaoping, from the time he took office in September 1976, made an effort to steer the country away from the excesses of the Great Proletarian Cultural Revolution that Mao had instigated and put it on a more pragmatic course. Deng not only managed to reinstitute a proper education system and then expand it massively, but also forced through economic reforms aimed at promoting private initiatives and the achievement principle. State-owned enterprises were given greater decision-making autonomy, small family-run farms became the preferred model in agriculture, and Special Economic Zones were created to attract international trade and investment. These reforms resulted in an annual growth rate of 7 percent, increasing industrialization, and huge imbalances in income and lifestyle among the population. By 1987 the average income in China was double what it had been in 1976.[72]

In 1986 General Secretary Hu Yaobang and Prime Minister Zhao Ziyang concluded that greater political freedom would be necessary to ensure the long-term success of the economic reforms. A program was put in place to disengage local government and companies from Party and state control; intellectuals and scientists were allowed more freedom to express divergent viewpoints. The reforms immediately led to the growth of a democracy movement among students, who were angry about widespread corruption and the lack of career opportunities. In

December 1986, major demonstrations were held in Wuhan, Beijing, and Shanghai, with protestors demanding power sharing, democratic elections, and an end to human rights violations.

The Party leadership reacted by putting the brakes on the reform process. Hu Yaobang was forced to resign as general secretary in January 1987; tens of thousands of students were sent to the countryside on work details. But all this failed to quell the democracy movement. When Hu dropped dead from a heart attack during a heated debate in the Politburo on April 8, 1989, demonstrations flared up once more. On April 27, five hundred thousand to a million students occupied Tiananmen Square (Square of Heavenly Peace) in Beijing; on May 13 a hard core of demonstrators began a hunger strike. Faced with the threat of losing their monopoly on power, and disregarding opposition from Zhao Ziyang, on May 19, under the influence of Deng, the Politburo decided to impose martial law. From all around the country, troops were assembled outside Beijing. The protestors attempted to impede their advance by erecting barricades and organizing sit-down protests, but on July 3 troops entered the city in tanks and armored vehicles. Between eight hundred and twenty-six hundred civilians who stood in their way (the exact number will likely never be known) were brutally mowed down. The clearance of Tiananmen Square itself, which took place in the early morning of July 4, passed off relatively peacefully; the regime was concerned to avoid the appearance of unchecked brutality.

The breakup of the demonstration was followed by a wave of arrests and death sentences passed on "troublemakers." Zhao Ziyang and others who advocated a dialogue with the students were relieved of their duties. But the crushing of the democracy movement did not spell an end to the economic reform program. The new general secretary was Jiang Zemin, who in his former role as mayor of Shanghai had shown how to effect economic modernization without relinquishing control over students and other sectors of the populace. Following a brief phase during which central state control was reasserted, in 1992–1993 Deng was able to force the pace toward a socialist market economy. Jiang Zemin was elected state president and chairman of the Central Military Commission (thus becoming the chosen successor to Deng, who died in 1997 at the age of 92). The regulations relating to the Special Economic Zones were extended to the underdeveloped inland provinces, bringing a new influx of foreign capital into the country. Investors now included not just members of the Chinese diaspora from Hong Kong or Singapore, but above all the Japanese.

These measures all combined to boost economic growth still further. Whereas it took eleven years for the first spectacular doubling of the country's per capita income, the second such increase had occurred by 1995, after just eight years.[73] In the second half of the 1990s, China developed into the new workshop of the world, with export rates that, after entry into the World Trade Organization in 2001, reached daily levels corresponding to a whole year's worth of exports in 1978, along with rapidly growing investment in research and development. At the same time, Chinese businesses began investing in Central Asia, Indochina, and sub-Saharan Africa, with an eye to both securing supplies of raw materials and spreading political influence. A succession of African countries, along with Iran, Pakistan, Burma, and North Korea, received Chinese military aid. With scant concern for the safeguarding of humanitarian or environmental standards, Chinese state capitalism thus became an unwelcome rival to Western development policies and an economic player of global significance.

Overall, the modernization of Chinese communism took a turn quite different from the roughly contemporaneous reform of Soviet communism. A comparison of the two processes reveals that the attitude of the leaders was the principal factor in overcoming the legacy of regimes structured along Marxist-Leninist lines. At the key moment, Deng chose a path different from Gorbachev's. The question of which course was the more appropriate depends on one's own political standpoint. What is beyond dispute is that each option had its price and that in both cases, many other options were available.

Imbalances and Multipolarity

After China, there appeared on the scene several other anchor countries: major states caught up in a process of dynamic economic development that impacted on the global economy, which guaranteed them an independent role on the international political stage. In India, economic reforms in the first half of the 1990s stimulated a level of growth comparable with the situation in China, with equally strong investment in research and development enabling Indian firms to likewise become competitive players in global markets. In Indonesia, which was particularly badly affected by the Asian economic crisis of 1997–1998, the fall of President Suharto in May 1998, after more than twenty-two years of military rule, and the ensuing struggle against corruption and nepotism, heralded a transition toward a more stable economic course. Similarly, in Brazil the progressive dismantling in the first half of the 1980s of a military dictatorship that had lasted for more than two decades paved the way for economic modernization and stable growth. Through several changes in political direction (in 1992–1994 from the liberal Fernando Collor de Mello to the social democrat Fernando Henrique Cardoso, and in 2002 from Cardoso to the socialist Luiz Inácio Lula da Silva), the country has become a driving force in Latin American economic development. In Mexico, vigorous measures from 1990 on to reduce the country's crippling foreign debt went hand in hand with encouragement of private entrepreneurship, the ongoing fight against drug barons, and a move away from a one-party state. After weathering two severe economic crises, Mexico, by the late 1990s, once again had high growth rates and increasing competitiveness. In South Africa, the participation from 1990 on of the United States and Great Britain in the UN trade embargo helped bring about the end of the apartheid regime. The presidency of Nelson Mandela (1994–1999) saw all the country's major political forces embrace a free market economy with welfare state provisions; as a result, South Africa rose to become by far the strongest economy in the region.

After the millennium, the anchor countries began to augment their influence through cooperation. In August 2003 Brazil—with the support of India, China, and South Africa—seized the initiative in establishing a G-20 group of developing countries, which opposed the program of the OECD countries for the Doha Round of the World Trade Organization's negotiations. The industrialized states responded by steadily broadening their mechanisms for cooperation. In 2006, for instance, Russia was accepted as a member of the Group of Seven, which, following a drastic economic recession in the early 1990s that slashed industrial output and GNP in half, was itself beginning to take on the characteristics of an anchor country. At the G-8 summit at Heiligendamm in northern Germany in June 2007, it was agreed that constructive dialogue should begin with China, India, Brazil, Mexico, and South Africa; subsequently these countries have taken part on an informal basis in the yearly G-8 meetings.

The bipolar world order that existed during the Cold War was supplanted neither by American hegemony nor by a "global village" in which sovereign states and imbalances of power no longer played a role. Rather, what came about was a complex world order to which the concept of multipolarity scarcely does justice. Aside from an American-European duopoly of extremely diverse but mutually dependent partners, there is a whole range of countries that to varying degrees exert regional or supraregional influence. A general trend that can be observed is the growing strength of Asian players within this power structure. However, in the foreseeable future this does not mean that there is any danger of the West relinquishing its leading role. Among the factors militating against this are the American system's continuing dynamism in acquiring new resources and the inevitable economically driven convergence of the Russian Federation with the European Union.[74]

If they are to safeguard peace, promote prosperity, and conserve the natural environment, the world's states will be increasingly dependent upon cooperation. Whether and to what extent they and the societies they are grounded in will be shrewd enough to recognize and act on this remains to be seen.

Translated from the German by Peter Lewis

·[two]·

Opening Doors in the World Economy

Thomas W. Zeiler

Introduction

JAPANESE pitcher Hideo Nomo's contract with the Los Angeles Dodgers in 1995 initiated the globalization of baseball; the sport embraced market forces that heightened worldwide economic exchanges, integrated this business around the planet, and boosted global cultural convergence. These consequences arose from a world economy designed by the United States after the Second World War. Nomo served as the connective tissue that brought together various drivers of globalization, a process encouraged by the American transnational corporate entity Major League Baseball (MLB). While the confluence of satellite technology and entrepreneurial broadcasting companies extended MLB's world reach, the corporation also strategized that a global pool of labor and consumers would revive the game, help it compete with other sports, and boost revenue (by 2009, revenue exceeded $6 billion). The downside to this process became clear: poor and young talents from Latin America, for instance, were targeted by a voracious system of recruiting outside the bounds of international labor protections. Because foreign players represented over one-quarter of players on Major League rosters, however, the baseball market flourished as an example of the benefits of globalization.

Having coaxed other nations to send their players to the "big show" in the United States, the Major Leagues wanted them, above all, to buy into its vision of expansion and convergence, all under an American brand. Fans around the world had satellite feeds to the games, in which broadcasts were translated into over a dozen languages (including Hindi, Papiamento, Arabic, and Korean). Complex and extensive licensing deals between MLB and foreign companies and business networks forged lucrative local, regional, and global partnerships. That idea, simply, was "of a day when its game is played on multiple continents and the demand for the major league brand—think programming, advanced media, international corporate sponsorship, and yes, T-shirts and hats—cover the globe," wrote columnist Tom Verducci after the conclusion of the first international

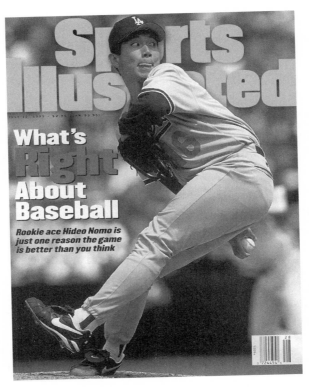

Hideo Nomo, Coors Field, Denver, May 7, 1995. The Los Ange-les Dodgers' ace was the first Japanese player to join Major League Baseball, thus creating professional sports synergies across national borders that epitomized the modern era of glo-balization. (Sports Illustrated/Getty Images)

tournament of professional players in 2006.[1] The only remaining barriers to MLB's growth were distance (and supersonic passenger jets were on the drawing board) and vestiges of nationalism that restricted the movement of players. Yet clearly, nations had to play by American rules, even if they beat the United States at its own game, as Japan did in the 2006 and 2009 World Baseball Classic tournament.

Nomo's case illustrates a central fact that since the Second World War, the world economy reflected the power of the United States, and the reception of that power. Although US power was significant, however, it was not always hegemonic. This chapter examines the co-optation, absorption, and rejection of the US market model by states, transnational entities, and people over the decades as globalization emerged to dominate the world economy. America remained the globe's dominant baseball arena, for instance, but that market accommodated a foreigner whose appearance portended changes in the quintessential American pastime. After the war, US leadership served as the foundation for recovery and growth, but in ensuing decades, rule from Washington was eroded—but not replaced—by multilateral governance of the world economy. The consequence was a world economy shaped by American free-market principles and power that fueled growth for many rich and poor nations alike, brought inequities to a large portion of the world, and integrated the planet into a system in which goods, services, money, and people flowed across national borders to a greater degree and intensity than ever before. The following is a history of postwar globalization's development under American influence. Though the United States was at the center of the picture, it was not alone in the global economy, of course. The Great Depression had devastated international capitalism and factored into the eruption of the most destructive war in human history, a cataclysm that propelled the United States to a position of hegemony atop the global economic hierarchy. From that point until today, competitors have threatened to knock America off its perch; repeated crises have certainly eaten away the country's foothold.

Market forces were always at the heart of this trend, because the hegemonic United States insisted that doors to global economic exchange be pried open and remain ajar, unfettered by barriers that were to be reduced on a multilateral basis. This approach (in ideology and practice) is referred to here as the "open door" doctrine, market precepts or policy, or free enterprise. The open-door concept should not be confused with British commercial policy in the mid-nineteenth century or American approaches to China after 1899, although there are similarities. Here the meaning addresses market access, the freeing and expansion of trade and financial exchanges, and intimate economic relations that led to interdependence the world over. Whatever it is called, this open, sprawling, and integrated system of globalization affected nations, territories, organizations, networks, and people around the world in different ways. It also prevailed—in a world torn by war, diplomatic tensions, poverty, and economic turmoil—because of America's projection of power through market capitalism, either imposed or negotiated through a multilateral process among governments. Thus, a key theme of this chapter is that state-to-state relations guided the process of globalization, although the agents were transnational entities that thrived on private exchanges.

The path to globalization was neither easy nor profitable for all, nor was it always pluralistic. That is, the United States was the predominant force in the world economy, but its power was most concentrated during the early postwar years and then gave way to other competitors in ensuing decades. Also, since 1945 the world economy has been shaped by such seismic shocks as the British financial collapse, the end of colonialism, hot and cold wars, sharp rises in energy costs, revolts against the open door in a Third World, abject poverty and tremendous debt, the advent of Japanese, European, Chinese, oil-state, and Indian power, the demise of the postwar monetary system, and periodic collapses in credit, investment, and commercial markets that have increasingly enmeshed the entire world in their clutches. The story of those setbacks, as well as the successes, reflected the American market model that, for better or worse, led the world into a dynamic era of globalization.

1. *Closed Doors*

IN THE MIDST of the Second World War, as the Allied powers struggled to cut off strategic materials to the Axis powers and boost the supply of goods from American production, the United States and Great Britain began shaping postwar world economic institutions. The goal fixed on promoting a multilaterally run global economy that opened Europe and other key trading areas to US goods, money, and influence, which required exposing the American economy to competition from abroad. Washington took aim on British imperial commercial arrangements that discriminated against the products of nonmembers. Although largely in accord with the idea of open global economic networks, Britain defended its semiclosed system of preferential trade for members in its empire. The British went into survival mode, trading a gradual weakening of imperial protectionism for American largesse to help float their economy during the dire times of war and postwar reconstruction. Negotiations over the outlines of new international economic institutions and the shifting Anglo-American power relationship reflected the ascendancy of the United States, even though a truly multilateral process would have to wait until partner nations had gotten back on their feet. In the immediate postwar period, US unilateralism in the world economy, rather than globalization, entrenched American market hegemony.

This power derived, quite obviously, from the ravages of war around the world. Much of Europe and Asia lay in ruins. Although US observers in particular pronounced optimistic assessments that the European economies would spring back quickly, those hopes were dashed by both the magnitude of the war's destruction and the ineffectiveness of piecemeal aid and stimulative fiscal measures to prime the capitalist pump toward permanent recovery. The combination of the catastrophe of war on others, and America's own productive capacity, gave the United States a huge economic advantage—and presence—abroad. The figures are staggering; the country was a production and consumption monolith on a scale never witnessed before, or since. With just 6 percent of the world's population in 1945, America produced nearly half of the world's energy, and consumed 40 percent of it; and due to its domination of global oil reserves (59 percent), it is not surprising that the United States manufactured eight times more cars than Britain, France, and Germany combined (and one hundred times more than its new rival, the Soviet Union) and that 60 percent of cars worldwide drove on American roads. By 1950, American consumers enjoyed the lion's share of refrigerators, telephones, and televisions (regarding the latter, nearly 100 percent were owned by US buyers). Of course, income levels drove this purchasing power; by the end of the 1940s, Americans earned two times more than the British worker, three times more than the French, five times that of Germans, and seven times the salary of a typical Russian. Added to its predominance in world trade and its hold of nearly half of all global currency and gold reserves, the United States was truly, as a historian has concluded, "the land of milk and honey" amidst the despair and struggles of other economies.[2]

In part, the United States faced an enormous task due to the conditions of war; the times were not right to impose multilateral, open-door prescriptions. The country had long run sizable trade surpluses with Europe and the British Commonwealth, and harmlessly small deficits with Asia and Latin America, but by 1946 its trade surplus boomed—to a $3.3 billion total with Europe, over $1 billion with the British nations, nearly a half billion dollars with Asia, and $320 million with Latin America. These trade partners might grow their way toward correcting their commercial imbalances with the United States—and for some, like Germany and France, recovery was relatively quick—but the calamity of war stymied reconstruction and, therefore, a balanced global economy.[3]

World War II destroyed territory and property, political systems and ideologies, and livelihoods and lives in Western and Eastern Europe and China and Japan, while Britain, the financier of capitalism, was bankrupted by its effort to defeat fascism and survive thereafter. Whole economies ceased functioning or sputtered along, tens of millions of people lay dead or injured, and hundreds of millions of homes and businesses were eviscerated. Famine plagued large swaths of the world, acutely so in Europe and Asia. Major cities—Hamburg, Manila, and Warsaw—had been destroyed, and aerial bombing campaigns had leveled factories in Germany and curbed commercial traffic in key ports, such as Rotterdam, London, and Tokyo. The European transportation system was in tatters,

The battle for the Philippines, March 2, 1945. This platoon of American soldiers patrols the Walled City of Manila in an epic World War II battle. The destruction signaled the need for tremendous reconstruction aid in the postwar era. (Time & Life Pictures/Getty Images)

leaving the countrysides isolated from commercial centers. Japanese and German merchant fleets did not exist to carry goods. The Soviet Union, for its part, seized territory, factories, and farms, and compelled workers to toil for the USSR's gain. This system of compulsion further weakened Germany and gave the USSR preeminence in central Europe. The brutally cold winter of 1946–1947 punished all of Europe, a region prostrate from war and with no good prospects in sight.

The need (and opportunity) for salvation by the United States was apparent. Lend-Lease aid, a grant of $42 billion in goods and services to the Allies during the war, revealed rising American dominance over the international economic order. Although the main goal of the program focused on military victory through aid, US negotiators insisted that the United Kingdom ease imperial restrictions on trade and finance for outsiders in return for billions of dollars in Lend-Lease assistance. By no means would President Franklin Roosevelt exploit London's hour of need by withholding aid, but the goal of placing market forces on a firm footing after the war was clear, and Britain reluctantly understood this reality. As a result, wartime aid (and the 1946 discussions over a $3.75 billion loan to England) was engulfed in testy negotiations that elicited howls from defenders of the imperial system. Lend-Lease served American interests—the main one being defeat of Nazism and Japanese militarism—yet that aid provided a platform for US ideas of free enterprise and their projection in the postwar world.

What catapulted the United States to predominance was wartime production. The output and shipment abroad of military goods led to a more than tripling of the value of US exports, which in turn helped double the nation's gross domestic product. Manufacturers, farmers, and workers counted on continued growth for their livelihoods, and to avoid a return to the Great Depression years of insolvency and unemployment. Overseas trade appeared more important for domestic economic stability and growth. Thus, US leaders focused on ensuring that the world economy had enough money for liquidity and investment, and also as few obstacles as possible to trade in goods and services, so that all nations could thrive and buy US goods. America's self-interested championing of market mechanisms not surprisingly undergirded the establishment of the governing postwar world bodies for monetary and commercial affairs.[4]

Financing Hegemony

In July 1944, over seven hundred delegates from forty-four Allied nations gathered at a resort in New Hampshire to hammer out the Bretton Woods agreements that established the postwar international monetary system. Two years of Anglo-American wrangling over the extent to which the market or state oversight should dictate economic relations resulted in a plan that addressed three cardinal issues: what regulations were necessary to stabilize global economic exchanges, how they would be enforced, and who would safeguard the system. In the past the gold standard had permanently fixed exchange rates to prevent financial fluctuations deemed hurtful to stable commercial relations, but this rigid approach had obligated nations to deflate their currencies when bad times hit or to simply abandon the gold standard altogether (as the United States did during the Great Depression). The Bretton Woods system maintained the high profile of gold, but Washington agreed to back it with the dollar, which became the world's dominant currency.

Granting America such unprecedented influence was not accomplished without a fight, but it should be stressed that all nations sought a multilateral world economy, or a system in which several nations, rather than one or two hegemons, worked in concert toward agreement. They just disagreed on how to set it up. This was especially so for the British, who, led by the noted economist John Maynard Keynes, understood that New York City had secured from London the title of the world's financial capital, which would weaken the empire, and compel it to carefully regulate the domestic economy. Regardless of these pressures, under the Bretton Woods accords put into effect in 1947, nations established the International Monetary Fund (IMF, or the Fund) to provide sufficient liquidity for commercial transactions. The agreement also created the International Bank for Reconstruction and Development (one of five institutions incorporated today into the World Bank Group), capitalized at $10 billion and designed to make loans for economic development and specifically speed the recovery of war-torn areas. Critical to both institutions in the Bretton Woods system was the predominance of the United States, which contributed the largest subscription to the Fund and, in return, received power commensurate to its size in the pool of currencies and gold that constituted the IMF reservoir of credit. The IMF and World Bank ensured that the American dollar would act as the postwar world's reserve currency.

Concerned about the menace of inflation that could destabilize prices, the Americans used their overweening leverage. As the world's largest creditor, the United States imposed rules to guard against price fluctuations by demanding domestic austerity measures from IMF members. To give nations an initial period of adjustment by permitting them to restrict trade and payments until they recovered from the war, the United States insisted that members limit their currency manipulation and take other measures, such as deflation or selling off assets, to participate in a multilateral, market-driven world. The exception was the Soviet Union. Although Moscow initially agreed to join the Bretton Woods system as the third largest subscriber to the Fund, the Western nations welcomed

Russian membership to encourage diplomatic friendship rather than for economic reasons. By December 1945, Moscow backed away from the IMF, partly out of recognition that the system further strengthened the capitalist community of nations and the USSR's potential rival, the United States.[5]

American conservatives in the banking industry and the US Congress did not mind the Soviet exit, but they did focus on a monetary deal that played to US strengths and interests. Promised that Bretton Woods would allow the nation to forgo major, potentially wasteful foreign aid programs, they got their way by elevating the dollar as the monetary system's "key currency." In reality, this meant that although nations were to "peg" their currencies to gold (fix them within an agreed-upon parity of exchange rates within the IMF regime), the dollar actually determined exchange rates. In essence the dollar became the new gold standard—international transactions were based on the greenback, and all nations defined their currencies in relation to the dollar ($35 could be traded for one troy ounce of gold). That system would not truly function until the postwar reconstruction period had ended in the early 1950s, but payments for goods and services around the world, and thus the basis of the multilateral regime, were made in dollars. As Treasury Secretary Henry Morgenthau told the State Department, "The financial center of the world is going to be New York. The advantage is ours here, and I personally think we should take it."[6] The Americans did, and they exercised supremacy over the global economy.

Pursuit of Trade Multilateralism

As in the Bretton Woods arrangement, so in establishing the trade regime under the General Agreement on Tariffs and Trade (GATT), the United States labored to shape a globalized market system. American secretary of state Cordell Hull was a staunch believer in the link between liberal trade and national security. He did not pursue the impossible dream of outright free trade (a regime bereft of protectionist obstructions), for politics in all nations would not permit the lifting of tariffs and other protection for domestic producers. But Hull did tie fair treatment (nondiscrimination), equal opportunities, and orderly exchanges in national markets to the promotion of peace. In his view, an open-door commercial system, based on multilateral negotiations of trade barriers and a market ethic, would prevent a headlong descent into regimentation, "to the suppression of human rights, and all too frequently to preparations for war and a provocative attitude toward other nations."[7] He frowned also on restrictions on the flow of gold, but detested even more the economic nationalism implied in the British system of imperial trade preferences. As the chief trade negotiating arm of the government, the Department of State followed his lead in working to pry open the closed doors to trade around the world. Hull set the standard for the pursuit of market capitalism as a pillar of US trade policy and as a foundation of the process of globalization.

What evolved in the postwar period was less an assault on national sovereignty, for recovery and reconstruction demands required countries to protect their economies, but a planting of the seeds of globalization in the trade and monetary regimes. In other words, the doctrine of the open door set down roots to flourish in a later time when the world economy had reached a more normal stage than the mid-1940s era of destitution and instability. The British, in particular, but essentially all nations, did not pretend to seek unregulated commercial relations. Each had domestic constituencies vulnerable to import competition, each struggled to normalize their economies during peacetime, and each had interests that superseded the theory behind market ideology. In short, there was never a chance for pure economics to dominate the politics and diplomacy of trade; globalization emerged between visionaries and pragmatic politicians. The advent of GATT in 1947 involved a multilateralist drive for installing free-enterprise practices, which themselves were buffeted by protectionism but guided by the state's adoption of Hull's hope for peace through prosperity propelled by the market.

The multilateral trade order reflected a compromise between unfettered commercial relations—the unattainable but ultimate goal of market capitalism—and narrow economic interests of profits through exports or regulation of imports by protectionism. The upshot of dealings, hedging, and the like—by the British preserving imperial preferences, the Australians backing wool tariffs, the Soviets structured by antimarket state-trading mechanisms, the Europeans and Japan endorsing cartels, and colonies in the Third World demanding protection for nascent domestic producers and more access into the advanced world—as a trade system (like the monetary system) reflected less the market and more muted free enterprise. Even the United States would not permit a sweeping aside of tariffs by sectors of the economy, on a percentage basis; US trade law allowed for only selected cuts on a reciprocal basis when other nations agreed to reduce their duties. The renewal of the Reciprocal Trade Act in 1945 (the US authorizing legislation for trade negotiations to this day) did push the country toward global multilateralism by calling for large cuts, but not by a sectoral process. The British insisted on large-scale American tariff reductions in return for easing quotas and closing some preferential trade deals within the British Empire, but like Canada, Australia, and other Commonwealth partners, London preferred to seek a regulated trade order that balanced imports and exports of all nations rather than focus on expansion through the open door. The result of continual discussion during the immediate postwar years was a compromise on tariff negotiations in which each country sought a bilateral deal on an item-by-item basis and then applied (or multilateralized) the concessions to the broader community of trading nations who joined the bargaining process under GATT.

Yet Anglo-American officials envisioned a more ambitious institution than just GATT's negotiating forum, as well as a commercial complement to the Bretton Woods monetary system. They hoped to subsume every issue related to trade—employment, subsidies, export taxes, quotas, cartels, preferential trade agreements, development, and tariffs—under an agency to oversee commercial relations and, in the American view, ensure that market precepts prevailed. The idea developed into the Charter for the International Trade Organization (ITO), the outlines of which were hammered out in numerous conferences from 1945 to its completion in Havana, Cuba, in 1948. Yet while the Americans sought as few impediments as possible in the ITO, they met the same resistance against market multilateralism as before. Nations tacked on amendments that watered down their commitments to trade liberalism. Some allowed for countries to escape from prior tariff-reduction deals, others blocked US banking efforts to protect its investments in the less-developed world by shifting the burden on bankers from profit seeking to boosting industrialization. A loose coalition of Latin American nations demanded that the philosophy of protectionism and anti-imperialism be enshrined in the ITO.

The modifications eventually doomed the Charter. Cold War ideology impinged on the ITO, because the US Congress (in conservative hands at the time) and free-trade purists in the business community deemed it a danger to American free enterprise, which they saw as being challenged by the communist menace. Business executive Philip Cortney warned, "We shall drift into Communism and finally to war" because the Charter promoted discriminatory trade arrangements and, therefore, "socialism the world over."[8] Thus, the United States turned on its own creation. Anathema to the market ethic, the ITO was stillborn; President Harry Truman eventually withdrew it from congressional consideration in 1950. A kernel of its idea resurfaced in the mid-1950s but disappeared, too, until the World Trade Organization championed a similar holistic approach to commercial relations during the renascence of globalization forty years later.

A good example of the difficulties facing the open-door approach in this period of transition from war to peace arose from one of the most globalized of industries—Hollywood. Facing the worst financial crisis in its history, Britain saw its international payments shortfall (the "dollar gap") reach an alarming $2 billion by 1947. London simply could not afford its overseas commitments (and thus began to back out of the Middle and Near East in a process that culminated in its withdrawal from imperial commitments by 1956), nor, leaders feared, could it support the domestic economy. However much Britain might embrace the market, this was no time for free enterprise. Because film and tobacco comprised 40 percent of the value of British imports from the United States, the government turned to an austerity program—the kind prescribed by the IMF on consumer goods—to buy "food before fags [and] films." A quota on the number of American movies shown in Britain tightened; at one point, 45 percent of the movies shown in the country had to be domestically made. The Americans cried foul, arguing that the screen quota violated trade rules as a discriminatory internal regulation. Motion picture executives offered an open-door solution: instead of curbing consumption of this luxury good, US industry would promote British film exports to earn London $30 million in 1948. Britain brushed aside the remedy as a false promise, for American studios dominated the industry at home and abroad, and proceeded a step farther along the road of protectionism by imposing a special tax on US films alongside the screen quotas. The tax was eventually repealed in March 1948 but not before American producers issued a boycott on exports to Britain. The British would not allow the market to decide the fate of their struggling film sector, and screen quotas remained in place for decades.[9]

Such trade disputes, and the complexities inherent in linking global markets to domestic economies, boded ill for a complicated rule-making body like the ITO, so GATT became the fallback institution for a world trade organization. Yet GATT met with some success in this period by maintaining modest momentum toward lowering or freezing tariff levels. In three "rounds," or negotiating conferences, between 1947 and 1951, dozens of nations exchanged nearly seventy thousand tariff concessions. By the end of the third round, duties had been cut by one-quarter of their level in 1948. To be sure, the market-oriented drive, particularly against British imperial preferences, sparked tensions at the first round, in Geneva; US negotiators had fits about London's unwillingness to give way due to its dollar gap, which made "multilateral trade almost an impossibility," confessed one British official.[10]

The saving grace for Britain was the Soviet specter. In a pattern that emerged from the early Cold War and persisted until its end, US officials cast trade negotiations within the larger context of the struggle against global communism. One of many instances of politics subsuming economics arose during the Annecy Round of GATT in 1949. American lemon producers lobbied hard against reducing tariffs in the face of Italian lemon imports, only to be told that to guard against a peasant revolt in Sicily and promote Italy's allegiance to the North Atlantic Treaty Organization (NATO), the concession would be granted.[11] During the Cold War, trade was used as a tool of diplomacy. America often opened its markets to aid its trade partners while it permitted discrimination against its exports abroad, all in the name of promoting stability within the capitalist world and seeking a liberal, open commercial order in the long run.[12]

Free Enterprise in a Time of Crisis

American leadership had ever greater urgency as the West confronted the threat of communism alongside the difficulties of reconstruction. The Bretton Woods institutions were inapplicable in a time of economic crisis. Unstable national currencies were inconvertible into dollars, and the Wall Street–led IMF insisted upon rigid standards of sound banking and production practices rather than easing terms of lending. Faced with feeding and housing 120 million people in the former Axis nations and aiding those Allied areas devastated by war, the

United States also organized costly occupation governments in Germany, Japan, and Austria that belied optimistic forecasts of quick recovery. For instance, Japanese industrial production crawled along at one-fifth its 1913 level, and Germany's sputtered at half that rate. The USSR, meanwhile, seized some of Germany's economic assets as reparations, thereby further dousing an industrial resurgence by this engine of the European economy. As the split between the Soviets and the West widened due to territorial disputes, diplomatic tensions in a host of issues ranging from sharing atomic technology, the joint administration of occupation zones of former enemies, and Russian sponsorship of socialist parties and subversion in Western Europe, Greece, Turkey, and elsewhere compelled the United States toward the containment of Russian influence and power.

Economic containment was the initial answer to the USSR's suspected expansionist and threatening foreign policy. Because this new American approach divided the world into two camps, installation of a multilateral market system was further delayed. In fact, the emerging Cold War so transformed the world economy that it set in motion a process of deglobalization of markets, in which the unilateral leadership of the United States and regional economic organization became the rule for decades. Within this circumscribed system, the Americans adopted an ever more market-oriented ideology as the confrontation against the anticapitalist ideology and practices of the Soviet (and soon Chinese) bloc became a fixation in Washington and in corporate boardrooms. Globalization would surface decisively only after the priority of security over the world economy ended some four decades later.[13]

Economic containment endured until Cold War tensions had so split the world in 1948 that militarization, and the subsuming of trade under diplomacy, replaced economics as the means of promoting national security. Initially this was not a coherent effort, as the Americans loaned France $650 million in 1946, followed by more through 1947, but gave a paltry amount of credits to Italy even though the political viability of its democratic system was just as precarious. Unfortunately, US leadership quelled neither the chronic economic crises in either country, nor communist intrigues. Neither did insistence, at the Geneva Round of GATT, that Europe allow in more US exports, which further worsened the European trade deficit as well as the dollar gap.[14] The World Bank held $15 billion in assets that could supplement US aid, but none was forthcoming during the dollar crisis. The United Nations offered humanitarian aid financed from US coffers, but this was simply insufficient. Any hope of market policies was still-born. The more direct unilateral approach of the Truman Doctrine, in 1947, offered a remedy. This granted congressionally mandated, direct assistance of $400 million to stem communist inroads in the Middle East. Most pointedly, the Truman Doctrine sparked both the administration and Congress, in tandem, to end the piecemeal approach to European reconstruction and launch a comprehensive program of recovery, regional capitalist integration, and the containment of communism.[15]

This European Recovery Program (ERP), or Marshall Plan, offered a solution to the economic deprivation in Western Europe and communist political and security threats. The situation was dire in the region for American friends. The Western Allies' German zones of occupation suffered from slow starvation and feeble industrial production, due to both Soviet-imposed barriers and the deindustrialization policies of all the occupiers, which was exacerbated by the dismantling of factories for shipment to the USSR. A shortage of coal arising from stalled German mining meant death by freezing and cold homes throughout Western Europe, particularly in Germany, for many in the winter of 1946–1947. As a result of the "hunger winter" and the desperation instigated by bad heating, difficulties in procuring water, and struggles to maintain basic hygiene, Berliners turned to a vigorous black market when it became clear that concrete international aid was not forthcoming. Mothers resorted to illicitly trading the family cigarette ration or milk card to farmers for food; as one woman recalled in explaining her response to starvation, "I was no great black marketer but an advanced forager." Youth in particular were skilled at illegal trade. In their occupation zone, the Americans tried to curb black market practices by opening a Barter Center in which Berliners could sell their goods for certificates to buy other products, but even the occupiers were often seduced into trading cigarettes for sex. In Germany, "an ambiguous moral economy" appeared next to the legal one and oftentimes was a more effective means of survival.[16]

In addition, European agricultural production in 1947 was just 83 percent of 1938 capacity, industrial output was not much better, and exports ran just 59 percent of the prewar numbers. These figures explained the growing dollar gap and consequent dysfunction of multilateral trade and financial arrangements.

Although America's economy did not rely on exports, which amounted to just 6.5 percent of the gross national product in 1947, farmers, steelmakers, and auto factories sold a sizable percentage of their goods abroad, and 2.4 million workers depended on exports. But even though economic arguments might win over the US Congress and business to full-scale aid for European recovery, the threat to democracy in the region was the administration's trump card. Plans went forth to draw on World Bank reserves, private loans, and credits, but the need for a large, formal program was in order.[17] Without it, hunger and hopelessness might lead to revolution; politics reflected economic realities as millions slowly starved and the communists exploited the distress.

The Marshall Plan by itself did not solve Western Europe's economic crisis, nor did it immediately jump-start the world economy into a condition of market exchanges, but it did lay the foundation for a rebirth of free enterprise by the time the five-year aid package expired in 1952. The assistance totaled $13 billion, giving Europeans the resources to promote production, curb distribution bottle-necks, and generally regain confidence in their economic institutions.[18] It certainly added to the momentum of the division of Europe, particularly the Soviet bloc of nations, which was offered but rejected Marshall Plan aid. As it stimulated the recovery of the region, the Marshall Plan also united the capitalist world into an integrated, market-oriented framework of exchanges that kept alive elements of globalization. To be sure, the ERP nations were not subject to the dictates of the open door; they molded the Marshall Plan to suit their own traditions and obstruct many US designs, such as the attempt to restrict British trade with Eastern European socialist nations.[19] The Americans got their way, however. They initiated and furthered the integration of Western Europe by stressing production (a market ethic) rather than the redistribution of income (a socialist objective). Productionism would allow for the normalization of world economic relations, a step toward the operation of a truly multilateral system of American free enterprise.[20] Such success would also, of course, serve US interests. The former cotton marketer and State Department official Will Clayton argued, "Let us admit right off that our objective has as its background the needs and interests of the people of the United States. We need markets—big markets—in which to buy and sell."[21] America would use its muscle for the greater good and, in no uncertain terms, for its own.

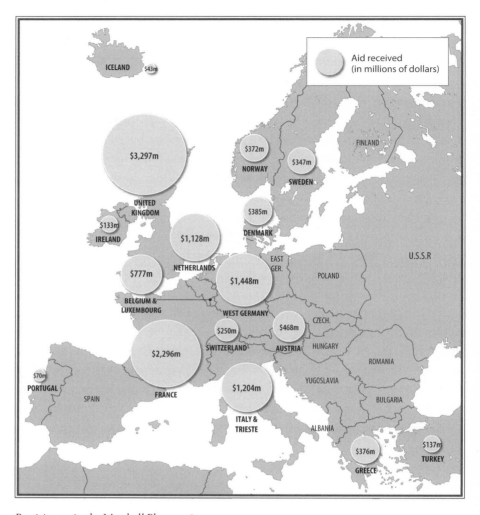

Participants in the Marshall Plan, 1948–1951.

The saplings of market policies were actually nourished by a transnational combination of the Economic Cooperation Administration (ECA), the US agency in charge of the aid program from the American side, and its European counterparts. Staffed by prominent corporate leaders brought into government to run the aid effort, the ECA sponsored advisory boards for all sectors of the international economy that not only studied remedies for recovery but created partnerships with Western European "productivity teams" that represented industry, labor, and government leaders. For instance, ECA leaders and the US Chamber of Commerce teamed with British technicians, foremen, and managers who themselves collaborated with civil servants in the National Joint Advisory Council. French business and labor formed into "modernization commissions" to coordinate various sectors of France's economy under the guidance of the father of European integration, Jean Monnet, and similar organizations evolved in Western Germany and Italy. These efforts furthered production goals and economic integration in ways that laid the foundation for future multilateral ties, yet they also indicated that the Americans had to compromise in their goal of reshaping European economies in the image of the New Deal, in which government encouraged a grouping of industry, labor, and agriculture into cooperative networks. For now, the Europeans preferred their own model—that of redistributing wealth rather than growing the economic pie, although transnational links fostered by the Marshall Plan stimulated regional integration.[22]

The impact of the Marshall Plan on the world economy was significant in this regard. In the effort to promote European integration as a basis for permanent recovery, which itself would make possible a global regime of open doors, officials established the Organization for European Economic Co-operation (OEEC) to administer the ERP. The OEEC eventually, in 1961, merged into the Organization for Economic Co-operation and Development (OECD), a thirty-nation body aimed at promoting a free-market global economy. The OEEC, as well as the ECA under Studebaker Corporation's Paul Hoffman, encouraged supranational and transnational economic integration under a European Payments Union in 1950 and a European Coal and Steel Community (ECSC) the following year. The latter joined France and West Germany in a cooperation based on selling this key but politically charged product, and thus won American backing even though the ECSC was really a cartel that contradicted free-market principles.[23] These institutions reflected the limited form of multilateralism that had come to characterize global economic structures; the European Payments Union, for example, allowed continued unilateral discrimination against the dollar and depended on dollar aid rather than a Europe-wide unified monetary regime. These efforts also led to the establishment of the European Economic Community, or Common Market, in 1957, although that body, too, discriminated against nonmembers' exports. The open door remained circumscribed by such regional economic integration, but the effort prompted political cooperation (and eventually, greater trade liberalization) within Europe, diplomatic unity among Cold War allies, and the potential for market globalization once conditions were right.

One important seed of the market approach had been planted in Western Europe: the overriding importance of consumption as an economic driver. If Europeans had their own ideas about the structure and policies to guide their economies (and, after all, they had long held a tradition of market economics before the war), they also gravitated toward the American view that a high standard of living was a right. Europeans became citizen-consumers—"children of Marx and Coca-Cola"—who sought private gains as well as government-generated higher wages to secure their well-being. Americans pushed Europeans to embrace the "politics of productivity," in which workers sacrificed high wages and job security to revive export-driven growth. This involved mass-marketing techniques to build a consumer economy and culture that bypassed politics for economics. In other words, the "American assembly line" would bring a "full dinner pail" instead of the "communist party line" of the "free lunch."[24] The most far-reaching consequence of the Marshall Plan, then, was in the creation of a transatlantic alliance of consumption—a bloc of nations aligned as consumer democracies—which served as the basis for the Americans' market designs for the world economy.

Cold War Economics

As US assistance poured into Western Europe, the United States led an effort to shore up and strengthen the capitalist bloc against the Soviet Union, its satellites in Eastern Europe, and other potential members. The goal was to limit Western economic ties to the socialist world, in the hope that this would deny these Cold War enemies such strategic goods as sensitive technology and critical military hardware but also would increase the dependence of these satellites on the USSR and thereby force Moscow to divert precious energies to its regional allies and away from its military. In addition, the United States had long frowned upon socialist planning, state trading and government monopoly practices, manipulation of currency values, and other intrusions in the market economy. The Soviet side simply did not want to play by the rules of multilateralism and the open door, as evidenced by the Russian refusal to join the Bretton Woods institutions, GATT, and the Marshall Plan. Once it was clear that the international politics of the Cold War had destroyed the World War II grand alliance by mid-1947, the ERP nations—led by the United States—began to curb and embargo exports to the communist world.

The ever-tightening noose of the strategic trade embargo, which became a pivotal part of the West's containment of the East, had profound implications for the global economy. For instance, the Allis-Chalmers Manufacturing Company canceled a machinery sale for a Czechoslovakian steel plant in 1947 on the grounds that the mill would serve the economic interests of the Soviet Union. The list of goods denied to the East soon extended beyond military equipment to technology transfers and civilian-use products, although European governments increasingly chafed at the wide scope of the sanctions, concerned as they were about recovery. By 1948, trade between Eastern and Western Europe had fallen to one-third of its prewar level, a worrisome development because expansion was necessary for reconstruction, stability, and growth. Western Europeans needed Polish coal, which Poland exported in large quantities despite having been rejected by the World Bank for a loan to help the country overcome its dearth of hard currency to buy consumer goods. Poland resigned from the World Bank in 1950, but the issue clearly showed that Europe's economies were interwoven. Sanctions expanded steadily, but the OEEC nations were oftentimes not willing to make the sacrifices demanded by the United States. Thus, when London and Washington established long lists of prohibited goods, the OEEC countries, including Britain, undermined the effort by maintaining their bilateral trade arrangements with the Soviets and the satellites.[25]

The British were certainly not passive followers of the American lead. In the critical field of aviation, for instance, they directly competed with US producers for the burgeoning international aircraft market. This effort, of course, related to their need to export and overcome their dollar shortage and domestic economic crises, but it also reflected the discomfort with American controls on East–West trade. London had the new air transport model, the Brabazon, on the drawing board, and as early as 1945 it turned to exporting its cutting-edge jet engines to nations eager to build up their civil aviation fleets. The decision was unusual in the sense that the Attlee government allowed companies to sell the most advanced engines, including Rolls Royce's Nene and Derwent state-of-the art military models, to whomever they wished and with minimum government oversight. Aware that making such engines available even to enemies weakened their hold on technology leadership, the British nonetheless sacrificed their advantage on the altar of economic need. Thus, in 1946 Britain sold civilian aircraft to Argentina, a former Nazi sympathizer excluded from the United Nations, and then turned to selling jets to Josef Stalin himself. The Americans protested, recognizing that British competition menaced their monopoly on the postwar aviation business, but they also played the Cold War trump card, arguing that even technology directed toward a nonmilitary use could increase the war-making potential of an enemy. Even worse, by 1948 Britain exhausted its supply of Nene and Derwent engines by fulfilling Moscow's large bid, and thus depleted its own Royal Air Force fleet. Americans criticized the sales as immoral, stupid, and risky, although high-level talks yielded a British promise in 1947 that subsequent aeronautical exports would come under the scrutiny of the government's military and security advisors.[26]

The creation in 1949 of CoCom, a permanent Coordinating Committee of technical experts with a policy-making executive to provide oversight, were the upshots of continued wrangling among the Western allies over such security-sensitive items as aircraft in East–West trade. In establishing their multilateral embargo, the Western nations created categories or lists of items, ranging from 129 military and strategic exports to a handful reserved for future scrutiny. From this point onward, the Americans insisted on adding goods to the lists while the Europeans, in general, wanted them reduced. This was certainly not in keeping with America's market ethic of opening doors to trade, but it reflected the overwhelming effect of the Cold War. The Department of State understood the need to reconcile the embargo with ERP nations' economic needs, but the Department of Commerce, Congress, and the newly created National Security Council (NSC) tended to equate these exports with Cold War security policy. By the mid-1950s, after the Cold War standoff had frozen the world into two military camps, even the State Department toed a stricter line toward sanctions, including endorsement of a more extensive East–West trade embargo. The British refused to expand the CoCom lists when it came to nonstrategic trade with Eastern Europe, at least up to the outbreak of the Korean War in June 1950, and thus preserved their industrial trade with the communist world. Still, politics trumped economics. Prime Minister Clement Attlee's economic policy committee warned that "it was necessary not only to limit the short-term striking power of the Soviet bloc but also to retard the development of its war potential in the longer term."[27] That the postwar trade and payments system in Europe could reach the point of economic warfare dismayed one-world idealists, humanitarians, and globalizers, but the Cold War took precedence over open-door dreams.

In contested Berlin, for example, the Soviets charged that interzonal economic contact allowed Westerners to plunder the city while the democracies pledged to defend inhabitants from a communist scourge. The Soviets claimed that they, not the West, actually were more interested in unifying the European economy, for they noted how the Anglo-French-American position on Germany was predicated on establishing a separate German state.[28] Frustrated by their inability to control trade coming into and emanating from Berlin, the Soviets decided to blockade the city, beginning in June 1948, to halt the outflow of wealth and adopt a new currency to separate the zones even more. Faced with a dangerous Soviet military presence that shut down all land transportation across Germany into Berlin, the Americans turned to airlifting supplies to their forlorn zone. As a result, they outlasted the blockade for nearly a year. This first Berlin crisis proved a hot point of the Cold War, convincing both sides that economic tools were insufficient to confront the enemy. Both turned to military options, in the form of alliances, weapons, and confrontation. If the United States did not achieve its goal of multilateral exchanges dictated by market capitalism, it did assert its rights and power in Germany in the Marshall Plan era.

Ironically, the Soviet counterpart to the ERP was a fairly multilateral organization within the borders of this emerging bloc of socialist nations, of which the German Democratic Republic, or East Germany, was a key member. In a defensive measure to counter the Western economic challenge and the lure of the ERP, the Soviets mobilized their satellites to face the CoCom export control regime of the West by establishing the Council for Mutual Economic Assistance (CMEA, or COMECON) in 1949. This socialist economic bloc, which stretched from Berlin to Vladivostok on the Pacific, lasted until 1991 and included more territory than the Marshall Plan or the European Economic Community a decade later. Although it was built on coerced bilateral arrangements between the six original members—the Soviet Union, Poland, Bulgaria, Romania, Czechoslovakia, and Hungary (East Germany and Albania joined by 1950)—it actually engaged in multilateral exchanges and practices in all the key categories of the economy, including production, trade, and finance. As its organizers announced, the CMEA would "establish still broader economic cooperation among the countries of the People's Democracy and the USSR," based on the principle of "equal representation, and having as its tasks the exchange of experience in the economic field, the rendering of technical assistance to one another and the rendering of mutual assistance in regard to raw materials, foodstuffs, machinery, equipment, etc."[29]

Just as the Cominform linked the world's communist parties and the Warsaw Pact served as the Soviet bloc's military organization, so COMECON coalesced the socialist economies across the globe. For instance, by the mid-1950s the People's Republic of China, Cuba, and Vietnam served as observers, but Finland, Iraq, Nicaragua, and Mozambique, among others, participated indirectly in COMECON through commissions in which their government and business communities took part. Such global reach showed that, at least in intention and name, the communists could offer a viable alternative to free-enterprise capitalism.[30] The Western powers ridiculed the CMEA as an artificial means of disguising Soviet domination, but in fact COMECON derived from a long history of organizational economic planning in Eastern Europe, as well as a necessary counter to the GATT's regime of nondiscriminatory, open-door trade treatment in the West. It should be noted, however, that socialist states like Czechoslovakia, Poland, Romania, and Hungary joined GATT over much opposition by Washington, which invoked discriminatory measures against their trade. The People's Republic of China also tried to be seated. But the complexity of socialist trading practices required a truly multilateral federation like the CMEA that relied not on the market to mediate economic relations but on agreements between governments to fix prices (usually at artificially high levels) and to adhere to varied approaches in trade—from reliance on the market to state trading monopolies. In addition, COMECON was also a response to the provocation of Western sanctions against CoCom, which only reinforced the impulse to collaborate in a regional economic policy under Soviet rule.[31]

To be sure, this was also a closed system with no pretense to market precepts, and although it had the potential to evolve into a truly supranational organization to harmonize national plans and practices into a common policy, such a result threatened the authority of communist parties and that of Stalin himself. COMECON served at the whim of Stalin in this period. By 1950, after a brief honeymoon when member states made decisions without centralized coercion, the Soviet dictator abruptly halted the organization's deliberations and converted it into merely a facilitator of trade. He did so to prevent his allies from ganging up on the Soviet Union, and to enhance his own power. Whatever the motives, the USSR curbed multilateral exchanges in Eastern Europe and the Balkans and forced through a principle that gave easy access to technology for those countries (the Soviet Union being one) that lagged behind the more industrialized Eastern European nations. The CMEA also did not prevent corrupt state trading practices; monopolies dictated the economies in each member nation. Yet it was effective in hording scarce hard currencies, stabilizing economies, and protecting them from the world market—COMECON operated by state trading and barter and not on the basis of free enterprise or the use of meaningful exchange rates. As a result of shutting out its members from foreign competition due to the prevalence of state trading monopolies, COMECON's international trade gradually declined through the decades. Still, the organization structured economic relations in the communist world, provided the USSR with an answer to the Marshall Plan in terms of institutionalizing trade relations and boosting postwar recovery in Eastern Europe, and, above all, armed the Soviet bloc with economic tools with which to survive, and even expand, in the divided world of the Cold War.[32]

Once the Korean War began, in the year following the end of the Berlin airlift, the shared logic of the two sides of a purposively discriminatory economic order rendered a freezing of East–West trade more possible, just as the Cold War itself froze in its tracks the development of a truly open multilateral world economy. Indeed, in 1951 American sales to the USSR declined to just $2 million worth of goods, while Western European exports to the Soviet bloc rose to $682 million, or more than one-half of the 1938 level. These figures represented only a partial defeat of US stringency, for the total for America's allies had fallen by a third from its 1949 peak of $994 million.[33] Add in the ongoing recovery of the Marshall Plan nations and modest trade liberalization under GATT, as well as the solidifying military alliance under NATO, and the United States could claim that a pulse of momentum existed toward the market ideal even within the rigidities of the Cold War.

Asian Battleground

At the time when crises in Europe were elevating military containment over economic diplomacy, Asia emerged as a testing ground for the securitization of the world economy and the consequent threat to the multilateral market vision. Actually, although preventing future aggression by Japan and trying to mediate a civil war in China were the top concerns of world leaders, the Cold War stimulated concerns over the Asian region's impact on global markets. As in Europe, the United States took the lead in attempting to reintegrate Asia back into a multilateral system of trade and payments, but guns often supplanted butter as the driving force of regional policies.

This trend was clear in the American occupation of Japan, as the United States switched in 1947 from a focus on demilitarization and liberalizing Japanese political institutions to a focus on placing the nation within the context of American strategic interests by curbing reforms and pursuing economic reconstruction. In a sense this was similar to the American experience in Europe when the quest for the open door was shoved aside for the pragmatics of economic recovery. The parallels did not end there, either. Japan lay prostrate after the war, having suffered over 1.8 million dead and damage to roughly 40 percent of its urban areas. Six million soldiers and repatriated colonists joined their compatriots to face the challenges of large unemployment, which jumped to 13 million in 1946. The country became dependent on the United States, for Japan had also lost its overseas territories by war's end and had no access to food and raw materials, and its industrial production plummeted severely. Like Germany, Japan had once been a great world workshop, but it no longer held that status. Starvation ensued as agriculture was plagued by bad harvests. Looting and other crimes were rampant, catalyzed by shortages combined with spiraling inflation that punished the citizenry. By 1948, 3.7 million families had no homes of their own. As in Germany, a black market (called the "free market" in Japan) thrived, although prices came down from roughly 34 times the official price for goods to double that level by 1949. Initially, Douglas MacArthur, the supreme commander for the Allied powers who oversaw the occupation, feared a resurgent militarism more than the impoverished state of the country.[34]

In his pursuit of democratization, MacArthur set out to eliminate the closely knit financial and industrial combines that controlled entire sectors of the Japanese economy. This assault on the *zaibatsu* mimicked the Roosevelt campaign against cartels; concentrated wealth, believed the Americans, suppressed individual rights, liberties, and free enterprise, and thus pushed nations toward aggression. The behemoth Mitsui alone was estimated to be the size of several of America's largest companies, including U.S. Steel, General Motors, Standard Oil, Alcoa, IBM, National City Bank, and DuPont. The reforms gave heart to leftist agitators and labor unions, which further upset Japanese conservatives, who defended the cartels as well as their own elite positions within the political system. When MacArthur fired fifteen hundred businessmen and bankers, the conservatives exaggerated the firings twentyfold. Although many had initially welcomed the American occupiers as fellow capitalists bound to embrace the *zaibatsu* as critical to recovery, they turned out to be naive. The Americans focused on punishment, and Japanese business bore the brunt. As well, Premier Yoshida Shigeru, although a conservative, agreed to redistribute land to farmers, who mostly still paid rent to rich holdovers from the feudal period. Yet inflation in 1947–1950 ruined the rural economy, and the tenant rate plummeted to 8 percent.[35]

These internal stresses, reparations payments, and underestimations of domestic consumption requirements that left the population hungry and poor—plus the sputtering global economy—resulted in a feeble output and stymied economic recovery by the end of 1947. Industrial production stood at less than half of the early 1930s average, while exports totaled just 10 percent. Income levels also remained at just half of the 1930s level, despite $400 million in American spending in 1947 alone for the occupation. American officials concluded that reparations had to end, along with the assault on the *zaibatsu*, to prevent Japan from sliding into permanent depression and socialization of the economy. As policy planning staff and containment policy author George Kennan put it, just as Spain occupied a critical strategic position for the Western allies in the Mediterranean, so Japan was a linchpin in Northeast Asia, but economic disaster was so imminent that turning over the reins of power to the Japanese themselves at this point "would be precisely what the communists want."[36] The fear of a communist revolution replaced worries of Japanese militarism.

As a result of strategic concerns, the Americans reversed the course of their policies. They curbed the decartelization process and endorsed a peace treaty to end the costly occupation, but they also pushed Japan toward embracing freer trade policies to prod the country's integration into the GATT and Bretton Woods systems. In 1948 MacArthur agreed to end his trustbusting of the *zaibatsu*, phase out reparations (they were halted by May 1949), and generally relax controls over the economy. Restraints were not wholly lifted, and Japan continued to discriminate against American exports, but it was allowed to do so in order to strengthen its economy and stabilize its political system as an American ally in the anticommunist alliance in Asia.[37]

Cold War strategists argued that Japan should be encouraged to expand its trade in Southeast Asia to enjoy a surplus with its less-developed neighbors that could be used to fund its recovery and pay off its dollar debt to the United States. The Americans then would recirculate these funds into the occupation economy to purchase raw materials for Japan, thus building a strong regional economy. To effect an export-driven economy rather than restore Japanese heavy industry through neomercantilism, the Yoshida government established the Ministry of International Trade and Industry (MITI) in 1949. MITI embraced the ideas of the Bank of Japan's governor Hisato Ichimada and Nissan conglomerate founder Ayukawa Yoshisuke to focus on light, labor-intensive industries. These were more easily produced and sold (because of their cheapness) than chemicals and other heavy industrial products, and could better compete overseas to earn foreign exchange.[38] There would be no Marshall Plan for Asia, but American capital investment blossomed during this period. The Japanese embrace of light industry and export expansion also connected Yoshida and his Liberal Party, which dominated Japanese politics into the 1990s, to American free-enterprise doctrines and the multilateral global economy. The "reverse course" of 1947 would be entrenched by the Korean War. In 1951, following the outbreak of that war,

Japan and the United States signed a peace treaty in which the United States received military bases and responsibility for Japanese security. In return, Japan got its independence, although within an American framework of governance, economic structures, and protection.

Tokyo was well on its way to becoming a key member of the American economic system in Asia; recovery and self-sufficiency would only last once the United States had improved the Far Eastern area's economy as a whole so that Japanese exports could be bought by productive regional buyers. This was no worldwide regime of market capitalism and cooperation but a regional product of the Cold War division and fear of communism. Regionalism was the stepping stone to greater economic integration, sustainability, and security. For instance, the Southeast Asian colonial outposts of Indochina for France, Malaysia for Britain, and Indonesia for the Netherlands had long been viewed as cornerstones of European recovery. Nationalist rebellions and insurgencies were potentially dangerous harbingers of communist takeovers. Now Americans placed the entire region in the context of preventing the Soviets from seizing mineral wealth and dividing the area into polar camps. The impending victory of the communists in China already foreboded of this danger, but despite America's long involvement there, the Chinese, unlike the Japanese, lacked both a developed economy and a history of integration in the global economy. Thus, in part, American involvement in Southeast Asia evolved from the need to maintain sources of raw materials and markets for Western Europe and Japan.[39]

In essence, while regionalism undermined globalism, the crises in Europe and Asia were related, because the United States expended great effort and fortune to combat forces that could destroy democracy and capitalism worldwide. Washington determined to keep both regions open to American interests and the market idea in the future. As Kennan noted, Japan and West Germany, "the two greatest industrial complexes of East and West," had to be saved from communism. So immunized, they could both serve as regional bases of the anticommunist coalition.[40] This also meant that Japan was treated as a second-rate economy; it would compete, not in the US or European markets, but in the developing world instead. That Japanese central planners envisioned a cutting-edge economy based on long-term investment in science, advanced technology, and high-end manufacturing was not noted by the Americans at the time. The confluence of the dollar gap and the open-door doctrine, both laboring in the shadow of Cold War security threats, compelled the United States to push Japan toward expansion in Southeast Asia—an irony in light of the rationale behind the Greater East Asia Co-Prosperity Sphere of the 1930s and wartime period. It also converted the United States from a vocal opponent of colonialism to an evolving backer of a formal European presence in Asia, as well as from a long-time friend of China to a vociferous opponent.[41]

China proved to be a lost cause for the open-door campaign. The Truman administration, under pressure from Nationalist leader Jiang Jieshi's lobby in Congress, had actually granted the Chinese a $463 million assistance package as an add-on to the European Recovery Program bill in 1948 to prosecute the civil war against communist forces led by Mao Zedong. Aid was contingent on Generalissimo Jiang reforming his corrupt government and leadership, which never happened. Events turned against Jiang, who received only a small amount of the assistance before Mao conquered his Nationalist government and banished it to Taiwan in 1949. This development came as a devastating blow to the American psyche as well as to foreign policy interests, although at least before the Korean War the United States did not restrict trade with the new communist government as much as it had with Eastern Europe. In part this was because of British concerns with safeguarding banking, investment, and shipping interests in Hong Kong and mainland China.[42]

While the Americans viewed the advent of communism in China as another example of the menace of the Soviet bloc, the British had different ideas. The United States set out to drive a wedge between Moscow and Beijing by closing off all economic contact with Mao in the hope that he would become a burdensome dependent on Stalin, but the British held to a more realistic policy of establishing relations with the new government in order to keep a foot in the Chinese economic door. This approach became apparent even before the communists took power in October 1949, and it became a sticking point in Anglo-American relations by early 1950 when London withdrew support for Jiang's Taiwanese government and recognized the People's Republic of China. Those moves had implications not only for American security policies—Washington withdrew military backing for Hong Kong—but for diplomacy and economics. By the spring of 1950, US policy makers issued NSC-68, a secret, high-level review of security options prompted by the clash with international communism. China was hardly mentioned in the document, but it was clear from the document that the Americans were prepared to contest communism throughout the world, even in areas deemed peripheral. Secretary of State Dean Acheson also tried to cover up differences with America's closest ally, Great Britain, over such hot issues as supporting an independent Taiwan and trading with "Red" China.[43]

Britain turned increasingly to the notion that more trade with China not only would promote peace but would help Britain regain its edge in such lucrative industries as the aviation business; but the Americans vociferously disagreed and held to their wedge theory of isolating Beijing to stimulate Sino-Soviet tensions. Like the other Western powers, however, Britain refused to embargo China, although by 1953 (as a result of the Korean War) CoCom applied to China a larger list of restricted goods than existed for Eastern Europe. The economics of the market continued to clash with international politics. The People's Republic did not figure decisively into the US market ethic at this time. American trade with China had never lived up to the half-century of dreams of the open-door proponents; US exports to China were small compared to exports to Europe or even Japan. Aid to Jiang's Nationalist exile government in Taiwan grew from $18 million to $80 million from 1950 to 1952, but that was due to the Cold War and not simply to business expansion. Still, even some corporations such as General Electric and Bank of America favored recognition of Mao's government in order to save their investments (Americans still had $180 million in mainland assets in 1950), and they were encouraged when Chinese authorities quickly restored order after the civil war and welcomed foreign capital. But the Truman administration and Congress compelled such firms to back out of China; the People's Republic would not be part of the American multilateral global economic order until Mao and communism fell from power.[44] Taiwan would take its place as the Chinese representative on the global capitalist stage. China was frozen out of the American economic system for over two decades.

War and Trade

If the late 1940s witnessed the decline of multilateralism in the world economy, the Korean War solidified the move toward a state of permanent confrontation with enemies and, thus, hindered market-led globalization. Unilateralism and protection replaced openness and internationalism in the minds of Western leaders once war broke out on June 25, 1950. The Truman administration had already largely abandoned the hope that trade and aid would contain communism, as military assistance to allies quintupled to $523 million in the four-year period ending in 1950. The war clinched the conversion of export control policy into an immutable instrument of the Cold War, rather than as a means to ease shortages among allies or prevent the Soviets and their satellites from obtaining vitally strategic goods. The Korean War brought into greater clarity the national security state and, arguably, represented a low point of American market practices.

While it clarified the capitalist and communist security structures, the war had a significant effect on Asian economies. South Korea went through a postwar downturn, but North Korea boomed for a time as Sino-Soviet aid poured into the country. The "workshop" of the region—Japan—had a similar experience due to outside assistance. Japanese recovery received a tremendous shot in the arm, and the economy got a much-needed boost in the midst of a serious recession, when the country became a staging area and depot for American troops and supplies. Two years into the reverse course by mid-1950, Japan had suffered a severe recession in which half a million people were unemployed, stock prices plummeted, and small businesses failed in large numbers. The Toyota Company produced just three hundred trucks in June 1950, faced as it was by strong unions and a credit squeeze. Then war erupted in Korea, and like other producers, Toyota saw its fortunes reversed and Japan enjoyed a shift in its position in the global economy.

As a source of supply for the United Nations military effort in Korea, Japan earned critical dollars. So influential was this procurement activity that by the end of 1950, after a half-year of fighting, the Japanese trade position dramatically soared as Europeans and the United States faced critical shortages of military goods. From 1950 to 1954 the United States spent nearly $3 billion in Japan on such purchases as weapons, vehicles, ammunition, and clothing, more than its expenditures during the five years of the Occupation. The windfall reversed Japan's dollar shortage, and for the first time since the end of World War II Japan could compete in the world economy—which had become a seller's market that profited Japanese business. No longer was Japan a minor producer of high-priced goods; instead it became a major manufacturer of competitive products in a global economy stimulated by the war. The economic manna prompted by the conflict was "sent from heaven," exalted Japanese policy makers, and Prime Minister Yoshida saw his government saved by "divine aid" that stabilized the economy and propelled it on a trajectory of growth.[45] Toyota sprang back from the brink of bankruptcy, registering a 40 percent boost in vehicle orders. Selling five thousand trucks within a year, the company boosted its monthly production to two thousand units, doubled wages, and paid its first dividend since the Second World War. Steel production rose by 38 percent, exports tripled during the first eight months of the Korean War, and the stock market increased 80 percent. From textile to construction sectors and metal to communications firms, the boom ignited 10 percent annual growth for the next two decades.[46]

The military procurement stimulus did not place Japan on a permanent footing of trade recovery, yet it did provide the mechanism that primed the pump and allowed for significant investment in basic industries as well as expanded credit for capital goods and export growth. But two significant transformations also occurred, one in Japan's economy and the other in the global economy. First, labor and factories underwent upgrades in technology, and the pace of modernization quickened. At America's behest, Japan acquired patents and commercial licenses that helped its capital-intensive firms emerge, develop, and prosper. The government teamed with the nation's most powerful business federation to import American technology that could be used for both military and civilian purposes. Such dual-use goods included steel products produced by Mitsui, which also made arms, and communications equipment that allowed Japanese producers to cross over into making transistor radios and cameras. For instance, Radio Corporation of America (RCA) fostered the Japanese consumer electronics industry by licensing patents to firms that transferred technology to Japan. Between 1951 and 1984, Japanese companies signed more than 42,000 contracts to import such technology at a cost of $17 billion. The investment was well worth the price, as it planted the seeds of later dominance in trade of high-end goods for Japan.[47]

The second transformation wrought by the Korean War came in the geography of trade. The Americans understood that the end of their occupation of

A Toyota auto assembly plant, June 1952. The Korean War stimulated the Japanese economy, boosting production through exports such as these cars, stabilizing employment, adhering the country to the US alliance, and pointing Japan toward a future of growth. (Time & Life Pictures/Getty Images)

Japan required a shift from maintaining the Japanese economy at subsistence levels to an engagement in economic cooperation fueled by incentives, subsidies, and support for Japanese trade expansion in Southeast Asia. Negotiations over the peace treaty of 1951 involved a reconceptualization of the economic relationship between Japan and the United States, in which American trade and industrial orders replaced American aid. The Japanese economy would be oriented away from China and toward Southeast Asia as well as the US economy. Japan joined CoCom in 1952 and issued strict export controls on trade with China that diminished its trade with the communist nation to just 0.04 percent of its total exports (in 1941, by contrast, 27 percent of its exports had been sent to China). The payoff for permitting increased exports to the US market for textiles and other goods—a policy that infuriated congressional protectionists—would be Tokyo's adherence to the Cold War alliance. Likewise, when the British complained about the potential of dumping cheap Japanese goods in Southeast Asia, Washington replied that the British should "face the realities of the situation and be prepared to meet Japanese competition if Japan is to be kept oriented toward the West and free from Communist pressures."[48] Japan thus recognized its stake in the "Free World" by developing close ties to the West and its allies in Asia, binds that promoted an adherence to competitive market policies later on.

Underdeveloped Economies and Aid

The American effort to combat communism by creating a world capitalist order based on new trade patterns, economic integration, and heightened consumption stabilized specific areas deemed under threat, such as Western Europe and Japan, but it also broadened the American gaze into what became known as the Third World, or the underdeveloped, developing, or emerging economies. In Asia, Latin America, Africa, and the Middle East, the Cold War brought American economic (and military) power to bear, with oftentimes grave consequences for tens of millions of subject peoples. Colonialism had undergirded the prewar global economy, but the United States denounced imperialism after 1945. Yet security concerns permitted European allies to retain their colonies for a time (Washington granted the Philippines its independence in 1946), and America insinuated itself into a position of economic dominance without having to occupy territory. The open door made America an imperialist in disguise; the United States tried to infuse the Third World with Western market policies that served the three purposes of profit, stability, and security.

These aims were clear in the guidance of Japan into Southeast Asia. The irony of renewing a postwar version of the Greater East Asia Co-Prosperity Sphere was not lost on some observers, but the need for new trade outlets to turn the Japanese away from China and maintain its position in the free world orbit subsumed such concerns. This policy had foreign policy and geopolitical implications for the United States. Washington decided to support France's defense of its Indochina colony against a nationalist-communist insurgency led by Ho Chi Minh to provide Japan and other Asian allies with a secure source of resources and trade. Although the eventual American war in Vietnam would become a crusade against communism, the initial objective was to convert a recovering Japan into the centerpiece of a multilateral Asian system of trade and finance that would stabilize the region, pacify Japan, and strengthen the larger global capitalist order in its fight against communism.[49] American development policies in the Third World reflected as much security concerns as free-enterprise impulses.

To be sure, America determined to keep open the door to access to the world's raw materials as a means of maintaining the health of the global and American economies, but Washington also sought to dominate the underdeveloped markets in order to shield them from Sino-Soviet influence. A synergy existed between the interests of investment and export expansion by government and business, especially those of multinational corporations. And the consequences of this close relationship were usually uneven, at best, as development for the host nation was less common than the exploitation of the bulk of populations by authoritarian regimes that served Western investors and governments. In short, the recipients of aid from the advanced nations experienced mixed results: some modernized and prospered, but most became locked into a system in which they provided raw materials, agricultural goods, and cheap, light industrial products to the Western and Eastern blocs while foreign corporations or socialist governments so dominated local economies that they distorted development and delayed democratic reforms. The Cold War brought security, in a sense, but not freedom, rights, privileges, and riches for the general populations in the emerging world.

The advanced nations and their capitalist institutions such as the World Bank and IMF actually did not welcome the developing world being used as a stomping ground for exploitation of resources and cheap labor. The American hegemon stomached undemocratic practices and human rights abuses to procure supplies of critical materials, but foreign investment and trade (except for oil) with the Third World were neither robust nor consistently profitable during the Cold War. By and large, business proved reluctant to invest in the developing areas, which compelled Americans and Europeans to send in direct and indirect aid rather than rely on multilateral market mechanisms of exchange.[50] In addition, the advanced countries also restricted the cheap products of the Third World—from textiles and steel to agricultural goods—in fits of protectionism that undermined development and also, ironically, made the "peripheral" nations more dependent on trade with the "core" capitalist nations. The terms of trade simply favored the advanced nations that consumed raw materials and produced high-cost manufactures, while the opposite was true for emerging economies. Global bankers and bureaucrats might plead for a nonpolitical, internationalist approach to development that they believed would usher in an era of prosperity, modernization, and peace, but statesmen in the core put nationalism—including protectionism against Third World products at home and military aims abroad—above one-world ideology and even market practices. Besides, even the World Bank, the leading nongovernmental organization pursuing development, targeted the economic realm rather than political reform to such an extent that no basic transformation of the international division of labor ensued, regardless of the quest for integrating the poor nations into an open global market.[51] Thus, while there was a growing awareness of the humanitarian burdens and political excesses in the Third World, policies and patterns of economic relationships remained inconsistent and uneven as globalization proceeded through the decades.

Because security overwhelmed the profit motive in American policies during this period, the impetus for higher investment and trade derived from the Third World nations themselves, who looked to the United States as the cardinal source of modernization. They sought protection for their infant industries at the Havana conference on the ITO in 1947, which Americans saw as inimical to a nondiscriminatory trade policy, but when the ITO was rejected and US tariffs still remained relatively high despite their lowering at GATT rounds, these nations turned to foreign aid. However, the United States preferred the supposed benefits of reliance on open doors and private investment to aid, as the record on the Point Four program of 1949 revealed. Congress approved only $34.5 million of this technical assistance requested by the Truman administration, an amount that fell well short of needs and highlighted the gap between Western promises of development and actual practice. Placing aid within the context of security, defense, and diplomacy did not always work for the poor nations.[52]

Americans proudly lectured on the benefits bestowed on their own country by the free-enterprise system, and developing nations took note. Besides, many of these nations sent a flow of immigrants into the United States in search of the American dream of prosperity. The United States enjoyed a certain cachet that rendered its campaign for market capitalism all the more powerful, and in the immediate postwar period there were few competitors to the American way. The Soviets provided an alternative means and template of development—through state guidance of the economy and direct aid—but Moscow did not focus attention on the Third World until the mid-1950s, after Stalin's death. European colonial powers were bankrupt, and although some reasserted their power, the days of imperialism were numbered as a wave of independence movements swept the world. The *idea* of Americanism—of "the freedom offered by washing machines and dishwashers, vacuum cleaners, automobiles, and refrigerators"—captivated the emerging nations as the United States reshaped the world economy.[53]

To claim that open-door enterprise appealed abroad is not the same as arguing that the Third World embraced multilateralism and free-market capitalism. India was a case in point. The Nehru government planned for a mixed economy, but its five-year plan to raise agricultural production (especially to end a famine), rural development, and promotion of electric power and industrialization followed along Western capitalist lines. There was little land redistribution, and nationalization of industry was limited to the commanding heights of communications, electricity, arms, and transportation. Free enterprise oversaw the rest. American officials preferred more food production and a focus on consumer goods such as radios, bicycles, and apparel; as Ambassador Chester Bowles exclaimed in 1952 in pushing for a liberal, market-driven rural development scheme, "How I would love to see Sears and Roebuck come out here and really tackle the problem of inexpensive distribution of consumer goods, keyed to the Indian market."[54] Yet differences in economic outlooks, planning objectives, capitalist behavior, and culture showed cracks in the free-enterprise dream. In general, Indians thought of Americans as greedy materialists who consumed too much but who had hegemonic trade and financial power, and thus merited recognition. While Americans cringed at Indian economic practices such as hoarding as immature, Indians needed food and money. The United States was the place to turn after the country earned its independence, split into Pakistan and India in 1947, and could not count on heavily indebted Britain for help.

The United States did not rush in to South Asia to replace Britain, for Washington understood that Europe and Japan needed their former and existing colonies as sources of raw materials and markets. Thus, American trade with India and Pakistan ran surpluses between 1948 and 1953, although this commerce was not tremendous for South Asia and it was of peripheral economic interest to Washington for the time being. Still, India possessed certain strategic materials, like manganese and beryl, and American attempts to add these items to its security stockpile ran up against hoarding by New Delhi as well as the Nehru government's resistance to the extraction of raw materials by foreigners. The government created a maze of restrictions that scared off investors; Indian discomfort with foreign capital curbed the inflow of American money into the country. Such problems, as well as the perception that India simply was too old to modernize, led Americans to believe the country could never be integrated into a dynamic world economy run by the dictates of the market.

Finance to promote Indian food development started to flow once the Korean War broke out, and a loan of two million tons of wheat followed as the United States focused on Asia. But the specter of famine appeared ever more threatening during the delay that occurred before help arrived, delays prompted by arguments over the American Cold War agenda in Asia. While the Americans sought a regional military pact between India and Pakistan, an end to both new nations' dispute over the Kashmir region, and prosecuted the war in Korea, India balked on all three goals despite its failed attempt to help settle the thorny issue of prisoner repatriation through talks with Beijing. As the Indian aid program experienced cutbacks and the United States focused more on military than economic assistance to the region, tensions were exacerbated. New Delhi was a difficulty for the American model of global economic governance mainly because Washington focused not on regional development but on placing India within a global Cold War context.[55]

The nexus of the Cold War and international economy was also apparent when it came to the procurement of natural resources, and particularly the world's minerals. The beneficiaries of national security policy were the large multinational petroleum companies that profited from Anglo-American efforts to back pro-Western monarchies in Saudi Arabia and Iran, secure the Persian Gulf area, and maintain the traditional US lock-hold over Latin American economies. It was oil that prompted a sharp upswing in private and US direct foreign investment in the 1950s, a change from the period 1945 to 1950 when the figures rose only about 20 percent. American investment in extractive industries exploded, however, more than doubling over these five years to $1.2 billion, and doubling again by 1960, yet it was offset in Latin America by a decline in British investment. Cheap oil and some minerals deemed necessary for national security (rubber) or consumption (coffee) were available only abroad; others were deemed to be in scarce supply after World War II and in need of stockpiling through imports that were oftentimes cheaper than domestic sources. As a result of the latter concern, by 1948 the world's biggest consumer of oil—the United States—became a net importer of petroleum for the first time. The two Cold War blocs competed for oil supplies.[56]

This was one commodity and one area of the Third World—the Middle East—where the United States took aggressive action to assert its interests. With shrinking reserves (America held about 15 percent of global supplies of oil), the United States became dependent on foreign sources of energy. American foreign investment in petroleum shot up by 550 percent in the decade beginning in 1946, to $9.05 billion. The government allied with a coalition of private companies led by the partnership of Standard Oil Company of California (Socal) and the Texas Company (later Texaco) under the banner of the Arabian-American Oil Company (Aramco). This entity drew on financing from Socony-Vacuum and Standard Oil of New Jersey to arrange a profit-sharing deal with Saudi Arabia in 1950 that developed oil fields and resulted in the shipment of petroleum to America at a cost of roughly 40 cents under the price sold from US and Latin American wells. Before, in 1947, Aramco had contracted to build the Trans-Arabian Pipeline (TAPLINE) from Saudi Arabia to Lebanon, which could move three hundred thousand barrels a day onto ships headed for the West. This involved the kind of heavy-handed "diplomacy" in which economic imperatives compelled tough political decisions that enraged Third World leaders. Aramco had to secure rights-of-way for the pipeline. Lebanon was amenable, but militant Arab nationalist Syrian leader Shukri al-Quwatly was not, and the Truman administration secretly backed the army chief of staff to overthrow him in March 1949. The way was clear for TAPLINE. A year later, an agreement to split profits evenly between the Saudis and Aramco gave the kingdom skyrocketing revenues, as had been the case when Venezuela forced Royal Dutch Shell and Jersey Standard to give the country a 50 percent share in profits. The American government waived antitrust and IRS rules and granted the US corporations a foreign tax credit to offset their loss of half their profits to Venezuela and Saudi Arabia. In return the United States not only had a growing supply of inexpensive oil through wells and the Arabian pipeline, which fueled development in other pro-Western Middle Eastern nations as well as European recovery, but a stable ally in Saudi Arabia in the region. Aid and arms supplies to friendly oil states followed, along with tax breaks for the oil companies because they served the US national interest. Saudi production increased by 60 percent and royalties to the kingdom by 135 percent; by 1954, Aramco paid King Ibn Saud over $250 billion, four times the total of 1949.[57]

The American hold over Middle Eastern oil expanded and tightened further due to the Soviet threat in Iran. After bolstering the British position in Iran against Soviet incursions just after the war, the United States teamed with London to block attempts to nationalize the Iranian oil industry by forces led by Mohammad Mosaddegh, who detested Western imperialism. When he seized a British refinery at Abadan in 1951, Britain issued a boycott against Iranian oil that effectively barred its distribution abroad. A World Bank economic plan, to provide funding to resume operations and act as a trustee over the oil fields and Abadan refinery until the British and Iranians reached an agreement, foundered on the vagaries of politics. Mosaddegh staked his regime on chasing the British out, and London dug in to salvage its imperial claims and prevent a supposed radical from destabilizing the Middle East. Fearing a wave of expropriation attempts across the Third World, Washington rejected Mosaddegh's request for financial assistance during the boycott and instead engineered a coup that brought

Mohammad Mosaddegh of Iran, November 10, 1953. After his government was overthrown by the CIA, the former prime minister was put on trial, accused of attempting a coup against the shah of Iran, America's longtime ally. Mosaddegh had confronted oil companies in Iran, while the shah permitted them the freedom to exploit the critical energy supply. (© Bettmann/CORBIS)

the shah of Iran to power and gave five big American corporations 40 percent of Britain's historic concession, formerly controlled by the Anglo-Iranian Oil Company.[58] Iran and its oil supplies remained out of Soviet hands and firmly in America's grasp for the next two decades. For the moment, oil companies appeared to be tools of US foreign policy in the region. Still, as one historian has noted, cooperation between them and the US government had added Iran to "the growing list of Middle Eastern nations whose oil fields were integrated into America's national security empire."[59]

2. *Shut and Unlocked Doors*

INTEREST in the emerging world on the part of both superpowers revealed that the Cold War became a battleground for markets and ideologies as much as a military standoff. After the death of Stalin in 1953, the Soviets not only launched a trade and aid offensive throughout the developing world from 1954 onward, but Moscow forced the United States to reconceptualize its open-door tactics. Washington grew increasingly concerned about the rising tide of communist threats, expressions of anti-Western sentiments, the pursuit of neutralism in the Cold War, and the chafing for modernization, improved living standards, and better terms of trade as struggling people around the world blamed American policies for their poverty. It was also apparent that the private investors had only a tepid interest in helping the Third World. The United States needed an answer to the Soviet challenge. Blocking communist inroads had been the primary goal behind US recovery prescriptions and development in the world economy for the past decade. Now the effort shifted to meeting the competition for the hearts, minds, and stomachs of three-fifths of the world's population.

The USSR sparked this economic rivalry by augmenting aid to the Third World by 70 percent, from $850 million in 1954 to $1.44 billion two years later. Credits, barter trade, and technical assistance with no demands for austerity measures or other strings attached (as the United States or World Bank insisted) shot up even more. Moscow had a public relations problem to overcome, because many nations, especially those in Asia, disagreed with Stalin's view that those allied with his side should cooperate only with other self-declared socialist countries.[60] The new Soviet leader, Nikita Khrushchev, accepted ties to nonsocialist Third World countries to build unity and confront the imperialist world, led by the United States. Multilateral cooperation, along American lines, was the key.

The effort was neither seamlessly successful nor without its detractors. Economic ties strengthened, and most significantly, aid to China rose sevenfold to 7 percent of the Soviet national income from 1953 to 1960. Using this assistance, a strong People's Republic would link with Asian communism, the Eastern Europeans, and leftist activists throughout the world to standardize production lines, transportation systems, research and training, and technology innovations "from Berlin to Shanghai" through periodic international congresses. This followed the Western capitalist model of economic integration. Beijing resisted, however, seeking less caution and more instant takeoff in development and certainly less guidance from Moscow to chart its own course. The Sino-Soviet rift was apparent by 1959, especially as Mao angrily denounced the Russian stance of peaceful competition with the West and relations with nonsocialist neutrals like Egypt and India. The Soviets disagreed, claiming that substantial aid had prevented these neutrals and others from economically allying with the West. By the early 1960s, the Soviets had withdrawn technical experts from China and the alliance was dead.

This Sino-Soviet fissure was a blow to Moscow's orchestration of socialist multilateralism, but the USSR focused on a myriad of other places in the Third World to promote its brand of modernization. Like the United States, which tutored its allies to mimic its course of development through the fruits of free enterprise, the Soviet Union counseled nations to note the great successes of Russian development during the 1950s. Emerging countries should link their national liberation movements seeking to cast off the yoke of colonialism to the dream of ever-growing socialist production that would lift them out of poverty and ensure their independence. The USSR offered an alternative, proclaimed Khrushchev, to Western subordination by foreign capitalist monopolies and stunted industrialization. Capitalists thought of the Third World as merely hewers of wood, not as modern, dynamic countries. On the contrary, under Soviet instruction these nations would become independent and use their natural resources to spur industrialization, thus beginning "a better life" for their people while also strengthening the socialist world as a whole and nailing down the coffin of colonialism. The inevitability of socialism sweeping over the world in a generation was mantra for the Soviets; as long as the West did not try to prevent revolution in the Third World, the global economy could become a tool for progress for the masses once in the hands of the communist bloc.[61] Globalization could be dictated along socialist rather than capitalist lines.

The sea change in the Soviet approach to the world economy paid dividends. When just a few years before, local communist parties were isolated throughout South Asia and the Middle East, by 1954 the USSR courted leaders in India, Burma, and elsewhere with promises of massive multipronged economic assistance. In February 1955, for instance, the Soviets contracted with India to build a huge steel mill at Bhilai in the state of Madhya Pradesh. A long-term $112 million low-interest government loan funded the deal, accompanied by an offer to expand trade by sending India industrial goods in exchange for raw materials and local currency. A high-level Russian state visit later in the year drove home the new policy of state-to-state economic cooperation. These types of targeted economic plans galled the Americans, who had largely neglected India's industrial development. Washington scrambled to grab its share of India's steel by seeking to aid in the expansion of the country's largest private producer, Tata Iron and Steel Corporation. The US Treasury balked at the special interest rate terms offered by the American Export-Import Bank, however, not wishing to favor one borrower over another, and Tata eventually turned to the World Bank for financing. The Soviet economic offensive was now in full swing, and not just in India. By mid-1956 the USSR had made credit arrangements with fourteen emerging nations amounting to $820 million, with another $180 million on the way. Washington noted that, ominously, nearly all of the loans were aimed at Yugoslavia, Egypt, India, and Afghanistan, four nonaligned nations that might be seduced to the socialist side by skillful Soviet oversight of impressive public sector projects. As Russian military "frowns have given way to smiles" of economic largesse, wrote Secretary of State John Foster Dulles, the American appeal to the Third World based on market ideology had disappeared.[62]

Moscow was just as bold in Latin America, the United States' supposed sphere of economic influence. After sloughing off President Dwight D. Eisenhower's warning that they would escalate superpower tensions if they shifted their gaze toward the developing world, in January 1956 Russian leaders offered more trade and technical assistance programs to Latin America "on the basis of mutual advantage" as part of an offensive to capture hearts and minds in the region.[63] Soviet trade with Latin America had risen by one-third the year before, with a special focus on Cuba, which sold over a half million tons of sugar to the USSR.

Actually, trade fell thereafter between the Soviets and the region, but the expressions of interest caused the United States concern.

The region posed challenges for both superpowers as well as for international aid agencies. The Cold War was a burden to Latin America; the United States fixated on the threat of Soviet communism, but the Latin nations focused on their historic rivalries (such as tensions between Ecuador and Peru) or rampant poverty. Yet they also realized that the United States especially, but the USSR as well, would pay more attention to issues of political stability and development issues. Of course, this also meant the possibility of heightened meddling in internal affairs by the colossus to the north. In Guatemala, the nascent Central Intelligence Agency (CIA) joined with conservatives and the multinational United Fruit Company in 1954 against the land reform programs of a moderate liberal government. United Fruit protested a compensation package offered by the government. Washington viewed nationalization as a dangerous tendency toward socialism and thus a threat to its open-door ethic. A CIA-assisted coup prompted the reformist Jacobo Árbenz to flee Guatemala. A military junta replaced him and oppressed the population (with tacit support from the United States) for the next three decades. Dulles departed the region without considering requests for economic assistance that might head off similar reforms and rebellions in the future, but the merger of the Cold War with market doctrine could not have been clearer.[64]

Historians debate whether the Soviet offensive really changed US policies in Latin America. It sounded alarm bells in Washington that led to more state visits (markedly, Vice President Richard Nixon's tour in 1958 and a frenzied response to revolution in Cuba). But security agencies were already focused on places like Guatemala before the Russians issued their challenge. In a more profound way, the Americans began to realize that the assumption that economic modernization would lead to democracy and pro-Western policies was valid only if no outside threat was present. The Soviet offensive changed the equation, compelling the United States to consider trying to raise standards of living in the area by pursuing more vigorous economic policies that did not rely merely on free-market pronouncements. Latin American governments responded positively to initiatives that, for instance, established an Inter-American Committee to discuss economic development. The Eisenhower administration urgently con-

Guatemalan rebels stand guard, 1954. These soldiers sided with conservative forces (symbolized by the church) that unseated the president of Guatemala, Jacobo Árbenz. Aided by the CIA, the rebels ended the Árbenz democracy and brought to a halt Árbenz's expropriation of land from multinational fruit corporations. (Popperfoto/Getty Images)

sidered augmenting aid outlays in order to bolster free enterprise. In the end, though, the pursuit of free enterprise won out over meaningful reform by government fiat; Washington's traditional approach of insisting on development through noninterference in markets persisted into succeeding administrations. The region still struggled.[65] The Soviet offensive also fizzled, but it had nonetheless marked US development pledges to Latin America as hollow.

The reception to its economic offensive in the Third World encouraged the USSR and converted economic policy into political gain. Moscow granted easy credit terms (usually at 2 or 2.5 percent interest) paid out over the long average period of forty years, better than nations could get from the Western powers. Barter arrangements such as Egyptian cotton or Burmese rice for industrial goods also sped development. The variety of development programs—from sugar-processing plants to textile mills—also spread modernization to critical sectors, and quickly, to the delight of leaders and businessmen. In addition, the economic aid allowed emerging nations to leverage better terms from both the Soviets and the Americans; Indonesia received more agricultural aid from the United States, and Afghanistan drew on Soviet geopolitical interests to obtain military assistance that strengthened its position in the region. Third World bargaining also led to foreign policy losses for the Americans. Burma evicted the US aid mission from the country after signing a deal with the USSR, although the Americans were later invited back in. Assistance to Egypt gave Moscow a cherished foothold in the Middle East and at the Suez Canal. Khrushchev traded arms to Cairo and Syria in return for Egyptian cotton and thus heightened Cold War tensions. Russia also entered the Arab-Israeli fray on the side of the raw materials producers in the region. In general, as one historian has concluded, the recipients "were generally impressed by this Soviet effort" while the aid injected socialist influence into the global economy.[66]

Aid

The president of the United States knew it. Eisenhower had referred to the Cold War as the ultimate struggle of humankind for freedom and dignity, but now, as one aide warned, "the Soviets are muscling in on Santa Claus" to the detriment of US interests. Clearly recognizing that the USSR intended to economically penetrate the Third World in a "sinister" ploy to secure political domination, Ike asked for higher aid appropriations from Congress under the mutual security program. The request was $2 billion higher for fiscal 1957 than the authorization for the previous year. This earmark included a total of $100 million for the Middle East, Africa, and Asia. Provoked by the Soviet economic offensive, the United States finally inched toward a sort of Marshall Plan for the emerging nations. Congress hesitated at providing massive aid, and remained skeptical that results would meet expectations once assistance arrived at the doorsteps of such uncertain allies as India, Yugoslavia, and Spain. Conservatives looked on the aid as bribery with no assurance of working, and liberals viewed it as support for dictatorships or feared that the aid would be used to purchase arms and not to promote production or alleviate poverty. Others simply believed that the United States could not outcompete the focused Soviet plans in the Third World, for the USSR could "offer a sales program that promises the moon or everything that the people of Asia desire," claimed a congressman.[67] Congress merged the special funds into a development assistance program and cut the request by $1 billion, although most of the reductions came in military aid. The administration undertook a study that showed that many nations were interested in both economic development and remaining neutral in the Cold War. Thus, America needed to reconceptualize its security-grounded approach to the world economy by showing that it could provide the poor with better products on better terms than could the Soviets. When Indian premier Nehru visited the United States in 1956, he found American leaders much more accommodating than ever before, and aid more forthcoming.

Like Western trade policies, aid programs in general played to the advantage of entrenched elites who controlled resources and succeeded in alleviating problems only in the short run. This was so because assistance given for strategic reasons (rather than economic ones) fell short of funding the rise to modernity in most cases (the most notable exceptions being Egypt and Israel, top recipients of American direct aid). Cold War–driven assistance struck against the changing and more assertively expressed aspirations of the Third World, which desired aid for purposes of development. American administrations certainly realized the emphasis on economics, but numerous government studies from the 1950s onward placed aid in the context of how growth would serve the ends of a stable world order, democracy, and victory over communism. Yet Washington also evolved away from purely market considerations when granting aid. Although the United States relied on the World Bank ($3.8 billion in investments by 1958 in forty-seven countries, most in the Third World) and the US Export-Import Bank to finance development on a commercial basis, the Eisenhower administration also turned to soft loans on easier terms, such as longer repayment periods at lower interest rates. Under the Mutual Security Act during mid-decade, nations could repay the United States with strategic materials rather than currency, for example, and Bolivia, India, and many nations in the Middle East and Africa owed the United States at least half of their debt on a soft-loan basis.[68]

Still, America preferred bilateral assistance programs to the multilateral Special United Nations Fund for Economic Development, created in 1956 at the behest of emerging nations, and thus moved to capitalize a development loan fund at $2 billion in order to foster economic growth. This program arose in direct response to the Soviet economic offensive as well as crises in Hungary and the Suez Canal, but Eisenhower also had to overcome opposition within and outside of his administration to public financing of development. Congress almost instantly cut his appropriations request by one-third in 1957 and refused to separate military from economic aid programs. Ike nevertheless linked a long-term commitment to economic growth to national security policies and did so by pushing the government into the credit arena rather than relying solely on private investment or the generation of funds through sales of surplus American products.[69]

Again Latin America emerged as a main target of a shift in thinking. Rioting in Venezuela against Vice President Nixon in 1958 and pressure from liberals in Congress to aid neighbors led to the establishment of the regional Inter-American Development Bank (IADB). This institution made loans and technical aid available and gave investors confidence to inject capital into these poor nations, although Congress would not provide the massive $5 billion capitalization of the Bank as called for by Brazil and other nations. Contributing just $450 million, the United States kept the IADB relatively small. In addition, Latin America received a minuscule percentage of the total US world economic assistance package of $2.1 billion in 1958, with approximately $60 million allocated for the region (just more than the $54 million spent on military aid). Still, the market ideology of a global economy run by private enterprise bent to accommodate new realities in the Cold War in this conservative administration. Attitudes, at the very least, had begun to change as American administrations became more aggressive in rounding up private and public capital for investment, but state intervention clamped down on the trajectory of globalization.

Driven by the revolution in Cuba, which brought socialism to the region, President John F. Kennedy greatly expanded the Eisenhower aid program. Just days before the aborted attempt to overthrow Fidel Castro a few months into his administration, Kennedy determined to make the 1960s a "decade of development" by launching a hemisphere-wide "vast cooperative effort, unparalleled in magnitude and nobility of purpose, to satisfy the basic needs of Latin American people for homes, work and land, health and schools."[70] Kennedy learned from modernization advocate Walt Rostow that at least four Latin American nations—Venezuela, Brazil, Colombia, and Argentina—stood poised for takeoff and self-sustaining growth by 1970. A renewed Soviet offensive, in which Khrushchev welcomed national revolutions against the capitalists, prompted JFK to ask for a special $500 million package of food aid for Latin America as well as loans and other funding to stabilize commodity prices. He then announced the Alliance for Progress, initially pledging $1 billion in US aid to Latin America for 1962, followed by $20 billion over the next ten years to promote a doubling in the standard of living by 1970 at an annual rate of 2.5 percent. He counted on another $80 billion in internal investment by Latin American nations themselves to accomplish these goals as well as stimulate land reform, end adult illiteracy, stabilize prices of raw materials, and promote democracy.[71]

The short-term success of this bold and popular program belied the fact that ultimately both the Cold War and US market dogma crimped the Alliance for Progress. Results never matched the rhetoric, because elites in the region would not reform and such structural problems as large populations stymied gains in education, health care, and housing. Democracy also declined, as the US government favored anticommunist strongmen over improving welfare.[72] Latin American economies grew at an anemic 1.5 annual rate (only seven hit the 2.5 percent target), although from 1970 to 1974 the increase in the region's gross domestic product reached 3.8 percent. Yet unemployment rose and the landed oligarchy remained entrenched. US funding amounted to $1.4 billion a year until 1968 (afterward, the Nixon administration cut appropriations), and annual total aid reached an average of $3.3 billion when private investment is included. The Alliance sent $22.3 billion to Latin America during its tenure, yet the assistance reached very few people in a meaningful way. The poorest got very little assistance; each Latin American received an average of $10 during the program. Latin American exports grew from $8 billion to $12 billion from 1960 to 1968 but did not keep pace with world trade expansion as a whole. As well, the region's share of the lucrative US market was cut in half by the early 1970s.[73]

Meanwhile, the free-enterprise ethic was alive and well, especially under the umbrella of the international campaign to blunt communist expansion. US business persuaded Washington not only to put pressure on regional government to increase private capital flows but also to restrict competition from Latin American exports and channel foreign aid recipients toward purchasing from American corporations. The power of US firms manifested itself by the overthrow of the socialist Allende government in Chile in 1973 at the behest of International Telephone and Telegraph. That same year the Organization of American States terminated its permanent committee that administered the Alliance for Progress and the program disappeared into history. American direct investments in the region actually rose and moved from extractive industries to manufactures, thereby helping to diversify economies. But US investors went elsewhere searching for open doors. As a result, many Latin American nations remained either dependent on Washington or mired in poverty.

Anticolonial Era

Not willing to count on foreign aid programs from either of the superpowers for their salvation, emerging nations drew on a template for mutual cooperation and respect that Jawaharlal Nehru had enunciated in 1954 when addressing Sino-Indian tensions. Twenty-nine, mostly newly independent, nations in Asia and Africa, representing half the world's population, gathered in Bandung, Indonesia, in April 1955 to demand an end to Western imperialism and what many saw as the neocolonialist Soviet offensive. This meeting was the first time the decolonizing world struck a position as nonaligned neutrals in the Cold War. The participants took aim on a host of regional disputes, lobbied against the supposed "color curtain" that structured global relations along a racial hierarchy, and sought ways to bring world peace. In the area of economic developments, the Bandung Conference sought cooperation among participating nations, although this did not preclude ties to outsiders, including foreign capital. The goal was to create a regional economic bloc and consultation mechanism based on self-help through intraregional trade fairs, banks, and exchanges of information while encouraging outsiders to help. The Bandung conferees stressed the need for the United Nations and the World Bank to undertake equity investments, stabilize commodity prices, and aid in the diversification of trade. In sum, economic cooperation would curb unequal trade relationships, predatory financial arrangements, and inadequate aid and development efforts. Pledging to take world economic matters into their own hands by enhancing trade and exchanging technical know-how among themselves, the Bandung participants led the Third World toward a multilateral economic movement for the developing nations.[74]

Their efforts sparked the 1961 Belgrade summit of the Non-Aligned Movement, an organization that by 2007 included some 118 nations, likened to NATO or the Warsaw Pact, in which members oftentimes clashed with each other as much as cooperated, sided with one or the other superpower rather than maintaining their neutrality, or split off from the movement rather than working together. Yet in relation to the world economy, a general thrust occurred toward changing the unfair terms of trade that had been perpetrated by the superpowers in colonial times in order to exploit poor countries. The results of their protests were mixed, judged from the angle of economic gain and development (and their struggle persists in the present-day globalization period), but the nonaligned nations transformed the dialogue, if not the structure, of both the socialist and capitalist economic orders.

The Soviets executed an economic offensive to appeal to the Bandung Conference members, and the US response ran the gamut from cynicism to concern. Some in Washington viewed the Bandung Conference as a communist conspiracy, while others, including Eisenhower, were frustrated by the ability of both these neutralists as well as the socialists to score public relations points by merging colonialism with Western capitalism. The administration struggled to join the propaganda battle with reminders that the USSR acted like an imperial power and that such nonmarket approaches to development as those followed by

Nehru's India had largely failed to help the people. Americans also understood that the Bandung dialogue (and Soviet offensive) represented a transformation in the world economic power structure, but they did not quite know how to deal with the dying out of colonialism, because their allies were imperial powers themselves. The answer was to try to push the West toward adopting an orderly, stable phasing out of colonialism, which also meant preserving the American open-door approach and the inadequately glacial—in Third World eyes—reforms of the global economy.[75]

America and the Soviets were now operating in the "market" of a global Cold War. To preserve and encourage market ideology and practices within the challenging changes in the world economy, the United States considered various options when it came to winning over the emerging nations. What Washington required was a theoretical foundation to its free-enterprise leanings beyond multilateralism and the open door, particularly because those prescripts were greeted with suspicion in the Third World, where the doors had long been forced ajar by predatory capitalists.

Such pressures led policy makers to W. W. Rostow's basic explanation of Western-oriented modernization theory. This posited that modernization proceeds on a linear progression of development, along predetermined stages of growth, that decades later culminated in the integration of economies under a world regime of globalization. In this structuralist view of how nations climb from primitive poverty to the heights of sophisticated capitalist wealth, development is most influenced—or should be most influenced—by economics and institutions (modernity) rather than by customs (traditions). Nations and peoples simply advance stage by stage to modernization, to be helped along by the United States and other big powers. Adopting such modern economic accoutrements as a banking system, an entrepreneurial class, and use of technology, nations advance through a "takeoff" period in which industrialization fuels growth and diversifies the economy. A mature society will emerge characterized by a high standard of living made possible by mass consumption and reduced rates of poverty. Rostow posited that modernization will build "a new post-colonial relationship between the northern and southern halves of the Free World" through "a new partnership among free men—rich and poor alike."[76]

This Rostovian model was not, and has never been, without its detractors. Some claim it neglects small nations in favor of big ones, state-controlled economies for market-driven ones, and development by fits and starts rather than linear. It is not only Western-oriented but American-centric in espousing the success of the US economy and its evolution into a mass-consumption society. Rostow was not that rigid, but his noncommunist "capitalist manifesto" appeared in 1960 with the Cold War struggle foremost in his scheme. Thus, he did have in mind the United States, which had with great success followed this linear path to modernity to the "highest stage" of development (mass consumption), although the communist route of totalitarian guidance of the economy was another. This battle over the process through the stages of growth underlay the Cold War competition in the global economy, especially in the Third World. In short, this liberal economic theory was the underlying alternative vision to socialism offered to the underdeveloped world, and it hinged on preserving market forces to effectuate modernization.[77]

Third World Revolt

Many poor and developing nations simply did not accept US modernization plans, for they had experienced the meager or deleterious effects of free-market growth strategies. At midcentury, other theories than the positivism of liberal modernization weighed in on the debate regarding the reasons behind poverty. Marxism argued that the world capitalist system was stacked against the South because monopolistic foreign financiers and merchants, backed by a nexus of foreign governments and elite client states, locked the emerging nations into a permanent condition of unequal exchange. Indebted to capitalist finance and suffering economic distortion because of terms of trade (export prices divided by import prices) that mired them in agricultural, raw materials, or light industrial production, the underdeveloped nations could not climb out of poverty except by leaving or changing the system, or destroying it through revolution. Few took this latter path, however, although nationalist rebellions in Vietnam, Cuba, and Angola brought Marxist regimes to power. Instead, the Third World turned to structuralism to critique their predicament. Structuralists agreed with Marxists such as Paul Baran that global capitalism favored the rich North and perpetuated backwardness in the South by unequal terms of trade. Argentine economist Raúl Prebisch, a member of the United Nations Economic Commission for Latin America, was one of the first thinkers to react against liberalism by adopting dependency theory to explain why wealth flowed from the Third World periphery to the advanced capitalist core. Immanuel Wallerstein later dubbed this process the "world system." Cheap primary goods exported by the developing countries faced competition in the world market as well as constant, but not necessarily growing, demand from the North, while the rich nations sent their high-priced manufactured goods to the South, which was compelled to buy them for their own development. Unequal trade relations thus transferred income to the advanced nations, and foreign investors either avoided the Third World or concentrated in export sectors that further drained profits from the South to the North.

The difference between Marxists and structuralists lay in the solution to this cycle of trade-induced poverty. While Marxist dependency theorists preached revolution, Prebisch and others advocated altering the global economic rules through regional integration, expanded intra-Southern investment and commerce, and a policy of import substitution. This latter prescription was the key to the structuralist protest against market multilateralism, although at times poor nations also had to resort to nationalization of foreign investment holdings, prohibitions on foreign capital, or subsidies to domestic producers to diversify their monoculture economies. Pushed by Latin Americans since the 1930s and adopted by African countries by the late 1950s, import substitution called for diversification from primary goods to manufacturing and services and the nurturing of infant industries. Specifically, it involved protecting local industries by tariffs, import quotas and other quantitative barriers to trade, restricting production to home consumption rather than for export, and directing growth through state control of trade, production, and consumption patterns. This protectionist tool might have punch, for the South wielded it against the Western capitalist regime just as the United Nations was transformed by the addition of dozens of countries newly unshackled from colonialism. Import substitution did not mean isolating the Third World from the multilateral market economy, for it encouraged development by foreign investment by multinationals and welcomed foreign aid. But the emphasis was on the home market and not on the open door in trade.

The drive for inward-looking industrialization attacked the multilateral market system but had mixed results. It worked for some of the largest nations in Latin America, such as Argentina, Brazil, Mexico, and Venezuela, because they enjoyed sizable consumer markets for their home-grown manufactures. Smaller nations had less success, and East Asian economies, such as high-tariff South Korea and the Philippines, were fueled by American Cold War aid and investment and a vigorous export trade, so they had little need for import substitution. The Latin Americans, meanwhile, tried to develop their industrial base by protectionism, a strategy that largely failed because they could not escape the advanced nations' domination of world markets or open-door rules that guided exchange relations. By 1960, total exports from the South had risen by nearly a third of their 1950 mark, with Latin America registering a 22 percent increase and Africa a 42 percent expansion (though Asia climbed just 10 percent). These figures hid the fact that Asia dominated in manufactured exports, such as textiles, which accounted for just 15 percent of Third World sales in the world economy. Import substitution generally failed to develop economies and did not augment the Third World's share of global exports, which actually declined as a percentage of the world's total exports. Multinational corporations maintained and enlarged their dominating roles in local economies while high tariffs stifled competition and promoted inefficiency at home.

Emerging nations issued their challenge nonetheless, and with some effect. For starters, they welcomed modernization programs because they came with aid, but many, such as Kenya's Tom Mboya, insisted that assistance come with no strings attached. "Remember, we are also capable of gauging the ulterior motives of all those who offer help to us," he instructed the British in 1961.[78] In addition, in 1958 the struggling countries took aim on the trade system. A panel of GATT experts recommended that the North not insist on reciprocal, multilateral trade terms and instead try more one-sided purchases of goods from the less-developed countries. Structuralism resulted in a campaign that became the economic equivalent of the diplomatic Non-Aligned Movement of neutrals. It awakened the advanced nations to Third World needs and expectations, and even its failure prompted the South to shift from domestic answers to development to

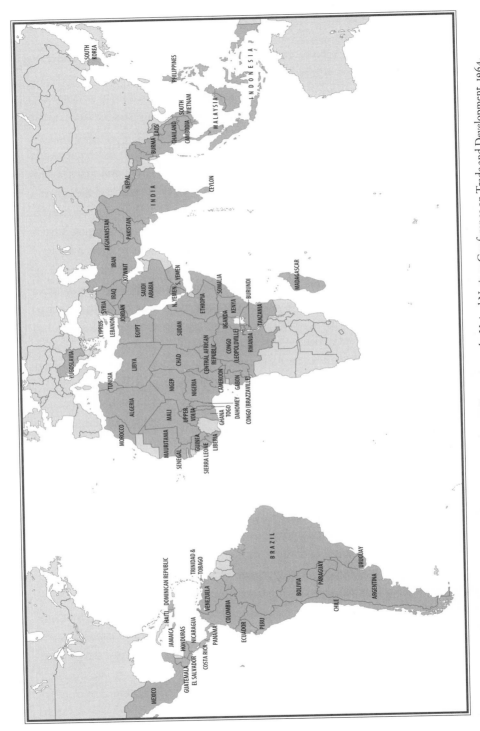

Signatories of the Joint Declaration of the Seventy-Seven Developing Countries at the United Nations Conference on Trade and Development, 1964.

international solutions. This meant, in short, a rebellion against the American-led global capitalist order in finance and trade. Because GATT did not focus on development needs, emerging nations like South Korea, Mexico, Jamaica, and Argentina rejected membership in the trade forum. They turned to the United Nations for help and created the Group of 77 in 1964 at the United Nations Conference on Trade and Development (UNCTAD). The G-77 became the permanent bloc to represent the economic interests of the South. After the first official meeting in Algiers in 1967, the G-77 had chapters in all of the United Nations' agencies as well as the IMF and World Bank. A foremost goal was for UNCTAD to persuade GATT to target development in the international trade system. In the end the structuralist model informed UNCTAD, which was led by its first secretary general from its inception in 1964 to 1969, the longtime reformer Raúl Prebisch.[79]

After institutionalizing the organization to meet every four years as an intergovernmental consultative, research, policy analysis, and technical assistance body—with 191 members by 2009—UNCTAD notably assailed GATT's multilateral market system. The obstacles were immense, because the advanced nations had long focused within GATT on their own trade, and at the Kennedy Round from 1963 to 1967, they concentrated on the new European Common Market. In 1962 twenty-one nations responded with a recommendation for the North to remove or reduce barriers to tropical commodities and semiprocessed goods as well as eliminate new tariffs and quantitative limits on Third World exports. This idea ran up against resistance from the Common Market. These six European countries already provided preferential trade treatment to associated former colonies by granting them concessions (lower barriers to trade than given to others) on many of their exports and not requiring reciprocity in return. Such trade preferences created a discriminatory system against those outside of the arrangement, but the French especially wished to preserve the system because Paris reached a somewhat closed agreement in 1963 in Yaoundé with eighteen of its Associated Overseas Countries (AOC) in Africa. The Third World action program of 1962 threatened this Yaoundé Convention that gave France franc-based cheap food imports and enhanced its image in Africa as a champion of decolonization just as it was losing Algeria. Latin Americans protested their exclusion from the Yaoundé Convention, and the United States backed them, in part because the Convention discriminated against most emerging nations and also because the deal restricted Western Hemisphere exports of bananas and coffee to Europe, thereby compelling the United States to buy more at a time when its international payments balance was suffering a growing deficit.[80]

A system of generalized preferential treatment to all Third World commodities was also unpalatable to the free-trading United States. Although Washington recognized the need to correct an ever-increasing Third World trade disadvantage, preferences threatened both US open-door doctrine and the delicate political support of Congress for liberal commercial policy. Protectionists at home did not take kindly to free entry of competitive commodities like sugar, for instance, while preferences trended away from market processes in the world economy. The United States preferred to help poor nations diversify their economies through aid, individual (rather than generalized) commodity agreements, and regional integration. Preparing for the Kennedy Round, the new administration of Lyndon Johnson offered to halve certain US tariffs for all nations and insisted on a bland "commercial basis" (meaning reliance on the market rather than intervention) for trade between the North and the South. Seeing the writing on the wall, GATT ministers scrambled to soothe the Third World nations by studying preferences on exports of light manufactures. Frustrated Southern nations threw up their hands and turned instead to revising the international trade rules under UNCTAD.

More than two thousand delegates from 120 nations and several international organizations at UNCTAD pushed the "core" group of Western advanced countries not only for preferential treatment for their exports but, in the event that the terms of trade deteriorated further, also for compensation so that the South could recover its losses. Scoring political points (even though prior East–South economic deals had gone sour), the Soviet bloc warmly embraced these ideas, denounced the "imperial powers" for their resistance to them, and added specific criticism of the Common Market's postcolonial relationship with the African nations. The communist nations offered to buy commodities at fixed, stable prices, thereby allowing the Third World to avoid the uncertainty of profits in the free-market system of the West.

The capitalist core geared up for a fight. The Western Europeans largely bowed to the demand for "selective and controlled" North–South trade to replace the free-enterprise multilateralism of the United States–led GATT regime, and when both Great Britain and GATT leaders themselves agreed that trade relations had been guided by an overly doctrinaire adherence to the open door, America had to choose sides. Domestic protectionist pressures, lack of negotiating authority to embrace such a regime, and overall principles prevented Washington from boarding the preferences train. They struck at the heart of US most-favored-nation policy, a nearly two-centuries-old policy of upholding nondiscrimination as a rule, although the US-Philippines trade agreement amounted to a preferential system (it ended in 1974) and the Canada–United States Automotive Products Agreement of 1965 also played favorites but was not prejudicial to others. Preferences also seemed like a modification of colonial relationships. The first UNCTAD conference actually only created a secretariat, to the satisfaction of the Americans, but clearly the United States stood alone. In order to head off the discriminatory Yaoundé Convention and rising negative press, Washington turned to the Organization for Economic Cooperation and Development (OECD) in 1966 to create a system of preferences generalized to all nations.[81]

When France agreed to let go of its special accord with the African nations and join the generalized system, the Americans gave the Third World a head start through special tariff treatment. Most of US business and labor organizations at this time supported the arrangement as long as American producers and workers were not hurt. While Latin Americans sought a distinct hemispheric preferential system, the United States endorsed the global one. In 1968 the Second United Nations Conference on Trade and Development (UNCTAD II), meeting in India, approved the generalized system of preferences for a variety of products seeking entry into Northern markets. Still, Third World squabbling and growing resistance in the North to a demand for duty-free treatment of manufactures and preferences for certain commodities weakened the commitment to helping the South. In the long run, the Generalized System of Preferences, which took effect in 1976 and became permanent three years later, emerged as only a temporary deal that exempted key Third World exports but limited gains for others. To be sure, rich nations granted preferences to nearly all non-OECD countries, yet there were exceptions. The United States refused to grant tariff waivers to Vietnam until the mid-1990s. In addition, protectionism in the North prevented preferential treatment for exports of key manufactures such as textiles, glass and steel, and leather goods—products that emerging nations made well and traded competitively. Preferences were generalized across products; a truly globalized system of trade arrangements with the emerging countries never evolved. In addition, more-developed nations benefited from export favoritism. By the 1980s the attempt to restructure world trade for the gain of the South had largely failed. Generalized preferences, a bold idea nursed by structuralism of the 1950s, fell short of its promise.[82]

North and South in the Cold War

In this era of rising expectations in the world economy, the emerging nations set out to use the US-Soviet Cold War competition to their advantage. One way was to work with nongovernmental organizations (NGOs) such as the World Bank to procure financing for development projects. Another alternative focused on keeping multinational corporate profits at home.

In 1954 the new revolutionary government of Gamal Abdel Nasser of Egypt sought financing to build the Aswan High Dam in order to generate electricity from the Nile River, promote agricultural development, and control annual flooding. The massive project would raise the country's living standard and solidify Nasser's revolution. The World Bank quickly drew up plans for financing the dam's construction, but Nasser balked when the $400 million loan came with a condition that Sudan, a British holding downstream from the Dam, must acquire an equitable share of the water and compensation for its displaced population whose villages would be flooded. The nonaligned Egypt saw Anglo-American collusion and imperialism behind the World Bank's demands, but the international bureaucrats countered that their qualified endorsement of the loan arose from economic and technical concerns. Further complications arose in 1955 over bids for construction, but the Cold War always hovered above the project. The Suez Canal, a strategic waterway that connected the Indian and Mediterranean Seas and through which two-thirds of Europe's oil was shipped from the Middle East, ran through Egypt. When Nasser announced that he would buy arms from Czechoslovakia, the British and Americans feared that the communist bloc might penetrate this part of the Middle East, jeopardize the canal's security, and undermine British prestige. In addition, Nasser soon recognized the People's Republic of China, supported the ouster of British officials from Jordan, and expressed dislike for Israel. To boot, southern American congressmen worried about the specter of competitive Egyptian cotton entering the United States. Detesting neutralism in the Cold War, Secretary of State Dulles fostered an anti-Nasser bloc of Middle Eastern nations while publicly supporting the World Bank's financial support for the dam.

Both governments rushed to underwrite half of the cost of the Aswan Dam in order to woo Nasser; eventually the Americans stepped in with a $270 million offer. Meanwhile, the World Bank worked with the US Treasury to pressure Britain to release Egypt's large accumulation of pound-sterling reserves held in London and negotiated an acceptable agreement on Sudan's demands.[83] Yet global bankers insisted on standards of international lending by encouraging competitive bidding for the project, rather than permitting Nasser's favored German company to construct the dam. Nasser chafed under these strictures as violations of Egyptian sovereignty, but the United States precipitated a major crisis by canceling the loan in 1956 on the grounds that Egypt would be unable to complete the project. This was untrue, as the World Bank attested to Nasser's economic viability. Nasser reacted by dramatically nationalizing the Suez Canal in order to use the tolls to fund the Aswan Dam and to enthrone Cairo as the leader of the Arab world against the imperialist nations and their corporations. In the ensuing crisis, Israel, France, and Britain invaded Egypt in October and November 1956, only to be condemned at the United Nations by several nations, including the USSR and the United States. Worried that the crisis would inflame emotions against the West and allow the Soviets a foothold in crucial areas of the Middle East, an infuriated Eisenhower used economic diplomacy against Britain, threatening to cause the collapse of the pound sterling by selling off sterling reserves. Hegemonic America held the purse strings of the Western alliance. Meanwhile, Saudi Arabia issued an oil embargo against Britain and France.[84] The Europeans and Israelis found themselves cornered by friends and enemies and backed away from the canal.

The Suez Crisis had major repercussions for the world economy and the standing of the Third World within it. Nongovernmental organizations such as the World Bank continued to make loans (in this case, extending a credit to help widen and deepen the Suez Canal for passage of larger ships), but they could not

Construction of the Aswan High Dam in Egypt, May 14, 1964. Nine years before, the clash between the revolutionary Gamal Abdel Nasser and European financiers and bureaucrats over this massive project prompted Nasser to turn to socialist nations for aid. The conflict led to the Suez Crisis of 1956, when Nasser nationalized the Suez Canal. The United States ended the crisis by halting an invasion by Britain, France, and Israel that had escalated tensions in the Cold War. The project went forth some years later. (Getty Images)

prevent Cold War politics from overwhelming their economic and social reforms so embraced by Egypt and other nations. The crisis hastened the end of French and British colonization, particularly in the Middle East and Africa, and also destabilized the NATO alliance, for Paris especially grew suspicious of America's reliability. And the balance of power in the region tipped a bit more toward the Soviet Union, which stepped in with financing for the Aswan Dam in 1958. Aided by Russian heavy machinery and technicians, construction began in 1960, the dam started to fill four years later, and it reached capacity for the first time in

1976. Meanwhile Egypt became a major player in global diplomacy and regional disputes, aided by the development provided by the dam, which initially provided half of the country's electricity. Nasser emerged victorious as the leader of the pan-Arab movement. His emerging nation had successfully played the Cold War game.[85]

Victories such as Nasser's and UNCTAD's were impressive, but the developing world still remained impoverished and the North remained in control. Third World nations struggled with strict, conservative loan terms set by the IMF, which believed that these nations had to be micromanaged because they did not honor their agreements due to bureaucratic unaccountability or corruption. Abetted by a dependence on multinational corporations and a lack of substantial domestic markets, a cycle of poverty dictated underdevelopment. For example, Ecuador tried to ignore the strictures, but loans from the US Export-Import Bank and the IMF came with strings attached, requiring austere fiscal policies such as higher prices for gasoline and electricity and currency devaluation as well as allowances for multinational corporations to gain more business in the country. Even the tapping of large oil deposits in the Ecuadoran Amazon by the Texaco-Gulf Corporation in 1967 and subsequent finds of petroleum riches did not provide a solution to the country's economic woes. Revenue generated from the oil fields and a pipeline augmented exports sevenfold by 1977, and the rise in global oil demand and prices during the decade further augmented the gross domestic product. But foreign capital invested by multinational companies dominated production and export and even led to the fall of Ecuador's military government when Texaco-Gulf boycotted selling the nation's oil abroad in protest of tightening regulations.

Ecuador offers an example of the complex relationship between multinationals, NGOs, and the emerging nations—laying bare the basic inequities in the global economic system. When competition from abroad lowered prices for cacao and rice in the 1950s, Ecuador turned to bananas and became the world's top producer due to growing demand driven by America. Banana exports rose in value from $2.8 million in 1948 to $90 million by 1960, constituting nearly two-thirds of the nation's exports in 1961. Roughly three thousand domestic banana producers flourished, although exporting and marketing remained in the hands of the five largest foreign firms. At the United Fruit Company's plantation, workers received many benefits, such as low-cost housing, safe drinking water, cheap food, hospital care, paid vacations and sick leave, and high wages relative to the rest of Ecuador. Yet bananas did not bring widespread well-being or modernization, because Ecuador's economy, like that of other countries in the Americas, relied on the big export companies. The nation made little progress toward industrialization or developing the middle class needed for urban development, management, and growth. Overall, industry's share of the gross domestic product in 1970 remained the same as it was in 1940, despite Quito's embrace of the UN Economic Commission for Latin America's recommendations for import substitution in the early 1960s.[86] This was so because the Cold War continued to deglobalize the world economy, curbing America's effectiveness in pursuing traditional free enterprise.

East–West

Trade relations with and within the Soviet bloc reflected these security strictures on the world economy. Earlier Stalin had ruthlessly unified the COMECON countries by dictating that their production and trade be directed inward. Now Moscow sought to expand commercial exchanges with the West. Peaceful coexistence brought a defrosting of the Cold War. Supported by American farmers seeking to sell their surpluses, Eisenhower pledged at a summit meeting in 1955 to lift some of the trade sanctions that were restraining East–West trade and liberalized the three lists of CoCom controls. He counseled against preconceived notions of Soviet hostility and instead sought to encourage peace and security through the exchange of goods. Congress largely agreed, and the administration relaxed restrictions on the embargo lists. Two years later Ike ran smack up against the wall of virulent anticommunism when the British asked the United States to loosen controls on some machinery trade related to the People's Republic of China. Eisenhower advocated careful study of the issue, not so much to encourage diplomatic relations, but to facilitate natural patterns of trade between Japan and "Red" China. Congress and a concerned Commerce Department compelled him to retreat when he was accused of violating the Battle Act, which prohibited aid to nations that knowingly traded with communist countries. The Commerce Department rejected an attempt by Dresser Industries of

Dallas, for instance, to exchange data on rock drill bits for rights to manufacture a new Soviet turbo-drill. The message was clear: there would be no easing of lists of banned exports to the Sino-Soviet bloc.[87]

This rigidity began to change in the 1960s as the Cold War reshaped the dialogue on economic relations. The Kennedy administration counseled the use of East–West trade as a vehicle to improve superpower relations after the harrowing Cuban missile crisis of 1962. Specifically, the United States approved a large sale of wheat to the USSR in 1963 and advocated expanding trade with Eastern Europe. President Johnson furthered the process of liberalization of East–West trade by centralizing decisions in the White House and State Department, both of which were prone to seek détente with the Soviets. Thus, LBJ committed to bridge building by forging trade deals supported by American business and labor, and noting endorsement by the CIA and the Department of Defense. Co-Com controls had not prevented the Soviets from infiltrating the Third World or building an economic base for the development of high-tech weapons systems. Limits and bans on strategic items remained because the United States was fighting a hot war against communism in Vietnam, but the administration was determined to extend most-favored-nation treatment to communist bloc countries as bargaining tools to effect change and to encourage them to engage in the free-market global economy.

America's wielding of East–West trade as a carrot or stick in shaping communist bloc behavior became the rule. The trend toward liberalization reached its apex during the administration of Richard M. Nixon, who moved toward détente with the communist bloc. As restrictions gradually diminished with China, trade rose from $5 million in 1971 to $900 million three years later. A sweeping US-USSR trade pact in 1972 led to numerous industrial contracts, totaling about $1.1 billion of imports into America, and sales of grain to the Soviets amounting to over $1 billion. The Commerce Department reduced its list of controlled items from 550 to 73 in just months, and rather than continually updating changes in strategic lists, CoCom relied increasingly on waiving items. The US requests for exemptions grew from two in 1962 to more than a thousand in 1978. Trade thrived between East and West as Moscow gained entry into the global capitalist market and the United States used trade to woo both estranged China and the USSR. Talks even began about cooperation in oil drilling, particularly after war broke out in the Middle East to threaten American oil supplies. Politics progressively intruded on East–West trade relations, however, as Congress proposed in 1974 to withhold trade privileges to the Soviets as punishment for human rights violations and restrictions on Jewish immigration.[88]

Successors applied controls according to their gauge of Soviet foreign policy. The administration of Jimmy Carter further linked diplomacy to Soviet behavior, and as a result trade began to plummet after the Soviet invasion of Afghanistan in 1979. Carter imposed a grain embargo, boycotted the Olympics, and tightened controls on technology. Ronald Reagan tried to trade as little as possible with his Soviet nemesis in order to bankrupt Moscow. Yet such punishment could not change the fact that the communist and capitalist worlds were closer than ever before, which lay a foundation for Russia's engagement in globalization after the fall of communism.

The path to integration was also furthered by the fissures within the communist system itself. It was clear that the COMECON regime represented a somewhat false economic union among the European socialist states. Many of the Eastern European satellites chafed at Soviet domination and the suppression of the market socialist reforms of the late 1960s; historic rivalries and suspicions added to Moscow's hegemonic policies that made a mockery of the push for integration. Attempts to replace CMEA centralization with planning and decision making by industrial associations also fell flat, for even such horizontal chains of command proved unwieldy and overly bureaucratic, unable to generate the financial and administrative infrastructures necessary for integration of disparate economies.[89] In essence, by the mid-1970s the American-led capitalist global economy had survived the Soviet economic offensive and stood as the hegemonic structure, although it was on rather shakier legs than before.

European Challenge

The American open-door doctrine ruled in part because of the sheer power of the United States, but also because of the surging economies of Western Europe and East Asia, which, ironically, placed US hegemony under threat. After gluing together their coal and steel markets in the early 1950s, the Western Europeans followed the pragmatic visions of Robert Schuman and Jean Monnet along a course of unification. The Americans looked on this European Economic Community (EEC) of six countries in 1957 as serving to contain West Germany within the democratic and anticommunist fold of nations and stimulating peace through prosperity on a continent so often torn asunder by war. In an economic sense, the Common Market of France, West Germany, Belgium, Luxembourg, the Netherlands, and Italy meant the creation of a potentially vast multinational customs union supportive of free enterprise and an open door to outsiders. So influential was the Common Market (the British term for the EEC) that its powers soon eclipsed those of the European Atomic Energy Community as well as the European Coal and Steel Community, both of which fell under its jurisdiction. By 1973 the EEC had been enlarged by four members (the United Kingdom, Greece, Denmark, and Ireland); it would add more members thereafter, totaling twenty-seven by 2009.[90] The EEC became the economic engine of Europe.

Its advent also came as a direct challenge to the extant global economic power structure. The EEC comprised 168 million people in Western Europe and 63 million in associated areas—a sizable trade bloc. The founders expected not only that the customs union would become the largest commercial entity in the world within a decade, but also that the economic organization would spill over into the establishment of a supranational political federation in which decision making would rest with the bureaucratic executive arm, the European Commission and not individual national ministers under the governing council. President Charles de Gaulle of France, who sought to elevate French power at the same time as that of the Common Market, blocked this European Commission initiative. As well, he prevented Britain from joining the Inner Six, because he viewed London as a proxy for America, which he feared would infiltrate the EEC. European supranationalism did not come to pass until the 1990s with the development of a single currency, but the Common Market emerged as a trade monolith in the 1960s by building an effective customs union.

After considerable debate within the EEC, the result was the substitution of national commercial policies with a unified approach to the world that defied America's postwar policy of nondiscriminatory trade and undermined the US hold on the global economy. The Inner Six installed a common external tariff (rather than separate national duty schedules) that governed trade in industrial goods between the Common Market and the outside world, thereby purposefully discriminating against the multilateral open-door doctrine of the United States. They harmonized their duties—France and Italy dropped tariffs, and the Benelux nations and West Germany raised theirs—and then applied this common tariff to imports while maintaining duty-free industrial trade among themselves. In addition, the bloc established a protectionist levy and quota system on food imports, called the Common Agricultural Policy, that led to major disagreements between the French and its European trade partners over the extent of farm protectionism in agriculture-rich France. Regardless of the fracas (much of it provoked by de Gaulle's drive for French recognition as leader of the new Europe), Western European trading rights took precedent over those of non-Europeans, particularly the United States. Americans actually welcomed this Eurocentric policy for political reasons, which outweighed the economic rationale for multilateralism; after all, the unification of Europe (and the linkage of Japan to the West) was a great success story of US foreign policy. But the potentially harmful effect of European trade and consuming power on US economic prospects could not be ignored.

In every economic category, the EEC emerged as a powerhouse that challenged US leadership and hegemony. The gap between American and European production was fast closing, even in the 1950s. European steel production rose to an annual level of 62.9 million tons by 1959 (up from 36.6 million seven years earlier), while US output stagnated at 84.5 million. By 1960 Common Market industrial production outpaced American manufacturing, decreasing the United States' share of global gross national product while the EEC's rose throughout the decade. America remained the single largest trading nation, but by 1960 the combined Inner Six outstripped the United States in trade volume. The Europeans also caught up in exports, as the American trade surplus with the region began to wane. Of course, this was all largely inevitable as recovery from World War II took root by the late 1950s, and the United States could not possibly maintain its tremendous economic edge of the immediate postwar years. But the Inner Six and the British-led seven-nation European Free Trade Association—a looser association than the EEC that resisted political integration—threatened to become inward-looking trade blocs that might close the door to the United States. Indeed, exports to both entities began to decline, raising alarms across the Atlantic about European protectionism. At the same time the United States suffered from inflation at home, incurred in part by unsustainable domestic economic expansion paid for by seemingly unsustainable exports to Western Europe.

American salvation lay, in part, in trade negotiations to deal with Common Market protectionism. During the Kennedy Round of GATT (1964–1967), the United States tried to reassert its leadership over the Western economic system by promoting traditional trade liberalization toward Europe and Japan. Of particular importance was liberalizing the EEC's Common Agricultural Policy so that America could benefit from its comparative advantage in farm trade and sell its surpluses. Washington also sought to lower the external industrial tariff so that American firms would manufacture at home and export rather than try to jump trade barriers and invest and produce in Europe. The French refused to play, for they understood that the Common Market rested on their access to German agricultural markets in exchange for opening to West German industrial products. When the Americans tried to sneak Britain into the EEC to undermine French intransigence, de Gaulle vetoed British membership, reading the ploy as an attempt to halt integration of the Common Market itself. The Europeans did lower industrial tariffs at the Kennedy Round, although trade in chemical products and steel remained plagued by ingenious nontariff barriers. Furthermore, transatlantic agricultural trade remained stymied by the Franco-German quid pro quo as well as longtime protectionist tendencies, as it does today. The effect was clear on the United States. American grain sales to the Inner Six in 1969 totaled less than half the figures from just three years before.[91] The EEC hindered US trade policy, despite a massive effort by Washington to maintain the open door.

The figures on the Western European economy were remarkable, but regional economic behavior turned out to be even more transformative for the global economy. Although the Inner Six generated just one-third of US production by the mid-1960s, the real purchasing power of the customs union reached half that of the United States. The region had begun to shift from the hierarchies of production and workers to a consumer area in which workers enjoyed rising incomes and spending power. Europe became a magnet for American multinational enterprises that injected mass-marketing techniques into the workplace and literally changed Europeans from their social stratification as laborers, homemakers, salarymen, and conservative executives into affluent and chic consumers. Advertisements depicted managers as well as workers skiing, eating at fast-food restaurants, and driving sleek automobiles. By 1965, 4.2 million color televisions were sold in France, where only five thousand had been bought in 1954—the consumer revolution brought Europeans into stores. Belgians abandoned bicycles to travel by car, German washing machines and Italian refrigerators sold in Holland, and EEC members shared in markets ranging from shoes to food, thanks to lower national tariffs that unsealed borders and allowed trade in consumer goods to flourish. Buying on credit became more acceptable. As Jean Monnet noted, Europeans would equal the US standard of living within fifteen years of the EEC's creation. His prediction was fairly accurate; the EEC's gross national product rose by an average of 3.5 percent per year until 1974, while American growth amounted to 2.1 percent over the same period. US consumption figures also lagged European. As disposable income doubled for wage and salary earners, the volume of trade tripled within the Common Market, showing that European purchasing power (and habits) had changed dramatically.[92]

Multinational Enterprise

One way to take advantage of this departure from the old productionist ethic to the new consumer model, as well as hop over European trade barriers, was for US companies to invest in plants in the region. In other words, they could engage in trade from inside the Common Market and Free Trade Area rather than attempt to penetrate Europe from the outside. Multinational enterprises expanded rapidly in the region. Canada still remained the top place for US investments, with Britain second, but the EEC (with the addition of the UK in 1973) surpassed America's northern neighbor in the 1970s. Capitalizing on opportunities in the region, firms nearly tripled their investments in the Common Market—despite rather tepid support from Washington, which viewed foreign investment as a drain on US international payments and a diversion of capital from the domestic economy. The Johnson administration eventually forbade large-scale foreign investments because of the ever-worsening payments imbalance—a shortfall caused by trade deficits and capital exports. Yet multinationals also planted the structural and ideological seeds of globalization; academics viewed them as an alternative to nation-states and their mercantilist policies. The move of American corporations abroad shrank the world's geography, sending business, people, and technology around the globe in ways that bypassed, negotiated with, or simply overwhelmed nations. Market advocates applauded the advent of these globe-trotting business firms as carriers of dynamic private enterprise, mutual prosperity, world federalist government, and ultimately peace, regardless of their reputations as profit-seeking, uncontrollable, cowboy capitalists lacking moral and social consciences—unlike their European counterparts.

While EEC multinationals seemed to invest in social causes, the American multinational offensive saturated Europe with consumer products, provoking a backlash that had more political consequences than economic. European anti-Americanism, perception of overregulated economies, and labor turmoil had scared off most big potential investors, but the easing of restrictions and the recession in America jump-started multinational activity abroad. American corporate direct investment in Europe nearly quadrupled, from $4.6 billion in 1958 to $16.2 billion eight years later, a sum roughly one-third of all US direct investment worldwide and the peak of the American share of the world market. Companies targeted visible and rapidly growing sectors, such as food, cosmetics, and household appliances, that brought high profits. In automobiles, the Americans sold low-cost cars with new gadgets and decent power that competed well against European companies, especially French low-cylinder models. Chrysler alone made more than all French car producers combined, and General Motors' annual sales outpaced Holland's total gross national product by 10 percent. American marketing agencies such as J. Walter Thompson set up shop in rebuilt Frankfurt and ran accounts across Europe for 117 items, ranging from Kraft foods to De Beers diamonds. General Electric's two hundred thousand products overwhelmed European industry, while American-style supermarkets cropped up in major cities, replacing the regulated individual sellers with the practice of self-service under one roof. So effective were the US corporations, their techniques, and their advertising that de Gaulle and other European (especially French) voices warned of Washington's imperialism through the "Americanization" of Europe or the "take-over" of Britain. Even in Canada, where US companies developed raw materials resources under few restrictions, a wave of nationalism led to criticism of American corporate domination and calls for independence from the continental integration of North America.[93]

Realizing that American multinationals produced more than the EEC itself, experts counseled Europe to organize its own such corporations across the Inner Six nations and mobilize capital to meet the American challenge in the oncoming high-technology markets of telecommunications and information. Europe could not shut out the tide of investments from across the Atlantic, so it adapted. European firms partnered with US know-how, such as the old French perfume industry with synthetic scent makers in New Jersey, and allowed Americans to take over eleven of France's leading perfume companies by 1970. Britain, Germany, Switzerland, and Italy were swept by chain and self-service stores (85 percent of Americans bought from such entities), and Kraft, Kellogg's, and other companies gained major market leverage in Europe. This did not mean that small provisioners disappeared, but their numbers began to wane as multinationals could cut prices by just 10 percent and bankrupt local concerns. Meanwhile, decrying violations of the capitalist ethic of competition, American tire makers like Goodyear and Firestone got around regulations by offering French car producers discounts on tires. In the end there was much grousing about the American challenge, but even the French drank cokes and bought Mobil gasoline. And US corporations turned increasingly to the German market by the early 1970s, deterred in part by French regulations even after de Gaulle's departure had the government scrambling to attract US dollars. Multinationals dodged the national label for regional and global identities.[94]

Despite the clash of economic civilizations, simultaneous with the birth of the European Common Market a virtual global revolution in transportation and communication greatly facilitated the expansion of multinational corporate activity. Multinationals (with Washington's backing) oriented much of their investment activity toward the Third World, especially as Congress frowned on foreign aid. In the North the dynamism of multinational enterprise blossomed in large part due to new technology generated by the United States. America accounted for 69 percent of the research and development in major countries. International Business Machines (IBM), for example, dominated the computer market in Japan and Western Europe as it used regional marketers to promote its products. Foreign sales accounted for 20 percent of IBM's revenues by 1960, and

54 percent by 1979; in 1964 the company had installed 62 percent of the computers in Western Europe. IBM retained total control of its foreign affiliates even in the face of governmental pressure to sell to locals.

In transportation, people and freight advanced around the globe at an ever-quickening pace. After investing a quarter of its net worth on developing a long-range passenger jet, Boeing sent the 707 across the Atlantic in 1957. The flight shrank time and space, allowing American businesspeople, in particular, to travel rapidly, comfortably, and cheaply to Western Europe in half the time of previous, multistop flights. Passenger numbers rose from 4.3 million to 18.9 million from 1957 to 1973 (and tourists numbered 278 million by 1980, and 880 million in 2009, with total passengers amounting to over 2.3 billion by the latter date) as tourists also took advantage of low-cost fares. In 1969 the Boeing 747, a widebody plane designed to carry cargo, made air travel even more efficient by nearly halving the seat-per-mile cost. Subsequent models boosted capacity to 233 passengers traveling between New York and Tokyo, and by 1989 commercial jets flew 412 people for twenty hours at subsonic speeds. Charter flights dropped costs even more, and it became common to see young people setting out for Europe or America and Canada. For first-class travel and business flyers, an Anglo-French consortium built the Concorde, which began the first regularly scheduled supersonic flights in 1976 from London and Paris to New York and Washington, DC. For more than twenty-seven years the Concorde flew across the Atlantic in just four hours; its routes expanded to include Asia and Latin America; but a crash in Paris in 2000, and prohibitive operating costs, stopped Concorde service altogether. By this time the air travel revolution, as one historian has noted, allowed for "the translation of prospects into actual foreign investments" by furthering the process of globalization.[95]

Commercial transport also followed this globalized pattern of expansion through efficiencies wrought by new technology. Air service expanded as the number of revenue-ton-miles for air cargo on international flights grew 866 percent between 1957 and 1973. This set the stage for vast market growth in jet freight in the following decade, but there were also other options available for trade and multinational commerce. In 1960 two American trucking lines standardized trailers for moving goods between ports, and other companies soon jumped into this container shipping business. Soon container ships plied the seas and sped

Flight attendants on the new Boeing Jet Stratoliner, March 21, 1956. Introduced in 1937, the Boeing 307—this is a model used for training—sported a new interior. This jet held ninety-eight passengers with comforts such as air conditioning and individual air vents, running water, and reading lights. The Stratoliner preceded the larger jets, such as the 707, that soon crossed the Atlantic with business executives on board. Air travel became less costly and more efficient, thus shrinking the business world. (© Bettmann/CORBIS)

the flow of trade across the Pacific and Atlantic Oceans, although by the 1980s many were too large to transit the Panama Canal. In addition, large vessels specially designed to hold up to two thousand automobiles, and tankers built to carry vast stores of oil and liquefied gas, expanded the shipping industry and integrated transportation systems around the world. The transportation revolution fueled the surge of enterprise across the Atlantic and beyond; by 1966 the volume of international trade in manufactured products more than doubled the rise in global production, accelerated in large part by plummeting freight costs that led to further integration of the world economy. Container ships spread from the Pacific to the North Atlantic, Mediterranean, and beyond by the 1980s, and containerization was so ubiquitous that long-distance trade skyrocketed. Capacity expanded by 10 percent per year in 2001–2005, and the vessels grew to such enormous sizes that many could carry four thousand 40-foot containers. Put another way, South Korean, Japanese, and Chinese companies launched container ships capable of carrying 1.3 million 29-inch color televisions or more than 50 million mobile phones. Plans existed to more than double the number of boxes, enough to create a sixty-eight-mile-long line of trucks for off-loading. The only constraints were geographic, for the world's busiest shipping lane, the Straits of Malacca between Malaysia and Indonesia, as well as the Suez Canal, placed natural limits on these behemoths.[96]

New communications technologies also aided the explosion in multinational enterprises. The telex made possible fast and clear communications to orchestrate deals and manage affairs in faraway places, while transatlantic telephone calls—using the first microwave amplification cable—soared from 250,000 in 1957 to 4.3 million in 1961. Both telex and telephone allowed American corporations to monitor their holdings overseas from US headquarters, and metropolitan centers around the world were increasingly linked through communications networks. In the decades to come, satellites provided the means of integrating remote areas of the globe into the world economy. Furthermore, television (in the midst of a boom at this point) provided visual perceptions that both introduced people to the exotic and also transformed the foreign into more familiar images. The thinking of executives changed as their vision and knowledge of opportunities overseas broadened. Managers the world over shared an image of the world that defied borders and distances. Technology started to collapse time and space by making even politics and diplomacy instantaneous. By the 1970s, technology empowered people with information through such personal electronic media outlets as radio, VCRs, cassette tapes, CDs, and person-to-person video links through satellite. By the beginning of 2010, more than 4.6 billion subscribers worldwide—or 90 percent of the planet's population—had mobile phones (up from 55.5 million just fifteen years earlier). In Canadian media theorist Marshall McLuhan's terms in 1962, a "global village" had arisen in which innovations in communications and transportation not only increased movement of goods and services but created interactive bonds that harmonized and even homogenized tastes and cultures.[97]

The Demise of Bretton Woods

Although the United States took pride in its role in promoting European integration, prosperity, and competition, the rise of its friends boded ill for its overall international accounts. These paid for the US presence overseas in the Cold War. A direct result of Western Europe's recovery, the American balance-of-payments deficit reflected both a dwindling US export surplus, the outward flow of direct investment, and Cold War military and aid expenditures. Under the rules of the Bretton Woods exchange system, nations holding stashes of dollars could cash in their growing reserves for American gold upon demand rather than hold dollars entirely as interest-bearing notes. The United States honored this agreement because gold was the economic and psychological foundation of the international monetary system, and the dollar was the key currency that undergirded American power and leadership.

By 1958 ten European governments allowed their currencies to be converted more freely into dollars. This signaled the health of regional economies (and thus the success of American postwar recovery policies), but convertibility quickened the drain of gold from the United States. America's gold stocks dropped by $2 billion that year and plummeted further the next. Deemed the price to pay for its leadership of the Western alliance, this conversion process led to the loss of nearly half of US gold reserves between 1958 and 1968. Washington tried to maintain the dollar's value by trade promotion and other measures. Instead of devaluing the dollar, the US Treasury stomached stopgap remedies and urged more multilateral burden sharing within the alliance. Yet the payments imbalance grew worse, giving de Gaulle and others leverage over US foreign policy, because they could threaten a run on Fort Knox.[98]

Spending on the Vietnam War exacerbated the deficit, as inflation wracked the US domestic economy while global economic instability continued. With expenditures for the war in Southeast Asia running at $10 to $14 billion a year, Congress worried that the conflict could destroy the world monetary system. At home, the negative impact was clear. Wages rose with prices, as war spending doubled the consumer price index in 1966 and 1967 and almost tripled it the following year. Lyndon Johnson was well aware of the impact of the Vietnam War on inflation, the bogeyman of the American economy for decades afterward. War and aid expenditures added to tensions within the Western alliance. As central banks persisted in trading dollars for gold, allies intensified their questioning of America's role in the world and especially in overseeing the defense of Western Europe. The economic situation now threatened American foreign policy; Washington seemed headed toward a tough choice of either defending the dollar or defending Europe.[99]

Clearly the bottom was fast falling out of the Bretton Woods system. A financial crisis in Britain in 1967 finally led to the devaluation of the pound, a currency long under pressure but saved by periodic American bailouts to prop up its value. When the Suez Canal closed during the Six-Day War in the Middle East, British exports plummeted and Arab countries exchanged their large sterling holdings for dollars, thereby fleeing the pound. This led France to demand that the dollar be complemented by some other form of currency in order to stabilize the monetary system and end America's practice of paying for inflation at home by running deficits overseas. The result was the Eurodollar, an expatriate currency market bigger than the reserves of America and all central banks combined, as well as an IMF-sponsored system of special drawing rights that provided more international liquidity and overcame the national payments deficit. Neither measure sufficed. As the gold drain continued into early March 1968 (in one day, the United States lost $179 million in gold), hopes waned for the Bretton Woods system's continuation. When bankers agreed to sever the dollar's link to gold in private markets, gold prices began to rise. This tenuous new deal was dependent on confidence that the overvalued dollar could be defended even as private capital flows soared upward. The Americans barely contained the instability by clamping down on outflows of capital, but much tension existed within the Western alliance over whether dollar-rich nations, such as West Germany, should revalue or whether the French should devalue the franc, which de Gaulle ultimately refused to do. Experts broached the idea of ending altogether the fixed exchange-rate regime of Bretton Woods and allowing the dollar to "float" against other currencies. Essentially, this meant that the United States would go off the gold standard, ending the link of bullion to dollars and possibly issuing a blow to American hegemony.

After neglecting the monetary system in its first two years, the Nixon administration turned to a more dramatic fix that midwifed the modern era of globalization. A debate emerged as to whether domestic inflation was the culprit, as monetarists believed, or whether the American payments deficit—worsened by aid burdens—needed to be addressed. Nixon focused on inflation, which was spiraling out of control and threatening both the trade surplus and monetary convertibility. He also told frustrated world bankers that the "dollar may be our currency but it's your problem."[100] Actually, the president continued previous US policy of fiscal restraint, and such austerity measures resulted in an international payments surplus in 1969, the first in nine years. The accomplishment never occurred again, however, and mounting unemployment and debt worried the administration. Losses in Congress for Republicans during the midterm elections of 1970, moreover, alarmed a White House looking toward reelection in 1972. It was time to reflate the economy, but this brought a wave of speculation against the dollar in global currency markets in 1971.[101]

Bretton Woods had made the dollar the world's key medium of exchange, against which all other national currencies were measured, but under international monetary rules the dollar could not be devalued to correct a payments deficit. This left the conversion of dollars to gold, yet the process was clearly dysfunctional and unworkable. After the American payments deficit was projected to reach a huge $22 billion for the year, Nixon acted. Rather than focus solely on Europeans, especially the West Germans, to increase their share of the NATO defense burden, recommendations emanating from the Treasury Department counseled an overhaul of the Bretton Woods system. This could be done in a variety of ways, many of them already on the table, but most effective would be forcibly realigning currencies and, in the event that the European run on the greenback continued, suspending the convertibility of dollar reserves into gold and negotiating a new, flexible monetary regime entirely.

The subsequent actions that gutted the Bretton Woods fixed system of exchange were less revolutionary than evolutionary, although the unilateralism followed by the United States certainly jarred America's allies and tested the multilateral ethic. The new policies announced by the administration after a historic meeting of officials on August 15, 1971, were tough, and the rhetoric was even harsher. Ominously, no State Department member was invited, and even National Security Advisor Henry Kissinger was unaware of the gathering. Instead, economic nationalists ruled the day. Led by Treasury Secretary John Connally, who had informed international bankers that the United States would no longer engage in a system that did not achieve America's long-term interests, the administration imposed its bold New Economic Policy of wage and price controls, a tariff increase, and, most important, a suspension of dollar convertibility into gold. By slamming shut the gold window, Nixon appealed to a domestic audience but alarmed those at home and abroad who cherished monetary and trade liberalization. Later he admitted his hasty error, but the president sought a new international monetary system to prevent the dollar crisis from interfering with his domestic economic program and reelection bid. Such crude mercantilism shocked those who looked to the United States as the proponent of the open-door capitalist system now that the quarter-century-old Bretton Woods system was on life support.

Nixon stunned global financial networks into abrupt change. He refused to depreciate the dollar, so central banks largely went along with the new approach by letting their currencies float downward. France initially imposed controls on capital in order to bolster the franc before giving way. Japan proved to be the staunchest defender of the old system, as Tokyo attempted to maintain the rate of 360 yen to the dollar by purchasing $4 billion in reserves in the first two weeks after the Nixon announcement. Japan looked like a dollar hoarder, but it could also be browbeaten into accepting the floating regime as a country dependent on trade and defense support from the United States. Like the other nations, Japan succumbed to the realities of US power.

In November 1971 the ten big capitalist powers met in Washington to sign the Smithsonian Agreement. In return for America devaluing the dollar to $38 per ounce of gold, Japan appreciated its currency (making its exports more expensive) by a whopping 16.9 percent and West Germany revalued upward by over 13.5 percent. Whereas the Bretton Woods accord permitted nations to trade currencies within 1 percent of each other as a stabilization mechanism, the Smithsonian Agreement widened the bands to 2.25 percent. Even this arrangement turned out to be temporary, as the entire monetary system soon turned ever more volatile. Over the next two years dollars poured out of the country again. This prompted more diplomacy to force appreciation of foreign currencies as the dollar was revalued again from $38 to over $42 per ounce of gold. After European currency markets closed in early 1973, the market took over by allowing free-floating of currencies that moved up and down against the dollar. The Europeans and Japanese opposed this direction, viewing a declining dollar as a burden on their trade. Yet they also were importing American inflation if they stayed the course (something that they were to suffer anyway because of their dependence on the US economy). Above all, the United States refused to support the dollar by artificial means. When new treasury secretary George Schultz announced that "Santa Claus is dead" in 1973, Bretton Woods was buried.

The overhaul of the monetary system had immediate success for the Americans and a lasting impact on global economic governance. Clearly the United States had become less competitive as the dollar had become overvalued, and thus the Nixon economic shock had been designed to keep investments at home and sell exports abroad. The Bretton Woods institutions—the IMF and World Bank—saw their job descriptions altered. The former was no longer needed to oversee national controls and supply payments assistance to developed nations. Instead, the Fund turned to integrating Third World nations into the global economy, training officials in the practice of opening markets and joining the GATT trade regime. In short, the institution emerged as an agent of neoliberal, free enterprise, market ideology. The World Bank joined in this movement, continuing its focus on financial and technical assistance to developing countries and also seeking safeguards for international investors in the Third World. Meanwhile, as capital controls were eased, US multinationals resumed their headlong rush into overseas markets to add to their dominance. And because the Europeans were still a quarter century away from establishing their own single currency to compete with the Americans, the dollar resumed its privileged position as the world's medium of exchange. The floating dollar set the foundation for multilateral openness; global trade and financial expansion underlay the market revolution and globalization process of later decades.[102] In the short haul, the Nixon team and the world faced a world economy in trouble.

3. *Prying Open the Door*

AT roughly the same time as market forces emerged in the international monetary regime, the advanced nations experienced the worst downturn in their global economic fortunes since the Great Depression. In the United States, inflation shot up followed by interest rates at record levels. Unemployment also jumped, while the real gross national product dropped by 2 percent. Similar problems occurred in the rest of the industrial world as inflation accelerated in the early 1970s and hit an average rate of 13 percent in 1974 in the ten largest noncommunist nations. While prices had risen roughly 2.5 percent during the mid-1960s, from 1968 through 1975 consumers from these countries paid between 47 percent and 127 percent more for goods. Experts blamed an overregulated economy (prompted in part by new environmental protections), self-indulgence, government entitlement programs, and America's monetary hegemony that allowed for inflation to be transferred across borders by other nations' addiction to cheap US credit. One major factor in inflation and the downturn arose from the explosion in the prices of raw materials—namely food but most notably petroleum. The skyrocketing cost of oil seemed to defy standard economic predictions of correlating prices to boom and busts in the business cycle as well as American effectiveness to control the global economy and gain from its open-door ideology.

The United States' plunge due to soaring oil prices had a ripple effect on the world economy. Americans represented just 6 percent of the world's population but consumed nearly a third of the world's oil. After World War II, US suppliers managed to limit imports, dominate the tremendous domestic market, and keep prices low through modest excise taxes. As a result, low retail costs sparked consumption. The gap between US consumption and global use widened, although overall world oil demand doubled every decade since the war. Lacking oil fields of their own, Western Europe and Japan imported vast amounts, but in 1950 even the United States became a net importer. The simple equation of demand combined with insufficient supply led to price increases. Sensing an opportunity for tremendous profits, oil-rich nations formed the Organization of Petroleum Exporting Countries (OPEC) in 1960. This producer cartel aimed to control supply and raise prices in pursuit of high revenues.

OPEC posed the most significant economic challenge ever to the nations of the North by a Third World entity. The advanced nations had long dominated world oil markets, helping to ensure a favorable political environment, military protection, and profits for the major oil companies—the Seven Sisters (five US companies along with British Petroleum and the Anglo-Netherlands firm Royal Dutch Shell). These "majors" built an oligopoly to divvy up oil fields, set prices, and undersell competitors. They held the producer nations hostage, granting small, fixed royalty payments in return for total control of global markets. Host governments managed to increase royalty and tax revenues as imports into industrialized nations rose, but the Seven Sisters continued to dominate noncommunist petroleum production, blocking any other companies from entering any part of the exploration, refining, distribution, and marketing processes. Yet such hegemony was in jeopardy. High Western demand, rising Arab nationalism, and emerging nations' discontent with their paltry returns in the American-led global economic system led the CIA to conclude in 1960 that "there may develop a kind of 'creeping' nationalization under which the companies gradually retreat to a position where they are little more than managing agents of the local governments."[103]

Several factors led to OPEC's ascendancy. New oil-producing players like Algeria, Libya, and Nigeria entered the game, more refineries were built to increase competition for the Seven Sisters, and skyrocketing demand reduced the oligopoly's ability to control prices by restricting supply. In addition, when the Eisenhower administration slapped quotas on imported oil in 1959 in order to protect domestic producers from cheap competitive foreign oil (a betrayal of its market dogma), the Seven Sisters saw the oil business slipping away. They produced 90 percent of non–North American and communist nation crude oil in 1952, but by 1968 they accounted for only 75 percent of the total. Competition and protectionism forced the majors to drop the official posted price of oil, which meant that royalty payments would fall for host nations. In self-defense these states, led by Libya and Saudi Arabia, renegotiated royalty deals with the majors and accumulated growing foreign exchange reserves as a result. Infuriated by the American quotas, five countries—Iran, Iraq, Kuwait, Saudi Arabia, and Venezuela—formed their OPEC petroleum bloc. The cartel managed to keep the posted prices from falling throughout the 1960s, but it could not force America to ease quotas or convince companies to reduce production and thus raise prices. OPEC's weak hand changed in 1970, however, for the Western industrial nations had exposed their dependence upon oil for energy use. By this time the cartel controlled the flow of the most important commodity in the world.[104]

OPEC seized the opportunity presented by the vulnerable industrialized nations. By 1972 Western Europe and Japan relied on oil for about 60 percent and 73 percent, respectively, of their energy needs (and the Americans for nearly half), four-fifths of which came from the Middle East and North Africa. Libyan dictator Muammar Gaddafi precipitated the oil revolution in 1970 by threatening to nationalize independent giant Occidental Petroleum and then cut production. Unable to gain backing from Western governments or the Seven Sisters, Occidental caved and not only raised its prices but also granted Libya a 20 percent increase in royalties and taxes. Other independents bowed, too, and OPEC made similar demands to the majors at the end of the year. Faced with a unilateral severing of oil supplies, the Seven Sisters signed a five-year agreement in 1971 that raised Persian Gulf oil from $1.80 to $2.29 per barrel with a requirement for an annual rate hike to offset inflation and an increase in royalties. The majors received a five-year lock on prices in return. The falling dollar during the demise of Bretton Woods undercut the price of oil; a new oil accord took account of fluctuating exchange rates and adjusted the posted price upward to $2.48 per barrel. Occidental's owner, Armand Hammer, warned, "Everybody who drives a tractor, truck, or car in the Western world will be affected" by OPEC.[105]

This was just the beginning of OPEC's muscle flexing. Independent oil companies joined Saudi Arabia, Qatar, and Abu Dhabi to discuss augmenting host-nation ownership of production facilities. Such nationalization would begin at one-quarter ownership and rise to 51 percent by 1982. By 1973 Libya seized total control of a dozen oil companies. The next year the shah of Iran expropriated all petroleum production facilities, and then Kuwait compensated British Petroleum and Gulf Oil $50 million for their joint concession in the country. By mid-decade, the long-standing ARAMCO holdings of Exxon, Mobil, Socal, and Texaco were handed over to the Saudis in exchange for marketing rights for the Dhahran fields; Baghdad took over the Iraq Petroleum Company holdings; and Venezuela completed expropriation of foreign oil concessions. Qatar and Dubai nationalized foreign holdings by the end of the 1970s. The Seven Sisters' oligopoly ceased to exist in reality.

Consumers, not companies, were the real victims of the OPEC revolution, however. The majors continued to benefit, because the posted price was frozen for five years, despite surging demand for oil that naturally inflated prices. In addition, inflation in the West and dollar devaluation kept real earnings at modest levels. Thus, in early October 1973, OPEC and the Seven Sisters entered into negotiations to raise the price of oil. The cartel demanded a 15 percent increase in prices to offset the dollar's recent depreciation. The majors delayed the talks, which turned out to be a big mistake. Just two days before these meetings, the Yom Kippur War erupted, pitting the Organization of Arab Petroleum Exporting Countries (a complement to OPEC born in 1968 after the Six-Day War to use oil as political leverage) against the Western states, consumers, and companies who sided with Israel. When the majors jumped at the 15 percent price rise, Saudi oil minister Ahmed Zaki Yamani told them that now OPEC sought a 100 percent hike. The multinationals adjourned for two weeks to consult their governments. In their talks with the Nixon administration, they warned that backing Israel might jeopardize the "whole U.S. oil position in [the] Middle East."[106]

Sure enough, within days the Arab OPEC states more than doubled crude oil prices to $5.12 per barrel, and Libya and Iran went beyond that figure by auctioning their supplies to the highest bidders. The cartel then decided to cut back production by 5 percent a month and slapped an embargo on exports to the United States until Israel conceded territory in the war. By December 23, OPEC unilaterally doubled the price of Persian Gulf oil to $11.65 per barrel. The Seven Sisters consented, knowing that Western consumers would bear the brunt of the higher cost and that Latin American and African output could fill any shortages. President Nixon warned Americans of impending energy shortages, even though, like previous administrations, his had allowed the majors to run the international oil business.

Sheikh Ahmed Zaki Yamani, oil minister for Saudi Arabia, December 1973. Yamani led the OPEC nations in their successful demands to raise oil prices. The oil-producing countries and kingdoms rewrote the rules of the world economy, and reshaped the power structure, after the first oil crisis of 1973. (Getty Images)

The oil-exporting nations could not lose in playing pure market economics as long as demand stayed firm and supplies remained limited. They completely controlled prices, negotiating among themselves over production rates in a show of producer unity. Saudi Arabia and Kuwait, the major producers, led the way in cutting production (and absorbing the costs) to keep up the price. Market conditions remained so tight that companies capitulated to OPEC, receiving technology and transportation contracts for their loss of ownership to the oil states. As for the consumer nations, in 1974 the United States tried to persuade Japan and Western Europe to form a consumer cartel to boycott purchases of oil and take economic or even military action against anti-Israeli producer states. America's allies refused, preferring dialogue with the nations on which they depended for foreign oil. They did agree to an American plan to create the International

Energy Agency to stockpile and share oil and looked to develop alternative sources of energy, but by and large the industrialized countries did not cooperate with each other. While Washington placed faith in the new agency and proposals to break the unity of the producers, the Europeans and Japanese signed bilateral agreements with OPEC that undercut a consumer bloc. The Americans resorted to warning or persuading their friends to end the destabilizing impact of price increases on the world economy, but even such allies as the shah of Iran sought to make as much profit as possible on the backs of US consumers. Oil had opened the door to economic blackmail over the North.[107]

The entire global economy had been restructured by the OPEC oil crisis. OPEC spurred a massive transfer of wealth that boosted the international payments position of the producer states, undercut the finances of the industrialized world, and further impoverished Third World countries not blessed with oil by sticking them with higher import bills. By 1977 America imported over one-quarter of its energy supplies from abroad, nearly triple the portion from 1960. Like its Western European and Japanese counterparts, the United States relied on OPEC, which enjoyed earnings of $140 billion, a sevenfold boost in revenues since 1973. The oil sheikhs spent into deficit by the late 1970s, but they were assured of revenues because they owned the oil. Throughout the world, dependence on oil depressed economic growth due to higher prices. The situation most hurt the Americas and Africa, though less so Asia because many of the developing nations (as well as Japan) paid for their petroleum by augmenting exports of manufactures to the West. Doing so, however, instigated protectionist pressures from manufacturers in the United States, such as automakers who now faced a tide of cheap but well-made and appealing smaller cars from abroad. Less enamored with American power after the Nixon monetary shock, Western allies turned increasingly to selling Arab nations arms and goods in order to placate the oil ministers in OPEC's headquarters in Vienna. Meanwhile Japan embraced the Arab world, receiving oil in return for Nissan's becoming the auto sales champion in Saudi Arabia. The world economy entered an era of transformation to globalization, in which America remained dominant but increasingly only one power among many.[108]

Under the leadership of Saudi Arabia (OPEC's biggest producer and exporter, holding the world's largest petroleum reserves), the oil nations ably manipulated output according to whether the world was in a period of excess or tight supply, and amassed huge financial reserves accordingly. The Gulf States did not seek inordinately high prices that might choke off consumer demand and undermine the oil-based world economy. They also noted that the North sought other sources of oil in the North Sea, Alaska, and the Soviet Union and engaged in conservation efforts by buying smaller cars. The Saudis clamped down on the efforts of aggressive OPEC nations with smaller petroleum reserves but ambitious development plans, such as Venezuela, Iran, Iraq, and Nigeria, to curb production by either absorbing reductions in output in slack times (1978) or increasing output when supplies were restricted (1979–1980). They also worked to moderate radical political policies. By and large the West adapted to higher gasoline prices and grudgingly accepted stabilized prices. There was a price to pay for this approach, however, as auto factories closed throughout the US Midwest, and employment (as well as prices) rose. President Jimmy Carter declared war on energy crises and urged Americans to moderate their consumer habits, but the United States was unable to shirk its addiction to imported oil.[109]

Revolution in Iran in 1978 brought a crashing end to Saudi-led moderation. The West had emerged from the worst of the recession by late 1975, and demand for oil resumed. But Iran, which exported 17 percent of OPEC's oil, fell into turmoil that resulted in the overthrow of the shah and the cutoff of petroleum supplies to the West by 1979 under an Islamist government. The Gulf States largely filled the gap, but companies and consumer nations began stockpiling oil to offset predicted shortfalls in supply. Prices shot up on turbulent world oil markets. OPEC raised prices in December 1978, the first significant increase in five years, and both long-term contract and short-term flexible "spot" markets panicked after the Iranian revolution. All oil not under contract was sold on this spot market, which adjusted to market conditions, and volatility around the globe spurred spot sales well above the set contract price of $13.34 per barrel of Saudi Arabian light crude in early 1979. Even Saudi Arabia could not prevent free-for-all price hikes and disorder in the world oil economy. By March 1979 OPEC announced a 14.5 percent increase in the cost of a barrel of oil. In July prices rose again. The departing US secretary of energy, James Schlesinger, announced, "We face a world crisis of vaster dimensions than Churchill described a half century ago—made more ominous by the problems of oil. . . . The energy future is bleak and is likely to grow bleaker in the decade ahead."[110]

The seller's market soon turned, although the reprieve for consumer nations was temporary. By mid-1980 Saudi production and world consumption leveled out, but war between Iraq and Iran in September led to the cessation of oil exports from both nations. World supplies fell by 10 percent, allowing OPEC to raise contract prices to $33 per barrel and the spot price to $41. This second oil shock precipitated soul-searching about America's coddling of the shah and Israel and whether consumer interests (the market) should prevail over foreign policy concerns. Saudi Arabia and other OPEC nations lost some faith in the reliability of the United States to lead the world and specifically stabilize the Middle East, particularly during the fifteen-month hostage crisis in Iran. In these dark days for consumer nations, experts began to predict years of uncertainty ahead for the global economy and an end to American open-door multilateralism.

By the early 1980s, OPEC proved its own worst enemy as its members' wealth and diversity tore apart the consensus that had so enriched the organization. Substitutes for oil, such as natural gas, nuclear power, and coal—stimulated by high energy costs created by OPEC—combined with recession to meet global demand. Conservation efforts within industrial nations also helped lower prices, as did the dumping of oil by companies eager to avoid high interest rates that accompanied large inventories. Furthermore, new suppliers jumped into the market to whittle away at OPEC's dominance. The USSR raised its exports to the capitalist countries to earn more foreign exchange; Britain and Norway entered the oil business with discoveries in the North Sea; Brazil, India, and China raised their output; Americans looked closer to home for secure suppliers in Canada, Mexico, and Venezuela. Between 1980 and 1990, oil imports from the Western Hemisphere swelled by 240 percent, to 729 barrels, while those from the Middle East dropped by one-quarter to 681 barrels. Whereas OPEC held 63 percent of the world market in 1973, its share fell to less than a third ten years later. As a consequence, revenues for Saudi Arabia tumbled from $102 billion in 1981 to just $37 billion in 1983, and the Gulf states suffered equally. In 1983, after the Saudi oil minister Yamani noted that the organization's prices were too far above what the world market could bear, OPEC, for the first time, cut prices.

During the 1980s the cartel began to fall apart as several OPEC countries began to cheat by producing above the agreed-upon limits and moderate nations could not completely halt the chaos. The result was a leaning toward American market forces rather than prices fixed by governments. Algeria, Iran, Libya, Venezuela, and Nigeria all raised their output over OPEC ceilings while cutting separate deals on freight costs and credit terms with consumer nations. Saudi Arabia and the Gulf states threatened to lower their prices to punish the cheaters, and a new intra-OPEC agreement limited production by reducing output and making Saudi Arabia responsible for regulating supply. But more oil was traded on spot markets as oil companies no longer feared price hikes. Prices eventually stabilized, but price wars during the decade prompted by oil gluts kept revenues flat or only slightly on the rise. In mid-decade, Britain, Mexico, and Norway actually lowered prices below the price set by OPEC. This forced OPEC to cut prices to $28 per barrel, and Saudi Arabia reduced its production to one-fourth of normal levels (2.5 million barrels per day) before abandoning its role as the cartel's regulator. By the end of the year, OPEC decided to permit the market to determine the cost of a barrel of oil. Production increased during 1986, but the new price target of $18 was much lower than earlier in the decade. In fact, adjusted for inflation, that price was one-quarter less than the $11.65 that OPEC had imposed in 1973 while production fell by two-thirds of the level of just five years before.[111]

The end of the Iraq-Iran war in 1988 affected oil markets. Both nations sought to produce more oil in order to rebuild their economies, but when OPEC could not agree on a production arrangement, the Saudis glutted the market. Prices fell to $13 a barrel, below the level of 1974 in real terms. OPEC discipline on output and pricing was shattered, and conflict ensued. Iraq exacerbated the dysfunction by seeking high oil prices in order to pay off huge debts incurred during the war. Neighboring Kuwait sought to lower prices as a way to discourage non-OPEC production and deter unfriendly Iraq from retooling its military. Thus, Kuwait refused to prop up prices in 1989 under a new quota arrangement. After OPEC tried to resolve the two nations' differences over production and prices, Saddam Hussein's Iraqi troops invaded Kuwait in August 1990. Both producer and consumer nations rushed to Kuwait's side, because the kingdom accounted for one-fifth of known world oil reserves and occupied a position from which the Iraqi dictator could also threaten Saudi Arabia and interrupt the flow of OPEC oil. A large coalition of nations issued an embargo against Iraqi oil that halted exports of 4.3 million barrels a day, or 7 percent of the world total. Oil prices spiked upward as a result, but the coalition drew on stockpiles of oil and increases in output from OPEC and other producers to draw down prices from $40 to $33 by the time Kuwait was liberated, by a US-led coalition of military forces in an action mandated by the United Nations, in January 1991.

The war's end exposed OPEC as an unmanageable organization. Despite Saudi influence, OPEC members headed in divergent directions. Besides, the cartel also failed to cooperate with nonmembers such as Mexico and Britain, both of which also went their independent ways when it came to production and setting prices. For the former, the 1994 peso crisis further restricted its ability to make arrangements with OPEC. The Gulf War, therefore, added to the turmoil in the world oil market that benefited the consumer countries in the 1990s.

OPEC hinted at the power of globalization to trump security politics. Cold War dogma had pushed the United States to privilege private enterprise over regulation for security reasons. But Washington had granted the oil multinationals great freedom to run world petroleum markets without fear of antitrust prosecution or congressional intrusion. This system lasted until the producer nations exercised their power, bringing privatization to a screeching halt by the 1970s. By that time it was too late for the United States to reform its pseudomarket policies that elevated the Seven Sisters to oligopolistic status. The North paid the price in punishing oil costs and lost revenues for decades thereafter.[112]

Third World Dreams

Ominously, the soaring "OPEC tax" burdened non-oil-producing Third World treasuries even more than the advanced nations. The price shock halted development efforts by curbing growth through trade expansion. In short, high prices for energy crippled payments balances, as the value of oil imports overwhelmed export profits. In Latin America, Guatemala and El Salvador experienced trade deficits that rocketed from $12 million in 1972 to $112 and $104 million, respectively, in 1975. The answer for some was to borrow from OPEC nations or the

North and thus enter a cycle of debt. These nations really occupied a "Fourth World" of nations, so hopelessly indebted that they could not climb toward the sorry status of Third World.[113]

For others, desperate times provided an opportunity. Producers of copper, bauxite, iron ore, bananas, and coffee organized against the American liberal trade system by forging cartels in attempts to limit supplies and raise prices during the 1970s. The North was reliant on imports of tin and coffee, and Western Europe and Japan, which lacked resource endowments, needed Third World copper, phosphates, and other goods. Thus, Jamaica succeeded in raising taxes and royalties on bauxite, and Morocco unilaterally hiked prices for phosphates. In the short term, market conditions favored producer cartels, and the structure of some sectors (bananas, bauxite) allowed for taxing multinationals or even nationalizing production. In the long run, however, cartels did not possess commodities with the value and inelastic supply of oil. Buyers of copper could use aluminum instead, and tea might be substituted for coffee. There was no replacement for petroleum. In addition, few producer cartels took a long-term perspective to building monetary reserves, preferring short-term gain. Finally, in the event of a true threat to adequate supplies in the North, advanced nations might act politically or militarily to prevent nationalization.[114]

Some struggling countries, recognizing the iron grip of multinational enterprises on their resources and observing the success of OPEC's nationalization efforts, turned to expropriation as the response to poverty. One example arose from the election of the avowed Marxist Salvador Allende in Chile, whom the Nixon administration feared might provide an entry point for Soviet and Cuban operatives in the Western Hemisphere. Chile suffered from low growth, underdevelopment, and the oligopolistic hold of foreign companies on its economy, particularly its copper mines. Allende set out to correct the disparities, singling out International Telephone and Telegraph (ITT) for nationalization. ITT accounted for $200 million of American investors' total of $964 million of holdings in the country. The United States, fearing the move was a prelude to expropriating the facilities of Kennecott Copper and Anaconda Copper Mining Company, decided to oust him. This successful operation (Allende was killed in September 1973) not only involved illicit CIA activity but used economic measures such as preventing IMF credits to Chile and fomenting strikes to destabilize the

Salvador Allende, president of Chile, September 1973. The socialist leader was overthrown and as-sassinated in a coup by a military junta. The Americans feared that his nationalization of interna-tional copper companies would set off more Third World revolts against the market economy. (© Luis Orlando Lagos Vázquez/The Dmitri Baltermants Collection/Corbis)

socialist government. The Cold War continued to take precedence in these mean economic times; the emerging nations would have to seek other ways to promote their interests.[115]

The United Nations called the 1960s the Decade of Development, but the next ten years were a decade of despair and debt. The situation prompted a campaign for a "North–South dialogue" to redress world economic relationships. New on this score was the tying of oil prices to development programs; what was not original was the persistent demand for special consideration for the South within the American free-enterprise system. After the UNCTAD revolt in the mid-1960s, the Group of 77 developing nations demanded a reordering of global wealth. The oil crisis highlighted the ongoing trend of impoverishment within a capitalist order that promised but did not always deliver robust growth and modernization, and elevated anticommunism over attacking international poverty. Protests percolated into a strategy of seeking change through the Declaration for the Establishment of a New International Economic Order (NIEO), a set of proposals announced by the Group of 77 in May 1974. The effort became another forum of opportunity to redress the inequities of the open-door trade and financial system. The South called for unilateral sacrifices by the North. Under the NIEO these included the old demands for one-sided commitments to provide aid and technology transfers with no strings attached and to grant generalized tariff preferences with no insistence on reciprocity from the developing world. The G-77 insisted on regulation and control of multinational corporations operating in their nations and on the freedom to expropriate or nationalize foreign holdings. Producer cartels were suggested, and to ensure their success the NIEO wanted the North to pledge not to interfere with them. In sum, the measures not only spoke to restitution for past ills but took a more confrontational stance to address the new realities caused by high oil prices and the inspiration of OPEC. The NIEO directly challenged the power of the United States, Western Europe, and Japan.[116]

Although the UN General Assembly approved the Declaration, the effort faced major obstacles. First, emerging countries shared a vision but not common strategies to achieve global economic reform. This weakness had long undermined concerted efforts to change the system. Newly industrializing countries, such as Brazil, Chile, and Mexico in Latin America and the four "Asian Tigers" of Taiwan, South Korea, Hong Kong, and Singapore, had different outlooks, needs, and objectives than the poorest nations. All but Hong Kong had adopted import substitution policies after World War II in order to develop manufacturing bases, but by the 1970s they sought more open export and capital markets and not more regulated trade, finance, aid, and investment projects. The Tigers wished to jettison the import substitution plans, which led to discrimination against their export drives. Furthermore, little unity with OPEC states existed; the world was divided by oil haves and have-nots. Third World nations not in the industrialization stage found themselves isolated in the wilderness of a punishing world economy. Added to the differential impact of the recession and energy (and food) crises as well as their different trajectories in the global economy were traditional political and economic rivalries that simply rendered consensus on the Declaration next to impossible.

Just as critical to the NIEO's prospects was the response of the North to this strategy of confrontation. Countries in America's circle of capitalist friends willingly engaged in a dialogue regarding the transformation of the international economy, particularly after recognizing that the first oil shock had ushered in a new era of relations in trade and monetary affairs. The North realized that inflated prices of grain, metals, fertilizers, cotton, wool, and rubber had increased the price of food for such desperately poor nations as Bangladesh, Vietnam, and many African countries. Initially resistant to an IMF plan to provide loans on easier terms to the less-developed countries because they might encourage producer cartels to opt out of the multilateral trade system, Washington reluctantly allowed the Fund to act like a bank under a special petroleum scheme by borrowing from surplus nations and lending to debtors. By August 1974, nine oil-rich states lent $3.6 billion to establish IMF special drawing rights. Eventually forty-four nations (most of them Third World but including Greece and Italy, both hard hit by the oil crisis) borrowed under this 1974 facility, which required an annual 7.7 percent interest rate. The next year, central banks in Europe and oil-producing countries donated funds again to Italy, Britain, Finland, Greece, New Zealand, Spain, and a handful of developing nations. The Americans remained tepid supporters, preferring aid (which diminished over the decade) to this multilateral lending effort. The United States balked at the restructuring of the world financial regime by the G-77 members.

Twenty-seven nations—nineteen emerging and eight from the North, including the United States—attended the Paris Conference on International Economic Cooperation in 1975 to discuss the NIEO. Angered by America's request for a confrontational oil consumer bloc rather than cooperation with the Middle East, France banked on the Conference for alternatives to US rule over the global economy. Washington hoped to sever the tightening bond between OPEC and developing nations, limit producer cartels, and keep industrialized economic allies in line with market policies. Secretary of State Henry Kissinger held the conference in contempt, but he felt compelled to attend a follow-up session in Nairobi in 1976 to head off a mutiny against American interests. To this end he suggested the establishment of a multilateral lending agency under the jurisdiction of the World Bank to direct private capital into mineral resource sectors. OPEC also initiated its own funding programs, including the Arab Fund for

Economic and Social Development, the Islamic Development Fund, the African Development Bank, and another that set a target pool of $5 billion run by OPEC ministers.[117] Yet global recession persisted, requiring ever higher infusions of capital from these lending institutions (which provided more loans by the second oil shock in 1979). And developing nations could not overcome US-led opposition to many key elements of the Declaration. When the Soviet Union did not step into the breach, due to its own economic problems, and countries within the Southern coalition split, the NIEO was clearly in trouble.

The conference did not even issue a communiqué. There was agreement to establish a common fund to stabilize commodity prices and reach a higher target of aid, and a pledge to provide $1 billion to the emerging nations. UNC-TAD created the common fund in 1980, but not enough countries ratified it into existence. The aid target of 0.7 percent of each advanced nation's gross national product was never attained, and the $1 billion promise was window dressing because that amount had already been committed. The quest for the NIEO waned by the late 1970s, replaced by efforts at self-help, privatized lending, and market prescriptions—in other words, American multilateral and free-enterprise programs.

Still, many of the NIEO's aims materialized both institutionally and in economic terms. The European Community (renamed from the EEC in 1967) signed the Lomé Convention with forty-six associated African, Caribbean, and Pacific states in 1975. Because the Western Europeans were more reliant on trade than the United States was, they acknowledged the need to prevent supply interruptions in the hard times of the 1970s. Thus, the EC pledged to increase aid, committing billions of dollars through the European Development Fund over the lifetime of the Convention. The Lomé Convention was renewed three times, until replaced by the Cotonou Agreement in 2000. Investment assistance was also forthcoming. In addition, the Lomé Convention provided preferential treatment for these nations' exports to the EC without reciprocity based on a quota applied to competitive goods like beef and sugar. Finally, the Convention created a financial arrangement, STABEX, to stabilize export earnings on twelve commodities particularly subject to price fluctuation on the world market. In typical open-door fashion, the United States protested the Lomé Convention, arguing that the preferential deals discriminated against nonmember goods. In the mid-1990s the World Trade Organization agreed with the Americans, and the EC and United States negotiated a settlement. Disputes on commodities—most famously on favored Caribbean banana exports to Europe—continued to show that Washington seemed to care more for principles and free markets than for radical programs.[118]

The Americans preferred that the South work through GATT, the traditional liberal-trade forum, for their development needs, although US policies could be hypocritical, owing to the economic downturn in the country's manufacturing sectors. At the Tokyo Round (1975–1979), emerging nations won exemptions from reciprocity and nondiscrimination rules, permanent legal status for the generalized system of preferences, and special treatment for the poorest among them. In return, the South would gradually lose its preferences as development took off, after which GATT obligations would be in force. The American campaign against preferences continued into the Uruguay Round (1986–1994), at which forty-six developing countries participated, more than ever at GATT forums. Of special significance for Washington were the Asian Tigers, whose export-led growth policies made them effective competitors.

These Asian nations highlighted a new approach to the global economy: a pragmatic engagement that focused on GATT multilateralism and the open door. The Tigers targeted light manufactures as a means of development, but such goods as textiles had influential constituencies in the United States. Advanced nations complained that the Tigers engaged in unfair trade practices such as dumping, export subsidies, and mercantilist import restrictions and that they did not need the coddling of preferences. As the South emerged by the mid-1970s as the most important source of manufactured goods for the North, the protests against cheap-labor Third World exports became louder. The Americans compelled the signing of numerous pernicious voluntary restraint agreements on many products, including textiles, as a protectionist response that defied its open-door principles. By 1978 nearly half of the agreements applied to Third World exports. By the Uruguay Round the EC, Japan, and the United States had increased nontariff barriers on their imports, including 55 percent of iron and steel imports, 80 percent of clothing imports, and more than 25 percent of footwear from abroad. The emerging world thus lobbied for more market access and a rollback of protectionist measures. Indeed, textile quotas were elimi-

nated over the ten years after the Uruguay Round, while the South won a promise of 20 percent cuts in agricultural subsidies by the new millennium under an
ambitious proposal offered by the United States and backed by the Cairns Group
of fourteen smaller producing countries. The promise was not honored in 2000,
and there was also suspicion that its terms were circumscribed by both the EC,
which opposed an end to subsidies, and US negotiators, among them representatives from the big agricultural food-processing and distribution companies like
Cargill.[119] Thus, real progress for the average developing nation dependent on
trade in agricultural goods was hard to come by.

For their part, the Asian Tigers and other developed Third World nations
aggravated protectionist sentiment in the North, but they also exposed the hy-
pocrisy of preaching but not living by the open-door doctrine. They gained market access but also resisted pressure to open their financial services markets, ease
restrictions on foreign investments, and implement intellectual property rules
(both new areas for GATT). They also used the Uruguay Round as a springboard to explore regional groupings that were created in the 1990s. Still, the
Uruguay Round barely made it to the finish line. Signed by 125 countries in
April 1994, the trade accord involved such contentious disputes over agricultural
subsidies and other issues that the new American president, Bill Clinton, focused
attention on jump-starting the talks. Barriers to trade in farm goods remained
high regardless of the antisubsidy pledge, and this challenge most affected the
Third World. Although the GATT director hailed the Uruguay Round as vital
to sustainable development, reporters countered that while the United States
and Europeans dickered over their slices of the "world-trade pie, developing
countries have wondered what's in it for them. Now, for some, the answer is
clear: the crumbs."[120]

Debt and Interdependence

Pragmatic reform arose in part due to an economic nightmare over financing
development. Because oil-shocked industrial nations were strapped for cash,
emerging countries could not count on flows of publicly financed aids and loans.
After the onset of the second oil crisis in 1978 and the advent of the fiscally conservative Reagan administration in the 1980s, the North looked for ways to assist

in development. Multilateral aid projects were one way, though Reagan frowned upon the expense and principle of handing out assistance. The Americans turned instead to an expansion of World Bank and IMF loans and increasingly to private bank credits. The Great Depression had witnessed massive international bank defaults, but by individual creditors. That memory, combined with debt restrictions in Argentina, Brazil, and Peru in the 1960s and general limits on predatory private commercial loan activity by Third World nations, had stymied such credits. In 1965, Mexico altered its laws to allow foreign private loans for public and private borrowers, and other countries followed. A younger generation of American bankers with no recollection of the Great Depression salivated at the prospects of opening new global capital markets. They took hold of private international lending policies. Deregulation of capital markets after the Bretton Woods system ended also gave commercial lenders freedom to compete effectively abroad without the burden of higher interest rates charged by local banks. And because Islam prohibited interest-bearing loans, these bankers commandeered huge deposits of OPEC petrodollars to satisfy the needs of developing nations, who themselves were willing to pay high interest rates to obtain loans. Bankers stepped in to globalize lending at great risk but also at great profit.[121]

The flow of money surged into the developing world as lenders and recipients grew increasingly optimistic about this system of privatized finance. Flush with OPEC cash, banks flooded markets in Latin America, Africa, and Asia. Between 1973 and 1981, annual borrowing by the non-oil-producing importers of the South rose from $6.5 billion to $293 billion. Their exports also shot up, and their gross domestic products were more than twice that of the North. Thus, emerging nations seemed able to service the debts. Roughly two-thirds of US private loans went to Latin America, due to proximity and bankers' familiarity with Latin American elites who had been educated in the United States. Literacy and life expectancy in the region went up. Multinational lending agencies and OPEC helped out the poorest of the poor. American and European financial institutions feasted at the till of the private lending market. They charged Third World borrowers a "risk premium" of a higher interest rate to safeguard their loans, and soon smaller banks jumped into the market to reap the abnormal profits of their larger counterparts. New debts piled on top of old debts month after month, as borrowers prepaid their existing loans so they could obtain more favorable terms on new ones. Seeking repayment, private bankers were compelled to make more loans so their clients could pay off old debts in an escalating cycle of mutual dependence built on paper. By 1982, external Third World debt reached 264 percent above its 1975 level. As long as interest rates remained low relative to inflation, borrowers could service these debts and the house of cards would stand.

Then the second oil shock and rising interest rates blew through the deck, prompting a massive Third World debt crisis. At each dollar hike in oil prices, the non-petroleum-producing nations had to come up with almost $2 billion per year in funds for their budgets. Private capital provided nearly half of the credits. The situation locked international bankers into riskier but enticing loans. As service costs rose to an average of 21 percent for all Third World nations (and to nearly 39 percent for the worst off) by 1979, lenders became more cautious and turned to short-term credits at interest rates that floated ever higher as inflation soared in the United States and Western Europe. Borrowers needed the money, oftentimes for consumption and not for investment and productive capital. In the case of Mexico, the country built steel mills, oil installations, and electrical power plants controlled by inefficient state agencies and corrupt companies. In other instances, aggressive bankers pushed loans on naive clients. As a result, Mexico's bill to foreign banks tripled between 1978 and 1982, while Argentina's and Chile's indebtedness rose 500 percent. Brazil salivated at financing huge public projects after a period of economic reform had led to vigorous growth. The country welcomed foreign credit with open arms, and loans flowed from Citibank, Bank of America, Morgan Guaranty, and Manufacturers Hanover, among others, in a process reliant on OPEC reserve surpluses.[122]

This regime could not last. Higher interest rates prompted capital flight from Latin America and elsewhere. Behind debt servicing, capital exports amounted to the second largest use of foreign exchange of these nations. Over a third of the $252 billion rise in the debt of Argentina, Brazil, Chile, Mexico, and Venezuela ended up in foreign bank accounts; Latin America held the largest and most rapidly rising portion of debt of all developing nations. In 1981, Latin America as a whole borrowed $34.6 billion but paid interest of $28.2 billion, giving it a net benefit of just $6.4 billion. The region as a whole sent abroad a net transfer of $106.7 billion between 1982 and 1985, more than it had received in the previous nine years combined. Chile suffered worst of all as its per capita gross national product decreased by one-fifth while unemployment shot up by nearly a third and the entire private sector nearly disappeared into bankruptcy. So ferocious was the downturn that some Third World banks borrowed money from foreigners and then reloaned it abroad to make a profit. That practice soon ended, however. After its defeat in the Falkland Islands by Britain in May 1982, Argentina defaulted on its $37 billion debt. In its fourth year of stagnation when the crisis hit, Venezuela sunk deeper in misery. Dependent on foreign finance, Brazil's economic fortunes so completely reversed that opposition parties joined with industrialists to oust the military from power and bring in a civilian government in 1985. After word in August that some American lenders were bankrupt, the Mexican government stunningly announced that it could no longer service its debts. Oil prices began to fall, which undermined the oil-rich Mexican economy. The US government rushed in with aid and credits to this important neighbor, and private bankers issued a moratorium on loan repayment from Mexico. The debt crisis was in full swing; a chain reaction of defaults swept over nearly the entire region.[123]

In the ensuing years, nations condemned higher interest rates while the Americans came up with the Baker Plan of 1985, named after the Treasury secretary, which provided an infusion of US government loans to debtors, curbed capital flight, and urged austerity measures to limit spending on consumption. Over the rest of the decade private banks wrote off their losses—Citicorp lost $1 billion in 1987—as they generally disengaged from the international lending market. Absorbing the losses lowered the outstanding loans of America's nine largest banks in the region from 177 percent of capital in 1982 to 84 percent, but the Baker Plan merely bought time. In 1989 the new Treasury secretary, James Brady, took measures to end the debt crisis altogether by calling for banks to reduce and reschedule debts on a voluntary basis in negotiation with each country. Private bankers restructured Mexico's debt of $69 billion by swapping old loans for new "Brady" bonds at reduced interest rates. The IMF, World Bank, Mexican government, and Japan guaranteed interest payments for eighteen months. This was the first instance of international debt forgiveness by commercial bankers. In 1994, after Brazil became the last major debtor nation to sign an agreement with 750 creditor banks, the crisis ended.[124]

International lending agency oversight replaced the private banking network of loans, but the IMF and World Bank became the instruments to encourage market doctrine. With support from the United States, Japan, and Western Europe, they set lending terms according to free-enterprise, conservative macroeconomic policies as the Cold War gave way to the era of globalization.[125] Under Structural Adjustment Programs, these institutions insisted upon domestic deregulation, privatization of state properties, austerity measures at home, trade liberalization, and more open investment climates. Debtor nations returned at least temporarily to a period of modest growth as private investments soared and privatization made millionaires (and even billionaires) out of local entrepreneurs. Yet the poorest nations remained mired in stagnation created by debt-servicing obligations, unequal terms of trade, and lack of control over markets.[126]

African Doldrums

Africa was a textbook example of this sad and alarming situation, particularly the region south of the Sahara, which was the most destitute area of the world. Despite the end of colonialism, much of Africa teetered on the brink of complete financial collapse from the 1980s onward. Many experts believed that the plagues of economic, political, and social turmoil removed the continent from the dynamism of world markets and the benefits of globalization. The causes were both internal corruption and inefficiency and the externally driven effects of unfavorable terms of trade, unequal exchange relationships, and Structural Adjustment Programs. Africa became a poster child of the worst conditions existing in the global economy.

Compared to the economies of other areas of the world, the African continent's economies were largely dysfunctional. To be sure, Nigeria, Angola, the Congo Republic, Gabon, and Cameroon enjoyed windfall profits from the oil crises. South Africa had exceptionally robust growth after World War II, due to its mineral resources, skilled management over the industrialization process, a sophisticated system of import substitution, and a favored position within the American Cold War orbit, which provided the country with capital. By the difficult economic times of the early 1970s, however, import substitution had run its course and South Africa's switch to an export-oriented strategy was ill-timed. In the 1980s the racist apartheid system instigated an outflow of capital as overseas investors either worried about violence or divested their holdings under pressure from civil rights constituencies at home. Wracked by the oil crises, inflation, plunging investment, and the end of cheap black labor once apartheid disappeared by the end of the decade, South Africa became a chapter in the story of general African economic decline in postwar history.[127]

The other forty-two nations of sub-Saharan Africa fared even worse. In 1995 the per capita gross national product of that vast region was fifty times smaller than the economies of the West. Whereas Americans registered average incomes of $26,980 per head, a citizen from a median African nation such as Mauritania earned just $460, and the poorest, such as Mozambique, suffered with just $80 per capita. Demographic trends exacerbated the economic problems; population bursts coupled with a high infant mortality rate, starvation, and disease hindered the development of a stable working class. By the mid-1990s, with illiteracy at over 40 percent, an educated workforce also was hard to find.[128]

The reasons behind such a depressing record are many, but Africa was a prime example of the unequal exchange system suffered by the South. Dominated by a monoculture of coffee, Rwanda depended on the vagaries of world market prices and could not generate any additional income should the crop fail, overseas demand slacken, or global prices weaken. Fourteen countries were in the same boat; Burundi and Uganda produced only coffee, while Zambia relied on copper and Somalia on livestock. Others produced only two, three, or four commodities. Some nations were luckier, for they possessed oil or possessed valued minerals such as uranium (Niger), bauxite (Guinea and Ghana), or diamonds (Sierra Leone), but even they were subject to periodic downturns that prompted political instability and interrupted development. Only eleven nations—South Africa, Tunisia, Lesotho, Zimbabwe, and Tanzania among them—enjoyed more diverse export economies, but they were often at the bottom of the global pecking order.

As a result, Africa remained dependent on the North in a neocolonial relationship that depressed prices because buyers essentially set prices in a closed system. For example, the French Sucden corporation purchased the entire cocoa harvest from the Côte d'Ivoire in 1988 at a bargain price because there were no other buyers. This pattern repeated throughout the continent resulted in a drop in African exports by 20 percent between 1980 and 1995. Compounding these difficulties were classic terms of trade disadvantages in which Africans not only sold abroad their cheap commodities at basement prices but had to import much higher-priced manufactured goods. Because foreign investors hesitated to sink capital into development projects, the unequal terms of trade meant that only 15 percent of the value of manufactures made with African raw materials returned to the continent—the North kept the rest. GATT trade negotiations did not seem to help; after the Uruguay Round in 1994, "like sheep being led to the slaughter," African delegates "went along and rubber-stamped the deal," even though they knew the continent "had nothing to gain from it."[129] The American market system trapped the continent and even put their survival at stake.

Despite trying to finance development through numerous measures, including foreign loans, by the 1990s Africa drowned in debt. The sub-Saharan region owed a whopping 90 percent of its GNP to international bankers. Prices for a variety of crops dropped; in 1981 cocoa exports were worth just a quarter of their 1973 value. For the dozens of countries without petroleum, the costs of energy added to the bad terms of trade and thereby sunk them further into debt. By 1994, fuel-importing Zambia owed $5.2 billion in debt, or 161 percent of its gross domestic product. As in Latin America, banks kept reissuing credits in the hope that Zambia could service its debt. The nation could not climb out of the hole. In all, Africa spent 21 percent of its export income in debt servicing each year, and by 1991 sub-Saharan Africa's external debt exceeded its annual GNP, or twice the proportion of any other region in the world. The World Bank and International Monetary Fund stepped in with Structural Adjustment Programs to rescue the continent.[130]

In return for these loans Africans had to liberalize their economies, both by opening them to investors and curbing the presence of the state. The process began with Kenya, Malawi, and Mauritius in the 1980s, and by 1995 all nations—even socialist Zambia and Tanzania—had come to terms. Governmental programs were dismantled, replaced by the market or made more efficient through privatization and reallocation of resources. Urban centers had received the most benefits from the state under inefficient import substitution planning, which compelled farmers to sell their crops below market value in order to maintain low food prices for bureaucrats, industrial workers, businessmen, and politicians in cities. The IMF now required that farmers receive full prices for their food so that they, not the industrialists, would become the drivers of export growth. Structural Adjustment Programs lifted state restrictions on imports and exports, removed tariffs, and reduced government spending as the market imposed discipline, even though the client-state was a deep-rooted sociopolitical phenomenon that could not be eradicated as easily as in liberal Europe and the United States. Tensions were bound to rise, therefore, between foreign capitalists and ensconced bureaucrats and their bourgeois backers.[131]

The results of liberalization were disappointing, tragic in some cases, and even dangerous. A 1994 World Bank study found that six sub-Saharan nations registered solid improvements and nine experienced modest positive changes but eleven ended up in worse shape. Seventeen countries carried such tremendous burdens of debt that the program was simply irrelevant without massive infusions of outside capital. The emphasis on expanding primary goods for export from rural areas meant a new reliance on world markets, which, under pressures of globalization, responded to higher supply by lowering commodity prices. The plans did not attract more external capital, for transnational corporations shied from these vulnerable economies. Furthermore, urban areas suffered rising unemployment as reforms cut protection for industries and funding for the public sector. As food became more expensive without state subsidies, the World Bank added "poverty alleviation programs" into the structural adjustment regimes in order to stave off starvation. Economic crisis actually spurred democratic change as people overthrew the now-bankrupt client-based system of the state (in Zambia and Malawi) in their demand for help. But it also generated such political strife as strikes, loss of faith in government, new ethnic tensions, rebellion (in Sudan and Liberia), and the collapse of states (Zaire and Somalia).[132]

Two examples of the downside of the World Bank effort showed that the American open-door regime had unintended consequences. In Zambia, 8,500 textile workers lost their jobs and clothing factories operated at no more than 20 percent of their capacity after 1989. The national airlines, bus company, hotel corporation, and other enterprises were eliminated, leading to 25,000 unemployed who joined 60,000 laid off from the public sector. In Ghana, a Structural Adjustment Program raised producer prices for cocoa by 67 percent. Privatization of 195 state-sponsored concerns followed. Many enterprises, such as the Ashanti Gold Fields, were sold to foreign corporations and then refurbished into viable commercial concerns once again. Ghana's economy stabilized by the mid-1980s as export earnings rose, but there was no Rostovian "takeoff" into sustained development. Currency devaluations and increased production worldwide caused cocoa prices to decline, and thus Ghana's debt grew. Industrial workers were laid off, and many could no longer afford higher education or health care, because of new user charges that covered former state subsidies. Rising food prices added to the burden. Calls for change ushered in multiparty elections in 1992, although the incumbent military dictator, Jerry Rawlings, a darling of the neoliberal market reformers, won a majority of the votes. In sum, Africa was not only running in place (in the best scenarios) but remained "uncomfortably close to the economic brink" in many other cases.[133]

Also evident on the continent and elsewhere was an emerging trend of marginalization of large numbers of people, especially along gender lines, due to the impact of economic globalization. In many societies, especially in the emerging world, poverty was borne predominantly by women, because the economic restructuring wrought by the market led to high rates of unemployment—and the first to lose work were those at the bottom of the social scale: women. New technology, flexible and insecure labor markets, and market processes that undercut traditional work patterns increased poverty and placed increasing pressure on gender distinctions. Restructuring under structural adjustment regimes dictated by international banks and institutions, and states unable to serve their people, placed poor women in ever worse economic situations. Their lack of access to education and their illiteracy, combined with a gender bias in development policies and the distribution of work (more than 75 percent of women's work in poor nations was unpaid), subjugated females to declining incomes and a male-dominated system of exploitation. Women took on a greater responsibility for manual labor once globalization's open-door ideology and practices restructured Third World economies away from social services provided by the state and toward subsistence activities bereft of government safety nets. Since 1975 and the first UN Conference on the Decade of Women, activists demanded solutions to better the plight of poor women around the world and empower females in the workplace. But critics of liberal trade noted that ingrained discrimination against women and traditions of male domination combined with a regime of exploitation to divide the labor market along gender lines. This actually enhanced globalization, and its downsides.

For example, in the world's poorest country—Mozambique—women shouldered the burden of farm labor to provide for their families. In 1994 the country ran a huge debt of $5.4 billion, or nearly five times its gross national product, as it was virtually cut off from the world financial and manufacturing systems. Foreign aid trickled back to donors who were owed this debt, and food aid did not reach the entire population, leading to massive hunger and a food riot in October 1995 in the capital of Maputo that highlighted the magnitude of the problem. Women farmers in Mozambique, who constituted nearly half of the labor force in the country, bore the brunt of this crisis, because they remained in the countryside as heads of household while males had migrated to the cities and abroad looking for work as the processes of globalization ground on. But their access to land and loans was limited by societal traditions and circumstances; women could only occupy land through male relatives, and rising privatization further relegated them to marginal land. Plagued by high food prices, low wages, and declining state support (the removal of subsidies to maintain low food prices and affordable transportation, and privatization of health care, for example), women turned out of desperation to provisioning their families by working on small farms near the capital. Structural Adjustment Programs did not lead to rural recovery (especially after Mozambique's seventeen-year civil war ended) but instead led to limits on government spending for a host of services that consigned women to basic chores such as gathering fuel and water after long and arduous journeys on daily transportation just to get to work. Denied access to resources, women more than men became victims of the market, which privatized land and reduced state programs at the same time that the demands on them for family care (child rearing, education, and elder care) remained. Their own health suffered as a result. Women were marginalized in Mozambique due to labor conditions propagated by globalization and the free-enterprise system urged on the South by the North.[134]

Pacific Century

If the African nations were losers in the American market system, then most of the East Asian nations—the Four Tigers, Japan, the People's Republic of China—were winners. But gendered poverty also became a norm for millions in this region, too. Like Mozambique, the Philippines, for instance, was also caught in a debt cycle trap, but while a dearth of social spending was partly to blame, so was the creation of export zones. These were a product of incentives given to multinational corporations in the 1970s onward to help the country develop and, in the 1990s, the draw of globalization. Export zones gave foreign firms tax-free total ownership supported by government-backed loans to sidestep trade restrictions abroad; investors from Japan, South Korea, Hong Kong, Taiwan, and elsewhere in Asia who faced export quota limits abroad fabricated electronics, textiles, and other light manufactures in the Philippines and then sent them to the American or European markets through Filipino quotas. These enclaves drove export-oriented growth and a market ethic for the country, and they also propagated female exploitation.

Export zones offered an escape from poverty that was more promise than reality. Work in assembling semiconductors and the like was considered low-skilled, which meant that most employees were women. Upward of 90 percent of the employees in these export zones were women drawn from the surrounding rural areas, thereby escaping traditional social systems and poverty but also encountering the high social and economic costs of Structural Adjustment Programs. Families faced with high unemployment and poverty in the Bataan countryside, for instance, sent their daughters (many of them young—the average age of the workforce was between 17 and 29 years old) to work in the zones, but the wages were lower than in the industrial areas of Manila. In fact, about 40 percent of the women worked under the legal minimum wage (just 17 percent of the men earned such paltry salaries), because females were deemed to endure poverty. Living and work conditions were often appallingly overcrowded, pricey, and dangerous. Women also faced a patriarchal system that gave them no opportunity for redress of these conditions; their every movement, from using the bathroom to traveling to work, was restricted by males. And sexual harassment and stereotyping were rampant. Filipino women in the export zones, therefore, were marginalized economically and alienated socially, much like others encountering the forces of globalization and American market policies.[135]

Yet the successes in Asia eclipsed these stories, which only lately came to light after digging by anthropologists and social commentators. The story of economic growth and emergence from poverty for many nations (including the Philippines) was stunning and seemed to validate the neoliberal market doctrines of free enterprise and the open door. South Korea, for instance, experienced a remarkable period of growth. One of the world's poorest nations in 1960, with a per capita gross national product ($78) lower than that of its basketcase cousin to the north, South Korea adapted modernization theory from the Americans by veering from Western concepts and grounding takeoff policies in religious and family traditions.[136] The development process hinged on an outward-looking industrialization strategy led by General Park Chung Hee, who overthrew a democratic government in 1961 and turned to *chaebols,* family-owned companies that monopolized production and industries. This plan focused on urban-based, labor-intensive, export-oriented growth through sales of cheap manufactured products like textiles, chemicals, electronics, and machine tools, and eventually automobiles. Foreign investment, mainly from the United States and Japan, as well as international lending agencies and commercial banks, financed the development until the domestic savings rate rose and the home market became substantial enough to support growth. The results of Korea's "catch-up" to the advanced nations were breathtaking. Between 1962 and 1989, the export drive netted 8 percent growth per year through commodity trade that increased sales abroad from $480 million to over $127 billion. Despite the burden of inflation and having the fourth largest debt in the Third World during the 1980s, South Korea ran an international payments surplus by 1986, thanks to skilled government direction and educated management. Per capita income reached $4,380 (a whopping 52-fold rise), and domestic savings increased ten-fold. South Korea earned its status as a Tiger, a nation that developed into a trillion-dollar powerhouse in less than a half century.[137]

If Seoul's development was remarkable, Tokyo's climb to the second biggest economy in the world was transformative to the global economy. Provided virtually "free security" by the Americans from the 1950s onward, the Japanese drew on US financing and the boon of Korean War expenditures to modernize and expand their economy. Reformed *zaibatsu* corporate conglomerates like Mitsui and Mitsubishi emerged as huge trading companies financed by banks and overseen by the government. Believing that Japanese markets were too small to develop, US firms sold their technology to Japanese companies, which modernized the industrial base and adopted a high-tech exporting strategy.[138] American outcries led to voluntary export restraints by Tokyo's ever-sensitive Ministry of International Trade and Industry (MITI), but by the late 1960s Japan was an increasingly burdensome competitor. Still, Japan complained that restrictions on its products gave Asian Tigers such as Hong Kong better opportunities in the United States. As well, Washington only feebly demanded, on Japan's behalf, that Europeans open their markets. Crisis loomed, and perceptions of Japanese free-riding intensified. The undervalued yen boosted exports abroad. As a historian has noted, Tokyo "dined at the world trade buffet but declined to share the bill."[139]

Yet no observer could deny that Japan had taken the teachings of US business management guru W. Edwards Deming to heart (while Americans largely ignored him) and produced goods of superior quality for discriminating foreign consumers. Japan gained from a long-run international marketing strategy that stressed labor-management cooperation and zero-sum neomercantilist policies versus the market philosophy of the United States, which counted on open doors, competition, and unfettered economic growth. Combining competitive firms with government guidance added to a culture of conformism, but it worked wonders in terms of productive efficiency and export potential. The consequences of this export-plus-protectionist approach were apparent. A stable labor pool rewarded by lifetime employment and bonuses, tight control over imports and labor costs, high taxes and state industrial policies that strategically favored new industries, and the state's long-term provisioning of capital for firms and industry, rather than reliance on short-term profits in the stock market, expanded the economy. Japan produced a half million autos in 1960 but made over 3.5 million by the 1970s, even more than West Germany, the world's second biggest manufacturer. Japan's shipbuilding industry was twice the size of its three closest competitors. America and the Europeans began running larger trade deficits with Japan; by the late 1970s Tokyo enjoyed $10 billion annual trade surpluses with the United States. The country obviously made more than transistors, as Charles de Gaulle had disdainfully quipped in the 1960s. It marketed with a sensitivity to overseas consumer tastes, such as making fuel-efficient cars during the oil crises.[140]

That Japan greatly profited in the global market economy, even though it did not necessarily play by the rules of market capitalism, posed a huge challenge to the United States. Japan beat America at its own game of innovation and market control through vision, trained management and bureaucracies, and strategy. Because Tokyo also exported more capital than it imported as it sought raw materials and minerals abroad, the yen transformed into a powerful currency. Meanwhile, America spent on military commitments—Vietnam, bases in South Korea and Japan, NATO programs in Europe—that drained away money. When Washington insisted that Japan open its trade and capital markets, the Japanese allowed 78 of America's biggest 200 corporations by 1970 but only under bureaucratic control. There would be no free flow of investment into Japan. The country also capitalized on American spending on the Vietnam War to the tune of as much as $4 billion a year by making military goods for US troops. Tokyo might have been shocked by Nixon's announcement in July 1971 that the United States would open diplomatic relations with communist pariah Beijing, but Japan had already become China's top trade partner through special commercial deals and credit arrangements. As well, Japanese investments poured into South Korea, capturing 64 percent of that market and nearly quadrupling America's capital there. The Japanese, in short, were changing the patterns of the global economy. Americans talked of the shifting balance of power away from the Atlantic (and the United States) and toward the Pacific.[141]

Tokyo had become a dynamo in the emerging age of globalization and as much a rival as ally to the United States' rule of the world economy. American businessmen warned President Nixon in 1971 that because Japan bought only raw materials from America but sold to Americans lucrative, high-priced finished goods—and all the while kept its markets closed to US exports—the Japanese treated the United States like an emerging nation. It was time to stop coddling a country a corporate leader compared to "the golfer who is shooting in the 80s with the same 25 handicap he used when he was shooting in the 100s."[142] But American manufacturers also noted the success of Japanese industrialists who pooled their resources under MITI coordination and teamed with government and labor to overcome inefficiencies and seize markets. This was the case in the semiconductor sector. Over a three-year period in the late 1970s, government tax breaks and subsidies fueled a research association comprising Mitsubishi, NEC, Fujitsu, Toshiba, and others that developed patents to pull the Japanese computer industry even with its American counterparts. To be sure, the government-corporate conglomeration soon belittled as "Japan, Inc." by Americans played unfairly; Tokyo locked out US semiconductor manufacturers from competing in the home market. But the Japanese blamed Americans for not improving their own management and production.[143] It was just this sort of neomercantilist behavior and cold-blooded (market) attitude that had spurred Treasury Secretary John Connally, a Texan, into announcing, "This cowboy knows that you can ride a good horse to death, and the world has been riding the United States, a good horse, to death in the postwar years, and this has got to stop."[144]

Staying in the saddle got harder during the years of oil crises and energy inflation, but Japan adjusted to the new conditions much more effectively than did the Americans. Nixon and his successors complained, cajoled, and even threatened Tokyo for veering from market doctrine, but such an approach blamed the symptoms—unemployment, reduced profits, and bankruptcies—rather than the diseases of American complacency and maladjustment. While Americans looked for scapegoats for ballooning oil prices, MITI bureaucrats vigorously established a national energy policy of conservation by heavy industry, development of nuclear power, bilateral deals with Middle Eastern producers, and increases of imports of refined oil from China. As Japan turned to services and knowledge-based sectors such as electronics, its energy consumption grew by only 7 percent between 1973 and 1986 even though its GDP soared by half.[145] Japan and the United States remained friends despite the trade and monetary frictions, but Japan was branded as an unfair competitor and became the focus of political and popular recrimination.

The venerable US auto industry dished out the criticism. Imports of Toyotas and Hondas sparked protests in the American Midwest. In 1992 an editorial cartoonist depicted a hulking football player wearing a "DETROIT" jersey whining to a US government referee that a trim player celebrating in the end zone with "JAPAN" emblazoned on his shirt was playing unfair. But Japanese carmakers made fuel-efficient and durable autos. Hard-pressed consumers facing high prices at the pump wanted these imports. As a result, the market doubled Japanese imports between 1975 and 1986, this despite a voluntary export restraint agreement forced on Tokyo in 1981 that raised prices on these cars. Fearful of rising protectionism and a strong yen that would boost export costs, the Japanese built "green-field" assembly plants in Ohio, Tennessee, and Kentucky. These overseas facilities avoided tariffs and won American labor to their side by employing locals. In 1978 Japan made no cars in the United States. Ten years later, green-field "transplants" delivered 695,000 autos. By the 1980s Japanese carmakers owned over a quarter of the US auto market, more than Ford and Chrysler, and were selling well in Europe as well.

That percentage rose to a third by the 1990s as the Japanese juggernaut cleverly retooled to changing global conditions while American carmakers seemed a step behind. To no avail, the Big Three and the government focused on looks and performance and the traditional strategy of buying up components manufacturers at home and investing in smaller Japanese companies (Mazda, Suzuki, Mitsubishi) abroad in order to control production. Chrysler declared bankruptcy in 1979 before receiving a federal bailout loan and returning to profitability three years later. When gas prices fell in the 1980s, Japan turned to the higher end of the market with the Lexus, Infiniti, and Acura models. When supposed free-trader Ronald Reagan imposed the export restraint in 1981, for public relations purposes Honda, Nissan, and Toyota actually continued to adhere to the limits after they lapsed four years later. Regardless, their imports rose to an annual 2.3 million cars, up from 1.85 million. American protectionism failed to hold back Japan's dominance. As Americans thought about short-term profit, Japan followed a long-haul strategy that internationalized the US market.

That strategy finally led the United States to concede a large segment of the field to Japan. Imports into the US market amounted to 43 percent of America's overall trade deficit of $49.4 billion with Japan in 1992. American auto parts manufacturers sought to cut into that deficit by opening the Japanese market to their products. President George H. W. Bush championed their cause on a trip to Japan in 1992 and insisted that US cars gain a greater market share in the country. He returned with little to show for his effort. Even with export prices bolstered by a weak dollar, Big Three sales in Japan did not go beyond the previous year's meager total of thirty thousand cars. US carmakers refused to make changes that might have stimulated Japanese demand, such as reducing vehicle sizes or switching the steering wheel to the right side. Meanwhile, the transplant strategy led to nearly 2 million Japanese models being made in the United States by 1995, which more than filled the gap when imports dropped off to around 1.3 million a year. General Motors brought out its novel and popular Saturn, but Detroit soon returned to making larger cars and sport utility vehicles. Nearing the end of the first decade of the new millennium, the Big Three's demise grew in proportion to the increasingly iron grip that Japan's three largest automakers had on the US market. By 2009 the American carmakers pleaded for their very survival by asking for government bailout funding.[146]

The second largest economy in the world beat the biggest in auto trade competition, but the US Big Three were not the only ones to feel the winds of change of Japan's open-door policies. The US semiconductor industry also experienced a shock from Japan that was ameliorated only by a government willing to shove aside market dogma. Japanese exports repeatedly cut the legs out of US industry— cars, steel, computers, and televisions. Americans made 82 percent of TVs for the US market in 1969; by 1988 a domestically made television could hardly be found. Imports of color sets and then Japanese wide-screen televisions had essentially erased all US competitors by the year 2000.[147] As the modern era of globalization dawned at the end of the Cold War, Americans foraged for answers to the Japanese commercial challenge to their hegemony.

If Japan issued blows to American dominance in trade, it hammered the US psyche when it came to investments. In 1985 the five leading global economic powers signed the Plaza Agreement, which appreciated other currencies against the dollar, and in particular the yen, which doubled in value. This was one reason the Reagan administration saw fit not to insist on the voluntary auto restraint, for Japanese car exports would rise in cost under the new exchange regime. In Reagan's worldview, the economic freedom of the marketplace was critical to obtaining foreign policy and domestic objectives. Freedom included allowing foreign investment and substantial overseas borrowing, which were rising already due to the attraction of high interest rates, to finance large budget deficits. Just as the OPEC nations had recycled their dollars earned from sales of oil in the West into investments abroad, so did the Japanese use their considerable earnings to buy American assets. With the dollar's fall during the late 1980s,

Japanese holdings of US securities also fell in value, but the yen bought twice as many dollar products as before. Japan turned instead to purchasing property at fire-sale prices.[148]

This shopping spree scooped up some marquee sites and names, although Americans were no strangers to high-profile investment abroad, including in Japan. McDonald's, IBM, Apple Computers, and firms ranging from beverages to electronics and chemicals owned more market shares in Japan, and Disney's theme park in Tokyo Bay captivated hearts and wallets from the time it first opened the doors to Cinderella's Castle in 1983. But Japanese companies invaded the sanctums of American culture and economy. They bought such icons as Universal Studios, CBS Records, MCA Entertainment (including commercial rights to Yosemite National Park), Rockefeller Center (and its Christmas tree), Columbia Pictures, and the trademark for the Indianapolis Motor Speedway in order to build an oval near Tokyo. Snapping up condominiums, houses, ranches, ski areas, racetracks (and racehorses), golf courses, and Hawaiian beachfront properties, real estate purchases by the Japanese between 1985 and 1990 totaled $65 billion. When added to the $170 billion in sales of American securities—about 40 percent of Treasury bonds over the same period—the purchases had a psychic impact. Americans were stunned, depressed, and prone to characterize the Japanese spree in sinister and even sensationally racist terms, even though Britain and Holland still surpassed Japan as the top sources of foreign investment in American real estate.[149]

Yet even the mighty Japanese had to pay the consequences of the market economy. The flow of investment capital helped the United States by floating American pensions and reenergizing localities hard up for cash in a recessionary economy. Investments proved to be jumbo-sized financial follies as Japan's economy tanked in the mid-1990s. A strong yen, slumping exports, and sluggish demand at home, along with an aging population unwilling to spend on consumer goods and crushed under mortgage debts, reversed Japan's fortunes. Workers were laid off, and the country assumed the largest debt in the world. American carmakers even started making better and cheaper automobiles in the 1990s, although Japan retained its hold on the market. The Nikkei stock market plunged by the end of the decade; one indicator of the distress was that Sony's earnings dropped by a third in 1999 despite robust worldwide demand for electronics. The country incurred losses of roughly $7 trillion in assets. With the Cold War's end, the security alliance that cost the United States dearly no longer was an imperative. Japanese policies of lifetime employment, government guidance, and closed networks of suppliers seemed unsuited for the new era of deregulation and global competition. Japan still ran a trade surplus with the United States and remained the second biggest economy in the world, but the nation looked both foolish and unprepared for new, wide-open-door realities.

Tokyo had launched a trade offensive around the world and changed the power structure of the global economy. But what appeared as a massive challenge to American power ended up as well-orchestrated opportunism. Belatedly, NASDAQ Japan linked to the world's stock markets for the first time in 2000, and Sanwa, Asahi, and Tokai banks merged that year to form the biggest global banking concern ever. Still, Tokyo did not abandon its directed economy and it opposed American and IMF market fundamentalism. Plans were set forth by the government to seize control of high-speed Web service by 2005, although the competition remained fierce from the United States and Europe. Japan's lucrative telecommunications market remained closed to outsiders. Targeted industrial policies were still on the table, but Japan's effective mercantilism of past decades was a memory in the era of global integration.[150]

China and India

Like America, Japan also faced new competition as the People's Republic of China became a force in the world economy. The establishment of diplomatic relations between Washington and Beijing in 1979 stimulated China's economic ties to the West and the global arena. The country engaged in a combination of import substitution and export-oriented industrial development, seeking to overcome the errors of its self-seclusion during the Cultural Revolution of the previous two decades, which had stagnated growth. Bilateral trade with Japan and the United States rose during the 1970s to approximately $4 billion with each country. Despite Sino-Japanese political tensions, trade between the two nations multiplied fifteenfold into the mid-1990s. Japan bought Chinese oil while it invested in chemical and steel plants. During the 1980s China's trade with communist countries declined to 8 percent of their value in the 1950s, and by the

1990s, when the communist world lost most of its members, the capitalist nations naturally rose in prominence. Japanese officials noted that the future rested with China, a nation predicted to grow into the world's biggest economy as early as 2010. Armed with apologies for its wartime occupation policies, but more importantly with foreign aid tied to purchases in Japan, Tokyo penetrated Chinese markets.

Japan was China's largest trade partner, followed by Hong Kong (due to indirect commerce with the 55 million overseas Chinese living in Taiwan and South Korea) and the European Union. Trade with the United States climbed above that of any single European country; China became the top communist commercial partner with the Americans by 1981. Coca-Cola opened a bottling plant in China that year, but in actuality the trade largely went one way. Although dreams of the China Market had existed since the nineteenth century, trade was asymmetrical as Chinese shoes, apparel, electronics, and consumer goods flooded the US market while China bought fewer technology goods than hoped. Both America and the Europeans ran trade deficits with China (by 2000 the United States bought $84 billion more than it sold), though Japan enjoyed surpluses.

The decentralizing reforms of Deng Xiaoping were the stimulus to this growth. Chinese farmers were given the right to buy and sell land-use rights. This stopped short of private ownership in the world's largest socialist country, yet it led to the expansion and more efficient allocation of resources in agriculture, and eventually in fishing, light industry, and restaurants. By the late 1980s, industrial reforms included a turn to light industry, more focus on customers, and profits made on the open market. Stock markets developed, and the banking system diversified. Deng also decentralized state-owned trading corporations and manufacturing enterprises to the extent that both engineered their own export and import policies and retained export earnings when they exceeded government targets. In the new market regime of augmenting consumption over state-driven production, they also suffered the losses. In any case, the consequences of these changes were staggering. China's gross domestic product surged at an annual rate of 9.5 percent between 1978 and 1999. Per capita income followed this growth, although it was still less than $800 in 1999—China remained an emerging country.

Deng was determined to end China's isolation by opening its doors to trade and investment as well as to earn hard currency by exporting. "One important reason for China's backwardness after the industrial revolution in Western countries was its closed-door policy," he noted. Embracing the American free-enterprise model, he believed history showed that "if we don't open to the outside, we can't make much headway."[151] While importing heavy capital goods, steel and iron, oil and gas equipment, and grain, China exported textiles, petroleum, toys, and other consumer goods. Deng and his successor, Jiang Zemin, also opened to the world by joining global institutions. In 1980 China joined the IMF and World Bank, becoming a large recipient of aid from both bodies. Through bilateral deals (the biggest with Japan) with developing countries, Beijing incurred a sizable but not excessive $154 billion in debt by 1999. The Chinese also applied for GATT membership in 1986, even though the capitalist world took fifteen years to accept the communist nation.[152]

In its quest to engage the world economy, China also encouraged foreign investment and joint ventures with the capitalist world by creating 124 Special Economic Zones around the country, particularly in coastal cities, through inducements such as tax breaks and guarantees of profit repatriation. Wholly Foreign Owned Enterprises, foreign companies, and contractual ventures invested in market-oriented "micro climates" that induced foreign outlays amounting to $40 billion by 1998, quadruple the sum from just eight years earlier. Although barriers remained, due to the inconvertibility of Chinese currency, bureaucratic restrictions, and worker and management attitudes, direct investment in export-oriented goods poured into the northeast and coastal areas from overseas Chinese and multinational corporations. These arrangements then connected inland China with global markets by a multiprong development effort that focused on traditional trade routes into Southeast and South Asia along the Yangzi River Valley, from the new Pudong District of Shanghai to all directions following the railway through the "continental bridge" from eastern to western China.[153]

The case of Suzhou Industrial Park illustrates the penetration by global capitalism. Founded in 1994 in an agreement between Singapore and China, the Suzhou Industrial Park hosted 103 foreign-invested enterprises capitalized at over $16 billion by 2002. Under the mantra "small government, big community," an efficient service-oriented staff attracted overseas investors by minimizing state interference and pursuing a pro-business agenda. Workers adopted the Singaporan model of a robust but reasonable social security system that provided employer contributions into personal employee accounts. Community services and public housing abounded. The market determined the workforce, as an administrative committee, not the state, recruited talent. Companies flocked to do business there; Philips Semiconductors chose the Park as its site for a new factory. It was a model of transnational financial strategies and regional business networks—Singapore shipping and engineering behemoth Keppel and United Industrial Suzhou, both controlled by the Salim Group, Indonesia's largest transnational corporation—operated in alliances with state and private capital. A question of its expansion arose after opposition emerged to the large-scale development of arable land in China in the mid-1990s (and globalization itself provoked discontent among Chinese intellectuals, who viewed it as a false identity for China and a tool of Western neo-imperialism). Yet Suzhou Industrial Park became a model of a world-class infrastructure supported by abundant human resources—a "garden-like township" lauded worldwide for the creation of an internationally competitive, high-tech industrial complex.[154]

That both history and foreign policy entered the economic picture was clear throughout this globalization period, as evidenced by the confrontation at Tiananmen Square in June 1989, human rights violations (Tibet), political tensions (with Taiwan, Japan, and so on), and exploitation of workers (especially women, as export-led industrialization became increasingly feminized). Protests against Chinese policies caused American automakers to lose a contract to build plants in China in 1995; a German company free of political dissenters won the day. Still, globalization swept China and the advanced nations along on a rising tide of commerce. In 2000, Chinese leaders announced a proactive policy of "going global" by opening doors to foreigners. The goal was to profit aggressively from the world economy and transform enterprises into transnational corporations.[155] Regardless of politics, China emerged as a gold mine for business expansion in the minds of executives throughout the world—the biggest retailer in the world, Walmart, based much of its manufacturing and assembly base in the country. After the US Congress and President Bill Clinton overcame their reluctance toward the repressive government and decided to grant China permanent most-favored-nation status in 2000, China acceded to the World Trade Organization (GATT's successor) under rules requiring more openness, fewer state restrictions on imports and foreign firms, and Western standards of worker safety and health conditions.[156]

China also engaged in a parallel trend of regional economic integration, joining Japan, Singapore, South Korea, and others in joint banking ventures and in lowering tariffs on Asian goods. By 2006 the "going global" campaign, incorporated into the Communist Party's Five-Year Plan, yielded a huge boom in foreign-financed projects at home. Meanwhile, 3.45 million workers labored overseas and thirty thousand enterprises operated in more than two hundred overseas countries and regions, in sectors ranging from construction to tourism. Parts of some of the largest firms were listed on the Hong Kong and New York stock exchanges, which raised billions of dollars for Chinese parent companies to acquire and merge foreign holdings.[157] At home, the Chinese witnessed over a 954 percent increase in per capita growth in personal income between 1980 and 2008, triple that of the next regional competitor, South Korea.[158]

The global market converted the communist dragon into a key member of the world economic community—an arena that favored China and transnational businesses but not the market advocate, the United States. In 2008, lagging exports to China and booming imports from the Asian giant led to a $266.3 billion deficit, the largest shortfall with a single nation ever recorded by America. Retailer Walmart was responsible for a big proportion of this deficit, but ominously for the United States, both advanced technology sales as well as cheap manufactures accounted for the twenty-year trend of the trade imbalance. By 2009 China had accumulated over $2 trillion dollars in reserves from this lucrative commerce, and it reinvested much of this treasure into US assets to keep interest rates low and maintain American consumer purchasing of its goods.[159] Transnational corporations such as Walmart welcomed the surge, but smaller competitors and US labor did not, and as the latter urged an increase in the value of China's artificially low currency to dampen down the export advantage, others noted that the issue was not about China itself but about the process of globalization that benefited transnational corporations (including many American ones). "Made in China" indicated only that the country was the final assembly point for goods that had wended their way through Japan, the United States, the Asian Tigers, and others in a global supply chain dictated by competitive market forces.[160]

Corporate proliferation in the new India, February 1994. Globalization and market potential arrived in India after the country deregulated its economy. Roadside signs carrying corporate logos indicate some of the more than 160 companies that staked out claims in Bangalore, a dynamic technological hub city. (Time & Life Pictures/Getty Images)

India, too, became an Asian giant during this burst of globalization, although at a slower speed than China. The world's largest democracy had long adhered to a mixed economic model between socialism and capitalism—market mechanisms controlled by state regulations. Unlike China's rather haphazard and dramatic opening to the capitalist world, India leaned toward the market in an orderly fashion. Prime Minister Rajiv Gandhi removed internal industrial controls in the 1980s, but more boldly, Manmohan Singh, the finance minister, followed with changes to exchange rates and taxes in the early 1990s, prompted by rising oil prices and the collapse of its top trade partner, the USSR. Overborrowing from the IMF caused a balance of payments crisis and pushed leaders toward liberalization. The government disposed of the License Raj of import, investment, and industrial licensing, curbed state monopolies, and encouraged foreign direct investment. What had been the most regulated country in the noncommunist world became one of the most "market-friendly, outward-looking" nations, noted the government.[161]

The southern city of Bangalore epitomized the riches of market-oriented development and the effects of globalization. This city of oxen, rickshaws, and avant-garde architecture hosted Electronics City, an industrial park with more than one hundred high-tech firms that served as the epicenter of globalized India linked to the world market. Software designers and engineers—the brightest young minds of the information technology revolution—found homes in Bangalore, which became the birthplace of IT giant Infosys in 1981. This multinational firm helped companies and people around the world program, manage, and integrate their personal computers. Infosys became a software and outsourcing giant with over one hundred thousand employees in nine centers in India and thirty worldwide offices, with revenues topping $4 billion by 2008.[162]

The IT revolution in Bangalore transformed the entire country and branded India as a source of innovation and service. Call centers serviced international clients seeking assistance for phone use, household appliances, and computers, while research and development facilities cropped up in English-speaking college-educated Bangalore rather than China. India had caught the wave of globalization, or at least overseas business had identified India as a prime place to outsource engineering, research, and manufacturing operations to cut costs. Growth skyrocketed in manufacturing, aviation, real estate, and film, among other sectors. Consumer spending rose steeply, and six million luxury buyers bought up pricey goods, including homes and land that placed thirty-seven Indians among the world's richest people. Deutsche Bank, Citigroup, Goldman Sachs, Barclays, and other foreign investment banks paraded into the country. Consumption boomed; in the telecom sector, India added seven million mobile phone subscribers every month in 2006, surpassing even the explosion in China.[163]

While India profited from the fuel of globalization, however, it could not be denied that one-quarter of the planet's poor inhabited the country. Thus, India like other nations experienced a considerable amount of unease over the effect (or ineffectiveness) of the market on poverty in the emerging nations. A battle persisted into the new millennium regarding the costs and benefits of the open-door doctrine, especially as a trend toward unfettered market capitalism took hold in the post–Cold War world economy.

4. *The Open Door*

BY 1989 the Soviet empire collapsed, violently in some places and less noisily in others. The USSR itself went out of business in 1991 in some turmoil. Away from the glare of media attention, the post–Cold War age of globalization sprang to life. It was a product of advances in communications and transportation, an environment particularly in the United States of deregulation, the opening of borders and freer movement of people, money, and goods, and a revival of open-door market ideology led by American and European business, political, legal, and academic leaders. The process of globalization promoted convergence, growth, transparency, and democratization of the world economy. The nation-state came second to the transnational corporation; the agent of change was no longer government but firms, producers, bankers, immigrants, travelers—in short, private citizens of the world. The market became the single authority that unified producers and consumers, shaped by nations, international institutions, individuals, firms, and business networks to promote integration and harmonization worldwide. The Trilateral Commission of the 1970s and the World Economic Forum (WEF), meeting in Davos, Switzerland, since 1982 voiced the plan of free-enterprise to replace regulatory capitalism. Monetary management of the economy, tax relief, containment of unions, deregulation, fluctuating exchange rates, and free trade were the policies of the globalizers. More rapid and massive flows of products, money, information, people, and technology were the mechanisms they encouraged. The demise of the Cold War created the political and diplomatic circumstances for economic globalization to assume its paramount status.

Before the superpower standoff ended, the Americans—and notably Ronald Reagan—provided the political impetus to globalization and the spur to worldwide economic integration by a mantra of freedom. While he took aim on the corrupt and destitute Soviet Union through his strident anticommunist rhetoric, a huge military buildup, and intervention in the Middle East and Latin

America, Reagan also pursued an agenda of deregulation and privatization at home, free markets abroad, and business expansion around the globe. He rejected the framework of the subordination of economics to security concerns (although he certainly prosecuted Cold War policies of containment and rollback of communism) and instead embraced free enterprise in the marketplace— itself transformed by technology and the withering away of constraints placed on it by the superpower rivalry. Falling oil prices in the 1980s aided his program of stripping the US economy of regulations; with more money in their pockets due to cheaper oil and lower taxes, and well-made imports arriving from Japan and elsewhere, consumers were inclined toward getting the government out of the market and freeing up the genius of American capitalism.

The revolution began at home. For instance, Reagan hastened the deregulation of the communications system in the United States by breaking up the world's largest corporation, AT&T. The advent of the so-called Baby Bells privatized the telephone system and opened up the country to foreign competitors, who seized the US market (though they did not grant American concerns equal access to their communications systems). In information technology, antitrust action against computer giant IBM led indirectly to the company joining Intel microprocessors and Microsoft's operating software with its own hardware to produce the personal computer. By not relying solely on IBM parts, the company's PC system was not proprietary, and soon spinoffs of components, chips, drives, and the like cropped up around the world, especially in developing Asian nations. The US computer manufacturer gave way to marketing organizations for foreign producers, or "hollow corporations" with no production base but heading networks that drew on cheap labor to produce efficient, cutting-edge technology. From the mid-1980s to 1998, the information technology sector augmented its share of the gross domestic product from 4.9 percent to 8.2 percent as the number of people using computers doubled to half of the workforce. By Reagan's second term, America enjoyed a growing export surplus in services, thanks to its competitive advantage in technology, even as its merchandise trade deficit blossomed under pressure from Japan, China, and others. This growth led efforts by the government to inject US private capital and business into overseas markets and provide rules against piracy and copyright infringement to protect their ideas and services.

Globalization was clearly visible in the world financial system. For starters, services became ubiquitous and grander in scale. The VISA credit card became a global brand with thirty million cards in existence in 1970, expanding to one billion by 2000, when this transnational company controlled 57 percent of world market share of financial services. Accepted in over 130 countries where transactions occurred over an average of just five seconds, VISA generated $2.1 trillion in annual business. Second, the abandonment of fixed exchange rates and deregulation of capital controls by Canada, Germany, the Netherlands, Switzerland, and America during the mid-1970s (followed by Britain and Japan a few years later) aided the globalization process. Also, with the cost of transatlantic phone calls dropping by 90 percent between 1970 and 1990—as well as price declines in computers—stock market traders, investors, and capital managers planned, organized, and executed transactions around the world on a continuous basis. Global financial dealing skyrocketed as cross-border transactions in bonds and equities climbed from 9 percent of the US gross domestic product in 1980 to 164 percent by 1996. Americans held foreign securities totaling $2.38 billion in 2000, up from $89 billion in 1984, while foreign ownership of American equities and debt shot up from $268 billion to a staggering $3.65 billion over the same period. And American private capital increasingly dominated loans and other exchanges to the Third World; by 1994, 78 percent of the investment money came from banks, while 4 percent hailed from international institutions. World finances were increasingly integrated and expanded under the regime of globalization; national banking systems were so intimately tied to each other that policies and events affecting one influenced all.

A demographic and cultural synergy occurred alongside this economic convergence. More people than ever before crossed borders as tourists, migrants, or students. The number of people who flew on international flights from US airports rose 240 percent to 55.5 million during the quarter century ending in 2000. Meanwhile, in 1970–1990 about a half million people per year entered the United States; in 1989 the figure reached a million, and an undetermined but sizable number poured across American borders as undocumented aliens thereafter. Reflecting regional and global migration trends, Latin Americans shifted from immigration to emigration, much of it to the United States. They were one-quarter of California's population in 1991. Asian immigration doubled during the 1980s. Furthermore, the number of foreign students studying in the United States numbered nearly 454,000 in the mid-1990s, about five times the number of Americans enrolled in schools abroad. And all of these globalized travelers and the millions who were "virtual" tourists found themselves linked together and sharing common experiences through the Internet. In 1997 fewer than 40 million people were connected across the planet but just a year later over 100 million communicated on the Internet. The world had entered the Information Age, which drove the globalization process and revolutionized culture, economies, and politics.[164]

Integration

Curiously, a result of this upsurge in integrated markets and peoples before and after the Cold War was a movement away from the multilateral universalism championed for decades by the United States, and toward regionalism. This was a product of GATT's struggle in the 1980s to maintain trade barrier-reduction negotiations, but it also reflected the success of the world's largest economic bloc, the European Union (EU), renamed from the European Community under the pivotal Maastricht Treaty of 1993. As of 2009, twenty-seven Western, Eastern, and Southern European states composed the EU, with several Balkan nations and Turkey candidates for admission. After the EU agreed to the Single European Act, which focused on forging a single (or common) market in which goods, money, services, and people circulated freely, the Maastricht Treaty enhanced that unity. Although the Americans feared protectionism and discriminatory treatment (inherent in a customs union), the Europeans largely adopted industrial policies that favored their enterprises (such as the subsidized commercial aircraft manufacturer Airbus Industrie) over a fortress Europe mentality.[165]

The Americans need not have worried. Further unification occurred in 1999 with the introduction of a single currency, the euro, in many of the member states, followed by the phasing out of national banknotes three years later in all but Britain and Denmark. The process of adopting the euro was politically difficult, and differences among member states in terms of economic policies remained hurdles to further integration, but there was no doubt that the euro rivaled the dollar as the world's reserve currency. The magnitude of the EU promised to change global economic patterns, as its 500 million citizens accounted for nearly a third of the entire world's gross domestic product, or nearly $17 trillion by 2007. From the mid-1980s onward, American-style grassroots consumerism swept the region, undermining traditional society along with the socialist mantra of producerism and the bureaucratic state. The EU also ranked as the planet's largest exporter and trade partner with the most dynamic Third World countries, India and China, while it was the second biggest global importer and hosted the headquarters of 170 of the Fortune Global 500's corporations. Despite American economic successes in the 1990s, the Europeans developed their own rival transnational networks in finance capital that linked horizontally with each other across the region through myriad interlocking directorates.[166] That is, market forces were increasingly privileged in Europe.

Under directives worked out in Lisbon in 2000, the EU determined to step up privatization, technological innovation and modernization, and worker productivity in order to strengthen its economic power and rival the United States. Some talked of a new European imperialism as ruthless as the old but aimed this time as much at the Atlantic world as at the Third. The EU defied the American open-door model with its customs union, yet it also resisted the temptation to veer from multilateral trade. The eventual passage of a major internal reform of the EU, embodied in the Treaty of Lisbon, which was finally ratified, after some dissension, by all twenty-seven member states and went into effect on December 1, 2009, showed a new Europe ready for competition. The Treaty of Lisbon, or Reform Treaty, streamlined decision making in the union to promote further interdependence through a more efficient institutional structure, strengthened executive powers without diluting the democratic process, and created a new post, High Representative on Foreign Affairs and Security, to coordinate EU external relations. This latter innovation directly addressed the longtime problem of a lack of cohesion in foreign affairs among the member nations. This lack of cohesiveness had weakened Europe's external influence, because it spoke with several voices, rather than with a unified one, and therefore its impact was marginalized when compared to that of the United States, China, and even emerging powers like Russia, India, and Brazil. The financial crisis that swept the world beginning in the summer of 2008 revealed the opportunity to junk this fractured external policy-making procedure and move toward further integration, as the Europeans would unify their trade, monetary, investment, and aid programs in international negotiations.[167] Europe, like America, thus encouraged the process of globalization, even in the midst of a severe downturn.

The movement toward regionalism accelerated around the world during the 1990s, especially in the South, which continually searched for development options after its decades-long disappointments with import substitution, trade preference systems, and debt. Latin America and Asia looked to growth in intraregional trade, while the many African nations associated with the EU renegotiated their trade relationship in the late 1990s, leading to the Cotonou Agreement in 2000 that supplanted the Lomé Convention with a more vigorous effort at reducing poverty and increasing aid by improving access into European markets.[168]

In response to the competitive potential of the European Union, Canada, the United States, and Mexico established the North American Free Trade Area (NAFTA) in 1992. This trilateral bloc of neighbors promoted investments, trade liberalization, and multilateral cooperation. It was vigorously opposed by environmentalists, small business, and labor, who feared a gutting of US and Canadian protective laws for endangered species, child and prison workers, and unions, along with predatory actions by big corporations. The Canadians accepted freer trade as a permanent condition of the budding era of globalization and approved the pact.[169] Mexico, as the weakest economic link, saw much to gain by NAFTA's supposed spur to development and access into rich nations. The Clinton administration fought tooth and nail to get its approval, however. Opponents used the NAFTA accord as a springboard to protest trade negotiations and globalization in the 1990s. The accord, which included side agreements on the environment and labor practices to appease foes, called for gradual elimination of barriers on sensitive goods like textiles, autos, and car parts as well as access to closed Mexican financial services and land transportation. Supporters and critics contended with each other over the impact. Some claimed that NAFTA was a foreign policy success as well as a boost to trilateral investment and trade, well above that recorded by the three nations with the rest of the world. Others countered that NAFTA sent US manufacturing jobs south. Opponents also focused on Mexico. Small farmers were chased off the land and emigrated illegally to the United States, because heavily subsidized American agribusiness depressed

Signing the NAFTA treaty, San Antonio, Texas, December 17, 1992. The leaders of Mexico (Carlos Salinas de Gortari), the United States (George H. W. Bush), and Canada (Brian Mulroney) stand as the North American Free Trade Agreement is signed. NAFTA prompted liberalization of trade and investment to spur development, profits, and globalization on the continent. It became a target for protest by protectionists, environmentalists, labor, and other groups, some of whom were opposed to market globalization. (Time & Life Pictures/Getty Images)

corn prices (though the cost to locals of processed corn tortillas rose, further impoverishing them). Business elites in all three countries profited, as megafirms like low-price Walmart (drawing on cheap Chinese labor) entered Mexico and bankrupted thousands of small manufacturers of toys, candy, and shoes. Suffice it to say that NAFTA exhibited the benefits and perils of American-style free-enterprise capitalism.[170]

A notable effort at regionalism arose when Argentina, Brazil, Paraguay, and Uruguay formed Mercosur in 1991 to promote freer trade among themselves as well as with six associated South American nations. Wielding a gross domestic product of $1.2 trillion by 1999, the customs union also aimed for cooperative free trade agreements with outsiders. Mercosur signed a free trade agreement with the five countries of the Andean Community in 2004 and with Israel three years later. The combination of the Andean members Ecuador, Peru, Bolivia, Venezuela, and Colombia with Mercosur created a potential trade bloc of 341 million people with the fifth largest economy in the world. Intraregional trade within Mercosur and the Andean Community, which climbed to around $2.3 billion in 1991, shot up above $35 billion ten years later. Latin Americans as a whole experienced a rise in commerce among themselves to 19 percent of their total trade by 2005.[171]

However, they could not ignore the fact that nearly half of their total trade focused on the United States. For some the ultimate goal was to balance the power of NAFTA and the EU by blocking the US-inspired creation of a Free Trade Area of the Americas. This arrangement planned to extend NAFTA to thirty-four countries to form a super-regional area of trade and investment and promote free trade and investments in lieu of the world trade negotiation forum. Many South and Central American countries balked at the idea, fearing it as an agent of US imperialism in the hemisphere, while the leaders of powerful Brazil and Mexico thought it a useless organization without an American commitment to lower its trade barriers to exports from the region. On the contrary, Washington looked to the Free Trade Area as a means of maintaining the openness of Mercosur and the Andean common market and thus placed less emphasis on reducing US tariffs. With the United States not forthcoming, the Free Trade Area remained on the drawing board as talks on integration, bending the American colossus to the needs of emerging nations, and development continued in the first decade of the new millennium among Latin and North Americans. Still, the "Washington consensus" of market-friendly internal reforms and open doors to the world remained strong. Consequences both favorable (inflation declined, debts repaid, fiscal imbalances righted) and unfavorable (poverty, underperforming commodity markets, financial turbulence at home, lagging terms of trade) for the region were the result.[172]

The wave of integration also swept Asia and the Pacific region. In 1992 the quarter-century-old Association of Southeast Asian Nations (ASEAN) created a Free Trade Area whose six members (projected to ten by 2012, along with several observer countries) originally sought to cut all internal tariffs to between 0 and 5 percent on certain products and eliminate nontariff barriers on these items by 2008. They moved up the deadline to impose this common preferential tariff in 2003, and average tariffs fell to 3.87 percent as intraregional trade more than doubled to $95 billion by the year 2000. By 2006, tariffs stood at 1.74 percent. Meanwhile, each nation retained its national duty schedules that applied to outsiders.[173] In 2001, ASEAN and China began talks on a free trade area that also drew the interest of Japan, and trade surged to $200 billion by 2008. In 1994 an even larger grouping of twenty-one developed and developing nations of the Asia-Pacific Economic Cooperation (APEC) organization set out to achieve free trade, investment, and cooperative ventures in industrial, resource, and banking management by 2010 for the advanced countries (including Canada, the United States, and Japan) and ten years later for the emerging countries in the group.[174]

Regionalism thus engineered a takeoff period in trade, but there was concern that the multilateral system developed under GATT would splinter into preferential blocs. This might undermine the American open-door system through exclusive arrangements that distorted trade. A world umpire to guide all of the regional groupings along the road of multilateral trade liberalization was needed. This idea had first been broached way back in 1948 with the aborted International Trade Organization and then tried and rejected again in scaled-back form with an Organization for Trade Cooperation in the mid-1950s. In order to institutionalize a comprehensive set of trade rules and update the international commercial regime so it addressed the full range of trade and trade-related issues, the EU and 75 members of GATT incorporated the negotiating forum into the World Trade Organization (WTO) in 1995 after the conclusion of the last GATT Round in Uruguay. The remaining 52 GATT members joined within two years. By 2007, the WTO had 151 members on its rolls. It monitored and enforced the principles of liberal trade, served as the barrier negotiation forum, and oversaw the implementation of all agreements.[175]

Essentially policing national trade policies to ensure their compatibility with liberal trade rules and to maintain open doors in the world economy, the powerful bureaucracy of the WTO had a myriad of functions that quickly drew attention from critics and supporters. The organization served as a research and analysis center, as a training forum for the developing world's leaders to engage in effective trade relations, and as the global commercial regime's link to the IMF

and the Bretton Woods system. Because of its high profile and sweeping responsibilities, the WTO became a lightning rod for grievances against the inequities
in the trade regime, the power of corporations, globalization, and the hegemony
of the North. Such nongovernmental organizations as the Sierra Club and the
World Wildlife Federation demanded a seat at the WTO table to shape global
economic policies that would protect the environment. On the other side, however, were nations arrayed against US regulatory policies that were dominated by
interest groups; in a reversal of roles, several Asian nations won their appeal in
the WTO in 1998 against a US ban on imported shrimp from nations that did
not protect sea turtles from dying in fishing nets. In this case, the market advocate turned state regulator, but it was compelled to change its laws to accommodate business forces. Conservative (and some liberal) groups, meanwhile, found
the institution undemocratic because unelected bureaucrats dictated rules to
which national governments had to adhere. This intergovernmental agency
emerged at odds with many interest groups, as well as the Third World, which
sought to wrest the WTO from the North's control. Yet undeniably this global
economic umbrella organization pushed nations toward embracing the ideal of
"one world" in which goods, money, and services were exchanged across borders
regardless of national origins, and with consequences both good and bad for the
integrative process.[176]

One upshot of the new regionalism and the advent of the WTO was an increase in international exchanges and thus the integration of the world's biggest
economies. Because of growth by 17 percent in merchandise exports from 1950
to 1999, the seven major industrial economies (the United States, Canada, Japan,
West Germany, France, Britain, and Italy) became more integrated in world
markets. Even the United States, historically a self-sufficient economy, saw its
imports and exports grow to equal nearly a quarter of its gross national product.
Economic linkages became more pronounced in the 1990s and beyond, as China
became a major investor abroad as well as exporter. Japan committed to trade
expansion and also to direct investment abroad (building Toyota and Honda assembly plants in the United States, for instance), and Americans worked abroad
for global companies that sold goods around the world (General Motors made
cars in Germany to export to Japan; Compaq purchased hard drives from Taiwan; IBM produced goods in South Korea and the Philippines; and seventeen

nations supplied Boeing with aircraft parts). The resurgence of trade after 1950 led to higher levels of integration among advanced nations and between them and the Third World and greater growth than during the so-called Golden Era of European-led capitalist fusion from 1870 to 1913. Such open doors and market-driven cohesion led analysts to applaud the salutary effects of globalization on world politics; economic interdependence, opined some, prevented war, because nations would not doom their lucrative trade and financial relations through conflict with a close commercial partner. Of course, others believed that integration heightened chances for disagreements or merely focused democracies too much on economics and not enough on their security, thus making them susceptible to pressures from authoritarian regimes. Whatever the theory, globalization had undoubtedly been spurred by the enhanced economic contacts in the era of integration.[177]

Trade Battles

Due to its growing dependence on world markets, the United States (as well as the New Labor government of Prime Minister Tony Blair, which broke with British socialism upon his election in 1997, in a trend that continued the free-enterprise policies of Conservative Margaret Thatcher in the 1980s) also endorsed a policy of liberal trade that abetted the market revolution. Both America and Britain pushed the process of globalization, which itself fueled more commerce, just as they had overseen the reconstruction of the post–World War II global economy through a mix of market and statist approaches. Entry into overseas markets would sustain and expand growth. The United States and Britain embraced the open-door doctrine as both an opportunity and a necessity, particularly as the oil, debt, and Japan shocks reverberated in the global economy. Historically the United States had not relied on exports and imports for its income; foreign trade in goods and services never reached higher than 10.8 percent of the gross domestic product from 1945 to 1970, and averaged 8 percent annually. During the 1970s the ratio doubled to 20.5 percent, and by the turn of the century imports and exports amounted to 26 percent of gross domestic product. With improvements in transportation and communications, a strong dollar, and rising overseas investment (which doubled during the 1980s and tripled from 1990 to 2000 to $2.2 trillion), the advanced nations led by the Americans turned to negotiating down trade barriers in GATT and the WTO.[178]

This meant that established labor-intensive industries fell by the wayside, replaced by the globalization of production in which cheap-labor emerging nations manufactured the goods the Americans, Europeans, and Japanese once made. The transformation wrought by the world market revolution not only meant more competition from abroad for the advanced nations but structural changes that did not necessarily privilege the powerful countries. That is, although most of the biggest transnational businesses were headquartered in the United States, they advocated vigorously for a free trade regime. Free trade would encourage imports on behalf of consumers, job growth in the service sector, and US manufacturers who obtain cheap components that lower costs for domestic production, enabling them to compete better globally. Market liberalism also favored fewer internal regulations on investments and more regulations to protect property, product standards, and the like to boost capital flows around the world and, with them, exports. Thus, cheap imports flooded into US markets, raising howls of protest in Congress and among an emerging coalition of small and medium-size businesses, organized labor, consumers, small farmers, and others as the industrial and work landscape transformed. Outmoded industries went bankrupt and injected efficiencies in the market. Automakers met the competition by modernizing and becoming leaner. Untrained or uneducated workers, and older workers who lived in the beleaguered manufacturing areas of the country, were unable to participate in the booming high-tech service sector and other romping grounds of the transnational businesses. Steel, textile, auto, and electrical unions, among others, lost hundreds of thousands of jobs, and wages plummeted for the jobs that remained. The dislocations caused by freer trade were painful for former union members, who had to take jobs in the low-end service sectors—security guards, fast food, janitors. Such conditions provided grist for the anti-globalization protests beginning in the late 1990s by organized labor forces. In fact, although the United States created 44 million net jobs between 1972 and 1992, none arose from internationally traded industries. Those went to Japan and industrializing countries like Taiwan, Brazil, and South Korea, which were not so much free traders as single-minded export boosters who had access to the open American market.[179]

The flipside of the statistics was that international trade had become more lucrative and expansive than ever before in the postwar world economy, due to negotiations and integration. The history of globalized trade reveals a complicated process of winners, losers, and power. For instance, a study of the "travels" of a T-shirt from its origins in the cotton fields on a Texas farm to its fabrication by mobile sweatshop labor in Shanghai's Number 36 Cotton Yarn Factory and Brightness Number 3 Garment Factory to its selling point in a drugstore in south Florida and its final destination as used clothing worn by poor Africans revealed both exploitation and opportunity. The $1.42 T-shirt (which included 24 cents in tariffs) fought off obstacles such as US trade barriers, Chinese bureaucrats who regulated Shanghai's apparel manufacturing, and American politicians who granted subsidies to farmers and protectionism to the textile industry. By the time a consumer put it on, the shirt had benefited foreign firms, by assuring them of a set amount of business under quotas, as well as workers abroad who preferred underpaid, sometimes dangerous, and tiresome factory work to the grueling drudgery and cultural backwardness of life on a farm. This system lasted until the structure of apparel protectionism under the oft-renewed 1974 fiber international trade system of quotas on less-developed nations ended thirty years later. Up to that point, a perverse consequence of protectionism emerged as actual aid to industrial development in many small countries. After the demise of the quota regime, however, the monolith China took over the manufacturing process, and its apparel exports surged after it reached deals with Walmart, the world's biggest retailer, which rewarded US consumers with the lowest prices. American retailers pressured Congress to lower trade barriers, and while other Third World countries lost jobs, former textile workers in the United States found new jobs at Walmart, Target, J. C. Penney, and other stores. Such employment paid less, with far fewer insurance benefits, than their textile jobs. These were the hard realities of the global trade network, whose diverse participants registered gains and losses depending on luck, perseverance, and entrepreneurial skills. The history of a T-shirt rendered debates between friends and foes of globalization both complicated and, as the system of manufacturing and distribution wound its way through the world, increasingly irrelevant.[180]

The compromises between freer trade and protectionism inherent in the GATT regime, which both encouraged and limited open-door access to national markets, were partly responsible for these conditions. At the end of the Tokyo Round in 1979, the advanced nations moved beyond tariffs to address ways to enhance market access, protect intellectual property rights, and settle disputes that marked the modern trade era. Duties on manufactured goods continued their fall from the Kennedy Round of the 1960s, but most important, codes on such nontariff barriers as subsidies, countervailing duties, dumping, and government procurement were drawn up for the first time. Such protectionist obstacles had proliferated as tariffs fell in significance. In sum, these codes allowed nations to impose countervailing tariffs or seek fair treatment if hurt by domestic "safeguard" measures. A system of surveillance, consultation, and dispute settlement was established in the nontariff barrier negotiating process, but only for signatories to the agreement. Thus, the many developing nations that did not sign the codes remained exposed to discrimination. The Tokyo Round also failed to address voluntary export restraints, targeted and discriminatory safeguard measures by the European Community, and agricultural protectionism—the latter the bane of the previous GATT negotiations. Neither the Europeans nor the Japanese would end their protectionism in agriculture.[181]

In the interim between the Tokyo Round and the new set of talks in Uruguay that began in 1986, the forces of globalization had added to the list of potential obstacles to the liberal trade order. These included trade in services, such as banking, telecommunications, securities trading, insurance, advertising, and data processing, that often faced stiff national licensing and tax regulations (and discrimination). Services were not addressed in GATT but amounted to an estimated 30 percent of world trade in the 1980s—and double that for the United States. As well, intellectual property rights emerged as a new trade issue, especially as Third World nations copied computer software and audio and video materials to avoid the expense of developing these products or paying copyright costs. Furthermore, GATT needed to devise an agreement on trade and investment issues, because governments had adopted means to protect their markets through domestic sourcing requirements, special licenses favoring local factories, and demands that investors export a percentage of their production or balance imports with exports within the host country.

These problems were among the issues discussed at the Uruguay Round (1986–1994), the last GATT meeting before the nearly half-century-old forum was folded into the comprehensive WTO in 1995. The pressures of globalization had so complicated and burdened trade rules that nations had formed the aforementioned regional groupings to defend their interests and undertook bilateral, trilateral, and quadrilateral (the United States, Canada, EC, and Japan) negotiations to manage trade, seek access on particular items and sectors, and resolve disputes. Such talks outside of the GATT framework undermined the multilateral regime; the postwar international trade system faced a collapse in the 1980s similar to that experienced by Bretton Woods a decade before. The global economy's American-led trade principles were in jeopardy. The Uruguay Round thus addressed not only substantive trade issues but also an update of GATT itself by enhancing surveillance and review mechanisms, strengthening links to the IMF and World Bank, and expanding its scope into new areas.

The negotiations were difficult, oftentimes rancorous, and dragged along for eight years with no resolution in sight until the 124 countries decided to conclude this most comprehensive GATT round in 1994. Industrial tariffs fell by a third, and textile quotas were phased out. Barriers to agriculture remained, but for the first time in a GATT round there was agreement on improving market access, replacement of insidious quotas with tariffs, and limits on subsidies. The safeguard codes were tightened to define harmful trade and regulate resort to protectionist measures. Contracting parties also wrote an agreement on trade in services that committed members to apply treatment on a nondiscriminatory basis and provide a formal list of policies such as limits on the number of foreign branch banks allowed to operate in a country. Rules now protected patents, trademarks, and other intellectual property rights, although they would be phased in over a long period to satisfy developing countries. Negotiations also took a first step toward a trade-investment code as well as on a telecommunications accord that was completed in 1997.[182]

The Uruguay Round exposed new issues, such as the need for rules on electronic commerce to allow access to national infrastructures, competition policy to curb cartels that unfairly aided domestic over foreign producers in home markets, and environmental and labor regulations. Regarding the environment, Americans tried to restrict tuna imports from Mexico, because that nation's fishing nets killed porpoises, which could not escape the nets. US tuna producers were forbidden from using such nets, so Washington banned sales of Mexican tuna, to the applause of environmentalists. Mexico protested and the WTO eventually ruled in its favor, arguing that trade rules applied only to the content of the product and not the methods of production. Saying otherwise could set a precedent that might gut the goal of curbing discrimination in an open-door system by allowing nations any excuse to restrict trade. This was a victory for the Third World. Developing nations were ever more on guard, for they believed, like the European corporate-raider-turned-politician James Goldsmith, that the Uruguay Round would end up punishing the Third World as the "poor in the rich countries would subsidize the rich in the poor countries."[183] The emerging nations proved to be a problem, an indication that the international trade order had shifted its focus and would face challenges in the future.

Activists in the core nations recognized more than ever before that the struggles of the poor nations required more attention than they were given by the WTO and other institutions. In the age of globalization, in which people engaged in transnational, private exchanges across national borders without reliance on the state, many groups, nongovernmental organizations, and individuals got involved in helping the economic development of the emerging nations. Scholars and experts began to speak of the movement of "civil society" in which thousands of volunteer civic and social organizations cropped up between government agencies and corporations—filling a gap left by the state and the market—to effect change in the world economy. Their efforts ranged from security to social reforms and took on the characteristic of correcting the wrongs of and damage done by rampant free-market globalization.[184]

Much of this work crossed over into the realms of peacemaking, diplomacy, and social reform, as in the work with children, adoptions, and refugees undertaken by movie stars Audrey Hepburn, Brad Pitt, and Angelina Jolie (the latter worked closely with economist Jeffrey Sachs in villages throughout Africa, engaged the WEF on global economic and social issues, and donated millions of dollars to causes). The WEF itself provided a forum in which to discuss and plan measures to alleviate health and economic scourges around the world. It served to alert the public to major initiatives in health programs, for instance; the Bill & Melinda Gates Foundation offered substantial funds to fight disease worldwide at Davos meetings of the WEF. And the private Gates Foundation itself—its money earned from ownership of the Microsoft Corporation—donated some

$1.4 billion annually to health causes, more than the annual budget of the World Health Organization. The efforts went back a few decades but really accelerated in scope and effectiveness because of the communications wrought by the process of globalization. Ex-Beatle George Harrison had raised money for Bangladesh in 1971 by assembling a group of famous stars, but Bob Geldof's 1984–1985 Band Aid/Live Aid concerts, and his ten-nation Live 8 event in July 2005, which some 3 billion people watched around the world, drew on satellite technology to garner big rewards. Band Aid/Live Aid, undertaken to fight poverty in the Third World, occurred over fifteen hours with 1.7 million watching, and raised $100 million. Geldof designed Live 8 to pin down commitments of much more massive aid to the South by politicians to save the lives of an estimated 4 million people a year. In his characteristically undiplomatic fashion, he demanded that First World countries provide $50 billion per year until 2010 as well as efforts to combat AIDS and other maladies, cancel debts for thirty-eight nations (and eighteen alone in 2005), and provide free education and health care to millions of poor children, by accusing the current generation of politicians of immorally allowing world poverty to persist in times of great wealth in the North.

Other celebrities often stepped into the wake of natural disasters to help with the survival and recovery of areas. Princess Diana was well known for her efforts with victims of war. Soccer star David Beckham appeared as a UN goodwill ambassador in Thailand after the 2004 tsunami as well as in Africa. Media mogul Ted Turner of CNN offered $1 billion to the United Nations over a ten-year period beginning in 1998 for humanitarian purposes, and the funding was used in health and educational campaigns. Former US president Jimmy Carter's foundation was active in trying to stamp out guinea worm and other diseases in Africa that burdened national and local economies and hindered the development of a healthy workforce throughout the continent. The William J. Clinton Foundation did similar work, including a campaign in Malawi and Rwanda to stamp out diseases but also bring fair prices and market access for farmers. These Clinton global initiatives actually drew upon the forces of globalization by seeking finance from governments but mainly from persons who were rich and well connected in world civil society, such as Hollywood movie tycoons, petroleum-state royalty, and wealthy entrepreneurs in India. The former president enlisted some fourteen hundred paid staff and volunteers in over forty countries with a mantra of alleviating poverty and distress through market-based programs run by business, government, and nonprofits. Clinton epitomized a new process in the globalization trend—a middle way between corporations and the state.[185]

Nobody exerted more effort in the Third World, however, than the rock star Bono, who parlayed his celebrity and innovative thinking into relationships with top politicians. These connections earned him a presence at the G-8 summits of the richest nations at Gleneagles in 2005 and Heiligendamm two years later. Earlier Bono had demanded that the North cancel the debt obligations of the South. He then requested that the advanced countries contribute 7 percent of their gross national incomes to his antipoverty program in Africa. The civil society campaign in this regard did not exclude stars from the Third World. African musicians like Youssou N'Dour, Baaba Maal, and Angélique Kidjo joined Geldof on stage at Live 8.[186] Clearly, people around the world were mobilized, not just to wait for nations to negotiate trade and aid deals, but to do something on their own, and the technology and integration of economic globalization would assist them in doing so.

The next set of trade talks—the Doha Development round scheduled to begin in Qatar in 2001—was the first to occur under the WTO regime. It came on the heels of antiglobalization protests and the terrorist attacks on the United States on September 11, both of which wrought changes in the global economy. The multilateral negotiations had been slated to start in Seattle under the name Millennial Round in 1999, but the developing nations balked when the United States and European Union excluded them from talks on the traditionally difficult issue of agricultural trade barriers. They resentfully walked out of the forum, and the Seattle talks collapsed. Massive street demonstrations erupted simultaneously, led by an unlikely coalition of organized labor, environmentalists, anarchists, students, religious groups, consumer advocates, and political activists. They lobbied against corporate repression, the power of multinational firms to curb government safeguards and push for unfettered capitalism, a weakened union movement, poverty in the Third World, elitist international governance, and degradation of the Earth. Several corporations had already felt the wrath of the protesters.[187]

The Nike Company was a case in point. Drawing on various strands of the process of globalization, Nike had branded professional basketball star Michael

The Live 8 concert, London, July 2, 2005. Musician and activist Bob Geldof (in white shirt with finger in air) is joined by singer George Michael and children to perform the Beatles' tune "Hey Jude," part of the campaign by celebrities to promote aid to the impoverished poor nations of the world. (Getty Images)

Jordan himself throughout the world. The company's "swoosh" logo, coupled with "Air" Jordan's magnificent maneuvers on the court, had joined together a global sports craze with satellite communications, advertising, a foreign investment boom in China, and cheap labor in Asia to elevate Jordan to iconic status throughout the world in the 1980s. At the same time, however, tens of thousands of American laborers had lost decent-paying jobs at $5.95 an hour as Nike and other shoe companies moved production overseas. Nike paid workers in Indonesia just 14 cents an hour for shoes costing $49 to $125. By the mid-1990s this transnational came under withering attack for exploiting foreign workers by not paying a livable wage, forcing them to work overtime, preventing unionization, and overall subjecting them to subhuman conditions. In Indonesia, Vietnam, and China, it was the same story—bad wages and worse conditions. In 1997 a member of Vietnam Labor Watch, a US-based activist group seeking to protect workers abroad from predatory transnational corporations, noted after a visit to a

Nike plant in Vietnam that the supervisors humiliated women by forcing them to kneel or stand in the heat and sun as punishment for not working diligently. In another indication of the gendering of globalized work in the market economy, 90 percent of the Nike workforce of thirty-five thousand laborers were exhausted and malnourished women, who worked twelve-hour days to earn $2 for each pair of shoes made, which eventually sold for forty to fifty times that amount in the United States.

The resulting press and uproar prompted the Clinton administration to haul in Nike, L.L.Bean, Reebok, and other manufacturers (and their spokespeople) to sign a code of conduct limiting work weeks to sixty hours and requiring wages at national levels. The protesters wanted even more—recognition of unions and higher minimum wages, because the established wages were insufficient to pay for adequate food and housing. The criticism continued, but by 1997 the Asian economic crisis, along with the backlash, caused Nike sales to plummet by nearly half its record sales of $9.6 billion. Michael Jordan remained a selling point, and this corporation's profits stayed high, but the image of globalization itself had been sullied.[188]

Additional protests followed in ensuing months after the Seattle outburst. Even before Seattle in 1999, there were frequent displays of discomfort and anger over the effects of the open door in permitting transnational companies to dominate economies and even change cultural habits. Unlike Nike, which owned no factories but depended on specialists to negotiate production and costs with hundreds of manufacturers and shippers in several nations, the fast-food giant McDonald's allowed locals in over one hundred countries to operate, staff, and supply its thousands of restaurants. The headquarters in Illinois retained half ownership of these concerns. The problem was not its profits, but its detrimental influence on children's eating habits and health (weight gain, teenage mania, consumerism), family customs, and structures that trended away from networks to individuals and embraced new forms of togetherness (birthday parties at McDonald's rather than traditional celebrations at home), and a change to market values and entrepreneurship.[189]

These transformations wrought by this powerful transnational corporation were fodder for antiglobalization protesters who found the open door to be a means for predatory capitalists to alter traditions and destabilize societies, all in the name of modernization and consumerism. Other protests were more concrete. These involved, at times, tens of thousands of people (and multiple arrests, injuries, and even a death) in Prague, Quebec City, and Genoa in 2000 and 2001, during, respectively, meetings of the IMF and World Bank, Summit of the Americas (which planned for a free trade zone of the hemisphere), and the Group of Seven industrialized powers. Trade delegations reconvened in Doha two years later, just two months after the 9/11 attacks. This horrific event gave impetus to negotiators to succeed in order to help the world economy recover and provide a show of unity among peaceful trading nations who opposed terrorism.

The seven-year Doha talks became a contest of wills between the North and a large contingent of angry traders from the South. At a Cancun gathering in 2003, a new Third World trade bloc called the G-20, led by Brazil, China, India, and South Africa, prevented resolution of four so-called "Singapore issues" (trade and investment, competition, government procurement, and customs issues) that had arisen from WTO meetings the year before and that now created controversy at the Doha Round. The developing and developed worlds were also at loggerheads over nearly every trade item, the most prominent being agriculture and more specifically export subsidies that allowed an edge over Southern commodities to European and US farmers by an artificially priced world market. Although the European delegation pledged to end subsidies, its member states— namely France—refused to go along, out of their traditional embrace of EU agricultural protectionism. By mid-2006 the Doha talks were in trouble, and the crisis deepened when the US Congress renewed farm subsidies for five years. After India's commerce minister announced that he was not "risking the livelihoods of millions of farmers" by allowing subsidies, and China backed him with a call for tariffs to protect poor producers in the South, the Doha Round collapsed in July 2008. Recrimination passed all around, and hopes for the talks to restart foundered in the ensuing global economic meltdown.[190]

That the WTO's first round of trade talks stalled signified neither that the negotiations had aborted nor the end of liberalization efforts and a crimping of globalization. Resolution was possible, for never had a major multilateral trade round failed to produce an agreement, but negotiators discussed Doha issues on the sidelines of other economic conferences throughout 2009 and not in formal ministerial sessions in the WTO until the late fall. Globalization continued despite the trade discussion breakdown, but the process was infused with qualifications and regulations from all nations, and particularly those from the South, and especially as challenging world economic conditions made negotiators less amenable to compromise.

One area that clearly displayed the force and effects of market globalization was the environment. By the first decade of the twenty-first century, people around the world had become knowledgeable about the relationship between the global economy and the environment in which they lived. Declining quality of air, water, and ground affected all nations, and dealing with the detrimental effects of climate change—or the buzzwords "global warming"—became a top priority of the international community. The Kyoto Protocol of 1997 was an attempt to reduce greenhouse gas emissions to an agreed-upon level by 2012. The United States, the most notable polluter, accounting for over 36 percent of emission levels before the Protocol was negotiated, signed but did not ratify the accord, out of fear it would overregulate, and thus crimp, its economy. Emerging nations like China and India also were not parties to the Kyoto Protocol—these big polluters claimed that they were exempt from the requirements because their development took precedence over the environment. The Third World argued that the advanced nations should shoulder the burden of cleaning up the world and keeping it safe.[191]

Nonetheless, later accords, such as one at Montreal in 2005 and the Copenhagen agreement in 2009, pledged cutbacks in emissions (even if levels and deadlines to do so were left vague), and many localities adopted their own compliance levels. Negotiations for voluntary international partnerships to develop alternative energy sources sprang up around the world. Corporations and transnational businesses also jumped in: a group of twenty-four companies, including British Telecommunications (BT), Hewlett-Packard (HP), Toyota, Siemens, and Volkswagen, proposed a global emissions trading scheme that would set limits on how much greenhouse gas countries could emit and would define "emissions rights." This carbon "cap-and-trade" scheme assigned to corporations and other groups a certain amount of "allowances" or credits on emissions, which could be sold to big polluters who exceeded their cap. Businesses that polluted less earned profits from the credits; those that did not had to pay for polluting. Companies sought these types of limits out of an interest in more certainty for long-term investments and a more level playing field. In other words, market principles and practices entered the environmental field.

So did technology. A leading business that focused on reducing its "carbon footprint" was coffee retailer Starbucks (which had emitted an estimated 295,000 tons of carbon in North America alone in 2003); it focused on gauging more precisely its sources of power for transport and roasting, and committed itself to generating 20 percent of its energy use from wind power. Starbucks also engaged in high-profile campaigns, such as "Green Umbrellas for a Green Cause" and the online Planet Green Game to encourage consumers to "go green." In 2009 Google also helped create a market for eco-friendliness by leading a group of forty companies (including Starbucks) in kicking off the "Climate Savers Computing Initiative," a project aimed at building and buying computers that were more energy-efficient. Neither Google, Starbucks, nor many other firms wished to disclose their carbon footprint data, because this would reveal competitive information; nevertheless, Google kept watch on the size of its emissions and sought to use noncarbon energy sources for much of its power needs, and purchased carbon offsets for the rest. Recently Google flipped the switch on 1.6 megawatts of solar power modules on the roof of its Mountain View headquarters.

Some European nations, and the Obama administration in 2009, considered imposing a "carbon tax" on "dirty" imports, although this would amount to protectionism and would have violated the market precepts of the WTO.[192]

In the poor and developing world, remedies to the plight of indigenous populations, who were often the victims of environmental degradation, sprang up as a result of the melding of market and nature. Eco-tourism and sustainable tourist initiatives flourished globally to save forests, islands, seas, and wildlife that were being damaged and depleted by globalization's thrust of transportation and communication networks into remote areas. Furthermore, many poor countries lacked the capacity for new sources of energy or the money to import them; an estimated one-third of the world's population went without the modern energy services of lights, refrigeration, and transport (let alone telecommunications and information technology). An impending population explosion in the world's poorest areas boded ill for finding solutions. Yet the World Bank did not see hopelessness, because roughly a billion people could afford commercial rates, if the rates were reasonable and people were given aid to help pay for services. They could be turned away from such dirty, and costly, energy sources as kerosene and batteries, and toward subsidized electricity grids that already allowed the rich to live more cheaply.

As a direct result of market thinking, a "micropower" approach swept the world, in which small systems and facilities that were initially expensive could provide cheaper energy over time, as well as autonomy for poor people and groups. In Yemen, locals set up small, privately owned and operated electric generators to service households not reached by the country's inadequate grid system. In India, the Tata Energy Research Institute developed energy supply links across many small villages and focused on the efficiencies of conserving kerosene, diesel, and biomass to "green" the village. A nonprofit organization called Preferred Energy Incorporated initiated efforts in the Philippines to build a micro-hydroelectric facility on a creek to service neighboring villages. The project was jointly undertaken by several donor agencies and local residents. The donors supplied the necessary equipment, while villagers provided labor, materials, and organization. Evidence of the power of globalization was clear in the most remote and strapped areas of the world.[193]

Crisis

In fact, trade frictions stemmed also from repeated financial problems with the post–Cold War global market system. In 1994, for instance, the sudden devaluation of the Mexican peso precipitated a currency crisis as American banks faced defaults on their enormous loans to Mexico. Only a $50 billion loan by the US government in tandem with international lending agencies stabilized the peso and prevented the collapse of many American banks. Across the world, the dissolution of the Soviet Union and its empire led to lackluster economic performance at best and sheer crisis at worst. In Eastern Europe, new democracies found themselves bereft of needed large-scale aid from Western Europe and North America in their transition to liberal capitalism. Instead, the United States and the IMF, coached by advisors such as Harvard economist Jeffrey Sachs, advocated marketization by "shock therapy" rather than by gradual stewardship—as had happened in China after the fall of Mao Zedong. The goal was to break with the communist system through a decisive switch to free-enterprise capitalism and to promote a permanent turn to democracy. Although Poland thrived under the radical overhaul, and most of the Balkan nations fared well, the Western European investors who provided the bulk of the capital cared less for long-term growth in the region and more for quick profits. The former Soviet satellites counted on integration into the EU for their development when big aid packages were not forthcoming from a rather visionless Western Europe, which was preoccupied with its own problems and fearful of weakening their union by admitting southern Europeans susceptible to Islamic fundamentalism. EU enlargement took place, but only after the damage of shock therapy was done. For Russia, the experiment turned out to be most challenging.[194]

The advent of Russian Federation president Boris Yeltsin's plan for radical market reforms through austerity programs advocated by the United States and the IMF in late 1991 plunged Russia into economic crisis. Shock therapy's ripping apart of the socialist system by rapid privatization and termination of price controls pushed an estimated one-third of the population into poverty. Both the gross domestic product and industrial output contracted by half. By 1995 the neoliberal market jolt prevented Russia from paying off its external debt, and privatization handed over state enterprises to corrupt officials with ties to organized crime. An enriched Russian mafia exported much of their newfound wealth from the country in an outpouring of billions of dollars in capital flight. Meanwhile, Russia decayed into depression, environmental degradation, and occasional violent lawlessness as strongman rule clamped down on the commanding heights of the economy. As a result, the capitalist world abandoned its policy of rapid change, searching for ways to create "less shock and more therapy for the Russian people," noted a Clinton administration official.[195] Communism was surely dead in this pillar of Marxism, but the process of globalization undercut the very fabric of Russian society and placed in question the country's viability.

The global market economy again revealed its vulnerabilities and interdependence, and the tension between American market ideas and American power and leadership, during the so-called Asian crisis of 1997–1998. Investors in Thailand had borrowed in foreign currencies to finance stocks and real estate, but when values went sour they began to sell Thai currency (the baht) and seek cover in dollars or yen. In short, the government tried to buy up the baht to the tune of

$20 billion, in order to maintain its value against the US dollar, but the effort failed and the currency was allowed to float. As a result it lost nearly half of its value in a matter of days, despite massive government purchases, and by September 1997 the baht had been devalued by 70 percent relative to the US dollar. Due to the integration of the ASEAN nations, the lack of confidence in Thailand's economy spread anxiety to neighboring Malaysia, South Korea, Indonesia, Singapore, and the Philippines. They witnessed tremendous selling sprees of their currencies as capital sought haven elsewhere. Stock markets plunged, losing one-third to one-half of their values, for investors understood that firms would be unable to repay debt due to the plunging values of regional currencies. Indonesia's stock values fell by 46 percent and Malaysia's by half. Exchange rates followed downward; the Filipino peso dropped in value by one-fourth. About 150 financial institutions in Asia closed or suspended operations, were nationalized, or came under IMF control.

A sudden and severe recession swept over a region that had been noted for its vigorous growth through globalization. South Korea, for one, saw its eleventh-place world economic ranking, based on gross domestic product, fall to seventeenth, behind India, Russia, and Mexico, in a matter of two months. The Four Tigers were tamed (South Korea accepted an IMF bailout in return for laying off millions of workers) and Japan—already suffering economic woes—also felt the sting. The effects lingered for a year or so. For instance, the Philippines experienced zero growth in 1998. The Asian contagion then spread beyond the region into Russia, Brazil, and Argentina and threatened to infect the entire world. In late October 1997, the US stock market fell by 7.2 percent on worries about the Asian crisis. Indonesia erupted in riots to protest the suffering caused by the downturn, its dictator fell from power after a thirty-year reign, and Thailand's prime minister also resigned.[196]

Globalization had been trumpeted as ushering in the end of history—meaning the arrival of liberal democracy, including open-door capitalism, as the final form of human governance. But now American free-market ideology and its Washington/Wall Street advocates were branded as dangers to the world economy. As money flowed around the globe through financial liberalization in a borderless world, the IMF had joined purveyors of American free-enterprise to demand that nations liberalize capital accounts in order to right their payments deficits. Washington, for its part, blamed foreign corruption and inadequate accounting standards for the crisis and pushed for even more liberalization as the remedy. Treasury Secretary Robert Rubin, who had coordinated the bailout of the Mexican peso four years earlier, and Federal Reserve chairman Alan Greenspan turned to the IMF to quell the turmoil, much like the United States had done during the Latin American debt crisis of the previous decade. They demanded heightened free-market practices in every nation. Thus, beginning in October 1998, Greenspan lowered American interest rates six times to stimulate imports from Asia. This helped nations of the region repay debt obligations but placed further stress on vulnerable US industries like apparel manufacturing, which closed up shop and moved abroad to Mexico, Pakistan, or China, where labor costs were cheaper. In Asia, Thailand and Malaysia led others in tough reforms of their domestic economies by imposing regulations on banks and austerity measures to attract international investors. Clearly, crises stemmed from greed and overreaching but also from the fundamentals of transnational production, vast capital transfers, and other elements of the globalization process that enriched hundreds of millions of people but did not help billions more.[197] The Asian financial fiasco abated, although the upturn would not endure for long once the 9/11 tragedy rocked the global economy and exposed the vulnerabilities of supply chains that stretched around the world.

Market or State?

The terrorist attack orchestrated by Osama bin Laden showed the dangers and pitfalls of market doctrine, in that globalization fulfilled the long-held postwar American hope for openness, which by its very nature, ironically, facilitated such deeds. Open borders not only boosted access for corporations around the world but allowed criminals and terrorists ease of entry. Nations had been dealing with drug networks and transnational gang and criminal violence for decades; narcotics trade amounted to an estimated $500 billion a year by the new millennium, and gangs raked in somewhere around $7 billion as they annually moved four to five million people across borders. Criminals mimicked corporations in forging alliances to maximize efficiency, promote cooperative endeavors to enhance profits and opportunities, and include people of diverse backgrounds who could operate within the dominant culture. Bin Laden took advantage of the Information Age, with its easy access to technological know-how, by obtaining instructions from the Internet on making explosives. The migration of millions of people across borders allowed his suicide teams to pose as students and tourists in this jet-set era of expanding, cheap travel. The boom in container shipping in the integrated transportation system wrought by the global economy and lax security procedures on the part of overwhelmed American customs officials allowed the relatively unchecked entry of tens of thousands of containers flowing in and out of ports daily. Terrorist networks, along with drug-runners and gangs, thrived in such an accessible, permeable, and huge open market that was difficult to police due to its sheer size and volume of commerce.[198]

Signs of global recovery from the September 11 attacks were apparent as early as 2002, and international trade and investments resumed amidst the sober realization that globalization would continue despite the subsequent turn toward reliance on the state, national security concerns, and war. In essence, although the world could not return to the Washington-led framework of a half century before, it was evident that the market had not replaced the nation as the only dynamic actor in the world economy. And history could repeat itself in another way, as global economic downturns did not seem to be products of a dusty, irrelevant past. By late 2006 the world headed once again toward a collapse of banking and manufacturing, as it had faced seventy years prior. And once more the market leader—the United States—stood at the fore of the problems.

When American home prices began to fall, a rash of defaults on subprime home mortgages (loans made to low-income homeowners with troubled credit histories) ensued and triggered a massive number of foreclosures. Loans and securities backed by subprime mortgages lost their value, straining the banking and insurance systems in the United States and then worldwide. A global credit crunch followed. By mid-2008 the world economy was rocked by a sharp rise in gasoline prices to levels not seen since the oil crises of the 1970s. By October the IMF issued a bleak forecast, predicting that the advanced nations were already in or approaching a severe recession and that growth for the following year would be the slowest since the 9/11 tragedy. Risk taking and major players in investment markets—Bear Stearns, American International Group, Lehman Brothers, Merrill Lynch, and Citigroup—went out of business or were acquired by competitors for a fraction of their previous value. The two big US government lenders, Freddie Mac and Fannie Mae, saw their $5 trillion in mortgage-backed securities placed in conservatorship by the government.[199] As central banks scrambled to pump liquidity into frozen money markets, the IMF warned that not only would the housing slump in America, Spain, and elsewhere crimp the North, but developing nations would also suffer from soaring food and fuel prices and slackening demand. "The world economy is now entering a major downturn in the face of the most dangerous shock in mature financial markets since the 1930s," noted an IMF report at the end of the year.[200]

That statement proved prophetic; by March 2009 the economic news was bleak around the world. Taiwan's output had shrunk by over 8 percent in the last quarter of 2008 alone, Russian and American unemployment rose to above 8 percent, the currencies of Eastern Europe plummeted against the euro and the dollar, Japan faced its worst recession in decades (including the "lost decade" of the 1990s), and automakers around the world were heading for bankruptcy. Some observers even saw a complete failure of capitalism and America and the world descending into a prolonged depression.[201]

Iceland's experience with privatized banking speculation gone mad showed the dangers of both greed and a shaky world credit system so integrated by globalization that tremors in one economy affected many others. The country's finances literally collapsed, but not because of exposure to the American subprime mortgage crisis. Rather, the sickness was due to excessive leveraging—too much reliance on debt as a means to enhance returns on investments. Borrowing heavily from foreign lenders and depositors, banks lent freely to investors who leveraged their capital in a buyout spree across Europe on the notion that the stock market would forever rise, rather than on basing their accounts on adequate reserves. Icelanders became affluent by running up tremendous debt by borrowing from foreign banks that offered lower interest rates than they could receive at home. As long as the Icelandic króna remained strong, repayments of these loans were feasible. As insolvency hit worldwide financial markets in 2008, however, foreign banks stopped lending and the króna lost 43 percent of its value against the dollar. Soon no traders would buy it; interbank lending halted. Bankruptcies swept the world and over the country and the stock market shut down temporarily. The government nationalized the banking system. Yet thousands of individual depositors in Britain, Denmark, Germany, the Netherlands, Austria, and Norway who had invested heavily in Iceland's banks (Britain had deposits of $1.3 billion, for example) now demanded repayment. When it was not forthcoming some agreed to temporary loans to Iceland, whereas the Netherlands and Britain froze Iceland's assets in their countries and sued Iceland. The meltdown that came to pass in 2008 and 2009 hinged, at bottom, on disproportionate global debt that threw the world credit markets into crisis.[202]

As stock markets embarked on roller-coaster rides, plunging by hundreds of points in a single day then rising just as sharply the next, governments and financiers around the world huddled to strategize about solutions. Central banks coordinated interest-rate cuts, although the tumult continued in the economy. In Asia, which was experienced with such turmoil, the free-falling dollar posed worries. Critical exports abroad slowed; Japanese carmakers witnessed such a falloff in consumer demand in the United States, and a world mired in the worst auto downturn in a quarter century, that Toyota suffered its first losses since its birth in 1937. Like others in the industry, it turned to belt tightening by curbing worker benefits and even pondering layoffs. Indonesia's stock market halted trading repeatedly during these years, and investors looked for safe havens in banking systems in precarious situations at best. There were not many safe places to deposit money. Analysts agreed that interest-rate cuts would not be sufficient; conventional macroeconomic tools could not prevent violent market gyrations that threatened the biggest global economic collapse since the Great Depression.[203]

Soon most nations announced huge financial aid packages (the administration of George W. Bush stepped in with tax rebates and then a huge bailout of the financial sector totaling $700 billion, and President Barak Obama added billions more to the emergency aid to institutions and consumers alike in 2009) to rescue failing banks in a move that amounted to the nationalization of the global financial network. The "Big Three" American carmakers also trooped to Capitol Hill, requesting government assistance for the beleaguered US auto industry. Bush stepped in with minimal assistance when Congress refused to help, and then the Obama administration shored up Detroit with funds while it oversaw bankruptcy deliberations by General Motors and Chrysler to compel reorganizations that might save millions of jobs. Whether these fixtures in the

The Great Recession begins, November 15, 2008. Protesters rallied in Reykjavik against the Icelandic government's inept and permissive policies toward banks. As bankruptcies mounted and the Icelandic króna lost its value with the onset of the global financial collapse, the government nationalized the banking system. (AFP/Getty Images)

American economy would survive remained in question as globalization took its toll.[204]

The outlook slowly improved but it was clear that in many cases, the world economy had changed for the worse. By spring 2010, US banks had lost about $885 billion, British financial institutions suffered a drain of $455 billion, euro zone banks saw their accounts plummet by $665 billion, and Asian losses amounted to $2.3 billion. Spain, Hungary, and Greece threatened to default on their debts; overextended banks in France, Germany, and Austria created fears of more turmoil and instability ahead, and even an undermining of the euro. Leaders at G-20 summits pledged to reform finances and trade, and seek to create more employment, but they undertook few specific measures to address their growing public debts and balance-of-payments imbalances. Still, by late 2010 the global economic signs improved for sustained growth; into 2012 the employment picture picked up in America, even as it sagged in Europe.

Regardless of the better forecasts for international recovery, nations and transnationals around the world were entering, many feared, their own lost decade. Iceland's experience was one example, as was the ouster, due to the Japanese people's frustration with fifteen years of prolonged recession, of the political party that had long been predominant in Japan. The number of "failed states" in the emerging world also increased: in Somalia, so few people benefited from the agricultural export economy that many turned to piracy. Zimbabwe's corrupt government provoked violence and left that country bereft of a workable economic structure, and its people with a lower per capita gross domestic product ($200) than Somalia's pathetic level of $600 (the US figure was $49,900 in 2009). Inflation soared; outsiders estimated that four out of five Zimbabweans lived in abject poverty, and the country perched on the brink of total collapse. Africa had, on average, never fared well under the market regime of globalization, but the economic crisis of 2008–2009 worsened its prospects even further.[205]

Giant stimulus plans in Europe, North America, and Asia showed, at least, how interlinked the global economy had become and that no nation, institution, or investor could make a move independently of another. Like India, Brazil, and South Africa, China went on a stock-trading spree in the first decade of the 2000s; stock trading amounted to 230 percent of the nation's gross domestic production in 2007 (quadrupling over seven years). The country's merchandise trade also skyrocketed over the same period. And China, which held a significant portion of US debt, warned the Americans on this score. For their part, Americans worried about China's growing presence in their economy. They were unable fully to accept that financial markets were so globalized that there was no escaping the influence of another big power.[206] As American economist and Nobel Prize winner Paul Krugman noted, the need for international cooperation was imperative, "because we have a globalized financial system in which a crisis that began with a bubble in Florida condos and California McMansions has caused monetary catastrophe in Iceland. We're all in this together, and need a shared solution."[207] Such sentiment was widely shared and acted upon.

In September 2009 the G-20 summit of the twenty largest economies in the world met in Pittsburgh, Pennsylvania, to discuss the economic crisis and how to reshape policies to safeguard the global market. Leaders debated a host of transnational problems, including security and environmental issues alongside the weak economy. They focused on the current recovery agenda but also acknowledged a significant transformation, agreeing that for future discussions of the agenda for global economic matters they would replace the exclusive G-8 gathering with the G-20 group, which included emerging powerhouses like China, Brazil, and India. Some experts looked on this development as a watershed, a point in history where the power to arbitrate world market forces shifted beyond the United States and Europe.[208]

Forecasters soon looked more positively on the world economy, although they were not greatly excited. High-income nations were expected to grow by about 2.7 percent between 2010 and 2012, while poorer nations' economies, having not suffered from the downswing in stocks and credit defaults, were fairly stable. Outside of the Eurozone, recovery and growth appeared to be in the cards; in China, Russia, Brazil, Mexico, and India, growth would be robust (although not as stellar as before, as, for instance, in China), and even the US economy was deemed to return to some dynamism as losses in bank assets declined below expectations. Great Britain suffered through extreme austerity measures to position itself for recovery in the future. However, the uncertainty in Europe due to the continuing debt crisis, which had spread to Ireland and Spain, troubled economists. Even the strongest economy in Europe—Germany—grew anemically at 1.2 percent in 2010, a rate that would rise the next year only to 1.7 percent. As a whole, the Eurozone nations had growth rates at a feeble 1 percent in 2010. And although capital flows rose to the developing nations, fiscal restraints in the rich nations would likely reduce the amount of aid to the Third World. This would have serious consequences for Third World economies and modernization. Subtracting the solidly growing countries like China and India, the developing world was still in the doldrums.

In short, the record indicated a slow but steady uptick in economic activity worldwide, but that the global economy would remain fairly sluggish—and especially unable to provide the necessary large percentage increases in employment activity—for the medium term.[209] In response, bankers were heartened, as were stock exchanges around the world, but the optimism was tempered by a wave of protests, beginning in Spain and spreading worldwide by October 2011. Spurred by demonstrations at the capitalist system's ground zero—Wall Street—protesters demanded an accounting by the supposed richest "1 percent" of the population, who profited at the expense of the "99 percent," the middle and lower classes. That the powerful recovered, abetted by politicians, while the vast majority of the middle and working classes remained mired in recession, was not too hard to fathom, just as the Arab Spring, beginning in 2010, showed that a large percentage of, say, Egyptians barely subsisted while a fraction of the elites prospered. For decades the working and middle classes have been undermined by distant global—and unelected—bureaucracies and financiers, whom protesters believed were held unaccountable to the common voter, and who were beneficiaries of the great movement of the times—market globalization.[210] Any improvement in the global economy was a welcome development, although paradoxically it took another world financial contagion to show both the perils and the possibilities of the post–World War II American march through the open door to a regime of free enterprise and globalization that guided the economic hopes, political protests, policies, and prospects of a host of nations and transnationals.

The Record

Even though the severe recession of 2008–2009 put in question the merits of deregulation of the global economy, that downturn signaled the integration of stock markets, banks, and producers around the world. The open-door model was under stress but trundled on as a paradigm, in part by default but largely because it offered the potential for growth, profit, and development, just as it had since 1945. American leadership weakened as new powerhouses in Europe and Asia challenged Washington's hegemony. Thus, perhaps the most marked success of US stewardship paradoxically undermined American strength at the same time. That is, the United States created and engineered a global capitalist economy, based on free enterprise precepts, that was so open and expansive that it led to democratization in the management of trade and finances. Pluralism and power sharing signaled true globalization—the objective of the United States for decades. In the world economy, there was no longer any room for the unilateralism of the immediate postwar era or even the heavy-handed policies of the Nixon period. Globalization required global collaboration; no person, corporation, or country was an island.

While globalization endures as a work in progress—mainly because it is a process and not an end result of exchanges in the world capitalist order—the record since 1945 reveals winners and losers under the American regime of open doors and multilateralism. All traders and investors enjoyed ups and suffered downs during this long period; the miraculous rise of Japan and then its spectacular slide in the 1990s was a case in point, as is Germany's ascent from barbarity and utter destruction in World War II to the heights of European capitalism and then its recent struggles with high unemployment. The United States reigned supreme over the global economy just after the war and fell into the doldrums of the 1970s but emerged as the champion of globalization in the 1990s. Thailand turned out to be richer than most developing countries, but its quality of life was lower than most—Thai citizens enjoyed high incomes but lacked proper sewage systems, suffered from flooding, and played catch-up in the Information Age because they lacked sufficient high-tech expertise. Some nations never recovered their economic grandeur in the postcolonial era, yet European imperialists such as Britain, France, and Holland found success in regional integration. In Africa, Latin America, areas of the Middle East, and parts of the old European communist bloc, the ills of economic mismanagement, debt, natural crises, insecurity, doctrinaire market policies, inadequate generosity and patience with diverse models of development in the North (and especially on the part of the United States), and a lack of self-sufficiency mired hundreds of millions of people in poverty (although the United Nations found that the number of people living in extreme economic duress worldwide dropped from 1.8 billion in 1990 to 1.4 billion fifteen years later—much of this due to prosperity in China).[211] It should also not be forgotten that one of the golden eras of globalization—the late nineteenth century and early twentieth century, which witnessed improved communications, high growth rates, financial and investment stability, and world economic integration—ended abruptly with the disaster of a world war in 1914. Politics and power can interfere again with the process of globalization.

Although the world economy benefited some and hurt others, and although people around the globe could hope but also despair, it was clear that leaders would continue to wrestle with economic theories, models, and results. Just like during and after the Second World War, experts and politicians would continue to debate the problems of economic structures, processes, and power-sharing struggles, and even issues of morality in the global economy. People, corporations, and other transnational entities would carry seeds of change, protest, and growth with them as they crossed national boundaries. Countries would put forth new plans and negotiate agreements to forge an ever-expansive system of profit that met needs and ambitions. The United States showed no signs of succumbing to the status of a second-rate has-been, even as it struggled to influence the world economy. At the heart of American designs lay the force of the market that the United States injected across the globe, along with its sheer size and economic power. Postwar American free-enterprise ideology and practices opened the door to the explosion of globalization, which would be battered and contested as well as nurtured and applauded by nations and peoples around the planet. Market forces proved transformative in various ways and with many consequences, as the United States unleashed the power of free enterprise that shaped the lives of billions in negative and positive ways.

THREE

Into the Anthropocene:
People and Their Planet

J. R. McNeill and Peter Engelke

Introduction

SINCE the nineteenth century, geologists, earth scientists, evolutionary biologists, and their colleagues have divided the history of the Earth into a series of eras, periods, and epochs. These are based, in a loose sense, on the environmental history of our planet, especially on the twists and turns in the evolution of life on Earth. We are (and have been for a long time) in the Cenozoic era and within that the Quaternary period. And within the Quaternary period, we are in the Holocene epoch, meaning the last twelve thousand years or so. It is defined above all by its climate, an interglacial moment that so far has been agreeably stable compared to what came before. All of what is conventionally understood as human history, including the entire history of agriculture and of civilization, has taken place in the Holocene. Or perhaps one should say it all *took* place in the Holocene.

This chapter takes the view that a new era in the history of the Earth has begun, that the Holocene is over and something new has begun: the Anthropocene. The idea of the Anthropocene was popularized by the Dutch atmospheric chemist Paul Crutzen, who won a Nobel Prize in 1995 for his work on depletion of the ozone layer in the stratosphere. The changing composition of the atmosphere, especially the well-documented increase in carbon dioxide, seemed to Crutzen so dramatic and so potentially consequential for life on Earth that he concluded that a new stage had begun in Earth history, one in which humankind had emerged as the most powerful influence upon global ecology. The crux of the concept is just that: a new era in which human actions overshadow the quiet persistence of microbes and the endless wobbles and eccentricities in the Earth's orbit and therefore define the age.[1]

Crutzen and colleagues argued that the Anthropocene began in the eighteenth century, with the onset of both the fossil fuel energy regime and the modern rise of global population.[2] The use of coal was becoming integral to economic life in Britain by the 1780s, and it would thereafter play a larger and larger role in the world economy. New technologies and new energy demand led to the exploitation of other fossil fuels, namely oil and natural gas. By the 1890s, half of global energy use came in the form of fossil fuels, and by 2010 that share had climbed to nearly 80 percent. Modern history has unfurled in the context of a fossil fuel energy regime, and of exponential growth in energy use.

Modern history also played out amid runaway population growth. In 1780 about 800 to 900 million humans walked the Earth. By 1930 there were some two billion, and by 2011 just short of seven billion. No primate, perhaps no mammal, has ever enjoyed such a frenzy of reproduction and survival in the history of life on Earth. There is nothing in the demographic history of our species anything like the modern rise of population, nor will there be again.

How these surges of energy use and population growth will evolve in the future is anyone's guess. In any case, since the eighteenth century the human species has embarked on a bold new venture with no analogues anywhere in history. Within that span, the last two or three human generations have seen a screeching acceleration of most of the trends that define the Anthropocene. For example, three-quarters of the human-caused loading of the atmosphere with carbon dioxide took place between 1945 and 2011. The number of motor vehicles on Earth increased from 40 million to 800 million. The number of people nearly tripled, and the number of city-dwellers rose from about 700 million to 3.5 billion.

This period since 1945 corresponds roughly to the average life expectancy of a human being. Only one in ten persons now alive can remember anything before 1945. The entire life experience of almost everyone now living has taken place within what appears to be the climactic moment of the Anthropocene and is certainly the most anomalous and unrepresentative period in the quarter-million-year history of relations between our species and the biosphere. That should make us all skeptical of expectations that any particular current trends will last for long.[3]

Nonetheless, the Anthropocene, barring catastrophe, is set to continue. Human beings will go on exercising influence over their environments and over global ecology far out of proportion to their numbers and far overshadowing that of other species. But just how, and for how long, humans will do so is uncertain. In the fullness of time the Anthropocene may prove too brief to seem worthy as a geological epoch. The International Union of Geological Sciences is wrestling with whether or not to recognize the Anthropocene formally in its scientific scheme. Time will tell. With luck and restraint on our part, the Anthropocene might last as long as some earlier geologic epochs.

The Shift to Fossil Fuels

All historical developments have tangled roots. Those of the Anthropocene extend deep into the past, although just how deep is open to question. People in China and England used fossil fuels in medieval times. But as late as 1750 there was no sign that fossil fuels would become, within 150 years, the centerpiece of the world's energy system. According to one controversial hypothesis, human action—land clearing for agriculture—has affected climate for eight thousand years, preventing a return to Ice Age conditions. If true, this is a deep taproot of the Anthropocene.[4]

We will skip over the deepest (and most tenuous) roots of the Anthropocene, such as the harnessing of fire and domestication of plants, to focus on the transitional stage from 1700 to 1950, during which time humankind shifted from an organic economy to one driven by fossil fuels, from slow and spotty demographic and economic growth to rapid and persistent growth, from mainly modest and localized impacts on the environment to deep and pervasive ones.

In 1700 the Earth was home to perhaps 600 or 700 million people, roughly half the population of China today, or twice the population of the United States. Nearly 80 percent of them lived in Eurasia. Almost all were by today's standards desperately poor, more at the mercy of the environment than masters of it. They lived in fear of bad harvests and brutal epidemics, over which they had scant control and which they typically understood as divine retribution.

They did their best to shape the world to suit their preferences. The only efficient means they had for this task was fire. They routinely ignited forests or bush to prepare the way for fields or pasture, as their ancestors had long done before them. Beyond fire, they had the muscle power of domesticated animals and their own limbs with which to sculpt the earth, drain marshes, build cities, and do all the things people then could do that changed the environment. Their direct impacts were for the most part slow and small, mostly amounting to further extensions of agriculture into lands formerly left uncultivated: newly terraced mountainsides in Morocco, drained fenlands in England, crops in place of jungle in

Bengal, rice paddies carved out of South China hillsides, new clearings for cassava in Angola, and sugarcane fields installed in Jamaica.[5] These changes could seem dramatic on the local scale. Globally they were tiny and were sometimes offset by land abandonment resulting from war or epidemics. In the Americas, for example, the demographic catastrophe that followed the arrival of Europeans in 1492—a population decline of 50 to 90 percent within a century—meant that many formerly agricultural landscapes were turning to wilderness in 1700. Or put more precisely, they were supporting new patterns of spontaneous vegetation and wildlife in accord with the processes of ecological succession. Similar things happened more locally wherever protracted wars drove farming folk away, as in many patches of Central Europe during the Thirty Years' War (1618–1648).

Despite their limited technologies, these 600 million earthlings had some powerful, if indirect, environmental effects. The main reason for that was early modern globalization, the knitting together of the world's coasts through oceanic navigation. In the sixteenth and seventeenth centuries, maritime voyaging—especially in the Indian and Atlantic Oceans, but to some extent in the Pacific too—linked societies and ecosystems formerly kept separate by the broad expanses of blue water.

The most dramatic consequence of early modern globalization was the spread of infectious diseases to new lands and populations. In the Americas, South Africa, Australia, and New Zealand this led to horrific epidemics and radical depopulation. Gradually, however, diseases spread so widely that more and more infections became endemic—or childhood diseases—and epidemics grew rarer. This "microbial unification of the world" often brought higher infant and child mortality, but because many diseases are more dangerous to adults than to children, over time it lowered overall disease mortality. In addition, it may have led to improved genetic resistance to infections, as survivors reproduced more often than those most susceptible to disease. The rate of global population growth began a long upswing in the eighteenth century, partly as a result.[6] No one understood the process at the time, no one intended it, and no one could predict that microbial unification would help pave the way for the Anthropocene.

The upturn in population growth also owed something to the early modern globalization of food crops. The peoples of the Americas suffered heavily from the globalization of infection, but they benefited from the arrival of wheat, barley, bananas, oranges, apples, and dozens of other foodstuffs. Some of these could grow where no native American species would, and others yielded far better than did indigenous crops. So the food supply of the hemisphere improved, and conditions were set for rapid population growth—much of it in the form of immigrants, voluntary and involuntary, from Western Europe, West Africa, and Angola.

At the same time, newly introduced American crops improved the food supply in Europe, Asia, and Africa. Potatoes, maize, and cassava (also known as manioc) did well in environments that were unsuitable for native crops in Eurasia and Africa. Potatoes sustained population growth in northern Europe, and maize had similar effects in hilly parts of China. Maize and manioc became important crops in Africa, although what the possible effects may have been upon population remain uncertain due to lack of data.

In the nineteenth century, medicine and science too came to have a strong impact on population growth. The earlier improvements in food supply and the reduction in the roll of epidemics had owed very little to science. Now improved knowledge of disease transmission, and of the chemistry of soils and plants, led to a train of developments that relaxed constraints on population growth. Probably the most important was sanitation and the control of waterborne diseases such as typhoid, cholera, and dysentery. Improved transport played a role too, as railroads and steamships made it practical to ship grain from distant frontiers in America or Australia to lands where population threatened to outstrip local food production. Population crept ever upward in the nineteenth century and the early twentieth. Even the death tolls of the world wars could scarcely slow this trend.

Economic growth as well as the modern rise of population helped push us into the Anthropocene. The world economy grew timidly before 1700, at which point it was only about half the size of Mexico's today.[7] It thrived in the following centuries, due partly to population growth, partly to technological advances, and partly to the efficiencies arising from specialization and exchange on an increasingly global scale—what economists often call Smithian growth. By 1950, despite the setbacks of the world wars and the Great Depression of the 1930s, the world economy was about fourteen times bigger than it had been in 1700.

Economic growth on this scale required considerable environmental change. Lumberjacks felled forests to provide timber for construction of all sorts. Peasants and slaves toiled to convert land into cotton plantations to feed textile industries.

An Indian coal miner carrying a basket-load of coal, ca. 1950. Coal and other fossil fuels, such as oil and natural gas, powered the world's economy after 1945 but entailed major public health and environmental costs associated with extraction and use. (Getty Images)

Miners scraped the bowels of the earth to provide tin, copper, iron, and other ores for metallurgy. Engineers straightened rivers for navigation and diverted their waters for agriculture as never before. And of course, farmers plowed more and more land around the world to feed themselves and their ever more numerous neighbors. By dint of our economic activity, humankind had inadvertently become a geological force, shaping the face of the Earth.

Much of that economic activity resulted from the adoption of fossil fuels. In 1700 people used almost no fossil fuels. But that soon changed. Although used only in parts of the world, coal gradually became the most important energy source, in the aggregate, over the century between 1790 and 1890. By 1910, oil had also entered the energy picture. Together, coal and oil soon amounted to three-fourths of human energy use. They allowed far more economic activity, wealth, consumption, and ease than people had ever known—and far more disruption to the biosphere. By 1945, although most people had still never seen a lump of coal or a drop of oil, the world was firmly in the age of fossil fuels. The adoption of fossil fuels, more than any other single shift, inaugurated the Anthropocene.

1. *Energy and Population*

ENERGY is a vexingly abstract concept. The word is derived from a term apparently invented by Aristotle to signify movement or work. Modern physicists have gotten only a bit further than the venerable Greek. They believe that energy exists in finite quantity in the Universe but in several different forms. Energy can be neither created nor destroyed, but it can be converted from one form to another. For instance, when you eat an apple, you convert chemical energy (the apple) into bodily heat, into muscular motion, and into other forms of chemical energy (your bones and tissues).[8]

The Earth is awash in energy. Almost all comes from the Sun. For human purposes, the main forms of energy are heat, light, motion, and chemical energy. The Sun's payload comes chiefly in the form of heat and light. A third of this is instantly reflected back into space, but most lingers for a while, warming land, sea, and air. A little of the light is absorbed by plants and converted into chemical energy through photosynthesis.

Every energy conversion results in some loss of useful energy. Plants on average manage to capture less than 1 percent of the energy delivered by the Sun. The rest is dissipated, mainly as heat. But what plants absorb is enough to grow, each year, about 110 billion tons of biomass in the sea and another 120 billion tons on land. Animals eat a small proportion of that, converting it into body heat, motion, and new tissues. And a small share of those new animal tissues is eaten by carnivores. At each of these trophic levels, well under 10 percent of available energy is successfully harvested. So the great majority of incoming energy is lost to no earthly purpose. But the Sun is so generous, there is still plenty to go around.

Until the harnessing of fire, our ancestors took part in this web of energy and life without being able to change it. The only energy available to them was what they could find to eat. Once armed with fire, perhaps half a million years ago, our hominin ancestors could harvest more energy, both in the form of otherwise indigestible foods that cooking now rendered edible, and in the form of heat. Fire also helped them scavenge and hunt more efficiently, enhancing their access to chemical energy in the form of meat. This low-energy economy remained in place, with some modest changes, until agriculture began about ten thousand years ago.

Growing crops and raising animals allowed ancient farmers to harvest considerably more energy than their forebears could. Grain crops are the seeds of grasses such as rice, wheat, or maize, and are packed with energy (and protein). So, with farming, a given patch of land provided far more usable energy for human bodies than it could without farming, perhaps ten to one hundred times more. Big domesticated animals, although they needed huge quantities of feed, could convert the otherwise nearly useless vegetation of steppe, savanna, or swampland into usable energy, helpful for pulling plows (oxen, water buffalo) or for transport (horses, camels). Farming slowly became widespread, although never universal.

Eventually, watermills and windmills added a little more to the sum of energy available for human purposes. Watermills might be two thousand years old and windmills one thousand. In suitable locations, where water flowed reliably or reasonably steady winds blew, these devices could do the work of several men. But in most places, wind and flowing water were either too rare or too erratic. So the energy regime remained organic, based on human and animal muscle for mechanical power, and on wood and other biomass for heat. The organic energy regime lasted until the eighteenth century.

Then in late eighteenth-century England the harnessing of coal exploded the constraints of the organic energy regime. With fossil fuels, humankind gained access to eons of frozen sunshine—maybe 500 million years' worth of prior photosynthesis. Early efforts to exploit this subsidy from the deep past were inefficient. Early steam engines, in converting chemical energy into heat and then into motion, wasted 99 percent of the energy fed into them. But incremental improvements led to machines that by the 1950s wasted far less energy than did photosynthesis or carnivory. In this sense, culture had improved upon nature.

The enormous expansion of energy use in recent decades beggars the imagination. By about 1870 we used more fossil fuel energy each year than the annual global production from all photosynthesis. Our species has probably used more energy since 1920 than in all of prior human history. In the half century before 1950, global energy use slightly more than doubled. Then in the next half century,

TABLE 3.1
Global commercial energy mix, 2010

Type of energy	%
Oil	34%
Coal	30%
Natural gas	24%
Hydroelectric	6%
Nuclear	5%

Data source: BP Statistical Review of World Energy, June 2011.

it quintupled from the 1950s level. The energy crisis of the 1970s—two sharp oil price hikes in 1973 and 1979—slowed but did not stop this dizzying climb in the use of fossil sunshine. Since 1950 we have burned around 50 million to 150 million years' worth of fossil sunshine.

The fossil fuel energy regime contained several phases. Coal outstripped biomass to become the world's primary fuel by about 1890. King coal reigned for about seventy-five years, before ceding the throne to oil in about 1965. Lately natural gas has grown in importance, so that in 2010 the world's energy mix looked as shown in Table 3.1.

These data do not include biomass, for which figures are sketchy. But the best guess is that it accounts for perhaps 15 percent of the grand total, fossil fuels for about 75 percent, and hydroelectricity and nuclear power together for about 10 percent. King oil's reign, now forty-five years in duration, will likely prove as brief as coal's, but that remains to be seen. We have used about one trillion barrels of oil since commercial production began around 1860, and now use about 32 billion barrels yearly.[9]

The global totals belie tremendous variation in energy use around the world. In the early twenty-first century, the average North American used about seventy times as much energy as the average Mozambican. The figures since 1965, in Table 3.2, speak volumes about the rise of China and India, and about the distribution of wealth within the world.

TABLE 3.2

Annual energy consumption, 1965–2011
(in millions of tons of oil equivalent)

Year	World	China	India	USA	Japan	Egypt
1965	3,813	182	53	1,284	149	8
1975	5,762	337	82	1,698	329	10
1985	7,150	533	133	1,763	368	28
1995	8,545	917	236	2,117	489	38
2005	10,565	1,429	362	2,342	520	62
2009	11,164	2,177	469	2,182	464	76
2010	11,978	2,403	521	2,278	503	81
2011	12,275	2,613	559	2,269	477	83

Data source: BP Statistical Review of World Energy, June 2010 and June 2012.

Note: Amounts are for commercial energy only, not biomass, which might add 10 to 15 percent.

In 1960, most of the world outside of Europe and North America still used little energy. The energy-intensive way of life extended to perhaps one-fifth of the world's population. But late in the twentieth century that pattern, in place since 1880 or so, changed quickly. In the forty-five years after 1965, China increased its energy use by 12 times, India by 9, Egypt by 9 or 10. Meanwhile US energy use rose by about 40 percent. The United States accounted for a third of the world's energy consumption in 1965, but only a fifth in 2009; China accounted for only 5 percent in 1965, but a fifth in 2009, and in 2010 surpassed the United States to become the world's largest energy user.

In sum, the burgeoning rate of energy use in modern history makes our time wildly different from anything in the human past. The fact that for about a century after 1850 high energy use was confined to Europe and North America, and to a lesser extent to Japan, is the single most important reason behind the political and economic dominance these regions enjoyed in the international system. Since 1965 the total use of energy has continued to climb at only slightly diminished rates, but the great majority of the expansion has taken place outside of Europe and America, mainly in East Asia.

Fossil Fuel Energy and the Environment

The creation and spread of fossil fuel society was the most environmentally consequential development of modern times. Part of the reason for that lies in the direct
effects of the extraction, transport, and combustion of coal, oil, and (to a much
lesser extent) natural gas. These were (and are) mainly a matter of air, water, and
soil pollution. The other part resides in the indirect effects of cheap and abundant
energy: it enabled many activities that otherwise would have been uneconomic
and would not have happened, or perhaps would have happened but only much
more slowly.

Extracting fossil energy from the crust of the Earth has always been a messy
business. Coal, mined commercially in over seventy countries since 1945, had the
most widespread impacts. Deep mining brought changes to land, air, and water.
Carving galleries out from beneath the surface honeycombed the Earth in coal
districts such as South Wales, the Ruhr, eastern Kentucky, the Donetsk Basin,
and Shaanxi Province. Occasionally underground mines collapsed, as in the
Saarland (Germany) in 2008, producing a small earthquake. In China, as of
2005, subsidence due to coal mines affected an area the size of Switzerland. Mine
tailings and slag heaps disfigured the landscape around coal mines. In China (by
2005) coal mine slag covered an area the size of New Jersey or Israel. Everywhere
tailings and slag leached sulfuric acid into local waters. In some Pennsylvania
and Ohio waterways, acidic liquids from mine drainage had killed off aquatic
life by the 1960s, although in some spots life has since returned. Deep mining
also often put extra methane in the atmosphere, adding perhaps 3 to 6 percent on
top of the natural releases of this potent greenhouse gas.

Deep mining has always put people in dangerous environments. In China,
for example, where roughly one hundred thousand small mines opened up during the Great Leap Forward (1958–1961), mining accidents killed about six thousand men annually at that time, and at least that many yearly in the 1990s. In the
United Kingdom in 1961, about forty-two hundred men died in mine accidents.
In the United States, the most dangerous year for coal miners was 1907, when
more than three thousand died; since 1990, annual deaths have ranged from 18
to 66. Today about two thousand coal miners die from accidents each year in
China, several times the figure for Russia or India. Black lung disease, a conse-

quence of years spent underground inhaling coal dust, killed far more wherever coal was mined.[10]

Surface mining, often called strip mining in the United States, was far safer for miners. It began with simple tools centuries ago, but steam technology made it more practical in the early twentieth century. After 1945, new excavation equipment and cheap oil ushered in a golden age of strip mining. Today it accounts for about 40 percent of coal mining worldwide, and outside of China is usually much more common than deep mining. In surface mining, which is practical to depths of nearly 50 meters, big machines claw away earth and rock above coal seams, destroying vegetation and soils. In the United States it aroused fervent opposition in many communities, which provoked federal regulation after 1977. Since that time, mining companies have been legally obliged to fund landscape restoration.

One particularly unpopular variant of strip mining was "mountaintop removal," practiced especially in those parts of Kentucky and West Virginia that had low-sulfur coal. High energy prices in the 1970s made these procedures lucrative as never before. Tighter air pollution laws in the 1990s, which made using high-sulfur coal more difficult, added to the economic logic of mountaintop removal. Blasting the tops off the Appalachians had many environmental consequences, none so important as the filling in of streams and valleys with waste rock ("overburden"), which buried forests and streams and led to accelerated erosion and occasional landslides.

Mountaintop removal, and surface mining generally, aroused spirited opposition from the 1930s onward and made environmentalists out of ordinary rural people throughout Appalachia. Their farms, fishing streams, and hunting grounds were sacrificed for coal production. In the 1960s and 1970s, opposition to strip mining reached its height in Appalachia, proving divisive in communities where mining companies offered most of the few jobs around. But the practice of mountaintop removal remained economic, and lasted into the twenty-first century.[11]

Drilling for oil brought different environmental issues but no less discord. In the early twentieth century, oil drilling occurred in many heavily populated places, including East Texas, southern California, central Romania, the city of Baku, and the then-Austrian province of Galicia. Gushers, spills, and fires menaced hearth and home. But by midcentury the technologies of drilling and storage had improved, so that oil fields were no longer necessarily the oleaginous equivalent of the Augean stables. And production increasingly shifted to places where people were few, such as Saudi Arabia and Siberia, so the consequences of oil pollution became less costly—at least in economic and political terms.

But the hike in energy prices of the 1970s inspired oil drilling in new and often challenging environments, including the seafloor, tropical forests, and the Arctic. Leaks, accidents, and blowouts became more common, thanks to Arctic cold and deep-sea pressures. Crude oil except in small concentrations is toxic to most forms of life and is extremely hard to clean up. By 2005 the world had some forty thousand oil fields, none of them free from pollution. Routine drilling involved building new infrastructure, moving heavy equipment sometimes weighing thousands of tons, and splashing vast quantities of oil and contaminated water into the surrounding environment. In the decades after 1980, about 30 million tons (or 240 million barrels) of oil dripped and squirted into the environment every year, about two-fifths of it in Russia.[12]

Offshore drilling, pioneered in California waters in the 1890s, remained confined to shallow waters for many decades. In the 1920s the practice spread to Lake Maracaibo in Venezuela, and to the Caspian Sea—both enduringly polluted as a result—and in the 1930s to the Gulf of Mexico. Technological advances, and the huge pools of investment capital available to oil companies from the 1940s on, opened new offshore frontiers in deeper waters. By the 1990s deepwater platforms dotted the North Sea, the Gulf of Mexico, and the coasts of Brazil, Nigeria, Angola, Indonesia, and Russia, among others. Big platforms stood over 600 meters above water, rivaling the tallest skyscrapers.

Offshore drilling operations were inherently risky. When hit by tropical storms or errant tankers, rigs splashed oil into the surrounding seas. The worst accidents occurred in the Gulf of Mexico. In 1979 a rig operated by the Mexican state oil company suffered a blowout and spewed oil for more than nine months before it was successfully capped. Some 3.3 million barrels escaped (equivalent to about six hours' worth of US oil use in 1979). It resulted in a surface oil slick roughly the size of Lebanon or Connecticut that ruined some Mexican fisheries and damaged Texan ones.[13]

In April 2010 the *Deepwater Horizon*, an oil platform leased by BP, exploded and sank, killing eleven workers and springing a leak some 1,500 meters below the waves on the seafloor off the Louisiana coast. It defied all containment efforts for more than three months. Some five million barrels in all spewed into the Gulf, the largest accidental oil spill in world history. The coastal wetlands ecosystems and what in previous years had been tourist-filled beaches of the Gulf Coast sopped up some of the wandering oil. Tar balls and oil washed up on the coasts of Louisiana, Mississippi, Alabama, and Florida. Fisheries ceased operations, and dead and damaged birds began to pile up. One of the victims was the Louisiana brown pelican, once brought to the edge of extinction by DDT in the 1950s and 1960s. Conservation work had given the brown pelican second life to the point where in 2009 it migrated off the federal endangered species list. In the first two months of the BP spill, 40 percent of the known population of brown pelicans died oily deaths. Some forty-eight thousand temporary workers and an armada of vessels not seen since D-Day tried to limit the ecological damage. Oceanographers and marine biologists will be assessing the spill's impacts for years, and lawyers will be kept busy for decades ascertaining who will be held responsible and just how tens of billions of dollars will change hands.[14] In the Gulf of Mexico, small spills occurred daily, huge ones every few years, but nothing yet matches the *Deepwater Horizon* disaster.

Drilling for oil in the forests of Ecuador presented different challenges from offshore environments. In the remote upper reaches of the Amazon watershed, in northeastern Ecuador, a Texaco-Gulf consortium struck oil in 1967. Over the next half century, the region yielded over two billion barrels of crude oil, most of it sent by pipeline over the Andes, making Ecuador the second largest oil exporter of South America and keeping its government solvent. To operate in the rainforest, the consortium, and Ecuador's national oil company, which took over all operations by 1992, had to build new infrastructure of roads, pipelines, pumping stations, and so forth. Almost unencumbered by regulation, drilling in Ecuador took an especially casual course. Vast quantities of toxic liquids were dumped (or leaked) into the streams and rivers, creating the unhappy irony that in one of the most water-rich provinces on Earth, many people have no potable water. Inevitably, accidents happened. In 1989 enough oil spilled into the Rio Napo, which is about 1 kilometer wide, to turn it black for a week.[15]

Part of the local indigenous population, mobile forager-hunters called Huaorani, tried to fight off the oil invasion. Armed only with spears, the Huaorani

An exploratory oil-drilling site in the Ecuadorian rainforest. Pollution from oil extraction in Ecuador and other oil-producing regions led to fierce environmental struggles between foreign companies and local populations. (© G. Bowater/Corbis)

failed and were relocated by the government. Other indigenous groups in Ecuador have struggled, usually unsuccessfully, to keep oil production at bay. According to some epidemiologists, the populations living near the oil fields have shown elevated rates of diseases, notably cancer.

Oil revenues proved so tempting to the Ecuadorian state that it scheduled two-thirds of its Amazonian territory for oil and gas exploration. By 2005 it had leased most of that, including blocks within the Yasuni National Park. In conventional calculations, it made sense for Ecuador (and for oil companies) to make money from oil drilling in Oriente (as Ecuadorians call it), because the indigenous peoples whose lives it disrupted contributed next to nothing to the state. Likewise the ecosystems of western Amazonia, among the world's most biologically rich and diverse, produced little that the state valued. Identical logic prevailed in Peru, although its government did not permit drilling in national parks. In 2010, Ecuador and the UN Development Program (UNDP) cut a deal whereby a trust fund would pay Ecuador $3.6 billion not to produce oil in one of the Yasuni National Park blocks, where nearly a billion barrels of oil lay, preserving (for the time being) broad swaths of rainforest. Nigerian authorities showed instant interest in this novel arrangement, and with good reason.[16]

The Niger Delta region of southeast Nigeria, a patchy rainforest area, and one of the world's biggest wetlands, is a maze of creeks, marshes, and lagoons with once-rich fisheries. As in Oriente, the population of the Niger Delta is divided among several ethnic groups, notably the Ijaw, Igbo, and Ogoni. Unlike Oriente, it is densely populated, home to several million people. Shell and BP began oil operations here in the 1950s, happy to find a low-sulfur crude that is easy to refine into gasoline. Other companies followed, creating some 160 oil fields and 7,000 kilometers of pipelines. For decades, tankers filled up on crude where centuries before wooden ships had loaded slaves.

The Nigerian government, in what could well be an understatement, recorded about seven thousand oil spills between 1976 and 2005 in the Delta, involving some three million barrels of crude.[17] Some of the spills resulted from routine accidents, normal in the industry but especially frequent in the Delta due to poor maintenance and challenging conditions, both geographic and political. Others were acts of sabotage undertaken by locals, some of whom were seeking revenge for something, others of whom sought extortion or compensation payments from oil companies. The Niger Delta was, and remains, one of the poorest parts of Nigeria despite the several billions of dollars' worth of oil pumped out. For most residents, oil production made life harder. Dredging canals for oil exploration eliminated much of the mangrove swamp in which fish spawned, which together with oil pollution undercut a long-standing source of sustenance in the Delta. Air pollution and acid rain, largely from gas flares at oil wells, damaged crops. In the early 1990s the United Nations declared the Niger

Delta the world's most ecologically endangered delta. Locals felt (and feel) that their natural wealth has been either destroyed or stolen by foreign companies and the Nigerian state, whose leadership has shown remarkable persistence in skimming off oil wealth. Resulting frustrations fed both liberation movements of local minorities and criminal syndicates. Lately Nigeria and its multinational partners have emphasized drilling offshore, where there is no local population to consider.[18]

The quest for oil led to new drilling in the chilly latitudes of Siberia and Alaska as well as in rainforests. The Soviet Union developed the huge oil and gas fields of western Siberia beginning in the 1960s (the Soviets used nuclear explosions to help in seismic explorations between 1978 and 1985, so some Siberian oil is slightly radioactive).[19] The much more modest fields of northern Alaska opened up in the 1970s. Both regions, but especially Siberia, had their normal accidents and intentional releases of oil, "produced water," and other toxic substances. In high-latitude wetlands, taiga, and tundra, where biological processes move slowly, the ill effects of spills as a rule lingered longer than in the tropics, as we shall see.

Oriente and the Niger Delta are extreme examples of sacrifice zones, where the cost of energy extraction included pervasive ecological degradation. Among local species, only oil-eating bacteria benefited from the fouling of the soils and waters of these regions. But people far away also benefited, in the form of cheap oil for consumers, tidy profit for the companies involved, and luxurious revenue streams for state officials. The world enjoyed great benefits thanks to oil extraction, but specific places paid a high price. People living near strip mines would likely say the same of the history of coal extraction.

Coal and Oil Transport

While extraction of coal and oil exacted an environmental price upon a fixed archipelago of mining districts and oil fields, the transport of fossil fuels had a scattered impact. Coal transport took place mainly in rail cars and barges. Very few accidents occurred, and when they did what coal toppled out onto land or into canals and rivers led to minimal consequences.

Oil was a different matter. Part of the appeal of oil over coal is the ease of transport. As a liquid, oil (except for the heaviest varieties) can ooze through pipelines. Even more glided over the seas in tankers. After 1950 oil increasingly was drilled in one country and burned in another, a reflection of the emergence of the Persian Gulf giant fields. So tankers plied the high seas in ever greater numbers. Today oil makes up half the tonnage of maritime cargoes, and there are more miles of pipeline than of railroad in the world.[20]

Pipelines and tankers proved remarkably susceptible to accident. One reason tankers had so many accidents is that they became too big to stop. In 1945 a big tanker held 20,000 tons of oil, in the 1970s about half a million, and today 1 million tons. Supertankers are 300 meters in length and the least nimble vessels on the seas. They need several kilometers in which to slow to a stop.

Fortunately, in the same decades tankers became harder to puncture. In the 1970s most new tankers had double hulls, which sharply reduced the likelihood of spills resulting from collisions with rocks, icebergs, and other ships. But when spills occurred, they could be large, and they always happened near shore where oil could foul rich ecosystems and valuable property.

Though small tanker spills happened almost every day, most of the escaped oil came in a few big accidents. The English Channel witnessed two giant tanker spills, in 1967 and 1978. The biggest spill of all occurred off of Cape Town in 1983, leaking more than six times as much oil as did the famous *Exxon Valdez* in 1989. Tanker spills could happen almost anywhere, but they were most numerous in the Gulf of Mexico, off the eastern seaboard of North America, in the Mediterranean Sea, and in the Persian Gulf.[21] The most recent big tanker spill, in 2002, occurred when a single-hulled vessel broke up in a storm off the northwest coast of Spain.

Pipelines carried a smaller, but growing, share of the world's oil after 1945. Their builders intend them to last fifteen to twenty years, but many, perhaps most, pipelines are asked to serve beyond that span. They corrode and crack, especially when subject to extreme ranges of climate. By and large, pipeline design improved over time, but accidents increased because the world's network of pipelines grew so quickly.[22]

The most affected landscapes were in Russia. The most serious single pipeline leak occurred near Usinsk, in Komi Republic, Russia, about 1,500 kilometers northeast of Moscow in 1994. Outsiders estimate the leak at six hundred thousand to one million barrels. Officials initially denied any leaks, a position they soon had to abandon.[23] Another large one occurred in 2006. Altogether, about 7 to 20 percent of Russian oil production leaked out of faulty pipelines in the 1990s, a reflection of oil's low price, a business culture that put scant value on routine maintenance, especially in an economically disastrous decade, and the challenges of both remoteness and climate. Thousands of leaks and spills, large and small, happened every year in the 1990s. The subzero winter cold of regions such as the oilfields of Komi Republic—most of which lie north of the Arctic Circle— was hard on pipelines and other components of oil infrastructure.[24] Some indigenous Siberians, not surprisingly, tried to organize themselves against oil and gas development. Pipeline leaks imperiled their hunting, fishing, and reindeer herding. On at least one occasion some attempted armed resistance, which succeeded no better than the efforts of Ecuador's Huaorani.[25]

In human terms, the worst oil pipeline accident occurred in the Niger Delta in 1998 when a line maintained by Shell and the Nigerian state oil company sprang a leak. As villagers gathered to help themselves to free oil, an explosion and a fireball incinerated more than a thousand people. Two villages burned to cinders. In 2006 two additional oil pipeline fires elsewhere in Nigeria killed about six hundred people. As a means of ferrying energy from point of extraction to point of use, oil tankers and pipelines were both more economical and more hazardous than coal transport.[26]

Fossil Fuel Combustion and Air Pollution

Coal mine accidents and oil pipeline explosions took many thousands of lives in the decades after 1945, but nowhere near as many as the routine, peaceable combustion of fossil fuels. Air pollution, mainly from coal and oil burning, killed tens of millions of people.

To get an idea of the air pollution resulting from coal combustion, consider the annual pollution output of an average American power plant in the early 2000s, after decades of regulation and technical improvements. The average plant annually releases millions of tons of carbon dioxide, the main greenhouse gas, and thousands of tons of sulfur dioxide, the main ingredient in acid rain. It puts a few dozen kilograms of lead, mercury, and arsenic into the air as well. This is part of the price of turning coal into electricity, and forty years ago the price was much higher because coal combustion was much dirtier. And this does not include ash and soot.

Urban air pollution has a long history. In the twelfth century, Maimonides—no doubt justly—complained about air quality in Cairo, a dung- and straw-burning city. A century later London enacted the first recorded ordinances aimed against air pollution. The adoption of coal as a basic fuel made matters much worse, never more so than in London in the second week of December 1952.

When a cold air mass settled over the Thames valley in early December, bringing temperatures below freezing, Londoners added more coal to their hearths. Each day their million chimneys spewed out a thousand tons of coal soot and nearly 400 tons of sulfur dioxide. People could not see to cross the street at noon. Natives who knew the city like the back of their hand got lost on daily errands. A few walked into the Thames and drowned. During December 5–9, some forty-seven hundred people died, about three thousand more than normal. Over the next three months mortality remained well above normal for London winters, so that epidemiologists now attribute twelve thousand deaths to pollution during the December episode.[27] In the winter of 1952–1953, coal smoke, soot, and sulfur dioxide killed Londoners at roughly twice the rate the Luftwaffe managed during the blitz of 1940–1941. Undertakers ran out of caskets.[28]

The public and press raised a hue and cry, prompting one cabinet minister, Harold Macmillan, to write in a memo he wisely kept secret during his lifetime: "For some reason or another 'smog' has captured the imagination of the press and people. . . . Ridiculous as it appears, I suggest we form a committee. We cannot do very much, but we can be seen to be very busy."[29] Macmillan, whose insouciance about air pollution and its effects was characteristic of his time, went on to have a distinguished political career, including a stint as prime minister from 1957 to 1963. Pea-soupers, as Londoners called their densest fogs, persisted in London for a few more years. But between 1956 and the mid-1960s, mainly on Macmillan's watch, air pollution laws and fuel switching (to oil and natural gas) made London's killer fogs a thing of the past.[30]

Oil burned cleaner than coal. Combustion of oil and its derivatives, such as gasoline, releases lead, carbon monoxide, sulfur dioxide, nitrogen oxides, and volatile organic compounds (VOCs). VOCs together with sunshine help brew photochemical smog. Oil made its main contribution to urban air pollution through tailpipes rather than chimneys. Vehicle exhausts provided the raw material for photochemical smog, which was first observed in Los Angeles during World War II. Photochemical smog developed where motorization took hold and where the Sun shone brightly. Cities at lower latitudes, especially those with nearby mountains that keep pollution from drifting off with the winds, were especially affected: Los Angeles, Santiago, Athens, Tehran, and the world champion, Mexico City.

Mexico City had one hundred thousand cars in 1950, when it was still renowned for its clear vistas of distant volcanoes. By 1990, by which time it was enveloped in a near-permanent haze, four million cars clogged its streets. Trucks, buses, and cars accounted for 85 percent of Mexico City's air pollution, which by 1985 was occasionally so acute that birds fell from the sky in midflight over the central square (the Zócalo). After careful monitoring began in 1986, it emerged that Mexico City exceeded legal limits for one or more major pollutants more than 90 percent of the time. In the 1990s, estimates suggested some six thousand to twelve thousand annual deaths were attributable to air pollution in the city, four to eight times the annual number of murders. Various efforts to curb air pollution since the 1980s have produced mixed results, but the death rate seems to have declined slightly since the early 1990s.

Both coal and oil turned out to be mass killers in the world's cities. In Western Europe around 2000, vehicle exhausts killed people at roughly the same rate as vehicle accidents.[31] Meanwhile, in China air pollution from all sources killed about five hundred thousand Chinese annually and, due to pollutants wafting eastward with the winds, another eleven thousand in Japan and Korea together.[32] In the 1990s, estimates put the global annual death toll attributable to air pollution at about half a million. One study from 2002 put it at eight hundred thousand per year.[33] From 1950 to 2010, air pollution probably killed about thirty to forty million people, lately most of them Chinese, roughly equal to the death toll from all wars around the world since 1950.[34] Many millions more suffered intensified asthma and other ailments as a result of the pollution they inhaled. Fossil fuel combustion accounted for the lion's share of these deaths and illnesses.

In addition to these unhappy effects upon human health, fossil fuels, especially coal, were responsible for widespread acidification. Volcanoes and forest fires released quantities of sulfur to the atmosphere, but by the 1970s coal com-

bustion emitted about ten times more. Sulfur dioxide in contact with cloud drop-
lets forms sulfuric acid, which returns to Earth with rain, snow, or fog (commonly
called acid rain). Acid rain often contains nitrogen oxides too, from coal or oil
combustion. High-sulfur coal of the sort found in the Midwest of the United
States, in China, in Bengal, and elsewhere, acidified ecosystems far and wide.
Mountain forests and freshwater ecosystems showed the most acute effects, and
some sensitive species (brook trout, sugar maple) disappeared altogether in high-
acid environments. Broadly speaking, by the end of the twentieth century the
world had three acidification hot spots: northern and central Europe, eastern
North America, and eastern, especially southeastern, China.

Acid rain became a policy issue by the end of the 1960s. For local communities the easiest solution was to require tall smokestacks that lofted the offending
gases farther afield. In the 1970s acid rain became an international issue, as
Canadians objected to the acidification of their lakes by (mainly) American
power plant emissions, and Scandinavians discovered damage to their waterways
attributable to British and German coal combustion. Poland and its neighbors,
which used coal that was especially high in sulfur, splashed one another's landscapes with acid rain that occasionally reached the pH level of vinegar. Railway
trains had to observe low speed limits in parts of Poland because the iron of the
train tracks had weakened from acid corrosion. With the dramatic rise of coal
use in China after 1980, transboundary acidification became a source of contention in East Asia too, as Koreans, Japanese, and Taiwanese felt the consequences
of Chinese power plants and factories.

Beyond sensitive ecosystems, acid emissions also had modest effects on human health and major ones on buildings made of limestone or marble. Greek
authorities found it advisable to put the most precious statuary of the Acropolis
indoors to save it from corrosion by acid rain. In the Indian city of Agra, pollution from a nearby oil refinery, among other sources, threatened the marble of
the Taj Mahal.[35]

Acidification, happily enough, turned out to be one of the easiest of environmental problems to address. In Europe and the United States, after some delay
occasioned by the objections of coal utilities and their political allies, cap-and-
trade schemes were devised that allowed polluters to choose their means of reducing emissions and to buy and sell permits to pollute. Beginning around 1990

this reduced sulfur emissions by 40 to 70 percent in short order, at a cost that turned out to be a small fraction of that anticipated. It takes a while for ecosystems to rebound from acidification, but in northern Europe and eastern North America, by 2000 the recovery had begun to show. China, awash in acid rain, tried to address its sulfur emissions, but its heavy reliance on coal hamstrung the effort until 2006, after which date a tiny reduction in sulfur emissions occurred. In northern China the consequences of acid rain were checked by the prevalence of alkaline dust (neutralizing acid), but in the south, soils and ecosystems proved as vulnerable as those of northern Europe and eastern North America.[36]

By and large, the rich world after 1970 achieved healthy reductions in its emissions of sulfur dioxide as well as other coal-based pollutants. Copenhagen, for example, reduced its SO_2 concentrations by 90 percent between 1970 and 2005.[37] London lowered its smoke and soot levels by 98 percent between the 1920s and 2005.[38] In 1950 the residents of Glasgow, Scotland, each inhaled about 1 kilogram of soot each year; by 2005 their lungs received almost none. In Japan, a polluter's paradise until the mid-1960s, even hotbeds of sulfur emissions such as the industrial city of Osaka managed to clear the air by 1990.[39] These remarkable changes in urban air pollution came about because of fuel switching (less coal, more oil and gas), deindustrialization, and new technologies made economically practical mainly by new regulations. In most cases, citizen agitation lay behind the new regulations. Germany shows the importance of citizen activism: In West Germany air pollution levels declined markedly from the 1960s onward; in East Germany, where the secret police provided citizens with good reason to keep their views to themselves, air pollution remained unchecked through to the end of the communist regime in 1989.

Fossil fuel combustion played a central role in another modification of the atmosphere, the relentless buildup of carbon dioxide. Here, in contrast to the story with sulfur dioxide, public policy to date has been ineffective. High-level international efforts, such as the negotiations at Kyoto (1997) and Copenhagen (2009), led to no significant reductions in carbon emissions. China's emissions alone after 1990 swamped what minor reductions could be achieved here and there around the world. The spectacular climb in fossil fuel use since 1950 is the main reason behind the parallel rise in atmospheric carbon.

The Strange Career of Nuclear Power

Unlike other forms of energy use, nuclear power has a birthday: December 2, 1942. On that day the Italian émigré physicist Enrico Fermi oversaw the first controlled nuclear reaction, in a repurposed squash court under the stands of a football stadium at the University of Chicago. The power of the bonds within atoms dwarfs that of other energy sources available to humankind. A fistful of uranium can generate more energy than a truckload of coal. This astonishing power was first used in bombs, thousands of which were built, and two of which were used, both by the United States and against Japan in August 1945, bringing the Second World War to a close.

Peaceful uses of atomic power soon followed. By 1954 the first reactor providing electricity for a grid, a tiny one near Moscow, opened. Much bigger ones started up in the United Kingdom and the United States in 1956–1957. In the middle of the 1950s the prospects for nuclear power seemed bright and endless. Scientists foresaw nuclear-powered visits to Mars. One American official predicted that electricity would soon be "too cheap to meter." In both the United States and the Soviet Union, visionaries imagined vast engineering uses for nuclear explosions, such as opening a new Panama Canal or smashing apart menacing hurricanes.[40] Nuclear technology enjoyed tremendous subsidies in many countries— not least a law in the United States that fixed a low maximum for lawsuits against nuclear utilities, allowing them to buy insurance, which otherwise no one would sell them. Between 1965 and 1980, the share of the world's electricity generated in nuclear power plants rose from less than 1 percent to 10 percent. By 2013 that figure approached 13 percent.

Countries with scientific and engineering resources but minimal fossil fuels converted most fully to nuclear power. By 2010 France, Lithuania, and Belgium relied on it for more than half their electricity; Japan and South Korea for about a quarter of theirs; and the United States for a fifth.

The rosy expectations for a nuclear future withered in the 1970s and 1980s due to well-publicized accidents. Civilian reactors had suffered dozens of accidents large and small in the 1950s and 1960s, the worst of them in the USSR. But they were kept as secret as possible. The 1979 accident at Three Mile Island in Pennsylvania attracted public scrutiny. It turned out to be minor, as nuclear accidents go, but came close to being much worse and was not hidden from view. It served to turn US public opinion away from nuclear power.[41] In the rest of the world the public at large took less notice, although the mishap invigorated antinuclear movements and watchdog groups in every country that had a nuclear industry. Their concerns about nuclear safety led to reforms, more stringent controls, and higher construction and operation costs. In March 1986 the British highbrow magazine *The Economist* opined, "The nuclear power industry remains as safe as a chocolate factory."[42]

Four weeks later, at Chernobyl in Ukraine (then in the USSR), a three-year-old reactor vessel exploded. The ensuing fire released a plume of radioactivity hundreds of times greater than those over Hiroshima and Nagasaki in Japan some forty-one years earlier. For days the Soviet government, led by Mikhail Gorbachev, tried to keep it secret and declined to warn local populations of the risks of venturing outdoors or drinking milk (one of the pathways of radioactivity goes from grass to cattle to milk). Radioactivity spread with the winds over Europe and eventually in small amounts over everyone in the Northern Hemisphere. Some 830,000 soldiers and workers ("Chernobyl liquidators") were dragooned into the cleanup effort; radiation poisoning quickly killed 28, another few dozen soon after, and in the course of time, many thousands more of these unfortunate liquidators died than actuarial tables would predict. Some 130,000 people were permanently resettled due to contamination of their homes, leaving a ghost zone that will host unsafe levels of radioactivity for at least two hundred more years. A few brave and stubborn souls still live there.

The Chernobyl Exclusion Zone has since become a de facto wildlife reserve teeming with wild boar, moose, deer, wolves, storks, and eagles, among other creatures. They roam in areas with radioactivity levels deemed unsafe for humans—because of the risks of predation and starvation, few wild animals live long enough to develop cancers. But from beetles to boars, all species show unusual rates of tumors, accelerated aging, and genetic mutations. Plant life in "the zone"—as locals call it—also shows high mutation rates. So do the tiny proportion of soil microorganisms so far studied. Because the average human body contains about 3 kilograms of bacteria, viruses, and microfungi, their modification by Chernobyl may prove to have interesting effects upon human beings. The zone became a curious biological contradiction in the wake of the catastrophe of

1986: abundant wildlife and resurgent vegetation, far more prolific than in surrounding precincts because free from quotidian human actions such as mowing, weeding, paving, and hunting—but at the same time less healthy than wildlife and vegetation elsewhere precisely because of the accident.[43]

The human health consequences of Chernobyl remain controversial. Cancer rates spiked in years after the disaster, especially thyroid cancers among children, leading to perhaps four thousand excess cases up to 2004. The toll could have been much lower without the government attempt to hush up the accident. This much is widely accepted. The full extent of Chernobyl's health consequences is much disputed.

Epidemiologists, often extrapolating from the experience of survivors of Hiroshima and Nagasaki, ventured many estimates of the likely mortality from Chernobyl. A conglomerate of UN bodies called the Chernobyl Forum in 2006 estimated nine thousand deaths and two hundred thousand illnesses related to Chernobyl, totals its spokesmen found reassuring. These figures are at the low end of the spectrum of expert opinion. More recently, researchers from the Russian Academy of Sciences and Belarus Laboratory of Radiation Safety reported a welter of insidious effects. For example, they noted early aging and signs of senility among irradiated people, and spikes in the rates of Down syndrome, low-birthweight babies, and infant mortality all over Europe in the months after Chernobyl. In Ukraine by 1994 more than 90 percent of the Chernobyl liquidators were sick, as were 80 percent of the evacuees and 76 percent of the children of irradiated parents. So many people suffered weakened immune systems that health workers spoke of "Chernobyl AIDS." The most affected populations were those who received high doses of radiation because they lived near Chernobyl; the Chernobyl liquidators; and babies born in the months following April 1986—in utero was a very dangerous place to be that spring. Based on the elevated mortality rates in irradiated parts of the former Soviet Union, these researchers calculated that by 2004 Chernobyl had already killed some 212,000 people in Russia, Ukraine, and Belarus, and, they estimated, caused nearly one million deaths worldwide. These figures are toward the high end of the spectrum. But thanks to inherent difficulties in assessing causes of death and deliberate Soviet falsification of health records among Chernobyl liquidators, no one will ever know the true human cost of Chernobyl.[44]

Chernobyl came at the same time as a collapse in world oil prices. The ecological and economic logic of building nuclear power plants suddenly seemed less persuasive. The share of the world's electricity derived from nuclear power, which had been rising fast, leveled off for the next twenty years.

The chilling effect of Chernobyl on the nuclear industry lasted for decades, but not forever. In 1987 Italy had passed a referendum against nuclear power; in 2009 it revoked it. The ever-growing demand for electricity, especially in China, led authorities to build more nuclear power plants. As of 2010 about 440 were in operation around the world (in forty-four countries) and about 50 more were in the works, 20 of them in China, 10 in Russia, 5 in India. The fact that nuclear power contributes very little in the way of greenhouse gases made it popular with many people who took global warming seriously, despite concerns over safety, the dependence on government subsidies, and the as-yet unresolved problem of what to do with dangerous nuclear wastes. By 2010 the United States had accumulated about 62,000 tons of spent nuclear fuel and had nowhere to put it.[45] According to the US Environmental Protection Agency, after ten thousand years the problem would solve itself because the fuel would no longer pose a threat to human health. Despite arousing environmental anxieties and requiring subsidies to compete in the marketplace, nuclear power rose from the ashes of Chernobyl to become politically viable almost everywhere in the world by 2010.

Then came Fukushima.[46] In March 2011 a powerful earthquake, 9.0 on the Richter scale, launched a tsunami toward the northeastern coast of Japan. Towering waves—about 14 meters high—crashed ashore, killing about twenty thousand people and wreaking destruction on a scale likely to make it the most expensive natural disaster in world history.

The Fukushima Daiichi nuclear power plant, one of the world's biggest, had opened in 1971. It survived a 1978 earthquake. It was operated by the Tokyo Electric Power Company, known as TEPCO. But in 2011 the waves easily topped retaining walls built to withstand a tsunami less than half the height of this one. The six working reactors shut down, generators and batteries failed, and the plant lost all electric power, and thus the capacity to pump cold water over fuel rods—which generate heat even when a reactor is not functioning, due to the continuing decay of fission products. Fires and explosions followed. Three reactors melted down. TEPCO workers drowned the fuel rods in seawater, hoping to forestall the worst. The quantities of radiation leaked into the environment in the first month after the tsunami were about 10 percent of those from Chernobyl. Dozens of workers at Fukushima Daiichi absorbed heavy doses of radiation.

The government, which had initially sharply underestimated the severity of the disaster, eventually created an exclusion zone extending 20 kilometers from the plant. Some 350,000 people departed for safer ground. Just where that was initially seemed hard to specify. The government also officially determined that the water supply in Tokyo, some 200 kilometers south, was unsafe for infants due to radiation. Both TEPCO and the government came in for withering criticism in Japan for their unpreparedness and dishonesty.[47]

Small amounts of radiation floated around the Northern Hemisphere, tainting milk in North America and arousing anxieties everywhere. The German government announced a shutdown of some of its elderly reactors, and several countries announced reviews of their nuclear safety procedures. China, although closer to the catastrophe than most, kept up its record pace of nuclear power plant construction.

In Japan itself, sentiment surged away from support of nuclear power, and all fifty-four of the country's reactors were gathering dust within fourteen months after the disaster, although two have since returned to duty. Few local communities wished to host an active nuclear power plant. To make up for the resulting shortfall of electricity, Japan increased its fossil fuel imports by half, substantially raising its energy costs. Whether or not the tsunami at Fukushima's power plant will dampen enthusiasm for nuclear power for long remains to be seen.

The Contentious Career of Hydropower

In terms of output, hydroelectric power matched nuclear. In terms of controversy and tragedy, it trailed not far behind. People had used water power from ancient times for grinding grain, and for powering factories from the eighteenth century, but it was not until 1878 that water sent through turbines produced electricity. In Europe and North America, hundreds of small-scale hydroelectricity stations were built between 1890 and 1930. The United States—quickly followed by the USSR—pioneered giant hydroelectric stations in the 1930s. These behemoths became, like nuclear power plants, symbols of technological virtuosity and modernity. Jawaharlal Nehru, India's prime minister from 1947 to 1964, often called hydroelectric dams "the temples of modern India." The world went on a dam-building spree after 1945, peaking in the 1960s and 1970s, by which time most of the good sites in rich countries had been taken.

Hydropower offered great attractions. For the engineers, it held the advantage that it could deliver power at any time (except in the event of big droughts that starved reservoirs). The potential power, captive water, stayed put and available at no cost (except where evaporation rates were high, as in the case of Egypt's Aswan Dam reservoir, Lake Nasser). Moreover, reservoirs could serve multiple purposes, as sources of irrigation water, sites for recreation, or fisheries. For environmentalists, who often found big dams objectionable on many grounds, hydropower held the charm of releasing no greenhouse gases in operation. Dam construction was another matter, but even taking all phases into account, hydroelectricity was probably the best form of electricity generation from the climate-change point of view, and certainly far, far better than using fossil fuels.

Its drawbacks, however, were legion. Big dams could bring big accidents, as at the Banqiao Dam in China's Henan Province in 1975. During a typhoon the dam broke, unleashing a wave—an inland tsunami—that drowned tens of thousands. Subsequent starvation and waterborne epidemics killed another 145,000. Hundreds of other dams failed less catastrophically. More prosaically, dam reservoirs silted up, so that the useful life of a hydroelectric plant might be as little as ten or twenty years in some poorly designed cases, most of which were in China. Reservoirs also sometimes desecrated cherished landscapes, as when Brazil inundated a national park to cooperate with Paraguay on the Itaipu Dam, opened in 1982 on the Paraná River. Its power station is the world's second largest. Archeological treasures were obliterated by some reservoirs, notably the Aswan Dam in Egypt and Turkey's several dams on the Tigris and Euphrates in eastern Anatolia. "Salvage archeology" usually could rescue only a fraction of what disappeared beneath the rising waters.[48]

The most politically volatile aspect of dam building was the displacement of people. Reservoirs took up a lot of space—about twice the area of Italy in total. Some of the big ones, in Ghana or in Russia, are the size of Cyprus or Connecticut. Globally, some forty to eighty million people—twenty million in India alone—had to get out of the way for reservoirs, in rare cases fleeing for their lives without any advance warning.[49] In many cases ethnic minorities living in hilly districts with swift rivers were the ones relocated in the interests of electric power wanted elsewhere in their countries.[50]

In India, where dam building (for irrigation as well as electricity) formed a major part of the state's development plans after independence in 1947, peasant resistance to dams became a widespread movement by the 1980s. Resistance rarely deflected the state's ambitions, but in the case of dams along the Narmada River in western India, it led to huge protests, political tumult, and lengthy lawsuits. The Narmada scheme involved thousands of dams, large and small, on which construction began in 1978. Local resistance, occasioned mainly by displacements, grew more and more organized throughout the 1980s, and successfully reached out to international environmental organizations for support. In 1993–1994 the World Bank, a longtime supporter of dam building in India, withdrew its support. Foreign criticism stoked the fires of Indian nationalism. Indian novelists and actors got involved, both for and against additional dams. But India's Supreme Court stood by the government and the engineers, the work continued, and so another hundred thousand or so Indians—"oustees" as they are known in India—moved to accommodate the Narmada's reservoirs.[51]

While Europe and North America had exhausted their best sites for hydroelectric development by 1980, the rest of the world continued to build dams apace. Half of the big dams built in the world after 1950 are in China. Between 1991 and 2009, China built what is by far the world's largest hydropower installation, the Three Gorges Dam on the Yangzi. Like the Narmada project, it too attracted environmental controversy, as roughly 1.3 million people had to make way for its reservoir. As the dam trapped most of the enormous silt load behind it, the downstream Yangzi delta began to erode while the reservoir slowly filled. The reduction in organic matter delivered to the East China Sea imperiled China's richest fishery.[52] Moreover, the potential for instant disaster should the dam break—it is built on a seismic fault—is beyond imagination. But the Three Gorges Dam illustrates the environmental tradeoffs of hydropower: without it China would burn tens of millions more tons of coal annually.

As of 2013, enormous possibilities for hydropower remained in Africa and South America, unexploited because of the weak markets for electricity. But the growing concerns over climate change raised the odds that the remaining

Members of the Save Narmada Movement demonstrate against the US utility company Ogden Energy Group near the American Embassy in New Delhi, April 4, 2000. Hydroelectricity generated little pollution but typically required the construction of reservoirs that uprooted local people, as in the case of a string of dams on India's Narmada River. (Getty Images)

opportunities for the development of hydropower would not go begging, population displacement and other problems notwithstanding.

The (Tentative) Emergence of Alternative Energies

The manifest environmental drawbacks of fossil fuels, nuclear power, and hydropower made people long for healthy and "green" energy sources. Long-standing anxieties about exhaustion of fossil fuel supplies added to the urge to find alternatives. In 1917 the Scottish American inventor Alexander Graham Bell championed the cause of ethanol, a fuel made from crop residues, on the grounds that coal and oil would one day run out. Falling prices for fossil fuels and the optimism of the early years of nuclear power, however, discouraged work on energy alternatives until the 1970s. Then the oil price hikes of 1973 and 1979, and the disillusionment with nuclear power that climaxed with Chernobyl in 1986, sparked a surge of interest in solar and wind power, as well as tidal, geothermal, and a few other as yet less important possibilities. Ethanol, for its part, became a major fuel in Brazil beginning in the 1970s. Sugarcane stalks supply the basic energy for an automobile fleet that burns a blended fuel that is about 75 percent gasoline and 25 percent ethanol.

Nothing is more renewable than the wind. Windmills for grinding grain originated in Iran or Afghanistan. Fantail windmills for pumping up aquifer water became common more than a century ago, especially on the Great Plains of North America. Wind power as the basis for electricity became practical in 1979 with the work of Danish engineers who built modern wind turbines. Technical improvements followed quickly, so that with the help of government subsidies, by 2010 wind power supplied about a fifth of all electricity in Denmark. In Spain and Portugal, the figure came to around 15 percent. In the United States, less than 2 percent of electricity came from wind power, but the figure was rising fast, as it was in China. After 2008 more new capacity was installed globally each year for wind power than for hydroelectricity.

Everywhere, the attraction of wind power was chiefly environmental. Although big wind farms aroused minor controversies here and there because they changed the look of landscapes and in some cases killed birds and bats, by and large wind power had negligible environmental consequences. For green citizens and governments it seemed to promise a way out of the climate change morass. More precisely, it seemed to offer a partial solution, because wind power requires wind, and even in Denmark and Portugal the wind does not always blow when electricity is needed. It is hard to store power for those times when the winds are calm.

The same limitations applied to solar power, the other darling of green citizens. Clouds and night interfered with the steady delivery of solar energy. But the potential of solar power was hard to resist. The Sun donates more energy to the Earth in an hour than humankind uses in a year. And a year's worth of the Sun's bounty is more energy than all that contained in all the fossil fuels and uranium in the Earth's crust. More than any other energy source available, solar power promised an infinitude of energy.

The technologies of photovoltaic cells emerged in the late nineteenth century but languished for decades. Like wind power, in the 1970s solar appealed to many people due to the high oil prices. For remote places not connected to a power grid, solar panels proved very practical. After several slow years, resulting mainly from the oil price collapse of 1985–1986, investment in solar power surged ahead again after 2000. European countries that provided subsidies played a large role, notably Germany. The biggest single solar energy projects under construction in 2010, however, were in China, where western regions such as Xinjiang and Tibet have plenty of sunshine but are a long way from China's coal.[53]

Worldwide, wind and solar power together in 2010 accounted for less than 1 percent of energy consumption, despite their recent exponential growth. Unlike fossil fuels, they are hard to store. They may be the best hope for cutting greenhouse gas emissions, but they have a very long way to go to challenge fossil fuels—especially in the transport sector, where oil's advantages are strong.

Indirect Effects of Abundant Energy

The fossil fuel energy path brought profound consequences for the world's air, water, and soil, as well as for human health. Beyond all that, the mere fact of cheap energy (cheap by the standards of the past) led to all manner of environmental change. Cheap energy, and the machines that used it, remade timber cutting and farming, among other industries. By and large, cheap energy expanded the scope of what was economically rewarding, thereby extending the scale or intensity of these energy-guzzling activities.

Consider timber harvesting. The surge of deforestation around the world since 1960, especially in moist tropical forests, is one of the great environmental transformations of modern history. Cheap oil enabled it. Had loggers used axes and handsaws, had they transported logs only by animal muscle and via waterways, they would have deforested far less than they did. Loggers with gasoline-powered chain saws became one hundred to one thousand times as efficient at cutting trees than men with axes and crosscut saws. From the 1990s, huge diesel-powered machines that look like "insects from another planet" snipped off tree trunks at the base, allowing timber cutting with no human feet on the forest floor.[54]

Oil transformed agriculture even more fundamentally. In the 1980s one person with a big tractor and a full tank of fuel in the North American prairies could plow 110 acres (50 hectares) in a day, doing the work that seventy years before had required 55 men and 110 horses. Mechanization of this sort emptied the farmlands of North America and Europe of horses and people. In 1920 the United States had devoted nearly a quarter of its sown acreage to oats for horses; in 1990, almost none. Tractors transformed agriculture in parts of Asia too, where there are now more than five million tractors (Africa has perhaps two hundred thousand).[55]

Mechanization is only the most obvious change cheap energy brought in agriculture. The enormous use of nitrogenous fertilizers also depended on cheap energy. About 5 percent of the world's natural gas is devoted to fertilizer production. Many pesticides used oil as their chemical feedstock. Irrigation, too, especially when it involved pumping water up from aquifers, relied on cheap energy. All these practices of modern farming had profound ecological effects, and all of them needed cheap energy.

Cheap energy transformed the scale, intensity, and environmental implications of several other arenas of human interaction with nature, including mining, fishing, urban design, and tourism. Without cheap energy, it would not be practical for machines to grind through tons of Australian hillscapes in search of a few grams of gold. Nor would trawlers be able to scrape the seafloor with nets several miles across. Nor would cities such as Toronto and Sydney have sprawled over landscapes to the extent they have, gobbling up forests and farmland. Nor would millions of North Americans routinely fly to places such as Cozumel, or Europeans to the Seychelles, or Japanese to Saipan or Guam—all of which in the past forty years were transformed, environmentally as well as economically and socially, by mass tourism. In these and dozens of other cases, the cheap energy involved usually came from fossil fuels, but had it come cheaply from any source, the outcome for mountains, fish, forests, farmland, and beachfronts would have been much the same. The indirect effects of energy upon the environment resulted from the massive deployment of energy, from its abundance and low cost, not from any specific attributes of the energy source.[56]

Although one cannot hope to disentangle all the forces and processes that shaped the Anthropocene, from almost any viewpoint energy seems to be at the heart of the new epoch. The quantities of energy in use after 1945 became so vast, they dwarfed all that went before. The specific qualities of fossil fuels, of nuclear energy, and of hydroelectricity etched themselves into the biosphere through pollution, radiation, reservoirs, and so forth. Cheap energy gave people new leverage with which to accomplish things, move fast and far, make money, and, if inadvertently and often unknowingly, alter the environment. Almost everyone who could take advantage of cheap energy did so.

The Population Bomb

The demographic history of humankind in the years after 1945 was unlike anything that came before. The increase in human numbers impressed contemporary observers from the late 1940s onward. Most of those who paid attention to the question decried population growth—sometimes, but by no means always, on environmental grounds. Perhaps the classic statement of population anxiety came from Paul Ehrlich, a Stanford University biologist who popularized the term *population bomb* in a book of that title published in 1968. Ehrlich was wrong in many of his predictions, but he was right that the human animal was then in the middle of a population explosion, by far the biggest in its long history.

The Second World War brought early death to about sixty million people. During the war, the world contained well over two billion people, and each year some sixty to seventy million babies were born. In China, Japan, the USSR, Poland, Germany, Yugoslavia, and a few other countries, wartime mortality, and suppressed fertility, did leave a sharp imprint on demography. But in global terms all this death was swamped by a rising tide of births.

Still, the war had some delayed demographic effects. Its end triggered baby booms in several parts of the world. More importantly, medical and public health techniques and procedures, learned or refined during the war, helped launch a boom in survival, especially among infants and children. War's exigencies had legitimated massive public health interventions and taught administrators and health professionals how to deliver vaccines, antibiotics, and sanitation to the masses at modest cost, even in difficult conditions. So after 1945 human demography entered upon the most distinctive period in its two-hundred-thousand-year history. In the span of one human lifetime, 1945 to 2010, global population tripled from about 2.3 billion to 6.9 billion. This bizarre interlude, with sustained population growth of more than 1 percent per annum, is of course what almost everyone on Earth now regards as normal. It is anything but normal.

The first billion was the hardest. It took our species many thousands of years, including a brush or two with extinction, to become one billion strong. That came around 1800 or 1820. By 1930 the human population had doubled to two billion. It took only another thirty years, until 1960, to add the third billion. Then the crescendo came. The fourth billion arrived in 1975, joined by another by 1987, and then another by 1999. By 2011 or 2012 the world counted seven billion people, and had been adding a billion every twelve to fifteen years for two human generations. Between 1945 and 2010, some two-thirds of the population growth in the history of our species took place within one human lifetime. Nothing like this had ever happened before in the history of humankind.

One way to look at this extraordinary burst of population growth is to consider the absolute increase in the number of people per year, the annual increment or the net of births minus deaths. From 1920 to 1945 the globe had added, on average, a little over twenty million people every year. By 1950 the annual increment approached fifty million, after which it surged to about seventy-five million by the early 1970s, stabilized briefly, then in the late 1980s reached what is likely to be its all-time maximum at about eighty-nine million per year—equivalent to adding a new Germany or Vietnam (at their 2010 populations) every twelve months. Table 3.3 summarizes this record from 1950 to 2010.

A further way to look at the great surge in population is to focus on growth rates. For most of human history, growth rates were infinitesimal. By one careful estimate, for the seventeen centuries before 1650, annual growth came to about 0.05 percent per annum. In the nineteenth century, growth attained a rate of about 0.5 percent per annum, and in the first half of the twentieth, about 0.6 percent.[57] A great spike followed the Second World War (summarized in Table 3.4). Growth reached its apex about 1970, at some 2 percent per year. Then the rate of growth declined again, very fast after 1990, so that by 2010 it came to 1.1 percent per year. What the future holds is anyone's guess, but UN demographers project that the growth rate by 2050 will slacken to 0.34 percent, slower than in 1800. In any case, the era from 1950 to 1990, when global growth exceeded 1.75 percent per year, amounted to a burst of reproduction and survival, never before approached and never to be repeated in the history of our species. If we did somehow keep it up for another few centuries, the Earth would soon be hidden inside

TABLE 3.3

Global population increase per year, 1950–2010 (in thousands)

Period	Population increase per year
1950–1955	46,822
1955–1960	51,981
1960–1965	61,663
1965–1970	70,821
1970–1975	75,108
1975–1980	75,258
1980–1985	81,728
1985–1990	88,841
1990–1995	84,524
1995–2000	80,459
2000–2005	79,382
2005–2010	79,282

Data source: UN Population Division.

a giant ball of human flesh expanding outward at a radial velocity approaching the speed of light—an unlikely prospect.[58]

So we are in the waning stages of the most anomalous episode in human demographic history. The main reason (there are several others) for the steep fall in fertility is essentially environmental: urbanization. City people almost always prefer to have fewer children than their country cousins. As the world has urbanized at a dizzying pace, our fertility rates have slipped.

Nonetheless, our recent biological success is remarkable. As of 2010 we outnumbered any other large mammal on Earth by a large margin. Indeed, our total biomass (about 100 million tons) outweighed that of any mammalian rival except cattle, of which there were about 1.3 billion, weighing in at 156 million tons. Humans (whose average body size increased by half between 1800 and 2000)[59] now account for perhaps 5 percent of terrestrial animal biomass, half as much as all domestic animals combined. Ants, however, easily outweigh us.

Why did this bizarre episode in our demographic history happen? On the most basic level, it happened because the global death rate fell rapidly, from

TABLE 3.4
Global population growth rate, 1950–2010

Period	Population growth rate (%)
1950–1955	1.77
1955–1960	1.80
1960–1965	1.94
1965–1970	2.02
1970–1975	1.94
1975–1980	1.77
1980–1985	1.76
1985–1990	1.75
1990–1995	1.54
1995–2000	1.36
2000–2005	1.26
2005–2010	1.18

Data source: UN Population Division.

about 30 to 35 per thousand per year in 1800 to about 20 per thousand in 1945, before plummeting to 10 by the early 1980s. It now stands at 8.4. The birth rate fell also, but more gradually. Globally the crude birth rate slid from 37 per thousand in 1950 to 20 per thousand in 2010, a notable fall, but less so than the precipitous decline in the death rate.

On a less elementary level, what happened was that techniques of death control temporarily outstripped techniques of birth control. In the course of the eighteenth century in some parts of the world, notably China and Western Europe, better farming techniques, improved government response to food shortage, combined with gradual buildup of disease resistance, slowed death rates. In the nineteenth century, these processes continued and were joined by revolutionary changes in urban sanitation, mainly the provision of clean drinking water, and in the early twentieth century by vaccinations and antibiotics as well. States (and colonial administrations) created public health agencies that sought to impose vaccination and sanitation regimes wherever they could. Medical research also identified several disease vectors—lice, ticks, and mosquitoes, for instance—and in some cases proceeded to find ways to keep vectors and people apart. Successful mosquito control sharply curtailed the domain of diseases such as yellow fever and malaria. Moreover, food scientists in the 1920s and 1930s figured out the role of specific vitamins and minerals in checking malnutrition diseases, and agronomists figured out how to help farmers double and triple crop yields per acre.[60]

After 1945 all of these developments came together to lower death tolls very quickly in most parts of the world—hence, a tremendous surge in life expectancy, derived mainly from the survival of billions of children who in earlier times would have died very young. In the second half of the twentieth century, even poor people lived far longer (on average, about twenty years longer) than their forebears had a century previously. The gaps between rich and poor in life expectancy narrowed almost to nothing.[61]

This rollback of death was a signal achievement of the human species and one of the greatest social changes of modern times. The end of the twentieth century brought two exceptions that proved the rule. First, in Russia, Ukraine, and some of their smaller neighbors, life expectancy (which in the Soviet Union had lengthened rapidly between 1946 and 1965) declined after 1975, at least for males. This departure from the prevailing trend is usually attributed to alcoholism. Second, after 1990 in the most AIDS-ravaged parts of Africa, a parallel reverse of lengthening life expectancy occurred. These two exceptions had only a slender effect on the overall pattern of longer life and faster population growth. It was a pattern that provoked considerable worry, partly on environmental grounds.

Attempts to Curb Population

Even long ago some people worried about overpopulation. Around 500 BCE, the Chinese sage Han Feizi fretted, "Nowadays no one regards five sons as a large number, and these five sons in turn have five sons each, so that before the grandfather has died, he has twenty-five grandchildren. Hence the number of people increases, goods grow scarce, and men have to struggle and slave for a meager living."[62] The Latin author Tertullian (a North African and early Christian apologist) wrote around 200 CE: "The earth itself is currently more cultivated and developed than in early times. . . . Everywhere there is a dwelling, everywhere a multitude.... The greatest evidence of the large numbers of people: we are burdensome to the world, the resources are scarcely adequate to us ... already nature does not sustain us."[63] For many centuries occasional voices repeated these concerns, and in 1798 Hong Liangji and Thomas Malthus each published essays giving a plausible theoretical underpinning to notions of overpopulation.[64]

Modern versions of these ancient anxieties gained currency in the 1940s, giving rise to sustained efforts to check population growth. For most of human history, when rulers concerned themselves with population in their domains, their aim was to maximize the number of their subjects in the interests of military strength. With the rise of social Darwinism after the 1870s, some thinkers developed doctrines of eugenics, in essence arguments that other (and "lesser") people should reproduce less. But after World War II, a chorus of voices arose warning of excess population, of impending mass starvation, of violent social unrest, and in some cases of environmental degradation—and their views attracted interest in the corridors of power.

These voices, the most prominent of which came from Europe and America, urged population limitation mainly upon the rest of the world, above all upon Asia. The motives involved were decidedly mixed, but in any case, in several Asian countries the same goal made sense to people coming into power as colonial rule gave way.

India, for example, an independent nation after 1947, by 1952 undertook to limit its own population. In the 1970s India even put a birth rate target in its economic five-year plan and tried to mandate sterilization for people who already had three children. This last measure encountered robust resistance, provoking violent incidents and contributing to the downfall of Indira Gandhi's government in 1977. Fertility reduction in India (see Table 3.5) happened much more slowly than its backers wished.[65]

In China, sterner measures brought stronger results. The People's Republic of China, born in revolution and civil war in 1949, traveled a meandering road to birth control. For millennia Chinese emperors had favored high fertility, and later Chinese nationalists such as Sun Yat-sen and Chiang Kai-shek were equally pro-natalist. At the time of the revolution, Mao Zedong agreed, feeling, as most Marxists did, that birth control would be unnecessary in communist society because communes would unleash productive forces hitherto constrained by

TABLE 3.5

**Crude birth rates (number of births per 1,000 people per year),
India and China**

Year(s)	India	China
1950–1955	43	44
1970–1975	37	29
1990–1995	31	19
2010	21	14

Data source: UN Population Division (http://esa.un.org/unpp/p2kodata.asp).

capitalism, yielding a cornucopia of food. Soon after, he also judged that World War III was imminent and reasoned that China would need all the people it could get. In 1958 the Communist Party's second in command, Liu Shaoqi, looked forward to the day when China might have six billion people, but allowed that in this rosy future everyone would have to share beds. Others among Mao's lieutenants saw matters differently, thinking that further growth of China's huge population imperiled the economy, and after the horrendous famine of the Great Leap Forward of 1959–1961 their views acquired greater weight. But the Cultural Revolution (1966–1976), the violent political movement that plunged China into administrative and economic chaos, prevented any effective policy. In 1970 China began to encourage birth control by distributing free contraceptives. In the course of the 1970s, engineers trained in cybernetics (rocket guidance systems in particular), influenced by the dour ecological forecasts of the Club of Rome, worked out the scientific rationale for drastic reductions in fertility. Through personal connections with party leaders, their views gradually prevailed, first in a series of carrots and sticks devised to encourage small families, and in 1979 in the "one-child policy." This gave party cadres great power to determine who would be allowed to have children in any given year, and imposed stiff penalties (loss of job, loss of apartment, loss of educational opportunities) on couples who did not follow instructions. Urban couples by and large fell into line; villagers sometimes did not and eventually were permitted greater leeway. The policy made exceptions for ethnic minorities, who likely would have resisted

A billboard promoting China's "One Child Policy," Chengdu, 1985. Implemented in 1979 by Chinese leaders fearful about overpopulation, China's program is the largest-scale effort in world history to restrict demographic growth. The policy has had many critics, but without it the world would have several hundred million more human inhabitants. (LightRocket/Getty Images)

it strenuously. In China, extended families and heads of lineages had long exercised influence over when couples might have a child. This tradition made the concept of state-regulated fertility easier for Chinese to accept than it was for Indians. With these measures, among the most forceful efforts at social engineering anywhere in modern history, China reduced its annual population growth from about 2.6 percent in the late 1960s to 0.6 percent by 2010. The success of its population policy assisted China's economic miracle.[66]

Other East and Southeast Asian societies, notably South Korea, Singapore, and Malaysia, introduced less-draconian population limitation policies in the 1970s and 1980s, and also saw their demographic growth rates decline precipitously. This has probably helped them become much richer on a per capita basis than they otherwise would be, a matter of some consequence for their environmental history. They were swimming with the tide: Fertility declines happened almost everywhere in the post-1970 world, with or without state policies. They happened fastest in East Asia, and fastest of all in China, where unquestionably state policy played a large role.

By the 1980s the great majority of countries around the world had some sort of population policy. In Europe it usually consisted of ineffective measures to raise fertility. In most of the rest of the world, it consisted of measures, sometimes in vain, sometimes powerful, to defuse the population bomb by lowering fertility. Without these policies the world would likely have several hundred million more people, many of them Chinese.

Population and Environment

At first glance it stands to reason that population growth, especially at the rampant pace of 1945–2010, is disruptive to the environment. This has been an axiom in most strands of modern environmentalism. Its logic is straightforward: more people mean more human activity, and human activity disturbs the biosphere. As a first approximation this is true. But it turns out that it is not true always and everywhere. When and where it is true, the degree to which it is true is extremely variable. The main reason for this is that the notion of "environment" is capacious, so what may be true for soil erosion may not hold for air pollution. For example, population growth probably had a great deal to do with the clearing of West African forests since 1950 but almost nothing at all to do with nuclear contamination at the Soviet atomic weapons sites.

Population growth played its strongest role in the environment through processes connected to food production. The threefold growth in human population (1945–2010) required a proportionate expansion in food production. But even here the matter is not straightforward. Soils provide a fine example. Without a doubt, population growth pushed upward the demand for food, and also the demand for agricultural land. In China, for example, growing population and food requirements helped inspire a state-sponsored push onto the grasslands of the north, converting steppe pasture into grain fields. Frontier expansion had a long tradition in Chinese history, but rarely did it proceed at the pace achieved in the decades after 1950.[67] As is often the case when year-round grass is replaced by annual crops, the Chinese surge onto the steppe led to heightened rates of soil erosion, desertification, and downwind dust storms. Population pressure also helped push farmers onto semi-arid lands in the West and Central African Sahel (the southern fringe of the Sahara), a strategy that worked well enough in the 1960s, when rains in the region were plentiful, but turned disastrous in the 1970s when rains failed.

Population pressures also played a role in driving people to cut and burn tropical forest in search of new farmland. In Guatemala, Côte d'Ivoire, Papua New Guinea, and a hundred places in between, frontier farming edged into old forests. The effects on soils were often profound and enduring. Wherever the farmers cleared sloping land, they invited spates of soil erosion, not via the wind as on the world's grasslands, but via running water. Moreover, in many settings soils with high concentrations of iron oxides quickly turned to laterite, a brick-hard surface, when exposed directly to strong sunshine. Tropical deforestation, with its attendant effects upon soils, was not always mainly a matter of population pressure. Indeed, in Latin America and Southeast Asia, quests for ranch land and timber played a larger role. But everywhere, especially in Africa, population was part of the equation.

In a few places matters worked out very differently, because population growth actually helped to stabilize landscapes. Where farmers had carved new fields out of sloping lands, they put soils at high risk to erosion. But where there was enough labor, farmers could secure their soils by cutting terraces into the hillsides. In the Machakos Hills district of Kenya's highlands, for example, rapid population growth provided the labor power for the Akamba people to build and maintain terraces and thereby reduce erosion from their fields and plots. (The soil conservation service of Kenya helped out too.) Agricultural terraces, ancient and modern, are widespread around the world, especially in the Andes, the Mediterranean hills, the Himalayas, and East and Southeast Asia. In these settings, high population densities could keep terraces and soils in place. Where population thinned, as in southern European hill districts after 1960, soil erosion often spurted.[68]

Population, Water, and Fish

Population growth was also a major factor behind the rapid climb in the use of fresh water. As Table 3.6 shows, between 1950 and 2010, when population tripled, water use did as well. Most of the additional water, perhaps as much as 90 percent,

TABLE 3.6

Global freshwater use, 1900–2009

Year	Use (km³)
1900	580
1950	1,366
1980	3,214
2011	3,900

Data sources: Peter H. Gleick, "Water Use," *Annual Review of Environment and Resources* 28, no. 1(2003): 275–314; World Bank, http://data.worldbank.org/indicator/ER.H2O.FWTL.K3/countries?display=graph.

went to irrigation. Most irrigation water nourished food crops, although a fair bit went to cotton and other fiber crops. The world's irrigated area also tripled (1945–2010), led by India, China, and Pakistan. But in some places, including the United States, after 1980 water use leveled off (due to improved efficiency) while populations and economies continued to grow. Nonetheless, it seems a reasonable conclusion that the main reason behind the tripling of water use was the tripling of population, because irrigation for food production took the lion's share.[69]

In the seas, a similar story played out. Between 1950 and 1960, the global marine fish catch doubled, and then doubled again by 1970. It stagnated in the 1970s, grew by a quarter in the 1980s, and ever since has remained fairly steady—because all the world's major fisheries by then were fished at or above their capacity. Most famously, the historically abundant cod fisheries of the North Atlantic, from Cape Cod to Newfoundland, crashed and never recovered.[70] But the fastest expansion in marine fishing took place in Asian waters, in part because those were closest to the region of fastest-growing food demand. Indonesia, for example, which in 1950 landed less than half a million tons of fish, by 2004 brought in over four million tons. Fishermen almost everywhere had incentives to catch as much as they could as fast as they could, lest someone else get the fish first. Management regimes for fisheries that would conserve fish for another day proved especially hard to implement and enforce.[71]

Again, as with the changes to forests and soils, population was only part of the story with fisheries. The global marine fish catch quintupled between 1950 and 2008, while population growth nearly tripled. As a rough estimate, one can say that 60 percent of the expansion of the marine fish catch derived from population growth.[72] But this arithmetic remains rough, and in any case does not capture cases in which tremendous expansions of fishing took place because of new technologies that lowered costs. The humble menhaden of the western North Atlantic, fished for centuries, after 1945 became the target of intensified industrial fishing efforts, abetted by airplane spotters that made it easy for fishing boats to follow the schools. Population growth had little, if anything, to do with the rapid exhaustion of menhaden fisheries.[73]

Population and the Atmosphere

Some environmental changes had no direct relationship with food production. In these cases the role of population pressure is harder to specify. Consider, for example, the accumulation of carbon dioxide, the most important greenhouse gas, in the atmosphere. Over the past two hundred years, carbon emissions have come from two main sources, fossil fuel use (about three-quarters) and the burning of forests (one-quarter). Population growth no doubt increased demand for fossil fuels and helped drive the encroachment on the world's forests. So to some degree, population growth has led to growth in carbon emissions. But how much?

As we will see later in more detail, carbon dioxide concentrations in the atmosphere climbed after the Industrial Revolution. By 1945 they stood at about 310 parts per million, and in 2010 at about 385. In that span, carbon emissions (not concentrations) increased about eightfold. So at a first approximation, given the tripling of population in the same time period, one might suppose that population growth is responsible for about three-eighths, or 37.5 percent, of the accumulation of carbon dioxide.

But that can stand only as a first approximation. Afghanistan, which showed high population growth, emitted very little carbon, less than 2 percent of the United Kingdom's total. The carbon consequences of population growth depended heavily on where it happened. Not only did an additional person in the UK lead to more carbon emissions than the addition of a person in Afghanistan, but there was a difference between an Afghan in Kabul (more likely to use more fossil fuel) and one in a remote village. And when population growth happened mattered too. In the rich countries after 1980, programs of energy efficiency, fuel switching away from carbon-rich coal, deindustrialization, and other developments meant that the impact of each additional person was less than it had been in the 1950s. For the years 1975–1996, one mathematically inclined scholar found that population growth was a major force behind carbon emissions, but, interestingly, least so in both the very poor and the very rich countries. The sad truth is that there is no reliable way to calculate the impact of population growth upon carbon emissions over time.[74]

Sometimes Population Did Not Matter at All

While the important case of carbon emissions is an elusive one, it is easy to find examples of environmental change in which one can confidently say population growth scarcely mattered at all. Whaling, which in the years after 1945 brought several whales—blue, grey, humpback, for example—to the brink of extinction, bore only the smallest relationship to population. The great whaling nations—Norway, Iceland, Japan, the USSR—had slow population growth rates, and their whalers were responding to long-standing cultural preferences for whale meat rather than seeking more food due to population growth.

The corrosion of the stratospheric ozone layer, which occurred almost entirely after 1945, also had virtually nothing to do with population growth. The chemical releases that destroyed stratospheric ozone, mainly chlorofluorocarbons (CFCs), were used chiefly as insulation, refrigerants, aerosol propellants, and solvents. Very little in the way of CFC releases occurred where population growth was high. The only ozone-destroying substance used in agriculture, a pesticide called methyl bromide, was used mainly in places such as California for high-end crops such as strawberries and almonds, demand for which had everything to do with elevated tastes and improved shipping capabilities and almost nothing to do with population growth.

To take a final example, environmental disasters, frequent enough in the decades after 1945, had no discernible relationship to population growth. The great industrial accident near Seveso in 1976, which splattered dioxin over the countryside north of Milan, occurred in a region of extremely low population growth. In the worst industrial accident in history, in 1984, a Union Carbide chemical plant spewed 40 tons of lethal methyl isocyanate onto Bhopal, a city of one million in central India, killing several thousand people and sickening many more. It too had nothing to do with population growth.[75] The Chernobyl catastrophe occurred in 1986. The reactor existed to provide electricity; the accident occurred because of design flaws and human error. In the 1980s population growth in Ukraine was negligible.

Migration and Environment

Like population growth, migration had variable impacts upon the environment. The largest migration after 1945 was the stampede of villagers to cities, with myriad environmental effects. Migration from one city to another had much smaller effects, except in cases where new cities bloomed in formerly sparsely inhabited places. Migration from one rural area to another, however, often triggered profound environmental changes.

The decades after 1945 were an age of migration. Tens of millions moved from one country to another.[76] Even more moved within their countries, although often to very new environments. Millions of Americans moved from the "Rust Belt" to the "Sun Belt," to Florida, Texas, and California in particular. San Antonio, which had a quarter million inhabitants in 1940, by 2010 had nearly 1.5 million and had become the seventh largest city in the United States.[77] Cities such as Phoenix and Las Vegas grew from almost nothing into major metropolises, sprawling into surrounding deserts and siphoning off all available water for many miles around. Residents air-conditioned their homes and workplaces for most months of the year, leading electricity-intensive lives that encouraged additional fossil fuel use and the building of more hydroelectric dams, especially on the already overdrawn Colorado River.

A smaller, Chinese sunbelt migration took place into the even drier regions of Xinjiang and Tibet after 1950. Government policy had more to do with it than air conditioning. Millions of Chinese went to Xinjiang in northwest China, an autonomous region consisting of a string of oases thinly populated with ethnic minorities. Many of the migrants were compelled to go, especially during the Cultural Revolution (1966–1976). In Xinjiang, ethnic Chinese are now probably a majority, despite having a much lower birth rate than the Uighurs and other local populations. These migrations led to cultural and ethnic frictions, but also to new environmental stresses such as water and fuelwood shortages and desertification. Increased water demand, partly due to the influx of migrants, has reduced Xinjiang's lake area by half since 1950.[78]

In Mao's time, few Chinese moved to Tibet, the elevated plateau region bordering on the Himalayas that was incorporated into China in the 1950s. But in the 1980s and 1990s several hundred thousand went, often as laborers on road and railway projects. Since the 1980s the government has encouraged Chinese migration. According to the official census, ethnic Chinese made up 6 percent of Tibet's population in 1953 and slightly more by 2000. But unofficial estimates suggest Han Chinese now outnumber Tibetans in Tibet—if one counts their actual rather than official residence. Unlike in Xinjiang, the migrants flocked mainly to the cities of Tibet, but also to mining enclaves and labor camps around construction projects. The delicate high-altitude ecosystems of Tibet are easily disrupted, and wetlands, grasslands, wildlife, and air quality all suffered from the population expansion and development projects. In recent years the government has tried to check the environmental disturbance caused by railroads, by, for example, building overpasses for migratory wildlife. It has also tried to settle Tibetan nomadic herders into villages in the name of ecological stability, on the grounds that Tibetans and their herds were degrading grasslands.[79]

Migrants altered rainforests in Brazil and Indonesia at least as much as they did arid lands in the United States and China. Again, state policies played crucial roles. Many states, including Brazil and Indonesia, often encouraged and subsidized migration. Moreover, states obliged or encouraged migrants to engage in certain activities that just so happened to carry powerful environmental consequences.

For centuries, outsiders had seen in Amazonia—nine times the size of Texas and nearly twice the area of India—a sprawling storehouse of riches and resources, awaiting development. A rubber boom (ca. 1880–1913) gave tantalizing evidence of the wealth one might tap. But even businessmen with the savvy and resources of Henry Ford failed in their quests to convert Amazonian nature into money. Ford tried to build an empire of rubber plantations, called Fordlandia, beginning in the mid-1920s, but fell afoul of his own delusions and uncooperative local conditions, especially a rubber-tree fungus. When Ford's grandson sold off the ruins of Fordlandia in 1945, Amazonia had only about thirty thousand people in it.[80]

In the 1950s and early 1960s, the Brazilian government undertook another development scheme for the two-thirds of Amazonia that falls within Brazil. It was, as the saying went, a land without men for men without land. The government—a military regime from 1964 to 1985—intended to relieve poverty (and

A section of rainforest in the Amazon Basin, Brazil, clear-cut for transformation into farmland, 2009. Forested area in Amazonia shrank by about 20 percent from 1965 to 2012. (© Ton Koene/ Visuals Unlimited/Corbis)

deflate the recurrent pressures for land reform) in the dry northeast of Brazil. It also wished to populate the country's border regions with loyal Brazilians, and to mobilize the presumed natural wealth of the world's largest moist tropical forest. Thousands of miles of highways soon pierced the forest, and millions of migrants flowed into the region. They cut and burned patches of forest, mainly in order to run cattle on the newly cleared land. Parts of Amazonia increasingly became a land without trees for men with cattle. Soils in most of the region are low in nutrients, so ranchers usually found that after a few years they needed to move on, to cut and burn more forest to keep their cattle in pasture. Soybean farmers, increasingly prominent since the 1990s, found the same conditions. By 2010 about 15 to 20 percent of the forest area of 1970 had been cleared for grass or crops, but the rate of forest clearance had dropped sharply. The issue of Amazonian deforestation had become a perennial one in Brazilian politics and in global environmental politics as well.[81]

Indonesia became an independent, if rickety, country in 1949. Most of the population, and all of the leadership, lived on the fertile volcanic island of Java. Most of the other islands had poorer soils and scant population, usually of minorities with no love for Javanese rule. Building on a small program pursued by their former colonial masters, the Dutch, the rulers of independent Indonesia launched the so-called transmigration scheme in 1949. Military men (like their counterparts in Brazil), they hoped that some fifty million politically reliable Javanese would resettle on the other islands, notably Borneo and Sumatra. The plan was to relieve population pressure and poverty on Java, harvest the natural resources of the outer islands, and swamp the local populations with durably loyal Javanese.

By 1990, when the transmigration program had wound down, something under five million Javanese migrants had taken the lure of free land on the outer islands. They found their rice-farming skills did not yield encouraging results on the poor soils of Sumatra and Borneo, and until 1984 the government decreed that they should raise only rice. Like ranchers in Amazonia, they had to move to new land frequently, burning as they went, in order to gain access to the nutrients stored in the ash of former forests. Coming from a thoroughly deforested island, the Javanese often found it comforting to eliminate what felt like an alien habitat. Their efforts added to the pace of deforestation in Indonesia, which from 1970 to 2000 was one of the world's most active frontiers of forest destruction.[82]

These great migrations, and others like them, led to environmental changes of considerable magnitude. The changes were mainly local and regional in scope, although deforestation anywhere added appreciably to the carbon dioxide loading of the entire atmosphere. Despite their limited scope, the environmental changes provoked by migration were often thorough and of much more consequence, where they occurred, than greenhouse gas accumulation or climate change—at least up to the present.

Migration also contributed to heating up the global greenhouse through the relocation of people to places where they could lead much more energy-intensive lives. Tens of millions left Central America or the Caribbean for the United States and Canada, or North Africa for Western Europe, or South Asia for the Persian Gulf. To the extent that they succeeded in adopting the lifestyles of their new homes—driving cars, heating and cooling their dwellings with fossil fuels—their migration added to global energy consumption and thereby to greenhouse gas accumulation and the warming of the planet.

The period 1945–2010 witnessed a great crescendo in the human population history of the world. No period of similar duration—one human lifetime—was anywhere near as peculiar as this one. If population growth ever mattered for environmental change, it surely should have done so in these decades.

And it did matter. But not always and everywhere, and not necessarily in clear and obvious ways. For some forms of environmental change, such as West African deforestation, population growth played a leading role. For others, such as whaling, it played only a small role at most. As is normal in human affairs, population growth was never the sole cause of anything, but always operated in concert with other factors.

The same was true of migration. The decades after 1945 saw an upturn in rates of long-distance migration. This too brought environmental consequences, especially in those cases where people went from one sort of environment to a very different and unfamiliar one. Their accustomed ways of doing things, whether growing rice or raising cattle, often carried unforeseen and dramatic environmental consequences in their new homes.

For more than fifty years now, environmentalists have anxiously pointed to population growth as a major cause behind environmental change. That claim has often been justified, but it falls well short of a universal truth. By unpacking the concept of "environment" into specific biomes and processes, one can get a little further than this blanket proposition. In fifty more years, if the demographers are right and population growth has slowed to zero or close to it, we shall have a firmer idea of its significance for environmental change, both in general and for the exuberant age of 1945–2010. Let us hope that no gigantic ecological catastrophe intervenes to complicate the analysis.

2. Climate and Biological Diversity

THE Earth's climate is enormously complex, involving subtle and imperfectly understood relationships between the Sun, atmosphere, oceans, lithosphere (Earth's crust), pedosphere (soils), and terrestrial biosphere (forests, mostly). But over the course of the twentieth century, in particular from the late 1950s onward, knowledge of the Earth's climate advanced very quickly. By the late twentieth century, scientific research had reached near-consensus on the accuracy of a long-advanced and troubling forecast for the Earth's climate. This, of course, was the idea that human activities since the beginning of the Industrial Revolution had altered climate and begun heating the Earth. Variously labeled the "enhanced greenhouse effect," "global warming," or "anthropogenic climate change," the problem centered mostly on human interference in the planet's carbon cycle. By burning fossil fuels and emitting carbon dioxide (CO_2) and other gases, humans were increasing the concentrations of powerful heat-trapping gases in the atmosphere. Scientists feared potentially catastrophic consequences for the world's climate if these trends were left unchecked. Spurred by the increasing volume and quality of research on the subject, as well as by new technologies that enabled improved monitoring of the Earth's climate, these predictions became increasingly dire. Yet there was an enormous gap between what scientists thought needed to happen to avoid catastrophe and the reality of global climate-change politics. By 2013 there was increasingly strong evidence that the Earth's climate and the operation of its many ecosystems had already begun to change in response to higher CO_2 levels.

Climate and the Industrial Revolution

The Earth's atmosphere is the reason the planet is neither freezing cold nor burning hot. In highly simplified terms, almost one-third of solar radiation is instantly reflected back into space. A bit more than two-thirds of the incoming solar radiation that strikes the Earth is absorbed and converted into infrared energy (heat) by the Earth's surface, oceans, or atmosphere, and re-radiated in all directions. Greenhouse gases (GHGs), of which there are several types, absorb most of this infrared (or long-wave) energy. Naturally occurring greenhouse gases include water vapor, methane, carbon dioxide, and nitrous oxide. There are also several that do not occur in nature but that have been created by humans. The most important of these are CFCs, first invented in the laboratory in the 1920s. Each gas captures energy at different wavelengths, and each has different characteristics, such as absorptive power and duration in the atmosphere. Each, moreover, exists in the atmosphere at different concentrations, and the concentration of each gas has varied substantially over geological time. Very recently, at the onset of the Industrial Revolution, the naturally occurring concentrations were about 0.7 parts per million (ppm) for methane, 280 ppm for CO_2, and 288 parts per billion (ppb) for nitrous oxide. The concentration of every one of these has risen since.[83]

Atmospheric gas concentrations are not the only determinants of climate. Other factors influence the amount of solar radiation that reaches the Earth's surface and the amount absorbed or reflected. Developments that occur in and on the Earth itself also have an influence on climate. These, in turn, can interact in complicated fashion with GHG concentrations. The output of the Sun itself can vary, which influences the amount of solar radiation reaching the Earth. Slight oscillations of the Earth's axial rotation and orbit about the Sun are other factors affecting climate. These oscillations, known as Milanković cycles, occur over many thousands of years and help shape the timing of the Earth's ice ages. The amount of solar radiation that reaches the Earth's surface is also influenced by aerosols, which are airborne particles that block incoming radiation. Volcanic eruptions can influence global temperatures. The ash and soot emitted by volcanoes can reach the stratosphere and encircle the globe, increasing the amount of aerosols. If large enough, a single volcano's eruption can be sufficient to reduce global temperatures, albeit temporarily (a few years), until rain washes the particles out of the atmosphere. The largest recorded eruptions in world history have had significant short-term temperature effects in just this manner, as occurred after the Laki eruption of 1783 (in Iceland) and the Tambora eruption of 1815 and the Krakatau eruption of 1883 (both near Java).

Although more stable than what occurred before, the Holocene climate (which began roughly twelve thousand years ago) has had marked fluctuations. Temperatures in the early Holocene were as much as 5 degrees Celsius warmer than during the trough of the previous ice age. During the Holocene, the peak occurred between eight thousand and five thousand years ago, when temperatures ranged up to 3 degrees Celsius warmer at the highest (most northerly) latitudes than the average for the Holocene. Natural temperature variation has occurred in more recent history as well. Between 1100 and 1300 CE, Europe experienced something called the medieval warm period, followed by the Little Ice Age, which lasted from roughly 1350 to 1850 and had temperatures almost a degree Celsius colder on average than currently.

The concern about anthropogenic climate change centers primarily on human interference in the natural cycling of carbon during the industrial era. The world's store of carbon is cycled between the lithosphere, pedosphere, biosphere, atmosphere, and oceans. However, human activities since the Industrial Revolution have altered the distribution of carbon across these spheres. In essence, the climate change problem arises from the fact that humans have removed carbon from the Earth and placed it in the atmosphere at rates much faster than occurs naturally. Humans have also increased the concentration of other carbon-containing greenhouse gases. Methane (CH_4), also known as natural gas, when burned is transformed into CO_2 and water. The main problem with methane, however, stems from direct release into the atmosphere. On a per-molecule basis, methane is far more powerful than carbon dioxide at trapping heat.[84]

There are two basic ways humans have added carbon to the atmosphere. First, carbon is released through deforestation, via burnt or decaying wood and from newly exposed, carbon-rich soils. Deforestation is an ancient phenomenon, but the greatest acceleration of deforestation on a global level has occurred since 1945. Conversely, intact forests absorb carbon from the atmosphere. Hence, the amount of carbon added to the atmosphere through deforestation is always a net figure, in effect deforestation minus afforestation. Net deforestation and other land-use changes currently add about 15 percent of total anthropogenic carbon into the atmosphere.[85]

Second, and more importantly, carbon is released through the burning of fossil fuels. Humans have shifted carbon stored in the lithosphere (in the form of coal, oil, and natural gas) to the atmosphere and thereby to the oceans. Consider the amount of carbon released into the atmosphere from fossil fuel burning. In 1750, before the Industrial Revolution began, humankind released perhaps 3 million metric tons of carbon into the atmosphere in this manner annually. A century later, in 1850, the figure was around 50 million tons. Another century later, at the end of World War II, it had increased more than twenty-fold, to about 1,200 million tons. Then after 1945 humankind embarked upon a fiesta of fossil fuel combustion. Within fifteen years after the war ended, humans were putting around 2,500 million tons of carbon into the atmosphere each year. In 1970 this figure increased to over 4,000 million tons, in 1990 to over 6,000, and in 2006 to some 8,200 million tons—about 2,700 times more than in the year 1750 and eight times the total in 1945. By the turn of the twenty-first century, fossil fuels had become responsible for around 85 percent of anthropogenic carbon added to the atmosphere.[86]

Increased anthropogenic carbon emissions translated into increased atmospheric CO_2 concentrations. Carbon dioxide concentrations are now around 400 ppm, compared with the 280 ppm preindustrial baseline. This concentration is the highest CO_2 level reached in the last several hundred thousand years and possibly the last twenty million years. In 1958, when the first reliable, direct, and continuous measurement of atmospheric CO_2 began, concentration levels stood at 315 ppm. Since then the measured concentration has increased every year. It is unlikely that at any other time in the long history of the atmosphere CO_2 concentrations have jumped by one-fourth within fifty years.

Recent emission trends have been especially noteworthy. The rate of increase in carbon dioxide emissions during the 2000s was more than twice that of the 1990s (3.3 percent versus 1.3 percent global annual growth). The continuing economic growth of the global economy provided only part of the explanation. More troublesome was the carbon intensity of the global economy (CO_2 emissions per unit of economic activity). The global economy had been decarbonizing since about 1970, yet after 2000 the process went into reverse. Economic growth became more, rather than less, dependent on carbon-heavy fuels, in particular coal burned in China.[87]

By the last decades of the twentieth century, it appeared as if the world's climate was indeed shifting as a result of increased atmospheric carbon dioxide, methane, and other GHGs. Temperature data showed a mean surface atmospheric warming of about 0.8 degrees Celsius over the average of the twentieth century. The rate of change was greatest at the end of the century. Roughly three-quarters of the increase occurred after the mid-1970s, the remainder before 1940. Since the 1970s, each successive decade has been warmer than all previous recorded ones; in 2010 the National Aeronautics and Space Administration (NASA) in the United States announced that the decade of the 2000s was the warmest on record. Temperature increases were greatest at the highest latitudes in the Northern Hemisphere, consistent with climate models that forecast the greatest warming at the poles and the least in the tropics.[88]

Increased carbon dioxide in the atmosphere also had important consequences for the world's oceans. As with the atmosphere, measurements showed that the oceans had warmed during the second half of the twentieth century. The upper 300 meters of the oceans warmed a bit less than 0.2 degrees Celsius after 1950, while the upper 3,000 meters warmed just shy of 0.04 degrees. This may not sound like much, but given the density of water and the immense volume of the oceans, these small increases represented an enormous amount of thermal energy. Since 1950 the upper 3,000 meters of ocean had absorbed more than fourteen times the amount of energy absorbed by the continents.

Increasing oceanic temperatures began to have real effects, especially on sea levels and sea ice. Sea levels rose slightly over the twentieth century—about 15 centimeters, roughly half of which was from the thermal expansion of water and the other half from melting ice sheets in places such as Greenland. Arctic sea ice also began melting. Spring and summer sea ice cover in the Arctic Ocean retreated perhaps 10 to 15 percent over the second half of the twentieth century. As with atmospheric temperatures, the rate of change was greatest toward the end of the twentieth century and the beginning of the twenty-first. Trends for the sea ice surrounding the Antarctic were less clear. A disconcerting event occurred in April 2009, when a part of the enormous Wilkins Ice Shelf collapsed; but while some areas around the continent were losing ice, others appeared to be gaining. The total amount of Antarctic sea ice may even have increased since 1970.[89]

Increasing temperature was not the only consequence for the world's oceans. Part of the atmosphere's CO_2 is absorbed by the world's "sinks," meaning soils, forests, oceans, and rocks. The precise functioning of sinks is still debated, but roughly half the CO_2 emitted through burning fossil fuels winds up in various sinks. Oceans are responsible for about half of this figure. Without this service provided by the oceans, atmospheric concentrations of CO_2 would be far higher. Unfortunately, this service is not without consequences. By the turn of the twenty-first century, there was good evidence that the cumulative, additional CO_2 taken up by the oceans had begun to alter their chemistry. Increasing carbon dioxide levels acidify the oceans, which makes it more difficult for some organisms to manufacture their skeletons and shells. A few of these imperiled creatures are critical food for whales and fish. Even more ominously, there is some concern that oceans and other sinks such as forests may be having an increasingly difficult time absorbing atmospheric carbon dioxide. It is possible that some sinks could switch to net producers rather than absorbers of CO_2, as might occur if tropical forests dry out due to higher temperatures.[90]

The potential risks of climate change are numerous, few more threatening than the alteration to the world's water supply. Increased atmospheric temperatures likely will alter a great many of the world's ecosystems, change regional precipitation patterns, cause more frequent and extreme weather events, raise sea levels and erode coastlines, harm the world's biological diversity, enhance the spread of infectious diseases, and cause more heat-related human fatalities, among many other effects. By the onset of the twenty-first century, most scientists believed that increasing atmospheric temperatures had already begun to have such impacts. Glacial melt was one example. During the twentieth century there was increasing evidence that the world's glaciers were retreating, with the rate of decline much quicker at the end of the century than at the beginning. Glaciers in the European Alps, for instance, melted at the rate of 1 percent per year between 1975 and 2000, and at a rate of 2 to 3 percent since 2000. This was a global trend. Scientific tracking of thirty "reference" glaciers scattered around the globe revealed that melting after 1996 was four times as great as between 1976 and 1985.[91]

Concerns about glacial retreat might seem esoteric. Glaciers are far away in both mind and geography. The great majority of the world's ice is locked up at the poles, within the glaciers covering Greenland and Antarctica. Nearly everyone has heard of the risks of sea-level rise from the melting of these polar glaciers, but this particular problem seems to be a concern for the distant future. As for the world's glaciers that are not at the poles, what does it matter if they melt? How important is it to most Americans, for instance, that the glaciers in their soon-to-be-inaccurately-named Glacier National Park (in Montana) are almost gone? Not much, perhaps, outside of some aesthetic lament. Yet in many parts of the world, the spring and summer melt from glaciers is a matter of life and death. A critical illustration of this is provided by the Himalayas and nearby Central Asian mountain ranges, which hold the largest amount of ice outside the polar regions. These ranges are the source of Asia's most important rivers, including the Indus, Yangzi, Mekong, Ganges, Yellow, Brahmaputra, and Irrawaddy, which collectively sustain more than two billion people. Higher temperatures in the Himalayas, in particular at high elevations, has meant increased glacial melt over the past several decades. The fear is that decreased glacier sizes and snowpack will alter both the amount and the seasonal timing of river water, with dramatic and negative effects for downstream communities that depend on these rivers for irrigation agriculture, for drinking water, and for much else. Indeed, the ecosystems that support these two billion people are likely to undergo major changes.[92]

While the melting of glaciers that people have come to depend on has filled some observers with foreboding for the future, millions of people unconcerned with climate change likely have felt its indirect effects. One indirect effect of a warmer atmosphere is the increased capacity of air to hold water vapor. This, paradoxically, has improved the odds of both droughts and downpours. In dry parts of the world, warmer air can hold more moisture and so less falls as rain. In places already given to heavy rain, warmer air allows still greater rainfalls, because there is more moisture to be squeezed out of the clouds. Thus, areas such as the American Southwest have become more subject to drought, while drenching monsoon rains have brought more drastic floods to the Himalayan foothills.[93] Meanwhile, warmer sea surface temperatures have probably spawned more tropical cyclones. Even though one cannot attribute any specific weather event, whether Hurricane Katrina in 2005 or the Pakistan megaflood of 2010, to climate change, over time such events became more likely as a result of warmer temperatures. Trotsky is credited (probably wrongly) with saying, "You may not be interested in war, but war will be interested in you." So it has been with climate change and the world's vulnerable populations, whether in the low-lying

An empty chasm left behind by the retreat of the South Annapurna glacier in the Nepalese Himalayas, 2012. Since the end of the nineteenth century, many glaciers around the world have retreated due to rising average temperatures. Rapid glacier retreat in the Himalayas since 1980 threatens to create water shortages in South, Southeast, and East Asia. (© Ashley Cooper/Corbis)

wards of New Orleans or along the Indus River: they may not be interested in climate change, but climate change will be interested in them.

Climate Change and the History of Science

Given the complexity of the Earth's climate, it should come as no surprise that advanced scientific understanding of climate is very recent. Scientific understanding has required a high degree of interdisciplinary cooperation involving geophysicists, oceanographers, meteorologists, biologists, physicists, geologists, mathematicians, and specialists from a host of other disciplines. As a global phenomenon, climate change has provoked scientific collaboration across international boundaries. The history of climate science thus has been marked by both of these forms of cooperation. Although there is much yet to learn about how the climate changes, the past half century has seen enormous scientific progress. Concern about rising CO_2 levels has motivated a good part of the increased scientific attention to the problem. Technological instruments, such as satellites that became available only after the onset of the Cold War, helped translate that attention into information and understanding. These instruments have been fundamental to gathering and assessing the data needed to map the history of the Earth's climate, to model its workings, and—within sharp limits—to predict its future.

The first attempts to explain why the Earth has a habitable atmosphere occurred during the nineteenth century. The French natural philosopher Jean-Baptiste Joseph Fourier, writing in the 1820s, argued that the atmosphere traps a portion of incoming solar radiation, thereby raising its temperature far above what would otherwise be the case. He likened the atmosphere's influence on temperature to the glass covering a greenhouse, an imperfect analogy that nonetheless stuck. Over the course of the nineteenth century, scientists in other parts of Europe wrestled with basic questions about how the Earth's climate functioned. They were provoked in large part by the Swiss polymath Louis Agassiz, who wrote in 1840 that the Earth had experienced past ice ages. Hence, much of the subsequent scientific work centered on understanding how the climate could change so dramatically over time. Among these curious scientists was John Tyndall, a British physicist who in the 1850s discovered the infrared absorptive capacity of CO_2. Even more important was the work of the Swedish scientist Svante Arrhenius, who published a groundbreaking paper in 1896 that outlined the basic relationship between CO_2 and climate. Arrhenius calculated the global temperature changes that might result if levels of the gas were to increase or decrease. He estimated a temperature increase of 5.7 degrees Celsius if CO_2 levels were to double, but dismissed the possibility that humans could emit so much carbon into the atmosphere.[94]

Arrhenius's paper sparked considerable debate, but its impact was limited by a lack of basic scientific understanding of various Earth systems, poor data, and a conceptual lens that refused to consider that humans had the power to alter the Earth's climate. For instance, Arrhenius could only estimate the concentration of atmospheric CO_2, as no one had yet been able to measure it reliably. But the early decades of the twentieth century nonetheless were marked by scientific progress in other areas relevant to the study of climate. In interwar Europe, the Serbian mathematician Milutin Milanković refined the theory that the Earth's oscillations and solar orbit were responsible for the ice ages. His painstaking calculations resulted in an understanding of the cycles that bear his name. At about the same time in the Soviet Union, the geochemist Vladimir Vernadsky was working on the natural carbon cycle. He argued that living organisms in the biosphere were responsible for the chemical content of the atmosphere, adding much of its nitrogen, oxygen, and CO_2. Hence, plants and other living organisms were foundational to the Earth's climatic history.[95]

The basic understanding of Earth systems developed in the nineteenth and early twentieth centuries, but one big breakthrough in climate science occurred after 1945. As the Cold War spurred increases in public funding of the hard sciences, it was not surprising that American scientists became important figures. In the 1950s a group of scientists at Scripps Institution of Oceanography, near San Diego, funneled small amounts of defense-related funding toward their studies of CO_2 in the atmosphere and oceans. Two of them, Charles Keeling and Roger Revelle, created the first reliable atmospheric carbon dioxide monitoring station. They placed newly developed, sophisticated equipment atop Hawaii's Mauna Loa volcano, chosen because the air circulating about the remote location was not contaminated by emissions from local power plants or factories. The Mauna Loa station gave scientists their first true and reliable measurements of atmospheric CO_2 concentrations. Within a couple of years, the station established that concentrations were indeed rising. The Mauna Loa time series has produced data continuously since 1958; in the process, its sawtooth upward curve has become one of the most widely known visuals of anthropogenic climate change.[96] The sawtooth pattern represents the seasonal changes in CO_2 in the Northern Hemisphere: in the summer months when the leaves are out, more carbon is in trees and bushes and less in the atmosphere. In the winter the atmosphere has a little more CO_2.

The Mauna Loa initiative occurred within the context of the International Geophysical Year (IGY), a collaborative global research effort that highlighted both US and Soviet technical and scientific capabilities. But the IGY also spoke to scientists' desire to develop geophysical monitoring and assessment systems using the powerful new tools that had recently become available to them. Between the 1950s and 1970s, scientists could take advantage of the first satellites to study

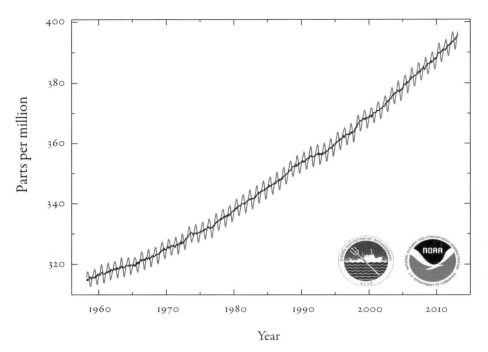

Atmospheric CO_2 at the Mauna Loa Observatory, Hawaii.

the Earth and the first mainframe computers to develop and run crude models of the Earth's climate. Cold War–driven exploration of the polar regions generated the first ice core drilling programs. These enabled scientists to analyze air bubbles buried in the polar ice caps that were hundreds of thousands of years old, thereby discovering information about past climates. The Americans drilled the first ice core in the late 1950s, for purely military reasons, at Camp Century in Greenland; it gave scientists useful data anyway. The Soviets had their own program at Vostok Station in the Antarctic. Starting in the 1970s, their drilling eventually produced cores extending back more than four hundred thousand years, giving scientists access to air pockets over several glacial periods.[97]

Cold War–related research overlapped with increasing scientific effort in other international contexts. The scale of the research problem, the resources needed to tackle it, and a desire to share expertise meant not only increasing scientific cooperation but also greater support from international institutions such as the World Meteorological Organization (WMO) and, later, the United Nations Environment Programme (UNEP). By the 1960s a number of prominent scientists had begun to address the possibility that anthropogenic climate change was possible. Research was sufficiently advanced to place the issue on the agenda of the UN-sponsored 1972 Stockholm environmental conference. Scientific advances continued through the 1970s, prodded by continuing technical and methodological improvements, better data, and more sophisticated research networks. American scientists continued to be leaders in the field, owing in part to support provided by organizations such as the National Academy of Sciences. The 1970s closed with the first international conference dedicated exclusively to climate change, held in Geneva in 1979 and organized by the WMO and UNEP.[98] Climatology, hitherto a domain of specialists trained in the precise sciences, would soon enter the messy arena of politics.

Science Meets Politics

Until the 1980s, discussion of anthropogenic climate change had been confined largely to the scientific community. There had been some political awareness and media coverage during the 1970s, but the issue was too new and abstract to receive much of a hearing. Moreover, the scientific consensus about warming was relatively weak. But the 1980s were a watershed decade, as scientific agreement about anthropogenic warming strengthened and the issue became political for the first time.

Partly this change stemmed from heightened awareness of atmospheric environmental problems. Acid rain became an important political issue regionally, in Europe and eastern North America, from the late 1970s. Political concern about the thinning of the ozone layer suddenly emerged during the 1980s, but, in contrast to acid rain, on a global level. The 1986 discovery of an ozone "hole" over the Antarctic stimulated public interest and gave a major boost to negotiation of the Montreal Protocol in 1987. This agreement, which committed signatories to reduce their emissions of CFCs, brought scientists into global atmospheric politics. Public awareness of the ozone hole was still fresh in 1988, when record-breaking heat and drought in North America helped stimulate public and governmental interest in institutionalizing climate change politics at the global level. That year the WMO and UNEP helped to create the Intergovernmental Panel on Climate Change (IPCC), a scientific body charged with arriving at a consensus position on anthropogenic warming. Since then the IPCC has produced four large assessment reports, in 1990, 1995, 2001, and 2007, with a fifth one due in 2014. All were based on comprehensive reviews of the scientific evidence surrounding climate change. These became increasingly assertive in linking climate change to human activities and in warning of the urgent need for a global political response. The 2007 report used the most explicit language, calling the evidence for global warming "unequivocal" and forecasting "best estimate" increased temperatures by the end of the twenty-first century of 1.8 to 4.0 degrees Celsius, depending on future carbon emissions scenarios. The IPCC leadership had to defend each report, in particular from a small but vocal and well-placed group of climate skeptics who attacked the IPCC's approach, evidence, motives, or legitimacy.[99]

The IPCC's work occurred in parallel to global political negotiations aimed at lowering anthropogenic CO_2 emissions. The process began in earnest in 1988, when the UN General Assembly labeled climate change a "common concern of mankind." In a startlingly short period, diplomats hammered out a Framework Convention on Climate Change, signed at the Rio Earth Summit in 1992. Although its provisions were nonbinding, the treaty put into motion regular diplomatic negotiations aimed at creating a more substantive agreement. Follow-up meetings over the next few years set the stage for negotiation of the Kyoto Protocol in 1997, a binding agreement that mandated small emissions cuts (compared with the baseline year established in the Protocol, 1990) by the world's rich countries.

But trouble was apparent immediately as rifts among the world's largest greenhouse gas emitters threatened to undermine the Kyoto agreement. These divisions have cast a pall over all subsequent diplomacy. The problem began with the two largest polluters, the United States and China. Since Kyoto, both have resisted aggressive and binding agreements on emissions. In the American case, domestic political resistance made it exceptionally difficult for even the most willing administrations to commit the United States to deep emissions cuts, which almost everyone expected would be expensive in the short run. Since 2006 the United States has been the second-largest source of GHG emissions, behind China, and its per capita emissions stand among the world's highest. The

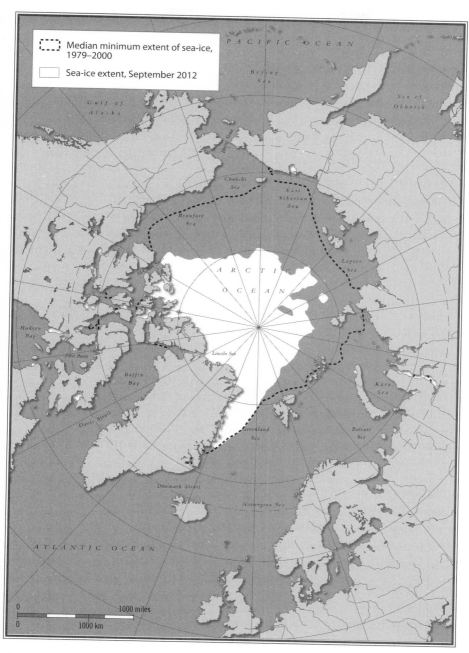

Sea-ice cover at the Arctic Circle, 1979–2012.

American position has emphasized a need for the largest developing countries, in particular China, India, and Brazil, to be included in the mandatory emissions cuts framework. China, on the other hand, has argued that the industrialized countries should make the first, deep cuts. China's intransigence has become increasingly critical, in large part because its economy relies heavily on coal, a dependence that has deepened since 2000. However, the Chinese have pointed to America's per capita emissions rate, which in 2012 was more than twice China's, as the key measure of responsibility and the reason why the United States should have to move first to cut emissions.[100]

Other large developing countries have taken similar positions on the matter. India, for instance, has argued that the world's rich countries have a moral obligation and greater capacity to make emissions cuts. Like China, India has argued that poorer countries have the right to increase emissions for the sake of economic development. Moreover, developing countries have lobbied hard for mechanisms to transfer mitigation technologies and expertise from the rich to the poor world.

On the other side of the equation have been a few rich countries, led most notably by those in the European Union, plus a group of small island states that stand to be swamped by rising sea levels, which together have lobbied for a strong, mandatory emissions reduction regime, starting with the rich world. European countries such as France, the United Kingdom, and Germany now have much lower emissions per capita than the United States, due in part to fuel shifts over the last several decades away from coal toward natural gas and nuclear power.

In the middle have been countries such as Japan, Canada, Russia, and Australia, which have entered into negotiations with varying levels of enthusiasm over time. In 2004, for instance, the Russian parliament ratified the Kyoto Protocol. It did so in part because the country's economy imploded during the 1990s, so Russia's emissions were already far lower than the Protocol required—a fact that might allow Russia to profit from any emissions trading scheme set up under the Protocol. Yet at the same time Russia was a major oil and gas producer, hence Russian leadership's support for international climate agreements has been lukewarm at best. Many Russians, not least President Vladimir Putin, anticipated that a warmer climate might bring them more benefit than harm. (In the summer of 2010, however, Russia experienced a heat wave so severe that it eclipsed all historical comparison.) Other countries also have altered their positions as domestic political and economic conditions have warranted. A 2007 election in Australia, for instance, brought to power an administration that appeared less hostile to climate agreements. Canada, on the other hand, ratified Kyoto in 2002 but failed to meet its targets, in 2006 elected a prime minister hostile to restriction on emissions, and withdrew from the Protocol in 2012.[101]

As the second decade of the twenty-first century wore on, there was a sizable gap between scientists' warnings about climate change and the political will to address it. A number of prominent scientists had grown skeptical that there was sufficient time left to prevent dangerous or even catastrophic anthropogenic warming. For them, the only remaining questions seemed to be how much the global temperature would increase and what effects this would have on the planet's ecosystems. The prospects for a diplomatic breakthrough on a scale corresponding to the scientific prognosis seemed very small. For more than twenty years, climate politics ran into the same roadblocks. First, for politicians focused on staying in power, addressing climate change held little charm: the costs of inaction would in most cases be felt only long after they left the political stage, whereas any reduction in carbon emissions entailed sacrifice that would cost officeholders popular support. Thus, it was one of those political problems that seemed to reward procrastination. Second, climate stabilization was (and is) a public good, meaning that all parties can benefit from it regardless of who sacrifices to achieve it—so negotiators were tempted to "free ride," that is, to encourage others to make sacrifices that would allow all to benefit.

Optimists placed hope in renewable energy sources, which were becoming more competitive in the marketplace with fossil fuels. Others thought that the best alternatives were geo-engineering schemes, wherein arrays of mirrors might be placed in the atmosphere to reflect incoming solar radiation or, less spectacularly, carbon might be sequestered in the soils or underground. Whether any of these alternatives will provide a way out of the climate quandary is perhaps the greatest question of the twenty-first century.

Biological Diversity

Scientific, philosophical, and occasional public concern about certain vanishing species can be traced back centuries, but until recently few people worried that humankind was capable of systematically decreasing the Earth's living heritage. This began to change only in the postwar era, when a small number of scientists started to ponder cumulative human impacts on the world's biomes. These concerns, first articulated sporadically by a few in the 1950s and 1960s, took roughly two additional decades of observation and argumentation to ripen into a critical mass. The terms *biological diversity* and the shorthand *biodiversity* were largely unknown within the scientific community until the 1970s and 1980s. But the scientific and popular use of both exploded during the 1980s, especially after a 1986 conference on the topic organized in Washington, DC, by the eminent biologist E. O. Wilson. The conference proceedings, published as a book under the apt title *Biodiversity*, sounded an alarm. The volume, Wilson wrote, "carries the urgent warning that we are rapidly altering and destroying the environments that have fostered the diversity of life forms for more than a billion years." This message, picked up and broadcast by the world's press, fed on increasing popular and scientific fears about global environmental conditions, from tropical deforestation to ozone depletion. Within a remarkably short time, concern about global extinctions had become a key feature of environmental politics and the word *biodiversity* had become a part of the world's popular lexicon.[102]

Biodiversity had great appeal, but in scientific practice it proved a difficult and blunt instrument. What, exactly, did it mean? What would be measured and how? Did biodiversity mean, for instance, genetic diversity, species diversity, or "population" diversity (meaning geographically distinct populations of animals or plants within a species)? Even if a measure was agreed upon, how did it matter? It would be far better, many scientists claimed, to focus on measuring and maintaining ecosystem functioning and healthy biotic landscapes rather than to obsess over the number of species or quantity of genetic matter. These issues are still hotly debated, but scientists acknowledge that species diversity is a simple, readily understandable measure that has powerful popular resonance. Even if flawed, so the argument goes, species extinction is still the most tangible way to measure global biotic decline.[103]

Attempts to identify and catalog the world's species go back several decades, but despite intense and sustained attempts to do so, biologists can only guess at the total number of extant species. Estimates vary widely, ranging from a few million to one hundred million species or more. Biologists have tended to settle toward the lower end of this spectrum, but they freely admit that their figures are rough estimates. Part of the variation is due to what is included in the count—for instance, whether to include microorganisms such as bacteria—but the problem arises from the simple fact that most species remain unknown to science. Fewer than two million species have been identified and "described" by scientists, and only a small percentage of these have been thoroughly assessed. Of the described species, invertebrates dominate (about 75 percent of all species), followed by plants (18 percent) and vertebrates (less than 4 percent).[104]

There is more agreement about where most life forms are located. Tropical forests in South America, Africa, and Southeast Asia contain the bulk of the world's species. Just 10 percent of the Earth's terrestrial surface is thought to hold between one-half and two-thirds of its species. The broadleaf rainforests have the most. By far the greatest number of described species of mammals, birds, and amphibians are found there. Rainforests are also richest in plant species, although there is wide plant biodiversity in other regions and biomes, such as the Mediterranean basin and South Africa's Cape Province. Stadium-size plots of Ecuador's lowland rainforest, for example, contain more than one thousand species of plants, shrubs, and trees. Ecuador alone (a small country roughly the size of Great Britain) is thought to have 40 percent more plant species than all of Europe. At the low end of the plant biodiversity scale are the world's deserts (although, counterintuitively, a very few deserts are relatively rich in plant biodiversity) and landscapes at very high (northern) latitudes.[105]

Terrestrial species form only a portion of the world's biodiversity. The rest exists in the world's oceans and seas and, to a lesser extent, in its freshwater. Some scientists have estimated that perhaps 15 percent of the world's species live in the oceans, but this is admittedly guesswork. Although freshwater systems represent only a fraction of the world's total surface area and water, they too contain a relatively high number of species, by some estimates as much as 7 percent of all described species. The problems with estimating species numbers and abundance are compounded by the nature of underwater environments: the oceans and seas are vast, and marine environments can be exceptionally difficult to reach and study. As a result, knowledge of marine species diversity and abundance lagged far behind that of terrestrial species through the twentieth century. Only recently has this begun to change.[106]

Oceans and lakes seem to show some similarities with terrestrial ecosystems. For instance, aquatic life is not uniformly distributed across the globe's waters. As with tropical rainforests, some aquatic ecosystems are incredibly rich in species. The continental shelves, coral reef systems, and those parts of the oceans exposed to nutrient-rich currents (such as Newfoundland's Grand Banks) possess enormous species abundance and/or diversity. (One attempt to count all the mollusk species at a single site in tropical waters off New Caledonia, for instance, uncovered 2,738 different species.) Otherwise, much of the ocean is relatively barren, akin to the world's land deserts. Further, as is the case with terrestrial species, a great many aquatic species are not highly mobile. Certain species, in particular the largest pelagics (some species of whales, dolphins, sharks, and fish that are found in deep water), do migrate over very long distances. This is not the case, however, for a great number of others. Many species can exist only in specific habitats and are therefore found in only a few places. Thus, as in terrestrial systems, endemism is an important feature of both freshwater and saltwater ecosystems. Grouper, for example, is a fish that survives in tropical and subtropical waters, with individual species of grouper found only in certain locations.[107]

Concern about species decline has been the primary motive behind attempts to estimate the number of species globally. Over the last three decades in particular, scientific concern increasingly has focused on whether humankind has begun the "sixth extinction," meaning a mass extinction of species that would rival in scale the five known such events in planetary history, the last of which occurred sixty-five million years ago. Scientific worry about mass extinctions emerged coincidentally with heightened concern about tropical deforestation and its effects during the 1970s and 1980s. Biologists began to speculate that human activities were forcing large numbers of species into extinction, far faster than the normal or "background" rate. Again E. O. Wilson was one biologist at the forefront in mainstreaming the idea, calculating in 1986 that extinctions in the world's rainforests were one thousand to ten thousand times greater than normal due to human activities. Many other biologists since have arrived at different estimates of the true extinction rate, with discrepancies once more explained by a combination of unknown species numbers and inexact assessments of human impact. All, however, concede that current rates are many times higher than background. Moreover, they generally agree that increased human interference in the planet's ecosystems was the reason for rapidly increasing extinction rates during the last half of the twentieth century. By 2000, some scientists estimated that perhaps as many as a quarter of a million species had gone extinct during the twentieth century, and feared that ten to twenty times as many might vanish in the twenty-first. Because most species disappeared before they could be described by scientists, the great majority of extinctions in the twentieth century were of creatures unknown to humankind.[108]

Though the idea of listing the world's threatened species had been floated as early as the 1920s, it was not until 1949 that European conservationists produced the first tentative list, which contained fourteen mammals and thirteen birds. That same year these conservationists, including the first UNESCO director, Julian Huxley (brother of the writer Aldous Huxley), created the International Union for the Protection of Nature (IUPN). Headquartered in Switzerland, the organization charged itself with preserving "the entire world biotic community." During the 1950s the IUCN (in 1956 "Conservation" replaced "Protection" in the organization's title) began producing lists of threatened species, and in the 1960s it began publishing them. Now known as the Red List of Threatened Species, these are the most highly respected global assessments, compiled by thousands of scientists. Nonetheless even the prodigious efforts made to produce the Red List could yield insights into the status of only a small fraction of all species. The most recent list, issued in 2012, contained nearly sixty-four thousand species, of which about twenty thousand (32 percent) were categorized as threatened. The list contained a heavy bias toward terrestrial species, with much more known about birds, mammals, amphibians, and some categories of plants than about aquatic species.[109]

Changes in Terrestrial Biodiversity

As with so many areas of environmental change during the last decades of the twentieth century, population growth, economic development, and technological capabilities combined to drive the decline of biodiversity. On land, the leading cause was habitat destruction. During the twentieth century the area devoted to cropland and pastures on Earth more than doubled, with roughly half of that occurring after 1950. This increase occurred at the direct expense of the world's forests and grasslands. This was the greatest threat to terrestrial species, because heterogeneous landscapes containing great plant and animal diversity were replaced by highly simplified ones managed by human beings for their own purposes. Such landscapes could and did continue to support some indigenous species, but a great many other species could not prosper in these modified landscapes. Replacing native habitat with other land uses systematically reduced the spaces for wildlife. Cropland and pastures, for instance, host only a fraction of the birds counted in the world's remaining intact grasslands and forests. Landscapes already long ago biologically simplified by conversion to farm or pasture grew still more simplified after 1945. Farmland almost everywhere was increasingly subjected to mechanization, intensive monocropping, and chemical pest control. After land-use changes, the next biggest threat to biodiversity came from exploitation due to hunting, harvesting, and poaching for subsistence or trade. In addition, invasive species were a major problem for biodiversity. Invasives preyed upon or crowded out indigenous species, created "novel" niche habitats for themselves and other exotic intruders, and altered or disrupted ecosystem dynamics in general. Finally, by the end of the century some scientists reported instances of species beginning to suffer from the adverse consequences of climate change.[110]

Global deforestation was the most important type of land-use change after 1945, especially in the tropics where the bulk of the world's species lived. The clearing of tropical rainforests spurred scientists to put biodiversity on the international agenda during the 1980s. Yet the exact amount of tropical forest lost in the postwar decades remained unknown. Analysts arrived at different figures for tropical deforestation, as they did with species estimates, because they used diverse methodologies and data sets. While deforestation remains a subject of intense debate and disagreement, the consensus is that it has proceeded rapidly. One estimate, for instance, put the total loss of tropical forest at 555 million hectares, an area a bit more than half the size of China, in the half century after 1950.

In contrast, over the same period temperate forests (largely in the Northern Hemisphere) were roughly in balance, losing only a bit more from clearing than they gained in regrowth. This difference represented an abrupt shift in relative fortune. In the eighteenth and nineteenth centuries, deforestation had been much faster in the Northern Hemisphere than in the tropics. This imbalance remained even into the early twentieth century, as North American forests became the world's largest suppliers of wood and forest products. By then, however, a shift from temperate to tropical forests was under way. The specter of wood shortages had induced reforms in the United States and elsewhere, which meant that large tracts of forest acquired protected status and aggressive afforestation measures began. The European empires also had taken advantage of rapidly decreasing transportation costs to increase logging for export in their colonial possessions in tropical Africa and Southeast Asia, for example, and to relieve pressure on their own forests.[111]

By World War II the global deforestation shift from temperate to tropical forests was largely complete. After the war, economic expansion further increased pressure on forests, especially those in tropical regions. Newly independent governments in equatorial regions were happy to supply timber to North America, Europe, and Japan; converting forests into lumber for export was a quick and simple means of gaining much-needed foreign currency. Rapidly growing human population in the tropics was also an important driver of deforestation, leading to greater migration into tropical forests. Governments often encouraged such migration, preferring that landless workers claim new cropland and pastures rather than enacting politically contentious land reforms. Finally, technological changes after the war made it much easier to deforest the tropics. The spread of trucks, roads, and chain saws allowed even the smallest operators to work with greater efficiency. All of these factors worked in combination. By the late 1970s and early 1980s, much scientific concern about the tropics centered on the clearing of the Amazon rainforest. Although Southeast Asian forests also had been cleared at a prodigious rate, the deforestation of the Amazon became the focus of global attention, due to its enormous size, perceived pristine state, and symbolic importance.[112]

Island ecosystems were as severely affected as tropical forests, if in different ways. Islands are home to isolated ecosystems containing many endemic species of plants, mammals, birds, and amphibians. Island species have no place to escape to when humans hunt them, alter their habitat, or introduce invasive species. Island nations therefore routinely appear at the top of the IUCN Red List of Threatened Species for having the highest percentage (but not the highest absolute numbers) of threatened species. Madagascar, for instance, contains thousands of endemic species of plants and animals. After 1896, when the French annexed the island, its forests were systematically logged. Deforestation and habitat alteration continued through independence in 1960, much of which owed to the country's high rate of population growth and consequent pressure to clear more land for farming. The result was that by century's end, more than 80 percent of the island's native vegetation had been removed, placing its endemic species under relentless pressure. Isolation also makes islands highly susceptible to invasive species. Islands have been home to the majority of the world's known bird extinctions, from the great auk to the dodo. On Guam, the brown tree snake, introduced by accident around 1950, found the Micronesian island to its liking and reproduced prolifically. In the following decades, snakes consumed a good portion of the island's endemic bird species and a few of its mammal species to boot. Efforts to eradicate the snake on Guam have failed, and biologists remain concerned that it will be inadvertently exported to other vulnerable Pacific islands. Small and remote islands, of which the Pacific has its full share, were the most vulnerable to biodiversity loss in general and through invasive species in particular.[113]

Changes in Aquatic Biodiversity

The decades after 1945 witnessed dramatic alterations to freshwater and marine ecosystems. After World War II humans accelerated their campaign of taming the world's rivers, to the point where few big ones anywhere were left in their original states. Engineers built tens of thousands of dams, reservoirs, levees, and dikes. The Nile's Aswan High Dam, installed during the 1960s, symbolized the world's infatuation with colossal dams. Engineers dredged streambeds and river bottoms and rerouted entire rivers, changing water flow patterns and temperature levels. Pollutants from cities and industry added chemicals of many different types and toxicities. Agricultural runoff increased the load of organic nutrients in streams and rivers. This led to the eutrophication of downstream water bodies and the creation of oxygen-deprived "dead zones," as in parts of the Gulf of Mexico, the Baltic, and the Yellow Sea. Increased siltation from mining, agriculture, and deforestation also reshaped stream, river, bay, and estuarine habitats. Finally, the world's marshes and wetlands, home to rich collections of unique fish, birds, amphibians, mammals, plants, and insects, shrank dramatically. This occurred nearly everywhere, although rates varied substantially. Marshes and wetlands were converted into other types of uses, filled in to make land for agriculture or cities. River diversions, especially in arid regions where freshwater for irrigation was precious, starved marshes and wetlands of water. Water diversions in some rivers, like South Africa's Orange or America's Colorado, reduced flow to the point of seasonal dryness, endangering species-rich wetlands at the river mouths.[114]

As on islands, invasive species in freshwater ecosystems proved increasingly disruptive after 1945. While invasives were nothing new, the accidental or deliberate introduction of such species became a commonplace thereafter. The Nile Perch, introduced from other parts of Africa into Lake Victoria sometime during the 1950s, was a dramatic example of what could occur when exotics encountered endemic species. By the 1970s this large predator reproduced exuberantly in Lake Victoria. It fed on the lake's endemic fish species, including many of its tiny and beautiful species of cichlid, and put the entirety of the lake's ecosystem in jeopardy. Biologists debate the perch's exact role in changing Lake Victoria, but they are in agreement that the fish was a major contributor to biodiversity decline in Africa's largest lake.[115]

Invasive species may have had their greatest effects on the world's estuaries, which are transition zones between freshwater and saltwater ecosystems. Estuaries are also natural harbors and provide the global economy with many of its ports. During the twentieth century estuaries felt the destructive effects of several combined forces. Changes made to upstream river systems altered sedimentation and temperature levels, among other things. Agricultural runoff changed nutrient balances. Urban and industrial centers added pollutants. Wetland conversion reduced animal habitat in estuaries. With estuaries so disturbed, exotic species, often introduced via ships' bilge tanks, easily colonized these habitats. San Francisco Bay provides a good illustration. By the end of the twentieth century, the bay had been subject to more than a hundred years' worth of urban growth, agricultural runoff, and replumbing of its rivers and wetlands. The ports of Oakland and San Francisco, moreover, were among the most important on the American West Coast, which meant that thousands of oceangoing vessels traversed the bay every year, each one a potential carrier of invasive species. As a result, San Francisco Bay is now home to over two hundred exotic species, including some that have become dominant in their new ecological niches.[116]

After 1945 the human impact on oceanic biodiversity intensified, just as it did in the world's freshwater and estuarine environments. Humans began interfering in the ecology of the deep ocean, which until then had felt little or no human presence of any kind. Commercial fishing was by far the most important activity. Humans had fished the oceans and seas for millennia, but the postwar era saw unprecedented increases in the scale, location, and impact of oceanic fishing. Global demand for fish increased rapidly along with rising wealth and growing world population. Supply increased in large part because postwar technologies allowed fishers to catch ever-larger quantities of fish in ever-deeper waters. Much of this technology had been developed initially for military purposes. Sonar, for instance, had been refined during World War II to track and hunt submarines, but after the war it was also used to locate schools of fish. Over the subsequent decades, improved Cold War–era sonar systems eventually enabled fishers to map the seafloor, giving them the ability to place trawls and nets in the most lucrative locations. When married to other postwar technologies such as shipboard computers, global positioning systems, and monofilament nets, fishing vessels became highly lethal machines. Moreover, states subsidized the construction of oceangoing vessels that were capable of not only catching greater amounts of deepwater fish but also processing and freezing the fish on board. These "factory" ships could stay at sea for long stretches, giving their prey no rest. By the 1980s and 1990s, fleets of massive vessels equipped with these technologies were plying the seven seas, fishing the deep waters of the Indian, Pacific, and Atlantic Oceans and venturing into polar waters as well.[117]

At the outset of the postwar era, almost everyone believed that oceanic fisheries had a near-infinite capacity to replenish themselves. Pushed by the United States in the 1940s and 1950s, fishery managers around the world adopted a model known as maximum sustainable yield (MSY) that reflected this faith in oceanic abundance. MSY elaborated the view that fish were resilient creatures capable of replacing their numbers easily, at least up to a point (the maximum yield), before they declined. By taking older and larger fish, so the argument went, commercial fishing opened up more space for younger fish to find food, grow to maturity faster, and reproduce quicker. Proponents of MSY thus placed the emphasis upon harvesting, essentially mandating that a species show signs of decline before conservation policies were considered. The MSY approach presumed that scientists could estimate fish populations, assign appropriate quotas, and thereby manage fisheries sustainably. This confidence ignored the fact that marine ecosystems were very poorly understood and always in flux, and that fish are impossible to count.[118]

Increased fishing effort substantially increased the global catch after 1945, but it also had major consequences for the oceans. Deepwater fishing, made ever more efficient by the new methods, severely reduced the number of top predators such as bluefin tuna. Pelagic net fishing took huge numbers of unwanted and unlucky species, euphemistically termed the "bycatch," including seabirds, dolphins, turtles, and sharks. Trawling reached increasingly deeper areas of the seafloor, scouring and removing everything. These benthic environments contained rich marine life that was hauled to the surface, the unmarketable portion of which would be thrown overboard. By the 1980s and 1990s, the world's major fisheries were showing signs of stress, with most going into decline and a few into collapse. The fishing industry was able to keep up with demand by using ever more sophisticated technologies to chase ever fewer fish in ever deeper waters and by investing in aquaculture, which by 2000 accounted for 27 percent of the fish, crustaceans, and mollusks eaten worldwide.[119]

The whaling industry did much the same thing. During the late nineteenth and early twentieth centuries, inventive whalers (many of whom were Norwegian) began to use a range of new technologies, including the cannon-fired harpoon, steam-driven chase boats, and huge factory ships that allowed whale carcasses to be quickly hauled aboard for processing. Together these technologies enabled whalers to expand their efforts into remoter waters and to target species that had heretofore been too fast to catch. Norwegian, Soviet, and Japanese whalers (among others) now targeted blue, fin, and minke whales in addition to the species such as sperm and right whales that had been hunted with abandon during the nineteenth century. Driven by the profits from selling whale oil, meat, bone, and other products, hunters took more than a million whales worldwide during the twentieth century. The industry was entirely unregulated until 1946, when a conference of the main whaling nations resulted in the founding of the International Whaling Commission (IWC). Ostensibly dedicated to assessing and managing the world's stock of whales, the IWC proved to be more interested in coordinating the industry's effort than anything else, a team of foxes guarding the henhouse. This only began changing after whaling economics worsened, forcing many nations out of the industry (by 1969, for instance, only

A green sea turtle (*Chelonia mydas*) and several species of butterfly fish swim along the Great Barrier Reef, off Queensland, Australia, 2008. In the late twentieth century, ocean acidification had begun to damage the world's coral reefs, which are home to an enormous diversity of marine life. (Jeff Hunter/Getty Images)

Japan and the Soviet Union continued hunting in the most lucrative waters around Antarctica). Just as critically, after 1970, pressure from environmentalists and the wider public forced the IWC to adopt ever-stricter quotas. Ultimately the IWC agreed to a complete hunting moratorium (passed in 1982, implemented in 1986). But the issue never went away entirely. A very small number of nations with populations having strong tastes for whale meat campaigned to get the IWC to partially lift the moratorium. Japan, Iceland, and Norway continued hunting a few species of whales in small numbers under Article VIII of the IWC's 1946 convention, which allowed hunting for "scientific" research purposes. Japan's actions have been the most aggressive and controversial, taking several hundred minke whales in Antarctic waters annually. The net effect of whaling and its modern regulation was to keep all marketable whales near the edge of extinction without (so far) tipping any over that edge.[120]

Beyond the challenges to life in the deep oceans, human activity menaced shallow-water environments such as coral reefs. Among the planet's most biologically diverse habitats, coral reefs were built over the ages by the accumulation of skeletons of tiny creatures called coral polyps. Relatively untouched in 1900, reefs over the next century came under heavy pressure. They were fished more intensively for food and for the aquarium trade, because many of the fish that lurk around reefs are brightly colored and popular among collectors. In many locales, accelerating erosion sent river-borne sediments onto nearby reefs, suffocating the coral polyps. In the Caribbean and the Red Sea, tourist resort pollution damaged still more reefs, as did the skin-diving tourists themselves who enjoyed them. The gradual acidification of the oceans (a result of pumping extra carbon into the atmosphere) also proved hard on coral reefs. In the early 1980s scientists who studied reefs began to notice general damage patterns, resulting in the first conferences on reef protection. By the 1990s the worries included coral-killing diseases and predators as well as coral "bleaching" (signifying reef stress), especially from higher ocean temperatures. A 1998 global bleaching outbreak was particularly worrisome, destroying an estimated 16 percent of the world's coral reefs, mainly in the Indian and Pacific Oceans. In 2005 a severe coral bleaching killed many reefs in the Caribbean. Worldwide, about 70 percent of coral reefs showed signs of ill effects by 2010. Although reefs sometimes showed remarkable resilience, the weight of evidence showed that climate change and other forces damaged reef habitats and thereby diminished the oceans' biodiversity.[121]

Solutions and Prospects

Given the pressures on the world's species during the twentieth and early twenty-first centuries, it is tempting to adopt a gloomy narrative. Yet the period also witnessed intense activity aimed at conserving species and habitat. Wildlife-themed television programming became popular in North America and Europe from the 1950s. New conservation organizations emerged, such as the World Wildlife Fund, spun off by the IUCN in 1961. Within another decade the mass environmental movement had succeeded in placing species conservation on the popular agenda in some parts of the world. In 1973 the United States passed the landmark Endangered Species Act (ESA). The ESA has been controversial, but it has succeeded in reintroducing some species, such as wolves, to some of their former habitats. Similarly, in 1973 India launched the Project Tiger program, designed to save the country's remaining wild tigers; unlike the ESA, Project Tiger focused its primary effort on setting aside large tracts of land (reserves) as protected tiger habitat. During the 1970s organizations such as Greenpeace spearheaded global campaigns to ban whaling, leading to the global moratorium in 1986.

Diplomatic activity matched these national efforts. Major international agreements and initiatives focused on biodiversity conservation, beginning when UNESCO hosted a 1968 biosphere conference. Others included the 1971 Ramsar Convention on wetlands, the 1973 Convention on International Trade in Endangered Species (CITES), the 1979 Bonn Convention on migratory species, and the Convention on Biological Diversity (CBD), negotiated at the 1992 Rio Earth Summit. Since the 1970s, biodiversity concerns have increasingly garnered political attention, both domestically and internationally.[122]

Nature reserves and national parks were the most common conservation tools. A legacy of the nineteenth century, reserves and parks were created the world over during the twentieth and twenty-first centuries. Game reserves in Africa, for instance, had been established in Great Britain's colonies starting around 1900 in order to protect species favored by aristocratic white hunters. While these sportsmen correctly surmised that hunting had reduced or eliminated some species, they tended to blame African and nouveau-riche and plebian white hunters for undisciplined slaughter of wildlife. Gradually the idea of turning thinly protected reserves into national parks along American lines took hold. Several such parks were created between the 1920s and 1940s, including South Africa's Kruger and Tanganyika's (now Tanzania's) Serengeti. After independence, new African governments supported the parks, and in fact created several new ones, seeing them as sources of national pride and identity as well as of tourist income. In 2002 Gabon created thirteen national parks covering 10 percent of its territory, much of it lush rainforest. Gabon thereby hoped to emulate Costa Rica as an ecotourism destination, but thus far success has proven elusive.[123]

Toward the end of the twentieth century the reserve idea was also applied to the oceans. The concept of marine reserves had been formulated in 1912 and largely forgotten until the 1970s, when biologists began conducting small-scale trials. These showed that marine reserves, areas where nearly all fishing was banned, might regenerate degraded ecosystems. Because there were few signs that commercial fishing could be regulated sufficiently to protect oceanic biodiversity, by the 1980s and 1990s biologists began pushing for large reserves. By the early twenty-first century many such reserves existed. Moreover, a few governments created several reserves of enormous size, including a large chunk of Australia's Great Barrier Reef and immense areas around the Pacific's Marianas and Hawaiian Islands and the Indian Ocean's Chagos Archipelago.[124]

Science informed the campaign to create marine reserves for fish, and it also contributed to debates about preserving whales. New research showed that the world's oceans might have been far richer before modern commercial whaling. This was more than an academic exercise, as it threw a wrench into whaling management. In 2010, for example, a dispute erupted at the International Whaling Commission (IWC) over plans to lift the 1986 whaling moratorium. The longtime whaling nations Japan, Iceland, and Norway backed IWC models showing that whale populations had rebounded enough to resume hunting. Critics, however, pointed to genetics-based evidence suggesting that historical whale populations might have been much higher than the IWC models showed, implying that whale populations were nowhere near robust enough to resume hunting.[125]

Biodiversity conservation has become a global norm in a very short period of time, in reaction to mounting evidence of biodiversity decline. Despite real conservation successes, human activities since 1945 greatly intensified the number and severity of threats facing the world's living organisms. Human beings increasingly order the world. We have selected a handful of preferred plant and animal species, living in managed and simplified landscapes, and have unconsciously selected another handful of species that adapt well to these landscapes (rats, deer, squirrels, pigeons, and such). In so doing we have greatly reduced or eliminated the number of other plants, birds, mammals, insects, and amphibians that lived in and on these landscapes just a short time ago. In this regard the ethical question is much the same as ever: Are we content with a world containing billions of humans, cows, chickens, and pigs but only a few thousand tigers, rhinoceroses, polar bears—or none at all?[126]

The twenty-first century portends still greater pressure on biodiversity than did the twentieth. Rising affluence, at least for some, plus three to five billion additional people, will menace the world's forests, wetlands, oceans, seas, rivers, and grasslands. But climate change likely will set the twenty-first century apart. Scientists fear that even modest temperature rises will have serious negative effects on all types of ecosystems. Some have estimated that a 2-degree Celsius increase might send one-fifth to one-third of the world's species into extinction. Such studies, it should be noted, often optimistically assume that species will have perfect "dispersal capabilities," meaning the ability to retreat to adjacent cooler environments. But perfect dispersal is usually no longer possible. There are now so many human-dominated landscapes—farms, roads, fences, cities, dams, reservoirs, and so on—that many species attempting to flee warming climate will have no migratory option whatsoever. Protectors of biodiversity in the twenty-first century have their work cut out for them.[127]

3. Cities and the Economy

WE LIVE on an urban planet. In 2008 demographers at the United Nations announced that more than 50 percent of humans were living in cities. This symbolized a profound change in human history. Never before had a majority of the world's population lived in urban areas. The world today has five hundred cities with populations of at least a million people, seventy-four with at least five million, and twelve with at least twenty million. The largest city in the world, Tokyo, has over thirty-four million people if one includes attached areas.[128] The full effects of so many cities and of so many people living in cities are as yet unknown. What is known is that cities have always depended upon and shaped their natural surroundings.

Cities concentrate people to levels far higher than the immediate environment can support. As they cannot exist in isolation from their surroundings, cities require access to natural resources and to waste sinks beyond their borders. Natural resource inputs consist of materials and energy. Materials range from food, clean water, ores, and basic construction materials (stone, wood) to an enormous range of manufactured goods. Energy resources are contained in some of the raw materials shipped into the city, in water that may flow through a city and that is captured by a mill or turbine, or electricity that is transmitted by wire from outside the city's borders. Before the onset of the Industrial Revolution, energy from raw materials entering the city took the form of wood and coal and of food for human or animal consumption. After the Industrial Revolution, cities required far greater amounts of energy, initially for factories and later for the technical innovations that have since become synonymous with urban living (electric lighting, trolleys and subways, automobiles, and such). Fossil fuels have provided the bulk of this energy. During the nineteenth century, coal became the dominant energy source used in the rapidly industrializing cities of Europe and North America. Petroleum became an increasingly important energy source for cities only much later, during the first half of the twentieth century in a few cities, then globally after World War II. During the twentieth century, cities also began to draw electricity from nuclear and hydroelectric plants.

The urban consumption of materials and energy produces waste. While mills process ores into desirable metals (iron and steel, for instance), they also produce slag, slurry, and wastewater. Urban residents (human and animal) benefit from the food that is brought into a city, but they also produce excreta, which has created major health problems for cities throughout history. Cities use energy for productive purposes, and its utilization generates pollutants and toxins. All of this waste has to go somewhere. Some waste is deposited inside a city's boundaries, in which case city residents have to tolerate it as a nuisance. In the case of some waterborne pollutants and airborne toxins, residents are forced to suffer potentially deadly consequences.

But for the bulk of urban wastes, cities require sinks outside their borders. Many cities sit along rivers and use them as waste dumps. Where cities are located along coastlines, the oceans and seas often are afforded the same treatment (until the 1930s, for instance, much of New York's garbage was dumped at sea). Waste can also find its way into the soils surrounding the city. Finally, burning fuels produces waste that we call air pollution. Indoor air pollution, still a major problem in poorer cities, arises from burning fuels such as wood, coal, kerosene, and dung in domestic stoves and fireplaces. Local air pollutants include toxic gases produced in metallurgic operations, smoke and soot from coal (an enormous problem through much of the nineteenth and twentieth centuries), and ground-level ozone from automobile exhaust. Urban air pollutants can be a regional problem as well, due to the wind. Acid rain and the deposition of toxins onto soil far away are two examples of pollution on a regional scale. By the second half of the twentieth century, cities had also become significant sources of global air pollution, contributing heavy amounts of chlorofluorocarbons and greenhouse gases to the atmosphere.[129]

The relationship between cities and their surroundings is not a simple process. Cities are dynamic entities, "ever-mutating systems" in the words of one environmental historian, that grow and contract depending on myriad factors. Their human and animal populations as well as their economic and political bases are in constant flux. This extends to their claim on extraterritorial sources and sinks, which can also shrink and expand as conditions change. In such a fluid context, cities have struggled for millennia to secure and maintain access to critical resources. Medieval Nuremberg, for example, imposed municipal control over nearby forests and systematically pushed out rivals in order to preserve the city's fuel supply.[130]

Cities transform nature. They interfere with natural water cycles. Pavements keep water from percolating into the Earth, resulting in more water running off into rivers and sewers. Drawing water from wells depletes aquifers. Canalization of rivers changes streamflows. Most importantly, cities dump masses of pollution into nearby waterways. Streams, rivers, and coastal waters close to cities therefore suffer from many types of degradation, such as decreased biological diversity and eutrophication. Cities' impact upon air quality is simpler than that upon water quality: they pollute it and to a small degree warm it up as well. Cities alter land use and soil characteristics, too. Farmland required to feed growing cities replaces forests and grasslands with simplified, managed, and less diverse ecosystems. Mines dug to satisfy urban demand for metals and fossil fuels often damage surrounding landscapes with pollution and tailings. Urban growth also creates "edges" that have dramatic effects on wildlife habitat and numbers.[131]

The relationship between cities and nature is more nuanced than this roster of direct effects suggests. Cities, of course, have been centers of ingenuity, creativity, and wealth since their origins more than five thousand years ago. If well designed, they can require fewer resources per capita than rural areas. Higher population densities in cities can translate into the more efficient production and distribution of goods and delivery of social services. Densely packed populations require less fuel to keep warm (or to keep cool). Moreover, cities help lower fertility rates. Although the decision to have children is always a complex one involving many factors and there is substantial variation across time and place, women who live in cities tend to have fewer children than their country cousins. Urban couples have better access to birth control, and urban women have greater economic, educational, and social opportunities compared with women in rural areas. By and large, children in urban settings can perform less useful labor for their families and require larger and longer expenditure to raise (and educate). So urban populations choose to have fewer of them.[132]

The Rise of Cities

Cities were unusual prior to the onset of the Industrial Revolution. Few of the world's inhabitants lived in them. Before 1800 only a very small number of cities had ever approached a million inhabitants. Ancient Rome might have come close for a century or two at the zenith of its empire. The same might have been true for a very small number of cities thereafter: Baghdad during the ninth century CE, Beijing from the sixteenth, and Istanbul from the seventeenth, for example. Few, if any, had been able to sustain these populations for very long. Even as late as the eighteenth century, only a handful exceeded a half million residents. About the only cities that could reach large size before the modern period were imperial centers, whose trajectories waxed and waned with political fortunes, and mercantile centers that depended on overseas trading networks.[133]

There were some basic reasons why there were few large cities, and few cities at all, for that matter, before the modern period. Cities depend on an agricultural surplus to survive. For much of human history, low agricultural productivity required that most people engage in growing and harvesting food, hence most lived on the land. Limited transportation technology compounded this constraint, making it costly to ship goods such as food over long distances. Cities located along navigable rivers or coastlines had a distinct advantage, in that ships, boats, and barges were the easiest and cheapest means of transport. This was especially true for bulky goods. Timber, for example, could be floated downriver to cities at low cost but was very expensive to move short distances overland or upriver. Cities required the agricultural surplus of areas far greater than their own to survive. And they needed the fuel, typically in the form of wood and charcoal, of an even larger space. They were like big carnivores in any ecosystem: they drew their sustenance from over a large space and therefore could only be few in number.[134]

Cities were also unhealthy places. Generally cities suffered from unsanitary conditions and crowding. The result typically was higher mortality in cities than in rural areas. Early death was routine, in particular for infants and toddlers from childhood diseases and, for the general population, from epidemics that ravaged cities with frightening frequency. For centuries cities had little recourse to countermeasures other than quarantine. Owing to their connections with the outside world, trading cities were often struck first and hardest by epidemics.

During the early nineteenth century, cholera spread from the Indian subcontinent to port cities across Europe and North Africa. Bubonic plague also struck ports and cities generally more severely than villages. It is important to note that not all cities were alike in their lethality. Japanese cities in the seventeenth and eighteenth centuries, for instance, may have been substantially healthier than their European or Chinese counterparts. Their systems for water supply and sewerage were more advanced, and their cultural practices were more hygienic. Japanese cities suffered from fewer epidemics as a result.[135]

After 1800, however, cities broke through the many constraints on their growth. The world's richest countries urbanized rapidly in the nineteenth century. The first megacities appeared during this period. London led the way, growing from fewer than a million people at the start of the century to more than five million at its end. New York's growth was even more impressive, from a small city in 1800 to the second largest in the world a century later; by 1930 it was the first metropolitan area in world history to have ten million residents. Its pace so impressed H. G. Wells that he expected New York would be home to forty million people by the year 2000.[136] London owed much of its growth to its role as political center of the world's leading imperial power. It benefited greatly from Britain's centrality in a rapidly growing global economy, allowing it to acquire goods from all over.[137] As Europeans built their empires, they also created new cities in their colonies. The British, for example, founded the East Asian trading cities of Singapore and Hong Kong and most of the major Australian settlement cities during the first half of the nineteenth century. As with so many aspects of colonization, locals played little part in siting cities. Nairobi sits where it does because the British found the location suitable for a refueling depot on their railway between Uganda and Mombasa.[138]

But the Industrial Revolution, rather than imperialism, drove most nineteenth-century urbanization. Agricultural modernization in Great Britain during the seventeenth and eighteenth centuries had increased food production. This meant that more people could eat, but it also created surplus labor in rural areas. Landless and jobless people fled to the cities, where by 1820 the Industrial Revolution was in full swing. Places such as Manchester became major cities almost overnight, driven by a combination of rural-to-urban migration and factory output powered by cheap British coal. Similar processes occurred a bit later in mainland

Europe, in particular where coal was found in abundance. Politics spurred industrialization in still other places. While Japan was already one of the most urbanized countries in the world, the 1868 Meiji restoration initiated a period of heavy industrialization encouraged by the state. Huge numbers of people were drawn into the cities during the decades that followed. In 1868 about 10 percent of Japan's population lived in cities; by 1940 this percentage had nearly quadrupled. Japan in 1940 had forty-five cities with populations over one hundred thousand, and four of these (Tokyo, Kyoto, Nagoya, and Osaka) had more than a million.[139]

The Industrial Revolution also brought significant changes in transportation. The steamship allowed faster and cheaper oceanic transport, which bolstered global trade among cities. The steamship also enabled mass transoceanic migrations in the second half of the nineteenth century, which contributed greatly to urban growth in the United States, Canada, Argentina, Brazil, South Africa, and Australia. Perhaps even more important was the railroad, which like the steamship went from being a curiosity at the beginning of the nineteenth century to having become a dominant means of transport at the end. By dramatically reducing overland shipping costs, the railroad allowed cities to extend their geographic reach well beyond the constraints imposed by the horse, foot, and wagon. Chicago's unparalleled growth after 1850, for instance, owed much to the fact that it became the hub of a railroad network extending far to its north and west. (Wells in 1902 also thought that Chicago, like New York City, would one day top forty million inhabitants.)[140] The railroad enabled the city to develop long-distance trade in the grain, livestock, and timber of North America's vast heartland. Chicago parlayed this geographic reach into enormous power, dominating a region that extended for hundreds of miles around. Chicago thus played an important role in organizing and transforming the forests and grasslands of this region into the highly productive, thoroughly commodified, and ecologically simplified landscapes of the American Midwest.[141]

Industrialization had a number of other important consequences for cities. It increased urban wealth but it also in the short run aggravated the problems of pollution, filth, disease, squalor, and crowding. The scale and rapidity of growth itself caused massive problems. The industrial working class, newly arrived from rural areas, most often had no choice but to live packed together in dank and dingy housing. New York's infamous tenements and Berlin's equally notorious *Miets-*

kasernen (literally, "rental barracks") were among the worst examples, but substandard housing accompanied industrialization nearly everywhere. Housing problems were overlaid upon a backdrop of intense pollution and poor sanitation. Working-class housing stood in the shadow of factories, which spewed coal smoke into the air and dumped toxic sludge into streams and rivers. Tanneries, slaughterhouses, and meatpacking houses operated in the very center of cities, adding all manner of chemical and organic pollutants to urban water supplies. Waste disposal became an even more nightmarish problem. Few cities had municipal services for collecting and disposing of solid wastes, which left streets littered with myriad wastes, including horse manure and dead animals. Rudimentary systems for collecting and disposing of human waste soon became overwhelmed by the scale of urbanization that came with industrialization.[142]

Public authorities struggled to address these problems resulting from swift urban growth. Sanitation became an important public goal in Europe and North America from the middle of the nineteenth century. Reformers such as Britain's Edwin Chadwick, who strove to establish an empirical relationship between cleanliness and disease, drove the process. During the 1850s Chadwick's influence led London and other British cities to build and improve sewage systems. French planners did the same. Baron von Haussmann's famous reconstruction of Paris in the 1850s and 1860s included a thorough rebuilding and upgrading of the city's water supply and sewer systems. Public sanitation measures received another boost from the bacteriological discoveries of the 1880s, which substantiated the germ theory of disease. Bacteriology overturned the prevailing understanding of disease origins and transmission, and gave scientific legitimacy to sanitation efforts, in particular attempts to clean and purify water. After 1880, American cities made major investments in public water supply and sewer systems.[143] The modern discipline of city planning also emerged in the late nineteenth and early twentieth centuries, as planners searched for ways to improve the industrial city. America's Frederick Law Olmsted, Britain's Ebenezer Howard, Scotland's Patrick Geddes, Austria's Camillo Sitte, and Germany's Reinhard Baumeister were a few of the iconic figures in the early history of city planning and related disciplines.

In the first decades of the twentieth century, automobiles started to reshape urban spaces in North America, while big cities began to proliferate on every continent. The United States and Canada built a booming automobile industry. Oil became an increasingly important energy source after enormous quantities were discovered in Texas in 1901, while Ford's Model T (introduced in 1908) greatly reduced the cost of the private automobile. Mass motorization, and with it the emergence of the automobile suburb, began in the United States during the interwar decades. Meanwhile, urbanization was accelerating in other parts of the world. Larger cities began to emerge in Africa, Latin America, and Asia, driven by processes not unlike those already experienced in Europe and North America. Cairo, for example, began to grow faster than Egypt as a whole during and after World War I. Migration to Cairo picked up, due mostly to economic depression in rural areas, at the same time as improved sanitation caused urban mortality rates to fall. By 1937 the city had 1.3 million people, more than three times its size of a half century before. Thanks in part to immigration from Europe, Buenos Aires mushroomed from under 200,000 people in 1870 to 1.5 million in 1910 and 3 million by 1950. Mexico City experienced similar growth at about the same time. Migration from rural areas to most Mexican cities sped up during the revolutionary period (1910–1920), driven by political conflict, changes in the rural economy, and industrialization. By 1940 the greater Mexico City area was more than twice its size of 1910.[144]

Cities since 1945

The period after World War II witnessed a crescendo of urbanization. The share of the world's population living in cities jumped dramatically, from 29 percent in 1950 (730 million people) to its current half (a bit more than three billion people). This was one of the signal characteristics of the Anthropocene: the majority of humankind now lived within environments of its own creation. Our species had become, in effect, an urban animal. Cities grew faster than rural areas in every part of the world. In 1950 there had been only two cities with populations greater than ten million; by the end of the century there were twenty such megacities.[145] Urbanization thus occurred everywhere, but the pace, nature, and consequences were different depending on location.

The most spectacular theater of urbanization in the postwar era was in the developing world. The share of people living in cities in the developing world

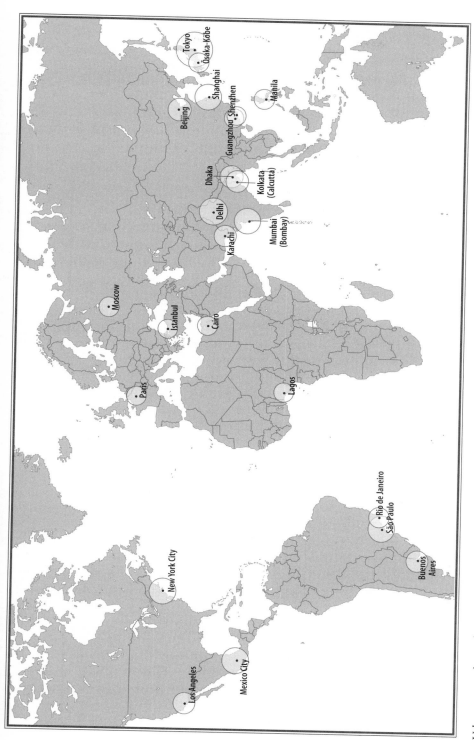

Urban areas with populations of more than 10 million people, 2011.

more than doubled between 1950 and 2003, from 18 percent to 42 percent of the population. This represented an absolute increase of nearly two billion people (from 310 million to 2.2 billion). From 1950 to 1975, the urban population in the world's poorer countries grew at an average annual rate of 3.9 percent. This was a rate nearly double that of cities in the rich world and more than double that of rural areas in the developing world. For the period 1975–2000, this disparity was even more pronounced. Even though the annual growth rate for poor cities declined to 3.6 percent, it was still about four times that of rich cities (0.9 percent) and more than three times that of poor rural areas (1.1 percent).[146]

Migration from rural areas fueled urban expansion in the developing world after 1945. Agricultural modernization drove many peasant farmers off the land. They had nowhere else to go but cities. The possibility of finding employment was one attraction, although opportunities were often few and sometimes only in the informal sector. Another attraction was access to social services such as schools and hospitals, however limited in the cities of the developing world. Familial ties and other social networks in cities smoothed the path for many rural migrants.[147]

Economic, political, and military developments had an influence on the process of urbanization as well. Burgeoning economies in some regions drew in urban populations. Villages in the oil-rich Persian Gulf, for instance, mushroomed into cities almost overnight, especially after the 1973–1974 oil price hikes brought enormous revenues into the region. Showcase cities such as Dubai and Abu Dhabi emerged, characterized by immense wealth and in-migration from nearby rural areas and from abroad, especially South Asia. National politics influenced urbanization processes, as in China both before and after the 1949 Revolution. The state's policies sometimes drew people into the cities, as was the case in the 1950s when Chinese ambitions focused on industrialization, and at other times deliberately slowed urbanization, as occurred during the Cultural Revolution. Wars (both international and civil), independence struggles, and guerrilla insurgencies also played a role. These made rural areas less secure, helping to spur migration to cities in some places. Karachi, for example, received several hundred thousand Muslim refugees fleeing sectarian violence in the wake of Indian independence in 1947.[148]

As was true of the Industrial Revolution in the nineteenth century, these processes led to rapid urban growth on a scale that overwhelmed local governments. Dhaka in Bangladesh, to give only one example, grew from a small city of four hundred thousand people in 1950 to over thirteen million in 2007. Poor migrants to Dhaka and other such cities found insufficient housing, and what did exist was often unaffordable for them. A great many thus were forced to squat on any marginal land they could find—on abandoned lots, alongside roads or railroad tracks, next to swamps or city dumps, or on steep hillsides. Developing cities all over the poor world teemed with squatter settlements, which commonly housed a third or more of all urban residents. The absolute numbers of people living in such settlements reached astonishing proportions: over nine million in Mexico City and three million in São Paulo around 1990, for instance. In Mumbai, over half the population was housed in these settlements, and anywhere from three hundred thousand to a million people lived on the streets. Many cities exhibited extreme spatial segregation, as the relatively few rich sought to insulate themselves from the many poor. In Karachi the wealthy began segregating themselves with renewed determination after squatters settled in large numbers in the 1960s and 1970s.[149]

In these settlement conditions, health and environmental problems deepened. Again these issues were similar to those in nineteenth-century Europe and North America. Substandard housing combined with inadequate public infrastructure meant wretched living conditions for large numbers of people in developing cities. Many squatter settlements had little or no access to clean drinking water, proper sanitation, or refuse services. Public infrastructure systematically favored wealthier residents. In Accra during the 1980s, for example, poor households had much worse service provision than richer ones. A majority of poor households had to share toilets with many other households, a condition the rich did not have to tolerate. There were predictable health effects of these types of arrangements. While the overall disease burden in the world's poor cities was slowly shifting from communicable to chronic diseases by the end of the century, communicable diseases maintained their grip on the poorest residents and were major causes of mortality. Infectious and parasitic diseases continued to strike poor children particularly hard. Every squatter settlement suffered these grim circumstances, but each had its own particular character.[150]

Over time, conditions in many settlements improved. Jerry-built housing gradually evolved into permanent neighborhoods. Residents converted flimsy structures made out of cardboard or plastic into more durable ones made out of metal, wood, and concrete. Local and national governments managed over time to extend public services—including electricity, sewers, piped water, paved roads, and schools—to many settlements. Where politics involved elections, politicians quickly figured out that many votes could be won by providing these basic services to squatter settlements. A prime minister of Turkey, Recep Tayyip Erdoğan, made his political reputation by delivering water, electricity, and sewerage to urban neighborhoods while mayor of Istanbul (1994–1998). Where these improvements took hold, older settlements had fewer problems than newer ones.[151]

All neighborhoods, old and new, in the burgeoning cities of the developing world suffered from air pollution. Because coal remained a cheap fuel, rapidly growing countries turned to it for industry and electric power generation. In the last decades of the twentieth century, Asian megacities in particular became notorious for severe air pollution from burning coal. Beijing and Shanghai suffered very high soot and sulfur dioxide concentrations, due in large part to coal combustion. Xi'an and Wuhan were worse still. Unfortunate geography compounded air pollution problems for yet other cities. Mexico City developed some of the worst air pollution in the world partly because it was ringed by mountains and sat at high altitude. Similar geography plagued Bogotá. Coal-based pollution dogged thousands of cities.[152]

Cities in the developing world suffered from the environmental consequences of both extreme poverty and concentrated wealth. Often these existed cheek by jowl, as in Jakarta. Once the sleepy capital of the Dutch East Indies, Jakarta (then known as Batavia) became a boomtown after Indonesian independence in 1949. Two aspects of growth characterized its recent history. On the one hand, as Jakarta was Indonesia's capital, the country's leadership saw it as an economic engine and the site for large show projects. The government invested heavily in Jakarta's infrastructure and encouraged rapid industrial and commercial development. Over time Jakarta came to possess all the trappings of the most modern and global of cities—many industries, an extensive highway system, and a glittering downtown of office towers and luxury hotels. On the other hand, Jakarta's growth attracted millions of new and poor migrants from the countryside. Many of these were obliged to live in *kampungs* (squatter settlements or "villages"). Together, these elements shaped Jakarta's environmental history after

1949. The city's poor suffered from the unsanitary conditions found in squatter settlements everywhere. Although the government made some progress in up-grading conditions in them (especially under Jakarta's governor Ali Sadikin during the 1970s), its policies also worked at cross-purposes, as when it cleared some *kampungs* to make room for commercial development and real estate speculation—driving squatters into the now more crowded remaining *kampungs*. Meanwhile new industries poured pollutants into the city's waterways while cement factories coated parts of it in a fine dust. Increasing wealth, plus the government's heavy investment in highways, led to increasing motor vehicle use, which became the chief cause of Jakarta's thick air pollution. All these factors led to significant health problems for Jakarta's residents.[153]

As in Jakarta, in cities of the richer parts of the world, increasing prosperity fueled urban environmental problems after 1945. Urban growth continued in absolute terms. Between 1950 and 2003, the number of city dwellers in the rich world grew from 430 million to 900 million.[154] But population growth arguably was less important in environmental terms than was the transition to the consumer society.

Reformers in industrializing countries had made sporadic efforts at air pollution control during the nineteenth century, but for several reasons their efforts bore fruit only after World War II. Widespread public pressure for reform intensified during the 1950s on both sides of the Atlantic, driven by increased impatience with coal smoke and mounting concern about the health effects of pollution. Several high-profile air pollution disasters that took human life, one in Donora, Pennsylvania, in 1948 and the far worse one in London in 1952, also helped to shape public opinion. At about the same time, some coal cities launched the first significant regulatory reforms. Just before and during the war, St. Louis and Pittsburgh began regulating coal smoke through civic ordinances that mandated smokeless fuels or smoke-reducing equipment. These reforms had immediate effects, which in turn helped to animate the first stirrings of reform elsewhere. West German bureaucrats, for example, watched with much interest, as did a good many in the West German press. During the 1950s that country began taking pollution control more seriously, as in the heavily industrialized Ruhr.[155]

In rich cities, fuel switching from coal to oil changed the nature of air pollution. Over the postwar era, air pollution in rich-world cities shifted from sulfur

Jakarta, May 1963. The surge of migration from villages to cities in the second half of the twentieth century caused explosive growth in the world's shantytowns. Jakarta had about six hundred thousand people in 1945 and about three million when this photo was taken. Today, greater Jakarta is home to twenty-five to thirty million people. (Time & Life Pictures/Getty Images)

dioxide and suspended particulate matter (smoke and soot) to nitrogen oxide, ground-level ozone, and carbon monoxide. These shifts occurred mostly during and after the 1960s and 1970s. Deindustrialization and the movement of industry from city centers to peripheries combined with fuel switching to propel these air pollution changes. By the 1970s as well, national air pollution legislation had become the norm in the world's wealthiest countries, adding to the local-scale regulatory reforms begun a few decades before.[156]

As pollution from coal smoke started decreasing, that from auto exhaust grew, accounting for an increasing share of rich cities' air quality problems. Photochemical smog was first identified in Los Angeles during World War II. Within a decade the city's smog had become famous and Los Angeles had become synonymous with the problem. As the automobile became much more common everywhere, so too did smog. In London, New York, and Tokyo, air pollution generated by cars increased even as other air pollution problems began to abate. Especially after regulatory interventions in the early 1970s, automobile exhausts became much cleaner in many places, hence air pollution levels in many cities fell. But the growing absolute numbers of vehicles on the roads also meant that photochemical smog remained a significant air pollution problem. By the last decades of the twentieth century, pollution from automobiles had become a serious problem in developing-world cities too, as in Jakarta, Beijing, and São Paulo. Even some of the world's poorest cities, such as Addis Ababa, suffered from automotive smog.[157]

Pollution from auto exhaust increased during the postwar era for two primary reasons. Motorization—meaning the share of the population owning an automobile—was the first of these. Before the nineteenth century, people traveled within cities on foot or by horse. During the early nineteenth century, omnibuses (horse-drawn trolleys) began appearing in Europe, then by the end of the century the electric tram. The first automobiles appeared at about the same time, but owing to their high price and impracticality they remained an extravagance for the rich. While several countries began investing in high-speed automobile highways during the interwar period (such as the Italian autostrada and the German autobahn), auto ownership remained low everywhere except the United States and Canada. After World War II, America's wealth, increasing suburbanization, and massive public highway investment entrenched this pattern. North

Americans owned far more cars than anyone else, both per capita and in absolute terms, and American automakers dominated the global market. For consumers elsewhere in the world, the American car culture became an object of fascination; for engineers, American transportation planning was an object for emulation. The car became a mass consumer item in Western Europe, Japan, and Australia in the 1950s to the 1970s, later than in the United States and Canada. By 1990 Americans still led the world in car ownership, but other rich nations were not far behind.[158]

Suburbanization was the second reason automotive pollution rose in rich cities after World War II. Though suburbs had existed long before 1945, mass motorization was the primary reason they multiplied so after the war. Again there were significant differences across national contexts. The United States set the precedent in terms of scale and cultural weight. The large, freestanding house with a yard and one or two cars became the iconic and global symbol of suburbia. In 1950 around two-thirds of the American urban population lived in central cities, with a third in suburbs. Forty years later these figures had switched. Over the same time period American cities more than doubled in physical size. Predictably, given the amount of available land, North American, Canadian, and Australian cities also grew outward faster and at lower densities than cities elsewhere. European suburbs were more than three times as dense as North American and Australian suburbs. Japanese cities decentralized as well, but their densities remained far higher than those in other wealthy countries. Japan's mountainous terrain meant that cities had to be concentrated onto narrow stretches of coastal land. Despite this constraint, Japan's private automobile fleet still increased dramatically; Tokyo's alone leaped by 2.5 million from 1960 to 1990.[159]

Together, suburbanization and auto ownership had important consequences. Increased driving was the first and most predictable. Driving was most common in North America, owing to the extent of suburbanization, low average suburban densities, plus other factors such as the low price of gasoline relative to other industrialized countries. In 1990, on average, Americans traveled more than twice as far per year in private cars as Europeans, and significantly farther than Australians. Conversely, Americans walked, bicycled, and used public transit far less often than other peoples, especially compared to urban Europeans. Nor was this all. American (and Canadian) cars were also consistently larger than those elsewhere throughout the twentieth century. Their larger size and weight made them less fuel-efficient. American motorists thus consumed more fuel and produced far more carbon dioxide than their counterparts anywhere else.[160]

Increasing wealth had a number of other consequences in the world's rich cities. While rapid outward growth consumed only a small percentage of available land in sparsely populated rich countries (Canada, Australia, and the United States), it still transformed millions of hectares of rural land into cityscapes. In places that were already crowded, such growth carried with it heavier consequences for a country's rural heritage. These places tended to have tougher land-use controls and allowed planners more say in how land was allocated, as in Great Britain after 1945. Urban wealth also increased the demand for energy and water, as people acquired the creature comforts that were developed during the postwar era. Only a very small part of the huge American appetite for residential water was for drinking and cooking. Water for lawns, cars, household appliances, showers, and flush toilets accounted for almost all of the rest in cities. The automatic dishwasher alone could increase household water use by up to 38 gallons (144 liters) a day. Finally, the consumer economies of the postwar world also generated tremendous amounts of garbage. Again the United States generated the most in per capita and absolute terms. Wealth was a major factor in increasing the amount of garbage, as were new materials (especially plastics) that became more important in the consumer economy. Cities therefore produced rising tides of garbage, forcing local governments to search endlessly for disposal solutions.[161]

In Search of the Green City

From the 1970s onward, more and more people increasingly sought to revisit the basic ecological arrangement of cities. They wondered whether modern cities must continue to be the grasping, all-consuming metropolises characteristic of the twentieth century, or whether they can be transformed in some way to reduce or eliminate the environmental damage they cause. The urban claim on global resources had increased many times over since the onset of the Industrial Revolution. Cities now acquired enormous amounts of resources from every part of the globe: Brazilian soybeans, American corn, Saudi Arabian oil, Bangladeshi cotton, Australian coal, Malaysian hardwoods, South African gold. Cities had also globalized their waste streams, becoming the source of most anthropogenic carbon emissions.[162]

In the early 1990s the ecologist William Rees, working at the University of British Columbia, and his Swiss student Mathis Wackernagel formulated the "ecological footprint" idea to give conceptual and quantitative expression to the global reach of cities. Every city, Rees argued in an early (1992) and groundbreaking paper on the concept, "coopts on a continuous basis several hectares of productive ecosystem for each inhabitant." Rees estimated that every resident of his own city, Vancouver, required 1.9 hectares of productive agricultural land for food. Rees calculated that the city consumed enough resources (including food, fuel, and forest products) and emitted enough wastes to "occupy" a land area about the size of South Carolina or Scotland. He thus demonstrated that Vancouver, by most standards one of the greenest cities on Earth, had an enormous ecological footprint.[163]

Despite challenges on theoretical and practical grounds to the ecological footprint concept, nonetheless it conveyed a fundamental idea—and anxiety— about cities that was becoming more common. Ecologists and planners such as Rees and Wackernagel had begun to ask whether there was enough nature to go around in a world increasingly dominated by cities. Rising concerns about climate change, ozone layer depletion, and other global environmental issues prompted much of this anxiety. So too did the rash of international environmental conferences that occurred at about this time, most especially the Earth Summit in Rio de Janeiro of June 1992. Similar concerns inspired some urban planners to call for refocusing their profession around environmental themes and some architects to develop green building standards.[164]

A fair number of cities, especially in central and northern Europe, had been experimenting with wide-ranging green policies since the 1970s. They built efficient cogeneration plants (these recycled waste heat from electrical generation) and encouraged alternative energy. They funneled new urban growth to designated areas adjacent to existing cities. They tried to increase, rather than reduce, densities in new developments. They created programs for recycling, community gardening, green roofs, and ecosystem restoration.[165]

Many of these initiatives became common practice in Europe, as in Freiburg (in southwestern Germany). Now recognized as one of the world's environmental leaders, Freiburg began emphasizing solar energy production in the 1990s as central to the city's long-term economic development. The city government installed solar panels on public buildings, made land available to solar firms at low cost, introduced solar power as a theme in public school curricula, and established cooperative programs with local research institutions. The city integrated solar power into new residential development, including high-profile green showcases such as the Vauban district on the city's outskirts. Freiburg's identity now reflects its great success in establishing itself as a solar city. The city markets itself as Germany's greenest city, where solar energy makes good business as well as environmental sense.[166]

After 1970 a number of European cities also broke with postwar planning trends centered on the automobile. For political or cultural reasons these cities decided to encourage other means of transportation in order to preserve their historic centers and avoid the worst consequences of auto-centric development, especially air pollution and sprawl. During the 1970s and 1980s, for instance, Zurich's leaders decided to expand and improve the city's tram system, which significantly increased ridership while slowing growth in auto use. Because the trams enlivened the streetscape, the effort also helped to revitalize the city center. Other European cities arrived at similar ends using different tactics, as was the case in some Dutch, Danish, and German cities with the bicycle. Popular support for bicycling in cities like Amsterdam and Copenhagen spurred their city governments to invest in cycling infrastructure, contributing to widespread usage of the world's most energy-efficient transportation machine.[167]

Environmental innovation was not limited to wealthy cities, as the case of the southern Brazilian city of Curitiba shows.[168] From the early 1970s, when it began implementing some innovative planning ideas, the local government created a city that won praise worldwide for its environmental credentials and high standard of living. Curitiba's government tried innovative approaches to just about every problem, preferring to focus on practical, low-cost projects over the expensive showpieces that characterized most other developing cities. For instance, the government took an unusual approach to tackling chronic flooding in Curitiba. Instead of building levees alongside the rivers running through the city, it constructed small dams to create lakes. The areas surrounding the lakes were then turned into large urban parks. This approach had two effects. The lakes absorbed the summer rainfall, reducing flooding in the city, and the amount of public green space increased dramatically.

While Curitiba could boast many other programs just as innovative and as important in burnishing the city's international reputation, its most famous success story was its bus transit system. Curitiba's decision to prioritize public transit in the 1960s flew in the face of the dominant planning trends of the period. City planners all over the world, including Brazil, were designing or redesigning cities around the automobile. Curitiba's planners rejected this model, believing it favored the wealthy motorist over the majority of the city's inhabitants. In addition, they thought the model would create traffic congestion and destroy the vibrancy of the city's historic center. They opted instead to revamp the city's bus network, beginning in the early 1970s. Five main axes running into the city center were identified as express transit routes, upon which only buses were allowed; cars were shunted off to side streets. An efficient system of color-coded feeder routes completed the network. Simple but ingenious design improvements were added. One of these innovations, the elegant glass-and-steel "tube stations" that enabled buses to be loaded much more quickly, became iconic symbols of the city's success. Curitiba's planners complemented these efforts through land-use regulations (allowing housing densities to be higher along the bus routes) and building infrastructure in the city center for pedestrians and bicyclists. These measures quickly generated results. By the early 1990s Curitiba's residents owned more cars per capita than the Brazilian average but the bus system carried a large share of the city's traffic, well over a million passengers a day. The city's residents also used less fuel and created less air pollution than would otherwise have been the case.

In Havana, inadvertent measures rather than deliberate planning provided an example of the greening of a developing city.[169] Like other countries, socialist Cuba had built its agricultural economy on mechanization (tractors and trucks), chemicals (artificial fertilizers and pesticides), and specialization in cash crops for export. By the 1980s Cuba imported a large share of its food while producing and exporting sugar. The country relied on Soviet oil and markets, both of which disappeared immediately after the USSR vanished. A sudden and dramatic decline in imports of all kinds, including oil, agricultural equipment, and fertilizers and pesticides, meant that Cuba could no longer produce enough sugar to afford imported goods. This was an even more serious problem given the continuing American trade embargo. Put simply, the country faced starvation, as it was not self-sufficient in food production.

With little choice, starting in the 1990s Cuba embarked on a massive experiment in organic agriculture. Farms shifted from tractors to oxen and from artificial fertilizers and pesticides to organic ones. Both generated unexpected positive developments. Oxen, for instance, did not compact the soil the way tractors had, and organic pesticides were far less toxic than chemical ones. With little oil for long-distance transportation, Cubans had to produce food closer to where it was eaten. Facing hunger, Havana's two million residents took matters into their own hands and began planting gardens on every square meter of land they could find. Over the decade, habaneros created thousands of such rooftop, patio, and backyard gardens. Neighborhood cooperatives emerged to acquire and garden larger parcels of land, such as baseball diamonds and abandoned lots. Recognizing a good thing, the state made tools, land, seeds, and technical advice available to Havana's residents, and allowed the formation of street markets. By 2000 these efforts had paid off. Havana and other Cuban cities produced a large share of the food they needed to survive.

Havana's experiment is astonishing for the rapidity and scale of its agricultural transformation, but "urban agriculture," as it has come to be known, is widespread globally. In the last decades of the twentieth century, as poor cities expanded, the scale of urban agriculture grew rapidly. Often unable to afford food provided through commercial systems, the urban poor turned to informal production and food networks. During the 1990s the United Nations estimated that some 800 million people worldwide depended on informal urban agriculture for sustenance or income, supplying a sizable share of all food consumed in poorer cities. At century's end, urban agriculture provided Accra with 90 percent of its fresh vegetables, Kampala with 70 percent of its poultry, and Hanoi with about half of its meat.[170]

Cities such as Freiburg and Curitiba are cases of real progress. They show again that cities are not uniform and can be places of enormous ingenuity and problem-solving creativity. Yet even these examples are not beyond criticism. Skeptics question whether any city can be made ecologically benign. The urbanization process has not stopped. Most cities will continue to grow in absolute terms well into the twenty-first century. In addition, increasing wealth around the world will mean that cities will continue to demand a wide range of luxury goods that they cannot possibly create within their own boundaries. The world's supply of automobiles, for example, is predicted to increase several times over, driven by rising prosperity in countries such as India and China. Improved technologies and approaches to design have bettered environmental conditions in many cities (not just in the greenest examples cited here), but the question is whether these efforts will be enough to alter the trajectory that cities have followed for centuries. As centers of population, consumption, and industrial production, they have long had an impact on environmental change far out of proportion to their size. As centers of creativity and innovation, they have lately also had a disproportionate role in checking human environmental impacts.[171]

Ecology and the Global Economy

In terms of ecological consequences, the most important feature of the second half of the twentieth century was the performance of the global economy. After World War II the global economy rebounded from the severe problems of the interwar period and embarked on a long period of unprecedented growth. In the half century after 1950, the global economy grew sixfold. Annual economic growth averaged 3.9 percent per year, far outstripping the estimated historical averages for the industrial age up to that point (1820–1950) of 1.6 percent per year and for the "early modern," post-Columbian world (1500–1820) of 0.3 percent per year. Growth peaked between 1950 and 1973, a period that has been labeled the "golden age," a "*Wirtschaftswunder*" (economic miracle), "*les trentes glorieuses*" (the thirty glorious years), or "the long boom," depending on the nationality of the observer. For several reasons, including increased oil prices and higher inflation, world economic growth slowed but did not stop after 1973. The economic growth of the postwar era led to a resurgence of global trade, communications, and travel, increased international migration, and technological advances. The era was marked, at different points in time, by the integration or reintegration of large parts of the formerly colonized and socialist worlds into the advanced capitalist economy. Large swaths of Asia became much wealthier over the half century, to the point where levels of prosperity and occasionally political influence began to rival those of the historic economic leaders (mainly Western Europe, the United States, Australia, Canada, and Japan). After the revolutions of 1989–1991 in Central and Eastern Europe, former Soviet Bloc states also began this reintegration process, with varying levels of success. However, the era was also characterized by increasing gaps between the wealthiest parts of the world and those regions that remained poor.[172]

Several factors combined to sustain the postwar era's rapid economic growth. On a political level, the onset of the Cold War quickly reorganized much of the world into two major blocs. Each of these was ruled by a superpower that had an enormous incentive to stimulate economic recovery and growth, albeit using very different methods. By the late 1940s the Cold War and global reorganization were fully under way. American leadership provided the basis for the larger and what would prove to be more dynamic of the two systems, the capitalist order. During World War II the Western Allies (led by the United States and Great Britain) had laid the groundwork for this system. Fearing a return of the Great Depression, the Allies created a series of institutions designed to encourage cooperation in finance, trade, and politics and to discourage autarkic solutions. These institutions included the United Nations and those that grew out of the Bretton Woods Conference in 1944—the International Monetary Fund and the International Bank for Reconstruction and Development, later the World Bank. They were designed to help finance the reconstruction of national economies ravaged by the war. Within a few years negotiations also produced the General Agreement on Tariffs and Trade (GATT), designed to reduce tariffs, quotas, and other trade restrictions.

The political and economic position of the United States made all this possible. America had emerged from the war with an intact economic base and undamaged cities, in contrast to Japan, China, the Soviet Union, and Europe. It had suffered only a fraction of the human losses endured by all of its potential rivals. As after World War I, it had emerged from the second global war as a creditor rather than a debtor nation. Perhaps most importantly in an economic sense, American industrial power was unmatched. The American economy had overtaken Great Britain's decades before and had since extended its advantage. The country's vast resources and large population contributed to this lead, as did the vigor and innovativeness of its industry. Its firms had perfected the assembly line technique, for example, starting in the early twentieth century, while the relatively high wages these firms offered allowed the world's first mass consumer society to emerge, even before the American entry into the war in 1941. In the immediate postwar world, when the United States alone accounted for more than one-third of the global economy, its financial strength allowed the United States to underwrite a massive worldwide reconstruction program that had the dual aims of stabilizing the global economy and containing communism. America's huge financial resources meant that it could funnel billions of dollars in aid to reconstruct both Europe (via the Marshall Plan) and Japan, thereby stabilizing both and contributing to their rapid economic takeoff during the 1950s, while simultaneously building political and military alliances around the world. On top of all this, the strength of the dollar stabilized the global financial system, at least until the early 1970s.[173]

The story was a bit different in the socialist world after 1945. The Soviet Union suffered the most of all major combatant nations during World War II, having lost upward of twenty million people. With Russia and the Soviet Union having been on the receiving end of three invasions from the west in a bit more than a century, Stalin was in no mood to withdraw the Red Army from Eastern Europe at war's end. The Soviet Union, like the Western Allies, therefore set out to mold its sphere of influence. Among other things, the Soviets attempted to forge an economic bloc in Eastern Europe through the creation of the Council for Mutual Economic Assistance (COMECON), established in 1949. COMECON sought to coordinate economic development among member countries, but unlike the relatively free trading regime eventually established in the West, the organization scarcely furthered economic integration. Rather, it served to facilitate bilateral trade between the Soviet Union and its Eastern European clients.[174]

During the interwar period, the Soviets' crash program in state-led, centrally planned gigantism—the hurried, even frenetic, construction of huge metallurgical complexes, dams, mines, new industrial cities, enormous collectivized farms, and the like—had enabled the country to transform itself quickly from a low level of industrialization to a relatively high level, sufficient to defeat Nazi Germany when war came. This development model therefore had been a success, if one defines success narrowly in a productivist sense and ignores the violence to human beings and the natural world that state-driven industrialization on such a vast scale and in such a compressed time frame seemed to require.

After World War II the Soviets continued to follow the same model. They rebuilt those parts of their industrial base that had been ravaged during the war, a cause helped by their ability to extract reparations from their former enemy (in the form of heavy machinery and equipment that was hurriedly stripped from occupied Germany and shipped eastward). Moreover, they continued to focus on increasing the country's heavy industrial output, concentrated in large state enterprises, as opposed to developing a more flexible, consumer-driven economy like the West's. This was in part a result of ideological preferences, which fetishized heavy industrial output (such as iron and steel production), and in part a result of the Cold War, which required massive and continued investment in armaments. But part of the explanation also rested on the success and prestige of the Soviet model, which had led to industrialization and defeat of the Nazi war machine. Although from a much smaller total base, the Soviet Bloc economy grew nearly as fast as the West's during its golden age. Annual per capita GDP growth averaged 3.5 percent in the East versus 3.7 percent in the West (including Japan). From 1928 to 1970 or so the USSR was an economic tiger—war, terror, purges, and state planners notwithstanding. As there appeared to be little reason to alter their system, during these decades Soviet leaders continued to emphasize heavy industrial development via top-down, bureaucratic, and highly centralized planning.[175]

Global economic growth everywhere also depended on a critical physical factor, energy. Over the twentieth century, energy use and economic expansion proceeded in lockstep, meaning that economic growth required expanding energy inputs. During global economic booms such as the periods before World War I and after World War II, global energy use also increased at high rates. During periods of slower economic growth or contraction, as during the interwar decades, energy use likewise increased much more slowly. During the decades after 1945, the enormous scale of the global economy required energy inputs far in excess of all previous periods.[176]

There were large regional variations in the production and use of energy. The leading producers benefited most of all from good geological fortune. In the nineteenth century, its huge coal reserves helped to make Great Britain the world's largest fossil fuel producer. From the 1890s, however, the vast coal, oil, and natural gas reserves of the United States enabled it to surpass Great Britain, a position it has never relinquished. After World War II, the Soviet Union also overtook Great Britain and held on to second place behind the United States until the USSR disappeared in 1991. At century's end, China, Canada, and Saudi Arabia joined the United States and post-Soviet Russia as the largest energy producers.

Energy consumption was another story, bearing scant relation to geology. Generally speaking, more wealth required more energy for comfortable levels of consumption, while at the same time more energy deployed productively led to more wealth. In 1950 the rich industrialized world consumed the vast majority (93 percent) of the commercially produced energy on Earth. This percentage fell over time as industrial production, accompanying wealth, and population increased in other regions of the world. By 2005 the proportion was down to a bit more than 60 percent. Nonetheless, throughout the postwar period absolute levels of energy consumption were always highest in the world's richest countries. Canada and the United States stood atop the list in annual per capita energy use for most of the period after 1945, joined lately by some small states of the Persian Gulf. Energy consumption did not always depend on possession of fossil fuels. Japan, for instance, has almost nothing in the way of coal or oil, yet it remains toward the top end of the global scale in energy consumption. At the opposite end were the world's poor countries, with energy consumption rates a tiny fraction of those of the world's richest countries.[177]

The contrast between Canadian and Japanese energy use points to another important issue: efficiency. At the end of the twentieth century, Japan required about a third of the energy needed to produce a dollar's worth of GDP, compared with Canada. European economies were almost as efficient as Japan. At the other extreme were rapidly industrializing countries, including China and India, whose economies were five to six times less efficient than Japan and two to three times less efficient than Canada and the United States. Such figures underscore two distinctions. First, the energy efficiency of national economies has tended to follow a historical pattern. The typical economy's energy use per GDP (energy intensity) rose quickly as it entered a period of rapid and heavy industrialization. This spike in energy intensity would normally be followed by a long and gradual decline as the economy began to use energy more efficiently. This was the historical experience of Great Britain, which peaked in the 1850s, Canada (peaked around 1910), and the United States (peaked around 1920). Not all economies have functioned in this fashion, however. Japan's economy maintained stable but comparatively low energy intensity throughout much of the twentieth century. Second, significant efficiency variations *within* the rich world showed that it was possible to become wealthy using energy at much lower levels than did Canada and the United States. There were many factors that explained why national economies in the rich world diverged, ranging from industrial mix to regional climate to suburbanization patterns. Comparative data showed that core quality-of-life indicators (including infant mortality, life expectancy, and food availability) did not improve substantially beyond annual energy consumption levels of roughly one-third to one-quarter those of the United States and Canada.[178]

As we have seen, the postwar era also saw the highest rates of sustained population increase in world history. Rising populations help explain global economic growth, almost by definition: more people usually meant more economic activity. But otherwise the relationship was not straightforward. In some places at some times, population growth occurred within countries that were experiencing strong economic growth. But in other times and places, population growth rates were so high as to cause problems, wiping out any per capita economic gains. If any generalization can be made about the relationship, it is that rapid industrialization and modernization and their effects, including urbanization and wealth accumulation, tended to reduce fertility rates, and thus population growth rates, over the long run. In 1945 this process had been ongoing in the rich world for a century or more. In the postwar era it continued, resulting in societies with slow population growth or none at all. This occurred despite longer life expectancy. Australian life expectancy increased from 69.6 years in 1950 to 76 years in 1987. Sweden's increased by six years, Italy's by ten, Japan's by almost twenty. Rich world economies thus had to face the economic complications associated with aging populations, including higher social security payments and fewer young workers to support the elderly. Declining population growth rates also marked the trajectories of those poorer societies that were undergoing rapid economic change. Large pools of cheap labor initially were of great assistance to economies in East Asia (South Korea and Taiwan, for instance), but over time their economic success led to lower population growth rates as well.[179] Thus, population growth both underwrote economic expansion after 1945, as it had done before, but when fast enough also imperiled per capita gains. When it slowed after 1975, issues of intergenerational equity (mainly unsustainable pension commitments) loomed ominously, at least in the rich world.

Technology, Economy, and Nature

Improved technology also enabled the rapid economic growth in the postwar period. Periods of intense technical innovation had marked the Industrial Revolution since its origins. Scientific research and its technical application to the postwar world, driven by both public and private investment, acted as an important spur to the global economy. Some postwar innovations, such as satellites and the Internet, were completely new; others simply improved upon earlier designs. The humble shipping container is a perfect example. Before World War II, oceangoing freighters were loaded with odd-size cargo that required legions of stevedores and considerable time to load and unload. After the war, however, shippers began improving the container, a device that had been invented but not used widely before the war. The container's great advantage was that it allowed odd-shaped cargo to be packed beforehand into a standardized box, which could then be loaded and unloaded by crane operators at much greater speed, without longshoremen. This dramatically increased shipping efficiency, hence greatly lowered costs. After 1965 the container became the standard means of shipping manufactured cargo, and probably did more to promote international trade than all free trade agreements put together. Eventually the container was married to railroad and trucking systems and to information technologies that allowed the millions of individual containers to be tracked in real time. By 2000 there were some 6.7 million containers in operation worldwide. The reduction in shipping times achieved through containerization proved especially critical to the rise of export-oriented economies in East Asia that were literally oceans away from their markets.[180]

Postwar technological innovation also created new types of environmental difficulties. Scientific and technological advances during the nineteenth century had produced a range of synthetic chemicals, compounds, and substances. But during the twentieth century in general, and the postwar period in particular, the use of artificial substances greatly proliferated. Laboratories churned out countless new chemicals, ranging from household cleaners to industrial lubricants to agricultural pesticides, herbicides, and fungicides. Because there was little awareness of the possible health and environmental consequences of so many new substances, a great number of these were originally used without any precautionary testing or regulation. This began to change only during the 1960s and 1970s, with the emergence of the mass environmental movement.[181]

The production and use of plastics provided a good example. Polymers (molecular compounds consisting of linked chains of simpler molecules) based on natural materials such as cellulose had been invented in the late nineteenth century. Synthetic polymers were created shortly after 1900. Then during the interwar period they were manufactured and marketed on larger scales. During the 1950s and 1960s, rapid advances in the laboratory enabled large chemical firms such as DuPont in the United States and Imperial Chemical Industries (ICI) in the United Kingdom to create a slew of improved synthetic polymers, enabling their rapid proliferation. Before 1960 the manufacture and use of plastics during these decades appeared to cause little, if any, anxiety about environmental consequences. As was typical of the period, this form of technical achievement was embraced without much reservation. A 1959 article in *The Science News-Letter* (an American publication), for example, gushed about polymer research. Polymers, the author wrote, would provide "lighter, stronger components for missiles and space vehicles and automobile bodies that are more rugged pound for pound than those in current use." In deference to the prevailing faith in (male) expertise to overcome any difficulty, the author argued that any problems could be solved by "technical men" who were "confident that important progress" was being made. The link between the technical mastery of plastics and social progress was considered a given; environmental considerations remained minimal. Global plastics production exploded at midcentury. World production rose from less than 50,000 tons in 1930 to 2 million tons in 1950 and 6 million tons a decade later. New types of plastics flooded the marketplace. Plastics substituted for materials such as glass, wood, and paper in existing goods or became the key substance in a huge array of new consumer goods.[182]

Production in such quantities invariably meant that plastics began to show up in the world's ecosystems. By the early 1970s the previously sunny narrative about plastics darkened as the mass environmental movement began to alter the way in which people thought about introducing artificial substances into the environment. Observers started filing disconcerting reports about plastics dumping, in particular in the world's waterways and seas. In 1971 the Norwegian adventurer Thor Heyerdahl caused a stir when he published a book containing the claim that the Atlantic Ocean resembled a vast garbage dump. The subjects of the book were the 1969–1970 transatlantic voyages of Heyerdahl's papyrus rafts *Ra* and *Ra II*, voyages that were similar in design and purpose to the 1947 *Kon-Tiki* expedition in the Pacific that had made the author famous. The transatlantic voyages had shown him that the ocean had become laced with oil and all manner of refuse, notably plastics. The Atlantic of the late 1960s, Heyerdahl said, was infinitely dirtier than the Pacific he had sailed in the late 1940s. "I had seen nothing like this when I spent 101 days with my nose at water level on board the *Kon-Tiki*," he wrote. "It became clear to all of us [on board the *Ra*] that mankind really was in the process of polluting his most vital wellspring, our planet's indispensable filtration plant, the ocean." A couple of years later, a large-scale study of the Caribbean Sea and western Atlantic Ocean, undertaken by scientists at America's National Oceanic and Atmospheric Administration (NOAA), confirmed the accuracy of Heyerdahl's claims.[183]

Yet the newfound concern for protection of the environment from plastics did not reduce the use of plastics in the following decades. The range of applications and general utility of plastics outweighed environmental concerns, so that by 2000 the world produced some 150 to 250 million tons of plastics annually (estimates vary), some 75 to 125 times as much by weight as in 1950 and perhaps 3,000 to 5,000 times as much as in 1930.[184] Despite some environmental regulation in some places, plastics continued to accumulate in the world's oceans and seas, not to mention its landfills (globally, in the early twenty-first century plastic constituted about a tenth of all garbage).

Early in the twenty-first century, scientists and sailors reported a new and frightening variant of the plastics saga, consisting of gigantic floating trash middens that plagued the world's oceans. One of these concentrations, a massive plastic soup slowly twirling in the Pacific Ocean between Hawaii and Califor-

A pile of trash removed from the North Pacific Gyre, October 2009. Ingenious chemistry in the twentieth century led to ever more durable plastics, but many plastic items end up in the world's oceans, bobbing in the waves for decades. (UIG via Getty Images)

nia, contained a good share of the last sixty years' worth of plastic production, much of it apparently from Japan. (No one knew its exact size, but by 2010 some estimates put it at twice the size of Texas.) The bulk of the gyre consisted of tiny fragments of plastic, sodden petrochemical confetti. But there were also rubber dinghies and kayaks, condemned to endless drift voyages, like the *Flying Dutchman* of yore. The South Pacific, Indian Ocean, and North and South Atlantic had their own, smaller patches of floating plastic. Although scientists do not know how ocean plastics affect ocean biology, it is well attested that seabirds and marine mammals get tangled up in plastic and often eat it. All recently examined seabirds of the North Sea contain plastic, as do a third of those in the Canadian Arctic. Tiny bits of plastic work their way through the food web of the oceans, collecting in the top predators such as killer whales and tuna fish. Happily, most plastics are not toxic, and only a few are dangerously so. Some birds have learned to use plastic pieces in making nests. It is early days yet in the history of plastics, but chemists expect the contents of the marine middens to last centuries or millennia, so the oceans' flora and fauna will for a long time be subject to a new selection pressure—compatibility with plastic.[185]

The history of plastics indicates that technologically driven economic change had enormous environmental consequences. But the relationship between technology, economy, and environment often was more complex than the plastics example showed. New technologies occasionally could be less destructive of the environment compared with what preceded them. On the other hand, such technological innovations might not have net environmental benefits if economic growth swallowed the gains. The history of electronic appliances such as refrigerators provides an apt illustration of this contradiction.

Modern refrigerator technology dates to the early twentieth century, in particular the 1920s, after a cheap and apparently harmless category of refrigerants, CFCs, was discovered in the laboratory. This discovery was the key that allowed refrigerator prices to fall rapidly in the United States, where the appliance was in half of all homes even before World War II. Postwar mass consumerism in the rich world drove sales of the appliance strongly upward for decades. After it had become clear in the 1970s and 1980s that CFCs were thinning the Earth's ozone layer, an insight that led to the signing of the 1987 Montreal Protocol, the world's largest refrigerator manufacturers embarked on campaigns to "green" their appliances and to market them as such. During the 1990s they phased out CFCs as other refrigerants came onto the market and began designing and building appliances that contained less material, used energy more efficiently, contained fewer toxic chemicals, and were more recyclable. In addition, firms worked with regulatory agencies and nonprofit organizations to create environmental standards and performance benchmarks. All of this activity had a real effect: the typical refrigerator made in 2002 consumed nearly 80 percent less energy than a unit produced in 1980. Meanwhile, global refrigerator sales expanded throughout the period. Households in the developing world, especially East Asia, bought their first refrigerator, while some households in the rich world acquired their second or third units. The environmental benefits of the improved refrigerators, in fact, became a key part of the marketing strategies of the major manufacturers and contributed to higher global sales. Eventually even a fivefold reduction in energy use per refrigerator was offset by the growing number of refrigerators in use, boosting total energy consumption. In China refrigerators account for 15 percent of total electricity demand. Household appliances are now enormous consumers of electricity on a global level.[186]

Regional Economic Shifts

In 1945 the great majority of the world's population lived outside of the consumer-driven, high-energy, and materials-intensive global economy that now characterizes much of the globe. The story of the succeeding six decades was one of the incorporation of ever-larger parts of the world into this economy. Only North America had emerged from the war in a condition that allowed a quick return to a peacetime consumer economy. The war itself had almost leveled the economies of both Western Europe and Japan, both of which had been at a much lower level of consumer development than the United States and Canada before the war. But these economies also transitioned quickly to mass consumerism, beginning with the onset of the "golden age" in the 1950s. Other world regions started their integration into this economy at still later dates. Perhaps the most important were Southern, Southeastern, and East Asian countries, beginning with the "tigers" Taiwan, South Korea, Singapore, and Hong Kong. These small economies utilized low labor costs and other advantages to service the richer parts of the world in an export-led strategy. Their success induced other states in the region to follow their example. China was the biggest and most significant of these later participants. It began a transition in the late 1970s from a statist, centralized, autarkic economy to one that incorporated some key capitalist features, a choice that by the 1990s began to produce some spectacular results. The socialist economies of Eastern Europe and the Soviet Union would have to wait until the revolutions of 1989–1991 to begin their transitions to a consumer society. Latin America and Africa also increasingly integrated into global circuits of trade and investment, but with mixed results that permitted only a narrow expansion of consumerism.

After some difficult initial years following the war, the economies of Western Europe began to grow quickly. Under the American security umbrella, European elites could focus on the linked processes of refashioning their economies around consumer-driven growth and on increasing the political and economic integration of the continent. They were successful on both fronts. The major European economies of the Western alliance—West Germany, France, Italy, and Great Britain—grew quickly after 1950, owing to a combination of government activism in guiding and stimulating the economy, high savings and investment rates, skilled workforces, and full access to the enormously wealthy American market. Economic activity was also enhanced by the spread of cheap energy, in particular oil, which gave European economies the basis for their postwar transition to high-consumption societies. After 1973, Western European economies ran into considerable difficulty thanks in large part to higher oil prices. But over several decades, from the 1950s to the 1990s, Europe's politicians and Brussels's bureaucrats managed to bind the continent's economies tightly together in the European Union, helping to underpin continued economic growth into the twenty-first century.[187]

Japan followed a similar growth trajectory. Flat on its back in 1945, Japan's economy under the American occupation soon rebounded to prewar production levels. By the early 1950s rapid growth was well under way, spurred by American military contracts as a result of the Korean War. Over the next two decades the country grew faster than any other in the world, averaging eight percent per year. Japan's success owed much to its well-educated workforce, high levels of savings and investment, and close cooperation between the government and big business on economic policy and technological development—for instance, through the powerful Ministry of Trade and Industry (MITI). Growth in Japan slowed after 1973, as it did nearly everywhere else, but it remained higher than in Europe or the United States into the 1990s. Mass consumerism reflected a rising Japanese standard of living. Within a few decades after the war, the typical Japanese household went from possessing almost no large durable goods to owning most of those goods that characterized the high-consumption economy. For instance, in 1957 only 3 percent of Japanese households owned an electric refrigerator. By 1980 nearly all of them did. In 1957, 20 percent of households owned an electric washing machine and just 7.8 percent a television set. In 1980, nearly all Japanese households had both these items. Automobile ownership also skyrocketed: from 22 percent in 1970 to 57 percent just a decade later. Japan by 1980 had joined the mass-consumption club.[188]

The European and Japanese economic revivals demonstrated the pull of American consumer culture. Europeans had alternatively feared or embraced the "Americanization" of their continent in the interwar period, but during the postwar era American cultural and economic power on the continent attained unprecedented levels. The broad-based prosperity enjoyed by Europeans enabled many more people to consume products and services that were exported by the United States. Even more critically, large numbers of Europeans had the desire and the means to approximate the high-energy, materials-intensive American lifestyle, embodied in the automobile, household appliances, the freestanding house in the suburbs, and everyday consumer products. Nor was this experience confined to Western Europe.

The Japanese also had their version of Americanization, having been directly exposed to American culture through the postwar occupation. As Japanese workers earned higher wages during the miracle decades, they eagerly snapped up the fashion, food, entertainment, and clothing that were regarded as quintessentially American. Advertisers discovered this taste for American products and tailored their messages and products to fit demand. Like Italians or Britons, the Japanese found new methods of consumption that mirrored American practice. By the late 1950s, for example, supermarkets had found their way into Japanese cities, as did 24-hour convenience marts and fast-food restaurants about two decades later. Americanization, it should be noted, is a construct that historians have debated for decades. Scholars now consider the historical production, transmission, and reception of American culture abroad to be highly complex, nonlinear, and constantly evolving. Nonetheless, it is reasonable to argue that it was a key factor in stimulating consumer desires around the globe.[189]

However, mass consumerism had little to do with the socialist economies of the USSR and, after 1949, the People's Republic of China. Mao Zedong had developed a worldview that in some respects mirrored that of Soviet leaders in the interwar years. He had a commitment to rapid industrial development, driven by a fear of Western encirclement and by a desire to catch up with and eventually overtake the Soviet Union itself. Mao believed that the Chinese Communist Party, through the force of superior organizational skill and a willingness to engage in mass mobilization, could force China to develop from a nation of poor peasants to an industrial power almost overnight. It was true that China did industrialize after 1949, a process that by the time of Mao's death in 1976 had both enlarged the country's economy and nearly doubled its per capita GDP (albeit from a low initial level).[190] Yet, as did the Soviet Union, China paid a heavy price for this in human and environmental terms, as we shall see.

Around 1960 the Soviet Union's economy appeared to be in better shape than China's. But by the 1970s it began to show signs of major structural problems. The constant emphasis on heavy industry and military spending worked to the detriment of the consumer economy, empowering central planners, the military, and large state producers rather than individual consumers. The Soviet economy thus was capable of churning out huge quantities of materials, including some categories of consumer items, but these rarely matched consumer preferences. The system provided factory managers with few incentives to use materials and energy sparingly and laborers with little reason to work hard. Moreover, despite having outstanding scientists, the Soviet economy seemed unable to keep up with Western technological improvements, at least in areas such as computerization that were beginning to reshape the global economy. In agriculture, collectivized farms proved grossly inefficient. The small plots that peasants were allowed to cultivate for themselves were far more efficient, because peasants could sell produce from them on the market. Large agricultural projects, such as Khrushchev's "Virgin Lands" scheme (1956–1963), wasted untold amounts of valuable resources, including soil and freshwater. On top of all this the Soviet Union faced serious social problems that hampered the economy, such as chronic alcoholism.[191]

In the 1970s, despite these problems, the Soviet leadership proved unwilling to engage in any serious reforms. Part of the reason stemmed from what appeared to be the system's success. The Soviet economy had been propped up by the discovery of enormous oil and natural gas deposits in the 1960s. This generated huge revenues for the state, in particular after the 1973 OPEC oil embargo caused global fuel prices to skyrocket. Oil prices stayed high through the 1970s, allowing the Soviets to paper over their system's shortcomings. While several Western countries, including the United States and Great Britain, were forced to engage in painful restructuring of their heavy industrial sectors during the 1970s, the Soviets did no such thing. The aging Soviet leadership, dominated by men who had come of age under Stalin, also refused to reconsider the country's increasingly difficult geopolitical position. The Cold War imposed a military spending burden on the country that was far larger than in the West in terms of the share of GDP spent on defense. The Soviet Union's sphere of influence contributed to the problem. Eastern Europe was as much a drain on resources as it was a benefit. Unlike the Western alliance, the Soviet Bloc had been held together through coercion more than anything else, as the violent uprisings in East Berlin and Poland (1953), Hungary (1956), and Czechoslovakia (1968) had shown, and as later mass resistance movements such as Poland's Solidarity would again demonstrate.[192]

By the 1980s the Soviet Union was in desperate straits. At mid-decade a global collapse in oil prices took away the state's windfall revenues, exposing the glaring weaknesses of the Soviet economy. In March 1985 things appeared a bit brighter after the fifty-four-year-old Mikhail Gorbachev became general secretary of the Communist Party, displacing the Kremlin's old guard. Having long recognized the shortcomings of the Soviet system, Gorbachev immediately embarked on a program of fundamental political, economic, and diplomatic reform. Glasnost opened up the Soviet Union's political system to freer exchange of information. Perestroika reforms were intended to reshape the economy. Gorbachev also sought a new relationship with the West that included deep cuts in nuclear arms, a decision motivated as much by Gorbachev's recognition that military spending was a major part of the Soviet Union's economic weakness as it was by a desire to defuse Cold War tensions. While these reforms produced positive results in a number of areas, in aggregate terms they backfired. Soviet citizens reacted to the unceasing reports of the state's incompetence and corruption with widespread cynicism and anger. Glasnost became a boon to nationalists in the country's peripheral republics. After Gorbachev allowed the Eastern European revolutions to proceed in 1989, the political integrity of the Soviet Union itself withered. Worse still, the economic reforms proved to be only halfway measures and failed to reinvigorate the economy. Attempts to stimulate consumerism and introduce profit motives to state-owned firms were more than offset by the system's bureaucratic inertia and by long-standing corruption.[193]

Gorbachev's efforts to remake the Soviet Union therefore succeeded, but not in the way he had hoped. He intended for his reforms to reinvigorate a moribund socialism, but what occurred was the end of the Soviet system. In 1991 the Soviet Union disappeared and a set of new republics took its place. During the 1990s all of these underwent very difficult transitions to market-based economies. So did those of the former Soviet Bloc, although some, such as Poland's, experienced fairly high growth. Russia, the core of the former Soviet Union, was hit the hardest, in part because it presided over the largest collection of obsolete heavy industrial plants, most of which could not compete in the global marketplace. A host of other problems beset Russia during the 1990s, including elites' redirection of much of the country's remaining wealth into their own hands. The Russian economy collapsed, shrinking by as much as 40 percent during the decade, although no one really knew the true extent, owing to reporting irregularities and the country's vast black market.[194]

China followed a much more successful path. By the mid-1970s China had gone through a series of convulsions, including both the Great Leap Forward and the Cultural Revolution, which had left the country exhausted. To make matters worse, China had become economically and politically isolated. Deepening ideological differences with China's Soviet mentors had resulted in Soviet withdrawal of aid in 1960, signaling an era of escalating tensions between the largest, most important, and most militarily powerful regimes in the communist world. Soviet withdrawal also effectively cut China off from its remaining political and economic allies. This began changing in the early 1970s, when both China and the Western powers began seeing opportunities for a realignment of global geopolitics. American policy had been antagonistic toward China for two decades. But in the early 1970s, seizing the advantage presented by the Sino-Soviet split of 1958–60, the Americans and the Chinese opened diplomatic relations. Economic reintegration with the global economy had to wait another half decade, until Mao's death in 1976. His successors, searching for ways to revitalize China's dormant economy, began reforms, including opening regions along the country's southern coastline to foreign investment and trade.[195]

Several neighboring economies had shown China the merits of capitalism. South Korea, Taiwan, Hong Kong, and Singapore, the "tiger" economies of the 1970s and 1980s, had engaged in a developmental strategy focusing on exports of manufactured goods. Starting in the 1960s these economies had benefited from a favorable strategic environment. The Cold War ensured continuous American attention to the region, in places such as Taiwan, Japan, the Philippines, and South Korea, as well as billions of dollars in economic aid. At about the same time, firms from the rich world came in search of low-wage investment opportunities. Japanese firms were the first to do this, becoming the most important external economic force in the region. For their part, the four tigers found ways to attract external investment, offering among other things cheap and well-educated labor plus stable, if frequently undemocratic, politics. The tiger economies grew quickly, becoming globally important in industrial sectors such as metallurgy and electronics. Average wages in the tiger economies rose, so other countries in the region with lower wage scales could now attract foreign investors. The process was thus repeated in Southeast Asian economies such as Thailand, Malaysia, and Indonesia.

By the 1990s China was a full participant as well. The Chinese leadership skillfully maneuvered the country into position to benefit from export trade, using its huge, low-wage population to attract massive foreign investment from all over the rich world. Since then the Chinese economy has mirrored the Japanese golden age, except on a far larger scale. China since 1995 has featured very high economic growth rates, rising per capita wealth, increasing technological capabilities, and an expanding consumer market. As in the other success stories, the state was critical to the success of the Chinese venture. Unlike the Soviet leadership during the 1980s, the Chinese Communist Party also showed it could retain tight control of the country's politics.[196]

Many developing countries suffered from a poor structural position in the global economy, wherein they exported primary commodities in exchange for finished (manufactured) goods from the rich world. This was in large part a legacy of the colonial era, when imperial powers' investment in their colonies went to little more than extractive enterprises such as plantations and mines. The commodities-for-manufactured-goods swap continued after decolonization swept across the world from the 1940s to the 1960s. Selling raw materials was no recipe for economic prosperity. Among other things, it could quickly devastate the natural resource base of a developing economy, undermining itself over the long term. Also, the rich world's demand for these commodities fluctuated. Changing consumer tastes half a world away had strong influence over the fortunes of entire countries. World prices for commodities, from bananas to copper to cocoa, fluctuated dramatically, imposing great uncertainty and reversals upon the economies of producing countries.[197]

Political leadership in the developing world struggled to find ways to escape from this primary commodity trap. Import substitution was one solution pursued in Asian, African, and above all in Latin American countries. This strategy was based on the theory that global trade systematically discriminated against poor countries. Developing countries therefore needed to build their own domestic manufacturing bases through protection from rich world competition. After much experimentation, this strategy proved largely unsuccessful. Yet the export-led growth model of the kind used by the East Asian tigers also was difficult for many developing countries to emulate, because they could not attract the high levels of foreign investment necessary to repeat the tigers' experience. Nor could many poor countries benefit from geography as favorable as that of the entrepôt economies of Singapore and Hong Kong.[198]

After decolonization, per capita GDP growth rates in Africa lagged behind other regions, although they were still around 2 percent per year. After 1973, however, the continent ran into more serious difficulties. Africa's problems became severe, with per capita GDP growth slowing to almost nothing between 1973 and 1998. Problems included high external debt levels, rampant official corruption, ramshackle educational systems, and political instability, including several civil wars. Africa's transport systems proved a particular obstacle to economic improvement. A good portion of the continent also faced severe social problems, including high illiteracy rates and public health crises such as HIV/AIDS. None of this encouraged foreign investment. The demographic dividend so important to East Asia's per capita growth was conspicuous by its absence in Africa, where fertility generally remained exuberant. But like other regions, Africa was and is a heterogeneous place. Some countries, such as Botswana, Namibia, and Côte d'Ivoire, were wealthier and more stable than others.

Latin America had a better record of success in the postwar period. Again the golden age witnessed relatively strong per capita economic growth (about 2.5 percent per year), based mainly on rising world demand for minerals, oil, wheat, beef, coffee, sugar, and other primary products but also on the early success of protected industries. Between 1973 and 1998, however, this rate dropped to around 1 percent. Inflation and heavy external debt quickly became major problems for many countries in Latin America. Sharp economic inequalities within Latin American societies limited the scope for the emergence of domestic markets for manufactured goods, and few segments of Latin American manufacturing proved internationally competitive. By the 1990s, economic stagnation inspired most countries to do as Chile had already done, and experiment once again with more open markets and less state direction. This helped the export trades to benefit from rising commodity prices (after 2000) associated with the roaring demand of the Chinese economy for raw materials and food.[199]

While considerable variation existed from one place to another, and from one decade to another, the conspicuous trait of the world economy after 1945 was fast growth. Cheap energy, technological change, and market integration all helped generate per capita growth never seen before in human history. No three consecutive generations ever experienced anything remotely like what those alive in the sixty-five years following 1945 witnessed. That spectacular growth raised the consumption levels of several billion people, and the aspirations of most of the rest.

Economy, Ecology, and Dissent

During the postwar era, dissenters emerged who saw the ecological consequences of, and social injustices in, the global economy. Two sets of critiques among many can serve as illustration. The first set fell under the heading of ecological economics. Its central idea was, and remains, that the global economy is a subsystem within the Earth's ecosystem, which is finite and nongrowing. The laws of thermodynamics were foundational concepts in this field. Energy, according to the first law of thermodynamics, can be neither created nor destroyed. While the first law implies that the Universe is in a state of perpetual stability, the second law does not. Rather, it states that matter and energy deteriorate from initially concentrated and more capable states (low entropy) to diffuse and weaker states (high entropy). Therefore, while the first law means that the total amount of energy in the Universe will always be the same, the second means that that energy is inevitably heading toward a less usable form. The ecological economists who applied these laws to human endeavors argued that any system that depends on infinite growth is impossible, for eventually it will exhaust the finite quantities of low-entropic matter and energy on Earth. At the same time, and for exactly the same reason, any such system will pollute the Earth with high-entropic waste. For ecological economists, the only question is how long the process will take.[200]

Although ecological economics had important intellectual roots in the late nineteenth and early twentieth centuries, it was not until the 1960s and 1970s that a coherent body of thought coalesced around these insights. Part of this coalescence was due to pioneering work by economists who had a dissenting view of their field's obsession with economic growth. These included the Romanian expatriate Nicholas Georgescu-Roegen, the English-born Kenneth Boulding, and the American Herman Daly, all of whom worked at American universities. Another part of the coalescence was due to the emergence of the mass environmental movement, which allowed this otherwise obscure intellectual exercise to gain some traction during the 1970s. It was not until the 1980s that a self-conscious field of study, defining itself as "ecological economics," came into existence. By the end of that decade the field had established an international society with affiliates in numerous countries around the world, a specialist's journal, and key texts introducing the field to outsiders. Over the course of the 1990s it developed rapidly. Scholars added to the field's theoretical bases and also developed alternative measures of economic performance that included the societal and ecological costs of growth. One well-known study, published in the journal *Nature* in 1997, attempted to estimate the total economic value of indispensable ecological "services" such as pollination, nutrient cycling, genetic resources, and soil formation. All of these are provided by the Earth free of charge to humans but are not priced in markets. The authors estimated these seventeen services were worth $33 trillion per year. Although the study aroused criticism for its attempt to put a price on nature, the point nonetheless had been made: the global environment provides humankind with enormous hidden and undervalued benefits.[201]

A second set of criticisms fell under the heading of sustainable development. While it had important intellectual linkages to ecological economics, the concept of sustainable development evolved mainly outside of academic circles, hashed out in countless international forums by practitioners, diplomats, and social and environmental activists. It was thus a political idea that eventually found its way into mainstream thinking. Since its inception, most iterations of the sustainable development concept have combined two big ideas: first, that the global economy as it operated in the postwar era was socially unjust, in particular for the world's poor; and second, that the global economy threatened to outstrip ecological limits, mainly due to the patterns of consumption in the rich world. Beyond these basic components, the idea has been redefined countless times.

As with ecological economics, one can trace the intellectual roots of sustainable development back to the nineteenth century, but its direct origins lay in recent decades. The paradigm's basic linkages between wealth, poverty, and ecology emerged out of the many environmental and development conferences held during the 1970s, in particular those under the aegis of the United Nations. The term *sustainable development* came into vogue in 1987 with the publication of *Our Common Future*, a report issued for the UN by the Brundtland Commission (named for its chair, Norwegian prime minister Gro Harlem Brundtland). Its definition of sustainable development as "development that meets the needs of the present without compromising the ability of future generations to meet their own needs" became the archetypal expression of the concept. The Brundtland report also helped to institutionalize sustainable development at the 1992 Rio Earth Summit and subsequent international negotiations.[202]

Yet despite the seriousness of these and other critiques, at the beginning of the twenty-first century the global economy operated in much the same fashion as it had since 1945. Billions of people in the developing world strove to attain the levels of comfort enjoyed by those in the rich world, while the latter sought to increase their wealth. These aspirations undergirded the continuity of the postwar global economy. In the decades after 1945, hundreds of millions of people, including most Japanese and Spaniards, and quite a few Brazilians and Indonesians, attained levels of consumption unimaginable to their ancestors. Although billions more remained on the outside looking in, this represented a major shift in human history. In some respects all of this amounted to great progress, as it lifted many out of poverty. But at the same time the global economy's aggregate effects on the planet became all too apparent, and that economy was deeply dependent on the use of nonrenewable resources such as fossil fuels and minerals. A central question for the current century is whether styles and patterns of consumption can be altered to fit within a finite ecological system.[203]

4. *Cold War and Environmental Culture*

WHILE historians, like the Cold Warriors before them, argue about who started the Cold War and when, its general outline is simple enough. During or soon after World War II, the victorious Allies quarreled and quickly found themselves enemies. Josef Stalin's Soviet Union and its Eastern European satellites formed a contiguous bloc in Eurasia stretching from the Elbe to Vladivostok. The Americans formed a rival, larger, but looser coalition, involving European allies, notably Britain and West Germany, Middle Eastern ones, especially Iran and Turkey, and East Asian ones, particularly Japan. The chief theaters of the Cold War were those of World War II: Europe and East Asia. While the Cold War featured many moments of peril and political shifts that at the time seemed portentous, it was remarkable for the stability that it brought, especially after the victory of Mao Zedong and the communists in the Chinese civil war in 1949 settled the question of the alignment of the world's most populous country.

It was a stability of armed and arming camps. One of the distinguishing features of the Cold War was its sustained militarism. In modern history, most countries, after major wars, reduced their military spending sharply, stopped buying mountains of materiel, and cashiered most military personnel. The United States and USSR did this—briefly—after 1945. During the Cold War, however, the major powers maintained high levels of military spending decade after decade. They sustained their military-industrial complexes, indeed nurtured them, even though this was extremely expensive. Probably it could only have been done because of the spectacular economic boom of 1945–1973. In the Soviet Union during the Cold War, for example, as much as 40 percent of all industrial production was military. A tenth of the world's commercial electricity production went to the building of nuclear weapons.[204]

The Cold War also justified, or seemed at the time to justify, heroic commitments of money, labor, and planning to gigantic state-sponsored infrastructure projects and development campaigns. The United States in 1956, for example, authorized unheard of sums for the world's largest engineering project. The building of the interstate highway system reshuffled American landscapes, hastening suburbanization and altering wildlife migrations, among other effects. Like most acts of government, this decision had many motives behind it, but prominent among them was military preparedness in expectation of war with the USSR.[205] In 1958 Mao's China launched a frenetic campaign to overtake Britain and the United States in economic production within only a few years, a quixotic quest known as the Great Leap Forward, and in 1964, as we will see, it undertook to build a new military-industrial complex from scratch. After the Sino-Soviet split, the Soviet Union for its part built a second Siberian railroad line, which provided a more secure link to its Pacific ports because it stood farther back from the Chinese border than the old Trans-Siberian Railway. This rail line opened up vast new possibilities for accelerated harvesting of timber, furs, and minerals in the Soviet Far East.[206]

The Cold War context also helped to motivate sustained efforts at economic self-sufficiency in China and the USSR; these carried environmental consequences. This ambition never became a priority for the United States, which relied on its navy and its allies to keep sea lanes open and goods flowing internationally. But Stalin and Mao usually felt they needed to be able to make everything they might need within their borders, a sentiment that US embargoes, sanctions, and quarantines reinforced. Both regimes went to great lengths to do so. In the late 1950s, for example, after Stalin's death, his successors chose to convert dry swaths of Central Asia into cotton land. This required massive irrigation works drawing water away from the rivers that fed the Aral Sea, so that by the early 1960s that salt lake began to shrink. Today it stands at a quarter of its 1960 size, with only a tenth of the volume of fifty years ago. The strangulation of the Aral Sea evolved into one of the twentieth century's signature environmental disasters, what with vanished fisheries, desiccated delta wetlands, a tenfold increase in the seawater's salinity, airborne salt blown onto croplands by dust storms arising from newly exposed lake beds, and a dozen other problems. But the Soviet Union needed cotton, and in the Cold War context importing it from India or Egypt entailed risk that Stalin's successors wished to avoid.[207]

Equally attracted by the vision of economic autarky, Mao's China concocted the ambition to grow rubber in the rainforest corner of Yunnan Province called

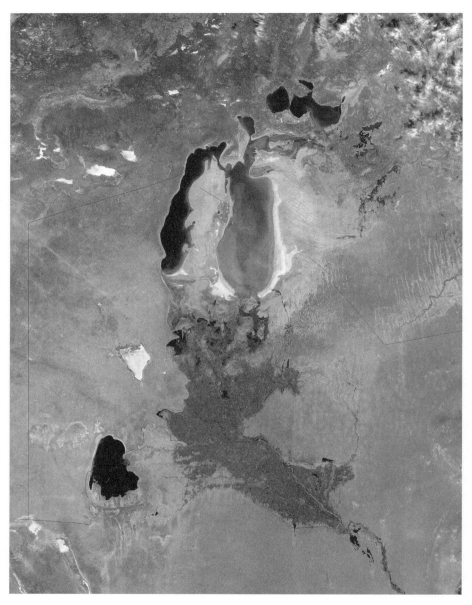

The Aral Sea, as seen from space in October 2008. Once the fourth-largest lake in the world, by 2008 the Aral covered less than 10 percent of its former area. Soviet irrigation projects built in the 1960s deprived the sea of most of its inflowing waters. (Getty Images)

Xishuangbanna, a prefecture in the Mekong River watershed near the border with Burma and Laos. In the early 1950s the USSR had requested that China provide rubber in the spirit of socialist solidarity. Rubber, derived from an Amazonian tree, could not grow in the frosty climes of the USSR. It was a strategic good, necessary for tanks and aircraft (all airplanes use natural rubber tires). Inconveniently for Moscow and Beijing, most of the world's rubber came from Malaya, then a British colony, and Indonesia, ruled by anticommunist generals allied to the United States. The first plantings in Xishuangbanna took place in 1956; after the Sino-Soviet split, the Chinese wanted all the rubber they could get for their own military purposes. Much of the brute labor involved was done by youths sent to the frontier during the Cultural Revolution to improve their political outlook. In China's most biologically diverse region, they cut trees over thousands of square kilometers, destroying animal habitat and obliging the local Dai population to migrate to higher elevations, which put them in conflict with other minorities. The rubber trees often froze because Xishuangbanna lies on the northern climatic margin of the possible range for the Brazilian tree, but eventually these efforts did manage to provide China with the prized supply of rubber. As the Chinese economy boomed from the 1980s, its demand for industrial rubber skyrocketed, and monoculture plantations spread over more and more of the region. After 2000 China needed ever more rubber for its own burgeoning fleet of automobiles. The replacement of forest by rubber plantations over an area the size of Lebanon even altered local climate, bringing a sharper cycle of drought and flood and far fewer days of fog. Rubber processing also filled the nearby rivers and lakes with chemical pollution, all of it destined for the Mekong River. The early quest for military self-sufficiency prepared the way for a thorough environmental transformation of Xishuangbanna.[208]

The Cold War also sparked and sustained guerrilla wars around the world. The United States and the USSR especially, but also China, Cuba, France, and South Africa from time to time, thought it cost-effective to support separatists, revolutionaries, resistance movements, and their ilk wherever that could weaken their rivals. Thus, in places such as Angola, Mozambique, Ethiopia, Somalia, Vietnam, Afghanistan, and Nicaragua, the Cold War superpowers waded into local power struggles, backing their preferred factions with arms, training, money, and occasionally troops. Guerrilla struggles normally involved a large component of environmental warfare—burning forests and crops, slaughtering livestock, flooding fields—because one side or the other typically used forests as cover, and because peasant populations had to be punished for supporting (or merely tolerating) one's enemies. Moreover, these wars produced legions of refugees, people fleeing combat zones or on the move because militias and armies had destroyed their livelihoods. Refugee movements, like other migrations, brought environmental changes both to the lands people left and to those where they settled. The section below on Southern Africa and Vietnam will explore some of these matters.

For its sustained militarism, its military-industrial complexes, its heroic efforts to mobilize or alter nature for political ends, its fueling of guerilla wars—for all these reasons the Cold War contributed to the environmental tumult of the post-1945 decades. None of it will have a longer-lasting imprint on the biosphere than nuclear weapons programs.

Nuclear Weapons Production and the Environment

Cold War anxieties motivated the United States to build about 70,000 nuclear warheads and to test more than a thousand of them from 1945 to 1990. The USSR built about 45,000 and tested at least 715. Meanwhile, Britain after 1952, France after 1960, and China after 1964 built hundreds more. Nuclear weapons require either enriched uranium or plutonium (made from uranium). The nuclear weapons industry led to a rapid increase in the volume of uranium mining around the world after 1950, especially in the United States, Canada, Australia, central and southern Africa, East Germany, Czechoslovakia, Ukraine, Russia, and Kazakhstan. In the early Cold War years, when safety regulations were few, miners routinely received abundant doses of radiation that shortened thousands of lives.[209] All nuclear powers developed atomic archipelagoes, networks of special sites devoted to nuclear research, uranium processing, and weapons manufacture and testing. These were shielded from public scrutiny by Cold War secrecy, and to some extent, especially in Russia and China, they still are. In the United States, this archipelago involved some three thousand locales, including the Savannah River Site in South Carolina and the Rocky Flats Arsenal in Colorado, both central to the bomb-making effort. The jewel in this crown, the Hanford Engineer Works (later called the Hanford Site), some 600 square miles of dusty, windy, almost-empty sagebrush steppe on the banks of the Columbia River in south-central Washington state, opened in 1943.[210]

Hanford was the principal atomic bomb factory in the United States throughout the Cold War.[211] In a little over four decades of operation, Hanford generated 500 million curies in nuclear wastes, most of which remained on site, and, both by accident and design, loosed 25 million curies into the environment, much of it into the Columbia River. Often the quantities in question exceeded those thought to be safe at the time (the limits of what is deemed safe have been ratcheted downward over time). For comparison, the 1986 explosion at Chernobyl released some 50 to 80 million curies into the environment, all of it into the atmosphere. The environmental and health dangers of radioactivity releases and wastes seemed large enough to require constant secrecy and, by some accounts, occasional dishonesty on the part of the responsible officials, but to decision makers the dangers also seemed small enough to be an acceptable cost for the acquisition of more nuclear weapons. Most officials believed Hanford's operations posed minimal risk to people and to local ranching operations, and in the early years at least did not concern themselves with broader ecosystem effects.[212]

The murky story of the Green Run shows the degree to which urgency and haste shaped the history of Hanford. The largest single release of radioactivity, known as the Green Run, took place in December 1949. It is still not entirely clear whether this was fully intentional or somehow got out of control (some pertinent documents remain secret more than sixty years later). It was probably an experiment prompted by the detonation of the USSR's first nuclear weapon, which registered on radioactivity monitoring equipment in western North America. American officials had reason to assume the Soviets were using "green" uranium, only sixteen to twenty days out of the reactor. If so, it indicated accelerated production schedules for Soviet enriched uranium. To test the hypothesis, it seems, they decided to release green uranium from Hanford's smokestacks and then see how accurate their monitoring might be. Some engineers involved now suggest the experiment went awry. In any case, the Green Run released radioactivity on a scale never matched before or since in the United States, quietly spattering downwind communities in iodine-131 (a radionuclide potentially dangerous to humans and implicated in cases of thyroid cancer). The radioactivity secretly released in the Green Run was about four hundred times that which escaped in the Three Mile Island accident of 1979, which put an end to the construction of nuclear power plants in the United States for three decades. The affected people learned of the Green Run only in 1986, after persistent effort to get the federal government to release relevant documents. The secret experiment vividly indicates the risks American officials felt obliged to run in the dark days of the early Cold War.[213]

Remarkably, in retrospect, statesmen often took a relaxed attitude toward radiation risks. In Oceania, the Americans, British, and French tested nuclear weapons beginning in 1946, 1957, and 1966, respectively. Atomic explosions shook various remote atolls again and again. The appeal of Oceania for atomic experimentation was that population was sparse, so testing did not immediately imperil many people—and most of the imperiled people were not citizens of the United States, Britain, or France. They were Polynesians and Micronesians with little formal education or political voice, which made it easier for statesmen to take risks with their health. Beginning eleven months after the end of World War II, American nuclear testing exposed the islanders of Bikini and adjacent atolls to repeated dangerous doses of radiation. Their experiences provided useful information about the susceptibility of the human body and its genes to radiation-related illness and mutations. They, and some US military personnel, were essentially human guinea pigs in the early days of atomic testing.

The French program of nuclear testing in the Pacific also occasionally put safety below other concerns. In 1966 General Charles de Gaulle, then president of France, ventured to Polynesia so he could personally witness a test on the Moruroa Atoll. Adverse winds that meant radiation resulting from the test would be scattered over populated islands held matters up for two days. De Gaulle grew impatient, and citing his busy schedule demanded the test proceed regardless of the winds. Shortly after the explosion, New Zealand's National Radiation Laboratory recorded heavy fallout on Samoa, Fiji, Tonga, and other population centers of the southwest Pacific. De Gaulle returned to Paris and state business forthwith. Since 1966 Polynesians have compiled a long list of grievances against the French nuclear program in the Pacific, as Marshall Islanders have against the American program since 1946.[214]

The Soviet nuclear weapons complex operated with even greater nonchalance toward environmental risks and human health. Stalin declared the creation of nuclear weapons to be "goal number one" as the Cold War began, and by 1949 he had what he wanted. The Soviet atomic archipelago consisted of uranium mines (in which hundreds of thousands of prisoners died), secret cities built for nuclear research, fuel-processing sites, bomb factories, and test sites. The chief plutonium- and weapons-making centers were near Chelyabinsk in western Siberia, and Tomsk and Krasnoyarsk, both in Central Siberia. These secret facilities were often cryptically referred to by their postal codes, such as Tomsk-7 and Krasnoyarsk-26. Their histories remain for the most part sealed in secrecy. Chelyabinsk-65, which also went by the name of Mayak (lighthouse) is the best known. Chelyabinsk region, once a landscape of birch and pine groves amid thousands of lakes, became a main cog in the Soviet military-industrial complex during World War II, when it produced half the tanks used by the Red Army. It was far from the vulnerable frontiers of the country and had plenty of water, as well as metallurgical and chemical industries, all of which recommended it for nuclear weapons production. For fifty years it has been the most dangerously polluted place on Earth.[215]

The Mayak Chemical Complex opened in 1948, creating the USSR's first plutonium. Over the years, at least 130 million curies (the official figure—others say billions of curies)[216] of radioactivity has been released at Mayak, affecting at least half a million people. Most of that occurred in its early years, especially 1950–1951, when nuclear wastes were dumped into local rivers, tributaries to the Techa from which thousands of people drew their drinking water. Several thousand villagers were evacuated; those who remained apparently suffered from elevated rates of leukemia.[217] As a result of an explosion in a high-level radioactive waste tank in 1957, about 20 million curies of radioactivity escaped and 2 million showered the Mayak vicinity. Some ten thousand people were evacuated (beginning eight months after the accident) and 200 square kilometers were ruled unfit for human use.[218]

A bit more radioactivity spattered regions downwind of Lake Karachay. A small and shallow pond used after 1951 as a dump for nuclear wastes, Lake Karachay is now the most radioactive place on Earth. It contains about twenty-four times as much radioactivity as was released in the disaster at Chernobyl in 1986. Today, standing at its shore for an hour would provide a fatal dose of radiation. As it is situated in an often dry landscape, its water level frequently subsides, exposing lake bed sediments. Fierce Siberian winds periodically scatter the radioactive dust, most damagingly in a 1967 drought. In addition to the 1957 and 1967 tragedies, several other accidents have befallen the Mayak complex. In all, the contamination from Mayak affected about 20,000 square kilometers.[219]

The human health effects of Mayak's contamination, if official Soviet and Russian studies are to be believed, were modest.[220] However, a local politician, Alexander Penyagin, who chaired the Supreme Soviet's Subcommittee on Nuclear Safety, once said the mess at Mayak was a hundred times worse than Chernobyl. Evidence offered by journalists and anthropologists who visited the region implies serious and pervasive human health problems.[221] So do some epidemiological studies, although their conclusions are often inconsistent.[222] In one especially hard-hit village, life expectancy in 1997 was twenty-five years below the Russian national average for women and fourteen years below for men.[223] The true human costs remain elusive at Mayak, and health effects of nuclear contamination are much in dispute, even where data are more complete.[224]

The atomic archipelagoes consisted of much more than Hanford and Mayak. Nuclear test sites, such as those in Oceania, Nevada, Kazakhstan, and the Arctic island of Novaya Zemlya, were especially active in the 1950s and early 1960s—and radioactive ever since. Atmospheric tests (of which there were more than five hundred) scattered about four hundred times as much radioactive iodine-131 to the winds as did Chernobyl. The Soviet navy used dumping sites at sea for its spent nuclear fuel and contaminated machinery, polluting inshore waters of the Pacific and the Arctic Oceans, especially around Novaya Zemlya. Surprisingly, perhaps, the world's most radioactive marine environment was not Soviet responsibility, but Britain's. The Windscale site (renamed Sellafield in an attempt to shed notoriety), which produced weapons-grade plutonium for the United Kingdom's nuclear arsenal, released radioactivity into the Irish Sea, especially in 1965–1980. The Irish Sea's currents do not disperse pollutants quickly, so the radioactivity lingers and turns up in British seafood. Windscale also caught fire in 1957, which the British government eventually acknowledged in 1982 and blamed for thirty-two deaths and a further 260 cases of cancer.[225]

The nuclear weapons industry created several "sacrifice zones" in a half dozen countries. The security demands of the moment seemed, to those in power, to justify lethally contaminating chosen areas for millennia into the future. Of all the mines, bomb-making plants, test sites, and waste dumps, none were sacrificed more thoroughly than the grasslands, birch groves, streams, ponds, and villages of the Mayak region, which was still in the twenty-first century acquiring additional radioactive contamination.[226]

In one of the many ironies associated with the Cold War, some of its nuclear weapons development sites became de facto wildlife preserves. The Savannah River Site, for example, produced plutonium and tritium, and its 300 square miles were kept free of routine human activities. As a result of banning humans in the interest of building bombs, ducks, deer, snakes, 250 species of birds, and the largest alligator ever found in Georgia (not an atomic mutant) flourished despite 35 million gallons of high-level nuclear waste scattered around. The Rocky Flats Arsenal in Colorado, which produced plutonium until the mid-1990s, became a prairie wildlife preserve, a protected home where the deer and the antelope play under the watchful eye of up to a hundred bald eagles. The Hanford stretch of the Columbia, where the first atomic bombs were built, hosted the healthiest population of chinook salmon anywhere along the River.[227]

In a further irony, one of the world's first international environmental agreements arose from nuclear testing. As evidence mounted that atmospheric testing sprinkled all ecosystems and earthlings with extra doses of fallout, as test explosions grew bigger and bigger, and as expertise in radiation medicine accumulated, politicians and scientists by the late 1950s developed some doubts about the prudence of continued testing. In some countries, where such things were permitted, citizen action helped to build pressure for a ban on atmospheric testing. In all countries the fear of nuclear annihilation, intensified by the Cuban Missile Crisis of October 1962, added to this pressure. In late 1963 the USSR, United States, and United Kingdom signed a partial test ban (meaning no atmospheric testing), and many other countries soon followed, although not France or China, each of which prized its own independence in matters of nuclear politics. As a result of the partial test ban, people born after 1964 carried much smaller quantities of strontium-90 and other radioactive isotopes in their bones than did their elders. Everyone alive in the 1950s and early 1960s, even those living in remote Tasmania or Tierra del Fuego, keeps a signature of the Cold War atomic weapons programs in their teeth and bones.[228]

In sum, the nuclear weapons programs of the Cold War probably killed a few hundred thousand people, at most a few million, slowly and indirectly, via fatal cancers caused by radioactivity releases.[229] Almost all were killed by their own governments in a Cold War version of friendly fire. French president François Mitterrand is credited with saying that the most essential quality for any statesman is indifference. He meant that leaders must at times take decisions that result in death and suffering for others. During the Cold War, leaders, including scientists heading atomic weapons research and development programs, made such decisions repeatedly. Some no doubt acquired troubled consciences in the process, but they all felt the politics of the moment required them to do as they did, even when it involved the likely sacrifice of some of their own subjects or fellow citizens.

Nowhere, not even at Mayak, did radioactive pollution kill many millions of people and lay waste to broad regions. Cigarettes killed far more people during the Cold War than did nuclear weapons programs. So did air pollution and road accidents. Cooler heads prevailed over those who wanted to use nuclear weapons to blast instant harbors in Alaska or new canals through Panama.[230] When an American B-52 exploded in midair and dropped four H-bombs on the coast of southeastern Spain in 1966, the bombs did not explode and only a little plutonium splashed on the countryside.[231] So one is tempted to conclude that the health and environmental effects of Cold War nuclear weapons programs were therefore modest.

But the story is not over yet. It will not end for at least one hundred thousand more years. Most radioactivity decays within hours, days, or months and quickly ceases to carry dangers for living creatures. But some radioactive materials used in nuclear weapons, such as plutonium-239, have half-lives of up to twenty-four thousand years. Some wastes created in nuclear weapons manufacture will remain lethally radioactive for more than a hundred thousand years. This is a waste management obligation bequeathed to the next three thousand human generations. If not consistently handled adroitly, this will elevate rates of leukemia and certain cancers in humans, especially children, for a long time to come.

To reflect on the significance of this obligation, it may help to remember that twenty-four thousand years ago was the height of the last ice age, long before cities or agriculture or the first arrival of humans in North America or Oceania. One hundred thousand years ago, mastodons, wooly mammoths, and giant saber-toothed tigers roamed the future territories of the USSR and United States, while hominins were just beginning their migrations out of Africa. Long, long after only a few historians know anything about World War II or the Cold War, people will either manage Cold War nuclear wastes through all the political turmoil, revolutions, wars, regime changes, state failures, pandemics, earthquakes, megafloods, sea level rises and falls, ice ages, and asteroid impacts that the future holds, or inadvertently suffer the consequences.

China's Great Leap Forward and the Third Front

Few, if any, Cold War leaders felt that the political climate justified manipulations of nature more strongly than did Mao Zedong. Mao came to power in 1949, self-educated in a Marxist tradition in which nature exists to be conquered by labor. The prestige derived from his success as a revolutionary leader, and his skill at destroying rivals, gave him an unusually powerful hand within China for most of his career as helmsman of the ship of state (1949–1976). Like many men whom luck and talent propelled to the heights of power, he acquired a firm faith in his own wisdom and was not easily swayed by evidence or apparent failure. His determination to outstrip the economies of capitalist enemies, for example, helped inspire him to disregard basic laws of chemistry, biology, and physics, not to mention human nature, in a campaign known as the Great Leap Forward, launched in 1958. In January of that year Mao announced, "There is a new war: we should open fire on nature."[232]

Scholars have yet to forge a consensus on the priority of motives behind the Great Leap Forward. But it surely involved, on Mao's part, a twin ideological urge to industrialize China as fast as possible and to build communism sooner than the "revisionist" Soviets, and a geopolitical ambition to make China strong in a hostile world. Scholars also disagree about the human toll it took: estimates of the number who starved to death as a result of the grain requisitioning and other features of the Great Leap Forward range from fifteen million to fifty million, some 2 to 7 percent of the Chinese population.[233]

For Mao, steel production had a special talismanic quality. It bespoke modernity and power. When confronted with disappointing economic performance in his first five-year plan (1953–1957), Mao made steel production a centerpiece of the second, fantasizing about overtaking British and American steel production in just a few years. When Soviet premier Nikita Khrushchev, visiting China in 1958, expressed doubts that China could meet its steel targets, Mao raised them.[234] His secret speeches to party cadres in 1958 reveal a persistent fascination with steel tonnage and China's rank among great powers in steel production.[235] Because China lacked the capital and technology to build modern steelworks, Mao insisted that each peasant commune and urban neighborhood would make steel with "backyard furnaces." Mao's lieutenant and sometimes rival, Premier Zhou Enlai, personally organized the students and faculty of Peking University for steel production. Nationwide, the scale of mobilization was heroic: ninety million people smelted steel and iron in six hundred thousand backyard furnaces, melting down cooking pots, bicycle frames, and doorknobs. Through stupendous effort they doubled China's steel output. Most of it, however, was brittle and worthless.[236]

Unsurprisingly, making steel in this fashion was extremely inefficient in terms of fuel and dangerous in terms of pollution. In those parts of China with plentiful coal, decentralized steelmaking simply meant wasted coal. Elsewhere it meant that all rail lines were clogged with coal and ore shipments, and that any and all wood and shrub was reduced to charcoal and fed to the furnaces. In Yunnan, Sichuan, and perhaps across the whole country, some 10 percent of extant forests vanished within a year. In some provinces, Hunan and Guangdong, for example, half or a third of forests were felled. This was surely the fastest retreat in the long history of shrinking Chinese forests.[237] Equally unsurprisingly, wherever backyard furnaces burned charcoal, they emitted intense air pollution. The city of Suzhou, near the mouth of the Yangzi, recorded a fall of 400 tons of soot and dust per square kilometer, and some places more than double that. Breathing air so laced with particulate matter, not to mention sulfur dioxide, did no one any good.[238]

The grain harvest was a second priority in the Great Leap Forward. Appropriately enough, Mao thought China needed to produce more food. However, he wanted it done instantly, and promoted quack science to that end. Party officials assigned peasant communes wildly unrealistic production targets, which the communes usually claimed to meet for fear of punishment. Peasants drained marshes and lakes to plant more rice and wheat. They terraced mountains up to the summits and plowed China's northern grasslands. They followed instructions to plant seeds close together because Mao believed plants of the same species would not compete with one another for water and nutrients but would somehow grow in harmony. In some parts of the country, the peasants plowed furrows deeper than they were tall, on the theory—another of Mao's passing enthusiasms—that this enhanced soil fertility and encouraged larger root systems. Everywhere they constructed jerry-built dams and dug new wells for irrigation water. Mao wanted each commune to collect and store its own water: as the slogan went, "Each piece of land has its own piece of sky." People who voiced doubt about the production targets and the absurd farming methods invited swift retribution.

Linked to the struggle for grain was a campaign against creatures deemed parasitic or unhealthy. Slogans urged Chinese as young as kindergartners to eliminate the "four pests"—rats, mosquitoes, flies, and sparrows. (Mao was under the impression that Japan had rid itself of insect pests.)[239] Party officials assigned communes and neighborhoods quotas of rats and sparrows—even flies—to be killed and counted. In seven months in 1959, the Chinese killed nearly two billion sparrows, whose crime was eating grain.[240]

All this frantic urgency brought fiasco.[241] Millions of peasants starved to death while party cadres requisitioned more and more grain for the cities, the army, and export. The agricultural policies were fully abandoned only in 1961 (when grain was purchased from Canada and Australia). The deep plowing, planting on mountainsides, and cultivating the steppe brought more erosion and dust storms. The hastily built dams often burst. The wells depleted groundwater in some places while reservoirs raised the water table in others, bringing salts to the surface and salinizing fields. In the North China plain in the late 1950s, the area damaged by salinization grew by 40 percent, mainly due to hastily engineered water impoundment schemes.[242] The assault on sparrows reduced predation on many kinds of insects, leading to infestations of crop pests (so in 1959 bed bugs replaced sparrows on the most-wanted list). In the city of Jilan, on the lower Yellow River, a successful antisparrow campaign was followed by a plague of caterpillars.[243] Pests of all sorts gobbled up a tenth of the grain harvest in Zhejiang Province in 1960; locusts helped themselves to a sixth of the rice crop in Hubei Province in 1961. In addition to short-run starvation, the agricultural policies of the Great Leap Forward hampered China's long-range agricultural potential.[244]

The failures of the Great Leap Forward dimmed Mao's star for a few years. But by 1964 he again had assumed the reins (which some historians believe he held all along from behind the scenes). Soon he launched another militarized, top-down campaign, the construction of the "Third Front." By late 1964 Mao concluded that China's international position had worsened. The Sino-Soviet rift, brewing in 1956–1960, had become a full breach by 1962, turning his patron and ally into an enemy. The Americans were preparing a massive escalation of their combat forces in Vietnam. Mao felt that China needed to prepare for all-out war. In particular, he felt China needed a new military-industrial complex deep within the country, well away from American bombers based in Taiwan, South Korea, or Okinawa, and well back from the Soviet frontier. The Soviet invasion of Czechoslovakia in 1968 and the weeks-long border clashes in 1969 further convinced Mao that Moscow might well unleash its Red Army—of which twenty-five full divisions were stationed on the border—into China.

To withstand this anticipated assault, Mao chose to build a secret armaments industry with all the trimmings in Sichuan, Guizhou, and Yunnan Provinces. It would include mines, smelters, steel mills, chemical plants, hydroelectric stations, and more, all linked by new railroads. In the 1930s the Chinese Nationalists had tried to build industry in Sichuan when the Japanese Imperial Army occupied China's coastal regions. Mao admired Stalin's response to the German invasion of the USSR in 1941, in which the Soviets had removed hundreds of factories behind the Urals. Now Mao would do the same thing, only before being attacked, on a much larger scale, and into much more remote and rugged country. Siting military industry in Yunnan had the added attraction that it would ease Chinese support of their North Vietnamese allies against the Americans: Yunnan had a rail link (its only rail link before 1965) to Hanoi.

Mao, not a man given to half measures, wanted this military-industrial complex built overnight. Beginning in late 1964, industrial plant in coastal provinces was disassembled, transported to the interior, and put back together again. In addition, just about all Chinese investment in new industry in the years 1965–1971 went to the Third Front. Construction brigades from the People's Liberation Army worked around the clock, laying railroad track, blasting tunnels, and building factories. Where possible, factories were put in caves and steep-sided valleys to make them less vulnerable to attack from the air. Altogether, the Third Front was the most intensive commitment ever made by any country to military industry. The centerpiece of this crash program was a giant steel mill at Panzhihua.[245]

Panzhihua, near the border of Sichuan and Yunnan provinces, sat atop mother lodes of minerals with military uses, including the world's biggest reserves of titanium. It had all the iron ore and coal needed for steelmaking. Its inhabitants before 1964 were mainly an ethnic minority, the Yi, who had long history of fractious relations with Han Chinese. Starting in 1965, hundreds of thousands of migrant workers flooded into Panzhihua. An indication of its priority in Chinese politics was that Premier Zhou Enlai assumed direct responsibility for getting Panzhihua up and running. By 1971 it was making steel—probably of better quality than that made thirteen years before under Zhou's direction by the faculty and students of Peking University.

In these frenzied times, no thought could be spared for the environment. Little enough was spared for safety: during its construction, upward of 5 percent of Panzhihua's workforce died each year. The steel mill generated vast clouds of air pollution. Its location in a steep-sided valley with frequent temperature inversions meant that sulfur dioxide and particulates sometimes accumulated for weeks before being swept off by the wind. In 1975 particulate matter at times reached concentrations three hundred times the national standard. A location that made sense from the military and mineralogical points of view proved a dismal choice from the air quality standpoint. The mill also poisoned the local rivers and soils. No environmental regulation took place at Panzhihua until 1979, well after the international situation had changed, China's isolation had ended, the Americans had left Vietnam, and no strategic logic remained for locating military industry in the remote interior of the country. Today Panzhihua is China's fourth largest steelmaking center, a quirk of economic geography derived (like the rubber plantations of Xishuangbanna) from the exigencies of the Cold War.[246]

In the campaigns of the Great Leap Forward and the Third Front, a sense of urgency pervaded everything. In the first case it derived only partly from Cold War international considerations. In the second, the Chinese sense of impending war with the Americans or the Soviets, or both, was the sole reason to build the Third Front. This urgency meant that environmental implications counted for nothing.

Mao was not always blind to environmental matters, however. He favored af-forestation, and at least once wondered aloud how it might affect groundwater supplies.[247] One of his stated reasons for trying to raise grain yields was so that one-third of Chinese farmland could be converted to forest, a proportion recommended for Russia by a Soviet agronomist whose work had come to Mao's attention. But Mao's outlook was normally what is sometimes called "instrumentalist." He took interest in the environment insofar as it provided resources for the political agen-das that mattered to him. What few environmental regulations China did have were declared "capitalistic, inhibiting, and revisionist" at the outset of the Cultural Revolution in 1966 and duly jettisoned.[248] Only in 1972–1973 did China's leader-ship start to develop doubts about its neglect of the environment—largely inspired apparently by the first international environmental conference in Stockholm.[249] But China's efforts to control environmental problems to date have been over-whelmed by the hectic urbanization and industrialization of the decades after 1980, a true great leap forward in economic terms. By 2010 China had far surpassed Mao's reckless dream of 1958, milling five times as much steel as the United States. Thanks to his penchant for autarky and his campaigns of mass peasant mobili-zation, Mao took a great toll on the environment of China. But perhaps by inad-vertently delaying the economic rise of China by a generation, he postponed a larger impact upon China's environment, and the global environment as well.

Hot Wars and Environmental Warfare in Southern Africa and Vietnam

Mao fretted about the designs of the imperialist camp in the 1950s and 1960s, but most of its members proved to be paper tigers as imperialists. They could not maintain their grip on their Asian and African territories. A surge of decoloni-zation (1947–1975) resulted, changing the landscape of world politics. Decoloni-zation presented the Cold War powers with an opportunity, or, as they saw it, an obligation, to compete for the loyalties of newly created countries. The Soviet Union in particular tried to portray itself as the champion of anti-imperialism, and often supported liberation movements seeking to end British, French, or Portuguese colonial rule. Mao did the same, and in the 1960s and 1970s China overtly competed with the USSR for the mantle of anti-imperialist champion.

In southern Africa, the Cold War intruded deeply into the politics of decolonization. Ongoing political and sometimes guerrilla struggles took shape in the 1960s, aiming to end Portuguese rule in Angola and Mozambique, white settler rule in Rhodesia (now Zimbabwe), and South African rule in what has since become Namibia. In addition, groups formed to contest white rule and apartheid in South Africa itself. The Portuguese, white Rhodesians, and white South Africans sought to portray their causes as anticommunist crusades, hoping for assistance from the United States and its allies.

In 1974–1975 a staunchly anticommunist Portuguese dictatorship collapsed at home and Portuguese colonial rule in Africa collapsed with it. Civil wars heated up in Angola and Mozambique, and competing factions found willing sponsors in the Cold War rivals. In Angola, the USSR, Cuba, China, the United States, and South Africa all got involved, supporting various factions. Here, and in other cases too, Cold War logic was only part of the motivation for foreign involvement. The South Africans, although they often offered anticommunism as the rationale for their incursions into Namibia, Angola, and Mozambique, and although they were in some cases egged on by the United States, were also fighting to preserve racial apartheid at home and to prevent the triumph of movements hostile to it in neighboring lands. Fidel Castro, although in many respects dependent on Soviet support, sent tens of thousands of Cuban soldiers to Angola without consulting Moscow and had his own agenda of promoting African revolution. The outside support, whether directly or indirectly motivated by Cold War strategies, made the wars in southern Africa more destructive than they could otherwise have been. Foreign powers supplied Angola with fifteen million land mines, eventually producing the world's highest rate of amputees.

In Ovamboland, a densely populated floodplain region of northern Namibia and southern Angola, warfare raged from 1975 to 1990 with frequent South African involvement. The South Africans were trying to destroy a Namibian militia that enjoyed support from an Angolan faction that itself was supported by Cuban soldiers and Soviet weaponry. Militias and armies terrorized the farming populations of Ovamboland for years, burning homes and farms, butchering livestock, and flattening orchards. The main grain crop, millet, grew tall enough to give guerrillas excellent cover, so anti-guerrilla strategies featured systematic burning of stands of maturing millet. Thousands fled, allowing their fields and homesteads to return to nature (often a dense cover of thornbush, of not much use to man or beast).

In southern Mozambique, where the anti-Portuguese struggle also gave way to civil war starting in the mid-1970s, rival factions again enjoyed outside support—from China, the USSR, South Africa and, after 1980, Zimbabwe. In some districts so many refugees fled that population fell by half. The refugee totals ran into the millions. Again, farms went untended and the bush encroached. Bush encroachment in Mozambique often led to infestation by tsetse flies, the carriers of sleeping sickness and nagana (a livestock disease). The widespread use of land mines discouraged people from returning to their farms after the fighting ended in the early 1990s, so the land-use patterns of the region continued to bear the imprint of war.

In Ovamboland, in southern Mozambique, and indeed throughout the zones of guerrilla war in southern Africa, fifteen or more years of fighting changed the land by making routine human management of it—pruning back the bush, tending flocks and herds, cultivating fields and orchards—too dangerous. Instead, fire, used to punish or intimidate, or to deny cover to enemies, became the principal tool of—often accidental—ecological management. Armies and militias frequently operated in parks and nominally protected areas, because they offered easy hunting and plentiful meat for armed men without secure supply lines. Moreover, animals such as elephants that offered marketable parts (such as ivory tusks) made inviting targets for cash-strapped forces. Refugees, too, often flooded into protected areas and survived as best they could off of wildlife and the fruits of the land. Wildlife and livestock both suffered in the independence war in Zimbabwe, because anthrax and rabies ran wild in the absence of veterinary services disrupted by war. The southern African wars proved very hazardous for the animal kingdom, human and nonhuman alike.[250]

In Vietnam, the clashes were more deadly and the involvement of Cold War powers more thorough than in southern Africa. After 1945 Vietnamese nationalists (some of whom were also communists) redoubled their effort to achieve independence from France. The French tried to hold on, but after a major defeat in 1954 they increasingly invited the Americans to help resist communism in Vietnam. Despite some ambivalence about ground wars in Asia, the United States in 1964–1965 committed itself heavily to preserving its flimsy client state in South Vietnam and combating the forces of North Vietnam, which was ruled by its communist party and supported by both China and the USSR. To President Lyndon Johnson, and initially to most Americans, Vietnam was worth fighting over mainly because it seemed to be part of the Cold War chessboard.

American firepower made it an asymmetrical conflict. While there were phases of conventional warfare, at most times and places the North Vietnamese forces, and their Viet Cong allies in South Vietnam, had to fight guerrilla style. In turn, the Americans fought anti-guerrilla campaigns, something in which they had scant recent experience. They converted their more traditional capital- and equipment-intensive way of war to the circumstances they faced, using the latest technologies against their enemies.

Much of Vietnam was tropical forest, which afforded good cover for guerrillas. The North Vietnamese even carved out supply lines hundreds of kilometers long through the jungle, such as the famous Ho Chi Minh trail, part of which traversed neighboring Laos. They inflicted damage on the Americans via ambush, snipers, booby traps, using the terrain and especially the vegetation to their advantage. To counter these tactics, the Americans turned to defoliants, various chemical agents that killed trees, bushes, and grasses. The most notorious of these—Agent Orange—contains dioxin, a particularly nasty and persistent chemical compound. This form of chemical warfare had been pioneered on a small scale in the British campaign against communist rebels in the 1950s in Malaya. The Americans used it far more widely. Conveniently, airplanes could spray these chemicals cheaply and easily over vast tracts. The United States sprayed about 80 million liters of defoliants on an area the size of Massachusetts (about 8 percent of Vietnam, mainly in the Mekong Delta) to try to save US soldiers from surprise attacks. Today the Vietnamese government claims four million people suffer from the effects of dioxin.

The United States also used mechanical means to try to deny forest cover to its enemies in Vietnam. Fleets of Rome plows, giant bulldozers wielding two-ton blades for scything down trees, could make short work of most vegetation. The United States developed them specifically for conditions in Vietnam, and used them especially for clearing the land alongside roadways. Rome plows shaved about 2 percent of South Vietnam's land area starting in 1967. From at least the time of the caesars, anti-guerrilla and counterinsurgency efforts had often involved deforesting strips adjacent to roads, but no one before could do it with the efficiency and thoroughness of the Americans with their Rome plows. Between the defoliants and the mechanical devices, the United States cleared about 22,000 square kilometers of forest (the size of New Jersey or Israel), roughly 23 percent of Vietnam's 1973 forest cover.[251]

In contrast to the wars in southern Africa, the conflict in Vietnam also featured a large bombing campaign, larger than all those of World War II combined. The US Air Force dropped over 6 million tons of bombs on Vietnam over nine years, leaving about twenty million craters, more than the moon has acquired in 4.5 billion years of bombardment by bolides. Some of these craters now serve as fish ponds. Some bombs, nicknamed "daisy-cutters," exploded aboveground and, when they worked properly, cleared away everything over a patch about the size of four football fields. They were designed to create space for helicopter landing sites or field artillery emplacements, again specifically for use in Vietnam.

Thanks to its firepower and technology, the US military was able to make rapid changes to the environment of Vietnam. No doubt the North Vietnamese and Viet Cong made some too, burning crops and villages when it suited them. But they did not have the Americans' technological capacity, or the persistent motive, to clear and poison forests.[252]

In addition to obliterating a goodly chunk of Vietnam's flora, the Vietnam War altered conditions for Vietnam's fauna. Scavenger species probably flourished thanks to extra servings of corpses. Rats, too, because of military food storage. Elephants, however, suffered, because the Americans often strafed them from the air, suspecting them of aiding and abetting the enemy as beasts of burden. The Viet Cong and other guerrillas tried to kill dogs, which might alert their enemies to impending surprise attacks. Forest animals lost habitat because in the wake of defoliation many landscapes supported only tough *imperata* grass, which few creatures can eat. Herbivores ate grass and leaves laced with toxins. Minefields selected for lightweight animals and against large ones (and continue to do so decades afterward). As in Southern Africa, in Vietnam warfare was hard on many animal species, if helpful for a few.[253]

In earlier centuries warfare had often created refuges in which wildlife could flourish, because people found it too dangerous to settle where violence reigned. In the late twentieth century, the effect of warfare on wildlife seems to have changed. Weapons had become so powerful and accurate that men with even

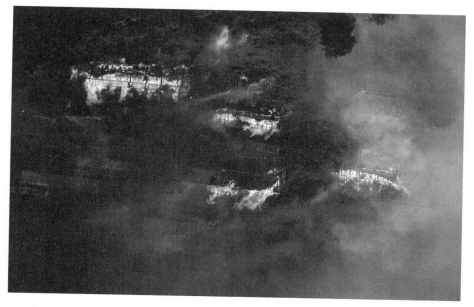

Fires burn a cluster of huts following napalm bombing by American planes, Vietnam, January 1966. Anti-guerrilla warfare often involved intentional deforestation in efforts to deprive enemies of cover. (Time & Life Pictures/Getty Images)

minimal hunting skills could easily bag big game. And after 1945, most warfare involved informal forces, militias, guerrillas, and so forth, which needed to live off the land because they had no bureaucracy of quartermasters and supply chains to rely on. Thus, theaters of war in recent decades became wildlife killing zones. Moreover, the effects of wars tended to linger on, and not merely in the form of land mines. The end of warfare might remove some of the immediate motives to hunt wildlife, but the postwar profusion of guns and vehicles, and in some cases a newly pervasive culture of lawlessness, often meant that edible or marketable fauna enjoyed no peace dividend.[254]

All in all, the Vietnam War, like the struggles in southern Africa, involved a large quotient of environmental warfare and much destruction of flora and fauna. This, it should be remembered, was probably true of all guerrilla conflicts around the world, those connected to the Cold War and those not. In the post–Cold War decades, insurgencies and guerrilla campaigns have diminished somewhat, but

Congo, Somalia, Liberia, Sierra Leone, Iraq, Afghanistan, and a few other unfortunate lands have seen their share of unconventional warfare with collateral damage to the biosphere.

From Iron Curtain to Green Belt

The Cold War also created a few war-zone wildlife refuges. These were not combat zones but corridors in the shadow of the Iron Curtain. Churchill in 1946 famously called the line that separated zones controlled by the USSR from those of the West "the Iron Curtain." It ran from the Baltic coast, where West and East Germany met the sea, to the Adriatic, although the defection of Yugoslavia from the Soviet camp made the southern reaches of the Iron Curtain no more formidable than tin foil. But from the border of Hungary with Austria all the way to the Baltic, the Iron Curtain was a no-go zone for forty years, bristling with barbed wire and military observation towers. Unauthorized human visitors risked their lives by entering.

As a result of exclusion of ordinary human activity, the Iron Curtain gradually became an unintended nature preserve, a north–south wildlife corridor in the heart of Europe. Border police served unwittingly as park wardens, maintaining ecosystems and wildlife through exclusion of humans. Rare insects survived because no pesticides were used. Deer and boar proliferated. Along the Baltic shores, where the Iron Curtain met the sea, coastal species flourished. Thanks to Cold War distrust, the Drava River, separating Hungary and Yugoslavia, remained in a more natural state, undredged and unstraightened, preserving aquatic life, floodplains, oxbows, meanders, and the wild, channel-shifting character of the river. The Rhodope Mountains form the border between Bulgaria and Greece, another prohibited corridor during the Cold War. Consequently, the mountains hosted a wealth of rare and endangered species, with perhaps the greatest biodiversity in the Balkans. In Berlin the area immediately around the wall became a de facto sanctuary for urban species.

When the Berlin Wall fell and the Iron Curtain parted in 1989, a German doctor gathered allies to campaign for the preservation of the unusually rich environment the Cold War left behind. With the help of nature conservation organizations in Germany, and eventually the IUCN, long stretches of the former frontier have been set aside as parkland in a project known as Europe's Green Belt.[255]

The same thing could conceivably happen in Korea. Since the end of the Korean War in 1953, a demilitarized zone (DMZ) has separated North Korea from South Korea. It amounts to about half a percent of the peninsula's area and is about 4 kilometers wide, a narrow belt across Korea's waist, guarded by barbed wire, booby traps, about one million land mines, and armed men instructed to shoot to kill. Farmed for more than five thousand years and then abandoned for more than fifty, the DMZ became another accidental nature preserve. It contains a broad cross-section of Korean ecosystems, from coastal marshlands to mountain moors. It is home to dozens of endangered species, some fifty mammals in all, including bear, leopard, lynx, and a very rare mountain goat. It hosts still more species of birds and fish. Many of East Asia's migratory birds, including several kinds of majestic cranes, use the DMZ as a rest stop on their travels between Siberia and warmer climes. Red-crested cranes, now exceedingly rare, are symbols of good luck and longevity in Korea and throughout East Asia. The DMZ, the last frontier of the Cold War, has given them a new lease on life.

Since 1998 a group of Koreans (and some foreigners) have sought to prepare for the day when the two Koreas reunite and the DMZ's ecosystems are no longer protected by political standoff. They fear, not unreasonably given the environmental records of both North and South Korea, that upon reunification the DMZ might be stripped of its wildlife and sheathed in asphalt and concrete. Their organization, DMZ Forum, proposes to convert the DMZ from an accidental nature preserve to a deliberate one, a peace park. Perhaps in Korea, as on the western edge of the old Iron Curtain, one of the environmental legacies of the Cold War will be a ribbon of nature sanctuary.[256]

During the tense decades of the Cold War, leaders of the great powers normally felt that their survival, and that of the populations they led, hung by a thread. Any and every action that seemed to promise improved security appealed to them, as did anything that promised to enhance the prosperity that underwrote expenditures on security. In this political circumstance, they thought it was justifiable, even necessary, to sacrifice select places such as Mayak or Hanford and to risk the health and livelihoods of many people, such as uranium miners or the Dai people of Yunnan. World leaders found it easy enough to summon the necessary indifference to the environment to act upon their plans to bolster security and prosperity.

Until the late 1960s their populations did too. But the Cold War, paradoxically, indirectly helped spawn a surge of modern environmentalism. Anxieties about fallout from nuclear testing in the early 1960s filtered into a broader environmentalism. Beyond that the years of détente (ca. 1972–1979), when Cold War tensions abated somewhat, opened a window of opportunity for people to voice environmental concerns. In Western Europe, North America, and Japan, and in the less regimented parts of Eastern Europe, more and more people expressed doubts about nuclear weaponry and unrestrained industrial development. Détente made them more likely both to think about the environment as an important issue and to feel more free to say so. Even after the end of détente, conventionally dated to the 1979 Soviet invasion of Afghanistan, the genie of environmentalism was out of the bottle. It could not be put back in when the Cold War entered a new frosty phase in the 1980s, despite the best efforts of some political and business leaders—such as the Bavarian politician who referred to the German Green Party as the "Trojan horse of the Soviet cavalry."[257]

The Cold War left its imprint on the biosphere on every continent and in every ocean. Many of its effects, such as the destruction of crops and villages in guerrilla wars, proved fleeting. Some effects will linger for generations still, such as the desiccation of the Aral Sea. Others will be with us, and our descendants, for time out of mind.

The Environmental Movement

The rise of the global environmental movement was one of the great stories in twentieth-century history. While there were many reasons why it occurred, not least anxieties about nuclear testing, the best explanation might be the most obvious. Economic expansion threatened environmental conditions in a great many places. This caused a reaction among those concerned about their lives, health, and livelihoods. A global economic thesis generated its own antithesis, environmentalism.

The beginning of the mass environmental movement in the United States is often tied to the publication of Rachel Carson's *Silent Spring* in 1962. Songbirds, Carson argued, were caught in a chemical web of contamination that might lead to their elimination. But behind the book's evocative imagery of lost birdsong stood a stark message for humankind, namely, how chemicals such as DDT were destroying the very basis of life itself. Modern chemistry was leading humanity to its own doom. This was the message that resonated with readers around the globe. The book made Carson famous overnight, both in the United States and in many other parts of the world (the book was translated into well over a dozen languages). It made DDT notorious. Before *Silent Spring*, the chemical had been considered a godsend in the twin battles against crop pests and insect-borne diseases. After, it became a symbol of humankind's ecological hubris.[258]

But as environmental historians point out, it is a gross oversimplification to pin the emergence of a mass, heterogeneous, and global movement on a single book.[259] Over half a century before Carson, the United States had gone through a debate about the proper use of public lands, in particular forests. It had created national parks and had busily expanded that system throughout the twentieth century. So had several European countries, both at home and in their colonies. Debates about industrial pollution also extended well back into European and North American history. In the United States, Progressives fretted about coal smoke from the end of the nineteenth century, leading to smoke control efforts in some of the country's biggest cities. After World War II, West German engineers followed the examples of St. Louis and Pittsburgh, in the hope that West Germany might also reduce smokiness for regions such as the industrial Ruhr.[260]

Moreover, the times were ripe for the message in Carson's book. The first two decades after the war had witnessed a blind faith in technology and a headlong quest for affluence. Nearly every state on Earth, rich or poor, bought into this consensus. Yet even at its height the consensus had shown signs of cracking. Anxieties about technology such as nuclear testing had crept into international discourse well before *Silent Spring*. During the 1950s the superpowers' atmospheric testing helped to create the initial wave of global fears about radioactive fallout and its effects on human health. Testing during the 1950s not only provoked much unease but also spurred some, such as Barry Commoner, to start thinking systematically about the relationships between technology and the natural environment. By 1960 some influential Americans were becoming increasingly uncomfortable with the side effects of prosperity. One was the Canadian-born economist John Kenneth Galbraith, whose best-selling book *The Affluent Society*, published in 1958, argued among other things that wealth entailed adverse effects upon nature. Grassroots groups across the country, many led by women, were linking suburbanization, the ultimate expression of American postwar prosperity, to the destruction of the countryside.[261]

Mass environmentalism in affluent countries emerged out of this background and in tandem with the "new social movements" (antiwar, students, women, hippies) of the late 1960s. The emergence of mass unrest in so many areas of life was critical for launching the nascent environmental movement from the margins of public consciousness into the forefront. All around the world, people began to question all types of authority, objecting to everything from racial injustice to gender relations to American behavior in Vietnam. Ironically the most materially comfortable generation in world history (to that point) was also the most revolutionary (at least while young). It did not take long for many in these mass movements to shift attention to the postwar consensus and its environmental consequences. Many of the youth involved in student and antiwar demonstrations ended up providing environmentalism with both energy and leadership.[262] But environmental protest did not take the same form everywhere, was not motivated by identical problems, and was not always a youthful phenomenon. Students and hippies may fit the stereotype of 1960s/1970s activism, but these were not the only participants in the new mass environmental movement. Middle-aged women had been among the vanguard at various times. So too, in many places, were intellectuals of all stripes. People of all social ranks around the world were occasionally aggrieved by the environmental degradation of their immediate surroundings, by the consequences of greater economic activity, and by inappropriate technology—and enlisted in environmental movements.

Japan provides a cogent example. After the flattening of Japanese factories in World War II, a ruling elite in government and big business joined in a headlong rush to reindustrialize the country. Their efforts met with spectacular success. Over three decades the Japanese economy grew fifty-fold, to about 10 percent of the entire global economy in the mid-1970s. Massive new industrial complexes drew huge numbers of people into Japan's cities. Unfortunately these also generated some of the world's worst air, water, and soil pollution. By the early 1960s, local opposition had emerged in several industrial cities, driven almost entirely by residents frightened for their health and lives. Toxic traces of lead, copper, mercury, zinc, asbestos, and other contaminants were widespread in industrial areas and were reliably linked to diseases and grotesque birth defects. Japan's economic miracle came at a hefty price. Citizen complaints induced some bureaucratic response, but it was not nearly enough, and by the end of the decade pollution had been turned into a national political issue. Motivated in part by the examples set by environmental protesters abroad, Japanese groups became an important factor in inducing the national government to enact tough pollution control legislation from the 1970s. By and large, Japan's environmental movement focused tightly on pollution and human health, rather than embracing concern for forests, wildlife, fisheries, or ecosystems generally.[263]

Global environmental activism intensified rapidly after 1970. For the first time, environmentalists could mobilize large numbers of people in mass demonstrations. While the most famous of these might have been the first Earth Day (April 22, 1970) and the mass protests against nuclear power in Western Europe later in the decade, such demonstrations occurred in a great many places and for a great many reasons. Older conservation organizations were put on the defensive as more confrontational groups formed, motivated by frustration over tactics and a more critical outlook based in the ecological sciences. David Brower resigned the Sierra Club presidency in 1969 to begin Friends of the Earth, a global organization dedicated to what he believed would be more radical social and environmental change. In the early 1970s a new wave of publications appeared that questioned economic growth itself. *The Limits to Growth*, a report issued in 1972 by the Club of Rome (a group formed in 1968 by Aurelio Peccei, an Italian industrial magnate), was by far the most significant of these. It sold twelve million copies in thirty languages and helped to trigger an intense debate among intellectuals about industrial society, pollution, and environment that would last for decades.[264]

The Cold War also fueled countercultural environmentalism. Although the 1963 Partial Test Ban Treaty had eliminated atmospheric testing, all the nuclear powers continued undersea or subterranean testing programs. In 1971 a small group of Canadian and American environmentalists sailed a boat toward a nuclear testing site in the Aleutian Islands, causing the US government to cancel a planned detonation there. Out of this act emerged a high-stakes brand of direct environmental activism and a new transnational environmental group, Greenpeace. Over the following years the group continued its confrontational methods in opposition to Pacific nuclear testing, a strategy that brought it into open

The first Earth Day, New York City, April 22, 1970. In the course of the 1960s, environmentalist social movements became increasingly popular around the world. The Earth Day tradition was launched in the United States by Gaylord Nelson, a Wisconsin senator outraged by a California oil spill. Earth Day eventually became a global observance, officially supported by the United Nations. (© JP Laffont/Sygma/CORBIS)

conflict with the French government. This resulted in the 1985 sinking of the Greenpeace ship *Rainbow Warrior* by French intelligence agents in the harbor of Auckland, New Zealand.[265]

The Cold War's nuclear shadow, not merely testing, motivated environmentalists. The many ecology or green parties that sprang up across Western Europe found common cause with the peace movement. This alliance became much stronger in the late 1970s and early 1980s, in particular after NATO's decision in 1979 to station Pershing II and cruise missiles in Europe, causing a dramatic escalation in popular fears of nuclear war. West Germany's Green Party became the exemplary case of the marriage between the peace and environmental movements, with the party's early history marked as much by its steadfast pacifism as its environmentalism.

Environmentalism of the Poor

The same developmental forces that had created the postwar consensus in rich countries were also at work in poorer ones. The rapid global economic growth from the 1950s required ever-increasing quantities of raw materials and foodstuffs—metals, oil, coal, timber, fish, meat, and agricultural commodities of all types. Heightened demand for these pushed commodity frontiers ever outward, into parts of the world that were not yet wholly integrated into the modern economy. This demand was matched by the goals and policies of national elites in poor countries, almost all of whom subscribed to the same ideology of economic growth as prevailed in wealthier parts of the world.

Economic intensification had practical and often very negative consequences for poor people in rural areas. More metals required more mines in more places, more timber required more felling in more forests. As extractive industries began their operations (or intensified existing ones), the worst outcomes fell on the poor residents of these places. These outcomes were of two types. One resulted from extraction processes, which produced all manner of unpleasant and even deadly problems. Mines produced huge piles of tailings and polluted drinking water for miles around. Timber extraction denuded steep mountain slopes, leading to soil erosion and mudslides. Hydroelectric projects flooded large areas where rural people lived. A second outcome concerned access to natural resources. The rural poor depended for their existence on the very same resources that were now being extracted by far more powerful (and rapacious) industries. Fishing villages that had relied on small boats and low technology, for example, were now confronted by industrial trawlers able to wipe out entire fisheries.[266]

These outcomes fueled what is known as "the environmentalism of the poor." The idea originated during the 1980s, when Indian intellectuals subjected environmentalism in the richer parts of the world to intense scrutiny. In their view, environmentalism in the United States and other wealthy countries had been motivated by concerns for idealized (and constructed) forms of nature such as wilderness. Thus, it failed to address the root causes of environmental degradation—in particular, consumption—whether in their own countries or other parts of the world. In addition, some North American and European intellectuals had subscribed to a "postmaterialist" theory of environmentalism's origins. According to this theory, people in the West had become environmentalists only because their basic needs had been securely met. Environmentalism, so this theory went, had begun in the rich world because wealth allowed people there to stop worrying about their next meal and start caring about whales, bears, and wilderness. Poor people in poor countries had other environmental priorities because they were busy trying to stay alive.[267]

The Indian critics refuted the notion that the poor had no awareness of nature, no desire for protection of their environment. Much of their intellectual ammunition stemmed from a deep understanding of protests that had been lodged by the rural poor in their country. The vigor and effectiveness that the Indian poor had brought to environmental issues not only had attracted scholarly attention to their cause, it also had helped to force a rethinking of environmentalism as an intellectual problem. The formative case occurred in the Indian Himalayas in the early 1970s, when villagers in the northern state of Uttarakhand pitted themselves against foresters selling timber concessions. State-supported logging had cleared forested hillsides, leading to flooding, and had also encroached on villagers' long-standing claims to forest access and use. Hence, logging threatened villagers' lives, property, and economic livelihoods. Things came to a head in 1973 when a group of villagers, including women and children, stopped a timber operation by threatening to bind themselves to the trees. This act gave the movement both its name, Chipko (roughly, "to hug") and everlasting renown. Chipko's initial successes allowed it to expand for a time to other parts of the Himalayas, after which it faded. Besides earning environmentalists everywhere the "tree-hugger" moniker, Chipko provided the iconic example of the environmentalism of the poor.[268]

Details and circumstances differed in every case, but around the world stories very similar to Chipko abound in postwar history. No global coordinated movement existed, but these examples had much in common. Many were localized protests that did not receive much attention elsewhere. A few attracted significant notice internationally. Almost all were rooted in struggles over access to nature's bounty. In the 1980s and 1990s the Indian cause célèbre shifted to protest over dams on the Narmada River. Other instances included indigenous people's uprisings over forests in Indonesia, Buddhist monks protesting deforestation in Thailand and Burma, and villagers' objections to gold mining in Peru. Several cases have ended in tragedy. The rubber tapper Chico Mendes became a global icon after he was murdered in 1988 for organizing opposition to ranching in the Brazilian Amazon. A further example was the case of the Nigerian playwright Ken Saro-Wiwa, who led his Ogoni people in mass protest against the degradation of the Niger Delta caused by oil drilling. The Nigerian government, threatened by the attention brought to the deplorable state of the delta, arrested Saro-Wiwa and his associates. In 1995, after a short show trial, they were all executed, against international objections.[269]

The environmentalism of the poor also extends to the plight of poor people who live in rich countries. Laborers and their families in grimy landscapes had protested sporadically against the pollution of air and water since the dawn of the industrial age. But they rarely had the power to achieve their goals, partly because their organizations typically were small, local, and short-lived, attuned to specific examples of environmental degradation rather than to the broader phenomenon. In the late twentieth century this too began to change. A key event occurred in 1982, when the governor of North Carolina decided to locate a toxic waste dump in the poor and mostly African American community of Afton. This triggered mass protest, out of which was born the environmental justice movement. Rejecting mainstream environmentalism as a middle-class white phenomenon with no interest in the poor, advocates in the movement sought to link environmental health and civil rights. They stressed the fact that toxic waste dumps and power plants, for example, were placed in poor minority communities much more often than in wealthier ones. Since the 1980s, environmental justice has become increasingly integrated into mainstream environmentalism in the United States. Elsewhere, shorn of its emphasis on racism in the American context, the concept of environmental justice has flourished in several of the many places where ecological sins seem disproportionately visited upon the poor, upon minorities, or upon indigenous peoples.[270]

Environmentalism and Socialism

Socialist regimes took the correction of nature's mistakes as a duty and put environmental protection near the bottom on their list of priorities. Ideology had much to do with it. Socialist orthodoxy simply defined environmental degradation as a capitalist problem. Pollution occurred under capitalism because profit-maximizing firms foisted their pollution on society as a way to save costs. Soviet theorists maintained that pollution could not exist under socialism.

Such blinders had consequences for the real existing socialist environment. Soviet orthodoxy after World War II defined population control, for example, as a reactionary concept. All such proposals were said to stem from Thomas Robert Malthus, a Briton who had explained poverty in demographic terms and had thus committed the sin of failing to blame capitalist exploitation. Mao Zedong refused to be concerned about China's rapidly growing population in part because he accepted Soviet orthodoxy on the matter. In the mid-1950s China's leading demographer, Peking University president Ma Yinchu, had warned of catastrophe if the country did not bring growth under control. Mao, sensing the hand of a dead Englishman, branded Ma a rightist, thereby silencing him and ending all talk of population control until the early 1970s. By that time, alarm about overcrowding overwhelmed socialist orthodoxy, and the state resorted to increasingly strict family planning measures, culminating in the desperate one child per family policy in 1978 (discussed above).[271]

Resistance to environmental protection stemmed from the theoretical underpinnings of Marxism and its twentieth-century variants. Marx had formulated a progressive theory of human history, running from feudalism, through capitalism, to socialism, before culminating in communism. Industry was the key to the last three stages of the process. Capitalist industrialization was necessary and good, but by definition socialist industry had to be better. When this theoretical perspective was combined with the very real imperative to match Western powers militarily, socialist regimes could not resist emphasizing industrialization as much as possible.

The result was a narrow and utilitarian view of nature. Although nature conservation had prospered in the Soviet Union's first decade, by the time of Stalin's first five-year plan (1929–1934) state policy had begun to shift dramatically toward using all available resources for productive purposes. Mining and logging operations began to encroach on the nation's extensive system of protected areas (*zapovedniki*), the collectivization of agriculture began in earnest, and the country's best conservationists were purged. After 1945, states within the Soviet orbit went to work on gigantic and, in retrospect, ill-conceived projects of all sorts. Engineers in Eastern Europe built countless hydroelectric projects and steel mills. Their Soviet counterparts dreamed of redirecting Siberian rivers from the north, where they emptied into the Arctic Ocean, to the south, where they were to be put to work irrigating Central Asian cotton fields. The Cuban government drew up plans to construct gigantic dikes between the mainland and surrounding islands, thereby walling out the Caribbean and allowing the interior to be drained for farmland. The biggest of these projects would have increased Cuba's land area by more than 15 percent. Lack of funds, rather than concern for ecology, shelved these plans to improve upon nature.[272]

Against this backdrop it was not surprising that environmental protection had a very low priority under state socialism. But *environmentalism* existed in a kind of netherworld in these states. Having defined environmental degradation as a capitalist phenomenon, socialist regimes could hardly acknowledge, let alone publicize, the severity of their own shortcomings. Instead their public rhetoric embraced environmental protection even as they suppressed information about environmental problems. Socialist regimes often claimed superior treatment of nature as a way of showing their merits to the rest of the world. As proof they would occasionally cite legislation that contained stricter standards than anything found in the West and trumpet the existence of state-directed or state-sponsored environmental organizations having enormous membership. Both types of claims were usually groundless. More often than not, environmental legislation was ignored in practice, while state-sponsored environmental organizations often had inflated membership lists and servile governing boards.[273]

In the dictatorships of the proletariat, speaking frankly on the environment could be a costly undertaking, but it was not always so. In the right circumstances, the authorities found it preferable to tolerate the few environmental organizations that emerged during the Cold War. As long as such groups remained small in size and apparently apolitical in goals, they did not constitute much of a threat. Even episodes of genuine national anxiety about the environment, as occurred in the case of the pollution of the pristine Lake Baikal in the Soviet Union from the late 1950s, could be kept in check. The Soviet government concealed information about Baikal's condition while permitting some public dissent about pollution in the "pearl of Siberia." Environmental critiques concerning Lake Baikal were deemed tolerable: they focused on a very limited geographic area and did not call into question state control of the economy.[274] Further, some regimes avoided harsh treatment of environmentalists out of a desire to maintain domestic peace. This was the case in East Germany, where a small environmental movement managed to form from the early 1970s. It originated within the Protestant church, one of the very few institutions in the country that had had enough power to negotiate some independence from the state. While the secret police, the Stasi, kept an eye on environmentalists' activities and tried to contain or deflect them, the state allowed the movement to survive because it feared a showdown with the church.[275]

In parts of the Soviet Bloc in the 1980s, the policy of containment of popular environmentalism failed. By the beginning of the decade, large swaths of Eastern Europe and Russia had been conspicuously degraded by air, water, and soil contamination. In the Soviet Union, the first ecology groups without official recognition started to form. Influential writers such as Valentin Rasputin and Sergey Zalyagin publicly questioned the state's handling of environmental issues. The biggest change followed in the wake of Mikhail Gorbachev's arrival and his political reforms, which allowed people to voice concerns about the environment openly and without prior approval. These voices became a chorus after Chernobyl in 1986, after which hundreds of new environmental groups emerged. Many originated in the Soviet Union's outlying republics, where environmental degradation became associated with the unaccountability of the Soviet state. In places such as Latvia and Estonia, environmentalism was put in the service of nationalism, thereby contributing to the eventual breakup of the Soviet Union. In Hungary and Czechoslovakia, too, in the 1980s, popular environmentalism escaped the control of officialdom and became a vehicle for the expression of political dissent.[276]

The 1980s also marked an important shift in China. Again the key change was the creation of space for an independent civil society. The economic reforms of the late 1970s and early 1980s had nudged the Chinese economy toward private enterprise and invited trade with foreigners. This had two effects. The first occurred in the wake of the massive economic growth that started in the 1980s. As had been the case in other countries after 1945, in China the government pursued growth at any price, whatever the environmental consequences. There followed the now-familiar story of China's blackened rivers, eroded soil, and unbreathable air.

The second effect took the form of environmental dissent. It emerged in the 1980s, centered at first in larger cities. By the end of that decade, nationwide networks had surfaced. As in other socialist states, in China the government attempted to channel environmental criticism into state-sponsored organizations. But independent groups managed to form anyway. The sizable and influential Friends of Nature, for instance, decided to register itself in 1994 with the state's Academy of Chinese Culture. This act defined the Friends of Nature as a cultural organization, which meant it could avoid conflict with state restrictions on environmental groups. Thereafter, environmental organizations proliferated. By the beginning of the twenty-first century, observers estimated that thousands of groups existed throughout China, in cities of every size and in rural areas as well. These groups became increasingly bold. When supported by China's Ministry of Environmental Protection (which diverged from the party line on occasion), some groups took up taboo matters such as dam construction. Indeed, during the 1990s the Three Gorges Dam project became a preeminent focus of Chinese environmental activism.[277]

Institutional Environmentalism

The early 1970s were marked, nearly everywhere, by a significant upswing in governmental activity on the environment. Within the OECD member states, the number of major environmental laws doubled in 1971–1975, compared to the previous five years. West Germany alone crafted some two dozen pieces of new legislation during this period. In 1970 the United States created the Environmental Protection Agency (EPA) and the United Kingdom reshuffled its bureaucracy to create a cabinet-level Department of Environment. Such changes were not limited to rich countries. Mexico, for example, passed comprehensive pollution control legislation at about the same time as Japan and the United States. A large number of Latin American countries followed, establishing environmental protection ministries, many of which were based on the EPA.

In the 1970s, governments of all political hues enacted progressive environmental policies. Richard Nixon, for example, was a Republican president who embraced environmentalism to help him win reelection in 1972. West Germany's Hans-Dietrich Genscher, of the centrist Free Democratic Party, made environmentalism his own partly to steal support from the enormously popular Social Democratic chancellor, Willy Brandt. Right-wing dictatorships had no such electoral motives, but some tried environmental reform anyway. In the case of Brazil's military government before 1985, early reforms were largely hollow, undertaken as much to look modern to the outside world as anything else. But reforms under the Dominican Republic's dictator Joaquín Balaguer, who reversed some of his predecessor's destructive forestry policies, were more substantial.[278]

International organizations of all types matched this flurry of national environmental policy making. Governments had held conferences and formalized treaties as early as the nineteenth century on such matters as wildlife conservation. This picked up a bit after World War II. In the late 1940s the youthful United Nations joined with a handful of conservationists to create the IUCN. It later spun off the World Wildlife Fund (WWF). During the 1950s and 1960s the UN oversaw a small spate of conferences, one of which produced the successful biosphere reserve program.[279] By far the most important international meeting of the period was the United Nations global environmental conference, held in Stockholm in June 1972. Attended by delegates from all over the world, the conference appeared to legitimize environmentalism at the highest diplomatic level. It brought some concrete results, such as the creation of the United Nations Environment Programme (UNEP), later headquartered in Nairobi. But the conference also revealed important fissures that would bedevil subsequent environmental diplomacy, as some in poorer countries saw environmentalism as a cynical trick by which rich countries could deny them the means to develop.[280]

After Stockholm, international environmental agreements became routine in global politics. States negotiated agreements on every conceivable topic, including ocean pollution, whaling, endangered species, hazardous waste, Antarctica, forests, regional seas, biodiversity, wetlands, desertification, and acid rain. Admittedly, some of these agreements were weak. Some, however, were not, such as the 1987 Montreal Protocol that laid the foundation for the sharp reduction in CFC emissions, which had depleted the ozone layer. Over the past two decades intergovernmental bodies have become key institutions in directing attention to climate change, which by 2000 was the most important and contested area in global environmental politics. The most significant of these bodies, the Intergovernmental Panel on Climate Change, took shape in the early 1990s under UN auspices. It has sought to digest the plethora of publications on climate change and present its consensus findings in a format suitable for policy makers. Its efforts have resulted in the most authoritative synopses of the relevant science but nonetheless aroused storms of controversy, fed by forces hostile to constraints on fossil fuel use.

The trajectory of the environmental movement intersected with that of national and international political developments. In many cases national environmental movements retrenched after enjoying an initial burst of activism, settling into a long period of institution building. Much activity centered on building the capacity and technical expertise required to deal with increasingly complex scientific and regulatory issues. This was important in some places because industries were becoming much better at organizing against environmental legislation. Yet even after suffering political setbacks due to environmental backlash, as occurred in Japan, Great Britain, and the United States at different points, the environmental movement often managed to retain all or much of its strength.[281] Political engagement by environmentalists also took on new forms with the emergence of ecology parties. New Zealand formed the world's first nationwide ecology party in 1972. A bit more than a decade later, several such parties had become fixtures in the political landscapes of many countries, especially in Europe. In Belgium, a green party won seats in the national legislature in the late 1970s, followed by West Germany's greens in the early 1980s. The Finnish green party took part in a coalition government starting in 1995.

Similar institutionalization occurred within poorer countries' environmental movements. Some environmental groups in these countries enjoyed institutional trajectories that mirrored those found in North America or Europe. A few of these groups grew into large, established organizations having influence well beyond their national contexts. Kenya's Wangari Maathai started planting trees in the 1970s with no more than a little money, a few contacts abroad, and her own formidable talents. Since then, Maathai's Green Belt Movement has planted tens of millions of trees in rural areas around Kenya and in other parts of Africa. The organization has grown into a global success story and become a model for emulation, for which Maathai was awarded a Nobel Peace Prize in 2004.[282]

Brazil's environmental movement illustrates the same process but on a larger scale. For much of the twentieth century Brazil had no environmental movement outside of a small number of scientists and conservationists who were concerned about protecting their country's astonishing natural heritage. Most Brazilian elites, including the military regime that ran the country from 1964 to 1985, subscribed to a consensus focusing on rapid economic development.[283] From the late 1970s, however, the regime began to bow to growing domestic pressures for political reform. As in other places, this opened up space for the formation of an environmental opposition. Over the next decade, a growing Brazilian movement widened the scope of its activities and deepened its professional and organizational sophistication. It also began building ties to other parts of the world, as when Brazilian and West German environmentalists started cooperating after their countries agreed to build nuclear plants together. This process received an enormous boost from the second UN-sponsored global environmental conference, held in Rio de Janeiro in 1992. Brazilian environmentalists traveled the globe in the run-up to the conference while groups from all over the world converged on Rio. The result, before and after 1992, was a much deeper integration of Brazilian environmentalism within a global activist network.[284]

The emergence of formal environmental movements, politics, and parties had grown well-nigh universal by 2013. Just about everywhere that electoral politics existed, so did green parties. A loose international coalition of green parties existed from 2001.[285] Unorganized, spontaneous, countercultural environmentalism survived here and there, bubbling to the surface in the aftermath of newsworthy ecological mishaps, such as the nuclear contamination at Fukushima. And environmental institutions disappeared from time to time, as in Russia in 2000 when President Putin abolished the environment ministry. By and large, though, by the twenty-first century environmentalism as a social movement had become a legitimate and institutionalized part of the political architecture on local, national, and international levels all around the world. But it remained, with few exceptions, a small part.

The Mainstreaming of Environmentalism

Environmentalism is now a lasting element in global culture—politically, morally, and socially acceptable to a great many people, although by no means to everyone. Political discourse is infused with environmental rhetoric, while environmentalism itself has become commodified. What are some of the reasons for this mainstreaming?

Disasters have provided nearly continuous fuel for environmentalists and graphic tragedies for public consumption. Some types of disasters, such as oil spills, generate particularly riveting images of destruction—beaches covered in thick black ooze and sea birds in wrenching death throes. One of the most important occurred in 1967 when the supertanker *Torrey Canyon* ran aground in the English Channel off Cornwall. Caught wholly unprepared for oil spill containment, the British government resorted to extreme measures that included aerial bombardment of the wreck in the hopes of setting it afire. This was the world's first catastrophic tanker disaster, drawing global attention to the risks attendant upon the new supertankers.[286]

Many high-profile disasters followed. The 1979 accident at the Three Mile Island nuclear power station in Pennsylvania caused a partial meltdown of a reactor core. Although the incident turned out to be minor in terms of actual damage, the fear it generated was very real. In 1983 in the Brazilian city of Cubatão, an industrial accident killed several hundred poor people living in a nearby shantytown. Ten months later a Union Carbide plant in Bhopal, India, exploded, killing thousands. The most serious and frightful of all, the Chernobyl accident, followed less than two years later. These and many other widely publicized ecological disasters helped to mainstream environmentalism.[287]

Electronic media assisted in the mainstreaming process. Environmental disasters became culturally and politically more important starting in the 1960s because television could beam visceral images into households around the world. But television's influence extended much further than coverage of disasters. Not long after television sets became a mass consumer item in North America and Europe, broadcasters discovered an immense popular interest in nature programming. By the mid-1950s, West Germans could watch *Ein Platz für Tiere* (*A*

Place for Animals), a series made famous by Frankfurt's zoo director Bernhard Grzimek. A few years later, Americans were introduced to the world's wildlife via Marlin Perkins and his *Wild Kingdom* series. But it was the French oceanographer Jacques Cousteau who became the most famous. Like Grzimek, in the 1950s Cousteau had produced a color film about nature that earned him public acclaim and an Oscar to boot (Grzimek's film was about the Serengeti, Cousteau's about Mediterranean marine life). Propelled by this success, Cousteau set about plying the oceans, gathering footage for countless films and television documentaries. These were broadcast the world over, turning Cousteau into a global celebrity and solidifying the grip on the public imagination held by the glories of nature.[288]

The Internet and the World Wide Web further entrenched environmentalism in the mainstream of culture and society. The Internet made it far easier for environmental activists to locate one another and make common cause. In addition, their ability to raise funds, research issues, and share legal expertise only grew thanks to the Internet and social media. Moreover, the new electronic media made it more difficult for anti-environmental states to prevent environmental organizing and limit the availability of information. Through the Internet, even under oppressive regimes environmentalism could escape the shadows and slip into the mainstream of societies.

The commodification of the environment has proceeded in tandem with heightened public interest in the subject. Corporations now market themselves and their products in the greenest possible terms. Much of this is simple public relations posturing with little relationship to actual behavior, but a good deal of it consists of a genuine interest in appealing to customers' green sensibilities. This development reflects the increasing power of consumers who demand products that are safe, clean, and energy-efficient. Consumer interest built a burgeoning organic food movement, for example, now big business in many parts of the world.[289] The list of green products and new green industries is almost endless: electric cars, energy-efficient appliances, Earth-friendly clothing, wind turbines, green buildings, solar-powered everything.

In many ways all of this represents a remarkable set of changes from the 1950s or even 1960s. It points to the increased breadth and vigor of environmentalism as a movement and to its staying power at the global, national, and local levels.

Environmental awareness and concern have become commonplace nearly everywhere, as have environmental institutions and politics.

What before 1950 was an issue mainly for aristocrats and blue-bloods anxious about birds, game animals, and property rights, and typically called "conservation," gradually became broader in its concerns. By slow degrees it became environmentalism and increasingly between 1950 and 1970 a cause of the political left and counterculture, at least in Europe and North America. In the following decades, however, environmentalism evolved into a more generic movement, important to people from various parts of the political spectrum and fully integrated into politics through lobbying groups, fundraising machines, political parties, and the like. Environmentalism continued to draw some energy from young volunteers and grassroots activists, and still had some supporters among the blue-blooded squires and landed proprietors, creating fractious alliances of strange bedfellows.

Despite the unquestioned successes of the environmental movement, the fact remains that the global economy continues to expand in ways that threaten all that environmentalists cherish. The postwar vision of unending economic growth and unbridled technological progress remains intact—if no longer unchallenged.

Modern environmentalism, perhaps, represents a stage in the development of the Anthropocene. For many decades people tinkered with the basic biogeochemical cycles of the Earth without recognizing that they were doing so. As the scale of these unwitting interventions grew, more and more people noticed that, in some ways at least, humans could have an impact on the Earth. By the 1950s, if not before, a few saw that human action could affect matters as vast and important as atmospheric chemistry and global climate. Popular environmentalism from the 1960s prepared the way for a fuller recognition of the scale and scope of human impact, to the point where, in the early twenty-first century, scientists and journalists began to adopt the term *Anthropocene*.

So far humankind has influenced basic Earth systems without consciously managing them. It is as accidental by-products of actions undertaken for other reasons that we have our powerful impacts on the global carbon and nitrogen cycles. If we elect to try to manage Earth systems, that is, if we undertake explicit geo-engineering, that will amount to yet another stage of the Anthropocene—whether it goes well or badly.

·[FOUR]·

Global Cultures

Petra Goedde

Introduction

AT the turn of the twenty-first century the major metropolitan centers of the world had much in common. Visitors to New York, Paris, Tokyo, Dubai, Mumbai, or Nairobi could find the same clothing brands, eat the same foods, stay in the same hotel chains, and sip the same beverages. Yet as people found more of the same in each of these places, they also encountered more diversity within a single locale. Urban populations, culinary habits, and cultural offerings, including music, film, theater, and literature, became multiethnic and multicultural. In these places homogenization moved in tandem with heterogenization, creating creolized global cultures.[1] Scholars have attributed these cultural transformations to the forces of globalization. Globalization, in turn, has remained an elusive concept, used at times to describe the more recent developments that have connected disparate parts of the world into ever more intricate webs of goods, people, and ideas; and at other times to describe the much longer history of premodern trade routes, migrations, military campaigns, and explorations.[2] To be sure, local cultures have always evolved in response to internal and external impulses through the production of knowledge and contact with other cultures. At the turn of the twentieth century, cultural anthropologists began to study more systematically the mechanisms of cultural evolution and change.[3] While they focused primarily on explaining patterns of cultural difference, the globalization literature of recent decades increasingly emphasized patterns of cultural assimilation and adaptation. Yet a close examination of the global transformations of cultures since 1945 reveals how assimilation and difference interacted with and complemented each other.

Debates about cultural globalization after World War II cannot be separated from debates about economic globalization. In fact, the term *globalization* emerged first in the 1970s among economists who described the effects of the increasing integration of business ventures worldwide.[4] Both critics and supporters saw cultural globalization as a consequence of economic globalization. Supporters argued that creative adaptation as well as wholesale adoption of superior economic and cultural practices would create more wealth and power for all who participated. They celebrated economic globalization at annual meetings of the World Trade Organization and the World Economic Forum in Davos, Switzerland, where government and corporate leaders discussed ways to foster and manage global economic cooperation. They lobbied national legislatures to lower trade barriers and supported international business ventures, promising economic growth in industrial countries as well as modernization in the developing world.

Skeptics warned that corporate greed and economic exploitation would destroy local self-determination. In their estimation, globalization created more wealth and power for those in control of the global marketplace, dependency for those on the margins, and greater inequality for all. Globalization, to these critics, meant little more than Western, primarily American, economic and cultural imperialism. It crushed indigenous economic development and local self-sufficiency, creating new postcolonial dependencies in its wake.[5] Businesses run by local merchants folded as larger and more cost-effective corporations moved in. Indigenous producers could not compete against the lower prices of these giants and thus faced either elimination or absorption into large impersonal corporate structures. George Ritzer has termed this process "McDonaldization," likening the greater rationalization, efficiency, and standardization in production and service industries to the techniques employed by the world's most successful fast-food chain.[6] Associating economic self-sufficiency with cultural distinctiveness, critics also predicted the loss of local cultural identity as a consequence of economic imperialism. They demanded the protection of indigenous cultures against the onslaught of what they identified as the cultural imperialism of corporate powers. In an effort to counterbalance the World Economic Forum, and to foster instead an alternative globalization that championed global causes like human rights and social justice, some globalization critics founded the World Social Forum (WSF). Since 2001 the forum has met annually, around the same time as the World Economic Forum in Davos, to discuss ways of strengthening global democracy, equality, and human rights.[7]

A parallel disagreement about the effects of globalization emerged in the political sphere. On the one hand were those who credited political globalization with fostering democratization and local empowerment. They usually pointed to international organizations such as the United Nations, which since its inception in 1945 has attempted to create and safeguard certain fundamental rules of global engagement among states and individuals. One of its first and most decisive acts was the Universal Declaration of Human Rights, which member states signed in December 1948; this declaration asserted that "the inherent dignity and . . . the equal and inalienable rights of all members of the human family is the foundation of freedom, justice, and peace in the world."[8] The United Nations and other international organizations were built on assumptions of universal laws and rights governing the interactions among people and nations, regardless of their cultural heritage and political ideology.

Even though international institutions embodying the ideals of universal rights and laws proliferated after 1945, they did not have the mandate to interfere in local governance.[9] Nonetheless, supporters voiced optimism about these institutions' ability to advance the process of political liberalization by making available to a growing number of people the tools with which to achieve both greater visibility and greater political and economic autonomy.[10] Those tools included new means of communication through radio, television, and, more recently, the Internet, as well as new opportunities for social and geographical mobility. Supporters hoped that advances in communication technology would lead to greater awareness of world affairs on the periphery as well as greater awareness in the metropole of the fate of those at the margins. They likewise hoped that mobility would allow people to escape oppressive regimes. International organizations, according to their supporters, were both a reflection of and motors for greater global connectivity.

Critics, on the other hand, blamed political globalization for the disenfranchisement of local communities. They claimed that multinational organizations such as the United Nations did not represent the interests of the world's poor nations. Instead the wealthiest nations and international economic and political conglomerates reached farther into the provinces, transforming local economic, political, and cultural power relations. The loss of political autonomy was often a direct result of the loss of economic autonomy, they argued. Thus, instead of greater self-determination and democratization, as supporters hailed, opponents of political globalization saw the opposite: a marked decrease in democracy and autonomy, as political centralization proceeded apace with economic centralization.

This chapter traces the emergence and evolution of the world's cultures since the end of the Second World War as they responded to the contradictory as well as complementary forces of homogenization and heterogenization. It does not attempt to provide a comprehensive overview of the cultures of the world since 1945. Instead it focuses on cultural transformations that transcended local and national boundaries to leave a global imprint. Cultural globalization after 1945 proceeded in three distinct phases. The first phase, from the end of the Second World War to the 1960s, was dominated by the competing cultural visions of the Soviet Union and the United States. This period saw the most heavy-handed state-sponsored attempts at achieving global cultural conformity according to the respective ideological premises of the two superpowers and their allies. However, the period also saw the most serious challenges to that conformity in the Soviet and American spheres of influence. Dissident countercultures challenged and ultimately undermined the power of state-sanctioned cultural conformity on both sides of the Iron Curtain and in the nonaligned world. The term *counterculture* as used here refers not only to the specific phenomenon in the Western industrialized world in the 1960s but more broadly to the proliferation of alternative, oppositional, dissident, anticolonial, and subaltern cultures that emerged throughout the Cold War world. The second phase, from the 1960s to the end of the Cold War, saw an increase in cultural diversification as newly independent former colonies asserted their cultural independence while residents in the metropole explored alternative cultural forms as never before. As travel, economic networks, and migration proliferated, so did the level of cultural transfer, creating greater exposure to foreign cultures and bringing more people of different cultural backgrounds into contact with one another. The third phase began with the end of the Cold War, when the movement of people, goods, and information accelerated exponentially. The political transformations brought about by the collapse of communism in Eastern Europe provide only part of the explanation. Technological changes in the communication industry, above all the inauguration of the Internet in the early 1990s, as well as an increase in global migration and travel, connected the most remote areas of the world and diversified urban areas. The pace of urbanization itself increased dramatically in the last two decades of the twentieth century, especially in Africa and Asia. The United Nations Population Fund (UNFPA) announced in 2007 that more than half of the world's citizens now lived in urban areas.[11] Newly emerging as well as old urban centers reflected the complex interplay between local idiosyncrasies and international practices, blending the local with the global and creating hybrid cultures that were both distinct and internationally recognizable.

Three central premises guide this chapter. First, although the process of cultural homogenization undoubtedly accelerated after 1945, the world at the beginning of the twenty-first century was still characterized by cultural diversity rather than uniformity. Second, a cultural history of the world, even if it covers only the relatively short span of sixty-plus years, inevitably has to paint with a broad brush. Thus, the objective of this chapter is to show the global convergences of the world's cultures rather than the persistent idiosyncrasies (of which there are, fortunately, still too many to do adequate justice here). For that reason this chapter focuses on broad transformations over the past decades. It will focus on clusters of cultural change that have expanded to global significance. Those include the cultural sources and consequences of global political developments, above all the Cold War and decolonization; the movement of goods, people, and ideas; and the cultural effects of economic globalization, particularly through the medium of consumerism. Third, increased local diversity forms an integral part of cultural globalization. Therefore this chapter will show how the continual emergence and proliferation of dissident forces and countercultures resisted pressures toward cultural conformity; how universalism and particularism remained constant cultural forces drawing the world's populations both closer together and pushing them farther apart; and finally how global homogenization and local heterogenization were mutually reinforcing processes. These took hold in remote places hitherto isolated from the global marketplace as well as in the metropolitan areas of the industrialized world.

To better understand the interplay among these three sets of forces—conformity/dissidence, universalism/particularism, and homogeneity/heterogeneity—the chapter will concentrate on particular cultural transformations in their global context since 1945. Some transformations occurred early in the Cold War period, others emerged only after the end of the Cold War, and still others are woven into the fabric of the entire period. The symbiotic relationship between homogeneity and heterogeneity, between universal and particular human experiences, and between conformism and dissidence will be a persistent theme throughout. The challenge of the twenty-first century will be to understand the centripetal and centrifugal forces of cultural change and to embed local distinctiveness within the network of cultural globalization in a meaningful way.

1. Cold War Cultures

FROM the end of World War II to the 1960s, Cold War politics dominated the international exchange of people, goods, and ideas. Both the Soviet Union and the United States, followed by their allies and client states, invested heavily in cultural diplomacy in an effort to win the political allegiance of nonaligned nations and to contain further advances—ideological as well as territorial—by their counterpart. Trying to overcome the cultural legacy left by the former colonial powers, these new nations were understandably reluctant to enter into any new international arrangement with either Cold War power. Between 1945 and 1970, sixty-four countries gained independence, some through the peaceful transition of power, others through violent uprisings.[12] Even before colonial empires crumbled after World War II, they had sought to redefine their cultural identity independent of the culture of the metropole.[13] These large-scale political transformations had a lasting impact on the evolution of cultural globalization since 1945.

The cultural aspects of the Cold War competition between the United States and the Soviet Union and the process of decolonization have to be understood in relation to the transformations generated by the Second World War. With an estimated death toll of fifty to seventy million, including six million Jews, the total human cost of the war was monumental and the level of destruction unprecedented in modern history.[14] The war also brought the world's populations into closer contact, as millions of civilians, forced from their homes by advancing armies, moved across Europe, North Africa, and Asia. On the European continent, authorities in Germany and in areas under German control deported into concentration camps Jews and other groups they deemed undesirable. In addition they pressed thousands of forced laborers into service at German factories. In Asia, the Japanese invasion of Manchuria in 1931 led to a massive exodus of Chinese nationals. In the United States, the government forced Japanese immigrants and their children from the West Coast into internment camps.[15]

Furthermore, the postwar redrawing of borders in Central Europe forced out Poles from the eastern part of their country ceded to Russia, Germans from territories ceded to Poland, and Germans from the Czech Sudetenland. Most Holocaust survivors left Europe after the war, looking for new homes in the United States, Israel, and Latin America. Eastern German refugees and expellees relocated in the central and western parts of the country, often encountering mistrust and outright hostility from local populations. Japanese nationals, in turn, were expelled from or fled Asian territories liberated from Japanese control.[16] Most of these postwar migrants tried to strike a balance between preserving their cultural heritage and adapting to the local customs of their new homes.[17] They did so within the context of renewed international tension, pitting the communist sphere of influence around the Soviet Union against the capitalist West, and demanding an unprecedented level of cultural and political conformity on both sides.

Within its own sphere of influence the Soviet Union showed little tolerance for political and cultural diversity. It surrounded itself with a cordon of buffer states in Eastern Europe and controlled their political, economic, and military affairs. It actively supported a communist coup in Czechoslovakia in 1947 and crushed uprisings and reform movements in East Germany in 1953, Hungary in 1956, and Czechoslovakia in 1968. It curtailed free speech, incarcerated dissidents, and exercised direct control over cultural institutions in Eastern Europe through an extensive domestic police apparatus.[18] The infringements on free expression led to a vibrant underground market in art and literature, some of which was smuggled to the West. Known as samizdat, the genre included world-class literature, such as Aleksandr Solzhenitsyn's *Gulag Archipelago*.[19] Outside its sphere of influence, the Soviet Union tried to project an image as the guarantor of international peace, protector of the underprivileged classes of the world, and advocate for those suffering under the yoke of colonialism and imperialism.

By contrast, the United States in the postwar period emphasized its international role as the protector of freedom and justice and as a model of modern consumer capitalism, promising prosperity to all who adhered to a democratic-capitalist ideology. At the same time, however, it supported authoritarian regimes in the name of anticommunism, particularly in Latin America. It repeatedly interfered in the affairs of other countries, both overtly and covertly, at times actively disposing of democratically elected leaders, as in Iran in 1953 and Guatemala in 1954, all in the name of national security.[20] Americans refrained from exercising direct control over foreign cultural institutions and instead actively engaged in cultural diplomacy. They also turned a blind eye to the censorship and persecution of political dissidents in countries governed by authoritarian dictatorships, as long as they were anticommunist. Even though the United States did not interfere directly and as deeply as the Soviet Union into the domestic political affairs of its client states, it aided local elites in their consolidation of power and suppression of opposition in exchange for a US-friendly policy.[21]

Decolonization complicated this bipolar rivalry, both in the political arena of the Cold War and in the cultural realm of identity formation. Intellectual and political elites in the newly independent countries of Asia and Africa often viewed the Cold War as the latest manifestation of European imperial rivalries. They were reluctant to accept the cultural offensive from either of the two opposing camps, but sometimes utilized their own leverage in this global competition. They had to weigh this newfound leverage against their efforts to re-create for themselves an independent postcolonial cultural identity that was both locally distinct and able to connect to other postcolonial identities. This negotiation between local particularism and universal postcolonialism played out in international forums throughout the 1950s and 1960s and significantly shaped the evolution of the Cold War system.

Spreading the American Dream

The United States at the end of the war was in a position to shape the future of world affairs more than any other country in the world. Unlike its European and Asian allies, its cities and industries had suffered little physical damage and its population was economically better off at the end of the war than at the beginning.[22] More importantly, Americans were willing to take on a leadership role in world affairs, in marked contrast to the aftermath of World War I, when congressional leaders and the public rejected President Woodrow Wilson's grand vision of a new world order.[23]

Prior to America's entry into the war, a small but influential segment of the American public advocated for a more activist involvement in foreign affairs.

Representative of this position was Henry Luce, owner and editor in chief of *Life* magazine. In an article ambitiously entitled "The American Century," he claimed that the United States had not only the capacity but the duty to "now become the powerhouse from which the ideals spread throughout the world and do their mysterious work of lifting the lid of mankind from the level of the beasts to what the Psalmist called a little lower than the angels."[24] He identified four areas in which America had to shape world affairs: enterprise, technical expertise, charity, and the defense of the ideals of freedom and justice. In all of these areas, he argued, the United States had to play a leading role in the second half of the century.

Luce saw America's cultural influence in the world as a foundation for its political influence. "American jazz, Hollywood movies, American slang, American machines and patented products," he determined, "are in fact the only things that every community in the world, from Zanzibar to Hamburg, recognizes in common." He concluded that "blindly, unintentionally, accidentally and really in spite of ourselves we are already a world power in all the trivial ways—in very human ways."[25] What America had left to do in the second half of the century, he surmised, was to channel its "human" influence into the political arena.

By the time Luce published his visionary blueprint, President Roosevelt had already laid the groundwork for pressing America's cultural influence into political service. In 1938 he created within the State Department the Division of Cultural Relations to coordinate and foster the spread of American culture abroad. The motive for the creation of the division emerged from a growing concern regarding Axis propaganda in Latin America and elsewhere.[26] After the United States entered the Second World War, the Roosevelt administrations established other propaganda agencies, among them the Office of Facts and Figures (OFF), later renamed the Office of War Information (OWI). In July 1942, the Voice of America (VOA), an American propaganda radio station, began broadcasting in Europe and Asia. OWI and VOA were dismantled after the war, only to be resurrected with the onset of the Cold War in 1947. A year later Congress provided funding through the Smith-Mundt Act, with the objective "to promote the better understanding of the United States among the peoples of the world and to strengthen cooperative international relations."[27] VOA resumed broadcasting into Russia a month after passage of the Act. By 1953 it had two thousand employees, a quarter of them foreign nationals who broadcast in forty-six languages. Most of its budget went toward transmitting into communist countries.[28]

In 1953 the Eisenhower administration established the United States Information Agency (USIA), which operated independently from the State Department and reported directly to the National Security Council and the president. Over the next four and a half decades, the agency funded educational and cultural missions abroad, distributed information material in foreign countries, and supported foreign information centers. The agency also took over the broadcasting of the Voice of America. Because USIA's main objective had been to combat communism in Eastern Europe and the nonaligned world, it had outlived its mission with the end of the Cold War. The Clinton administration finally dismantled it in 1999 and folded its remnants back into the State Department.

For much of the 1950s and 1960s the US government also engaged in covert funding of anticommunist organizations, most prominently the Congress for Cultural Freedom (CCF). One of the founders of the CCF was Sidney Hook, a professor of philosophy at New York University and one of the leading anticommunist intellectuals of the early Cold War. In the span of a decade Hook had made a complete intellectual turnabout from Marxist to anticommunist. Like other former leftist intellectuals, including George Orwell and Arthur Koestler, Hook had become disillusioned with the Stalinist version of repressive and authoritarian communism. After the war he watched with alarm as Soviet and communist intellectuals created international networks to advocate for world peace and against the atomic bomb. When internationalist communist and leftist peace advocates met in April 1949 at the Waldorf Astoria for the "Cultural and Scientific Conference for World Peace," he resolved to counter what he perceived as a Soviet propaganda campaign by organizing a protest meeting nearby. Out of this countermeeting emerged the CCF, which Hook, Karl Jaspers, Melvin Lasky, Tennessee Williams, Raymond Aron, Bertrand Russell, and others founded in Berlin a year later. The official mission of the CCF was to sponsor art and cultural endeavors that celebrated liberal democracy and countered Soviet efforts to portray communism as the champion of peace and civilization. But unofficially the CCF became part of America's cultural containment strategy. In the 1960s the American magazine *Ramparts* revealed that the CIA had funded the CCF since its inception, exposing the covert operations of the US government in liberal intellectual circles.[29]

For much of the Cold War, American initiatives, such as the sponsorship of the CCF, were designed not only to foster understanding of American culture and society abroad but also to loosen the ideological grip of communist-led countries on their populations. Those efforts ranged from open propaganda early in the Cold War, such as the Truman administration's resurrection of the World War II–era Psychological Warfare Division (now called the Psychological Strategy Board, or PSB) during the Korean War, to more subtle forms of cultural "infiltration" under USIA auspices.[30] Increasingly aware of the power of American popular culture, including jazz and Hollywood movies, American cultural diplomats shifted the program's emphasis to the export of music, films, and consumer goods. By the end of the decade the most popular program on VOA was Willis Conover's "Music USA," which played jazz for audiences in Eastern Europe, Africa, and Asia.[31] In addition, the USIA sponsored international jazz tours and made a special effort to recruit black musicians. Initially African Americans were reluctant to participate, because they suspected they were being used to deliver a far rosier picture of American race relations abroad than existed in reality. Ultimately, however, as the historian Penny von Eschen has shown, those who went, among them Duke Ellington and Louis Armstrong, used these tours to connect with new audiences (particularly in Africa) and to deliver independent and at times subversive messages at home and abroad. One of those subversive moments occurred in 1961 when Dave and Iola Brubeck teamed up with Louis Armstrong to write the musical *The Real Ambassadors*, which satirized the State Department tours and featured some blunt critiques of race relations within the United States.[32]

A principal weapon in the American arsenal of cultural diplomacy was consumerism. In the aftermath of World War II, the American economy shifted production from war machinery to consumer goods, unleashing an avalanche of spending among Americans who had suffered through a dozen years of Depression-era deprivations and war-era rationing. In the postwar period shopping became a patriotic duty, as policy makers linked consumer spending to national security.[33] Moreover, Americans used consumerism as a Cold War

Louis Armstrong plays the trumpet at a concert broadcast by the Voice of America, around 1965. VOA operated under the auspices of the United States Information Agency and featured popular jazz programs such as Willis Conover's *Music USA,* directed at audiences in Eastern Europe, Asia, and Africa. Armstrong's music featured prominently on those programs. (Getty Images)

propaganda tool. The July 1959 exhibition of American industrial products in Moscow, for instance, featured lavish displays of consumer products and household appliances, including a fully furnished American ranch house. The exhibition stood in glaring contrast to a Soviet exhibit in New York the previous month, which had featured primarily displays of heavy industry and space technology.[34] Americans found that kitchen gadgets, nylon stockings, Pepsi-Cola, jazz, and the latest women's fashion were far easier to sell to communist audiences than elusive promises of democracy and freedom.

Cultures of Anti-Imperialism

As Americans worked diligently toward the cultural infiltration of Eastern Europe, the Soviet Union struggled to maintain control over its sphere. After Stalin's death in 1953, the Soviet leadership under Nikita Khrushchev inaugurated a period of cautious liberalization, in which politicians and intellectuals were able to express themselves more freely. Aware of the growing gap between East and West, Khrushchev tried particularly hard to accelerate the production of consumer goods. However, these efforts were punctuated by moments of coercion and repression at home as well as military interventions abroad, particularly in East Germany in 1953, Hungary in 1956, and Czechoslovakia in 1968. The Soviet Union's violent suppression of dissident movements damaged its reputation even within the communist world.[35]

During Khrushchev's tenure, Soviet cultural propaganda focused increasingly on areas outside its direct sphere of control, above all in Southeast Asia and Africa. In its international campaigns, the Soviet Union capitalized on two essential weaknesses in the Western capitalist world: its close affiliation with colonialism and its history of racism. Many of the countries that advocated freedom and democracy in the postwar era had been at the forefront of colonization in the nineteenth century. In fact, most colonial powers, including France, Belgium, and Great Britain, were reluctant even after World War II to give up their colonial possessions. The West's rhetorical support for freedom and self-determination thus rang hollow in many parts of the world. Suspicion of Western imperialist ambitions continued to linger even after colonies gained independence, thus providing an opening for the Soviet message of anti-imperialism.

The Soviet Union was also able to point to the West's dismal record of racial discrimination. Colonialism was based on a sociocultural system of racial hierarchy, which Western powers had used to legitimize their dominance over nonwhite peoples. The Second World War exposed the gruesome consequences of a philosophy of racial hierarchies taken to its extreme. While the United States condemned in the strongest terms Hitler's policy of racial annihilation of the Jews, it supplemented its military campaign against Japan with a propaganda campaign of racial denigration.[36] In addition, America's domestic system of racial discrimination undermined propaganda messages postulating the links between democracy, freedom, and equality. Throughout the war black and white troops remained segregated within the US armed forces. Drawing on Lenin's 1917 treatise on the connection between imperialism and capitalism, the Soviet Union condemned both colonialism and imperialism, ignoring its own domination of neighboring states in Eastern Europe and Central Asia. Lenin's ideas had inspired many of the anticolonial activists of the interwar and postwar period.[37] Soviet propagandists' message of anti-imperialism coupled with the legacy of Western abuses of power in Asia and Africa sufficed to raise doubts about the American message of freedom and democracy.

The Soviet Union showed particular ingenuity in linking the postwar rhetoric of internationalism to the message of world peace. As Cold War tensions increased in the summer of 1947, the Soviets, through organizations like the Women's International Democratic Federation, the World Federation of Democratic Youth, and the World Peace Council, sponsored international gatherings designed to celebrate and foster the idea of world peace. One of the first such gatherings was a World Youth Festival in Prague in 1947, which convened under the banner "Youth United, Forward for Lasting Peace," and drew some seventeen thousand participants, mostly from Europe and the Americas.[38] Subsequent youth festivals continued with various combinations of the themes of internationalism, peace, and anti-imperialism. Most of the participants were young people from nonaligned and communist countries, but some noncommunist Western peace groups also attended.

The World Peace Council (WPC), in turn, attracted Western intellectuals with leftist political leanings, many of them communists. Emerging out of the "first World Congress of the Partisans of Peace" in Paris in 1949, the organization operated independently of the Soviet Union in name only and became increasingly partisan during the 1950s.[39] Because of its prolific utilization of the term *peace,* the Soviet Union succeeded in linking communism to the idea of peace in world opinion. For that very reason, Western political officials and pundits relentlessly condemned the World Peace Council and many other peace organizations as communist front organizations and their members as "fellow travelers." In 1951 Henry Luce called the World Peace Council "a coldly calculated master plan to sabotage the West's efforts to restore the world's free economies and to defend itself."[40] Others derided peace advocates and pacifists as subversive communists or naive victims of a communist propaganda plot.

Soviet officials significantly expanded international propaganda efforts in the non-Western world through the printed press and Soviet news services. By the 1970s the Soviet news agency Novosti regularly published abroad; these publications included weeklies and monthlies such as the English-language *New Times*, *The Soviet Weekly*, and *The Soviet Union*. In addition, propaganda officials blanketed the globe with a rich array of radio broadcasts. The area of broadcasts, the languages in which the broadcasts were read, and the number of hours of broadcasts increased steadily over the course of the 1950s and 1960s. Propagandists were determined to utilize all available means of communication to win over the nonaligned world. This included foreign translations of carefully selected ideologically acceptable Soviet literature, which rose from 28 million Russian books in eleven foreign languages in 1956 to 55.5 million books in thirty-six languages by 1970.[41] The Soviet efforts at foreign information dissemination mirrored those of the USIA in many ways, even if they were more unabashedly propagandistic than the USIA's. The Soviet Union, like the United States, recognized that the battles of the Cold War had shifted to the nonaligned world and that these battles were fought with not only military but also cultural weapons.

As Asian and African countries struggled to gain independence from the former colonial powers, they were receptive to the Soviet message of anti-imperialism, anti-racism, and peace, especially if that message was bolstered by offers of economic and financial aid. Yet as the case of Egypt's Gamal Abdel Nasser in the 1950s proved, the gains were often more elusive than real. Nasser was quite willing to turn to the Soviet Union to finance his Aswan Dam project after the United States exerted pressure on him to conform to US demands, yet he never subscribed to communist ideals. To the contrary: in 1958, two years after the Suez crisis, he actively cracked down on communists within his own country.[42]

The Soviet Union's twin rhetoric of peaceful coexistence and anti-imperialism sounded appealing to other newly independent countries as well. In India, the Soviet Union bolstered its claims of peace with offers of technical and financial aid as well as increased trade relations "free from any political or military obligations."[43] India and other former colonies remained acutely aware of the military might of the former colonial powers, and the potential for renewed economic dependency if they accepted aid from the West. Even though the Soviet Union was able to build temporary alliances with several newly independent countries, it rarely succeeded in establishing full-fledged communist regimes in any of them.

Cultures of Postcolonialism

Though decolonization shaped and in turn was shaped by the Cold War, its cultural impact can be understood only in relation to historical processes that long preceded the Cold War. The global system of colonial rule altered forever the cultural identity of people living within it. The economic-political processes of exploiting natural resources, consolidating power, and creating dependencies in the colonies were inextricably linked to the cultural processes of subjugation, assimilation, and resistance. European powers had long rationalized the economic exploitation of colonial possessions by claiming a cultural mission to civilize and raise the living standards of the nonwhite peoples of the world. Cultural conversion was never the primary objective of colonialism, but it nonetheless became an integral part of colonial politics in many parts of the world. Europeans set up schools and other educational institutions in the colonies to educate and train the indigenous elite for leadership positions in the local colonial bureaucracy. Some of these students moved to the metropole to continue their education at European universities, among them the Vietnamese leader Ho Chi Minh, the Martinique-born Algerian activist Frantz Fanon, both of whom studied in France, and Indian anticolonial leaders Jawaharlal Nehru and Mohandas Gandhi, who studied in Britain.[44] Western thought and values, not least of all the idea of nationalism, thus influenced the ways in which many indigenous leaders approached their political fight for independence. However, it would be misleading to assume that their political activism emerged only through exposure to Western thought. Rather, knowledge of those ideas allowed anticolonialists to develop effective strategies in their struggle against the overwhelming power of the metropole.

Politically, most newly formed states adopted the territorial boundaries set by the colonial powers, even though those boundaries did not necessarily overlap with cultural, tribal, or even ethnic boundaries. They also followed the European model of the nation-state in an effort to impose order and establish centralized control.[45] Indigenous elites struggled to forge independent national identities out of sometimes arbitrary conglomerates of tribes and ethnicities within the territorial confines of the new state, often clashing violently with competing ethnic groups for dominance. The French colony of Indochina, for instance, broke into three states: Laos, Cambodia, and Vietnam. After the disengagement of the French in 1954, the Geneva Accords split Vietnam into two zones, the communist-controlled Democratic Republic of Vietnam in the North and the Western-allied State of Vietnam in the South. In India, ethnic and religious divisions prompted the British to promote the partition of the Indian subcontinent into two separate states: Hindu-dominated India and Muslim-ruled Pakistan. East Pakistan, a territory disconnected from West Pakistan in the northeast corner of the Indian subcontinent, fought a bloody war for independence with support from India, becoming Bangladesh after independence from Pakistan in 1971. Likewise, tensions between Jews and Arabs in the Middle East permanently scarred the region after the creation of the state of Israel in 1948.

Ethnic conflict erupted in Rwanda and Burundi even before the two countries achieved independence from Belgium in 1962, exposing the political, social, and cultural rivalry between Hutus and Tutsis. In 1959 in Rwanda Hutus massacred Tutsis, who then sought refuge in Burundi and other neighboring countries. The monarchies in both countries were of Tutsi heritage and Tutsis enjoyed a higher social standing under Belgian rule. In fact, according to Mahmood Mamdani, the political rivalry between Hutus and Tutsis was a product of Belgian colonial rulers, who had designated Tutsis as cattle herders and given them privileged positions within the colonial regime.[46] In many colonies a centralized colonial bureaucracy had allied itself with one ethnic group or another and had suppressed cultural and ethnic tensions with an iron fist. The transfer of political control to indigenous groups therefore occasioned an internal power struggle among several competing political or ethnic groups, sometimes leading to violent clashes and even civil war.[47]

In areas with a significant white settler population, as in Algeria, Namibia, and Rhodesia, decolonization led to bitter, often violent racial confrontations. White settlers in these communities followed the model of South Africa, which had established a white-controlled centralized state in 1909 and had maintained close ties to the British mother country. Left without the military protection of the European colonial power after independence, whites often took drastic measures to preserve their privileged positions over a black indigenous majority. The white South African ruling class instituted a rigid system of apartheid and political repression in order to preserve its power vis-à-vis the increasingly well-organized

African National Congress.[48] Like South Africa, Algeria's white settler population retained close ties to the French mainland, and a significant portion of Algerians lobbied for inclusion in the French nation after World War II. Yet by the 1950s Algerian nationalists gained strength and organized the Front de Libération Nationale (FLN), a powerful and violent movement in opposition to French rule. The struggle for independence lasted from 1954 to 1962, when the French government gave up claims to the Algerian territory. Millions of European Algerians, known as the *pieds-noirs,* fled Algeria and settled in France.[49]

As former African colonies sought political independence, they struggled to redefine their cultural identity. Colonial rulers had introduced Western rituals, customs, and culture into these areas and often suppressed indigenous practices, setting up a false dichotomy between European modernity and colonial backwardness.[50] Though the anticolonial struggle had unified indigenous populations against their oppressors, the postcolonial era revealed new fissures among indigenous interest groups with competing visions of independence. Political leaders' success often depended on how well they were able to overcome this artificial juxtaposition between local tradition and cosmopolitan modernity, and how well they were able to transcend ethnic, tribal, and cultural differences among their own constituents.

In newly independent states in Africa, one way to reclaim cultural autonomy was to draw on the Afro-Caribbean *négritude* movement that had emerged in the 1930s. Its founders, among them Léopold Sédar Senghor, a Senegalese poet and essayist who in 1960 became Senegal's first president, and poet Aimé Césaire, from the Caribbean island of Martinique, provided the cultural rationale for the political drive for independence. Both drew inspiration from African and African American writers, particularly those of the Harlem Renaissance, including Langston Hughes and Richard Wright, who had celebrated black pride and black culture since the 1920s. Both also drew on historical precedents of struggle against white colonial rule, such as Toussaint Louverture, who in the 1790s had led a revolt against the French in Haiti.[51]

Each of them, however, developed their own practical application of the concept of *négritude.* For Senghor, *négritude* was "the whole complex of civilized values—cultural, economic, social, and political—which characterize the black peoples, or more precisely, the Negro-African world. . . . In other words, the

Léopold Sédar Senghor, a poet and linguist from Senegal, who became the country's first president after independence from France in 1960. Together with Aimé Césaire and Léon Damas, he developed the concept of *négritude*, which sought to reclaim Africa's cultural independence in opposition to the cultural repression of the colonial system. (Getty Images)

sense of communion, the gift of mythmaking, the gift of rhythm, such are the essential elements of négritude which you will find indelibly stamped on all the works and activities of the black man."[52] Senghor's *négritude* became a unifying force in the postwar Afro-Caribbean struggle for political independence. Césaire's idea of *négritude* relied on a less rigid notion of black cultural independence.

Like Senghor he called into question the validity of Western cultural dominance, yet he did so without denying the utility of Western texts to make the case for cultural independence. For instance, he appropriated the Shakespearian play *The Tempest* as a vehicle to assert the colonials' cultural emancipation, arguing for the adaptation of the 1610 play for black theater.[53] Césaire saw in the protagonist Prospero "a complete totalitarian," "the man of cold reason, the man of methodical conquest—in other words, a portrait of the enlightened European." His counterpart, the native Caliban, on the other hand, is "still close to his beginnings, whose link with the natural world has not yet been broken." Césaire equated Prospero, and by extension, enlightened Europe, with totalitarianism, Caliban with cultural authenticity.[54] More importantly, though, Caliban is able to traverse the world of the colonized and the colonizer. He speaks a European language, knows the Western ways, and thus has a cultural advantage over his master, Prospero. Like Caliban, Césaire turned his cultural knowledge of the West into a weapon for cultural liberation by reinscribing indigenous meaning into Western texts.

The concept of *négritude* encountered powerful critics. Frantz Fanon argued in *The Wretched of the Earth* that African and Caribbean intellectuals, including Césaire, whose call for *négritude* rested on the reinterpretation of European Enlightenment texts, were complicit in reinforcing the power of colonial culture. Rather than reviving indigenous national cultures, Fanon charged, they accepted the European label of all African and Caribbean cultures in monolithic terms. "The concept of négritude," he stated, "was the emotional if not the logical antithesis of that insult which the white man flung at humanity."[55] This insult was to lump all Africans, regardless of their national origins or cultural identity, together, to deny them the existence of an indigenous culture and to instill in them the values of Western culture. The fallacy of native intellectuals steeped in Western culture was, in Fanon's view, their attempt to prove that there was an African culture, rather than an Angolan, Kenyan, or Ghanaian culture. Fanon condemned the process as essentially an inversion of the colonial system of cultural oppression. *Négritude,* which emerged as much in the Americas as in Africa, signaled to Fanon the racialization of cultural identity.[56]

Fanon's critique revealed a crucial aspect of the process of cultural change and the idea of cultural identity. Contact with foreign cultures, whether by force or by choice, invariably altered the native population's own cultural matrix. It would have been a futile undertaking for native intellectuals to reverse the process of cultural transformation and to erase the impact of colonial domination. Even advocates of *négritude* did not propose a complete reversal. Instead they sought to integrate the Western colonial cultural canon in a way that met their own indigenous political and cultural needs. By the early 1990s, cultural anthropologists and sociologists labeled this process cultural hybridization or creolization.[57]

Though there existed no Asian counterpart to the African *négritude* movement, colonial engagement in Asia created in Europe a particular notion of Asia as the "oriental" other. In his 1978 book *Orientalism,* the Palestinian-American literary theorist Edward Said argued that notions of inferiority of Middle Eastern colonial subjects were deeply ingrained in the Western world's cultural and literary texts. He was interested primarily in showing orientalism as fundamentally a Western concept rather than exploring the ways in which ideas of orientalism might have become deeply embedded in the postcolonial identities of non-Western peoples.[58] Said's critique of orientalism sparked a new wave of scholarship, exploring the influence of Western notions of the East in popular culture and political relations, interrogating ethnic and national identity formation, and analyzing the ideological foundations of the Orient/Occident dichotomy.[59] Embraced by many, his writings also drew criticism from some academic scholars, who challenged his definition of orientalism, questioned the existence of a single orientalism, or accused him of polemicizing an academic problem.[60]

Said continued to develop his interpretation of the cultural consequences of imperialism, arguing in his later work that empire had created not just cultural subjugation but integration, hybridization, and heterogenization. This reading of the mutual reshaping of imperial and colonial cultures allowed him to claim writers like William Shakespeare for the decolonizing project as Césaire had done before him. Shakespeare's plays would thus lose their particular European identity and become global repertoires of human experience. Drawing on Césaire's version of *The Tempest*, Said laid out alternative readings of the play's main colonial characters Caliban, the rebellious slave, and Ariel, the assimilated and accommodationist spirit (in Shakespeare's version) turned mulatto (in Césaire's version). According to Said, the play offered answers to a central question for independence activists: "How does a culture seeking to become independent of imperialism imagine its own past?" The Ariel-Caliban dichotomy in *The Tempest* offered three distinct options, he suggested. The first was to take Ariel as the model and to accept one's subservient status as long as the colonialist rules and afterward resume the native self. The second option was to follow Caliban's example, which was to integrate the "Mongrel past" into an independent future. The third option was to view Caliban as fighting to shed the past oppression and return to a "precolonial" self. Said identified this last option as the radical nationalism that produced the ideology of *négritude*. Like Fanon, he expressed deep reservations about this form of colonial emancipation, because it could easily deteriorate into a simple form of "chauvinism and xenophobia" that mirrored the European colonial rationale for colonization in the first place.[61]

By the mid-1960s, leaders in many newly independent nations disagreed over whether there existed a common African or Asian identity and what the nature of that identity might be. Language, religion, and tribal customs significantly impeded the process of cultural unification. In addition, at least in Africa, the colonial legacy divided the former colonies into Francophone and Anglophone countries. Many prominent writers and poets expressed their search for a common African identity not in their native language but in the language of their former oppressors, among them Senghor, who wrote in French, and the Nigerian writer Chinua Achebe, who wrote in English.[62] Achebe, author of the internationally acclaimed novel *Things Fall Apart*, defended his choice by pointing to the importance of communicating across language barriers with other victims of colonization and with the colonizers.[63] But he also acknowledged that particular local experiences could not be expressed adequately in the English language and advocated extending the limits of English to accommodate those African ideas and experiences.[64]

These debates exemplified not only the scars left by more than a century of colonial domination but also the diversity of postcolonial experiences. Africans more than Asians had to renegotiate their identity within an increasingly heterogeneous environment where the recovery of a lost tribal culture held both great promise but also the threat of continuous conflict and war, which might create living conditions no better and sometimes worse than those experienced under colonialism. Cultural creolization was as much part of the process of decolonization as were ethnic strife, violence, and war.

The cultural debates accompanying the process of decolonization formed part of a broader challenge to the rigid structures of the Cold War cultural consensus in East and West and exposed the cultural diversity that had been suppressed by the Cold War rivalry. Others included the increasing movement of people and goods, the emergence of an international protest culture, and an international language of rights that transcended the East–West divide. Those challenges led to broad cultural transformations over the course of the 1960s, permanently changing the political, economic, and cultural relations among peoples and nations. Even though the Cold War heated up again in the late 1970s with the Soviet invasion of Afghanistan, the two superpowers no longer dictated the cultural terms of their exchange. These transformations represented, not so much a linear development from cultural conformity to cultural diversity, as a renegotiation of the relationship between the two.

2. People and Goods on the Move

THE transnational movement of people and goods accelerated after World War II, as national boundaries shifted, colonies gained independence, and means of transportation improved. Migrants, including refugees, tourists, and guest workers, played key roles in the global process of cultural heterogenization. As they moved, they brought with them cultural, religious, and material traditions that altered the cultural landscape of their new environment. They established restaurants, houses of worship, and cultural centers, which initially served the immigrant population, yet over time transformed neighborhoods into multiethnic patchworks of cultural diversity.[65] Wherever they went, these migrants created both greater tolerance of cultural difference and new fissures, bringing cultural conflict into every part of the world. As people moved, so did goods, creating a global marketplace of consumption. The material aspects of this global migration have often been associated with the rise of the multinational corporations, and thus the charge of cultural homogenization. But although there is some evidence to support this charge, not the least of which is the rapid proliferation of global brands, other evidence points toward greater material diversity within a single locale, such as the proliferation of ethnic restaurants in major urban centers. As the transnational movement of people and goods accelerated, so did the process of cultural hybridization, making places at once more familiar and more alien.

Migrants

The patterns of migration in the second half of the twentieth century were more diverse and multidirectional than before. North America remained a primary destination for people from all parts of the world, though the postwar level of immigration was never as high as the level at the turn of the twentieth century, when the immigration rate to the United States had been over 11 immigrants per thousand US population. It fell to 0.4 immigrants per thousand in the 1940s and reached its postwar peak of about 4 per thousand in the 1990s.[66] The ethnic composition of migrants changed dramatically as well. Most of the immigrants to the United States in the earlier wave had come from Europe; in the second half of the twentieth century they came primarily from Latin America, Africa, and Asia. The reasons for migration, however, remained the same: economic hardship, population increase, and violence.

Decolonization accounted for part of world migration since World War II. Sometimes called reverse colonization, the influx of former colonial subjects diversified the cities of the industrialized world as Africans and Asians migrated to England, France, Belgium, and the Netherlands; Filipinos moved to North America, the Middle East, and Japan; and Latin Americans, Asians, and Africans migrated to the United States and Canada. To be sure, the colonial world had intruded upon the metropole ever since the time of contact, largely through the import of raw materials, artisan goods, and foreign foods, including spices, grains, coffee, and tea.[67] As colonial peoples followed their products, they changed not only the metropole's ethnic composition but its cultures as well.

Decolonization generated three successive waves of migration. The first was the return of white settlers and administrators to the homeland. These returnees, some of whom had intermarried with the indigenous population, provided the incentive for a second wave of migrants: indigenous relatives and members of the colonial elites who had lost their positions of power and privilege in the newly formed independent state. A third wave of migration was internal as indigenous populations moved from rural to urban areas, from impoverished to prosperous land, from regions with low demand for labor to those with high demand, within or across national boundaries. An example of the latter was the large-scale seasonal migration within Africa of almost a million laborers to South Africa from areas to the north.[68]

Europe's migration patterns shifted considerably as well in the postwar period, beginning with the massive movement of people displaced by war and persecution. Between 1965 and 2000, the foreign-born population in Western Europe rose from 2.2 percent to 10.3 percent. Western Europe thus shifted from being a point of departure (mostly to the Americas) to becoming a destination for immigrants both from other European countries as well as from Asia and Africa.

Immigration to countries within the European Union reached an all-time high—over one million annually—between 1989 and 1993, largely as a result of the breakup of the Soviet Union. It had been around 200,000 for much of the 1980s and leveled off to a little over 600,000 annually after 1993.[69]

Intra-European migration shifted from political migration, during and immediately after World War II as populations were expelled from or fled the newly emerging socialist regimes, to economic migration, as labor shortages in Northern and Western Europe in the 1950s and 1960s drew workers from Southern Europe. For instance, between 1955 and 1968 Germany signed agreements with Italy, Spain, Greece, Portugal, Turkey, Tunisia, Morocco, and Yugoslavia to contract more than 2.5 million people for temporary work in Germany. By the time the government terminated the program in 1973, many of those workers had brought their families and established permanent homes within the major industrial cities, especially in the Ruhr area, home of Germany's coal and steel industry. Their children and grandchildren grew up in a cultural environment that was neither fully integrated into German culture nor closely tied to their parents' homeland. As Germany's economy went into recession in the 1970s and 1980s, xenophobia increased and violence escalated against foreigners, directed at both longtime immigrants from Southern Europe and more recent immigrants from Africa and Asia. Rising unemployment after Germany's unification led to fierce debates over immigration policy, integration of foreigners into German society, and Germany's own cultural identity.

The integration of a North African, largely Muslim population into French society after the end of the French-Algerian war proved difficult as well. Most immigrants lived in segregated neighborhoods on the outskirts of major cities and faced poor economic prospects and other forms of discrimination. Great Britain absorbed immigrants from Europe and the Commonwealth nations until the Commonwealth Immigrants Act of 1962 severely restricted the entry of nationals from the former colonies. The Act, which set an annual quota for immigration of British Commonwealth Asians of a mere fifteen hundred, was aimed primarily at reducing the influx of citizens from Asia and Africa, even though they made up a far smaller percentage of Britain's immigrant population than European and Caucasian immigrants from white-dominated commonwealth countries, such as Australia, New Zealand, and Canada.[70]

Latin America also saw a shift in migration patterns: once a destination for Europeans and Asians, it became a region of emigrants in the postwar period. Between 1960 and 1980, 1.8 million people left the region, most of them for the United States and Canada. Mexicans and Caribbean Islanders in particular took advantage of a 1965 liberalization of US immigration laws to move north. Most of them worked seasonally for the large fruit and vegetable conglomerates in California or as domestic workers in the urban areas along the East and West Coasts.[71] New ethnic neighborhoods emerged in all major North American cities. A large Cuban community settled in Florida after Fidel Castro's successful 1959 revolution. Over the next few decades the Cuban-American population not only transformed local Floridian culture, but also exercised considerable political influence in Washington, largely fueled by the anticommunist climate of the Cold War.[72]

In the Middle East, the oil boom attracted a large foreign labor force, primarily from Asia and Africa. Most of these workers were male and single, and they stayed for short periods of time only. Their social and familial ties remained in their homelands, and their wages, too, flowed mostly into the local economies of their home communities.[73] In the United Arab Emirates alone, the foreign population outnumbered the native population by a margin of nine to one in the 1990s.[74] The overwhelming presence of foreigners was both cause and consequence of the commercial boom in the country. At the same time it gave rise to concerns among Emirati political and intellectual leaders about their ability to preserve their Bedouin heritage.[75] As they sent their children to elite schools and colleges in Great Britain and North America, they found it even harder to preserve traditional customs.

Temporary migration was not a new phenomenon of the postwar period. At the turn of the twentieth century, about 30 percent of US immigrants returned to their homeland. Indeed, millions of workers in the early twentieth century migrated seasonally between harvesting work in southern Europe or Latin America and factory work in Northern Europe or the United States.[76] By the end of the twentieth century, migration, rather than a once-in-a-lifetime event with a remote possibility of a once-in-a-lifetime return, became for a sizable proportion of the world's population a lifelong process. Some of these transnational commuters belonged to a highly educated and fairly wealthy class of professionals who could afford to maintain more than one household on more than one continent, whose work was often in international business, and whose jobs demanded a high level of mobility.[77] Most had little opportunity and equally little desire to interact with the native-born population. They often preserved their national traditions through diasporic associations and set up international schools for their children.[78] Particularly Western business elites in the Middle East, Latin America, Asia, and Africa built transnational enclaves, provided housing, schooling, shopping, and other recreational amenities, which were financially out of reach for the indigenous population. They thus created a new social class of expatriates who felt more at ease with other business globetrotters than with the local communities of their host countries.

Less wealthy immigrants also began to take return trips to their homeland as air travel became more affordable. In addition, new developments in media and electronic communications allowed expatriates to stay personally and culturally connected to their homeland. By the late 1990s, for instance, Indian immigrants in New York and London watched Indian television via satellite and stayed in touch with friends and family on a regular basis. Brazilians, too, as Maxine S. Margolis noted, saw their time in New York as a sojourn rather than permanent immigration. They had become, in her words, "transnational migrants who sustain familial, cultural, and economic ties that ignore international borders and span the home and the host societies."[79] Telephone communication and the Internet became both more widespread and cheaper, even in the global South. Spatial distance no longer entailed cultural distance for late twentieth-century migrants. Their sense of belonging to a particular cultural community had become deterritorialized.[80] Diasporic groups in many parts of the world no longer faced the same pressures as their nineteenth-century predecessors to assimilate into a putatively homogeneous national culture. They often found cultural diversity if they moved to major urban areas, allowing them a choice between finding their particular cultural niche and liberating themselves from the cultural constraints of their homelands. For some, at least, cultural identity became as much a matter of choice as one of inheritance or locality.

Internal migration from rural to urban areas affected cultural diversity as well. Throughout the twentieth century the world population became increasingly urban, finally tipping the balance in favor of urbanites in 2008, even though, according to the 2005 *United Nations Demographic Yearbook,* definitions of "urban" varied greatly by country, making it a somewhat imprecise milestone.[81] Some countries measured population density, others the level of administrative government, and still others the total agglomeration of inhabitants in a particular locality.[82] Nonetheless, the figures show a clear and constant trend toward urbanization. In 1950 the UN identified only two cities with populations above ten million, New York and Tokyo. By 2005 there were twenty such cities, and only seven of them were in the industrialized world.[83] Most of the recent growth in urban populations occurred in Asia, Africa, and Latin America. According to a 2001 UN population report, the two cities with the largest growth rate between 1950 and 1975 were Mexico City, and São Paulo, Brazil. Their populations grew fourfold in this period, from 2.9 million and 2.6 million, respectively, to over 10 million by 1975. The highest average annual growth rate in that period—7.6 percent—occurred in Seoul, South Korea. Seoul grew from fewer than 1 million inhabitants in 1950 to 6.8 million in 1975. In the last quarter of the twentieth century, Riyadh and Jeddah in Saudi Arabia, Dhaka in Bangladesh, Lagos in Nigeria, and Guatemala City experienced average annual growth rates of over 6 percent.

Urban migration grew in tandem with population growth overall. Since 1950, Asia and Africa experienced higher growth rates than Europe and North America. Urban areas promised better health care and better education for their citizens. However, when cities grew rapidly in a short period of time, public sanitation, housing, and social services could not keep pace with the dramatic influx of people. For instance, the annual growth rate of Lagos, Nigeria's capital—over 14 percent in the 1970s and 1980s—was so large that municipal services could not keep up. There were regular shortfalls in the supply of electricity, water, and sanitation, as well as a lack of basic social services, including schools.[84] More than half of Mumbai's population, which grew from three million in 1950 to over sixteen million in 2000, lived in slums at the turn of the twenty-first century. The city was a model in contrasts. While the urban center provided about 20 percent of India's industrial output and showcased modern, cosmopolitan high-rise buildings, the majority of Mumbai's population lived in preindustrial, low-grade dwellings. While the highly educated professional minority of the city was engaged in the production of international capital as well as the production for India's cultural and movie industry, the urban poor on the city's geographic and social fringes sank deeper into poverty, making Mumbai a showcase for the polarizing consequences of globalization.[85] The stark divisions between wealth and poverty were no longer primarily visible along the North–South spectrum, but manifested themselves within the narrow geographic confines of single cities.

Economics accounted for part of the total migration in the second half of the twentieth century. War, natural disaster, and political and ethnic persecution accounted for the rest. World War II dislocated millions throughout Europe, via the deportation and killing of millions of Jews, gypsies, political dissidents, and the disabled across Germany and German-occupied territory; the importation of forced laborers from Eastern and Southern Europe to Germany and from Southeast Asia to Japan; and the expulsion of millions of citizens in Eastern and Central Europe as national boundaries were redrawn in the aftermath of the war. In addition, millions of people tried to leave war-ravaged Europe during and after the war in search of better living conditions and greater political freedoms.

Among those fleeing Europe were millions of Jews who managed to escape before their deportation or had survived the concentration camps. Their primary destinations were the United States and Palestine.[86] The influx of large numbers of Jewish refugees into Palestine—the immigrant population in Israel stood at 26 percent in 1949—dramatically shifted the demographics of the region and produced another refugee crisis, that of Arab Palestinians. Since the British Balfour Declaration of 1917, Jewish Zionists had sought to create a Jewish state in the British colony. The Declaration stated that the British government was in favor of creating a homeland for the Jewish people in Palestine, provided that the rights of the non-Jewish communities within Palestine were preserved.[87] After the British ended their mandate in Palestine in 1947, the United Nations stepped in to divide the area into separate Jewish and Arab states. The proclamation of the State of Israel in May 1948 immediately prompted the first of several Arab-Israeli wars, which led to the expansion of Israeli territory and the flight of roughly 330,000 Arabs to neighboring countries.[88] Many Palestinian refugees settled in camps that became hotbeds of political radicalism for decades to come. Israel, meanwhile, maintained a high level of immigration. In 1972 the vast majority of Israel's population, 91.5 percent, had been born abroad. The source

Palestinian refugees in Jordan, June 25, 1949. The proclamation of the State of Israel in May 1948 prompted the first of several Arab-Israeli wars, which led to the expansion of Israeli territory and the flight of roughly 726,000 Arabs to neighboring countries, including Jordan. Many Palestinian refugees settled in camps that became hotbeds of political radicalism for decades to come. (Getty Images)

of immigration to Israel shifted from Europe in the immediate aftermath of the Holocaust to Asia and Africa in the 1960s and Russia in the 1990s.[89] The Israeli-Palestinian conflict provided a stark reminder that closer proximity among members of different, cultural, ethnic, and religious groups did not automatically lead to greater understanding, but could also lead to greater tension, open hostility, and violence.

Africa also became the site of involuntary migrations as civil wars ravaged newly independent African nations, forcing people to seek shelter and food in temporary camps. Refugee crises occurred repeatedly after independence in places such as Rwanda, Burundi, Ethiopia, Sudan, the Congo, and Angola.[90] Located in the poorest regions of the world, these displacements often resulted in large-scale famines: Ethiopia experienced repeated famines from the 1960s to the 1980s, Nigeria (Biafra) in 1968–1970, and the Sudan intermittently since the 1980s.[91]

Some of those refugees sought asylum in Northern Europe and North America, unleashing spirited debates in those countries about the intersection of human rights mandates and immigration regulations. Countries with historically high immigration rates, such as the United States, Canada, and Australia, seemed less unsettled by the influx of new immigrants and asylum seekers than those with more homogeneous populations, among them Western and Northern Europe. In all of these countries, immigration remained a subject of continuous political debate, particularly when the immigrants came from the global South. The measure of success of integration often depended on the political will of the governing parties in each country.

Sojourners

While economic migrants and refugees often made a permanent home in an alien environment, travel for leisure, business, or education provided additional opportunities for cultural exchange, albeit of a rather fleeting nature. International travel rose in tandem with an increasingly prosperous and globalized economy after World War II. Members of national elites had traveled for leisure since the nineteenth century. In the second half of the twentieth century, international travel increased manifold, thanks to improved modes of transportation and affordability. This transformation resulted in a higher proportion of the world's population gaining greater than ever exposure to foreign peoples, languages, customs, and foods. Only recently have anthropologists, sociologists, and historians begun to explore in more depth the cultural impact of global tourism on travelers and indigenous cultures.[92]

In the early decades after World War II, American soldiers, tourists, and business managers dominated international travel. Wartime military deployment in Europe, North Africa, and Asia afforded most soldiers their first opportunity to explore foreign places.[93] At the end of the war the American military occupied Germany, Austria, and Japan and established permanent military bases in the Pacific, Asia, and Europe. The experience of overseas deployment altered their attitudes toward foreign cultures, but also brought America closer to the people living in the vicinity of the bases. GIs became major exporters of American popular culture.[94] They became Europe's first tourists during and immediately after World War II. As soldiers moved across France in the spring and summer of 1944, their curiosity about all things French often accompanied and at times interfered with their duties as combat soldiers. One soldier remarked that as he arrived in Normandy, his "thoughts were not so much of liberating, fighting, or helping to chase out the Germans as the thought of stepping foot upon the land of France, of saying one French word to someone French in France."[95] When combat duties transitioned into occupation duties in Europe and Asia in the aftermath of the war, soldiers increasingly took time to explore the region as regular tourists.

Mass tourism became an integral part of the postwar global economic recovery. As American, and later European and Asian, international travel increased, so did tourist spending on consumer goods, hotels, and transportation. International travel became so extensive that the US government created a travel branch under the auspices of the Marshall Plan in 1948. Known as the Travel Development Section (TDS), the branch set up shop in Paris with an initial staff of three, but soon expanded to seventeen with a representative in every Marshall Plan country in Europe. The task of the TDS was to facilitate international travel in Europe and encourage the local travel industry to improve standards. In addition, it developed a program to facilitate American investment in Europe's travel industry. American policy makers further tried to encourage travel and spending abroad by raising the duty-free import level from $100 to $500.[96] One of the first initiatives on a global scale was the United Nations' establishment of the International Union of Official Travel Organizations (IUOTO) in The Hague in 1947. The organization sought to ease travel restrictions and standardize passport and visa requirements across the world. Prompted by the IUOTO, the United Nations declared 1967 International Tourist Year (ITY), using the slogan "Tourism, Passport to Peace." The organization's mission lay at the intersection of promoting international understanding through easing the flow of people across national boundaries and promoting economic development and modernization through the increase in global consumption.[97]

As international travel became more affordable and Western European and Asian countries recovered from the wartime ravages, the social and ethnic profile of tourism changed. By the 1970s, international travel was no longer the exclusive domain of the upper classes. It brought a broader cross section of the world's population into contact with one another. According to the United Nations World Tourism Organization (UNWTO), established in 1974, international travel rose from 25 million in 1950 to 806 million in 2005. Global income generated through international travel stood at an estimated $680 billion in 2005, reflecting an average annual increase of 11.2 percent since 1950. As the number of travelers increased, so did their destinations. While in the early postwar period fifteen top destinations, most of them in Europe and North America, made up 88 percent of all travel, their share fell to 75 percent by 1970 and to 57 percent in 2005. Many of the new travel destinations were in Africa and Southeast Asia, indicating the global reach of international tourism.[98]

The tourism industry, according to Marc Augé, also created "non-places," places of transit exclusively designed for and frequented by tourists. These airport terminals, hotel lobbies, highway service stations, and so on were devoid of local cultural significance but nonetheless functioned as important cultural sites, signifying the culture of tourism rather than the tourists' experience of culture. They were the essential localities of cultural and geographic transiency, and as such were embodiments of cultural change as well as cultural diversity. According to Augé, travelers often reported a sense of being in a non-space even as they entered their local airports. In line at an airline counter, they already had mentally left their place of origin. The non-spaces of the traveling world were strangely unmoored from their actual physical locale. The local population rarely frequented these places. By the same token, those who moved through them rarely experienced the culture of the local environment.[99]

The cultural impact of the rise in international tourism is harder to measure than its economic impact. Although the United Nations and other international organizations promoted tourism as a path toward greater understanding and peace, tourism created new sources of friction as differences in standards of living and social customs among various cultures became visible. By the early 1960s, American government officials became increasingly concerned that some American tourists' rowdy behavior and conspicuous display of wealth abroad would damage America's image in the world. A 1960 *Parade* magazine article on tourism warned American readers: "Don't be an Ugly American."[100] The article's author, Frances Knight, was the director of the US Passport Office, and thus familiar with complaints from foreign law enforcement agencies about American tourists' delinquent behavior. Knight's rendering of the "Ugly American" as a spoiled and insensitive tourist inverted the meaning first put forward in the 1958 novel with the same title by Eugene Burdick and William J. Lederer. They portrayed the ugly American, a less-than-handsome American engineer named Homer Atkins, as the embodiment of the American spirit of grassroots entrepreneurship and benevolence. Burdick and Lederer's Ugly American helped the local population in a fictional Southeast Asian nation more effectively than any of the foreign service officials in the sheltered consulates of the capital.[101] Soon, however, Knight's version of the ugly American came to dominate the global public image: an image of Americans as loud, overprivileged, and demanding.

The rising tide of international tourism proved a mixed blessing for popular destinations. Local communities greatly benefited from the influx of foreign currency and the boost to their infrastructure, but they often chafed under the massive buildup of expensive hotels, restaurants, bars, and tourist attractions, most of which were beyond the means of local residents. In addition, many feared that these transformations undermined indigenous cultures. The problem became more prevalent in the 1970s when middle- and upper-middle-class Europeans and Asians joined Americans in their passion for travel, further internationalizing the world's prime resorts but also adding new sources of friction with local populations. In response, some communities began to regulate the expansion of the tourism business. Others were unable to counter the power of international hoteliers and travel agents. They stood by as their local communities turned into "non-places," tourist destinations without a cultural identity.

International travel was closely tied to international politics as well. The outbreak of domestic unrest or armed conflict in any region effectively shut down an area's tourist industry. In addition, for much of the Cold War, leisure travel between East and West was subject to tight control. Eastern Europeans who wanted to travel to the West were often in a catch-22. If their own country was willing to issue an exit visa, Western customs officials usually denied them an entry visa on the rationale that if their home country was willing to let them go, they must be at minimum ardent communists and possibly spies. Western Europeans and Americans also restricted their own citizens' travel into the Soviet Bloc, particularly those with known ties to the Communist Party. In the 1950s the United States confiscated the passports of leading communists and leftists, among them

Paul Robeson, W. E. B. Du Bois, the writer Albert E. Kahn, and Communist Party functionaries.[102] In 1958 the US Supreme Court ruled against the practice and reinstated the right of American citizens, communist and noncommunist, to travel abroad.[103] As Cold War tensions declined in the era of détente in the 1970s, both sides eased travel restrictions across the East–West divide.

Robeson and others on the political left, of course, were not tourists in search of places of leisure, but part of an increasingly active cohort of international political travelers. Their travel motives were twofold: to explore the political and social conditions in countries other than their own, and to transmit information abroad about social and political conditions in the United States. While the American government prevented leftists such as Robeson and Du Bois from engaging in this mission for much of the 1950s, it encouraged and promoted others who could transmit a benevolent image of the United States. In fact, the US government actively recruited artists, entertainers, and intellectuals to deliver America's message of freedom and democracy abroad. Bob Hope and the Harlem Globetrotters performed in front of mass audiences in the Soviet Union in 1959. Dizzy Gillespie, Louis Armstrong, Benny Goodman, and others played jazz in Africa, Asia, and Eastern Europe in the late 1950s and 1960s. US policy makers pursued two related objectives with these international tours. First, they sought to capitalize on the growing international popularity of American mass culture, and second, by including African American entertainers they sought to counter the damaging image of the United States as a place of racial discrimination. Seeing itself in a fierce competition with the Soviet Union for the allegiance of nonwhite peoples in Africa and Asia, the United States was acutely aware of its own shortcomings in advancing racial equality and tried to overcome those by sending its black artists on tours abroad.[104]

Those who participated in these goodwill tours often gained a new and sometimes more critical perspective on American foreign policy. Among them were young Americans who since the early 1960s had joined the Peace Corps. Inspired by Kennedy's message about public service, these young idealists—around seventy thousand of them in the first decade since the inception of the Peace Corps in 1961—embarked on two-year sojourns into areas the US government deemed threatened by communist agitation.[105] When they returned, they brought with them a new appreciation for the hardships in underdeveloped areas, and sometimes a new appreciation for leftist and egalitarian political values.[106] Within the charged atmosphere of 1960s student protests, many Peace Corps volunteers became vocal advocates for the rights of the countries in which they had served.

Students and academics made up another group of transnational sojourners. Since the end of World War II the number of official exchange programs grew exponentially, as individuals and governments sought better educational opportunities for their youth abroad. In the 1950s the United States became a major destination for foreign students and academics, because the top US universities, many of them private, invested heavily in research and development. This was a remarkable reversal—only a few decades earlier the flow of students and academics had gone the other way, when well-heeled American students flocked to prestigious European universities for advanced academic training.[107]

The US government fostered educational exchange as another weapon in the arsenal of the cultural Cold War battles, both to attract brain power from abroad and to influence the future elites of foreign countries. A cultural agreement reached between the United States and the Soviet Union in 1958 included a provision for the exchange of students between the two nations. However, during the first year of the agreement only twenty students from the Soviet Union and the United States participated in the exchange, well short of American expectations. The Soviets remained cautious about the program, fearing possible recruitment of their own students for US intelligence. Even though Eisenhower dismissed their suspicions as unfounded, he must have been aware that the CIA at that very moment was infiltrating the National Students' Association, a strong lobbyist for increased US-Soviet student exchange. Despite well-founded Soviet concerns, the exchange program expanded to over fifteen hundred students from either side within the next two years.[108]

Soviets and Eastern Europeans also made an effort to recruit students from nonaligned countries in Africa and Asia. The education of the political and social elites at the major schools and universities of the industrialized world had been an integral part of colonial regimes, which is why decolonization left many citizens in the newly independent states suspicious of the educational mission in those countries. Eastern Europe and the Soviet Union thus offered a welcome alternative to the former centers of imperial power.[109] However, funding for higher education in the Soviet Bloc lagged far behind the West, making it harder to recruit highly qualified students from the former colonies. The Soviet Union had to compete with the highly successful American Fulbright program, which brought thousands of students, academics, and professionals to the United States and sent thousands of American students and academics abroad. Established in 1946 through the efforts of Senator J. William Fulbright, Democratic senator from Arkansas, the program grew into a major government-funded organization with exchange programs in 144 countries. Throughout the Cold War, however, the Fulbright exchange program never transcended the Iron Curtain into Eastern Europe and the Soviet Union.[110]

The global movement of people since World War II both exposed a great number of them to foreign cultures and in the process altered their understanding of their own cultural identity in relation to others. Cultural traditionalists often tried to stem the tide of cultural hybridization through demands for restrictions on immigration as well as more stringent requirements for the assimilation of outsiders into the dominant culture of the homeland. Others, particularly those who themselves had traveled to foreign places, were more likely to accept and welcome the increase in cultural diversity around the world as a permanent and irreversible fixture of the modern world. In fact, by the end of the twentieth century the ability to live, work, and communicate in more than one cultural orbit became an important asset for personal advancement. International studies, business, and language programs proliferated in all major universities, accelerating the pace of economic and cultural globalization. Those very changes further illustrated globalization's simultaneous drive toward homogenization and heterogenization.

Global Consumption

Ethnic diversity in urban areas manifested itself in material ways through the accelerated flow of goods across national boundaries after 1945. In fact, the emergence of a global marketplace for consumer goods might be globalization's most visible feature. The global marketplace reached a symbolic pinnacle on November 4, 2008, when the residents of Dubai celebrated the opening of what was then hailed as the world's largest indoor mall. The mall boasted a record number of retail spaces (twelve hundred, of which only six hundred were occupied at the time of the opening), a record number of square feet (12 million), an indoor aquarium, a skating rink, a children's entertainment center, movie theaters, as well as restaurant and hotel facilities. The developers' promotional video dubbed the mall as the "new center of the earth."[111] Its opening came at a time when a global economic downturn and the precipitous drop in oil prices after an all-time high seriously jeopardized the financial viability of such grand-scale projects. Its location in the Middle East served as a manifestation of the shifting center of gravity of global capitalism, away from the old industrial powers of Europe and North America toward new areas of economic power.

The mall differed in scale but not in content from countless other retail malls in urban areas all over the world. The convergence of retailers from Europe, North America, and East Asia in a single space symbolized the globalization of consumption as well as the centrality of consumption in the evolution of a global culture. The mall represented not quite the world in a nutshell but the world on the equivalent of fifty soccer fields. The merchandise in the mall was as global as its clientele, because the majority of the mall's visitors were not native Emiratis. The array of stores within the mall—every major international retailer had moved in or reserved space—mirrored the array of international residents and tourists in Dubai. The mall epitomized the expansion of places of consumption beyond the industrialized North and West.[112] More significantly it seemed to confirm the worst fears of globalization's opponents, who had predicted that the overwhelming economic power of a generic Western consumer culture would crush indigenous cultures on the periphery.

Critics associate the rise of a global consumer culture with the rise of the United States to world hegemony and thus with the global spread of American consumer goods. But as the historian Kristin Hoganson has noted, the process of global consumption began before America's ascent to world power, at a time when the United States consumed more foreign products than it produced for foreign markets.[113] Americans had become avid consumers of imported goods already in the eighteenth century—so much so that some items, such as tea, became rallying points for political independence from Britain.[114]

Still earlier, Euro-Asian trade routes created a lively exchange of goods between the two worlds. Spices and tea brought from India and China transformed

European cooking and drinking. Coffee, a staple of Western society by the twentieth century, originated in Ethiopia and made its way through Turkey in the sixteenth century to Southern and Central Europe in the seventeenth century.[115] Travelers along the Silk Road, which stretched between Southeast Asia and the Mediterranean, transported fabrics, food, plants, earthenware, production techniques, and ideas. This exchange of goods and ideas established the patterns of cultural and material hybridization over three thousand years ago.[116] Consumption and the cultural transformations associated with it long preceded the rise of capitalism. Nonetheless, international trade expanded rapidly into Africa and the Americas during the age of exploration, and particularly since the emergence of mercantilism and capitalism.

The import of foreign goods into American households, which continued and even increased over time, has been overshadowed by the more dramatic rise in the export of American consumer goods worldwide in the twentieth century.[117] Selling America to the world became an integral part of US foreign policy by the end of World War II. Consuming America turned into a major pursuit in Western Europe in the early postwar period and across the globe by the 1970s. Yet while it is relatively easy to trace the spread of Coca-Cola or McDonald's branches abroad or to quantify the international proliferation of American movies and Starbucks coffeehouses, it has been far more difficult to determine the cultural and political impact of this proliferation.

Global consumption, more than any other development since 1945, has invited the charge of homogenization.[118] The sociologist Douglas Goodman postulated in 2007 that "to the extent that there is a global culture it will be a consumer culture."[119] If Goodman's premise is correct, then America as the leading producer and exporter of consumer goods in the world became the template for global culture. However, goods and cultural products such as music and film do not carry a fixed, normative meaning that is closely tied to their place of origin. Eating a McDonald's hamburger carries different cultural meaning for Taiwanese, Dutch, and American consumers. Sociologists, anthropologists, and cultural historians have only recently begun to explore in more depth the multiple meanings of objects in different cultural contexts, even though the global dissemination of goods began a long time ago.[120]

The German philosopher Walter Benjamin was one of the first scholars to ask about an object's relation to time and space. In a 1936 essay about the effects of mass production on the cultural meaning of art, he argued that through the new techniques of mechanical reproduction, art was losing its "aura," which he identified as its "presence in time and space, its unique existence at the place it happens to be." Through the process of mechanical reproduction, a work of art could be transferred in time and place and thus become "reactivated" in a vastly different context. This transfer, Benjamin concluded, represented a "tremendous shattering of tradition," commodifying but at the same time democratizing art by making it accessible to a broader audience.[121] From this critical perspective, the transfer of products of popular culture, especially film, from their place of original production in the United States to places of consumption anywhere in the world, stripped them of their "authenticity," their uniqueness in time and space. They became symbols of the generic nature of modern consumer culture. Benjamin was right about the epistemological unmooring of artifacts, whether art or consumer products, when removed from a specific time and place. But the loss of "aura" should not be confused with a loss of meaning. Consumers of art and artifacts reassembled the cultural meaning in ways specific to their own place and time.

Benjamin's analysis sheds light on European intellectual disputes over mass consumption and modernization since the beginning of the twentieth century. On one side were those who saw it as a tale of progress. Since industrialization, they argued, people had produced and consumed more, knew more, and lived longer and in greater comfort. In cultural terms, advocates associated modernization with a better-informed public, greater political participation (Benjamin's democratization), and greater equality of the sexes.[122] On the other side were those concerned about the loss of what Benjamin had called "aura" or authenticity. They saw in modernization the depersonalization of production, the loss of individualism in an increasingly technocratic and bureaucratic society, and the predominance of materialism and consumerism in people's lives. Spearheaded by the Frankfurt School in the 1920s and 1930s, this view became a major critique of Western industrial society in the period after World War II and helped spark the protest movements of the 1960s. Adherents of this view warned that the forces of materialism and the overwhelming power of the capitalist system would replace indigenous cultures with generic ones stripped of any authentic meaning.[123]

Once scholars looked closely at the reception of global, mostly American, products abroad, they found more diversity than critics had predicted. McDonald's became a favorite object of investigation for anthropologists and sociologists, perhaps because its rapid global proliferation made it a prime target for attacks by cultural traditionalists. Founded by two brothers in suburban Los Angeles in 1937, the chain expanded nationally in the 1950s under the management and later ownership of Ray Kroc. Kroc applied the methods of Fordism and Taylorism to the preparation of food. The burgers and fries were "assembled" along a line of production much like Ford's Model T automobiles earlier in the century. The process made the product more uniform, cheaper, and thus accessible to a new set of consumers with limited means. Aided by the changes in American demographics and infrastructure—suburbanization and the baby boom—McDonald's thrived as an affordable restaurant choice for lower- and middle-class families in the United States. In the 1960s McDonald's began its international expansion, reaching 120 countries by the end of the century.[124] More than any other international brand, McDonald's came to symbolize the globalization of American culture. Apart from burgers and fries, the company sold a way of life associated with America: cosmopolitanism to some, generic blandness to others. Critics charged that McDonald's represented the worst of global culture, devoid of local authenticity. They saw Max Weber's dire prediction realized, that rationalization would restrict "the importance of charisma and of individually differentiated conduct."[125]

Rationalization and modernization became McDonald's greatest asset. In Asia, for instance, customers frequently cited high sanitary standards, the predictability of food choices, reliable quality, and the professional courtesy of the staff as major benefits of the restaurant chain. While customers associated eating at McDonald's with American culture, researchers found little indication that the presence of these restaurants threatened local customs. Instead, they found that the restaurant chain itself engaged in a process of indigenization and hybridization. Franchises adapted to local culinary and service preferences, while nearby businesses emulated some of McDonald's innovations.[126]

McDonald's represented only the tip of the iceberg of a rapidly expanding network of global retail chains. These businesses became part of what George Ritzer has termed McDonaldization, a process that has moved beyond fast food and retail into areas as diverse as education, child care, health care, travel, and leisure. The essential elements of McDonaldization, according to Ritzer, were efficiency, calculability (the emphasis on quantifiable aspects of products sold), predictability (service and product are the same everywhere), and control through technology.[127] Together these elements created a powerful formula with which to catapult local businesses onto a global market. McDonaldization appeared to have become the economic vehicle for the cultural homogenization of the world.

Ritzer belonged to a group of scholars concerned about the leveling effects of global capitalism. Others, such as the political scientist Benjamin Barber, emphasized the resilience of local cultures as well as the process of hybridization that gave rise to new cultural forms.[128] Barber saw both universalizing and particularizing forces at work and found each of them equally alarming. He called the leveling forces "McWorld" (much like Ritzer) and the particularizing forces "Jihad," which he defined as an exclusionary system of religious and ethnic separatism. In his estimation, both were anarchic and ultimately destructive social instruments, undermining democratic liberalism.[129] The sociologist Roland Robertson coined the term *glocalization* for the competing, at times contradictory effects of global consumption. He emphasized the locally specific adaptation of global products, including the possibility of a reverse flow of influence, in which local mutations of products influence the way they are consumed in the metropole.[130] However, critics, among them Ritzer, charged that the concept of glocalization ignored the realities of the overwhelming economic imbalance between multinational corporations and local producers, and the cultural consequences of that economic imbalance.[131]

The Politics of Consumption

Considering its long history, why did consumption become a central focus of the historiography of globalization only in the second half of the twentieth century? One answer might be the politicization of consumption in the early part of the

Cold War. The United States made the freedom to consume a central part of its ideological battle with the Soviet Union. A promotional segment in an American newsreel in the early 1950s juxtaposed the "sparkling assortment" of goods in American supermarkets and strip malls with the dreary and empty shelves in Soviet stores, establishing a direct connection between American consumerism and democracy. The freedom to buy appeared as critical to Western democracy as the freedom to vote.[132]

Postwar Germany and Japan became laboratories for America's brand of consumer democracy. US occupation officials stressed the need for material security and economic recovery as prerequisites for the democratization of these wartime enemies. In Germany the contrast between the consumer-oriented economy of the capitalist West and the collectivized planned economy favored by the Soviet Union became visible in dramatic fashion during the 1948 Berlin crisis, when the Soviets blocked all traffic to Berlin and the Western allies supplied the western part of the city through an airlift of food, fuel, and other vital goods. The airlift symbolically linked consumption to the Western democratic system by delivering planeloads of material goods into the heart of the Soviet occupation zone. When the blockade ended almost a year later and Germany split into two separate states, West Berlin, like West Germany, was enjoying the fruits of consumerism along with the Western system of democratic capitalism. Indicative of the prevalence of consumption in the West German understanding of democracy was a 1949 campaign poster for West Germany's leading conservative party, the Christian Democratic Union (CDU), which bore the slogan "Finally we can buy again."[133] The West German political establishment built its state on the promise of consumption. It fulfilled that promise beyond all expectations during the 1950s, known as the economic miracle years.

In Japan, American GIs delivered the message of the close links between democracy and consumer culture primarily through the distribution of scarce foods and goods to the local population. As in Germany, American cigarettes, nylon stockings, chewing gum, and PX rations circulated on the black market, and served as payment for sexual favors or as gifts. The Japanese national economy began its transformation toward a consumer economy in the early 1950s during its first postwar economic boom, much like Germany.[134] Over the next three decades its economy expanded dramatically, becoming a leading producer

ENDLICH WIEDER KAUFEN KÖNNEN

WÄHLT CDU

A campaign poster of the Christian Democratic Union in the German state of North Rhine-Westphalia, 1948: "Finally, we can buy again." West Germany built its state on the promise of prosperity and consumption. It fulfilled that promise beyond all expectations during the 1950s, known as the years of the "economic miracle." (Konrad-Adenauer-Stiftung) of consumer goods, particularly cars and consumer electronics. Consumption became an integral part of Japanese postwar political culture.

As the Cold War intensified, Americans pushed their products into political service, often with the help of private corporations interested in the global distribution of their goods. Coca-Cola, for instance, launched international advertising campaigns that linked the consumption of its signature beverage with the pursuit of freedom and democracy. During World War II it shipped its product everywhere American GIs went and in domestic advertising campaigns drew a close connection between the consumption of Coca-Cola and patriotism, freedom, and support for American troops. During the Cold War, James Farley, the chairman of the board of the Coca-Cola Export Corporation and an ardent anticommunist, infused advertisements with anticommunist messages. For the 1952 Olympic games in Helsinki he shipped thirty thousand cases of Coca-Cola in a rebuilt World War II landing craft to arrive in spectacular fashion on Finnish shores. Farley's amphibious invasion of a country on the fault line between capitalism and communism, even if armed only with a soft drink, suggested the close association between military and cultural weapons in the Cold War.[135] It also mirrored the global proliferation of American consumer culture.

The Cold War politics of consumption moved center stage during the famous "kitchen debate" between US vice president Richard Nixon and Soviet premier Nikita Khrushchev at the American National Exhibition in Moscow in July 1959. A year earlier the United States and the Soviet Union had struck an agreement to mount national exhibitions in each other's country. The Soviet Union held its exhibition in New York in June and July 1959, while the Americans followed suit in Moscow the next month. The Soviets put on display samples of heavy machinery and space technology, including a model of the 1957 Russian satellite *Sputnik*.[136] By contrast, American exhibitors chose to present not heavy industry and high technology but ordinary consumer goods. Financed in large part by American corporations—the US Congress contributed only $3.6 million in federal funds—the exhibition included Sears sewing machines, Hoover vacuum cleaners, and the entire contents of a model ranch house, complete with a fully equipped kitchen, which became the backdrop for a spirited debate between Khrushchev and Nixon about the benefits of communism over capitalism: "Your American houses are built to last only 20 years so builders

Three Wayuu women wait for a bus at a gas station in Venezuela underneath an advertisement for Coca-Cola, ca. 1955. The brand symbolized the global proliferation of American consumer culture. The head of Coca-Cola's export division, James Farley, sought to put his product to work in the service of containing communism worldwide. (Getty Images)

could sell new houses at the end," the Russian premier charged. "We build firmly. We build for our children and grandchildren." Nixon retorted with a telling hint toward the primacy of consumption: "American houses last for more than 20 years, but, even so, after twenty years, many Americans want a new house or a new kitchen. Their kitchen is obsolete by that time.... The American system is designed to take advantage of new inventions and new techniques."[137] Nixon emphasized Americans' desire for new consumer products whereas Khrushchev emphasized Soviet production skills.

The debate symbolized the paradoxes of Soviet attitudes toward consumption during the 1950s. On the one hand, Khrushchev seemed to reject the conspicuous consumption on display in the US high-tech kitchen model. On the other hand, he claimed for the Soviet Union success in the area of mass consumption, thus validating mass consumption as a national goal.[138] For Nixon and the exhibition's organizers, the higher quality of American consumer goods and the superior living standard of ordinary Americans became the major argument for the superiority of the Western capitalist system. The exhibition also included a display of an American voting booth, but that symbol of democracy was overshadowed by the dazzling array of American consumer gadgets. The American company PepsiCo, one of the sponsors of the exhibit, distributed free soft drinks to visitors, further driving home the message of material abundance in the United States. The Moscow exhibit suggested that in the United States life was far more comfortable than in the Soviet Union, and that this comfort was grounded in the material goods available to ordinary citizens rather than the abstract freedoms and democratic privileges they enjoyed.

The American exhibition in Moscow put into sharper relief Soviet and Eastern European shortcomings in the development of consumer goods, despite Khrushchev's effort to conceal them. He had been aware of the potential political fallout from the widening material gap between East and West and had already delivered a promise at the Twentieth Party Congress in 1956 to increase living standards in the Soviet Union. Following his famous denunciation of Stalinism, he declared, "We are setting ourselves the task of overtaking and surpassing the richest capitalist countries in the matter of per capita consumption, of achieving a complete abundance in our country of every type of consumers' goods."[139]

The thaw that followed, however, did not produce the desired prosperity but instead accelerated disaffection in several Eastern European countries, culminating in strikes and riots in Poland in the summer of 1956, followed by a popular uprising in Hungary in October and November. Soviet troops intervened and crushed the revolt, demonstrating the limits of the post-Stalinist liberalization. Stalinist methods thus prevailed in the political realm, even though changes were under way in the cultural realm, particularly in the creative arts, where modernism took hold in industrial design and architecture.[140]

The push for consumer goods occurred in other socialist states as well. East Germany's ruling party, the Socialist Unity Party, announced at its Fifth Party Congress in July 1958 that by 1961 the GDR would not only reach, but surpass, the per capita consumption of its West German rival. The objective, declared party leader Walter Ulbricht, was to show the superiority of the socialist social order over the imperialist forces of the Bonn regime.[141] Manufacturers increasingly turned from housing to furniture, household goods, and fashion design in the 1960s. East Germany became the Eastern Bloc's leading manufacturer of plastics and other synthetic goods, relying on a well-developed chemical industry dating back to the prewar years.[142]

East Germans used thermoplastics in the manufacturing of a wide variety of products, from household goods to cars. These cars were meant to showcase East Germany's progress toward a consumer society. Instead they became symbols of socialism's failures in consumer manufacturing and marketing. East Germans had to wait an average of fifteen years for the delivery of a Trabant model. The design of the car and its sister model, the Wartburg, changed little over the years. East German officials hailed the longevity of the design as a sign of the superiority of the socialist over the capitalist system. "In the USA," one Socialist design analyst postulated in the late 1950s, "large amounts of plastics are produced. But they are made in the main into worthless, cheap and shockingly kitschy mass wares, into Woolworth products. Owing to their mania for ornamentation, these in turn tend to be rendered quickly obsolete by something new and more fashionable." Socialist production, by contrast, the statement continued, focused on long-term practicality, thus implicitly condemning America's wasteful consumption.[143]

Eastern European government officials proved only marginally more amenable to shifting tastes in clothing during the 1950s. Long production cycles and the five-year economic plan made it virtually impossible to keep up with the fast pace of changing designs offered in the West. By the end of the decade, however, officials were confronted with the increasing popularity of American-style casual clothing. Blue jeans and T-shirts became prized commodities in an underground market of Western consumer goods. Jeans in particular served as a symbol of youthful rebellion against the strict norms of traditional European society, in both East and West. While Western European conservatives ultimately accepted the commodification of youth culture, their Eastern European counterparts continued to deride it as evidence of capitalist materialism and decadence, and, worse still, as an incentive to juvenile delinquency and a threat to communist ideology.

Soviet officials uncoupled their disdain for Western materialism from their own push toward increased consumption and modernization. Khrushchev packaged higher living standards as a socialist goal. He acknowledged that shortages in consumer goods were a major source of dissatisfaction for Soviet and Eastern European citizens and resolved to build a consumer economy within the ideological parameters of the Soviet system.[144] This meant accelerating the production of domestic versions of Western consumer icons, including passenger vehicles and American-style jeans.[145]

The Soviet effort to create consumer socialism without ideological reform ultimately failed. Consumption championed individualism and private ownership. Ownership of automobiles and homes gave citizens more freedoms, more privacy, and more mobility, thus limiting the possibility of state surveillance and control. By endorsing consumption, communist states allowed limited free expression in material terms while still curtailing it in word and image. However, they soon discovered that objects could symbolize political rebellion against the state. Appearing in public in authentic American jeans, for instance, could symbolize political dissent in the context of the Cold War. Consumption in the communist bloc remained a highly politicized and contested arena throughout the duration of the Cold War.

More importantly, however, Eastern European governments could not deliver the goods. Despite public promises to outdo the West in the production of consumer goods, Eastern European manufacturers lacked the material resources to launch large-scale production of their new designs, whether jeans, household goods, or cars. Design and propaganda consistently outperformed real existing production in Eastern Europe. East Germans, in particular, became acutely aware of their own material shortcomings as they compared their own postwar living standard to that in West Germany.[146]

Even though political barriers kept Western consumer goods out of the communist bloc, advances in transportation technology facilitated their spread everywhere else. They allowed local products to reach a global market and respond to consumer demands faster than ever. International brands such as Coca-Cola relied on cheap production, an international distribution network, and global marketing. Advances in communication technology provided another vehicle for the globalization of consumer products, primarily through new means to advertise products to a global clientele. Advertising evolved as an industry in the United States in the 1920s and expanded rapidly in all major industrial countries in the postwar period. Advertising agents became major interpreters of popular culture and producers of popular desires. They fine-tuned their messages to local, national, and international markets, and tweaked a product's image to match the cultural, social, and economic environment of their target audiences. Advertisers proliferated their messages through print, audio, and, by the 1950s, television media. As new communications technologies reached larger audiences, advertising became increasingly profitable. The advent of television in particular offered the opportunity to broadcast visual messages to millions of people simultaneously, thus greatly accelerating a product's national and international recognition.

Although the webs of consumption drew an increasingly larger number of people from different parts of the world closer together, it is important to recognize that many of the world's poor remained outside of that globalized consumer society. Consumption signified and reinforced inequality and thus, by extension, difference. Most of the poor in the industrialized and the developing world had access to the images of luxury consumer goods through billboards, newspapers, and television screens, yet they did not necessarily have access to the goods themselves. The inequalities remained largely tied to the North–South differential, yet not exclusively so. In many places, particularly in the global South, abject poverty and conspicuous wealth existed side by side within a single locale. As urban elites became linked to a universal community of global consumers, they were separated from their impoverished neighbors by the inequalities of class.

Like other areas of globalization, consumption fostered both homogenization and heterogenization as consumers made individually, economically, and culturally determined choices in the marketplace. Middle- and upper-class consumers in major population centers enjoyed a greater choice of products, but that same diversity replicated itself in every other metropolitan area of the world. Whether consumers entered the Dubai Mall in the United Arab Emirates or the Mall of America in suburban Minnesota, they could count on finding a core group of global brands. At the dawn of the twenty-first century, class more than nationality seemed to separate people's experience as consumers.

3. *Challenging Cultural Norms*

AS the pace and volume of transnational exchanges of goods and people accelerated, challenges to dominant cultural norms and practices multiplied. Beginning in the late 1950s these cultural challenges burst onto the political stage,
undermining the power of cultural and political elites everywhere. Civil rights
advocates in the United States demanded racial equality before the law. Youth in
Europe, the Americas, and East Asia demanded greater cultural and political
freedoms, undermining the Cold War consensus in East and West. Women
challenged gender and sexual norms and demanded equal rights. And religious
groups demanded both greater tolerance of different belief systems and a return
to fundamental religious values in an increasingly secular world. These transformations raised important questions about the effects of the greater connectivity
of the world's cultures across vast distances. Did they create a better understanding
of and higher tolerance for cultural difference, or did they instead cause increasing
cultural fragmentation and the potential for cultural conflict?

Transnational Youth Cultures

Young people more than any other population group drove the postwar movement toward cultural globalization. Emerging first in Western industrialized
countries, but eventually spreading globally, young people began to identify
increasingly with a deterritorialized culture of shared tastes in music, fashion,
language, and behavior across national boundaries. They sought connections to
a transnational youth community independent of, and often in opposition to,
dominant regional and national cultures, provoking intergenerational conflict
within their own communities. They played a vital role in resisting and ultimately undermining the pressures toward conformity within their home societies. Their search for alternatives began in the cultural realm with the creation of
cultural niches within existing structures. By the 1960s the search turned into a

TABLE 4.1

**Crude birth rates (number of births per 1,000 people per year):
Germany, Japan, and United States**

Year	Germany	Japan	USA
1945	16.1	30.9[*]	20.4
1950	16.3	28.1	24.1
1955	15.8	19.4	25.0
1960	17.4	17.2	23.7
1965	17.4	18.6	19.4

Sources: Statistiches Bundesamt Deutschland, Genesis, table 12612-0016: "Lebendgeborene je 1000 Ein-wohner: Deutschland, Jahre," www.genesis.destatis.de/genesis/online; Japan, Statistics Bureau, *Historical Statistics of Japan,* chap. 2, "Population and Households," table 2-24, "Live Births by Sex and Sex Ration of Live Birth, 91872-2004," www.stat.go.jp/english/data/chouki/02.htm;Michael R. Haines, "Crude Birth Rate and General Fertility Rate, by Race: 1800–1998," table Ab40-51, in *Historical Statistics of the United States, Earliest Times to the Present: Millennial Edition,* edited by Susan B. Carter, Scott Sigmund Gartner, Michael R. Haines, Alan L. Olmstead, Richard Sutch, and Gavin Wright (New York: Cambridge University Press, 2006), http://dx.doi.org/10.1017/ISBN-9780511132971.Ab40-643.

[*] Data from 1943.

political challenge to those very structures, leading to political and cultural fragmentation.

The concept of a separate youth culture became identified primarily with American popular culture in the early postwar period. The reasons for the American predominance lay in the historical role of the United States in the production and dissemination of mass entertainment, dating back to the inter-war period, but also in key postwar economic and demographic developments in the United States. Economically Americans emerged from the Great Depression and war with unprecedented productive capacity. The manufacturing of consumer goods coupled with the social and economic consequences of the baby boom (see Table 4.1) fueled America's postwar economic prosperity and ensured the domi-nance of American products on the world market well into the 1960s.

Demographic changes influenced the evolution of a separate youth culture in the United States. Birth rates rose from 2.4 children per family during the De-pression to 3.2 in the 1950s.[147] Suburbs around New York, Cleveland, Chicago, and Los Angeles expanded rapidly, where a growing middle class raised the baby-boom generation. Suburban life revolved around the needs and desires of these baby boomers. As these children grew into teenagers in the 1950s, they became a major force in the development of a separate youth culture as their tastes in fashion, music, and entertainment began to diverge significantly from those of their elders and their purchasing power helped shape the national and international market in consumer products.

The postwar children confronted in their parents a generation that came of age during the Depression and war and retreated to the suburbs in search of security, financial stability, and middle-class status. The sociologist David Riesman presented a psychological profile of the Depression generation in his study *The Lonely Crowd* (1950). He identified the other-directed individual as the dominant social type of the postwar generation, a type that sought to fulfill the expectations of those around him or her, to fit into a social environment prescribed by others. Riesman's stinging critique of postwar society would resonate with youthful rebels over the next two decades.[148]

By the mid-1950s, Riesman's diagnosis had become embedded in fiction and nonfiction works. Sloan Wilson's 1955 novel, *The Man in the Gray Flannel Suit,* illustrated the struggles of middle management employees who needed to come to terms with work, home life, rising material expectations, and their wartime traumas.[149] The novel addresses two key social expectations of men: as successful breadwinners and caring fathers. Both were supposed to define the successful man in the postwar era, and both at times stood in direct conflict with each other. The 1959 book *The Status Seekers* by Vance Packard exposed the social constraints faced by an expanding middle class. Packard produced a meticulous analysis of the social stratification of American society, concluding that the rise of big corporations in the United States made the American ideal of social mobility and individual creativity ever harder to achieve.[150] The monotony and conformity of the workplace seemed to undermine some of the core values of the American dream.

America's postwar youth culture emerged in opposition to these social pressures toward conformity and rising expectations. The first to mount the challenge were working-class youth who felt excluded from the rising living standards and better employment opportunities afforded their middle-class peers. In the early postwar years they developed a distinct style of dress, language, and musical taste that drew on African American music and culture, and rejected middle-class conventions and codes of conduct. The look and language of working-class youth culture received national attention through the 1953 movie *The Wild One*, starring Marlon Brando as Johnny, the leader of a working-class motorcycle club. Johnny and his fellow motorcyclists wear blue jeans and black leather jackets, making them oddly conformist in their nonconformity. The plot was loosely based on a real-life incident in July 1947 when about four thousand motorcyclists terrorized the small town of Hollister in central California for several days.[151] Even though the movie was highly critical of the disrespectful and destructive behavior of the club members, it tried to provide a psychological and sociological explanation for their behavior. Johnny's rebellion seems random and unfocused at first. When one of the patrons in the local bar asks him what he is rebelling against, he answers: "What have you got?" But as he develops a close bond with Kathie, a waitress and daughter of the local police chief, he reveals his emotional scars, brought on by the physical abuse suffered at the hands of his father. He bonds with Kathie because she too has a difficult relationship with her father, who shows no backbone as a law enforcement official and is pushed around by both the townspeople and the motorcycle youth. The movie makes a statement as much about fatherhood as about youthful delinquency. It suggests that both abusive and spineless fathers are to blame for the troubled youth.

Two other films consolidated youth rebellion as a blockbuster genre in Hollywood. In *Blackboard Jungle,* a young Sidney Poitier plays an inner-city high school student who with his classmates challenges the authority of one of his teachers. *Blackboard Jungle* adds a layer of racial conflict to the theme of delinquent working-class youth who both rebel against and crave parental authority. *Blackboard Jungle*, like *The Wild One*, critiques as well as humanizes youth behavior and blames broken families and insufficient parental supervision.[152] That same year, the emerging youth icon James Dean played the role of a disillusioned high school student in search of love and parental guidance in *Rebel without a Cause*. Dean made youth culture attractive to white middle-class adolescents. The three protagonists in the film, Jim (James Dean), Plato (Sal Mineo), and Judy (Natalie Wood) all feel alienated from their parents—Jim because his father is not standing up to his overbearing and controlling mother; Judy because she

Marlon Brando leans on a motorcycle in a scene from *The Wild One*, 1953. The movie showcased American youth culture in the late 1940s and early 1950s. Brando became an international icon of youthful rebellion. (Getty Images)

feels rejected by her father, who seems emotionally cold and fails to relate to her since she has become an adolescent; and Plato because his father left him when he was a little boy and his mother is largely absent, leaving him in the care of a housekeeper. The three of them create an imaginary nuclear family with Jim and Judy assuming parental roles toward Plato. They search for authenticity, emotional support, and moral guidance, yet receive only material comforts and emotional rejection from their parents.[153] The movie's critique of the shallowness of the parents' lives foreshadowed the political and cultural critique of American materialism launched by the New Left in the 1960s.

The spiritual rift between the generations was amplified by the emergence of a new genre in music: rock and roll. In the postwar period, young Americans, many of them white, experimented with new forms of rhythm that drew on jazz, blues, and other black musical traditions. Bill Haley, Buddy Holly, Elvis Presley, and others drew on African American music to create their distinctive rhythm and sound.[154] The established industry at first rejected Elvis's music until he found fame through a little-known label, Sun Records. Still, because of the African American influence, white radio hosts in the South refused to play his songs. Some black radio stations also rejected his music because they knew he was white and felt he had pirated songs from black musicians.[155] After his breakthrough in the mid-1950s, conservative critics, mostly whites, were appalled not only by the sound of his music, but also by his sexually suggestive dance moves. They accused him of being both oversexed and effeminate. Because his public performances often generated uncontrollable screams and even riots among his fans, law enforcement officials saw him as a threat to public order. Despite the negative reactions, or maybe because of them, Presley's popularity quickly rose to phenomenal heights in the United States and abroad. Young people copied his dance moves, his hair (which Elvis dyed black to look like the actor Tony Curtis), and his way of dressing. His music as well as his public appearance had no precedent and therefore became easily recognizable when copied, and his style became a vehicle for challenging established cultural norms and social conventions.

Urban youth in Europe and Japan adopted the dress styles, music preferences, and even some linguistic terms from their American counterparts, and they did so for much the same reasons: to challenge the deeply conservative and conformist culture of their parents' generation.[156] Jazz, rock, blue jeans, cigarettes, and chewing gum became universal symbols of postwar youth rebellion. In the United Kingdom, the "Mods" embraced modern consumerism and stylish clothes, rode around on Italian scooters, and listened to rhythm and blues. Their model was not so much the American rocker as the American version of the Italian mafioso. They listened to jazz and congregated in urban coffee bars.[157] In Germany these youth became known as *Halbstarke*. They rode around on motorcycles, sported Elvis-like hairstyles, and wore jeans and leather jackets, emulating Marlon Brando and James Dean. More worrisome to their parents was the sudden spike in juvenile rioting and crime in the mid-1950s.[158] Rather than searching for indigenous causes, West German officials identified the riots as a problem imported from America, reviving the interwar debates about the evils of Americanization. They thus turned a domestic generational conflict into an imported cultural one.

America's youth culture seeped into Eastern Europe as well, where young people followed closely the trends of their peers in the West. East Germans had access to the latest trends in American popular culture through Western radio stations, such as West Berlin's Rundfunk im amerikanischen Sektor (RIAS) and the Voice of America. They also frequently crossed over into West Berlin to watch newly released American movies. East Berlin authorities estimated that in 1956 and 1957 around twenty-six thousand East Berliners attended West Berlin movie theaters every day.[159] American-style motorcycle gangs proliferated in the East as well. East German government officials condemned these youth trends in much the same ways as the West did: as a threat to public order and a foreign import. For East German authorities, however, ideological concerns were at stake as well. They interpreted the behavior and dress styles of the *Halbstarken* as a mindless adoption of the materialist culture of the capitalist West and therefore a threat not only to German traditions but also to the ideology of socialism.[160] By the late 1950s the East German state stepped up its assault on rock and roll. Party leader Walter Ulbricht and defense minister Willi Stoph declared that rock and roll was an anarchistic and capitalist invasion and a threat to East Germany's national security. Law enforcement officials meted out harsh punishments for fans who dared to advocate or listen to the music in public. In one typical incident in the fall of 1959, the courts sentenced fifteen Leipzig youth demonstrators to jail because they had marched through the streets demanding rock and roll rather than a watered-down domestic version called the Lipsi, and booing the Socialist leadership.[161]

In postwar Poland, American youth culture seeped into the domestic scene through a group called the *Bikiniarze* (Bikini Boys), named for the American atomic test site on the Bikini Atoll in the South Pacific. The *Bikiniarze*, primarily located in Warsaw, were easily identifiable in public by their Western clothes and public mannerisms. They listened to jazz, smoked American cigarettes, and called each other by American names. Polish authorities derided them as hooligans *(chuligani)* and accused them of sexually promiscuous behavior.[162] In Czechoslovakia, fans of American pop culture called themselves *pásek*; in Hungary they were the *jampec*.[163] Across Europe, socialist as well as capitalist, state authorities shared similar concerns about American materialism, cultural imperialism, and social disintegration.

For European youth Americanization meant something entirely different, however. It stood for emancipation, modernization, and in some cases democratization. They perceived their embrace of American pop culture not as cultural imperialism but as rebellion against the cultural conformity and authoritarianism of their parents' generation and the state. America thus became an integral part of the domestic intergenerational conflicts between cultural homogeneity and heterogeneity.[164] Local youth utilized the foreign as a way to challenge what they perceived as conformism at home. From their perspective American popular culture offered diversity rather than imposed conformity.

Not even the Soviet Union could prevent the spread of American pop culture among its youth, despite state officials' concerted efforts in the first decade after the war to keep Americanization at bay. In 1946 Stalin appointed General Andrei Zhdanov to oversee the propaganda campaign against Westernization. Zhdanov was a highly accomplished veteran of the Second World War, having led the defense of Leningrad during the German assault. By the early 1950s, after Zhdanov's death, the anti-American campaign zeroed in on a group called the *stilyagi*, or "style hunters," which had emerged in the late 1940s in Soviet cities. They dressed in stylish suits with long, broad-shouldered jackets and narrow trousers, reminiscent of the Zoot-suiters of Depression-era Los Angeles. *Stilyagis* wore their hair long, listened to jazz, and adopted American names. They took their stylistic cues from American movie actors whose films had made it past the censorship office, among them Johnny Weissmuller, whose masculine primitivism displayed in *Tarzan* appealed to the young, and James Cagney, whose underworld slang in *The Roaring Twenties* they soon adopted. Terms like *dudes, chicks,* and *groovy* became standard elements of the *stilyagis'* language. These youths were not only challenging the cultural conformity of the Stalinist system, they were also calling into question the traditional values of hard work and folk traditions of their parents' generation. Much like American psychologists and youth specialists, Soviet officials blamed parents for providing insufficient guidance to the youngsters who were "hanging around doing nothing."[165] They also frequently harassed the *stilyagi* by rounding them up for misdemeanors and petty crimes.

During Khrushchev's post-Stalinist thaw, attitudes toward Western music and Western-influenced youth groups gradually softened. Perhaps in an effort to co-opt Western music for Soviet political objectives, the Soviet government invited Eastern and Western jazz bands to the sixth World Festival of Youth in Moscow in 1957, thus effectively ending the ban on jazz. Along with jazz musicians came rock and roll aficionados who popularized hits like Bill Haley's "Rock around the Clock." By linking the popular music of the capitalist West to the ideological precepts of international communism and the youth festival's theme of Peace and Friendship, Soviet officials hoped to turn communism into a political doctrine acceptable to and even popular with youth. The festival might not have succeeded on the ideological front, but it did succeed in giving both jazz and American rock music their popular breakthrough in the Eastern Bloc.[166]

The Moscow festival was by far the biggest in a series of gatherings organized by the World Federation of Democratic Youth since 1947. It marked the first time that the Soviet Union had invited large numbers of foreigners into the Soviet heartland. According to official Soviet statistics, a record thirty-four thousand guests from 131 countries attended. Together with domestic participants, estimates of attendance at the opening ceremony alone reached as high as two million.[167] Western governments, including the United States, actively discouraged their youth organizations from attending the festival, portraying it as a giant political indoctrination camp. Those who ignored the warnings encountered in Moscow an openness that shattered their preconceptions about life in the Soviet system. American reporters who covered the festival noted the critical impact of the 160 American participants, who frequently engaged Eastern European and Soviet youth in debates about US and Soviet policies, including the recent invasion of Hungary.[168]

Throughout the duration of the festival, Soviet authorities and police exercised remarkable restraint, tolerating open access to Western popular culture, political debate, and the forging of personal relations. A surprising number of those personal contacts morphed into romantic relationships, as contemporary observers noted with a mixture of wonder and alarm.[169] Many young Soviets would later credit the youth festival with transforming their views about Western culture and politics and with leading them into political opposition in the 1960s and 1970s.[170] Although this and subsequent youth festivals had far less of an impact on Western youth, they nonetheless helped lay the foundation for a transnational cultural and political dialogue. Moscow strengthened the determination of an entire generation to overcome the Cold War divide, fleeting and illusionary as it may have been.

Political Rebellion

The politicization of international youth culture occurred at different moments in East and West in response to local as well as global concerns. In the United States, the civil rights movement became a major catalyst for galvanizing youth activism in the late 1950s. Organizations like the NAACP had fought racial discrimination since the early twentieth century, primarily in the courts and without significant grassroots participation. This changed in the 1950s when African Americans began to stage large-scale popular campaigns, such as the Montgomery bus boycott in 1956, the Greensboro lunch counter sit-ins in 1960, and the 1963 effort to desegregate the commercial district in downtown Birmingham, Alabama. These campaigns drew international attention and led to significant pressure on the federal government to address the problem of racial discrimination in the United States.[171] By the 1960s, America's civil rights struggle became deeply enmeshed in the decolonization movements in Africa and Asia, Cold War politics, and the American war in Vietnam.

Young activists not only played a critical role in the struggle for racial equality in the United States; they also began to challenge the international Cold War order. In the late 1950s they joined long-established groups of pacifists, leftist intellectuals, and concerned scientists in Japan, Western Europe, and the United States, calling for an end to the nuclear arms race, which had escalated since the Soviet Union acquired the atomic bomb in 1949.[172] By 1960 the antinuclear campaign had grown into a mass movement of young activists on college campuses across the industrialized North and West who questioned the ideological divisions of the Cold War and demanded the abolition of nuclear weapons. They advocated peaceful coexistence, borrowing vocabulary cultivated by the Soviet Union since the 1940s, but at the same time they rejected the ideological precepts of the Soviet system just as they rejected the Western system of unfettered capitalism. Their unique political position outside the traditional parameters of the ideological spectrum of the Cold War converged in the transnational movement of the New Left.[173]

Ideologically the origins of the New Left lay with the neo-Marxist theories of the Frankfurt School, led by Theodor Adorno, Max Horkheimer, and Herbert Marcuse. In the United States, students also drew on the sociologists David Riesman and C. Wright Mills and the French philosopher Jean-Paul Sartre. Sartre's existentialism admonished its adherents to rely on their inner consciousness to give meaning to their own existence rather than conform to outside expectations, much like Riesman's idealization of the inner-directed personality. Adorno and Horkheimer, in turn, critiqued the mindlessness of modern materialism, which, in their view, crushed cultural originality and rendered humanity susceptible to totalitarian indoctrination. They regarded the Soviet implementation of Marxist ideology as well as the materialist impulses of Western consumer society as failures, leading to the loss of political and cultural autonomy. Modern mass media collaborated by culturally indoctrinating and depoliticizing citizens.[174]

The philosophical and cultural critique of mass culture and Western democracy found expression in the 1962 Port Huron Statement, the founding statement of the American New Left organization Students for a Democratic Society (SDS). Its main author, Tom Hayden, had become involved in student politics at the University of Michigan. The Port Huron Statement advocated "participatory democracy," the return to direct citizens' engagement with the political process. Drawing on Horkheimer, Adorno, Sartre, and Mills, the statement observed the growing alienation among students and citizens, the increasing bureaucratization of everyday life, and the lack of autonomy of workers, managers, and students. It shifted the locus of radical political activism from the traditional base of the Left—the industrial workplace—to the university and the corporate office complex.[175] The statement reflected the generational transformation from the traditional political assumptions of the old Marxist Left to the grassroots activism of the New Left.

Racial equality, the prevention of nuclear war, and national liberation movements in the Third World emerged as core elements of the New Left agenda in the United States and Western Europe over the course of the 1960s. Some of the more radical groups began to conceive of their opposition against government restrictions in their own country as part of a global struggle against colonialism and imperialism. Militant activists were particularly inspired by Frantz Fanon, who argued in *The Wretched of the Earth* that violence was an inevitable part of the liberation of the colonized from the colonizer.[176] His writings offered a pragmatic rationale for their romantic notion of the militant Third World revolutionary, exemplified by figures such as Ho Chi Minh, Che Guevara, and Mao Zedong. Che Guevara in particular achieved iconic status among Western youth by the mid-1960s as he moved from one guerrilla campaign to the next. After helping Fidel Castro oust the Cuban leader Fulgencio Batista on New Year's Day 1959, he continued his revolutionary struggle first in the Congo and later in Bolivia, both without success. Che was captured in the Bolivian mountains on October 8, 1967, and executed two days later.[177] His death cemented his mythical status as a hero of the militant struggle for national liberation, a myth that endures to this day.[178]

It would be wrong to conclude, however, that violence was a foreign import into the Western world through revolutionary fighters like Che Guevara or radical writers like Fanon. Violence had been an integral aspect of the 1960s youth protests worldwide. In the United States, violence occurred among angry mobs of white segregationists who assaulted peaceful protesters at lunch counter sit-ins across the South. Police beat civil rights protesters or sent dogs to attack them at marches, as they did in Birmingham, Alabama, in May 1963. Militant segregationists bombed churches, lynched African Americans, and assassinated civil rights leaders, including Medgar Evers and Martin Luther King. By the mid-1960s, violence erupted frequently in American cities as frustration with police injustice and the slow pace of civil rights reform mounted. Some riots were sparked by instances of police brutality, others occurred in response to street violence and murder. In the aftermath of Martin Luther King's assassination in April 1968, riots occurred in cities across the country, including Chicago, Baltimore, and Washington, DC.[179] A few months later at the Democratic National Convention in Chicago, police chased and beat protesters in what an official report later called a "police riot."[180] The state thus both initiated and became the target of violence throughout the 1960s.

In Europe, too, state violence begat popular violence in a vicious cycle that escalated in the late 1960s. When German students took to the streets of Berlin in June 1967 to protest the visit of the shah of Iran, a police officer shot and killed a demonstrator, Benno Ohnesorg. The killing of an innocent protestor— Ohnesorg had been shot in the back of the head and thus could not have posed an imminent threat to the police as initially claimed—galvanized the student population across Germany.[181] It also catapulted Rudi Dutschke, leader of the Berlin branch of the German SDS (Sozialistischer Deutscher Studentenbund) to national prominence. Dutschke himself became the victim of violence a year later when a young radical rightist shot him in the head on April 11, 1968, apparently inspired by the hateful anti-Dutschke reporting in the sensationalist conservative German newspaper *Bild* and the assassination a week earlier of Martin Luther King. Dutschke narrowly survived the attack, but died a decade later from related health problems.[182] Already radicalized after the Ohnesorg killing, students turned their anger against the media and the government. The most radical among them joined or supported militant organizations, such as the June 2 Movement, the Baader-Meinhof Group, and the Red Army Faction (RAF). From the 1970s to the 1990s the RAF engaged in bombing attacks, kidnappings, and murders of leading industrial and political figures.[183]

Violence also erupted on the streets of Paris in May 1968, as student protesters clashed with police in what became known as the "night of the barricades." The clashes represented the culmination of months of unrest that had begun earlier that year at one of the city's suburban campuses in Nanterre. The initial protests were directed at university regulations, chief among them strict rules prohibiting men from entering women's dormitories. When administrators showed no sign of relenting, the protests intensified and the catalog of grievances expanded.[184] It ultimately encompassed a broad critique of the conservative social and political course of the de Gaulle government, a demand for greater democratic participation of students in the governance of the university and the state, and outrage over the increasingly aggressive measures of the local police in quashing student protests. By early May the protests had spread beyond Nanterre to the Sorbonne in the heart of Paris. The more the conflict escalated, the more support the protesters received from moderates who had become convinced of the authorities' abuse of power. During the night of the barricades on May 10–11, prompted by the arrest of more than two hundred students who were held without recourse to legal representation, several thousand students set up roadblocks and engaged in street battles with the police in the Latin Quarter of Paris. Several hundred suffered injuries and more activists were arrested.[185]

Building on the momentum of the student protests, French labor unions announced a general strike on May 13 that almost brought down the national government. Notably absent in this struggle were the French Communist Party and the Communist-dominated labor union, the Confédération Générale du Travail (CGT). They supported neither the students nor the workers' demand for autogestion (self-management). The French communists saw the rise of the New Left student movements as a threat to their dominance on the political left, and they were not altogether wrong. The students and workers challenged the regimented and hierarchical authority of the Communist Party elite. Daniel Cohn-Bendit, leader of the *enragés*, as the student protesters became known, often attacked the communists as authoritarian "Stalinist slobs."[186] The student-worker coalition in France challenged both state authority and the predominance of the Old Left in French politics. However, despite the pressure from below, little changed permanently in the French political system. The next French national election in June produced a decisive victory for conservatives under President de Gaulle.

State authorities on the other side of the Iron Curtain viewed the Western protest movements with increasing unease. They shared the French communists' concerns regarding the loss of control over the leftist political agenda. Rather than interpreting these protests as an encouraging sign of the imminent collapse of the capitalist system, Eastern European government officials feared that the spirit of protest could incite Eastern European youth against their own governments. Thus, when reform movements emerged in Poland and Czechoslovakia in the mid-1960s, Soviet and other Eastern European leaders reacted with alarm. The Prague Spring of 1968 became the Cold War era's biggest social, cultural, and political challenge to the Soviet Bloc system until its collapse in 1989. The Soviet response to this challenge—a joint military invasion by most of the Warsaw Pact countries—effectively crushed any hope for a reform of the system for the next twenty years.[187]

The initial impetus for reform in Czechoslovakia came not from students, as in the West, but from the country's literary elites. However, their critique of Czech socialism resonated with the nation's students, intellectuals, and professionals, who transformed the critique into a broader reform movement. Participants at the Fourth Writers' Congress of Czechoslovakia, June 27–29, 1967, openly criticized the Czech Communist Party's policies, particularly those concerning restrictions on free speech. One of the speakers, the poet Pavel Kohout, told listeners that it was "the duty of our congress, the congress of a union to which the great majority of writers and commentators belong, to demand an amendment to the press law so that each author should have the right to defend the freedom of their speech within the framework—I stress, within the framework—of the constitution."[188]

Czech leader and first secretary of the Communist Party Antonín Novotný roundly condemned the writers for their oppositional rhetoric and threatened a campaign against the liberalizing forces. However, Alexander Dubček, the first party secretary of Slovakia, adopted a more supportive position. At the Central Committee Plenum held at the end of October 1967, he called on the party leadership to "deepen intra-party democracy" and to loosen up the hierarchical top-down power structure.[189] Novotný, who held the nation's top military, governmental, and party functions, became increasingly isolated within the Communist Party structure. By January the party had decided on a fundamental restructuring that separated the party from the government. Novotný retained the title of president, a largely ceremonial post, while Dubček became first secretary of the Communist Party of Czechoslovakia (CPCz). This bureaucratic and personnel reform opened the path toward sweeping changes in the country. It brought to power the progressive wing of the Czechoslovak Communist Party, which had been pushing for more openness within the social and political structures of the state since the early 1960s.

In April 1968 the new party leadership under Dubček officially approved the "Action Program," a series of measures to allow for more political diversity and greater freedom of expression.[190] The Action Program officially sanctioned developments already under way within the country. Since March, newspapers had been printing an increasingly broad spectrum of political views, including commentaries critical of socialism. Noncommunist political parties reemerged from internal exile and publicized their own blueprints for reform. In June 1968 leading Czechoslovak writers and intellectuals published the "Two Thousand Words" Manifesto, which laid out the grassroots hopes and expectations of the reform movement and the ideas behind the concept of "socialism with a human face." It called on workers, students, and intellectuals to continue to push for reform in their immediate environments.[191] The Manifesto shared some common ground with the Port Huron Statement composed by the American New Left six years earlier. Like the American statement, it called for a coalition between workers and intellectuals and for mass participation of all citizens in the democratic process regardless of their political ideology.

Despite Dubček's assurances, hard-liners in both Czechoslovakia and neighboring countries expressed grave concerns about the reforms. Soviet leader Leonid Brezhnev pressured Dubček to rein in the popular wave of liberalism. East Germany's leader, Walter Ulbricht, was especially adamant about curbing the reform course, fearing that reform momentum from both the West German and the Czech sides might inspire youth in his country. Among the Eastern European socialist states, only Romania and Yugoslavia seemed unfazed by the Prague Spring. Both had followed an independent course toward socialism since the end of World War II and rejected foreign interference in what they regarded as the internal affairs of a sovereign brother state. Albania, already estranged from the Soviets, feared infringement on its own sovereignty more than a possible spillover of the Czech spirit of reform.[192]

The invasion of Czechoslovakia by five Warsaw pact states—Poland, East Germany, Bulgaria, Hungary, and the Soviet Union—on August 20, 1968, brought a sudden end to the reform spirit in Eastern Europe. Politically, the party leadership returned to a conservative interpretation of socialism that followed closely the ideological line of the Soviet Union. Thus, much like in France in the summer of 1968 and in the United States, challenges to the Cold War order appeared to have failed. Nonetheless, they left a cultural legacy that was nurtured in alternative communes in the West and in underground dissident groups in the East.[193]

Cultural Fragmentation

Even though politically the Prague Spring failed, culturally it brought about a vibrant underground culture of nonconformism in the 1970s and 1980s that gradually eroded the power of the communist regime. American bands like the Velvet Underground and Frank Zappa became a strong inspiration for Czech youth. Besides listening to foreign recordings of rock music, as early as the 1950s Czech musicians created their own rock groups, among them the Akord Club, which performed at the Raduta Club in central Prague, and The Plastic People of the Universe, who took their name from a 1967 Zappa song. While most of these groups were allowed to play in any number of prominent Prague nightclubs in the late 1950s and 1960s, they faced restrictions after the failure of the Prague Spring. The party leadership banned bands like The Plastic People, forcing them underground where they continued to nurture a dynamic collection of music groups called "the second culture." This "second culture" movement staged rock concerts in small Czech and Slovak towns away from the close scrutiny of the party bureaucrats, and thus succeeded in keeping rock music alive behind the Iron Curtain.[194] Vaclav Havel, one of the leading activists in the Czechoslovak dissident movement and the first democratically elected postcommunist Czech president, stressed the tremendous influence of Western music and youth culture on his own political and cultural growth.[195]

Even though youths' infatuation with rock music was not a political form of protest, state authorities interpreted it as such. Violent confrontations between police and rock fans erupted at several underground rock concerts in the mid-1970s. On one occasion young fans rioted in the small Bohemian town of Kdyně after organizers had canceled a concert for fear of rowdy behavior. Angry youth went on a rampage through the town, smashed car windows, and battled police at the local train station. The riot left more than one hundred people injured.[196] Moderate voices within the party hierarchy warned that the party's hard line against rock music was turning apolitical music fans into opponents of the regime. Undeterred by these cautionary detractors, the party leadership continued its campaign against the second-culture rock bands, thereby ensuring the repoliticization of a cultural opposition movement.

Youth in the West in the 1970s channeled their political activism into causes related more directly to their personal lives. This transformation reflected not so much a coming to terms with their own inability to change the political system as an effort to find local and personal solutions to global problems. The movements that emerged in the late 1960s and early 1970s—among them the environmental, women's, and gay and lesbian movements—expressed greater concern with the well-being of individuals regardless of nationality, gender, or race. In their universal applicability, they were at once local and global. Young Americans and Europeans experimented with alternative ways of organizing partnerships, families, and communities. Some created alternative work environments for adults and alternative learning environments for children.[197] This fragmentation diffused the power of the 1960s movements. At the same time it gradually transformed the social and cultural landscape of Western Europe and the United States.

The idea of personal fulfillment and cultural diversity manifested itself in education reform in many Western countries. Daniel Cohn-Bendit's post-1968 biography illustrates one aspect of this transformation. After being expelled from France for his role in the 1968 upheavals, he worked as a teacher in an experimental nursery school in Frankfurt. Together with other educators he followed the concept of anti-authoritarian education, developed in the 1960s and adopted by New Left activists as a rejection of the strict authoritarian parenting and teaching many of them had received as children and adolescents. Despite some controversial aspects, including the idea of permitting young children to explore their own sexuality as well as that of their peers and elders, the anti-authoritarian movement contributed to the establishment of a more cooperative learning environment in modern pedagogy. School curricula reduced rote memorization and encouraged more questioning, debate, and experiential learning.[198] Universities, too, gradually transformed their curricula as a result of the civil rights, ethnic, and women's movements, even though the pace of change was uneven across Europe and North America. North American universities led the way by establishing African American studies, women's studies, and ethnic studies programs in the 1970s.

The environmental movement had a far-reaching impact on late twentieth-century culture and society. The environmentalists of the late 1960s were very much a product of postwar consumer culture. Clean air, clean water, and unpolluted parks were consumer amenities for middle-class suburbanites.[199] But environmentalism also shared the antimaterialist philosophy of the New Left, and the antinuclear demands of the peace activists. The detrimental effects of consumption were revealed in *Silent Spring,* Rachel Carson's exposé on the dangers of pesticides and other harmful chemicals, published in the United States in 1962. The book galvanized opposition to chemical and industrial pollution of the global ecosystem and led to tighter environmental regulation.[200] It connected the local to the global environment, because contamination of land, air, and water in one part of the world had environmental consequences in other parts of the world. Pollution knows no national borders.

The publication of Carson's book came on the heels of heightened concern about nuclear war and nuclear waste. The antinuclear movements of the 1950s had already begun to conjoin their political message with an environmental one. Nuclear scientists had warned from the beginning about the long-term damage of nuclear war to the environment.[201] Yet the dangers of nuclear contamination did not enter the public consciousness in a major way until the mid-1950s, when fallout from a US nuclear test site in the Pacific reached populated islands and international fishing grounds. A Japanese tuna trawler, the *Lucky Dragon,* was fishing in the path of the radioactive cloud, and its crew and catch received high doses of radiation. The incident created worldwide public concern, boosted the antinuclear movement, and led to international campaigns to stop nuclear testing.[202] In 1963 the Soviet Union, the United States, and Great Britain signed the Partial Test Ban treaty, which abolished surface testing of nuclear weapons. Underground tests continued unabated.[203]

Fear of nuclear, chemical, and industrial pollution helped catapult the environmental movement to global prominence. In the 1960s and early 1970s Americans were at the forefront of the movement. In 1970 they designated April 22 as annual Earth Day in order to boost environmental awareness among citizens and encourage efforts to preserve the Earth's natural resources. Between the passage of the Wilderness Act in 1964 and the Superfund Act in 1980, American environmentalists achieved a number of important legislative successes in environmental protection.[204] Europeans, on the other hand, succeeded in creating enduring political parties focused on environmental issues, which gained moderate legislative success and helped pass stringent regulations against pollution. In West Germany, the Green Party entered into its first governing coalition with the Social Democrats in the state of Hesse in 1985 and joined a federal coalition government between 1998 and 2005. The emergence of environmental parties on the European political scene forced mainstream political parties to embrace at least some environmental policies, such as curbing pollution, subsidizing renewable energies, and limiting the use of nuclear power.

Nongovernmental environmental organizations also proliferated since the 1970s, reflecting a broad spectrum of environmental concerns and channeling the grassroots youth activism of the 1960s into a more focused vehicle of political advocacy. Most organizations operated on a regional and national level, yet several developed an international base, among them Greenpeace and Earth First.[205] Greenpeace in particular garnered international attention and support through its orchestration of spectacular and widely publicized protests. Founded in British Columbia in the early 1970s, the organization combined antinuclear with environmental protests. Its first action was a protest against nuclear testing on the island of Amchitka in southwestern Alaska. Further campaigns included protests against the French testing site on Moruroa Atoll in the South Pacific, leading the French government to order the secret bombing of the Greenpeace ship *Rainbow Warrior*. A photographer, unable to evacuate the vessel in time, was killed in the blast. In the late 1970s, after it had evolved into the leading activist environmental organization, Greenpeace moved its international headquarters to Amsterdam. This move symbolized the increasing strength of environmental activism in Europe. Since its emergence as an antinuclear activist group, the organization has taken on a broad range of issues, including whaling, global warming, and deforestation.[206]

The antinuclear movement reconnected with the international peace movement in the early 1980s in opposition to the 1979 NATO double-track decision, in which NATO countries proposed a mutual reduction of medium-range missiles while at the same time threatening to increase nuclear missiles in Western Europe should the Soviets and their Warsaw Pact partners turn down the proposal. As the deployment of those missiles in Western Europe neared, massive demonstrations and peace marches erupted in all major cities across Western Europe. The protesters charged that the doctrine of "mutually assured destruction" rendered additional nuclear weapons futile, because Europe already had enough nuclear warheads on its soil to destroy the Soviet Bloc multiple times. Even though most Europeans shared the protesters' concerns that adding more nuclear weapons to the arsenal would accomplish nothing, their governments proceeded with the deployment.

The youth cultures of the 1970s and 1980s proliferated into a myriad of political and nonpolitical subgroups, connected across vast distances through new technological means of communication. They epitomized the complex interplay between the forces of homogenization and heterogenization. Transnational youth movements and youth cultures challenged dominant cultures and became major producers of local and global countercultures. The result was, depending on one's viewpoint, either cultural fragmentation or cultural pluralism. Fragmentation meant loss, pluralism signified gain. Those who had been part of the dominant culture saw this diversification as a loss of cultural traditions and cultural unity. Others, however, saw diversification as an opportunity for greater choice. Most in the younger generation were at ease with the idea of multiculturalism, yet they also developed an acute sense of globalization's potential for crushing the very diversity it helped to create.

Challenging Gender Norms

One of the most far-reaching global challenges to cultural norms came from the revitalization and expansion of the international women's rights movement in the 1960s and 1970s. Throughout the second half of the twentieth century, women's rights advocates struggled to make women's lives visible in the public realm and to make their rights explicit in the political realm. They received a significant boost from the civil rights movement in the United States, and more broadly from the expansion of the human rights agenda in the early 1970s.

Women helped shape and were shaped by the cultural transformations of the postwar period. Since 1945 more women than ever before worked outside the home, participated in political processes, and became vocal advocates for their rights. Economic and cultural globalization, in turn, affected the ways in which societies defined women's roles and women's status. There remained huge differences, however, in the social and political spaces women occupied and the advances they achieved, depending on the prevailing gender norms in their respective societies. The debates about women's place in society rested on cultural assumptions about gender relations and thus formed an integral part of the discussion about global cultural change in the twentieth century. As women worked to overcome the inequalities within their own environments, they also struggled to define a universal understanding of the rights of women.

Ethnicity, class, and cultural customs shaped women's experiences in ways similar to men's, making them part of the global transformations brought about by the Cold War, decolonization, and migration. Nonetheless, conceptions of gender shaped women's engagement with these transformations in particular ways and thus warrant separate treatment. When exploring cultural change through the lens of gender, the competing forces of homogenization versus heterogenization, on the one hand, and universalism versus particularism, on the other, become visible. Women's lives became at once more alike in disparate parts of the world and more diverse in each particular local setting. Their roles and their rights were embedded both in the local traditions of their home communities and in the global debates over human rights.

Women's status within society became one of the battlegrounds in the emerging Cold War of the late 1940s and 1950s. Communists and capitalists each put forward an idealized image of women's roles in their respective societies, highlighting the benefits afforded women in their own society and denouncing the conditions in the other. Americans, and to a lesser extent Western Europeans, propagated the rising living standards in the West, which afforded women greater comforts in increasingly mechanized households that included washing machines, vacuum cleaners, and other modern amenities. The Soviet Union and Eastern Europe, in contrast, advertised the accomplishments of their women in production and research. What emerged in these idealized portrayals were two competing visions of women's lives and women's roles; one stressing women's role as consumers the other their role as producers.

In the United States women played a central role in the postwar creation of what Lizabeth Cohen has termed a "Consumers' Republic," which elevated consumption to a patriotic act that confirmed America's democratic ideals.[207] The ideological underpinning of the "consumers' republic" was that mass consumption fueled the postwar economy, which in turn strengthened the nation's security vis-à-vis the Soviet Union. In addition, higher living standards and an abundance of goods, consumer patriots hoped, showed the benefits of the capitalist system over socialism and communism in the international arena. The democratic consumer ideal went hand in hand with reconstructing women's place within the home. Though American women had joined the ranks of producers in factories during the war, they were now encouraged to return to their traditional roles as mothers, homemakers, and consumers. Shopping became a way to enjoy the benefits of the modern liberal-capitalist state and strengthen America's national security at the same time.

The gendering of consumer democracy was not confined to the United States. In postwar West Germany the private home became the source of the nation's postwar economic recovery and the housewife as rational consumer became the guarantor of postwar freedom and democracy. Through their conscious choices in the marketplace (weighing cost, benefits, and quality of products), women were seen as active shapers of the national economy, and thus fully vested participants in the civic project of nation building. The 1948 Christian Democratic campaign poster of a mother with a shopping basket served as a conscious reminder of women's patriotic duties as consumers.[208] By contrast, the Soviet-controlled socialist eastern part of the country, where economic recovery progressed at a much slower rate, measured women's participation in nation building by their level of participation in the workforce.[209]

The public emphasis in the Western world on women as consumers did not mean that they did not also contribute to society as producers. During the war women's participation in the workforce and public life was largely a result of necessity. Female employment outside the home, including military service, rose significantly in all countries affected by the war. In the United States, government propaganda portrayed women's employment as an extension of their duties as wives, mothers, and daughters of fighting men. In Germany, too, Nazi propagandists encouraged women's work outside the home as a service to the nation, yet with far less success than their American counterparts.[210] Most of those who did work outside the home regarded their jobs as a temporary arrangement to help the war effort and support their family through supplemental income in the absence of the male breadwinner. Some, however, saw new opportunities to branch out into occupations previously barred to them. Most of the women in traditionally male occupations such as welding and construction lost their jobs even if no male candidates came forward to take their place.[211] Despite these setbacks women's employment rose steadily in Western industrialized countries over the next decades, indicating changing attitudes among women about work outside the home and changing social attitudes toward working women. In the United States the percentage of women in the workforce stood at 34 percent in 1965, an increase of 9 percent since 1940.[212]

The communist regime in the Soviet Union took a dramatically different approach to women's participation in the workforce. Since the 1920s it had encouraged female employment outside the home. During the 1930s, when Soviet authorities actively began recruiting women for their push toward industrial expansion, female participation in the workforce reached 42 percent. Even though women's employment included traditionally male occupations, it did not necessarily translate into greater equality within Soviet society.[213] Men were often hostile to women in their workplace and subjected them to discrimination and harassment.[214] Nonetheless, the labor shortages of the war years pushed women into all areas of the labor force, including agricultural work in the countryside, where some acquired leading positions on large collective farms. Most of these women lost their positions of leadership after the war, much as American women did, yet the overall number of women in the workforce continued to rise, albeit at a slower pace.[215] By the end of the Khrushchev era, women's participation in the industrial workforce had reached 45 percent.[216] Other Eastern European states followed a similar trajectory. In East Germany, the percentage of women in the workforce was 45 percent in 1960 and rose to 48 percent in 1970.[217]

In public displays of art and culture, the Soviets propagated an image of the communist woman as producer. The Polish artist Wojciech Fangor's painting

Postaci (Form/figure) in the Socialist-realist tradition used gender to illustrate the contrast between capitalism and communism. The painting shows a robust couple, dressed in simple work clothes, on one side of the picture, and a fragile woman, wearing a white dress, pearl necklace, yellow sunglasses, and heavy makeup, on the other. The facial features of the working woman are muscular, serious, and similar to those of the man behind her. Her rolled-up sleeves reveal strong arms; one hand rests on her hip, the other on a shovel. In sharp contrast the Western woman's delicate hands with painted fingernails clutch a dainty purse. Her dress is printed with commercial advertisements, including for Coca-Cola and Wall Street. The contrast between the figures is amplified by the painting's background, a tall white building under a blue sky behind the working couple, a grey, possibly polluted sky and a brown landscape of ruins behind the capitalist woman.[218] The superficial, painted beauty of capitalism appears barely able to hide the decay and pollution in the background, whereas the clear, honest and hardworking face of socialism shines before an equally clear, modern, and productive urban landscape.

A 1959 picture by the Latvian painter Michails Korneckis celebrates both women's work and their femininity. It shows three female masonry workers on the scaffolding of a building. Two of the women wear overalls, the third a skirt; all wear headscarves. The women appear completely at ease with this traditionally male occupation.[219] These celebrations of gender equality in the workplace hide the reality of continued discrimination. Despite women's greater advances in the labor force under socialism, inequalities in pay and job placement persisted. In addition there was little willingness among men to take on traditionally female tasks such as housekeeping and child rearing, leaving women to balance wage labor, housekeeping, and child care on their own.[220]

The gendering of the consumer and producer ethos among the Cold War rivals became obvious in the 1959 Nixon–Khrushchev kitchen debate. Nixon invoked women's central position as beneficiaries of America's consumer culture. Showcasing the abundance of kitchen gadgets, Nixon declared: "In America, we like to make life easier for women." Khrushchev retorted: "Your capitalistic attitude toward women does not occur under Communism." Though Khrushchev did not elaborate further at the time, he alluded to the ethos of equality concerning gender relations. In his view, under communism things were not done *for* women, but women *and* men did things for the greater welfare of the community. In Khrushchev's communist society women produced *and* consumed goods.

In an ingenious publicity stunt, the Soviets showcased their idea of gender equality with the introduction of the world's first female cosmonaut in June 1963. The move added another level of humiliation to an already bruised NASA confidence and unleashed a transnational debate about gender and science. Valentina Vladimirovna Tereshkova's launch into space on June 16, 1963, was the latest in a long line of Soviet firsts. Six years earlier, on October 4, 1957, the Soviet Union had launched *Sputnik I,* the first satellite, into space. A month later, Laika, the dog, followed on board *Sputnik II.* Instead of acknowledging the launching of a living being into space as a great achievement, Americans highlighted the cruelty of the experiment: the Russians had not yet developed a mechanism for reentry into the atmosphere, leaving Laika to perish in space.[221] By 1961 the Soviets had solved that problem as well, launching the first man, Yuri Gagarin, into space and returning him safely to Earth.

The way the Soviet Union publicized Tereshkova's accomplishment and the way the Western world received the news illustrate how much gender relations were entangled in the Cold War conflict. Tereshkova was born in a small town in the Yaroslavl region in central Russia in 1937 and worked in a textile factory when Soviet officials selected her for the cosmonaut program in 1962. Her only qualification until then had been a training program in parachuting, which she had begun in the late 1950s at a local facility. [222] Khrushchev and the Soviet press immediately turned her into a symbol of women's equal status in communist society.[223] The successful launch of a male colleague two days earlier in a separate flight that would break the record for rotations around Earth was almost forgotten in the publicity surrounding Tereshkova. Soviets celebrated her return with pomp and circumstance in Moscow's Red Square. Khrushchev called her flight the pinnacle of Soviet achievement. "That's the weaker sex for you," he triumphantly declared. "The name of Valentina Vladimirovna will go down in world history. She has demonstrated once again that women raised under socialism walk alongside men in all the people's concerns, both in self-sacrificing labor and in heroic feats, which amaze the world."[224] She became a national heroine in the Soviet Union.

Tereshkova's space flight generated much publicity in the Western world as well. The initial reports, though overall positive, showed an undercurrent of sexism that would only increase over time. Because Tereshkova's flight coincided with that of her fellow cosmonaut Valery Bykovsky, American newspaper reports speculated on whether the two would attempt a "rendezvous in space." They also repeatedly commented on her physical appearance. One article described her as a "blonde" in space (though elsewhere she is described as having brown hair), another announced that she "loves spiked heels and long-haired music," a third called her a "space girl."[225] *Life* magazine subtitled its article "Blue-Eyed Blonde with a New Hairdo Stars in a Russian Space Spectacular."[226] Soviet propaganda agencies actually promoted the disproportionate attention to Tereshkova's looks by releasing pictures of her at a beauty parlor prior to the space flight.[227] Soviet officials clearly aimed at countering American portrayals of Russia's working women as lacking in femininity.

For American women who aspired to go into space, news of Tereshkova's launch was bittersweet. It proved what they had argued for some time, that women were as capable as men to join the space mission. But it also magnified the discriminatory treatment they received within their own program, because NASA officials continued to bar women from the astronaut training program. NASA pilot Jerrie Cobb expressed regret that "since we eventually are going to put a woman into space, we didn't go ahead and do it first." She had earlier joined nineteen other women in a privately funded test regimen equal to that of male candidates for the program. Even though thirteen of them had passed the tests, they were still excluded from the program. With the test results in hand, she had been lobbying Congress for two years to allow women into the astronaut training program

Cobb received support from Jane Hart, wife of the Democratic senator from Michigan, Philip A. Hart, and herself a pilot, who expressed her hope that NASA would soon change its policy.[228] Another outspoken supporter was Clare Boothe Luce, prominent Republican and wife of publisher Henry Luce, who wrote a spirited editorial in *Life* magazine the week after Tereshkova's flight. She took particular issue with the male establishment's insistence that women were inherently less qualified for the space program than men and that the Soviet move was little more than a publicity stunt. In a bold conclusion, considering her association with the Republican Party and its strong anticommunist ideology, she declared, "Soviet Russia put a woman into space because communism preaches and, since the Revolution of 1917, has tried to practice the inherent equality of men and women." After inundating the reader with a barrage of figures showing Russian women's advances in the technical and medical professions, occupations still overwhelmingly male-dominated in the United States, she declared that "the flight of Valentina Tereshkova is consequently symbolic of the emancipation of the Communist woman. It symbolizes to Russian women that they actively share (not passively bask, like American women) in the glory of conquering space."[229]

Efforts to rationalize the American decision to exclude women from the space program ranged from the scientific-technical to the cultural chauvinistic. Some American editorials called into question Tereshkova's qualifications—her aerial experience was limited to parachuting, and her technical training was limited.[230] Others dismissed the flight as a publicity stunt aimed at upstaging the Americans in the space race, because it did not produce any tangible scientific benefit.[231] A German article quoted a NASA official's facetious comment that in the future American space capsules would have more room and could therefore accommodate an additional 125 pounds of "recreational equipment."[232] Still others portrayed Tereshkova's and other women's successes in male-dominated fields as a loss. They argued that Russian women's multiple duties as mothers, housekeepers, and workers left them overworked and, worse still, deprived of their femininity. "For a generation and a half since the Revolution," Audrey Topping, the wife of the New York Times bureau chief in Moscow, wrote in an article, "Russian women have been torn between a drive for equality with men, a compulsion to prove their worth in building the glory of the state and a desire to be feminine." After women were initially told to reject Western-style femininity as "bourgeois," the article continued, they were now again interested in fashion and beauty. However, "the average Soviet woman has a long way to go before she reaches the standard in America and Europe." Topping's conclusion was reminiscent of the Nixon-Khrushchev debate four years earlier: "No number of space flights can free the average Soviet woman from household drudgery as could the good old clothes dryer, dishwasher or efficient diaper service. These things are not available in the Soviet Union."[233] Topping turned the advances of Russian women in the male-dominated fields of space exploration and technology into a deficiency in the areas women allegedly really cared about: fashion, beauty, home management, and consumption.

Though Luce and Topping belonged to roughly the same generation, they advocated diametrically opposed roles for women in postwar society. Topping held on to a traditional definition of women's roles. Luce's commentary expressed the growing frustrations of countless college-educated women who continued to encounter barriers to professional advancement—women who were the vanguard of the second-wave feminist movement that would emerge with full force by the mid-1960s.

The French existentialist writer Simone de Beauvoir, five years Luce's junior, provided the philosophical underpinnings for the new feminism. In *The Second Sex* she argued that modern society had defined women only in relation to men. Man was seen as the scientific objective self, woman as the subjective "other." Drawing on existentialist philosophy, de Beauvoir declared that women were not born as women but became women through a gradual process of social conditioning. By separating sex from gender and identifying the latter as a social construct rather than a biological fact, she provided the basis for a feminist critique of modern society. By altering the social construction of gender, women could make themselves into "subjective" selves.[234] Her writings energized the women's rights movement in Western Europe and the United States in the 1960s.

The American journalist and writer Betty Friedan built on de Beauvoir's articulation of the second sex with her 1963 book *The Feminine Mystique*. Published only months before Tereshkova's flight, the book documented women's frustrations with being relegated to the role of mothers and wives when their intellect would allow them to be so much more in public life.[235] The articulation of "the problem that has no name," as Friedan called it, played a critical role in sparking the second-wave feminist movement in the United States. However, critics blamed Friedan for focusing too narrowly on the plight of middle-class women and overstating the pressures toward female domesticity.[236] Nonetheless, her impact on the women's movement of the 1960s and 1970s was unequivocal.

The concerns raised in Friedan's book emerged at a time when more American women were entering college than ever before and when many of them participated in the civil rights and New Left movements. These women activists had not yet experienced the constraints of motherhood and domesticity of their elders, nor did they regard themselves as the "second sex." Nonetheless, as they fought for racial equality, they confronted gender inequality on a daily basis. During the day-to-day operations within their organizations, male colleagues often relegated them to menial positions, including secretarial work and household duties, such as cleaning and cooking. In 1965, Casey Hayden and Mary King, two white activists in the American Student Nonviolent Coordinating Committee (SNCC), articulated their frustrations in a pamphlet called "Sex and Caste: A Kind of Memo," in which they drew parallels between the discrimination faced by African Americans within a society dominated by whites and the discrimination faced by women in a society dominated by men.[237] Theirs was an expanded, updated, and in many ways more radical articulation of Friedan's "problem that has no name" and Beauvoir's "second sex." It created a male backlash within the civil rights movement and helped fuel women's resolve to form separate organizations dedicated to achieving equal rights for themselves. African American women shared many of those experiences but faced a crucial dilemma: would articulating, much less fighting, sexual discrimination derail the fight against racial discrimination?[238]

As in the United States, feminist movements in Europe grew out of the student protests of the 1960s. Young women began to demand greater participation within the power structures of their organizations and created advocacy groups to address gender inequality. In Great Britain the London Women's Liberation Workshop functioned much along the lines of the American consciousness-raising groups. At the same time, the Women's National Coordinating Committee organized conferences, formed consciousness-raising groups, and fought publicly for women's equality in the workplace as well as abortion rights.[239] In 1968, West German student activist Helke Sander, member of the newly minted Aktionsrat zur Befreiung der Frau (Action Committee for Woman's Liberation), articulated women's frustrations at a meeting of the German Socialist Student Association (Sozialistischer Deutscher Studentenbund, or SDS).[240]

In France the women's movement expanded significantly in the aftermath of the student protests of May 1968. A diverse conglomerate of organizations merged into the Mouvement de Libération des Femmes (MLF) around 1970.

One of the organizations within the MLF—Psychoanalyse et Politique, founded by the psychoanalyst Antoinette Fouque—soon charted its own path, in part by openly rejecting the label "feminist" as pejorative. Fouque rejected the struggle for equality, which she felt denied the feminine, and instead sought the empowerment of women by embracing difference. Much better organized than the other groups within the MLF, and much more vocal through periodical publications, among them *Le Quotidien des Femmes* and *Des Femmes en Mouvements Hebdo,* or *Psych et Po,* as it became known, soon overshadowed other feminist groups within France. Fouque's publicity campaign created the impression in France that *Psych et Po* was, in fact, the voice of the feminist movement in the country. Fouque herself fostered that misconception by officially changing her organization's name to MLF in 1979, thus effectively silencing other feminist voices within France.[241]

Women activists everywhere publicized their demands for equality through periodicals dedicated to the feminist cause. In the United States Gloria Steinem founded *Ms.* magazine; in West Germany, Alice Schwarzer founded *Emma;* British feminists founded *Spare Rib.*[242] As circulation grew and reached a wider audience, women's rights assumed a larger role in public and academic discourse. Universities gradually developed courses that dealt with women's issues, some blossoming into full-fledged women's studies programs.

As the movements matured in the West, they proliferated into a myriad of special interest groups that reflected the diversity of women's lives and political objectives. The fragmentation occurred along the lines of class, race, political conviction, professional affiliation, and sexual orientation. Gay and lesbian groups multiplied in the 1970s, creating their own political organizations to lobby for the elimination of discriminatory laws that criminalized homosexuality. Using many of the same strategies as the civil rights movement, gay and lesbian activists in the United States and Western Europe staged sit-ins, organized marches, and challenged the law through deliberate acts of defiance. The Mattachine Society, an American gay rights organization, staged a "sip-in" in New York in 1966 to challenge a New York State Law that prohibited serving alcohol to gays in bars. A year later Great Britain decriminalized male homosexuality through the Sexual Offenses Act.[243] By the 1980s most Western European countries had eased or eliminated laws banning homosexuality, though cultural reservations about homosexuality endured. In some countries, criminalization persisted into the twenty-first century.[244]

Key concerns among women activists in the Western world centered on sexual and reproductive rights. The emergence of the contraceptive pill in 1960 ushered in a sexual revolution in the industrialized world that gave women much greater control over the reproductive process. It effectively eliminated the threat of pregnancy as a result of casual sexual encounters. However, it did not protect women from continued sexual exploitation. To the contrary, some radical feminists argued that birth control increased male sexual exploitation of women, because men no longer had to fear becoming fathers.[245] The Canadian-born Shulamith Firestone, activist and founder of the New York–based radical group Redstockings, argued that women's biological reproductive function made them vulnerable to male exploitation. The sexual act was an expression of male domination over women and thus a root cause of female dependency.[246] While sexual violence was a major concern for all feminists, most preferred a less extreme assessment of sexual relations. They demanded for women the same right to sexual liberation as men, as well as an understanding of heterosexual sexual relations premised on the principle of equality. The phrase "the personal is political," popularized by second-wave feminists in the 1970s, captured the tremendous shift from the collective to the individual that had occurred in the rights movements of the 1960s.

Another major concern of Western women's organizations in the early 1970s was the right to an abortion. Most countries at the time prohibited or restricted the right of women to carry out an abortion. In the United States in 1973, the Supreme Court declared abortion a fundamental right under the US Constitution, after intense lobbying by women activists, including Gloria Steinem, who by the early 1970s had risen to national prominence.[247] Over the next three decades social conservatives and the Catholic Church in particular lobbied hard to overturn *Roe v. Wade* in the United States and prevent similar legislation elsewhere. The fight against abortion turned deadly as militant fringe groups attacked physicians who performed abortions. In 1993 Dr. David Gunn of Pensacola, Florida, became the first of several victims of deadly anti-abortion violence in the United States: an anti-abortion activist gunned him down outside his clinic.[248]

In Germany, abortion rights became a rallying point for feminists as well. The criminalization of abortion was enshrined in Clause 218 of the German Criminal Code. In 1971, prominent German feminists publicly claimed in a leading German political weekly to have had an abortion and challenged the courts to prosecute them.[249] The controversy generated by the article led to a public debate in Germany and in 1974 resulted in the legalization of abortion during the first trimester. A year later, however, Germany's Supreme Court declared the law unconstitutional, forcing legislators to restrict abortion rights to a narrowly defined set of conditions, such as medical and criminal grounds. The struggle over abortion continued in the courts until the 1990s, when German unification prompted the consolidation of the East and West German laws into a single code. East Germany had legalized abortion in 1972.[250] The new law permitted abortions in the first trimester after mandatory counseling and a three-day waiting period, but limited later procedures to those for medical reasons.

Beginning in 1971 feminists in France also demanded unrestricted abortion rights. They garnered publicity through the support of several prominent figures, including Simone de Beauvoir. In addition they staged public protests and formulated an abortion rights manifesto. With the 1975 Veil law (named after Minister of Health Simone Veil), abortion in the first trimester became legal.[251] Over the course of the 1970s, most other Western European countries followed suit, either legalizing or loosening restrictions on abortions.

Women's rights activists in the global South set different priorities. They had to contend not only with discrimination against women but also with a lack of economic and social rights that transcended gender differences. Particularly in Asia and Africa, the feminist cause was intimately connected to the project of decolonization and national self-determination. In India, women's organizations formed in the 1920s in tandem with the movement to gain independence from Britain. They were less concerned than their Western peers with issues of personal or sexual liberation, and often worked in concert with other organizations toward national liberation.[252] In Egypt, too, women had been active in feminist causes since the 1920s, and, after gaining the vote in 1956, they increasingly participated in public and political debates. One of Egypt's leading feminists, the physician Nawal El Saadawi, caused a national uproar with her publication of *Women and Sex* in 1972. The book addressed various forms of violence committed against women in Egyptian society, including the ritual of female genital mutilation. Saadawi's rights campaign was indicative of broader strategies among Third World feminists, namely, to focus on local conditions in their fight for equality.[253] Those included religious, social, and political contexts that required a locally specific feminist approach.[254] For women in Kenya, that meant organizing in rural communities to address specific problems concerning women and the poor, including child care, health, and economic development. For women's groups in Latin America, local causes often involved issues of labor, prompting women to collaborate closely with male labor activists. Their objectives were to gain better wages, better social services, and greater participation in the political process for both women and men.[255]

Non-Western women's struggles for equality have always been negotiated through the filter of racial and class domination. What separated Third World feminism from its Western counterpart, according to Indian-born sociologist Chandra Mohanty, was "the contrast between a singular focus on gender as a basis for equal rights, and a focus on gender in relation to race and/or class as part of a broader liberation struggle."[256] Because of the vast differences in women's experiences in the global South and the complexity of local social and political relations, women in Asia, Africa, and Latin America developed women's movements and organizations that articulated local concerns, which could not necessarily be transferred onto a continental, much less global, level. As women's groups began to converge on the global stage through the United Nations and other international venues, these differences became exposed.

Feminist Internationalism

For much of the twentieth century, feminist internationalism confined itself largely to the Western industrialized world. The Women's International League for Peace and Freedom (WILPF), founded in 1915 in the United States, became the first transnational women's organization, but its initial focus was the struggle for world peace rather than women's equality. The WILPF gradually expanded its platform to include racial and economic equality, issues of concern to non-Western women's rights advocates, even though its membership base remained largely in Europe and the United States.[257] In 1945 the Women's International Democratic Federation (WIDF) emerged as an alternative venue to the WILPF. Even though it drew members primarily from communist countries, it made a concerted effort to reach out to women's organizations in the Western and nonaligned worlds.[258] WIDF's self-proclaimed mission was to "win and defend national independence and democratic freedoms, eliminate apartheid, racial discrimination and fascism." Even though the WIDF's mission appealed to women's organizations in the global South, its close political affiliation with the Soviet Union prevented many from joining.[259]

State-centered international organizations like the United Nations were slow to establish subdivisions devoted to women's issues. This changed in the 1970s when, riding the wave of feminist grassroots activism, the United Nations designated 1975 as an International Women's Year (IWY). It then hastily convened an International Women's Conference in Mexico City in June, because the WIDF threatened to upstage the UN with an international women's conference in honor of the IWY in East Berlin.[260] The UN conference consisted of a formal venue attended by about one thousand official delegates from UN member nations (about a third of them men) and an informal venue across town of more than five thousand delegates, including women's organizations, NGOs, and individual activists. The official delegates included only one female head of state, the prime minister of Sri Lanka, Sirimavo Bandaranaike. The two other female heads of state in the world, Indira Gandhi of India and Maria Estela Peron of Argentina, declined attendance because of domestic unrest in their own countries. The Soviet Union sent Valentina Tereshkova as its official delegate. Other countries sent wives or female relatives of heads of states, including Leah Rabin of Israel, Jehan Sadat of Egypt, and Princess Ashraf Pahlavi, the twin sister of the shah of Iran.[261] The unofficial NGO tribunal included several prominent international feminists, among them Gloria Steinem and Betty Friedan from the United States, Australian feminist Germaine Greer, and Bolivian labor activist Domitila Barrios de Chúngara.

Even though the Mexico meeting was supposed to create the basis for a common global agenda, and was hailed, somewhat prematurely "the world's greatest consciousness raising event," it exposed as many differences as it found common concerns. The biggest and most open confrontations occurred at the site of the NGO tribunal. Ethel L. Payne, in attendance for the *Chicago Defender*, described

Delegates to the UN World Conference on Women in Mexico City listen to the speech of Mexican president Luis Echeverría, June 19, 1975. At center is Leah Rabin, head of the Israeli delegation. More than a thousand official delegates—about a third of them men—attended the conference, while more than five thousand other activists and representatives of women's and nongovernmental organizations met at an unofficial forum on the other side of the city. The meeting exposed as many differences as common concerns. (© Bettmann/CORBIS)

the spectacle as "a comic opera of female fury venting itself in the halls of the Centro Medico, where the rag taggle dissidents of all beliefs met in combat."[262] Delegates vented their disagreements openly at the tribunal, because its setting was less formal and delegates were not bound by their governments to represent a particular position.

The fiercest disagreements occurred between Western and non-Western feminists over a global agenda. While the majority of feminists in the industrialized world wanted to prioritize issues of social equality and sexual liberation, including abortion rights and rights of lesbians, their counterparts in the global South demanded a focus on economic development and redistribution of wealth.[263] Divisions occurred along class lines as well. In one of those altercations Domitila

Barrios de Chúngara confronted upper-middle-class Latin American delegates about their false sense of commonality with working-class women. She remembered exclaiming in exasperation: "Now tell me: Is your situation at all similar to mine? Is my situation at all similar to yours? So what equality are we going to speak of between the two of us? If you and I aren't alike, if you and I are so different? We can't, at this moment, be equal, even as women, don't you think?"[264] To Barrios de Chúngara, the problem of women's inequality was inseparable from the problem of poverty and economic inequality. She felt that her fight for women's rights had to connect to her fight for economic equality, a fight she shared with the men in her community.

Another division occurred along political lines. Tribunal and official delegates from communist countries declared confidently that their societies had already achieved gender equality. Thus, they reasoned, once women focused on achieving a new economic world order, gender equality would follow automatically. Vilma Espín, wife of Cuba's defense minister Raul Castro and sister-in-law of Fidel, declared at the official UN meeting where she served as Cuba's delegate: "We have already obtained for our women everything that the conference is asking for. What we can do here is tell other women of our own experiences and help them that way." For Western feminists, among them the French delegate Françoise Giroud, the emphasis on economic solutions to gender inequality amounted to a "diversion" tactic.[265] For Third World tribunal delegates, such as Chúngara, however, Cuba's success sounded a hopeful note, because the economic conditions in her home country were similar to Cuba's before the revolution.

The official conference's final declaration, the "World Plan of Action," reaffirmed the interconnectedness of the three objectives of the conference: equality, development, and peace. It called on governments to establish regulations that would ensure women's full equality and participation in public life and to allocate funds for economic development. Toward that end the UN set up the International Research and Training Institute for the Advancement of Women (INSTRAW) and the United Nations Development Fund for Women (UNIFEM).[266] The results of the conference and the tribunal disappointed everyone. Non-Western women's rights advocates criticized the lack of attention to economic inequality, and Western observers argued that the plan offered primarily solutions to problems that had already been solved in the West. "Feminism means little to the poor countries that dominate the United Nations," one Western commentator lamented. "The feminists come from rich countries that have little say at such meetings."[267] Tribunal participants were equally frustrated with the results. Germaine Greer, the Australian feminist made famous by her controversial 1971 book *The Female Eunuch*, called the meeting a "shadow play" of political posturing that obscured issues of common concern to all women.[268] The criticisms were at least partially justified. The concerns of women in Western and non-Western societies, as well as in communist and liberal-democratic societies, differed too much to consolidate them in a single document. In addition, political strategy influenced the agenda of official delegates as well as many unofficial tribunal attendees. Nonetheless, even if issues of development were pushed by a male-dominated contingent of representatives, or by women representatives who functioned as stand-ins for the male leadership of their countries, as some critics contended, the exchanges that took place in Mexico City gave rise to a transnational dialogue over what mattered most to women in different parts of the world and how universal equality could be achieved. The exposure of these differences marked the beginning of a process that would bring all sides closer together.

As the transnational debate evolved during the UN Women's Decade and beyond, the level of confrontation and mutual misunderstanding decreased. Subsequent UN women's conferences—Copenhagen 1980, Nairobi 1985, Beijing 1995—paid increasing attention to issues of economic development, thus giving Third World feminists a broader platform than in Mexico City. Reviewing the history of the international conferences since 1975, the Indian economist Bina Agarwal noted steady progress toward recognizing economic equality as a central feature toward women's equality. She called the Beijing "Platform for Action" a significant advance over previous ones. "The gender gaps in economic power, property rights, and poverty occupy centre stage [in the Beijing Platform]. It also clearly connects women's poverty and gender inequality." She highlighted a section of the platform that stated, "Women's power is directly related to the absence of economic opportunities and autonomy, lack of access to economic resources, including credit, land ownership and inheritance, . . . education, and support services, and minimal participation in the decision-making process." Agarwal thought of the transformation between Mexico City and Beijing as "romantic sisterhood" giving way to "strategic sisterhood."[269] In other words, if the idealism of Mexico had been crushed by the realization of the vast gulf among feminists from different parts of the world, the pragmatism of the Beijing conference produced the foundation for concrete solutions to specific forms of inequality in the world. The transformation occurred not so much in the overall agenda but in the shifting power distribution between Western and non-Western women's rights activists.[270] The latter had called for a greater emphasis on economic development since 1975, and over time they convinced at least some in the Western contingent.

Efforts to create a network of international women's rights advocates took root outside the UN institutional framework as well. In 1984 the American feminist journalist and co-editor of *Ms.*, Robin Morgan, founded the Sisterhood Is Global Institute (SIGI) to provide a permanent forum of intellectual exchange for international feminists. Morgan founded the institute after publishing *Sisterhood Is Global,* an 800-page anthology of writings by feminists from all over the world.[271] The contributors became SIGI's first fellows. Over time SIGI grew into a major organization for international feminists. It cooperated closely with the UN and with other transnational organizations, among them Women Living under Muslim Law (WLUML), founded two years later in Paris by Marie Aimée Hélie-Lucas.[272]

Third World feminists, whose voices became increasingly powerful in transnational women's organizations in the 1970s through the 1990s, significantly complicated Western feminists' understanding of "universal sisterhood." Many of the Third World feminists involved in the debate were Western-educated or had lived and worked for part of their lives in the Western world, leaving working-class women such as Barrios de Chúngara marginalized.[273] Nonetheless, these women used the language of Western feminism to articulate the perspective of non-Western women. Chandra Mohanty, who received her PhD in sociology at the University of Illinois, criticized her Western peers for constructing " 'Third World women' as a homogenous 'powerless' group often located as implicit victims of particular socio-economic systems." In this rendering of otherness, women in the global South were usually portrayed as victims and dependents without agency or individuality in their own right.[274]

Mohanty identified a central paradox embedded not only in the feminist discourse but also in the uses of gender as a category of analysis. If gender is the social construction of biological differences, as Joan Wallach Scott had postulated in 1985, then different social and cultural contexts produce different conceptualizations of gender.[275] While difference is common to gender relations in all cultures, the nature and definition of those differences are contingent upon the social and cultural context. Mohanty and others have charged that Western feminists' representations of women's inequalities in the Third World mirrored the representation of the colonial "other" in imperialist writing.[276] Western feminists claimed for themselves the right to define the social construction of gender and presented it as a fixed category. They measured progress toward women's rights according to this fixed Western standard. Simone de Beauvoir's "second sex" was thus replicated in the relationship between Western and non-Western women. The latter had become the "other" to the former "self." Third World women became "second" to the "second sex."

Third World feminists well-versed in the language of Western feminism also began interrogating their own assumptions of difference in relation to women within their own society. The upper-class Indian literary scholar Gayatri Chakravorty Spivak warned her colleagues (both Western and non-Western) that "in order to learn enough about Third World women and to develop a different readership, the immense heterogeneity of the field must be appreciated, and the First World feminist must learn to stop feeling privileged *as a woman.*"[277]

Two cases illustrate this heterogeneity as well as the consequences for the attainment of a universal feminist consciousness. The first is the international campaign against female genital mutilation (FGM). The practice of female circumcision, prevalent in parts of Africa and the Middle East, and to a lesser extent in Muslim Asia, became a major cause for Western feminists beginning in the late 1970s. Brought to national attention in the United States by the American journalist and activist Fran Hosken, who in 1979 published the *Hosken Report*, which documented and condemned the practice, FGM generated outrage and concern in the West.[278] Few women and medical experts defended the ritual, but many criticized Hosken's confrontational and at times paternalistic approach. In a 1980 article in *Ms.* magazine, editors Gloria Steinem and Robin Morgan tried to strike a different tone. They condemned the practice, but did so by letting the victims speak for themselves.[279] They included the testimony of Saadawi, who had been an outspoken critic of female circumcision in her own country since the early 1970s. Saadawi, already a powerful spokesperson for the anticlitorectomy campaign in her own country, described her procedure at the age of six and that of her younger sister, which ultimately led her on a path toward feminist rebellion.[280]

Considering their fundamental agreement on the barbarity of the practice, it seems surprising that at the 1980 UN conference in Copenhagen, Saadawi and other Muslim feminists clashed with Western women over the issue of FGM.[281] Yet when analyzing the dispute more closely and within the context of the global feminist agenda, it becomes understandable. Even though they were as outraged by the practice as their Western colleagues, Muslim women objected to the debate in this forum for two reasons. First, they felt that the issue detracted from the problems of economic exploitation and imperialism.[282] And second, Saadawi and others objected to the way in which the primary focus on FGM branded African and Arab cultures as backward and savage.[283] Third World women thus still found themselves battling First World women over the right agenda for their struggle and the particulars by which women's advances should be measured.

A second issue that illustrated the heterogeneity of women's experiences but also rifts within feminist circles was the controversy over the Muslim veil. Most women in the Western world interpreted the wearing of the veil in Islamic countries as evidence of female degradation. Feminists from countries in which the practice was common found themselves in a difficult position. Even if they did not support the custom, most felt compelled to either defend it or at least demand that it should be placed in the right context. For some Muslim women the veil became a way to resist pressure toward cultural assimilation in Western countries. The case of three students at a suburban high school outside Paris in 1989 is illustrative. School administrators banned the three girls, ages thirteen and fourteen, from attending classes because they violated a school rule against wearing headscarves.[284] When faced with vocal public protests from the Muslim immigrant community in France and from prominent liberals who favored cultural tolerance, the Socialist government backed down. In the ensuing debates the different types of head and face coverings—headscarf, veil, hijab, chador—were often used interchangeably, even though there were significant differences among them, ranging from covering only the hair to covering the entire face.[285]

More importantly, though, these debates exposed the different meanings people attached to the practice. In a poignant editorial in 1994, Germaine Greer, the Australian-born feminist, pointed out the multiple symbolic functions of the veil within modern society: "It [the veil] can be identified with oppression or liberation, with privilege or disability, with impotence or empowerment. One thing is certain, if the right to wear it is denied, it becomes a symbol of freedom. If the right to wear it is denied by authorities known to discriminate against the group that seeks to wear it, the veil becomes a symbol of rebellion, even a weapon of war."[286] The veil controversy thus grew from a battle over cultural norms and cultural integration to a battle over asserting individual rights, whether they were women's rights or minority rights. Greer recognized the multiple dimensions of the controversy and opted for the primacy of free choice.

The controversy in France addressed a larger conflict concerning both women's equality and cultural diversity. According to historian Joan W. Scott, "The head scarf is a tangible sign of intolerable difference. It defies the long-standing requirement that only when immigrants assimilate (practicing their beliefs in private) do they become fully 'French.'"[287] The headscarf was seen both as a symbol for an immigrant population's refusal to integrate into French society and a sign of women's degradation within Muslim society, and hence incompatible with French norms of gender equality. However, while for some it meant women's debasement, for others it meant women's empowerment. By insisting on their right to wear the headscarf, Muslim girls and women asserted their right to a cultural identity, and thus participated in a political debate about cultural diversity.[288]

The wide spectrum of symbolic meanings of the veil, and the disagreement even among feminists about how to approach the controversy, demonstrates that the dividing line between cultural universality and particularities did not run neatly between Western and non-Western feminists, or even between feminists and nonfeminists. It would be wrong, however, to assume that the diversity of women's experiences precluded a consensus on minimum standards of women's rights in the global arena. Rather, according to Chandra Mohanty, one needs to find an alternative universality that is not premised exclusively on Western conceptions of gender relations and women's equality, but takes into account differences in experiences and social contexts. "The challenge is to see how differences allow us to explain the connections and border crossings better and more accurately, how specifying difference allows us to theorize universal concerns more fully."[289] Difference and universality have to work in tandem, not only, and maybe not even most importantly, to create a new global feminist consciousness. They need to capture the diversity of women's experiences within a universal rights framework. Only by moving beyond the universalist-particularist dichotomy can the full spectrum of women's needs and objectives be addressed.

Continuity and Challenge in Religious Cultures

The headscarf controversy in France also ignited a debate about the role of religion in the public sphere. France had long embraced the principle of *laicité,* which demanded the preservation of a secularized public space. However, despite its embrace of secularism, France was a religiously and culturally homogeneous nation, whose Catholic heritage lay deeply embedded in its social, cultural, and political identity. The veil controversy arose in the context of far-reaching social transformations in France, as nonwhite, non-Christian migrants settled in France in greater numbers than ever before. Their different social, cultural, and religious practices stood in opposition to the secularism within French society, which was constructed on the basis of a single dominant religion and an abstract idea of civic unity.[290] The existence of different religions in close proximity to each other—a new phenomenon in Europe and North America in the postwar period—posed particular cultural challenges and tested the limits of religious tolerance. In the global arena, religion became a force for both cultural homogenization and heterogenization.

Despite the codification of religious pluralism in all modern democratic constitutions and the guarantee of religious freedom in civil law, most states in Europe and the Americas remained deeply rooted in Judeo-Christian practices and rhetoric. Two of Europe's largest postwar conservative parties were explicitly Christian in their political mission, the Democrazia Cristiana in Italy and the Christlich Demokratische Union (CDU) in West Germany. The US Congress, at the height of the Cold War in 1954, reinserted the words "under God" into the national Pledge of Allegiance and ordered the addition of "In God we trust" to all US paper money. Thus, although state and religious power had certainly separated, religious values and religious imagery remained integral to the business of state and the business of international relations.[291] Sociologists, who had regarded the process of secularization as an inevitable consequence of political, economic, and social modernization since the nineteenth century, began to reconsider their assumptions in the 1980s. The secularization thesis could not explain the resurgence of religious fundamentalism and the proliferation of diverse religious sects across the globe. As they began to explore the role of religion in modern societies in more depth, they discovered that the assumed secularization of earlier decades had been superficial at best.[292]

Throughout the Cold War, religious rhetoric played a central role in the rivalry between the Soviet Union and the United States, prompting one scholar to call it "one of history's great religious wars."[293] On the American side, notions of providentialism had been integral to the idea of American exceptionalism, which saw in the republic the realization of God's promised land.[294] By the early twentieth century Wilson infused his foreign policy with religious references to America's missionary obligations toward the world.[295] After World War II, the rhetoric intensified: political and religious leaders portrayed the fight against communism increasingly as a struggle for the defense of Judeo-Christian values against the atheist convictions of the communist state.[296] Leading American Cold War strategists, among them Dean Acheson and John Foster Dulles, both sons of protestant ministers, frequently resorted to religious imagery in their political statements.[297]

For the United States and its Western allies, religious symbolism became a major trope with which to transform the geopolitical conflict into an ideological-cultural one. It allowed politicians to cast the conflict in simple binaries of good versus evil and to mobilize their own people against communism. The distinction between democratic liberalism and Judeo-Christian values all but disappeared in the political rhetoric of the time. President Eisenhower was unabashed about the insertion of religion into politics. He mandated that all cabinet meetings began with a communal prayer, regularly consulted with the Protestant evangelical Billy Graham (who would go on to serve as spiritual consultant to every president, including Barack Obama), and declared in 1955 that "recognition of the Supreme Being is the first, the most basic, expression of Americanism. Without God, there could be no American form of government, nor an American way of life."[298] His secretary of state, John Foster Dulles, shared Eisenhower's deep religious conviction, making it a prominent factor in all policy decisions.

The widespread assumption in the West was that the communist state system was not only atheist but outright hostile to religious worship. According to the scholar Elizabeth Shakman Hurd, this was a misconception. She argued that the Soviet state had adopted a laicist model of secularism, which meant that its political system was devoid of religious references and that the practice of religion was confined to the private realm.[299] Even though Marx had called religion "the opiate of the masses," the Soviet system under Lenin did not ban religious practice. In fact, Lenin had in 1905 specifically sanctioned the private practice of religion as a right of every citizen. He did not, however, believe that religion should have a place in the public or political sphere.[300] In this respect his views were not all that different from those of his Western liberal adversaries. Both were heavily influenced by Enlightenment approaches to the role of religion in public life and the separation of church and state. Stalin initially took a much harder line toward religious groups. In the interwar period he persecuted religious leaders and restricted their ability to operate freely and independently. During the Second World War, however, he made concessions to the Orthodox Church in the interest of greater national unity. He sought to fuse the people's emotional attachment to the church with an equally emotional attachment to the nation. A similar accommodation occurred later in the socialist German Democratic Republic in the 1970s. In an effort to link the socialist present of the GDR with Germany's intellectual past, the political leadership launched a public rehabilitation of the sixteenth-century Protestant theologian Martin Luther, who had spent his life in several East German cities. Linking religious and national identity could inspire greater loyalty to the state, officials hoped.[301] Despite these accommodations, state officials in Eastern Europe and the Soviet Union maintained an uneasy relationship with the churches throughout the Cold War, alternating between repression and integration.[302]

The prevalence of religion in the Cold War discourse undermined core assumptions about the secularization of the modern world. Building on Enlightenment thinking, advocates of the secularization thesis had argued that modernization led to the decline of religion in politics and society. The logic was often reversed as well, with secularization of society and politics being seen as signs of modernization. The assumed nexus between modernization and secularization has been so deeply embedded in modern thought that progressive forces within societies have insisted on the secularization of public and political life, while religious leaders have at times resisted modernization because of the fear of religious decline.[303] These two positions were exemplified on one end of the spectrum by the efforts of Turkish leader Kemal Ataturk to modernize and secularize his country in the 1920s, and on the other by the efforts of the Taliban regime in Afghanistan in the 1990s to reverse the trend toward modernization in society and politics through the reinstitution of a strict religious code in public life.

Supporters of the secularization thesis can point to Western Europe, where religious affiliation and church memberships have steadily declined since the 1950s. Grace Davie argued, however, that decline in church membership in these countries did not necessarily mean a decline in religious belief. Rather she detected alternative forms of religious practice, focused on private noninstitutional worship, including a turn toward alternative religions and the practical application of religious beliefs in charitable institutions.[304] In addition, there existed wide variations in the practice of religion throughout Western Europe. In northern, predominantly Protestant countries, religious practice declined more than in southern Catholic and Orthodox parts. Ireland was a unique case, because religious affiliation was caught up in the political conflict between Protestants and Catholics in Northern Ireland. Furthermore, non-Western religious minorities expanded in most European countries, largely as a result of migration from former colonies. By the late twentieth century Muslims made up about 3 percent of Europe's population. France was home to about 3 to 4 million Muslims. Germany's Muslim population was estimated to be 1.6 million in the late 1980s, increasing to 3.2 million in 2008.[305] Britain had a Hindu/Sikh population of a little over a million.[306]

However, as the headscarf controversy in France illustrated, increasing secularization did not necessarily lead to a higher level of religious tolerance in Western Europe. Rather, it revealed a deep-seated secularized-religious foundation for everyday practices and customs in public life. The public display of religiosity through the wearing of headscarves upset both the appearance of cultural homogeneity and insistence on secularity. Some opponents of headscarves conflated homogeneity and equality. Homogeneity in dress and appearance, school officials argued, allowed for a more egalitarian learning environment that would not single out pupils for their different cultural, religious, or ethnic background. These officials failed to realize that their idea of cultural egalitarianism was also a prescription for a particularly French, Western, and Christian form of homogeneity, one that demanded public assimilation into the dominant Judeo-Christian cultural system.

Just as religion could encourage, even demand, cultural conformity, so it could fuel cultural and political rebellion. Religious activism became one of the key sites of opposition to the communist system in Eastern Europe. When the Polish cardinal Karol Wojtyła became Pope John Paul II in 1978, he inspired a religious revival in Poland that aligned itself with the labor organization Solidarity in 1980 to form a broad-based dissident movement against the communist state. Leading members of the Solidarity movement, above all Lech Walesa, acknowledged the decisive influence of the pope on the movement. Even though the Polish president, Wojciech Jaruzelski, declared a state of emergency and banned Solidarity in 1981, he was unable to crush the powerful church apparatus in this predominantly Catholic country. Throughout the next decade the Catholic Church provided a protective shield for the Polish dissident movement.

In neighboring East Germany the Protestant church came to play a key role in galvanizing opposition against the authoritarian state. Church leaders and the church buildings themselves offered refuge for dissidents in the 1980s. As antigovernment protests intensified in Leipzig in the fall of 1989, the St. Nikolai Church in the city center became a gathering point for weekly candlelight demonstrations. The crowds at the Leipzig prayers and demonstrations grew from around one thousand in September to more than five hundred thousand on November 6, just three days before the fall of the Berlin wall.[307] If religion had functioned as an ideological weapon of the West in the early Cold War, it had become a locus for political opposition movements in Eastern Europe by the end.

Religion played a role in anticolonial and civil rights struggles as well. In India in the 1940s Mohandas Gandhi developed his philosophy of nonviolent resistance based on the precepts of his Hindu faith. His philosophy, in turn, inspired Martin Luther King, a Baptist minister, in his civil rights campaign. King's public speeches in favor of equal rights for African Americans were heavily infused with religious rhetoric, and southern churches became centers of resistance against the system of racial segregation.[308] Malcolm X's calls for racial justice were inspired by his conversion to Islam and his membership in the African American organization Nation of Islam. Though he eventually distanced himself from the Nation and its leader, Elijah Mohamed, he remained a Muslim until his assassination at the hands of members of the Nation of Islam in February 1965.[309] Strengthened by their respective religious beliefs, King and Malcolm X shared a belief in the righteousness of their cause against the legal and political inequalities embedded in American society.

In Latin America, opposition movements drew on the spiritual precepts of liberation theology to protest the increasing social and economic dislocation of the poor in many parts of the continent. Since 1945, rapid economic growth and urbanization had dramatically increased the gulf between rich and poor in Central and South America. Prominent Latin American Catholic theologians, among them the El Salvadoran cardinal Óscar Romero, who was assassinated in 1980, the Peruvian theologian Gustavo Gutiérrez, and the Brazilian theologians Leonardo and Clodovis Boff, began advocating publicly for a new understanding of Christianity that reemphasized its obligation toward reducing the suffering of the poor.[310] Rather than engaging exclusively in charitable work, as had been traditional within the Catholic Church, these theologians openly criticized the political system that combined unfettered capitalism with repressive political authority. They demanded instead a system premised on the redistribution of wealth according to Christian morals, and on preserving human dignity through a minimum standard of living. Politically on the left, they also demanded better labor standards, regulation of industry, and the reduction of the power of foreign, primarily American, investors. Their campaign for more equity earned them censorship from the Vatican and persecution—in Romero's case fatal—in their own countries.[311]

Evangelical Protestantism provided an alternative to those disillusioned with the Catholic Church's dogmatism and deterred by liberation theology's leftist politics. Beginning in the 1950s, thousands of evangelical missionaries moved from the core areas of Europe and North America into Asia, Africa, and Latin America and converted local populations with spectacular success.[312] Evangelicals

Óscar Romero at his home in El Salvador, November 20, 1979. In the late 1970s he came to support the liberation theology espoused by Latin American theologians, which advocated publicly for Christianity's obligation to reduce the suffering of the poor. Romero also became an outspoken critic of the human rights violations and social injustices perpetrated by the military regime in his country. He was assassinated less than a year later. (Getty Images)

soon became the world's fastest-growing religious group, challenging the traditional predominance of the Catholic Church in many areas, particularly Latin America.[313] By 2000, evangelical Christians were 27 percent of Africa's population, 17 percent of Latin America's, and 5 percent of Asia's. At the beginning of the twentieth century, the average in those regions had been less than 2 percent.[314]

The proliferation of this particular brand of populist Christianity in the global South could be read both as a form of rebellion against the local establishment and a co-optation of the local population by wealthy, conservative, cultural imperialists. Liberation theologians themselves became the harshest critics of the movement, claiming—not altogether wrongly—that the missionary activities of North American evangelical churches in Central and South America reflected American business and foreign policy interests.[315] The failure of the Catholic establishment to support liberation theology's basic premises might have contributed to the tremendous success of Evangelicals and Pentecostals in the region. Unburdened by centralized control, these modern-day missionaries were able to adapt quickly to the needs and desires of local communities. They created a spiritual message that was deeply personal and focused on individual salvation. Yet at the same time they were connected to a global network of influential Evangelicals with vast financial resources and political clout in the industrial metropole.

Fundamentalisms and Pluralism

The fundamentalist version of Protestant evangelicalism emerged in the 1920s in the United States as a rural rebellion against modern industrial society and scientific-technological advances that shook the faith of many. The postwar revival of that movement, by contrast, embraced aspects of modernization, above all the latest advances in communication technology to spread the message of social and cultural conservatism.[316] By the 1970s evangelical preachers in the United States, among them televangelists Oral Roberts, Jerry Falwell, Jimmy Swaggart, and Jim Bakker, created actual and virtual communities of faithful and encouraged them to organize their personal and professional lives around the institutions of the church. Jerry Falwell built the Thomas Street Baptist Church in Lynchburg, Virginia, one of the first "megachurches" in the United States. Falwell utilized modern advertising techniques to rapidly enlarge his following, solicit donations, and create the Lynchburg Christian Academy in 1967 and Liberty University in 1971.[317] By 2010, Liberty University enrolled over 73,000 students, more than 60,000 of them in online degree programs. This and other megachurches functioned as religious enclaves for fundamentalist Christians who sought refuge from secular society.

It would be wrong to assume, however, that Falwell's goal was isolation from the secular world. Instead he sought to make the outside world more like his own. For that reason, in the late 1970s he founded a political lobbying group called the "Moral Majority," which openly supported conservative Christian candidates for public office.[318] The group gave rise to a host of politically conservative organizations collectively known as the New Christian Right. They made substantial financial contributions to Ronald Reagan's presidential campaign in 1980 as well as to the campaigns of countless other Christian conservatives running for state and national office. Thanks to the New Christian Right's lobbying efforts, religious conservatives began to assert real political influence in the United States by the 1980s. They shaped much of the debates about sensitive social issues, including abortion rights, homosexuality, and the teaching of evolution at public schools.

Fundamentalism took root in other major religions as well, particularly Islam. These religious movements have to be understood both as a critique against more liberal strands within their religious denominations and, as sociologist and religious scholar Peter L. Berger calls them, "populist" movements against a "secular elite."[319] Not all fundamentalists ventured into the realm of political protest, and even fewer turned to violence. But many of those who did belonged to the most disillusioned and disoriented segments of a population at odds with the processes of economic and cultural globalization. At the same time, though, as Peter Beyer and Lori Beaman have argued, "religion and the religious is an integral aspect of globalization and not an 'outside' respondent or victim."[320]

The term *fundamentalist* has been infused with heavy political baggage as well as pejorative connotations since the 1920s. The concept gained wide usage in the last quarter of the twentieth century as a label for a number of religious groups, including Muslim, Hindu, and Jewish denominations, and on occasion even for nonreligious movements. Its occasional polemical usage and its application to several quite distinct religions made a clear definition increasingly difficult. In an effort to gain clarity, the American Academy of Arts and Sciences in

1987 commissioned the Protestant religious scholar Martin E. Marty and the historian R. Scott Appleby to study and define religious fundamentalist movements. Over the next eight years, two hundred scholars participated in the production of a five-volume series on the subject.[321] When Marty attempted a first definition of fundamentalism in 1988, he began with what fundamentalism was not: it was not synonymous with conservatism or traditionalism; it was not anti-modern, or antiscientific; and therefore it was not a movement seeking a return to some static ahistorical ideal of religious practice. Fundamentalists were also not always activists, militants, or terrorists; and they were not necessarily poor or uneducated.[322] Instead, fundamentalism, Marty continued, was always reactive or reactionary; it drew on "selective retrieval," focused on certain aspects of its religion and ignored others; it was "exclusive or separatist." Marty even called adherents to fundamentalism "oppositional," "absolutist," and "authoritarian," unable to forge any form of compromise with those who think differently. As a result, fundamentalism was also "anti-evolutionary, anti-hermeneutical, and anti-permissive."[323]

Though comprehensive, Marty's definition of fundamentalisms (he later preferred the plural form) remained contested. Some scholars, particularly specialists of non-Christian religions, rightly argued that the religious and doctrinal elements within each of these movements were so different that it was impossible to compare them, much less to determine common sources or outcomes. Others believed with Marty that despite their differences fundamentalist religions had something in common, but provided a much more general definition. According to Peter Berger, they "suggest a combination of several features—great religious passion, a defiance of what others have defined as the *Zeitgeist*, and a return to traditional sources of religious authority."[324] The anthropologist Richard Antoun argued that fundamentalists of different religious denominations were united in their belief in the absolute authority of the sacred over every aspect of their private and public life, and that their strict adherence to a religiously inspired worldview determined their code of conduct.[325]

Religious absolutism was on the rise in the last quarter of the twentieth century. Explanations as to why diverged. Some analyzed it in primarily religious terms (as a disaffection of particularly faithful believers with the liberalization of religious practice within their faith); others in social or political terms, as a religio-political response to the experience of social and economic decline, including unfulfilled promises of decolonization, persistent poverty, an increasing gap between rich and poor, negative social consequences of urbanization, lack of opportunities for a young generation with rising expectations, and encounters with a secularized, homogenized, increasingly material global culture.[326]

The phenomenon of fusing religious and political identity emerged most prominently in the Middle East in the postwar period. The legal scholar Abdullahi A. An-Na'im defined political Islam as "the mobilization of Islamic identity in pursuit of particular objectives of public policy, both within an Islamic society and in its relations with other societies."[327] The association of modernizing leaders with both secularism and the former colonial powers provided a niche for religious fundamentalists to fuse the ideology and practice of Islam with the political causes of anti-imperialism and anti-Westernism.[328] The Iranian revolution in 1979 reflected this conflation of political and religious ideologies. It deposed the secularist and repressive regime of Shah Reza Pahlavi, who ended democratic rule after a CIA-backed coup against the populist democratically elected leader Mohammad Mosaddegh in 1953. After a coalition of liberal intellectuals and Islamic fundamentalists succeeded in ousting the shah in 1979, Islamic fundamentalists turned against the liberal wing and established a theocracy under Ayatollah Khomeini. The new regime limited freedom of expression, political rights, and women's rights. Moreover it turned decisively against Western cultural and political influence. Iran became a model state of political Islamism.[329]

Religion and politics also overlapped in the Arab-Israeli conflict after 1948. Arab neighbors saw Israel as a "colonial implant" protected by the former imperial powers of the West. Radical political Islamists made the eradication of the state of Israel a religious jihad. Begun as a nationalist movement under the leadership of Yasser Arafat, the Palestine Liberation Organization (PLO) and its political wing increasingly merged religion with political identity. On the Israeli side, too, the more radical political parties expressed their struggle against Arab neighbors in religious terms. The extreme religio-political voices often undermined efforts by more moderate and secularized politicians to forge a compromise. The conflict was exacerbated by the economic and social dislocation of populations left in

Ayatollah Khomeini, January 17, 1979. He became Supreme Leader of Iran after the successful revolution that deposed Shah Reza Pahlavi. The revolution conflated political and religious ideologies, leading to the establishment of an Islamist theocracy. (Getty Images)

poverty and without a political voice. For Palestinians, the dislocation was not just economic but spatial, because they had to settle in what started as temporary and then turned into permanent refugee camps in Syria, Lebanon, Egypt, Jordan, the Gaza Strip, and the West Bank.[330] The stakes in the conflict became, in Marty's words, "absolutist," and thus made compromise impossible.

Despite the polarization of religious identity in the Middle East, efforts were under way to increase cross-denominational dialogue. In 1948, shortly after World War II, the major Christian churches, with the notable exception of the Catholic Church, formed the World Council of Churches (WCC) in an effort to improve cooperation and communication on doctrinal, practical, and social issues. The Roman Catholic Church sent observers to the WCC meetings and gradually increased its dialogue with non-Christian religions over the next decades. The Second Vatican Council made some progress with its declaration, *Nostra Aetate*, which redefined the Church's relationship with non-Christian religions. Issued in 1965 under Pope Paul VI, the document promoted both dialogue and understanding for non-Christian religions, particularly Hinduism, Buddhism, Islam, and Judaism.[331] Ecumenical and interfaith organizations proliferated in the postwar period in response to the increasing geographic proximity of different religious faiths in many parts of the world. They sought to contain the potential for conflict and hatred that came with this close proximity and to promote among them a greater understanding and acceptance of religious difference.

The rise in interfaith movements was related to the general increase in popularity of non-Western religions among people in the industrial world. Beginning in the 1950s, interest in Zen Buddhism rose significantly in the United States and Western Europe.[332] By the 1960s Hinduism and Zen Buddhism became for many adherents of the counterculture a spiritual retreat from the technocratic and materialist realities of modern society. According to a 1970 US survey, 3 percent of the population of San Francisco claimed to have tried Buddhist meditation and 5 percent had tried Transcendental Meditation. Nationwide the figure was similarly high, with 4 percent having tried Transcendental Meditation, suggesting that the practice had found supporters beyond the core areas of the counterculture. Transcendental Meditation, or TM, as its practitioners called it, was a method of meditation popularized by the Hindu spiritualist Maharishi Mahesh Yogi. Traditional Hindu spiritual leaders looked with suspicion on the Maharishi's version of meditation because it was much shorter and less rigorous than the traditional process of Hindu religious meditation, which required weeks or months of discipleship and ascetic rituals. The Maharishi's method gained international fame when the Beatles went on a three-month retreat to his meditation center in Rishikesh, India, in 1968. They were joined by other celebrities, among them Mia Farrow and Shirley MacLaine. The Maharishi's appeal reached far beyond the celebrity level, however. He regularly toured Western Europe and the American West, where interest in non-Western religions was strong. TM met the needs of Western professionals in search of spiritual renewal.[333]

The search for alternative spirituality in the Western world continued throughout the 1970s and 1980s with the proliferation of experimental religious communities, many of them inspired by Hinduism. Among the more controversial groups was the Rajneeshpuram, which followed the leadership of Bhagwan Shree Rajneesh, an Indian professor of philosophy. In the 1970s he established an ashram in the Indian town of Puna, where he conducted meditations and lectured on spiritual matters. His liberal attitude toward sexuality and his criticism of Gandhi earned him powerful enemies in India and prompted him to relocate to the United States in the early 1980s. By then most of his followers were American. Within a year of taking up residence in the small town of Antelope in rural Oregon, the members of his group clashed with the local community and each other.[334] In addition, the Rajneesh himself came under scrutiny from federal authorities for tax evasion and immigration violations. In a 1985 plea bargain he agreed to leave the United States. After extensive travels in Europe and Asia, in 1987 he returned to India, where he died three years later at the age of fifty-eight.[335] His meditation center in Puna continued to attract international visitors in search of spiritual renewal, meditation, and stress management.

Interest in Hinduism, Zen Buddhism, and other Eastern religions became part of the New Age movement, which spread throughout the Western world in the last quarter of the twentieth century. The addition of "movement" to the term *New Age* might be somewhat misleading, because no central group or even cluster of groups existed to define or coordinate the practice of "New Age." Nonetheless, the phenomenon became significant enough to produce a large body of literature and an equally large number of workshops, commercial enterprises, and a health industry. New Age ranged from interest in the occult and astrology to psychotherapy, self-help, alternative medicine, and ecology. According to one definition, "the New Age movement is characterized by a popular Western culture criticism expressed in terms of a secularized esotericism."[336] Its adherents were predominantly middle-class and white, unified in their unease about materialism and their attempts to seek spiritual, esoteric alternatives. Yet rather than rejecting modern consumer society altogether, New Age adherents developed an alternative consumer culture. By the late 1980s, New Age had become a major global enterprise with particularly strong followings in Germany, New Zealand, Israel, Great Britain, and the United States, with a lucrative industry to sustain it.[337] At the same time, critics began to call into question some New Age practices, including interest in the occult, tarot cards, and efforts to communicate with spirits. Others began to see New Age less as a social or religious movement and more as a path toward personal fulfillment and spiritual improvement.

For New Age followers in the West who were in search of spiritual renewal, a major destination became India—including Puna, where the Rajneesh had set up a resort; Adyar, Madras, where the Theosophical Society, an early twentieth-century precursor of the New Age movement had its headquarters; and Puducherry, where the spiritual leader Sri Aurobindo and his collaborator Mirra Richards, known as "the Mother," had set up an ashram in the 1920s. Aurobindo's ashram attracted global attention when Richards, who became instrumental in sustaining and expanding it after Aurobindo's death in 1950, set up an experimental township called Auroville in 1968. The community, which won an official endorsement from UNESCO, included members from dozens of countries who sought to translate the spiritual precepts of Aurobindo's philosophy into practical living arrangements. Initially a Western adaptation of Indian religious ideas and practices, Auroville and other New Age communities gained new adherents among middle- and upper-class Indians, thus reconnecting the Westernized version of Hindu spiritualism with its indigenous Indian roots.[338]

Embrace of non-Western religious practices also merged with environmental concerns to create a new understanding of the relationship between the human body and its natural environment.[339] Homeopathy, yoga, holistic medicine, aromatherapy, and the Chinese practice of acupuncture gained popularity among middle-class intellectuals in Europe and North America beginning in the 1970s.[340] Practitioners increasingly stressed the links between physical and spiritual health. Western psychologists, psychiatrists, and medical scientists, too, began to study more systematically the relationship between the two. As a result,

TABLE 4.2

Number of adherents of major religions, as a percentage of the global population

Religion	1900	1970	2000	2010
Agnostic	0.19%	14.68%	10.70%	9.81%
Buddhist	7.84%	6.36%	7.32%	7.16%
Chinese Traditional	23.46%	6.16%	6.99%	6.30%
Christian	34.46%	33.24%	32.43%	32.81%
Hindu	12.53%	12.53%	13.47%	13.76%
Muslim	12.34%	15.62%	21.08%	22.51%

Data source: World Religion Database.

medical experts gradually began to integrate non-Western methods into their approaches to healing, including the use of ancient herbs and other natural remedies.

In many ways New Age was a response to the increasing dependence of humans on technology, but it was by no means an antimodern movement. Rather, it tried to channel the advances made in science and technology into projects toward the personal betterment of humanity. The objectives were distinctly personal rather than collective. The regeneration of body and soul was to be achieved through the attainment of harmony between modernism and tradition as well as between mind and matter. The global interest in this new spirituality was distinctly born from a life of affluence and comfort. As such it stood in marked contrast to the spread of other religious movements, among them liberation theology and Islamic fundamentalism.

As the concurrent rise of religious fundamentalism and religious pluralism shows, the world's religions were not static entities immune to cultural or even doctrinal change. Religious beliefs and religious practices evolved in tandem with and in reaction to larger social, cultural, and political forces. By the same token, evolving religious identities, practices, and belief systems contributed to the cultural transformations of the second half of the twentieth century. Two factors in particular defined religion's role in these cultural transformations. The first was religion's relationship to modernism. By the beginning of the twenty-first century it had become increasingly clear that the traditional assumptions about the secularizing power of modernism no longer held true. In other words, economic, social, and political modernization did not inevitably lead to a decline in religiosity. To be sure, certain functions traditionally fulfilled by religious belief systems and religious institutions had been taken over by other agencies—for instance, the spiritual function of explaining the mysteries of the natural world and the origin of life was increasingly taken over by science, and religion's practical function of creating communities and engaging in charity was increasingly taken over, at least in the Western world, by government agencies and secular humanitarian organizations. However, rather than rendering religious affiliation obsolete, both worshippers and religious organizations adapted to the changing functions of religion in the modern world. The more flexible religious organizations were in their adaptation to the changing spiritual and emotional needs of congregations, the better they survived or even prospered. Modernism thus affected religion in unanticipated ways. It encouraged a system of religious beliefs and religious practice that became more flexible, more fragmented, and more diverse. Within all major religions, above all within Christianity, Hinduism, Judaism, and Islam, a broad spectrum of subgroups emerged, ranging from liberal-progressive to fundamentalist-conservative.

Religion's second major contribution to the cultural transformations of the past sixty years was the consolidation of the idea of religious pluralism. Since 1945 religious boundaries had at once multiplied and become more diffuse. They had multiplied because many religious subgroups erected spiritual, if not territorial, barriers to the secular world. The process of creating religious enclaves occurred primarily within fundamentalist and conservative subgroups. However, boundaries also became more diffuse as fewer of them cohered with political or state boundaries. Conservative and liberal variants of a single faith coexisted within a single locale, often sharing the same urban space when recruiting worshippers. In all major metropolitan areas of the world, one can find representatives of every major faith, often subgroups within each faith as well.

Religious pluralism, as defined by Thomas Banchoff, is "the interaction among religious groups in society and politics." It emerged in the period after 1945, Banchoff argued, as a result of increased international migration, urbanization, and cultural globalization. "In the context of globalization and modernity, individuals constitute and reconstitute religious groups on a more fluid basis."[341] However, the idea of religious pluralism, in which individuals choose or "consume" religion, like they would other products offered in a pluralistic society, does not translate easily into reality. Even in the United States, which has a long tradition of religious tolerance, tensions arose between majority and minority religious groups over the inscription of oppositional values into state and national laws. Those include questions of public religious display, abortion rights, homosexuality, and same-sex marriage. In Europe religious pluralism created deep divisions, less about religious beliefs than about the outwardly visible cultural signs associated with religious practice. Other divisions have included the treatment of women within Muslim cultures or the practice of Sharia, which could bring Muslims in direct conflict with Euro-American law.

Even though pluralism is one of the core elements of any democratic system, religious pluralism has at times been seen as a threat to democracy. The root of this argument lies in the confrontation of Western religions, primarily Christianity and Judaism, with non-Western religions. How should a political system based on values forged in large part out of a Judeo-Christian heritage absorb and accommodate groups and individuals steeped in a religion and culture that in many ways contradict that heritage? Or as the legal theorist and philosopher Martha Nussbaum asked: "How can a respectful pluralistic society shore up its fragile bases of toleration, especially in a time of increased domestic religious pluralism and in a world in which we need to cultivate toleration not only internally, but also between peoples and states?" According to Nussbaum, a secularized civil religion, as first postulated by Jean-Jacques Rousseau, offered a flawed solution, because its consequence was intolerance toward those who did not adhere to the fundamental precepts of that civil religion, which in turn created even bigger problems in international relations. In fact, in 1762 Rousseau had declared, "It is impossible to live in peace with those one believes to be damned."[342] Nussbaum suggested another option, based on John Stuart Mill's nineteenth-century elaboration on the idea of a "religion of humanity," first suggested by Auguste Comte.[343] This religion embraced "compassion as a moral sentiment that can be cultivated by public institutions and public education." This new form of patriotism, as she called it, would contain within itself the idea of tolerance and compassion toward others and thus create pride in universal humanity. She argued that "a liberal society, without offending against respect for pluralism, can still employ a moral ideal of this sort [compassion] and promote a moral education aimed at underwriting it. This ideal would serve as a basis for public political culture, in connection with public norms of equality and respect."[344] Thus, rather than banning religious identity from public life, the tolerant state could embrace religious pluralism and tolerance as part of its national identity.

Nussbaum's proposal returns us to the idea of embedding particularism within a larger framework of universality. By incorporating religious pluralism and the diversity of values within a larger project of public education and ultimately national identity, the state places diversity at the core of its unification process. This unification process, whether at the state, regional, or global level, presupposes an agreement on certain basic human values and morals that might ultimately be difficult to achieve. It requires religious leaders and their followers to focus their doctrines on the fundamentals of human dignity and well-being rather than on more specific doctrines and practices. Ironically, it was often the fundamentalist branches of the world's major religions that lost sight of these fundamental values, and created instead an elaborate system of doctrines, rules, and social practices that made them incompatible with others.[345] At the turn of the twenty-first century the challenge remained of how to curb the power of those who wanted to abolish pluralism without resorting to coercive measures such as curtailing free speech and free expression of religious and cultural difference.

4. Human Rights and Globalization

IN many ways the postwar rise of human rights in the international arena became a secular religion of sorts for rational Enlightenment thinkers across the world. International legal experts, humanitarians, diplomats, and religious leaders could rally behind the idea of establishing a new world order in which the rights of individuals and states were guaranteed by a common set of laws. Begun as an idealistic vision of universal values applicable to all of humanity, the debates about the definition and scope of human rights since World War II showcased the major cultural dichotomies between particularism and universalism, and between homogenization and heterogenization.

Debates about rights had been part of state formation for centuries, focusing initially on concerns about citizenship and the rule of law within the state. However, as the world community suffered through two devastating wars in the first half of the twentieth century, the debate regarding rights shifted from the domestic to the international realm. The core question became whether human beings, despite cultural and political differences, could agree on a universal code of conduct that would guide their interactions and prevent future wars. Determining the substance of these values became part of an international discourse on rights: civil rights, women's rights, economic rights, minority rights. While participation in this discourse expanded, agreement on the nature and extent of these values remained elusive. The debates themselves illustrate the political constraints of reaching a global consensus on fundamental rights accorded all human beings and the practical constraints of enforcing a universal rights code around the globe.

The United Nations helped define the international rights debate at its first conference in San Francisco in 1945. Emerging from a devastating conflict that had claimed fifty to seventy million lives, most of them civilians, the delegates rallied around the core principles of international peace and justice. They agreed on a fundamental set of rules to guide relations among its member states, including, enshrined in the preamble to the UN Charter, "faith in fundamental human rights, in the dignity and worth of the human person, in the equal rights of men and women and of nations large and small."[346] The Charter deliberately neglected to define the meaning and extent of those rights, leaving states, individuals, and human rights advocates to argue over those issues for the next six decades. It also deliberately neglected to provide mechanisms of enforcement, leaving states free to determine the reach of individual rights within their own jurisdiction.

Even though scholars trace human rights discourses to early Enlightenment thinkers, concrete transnational manifestations of the realization of a human rights agenda remained rare.[347] Rights campaigns surfaced in different political and social contexts throughout the nineteenth century, among them the campaign against slavery, the women's rights movement, and the fight for workers' rights. The first Geneva Convention, ratified by twelve nations in 1864, established an international set of rules for the treatment of captured and wounded enemy soldiers.[348] The brutal colonial regimes of the late nineteenth century and the genocides and wars of the first half of the twentieth century, however, dispelled any illusion that these rights discourses led to a more just and humane world.[349] In the aftermath of World War I, Woodrow Wilson advocated a system of international laws to regulate relations among nations without recourse to war but he refrained from adding human rights to his Fourteen Points. Nongovernmental human rights advocacy groups, such as the Ligue des Droits de l'Homme, which was founded in the aftermath of the anti-Semitic Dreyfus affair in France in 1898, and which pledged to protect minorities, struggled to gain political attention.[350]

A global human rights agenda emerged gradually between 1941 and 1948 under US and UN auspices. In January 1941, Franklin Delano Roosevelt included the defense of human rights in his State of the Union address and repeated the pledge as part of the Allied Powers' statement of war aims on New Year's Day 1942, shortly after America's entry into the war.[351] Though human rights were not included in the Atlantic Charter of August 1941, six months later the declaration of the United Nations, consisting of the countries at war with the Axis powers, pledged to "preserve human rights and justice in their own lands as well as in other lands." There was no further elaboration on what these rights were or how they should be enforced.[352]

·[651]·

Because the UN Charter's definition of human rights was so vague, international human rights advocates pushed for a separate Universal Bill of Rights. The UN subsequently set up a human rights commission to draw up such a document under the leadership of the United States' former first lady Eleanor Roosevelt. The final product of the committee, the Universal Declaration of Human Rights (UDHR), included individual civil and political rights and collective economic and social rights. The preamble laid out the general principles of dignity, liberty, equality, and brotherhood, and the reasons for the declaration. Then followed articles relating to individual rights (Articles 3–11); rights of individuals in relation to groups (Articles 12–17); spiritual, public, and political rights (Articles 18–21); and economic, social, and cultural rights (Articles 22–27). Articles 28–30 placed the rights within the broader context of limits, duties, and order.[353] Clean and orderly as the organization of the Declaration was, it could not mask the ambiguities in the wording, which led almost immediately to contestations over the meaning of such concepts as freedom, the proper relationship among individual, community, and states' rights, and the obvious and most glaring gap in provisions for the enforcement of these rights. The document thus reflected idealistic aspiration rather than practical political application. The UN General Assembly approved the Declaration on December 10, 1948, by a vote of forty-eight states in favor, none opposed, and eight abstentions. The abstentions came from the Soviet Union and its satellite states Byelorussia, Poland, Czechoslovakia, and the Ukraine; from independent socialist Yugoslavia; and from Saudi Arabia and South Africa. They reflected a fundamental unease about the potential infringement on the sovereignty of individual states, even though the declaration included no provisions for the enforcement of the human rights agenda.

Cold War Human Rights

Despite its claim of universality, the UDHR would be at the center of all the major global political and cultural divisions over the next half-century, beginning with the Cold War struggle between East and West. In fact, at the very moment of the adoption of the declaration in New York, the United States brought accusations of human rights violations against the Soviet Union before the United

Nations. Five months earlier, the Soviets had blocked all traffic between the Western-controlled parts of Berlin and the Western zones of Germany in protest over the currency reform implemented by the Western Allies. The Soviets feared that the introduction of a new currency in the Western sectors of the city would destroy the old currency still in existence in the Soviet-controlled sector as well as the Soviet occupation zone surrounding Berlin. The US deputy representative to the United Nations, Philip C. Jessup, charged that the Soviet Union was depriving the citizens of Berlin of access to food, fuel, and health care, basic rights inscribed in Article 25 of the UDHR: the right to a "standard of living adequate for the health and well-being of himself and his family."[354] Ultimately the two parties resolved the crisis outside the venue of the United Nations, but not until the following May. Berlin marked the first of many Cold War clashes in which opposing definitions of human rights played a key role.

Anticommunists in the United States and Western Europe were determined to press the human rights agenda into service for their ideological battle against the Soviet Union. They charged that communism itself violated human rights, because it deprived those under its rule of the fundamental rights of freedom of expression, freedom of movement, and religious and political freedoms. They drew selectively on the Universal Declaration to hail the Western liberal democratic system as its champion and vilify the Soviet-dominated system as its direct nemesis. They could draw on some hard facts in support of their claims, including the persecution of political dissidents under Stalin. However, human rights remained marginal to their rhetorical campaign against the Soviet system, because they did not want to open themselves up to potential charges, particularly during the ideologically repressive era of McCarthyism in the United States. Led by Republican senator Joseph McCarthy from Wisconsin, policy makers and law enforcement officials launched a fierce campaign against political leftists in public life, destroying careers and incarcerating many suspected of subversive activities, including spying for the Soviet Union. The government's obsession with anticommunism led to substantial violations of individuals' rights to free speech and due process, in the interest and under cover of national security.[355]

The Soviet Union, in turn, focused on America's dismal human rights record regarding its African American population. It provided active support to African Americans who brought cases of systematic racial discrimination to the attention of the United Nations General Assembly. At a meeting of the UN subcommission for minority rights in Geneva in the fall of 1947, the Soviet delegates used a petition brought to the UN by W. E. B. Du Bois to charge that US support for international minority rights was undermined by US treatment of its own minorities. Du Bois and the African American civil rights association NAACP were at that time publicly lobbying for the inclusion of African American equality in the UDHR. Du Bois had presented to the General Assembly his "Appeal to the World: A Statement on the Denial of Human Rights to Minorities in the Case of Citizens of Negro Descent in the United States of America and an Appeal to the United Nations for Redress." His act met with strong disapproval from white liberal civil rights supporters, including Eleanor Roosevelt.[356]

US political leaders initially sought to deflect those criticisms by pointing to the advances, albeit elusive, made in the United States since the end of World War II. Yet soon they took a more calculated approach that sought to associate with communism the calls for some human rights, including the right to equal pay for equal work and the rights to housing and health care. The historian Carol Anderson has argued that the Cold War "blacklisting" of these human rights objectives seriously undermined African Americans' struggle for equality in the United States and forced them to settle for a much narrower fight for political and legal equality. Even liberal supporters of black equality, Anderson showed, refrained from championing social and economic rights on a national and global scale. By refusing to ensure the international enforcement of those two key rights enshrined in Articles 25 and 26, US human rights advocates severely compromised the declaration's potential to achieve universal equality.[357]

Divisions over the human rights agenda were also at the center of the struggle for decolonization in the 1950s and 1960s. European powers went to great length in the 1940s to exclude the populations in their colonies from the reach of universal human rights, particularly in the realm of civil and political rights.[358] Belgium, Great Britain, France, and other colonial powers, eager to hold on to their overseas possessions, argued for an exemption clause for colonial territories. They justified this exemption in terms of cultural difference, yet these justifications were little more than thinly veiled expressions of racial discrimination. Giving colonial subjects the same rights, advocates of the exemption clause argued, would endanger the public order in those territories.[359]

Conversely, anticolonial activists saw in the human rights agenda a vital tool for their struggle for independence. At the 1955 Bandung Conference of Non-Aligned Nations, where African and Asian nations—some of them newly independent—sought closer economic and political cooperation and a common strategy to fight colonialism and imperialism, participants defined self-determination as the "first right." Though human rights scholars later contested whether self-determination was in fact a human right, the delegates at Bandung clearly identified it as such and gave it a privileged position.[360] Self-determination, while not explicitly stated in the UDHR, clearly related to the collective rights of individuals to freely choose their form of government and to participate in the process of political governance.

The Bandung delegates debated individual human rights as well. For instance, the Egyptian journalist and publisher Mahmoud Aboul Fath, who had been forced into exile for his open criticism of Gamal Abdel Nasser, admonished delegates not to lose sight of individual human rights, among them the right to free speech. In an open letter to conference participants he implored delegates to adhere to the standards laid out in the UDHR. "The violation of human rights," he warned, "is certainly bad and intolerable when committed by imperialists against peoples on whom they force their authority, but it is also worse and more obnoxious [when] committed by a few nationals against their own people."[361] Fath's statement put into sharp relief the tension between individual and collective rights. The right to self-determination applied primarily to states, not to individuals. It harked back to the post–World War I focus on minority rights, rather than the United Nations formulation of the rights of individuals.[362] Fath warned against establishing a hierarchy of human rights that replaced one category of rights with another, arguing instead that adherence to both collective and individual rights was a necessary prerequisite for the creation of a just post-colonial world.

The universal language of human rights served Asian and African political demands for independence in the 1950s and 1960s. They claimed for themselves the same rights afforded the original signers of the Declaration. At the Bandung Conference, African and Asian states rejected not only the traditional political regime of colonial governance, but also the cultural system of human rights relativism. Their understanding of the interconnection between universal human rights and the anticolonial struggle found expression in declarations of independence across Asia and Africa. The African National Congress, for instance, that same year drew heavily on the language of human rights in its formulation of the Freedom Charter.[363] Individual rights, the Freedom Charter argued, long the prerogative of the white minority population in South Africa, should be extended to all citizens of South Africa, regardless of skin color.

Some of the debates over the meaning and scope of human rights were expressed in the language of cultural difference. In fact, cultural differences had already been a source of contention during the drafting of the declaration. Yet the mostly white Euro-American commission quickly dispensed with any argument in favor of interpreting or enforcing human rights differently in different parts of the world. The commission did, in fact, solicit the views of a few prominent non-Western intellectuals before it finalized the wording of the Declaration. Gandhi, who at the time was leading India's struggle for independence, declared that he preferred an emphasis on duties rather than rights. He explained that "the very right to live accrues to us only when we do the duty of citizenship of the world." Instead of a universal declaration of rights, he proposed "to define the duties of Man and Woman and correlate every right to some corresponding duty to be first performed. Every other right can be shown to be a usurpation hardly worth fighting for." The Chinese philosopher Chung-Shu Lo concurred: in Chinese social and political discourse, rights were enshrined within the language of duties to one's neighbor.[364] These critiques did not amount to a rejection of the concept of human rights, but instead challenged the way in which these rights were framed. Most importantly, however, they affirmed the universality of rights and duties across cultural divides.

In the 1960s the parameters of the human rights debates shifted from the international arena of intergovernmental agencies to grassroots activism on the local and transnational level. As student protesters in the industrial world challenged the Cold War order and charged their own governments with violating the principles of democratic governance, new organizations emerged that made the defense of human rights on a global scale their main objective. Most prominent among them was Amnesty International, founded in 1961 by the British lawyer and labor activist Peter Benenson.[365] Amnesty International's mission was to draw public attention to individuals who were incarcerated for political reasons. Benenson encouraged letter-writing campaigns to put public pressure on law enforcement agencies and governments to release political prisoners. Though its record was sketchy over the next decade, the organization grew rapidly into an international network and expanded its advocacy to women's rights, children's rights, and rights of refugees and torture victims. Its significance in the 1960s and 1970s lay in expanding human rights advocacy from a high-level intergovernmental diplomatic endeavor to a grassroots-level transnational movement. In the atmosphere of mass political activism of the 1960s, the organization's idealistic objectives appealed to many who had grown frustrated with the level of complacency among their own political leaders.[366]

Amnesty International focused on the plight of individuals. It tried to remain politically neutral in the public sphere, much to the dismay of those who felt that the human rights abuses in some regimes could not and should not be separated from their political context.[367] The organization went so far as to advise local branches to "adopt" political prisoners in equal proportion from Western countries, the communist world, and the Third World.[368] Furthermore it showed a marked preference for cases with sensationalist potential, in order to raise public awareness about Amnesty International's work. Critics charged that this method privileged publicity over the actual cases and possibly detracted from human rights violations that deserved equal or more attention.

Amnesty International's work epitomized the shift toward individual rights in the global human rights agenda of the 1970s. Their radius of operation also extended into the global South, where, despite Fath's earlier warnings, human rights violations mounted. Many postcolonial leaders resorted to political oppression and physical violence to consolidate their power. Throughout much of the Cold War these regimes justified political repression as a legitimate means to ensure public order and political stability, often receiving political cover from one or the other superpower. Even when US president Jimmy Carter pledged in 1977 to make human rights one of the core policy principles of his administration, geopolitical considerations interfered.[369] Carter put pressure on Chile and used human rights as political leverage in his dealings with the Soviet Union, yet he failed to follow through with countries that were important economic and political allies, including South Africa, whose apartheid regime was a flagrant violation of human rights but whose anticommunist policies made it a crucial Cold War ally of the United States.[370]

Even though the Carter administration's human rights policies remained burdened by Cold War considerations, progress occurred on the European stage with the multiyear Conference on Security and Cooperation in Europe (CSCE), attended by Western and Eastern European states as well as Canada and the United States. Eastern Europeans had convened the conference in an effort to gain Western acceptance of the existing system of postwar state boundaries. Western European states signaled their willingness to agree to the permanence of those boundaries, with the proviso that a series of human rights clauses be added to the final accords.[371] Those clauses included "respect [for] human rights and fundamental freedoms, including the freedom of thought, conscience, religion or belief, for all without distinction as to race, sex, language or religion," but also a section on "equal rights and self-determination of peoples."[372] The Helsinki Accords of 1975 led to the creation of the Helsinki Watch group, a nongovernmental organization that monitored compliance with the accords in Eastern Europe and the Soviet Union.[373] The Accords also encouraged Eastern European dissidents, among them prominent Russian physicist Andrei Sakharov, Russian writer Aleksandr Solzhenitsyn, and Czech playwright Vaclav Havel, to create movements that challenged their own governments and ultimately helped bring down the communist regimes in 1989.[374] The signing of the Accords established, at least on paper, a common understanding of the inviolability of human rights across the Cold War divide. Despite those efforts, repression in Eastern Europe persisted, demonstrating that the human rights regime would remain an ideal rather than a reality for years to come.

Defining Human Rights after the Cold War

The year 1989 offered new hope for the triumph of human rights in international relations. As communist regimes in Eastern Europe and the Soviet Union fell, the United Nations seemed poised to take a much more active role in guaranteeing peace, justice, and universal rights around the world. Funding for repressive leaders in the world dried up. South Africa released its most prominent political prisoner, Nelson Mandela, within two months of the fall of the Berlin Wall; Latin American insurgents and dictators lost financial backing. Nicaragua held multiparty democratic elections in 1990, which deposed the Soviet-backed Sandinistas. The end of the Cold War also coincided with the emergence and expansion of global communication networks, including the advent of the Internet and the launching of new communication satellites into space. Together, these developments filled people with optimism that the post–Cold War years could break down cultural barriers and foster a new era of global peace.

The global surge in optimism dissipated soon after 1989. The end of the Cold War did as much to expose ethnic, cultural, and political divisions as it did to forge new connections across ideological and cultural divides. An example of the former was the ethnic conflict emerging in Yugoslavia in the 1990s. Serbs, Croats, Bosnians, and Albanians, who had kept in check their historic animosities as long as they lived under communist control, now lashed out against one another with brutal force unseen on the European continent since World War II. Serbia's ethnic cleansing campaign in Bosnia in the early 1990s was a painful reminder of past atrocities in the region and revealed the inability or unwillingness of the international community to act on behalf of victims of human rights abuses. Around 2.2 million civilians in the region were displaced, some of them to refugee camps within the former Yugoslavia, others to European Union countries and North America. Only about half of them returned, according to a 2006 UN report.[375]

European Union countries, which absorbed many of the Balkan refugees as well as migrants from other Eastern European countries, struggled socially, economically, and culturally to integrate the newcomers. In Germany, France, Austria, the Netherlands, and elsewhere, ultraconservative political parties garnered votes through anti-immigrant and ultranationalist positions. For a while it seemed that the opening of the borders to the former communist bloc created a nationalist backlash rather than a rush to global integration. Western Europeans debated questions of citizenship, responsibility for language education, tolerance of nonindigenous cultural practices, women's rights, and access to social services like health care. Most of the governments developed a dual approach: they tightened restrictions on immigration and political asylum while simultaneously redoubling efforts to integrate and provide basic services for those they

In 1987, protesters in Johannesburg marched for the release of Nelson Mandela, who had been imprisoned by the South African apartheid regime since 1964. International pressure on South Africa to end its human rights abuses and discriminatory practices against black citizens increased in the 1980s. In 1994, four years after his release from prison, Mandela became the country's first democratically elected post-apartheid leader. (Getty Images)

permitted to enter. Even if international migration did not always translate into greater cultural understanding, it nonetheless led to greater cultural and ethnic diversity in all major European countries by the beginning of the twenty-first century.

Ethnic tension erupted into mass murder in Rwanda in 1994. The killing of the Rwandan and Burundi presidents in an attack on their airplane as it approached the Rwandan capital, Kigali, unleashed the genocide. Both men belonged to the Hutu ethnic group, which had for years agitated against the Tutsi minority in Rwanda. Over the course of three months Hutus murdered between five hundred thousand and one million Tutsis and moderate Hutus, while UN troops, who had been deployed to the region in a peacekeeping mission in 1993, stood idly by. As they explained later, they had no official UN mandate to intervene and thus were powerless to prevent the massacres.[376]

Tensions also continued regarding the integration of Muslim populations into Western, primarily Christian societies. In France the controversy over the wearing of the veil in schools and public venues intensified, creating a strange coalition between conservative anti-immigration advocates, who wanted to force cultural and social assimilation within the immigrant population, and liberal, leftist, and feminist politicians who saw the veil as an infringement on the secular traditions of the French state and an expression of women's degradation in the public sphere. The long-standing controversy resulted in a 2004 national law prohibiting the wearing of "ostentatious signs of religious affiliation in public schools," followed in 2010 by a parliamentary vote to ban veils "designed to hide the face."[377] The ban took effect in April 2011. Belgium followed suit with a similar ban that went into effect three months later.

Concern over the integration of Muslim populations were magnified after the end of the Cold War by the rise of political Islamism in the Middle East and more specifically the creation of informal regional and transnational groups of varying militant persuasions. These groups established bases in states with sizable Muslim populations—tolerated and supported by some, such as Sudan and Pakistan for much of the 1990s, and opposed by others, including Iraq, whose secular dictator, Saddam Hussein, saw political Islamists as a threat to his authority. The groups' militant wings engaged in acts of terrorism in the Middle East and beyond. Islam experts warned against conflating the religious practice of

Grim evidence of genocide: three hundred skulls sit outside a chapel in Rwanda on November 6, 1994, as authorities determine the extent of the killings. Over the course of three months in 1994, Hutus murdered between five hundred thousand and one million Tutsis and moderate Hutus. (Getty Images)

Islam and fundamentalist political tenets. They also warned against conflating religious fundamentalist Islam with militant-political Islam.[378] Those nuances, however, escaped most Western popular commentators, who fueled anti-Muslim sentiment, particularly in the United States.

Samuel Huntington's controversial 1993 thesis of a "clash of civilizations" articulated a new kind of cultural pessimism.[379] Huntington argued that "the great divisions among humankind and the dominating source of conflict will be cultural." He divided the world into seven or eight civilizations and saw evidence that current and future violent conflicts occurred primarily among different civilizations. He defined civilizations as cultural entities sharing a common "history, language, culture, tradition and, most important, religion. The people of different civilizations have their own particular views on the relations between God and man, the individual and the group, the citizen and the state, parents and children, husband and wife, as well as differing views of the relative importance of rights and responsibilities, liberty and authority, equality and hierarchy."[380] Not only did he deem religion as the most important foundation of those entities, but more importantly he predicted that religio-cultural differences were too deeply ingrained in each of these civilizations to allow for an accommodation across boundaries. Conflict, in his estimation, was inevitable.

Huntington rejected warnings about the homogenizing effects of cultural globalization. He acknowledged that there were more interactions among peoples from different religious and cultural backgrounds. But instead of producing greater understanding and tolerance for difference, Huntington argued, they produced the opposite: a higher potential for conflict, at times violent in nature. "As people define their identity in ethnic and religious terms, they are likely to see an 'us' versus 'them' relation existing between themselves and people of different ethnicity or religion."[381] Huntington could indeed point to several conflicts in the second half of the twentieth century in which religion became the focal point of what essentially were ethnic conflicts—Protestants versus Catholics in Northern Ireland, Orthodox Christians versus Muslims in Serbia, Croatia, and Bosnia, and Arabs versus Israelis in the Middle East.[382] According to Steve Bruce, religious identity "can acquire a new significance and call forth a new loyalty" when two cultures of different religion are in conflict or if a culture of one religion dominates another.

Critics accused Huntington of exhibiting a kind of cultural determinism reminiscent of the economic determinism advanced by Marxists in the nineteenth and twentieth centuries.[383] They also charged him with creating a stereotypically negative image of Islam and conversely an equally stereotypically positive image of the "West."[384] Particularly worrisome in their eyes was his idea that the political manifestation of Islam was incompatible with democracy, a belief he shared with several leading conservative intellectuals, among them Bernard Lewis and Daniel Pipes.[385] Huntington's monocausal religio-cultural explanation for global relations and global conflict left little room to explore in earnest the extent and limits of cultural influence on relations between peoples and among people. It also demonstrated that despite international pronouncements of an increasingly connected and unified global society, evidence of cultural differences and cultural conflict remained strong.

Huntington's thesis gained new momentum in the aftermath of the attacks on the World Trade Center in New York and the Pentagon in Washington, DC, on September 11, 2001. Planned and executed by the Islamist terrorist organization al-Qaeda under the leadership of Osama bin Laden, the attacks claimed almost three thousand lives. Vowing to hunt down bin Laden anywhere in the world, the US government launched a military campaign against Afghanistan, the country believed to be harboring leading al-Qaeda operatives. It followed with an invasion of Iraq in 2003, even though Saddam Hussein was a known enemy of al-Qaeda. The administration of US president George W. Bush justified its pursuit of Islamist terrorists in Afghanistan and Iraq in part by pointing to the Taliban's and Saddam Hussein's human rights violations. But with revelations of torture and physical abuse of prisoners in American custody at the Abu Ghraib Prison in Iraq in 2004, the United States itself came under fire for human rights abuses.[386] Legal advisers' attempts to justify abusive interrogation techniques such as water-boarding caused a domestic and international uproar. The incident gravely damaged the reputation of the United States as a champion of universal human rights and undermined hopes for enforcing global standards of human rights.[387] If the United States reserved for itself the right to define torture in contradiction to international conventions, it effectively undermined any efforts to arrive at an internationally recognized system of human rights enforcement.

Those efforts had been under way since the founding of the United Nations in 1945, but had stalled largely because of the ideological conflicts of the Cold War. Yet new opportunities for international cooperation in enforcing human rights on a global scale emerged in 1990. The United States had been a staunch supporter of the creation of international tribunals to bring to justice perpetrators of war crimes. The UN Security Council established the first of these in 1993 to deal with human rights violations in the former Yugoslavia. The International Criminal Tribunal for the former Yugoslavia (ICTY) tried individuals accused of human rights violations in that territory since 1991. The most prominent defendants to stand trial were the former Serbian prime minister Slobodan Milošević; former president of the Serbian Republic of Bosnia-Herzegovina, Radovan Karadžić; and former Serbian military commander Ratko Mladić.[388]

A year later the Security Council set up a second tribunal to deal with the 1994 mass killings of Tutsis in Rwanda, again with support from the United

States. The new spirit of post–Cold War cooperation in the UN allowed the Security Council to pass a resolution condemning the violence and set up the International Criminal Tribunal for Rwanda (ICTR). As in the former Yugoslavia, the international community failed to prevent the massacre. Yet it acted quickly to bring the perpetrators to justice. Beginning in 1996 the ICTR heard several dozen cases. Among its most prominent defendants were Rwanda's interim prime minister, Jean Kambanda, and Jean-Paul Akayesu, who at the time of the killings was mayor of the town of Taba, where Tutsis were systematically rounded up and killed. Both Kambanda and Akayesu received life sentences.[389] The Yugoslavia and Rwanda Tribunals showed that although the United Nations did not have the power to intervene directly in regional conflicts to prevent or stop human rights violations on a massive scale, it was gradually developing the mechanisms to bring to justice those who had committed crimes against humanity.

In 2002, UN member states went a step further toward an international criminal justice system by establishing the International Criminal Court (ICC). However, the United States under the presidency of George W. Bush refused to ratify the Statute and withdrew its support for the ICC. Despite US rejection the court thrived and gained new signatories. By the end of 2011 there were 119 state members of the ICC. The Court's jurisdiction, while broad in geographical scope, remained limited to the prosecution of nationals whose governments belonged to the Court and in cases where "the investigating or prosecuting state is unwilling or unable genuinely to carry out the investigation or prosecution." Most of the cases brought before the Court in its first decade of operation involved nationals from African states.[390]

The tribunals as well as the ICC operated on the assumption that a single set of laws should govern the national and international conduct of states and individuals. The success of these legal institutions rested on the willingness of member states to subscribe to and enforce those laws.[391] However, in the last decade of the twentieth century the global community was still far from united on what constituted human rights and which laws should be applicable to all of humanity. In fact, the very idea of the universality of rights was challenged anew at the United Nations in the early 1990s when the heirs of those who had fought for self-determination at the Bandung Conference thirty-five years earlier claimed for themselves a particularist interpretation of human rights.

The controversy emerged in 1991 in response to the publication of the United Nations Development Program's second annual report ranking countries according to a newly developed Human Freedom Index. The index took forty criteria of human freedom and ranked countries accordingly. UN ambassador Kofi Awoonor of Ghana, spokesperson for the Group of 77, objected to the list of criteria. "Freedom is a value-laden concept that finds expression in different shapes and forms from society to society," he protested. "To take the work of a particular scholar representing a particular culture seen by many in recent history as linked to the oppression and exploitation of a vast part of our world and develop an index that should be applicable to all societies and cultures, is to show a lack of sensitivity hardly acceptable in a universal body like the UNDP."[392] The Group of 77 objected in particular to the inclusion in the index of the freedom accorded to homosexuals. In several of the seventy-seven member states, including much of Africa and the Middle East, homosexuality continued to be punishable by law. Even in countries that no longer criminalized homosexuality, there was still spirited debate over issues concerning sexual and women's rights— including the right of homosexuals to serve in the military or to marry, as well as a woman's right to terminate a pregnancy.

A challenge of broader import emerged at the World Conference on Human Rights in Vienna in 1993, as several non-Western countries, including China, Iran, Syria, Singapore, Malaysia, and Cuba, questioned the universal applicability of the UDHR, dismissing it as an instrument of Western imperialism and demanding instead the primacy of the right to national sovereignty over universal claims of human rights.[393] Those spearheading the critique, among them Singapore and Indonesia, faced charges of human rights violations and therefore had a vested interest in redefining the parameters of the human rights agenda.[394]

The battle over cultural relativism had taken shape three months earlier in Bangkok, Thailand, where Asian countries had convened in preparation for the Vienna conference.[395] At the Bangkok conference, Asian countries stressed the culturally specific regional application of individual rights. Article 8 of the Bangkok Declaration stated that "while human rights are universal in nature, they must be considered in the context of a dynamic and evolving process of international norm-setting, bearing in mind the significance of national and regional particularities and various historical, cultural and religious backgrounds."[396]

This line of argument represented a significant departure from the Bandung Conference four decades earlier, which had endorsed the universal applicability of human rights to claim for Asians and Africans the right to self-determination. At Bangkok, in contrast, the particulars of cultural differences trumped the universality of human rights.

Asian human rights organizations and leading intellectuals immediately challenged the official Bangkok position. Meeting at the same time as their governments, they rejected the cultural relativism argument and reaffirmed their commitment to the universality, inalienability, and indivisibility of human rights in Asia. The NGO meeting concluded with a counterdeclaration stating that "universal human rights are rooted in many cultures," and that because "human rights are of universal concern and are universal in value, the advocacy of human rights cannot be considered to be an encroachment upon national sovereignty."[397] Asian human rights organizations were very much aware of the ways in which their governments were exploiting the debates over cultural relativism to justify human rights violations. While they acknowledged that cultural differences existed, they argued that universal human rights as defined in the 1948 UDHR applied to all cultures. Their view ultimately prevailed in Vienna. Not only did the conference conclude with a strong statement in favor of the universal applicability of human rights, it also succeeded in creating the office of the UN Commissioner for Human Rights, a move opposed by the government delegates and supported by Asian NGOs.[398]

Human rights advocates had to reconcile their belief in the universal applicability of human rights based on shared cultural values with an equally strong support for the preservation of cultural diversity. The Indian economist Amartya Sen provided the most articulate argument for the integration of particularism and universalism. He charged that the idea that all of Asia shared a particular value system different from "the West" repeated and reinforced an old Eurocentric vision. He embraced the existence of cultural diversity, because diversity existed within Asia as on every other continent. That diversity, Sen continued, did not preclude the existence of shared values. He particularly dismissed the argument made by Singapore's Lee Kuan Yew and China's Li Peng that Asian cultures had more appreciation for authoritarian rule and less appreciation for individual freedoms and civil rights and that Asia owed its economic success to that embrace of authoritarianism.[399] Because the regimes had been authoritarian long before economic progress occurred, Sen countered, the reasons for their success had to lie elsewhere. In addition, he pointed to specific Asian religious and cultural ideas, including Buddhism, that promoted civic and personal independence over blind obedience to authority. Conversely, he pointed to Western philosophical and intellectual traditions that showed a deep appreciation and valorization of order and authority. Diversity, he concluded, did not preclude the existence of common ground.

Debates about the universality of human rights were both locally distinct and globally recognizable. Rather than being mutually exclusive and in competition with each other, the particularist and universalist claims of human rights were mutually constitutive. In the era of post–Cold War globalization, these debates called into question the primacy of the nation-state, though they by no means abandoned the state as a locus of power and action. They fragmented national and international communities by linking the local to the global. They elevated to prominence the importance of new means of communication and information technology. Though imperfect and uneven, global networks of human rights activists broadcast testimony and visual images of human rights abuses, thus engaging a global audience in their campaigns against perpetrators.[400] These campaigns did not create an international consensus on the meaning and extent of the human rights regime. To the contrary, multiple groups and political constituencies continued to battle over how to define human rights, and these groups often operated in the interest of political expediency rather than moral principle. A decade into the twenty-first century our understanding of human rights might be more fragmented than ever before.

Cultures of Globalization

The post–Cold War period also generated heated debates over the meaning and consequences of cultural globalization. What most people agreed upon was that the world had shrunk significantly and that globalization was a real phenomenon that touched the lives of almost every human being on Earth. Depending on their political, economic, and ideological convictions, participants in the debate saw around them either homogenization or heterogenization, unification or fragmentation, particularism or universalism, and they had mixed feelings about both the forces that pushed them closer together and those that pulled them farther apart. The advocates on both sides battled each other in public demonstrations, in political forums, and on the pages of newspapers and journals. However, the battle lines were not drawn neatly along geographic, class, or even generational lines. At times the same people could embrace cultural globalization in one context and reject it adamantly in another.

As a demographic group, young people were most comfortable with the new opportunities offered by cultural globalization. They particularly embraced the Internet as a vehicle for communication across vast geographic distances and an amplifier for popular trends across disparate parts of the world. They became most adept at enjoying the fruits of cultural globalization through access to a broad spectrum of cultural and material offerings allowing them to transcend the confines of their physical environment. They were also less concerned than their elders about a loss of cultural tradition in their local environment. Through television, Internet, and other means of modern communication, they were able to connect to a virtual community of people with shared tastes, beliefs, and interests. They were thus able to find their very particular cultural niche independent of their geographical location.

The Internet democratized information and communication for those with access to the technology. But this universal access to information did not lead to cultural homogenization, as critics feared. And while it had the potential to lead to greater understanding of cultural diversity, and greater tolerance of cultural difference, this did not always occur either. As the virtual marketplace of ideas and communication expanded, it fostered all kinds of ideas indiscriminately. It enabled Islamist jihadists to spread their message of hate as well as helped organize the peaceful protests for democracy in Tunisia and Egypt during the Arab Spring of 2011. In both cases people utilized new technology to spread their messages instantly to a national and international audience.

Young people's easy embrace of new communication technologies did not turn them into fervent advocates of globalization, either. To the contrary, many of them joined protests against economic globalization at the annual meetings of the World Trade Organization, the World Economic Forum, and other economic summits in the late 1990s and early 2000s.[401] The international media were quick to label these activists antiglobalization protesters, though the activists' opposition focused on the particular neoliberal aspects of economic globalization embedded in the policies of the World Bank, the IMF, and the world's leading economic powers. Protesters charged that the policies advocated by these economic powers, particularly free trade and economic deregulation, gave an unfair advantage to the world's richest economies. They pointed to a series of international agreements in the early 1990s designed to facilitate international trade, which instead threatened local businesses who could not compete in the international marketplace. Those agreements included the North American Free Trade Agreement (NAFTA) and the latest General Agreement on Tariffs and Trade (GATT), which took effect in 1994.

The free trade agreements did indeed produce uneven results for national economies. They helped make the international exchange of goods cheaper, easier, and faster in the last decade of the twentieth century. Together with technological advances in international shipping, the pace of trade accelerated and the cost of moving goods from their point of production to the point of consumption decreased, a development that also enabled communist China to become a leading producer of consumer goods for the American market. More importantly, the production process itself became globalized, with parts manufactured in several countries and assembled in places far removed from the design and marketing centers. The multinational production process cut down on the cost of consumer goods in the international market.

But there were also negative effects, among them an overall decrease in wages in the manufacturing sector, as producers moved from high-cost labor markets, such as the United States, Western Europe, and Japan, to low-cost labor markets in Southeast Asia and Latin America.[402] According to the economist Jeff Faux, the winners and losers of this process were now separated not by nationality but rather by class. The worldwide decline in wages reduced workers' share in international wealth, whereas multinational corporate elites benefited disproportionately. It also pitted consumers against labor in the industrialized world. Consumers benefited by having better access to lower-priced goods, including everyday items like clothes and shoes, while workers suffered from stagnant or declining wages, or worse, lost their jobs altogether. Because they were also consumers, workers found themselves at once on the winning and losing sides of the equation.

The conflicts over NAFTA and GATT not only divided workers, consumers, and producers in each of the participating countries, they also created new solidarities across national and cultural divides. The protests led to the formation of transnational social movements such as the World Social Forum, whose goal it was to make globalization work toward global justice instead of economic stratification.

As globalization magnified difference in the economic realm through increasing social and economic stratification, it appeared to accomplish the exact opposite in the cultural realm, namely, the leveling of cultural difference. But evidence to the contrary can be found in the increasing multiculturalism in most major urban areas of the world, in the proliferation of international food everywhere, and particularly in the increase in travel to areas outside of Europe and North America. In fact, the experience of difference became a major selling point in the post–Cold War expansion of global tourism, as rich Western investors sought new opportunities for development in the global South and Far East. Many former political hot spots in Africa and East Asia, including Vietnam and Indonesia, became prime targets for tourist developments. Particularly in the 1990s there emerged a new wave of ecotourism, which required the controlled "cultivation" of areas previously inaccessible to outside visitors. The somewhat contradictory goal of ecotourism was to leave those newly cultivated areas as pristine as possible while at the same time introducing Western travelers to the region.

Ecotourism became so popular in the 1990s that the United Nations declared the year 2002 the International Year of Ecotourism.[403] At a World Ecotourism summit in Quebec that same year, the participants issued a declaration, known as the "Quebec Declaration on Ecotourism," in which they pledged their commitment to preserving the "natural and cultural heritage" of tourist destinations, as well as a host of other commitments designed to achieve what the participants called "sustainable tourism." The summit, as well as the International Year of Ecotourism, signified new post–Cold War environmental concerns as well as concerns over sustainable development. The summit organizers recognized that global travel provided a major source of income for parts of the world that had seen very little economic development. More importantly, however, the meeting exposed the deep paradox of tourism at the turn of the twenty-first century. Ecotourists were both rejecting and driving cultural and economic globalization.

They sought authentic cultural experiences in ever more remote areas of the world, but their expanding collective desires coupled with economic power invariably altered the cultural and economic dynamics of their destinations. In their search for difference, ecotourists linked the local to the global. They created hybridity at the very moment they celebrated authenticity.

Even though ecotourism was primarily a commercial phenomenon, it expressed a deep-seated desire to incorporate cultural difference into one's own life experience. The embrace of difference combined with a sense of interconnectedness across cultural and geographical divides found expression in the late twentieth-century philosophy of cosmopolitanism. One of its primary advocates was the philosopher Kwame Anthony Appiah, who thought it a useful alternative to the overused and ill-defined concept of globalization, "a term" he argued, "that once referred to a marketing strategy, and then came to designate a macroeconomic thesis, and now can seem to encompass everything, and nothing."[404] Appiah borrowed his idea of cosmopolitanism from Immanuel Kant's 1795 essay *Toward Perpetual Peace*, which expressed not so much the material interconnectedness of the world but "the idea we have obligations to others, obligations that stretch beyond those to whom we are related by the ties of kith and kind, or even more formal ties of shared citizenship." In addition, cosmopolitanism fostered an engagement with human existences beyond one's own cultural orbit, to "learn from our differences."[405] Cosmopolitans, according to Appiah, believe both in universally shared values that bind them to strangers outside their own familiar environment, and in the idea of cultural pluralism. In his own writing Appiah often stresses his own multicultural roots, which sensitized him to both cultural universalism and pluralism. His English mother and Ghanaian father raised their family in Kumasi, the provincial capital of the Ashanti region of Ghana, but Appiah felt equally at home in British and Ghanaian culture and eventually moved to the United States.

Cosmopolitanism, just like globalization, was not without controversy as a philosophical concept. The political theorist Seyla Benhabib identified three strands of thinking about the concept: as an "attitude of enlightened morality that does not place 'love of country' ahead of 'love of mankind'"; as a signifier of "hybridity, fluidity, and recognizing the fractured and internally riven character of human selves and citizens, whose complex aspirations" move beyond the national community; and thirdly as a "normative philosophy for carrying the universalistic norms of discourse ethics beyond the confines of the nation-state."[406] Benhabib associated herself most closely with the third variant. Her interest in cosmopolitanism lay in the concrete and normative manifestations of the concept in international laws and institutions. Those included definitions of human rights, humanitarian aid, refugee and asylum status, transnational definitions of citizenship, international criminal courts, tribunals, transnational human rights organizations, and, of course, the United Nations. Cosmopolitanism, in her view, provided the moral and ethical foundation for the ordering of the state's relationship with its people (the rights of individuals vis-à-vis the state) and the ordering of the relationship among people across state boundaries. Despite their different approaches, Appiah and Benhabib ultimately came to similar conclusions about the importance of cosmopolitanism in the globalized environment of the twenty-first century. While their variants of cosmopolitanism do not offer a solution to the continued struggle between the forces of universalism and particularism, they offer a clear idea of the challenges ahead.

Universalizing Difference

Difference provides the key to understanding the cultural conflicts at the turn of the twenty-first century. Difference also provides the key to a possible resolution to those conflicts. Integrating cultural difference into the process of nation building has become the biggest challenge of the post–Cold War period. It might be the project of nation building itself that will become a casualty of the inexorable advance of cultural globalization. Transnational economic conglomerates, political organizations, and cultural institutions are challenging the primacy of the nation-state. To be sure, sovereign states are nowhere near to relinquishing power to higher political institutions. But those same states are recognizing the increasing dependence of national economies and societies on global networks. While they are willing to facilitate the transfer of goods, people, and information across national boundaries, they remain uneasy about accepting the cultural consequences of that transfer.

The uneasiness stems from a peculiar understanding of cultural identity as fixed in time and place that is itself a product of early nineteenth-century

Enlightenment thinking about the centrality of the nation-state. Print culture, capitalism, and imperialism contributed to the emergence and strengthening of a national consciousness in Europe and the United States.[407] The more prescriptive and explicitly defined nationalism became, the more it relied on a linear myth of historical continuity. The past was reinvented to fit the identity of the present state. And the more the state relied on a linear myth, the more intolerant of difference it became. Two world wars in the first half of the twentieth century showed the terrible consequences of an ideology of extremist nationalism that defined itself in opposition to other cultures and, in the case of Nazi Germany, insisted on the eradication of entire segments of its population deemed as "other." The second half of the twentieth century was characterized, at least in the cultural realm, by the negotiation between the forces of nationalism and transnationalism. Embracing difference was as much part of the process as finding commonalities. "Difference is reproduced locally," the historians Michael Geyer and Charles Bright postulated in 2002, "not as an assertion of traditional meanings or practices, but as a product of engagement with the global processes of change that are played out in everyday life."[408] This does not render the idea of nationalism or national identity obsolete in the twenty-first century, but it assumes a new understanding of that identity as being forged and reproduced in continual interaction with—and not in opposition to—transnational impulses.

Even though cultural globalization is seen as a consequence of economic and political globalization, producers of culture—artists, writers, musicians—have been at the forefront of cultural hybridization. Some of these are well known, like Picasso and his works of art during his "African period." Others have only recently gained international attention, among them the conceptual artist Yinka Shonibare, whose installations epitomize both postcolonial and post–Cold War cultural hybridization. As an artist and an individual he defies easy categorization. His art installations build on cultural stereotypes in ways that demonstrate their absurdity. His preferred medium has been African batik print fabric, which, he discovered, was not really African in origin but imported from the Netherlands. The Dutch, in turn, had made these fabrics based on batiks they themselves had imported from Java, colonized by the Dutch in the seventeenth century. What whites, and many Africans for that matter, regarded as "authentically African" thus turned out to be a product of multiple layers of colonial conquest and interaction within the Dutch imperial system.

The story of how Shonibare came to these hybrid "African" fabrics illustrates the complex processes of postcolonial and ultimately post–Cold War cultural globalization. It also helps give practical meaning to what Appiah understands as cosmopolitanism. Shonibare was born in 1962 in England, where his Nigerian father was studying law. The family returned to Nigeria three years later, but Shonibare continued to spend summers in England, growing up in two worlds, bilingual and bicultural. At age eighteen he fell ill with transverse myelitis, which left him partially paralyzed. He later reflected on the peculiar circumstances of his evolution as an artist: "All of the things that are supposed to be wrong with me have actually become a huge asset. I'm talking about race and disability. They're meant to be negatives within our society, but they have liberated me."[409] His disability led him to depart from more conventional artistic expressions and focus instead on conceptual art, which allowed him to explore new media. The racial aspect of his liberation emerged from an exchange with one of his white tutors at the Byam Shaw School of Art in London, where he had enrolled in the mid-1980s. At the time he was interested in making "art about perestroika," but struggled to find the right approach. His tutor challenged the wisdom of his project and suggested instead that as an African he should focus on making "authentic African art." Once he overcame the affront not only of being racially stereotyped, but also having thrust upon him the artistic expression of an entire continent, Shonibare began to explore the question of what white imperialists (as well as postimperialists) might consider as "authentic African Art." That led him to the discovery of the Javanese-Dutch origins of the African fabrics and eventually the realization of the superficiality of the notion of authenticity in art and culture in general. "My tutor wanted me to be pure African," Shonibare later reflected. "I wanted to show I live in a world which is vast and take in other influences, in the way that any white artist has been able to do for centuries."[410] Through his art Shonibare refused to accept Euro-American projections of African identity or to engage in ethnic self-identification. Instead he inserted colonial themes into the repertoire of European representations of ethnic identity.[411]

His art plays with common stereotypes by turning them on their head. In one photographic installation with the title "Diary of a Victorian Dandy," he is lying in a comfortable bed in a Victorian-style room, surrounded by four white maids and a white butler, all of them apparently tending to his every whim. The scene is complete with classic landscape paintings of the English countryside on the walls. He has also created elaborate Victorian dresses out of his Dutch-Javanese-African fabrics, integrating the themes of colonialism, race, and class. The dresses are often worn by headless mannequins whose skin color defies easy racial categorization, located somewhere on the spectrum between white and black. With his installations, Shonibare interrogates cultural stereotypes, but also the concept of cultural authenticity. His artistic creations mix and at times invert cultural identities. This practice allows him to create a new cultural space that is authentic in its own right, by not adhering to any established national or continental "authenticity." He produces difference locally, in Bright and Geyer's words, by engaging "with the global processes of change that are played out in everyday life."[412]

Shonibare belongs to a group of artists from non-Western countries who have rejected the role, given to them by the international white art establishment, as representatives of an imagined ethnic art. Others include the Zairian artist Chéri Samba, Ghanaian Godfried Donkor, and Georges Adéagbo from Benin.[413] These artists provide a window through which to explore the possibilities and challenges of cultural globalization in the postcolonial and post–Cold War period. Their art exemplifies the lived experience of cultural hybridization by showing that it is more than a theoretical concept. It reflects, in concrete ways, the lives of those who have migrated between places and come in contact with more than one culture or draw on the cultural heritage of more than one country or region. According to the Dutch-born anthropologist Jan Nederveen Pieterse, that experience is "quite common: one way or another, we are all migrants."[414] Pieterse himself was born in the Netherlands after World War II, eleven days after his family arrived there from Java, where his ancestors had settled in the early seventeenth century as part of the Dutch East Indies Company. He described his heritage as mixed with "Javanese, Portuguese, French, Germans, and others, and steeped in Indo-Dutch mestizo-culture."[415]

Pieterse's own transnational biography was not as unusual by the end of the twentieth century as it would have been a few decades earlier. Nonetheless the vast majority of the world's population during their lifetime did not venture far from where they were born. The multinational experience had always been much more common among those engaged in cultural production and cultural analysis: intellectuals, scientists, missionaries, artists, musicians, writers, and even politicians. More importantly, the number of individuals combining Western with non-Western biographies has increased at a faster rate than at any time before. Their voices have grown in tandem with non-Western voices within international organizations, politics, art, and literature.

One indicator of the cultural shift toward greater inclusion of non-Western voices in the production of global cultures lies in a survey of the Nobel laureates in literature in recent decades. Between 1980 and 2012, the Nobel Institute awarded the Nobel Prize in Literature to writers from Asia, Africa, and South America twelve times. In the first eighty years of its existence, it had done so only five times. Moreover, in recent years the committee was more likely to choose authors who wrote about intercultural and interracial themes. Those included apartheid in South Africa (Nadine Gordimer, 1991), race relations in the United States (Toni Morrison, 1993), and colonialism and postcolonialism (Derek Walcott, 1992; V. S. Naipaul, 2001).[416] These authors reflect a broader transformation in the international literary landscape that included best-selling authors such as Salman Rushdie, Anita Desai, and Jhumpa Lahiri. The Indian-born Rushdie received his education in England and has since resided there. Desai was born in India to a German mother and a Bengali father. She was educated in India and has worked both in India and the United States. Lahiri, the 2000 winner of the American Pulitzer Prize in Literature for her collection of short stories, *Interpreter of Maladies*, was born in London to Bengali parents and moved to the United States when she was three.[417] The increasing presence on the international literary stage of writers with non-Western or transnational personal histories, as well as works that address multicultural themes, is a barometer of the growing intercultural networks. They have become part of a cosmopolitan cohort communicating in a common global language.

This language is not only multicultural but multilocal. It is by no means a new language, because cultural exchange and cultural borrowing have existed for centuries, if not millennia. However, since the 1990s its radius has extended from the elites to the middle classes and from the global North to the South.

This broadening has created greater diversity and increased the common cultural radius. But it has also created friction and cultural fragmentation as different cultural groups vie for dominance in local, national, and global settings. The emergence and evolution of global cultures since 1945 thus followed centripetal as well as centrifugal trajectories. Global cultures were marked by homogenization as well as heterogenization in the major urban centers of the world. Cultural interaction produced universal standards of conduct, rights, and values, while at the same time they revealed the particular local interpretations of those values. And finally those engaged in cultural exchange negotiated and continue to negotiate between the demand for conformity and desire for difference. Despite an ever tighter network of global exchange of people, goods, and ideas, the cultural landscape at the turn of the twenty-first century might be more multifaceted than it has ever been.

·[FIVE]·

The Making of a
Transnational World

Akira Iriye

Introduction

IN EARLY June 1940, as war had come to Western Europe, and the people of Paris—those who had not left for other parts of the country—braced themselves for the impending German invasion, the Paris Opera gave its scheduled performance of Jules Massenet's opera *Thaïs* (1894), a story of a religious zealot who tries to convert a profligate courtesan, only to be enticed and ensnared by her. Merely a handful of people—no more than fifty—came to see the opera, among them a young diplomat who worked for the Japanese embassy.[1] He had come from Japan to Paris to study the philosophy of Blaise Pascal at the Sorbonne, but when war broke out in 1939, he was recruited by the embassy to reinforce its staff. He served in the post for four years before leaving for Berlin when the allied powers successfully launched their counterattack in Normandy in 1944 and pushed German forces out of France. Before he left Paris, he visited various parts of France and ran into prison inmates who had been released and forced to march on the Nazis' orders—the phenomenon of what a later historian would call "death marches."[2] The marchers included men and women of many religions and nationalities. The diplomat never forgot his encounter with these people who had hitherto been hidden from public view. In May 1945, when Germany surrendered, the Japanese diplomat, his colleagues, their families, and several other civilians (including a female violinist who had been studying and giving concerts in wartime Europe and was to become world famous after the war) were all detained in Bad Gastein, Austria. But the State Department in Washington decided to move such personnel to the United States, and as a result they were brought over to Bedford Springs, Pennsylvania, in August, where they were confined in a hotel for several months before being sent back to Japan toward the end of the year.[3]

A story like this diplomat's may be understood in a number of contexts. At one level, of course, it is a story of war in which nations try to destroy and defeat one another. International relations inevitably impact on personal lives, and the diplomat's experiences were undoubtedly shaped by the vicissitudes of the Second

World War. But to end here would be unfair, both to the individual and to history. It would amount to defining history on the basis of national and international affairs and to consign such personal experiences, along with those of hundreds of millions of others, to a mere footnote. But what the diplomat saw, did, and thought about gains significance if it is put in other contexts, such as the history of music, the movement of people across borders, or encounters among individuals of different backgrounds. These themes do not always fit into the large story of war or diplomacy, but they may have a legitimacy and an integrity of their own. To trace some of these experiences would be to add another layer to the history of the world.

This chapter seeks to add such a layer, what may be termed a transnational perspective, in our understanding of global developments since the end of the Second World War. Transnational history may be understood to mean a look into the past in terms of phenomena and themes that cut across national boundaries and in which non-national actors (such as nongovernmental organizations and business enterprises) and entities (civilizations, races, for instance) play crucial roles. In such an approach, individuals and groups of people become involved in history not primarily as members of a national community but through other identities (such as migrants, tourists, artists, students, missionaries). Their interactions with one another differ from the usual "international relations" in which states engage with one another in pursuit of some national objectives, and they create their own networks and bridges that are not identical with territorial boundaries defined by nations. Transnational relations, then, are conceptually distinguishable from international relations, and transnational affairs from national affairs.

Transnational history so understood has existed for a long time. A spectacular example is the ancient trade route known as the Silk Road, connecting the Levant with East Asia, in which people of diverse races and religions met and traded.[4] In the modern world, however, particularly since the eighteenth century, the nation became the key unit of human activities, first in Europe and then in other parts of the globe. Individuals and even non-state actors were now enmeshed within territorial states. Nevertheless, global transnational connections were steadily being built throughout the nineteenth century, primarily thanks to technological innovations such as the telephone, the telegraph, the railroad, and other means of faster communication and transportation. Economically, a global market was emerging. Even so, nation-states retained their predominant roles as definers of history, in that how nations behaved, both internally and toward one another, defined the ways in which people lived. A transnational world was in the making by the beginning of the twentieth century, but its momentum was frequently lost because of the emergence of centralized states and of the rivalries among nations, in particular among those that were called "great powers."

One way to comprehend world history after the Second World War, then, would be to see how nations and international affairs fared and how, parallel to these phenomena, transnational forces developed. Did a transnational world that was making its appearance around 1900 survive the turmoil of national and international crises that dotted world history during the first half of the twentieth century? How would the world of 2000 compare with that a hundred years earlier in that regard? Here we will trace the transnationalization of the world, as it were, by focusing on a few themes—transnational encounters, activities, and thoughts—to see whether and how a more transnational world had developed by the first decade of the twenty-first century.

Transnational encounters—people meeting people across national boundaries—can, of course, take place in war as well as in peace. The young Japanese student who first went to Paris to study French philosophy in 1934 had encountered a wide range of people from other countries, in Japan as well as elsewhere. Once in Paris, he, his new wife (who also came from Japan), his children, and other members of the family daily met and interacted with students and scholars from many countries as well as with neighbors, local store keepers, and even maids. When war came, some foreign acquaintances (from the United States, for instance) steadily disappeared from France, while new ones, especially from Germany, arrived. Through the family albums and letters, it is possible to trace the changing patterns and contents of transnational encounters. After the end of the European war in May 1945, these encounters became much more restricted and, unlike earlier, most of the people the Japanese diplomat and others like him had contact with were Americans, both in Europe and in the United States. Such a story will, of course, have been duplicated millions of times through global transnational encounters before and during the war. It will be impossible to be numerically precise about the phenomenon and to say with certainty how much larger such circles of cross-border meeting grew after the war, but we can indicate some trends and characteristics in the post-1945 period.

Transnational encounters would be of only statistical interest, however, if they did not produce, or were not part of, transnational activities. Individuals from different countries could run into each other without producing any lasting effect. It is when they decide to participate in some common undertakings—ranging from engaging in a conversation to eating the same food, from enjoying each other's artwork to organizing themselves to promote a cause—that transnational encounters begin to take on significance. Historically, the best-known instances of transnational activities would include efforts to share and spread religions and ideas. To go back to the Japanese diplomat's example, his parents were both Friends (or Quakers) as a result of their encounter with American Quakers who had come to Japan in the early part of the twentieth century. There is, of course, a long history of religious accommodation as well as persecution, stories in which individuals and communities of different religions sometimes come together and develop an ecumenical environment, while in other instances they confront one another, even through violence. We may also add quasi-religious or secular ideological movements in the same category of transnational activities. After the French Revolution, revolutionary and reformist ideas and movements spread across national borders. As R. R. Palmer showed nearly half a century ago in *The Age of the Democratic Revolution*, ideas of democracy and freedom knew no national boundaries and became Atlantic, if not yet global, movements, being actively promoted by politicians and intellectuals.[5] From the middle of the nineteenth century, socialism and Marxism grew as transnational ideologies and won millions of converts who organized study groups, cells, and political parties to spread the new "gospel." In the twentieth century, cosmopolitanism, internationalism, and ultimately transnationalism were added to global ideologies that created advocacy networks operating with their own agendas and momentums.

Many of these religious and ideological activities had a political dimension and thus were part of national affairs and international relations. Nations often sought to spread their power and influence abroad through converting others to their faith or ideas. Christian missionary activities were inseparable from the great powers' colonial acquisitions and governance in the nineteenth century. A secular ideology—the notion of civilization and civilizing mission—served as a core underpinning for imperialism. However, not all religious or quasi-religious ideologies served the interests and objectives of a state. Some religious and secular movements remained outside the perimeters of national authority and at times even sought to influence the policies of individual governments. Adherents of some extreme ideologies, such as anarchism, revealed that transnational thought and action could be explicitly directed against the state. More often than not, however, transnational religious and ideological organizations joined forces with intergovernmental settings such as the United Nations to promote shared objectives. Many of these activities can be comprehended within the traditional frameworks of national history and international relations. The key, however, is to keep in mind the possibility that in a variety of settings and contexts, transnational activities steadily expanded throughout modern history, so that the history of the world after 1945 would be incomprehensible without paying close attention to developments outside the framework of national and international affairs.

Some activities, whether individual or group, would seem to enjoy greater autonomy and flexibility in building transnational bridges. Literary and artistic productions may be good examples. William Shakespeare is read worldwide, not because millions are forced to do so by their governments but because people everywhere enjoy, are inspired by, and share the virtual worlds created by the seventeenth-century English playwright. His plays are performed in many languages, thus making translation one of the most important means for creating transnational networks. For someone who is not a native English speaker to read something in that language is a transnational experience, suggesting that transnational communities are usually created through written and spoken words, in increasing instances through English. Indeed, a Chinese may communicate with a Japanese, not just with an American or a European, in English, which both may find easier to learn than the other's language. The growth of transnational readership and audiences may thus be taken as an important index of the increasing transnationalization of the world. The same will be true of fine arts, architecture, music, and other creative activities. No matter their nationalities, artists, architectural designers, and musicians create works that are meaningful across national boundaries. Not only do viewers of paintings and audiences at musical performances more often than not come from many countries, but increasingly since the last decades of the nineteenth century, art and music have become products of transnational influences and collaboration. When the French conductor of an American orchestra plays German music, and when the orchestra contains a large number of Chinese, Koreans, Russians, and people of many other nationalities, it is difficult not to see such a phenomenon as anything other than transnational. The same is true of scholarship. The study of history, literature, fine arts, and music grew steadily more transnational since the late nineteenth century, with historians from France publishing influential monographs on English history, and art historians from the United States making scholarly contributions to the study of Renaissance art.

But does a transnational activity reflect, give rise to, strengthen, or do little to enhance a transnational state of mind? This is the third facet of transnational history, what we may call transnational thought or transnational consciousness—the awareness of linkages across borders and, ultimately, a sense of shared humanity, a faith that people can indeed communicate with one another regardless of their diverse identities. To focus on transnational phenomena and themes in reviewing the past is, then, to consider whether the world became more, or less, transnational during a certain period of time.

The development of transnational consciousness may be examined through some personal experiences. For instance, in studying Pascal in Paris during the 1930s, the above-mentioned Japanese diplomat and his advisors exemplified the idea that philosophy, of whatever origin or character, has a meaning that transcends its national origin and that, more broadly put, scholarship knows no national boundary. Actually, some professors at the Sorbonne initially tried to discourage the future diplomat, saying that a quintessentially European thinker like Pascal could never be understood by an outsider. But others were more open-minded. A shared mental universe was created between them and the student, and indeed between the seventeenth-century French philosopher and a twentieth-century Japanese youth. By then, of course, scholarly transnationalism had been well developed in the West. Even though cultural nationalism sometimes stood in the way, the idea that in scholarly and academic undertakings national identity mattered much less than personal qualities (intellectual aptitude, willingness to learn, receptivity to unfamiliar ideas) had provided the basis for scholarly and academic exchange programs across national boundaries. Some of the philanthropic foundations established in the United States—such as the

Rockefeller Foundation (founded in 1909), the Carnegie Corporation (1922), and the Ford Foundation (1936)—explicitly promoted educational and cultural exchanges to foster what may be called transnational awareness. Where politics stood in the way of such transnationalism—as happened when foreigners and Jews were expelled from German universities and research centers after the Nazis came to power—many were able to go elsewhere to find a more receptive environment, as exemplified by universities and colleges in the United States that opened their doors to exiled scholars. Intellectual transnationalism was challenged by, but did not completely succumb to, political anti-transnationalism.

Likewise, the Japanese diplomat who went to see an opera in Paris in 1940 despite the impending crisis that was about to envelop the city may be said to have exemplified transnational consciousness in the field of music. There was a shared universe of music that defied national and international "realities." The Japanese violinist who traveled with him across the Atlantic in 1945 was one of many foreign musicians studying in Europe before and during the war, and in such instances, too, it may be said that both they and their teachers believed in musical transnationalism, as did German musicians, many of them Jewish, who continued to conduct and teach far away from Europe during the 1930s and beyond.[6] They shared the idea that art (in this instance music) was timeless whereas politics was temporary and transient. The view that art is eternally and universally valid would contrast with the narrower idea that each country and each culture had its own musical heritage that could never be transmitted to, let alone understood or shared by, others. Many states, most notoriously Nazi Germany and its ideologues, sought to promote their own music (as well as other art forms such as paintings and cinemas) to enhance national prestige. But such attempts did not stifle a transnational appreciation of culture independently of national policies or nationalistic propaganda. Yan Ni's study of Japanese film in China during the 1930s shows that, despite the obvious foreign policy implications of the making of movies by Japanese directors on the continent, their cooperative Chinese counterparts and the enthusiastic Chinese audiences knew how to separate propaganda from art, how to find room for artistic pursuits even while they were vehemently opposed to Japanese rule. In such instances, too, artistic transnationalism existed side by side with, and ultimately survived, political vicissitudes.[7]

In the case of classical European music, an extremely important realm of transnationalism, it was only around the turn of the twentieth century, as Jessica Gienow-Hecht has shown, that it came to be appreciated very seriously in the United States.[8] There was, as she notes, a shared sensibility, a common emotion, that bound Europe and North America together. What about the rest of the world? Classical music arrived in China in the 1920s when an orchestra was established by European residents of Shanghai, but at first only Westerners went to hear its performances.[9] (The Chinese were not even allowed into the concert hall.) Western melodies were introduced to Japan in the late nineteenth century as part of the school curricula and military training, and Japanese travelers sometimes went to concerts and operas in Western cities. Nagai Kafū, the Japanese novelist, is said to have been one of the first Japanese to attend the Metropolitan Opera's performances in New York in the early years of the century and to write about them. He found it a deeply moving experience and lamented that in his own country there was nothing comparable, appealing to universal audiences.[10] Outside of classical music, it is well known that jazz, whose origins were transcontinental (African and African American), gained its popularity abroad during the 1920s, including in the Soviet Union, which often invited African American musicians to perform.[11] Although the war put obstacles in its path, musical transnationalism never disappeared. For a vivid example, when Moscow was under siege by German forces, musical scores for Dmitri Shostakovich's *Symphony No. 7* were smuggled out of Russia and played all over Europe and North America. Operas like Richard Strauss's *Capriccio* and Benjamin Britten's *Peter Grimes* were composed and performed toward the end of the war and had little or nothing to do with nationalistic emotions but appealed to audiences all over the world with their universal themes—in *Capriccio* the delicate balance between music and literature, and in *Peter Grimes* the problem of alienation and social ostracism. When in *Capriccio* the heroine sings that the arts are for the whole world and that the opera has no ending, it was as if Strauss, despite the fact that politically he never distanced himself from Nazism, was transmitting the message of transnationalism to a world devastated by war, that the military conflict would soon come to an end, as did all temporal affairs, but that art would live on forever.

Transnational consciousness may be fostered by literature even in times of war. While patriotic writing was encouraged, Paul Fussell's study shows that in the United States many writers spoke the language of universal humanity.[12] In Japan, in contrast, novelists and poets adopted a nationalistic stance and spoke excitedly of the nation's new mission to expel the West from Asia. As Donald Keene has documented, their language was narrowly nationalistic and parochial, and many of them consciously rejected cosmopolitanism, considering it an outdated Western import.[13] It is interesting to note, on the other hand, that many Americans, including Keene himself, gained an appreciation of traditional Japanese literature during the war. Roger Dingman has pointed out that some US naval personnel who interviewed Japanese prisoners of war discovered facets of Japanese culture that intrigued them and decided, then and there, to study the subject further once the war was over.[14] That, too, shows a transnational awareness, the view that certain cultural legacies are of value to the whole world. Somewhat different in setting but no less transnational were literary works published in the United States by Chinese American writers. As Xiao-huang Yin has shown, by the 1930s several generations of Chinese in the United States had been writing stories, both in Chinese and in English, and the writers, while uniformly conscious of their Chinese background, had begun to strive to transcend their alleged Chineseness. They were influenced by the literary styles and experiments of other American writers and were coming to think of their work as both Chinese and American, a worthy addition to world literature, what in our context could be called transnational literature.[15]

Lastly, we may consider transnational memory. When the Japanese diplomat reminisced about the war, his personal memory was as much transnational as national, and he shared it with friends and acquaintances in many parts of the world. The same would be true of virtually everyone throughout the world who was old enough in the early 1940s to retain some memory of the global conflagration. Each individual involved in the conflict, whether directly or indirectly, would retain personal memories of the war, and the bulk of those memories might be framed within national dramas, the stories of being drafted and sent to the battlefield, killing enemies so as not to be killed by them, staying at home and being engaged in arms production, in teaching, and other pursuits to enhance national power, being invaded by enemy forces, seeing their homes destroyed. Such memories, while differing from individual to individual, also constitute national memories.[16] There are memories shared by all Americans, all Chinese, and so

forth, and these national memories are transmitted from generation to generation through history education, books, historical exhibitions, and so forth.

Can there be such a thing as transnational memory? May Americans and
Germans, or Chinese and Japanese, be said to have certain wartime memories in
common? Or, if not wartime memories, do they have a sense of a shared past,
whether going back for centuries or with regard to more recent experiences such
as September 11—the terrorist bombings against the United States in 2001? The
study of transnational history would have to raise such questions, for, after all,
memory constitutes an essential part of history. To ask whether there is such a
thing as shared transnational memory, then, requires dealing with fundamental
methodological issues in studying transnational history. Here Martin Conway
and Kiran Patel have made important suggestions in their edited volume, *Europeanization in the Twentieth Century*.[17] They, and the contributors to the book,
argue that there is such a thing as a "community of shared memory" that is transnational, at least in the European context. Europe for them may be defined as
such a community. This memory includes what Europeans remember of the past,
ranging from calamitous wars to cultural achievements. Both negative and positive records are part of the shared memory, and all Europeans "remember" them
as the key to their identity. Can there be other communities of shared memory?
How about East Asia, South Asia, the Islamic Middle East, Africa, or South
America? Does each of such geographically specific regions also constitute a zone
of common legacies? For that matter, can North America and Europe be also said
to share historical memory? Is there a Pacific legacy common to all countries and
regions that border on the ocean? Or, to get away from geography, can races, religions, or civilizations share memory? If Western civilization, for instance, may be
defined as a community of shared memory, how about other civilizations?

Ultimately such questions lead to shared global memory, or common human
heritage. Do all people, regardless of where they live or their national, religious,
or racial identities, understand themselves as belonging to a community with a
shared past? Is there such a thing as global history—or, to be more precise, global
world history, the history of the world in which globally shared developments
are the focus of inquiry?

It may be suggested that for those old enough to have experienced the Second
World War, there is a shared memory across national or other borders. To be

A Macedonian soldier carries an urn with the ashes of Macedonian Jews during the opening of the Holocaust Memorial Center in Skopje in 2011. This and other Holocaust memorial museums in various countries show how a human tragedy is shared worldwide. (AFP/Getty Images)

sure, even today, nearly seventy years after the end of the global conflict, the war tends to be remembered in nation-specific contexts. Personal memories are given meaning as part of national memories. Still, the very fact that the act of remembering the Second World War cuts across national boundaries makes it a transnational experience. More specifically, certain generations in different countries may remember the war in their own specific ways. Those born before 1925 or thereabout were old enough to be directly involved in the war, the male half of them having been combatants, while women experienced the conflict at home. This generation is now in their eighties and nineties, but regardless of where they live, they seem to retain the memory of the wartime experiences as the defining moment of their lives. In contrast, the majority of those who came into the world after 1925 but before 1940 seem to have their own memories of the war years that are somewhat different from their elders'. It may well be that there is such a thing as a globally shared generational memory. Whether or not the postwar generations have also developed transnational memories is a question that will be addressed in various places in the subsequent sections. Regardless of which generation one belongs to, however, there may be such a thing as transnational memory when individuals, whatever their nationality, age, or other identities, join in a cooperative effort to understand the past. When a teacher in an Illinois middle school asks his students to discuss how President Harry S. Truman made the decision to drop atomic bombs on Japan, and whether he might have chosen not to do so, both teacher and students are engaged in memory sharing, an activity that knows no national or other bounds. When the composer John Adams and the librettist Peter Sellars produce an opera—*Dr. Atomic*—in which the singer playing the role of J. Robert Oppenheimer remarks, seconds before the detonation of the first nuclear device over New Mexico, "There are no more minutes, no more seconds! Time has disappeared; it is Eternity that reigns now," they are inviting people of all countries to ponder the coming of the atomic age.[18] Historical memory is being shared transnationally.

A key framework for this discussion will be how, through such experiences, transnationalism as an idea and an attitude developed after the Second World War. The term *transnationalism* is used here rather than the more traditional *cosmopolitanism* and *internationalism,* concepts that are no less valid but perhaps more appropriate for other, less transnational ages. Internationalism may be seen as an idea of fostering cooperation among nations through inter-state cooperation, and cosmopolitanism usually refers to a state of mind among educated elites that seeks to appreciate different national traditions. Transnationalism as an ideology, in contrast, underlies the efforts by private individuals and non-state actors in various countries to establish bridges toward one another and to engage in common activities. It reflects, and strengthens, attempts at understanding historical as well as current developments as being made up of cross-border phenomena, shared concerns, and global human perspectives.

1. Postwar Transnationalism

WE MAY begin our inquiry into postwar transnational history by going back to the question of whether there are memories of the Second World War shared across national boundaries. Books and essays continue to be written on the war; the overwhelming majority of these focus on one belligerent or another. At the same time, however, attempts have been made to consider the experiences of the war as a global, human event in which moral dilemmas and tragic outcomes transcended national boundaries.[19] The development of a transnational perspective on the war constitutes an important aspect of post-1945 history. It is true that in the immediate aftermath of the conflict, in particular during the war crimes trials, separate national memories were pitted against one another. As German and Japanese military and political leaders were brought to trial, sharply contrasting histories of the prewar and war years were presented, prosecutors representing the victorious nations seeking to construct a past in which Germany, Japan, and their allies had engaged in a conspiracy to rule the world, while the defendants argued on the basis of a different historical memory, in Germany's case going back to the injustices of the Versailles peace settlement, and in Japan's even farther back, to the nineteenth century, which was recalled as the time when Western powers began their subjugation of Asia. And there were differing readings of international law. The United States and its wartime allies, for instance, cited the Hague conventions of 1899 and 1907 as well as later agreements such as the Geneva Protocol of 1925 and the Pact of Paris of 1928 to accuse Germany and Japan of having committed crimes of war (such as the mistreatment of prisoners of war) and against peace; the defendants' lawyers cited the same laws to argue that the prosecuting countries had themselves violated international law in attacking and killing unarmed civilians through their strategic bombing raids. Quite apart from such differences, the two sides represented conflicting memories of the past. Although in the end memories held by one side were rejected and war criminals were punished, these contrasting memories would remain. Even among the allies, sharply divergent national memories of the war soon came to be constructed, with Americans and Russians, for instance, producing separate accounts of how victory had been achieved. Nation-specific memories have not disappeared and will continue to be preserved through history education, national museums, and other means.

At the same time, however, there were innumerable instances of transnationally shared experiences in the immediate aftermath of the war, experiences that would eventually come to be remembered by people of victorious and defeated countries alike. Take, for instance, the story of Anne Frank, who had been hidden in a house in Amsterdam to protect her, as she faced deportation and certain death because she was Jewish. Her memory became widely shared when her diary was translated shortly after the war and read by hundreds of thousands, not simply by those belonging to the wartime generation but by the younger generation as well. Likewise, Viktor Frankl's account of his internment at a Nazi camp, which he published as a book in the early 1950s, served to arouse a global awareness of what had gone on in the camps. (It is reported that when it was published in Japanese translation in 1956, it immediately became a best seller and went through twelve printings in two months.[20]) Even before the 1960s, when a large number of books on Nazi Germany, in particular its persecution of Jews, began to be published, it may be said that, quite apart from political phenomena like the war crimes trials, something like a transnational memory of the Second World War was already in the making. Concerning the Pacific theater of the war, it would take much longer to develop a transnationally shared memory of the war, which went back to 1931 and lasted for fourteen years. There was no counterpart to Frank's or Frankl's writings to be shared across national boundaries, and even to this day, the failure to generate a shared community of memory militates against the establishment of an Asian counterpart to the European Union, as we will see. The Japanese attack on Pearl Harbor that began the Pacific phase of the Second World War almost instantaneously generated a shared memory for the American people that would continue for generations without evoking its counterpart in Japan, although in time veterans from the two countries would begin meeting together to commemorate the event.[21] About one of the momentous events in the Pacific War, the dropping of atomic bombs, there was at first little information, shared or not, about the secret weapon. Americans and Japanese, as well as people all over the world, of course wanted to know the impact of the atomic bombs on cities and individuals, but US occupation authorities did not at first allow civilians even to interview the victims. But the situation began to change after John Hersey's *Hiroshima* was published in the United States in 1947. (It had first appeared as an article in *New Yorker* in August 1946.[22]) Hersey was one of the first to visit Hiroshima, and his report almost overnight made nuclear war part of global consciousness, to such an extent that within ten years after the war a powerful transnational movement began to emerge against further uses of such weapons. Such consciousness grew in both sides of the wartime conflict and became a powerful instrument for reestablishing a sense of restored humanity.

The atomic bombing of Hiroshima on August 6, 1945. It not only led to Japan's surrender but also signaled the beginning of a nuclear age. (IWM via Getty Images)

Similar observations may be made about the occupation of Germany, Austria, Japan, and other countries by US, USSR, British, French, Chinese, and other forces. At least as far as Western Europe and Japan are concerned, there seems to exist a shared memory of the occupation in which the occupied population came into contact with Americans, British, French, and other occupiers, and in which both sides gained a knowledge of each other more closely than in the past. The same would not be true of Germans and Russians. As Norman Naimark has shown in *Russians in Germany*, the Russian zone of occupation was not conducive to creating a shared memory, certainly not a sense of transnational humanity.[23] Even here, however, the fact remains that, like the war that they had just fought, the Russian occupation of East Germany, Poland, Hungary, and other nations was an experience shared by the same generation in all these countries.

How an occupation experience may have given rise to transnational consciousness may be illustrated by taking a closer look at the American occupation of Japan. Transnational and transcultural encounters through military occupation were particularly revealing in Japan, where most of the occupying forces were US soldiers. Aside from American missionaries in Japan and Japanese immigrants in the United States, there had been little direct encounter between individual Japanese and Americans before the war. This changed literally overnight, however, upon the arrival of US occupation personnel in Japan in August 1945. After the surrender ceremony on the battleship *Missouri* in Tokyo Bay on September 2, American GIs became a common sight all across the country. Their primary task, of course, was to ensure peace and order, but in many other aspects as well the occupiers came into closer contact with the occupied. As in Germany, women often were the conduit between the two groups of people. As Naoko Shibusawa has shown, from the very beginning GIs were involved with Japanese women, initially mostly in prostitution but in time involving other types of association.[24] Of such associations, postwar reforms were of primary significance. The occupation authorities under the command of General Douglas MacArthur were determined to remake Japan, putting away its militaristic and authoritarian past to turn Japan into a modern democracy. MacArthur's staff included a number of officers who had been active in the New Deal era or otherwise involved in social and cultural changes in the United States. They were eager to help transform Japan, and in this process they came into contact with a large number of Japanese, both men and women, who would join them in the endeavor. It may well be that both occupiers and occupied shared a "memory" of the 1920s, which both saw as having been a promising period for democracy and peace for Japan, before it launched an aggressive war in the following decade.[25] Women's rights were a particularly significant issue inasmuch as Japanese women had not enjoyed the right to vote and had been reared in the traditional ethos of submitting themselves to their husbands and parents-in-law. The new constitution guaranteed gender equality, and soon women became active in Japanese politics as well as popular culture and education. Americans came to know a number of these women, and collectively they transformed their image of Japan, paralleling the developments in Germany.

All these may still be considered aspects of a geopolitical phenomenon, the occupation of Japan by the United States and its allies. The transnational connections in postwar Japan were not exactly between equals. Nevertheless, occupiers and the occupied gained knowledge of each other to an extent never seen before the war, and some of them developed transnational linkages that would in time form a basis for their shared memory of those years. A significant number in the US occupation personnel were attracted to the traditional Japanese theater, the *kabuki* and the *nō*, and became their enthusiastic introducers to Western audiences. Others translated modern Japanese literary works, thus incorporating them into the corpus of world literature. Many army and navy officers would in time go back to the United States and contribute to the inauguration and strengthening of Japanese studies in the West. This was not something that had been anticipated in the official guidelines for the occupation of Japan and may thus be seen as an important feature of transnational connections emerging out of the Second World War.

The same thing can be said of the Japanese reception of American culture. Apart from baseball, a limited number of Hollywood movies, and architectural gems (such as the Imperial Hotel) designed by Frank Lloyd Wright and other Americans, the average Japanese person's knowledge of the United States had been extremely limited before the war. Now, however, schools began to teach something about democracy, English textbooks introduced scenes from American life, scholars belatedly began to study US history and politics, and ordinary citizens came into contact with American food, such as canned corned beef, which was introduced to the Japanese diet for the first time thanks to MacArthur's determination to prevent a famine that threatened the country after the war. Japanese fondness for American food, just like a similar phenomenon in Germany and Austria, may initially have been a product of occupation policy, but it outlived the occupation and was to grow stronger in the subsequent years. Perhaps even more instrumental in familiarizing the Japanese with American society and culture were the Hollywood movies. As Hiroshi Kitamura shows in *Screening Enlightenment*, there were clearly political objectives behind the choices of films to be screened in postwar Japan, whose leaders also sought to take advantage of Hollywood productions to make their task of reforming the country easier.[26] But one should also note that the viewers who went to see these movies gained an excellent view of American home life, food, clothes, and all other aspects of middle-class living that would in time become a transnationally shared vision of the good life to aspire to.

For the generation from whose ranks the bulk of the US occupation personnel came and who, in Japan, experienced the occupation, there seems to have been generated a memory that is still fresh today, the awareness that their understanding of US-Japanese relations goes back to the immediate postwar years. The formation of such memory is one of the most significant aspects of transnational consciousness. To the extent that those involved in the occupation bequeathed their memories to those who came after them, much of how the postwar generation came to understand contemporary history would hinge on the transmission of these memories. How do the post-1945 generations in both the United States and Japan, and by extension elsewhere, view and react to their elders' transnational experiences? Do they share the memories of the older generation? Or have they developed their own understandings of the recent past? These are extremely important questions that remain to be explored.

Migration as a Shared Experience

Also important to transnational consciousness during the immediate postwar years were the experience and memory of cross-border migrations. The immediate postwar years are recalled by millions of people as having been the time when they crossed borders, often several times, before finally settling down in their new homes, or going back to their original lands. Such movements by definition create transnational individuals, but whether they share positive memories of the experience varies from people to people, from circumstance to circumstance. Still, the story of postwar migrations seems to constitute an important part of shared global memory.

At the end of the Second World War there were roughly two billion people on the planet, of whom about eleven million, or a little over 0.5 percent, were outside their own countries.[27] Strikingly, the number of such people—migrants, broadly put—did not diminish but increased drastically after 1945. Because the Second World War had involved far more military and civilian casualties than ever before, it left a staggering number of families who had lost someone in the war, and some of these families joined other migrants in search of a new home. Moreover, in many parts of the world the war's end signaled the beginning of conflict within empires where anticolonial forces sought to stop the colonizers from returning to the prewar systems of imperialism. In such areas violence continued unabated, in the process creating large waves of migrants. All in all, several years after 1945 were a period of unusual global migrations. Migrations, of course, did not end then but have continued to this day, but the immediate postwar years were unprecedented in that the bulk of migrants consisted of involuntary refugees, whereas after the 1960s a growing number of them would be associated with global economic opportunities.

The key question in this context would be to what extent migrations were viewed as shared experiences that constituted an important aspect of the postwar world. It would seem that the experiences of Jewish people came to be widely viewed as one such example. Arguably, Jews had been among the most transnational of ethnic communities, and so it was a brutal irony of fate that under the Nazis their transnationality had been confirmed in the concentration camps where they awaited their death. In the process they encountered many nationality groups—German, French, Polish, and others—almost always in an environment of mutual incomprehension and horror. This became even more pronounced in the last months of the war when Jews and other prison inmates were released and forced to march to uncertain destinations. They were not to be liberated by invading enemy forces, so ordered Adolf Hitler, but were to be taken to other (in many instances undetermined) destinations. In the process of their "death marches," they were taunted, abused, and even attacked by civilian Germans and others who came into contact with them. The fact that a significant minority of the death marchers were non-Jewish made these marches an even more tragically transnational phenomenon.[28] (It should be remembered that the victims of the Holocaust and targets of other exterminations included Roma or "gypsies," as well as communists, homosexuals, and the mentally ill—all of whom could also be considered transnational humans.)

From such tragic circumstances, a sense of common humanity emerged as some of the survivors recounted their experiences, making the whole world aware of them. The term *genocide* came to be used to describe what had been done to them, the underlying assumption being that what the Jews and others had gone through constituted a denial of their humanity, that the crimes committed against them amounted to the refusal to concede human existence to a segment of the world's population. As Bruce Mazlish has noted, the term *crime against humanity* was first used during the First World War to refer to the killing of hundreds of thousands of Armenians in Turkey.[29] The term was adopted at the Nuremberg Trials to indict the Nazi atrocities committed against Jews. The 1948 Universal Declaration of Human Rights promulgated by the United Nations was the final step in establishing the transnational concept of humanity. Quite clearly, then, the suffering of Jews and others had generated a new awareness, a transnational memory that went beyond separate national or ethnic memories.

It may also be added that many Jews who had left Germany and other parts of Europe after the Nazis came to power had had their own transnational experiences that, put together, came to constitute an integral part of postwar memory. Some left for Palestine and other destinations as early as 1933, while others stayed until the *Reichsprogromnacht* (which Nazi propaganda called *Reichskristallnacht*) of 1938 forced them to leave. Their destinations ranged from Britain to the United States, from Argentina to Manchuria, but the sum total of their migrations became part of the saga, the experiences of migrants who included many other ethnic and national populations, such as Estonians, Latvians, and Lithuanians who, having been ruled by Russians, then by Germans, and, once again after the war, by Russians, eventually settled outside Europe. And then there were Germans in Silesia and other provinces that became incorporated into Poland after the war.

Some ten million of them lost their homes in the process, being forced to be repatriated to what now was determined by the allies as the new, postwar Germany. They shared a transnational identity as wartime and postwar migrants, exemplifying a key theme in contemporary world history. Although fewer in number, hundreds of thousands of overseas Japanese, along with about two million soldiers on the Asian continent, were sent back to a Japan homeland that had now shrunk to four principal islands. Many died in the long trek home; some left their children behind, entrusting (or selling) them to Chinese families.[30] Their experiences were not drastically different from those of European migrants.

The construction of shared memory might become more complicated when we focus on waves of human migration that accompanied decolonization and nation building in Asia, the Middle East, and Africa. In the European colonies in Southeast Asia, local communities and their leaders organized anticolonial movements to prevent a return to the prewar condition. In French Indochina, the Dutch East Indies, and British Malaya, violent clashes broke out and continued for years between colonizer and colonized, in virtually all cases resulting in the repatriation of Europeans. The overriding ideology of those engaged in colonial independence was nationalism, which on its surface seems like an antithesis of transnationalism. However, as Sugata Bose and others have argued, anticolonial nationalism at least in South Asia could be comprehended within the framework of cosmopolitanism.[31] "If nationalism was the main political project of resistance in the anticolonial era, cosmopolitanism was the main ethical project—and both of these operated together."[32] The leaders of the anticolonial movement, such as Mohandas Gandhi, Jawaharlal Nehru, and Muhammad Ali Jinnah, saw themselves as representing universal principles, so that while they struggled for national independence, their nationalism was not only not incompatible with transnationalism but was very much a part of the world order emerging in the wake of the war.

Ironically, as indigenous populations successfully achieved liberation and set up their own states, they experienced the same problems of governance that the colonial powers had: the demarcation of territorial boundaries and the administration of a complex mix of ethnic communities, including their education and public welfare. As had happened in the wake of the First World War when new states (Turkey, Yugoslavia, Czechoslovakia, and many others) had to struggle with these problems, in the process creating millions of repatriates and stateless persons, after 1945 waves of migrants found themselves removed from their homes and often ending up in refugee camps. Even in the allegedly cosmopolitan South Asia, where three new states (India, Pakistan, and Ceylon) were created in 1947 out of the British Empire, there were no mutually recognizable boundaries and, to make matters worse, India and Pakistan were defined in part by the ethnic groupings within those uncertain boundaries. India saw itself primarily as a country consisting of Hindus and Buddhists, whereas Pakistan was established as an Islamic nation. As a result, millions of Muslims moved from what now became India into areas belonging to Pakistan, while Hindus and Buddhists trekked in the opposite direction. It is estimated that some 17.9 million people moved out of their original homes and that 14.5 million eventually settled in one of the newly established countries, indicating that over 3.4 million died or became missing in the process. Other religious groups, such as Sikhs and Christians, mostly preferred to live in the new India. Reminiscent of the ethnic exchange that took place after the Great War between Turkey and Greece, the South Asia resettlement uprooted people from the homes in which they had lived for generations. But the situation there was even more serious because of the ambiguous frontiers. Furthermore, even among the Muslim majority in Pakistan, those in the Bengal region remained restive, seeking to build their own country, separate from Pakistan. In Ceylon, in the meantime, where the majority were Buddhists, the Tamils, comprising nearly 20 percent of the population and embracing the Hindu faith, likewise sought to follow the principle of national self-determination. Many of those who were unwilling to be ruled by the majority crossed the sea to enter and live in southern India. In such circumstances, it would be difficult to create a community of shared memory in the region. And yet, to the extent that these issues were all aspects of post-1945 history, there was something transnational about their experiences; they were not unique to South Asia but became part of similar developments elsewhere. Nationalistic antagonisms, as it were, were transnationalized. It remained to be seen whether, in such circumstances, some overarching transnational perspective would in time develop.

Even more serious in this regard was the question of memory in Palestine. The birth of Israel and the consequent struggle between Israelis and Palestinian Arabs are, of course, key events in post-1945 international history and in Middle

Eastern history. But we can also put them in the framework of the search for a shared past. Both Jews and Arabs had a long sense of history going back for centuries, but unfortunately there was little that was transnational about their understanding of the recent past. Before the war there were fewer than 400,000 Jews in Palestine; by the time the new nation was proclaimed in 1948, the number had increased to 650,000, one of the most remarkable transnational migrations in modern times. In contrast, there were more than one million Arabs in Palestine in 1945, of whom 600,000 to 700,000 were expelled from their homes during and in the aftermath of the Arab-Israeli war that followed the creation of the State of Israel in 1948. Hundreds of villages were completely depopulated, and abandoned villages bulldozed or settled by Israelis.[33] These broad statistics are not contested, but the two sides had sharply contrasting views of what they meant, views that constituted an integral part of the remembered past. Generations of Palestinians had lived in the area, which had been part of the Ottoman Empire but became a British mandate after the First World War. Most of the Palestinian refugees, then, believed they had the right to expect to return to their lands. Jewish memory was of altogether different character, most crucial of which was the history of their persecution under the Nazis. Those who had moved to Palestine after 1933, now joined by waves of others after the war, believed that if modern history suggested anything, it was the absolute imperative of having a nation that people could call their own, a state that would protect them against internal and external enemies. The Arab refugees shared such a view, but their idea of a new Palestinian state differed sharply from what emerged as Israel that was defined by its founders as a Jewish nation, and it would have been an awkward situation if all the Palestinian refugees had returned to their homes in Palestine, constituting a majority of the population. Jews would have been outnumbered by Arabs, and although the former had a longer life expectancy—within a few decades, Israel would emerge as one of the world's leaders in this regard—the prospect for a Jewish state did not look promising unless the bulk of the Palestinian Arabs were kept out. (And the birth rate among Palestinians would remain extremely high until the final decade of the twentieth century.) The result was that the Palestinians would not have their own state but would continue to live in the refugee camps that were created for them on the west bank of the Jordan River. There would be no sharing of historical memory in such circumstances.

This did not prevent the Israelis or the Palestinians, however, from reinforcing their sense of transnational linkages to the rest of the world. The new state of Israel invited Jews around the world to join the new nation or else to support its existence and well-being. It should be noted, at the same time, that the recent fate of Jewish people became part of global memory. The images of the Holocaust, the Warsaw uprising of 1943 when Jewish residents in the city staged an organized resistance to the Nazi occupiers, and Jews scattered all over the globe both during and after the war quickly became part of shared, transnational history. The Palestinian Arabs, too, had their own transnational links to Muslims elsewhere. The majority of them were citizens of their own states, some old (Iran, Turkey), some new (Pakistan, Malaya, Indonesia). The new Arab states such as Libya, Syria, and Egypt refused to recognize the state of Israel. The series of military conflicts between these two was an important chapter in postwar international affairs, but in the history of transnationalism, at this time the worldwide community of Arabs and Muslims was less successful than the Israelis and Jews in imparting a sense of transnational solidarity. Why this should have been the case is one of the most critical questions in the history of the world in the immediate aftermath of the war that awaits investigation.

Despite all such contrasts, however, refugees, forced migrants, and stateless people were not just statistics but individual humans—living at the very moment when the notion of "human rights" was being enshrined as a basic value in the postwar world. No matter where they lived, they had to be cared for, at least in principle. Their livelihoods, their health, and their education were matters of public concern, not merely private affairs. Although these problems were primarily within the jurisdiction of separate states, and thus belong more in national than in transnational history, the whole conception of "welfare state" was becoming transnational. As Rana Mitter has shown, hundreds of thousands of wartime refugees in China, expelled from their homes during the war with Japan, confronted the Nationalist government with a major task, which it undertook within the framework of the incipient notion of the state's responsibility for society's well-being.[34] From Europe to North America, from the Middle East to East Asia, the immediate postwar years were notable because public welfare, just like human rights, was globally seen as a matter of public policy for all countries. And when governments failed to fulfill their obligations in this regard, international organi-

Unauthorized immigrants crossing the US-Mexican border during the night, April 1951. Migrations, both legal and illegal, have been a major transnational theme in world history since the end of the Second World War. (Time & Life Pictures/Getty Images)

zations such as the UN as well as a host of private nongovernmental bodies, could step in and undertake the task. Because migrations were by definition a transnational phenomenon, it is not surprising that migrants' well-being became the concern of international entities, most notably the United Nations Relief and Rehabilitation Agency (UNRRA). Here, too, was another instance where a transnational world was being constructed.

Intellectual and Cultural Exchanges

It is possible to raise the same kinds of questions about the transnational understanding and memory of the Cold War as those discussed in connection with the

Second World War and with postwar migrations. In the aftermath of the Cold War, it became possible for researchers from both sides of the geopolitical divide to explore together the evidence and to seek to construct a comprehensible, shared understanding of the confrontation between the United States and the Soviet Union, with their respective allies and satellites, that defines one facet of post-1945 history. With the opening of the archives in the former Soviet Union and its Eastern allies as well as in the People's Republic of China, the Cold War, too, may now constitute a chapter in the shared memory of all people.[35] At the same time, the Cold War fundamentally entailed international alliances and national security concerns, not global memory sharing. The essence of the Cold War was to divide the globe, and if possible to freeze the status quo on that basis, not to encourage the growth of transnational consciousness. A universal conception of humanity would have been difficult to sustain when the "Soviet" and the "Westerner" seemed to dominate and divide Earth's human population.

Frank Ninkovich, Volker R. Berghahn, Richard Pells, and others have shown that Cold War strategic thinking propelled the United States to engage in a cultural diplomacy in order to produce and preserve pro-American views in Europe, Asia, and elsewhere.[36] The Central Intelligence Agency, in particular, was eager to promote cultural activities abroad that gave people favorable images of the United States and spread negative ones of the Soviet Union. Voice of America (VOA), a foreign broadcaster established and funded by the US government during the war to counter Axis propaganda, became an arm of diplomacy in 1946 when it was transferred to the State Department. The languages that VOA transmitted in included Russian and Arabic. The Soviet Union tried to prevent its citizens from listening to VOA broadcasts by jamming the transmissions. Moscow was engaged in its own transnational cultural strategy, bringing students from Asia and Africa to inculcate in them Marxist orthodoxy and to turn them against Western colonialism and imperialism. Still, these activities should not all be subsumed under the rubric of Cold War history. Often, as will be seen, the very projects that were seeking to produce cultural warriors in the global geopolitical struggle betrayed the sponsors and developed their own agendas. In the West, moreover, governmentally initiated projects were just a part of the large-scale postwar undertaking in cultural and educational exchange aimed at fostering international understanding and transnational thought.

The Rockefeller, Ford, Carnegie, and other foundations in the United States were particularly active promoters of international educational and cultural exchanges in the aftermath of the war. The Rockefeller Foundation inaugurated the Salzburg Seminar in American Studies as early as 1947 in order to reestablish and expand contacts between Americans and Europeans, in particular Germans and Austrians, so as to promote postwar reconciliation. It is not surprising that the task of reconciliation was considered to be a fit arena for private foundations' activities. While official policy might be dictated by geopolitical interests, private, nonprofit organizations were in a position to fund and direct their own agendas. From modest beginnings the Salzburg Seminar grew into one of the longest-lasting and most successful exchange programs across the Atlantic. Cold War perceptions and policies did creep into such activities, but the geopolitical struggle did not define all aspects of exchange programs, which tended to move with their own momentum. Some nongovernmental organizations (NGOs) were aware of the danger that their work might be co-opted, even subverted, by calculations of state policy and strategy and were determined to maintain their autonomy as much as possible. There was ample space for private initiatives in their endeavor to promote postwar reconciliation and mutual understanding. As Rowan Gaither, president of the Ford Foundation, noted in 1951, "The ultimate conditions of peace include minimum levels of economic well-being and health, enhanced world understanding, and a world order of law and justice."[37] Of these various objectives, "enhanced world understanding" was particularly important as something that private foundations could undertake. Large and small foundations in the United States brought an increasing number of students, scholars, journalists, artists, and many others from Europe, Asia, and elsewhere, and at the same time provided funding for "international area studies" during the 1950s. (These private initiatives were matched by the federal government under the National Defense Education Act of 1958, which funded foreign language study at US universities, with an initial emphasis on Chinese, Japanese, Arabic, Portuguese, Russian, and Hindi-Urdu.)

These programs were by definition productive of transnational encounters. Statistically, the postwar years saw a spectacular increase in the number of exchange students and other personnel, at first centered in the United States but by the early 1960s in many other countries as well. The Fulbright exchange program, initiated in the United States in 1947, was the best known of such projects at that time, not least because thousands of German and Japanese students were among its first beneficiaries. Their presence in campuses across the nation did a great deal to bring about postwar reconciliation—and the effort at understanding their recent past better, at sharing historical memory, is a key aspect of such reconciliation.[38] Although a government-funded program, the Fulbright program was largely administered by nongovernmental bodies, both in Washington and at various universities and research centers. There were smaller-scale foundations that also promoted international student exchanges. One, led by the American Friends Service Committee, a Quaker organization, established seminars and work camps in Japan and other parts of Asia to bring Americans, Japanese, and others together to share common experiences and to explore the possibilities for an interdependent world. Their experiences were by no means uniform, but they invariably contributed to creating a sense of cross-border encounter and engagement. To meet students and educated people from other lands was to engage in a transnational experience, out of which developed a sense of common humanity.

In this connection, it is pertinent to note certain scholarly developments and cultural trends, broadly considered, that provided underpinnings for the emerging transnationalism. During the war and in the immediate postwar years, the United States began to emerge as the world center of scholarship, in part because of its principal role in mobilizing global resources for war, and also because it was the haven for many refugee scholars from Europe and (to a lesser extent) elsewhere. Noted scientists and humanities scholars, some but by no means all of whom were of Jewish background, had left their countries, especially Germany, to find refuge elsewhere to continue with their scholarly activities. A significant number of them, such as Erich Auerbach, a distinguished scholar of comparative literature, spent the war years in Turkey and then moved to the United States after the war. Others, such as Enrico Fermi and a large number of other scientists, came to the United States to work on nuclear arms and related projects and stayed after the war to teach and do research at various universities. Several scholars associated with the noted Frankfurt School, which had flourished as a center of learning in the social sciences, also ended up in the United States. Theodor W. Adorno, arguably the most influential of them, was at Princeton in 1938–1941 and at the University of California, Berkeley, for seven years afterward before returning to Germany in 1949. His writings on "the authoritarian personality," among other subjects, became very influential as they offered a way to understand the development of fascism, Nazism, and other forms of totalitarianism in prewar Europe. A large number of other refugee scholars from Germany were invited by the New School for Social Research in New York, whose graduate program in the social sciences became a new home for their research and teaching.

These exile scholars were exemplars of intellectual transnationalization in that they brought their scholarship to a large number of American colleges, universities, and research institutes and shared their ideas with students and scholars of the host nation. The latter, in turn, incorporated the fresh perspectives coming from Europe and expanded their intellectual horizons. Most of the voluminous writings by the German sociologist and political theorist Max Weber, for instance, became available in English translation for the first time after the war—the only significant exception was his *Protestant Ethic and the Rise of Capitalism,* whose English version had been published in 1930—and made an enormous impact on the study of history, in particular the rise of the modern capitalist West and the contrast between it and the rest of the world. What came to be known as modernization was frequently derived from Weber's thought, which stressed religious and intellectual preconditions for socioeconomic transformation. Such perspectives were welcomed in the West, as they seemed to challenge Marxism's emphasis on material factors and class relations as engines of change. Weberism and Marxism were both transnational perspectives, though, in that they offered theories for understanding social phenomena that cut across national boundaries. At a time when the Cold War was making Marxism, because of its anticapitalist implications, an alien ideology to shun, exiled scholars contributed to keeping it alive. In the meantime, Freudian theory spread to North and South America as well as Australia and other countries after the war and began to influence scholarly writings in history and the social sciences. Both Marxism and Freudianism had obvious ideological and political implications, but those implications transcended specific national limits, the former stressing the possibility of understanding modern world history in a global framework, and the latter the identities of subnational groups such as racial minorities.[39]

In other fields, too, transnational émigré scholars made a significant impact upon the postwar scholarship. The study of comparative literature, for instance, was given an enormous boost through the infusion of European scholarship brought to the United States by Auerbach, René Jasinzki, Herbert Dieckmann, and others. Although their field was called "comparative" literature, these scholars were promoting the study of literature, not nationally separate literary traditions. In time their ranks would be expanded by those who brought Asian perspectives, either by Chinese, Korean, and Japanese intellectuals who came to the United States after the war or by American and European scholars who applied their recently acquired knowledge of East Asian culture to their study of literature. Likewise, European émigré scholars dominated the field of musicology, the study of musical theory and history. As vividly recalled by one of them, Bruno Nettl, at first the bulk of them were Jewish scholars who had been expelled from their positions in Europe during the 1930s and the war years. As Nettl notes, whereas before the war the study and teaching of musicology hardly existed in the United States, after 1945 American universities came to rival "the grand institutes of Berlin, Vienna, Prague, Leipzig, and Munich, which considered themselves the cradle of musicology."[40] Although initially the focus of research was on Western music, soon the field expanded to include the study of other musical traditions, which came to be known as ethnomusicology, a truly transnational approach to the history of music. Curt Sachs, another émigré musicologist, who left Germany in 1933 and taught in Paris before moving to New York University in 1937, remained the leading scholar in this field until his death in 1958. There is little doubt that thanks to the activities of these and other scholars, the postwar intellectual scene in the United States and elsewhere grew more and more transnational.

The transnational scholarship in such fields as literature and music, of course, was amply supplemented and reinforced by postwar literary and artistic activities throughout the world. Although it would be difficult to be statistically precise, anecdotal evidence suggests that almost as soon as the war ended, transnational cultural activities, ranging from translations of novels and poems to art exhibitions, from musical performances to international film festivals, resumed. Some of these activities, to be sure, were initiated or sponsored by states for foreign policy purposes and were more in the realm of cultural propaganda than transnationalism. The Cold War deeply involved the governments in Washington, Moscow, and elsewhere in international artistic and musical events. During the height of McCarthyism in the United States, for instance, steps were taken to remove a large number of books from overseas libraries that had been established under the auspices of the State Department. The banned books included Ernest Hemingway's *Across the River and into the Trees* and D. H. Lawrence's *Lady Chatterley's Lover*. The Soviet Union, for its part, established Stalin International Prizes and in 1954 awarded one of the prizes to Paul Robeson, an African American singer who was virtually shunned in his own country because of his opposition to Cold War policies.

Examples can be multiplied, but it would be too easy to comprehend them merely in the geopolitical framework. Even when the state was involved in financing, directing, or dismantling such activities, it could not have controlled or anticipated the impact they would have on individuals across national boundaries. The International Tchaikovsky Competition, in piano, in Moscow, just to take one example, was held under the auspices of the Soviet Academy of Music, a state organ, but its awarding of first prize to an American, Van Cliburn, in 1958 had many transnational consequences, not the least of which was to confirm the view that music knew no national or political boundaries. The Japanese violinist who was mentioned at the beginning of this chapter remained in Japan, to which she returned from Europe via the United States in 1945, and became the principal violinist to reintroduce European music to her country. In the meantime, the revival of the Wagnerian festival in Bayreuth, a quintessentially German cultural event, in 1948—when Herbert von Karajan conducted Wagner's Ring cycle as well as *Meistersinger*—had political implications, but that did not prevent opera lovers from all over Europe and North America (and eventually from other parts of the world as well) to make annual pilgrimages to the city. The renowned orchestra conductor Wilhelm Furtwängler, who had remained in Germany during the Nazi era and was suspected abroad of being a sympathizer, soon resumed his activities, some of which were held overseas. (For instance, he took the Berlin Philharmonic Orchestra on a tour of Britain for the first time in 1951.) European soloists were once again a familiar sight in Japan after its occupation by US and other forces ended in 1952. A young musician from Tokyo, Seiji Ozawa—he was born in China in 1935—joined many others from other countries in Tanglewood, Massachusetts, and elsewhere for training. Japan's Kabuki theater troupe toured American cities in the mid-1950s, a first.

·[711]·

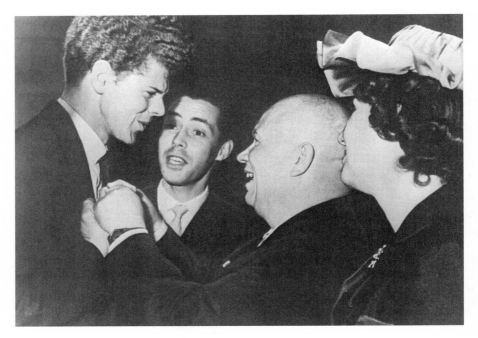

Van Cliburn congratulated by the Soviet leader, Nikita Khrushchev, upon winning the 1958 International Tchaikovsky Competition in Moscow—a moment of cultural transnationalism at the height of the Cold War. (© Bettmann/CORBIS)

The resumption and growth of transnational cultural activities was undoubtedly facilitated by postwar improvements and innovations in communications technology. For instance, international telephone calls had become less expensive, so that ordinary citizens could discuss and make arrangements for cultural events by telephone. (The cost of a three-minute conversation between New York and London, for instance, decreased from $189 in 1940 to $46 twenty years later, in 1990 dollars.[41]) Even more relevant was the prevalence of the tape recorder, a device for recording sounds by using magnetic tape. Developed initially for military use, it soon became a popular device for recording voices and music, with vast possibilities for circulating them transnationally. And then there was the television, which came to be found in an increasing number of homes in the United States after the war and, by the end of the 1950s, in other parts of the world. These devices made the transmission of cultural products across borders much easier than before the war and contributed to creating a sense of shared experiences.

These developments, in particular the spread of television sets, had particularly notable implications for the cinema. It was widely believed that the television would soon replace movies as a form of entertainment on the screen. But it did not happen, in part because Hollywood responded with wide screens ("cinerama") and "technicolors," to show what they were capable of doing to keep customers coming back to the theater. Moreover, the industry produced a number of movies that appealed to audiences in many parts of the world. In 1953, to take a single year, Hollywood productions such as *High Noon* with Gary Cooper, Charlie Chaplin's *Limelight,* and Gene Kelly's *Singin' in the Rain* were immediate sensations not just in the United States but also in Europe and parts of Asia. While these products exported Hollywood overseas, others, while also made in Hollywood, may have served to connect the American people to the rest of the world. *Around the World in Eighty Days,* a 1956 movie version of a French novel written in the 1870s, was one of the hits of the season and may have given theatergoers in the United States a taste of transnational experience. Equally important in the context of transnational history was the large number of films made outside the United States that helped connect people across national boundaries in a common visual experience—and a shared consciousness about life. Masterpieces such as the Italian *The Bicycle Thief* and the Japanese *Rashomon* appealed to audiences around the globe because they seemed to speak to universal themes, in these instances having to do with layers of morality and of memory. These and other movies won prizes at international film festivals, which were revived shortly after the war and whose number increased over the years, further contributing to transnationalizing cultural productions.

Lastly, we may consider the study of history as a transnational experience. To what extent may it be said that historical scholarship contributed to fostering an understanding of the past shared across borders? Like other fields of scholarship, the study of history in the United States was affected by immigrants, including émigré historians such as Hajo Holborn and Felix Gilbert, each of whom contributed a great deal to broadening the scope of American history by viewing it in the context of Western history or in some cases of Atlantic history. They all emphasized the critical importance of considering parallel developments in

Europe and North America as heirs to a shared historical heritage. Their influence became apparent in the emergence of comparative history, the study of a number of countries in terms of such themes as feudalism, social structure, and politics. (A book published in 1956 with the title of *Feudalism in History*, comparing European and Japanese feudalism, was a harbinger of what was to come.[42]) To be sure, some historians in the United States continued to stress the exceptional character of the American experience. David Potter's *People of Plenty: Economic Advance and the American Character* (1954), for instance, portrayed the history of the American people against the background of the nation's uniquely rich natural resources, while Louis Hartz, Richard Hofstadter, and others explored the meaning of the "liberal tradition" in the United States as a phenomenon distinct from European political developments.[43] Such works perpetuated the mono-national orientation of historians; even when they compared developments in the United States to those in Europe, there was little sense of how the two had interacted—even worse, no consideration at all of other parts of the globe. Other scholars, however, offered less parochial and more transnational perspectives. For instance, David Riesman's pathbreaking work *The Lonely Crowd* situated the well-known phenomenon of social conformity among middle-class American families in the context of the worldwide development of industrialization and urbanization, while W. W. Rostow's *Stages of Economic Growth* offered a way to read world history comprehensively in the framework of the stages of economic development that the author applied to all countries and societies.[44]

The popularity and the wide impact these works had indicates the growing influence of the social sciences in postwar scholarship in the United States and elsewhere. (Riesman was a sociologist, and Rostow an economist.) Anthropology and sociology had developed in Europe at the end of the nineteenth century, but until the Second World War most work tended to be parochial—both in the tendency to develop generalizations and hypotheses on the basis of European and American models, and in the tendency to "essentialize" the non-West, viewing Asia, Africa, and the Middle East as qualitatively different from the West. During the 1950s, however, various attempts were made to develop a comprehensive framework for understanding all societies. The theory of modernization, made popular by the sociologist Talcott Parsons and others, was a notable example of this new trend. If all societies were comprehensible as moving toward modernity, usually defined as industrialization, urbanization, and democratization, then it would become possible to establish meaningful comparisons across national boundaries. This sort of methodological transnationalism was characteristic of the postwar work of social scientists, many of whom had experienced military service abroad and postwar occupation duty, both of which contributed to deparochializing their outlook. Physical border-crossing, in other words, had resulted in intellectual and mental border-crossing. Not the least significant implication of such a phenomenon was that it contributed to fostering transnational thinking. Although some of the social sciences, such as political science, tended to dwell on the uniqueness of each country's system of governance and decision-making process, with an inevitable emphasis on national interest and a "realistic" assessment of available choices (this was the heyday of "realism" in international relations theory, popularized in the United States by an émigré scholar from Germany, Hans J. Morgenthau), others, notably economics but also sociology—in particular "historical sociology," which began to make its appearance during the 1950s, promoted by the sociologist Robert Merton, the historian John K. Fairbank, and others—encouraged efforts to establish more common, universalizable generalizations.

In such a situation, it is not surprising that the postwar years gave rise to a renewed interest in world history and world civilizations. Earlier in the twentieth century, Oswald Spengler, H. G. Wells, and several other (mostly European) writers had published books on world history, in the process seeking to present a perspective on history in which themes and chronologies were not all derived from European history.[45] Such pioneering work had not made much impact on the historical scholarship before the Great Depression, and the war brought back a more Western-centric perspective; the efforts to overcome the economic crisis and the fight against totalitarian enemies were conceived as a struggle for the survival of Western civilization. The same ideology would inform much of the Cold War as it was understood in Western Europe and North America. At the same time, in the aftermath of the war there was increased awareness that the fate of humankind knew no national or civilizational boundaries. Civilization as such was on trial, as Arnold J. Toynbee noted in the book he published in 1948 with that title.[46] Toynbee had long been involved in editing the *Survey of International Affairs* series for the Royal Institute of International Affairs, chronicling international relations on an almost annual basis. But he was also interested in the world's historical development, an interest that went back to his experiences on the European continent, especially in Greece and the Balkans, in the immediate aftermath of the First World War. In 1934 he began publishing *A Study of History,* a twelve-volume work that was not to be completed until 1961.[47] But the bulk of the work was completed shortly after the Second World War. In his approach to history, the units of analysis were civilizations, rather than nations, regions, or religions, although religion was seen to have played a key role in the development of civilizations. In this sense he was a transnational historian whose work was enriched by his extensive global travels, especially in the post-1945 years. In seeing civilizations as the key to the development of world history—he focused on the "challenges" presented to specific civilizations by changing natural and human conditions and on their "responses"—he emphasized spiritual and intellectual, rather than material, foundations of history. One of Toynbee's junior collaborators in editing *Survey of International Affairs*, William H. McNeill, was to carry on the enterprise by developing what proved to be an academically more respected history of the world. Their work undoubtedly reflected the awareness that the West needed to be historicized, that is, it should not be taken as the main definer of the history of humankind, which must be understood as an arena for the interplay of a rich variety of civilizations. In some such fashion, the study of history, too, was beginning to be transnationalized.

Transnationalizing the Third World

The story of decolonization and nation building in the postwar world belongs more in international, imperial, and national history. Even so, it is pertinent to note that efforts were constantly being made, both by leaders and citizens in the new nations and by those in the established countries as well as in international organizations, to link what was emerging as the Third World to the rest of the globe. The idea of the Third World itself reflected this, a transnational awareness that the decolonized and still colonized areas of the world were very much part of a conceptually identifiable world community. The globe would have to be seen, now more than ever, as consisting of all countries, regions, and peoples, and to divide them into those belonging to the "first world" (the principal Cold War antagonists), to the "second world" (advanced industrial countries, mostly in the West), and to the Third World appeared to reflect the reality better than a bipolar division of the world, whether in the earlier framework of the Axis versus the democracies or in terms of Winston Churchill's 1946 division between the two sides of the Iron Curtain. The Third World would comprise the bulk of humanity and would have its own identity.

During the 1950s much effort was made to conceptualize the Third World, to identify its position in the world community. One way was through what was by then a familiar dichotomy of colonialism and anticolonialism. Both could be transnational ideas, but in the wake of the Universal Declaration of Human Rights and the decolonization of most countries in Asia and the Middle East, the history of anticolonial struggles would come to constitute a more widely shared memory. Many in the West, such as Albert Camus and George Orwell, continued to publish scathing attacks on colonialism, and their writings were widely read throughout the still remaining colonies as well as formerly colonized areas and suggested a unifying scheme for comprehending the Third World. Anticolonialism came to constitute both a shared memory and a common vocabulary for understanding what had happened, and was happening, in the Third World. For instance, Chinua Achebe, a Nigerian novelist, was inspired by such thinking and in 1958 published *Things Fall Apart*, in which he described the effect that British colonizers and Christian missionaries had had upon the Igbo people.[48] The Third World, in this framework, was comprehensible as an arena of victimization by colonial rule that had fundamentally altered the indigenous ways of life.

Somewhat different was the idea of development through which public leaders and private individuals both in the West and elsewhere sought to integrate the Third World conceptually into the whole globe. "Development," as David Engerman, David Ekbladh, and other historians have pointed out, was a leading ideology of the 1950s that was found on both sides of the Cold War divide.[49] Until after the Second World War, as James William Park has shown, the adjective *underdeveloped* had been rarely used. Instead, those countries and people who had failed to undertake economic transformation had been referred to as "backward" or "retarded," implying that they had stopped growing.[50] To be sure, toward the end of the nineteenth century and the beginning of the twentieth, much was said and written about the "awakening" of Asia and other parts of the world, suggesting that even the "backward" areas that had remained dormant while the West had forged ahead might sooner or later awaken from their long slumber and bring themselves into the modern age. Before the Second World War, however, only a handful of countries, notably Japan and Turkey, could be recognized as having modernized themselves. In the postwar years, in contrast, developmentalism became a widely shared vision, a transnational way of understanding the world in turmoil. This was in part because both sides in the Cold War sought to promote Third World economic development to expand their respective spheres of influence. We should note, however, that the superpowers might not have had to turn their attention to Third World countries unless these latter had themselves been determined to undertake development in the process of nation building. In a sense developmentalism affected the Cold War, not the other way around. In any event, Washington and Moscow shared a commitment to the idea of helping other countries modernize their economies, and the newly independent states as well as older but less developed nations such as those in Latin America were anxious to look in all directions for developmental assistance.

Here was an interesting case of two transnational doctrines of modernization competing for influence. On one side was what historians have called "liberal developmentalism," which argued that economic development could best be promoted under conditions of free-market competition.[51] Although economic planning by the state would be a requirement, the private sector would remain vibrant, as it did in the United States, Western Europe, and other areas. As W. W. Rostow argued in *Stages of Economic Growth*, most societies pursued a standard pattern of economic development, from the hunting to the agrarian stage, and from there to the industrial phase, followed by a postindustrial consumer culture. Such theory itself was not new. In the nineteenth century, the British sociologist Herbert Spencer had already written about human society's steady development through stages. For that matter, Karl Marx had theorized the march of history from the primitive to the feudal to the capitalist phase as an inevitable and universal development. But the Marxists postulated the postcapitalist phase as socialist, in which industrial workers would seize control of the state and carry out a planned development of the economy to benefit all people.

"Liberal developmentalism" and the socialist variety, then, shared much in common and differed only with respect to future prospects. In reality, neither vision was realistic. Few, if any, postcolonial countries undertook modernization along either the US- or the USSR-prescribed path; indeed, some of them would not be "modernized" for many more decades to come, or not at all. Among the older countries of Latin America, some, such as Argentina, rebelled against modernization theory, which usually implied industrialization through capital accumulation, technological development, and urbanization, and chose a policy of import substitution, through which they would purchase manufactured goods from abroad and pay for them by shipping agricultural products, rather than adopting their own indigenous programs of industrialization. One Caribbean country, Cuba, opted for socialism when Fidel Castro's revolutionary forces seized control of the state in the late 1950s, but the new regime in Havana did not exactly fit the Soviet model of a proletarian dictatorship. Without having entered the stage of industrialization, to speak of the industrial workers seizing control of the state was unrealistic. The same was true of China when it came under the Communist Party's reign in 1949. It called itself a "people's republic," very much like the Eastern European "people's democracies," and it eagerly sought to industrialize through state planning and control. But one major experiment, called "the great leap forward," undertaken in the late 1950s, was a self-consciously Chinese— that is, Maoist—way of industrializing the country. The plan called for establishing people's communes where workers would try to manufacture goods, in explicit rejection of the Soviet model of urban industrialization. But the experiment resulted in the starvation of millions of people as "collectivization" denuded huge areas of the countryside, thereby diminishing food production. And yet the Chinese Communist leadership refused to shift to the liberal developmental model until much later. Despite such differences and gaps, however, by then the idea of development had become well established, providing a framework in which the relationship between the Third World and other, more industrialized countries could be comprehended.

Another way in which the Third World could be conceptually transnationalized was through the dichotomy of "the West and the non-West," "the West and the rest," or, more popularly at that time, "East and West." ("East and West" also referred to the Cold War geopolitical divide, against which the Third World would, in the 1970s, propose a "North and South" dichotomy.) Such a conception would bring the Third World into a transnational scheme of things so that this latter would represent "the other." The bifurcated view of humanity, divided between East and West, had long existed, going back to the ancient Greek division of the world between "Europe" and "Asia." Around the turn of the twentieth century, too, as Cemil Aydin has shown, the idea of Eastern civilization was powerful enough to bring together thinkers from Turkey and the rest of Asia all the way to Japan.[52] During the 1930s and the early 1940s, however, the East–West dichotomy had been appropriated by Japan to justify its war in Asia as a mission to expel the West from the East and to return the latter to its pristine stage before it had become invaded by Europeans and Americans. Amazingly, despite such misuse of the dichotomy, it survived the war and reemerged as a plausible framework in which to comprehend the emergence of the Third World.

In the new scheme, the Third World represented the East. Whether Japan fitted into the West better than the East was a question that was not settled then (or since, for that matter.) Countries like China, India, and Egypt seemed to represent the East better. Their leaders believed there was an Eastern civilization as the counterpart to Western civilization, and that these were the two halves of humanity. Just as Europeans and Americans were now, in the aftermath of their fratricide, dedicating themselves anew to their Western heritage, Asians were to reawaken themselves to their common identity. Africans were often included in such a conception of the East; if East and West were two halves of humanity, and if Africans were not part of the West, they must be viewed as belonging to the East, or at least they and Asians must work together to confirm what they had in common. In 1955, for instance, when delegates from twenty-nine countries from Asia and Africa—most of them having newly achieved independence—met in Bandung, Indonesia, one of their subcommittees focused on cultural cooperation, emphasizing the need to promote exchange programs within the Asia-African region as part of various global projects being promoted by UNESCO. The delegates were proud that Asia and Africa were where human civilization had originated and therefore that they had an important role to play in promoting global communication and understanding. In the same spirit, also in 1955, India's new leader, Jawaharlal Nehru, proposed that UNESCO initiate a project to promote mutual understanding between "the East" and "the West" through a systematic comparison of the two civilizations. Of course, the definition of "the East" was rather ambiguous, but it was significant that Nehru and those who participated in the project, which continued for ten years, succeeded in bringing the non-West as exemplified by "the East" to the same level as the West. This was a way of ensuring that henceforth the promotion of international understanding would have to be through such transnational efforts and conceptualizations.

The flourishing of "area studies" in the West may also be put in the context of the transnationalizing of the Third World. This phenomenon had an obviously geopolitical dimension, but it also developed with its own momentum, leading to the steady encroachment of Third World topics in school curricula and libraries in Europe and North America. For educators, scholars, and leaders of foundations, the civilizations and histories of Asia, Africa, the Middle East, and Latin America were worthy of study in their own right. Area studies, as these explorations came to be known in the United States, were mostly situated within the larger framework of "international studies," thus revealing the awareness that in order to understand world affairs, it was imperative to probe into the traditions and contemporary developments in non-Western societies. Much of this work may have been "Orientalist" in the sense of viewing these societies as "the other," with the presumption that the West provided the norm to which "the rest" were to be compared and by which their differences were to be explained.[53] A particularly influential approach during the 1950s was to trace the histories of non-Western countries in the framework of "challenge" and "response." Borrowing from Toynbee's earlier framework but applying it to the Third World's relationship with the West, many sought to understand the non-West's history by pointing to its encounter with the "challenge" of the West, to which they would "respond" through a number of ways. Such a conceptualization of world history— as exemplified by the influential documentary collection *China's Response to the West,* edited by two Harvard scholars—at least offered a way of understanding modern history not as consisting of disparate local and national histories but in terms of some globalizing momentum, and in that sense here was another instance of the transnationalization of the intellectual horizon.[54]

As seen in such developments, Third World identities ranged from the experiences of decolonization and nation building to a faith in common civilization. In all such instances, the non-Western areas of the world were developing transnational experiences with one another and with Western nations. The result was to foster further transnational thinking even as nation-specific issues and overall international affairs were defining the "realities" at one level. The vogue of "realism" in scholarly and nonscholarly quarters during the 1950s tended to obscure these transnational layers—but not for too long.

Transnational Organizations

Transnational encounters and thinking in the immediate postwar years and the 1950s were significantly fostered by an increasing number of organizations that cut across national boundaries. This may be one of the striking differences between the world after 1945 and the one preceding it. Although there had been innumerable and varied instances of cross-border encounters before the war, they now were fast becoming institutionalized; individuals joined together to form transnational organizations, while nations came together to establish international institutions with missions ranging from promoting the well-being of migrants or victims of contagious diseases to providing for the smooth functioning of worldwide economic transactions. Such institutional frameworks ensured that transnational movements and activities would remain more stable and less precarious than earlier. Transnationalism, it may be said, was being fortified with a strong organizational base.

Many of these institutions are more appropriately called intergovernmental organizations, in that they were established through agreement among a number of nations to promote certain shared objectives, such as disarmament or humanitarian relief. The United Nations and its affiliate bodies, such as the World Health Organization and the International Labour Organization, are examples, as are the International Monetary Fund and other constituents of the Bretton Woods system. They belong more properly in the discussion of international affairs rather than of transnational history, but those bodies provided spaces for the coming together of people from all over the world, and not just government officials. Individuals and private associations frequently met at these institutions and established their own networks, sometimes independently of more formal day-to-day affairs conducted by government officials and international civil servants.

Transnational organizations, properly called, refer to non-state actors. By definition, they do not represent any government, although the distinction between public authority and private activity is not always clear-cut in countries with authoritarian systems of governance. To the extent that one may distinguish non-state actors from the state apparatus, they include private, voluntary organizations formed to promote specific objectives, whether humanitarian, religious, or economic. There had always been private associations of people; most had been local or national in scope and membership, some were intentionally transnational from the very beginning, but after 1945 the number of such transnational networks increased. By 1951 the United Nations had officially recognized 188 transnational nongovernmental organizations, of which 64 had been established during and after the war. Among humanitarian transnational bodies, particularly prominent were religious organizations, such as the Catholic International Union for Social Service, the Council of Jewish Organizations, and the Friends' World Committee for Consultation. Among medical societies, the International Committee of the Red Cross, the International Council of Nurses, the World Federation for Mental Health, and the World Medical Association, among others, worked closely with the World Health Organization to rid the Earth of communicable diseases such as tuberculosis and smallpox.[55]

These organizations provided the opportunity and the space for individuals and associations of various countries to come together, enabling them to confirm their transnational orientation. For instance, telecommunications experts from sixty-six countries met in Moscow in 1946 to establish a transnational body, the International Frequency Registration Board, that served as the clearinghouse of information regarding the radio frequencies used in different countries. Despite the rising tensions in the geopolitical arena, this body continued to function, providing one area in which Americans and Russians met to discuss more mundane but arguably equally critical questions. The pace of establishing nongovernmental organizations did not slow even during the 1950s, the decade of the "high" Cold War. Some transnational bodies were created precisely to lessen Cold War tensions and help reunite the world. Various organizations formed to promote nuclear arms control provide a good example. On both sides of the geopolitical divide there were informal networks of scientists who were committed to cooperation to diminish the danger of nuclear war, and some of them established the Pugwash Conferences on Science and World Affairs in 1957 to promote nuclear arms control. They were joined by pacifists and humanitarian organizations of various countries, many of whom had come together in Hiroshima in the summer of 1955 and pledged themselves to mobilize the world against atomic and hydrogen bombs. As Lawrence Wittner, Matthew Evangelista, and others have shown, these initiatives ultimately led to international agreements to limit nuclear testing and to reduce strategic arms.[56] Transnational awareness and the anti-bomb movement reinforced one another and created a worldwide community consisting of global networks in the interest of peace. When President Dwight D. Eisenhower announced programs for peaceful uses of nuclear energy, the way was opened for transnational cooperation in ensuring the safety of nuclear power plants, which were to be built in many areas of the world, and for preventing their conversion into weapons factories. A conference of scientists organized by the UN in 1955 was attended by Soviet and Czech scientists as well as those from the Western allies and paved the ground for the establishment of the International Atomic Energy Commission in 1956. Here was a pivotal transnational moment that proved far more crucial for the future of humankind than Cold War geopolitics.

In a similar vein, several thousand Americans went to the Soviet Union during 1958–1961 to organize various exhibits, and an equal number of Soviet citizens came to the United States for similar purposes. Admittedly, these exchanges were made possible through an official agreement between Washington and Moscow, but it may be argued that such an agreement itself was a product of pressures from private associations to open up national borders for transnational exchanges.[57] In the meantime, some transnational associations became particularly active in helping newly independent countries with economic development and modernization of schools and medical facilities. For instance, in 1954 the Medical Assistance Programs International was established to bring doctors and nurses from Europe and North America for service in newly developing nations. In the following year Japan began sending specialists to countries in the Middle East and Africa to help them overcome tuberculosis. Toward the end of the decade, My Brother's Keeper was founded in the United States as "a volunteer, nonsectarian group dedicated to the purpose of linking America's vast medical resources to global health care needs."[58] In education, too, private groups, notably foundations in the United States, were involved in efforts in the developing countries to make primary schooling available to all children and thereby to increase literacy. These were formidable tasks, as critical as health care for newly independent countries, many of which lacked the resources and infrastructure to promote public education. Catholic and Protestant missionaries from abroad sought to fill some of the gaps, as did the Rockefeller, Carnegie, Ford, and other foundations. They worked closely with UNESCO, whose constitution declared, "The wide diffusion of culture, and the education of humanity for justice and liberty and peace are indispensable to the dignity of man." Education would remain one of the thorniest issues in the construction of nations, but it would be a vital component of transnationalism, just as transnational encounters would contribute to developing an awareness of shared humanity, certainly a cardinal objective of education.

Besides the issue-oriented transnational organizations, we may also consider those that were essential to the reglobalizing of the world economy. The international economy was not fully global in the 1950s. Although trade and shipping around the globe expanded rapidly—during this decade, the total combined volume of trade by all countries nearly doubled—the rates of growth were much faster for the United States, Western Europe, and Japan than for other countries. The dollar was the only international currency, the medium of exchange among different countries. Its strength was backed up by the huge gold holdings in the US Treasury. (In 1950 the United States possessed more than two-thirds of the total gold reserves in the world.) Moreover, a large portion of the countries' resources was being devoted to military expenditures. Out of the total world GNP of $71 billion in 1950, more than $13 billion, or nearly 20 percent, was spent on arms, including atomic weapons. In such a situation, the global economy was both US-dominated and driven significantly by geopolitical considerations.

Nevertheless, the world economy was buttressed by international and transnational organizations that had not existed earlier. Most obviously, the Bretton Woods system, designed to dismantle protectionist trade and investment policies and to establish a more stable system for promoting worldwide exchanges of goods and capital, was institutionalized by the International Monetary Fund, the key instrument for the smooth functioning of trade and monetary exchanges, as well as the World Bank, which was designed to help developing countries with their economic projects. These were intergovernmental organizations, but like the UN they provided spaces for the establishment of networks among bankers, industrialists, and economists from all parts of the world. More genuinely transnational were organizations that were created to provide standards of quality and safety for goods produced. One of the earliest such organizations was the International Organization for Standardization (ISO), established in 1947 to define universal standards for products. Each country had its own set of standards, but the ISO was the first to bring different national systems together to facilitate cross-national exchanges.[59] From this time on, ISO and similar bodies continued to add more such transnational rules, which were an important aspect of economic globalization. Together with intergovernmental organizations, such bodies may be considered to have reflected the development of transnational consciousness in the immediate aftermath of the Second World War.

2. The Transnationalization of Humanity

A SIGNIFICANTLY transnational moment in humankind's view of itself may be said to have arrived when Neil Armstrong, an American astronaut, first set foot on the moon on July 20, 1969. The episode, in which he and his two colleagues had been launched to the moon in a rocket, was, at one level, clearly a product of US strategy during the Cold War. President John F. Kennedy had made it a cardinal objective of his administration to send a man to the moon before the Soviet Union did, a feat that would enhance national prestige and would also have military implications in terms of the emerging competition in outer space. (The mathematics and technical skills for sending a rocket to the moon were considered equivalent to launching an ICBM to Moscow.) But that was not the only way the moon landing was viewed in various parts of the world. Those with access to television watched Armstrong as he set foot on the moon and declared, "That's one small step for a man, one giant step for mankind." He planted an American flag, but there was no presumption that the United States now claimed its ownership of the moon. Indeed, beside the flag, Armstrong left a plaque with a message in English signed by President Richard Nixon as well as the three astronauts: "Here men from the planet Earth first set foot upon the Moon— July 1969, A.D. We came in peace for all mankind."

The moon landing did indeed belong to all humankind, as hundreds of millions of people in Asia, Europe, Latin America, and elsewhere watched the feat and not only hailed the successful adventure but also came to share a perspective on the Earth as viewed from outer space. "Planet Earth," as it came to be called, was seen as consisting of mountains, rivers, and oceans, not of separate national entities and boundaries. All inhabitants of the globe, now numbering over 3.6 billion, shared the same "spaceship Earth," another term gaining popularity. It was by no means the first time that people realized the silliness of populations subdividing the Earth into arbitrary and mutually hostile units when Earth's inhabitants shared so much in common. Transnational awareness had steadily

The plaque that would soon be placed on the surface of the moon by US astronauts, July 1969. The message combines pride in a national achievement with an eagerness to view it also as humankind's shared experience. (Time & Life Pictures/Getty Images)

grown after the Second World War, but the moon landing further strengthened it, giving legitimacy, as it were, to the questioning of the primacy of territorial states as the key definer of human affairs.

Such questioning had started immediately after the war—indeed, much earlier—but during the 1960s it gained in intensity across the globe. The inspiration for the renewed questioning came from many sources, but at bottom there seems to have been the idea, as Albert Camus had put it eloquently in his 1951 publication, *The Rebel*, that to exist as a human being was to rebel, to question one's circumstances and to consider alternatives. Camus had in mind not only historical movements against slavery, colonialism, and other injustices, but also existing political and social institutions. Such a perspective fit with the protest movement against the Vietnam War in the United States, Europe, and elsewhere, which ultimately led to the questioning of the Cold War itself and the political system that had sustained it.

In the late 1950s the Committee for a SANE Nuclear Policy, founded in the United States to oppose nuclear war, had asserted, "The sovereignty of the human community comes before all others—before the sovereignty of groups, tribes, or nations."[60] This was the language of transnationalism pitting itself against a worldview that divided the globe into allies and enemies, each armed with destructive weapons. At bottom was an impatience with the ongoing Cold War, its definition of world affairs, and its zero-sum game of gains and losses. The Vietnam War seemed to confirm such a mentality. This is not the place to chronicle the antiwar movement of the 1960s, except to note that it was truly global. It began in the mid-1960s across college campuses in the United States where students (including male students, who were liable to the draft) and faculty held "teach-ins" to discuss, and frequently to denounce, the war; it soon spread to many other countries and merged with various other activities to develop as a transnational anti-establishment movement.

It was anti-establishment in the sense that those who protested against the Vietnam War began questioning the wisdom of their respective countries' leaders (allegedly "the best and the brightest"), who had guided their national destinies for a generation, from the 1930s to the 1960s.[61] These leaders were of the wartime generation who had overcome the Great Depression, fought the Second World War, and were now waging the Cold War, in the process establishing around the globe "national security states," where large portions of national budgets were devoted to strengthening military power and where the civilian economy tended to be dominated by manufacturers of weapons, including warships and airplanes. Above all, there reigned a mentality that viewed both world and domestic affairs through the prism of national security. National interest was the unquestioned guide to policy, and nationalism the ideological framework for preparing citizens for waging war, hot or cold.

Such ideological orientation and intellectual premises came to be sharply questioned by those who opposed the ongoing war in Southeast Asia as well as by others who were not directly affected by the conflict but who shared the same skepticism about what the "establishment" had to offer. Thus, from the United States to France, from Britain to Germany, voices of protest grew louder, to culminate in 1968, the year that saw massive demonstrations and strikes in these and other countries.[62] The leaders of such movements, many belonging to the postwar "baby boomer" generation who reached adolescence during the 1960s, often called themselves "radicals," "revisionists," "the New Left," and spokespersons of "counterculture," indicating their self-consciousness about going against the prevailing culture of the day that had been defined by the older generation.[63] As the movement's leaders asserted, and as later generations recalled, the basic ideology was to stress that "the cultural is the political." In other words, to search for one's identity apart from that defined by the nation's political elites, was a very political act and was destined to reshape national and international affairs. This was transnational self-consciousness both in being directed against state authority and also in beginning to be widely shared across state boundaries.

It is true that the "counterculture" held conflicting views about modernity. On the one hand, its advocates criticized industrialization as a polluter of skies and waters, a shared experience in the 1960s from London to Tokyo. At the same time, many young radicals embraced some products of technology, like automobiles, transistor radios, and electric guitars. But the fundamental key to the 1960s "radicals" was that they typically stressed humanity as against nation, people as against the state, and individuals "doing their own thing" as against following the prescribed paths of education, military service, and career development. Some applied such radicalism to domestic reconstruction, paying particular attention to racial injustice and gender inequality, while others went even further and began questioning the age-old foundations of social order such as marriage and family. Many lived together without marrying, some had abortions, and some gays and lesbians began to partner openly. As they did so, they were aware that theirs was a "cultural revolution" in which old premises were discarded and people's consciousness was being remolded. "Consciousness-raising" indeed became an objective of their movement, to call on people to revolutionize their behavior by transforming their views of themselves and of the world. In such an equation, there was little room for the state—or the state would become an object of assault, political and sometimes even physical.

The "cultural revolution" was thus a mental transformation, a new way of defining oneself and one's relationship with the world and the state. It is not surprising that the transformation was fundamentally transnational, both because it stressed the authenticity of the individual's existence, regardless of his or her national identity, and because leaders of the movement in one country were aware of what went on in other countries. Many established contact with one another. For instance, as Martin Klimke has shown, student radicals from the United States and Germany visited each other and sometimes coordinated their activities, notably for the promotion of racial equality and justice.[64] Even in Eastern Europe, beyond the Cold War divide, there were echoes of the turmoil in the West. In Czechoslovakia, for instance, anti-establishment forces had steadily developed throughout the decade, culminating in the Prague Spring of 1968, a short-lived democratization of the Prague regime. While that was primarily a national moment, it also indicated that transnational forces—in this particular instance, the popularity of rock music—easily crossed borders. Rock and roll, which had originated in the United States, particularly among African Americans, in the late 1940s and the early 1950s, swept across the globe when British musicians borrowed from it and organized bands such as the Beatles and the Rolling Stones that became extremely popular in the United States and elsewhere. Each country had its own brand of "rock," but there was also direct encounter between musicians and audiences of Western and Eastern Europe, and numerous testimonies since the end of the Cold War indicate the existence of a rather extensive network of popular music lovers across Europe.[65] To those in Eastern Europe, this was music with a message, because even in the West "rock" was considered revolutionary and anti-establishment. Its lyrics often spoke of people's yearning for free lifestyles as well as their solidarity across national and ideological boundaries.

Elsewhere in the world, the penetration of political and cultural revisionism was slower but was nevertheless real, further contributing to the transnationalization of consciousness. China, for one example, had its own Cultural Revolution, lasting for ten years after its inception in 1966. Its origins could not have been more different from cultural revolutions elsewhere; Mao Zedong and other leaders of the Communist Party determined to launch a nationwide campaign to restore the purity of the revolution by encouraging young people to assault established customs and institutions, including the family, schools, bureaucracies, and ultimately even the armed forces. Intellectuals were sent to the country, forced to live as simple farmers in rural villages. This reflected the Maoist perception that commerce, industrialization, and urbanization had corrupted the revolution, which must now regain its essence by driving urban dwellers, in particular intellectuals, back to the people. Higher education and high culture were useless and harmful in such a context. All that people had to have as a guide to living were some basic principles written down by Mao and described in the "Little Red Book" that everyone was obligated to carry and recite.

In time, China's "return to nature" movement made a profound impact on segments of the contemporary revolutionaries in the West, who began to call themselves Maoists and to assault capitalism and bourgeois culture. Few Americans or Europeans went to China, as formal diplomatic relations did not yet exist between the People's Republic and the United States and some European countries; and even where such relations existed—by 1970, Britain, France, and Italy, among others, had recognized the Beijing regime—Chinese authorities did not easily issue visas, preferring to isolate the country from the rest of the world. There were few concrete transnational moments connecting Chinese and Western revolutionaries. Even so, in its stress on simple lifestyles and its assault upon educational, business, military, and other national institutions, the Chinese Cultural Revolution had an affinity with cultural revolutions in the West. As Richard Wolin has shown, the connection between counterculture revolutionaries was particularly notable between Chinese and French radicals. Such prominent intellectuals as Jean-Paul Sartre and Michel Foucault embraced Maoism—or what they understood to be its essential messages—and, echoing the Chinese students in the throes of their revolution, declared that intellectuals everywhere must identify with "the people," with their struggle to free themselves from outmoded and decadent lifestyles.[66]

The transnational character of these political and mental upheavals was evident in other parts of the world as well. In Japan the 1960s began with a nationwide protest movement against the government, which was dominated by the conservative Liberal Democratic Party, whose leadership included some who had been closely connected with the war—and who now were proposing to revise the 1951 treaty of alliance with the United States to bring Japan's security more explicitly under the US "nuclear umbrella." Although the protest was an issue-specific movement, its leaders often spoke of China as an alternative to the United States and espoused the cause of "democracy," which to them meant people seizing power in their own hands against "conservative and reactionary" politicians, bureaucrats, and capitalists. In the end, the new security pact was ratified by the Japanese Diet (Parliament) and went into effect, but many of the original oppo-

nents as well as those who came of age during the 1960s became aware that theirs
was part of a growing worldwide protest movement. Thus, even while they opposed the US alliance, they came to admire the American people who, like their
counterparts in Europe, appeared to be trying to bring about a profound transformation of their political and social systems. A minority of Japanese radicals,
on the other hand, identified with China's Cultural Revolution and saw it as the
wave of the future, while still others, some extremist fringe groups, went their
own ways and engaged in violent behavior that proved to be their undoing. (The
Japanese diplomat who was mentioned at the beginning of this chapter was by
then teaching French philosophy at the University of Tokyo. Along with his colleagues, he witnessed student radicals taking over the campus and forcing classes
to be canceled. Such a story was duplicated nationwide through the early 1970s.)

What were the implications of all such events for transnational thought, in
particular transnational intellectual collaboration? Empirical evidence suggests
that the effects were both affirmative and negative. On one hand, international
scholarly exchanges continued unabated, and as the awareness of global interdependence grew through the spread of radical movements, they may have been
provided an additional impetus as a venue for bridging generational divides.
Representatives both of the older generation and of those too young to have experienced the war could come together from various countries to study the past
and to deepen a comparative perspective. One of the most successful instances of
this was the "modernization of Japan" project in which historians and social scientists from the United States, Britain, and Japan participated throughout the
1960s, producing a number of books in the process.[67] Another project, located at
Columbia University, held monthly meetings among Japan specialists to reexam-
ine the course of Japan's foreign affairs since the nineteenth century.[68] Perhaps
the most notable achievement in this connection was a conference held in Japan
in 1969 in which historians from the United States and Japan discussed "the road
to Pearl Harbor." It was a remarkable scholarly phenomenon that, less than a
quarter century after the end of the war, researchers from the erstwhile antagonists came together for a scholarly discussion of US-Japanese relations prior to
1941. The participants were not intent upon defending the decisions made by
their respective countries; instead, they jointly explored in a comparative framework how policy makers and the public had steadily paved their ways toward

war.[69] The gathering was marred only by the absence of a small number of scholars who had to cancel their participation because they had to deal with their respective campus crises. At this time there was nothing comparable to bring together Chinese and Japanese, or Chinese and American, scholars. The joint exploration of these bilateral relationships would have to wait until later. For that matter, despite the transnational waves of anti-establishment thought, there was as yet little intellectual engagement across the Cold War divide. That would come only as Russian and Eastern European intellectuals migrated to the West and contributed to enriching the vocabulary of historical and other studies, a development that would begin to take place after the early 1980s.

The picture was even more complicated in the rest of Asia. For most of the 1960s and the 1970s, the pivotal event was the war in Vietnam. Here it may be sufficient to note that both the North Vietnamese (and their allies in the south, the Viet Cong) and the South Vietnamese sought to present their cases in transnational language, not just in the framework of the Cold War competition for power between the two camps. Ho Chi Minh and other leaders in Hanoi sought to appeal to world opinion by speaking of freedom, justice, and self-determination, while the Saigon regime, led by Ngo Dinh Diem until his assassination in 1963, presented the southern half of the peninsula in the language of nation building and economic development.[70] After the north toppled the south and US forces left in 1975, the newly unified Vietnam combined both these approaches and, perhaps for that reason, gave the impression that it was less radical than China under Maoism. In contrast, its neighbor Cambodia embraced the Chinese-style cultural revolution in its extreme form while the Khmer Rouge ruled (1975–1978), arresting, expelling, and killing intellectuals and professional people in the name of returning the country "back to the land." The excesses continued until Vietnam invaded Cambodia and put an end to the regime, a development that in turn triggered a war between China and Vietnam. The story belongs in the history of Asian international relations, but it is pertinent to observe that in the end radical excesses in China and Cambodia led to the rejection of virtually all transnational connections and contact, until the situation gave way to something more acceptable to the rest of the world.

Thus, the global cultural revolution of the 1960s had both positive and negative aspects in terms of transnationalism. While the negative aspects—

anti-intellectualism, for instance, in many lands—deserve to be deplored, we should note that at its most promising moments, the cultural revolution helped deepen an appreciation for common humanity, for a universal vocabulary that brought people of different countries together. It is no accident that around this time Viktor Frankl's influence grew in Japan and other countries. (He visited Japan in 1969.[71]) Frankl's stress on universal humanity even in the face of unspeakable adversity perhaps appealed to those going through the turmoil of the 1960s and the 1970s.

On the surface, it would be difficult to find anything parallel, let alone universal, in the Middle East, where the predominant issue remained the Palestinian question, which resulted in the Arab-Israeli military confrontations in 1967 and 1973. Still, it is possible to detect transnational ideas and movements in the region. One of these is sometimes called "Arabism," the idea of Arab unity that was influential in many countries in the Middle East as they achieved independence. Powerfully promoted by Egypt's leader Gamal Abdel Nasser, it combined Third Worldism, Arab nationalism, and socialism and was a major ideological and political force in the region in the 1960s. But Arabism as a transnational force declined after the 1967 war and was eclipsed by more militant movements like the Muslim Brotherhood and sectarian Islam. These, too, were transnational phenomena but were notable because of their willingness to espouse the use of violence in the name of a "holy war," in particular against Israel and its supporters.

More successful in promoting transnationalism may have been the ideas of Frantz Fanon, Edward W. Said, and others who challenged the intellectual frameworks in which the Middle East, and Asia on the whole, had been understood in the West, and in which the non-West had also seen itself. Frantz Fanon, an Algerian writer, in 1961 published *Les damnés de la terre* (*The Wretched of the Earth*), calling on all people in the former colonies to liberate themselves—even through violence—from the language, ideas, and ways of life that had been imposed on them by the imperialists.[72] A mental revolution was needed to think for oneself in a way that was not a mere regurgitation of Western imports. These ideas strikingly resembled those being presented by the cultural revolutionaries in the West. Together, they were paving the way for the decentering of the West as the hegemonic ideology that defined and explained human activities, the past, present, and future. We shall return to this theme in Section 4.

Edward W. Said's influential book *Orientalism* was released in 1978, seventeen years after Fanon's.[73] Said, an American scholar born in Palestine, argued that the West ("the Occident") had imposed on the non-West ("the Orient") conceptual frameworks through which to view the world, even how to think about itself. The very idea of the "Orient" was a Western import, Said argued; it did not exist in the allegedly "Oriental" countries, and it connoted "the other," namely, the opposite of everything for which the West presumably stood: movement, progress, science, even beauty. The time had come, he implied, echoing Fanon, for "the other" to think for itself, liberating itself from the West's intellectual and ideological domination. Although Fanon's and Said's ideas at one level seemed to discourage the kind of dialogue between East and West that UNESCO, among others, had been carrying on, they also fit into the vocabulary of the global transnationalism of the 1960s and the 1970s that was forcing a reexamination of familiar ideas and assumptions throughout the world.

Edward Albee's 1966 play *A Delicate Balance* may be taken as an apt description of this state of affairs.[74] In this drama, a delicate balance has been maintained by a family whose core members are an aging couple living in a middle-class suburban home. Both the husband, a retired businessman, and his wife try to preserve some sense of order in their life, a task that has become complicated as the wife's sister, an alcoholic, has moved in. The couple have lost their only son, and their daughter, age thirty-two, has been divorced three times and is separating from her fourth husband. Not a very enviable circumstance, and eventually the "delicate balance," maintained by familial norms, certain words, even facial expressions and gestures that they all understand, breaks down when they are visited by another couple, close friends of the husband and wife, who have become frightened for no particular reason and decide to move in with this family. These circumstances are evocative of the breakdown of the familiar political order and mental universe that was experienced during the 1960s. Every established norm and system appeared to be being questioned, if not breaking down completely, with no end in sight.

Eventually, to be sure, the cultural ferment of the decade would run out of steam. The Great Proletarian Cultural Revolution in China slowed down and petered out even before Mao's death in 1976, and in the West, too, "the establishment" returned to positions of power.[75] The legacy of "the sixties," however, was not so easily erased—fundamentally because the transnationalization of mentality, which was integral to the global cultural revolution, confirmed the trend that had become evident even before the decade and was strengthened by other, concurrent developments during the 1960s and the 1970s.

A Global Civil Society?

Nowhere were these developments better summed up than by the phrase *global civil society,* which began to be used in the 1970s, first primarily by political scientists and international relations specialists but in time by others as well. There was no standard definition of the term, and even today scholars disagree as to precisely what it designates. From a historical point of view, it is clear that the adjectives *global* and *civil* were neatly combined to indicate what was happening to "society," which in this instance was analogous to "world community," even "humanity," rather than local groupings. Up to this time the phrase *civil society* had designated an existence within a country that was separate from the state. A modern nation was said to consist of the state apparatus and the citizens, existing in a "delicate balance," to go back to Albee's play, each performing its roles so as to ensure the country's survival and well-being. The dichotomy of state and society was not a new idea, but during the 1960s it gained currency because "people" in so many countries appeared to pit themselves against "the establishment." Influential writers such as Jürgen Habermas of Germany and Michel Foucault of France popularized the idea of "civil society" standing autonomously against the state.

During the 1970s the concept of civil society was transposed onto the international arena and came to be viewed as a global existence. The whole world, in other words, came to be seen as consisting of two layers; the layer made up of states and that constituting a "global civil society." In the absence of the world government or its equivalent, of course, the domestic analogy of state and society would not be literally transferrable to the international arena. Nevertheless, the experiences of the 1960s and beyond seemed to suggest that one could never understand the contemporary world if one ignored the emerging and growing movements and phenomena by non-state actors that cut across national boundaries.

Such thinking coalesced into the idea of global civil society, which many—at first political scientists but eventually other scholars as well—dated from the 1970s, making that decade an even more transnational time than earlier.[76]

Who were the global non-state actors? They ranged from cross-border migrants and refugees to tourists, from multinational business enterprises to nongovernmental organizations (NGOs). They had long existed, but it was during the 1970s that their significance came to be recognized. They were seen to constitute the world community just as did nations and intergovernmental organizations. This was both because their numbers grew steadily (and in some cases even exponentially) during the decade, and also because many of them promoted transnational interests that were not identical with separate national interests. Here a bare outline of such phenomena as migrations and multinational business corporations will suffice to indicate their relationship to the evolving global civil society.

International migration statistics that are periodically published by the United Nations are quite revealing in this regard. These data cover refugees as well as those who cross borders to find jobs and residence abroad. In 1960, for instance, there were 73 million such people, and by 1980 the number had increased to nearly 100 million. These were still a tiny portion of the total world population, which expanded from 3.023 billion to 5.279 billion during the same period.[77] (Such a phenomenal demographic increase had many causes, in particular the growing life expectancy resulting from improvements in health care in the advanced countries—itself a transnational phenomenon of major significance—which offset the still persistently high rates of infant death in less developed areas, as well as the spreading use of the birth control pill that had the effect of limiting the number of children in richer nations.) But the picture begins to change if we add tourists as well as students, businesspeople, and others who are not included in migration statistics but who were nevertheless border-crossing individuals. They would stay for brief periods of time abroad and have their own transnational experiences.

For instance, in 1960 there were only 69 million international tourists, or slightly over 2 percent of the world's population. Twenty years later, the number was 278 million, or more than 5 percent of the total population. That each year, one out of every nineteen individuals was visiting another country tells a great deal about the changing conditions of the world. These statistics are provided by each country from its immigration data, so it is possible that some individuals were counted more than once if they visited more than one country. The real number of people who traveled abroad, therefore, was lower. The important thing, nevertheless, is to note the impressive growth of tourism during those decades. (By the early 1980s, it is reported, international tourism was the second largest component of the total world trade.[78]) Moreover, whereas in 1960 Europe and North America were the destinations of the overwhelming majority of international tourists, twenty years later the ratio was down to 86 percent, as Africa, the Middle East, and especially Asia began to attract an increasing number of tourists. Comparable figures for other categories of temporary border-crossing people, notably businesspeople and students, all suggest not only that their numbers increased during this period but that they were now found in all parts of the world. The growing importance of the Middle East as a magnet for foreign investors, merchants, and workers because of its petroleum resources is a good example, but these decades also saw a significant number of Japanese bankers and businessmen arriving in North America and Europe as well as in other lands. They were soon followed by their counterparts from South Korea, Taiwan, Singapore, India, and elsewhere in Asia. The upshot of all such activities was the rise of multinational enterprises in which the capital, labor, and markets of many countries, and not just those in the West, came together to produce and sell products—as well as ideas. In the process, world trade expanded phenomenally and the Middle East and East Asia steadily increased their shares of the global market.

All such phenomena were instances of transnational encounters and contributed to the development of global civil society. How they may have furthered transnational thinking may be difficult to generalize, but it would be fair to say that their rapid growth served to alter drastically the traditional perception of the world as consisting of nations, especially the so-called great powers that had defined an international "order" at a given moment in time. Sovereign states and superpowers continued to exist, but their "international" relations operated at one level, whereas non-state actors were adding many layers of "transnational" connections.

One could even say that international refugees were now becoming more transnational, in that more were coming from all corners of the globe. In 1960 there had been just over 2 million refugees, or 2.9 percent of the total migrant population, whereas the number shot up to 9 million by 1980, or 9.1 percent of the nearly 100 million people crossing borders. Some had been refugees for a long time, such as the Palestinians who had been unable to return home because of the continuous tension between Israel and the surrounding Arab states. About 700,000 Palestinians lived in Israel in 1980, but more than a million Palestinian refugees remained in the surrounding Arab-speaking countries, such as Lebanon, Jordan, and Syria. There were more recent refugees in Southeast Asia, who numbered 390,000 by 1980, five years after the Vietnam War ended. Many of them had left South Vietnam when the country was unified by the Hanoi government and found new homes in the United States, Canada, and other countries who would accept them. Cambodia, too, produced its share of refugees when Vietnam invaded the country during 1978–1979 to overthrow the Khmer Rouge regime. Close to half a million Cambodians crossed the border into refugee camps in Thailand. A large number of Vietnamese and Cambodian refugees came to be known as "boat people," as they resorted to navigating the oceans in small vessels, trying to reach Australia, Malaysia, and elsewhere. These countries were also magnets for East Timor's refugees, who fled their homeland when Indonesia challenged its independence and invaded the country, engaging in a brutal war. The picture was just as appalling in Africa, where the Angolan civil war resulted in hundreds of thousands of its people fleeing to neighboring countries such as Zambia and Zaire. The long war between Ethiopia and Eritrea, lasting from the early 1960s to the early 1990s, caused half a million people to seek refuge in Sudan and Yemen.

The impact of such large-scale migrations on national and international affairs is not hard to see. The United Nations, which had from its inception defined one of its objectives as the promotion of human welfare, sought to deal with the problems faced by migrants and refugees—housing, health, education—through the Office of the United Nations High Commissioner for Refugees (UNHCR), but separate countries needed to help in the process. The UN was instrumental in having them agree to accept certain numbers of international refugees each year, and some, mostly in North America and Western Europe, voluntarily admitted them. The emerging global society was in part a product of such measures; nations and international organizations were now more than ever concerned with dealing with border-crossing, and sometimes even stateless, people. In the process the ethnic composition of sovereign nations began to change as nations admitted into their midst people of vastly different backgrounds. In the United States, the country that accepted the largest number of refugees, some began talking of diversity rather than unity or conformity as a national characteristic, and the same trend could be seen in other countries such as the Netherlands, Sweden, and Australia.

These phenomena clearly had transnational implications. For one thing, ethnic enclaves and communities could now be found all over the world. The Vietnamese population, for instance, was scattered in North America, Australia, and Europe to such an extent that their food became no more "exotic" than Chinese or Japanese cuisine. Vietnam, in other words, was not just a state with territorial borders but also a transnational existence represented by its people around the globe. The same would be true of other countries, notably China and the Chinese, after the country was opened to the outside world in the early 1970s.

What added to the momentum was the growing number of transnational workers, who might not move permanently from their home countries but who nevertheless came to constitute a significant portion of the labor force in the host countries. Wang Gungwu has called such people "sojourners," to distinguish them from immigrants who usually stay in a country of their destination and become permanent residents or citizens.[79] One striking fact about such temporary migrants was that, starting in the 1960s, the bulk of the world's sojourners—including those who eventually settled down in their host countries and thus became immigrants—began to consist of non-Europeans. This was particularly true of laborers in search of job opportunities. Hundreds of thousands of Turks moved to Germany, for instance, to fill job openings as Germany's economy expanded. Similarly, France was home to millions of North Africans, mostly originating in its former colonies, and the Netherlands began to attract former colonials from Indonesia and Surinam and others from Morocco. In these countries, the percentage of the foreign-born in the total population increased steadily, reaching nearly 10 percent by the 1990s. From East Asia, a growing number of Koreans left their homes for the United States as the latter revised its immigration laws in 1965 and eliminated the quota system that had, since the 1920s, favored Europeans over the rest. (People from Latin America had not been regulated under the quota system, whereas Asians, Africans, Arabs, and others deemed nonwhite had been totally excluded.) Now immigrants from Asia began to outnumber those from Europe. Although during the 1960s and the 1970s the largest numbers originated from South Korea and Taiwan, soon they would be eclipsed by those coming from China as well as South Asia (India and Pakistan). The result was to confirm further ethnic diversity in the United States and in some European countries.

Such phenomena quite clearly added another transnational layer to the world community, but how they might have reinforced transnational thought is more difficult to determine. Did the addition of unprecedented numbers of ethnically diverse populations, producing "hybrid" persons and communities, confirm and strengthen a sense of shared humanity, or did it give rise to narrower, more parochial attitudes? Was "hybridity," a term that scholars began to use to characterize the phenomenon, seen as a healthy development for a country, or did most people prefer to retain their societies' "purity," however that was defined? It is of course impossible to generalize about millions of individuals, but we might at least make note of two developments during these decades that would help explore the question—the "brain drain" and "multiculturalism."

The two reinforced each other. The brain drain consisted of the movement of doctors, scientists, and other scholars and educators from Third World countries to the United States and Europe. It created a very serious problem for the countries of origin, which were just then seeking to modernize their economies, education, and health care, but such waves were also an inevitable aspect of the growing transnational networks that enveloped all types of human pursuits. The same may be said of foreign students. A steadily increasing number of students from Asia, the Middle East, Africa, and Latin America sought educational opportunities in Western Europe, North America, and Australia. The United States, which attracted about one-third of all international students to its colleges and universities every year, had just under 50,000 of them in 1960, accounting for roughly 1.3 percent of the total student population in the nation. The number increased sixfold, to over 300,000, by 1980, or 2.6 percent of all students in the United States. No other country's universities had such a high proportion of foreign students, although those in Britain, France, and the Netherlands had sizable student populations coming from their still-existing or former colonies. Many of these foreign students would stay in the host countries, and eventually became a significant portion of the host country's academic personnel. Most dramatic was the slow but steady growth of students from mainland China who began to appear on European and US campuses during the 1970s, almost as soon as official (or even informal) relationships were opened up between Beijing and Western capitals.

Spurred in part by the brain drain, but also because of the social and cultural changes in the West and elsewhere during the 1960s and the 1970s, there was a growing influence of multiculturalism, or the idea that the nations and the entire world consisted of diverse populations living in close proximity to one another, each with its own traditions and ways of life, but sometimes blending with those of other groups. If formerly the prevalent view had been that the globe was divided into separate ethnic categories and civilizations, the new perspective brought these entities together so that there would be one human grouping, the human species, and one civilization encompassing all people. But humanity and human civilization were not seen as homogeneous or monolithic. Rather, they contained infinite variety. There was unity consisting of, or coexisting with, diversity. (Although precise statistics about "mixed marriages" are hard to come by, it seems possible that interracial households and children of different races became increasingly noticeable during these decades. Barrack Obama, born in 1962, would perhaps prove to be the most famous example. But in the early 1970s, when John Lennon, a former Beatle, said the United States was "the best place to bring up a Eurasian child"—his wife was Japanese—he may have been speaking on behalf of an increasing number of such children not just in the United States but elsewhere as well.[80])

The emerging global civil society, then, embraced the ideas of the unity of humankind and of respect for infinite varieties of ways of life and thought. The coexistence of the two—what Arthur Mann referred to as "the one and the many" in the context of American history—could foster the acceptance of hybridity, the living, working, and blending together of people and institutions of diverse backgrounds. One could see this in global cultural developments and in the phenomenal growth in the number of multinational business enterprises. Here a bare outline will suffice to put these developments in the context of transnationalism.

Global culture meant the sharing of cultural products, both "mainstream" and "peripheral," across national boundaries. The idea of a globally shared cultural product usually conjures up the phenomenal growth in popularity of rock and roll that easily surmounted the Cold War divide and became "hegemonic" in the sense of offering a novel and also universal way of combining words and tunes. Although there were national variations, this musical genre was intended as a new wave, to go beyond jazz, blues, and country music. It would be wrong, however, to focus on rock and roll as the single notable development in the global cultural arena in this period. In the realm of "high culture," too, these decades were notable for transnational exchanges. In classical music, the Cold War divide was frequently breached. Pianists from the United States and elsewhere continued to participate in and win competitions in Moscow, Prague, and other Eastern European cities, and there was movement in the opposite direction. For instance, in 1961 the Kirov Ballet performed in Paris, and a year later the Leningrad Ballet toured North American cities. (Rudolf Nureyev, a twenty-three-year-old soloist of the Kirov company, defected at the Paris airport and became a major force in ballet in Europe and the United States.) The Philadelphia Orchestra lost no time in visiting the People's Republic of China as soon as formal contact was reestablished between Washington and Beijing. The 1960s and the 1970s were the heyday of recorded classical music, made accessible to all people thanks to the spread of tape recorders and, in particular, Sony's Walkman, a device with which one could easily listen to one's favorite music while walking, bicycling, or riding on a train. In the meantime, hitherto peripheral cultural pursuits began to be introduced to wider spaces and intermingle. The Japan Foundation, established in 1972, the British Council, the Goethe Institute, the Alliance Française, and other semiofficial cultural agencies were designed to promote cultural exchanges across borders, and similar foundations were created in South Korea, Taiwan, mainland China, and elsewhere in Asia. Although provided with funding from official sources, these foundations functioned like such private organizations in the United States as the Ford, Carnegie, and Rockefeller Foundations, to promote cross-cultural exchanges.

Even those who did not participate in foundation activities became part of global cultural networks in such other areas as food, fashion, and movies. With expanding waves of migration, it is not surprising that non-Western cuisine

Subway riders in New York City listen to Sony Walkmans, March 1981. The convenient portable audio player, invented and produced in Japan, became a symbol of a mass culture that easily connected people in all parts of the world. (NY Daily News via Getty Images)

spread to Europe, North America, and Oceania. There had always been Chinese restaurants in Western countries, but most of them had been limited to Cantonese food. Now many other varieties were introduced, including Peking and Shanghai cuisines. Anecdotal evidence suggests that more and more Americans and Europeans became adept at using chopsticks, something that was helped by the growing popularity of Japanese, Korean, and Southeast Asian dishes. Businessmen from Japan and South Korea popularized their native cuisine, often cooked by chefs brought over from their countries. Raw fish, the main staple of Japanese food, was no longer looked upon as exotic, tasteless, or unsanitary. Not just Japanese residents but an increasing number of Americans and Europeans began appreciating the taste as well as the health value of raw fish and other items such as tofu. Similarly, the influx of Vietnamese and other Southeast Asians in the wake of the Vietnam War familiarized Westerners with Vietnamese and Thai food. At the same time, in Asian countries restaurants offering Western food, in particular American, French, and Italian cooking, rapidly increased in number. Hamburgers and hot dogs appealed to Asians as an aspect of American culture; the first McDonald's fast-food restaurants opened their doors in Japan in the early 1970s.

In fashions, blue jeans, popularized in the West after the Levi's brand was marketed aggressively in the United States, came to unify the world's youth and even older people as their favored daily wear. An increasing number of non-Westerners came to attend fashion shows in Paris, New York, and elsewhere, and some outsiders even opened their own boutiques in Europe and North America. One might also note the international popularity of "Barbie dolls," clad in the latest fashions. With the spread of television sets in all parts of the world, people everywhere were able to see what styles were in fashion and to emulate them.

Moviegoing added to the trend. The 1960s were remarkable for such nonconformist and even countercultural movies as *The Graduate* and *A Clockwork Orange,* the former a Hollywood production and the latter made in Britain. *The Graduate* starred Dustin Hoffman, who plays a college student who disrupts his ex-girlfriend's wedding and runs away with her. Earlier in the movie he had an affair with the girl's mother. These and other episodes illustrated the crumbling of traditional family values and moral standards, which were considered out of date and hypocritical. Instead, the principal driving force now would be the determination to be true to one's desires and beliefs. The film was widely acclaimed in the United States and shown in many other countries where the audiences shared vicariously in what the counterculture generation was producing in the United States. Likewise, *Clockwork Orange* (directed by American author Stanley Kubrick) showed British hooligans who disregarded all social norms and resorted to violence against the established order, in the process even indulging in mass rapes. They spoke an argot of cockney English mixed with Slavic words. The movie was an extreme depiction of the countercultural impulses of the younger generation, and resonated with some young men and women elsewhere. It inspired other antiheroes and anti-establishment actors such as Jack Nicholson, Warren Beatty, and Dennis Hopper.

Of course, such extreme expressions provoked resistance and opposition, sometimes just as extreme, among those who saw a threat to traditional order and national values. Multiculturalism, which its European and American opponents equated with the erosion of traditional values, appeared to doom Western civilization. The breakdown of sexual morals as exemplified by these movies alarmed conservatives and even liberals who felt the countercultural movement had gone too far. Many of them came together around the issues of abortion and homosexuality. The US Supreme Court legalized abortion under certain circumstances in *Roe vs. Wade* (1975), a decision that was denounced by the Catholic Church and others who viewed fetuses as living beings and considered an abortion the equivalent to murder. Certain countries, in particular the Protestant nations of Europe as well as China, Japan, and others, had legalized abortion, but *Roe vs. Wade* became a battle cry for the Vatican and the Catholics in Latin America and elsewhere to renew their commitment to the sanctity of life, which they insisted began at conception. Likewise with homosexuality. Same-sex marriage was still illegal in most countries, but some homosexual couples were more willing now to "come out of the closet." Movies and dramas with explicitly homosexual themes began to attract large audiences. For instance, Michel Tremblay's play *Hosanna*, a story of two gay men in search of sexual identity, was first performed in Quebec in 1973 and was soon staged in Toronto, New York, and other cities. Transnational networks of homosexual organizations grew, which in turn produced hostile reaction in many parts of the world. As AIDS began to appear in the 1970s, first in Africa and then in Southeast Asia, notably among homosexuals, the fear of contagion brought about a global reaction against homosexuality, even as NGOs and the UN began to grapple with the spread of the disease.

In some such fashion, there were now global cultural developments that produced numerous transnational encounters and movements. Vicarious transnational moments were being created everywhere, contributing to the sense that while nation building continued in various parts of the world and the Cold War developed with its own momentum, even more significant phenomena were appearing, impacting upon the consciousness and behavior of people everywhere. Their mentality had been thoroughly affected, even transformed, in the process.

If these were instances of transnational cultural phenomena that provided underpinnings, as it were, for the global civil society, they were reinforced by multinational business activities. In the background was the steady erosion of the hegemonic position enjoyed by the US economy in the immediate postwar years. This could be most graphically seen in the fact that steadily through the 1960s and into the 1970s, the dollar, the mainstay of the Bretton Woods system, lost its primacy. The pound sterling, the franc, the mark, and the yen, among others, had been increasing their value as the countries in which they were the national currencies had grown economically and expanded their foreign trade, thus obtaining more dollar reserves. Put another way, world trade and financial transactions were becoming more and more multilateral, and the dollar was just one among the major currencies. The value of these currencies would fluctuate from one day to the next, opening the way to currency speculation that would become widespread in the 1980s. Thus, economic transactions would become as much transnational (among individuals and private establishments across borders) as international (among business firms acting within legal and policy frameworks set up by their home countries).

The growth of multinational enterprises was a good indication of the trend. These were transnational business arrangements in which capital, technology, and labor of more than one country would be combined to produce goods and services that would be marketed throughout the world. Financiers, producers, workers, and consumers of several countries became transnational actors, finding the best and most profitable means of production, marketing, and consumption. The number of multinational corporations was less than one hundred in 1970 but grew to over nine hundred by 1980.[81] They were transnational not only in the sense of building bridges across boundaries but also because they were driven more by business than by national considerations. Multinational enterprises were inherently non-national in that sense; they were subject to the rules and guidelines of the countries in which they operated, but they did not necessarily follow or identify with the policies or objectives of particular nations. This contrasted with the situation before World War I, when business enterprises were far more rooted in specific countries and engaged in their own nationalistic competitions with one another. Nations, above all the United States, had sought to safeguard their domestic producers by erecting tariff walls. In the last decades of the twentieth century, in contrast, these businesses operated within a framework set up by various governments supportive of global economic transactions and competed among themselves without regard to where their components came from. Earlier, it may be said, there existed international economic activities but no global civil society, whereas now the two reinforced each other.

Globalization was a term that had not yet gained currency during the 1960s or the 1970s. Yet it was clearly the direction of world economic affairs during those decades. What was suggested by the "Nixon shock" economic measures of July 1971, which resulted in the devaluation of the dollar, was that economic globalization was now more than ever becoming transnational. That is to say, quite apart from the story of the growth of international trade and investment, the agents of globalization were becoming more and more widely scattered. The Bretton Woods system had operated on the basis of the major countries' intergovernmental cooperation, and this would continue in a limited way even after the devaluation of the dollar starting in 1971. However, increasingly, outside the framework of such state-level transactions, transnational linkages were developing. That may be one reason why world trade did not diminish despite the global economic downturn during the 1970s.

This downturn was caused primarily by the "oil shocks," the tripling and quadrupling of the price of crude oil, the bulk of which was produced in the Middle East. This was a result of a conscious decision adopted by the Organization of Petroleum Exporting Countries (OPEC) in 1973 in retaliation against Israel's attacks on the neighboring countries. Not just Israel but the United States, Western Europe, Japan, and other countries that had seemed to be behind Israel were to be punished by the Arab countries that accounted for a majority of the OPEC membership. They were aware of these other countries' dependence on imported oil, and they aggravated this vulnerability by reducing the output of crude oil and at the same time raising its price. These decisions were repeated again in 1979. As a result, the cost of energy increased tremendously, causing trade deficits in oil-importing countries for the first time in many years. The global energy crisis during the 1970s led various countries to seek alternative sources of power. The United States, the Soviet Union, and other European nations as well as Japan had been building nuclear power plants since the late 1950s and throughout the 1960s, but during the 1970s they impressed observers as perhaps the best alternative to imported oil. Still, at that time nuclear energy provided only a fraction of power needed for industrial and individual needs, and so the countries' oil dependence was not mitigated. The result was a steep inflation coupled with economic stagnation, as goods made in the industrialized nations became more expensive while the consumers' disposable income (after food and energy bills had been paid) declined. Unemployment ensued, and the rates of economic growth of most advanced countries plummeted, some even recording zero or minus growth. Perhaps the most telling symbol of how the oil shocks affected the world's richer economies was the sight of the British government applying for and obtaining a $4 billion loan from the International Monetary Fund in 1976.[82]

Despite such disasters, however, the volume of international trade actually increased, in sharp contrast to the 1930s when the Great Depression went hand in hand with diminished trade. One key reason for this was that during the 1970s, manufacturing firms and businesses began to resort to "offshore" procurement—that is, they sought to reduce costs by looking for cheaper labor abroad. Investment capital, saturated in the domestic economy, also went abroad, to industrialize hitherto underdeveloped economies. A related development was a reorientation of the US, British, and several other advanced economies from industrial production toward the service sector such as finance, insurance, and real estate. A new global division of labor was developing, facilitated by the floating exchange rates that came into existence by the end of the 1970s. Currencies kept moving transnationally; while, for instance, US, British, and Japanese capital would be poured into China and India to hire local labor for manufacturing, the emerging rich in these latter countries would invest their profits in purchasing bonds and securities in New York, London, or Tokyo. Add to such developments the phenomenal growth of "oil dollars," the petroleum-exporting countries' cash receipts that they could invest abroad as well as use to purchase luxury items, it is not surprising that there were many transnational transactions in capital, goods, and labor.

Transnational Justice

No aspect of the emerging global civil society was more dramatic than the explosive growth of international NGOs. Together with individuals (migrants, tourists, and others) and multinational enterprises, these organizations constituted non-state actors and shared the world with separate states and intergovernmental institutions.

Nongovernmental organizations typically were private associations of people who voluntarily came together to pursue certain shared objectives, and as such they were not incorporated into public systems of governance. It would be difficult to apply such a definition rigidly to an organization from an authoritarian state that controls even private activities. Not all private organizations, therefore, could be seen as authentic members of civil society. We may, however, take the listing in the Union of International Associations, itself a non-state actor, as a reliable statistical guide. According to its publications, the number of international NGOs grew from 2,795 in 1972 to 12,688 (79,786 if local branches were also counted) in 1984. This was a spectacular increase, unparalleled in the history of NGOs before or since.[83]

Why this phenomenon? It can best be understood as another aspect of the overall characteristic of the world of the 1960s and the 1970s, namely, that the overwhelming authority and prerogatives of the state that had informed postwar history began to be challenged by the emerging social and cultural forces as seen above. Particularly pertinent was the growing awareness that the existing states were not capable of dealing effectively with issues that were of transnational nature. Many of those issues involve considerations of justice. The concept of justice had long existed in international law and in separate national legal systems, but during the 1960s and the 1970s it was given wider significance as people in various parts of the world sought to protest against violations of human rights and against ecological deterioration. Although the movement for the protection of human rights and for the preservation of the natural environment had different origins, by the 1970s they had become merged as a global agenda for justice. It is no accident that among the rapidly increasing number of NGOs were those concerned with these two issues.

Human rights is a quintessentially transnational concept. When people in different countries lived at great distances from one another, the definition of who constituted the human community was rather limited. Even when one spoke of the rights of men, as the French did during the Revolution, "men" were not necessarily envisaged as people all over the world. Actually, the Revolution combined the rights of men with those of the nation so that they would reinforce each other. The same was true in most other countries. Human rights were to be safeguarded within the framework of a nation-state that would provide law and order for its citizens. Their rights, in other words, were usually comprehended as civil rights rather than human rights. But the years after 1945 provided greater opportunities than ever before for the encountering and intermingling of people of different nations. It is not surprising, then, that the idea of human rights should emerge as a major principle of people's interactions with one another, and of the behavior of states toward their citizens.

The significance of the 1960s and the 1970s in the history of human rights lies in the fact that in those decades human rights came to refer to people of all backgrounds and circumstances. During the 1960s the UN adopted a series of resolutions declaring that "the subjection of peoples to alien subjugation, domination and exploitation," "all forms of racial discrimination," and "discrimination against women" were violations of human rights. To ensure that the nations adhered to such principles, a number of NGOs were created, such as Amnesty International and Human Rights Watch. Amnesty International, established in 1961, became a major transnational force on behalf of "prisoners of conscience," to promote global public awareness of, and protest against, abuses of political prisoners that transcended "national, cultural, religious, and ideological boundaries."[84] Such language shows that to be human was now considered a superior condition of existence, over and above national and other identities. This organization received the Nobel Peace Prize in 1977, reflecting the emerging view that a peaceful world order and the respect for human rights were interdependent. Human Rights Watch, founded at that juncture, particularly played a crucial role in ensuring that the emerging détente between the United States and the Soviet Union would include considerations for human rights on both sides of the Cold War divide. (The Helsinki Accords of 1975, signed by all the states belonging to the North Atlantic Treaty Organization and the Warsaw Pact, made an explicit reference to human rights.)

In the 1970s human rights had particular relevance to the protection of women's rights. Not just in individual states but across national boundaries, women's voices were heard more clearly and strongly than ever, especially through the large number of transnational organizations created for the purpose. During the 1960s, women's rights movements were mostly confined to the West, but during the subsequent decade women in Asia, Africa, and elsewhere also became active. The UN declared 1975 "International Women's Year" and designated the years

1975 through 1985 the "Decade for Women." In 1975 the first World Conference on Women was held in Mexico City, and the participants resolved to establish networks of women's organizations throughout the world. In 1976 in Brussels, the International Tribunal on Crimes Against Women brought together two thousand women from forty countries who cited and denounced all forms of violence against women. Clearly, no definition of humankind would ever again exclude females, and transnational women's organizations and gatherings continued to remind men of this simple truth.

Did "being human" include those born with physical and mental disabilities, those unable to take care of themselves, or even to express themselves due to brain damage? The most famous of "handicapped" persons in the world may well have been Helen Keller (1880–1968), a woman who overcame her blindness and deafness through special training and perseverance and led a movement to help the deaf and the blind. Her life's story captured transnational attention through *The Miracle Worker,* a play (1959) and a movie (1962) based on her life. People with physical disabilities had constituted a significant minority in all societies, some of which had developed programs to look after their needs. But the transnational care of such people had been very slow to develop. Apart from several organizations that assisted veterans of war who had been seriously injured, humanitarian relief activities had not involved efforts to have the handicapped be treated as "normal" human beings. The 1960 Rome Olympics was a landmark in this regard in that the regular games were followed by the Paralympics, where men and women with physical disabilities, from various countries, could for perhaps the first time in history challenge one another in sports in significant numbers. The experiment brought such joy to the participants and their supporters that the practice was followed by the Olympics held in Tokyo in 1964, Mexico City in 1968, and in all subsequent events. Among transnational efforts less connected to states was the holding in 1970 of an international competition for physically disabled athletes in Aylesbury, England. Such sporting events soon came to include the blind and those with cerebral palsy.[85]

Notable as these events were, they covered only those with physical disabilities, ignoring the large number of persons with mental, emotional, psychological, or linguistic disabilities. The United Nations belatedly included the rights of the

The Italian team at the Olympic Village before the start of the first International Paralympics, held in Rome immediately following the 1960 Olympic Games. The Paralympics have since been held every four years, demonstrating the world's belated awareness and acceptance of the disabled. (Getty Images)

mentally disabled in its list of human rights in 1971, and four years later the world organization denounced discrimination against all types of disability. Even so, it was only in 1980 that "Special Olympics" were organized to bring together mentally disabled persons. This was surely one area where even expanded definitions of human rights left a large segment of humanity inadequately covered. Nevertheless, soon it was globally recognized that one could not except even the most severely disabled from the definition of humanity. If anything, such people needed a greater measure of "human security"—a term that gained currency at this juncture, indicating the view that as well as, or even more than, the traditional notion of national security, the well-being of humans as humans regardless of who they were must lie at the basis of any conception of justice.[86]

An important component of "human security" was environmental. The decades after 1960 were notable for the worldwide concern with the physical environment, in terms both of the quality of air, water, and food that humans consumed and of the preservation of the ecological system that sustained animals, birds, trees, and all living things. Both were transnational issues whose relevance cut across national borders. At bottom was a growing transnational concern with two phenomena that had characterized the postwar decades: population growth and economic change. With the world's population more than doubling between 1945 and 1980, with larger and larger percentages of people living in urban centers, and with industrialization spreading even to small cities and villages, the skies began to darken, the waters became impure, and the air was sometimes unbreathable. Of course, wars and armaments contributed to some of these phenomena. The atmospheric testing of nuclear weapons sprayed "ashes of death" on all living beings indiscriminately until they were halted in 1963—at least by the United States, Britain, and the Soviet Union, which signed a test-ban treaty in 1963. In the war in Vietnam, US forces were spraying the Vietnam countrysides with Agent Orange, an agent containing dioxin that not only destroyed forests and farmlands but also acted as a powerful carcinogen in the human body.[87] Up to three million children and grandchildren of Vietnamese exposed to the chemical were said to bear its effects. Outside of such battlefields, air and water pollution remained and even grew worse because of pollutants such as carbon monoxide, nitrogen oxides, and sulfur dioxide emitted from factories and automobiles, while rivers, lakes, and oceans were increasingly contaminated by sewage and industrial waste.

One notable moment in demonstrating environmental damage may have come in Minamata, a seaside village in western Japan, where starting in the second half of the 1950s babies began to be born deformed, mentally handicapped, and even unaware of themselves. "Minamata disease" was caused by mercury poisoning; a manufacturer of a substance known as acetaldehyde used mercury in the production process, and dumped it into the ocean. The appearance of these babies was so shocking that civic groups were formed in the 1960s to protest against the company and to call upon the government to do something about the situation, which by then was causing scores of deaths.[88] The news of Minamata disease spread to other countries, where similar incidents were reported, and in time worldwide concern with mercury poisoning became one of the major sources of transnational environmentalism. The Minamata syndrome seemed to demonstrate the danger of uncontrolled industrial development and thus fed the growing movement across national boundaries to stem the tide. As exemplified by the Club of Rome, a gathering of economists and others in the late 1960s in response to the growing seriousness of the consequences of industrialization, there arose a transnational movement to resist unlimited economic growth.

Theirs was not necessarily a universal voice. From the beginning, the idea of limited growth was opposed by Third World countries, which asserted that the world's environmental problems had been produced by the countries that had already undertaken industrialization, in the process making use of the rich resources of the poorer lands. The poorer lands, they insisted, should not be required to restrain their economic development, which would keep them forever in the state of underdevelopment, increasing the already large gaps between the two groups of nations. The collision between environmentalism and developmentalism was serious, and has remained so to this day. However, all countries, regardless of their degree of industrialization or urbanization, agreed on the necessity to protect endangered species and to improve the quality of air and water. To that degree there was a transnational consensus. The disagreement had to do with specific means of achieving these goals, the poorer countries insisting that the rich nations should do more to improve the natural environment and should help the poorer nations attain "sustainable growth," that is, economic development that was compatible with environmental conservation.

A landmark moment in the development of transnational environmentalism was the Stockholm meeting convened by the United Nations in 1972. This was a major international (rather than transnational) conference, but the road to Stockholm had been paved by many transnational NGOs. One of them, the International Union for the Protection of Nature, had been in existence since 1948 and organized international conferences for the protection of what came to be known as the "biosphere." The word *protection* was replaced with *conservation* in 1956, and similarly named bodies were created during the 1960s and the 1970s. One of the most influential, Friends of the Earth, was founded in the United States in 1969 and soon established branches all over the world. These organizations—according to a UN survey, at least ten of them were international in scale—dedicated themselves to protecting "planet Earth" from humans, insisting that human lifestyles, ambitions, and avarice no less than human wars played havoc with the ecological system.

The Stockholm meeting was attended by representatives of both industrialized and developing countries, and by government officials as well as spokespersons for NGOs. While the United Nations Environment Programme, established in 1973 to follow up on the conference, was an international institution, it provided the setting for the coming together of representatives of many private organizations with their shared agendas. The number of transnational organizations dedicated to environmentalism grew so rapidly that in 1975 a conference was held in Austria to review their interrelationships as well as their relationships to the United Nations and to independent states.[89] Nowhere was environmental activism inside and outside national and international frameworks more sensationally demonstrated than through the activism of Greenpeace, an organization established in 1970. Greenpeace not only advocated the conservation of the biosphere and the protection of endangered species, notably whales, but it often resorted to direct action. The organization's founders, Canadians and Americans in Canada, from the beginning were assertive in protesting against underwater nuclear testing and against the killing of whales, and they sent ships to disrupt such activities. But Greenpeace was not alone. In its campaign to save whales it was joined by other organizations, such as Friends of the Earth and the World Wildlife Fund, the latter having been established in 1971. As a result of their activities, international agreements came to be negotiated to ban the killing of at least certain kinds of whales. Norway, Japan, and some other countries that still practiced whaling—and ate whale meat—protested against such bans, but they could not silence the transnational voices that grew even louder with each success.

Very broadly put, then, both human rights and environmental concerns were broadening the conception of justice. Going beyond the traditional legal notion, there was a transnational awareness that people and the natural environment needed to be treated justly. Technically, transnational justice was a concept that was formally adopted by the United Nations much later and referred primarily to reconciliation and restitution after violent clashes or dictatorial rule in a country.⁹⁰ But the idea that justice must prevail globally and that transnational efforts must be made to pursue such an objective was quite evident before 1980. It is not surprising, then, that the unprecedented increase in the number and activities of international nongovernmental advocacy groups coincided with the growing awareness that all persons must be protected against abuse, regardless of their differences, and that the planet Earth, with all its living beings, must be treated justly. These were transnational concerns, and NGOs mushroomed because the authority of the state was weakening or because existing governments were incapable of dealing with those problems. Transnational organizations worked with individual governments and with international bodies in seeking to cope with them, but when these others were found to be inadequate, private associations would gladly take their place to exercise the initiative in the name of the whole of humanity.

It was just a step here to the idea that in order to ensure transnational justice, there should be established new legal frameworks, transnational courts of justice. Unlike the international courts of justice that dealt with war crimes committed by one nation or group of nations against another, the transnational courts would represent people everywhere and bring to justice even those who acted in violation of the human rights of their own citizens.

Ironically, precisely at the moment when notions of transnational justice were making headway, a new challenge to the vision appeared in the form of terrorism, which often was couched in the language of justice and was now more transnational than earlier. Acts of terrorism had always existed, but most of them had been national phenomena. During the 1970s, West Germany's Red Army Faction protested against the governing class, which it believed contained too many holdovers from the Nazi era, while the Irish Republican Army led a guerrilla war against British occupation forces in Northern Ireland.⁹¹ The Kurdistan Workers Party worked for a Kurdish homeland in northern Iraq and eastern Turkey, and in northern Spain the separatist group ETA was formed in 1968 to gain a homeland for the Basque people of the Iberian Peninsula. Both these organizations were willing to resort to terrorism, but arguably the most spectacular terrorist incident occurred in 1972 when the Palestine Liberation Organization (PLO) attacked and killed a number of Israeli athletes at the Munich Olympics. At the end of the decade, when Soviet forces invaded Afghanistan, Islamic jihadists known as mujahedin staged guerrilla-style attacks against them. These were politically motivated terrorist acts that were part of national (or nation-making) dramas. In the late 1960s and the early 1970s, however, a more transnationally oriented and organized terrorism made its appearance. Particularly notable were groups of Muslims who came together across national boundaries to target their enemies, who included both Arabs (most notably Egypt's Anwar Sadat, who was assassinated by the Muslim Brotherhood in 1981) and non-Arabs who were considered enemies of Islam. Because Muslims were particularly numerous in South Asia, Southeast Asia, and the Middle East, networks of clandestine organizations began to be created in these regions, out of which the most famous transnational terrorist group, al-Qaeda, would be created in the early 1990s.

Terrorism, whether local, national, or transnational, clearly violated universal human rights in its assault upon people whom its perpetrators considered their enemy, whether because of the victims' nationality, religion, or way of life. Equally seriously, terrorists disregarded the sanctity of their own lives when they turned themselves into suicide bombers. Like the Japanese kamikaze ("divine wind") pilots who crashed their small aircraft into US ships in what they considered a sacred mission to honor the emperor, Islamic extremists blew themselves up in a "holy war" in the name of the prophet—and in the name of justice. (It was unjust, in their view, for the West to support Israel at the expense of Palestinian Arabs.) But the terrorist acts were criminal deeds in violation of all declarations on universal human rights that the United Nations and other organizations, including religious bodies, had promulgated. They were as serious an offense against humanity as genocides and even more transnational in scope. Transnational, non-governmental terrorist incidents were, unfortunately, to grow more serious in the following decades. These headline-catching crimes, however, provoked global condemnation that was just as transnational in scope. Whether transnational terrorism could be suppressed only by national or international efforts through the use of military force, and whether, in responding with military power, the states might also be violating human rights, were questions that were to be bequeathed to the subsequent decades.

Religious Revival and the Limits of Transnationalism

There is another way to contextualize the appearance of Islamic terrorism in the 1970s. It was a dramatic demonstration of the fact that religion was noticeably gaining influence among individuals and nations, and in various regions of the world. While it is wrong to equate terrorism with a religious movement, the coincidental phenomenon of transnational violence and religious revival in the decades that saw notable developments in such areas as human rights and environmentalism is deserving of attention. Certain religious developments tended to stress national and parochial concerns. Even if religious faiths had traditionally stressed the unity of humans before God, that did not prevent sectarian, particularistic forces from developing agendas that were clearly against universalism.

In particular, during these decades there grew what Scott Thomas has aptly termed "religious nationalism," or religion in the service of a nation, and vice versa.[92] Iran after the revolution of 1979 is a good example: a nation ruled by a theocracy of ayatollahs, or religious leaders. Of course, one could point to the example of Israel as a Jewish state as an even earlier manifestation of a religion establishing a nation, but Israel was not quite a theocracy, and secular Jews shared power with the more religious. Others, such as Hamas in Palestine's occupied territories, the Hezbollah in southern Lebanon, and the Taliban in Afghanistan (until after the end of Soviet occupation in the 1980s) and Pakistan did not control a national government but were seeking to seize political power. In all these instances, religious revival manifested itself through politicization. "Political Islam" was a good example.

But Islam was not alone. The 1970s also witnessed the revival of fundamentalist tendencies among other religions. As Thomas Borstelmann has shown, in the United States the decade was characterized by both social diversity and religious resurgence.[93] The same phenomenon could be detected elsewhere as well. Christianity, which had mostly remained a personal faith and, within a nation-state, by and large passive and subordinate to secular authority, came to assert itself. Most of its influence, it is true, was in civil society, where church attendance began to grow and evangelical preachers and movements gained influence. But within the Christian church, there were significant new developments among both Catholics and Protestants. Throughout the 1960s and the subsequent decades, the Catholic Church became a major force for nuclear arms control and interracial harmony, while at the same time adhering to traditional perspectives on such issues as marriage and birth control. Moreover, Catholics, especially in Europe, became deeply involved in developmental and humanitarian activities abroad. In Latin America, where such efforts were particularly notable, there emerged what was called "Liberation Theology"—this came close to fundamentalism, as its followers strictly adhered to the teachings of Jesus as recorded in the Bible, but it also had political implications in that it drove its adherents to involve themselves in opposition to secular state authorities.

The Protestant counterpart to Liberation Theology was revivalism, or evangelicalism as it was sometimes referred to, stressing the impending "second coming" of Christ and the need for ardent prayers for personal salvation. Mainline Protestant churches in Europe and the United States declined in attendance during the 1960s, but nondenominational and charismatic sects surged. They stressed that the Bible was to be understood literally as laws passed down from God through Jesus. In the United States, for instance, a group calling itself "The Moral Majority" increased its influence during the 1970s, joining forces with traditional evangelicals whose roots went back to the Great Awakening of the eighteenth century. Billy Graham exemplified the mid-twentieth-century variety, exhorting all devout believers to bring Christian doctrine into their daily lives. These movements were the Christian counterpart to Islamic fundamentalism, not only doctrinally but also in their attempt to make an impact on political and social affairs. Some fundamentalists became actively engaged in protesting against birth control and abortions, while others resurrected the anti-Darwinian movement that had seen its heyday during the 1920s (especially in the United States) and argued that science, especially as taught at schools, should conform to the Bible. In opposition to Darwinian perspectives on the origins of human species, the adherents of what came to be called "creationism" insisted that the origins of humanity as well as of the world should all be attributed to God's work.

While Islam and Christianity were particularly notable in the renewed emphasis on fundamental doctrines, other religions, too, were affected by the trend and produced groups within them that were oriented toward fundamentalism, even extremism. For instance, in South Asia, where Buddhists and Hindus had existed side by side for centuries—a coexistence complicated by the fact that Buddhists tended to be a major influence among poorer classes—some individuals and groups resorted to violence against one another, or sometimes against other

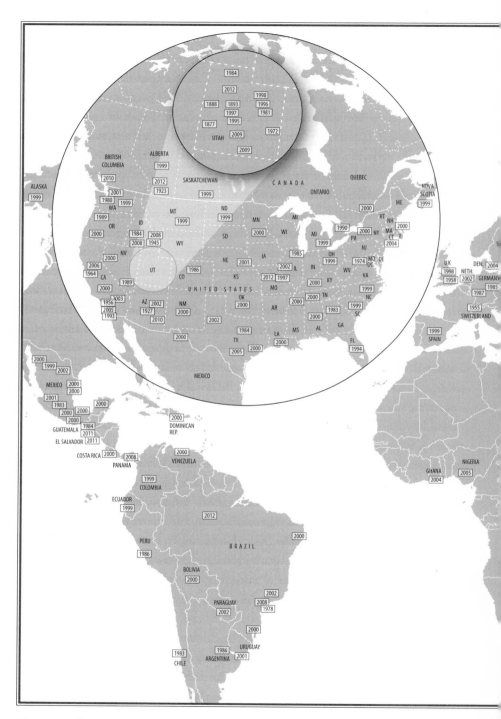

Transnational religion: temples of the Church of Jesus Christ of Latter-day Saints, 2013.

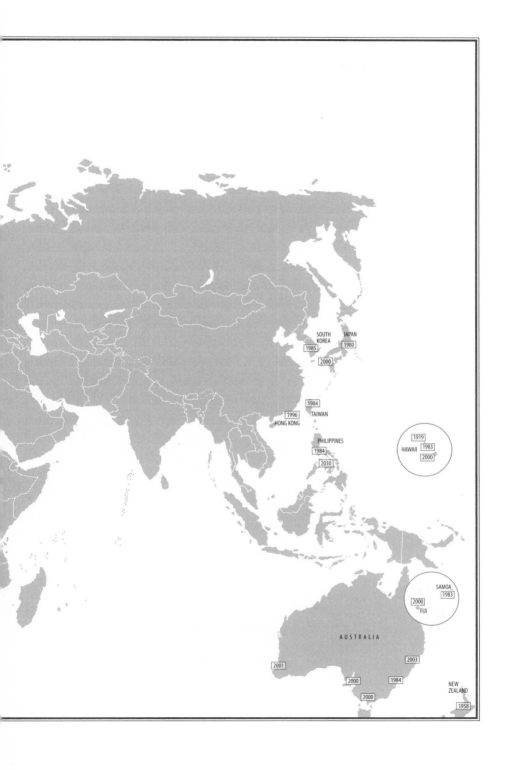

SOUTH
KOREA
1985

JAPAN
1980

2000

1984

1996
HONG KONG

TAIWAN

PHILIPPINES
1984

2010

1919
1983
HAWAII
2000

SAMOA
1983

2000
FIJI

AUSTRALIA

2001

2003

2000   1984

2000

NEW
ZEALAND

1958

religions. Such religious activism became serious when it was intertwined with ethnic conflict within national boundaries, as happened in Sri Lanka where the Tamil minority, espousing Hinduism, sought to achieve autonomy, if not complete independence, by struggling against the Buddhist majority. In Tibet, followers of the Dalai Lama accepted his doctrine of passive resistance to the Chinese government, which claimed that Tibet belonged to China, but a minority of radicals did not hesitate to use more direct means of protest. We may also add the example of Afrikaners, the white population in South Africa, the majority of whom professed faith in the Dutch Reformed Church while safeguarding their nation's policy of racial segregation, or apartheid, even as it came to be denounced by the transnational community as a gross violation of human rights. Religion in the service of the state, and vice versa, were in many ways an anomalous development in a period that saw so much evidence that transnational ideas and aspirations were being strengthened.[94]

The Dalai Lama and actor Richard Gere at the New York Lawyers Alliance for World Security's Annual Peace Award, April 1994. Exiled from Tibet when it was incorporated into China in 1949, the Dalai Lama has followers all over the world, symbolizing the spiritual leadership of a transnational individual. (WireImage/Getty Images)

Why such a development? It was clearly a reaction against the tendency of the age that exalted the transnational individual at the expense of the national community and that saw a steady erosion of state authority and the strengthening of non-state actors. Religious nationalism, in a sense, came to the state's rescue. One may see this most clearly in the United States, where religious revival was closely connected to nationalism and political antiradicalism, even antiliberalism. Those who were shocked by the challenges to state authority by the radical movement of the 1960s often sought refuge in religion, in most instances the Christian church. Many religious conservatives, on their part, saw eye to eye with political nationalists. The relentless assault on the government during the Vietnam War, as well as the growth of transnational movements, produced an inevitable backlash, coalescing those who sought to restore respect for the nation as well as the church. In this sense, religion and nation reinforced each other.

Religious revival in this period, however, may also be connected to another notable phenomenon: the self-assertiveness of non-Western countries and people. From the moment they came to power, Iran's ayatollahs did not conceal their disdain for modern Western civilization, in particular its secular lifestyles and democratic governance. Likewise with other Islamic fundamentalists, who castigated the West for its alleged domination of the world. Even less-politicized Muslims began to distance themselves from Western values or to assert that these values were not universally valid, that non-Western parts of the globe adhered to their own belief systems. We have noted the influence of such writers as Fanon and Said, who challenged the political and cultural terms that had been defined in the West and accepted unquestioningly by the non-West. Such thinkers as well as religious leaders were insisting on an equation between the West and the non-West, neither of which was of universal validity. Just at the moment when transnational forces appeared to grow with unprecedented speed, these views were calling for recognition of diversity, even of division of humankind into separate religious and other identities. Politicization of religion may be considered an aspect of such a phenomenon.

In 1963 the historian William H. McNeill published a widely acclaimed book, *The Rise of the West*. The title was misleading, because the book's aim was not to celebrate the triumph of modern Western civilization but rather to put it in the context of the long history of humankind. In McNeill's view, "the rise of the

West" was not foreordained. It was a relatively recent phenomenon, dating from no earlier than the mid-eighteenth century. The West "rose" and came to dominate the world because of its scientific and intellectual achievements during the Enlightenment, but, he argued, this dominance might not last any longer than that of other civilizations had. McNeill was only vaguely aware of the forces of what would come to be called globalization, let alone of transnationalization, but his emphasis, like that of his senior colleague Toynbee, was on connections among civilizations as a major engine of human history. Although McNeill was apparently unaware that these phenomena were even then challenging long-held ideas about the modern West, his insistence on viewing history as a world-embracing development, not just in terms of national or regional units, would, in two or three decades, come to seem commonplace.

In any event, to borrow from the title of McNeill's book, the 1960s and the 1970s did indeed mark the time when the non-West began to rise. We have seen some examples of this already during the 1950s, such as the Bandung Conference and UNESCO's ten-year project on mutual appreciation between East and West. Both challenged the traditional acceptance of the West as the norm and sought to place the West and the non-West on equal terms. We may likewise note the ways in which the idea of "development" became politicized and uncoupled from the West. No idea was more "Western," at least in modern history, than that of "development." And it had immense following among non-Western people. Economic development was a primary objective of the newly independent states during the 1950s and beyond. As more countries joined their ranks—by the 1970s more than two-thirds of the membership of the United Nations consisted of postcolonial states—development became an even more urgent imperative. Already in 1960 the UN General Assembly passed a resolution designating the new decade as the Decade of Development.

The situation began to change in the early 1970s, however, when the developing nations called for a "new international economic order" that would promote their development by giving them preferential treatment vis-à-vis the advanced countries of the West in trade, investment, and other areas. At the same time, reflecting the thinking of Fanon, Said, and others, some in the Third World came to challenge the prevailing thinking on economic development, which had postulated that agrarian societies would undertake industrialization and urbanization through some system of state planning, whether socialist or nonsocialist. The advanced industrialized countries were to provide capital and technology for this purpose. These ideas retained their influence after 1960. Indeed, they gained official recognition in the United States when President John F. Kennedy established an office devoted to foreign assistance (the Agency for International Development) and avidly promoted nation building and economic development in Asia, Africa, and Latin America. In addition, he also initiated the Peace Corps, a program for young American men and women to go abroad to serve as engineers, teachers, hospital workers, and in many other capacities to help modernize developing countries. The key theme was again development, which was now more firmly incorporated into official US policy, as exemplified by the appointment of W. W. Rostow, the preeminent theorist of development, as a member of the National Security Council. Even the Vietnam War, which grew in seriousness under Kennedy and was drastically expanded under his successor, Lyndon B. Johnson, was waged in the name of helping South Vietnam's self-determination and economic modernization.

This was the heyday of academic developmentalism. Theories of modernization were promulgated by political scientists and sociologists as well as by economists, and historians, too, avidly absorbed the social science literature on the subject. As noted earlier, modern Japanese history came to be understood in the framework of modernization, and the same conceptualization was applied to Turkey, China, and other countries, and not simply national histories but also international relations were frequently understood in the same framework. Often the Cold War came to be seen as a contest between the superpowers as to which of them was better equipped and more successful in helping Third World countries modernize themselves. But far more than global geopolitics was involved, as can be seen in the struggle between Moscow and Beijing to influence developmental strategies in such countries as North Korea and Vietnam. Recent research reveals that for Pyongyang or Hanoi, the Cold War struggle between the two superpowers was of much less interest to the political leaders than the question of choosing the ideology and methods that were best calculated to ensure their own, as well as their country's, survival.[95]

At this level, then, development was a widely shared, transnational ideology, as well as the basis for understanding national and international affairs. However, Third World doctrines against Western-style development also grew during the 1960s and became even more widespread in the subsequent decade. If we are to name a significant moment to mark the rise of counterdevelopmentalism, there would be no better landmark than the emergence of "dependency theory," first promulgated by Raúl Prebisch, an Argentine economist and statesman. During the 1960s he chaired the UN Economic Commission for Latin America and continued to take the advanced economic powers to task for pursuing their self-interest even when they undertook developmental assistance. Such assistance, he asserted, all had strings attached; the capitalist nations used it for solidifying their hold on less advanced countries, tying them to global trade and investment networks. The upshot was to keep these countries perpetually under the control of the industrial nations by making them dependent on the latter rather than freeing themselves from the chain. Like Fanon's treatises on the Third World's mental dependence on the West, Prebisch's formulation theorized about the same phenomenon in the economic area. Both questioned the prerogative of the West to present its own history as a model for others and sought to liberate the non-West from the advanced countries' seemingly perpetual control of the world's resources and markets. Soon dependency theory became widely shared among developing nations, who came to view themselves as victims of global economic forces.

Counterdevelopmentalism, however, was not confined to the non-West. As noted in the preceding section, an important aspect of the West's "cultural revolution" during the 1960s was the questioning of the premises of modernization and progress. The revolutionaries opposed their vision of a less developed, less urbanized world to the reality of a seemingly perpetually growing industrial world. But many of them also accepted counterdevelopmentalism as a viable concept to tie them and the Third World together. In their transnational universe, men and women from all over the world would work together, not for further promoting the world's economic growth but for combating poverty and inequality in different areas of the world. They would seek to eliminate injustice such as racial inequality and religious intolerance. They would put pressure on governments and corporations to stop doing business with South Africa until the latter gave up its policy of apartheid. For that matter, the transnational radicals would pay close attention to domestic affairs in all countries to ensure that the rights of women, children, and minorities were protected. It is fitting that, before he was assassinated in 1968, Martin Luther King always conceived of his struggle for equality at home in relation to similar movements abroad, including Gandhi's movement in India. Although the Indian leader had been assassinated twenty years earlier, King believed solid ties connected the two, as well as those struggling for justice in South Africa and elsewhere. They were against economic development for its own sake and gave priority to noneconomic objectives.

Such thinking was part of the story of the rise of the non-West. While modernization and economic development were quintessentially of Western origin, to stress racial equality or the Third World's liberation from dependency was to indicate that the non-West had arrived on the global scene. Their interests and ideas would now have to be taken seriously and their perspective incorporated into any view of the human condition and of humankind's future. As noted earlier, the term *human security* came to be used in this period among some officials and nonofficials to indicate the priority of human as against national interests. In their view, it was not enough to be concerned with national security, something that each country would define to fit its needs. Human security, in contrast, considered the welfare of all people in the entire world. Only when they were ensured a minimum of food, shelter, health, education, and dignity could there be true security for all, including individual states. There is little doubt that when people began couching their ideas this way, humanity was no longer equated with "Westerners," the symbol of modern civilization, but all people everywhere.

Religious revival of the 1970s may be put in some such context. It was not simply that certain religious movements gained influence or that they became ardent forces in support of nationalism. Many of these movements arose in non-Western countries, as if to indicate that the non-West was "rising" to challenge a world economy, a world order, and a world culture that had been part of the phenomenon of the "rise of the West." The resurgence of Islam and other faiths combined with Third World self-consciousness, the rise of China, antidevelopmentalism, and many other concurrent phenomena to challenge the power and influence of the West.

Whether such a situation fostered, altered, or damaged transnational networks is an interesting question to which no simple answer is possible. If the non-West had turned against the West, it would undoubtedly have led to a divided world, not an interconnected one. But that did not happen. The non-West did not amount to an anti-West coalition. People of Asia, the Middle East, Africa, and Latin America never stopped migrating to Western countries to seek jobs or to study. There developed transnational connections among countries in those regions, some of which may have been self-consciously parochial in promoting their identity as non-Western, but they were clearly outnumbered by multilateral networks that included countries from all parts of the globe. The incipient rise of the non-West, in other words, was a reality whose significance provided one layer in the evolution of transnational history. Just as non-national entities like religions, business enterprises, NGOs, and races were making their existence known in the world arena, non-Western people, faiths, ideas, and goods were intruding upon Western consciousness, in the process contributing to the making of a more fully global community.

3. Layers of Transnationalism

THE FINAL two decades of the twentieth century are usually characterized as having been a period of rapid globalization. It was in the 1980s that the term *globalization* came to be used widely, to refer particularly to a spectacular increase in the number and scope of activities of multinational enterprises. Globalization now more than ever came to embrace most countries of the world.

It is important to keep in mind that, as in the preceding period, the economic layer was just one of several that constituted the evolution of a transnationalizing world. One characteristic of the 1980s and the 1990s may well have been that some contradictions and even conflict among such layers became increasingly more visible.

In the economic sphere, perhaps the most significant development was that the People's Republic of China under the leadership of Deng Xiaoping in 1979 began to modernize the country by opening it up to international trade and investment. This resulted in a massive infusion of foreign capital and technology into the country as well as the establishment of manufacturing firms, combining such capital and technology with cheaper domestic labor.[96] By the end of the century, China was emerging as one of the fastest-growing economies, its rate of growth averaging 9 percent per year during the years 1980–2000. Its products, consisting mostly of agricultural and mineral goods initially but increasingly of manufactured items, began to flood the world market. From virtually nil in 1980, Chinese export trade was already accounting for 1.8 percent of the world's total in 1990 and 4.0 percent in 2000. China's exports as a share of the country's GDP rose from 13 percent in 1980 to 44 percent in 2000. Its foreign currency reserve, a test of how well a country is doing in its international balance of payments, already recorded $30 billion in 1990 and rose to $168 billion in 2000, among the highest in the world. In virtually all countries, the label "Made in China" could be found on a vast number of consumer products, including television sets, radios, air conditioners, and computer parts as well as kitchen utensils and clothes.

However, "Made in China" did not mean that an exported item had been manu-factured entirely by Chinese. It may have been designed by Americans or Euro-peans, and it may have been produced by Indian, Vietnamese, or Indonesian as well as Chinese workers. In other words, China was now being fully integrated into the global economy in which national labels lost their earlier, exclusive con-notations. Other countries, for their part, rushed their goods and capital to the partially opened China market, where people began to have the means to enjoy, or at least to aspire to enjoying, Western-style middle-class patterns of living. At the very least, the Chinese were less poor than they had been traditionally. For instance, the rural poverty rate was 42.8 percent in 1990, but it shrank to 24.2 percent by 1997. The percentage of China's population earning less than one US dollar a day fell from around 9 percent to less than 4 percent during the 1990s.[97]

It is true that state planning, rather than market forces, dictated the overall direction, size, and specific contents of the Chinese economy. The Beijing regime, controlled by the Communist Party, annually set goals for economic growth, made plans for industrial and agricultural production, and provided subsidies to export-oriented businesses. Even its population policy, which came to be known as the "one child per family" rule, was part of the state's attempt to increase the na-tion's productivity. By limiting the overall population, the leaders hoped to edu-cate and train those who were born so that they would become productive mem-bers of the country and succeed in the international arena. This was an integral part of China's strategy of modernization, launched in the early 1980s so as to catch up with the more advanced countries and to claim a larger share of the world economy. Even so, the state alone could not have carried on the task of trans-forming the country without the cooperation of the people, the more so because modernization entailed incorporating the nation into the global setting, which in turn meant providing a profit motive to ambitious and hardworking individu-als so that they would compete in both the domestic and external markets. An increasing number of Chinese willingly entered the global market and pursued their opportunities as well as interests, to such an extent that by the end of the century a small minority at the top of the economic ladder were emerging as mil-lionaires, to the envy of the rest of the population. The gap between the successful few and the rest created social unrest and political tension, which would never disappear despite the efforts by the governing elite to maintain domestic order.

The story could be duplicated in many other countries, so that there emerged a globally interconnected community of individuals and non-state actors with agendas that were not identifiable with formal state policies. Countries like India and Brazil were not far behind China, although their rates of economic growth in this period were lower. And in the wake of the ending of the Cold War and the collapse of the Soviet Union in the late 1980s and the early 1990s, Eastern European countries now entered the global arena and took advantage of the opportunities being opened up for economic liberalization and growth. Some of the formally socialist states did better than others, however. Poland, Hungary, and the Czech Republic made fairly successful transitions to the market economy, whereas Russia's economy shrank by 3.5 percent between 1990 and 2000 and Ukraine's rate of growth fell by nearly 7 percent per year. The fact remains that there were now far more numerous players in the drama of globalization. As a result, the United States, Japan, and the Western European countries that had dominated the world economy could no longer take their hegemonic position for granted and were forced to pay increasing attention to the newly globalizing states.

Such a nation-by-nation description of accelerating globalization, however, is somewhat misleading. The principal units playing their roles in the world economy were no longer just nations. One significance of globalization at the end of the twentieth century is that states were becoming less the determinants of economic activities and their traditionally central roles were being supplemented, if not supplanted, by non-state actors and individuals. This phenomenon had already become noticeable in the 1970s, but it was accelerated during the 1980s. Instead of focusing on the rise of China or of the entrance of Eastern European states into the global economic arena, therefore, we should pay equal attention to the flow of goods, capital, and labor, which was now much less restrained than earlier. Instead of seeing China as a monolithic economic entity, for instance, we should speak of individual Chinese as well as the country's profit-oriented firms. These were people and organizations that happened to be Chinese, but their roles were not bound by the territorial borders. They went all over the world in search of business opportunities.

Capital, too, was becoming increasingly more stateless, released from various restrictions that had regulated its movement. Perhaps the decisive moment in the transnationalization of capital came at the end of 1985, when representatives of central banks and finance ministers from the United States, Britain, Germany, France, and Japan met at the Plaza Hotel in New York City to liberalize currency transactions across national borders. The authorities in these countries had since 1971 sought to coordinate their monetary policies in order to sustain the value of the dollar at a certain level, but now they would minimize, if not eliminate altogether, such intervention. The Plaza Accord in effect withheld support for the dollar as the officially sanctioned currency of choice in international transactions and eliminated state-controlled rates of exchange, at least in theory. In reality, the central banks in various countries retained a measure of control over rates of exchange through buying or selling their respective currencies, China being a particularly notable example. Still, currency traders, speculators, and even ordinary citizens all over the world were now much less restrained than in the past to purchase, accumulate, or sell chunks of whatever national monetary units they chose. For the first time in the modern centuries, currencies began to float globally, which complicated business planning but was an inevitable aspect of the transnationalizing of the global economy.

The establishment of the European Union in 1991 and the decision in 1999 by most members of the regional community—Britain was a notable exception—to adopt a common monetary unit, the euro, was further evidence of the transnationalization of the global economy. One could now travel in most countries in Western and Central Europe without changing currencies at each border, while at the same time imports to, and exports from, the regional community waxed and waned as the rates of exchange between the euro and the dollar, as well as between the euro and the pound sterling and other currencies, kept changing.

Despite such developments, observers and academic specialists were slow to recognize them as a significant historical phenomenon. Although the term *globalization* began to be used by economists and social scientists during the 1980s—and its usage steadily spread to journalists, the business community, politicians, bureaucrats, and even foundations (such as the Center for Global Partnership, established within the Japan Foundation in 1991)—historians did not initially catch on. A cursory look at their writings indicates that few of them mentioned, let alone discussed, globalization until toward the end of the century. Even words like *global* and *globalizing* were rarely used by historians before the

1990s. But then, as if driven by some obsessive consensus, historians began writing books in which such words appeared in their titles.[98] Global history almost overnight became an acceptable way, a plausible framework in which to study history, especially of the modern period. World history, too, made a comeback. As noted earlier, McNeill's *The Rise of the West*, published in 1963, had been a path-blazer, but the author's passion for the history of the whole world and its various civilizations had not quite caught on, and historians continued to focus on national histories. This had been how they had studied the past ever since the discipline of history was established in nineteenth-century Europe. History meant the study of a nation's past (and present). Toward the end of the twentieth century, however, world history gained in popularity, making separate national histories less and less palatable, looking parochial. According to periodic surveys undertaken by the American Historical Association, whereas in 1980 only a tiny fraction of history departments in the United States had faculty teaching world history, twenty years later almost 20 percent of them did so.[99] The proportion of faculty and graduate students teaching and studying non-Western history continued to increase, challenging the once overwhelming presence of "Americanists" and "Europeanists." In this context, the term *global history* made its appearance. In most instances it meant the same thing as world history, but an increasing number of scholars came to prefer the term *global* rather than *world* to describe their work and their intentions, especially if they were teaching or writing about the modern period.

Whichever term was used, it is remarkable that in the 1990s more and more colleges began offering courses in world history, the assumption being that it was no longer sufficient just to study a particular country's past but rather that one should recognize the interrelatedness of all national histories. This was because, scholars and teachers now insisted, no country's history was self-contained but was a product as much of interactions with other countries as of internal dynamics. In a sense, then, there was no such thing as national history pure and simple, but only global history. However, because global history was a very awesome concept, assuming that one had to know something about all nations and civilizations, and because the term could give the impression that national borders no longer mattered, some preferred to refer to what they were advocating as "transnational history." Transnational history did not deny the existence and relevance of separate nations but emphasized interconnections and mutual influences among them. Nations still mattered, but there were many other players on the stage of history, creating constant flows of goods, people, and ideas across borders. Races, religions, and civilizations interacted with one another on a different plane from nations. Whereas most scholars continued to comprehend these phenomena as themes in international history, the term *international* tended to imply inter-state, rather than inter-civil-society and interhuman connections, and so, some argued, it was important to categorize these connections less as international and more as transnational.

Thus emerged the field of transnational history as a way to reconceptualize history, especially modern history. Because the modern period saw the ascendancy of the nation as the key unit of political governance, economic activities, and social order, and because the study and teaching of history were often bound up with the task of nation building, it was important to liberate oneself from such nation-centrism and pay equal attention to what was transnational in a nation's past and present. Thinking along some such lines, scholars increasingly began to refer to transnational themes and developments in the modern and contemporary world. It was no accident that the historians who led the way in this direction included scholars of US history, a subject that for decades had been dominated by writers focusing on domestic political, social, and cultural history, stressing its unique character. Scholars such as Thomas Bender and Ian Tyrrell began to emphasize the need to put US history in the context of world history and of global developments. Tyrell's 1991 article in the *American Historical Review*, "Transnational History," was among the first to use the phrase. The concept was still too underdeveloped to gain immediate currency, and it had to compete with "world history" and "global history" to find acceptance among scholars, teachers, and educated readers. Nevertheless, a transnational moment had arrived in the historical literature.[100] Scholars were willing to take note of the developing transnational consciousness and to seek to reconceptualize the study of the past.

How does one explain the gap between the reality—namely, the steady globalization of the world—and its scholarly perception? Quite clearly the study of history had lagged behind history. For instance, when a group of historians from Europe, the United States, and Japan met in 1983 to review the tumultuous events of the twentieth century up to that point, hardly anyone used the word *globalization,* but when the same group of scholars, with the addition of others, met ten years later, virtually every participant used that term and referred to various "global" themes in their understanding of the recent past.[101] It would be too easy to say that this gap was due to the fact that until the early 1990s the overwhelming attention of historians as well as the public had been paid to the vicissitudes in the Cold War. The decade of the 1980s did indeed witness dramatic turns of events in the geopolitical arena, starting with what some called the "second Cold War" in the wake of the Soviet Union's invasion of Afghanistan and the Reagan administration's response of dramatically increasing the US nuclear arsenal, which led to the summit conferences between Ronald Reagan and Mikhail Gorbachev, the Soviet leader. Gorbachev's domestic reforms under the principles of glasnost (openness) and perestroika (reconstruction), in the meantime, steadily undermined the stability and cohesiveness of the Soviet Bloc, which eventually led to political upheavals in Eastern Europe that brought about the fall of the Berlin Wall. All these breathtaking changes took place during the 1980s and were at first interpreted within the framework of the history of the Cold War. That story line has its own validity, but it conceals a great deal of transnational developments that were occurring simultaneously. The fall of the Berlin Wall, for instance, was preceded by the fall of the dollar following the Plaza Accord of 1985. That and many other developments in the transnational economic area may not have directly led to the ending of the Cold War, but this latter phenomenon should be understood in the context of the global transformations that were occurring in all fronts simultaneously, as will be discussed in the next section.

Historians as well as other observers of the contemporary scene were very slow to recognize these parallel themes because of their overriding commitment to, or habit of, viewing world affairs in the framework of the Cold War—or more broadly, comprehending history in geopolitical terms, which betrayed their nation-focused perspective. They missed the growth of transnational consciousness and focused on the US-USSR geopolitical relationship. It is true that an increasing number of observers became fascinated with the democratization movements in various parts of the world. Starting in the mid-1970s, waves of political liberalization spread from Greece, Portugal, and Spain to Argentina, the Philippines, South Korea, South Africa, Eastern Europe, China, and elsewhere. But these phenomena were initially understood as national developments, pro-

High school and university students demonstrating near Tiananmen Square in Beijing to support the pro-democracy protest, May 1989. The event was televised throughout the world and was seen as part of the global movement for democracy. Although this demonstration was brutally suppressed, reform movements have continued in various forms in China. (AFP/Getty Images)

duced by specific domestic circumstances, or else they were seen as by-products of the easing of great power tensions that reached a climax at the end of the 1980s. But it should have been obvious even then that the waves of pro-democracy movements were reflecting a shared concern across the globe with the well-being of all people. It was no accident that the protesters in Tiananmen Square in Beijing in the spring of 1989 built a replica of New York's Statue of Liberty as a universal symbol for the search for freedom. That the protest was brutally suppressed was a Chinese national affair, but its memory was transnational and never went away, so that the "Tiananmen moment" came to mean a betrayal of people's aspirations anywhere in the world.

Transnational Contributions to the
Ending of the Cold War

The dramatic ending of the Cold War at the end of the 1980s is usually attributed to geopolitical factors, in particular to the superiority of US military, economic, and technological power. The prevailing narrative postulates a teleology in which the bipolar struggle for power ended in one side's victory because it had greater military and economic power as well as intellectual and cultural resources—what Joseph Nye called "soft power"—which it used effectively against an opponent who may have had huge stockpiles of arms but not much else to counter that superiority.[102] If such a one-sided power equation was all there was to the Cold War, however, it would not have lasted as long as it did. We must remember that the Soviet Union as well as other socialist countries, including the People's Republic of China, had wielded as much influence as they did in the world because they appealed to anticapitalist and anti-Western opinion in various parts of the world, giving the impression that they, the socialist societies, were the wave of the future. It was the challenge posed to the ideological as well as the military underpinnings of the Cold War that contributed to undermining and altering the geopolitical map of the globe. The challenge was fundamentally transnational, ranging from global movements for human rights and for world peace to Islamic fundamentalism opposed both to the Soviet Union and to the West. The Cold War's end contained all such elements, and to single out the geopolitical "realities" would be fundamentally tautological. That is to say, if the Cold War is seen to have been defined by such "realities," to assert that it ended when the "realities" changed is merely stating the obvious. It would be more helpful to note that the arena in which the geopolitical game was played had been significantly transformed so that the game had steadily altered its character. While the nuclear-armed states remained, and while international relations and national rivalries continued to move with their own momentum on one level, transnational forces were steadily intruding upon their spaces.

Transnational contributions to ending the Cold War took many forms, but at bottom was the growth of non-state, non-national actors. NGOs and multinational business enterprises had spectacularly increased in number during the 1970s, and in the subsequent decade they continued to help promote a sense of global community. Some NGOs specifically aimed at resisting nuclear armament and strategy on the part of the superpowers, especially the introduction of medium-range missiles on European soil. The Catholic Church actively participated in the global call for reduction of tensions, and it joined other international NGOs in organizing protest marches and rallies in Europe, South America, and Asia. There was an atmosphere of transnational solidarity that even began to attract participation by some from the Soviet Bloc. In the meantime, multinational enterprises did their part in the process as well by expanding their business activities in Soviet-Bloc countries and in China. Although of modest scale, such activities created opportunities for contact between Western (and Japanese) business-people and their counterparts in the Soviet Union, Eastern Europe, and China. Soviet and Chinese leaders, exemplified by Gorbachev and Deng, understood that some personal engagement with capitalists from abroad was a necessary and inevitable aspect of their countries' economic modernization programs. The awareness of the growing business ties must have contributed to generating a sense of community driven by shared interests across what was left of the Cold War divide.

Another transnational factor in the drama of the 1980s was environmentalism. To recapitulate briefly, although the movement for protecting the planet from pollution and waste had begun to gather momentum in the 1970s, during the 1980s there was as yet little to show for it. The most graphic manifestation of this was in the Earth's temperature. It had arisen from the average of 56.5°F (13.6°C) during the first decade of the twentieth century to 57.0°F (13.9°C) seven decades later, but in the 1980s it rose at a more rapid tempo, to 57.4°F (14.1°C), indicating an alarming impact of the "greenhouse effect" caused by carbon dioxide and other gases that trap heat in the atmosphere. In 1980 the world emitted a total of 18,333 million metric tons of carbon dioxide from the burning of fossil fuels such as coal, oil, and natural gas, and by 1990 the amount had risen to 21,426 million.[103] The United States and the Soviet Union were the largest emitters of carbon dioxide, together accounting for 42 percent of the world's total in 1980 and 41 percent in 1990. China added another 8 percent in 1980 and 11 percent in 1990, so that these three large countries were significantly contributing to what came to be known as "global warming."

It would be far-fetched, of course, to argue that the increasingly serious greenhouse effect undermined and ultimately ended the Cold War. It is clear, nevertheless, that within the Soviet bloc no less than in the West, concern with the environment was growing, as was the realization that such concern was shared transnationally. Nowhere was this more dramatically demonstrated than in the horrendous nuclear seepage that took place in a nuclear power plant located in Chernobyl, Ukraine, in 1986. On April 26, reactor number 4 of the facility exploded, and the resulting fire spread contamination into the atmosphere, which winds distributed far and wide. It was a transnational tragedy as the nuclear gases spread beyond the Soviet borders. The elevated and potentially harmful fallout reached Western Europe and as far away as Greenland. (Even as late as 2011, it was reported that sheep-grazing pastures in Wales still recorded low levels of radioactivity.[104]) This was a civilian, not a military, disaster, but its impact was all the greater because the radiation released has been estimated to have been of far greater intensity than that produced by the atomic bombs dropped on two Japanese cities in August 1945, and because it caused the deaths of scores of people and the evacuation of the city's residents, many of whom have not returned there even today. In the United States, many had been traumatized by the depiction of nuclear fallout in the movie *The China Syndrome*, which together with the Chernobyl crisis and the less severe seepage in 1979 at a nuclear factory in Three Mile Island, Pennsylvania, served to confirm the transnational belief that environmental disasters knew no national boundaries. Gorbachev clearly understood this, and he turned to other countries for assistance in clearing up the debris from the Ukrainian nuclear plant. In such circumstances, maintaining a posture of confrontation with the United States and its allies must have seemed to make no sense. The Cold War, whatever meaning it had ever had, lost significance when the nuclear adversaries both contributed to, and suffered from, environmental disasters and global warming.

Human rights were another transnational issue that connected countries on both sides of the Iron Curtain. As Sarah Snyder details in her book *Human Rights Activism and the End of the Cold War*, since the 1975 Helsinki Accords, which included a provision about human rights, Western activists had been stepping up their efforts to contact similar groups, many of them clandestine, in the

Barbed wire surrounds the deserted town of Prypyat, Ukraine, adjacent to the Chernobyl nuclear plant, May 2003. An accident at the plant caused radioactive material to spread all over Ukraine and many parts of Europe, triggering a worldwide questioning of the wisdom of producing more nuclear energy. (AFP/Getty Images)

socialist countries in order to protect victims of political persecution.[105] Due in part to such efforts, Eastern Europeans increasingly became bolder in challenging their leaders. At first quite modest, steps toward democratization were nevertheless real. In Czechoslovakia, Hungary, East Germany, Poland, and other countries—even in Romania, which still had a particularly brutal regime—citizens organized themselves in opposition to those in power, and unlike earlier this time the Soviet leadership, under Gorbachev, did not send in tanks and troops to suppress them. After all, the Soviet Union itself was promoting the spirit of "openness." The result was that toward the end of the decade, one communist regime after another fell, and the borders between Eastern and Western Europe were opened up. Particularly dramatic was the fall of the Berlin Wall in November 1989—a fitting climax to the drama of democratization in Eastern Europe. While this event is often seen in the context of the ending of the Cold War, it would be more fitting to consider it a chapter in the history of human rights. It was democratization that, added to environmental and other transnational factors, led to the end of the Cold War, and not the other way around. Moreover, it would be too simplistic to assert that Eastern European democratization was a victory for the United States in the geopolitical contest. Human rights had been promoted by many people all over the world who had constructed non-state networks of activism, and the significance of this phenomenon went far beyond the ups and downs of international affairs. Rather, the story belongs in transnational history, and in that sense what happened in the 1980s demonstrated that conventional international relations were making way for transnational relations. What a study like Snyder's shows is that there exist several parallel histories: history of geopolitical affairs, history of human rights, history of environmental disasters and efforts to cope with them, and many others. What the 1970s and the 1980s showed was that human rights, perhaps for the first time in history, asserted its primacy and eclipsed other narratives. That, too, is an important theme in the making of a transnational world.

Transnational Nationalism?

Ironically, just as transnational waves were sweeping through the world, traditional forces of nationalism also appeared to be reviving. Nowhere was this phenomenon more striking than in Eastern and Southeastern Europe, where renewed assertions of national identity frequently led to calls for independent nationhood. During the 1980s, it took the form of Eastern European countries' assertion of greater independence from Soviet control, but in the aftermath of the Cold War, it became an even more extensive phenomenon, with various components of the USSR breaking away from Moscow and, with or without the latter's connivance, establishing (or, in most cases, reestablishing) autonomous nations, such as Lithuania, Estonia, Georgia, Uzbekistan, and Turkmenistan. Their separation heralded what would be the final demise of the USSR in 1991. Henceforth, Russia, too, would become a nation among nations, although even within the now smaller country there would be components seeking to achieve their own independence. The Islamic republic of Chechnya was the most notable example, where separatist rebels sought independence from the rest of Russia in 1994 and fought against Russian troops for a number of years, the Russian military in the process laying to waste the capital city of Grozny. The Chechen-Russian confrontation would continue into the new century.

In the rest of Eastern Europe, Czechoslovakia broke into two, the Czech Republic and Slovakia, but the most extreme case was in the Balkans, where Yugoslavia, which had been created in the aftermath of the First World War and consisted of regions with separate identities and religions, divided into a number of states after the 1980 death of Josip Broz Tito, who had presided over Yugoslavia after the Second World War. Like the Soviet Union and Czechoslovakia, Yugoslavia disappeared from the world map. The Balkans now consisted of the older countries Albania, Bulgaria, and Greece, plus Macedonia, Serbia-Montenegro (whose two constituting republics would be separated in 2006), Bosnia and Herzegovina, Croatia, Slovenia, and Kosovo. These were all very small countries, but each had its own distinctive history, religion, and ethnic identity. Inevitably there were problems in determining the precise boundaries and the ethnic composition of the new states. Serious fighting took place, for instance, between Serbia-Montenegro and Croatia. The worst crisis in this regard occurred in Sarajevo, the capital of Bosnia and Herzegovina, in 1992, when Serb militants in the city's surrounding hills declared themselves a "Serb republic" and attacked and laid siege to Sarajevo. The siege lasted until NATO aircraft bombed the Serb positions in 1995. In this and other instances, intense fighting among Serbs, Muslims, Croats, and others often led to "ethnic cleansing," as separate ethnic groups fought against one another with intense bitterness.

Elsewhere, too, ethnic nationalism intensified toward the end of the century. The African continent was scourged throughout the 1990s by a series of brutal conflicts. In Somalia, civil war broke out in 1991 between the central state and separatists in the northwest region. Sierra Leone was plagued with fighting to control the country's diamond mining region, recruitment of child soldiers, rape, amputations of limbs, and other cruelties. Central Africa, especially the mineral-rich areas of the Democratic Republic of Congo, was the site of what some have called Africa's "great wars." The fighting involved eight African states, involving dozens of militia groups, and killed at its peak an estimated one thousand people per day. As in West Africa, the Congo wars were characterized by mass rape, child soldiers, and massacres. In Rwanda, Tutsi and Hutu, the two principal ethnic

Protesters in London wave Serbian flags during a demonstration against NATO's bombing of Yugoslavia, April 1999, an instance of ethnic nationalism in conflict with an international police force. (Getty Images)

communities, engaged in fierce fighting, and the 1994 attack by Hutus against Tutsis was considered genocide.

In South Asia, Muslims, Hindus, Buddhists, Sikhs, Christians, and other religious groups periodically asserted power over the others, and in Sri Lanka, the Tamils, the island's Hindu minority who had opposed the rule by the Buddhist majority, rose in open revolt in 1983 and continued their struggle despite mediation efforts by the neighboring India.

Western European countries and even Canada were also roiled by waves of separatism. Most of these challenges to dominant national regimes were peaceful, but in Northern Ireland the Irish Republican Army periodically engaged in terrorist attacks on Protestants citizens, and the latter responded in kind, until a peace accord was concluded in 1998. In Spain the separatist Basque militants continued to agitate for independence, resorting to bombing raids through the first years of the new century.[106]

How do we interpret such occurrences? Clearly they indicated the depth of ethnic nationalism that went back to the nineteenth century and even earlier. Long suppressed while the Cold War rivalry between the Soviet Union and the United States had privileged the status quo over the aspirations of ethnic groups, such groups now felt released from any such constraint and sought to establish new nations to reflect their separate identities. It should be noted, however, that ethnic self-consciousness did not translate into an assertion of separate nationhood in most countries of the world, which after all were mostly multiethnic entities. Russia, even after the Soviet Union was broken up, continued to contain nearly two hundred nationality groups, while the People's Republic of China consisted of some fifty-five ethnicities, of whom nearly 10 percent were non-Chinese. In the United States, virtually all the races and religions of the world were represented. In the last decades of the century, non-African racial groups in the United States, particularly Latinos and Asians, grew rapidly in number, but there was no indication that any of the racial, religious, and other ethnically identifiable groups were seeking to create a separate nation. The United States was perhaps the best example where overall national consciousness had developed to such an extent that the nation's breaking up into fragments along ethnic lines would be unimaginable. Such was also the case with most other "established" countries, where, with the exception of a few like Spain, ethnic self-consciousness did not threaten the integrity of nationhood, at least in the last decades of the twentieth century.

Even in some of these countries, however, ethnic minorities were never free from a sense of national (or, perhaps more correctly, subnational) identity and did not integrate entirely into the larger community. The Turks in Germany, the Algerians in France, and the Pakistanis in Britain often chose to emphasize their ethnicity over assimilation into the larger national community.[107] Tibetans, Uighurs, Koreans, and other minorities in China remained cohesive and did not identify with the Han (Chinese) majority. These phenomena in turn provoked nationalistic responses from the majority populations, who sometimes organized themselves into ultranationalistic movements. If the second half of the twentieth century was the age of transnationalism, it also seemed to enhance nationalism, of both minority and majority groups. Perhaps the best way to understand these dual phenomena, transnationalism and nationalism, would be to view them as existing simultaneously at different levels or layers, inhabiting separate but not exclusive spaces. It was not so much that transnationalism and nationalism were competing for influence, but rather that they were simultaneous forces. For one thing, nationalism was becoming a transnational phenomenon. Along with everything else, nationalism was one kind of global development. Moreover, unlike the earlier "age of nationalism" that begot world wars and local wars, this time many of the nationalistic forces were oriented domestically, seeking their own separate identities and sometimes their own communities and even daring to break away from an established state. Nationalistic rivalries of the traditional sort remained, involving territorial, trade, and other disputes, but these international dramas were played out even while global forces were shaping another layer of transnational connections. Nationalism, in other words, was just like other "local" identities that grew hand in hand with forces of globalization. In that sense, there was no inherent contradiction or irreconcilable opposition between nationalism and transnationalism.

Not so much nationalism as mono-nationalism may be taken as having been a more serious challenge to transnationalism. Mono-nationalism in the sense of exclusionary loyalty to one's nation and of resistance to considering items beyond borders—be they goods, ideas, or individuals—was incompatible with transnationalism, and it was becoming rather rare. Even so, mono-nationalism sometimes made its appearance as if to revalidate the nation's sense of being. This can best be seen in historical memory. As suggested in the introductory section, how a nation remembers its past had always been central to its identity, but in a transnational age collective memories across borders could in theory have emerged so that ultimately they would become a shared memory of the whole of humankind. That was a development that was becoming discernible in Europe, as the next section will discuss, but more notable at the end of the century were competing memories that reinforced the mono-nationalism of many countries. China and Japan, for example, clashed over official memories of their modern wars, in particular Japan's invasion of China in the 1930s. Japanese history textbooks, written by nongovernmental writers but subject to official approval before course adoption, began to attract the attention of Chinese as well as Koreans and other Asians in the 1980s and beyond, who blamed the authorities in Tokyo for encouraging a revisionist teaching of the recent past, whitewashing the aggression and atrocities committed by Japan's military forces. Some in Japan, for their part, blamed their critics for distorting the record by publishing their own official histories, which, they said, exaggerated casualty figures and other aspects of the conflict. Japanese nationalists viewed the Asian-Pacific war as having been waged to "liberate" Asia, whereas Chinese nationalists, joined by those from Korea, the Philippines, and elsewhere, asserted that Japan's imperialism had been even worse than that of the European powers.[108] The history of the Second World War also engulfed the United States and Japan in controversy over the Smithsonian Institution's plans in the mid-1990s for an exhibition of the *Enola Gay* at the National Air and Space Museum in Washington. That was the aircraft that dropped the atomic bomb on Hiroshima in 1945, and the initial design of the exhibit had been to pay as much attention to the destruction caused by the atomic bombing as to the development of the new weapon. But the plans had to be drastically modified so as to present the nuclear attack as having been a completely justifiable means for bringing the war in the Pacific to an end without further casualties.[109] Japanese remembered Hiroshima in a sharply contrasting way, as an unjustifiably inhuman way to destroy a populace, and there could be no easy resolution of the two conflicting memories, indicating that even between allies, transnationalization of historical memory was no easy task. When it came to a nation's history, mono-nationalism seemed to trump transnationalism. It was as if the more transnational connections across borders grew, the stronger also became a sense of history and memory as constituting individual and group identities.

Transnational Regions

If there was to be a way to reconcile transnational and national layers of consciousness, the European example suggested that the construction of a regional community might be a possible solution. Nationalism and transnationalism—local and global forces—could perhaps be mediated through regional communities. As best exemplified by the European Community, which became the European Union in 1994, various nationalisms could be placed together in a regional framework in which all members would share certain policies, even a common currency. The story of the Union belongs in national and international history, but its transnational implications are obvious. Regarding such cross-border issues as migration, water resources, and environmental protection, the regional community would develop common approaches. By abolishing borders within the Union, citizens of all member states would be free to move across national boundaries, and foreigners would also be able to visit all countries within the regional community once they had been admitted into one of them. The Europeans were particularly concerned with their water resources. There are no arid areas within the European Union, but it is imperative to preserve its rivers and lakes in order to provide sufficient water for industrial, agricultural, and consumer needs. Since the 1960s the member states have cooperated in developing a strategy for controlling water usage.[110] The European states also worked together to protect the natural environment, defining a common approach to reduce carbon emissions and prevent deforestation.

Nowhere was transnational pan-European consciousness more graphically demonstrated than in the founding of the European University Institute in Fiesole, outside Florence, in 1976. There was clear awareness among the institution's founders—who came from all parts of Europe—that no regional community would be enduring without some shared intellectual and cultural experiences, and this would particularly be the case in education. Traditionally education had been a very national undertaking, as each country sought to create a future citizenship that would be cohesive, literate, and ready to serve its needs. As a consequence, not only primary schools but also institutions of higher learning had tended to be organized nationally. The new European leaders understood the imperative necessity to go beyond such a narrow focus, and, although they would still support national centers of pedagogical and academic excellence, they would also be willing to share their resources for bringing university-level students from all over Europe, and some even from the United States and other countries, to expose them to a more transnational environment of scholarship and research. Initially consisting primarily of programs in economics, law, history, and civilization, and in the political and social sciences, the European University Institute demonstrated Europeans' commitment to shared knowledge and to intra-European cultural exchange. Such a commitment was confirmed by the establishment in 1987 of the European Region Action Scheme for the Mobility of University Students, or the Erasmus Program, which enabled students to take classes across national boundaries, and by the Bologna Process of 1999, which established equivalency standards among higher education institutions within the European Higher Education Area. Although it is too early to evaluate the success of such programs, it would not be an exaggeration to say that in some such fashion, transnational lives were being created.

These moves within Europe paralleled the growth of regional communities elsewhere. Although far less systematically or thoroughly developed, the initial steps toward transnational communities were also taken by such transnational entities as the North American Free Trade Area (NAFTA), bringing Canada, the United States, and Mexico together; the Latin American Free Trade Association (LAFTA); and the Central American Common Market. Unlike Europe, however, it was not easy to go much beyond economic cooperation in bringing neighboring nations together. NAFTA, for instance, sought to establish common policies toward environmental and labor issues, but the three constituting members did not always see eye to eye on these matters. There was as yet no counterpart to the European University Institute. The key reason for this was that the United States continued to attract students from all over the world and was, in a sense, developing a transnational educational environment on its soil. Under the circumstances, less pressure may have been felt for establishing a specifically

North or South American oriented international university. (On the other hand, US and Canadian institutions of higher learning regularly exchanged faculty and students as a matter of course. The two countries' geographical proximity and shared language facilitated such transnationalism.)

Of fundamental importance in the successful launching of the European Union was the development of what some historians call "a community of shared memory."[111] In other words, Europeans had developed a common understanding of their past interactions. Some of the past events had been painful: wars, genocide, intolerance, and the like. At the same time, they shared more constructive pasts: the development of modern science, the Enlightenment, great works of art, literature, and music. European history had to be understood transnationally as having been a mixed record of tragedies and accomplishments, of evil and good deeds. They all took part in these divergent strands, but they were heirs to this often contradictory, both glorious and ignominious, past. The important thing was that they remembered the manifold shapes of the past as their common heritage. In the New World, however, Americans, Canadians, Mexicans, and South Americans had not arrived at a stage where such sharing of the past had become possible. At least between the people of the United States and Canada, there was a legacy of the common language and literary tradition; they could even be said to have a sense, however vague, that they belonged to the same past. (Broadway plays and musicals were brought to Canadian theaters as a matter of course, and audiences did not view them as alien or unfamiliar when they portrayed scenes from the American past.) Between these two peoples and the Mexicans, on the other hand, there was little such common consciousness, as exemplified by the fact that the war of 1846–1848, after which the United States acquired Texas, the Southwest, and California from Mexico, continued to be viewed in sharply divergent ways on opposite sides of the Rio Grande. On the other hand, in the last decades of the century, the regions bordering on the two countries began to develop a self-consciousness as a border community, part of the phenomenon that historians began to call "border history" that included many other regions of the world. In time, a new perspective might become more widespread, giving rise to the awareness that the world consisted as much of borderlands as of territorially marked national communities. This, too, was an instance of a developing transnational identity.

It is also pertinent to note that, because the American continent bordered both on the Atlantic and the Pacific, there was a dual sense of regional identity. Of the two, the idea of an Atlantic community of nations had long existed. Together, the United States and Canada had long defined themselves as part of a wider Atlantic, consisting of the legacy of Western civilization as well as geopolitical arrangements such as the North Atlantic Treaty Organization. The idea of a Pacific community was much slower to develop, but as Walter McDougall was already pointing out in a 1993 book, *Let the Sea Make a Noise*, countries and people of the north Pacific—ranging from Chinese and Russians to Hawaiians, Canadians, and Americans—had been interacting with one another for a long time.[112] As if to take a cue from such a perspective, historians in Australia, Canada, the United States, and elsewhere were beginning to conceptualize a Pacific community whose scale would be even grander than its Atlantic counterpart. However, no blueprint yet existed for a comprehensive Pacific community comparable to the European Union.

For that to develop, Asian countries would first have to establish their regional identities. But the situation in Asia continued to be complex. Several countries of Southeast Asia had already, in the late 1960s, created their own regional community, the Association of Southeast Asian Nations (ASEAN), which had begun to promote not only economic but also political interdependence among its members. Economically, they suffered a serious financial crisis in the late 1990s as Thailand and some other nations experienced a sudden shortage of foreign exchange, a crisis that had grown out of their increasing consumption of foreign goods. With a sharp increase in these countries' trade deficits, the value of their currencies fell. The worst possible development, like the global exchange crisis of the early 1930s, was averted by a timely intervention by the IMF, which provided temporary relief measures in return for these countries' pledges to reformulate their economic policies. But the experience showed that a regional community that focused almost exclusively on economic cooperation was insufficient. From around that time, ASEAN began to negotiate trade agreements with nonmembers such as China, South Korea, Japan, and the European Union, looking toward a more global engagement. Such undertakings were still within the traditional framework of international relations, but there also grew environmental and cultural regional consciousness transcending national boundaries, an identity that reflected a self-consciousness of the region's position vis-à-vis China in the north and Australia and New Zealand in the south. Leaders and the public in the region were making an attempt to develop a transnational identity that would enable them to define a common perspective on such issues as human rights and environmentalism. For instance, the seas surrounding the Southeast Asian countries were particularly rich in reefs, containing about one-third of the world's total. But it was reported in 1990 that virtually all these reefs were in danger of extinction because of pollution, and ASEAN provided a framework for transnational cooperation to cope with the critical situation.

However modest, the Southeast Asian countries' regional initiatives were far ahead of any development in East Asia. Consisting primarily of China (including Taiwan), South and North Korea, and Japan, the region remained divided not only because of the uncertain relationship between mainland China and the island of Taiwan, and between the two Koreas, but also because no shared memory comparable to that in Europe had emerged there. Koreans still resented the Japanese invasion of the peninsular kingdom toward the end of the fifteenth century and the rule by Imperial Japan during the first decades of the twentieth, while the Chinese retained bitter memories of their war against Japan. Unlike Europe, which had somehow managed to accommodate wartime German atrocities into a collective memory, in East Asia the Koreans, the Chinese, and the Japanese held on to their separate memories, nationalizing rather than transnationalizing history. North and South Koreans, for their part, dealt with their recent past, notably the Korean War, in sharply contrasting ways. Those in the Democratic People's Republic of Korea attributed the war's origins to South Korea's invasion in collusion with US imperialists, whereas in the Republic of Korea the conflict was remembered as a national tragedy perpetrated by the communist regime to the north that not only initiated the attack in 1950 but also retained a large number of people who were denied a chance to return to their homes in the south. Under these circumstances, it was very difficult to promote a sense of regional (or even of Korean national) identity.

Nevertheless, at least among China, South Korea, and Japan, there slowly developed a consciousness of shared regional concerns and destiny. This was most evident in their economic relations. Japan, the world's third largest trading nation during the 1980s and the 1990s (after the United States and Germany), increased its exports to China from $5 billion in 1980 to $30 billion twenty years later, and its imports from China from $4 billion to $55 billion in the same period. The United States still remained Japan's principal trading partner, but China was fast catching up. The "newly industrialized countries" of Asia, namely South Korea, Taiwan, Hong Kong, and Singapore, accounted for 8.9 percent of Japan's total export trade and 18.4 percent of its imports in 2000. East Asia on the whole was emerging as a major and rapidly expanding regional market; intraregional trade among East Asian countries as a percentage of their total world trade grew from 35.6 percent in 1980 to 46.8 percent twenty years later. These figures were still lower than those for the European Union or for NAFTA, which reached 73.1 percent and 55.7 percent, respectively, in 2000, but far higher than for ASEAN, whose members traded among themselves for only a quarter of their total trade. There was also much intraregional investment. A steadily increasing number of Japanese firms began to be established in China, where the number of business personnel and factory representatives from Japan jumped from 63,000 in 1990 to 567,000 ten years later. (The comparable figures for Japanese working temporarily in the United States were 479,000 and 661,000, respectively.) Conversely, more and more Chinese visited Japan; some stayed and added to the non-Japanese Asian population in the country, which numbered roughly one million at the end of the century.

There was also a deepening level of popular and elite exchanges among Chinese, South Koreans, and Japanese. Movies made in South Korea gained popularity in Japan, and Japanese television dramas were shown on Chinese television. Historians from the three countries began their initially modest attempts at studying the past together, in the process stressing the importance of transnational regional history. In other words, rather than studying the past in the framework of respective national histories, they explored the region's past as a whole, tracing the three countries' economic, social, and cultural interdependence. It remained to be seen if there would in time emerge an intellectually coherent idea of East Asian regional history, comparable to European history. There was little doubt, though, that the efforts by scholars, journalists, and others to undertake the task jointly were creating transnational moments and spaces that went beyond official relations.

The American Century as a Transnational Century

Toward the end of the twentieth century, especially after the end of the Cold War, many spoke of the United States as the sole superpower, as the new hegemon, or as an empire. All such expressions revealed a habit of mind that continued to see the world as fundamentally defined by sovereign states that maintained some order through their military and economic power. In the age of globalization and transnationalization, however, such traditional measurements of influence were no longer adequate. A nation would be a "winner" only to the extent that it reflected and reinforced global trends and furthered the networking of people and communities. It was perhaps because this key fact was recognized that many recalled Henry Luce's 1941 editorial in *Life* magazine on the "American Century," or that Francis Fukuyama's 2002 book, *The End of History*, gained so much popularity. A group of conservatives in the United States even began a movement called "For a New American Century." That, however, was a mono-nationalistic take on a fundamentally transnational phenomenon, for the writings by Luce, Fukuyama, and others emphasized not so much US geopolitical power as its "soft power," another term that gained currency after Joseph Nye used it in a 1990 book, *Bound to Lead*, pointing to the nation's technology, ideas, and sheer example as the keys to its global influence. And there was little doubt that at the end of the century the United States stood as the embodiment of the ideas and ideals that had transformed the world. That was what Fukuyama meant by the "end of history"—namely, that Enlightenment ideas such as democracy and freedom exemplified by the American example seemed to have been universally embraced so that history had in a sense been fulfilled.

Such optimism was, and has since been, severely criticized, but Nye, Fukuyama, and others were undoubtedly correct to link the destiny of the United States with the modern global transformation. What they could also have stressed is that this transformation had fundamentally entailed transnationalization, so that in contributing to it, the United States, too, had been changed. It had become increasingly more interconnected with the rest of the world, with the result that it was now less unique and shared many traits and phenomena with other countries. In that sense the American century had made the United States less "American" and more interchangeable with others. One could see such a process, Americanization of the globe and the globalization of America, occurring simultaneously, in population movements, technological developments, and many other areas.

For instance, international tourism was now becoming more and more transnational. Whereas earlier Americans, and then Europeans after they recovered from the war, had dominated the tourist scene, their numbers were being steadily augmented by travelers from other parts of the world. The overall number of international tourists increased from 278 million in 1980 to 687 million in 2000. These figures correspond to roughly one out of fifteen people in the world in 1980, and one out of nine in 2000. (The same individual may be counted more than once in such statistics, because, as we saw earlier, the statistics are compiled by the host countries independently of one another. Still, the trend is unmistakable.) What is equally interesting is the growing diversity both of the national origins of the tourists and of their destinations. In the last two decades of the century, middle-class Japanese and wealthy Arab tourists, and eventually Koreans and Chinese, joined American and European travelers, so that foreign traveling became a truly transnational phenomenon. Stores in New York, London, Paris, and other Western cities began to post signs in Japanese and other non-Western languages and hired native speakers of non-Western languages to cater to the new visitors. Equally significant, international tourists increasingly began visiting areas outside of Western Europe or the American continent. In 1980, for instance, about 23 million travelers visited Asia and the Pacific, accounting for less than 9 percent of the total number of tourists, the remainder visiting mostly Europe and North America. Twenty years later, however, 110 million people visited the Asia-Pacific region, another 28 million went to Africa, and 23 million went to the Middle East. Together, these areas hosted about a quarter of the world's tourists.[113]

The expansion of international tourism was reflected in the phenomenal growth of the money spent by the travelers all over the world. Tourism receipts grew from $104 billion in 1980, to $264 billion ten years later, to $475 billion by 2000.[114] These figures average out to nearly $700 per traveler in 2000—not including the cost of airfare and other transportation. Most long-distance travel was by plane, and the rising price of gasoline made air travel more expensive. Nevertheless, the tourist figures suggest that increasing numbers of people felt they could afford to undertake such trips, perhaps by joining tour groups and also by staying at less expensive lodgings. Although few people in the developing countries were earning sufficient income to enable them to undertake even the cheapest of foreign travels, international tourism was nevertheless becoming affordable for the majority in the advanced and advancing economies. And although Europe and America took the lion's share of tourism receipts, for countries of Asia, Africa, and the Middle East, the billions of dollars spent by visiting tourists were a growing portion of their national revenues.

That roughly one out of nine people in the world in the year 2000 was crossing borders every year as a tourist and spending so much money abroad was an important aspect of the transnationalization, and of the Americanization, of the world. But international tourism was also a major contributor to the growing global environmental crisis. Many travelers crowded big cities and provincial towns, putting pressure on water resources, polluting skies and lakes, damaging trees, even killing endangered species. African safaris, for instance, became so popular that already in the 1980s voices began to be heard, warning of the danger to the survival of elephants, lions, and other animals. The concern with protecting the natural habitat and preserving endangered species developed in tandem with the growth of international tourism. That, too, was something that Americans and people from other countries came to share.

When hundreds of millions go abroad and meet people in other countries, however fleetingly, innumerable transnational moments are created, often resulting in the development of transnationally shared ideas and attitudes. Literary writers were quick to incorporate this emerging phenomenon into their work. David Lodge's *Changing Places* (1975) and *Small World* (1984) perhaps best exemplified the trend. In these and other novels, college students and university faculty were described as basically stateless, engaging in their research, teaching, and social activities in which their national identities were of much less significance than the transnational spaces they created. Readers of these best sellers immediately recognized the settings, what some sociologists were beginning to define as "non-places"—airports, tour buses, shopping centers, and the like that were interchangeable anywhere in the world—where the principal characters intermingled and spoke common languages. Although many such novels were set in academic institutions where students and faculty from many countries mingled and created their transnational communities, the description of how different national intellectual landscapes and institutional traditions became merged, transformed, or reaffirmed could have been applied to all international visitors—and those staying home but interacting with them. It is, of course, impossible to generalize about the combined impact of such encounters, some of which were undoubtedly less friendly than others and confirmed existing prejudices and stereotypes about "foreigners." Nevertheless, it would be fair to say that through tourism the world's people were becoming more than ever conscious of human diversity as well as shared humanity. The question was whether such awareness would have a constructive consequence, such as the promotion of the spirit of tolerance, or whether it would do little to overcome traditional prejudices toward the unfamiliar. Most likely, both processes went on at the same time, as Jane Desmond's 1999 study of Waikiki tourism suggests.[115] All the same, tourism may be comprehended as yet another manifestation of one of the key phenomena in the contemporary world, the unceasing intermingling of people of diverse backgrounds and orientations.

Here, too, the United States as a nation remained more truly transnational than most others because of its tolerance for diversity. Global migrations continued unabated in the last two decades of the century, but migrating into the United States, whether as legal or illegal immigrants, on business, or for education, was a particularly striking development The percentage of the foreign-born population in the United States, which was as high as 14 percent at the beginning of the twentieth century, had been steadily declining, hitting the lowest point, or 4.7 percent, in 1970, but the trend began to reverse itself rapidly thereafter, and by the year 2000 more than one-tenth of the population consisted of those born elsewhere. By far the largest body of immigrants in the last decades of the century came from Central and South America. At the end of the century, they numbered over fourteen million, more than one-half of the entire foreign-born population in the country, followed by those from Asia, who now exceeded seven million. Europeans, who as recently as 1960 accounted for more than 50 percent of residents in the United States who had been born abroad, now fell to about 15 percent. Mexico, in particular, sent by far the largest number of people to settle north of the border. Already in 1980 there were over two million of them, or about 15.6 percent of the foreign-born population of the United States, but by 2000 the number had increased to over nine million, or close to 30 percent of this population. There was also a sizable Cuban population, as many people from that island nation, still under Fidel Castro's socialist regime, tried all means to cross the Gulf of Mexico northward. At one point, in 1980, the Havana government allowed 120,000 Cubans to move to the United States. But their status remained unclear for several years, and many of them were detained in federal prisons.[116] In any event, the number of Mexicans and other "Latinos" was increasing so fast that there were even predictions that within another half century they would be the majority population in the nation, surpassing even European Americans. Among the latter category of newcomers, too, there were significant developments in the aftermath of the opening of the borders dividing Eastern and Western Europe. An increasing number of Eastern Europeans, especially Poles, found their new home and employment in American cities. In the meantime, immigrants from the Philippines, Vietnam, and India joined those from East Asia who had arrived earlier, swelling the ranks of Asians in the United States.

While these remarkable demographic developments inevitably provoked domestic, anti-transnationalist opposition, with many traditionalists calling for more stringent control of immigration and some even arguing for denying schooling and medical services to illegal aliens, it must be noted that these issues were also being raised in other countries, especially in Europe. The fact remains that in the United States, Western Europe, Japan, and some other countries, immigrants, whether legal or clandestine, filled the needs of aging societies. These countries all recognized the problem and sought to cope with serious labor shortages in areas such as hospitals, nursing homes, and domestic services. In any event, the sheer number of recent arrivals, as well as their employment in certain categories of jobs—nurses, janitors, gardeners, apple pickers, house cleaners, babysitters, and so on—served to make the United States an especially transnational nation in the late twentieth century. Naturalization laws automatically conferred US citizenship on babies born in the country, with the result that the younger generations of citizens were more racially heterogeneous than their elders. (According to the US Census Bureau of 1990, the last year when individuals could report only one race, 80.3 percent of the American people considered themselves "white," 12.1 percent "black," and 2.8 percent "Asian." The bulk of people of Hispanic origin reported their race as "white," but considered separately they constituted 9 percent of the total population.) Intermarriages across racial lines were probably more common among Americans than other people—one reason why the Census Bureau allowed people to report more than one racial identity in 2000—contributing to the transnationalization of the population.[117]

Equally significant was the increasing number of foreign students in the United States. During the academic year 1977–1978 the proportion of foreign students at American colleges and universities for the first time exceeded 2 percent. By the end of the century, the ratio had reached 3.6 percent, or nearly half a million coming from abroad to study in the United States, where total university enrollment had reached fifteen million. What these figures indicate is that while more and more Americans were going to college, they were being joined by an increasing number of foreign students. Just to recall that as late as in 1959–1960 there were fewer than fifty thousand students from abroad is to become aware of the continuing attractiveness of the United States to college-age men and women from all over the world. So many of them would not have come to the United States to study if the quality of US higher education had not been recognized as being superior to that in other nations—and if job opportunities for foreign students, should they decide to stay and work in the country, had not been better. When we speak of the twentieth century as having possibly been an American century, then, we must not forget that it may have been in the area of higher education that the nation achieved undoubted supremacy. No other country could boast such a high ratio of foreign students or such a large number of foreign-born scholars, researchers, and educators.

This situation is well represented by the number of Nobel Prizes that were received by scholars in the United States, whether native or foreign-born. They had internationalized their scholarly work, turning the laboratories and classrooms into arenas for transnationally collaborative activities. Of roughly 120 Nobel Prizes in the sciences (including medicine) awarded during 1980–2000, over 70 went to the United States. Most of the rest of the laureates had spent at least part of their time in the country. Of course, many American winners of the prizes had conducted research and teaching abroad. To break down these scholars into nationality groups makes little sense, itself another indication that in the world of scholarship, border crossing had become routine. Nonetheless, the opportunities that US research institutions provided for transnational collaboration cannot be disputed. The Nobel Prize in Economics, which was established in 1969, was also dominated by American scholars; 46 were awarded through the year 2000, of which 27 went to economists in the United States. It would be safe to assume that practically all of these laureates had trained a large number of foreign economists. Milton Friedman and other University of Chicago economists, for instance, who were among the early recipients of the prize, were known to be exponents of "monetarism," stressing the critical importance of the free circulation of money as a mechanism for providing for the well-being of society, rather than governmental regulations. Such thinking, which rejected not just socialism but also New Deal–type national planning, made an enormous impact on foreign economists and government officials, who collectively turned the decades of the 1980s and the 1990s into an era of reduced state roles in regulating social and economic affairs. The "Chicago school" was particularly influential in South America, where economists trained at the University of Chicago and elsewhere in the United States set about dismantling edifices of governmental control.

It is also noteworthy, however, that the Nobel Prize in Economics toward the end of the century (in 1998) was awarded to Amartya Sen, a scholar from India who had conducted research in Britain and the United States. In sharp contrast to Friedman, Sen emphasized political and social aspects of all economic phenomena and stressed the need for education to bring impoverished people in all countries out of their predicament. He became a powerful voice for a new cosmopolitanism that would emphasize the interconnectedness of nations and espouse universal values adapted to local conditions. It is not hard to detect the influence both of Indian tradition and of American education on his thought. In that sense he typified the interrelationship between American educational achievements and transnational scholarly developments. One might even say that economists and other scholars worldwide were trying to grapple with the phenomenon of globalization and that, while Friedman and others were arguing for removing what they viewed as political and bureaucratic obstacles standing in the way of the smooth functioning of economic forces, those who thought like Sen were becoming aware of the social and cultural dimensions of the global transformation and sought to change the course of history through active human engagement. Both cases illustrated that the still visible American century was being particularly well demonstrated by transnationalism in education and learning.

In short, the key achievement of the American century was that it had trans-nationalized the world to an extent never seen earlier. The 1980s and the 1990s were above all an era of a rapidly interconnecting world. People everywhere in the globe were becoming connected to one another to an extent never seen before. Not just through migration, tourism, or education, but even more fundamentally through technological developments and material culture, notably food, they were beginning to share a vast amount of mental and physical products. It may be said that transnational networks were being built on many layers, some through people, others through goods and ideas, and still others through "virtual" connections, those made possible by rapid advances in information and communications technology.

People across the globe were becoming connected, or, as many started saying, "wired." With the Internet system of communication, initially developed for military purposes in the United States, being increasingly made available for civilian use, companies and individuals took to it in droves starting in the mid-1980s. Electronic mail was another remarkable instance of American technology facilitating the establishment of transnational links. It was found to be so easy to use and so quick in making connections that it steadily became a favored means of communication among those who could afford to own a computer. And their number kept expanding. In 1995, for instance, the total population online was 16 million, or 0.4 percent of the globe. By December 2000 the number had already climbed to 361 million, or 5.8 percent of the world's population. Graphically indicative of the new technology's transnational and global character is the fact that as early as in 2000, the largest percentage of Internet users was in Asia (114 million, or 31 percent), compared to 108 million in Europe and about the same number in North America.[118]

More than a novel means of communication, the Internet in time developed as a major transmitter of information. Organizations began to create their own websites, accessible to anyone who would type in the proper address. And it was just a matter of time before a device would be developed that collected all such information and made it available to Internet users. The Google system best exemplified the new phenomenon. Established in the late 1990s by a handful of young engineers in California, it amassed an immense amount of information

Mongolians playing computer games at an Internet café in Ulaanbaatar, Mongolia, July 2003, an example of a globally shared personal pastime. (Getty Images)

worldwide—on stores, train and air travel schedules, cultural events, weather, and just about every subject—that would be offered free of charge to anyone connected to the Internet. All one had to do was to type in a subject or a question, and Google would provide the answer. At first only a small number of Internet users took advantage of what Google had to offer; barely 100,000 uses were made of Google per day at the end of the 1990s. But already seeds were being sown for a vast expansion of the information network in the coming century.

Such a network confirmed the supremacy of the English language, at least for the time being. Because information technology was most rapidly developed and spread in the United States, what it had to offer necessarily came in English. Computer keys, terminology, and user manuals were written in English, and non-English clients had to get accustomed to them. Email addresses and links were likewise in English. The situation did not change immediately, even after Japan, China, and other non-English-speaking countries began manufacturing computers, although

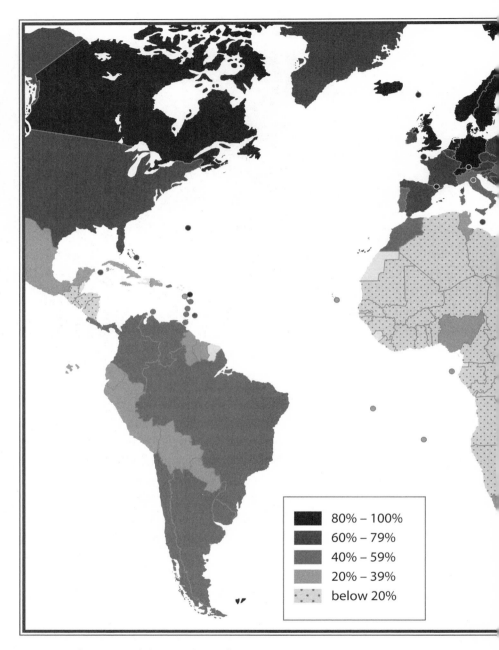

■	80% – 100%
■	60% – 79%
■	40% – 59%
■	20% – 39%
⋯	below 20%

Percentage of a nation's inhabitants who use the Internet, 2011.

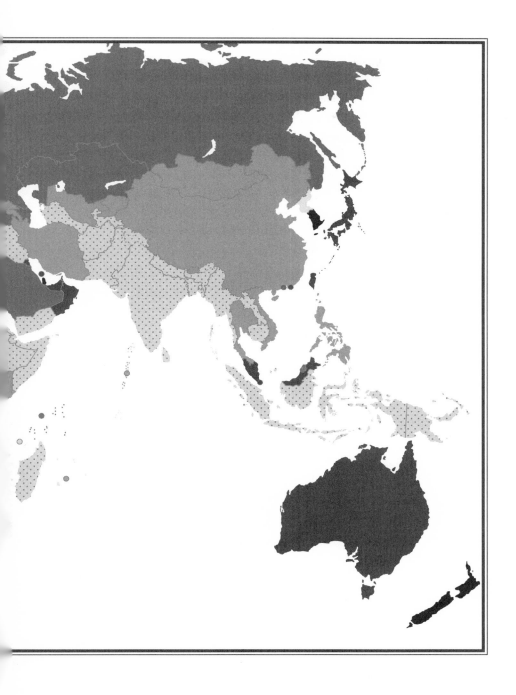

in the twenty-first century the number of websites written in Chinese, Spanish, Japanese, and other languages would increase. In any event, the spread of the Internet implied that the world was becoming interconnected through shared technology and information to an unprecedented degree.

The Internet was not the only way that people in different parts of the world established connections with each other. Another important technical breakthrough at the end of the century was the mobile phone, or the cell phone as it was known in the United States. Worldwide mobile phone subscribers jumped from just 11 million in 1990 to 740 million in 2000. That would mean, in the abstract, that one person out of nine used the new device, perhaps one person in seven if we exclude infants and small children. (Those between the ages of zero and fourteen accounted for about 30 percent of the world's total population in 2000.) The portable phone that one could carry in one's pocket anywhere was not simply a triumph of technology; it also implied greater mobility of people, as they no longer needed to be at home or in their workplaces to receive telephone calls. Added to email, the cell phone connected people in different parts of the globe more easily than ever before. Although some mobile phones would not work across borders, altogether international telephone calls made from traditional as well as cell phones increased from 33 billion minutes in 1990 to 118 billion minutes in 2000.[119] (It may well be that the widespread use of email and mobile phones around the globe resulted in a sharp decline in more traditional forms of correspondence. As fewer people wrote letters to foreign addresses, international postage rates skyrocketed, which may further have discouraged the practice.)

Individuals all around the world, in any event, came to know each other, vicariously if not directly. Their mutual knowledge may not have developed beyond an elementary level, but compared to their forebears, a far greater number of men and women—and even children—in virtually all parts of the globe became aware of each other's existence and shared information and their experiences. This could be seen in the spread of various kinds of cuisine all over the world. During the last decades of the twentieth century, there grew networks of "exotic" restaurants all over the world, to such an extent that in most large cities one had an enormous range of food to choose from: French, Italian, Greek, Ethiopian, Turkish, Indian, Thai, Vietnamese, Cambodian, Indonesian, Chinese, Korean, Japanese, and many others. This was in part a result of migrations; as people moved across borders, they brought their own cuisine, which was now seen by the local population as less quaint than interesting, something they would try themselves. Ethnic diversity and culinary variety reinforced each other. At the same time, it became more common for city dwellers to dine out. Restaurants and catering businesses seem to have multiplied everywhere in the world, no doubt reflecting the fact that more and more women were now working so that they would have less time than traditionally to devote to cooking at home. The point is that besides the familiar fast food, people were willing to try nontraditional dishes at a restaurant if not at home.

One consequence of such a development was that the major cities of the world began to look more alike. Shanghai and New York imparted similar impressions to visitors, and all cities faced the problem of accommodating their growing populations. Among the advanced countries, already in 1950 about half of their people lived in cities, but by 2000 the ratio had reached 70 percent. In the rest of the world, too, the urban population increased from 25 percent in 1970 to 40 percent in 2000. The kinds of issues that urban centers in Western Europe and North America had faced a century earlier—such as crime, social order, public education, garbage collection, street cleaning—now were all global problems. What is equally significant is that, in coping with such issues, national governments were proving to be inadequate instruments, and the initiative for urban governance was reverting to the cities themselves. Mayors and officials of the world's cities periodically met with one another to share ideas and to develop common strategies. Whether living in what Saskia Sassen has called "global cities" or not, urban residents all over the world were becoming transnational beings.[120]

Nowhere was the phenomenon of transnational interconnectedness more dramatically demonstrated than in worldwide sporting competitions, such as the Olympics and the World Cup for football (soccer). The teams in both events competed in the name of their respective nations, and nationalistic emotions were unabashedly enhanced during the games. But such nationalism was also a transnational phenomenon—it was manifest all over the globe, and nevertheless it was not an exclusionary, antiforeign sentiment that traditionally had exacerbated relations among countries. In World Cup games, while the spectators tended to be segregated by nation in the stands, the franchises were becoming steadily less "national" in their composition. During the 1990s, football leagues in Europe almost completely shed their associations with regional or national entities (except in name), and much like a prototypical transnational corporation (which they actually were), teams recruited coaching staff and players from around the globe. A glance at the winners of the FIFA (Fédération Internationale de Football Association) World Player Award in football since 1991 showed a very weak correlation between the player's nationality and the "nationality" of his team.

Seoul, Barcelona, Atlanta, Sydney—to list the cities where the summer Olympics were held between 1988 and 2000 is to name some of the fastest-growing urban centers in the world. The 1980 and the 1984 games, planned for two other large urban areas, Moscow and Los Angeles, were boycotted by some countries for geopolitical reasons, a striking example of how states overrode the aspirations of the world's athletes to come together for "a festival of peace." Even during the height of the Cold War in the 1950s and 1960s, the games had not been boycotted, so these were rather unusual developments, and in any event they did not prevent the resumption of the games after 1988. (The winter Olympics held in Lake Placid, New York, in 1980 and in Sarajevo, Yugoslavia, in 1984, were attended by athletes of all countries.) Young men and women congregated in urban centers, shared living quarters, and competed with one another, in the process further enriching their transnational experiences. Arguably the most dramatic illustration of the transnational reach of spectator sport came during the opening ceremony of the Nagano (Japan) Winter Olympics, held in early 1998. There Seiji Ozawa, the conductor, led a global chorus in singing from Beethoven's *Ninth Symphony,* the *Ode to Joy.* Groups of singers from Australia, South Africa, Europe, China, the United States, and other countries sang in real time, being coordinated via satellite television by Ozawa's baton in central Japan. It was a fitting illustration of the age of transnationalism.

Transnational Criminals

Unfortunately, not all layers of transnational activities contributed to the making of a more peaceful world. A significant number of individuals and groups, who were transnational in that they did not represent specific states but availed themselves of opportunities provided by cross-border connections, began to engage in criminal acts. International terrorists, drug smugglers, and traffickers in women and minors had always presented a serious threat to world order as well as to domestic well-being, but it was especially in the last two decades of the twentieth century that such criminals came to wreak havoc upon the global community.

It is customary to view the acts of terrorism carried out by Islamic fundamentalists in those decades as having been directed against the United States and against the West in general. Thus, a suicide bomber attacked the US marine headquarters in the Beirut, Lebanon, airport in 1983, and in 1998 the US embassies in Kenya and Tanzania were bombed, killing more than two hundred people. These were episodes in international affairs, but they did not pit one nation against another. The terrorists did not represent, or seek to promote the interest of, any particular country but were coming together to target the United States because of its support for Israel or its overall presence in the Middle East, or else because in their view the United States exemplified modern capitalism, bourgeois decadence, secularism, materialism, and many related sins. Thus the attack upon the World Trade Center in New York in 1993, carried out by a group of Arab extremists, was viewed as an exemplification of the fundamental conflict between two ways of life, one modern Western and the other traditionalist and anti-Western. Samuel Huntington, one of the most influential writers of the 1990s, presented such a dichotomous scheme in his widely read book *The Clash of Civilizations*, published in 1996. The modern West he viewed as defined by Christian civilization, which he argued was being threatened by other civilizations, especially Islamic and Chinese. That, he argued, would be a more serious problem for the United States and its Western allies than any old-fashioned geopolitical threat. He cited the terrorist attacks by Islamic fundamentalists as evidence that civilizations, not nations, were becoming the crucial determinants of world affairs. But he was also concerned with the rise of Asia, which he saw as a potentially anti-Western development. (Ironically, in the coming struggle that he predicted for the twenty-first century between the West and "the Rest," he was hopeful that India would take the West's side, as would Russia and any other country or civilization that had a modicum of "Western" ingredient.)

Huntington and many others who understood international terrorism in such a framework were correct to note the emergence of transnational challenges to world order, but their tendency to dichotomize between "the West and the Rest" did not go much beyond traditional thought—many of their ideas had been expressed by American and European thinkers at the turn of the twentieth century—and ignored the fact that East and West, Europeans and Asians, and different races of the world were now, at the end of the twentieth century, fast coming together, in some instances literally intermixing with one another and creating a new, hybrid, global civilization. Transnational connections and exchanges characterized that civilization, so that even the acts by the terrorists were one part of the new global drama, representing one layer of the emerging cross-border consciousness. They were not pitting one civilization against another, one nation against another, or even one religion against another. Rather, the terrorists were like alienated individuals who exist everywhere and choose to marginalize themselves from what they take to be the way things are moving. Instead of finding meaning in social and community affairs, they would seek to retain their sense of purity and to eradicate everything else that stood in the way. They were transnational beings in the sense that they did not identify with, or act on behalf of, a country, but at the same time they were trying to damage other transnational beings lest their efforts to establish bridges across the world's regions and civilizations should succeed.

The Islamic terrorists were also transnational in that few of them remained in their countries of origin. Several key terrorists came from Yemen, others from Saudi Arabia and elsewhere in the Middle East as well as South Asia. They went back and forth among these countries and regions, and some studied in Europe and North America. It was while spending time in the West that some of them fell under the influence of radical Islam. The reasons are not hard to guess. A sense of alienation living as guests in a country that espoused a different religion and a contrasting way of life, combined with frustrations at not being recognized as respectable members of the host community, frequently drove these foreign residents to despair and in extreme cases to hostility that seemed to justify any act of violence to express their anger. Such anger was provided with the teachings of radical Islamic theologians to generate a sense of mission ostensibly derived from a moral superiority. Such self-righteousness was fueled when would-be terrorists came together in congregations and seminaries where they were taught by those with a rigid faith in their doctrinal purity, correctness, and superiority.

Why some transnational persons embraced antisocial behavior that might (and did) provoke an opposition that could undermine the transnational resources at their disposal—for instance, through stringent immigration restrictions or a strict surveillance of foreign banking accounts—while the majority embraced or at least chose to live on a more peaceful level of transnationalism, is one of the key questions of contemporary society. Although the idea of jihad, or "holy war," was a fundamental tenet of the Islamic faith, for most of its sects and believers it did not mean a call for collective (and violent) action against all that stood in the way. But it did imply disregarding secular authority, especially any state not based on Islam (or one of its sects), so that Islamic terrorism at one level was an assault upon a world composed of independent nations. But whereas other transnational people challenged the authority of the state by setting up non-state organizations and building bridges among them, the terrorists envisaged a world in which not only secular states but also NGOs not related to Islam would be eliminated. Such, of course, was an impossibility, and the terrorists knew they had to make use of existing institutions. Thus, the distinction between them and the vast majority of people throughout the world consisted in the terrorists' unwillingness to envisage a transnational future other than that of their own apocalyptic vision. They were criminals in the sense that they refused to share the planet with other human beings. It should be noted, at the same time, that many of the terrorists were purists in a world that was increasingly becoming hybrid, and in that sense they shared a psychological oneness with other purists, whether religious, racial, or nationalistic. They preferred doctrinaire (and unrealizable) purity in a world that was becoming more and more ambivalent, as Kenneth Weisbrode has noted.[121]

The terrorists were far from alone, however, in posing a serious threat to the integrity of the global community. Arguably even more sinister challenges to transnationalism were posed by drug smugglers, traffickers in women and children, and other criminals. Drug smuggling took advantage of the global networks of producers and consumers and thus became more successful than ever before. Although opium smoking abated significantly in the twentieth century, the consumption of other narcotic drugs increased. It would be difficult to determine whether there was now more demand for drugs because of their increasing availability, or whether the supply was a response to growing demand, which may have been related to criminal activities in many countries where the selling of illegal drugs was a lucrative business and a source of income for crime syndicates. Globalization had something to do with the phenomenon, in that demand and supply data could be instantaneously communicated across borders and illicit transactions could take place via the Internet. There was in a sense a transnational brotherhood of drug traffickers against whom law enforcement bodies were often helpless—some in law enforcement even profited by taking bribes. The distinction between illegal and legal action was sometimes hard to make in such regions as the Afghanistan-Pakistan border and the areas adjacent to Myanmar.

Like international terrorism, drug trafficking across borders was difficult to control because it went beyond the jurisdiction of a single state and there was no nonmilitary mechanism sufficiently global in scope to control such abuses. In 1923 the international community established Interpol as a cooperative agency to coordinate policing activities across borders. Initially only a few countries were represented, but Interpol membership grew rapidly after the Second World War, with over one hundred countries participating by the end of the century.[122] But Interpol's effectiveness in controlling drug traffic varied from region to region. (In Europe, Europol was established in 1992 as the policing arm of the European Union, but there was nothing comparable in other areas of the world.) It may well be that because, unlike terrorists, drug smugglers did not espouse any violent ideology to remake the world, perhaps their presence was not considered an equally grave threat, although the problem would grow even more serious in the coming century.

Transnational humanitarian organizations that earlier in the century had been quite active in the movement to control opium traffic now were more concerned with human trafficking, especially of women and children, which grew in scale at the end of the century. (Statistics vary, but according to a UN estimate there were about one million trafficked people in 2000.[123]) Here was another aspect of the fast-globalizing world. With national borders becoming more and more porous, women were taken from Eastern Europe, Southeast Asia, and elsewhere and sent to other parts of the world to serve as "sex slaves." Even teenagers would be lured away from their homes by promises of jobs abroad, only to find themselves confined to tight spaces, with their passports taken away and forced to serve strangers as servants. There was a growing demand for services of such entrapped people, whose movement and activities were controlled by transnational

An Afghan farmer scores opium poppy buds in a field near Habibullah, Afghanistan, April 2011. Drug cultivation, consumption, and trafficking became serious transnational issues of the contemporary era. (AFP/Getty Images)

criminal syndicates that clearly violated all principles promulgated by the international community to protect human rights. It remained to be seen whether Interpol, Europol, and other police agencies as well as the regional communities and transnational organizations would in time succeed in coping with these violations of human rights.

The world at the end of the twentieth century, then, was a kaleidoscope of transnational beings, constituting layers of cross-border activities and emotions. Most of them took advantage of the new opportunities being provided by the lowering of territorial boundaries and the availability of cross-border information and communication to build a better future for themselves and for others, while a minority were a negative presence whose activities would move the world closer to violence and chaos.

What about those who never became transnational? There were, of course, many of them all over the world, some physically cut off from other countries and societies, others choosing to isolate themselves as a matter of principle, taste, or personality, or for other reasons. Many objected to some aspects of transnationalism but not to others. For instance, the massive demonstrations against the Seattle meeting of the World Trade Organization in 1999 showed that while the demonstrators expressed their opposition to economic globalization, they were united transnationally in pursuit of what they believed would be a less avaricious world order. Such people were part of an evolving global civil society. On the other hand, there were those who remained outside the networks of transnational connections not because they were necessarily anti-transnational but because they were fundamentally mono-national beings in the sense that their primary and overwhelming identity was with their respective countries and they saw no need to change. Even though they might run into foreigners in their midst, enjoy an occasional tasting of exotic food, or even set foot abroad, they would always think in mono-national terms. Their well-being, their education, and their life objectives all were bound up with the power, prestige, and interests of their own country. Probably the bulk of humanity combined transnational experiences with national perspectives. Only a minority may have considered themselves transnational individuals leading "transnational lives," to use a term some historians have begun to use.[124] Put another way, national sentiments and nationalistic attitudes did not disappear even as the world was coming to consist of transnational connections. Layers of transnational consciousness had been added to the traditional national consciousness. How these various layers would be transformed, amalgamated, augmented, or instead violently collide against one another was a question that the end of the twentieth century was bequeathing to the twenty-first.

4. The Twenty-First Century

THE YEARS since 2001 are part of contemporary history that began some time during the last decades of the twentieth century. That may explain why there was relatively little attempt at predicting the possible course of the twenty-first century. Compared to the last years of the nineteenth century and the early years of the twentieth, this time there were few confident depictions of human civilization that would usher in a world without conflict, war, or antipathy among groups of people. There was, to be sure, much concern over the transition from December 31, 1999, to January 1, 2000. Known as the Y2K problem, it involved the fact that all sorts of activities in the world, ranging from nuclear arms development to navigation, were programmed by computer but that computers might not recognize the transition to 2000 (because the number 2000 might be rendered as 100, 1900, and so forth), which might result in catastrophes. It was said that billions of dollars were spent worldwide to fight the "millennium bug." This, however, was less a prediction of the coming century than a pragmatic concern with specific technological questions—more or less in the same category were predictions about the rise of China as the new century's greatest power or of India as the most populous country. These were not particularly profound observations and may have revealed a lack of imagination on the eve of the new millennium.

Many observers assumed that globalization would continue, with all that it implied in people's lives as well as the fortunes of nations. Whether the United States would remain the sole superpower was a favorite subject that intrigued numerous observers, but such geopolitically framed questions were not particularly interesting in the age of globalization. What was more relevant was the view that the continued economic development of China, India, Brazil, and other countries could have dire environmental consequences, or that the unceasing increases in the world's population might create a new scramble for food and raw materials. Unlike a hundred years earlier, there was much less confidence that science would solve all these and many other problems. On the other hand, there was no widely shared belief that a military collision among some great powers was inevitable, as there had been in the early years of the previous century. Instead, there was some faith that cooperation among nations would continue and that through international organizations the pressing problems of the day might become susceptible of solution. In other words, many of the ideas that had characterized the decades since the 1960s continued to provide the key framework for the new century.

The situation did not change even after the terrorist attacks on key US targets on September 11, 2001, which most people recall even today as having been the key event of the first year of the twenty-first century. On that day, several Islamic terrorists seized two airplanes departing Logan Airport in Boston for the West Coast, took over the planes' cockpits, flew to New York City, and crashed the planes into the twin towers of the World Trade Center, destroying the buildings and causing death to nearly three thousand people, mostly Americans but also including a number of foreigners. Simultaneously, a third hijacked plane, departing from Washington Dulles International Airport, flew into and partially damaged the Pentagon building outside Washington, DC, and yet a fourth flew across the state of Pennsylvania to target another city, possibly Chicago, before the passengers, having become aware of what was happening in New York, assaulted the terrorists and diverted the aircraft to the western part of the state, causing it to crash in a field in Somerset County, destroying the plane and killing all onboard. All these attacks had been planned by al-Qaeda, the terrorist group headquartered in Afghanistan under the leadership of Osama bin Laden.

This heinous, extremely tragic incident traumatized not only the American people but the rest of the world. It was a transnational crime of the kind that some may have imagined possible before it happened, but few would have been able to foresee the sense of horror that it gave rise to across the globe. All over the world, leaders and ordinary citizens—save the minority who sided with the terrorists ideologically and gloated over the humiliation suffered by the mighty United States—expressed their utter disgust with the crime and their heartfelt sympathy with the American people. The victims as well as the culprits were transnational, and so the attacks were viewed by many as a harbinger of what was to come in an increasingly interconnected world. Some of the terrorists had studied in Europe, and others had learned how to fly in the United States. The perpetrators had exchanged messages with bin Laden, who remained in the remote mountains of Afghanistan. They had received funds from various sources channeled through legitimate bank accounts in the United States and elsewhere.

The terrorists' ideology, on the other hand, was anything but transnational in the sense of bringing people of the world closer together. Islamic fundamentalism divided all people into true believers and the rest, and the latter were considered enemies of the faith that needed to be destroyed. The ideology likewise had little tolerance for the diversity of religious interpretations within Islam itself. The West, in particular the United States, exemplified the enemy because it was materialistic, secular, and committed to the idea of global community consisting of people of all faiths. More specifically, the Islamic terrorists castigated the United States for its unflinching support of Israel and its alleged antagonism toward Islamic countries such as Iraq and Iran.

It would be wrong, however, to view the September 11 attacks as an act of war between the terrorists and the United States. That was President George W. Bush's perception, and he believed the world now consisted of supporters and opponents of terrorists against whom the nation would wage a relentless war. But how would a nation fight a "war" against a non-nation, an entity that existed apart from sovereign states? President Ronald Reagan, it is true, had already in the 1980s spoken of "war on terror," much as his predecessors had popularized notions of "war on poverty," "war on illiteracy," and the like. But traditional international law had made little provision for a nation waging war against an individual or an organization not connected to another state. (That was why the 2011 killing of Osama bin Laden by US forces, which was justified by the White House as an act of war, was not universally considered legitimate.) On the other hand, the world was witnessing increasingly ominous activities not just by terrorists but by drug smugglers, pirates, traffickers of women, and the like, so that some internationally coordinated action to deal with them was becoming a matter of urgency. The problem was how to arrange for such coordination and how to carry out such a "war."

Moreover, the perpetrators of the September 11 attacks were not waging war against a single nation. It would be more correct to say that the criminal acts were targeting the entire human community as it existed in reality and in perception. The whole idea of a transnationally connected global community would have been repugnant to the radical Islamists, who must not have anticipated the way that community responded in shared horror and outrage, thus in a way confirming the existence of a transnational world. If the terrorists really thought that through their acts they would intimidate or undermine the emerging global community, they were totally mistaken.

Ironically, the nation-centric response to the September 11 attacks by the United States government also tended to undermine the unity of humankind. The global outpouring of sympathy and support for the American people did not prove enduring for various reasons, but one key factor was surely the way the Bush administration handled the crisis. By framing it in a traditional manner, as a surprise attack upon an unsuspecting nation—the Pearl Harbor analogy came easily to the minds of many Americans—the president led the fight to punish the offenders, much as the nation had risen in unison against the instigators of Pearl Harbor. To say, as he did, "You are for us, or you are against us," was to divide the globe into two, but "us" in this case was the United States, and the image of the whole world either engaged in war against the nation or coming to its support was extremely nation-centric and unrealistic as well as insensitive to changing world conditions.

Indeed, it may not have been so much the terrorists as the unilateralist response of the United States that threatened to undermine the emerging transnationalization in the days and months following the September 11 attacks. Whereas the event only confirmed the existence of a global community, the Bush administration's countermeasures tended to revert back to a time when one power could, or believed it could, change the world. Actually, even before 9/11, in the spring of 2001, Washington had withdrawn from the 1998 Kyoto protocol on combating climate change and refused to ratify the convention for the establishment of an international criminal court, insisting that US military personnel be exempted from any such jurisdiction. Neither did the Bush administration ratify the 1997 Ottawa treaty banning antipersonnel land mines. It had been adamant from the start that national interest considerations alone should be the basis of its foreign policy and that any restrictions on the nation's freedom of action would be resisted. These decisions were clearly out of step with worldwide trends and showed that unilateralism was already becoming a mark of the new US government when the September 11 attacks took place. The gap between the United States and the international community had become so clear that the latter's overwhelmingly empathetic support of the American people in the aftermath of the terrorist assault could have provided an opportunity for the United States and the rest of the world to come together again. That this did not happen was a serious setback for the further growth of an interdependent, transnational world.

Some historians date the end of "the American century" to those attacks, but if they do so because the incident showed that even the mighty United States was vulnerable to transnational terrorism, they would be wrong.[125] It would be more correct to say, as noted in the preceding section, that "the American century" had been losing its meaning in an increasingly transnational world and that if the leaders in Washington now tried to bring it back, they were engaged in an anachronistic task. (A group of neoconservative leaders had organized a short-lived "project for the new American century" in 1997, calling for increases in defense spending, challenging "hostile regimes," promoting the cause of "freedom" abroad, and accepting the nation's "unique" role in keeping and extending the international order.[126] But the construction of such a "new American century" was an unrealizable dream, not because the nation was incapable of using all its military and economic resources to combat terrorism, but because the global community would not have accepted such a mono-national orientation and nation-centric definition of the world for the twenty-first century.)

There was a good deal of cooperation between Washington and other capitals, especially of the liberal democracies with sizable Muslim populations, to seek out and punish the culprits of the terrorist attacks and to prevent their recurrence. Some of these measures were readily concurred in by most other countries as well, including autocratic states and former Cold War adversaries. For instance, they cooperated with the United States in the policy of "rendition," in which terrorist suspects would be "rendered" to the CIA's secret prisons or to locations abroad where criminal suspects faced inhumane conditions and even torture. Most nations tightened border control, seeking to make it less easy for would-be terrorists to cross national boundaries. Many countries began instituting more stringent screening systems at airports, inspecting checked and carry-on luggage with greater care. At first even such items as fingernail clippers and sewing needles were confiscated; later, liquids over 3.4 ounces in quantity were banned unless they were put in checked luggage. When a small explosive was found inside the shoe of a would-be terrorist, several countries, including the United States, made it mandatory for passengers to take off their shoes when they went through the security check. The United States, Japan, and several other countries began requiring the fingerprinting of all incoming foreigners. Because some of the September 11 culprits had studied in the United States, it became more cumbersome to enter the country with a student visa, and there was a dip in the number of foreign students arriving on American shores. (It fell from some 586,000 during the academic year 2002–2003 to 564,000 three years later.) Many who might otherwise have studied in the United States now went elsewhere, in particular to Canada, Britain, and Australia.

Initially, European allies were willing to accept the US initiative to lead a punitive attack upon Afghanistan, whose Taliban regime was considered an ally of Osama bin Laden and the terrorist organization al-Qaeda. The NATO allies invoked Article 5 of the treaty, stating that an attack on one member was an attack on all. Believing that bin Laden was living in Afghanistan, the US government demanded that the Kabul regime surrender him, and when the latter refused, Washington and London began bombing the Afghan capital and surrounding areas. The result was a quick retreat by the Taliban to the peripheral areas, in particular the mountainous border with Pakistan. The new non-Taliban regime under Hamid Karzai was established by the end of the year 2001 and was recognized by more and more countries in the following years. It remained extremely unstable, however, and civil strife and Taliban attacks never ceased. As the situation continued, international support for the US initiative in Afghanistan began to erode.

This lack of enthusiasm for US policies became particularly clear in 2003, when Washington virtually ignored world opinion in launching a military expedition against Iraq. (It has been estimated that prior to the invasion, six to ten million people worldwide demonstrated their opposition to the coming war.[127]) The ostensible reasons for the attack were that Iraq under Saddam Hussein had harbored terrorists and that it had also developed nuclear and other "weapons of mass destruction." Neither of these allegations was substantiated, but George W. Bush was willing to act alone if necessary. Subsequent revelations were to show that his top aides were willing to ignore information—some provided by US intelligence officials—that contradicted these allegations, and that even the closest ally,

Britain, remained skeptical. It was very difficult to obtain UN concurrence in launching an attack on Iraq, but that did not prevent the United States from doing so, starting the bombing and invasion of Iraq in March 2003. Britain also sent its troops, but some NATO allies, such as Spain and France, openly criticized the war. (France did not allow overflight rights for US military aircraft in the assault on Iraq.) This sort of unilateralism alienated the international community, as well as significant portions of public opinion in the United States. But it seemed as if the more the world criticized Washington, the stiffer the administration's attitude grew. There was clearly a gap between the world, which remained transnationally connected, and the US government, which appeared to alienate itself from it, at least on this issue.

All wars are transnational as well as international. They establish connections among people across borders that might otherwise not have developed. But the wars in Afghanistan and Iraq proved much less so, for different reasons. Afghanistan's transnationalism was more internal than external; the country consisted of tribal groups who fought against one another, militarily as well as politically, and even those who had been opposed to the Taliban were not able to establish a stable system of national governance. Ethnic, tribal loyalties trumped any sentiment of nationhood in a country where the borders with its neighbor, Pakistan, were particularly artificial, even for that part of South Asia. Populations of Pashtuns, Hazaris, and Tajiks paid little attention to which side of the border they belonged to and even less to the dictates of weak central governments in Kabul or Islamabad. Transnational connections, to the extent that they were fostered, were mostly products of humanitarian organizations, both intergovernmental and nongovernmental, that sent aid missions to assist the country's nation-rebuilding efforts. But humanitarian activities were frequently frustrated by violence and instability. These were nothing like the transnational connections that were constructed in Germany, Austria, or Japan after the Second World War.

In Iraq the situation was even less conducive to transnational encounters. Little preparation had been made for the fact that the war would inevitably entail both military and nonmilitary tasks, the latter involving a range of issues from maintaining law and order in occupied areas to ensuring the establishment of a stable government that would replace Saddam's dictatorship. It was much easier to dispose of the regime than to reconstruct the country, in part because Iraq had been in a state of chaos for over ten years. Intermittent US bombings as well as UN sanctions during the 1990s had destroyed much of the infrastructure in the country as well as social and educational institutions. The restoration of order and social services would require a great deal of transnational cooperation at the civilian level, but much of this had to be established on the spot. There had been little preparation for such tasks—in sharp contrast to the careful planning for the occupation of Germany and Japan that had been made during the Second World War. US military and civilian officials had to shoulder the burden of post-Saddam reconstruction, but few of them had had training in Iraq's languages or culture. Their work was assisted by, and sometimes assigned entirely to, civilian contractors from the United States and elsewhere who also lacked prerequisite backgrounds. The UN did try to help in reconstruction work, but its efforts suffered grievously when, in September 2003, a truck bomb driven by a suicide terrorist exploded outside the UN's headquarters in Baghdad. The explosion killed UN special representative Sérgio Vieira de Mello. After a second bombing in the following month, the UN pulled its personnel from the war-torn country.

Under the circumstances, transnational encounters remained superficial. Although serious attempts were made by a number of NGOs, including the International Red Cross, Doctors Without Borders, and smaller groups committed to helping the people of Iraq, they had to spend much of their time protecting themselves from attacks by extremist groups that disdained any such attempts to promote transnationalism. In danger for their lives, humanitarian organizations and relief workers often had to turn to US and other military forces for protection. The weakness of the country's civil society made it extremely difficult to create and sustain transnational encounters.

Dialogue among Civilizations

Transnationalism was clearly on trial, but the September 11 attacks and the consequent wars in Afghanistan and Iraq did not mean that history was reversing the trends that had become evident toward the end of the twentieth century, such as economic and cultural globalization as well as efforts at increased communication and understanding among nations, religions, and civilizations. This latter objective might have been frustrated by the 2001 terrorist attacks on the

United States and the subsequent rise of anti-Islamic sentiment. The incident undoubtedly created fear of Islam in many parts of the world, especially in Europe and North America where there had been less experience with or knowledge of the Islamic religion than elsewhere, such as China and India, whose populations contained a significant minority of Muslims. In the West, many people were unable to distinguish between the extremists and the moderate (or politically uninvolved) majority among the followers of Islam. There was confusion as to who the extremists were, and many, including government officials, were prone to see all Muslims as potential terrorists.

Such fears might have seemed justified to some when the September 11 attacks were followed by similar, if less massive, assaults on civilians, such as the explosion at the resort in Bali in October 2002, the attempt to blow up a transatlantic flight in 2003 by a terrorist with explosives hidden inside his shoe, the subway and bus bombings in London in July 2005, the attack on Mumbai, India's largest city, in 2008, and a failed attempt to blow up a US civilian aircraft on Christmas day 2009 that was in transit between Amsterdam and Detroit. The majority of these attacks were cases of "suicide" assaults in which the terrorists blew themselves up along with their targets. The image of a fanatic blowing himself up in pursuit of an ostensibly higher cause reminded observers of the kamikaze bombings by Japanese pilots toward the end of the Second World War. But the Japanese analogy was not entirely fitting in that the kamikaze pilots were carrying out a military mission and mostly targeted US warships, whereas there was no national command behind the Islamic terrorists, who did not discriminate among their targets. In any event, both Islamic and Japanese suicide attacks were incomprehensible to the bulk of humanity and further confirmed the image of fanatics who were driven by irrational beliefs. It was easy to generalize from these instances and to consider the whole religion of Islam, or the bulk of Muslims worldwide, as abetting such a culture of irrationality. Few enjoyed the stringent system of airport security that became a transnational experience in the wake of these bombings, actual or attempted. Under the circumstances, pessimists might have believed that this was no time to start a dialogue with Islam, even to continue transnational efforts at cross-cultural communication and understanding.

In reality, however, efforts at such communication and understanding never abated after 2001. If anything, because of the very seriousness of the crisis, civilian organizations as well as international bodies redoubled their efforts at continuing the dialogue among civilizations. The United Nations had adopted a resolution in 1998 that the year 2001 would be called the Year of Dialogue among Civilizations. The UN and various international and national organizations were to sponsor meetings where this theme would be explored. One of the first such gatherings took place in Vilnius, Lithuania, in July 2001. Opening the conference, Kōichirō Matsuura, general secretary of UNESCO, noted that the emerging new global order must be solidly built on communication and dialogue among civilizations. Specifically, he and the conferees agreed on the need to intensify efforts to promote an understanding of the world's diverse cultures and civilizations. This and other gatherings that took place in 2001—for instance, UNESCO sponsored a meeting of scientists in New York to discuss biodiversity—were overshadowed by the much more dramatic events of September 11, but it should be noted that the terrorist attacks did not dampen the enthusiasm for or commitment to the cause of intercivilizational dialogue. During the remainder of the year, meetings similar to the Vilnius gathering were held in different parts of the globe, demonstrating that the terrorists did not succeed in intimidating efforts at promoting transnationalism.

As if to give moral support to such activities, the Nobel Peace Prize Committee in Oslo held a symposium in early December 2001 to commemorate the centenary of the peace award. Kofi Annan, secretary general of the United Nations, who received the prize for that year, as well as many former recipients of the Peace Prize came to the gathering, as did representatives of various organizations that had been so honored, including the American Friends Service Committee, Amnesty International, Doctors Without Borders, and the International Coalition Against Landmines. Coming barely three months after the September 11 attacks, the meeting was notable for its renewed dedication to the cause of world peace and mutual understanding. The overwhelming sentiment of the participants was against the ongoing military involvement in Afghanistan, and they feared that the US government was contemplating similar action against Iraq. Kofi Annan, in accepting the Nobel Peace Prize, reminded those present—and through them the whole world—that the construction of a peaceful world depended on far more than eliminating terrorism. For instance, he pointed out that some seven thousand people—more than twice the number who had been killed in the World Trade Center attack—were dying of HIV/AIDS every day in Africa. No stable world order would be possible until all such tragedies were coped with and eventually eradicated. (Fortunately, by the start of the second decade of the new century, the UN was able to report significant slowing down in the HIV infection rates among young people, even in sub-Saharan African states that had been the hardest hit by the disease.)

In the meantime, efforts at promoting dialogue among civilizations continued into the second year of the new century and beyond. The UN initiative resulted in additional gatherings to promote the cause. Such efforts proved often frustrating, and they sometimes came under severe criticism from those who insisted that no communication and understanding was possible with Islamic extremists. Islamic extremists also responded in kind, touting their own brand of purism in opposition to reconciling with the "devil." The continued influx of Arab, Pakistani, Afghan, Albanian, and other Islamic migrants into Europe, North America, and Australia frequently created social tensions, especially as the new arrivals tended to live in segregated, poorer sections of large cities. The riots that took place in the suburbs of Paris in the fall of 2005, in which crowds consisting largely of Arab immigrants attacked police vehicles, public buildings, and schools, seemed symbolic of the gaps among communities espousing different faiths and ways of life.

The conflict was often between the ideals of cultural diversity and pluralism, allowing each group of people its own belief system and way of life, and secularism, insisting that certain values, such as respect for women's rights, should be considered universally valid and accepted by all. For instance, in France, a country with a strong tradition of secularism, the government banned the wearing of *hijab* (headscarves, veils, burqas) in public places such as schools, and in Britain a member of Parliament (who was also foreign minister) criticized women constituents who met with him with scarves covering their faces. In 2005 Danish cartoonists' portrayal of the prophet Muhammad's face caused worldwide protest among Muslims. And in 2011 in Norway, an extremist with a rifle shot and killed a large number of young people, including several Muslims, who were among those attending an interracial, interfaith gathering on an island. The appearance of mosques in European cities impressed observers as incongruous, an Islamic intrusion upon Christian civilization, and in the United States plans to construct an Islamic culture center near "ground zero" in Manhattan seriously split the nation, although in this instance both the idea of cultural pluralism and the secular doctrine of freedom of religion seemed to stand on one side, and the memory of a national tragedy on the other.

Underneath the surface drama of such conflict, however, there continued to be quiet efforts to overcome simplistic notions of civilizational, religious, or ethnic conflict and incompatibility and to develop less extremist, less dogmatic worldviews. What was needed was an image of the world and of humanity as both divergent and united, both local and global. The energetic efforts by American, Canadian, Australian, British, and other European historians to teach themselves and their students to overcome traditional ethnocentrism and nation-centered perspectives on the past may be seen as one important example. During the first decade of the century, many universities added or expanded their programs in world, global, or transnational history. In 2008 Harvard University hosted the first global history conference with historians participating from all continents. The Mandelbaum Verlag book publishers in Vienna opened a new series titled Global History and Development Policy.[128] A number of superb textbooks were written, incorporating a global perspective into the study of the past. For example, Richard Bulliet and his colleagues published *The Earth and Its Peoples* in 1997 and subsequent years, showing how one might move away from the standard Eurocentric narrative. The authors did not just add other parts of the world to the narrative, but sought to keep the whole globe constantly in view so that readers would be able to trace how different peoples and regions had established connections with one another. In the twenty-first century, the book noted, "people increasingly visualize a single global community."[129] Another textbook of modern world history, *Worlds Together, Worlds Apart* (2002), discussed transnational developments such as "the Black Death, the influx of silver from the Americas into the world economy, and the rise of nationalism, that reverberated throughout the world." These phenomena "produced varying reactions in different regions," the authors argued.[130] The emphasis here was on the dialogue between interconnectedness and divergence, a theme that many scholars were adopting as a viable conceptual framework in their studies of world, global, or transnational history. The key was to move away from a focus on nations as units of analysis. Rather, these historians believed that one would arrive at a more balanced understanding of historical development if one focused on migrations, diseases, the circulation of gold and silver, and many other themes that transcended national boundaries.

Even when dealing with a single nation's history, writers were becoming more and more interested in situating that history in the context of worldwide developments. Thomas Bender's *A Nation among Nations* (2006), for instance, surveyed American history from Columbus to the present but always compared national to global developments so that the nation's politics, society, and culture would not be presented as unique.[131] The author was seeking to counter the "exceptionalist" presentation of the nation's history that had abounded in the literature, arguing instead that mutual influences and parallel developments across national boundaries explained much of what happened in the United States, or indeed in any other country. Likewise, the Australian historian Ian Tyrrell's *Transnational Nation* (2007) sought to place US history squarely in the context of global history, so that US history would be seen as a product as much of external forces (economic, cultural, social) as of domestic factors.[132] These examples show that, almost in proportion as the government of the United States tended to pursue a unilateralist foreign policy, US educators and scholars were seeking to turn the attention of the people to the wider world. It was clearly understood that if their education of the younger generation led to a citizenry more attuned to global issues and sensitive to other people and cultures, that would be one of the most promising developments of the new century.[133]

In Asia also, similar efforts were not lacking. In Malaysia, the Center for Civilizational Dialogue was established at the University of Malaysia, and in Osaka, Japan, Kansai University opened a new center for the study of cultural transmission in East Asia in 2007. Led by a Chinese historian, Tao Demin, the institute aimed at exploring the history of intraregional (as well as interregional) cultural diffusion and intermingling in the early modern times. Around this time, annual symposia began to be held both in Beijing and in Seoul to consider the state of human civilization and its future. While no simple understanding of civilization or even of dialogue among civilizations emerged from such efforts, they indicated that in Asia, too, there was a serious interest in going beyond mono-national frameworks in understanding the past. Along with contemporaneous endeavors by educators elsewhere, these examples were pointing to a transnationally shared perception that, in the words of the historian Bruce Mazlish, civilization now "encompasses all human beings, everywhere."[134]

The Transnational Reach of the Global Economic Crisis

In the meantime, globalization went apace—although starting in 2007 the world economy began to slow down and entered a period of profound crisis lasting for several years. Whether the world economy moved upward or downward, the vicissitude only confirmed that all parts of the world were tied together more closely now than ever before.

During the first decade of the new century, the world's total population grew from roughly 6.1 billion to about 6.9 billion. It was predicted that if the trend continued, world population could reach 8 billion by 2025 and even 9 billion by 2050. Considering that in 1900 there were just 1.6 billion, and in 1950 only 2.5 billion, people in the world, these were almost unmanageable increases, challenging the human environment, the Earth's resources, and the capacity of governments and communities everywhere to maintain a semblance of order. However, it should be noted that the rate of demographic increase was lower at the beginning of the twenty-first century than in the middle of the twentieth. The rate of natural growth—that is, the rate of birth less that of death as a proportion of the overall population—fell from 17.8 percent during 1950–1955 to 12.3 percent fifty years later.

What these figures indicated was that although the death rate had declined significantly, thanks to the absence of large-scale wars and to medical advances, the birth rate also diminished. It is a remarkable fact that these generalizations applied both to economically advanced countries as well as to developing nations. Although the latter continued to register higher birth rates and accounted for more than 80 percent of the world's people, their populations were increasing less rapidly by the first decade of the twenty-first century. There were many reasons for this, including the spreading use of birth control, a less traditional way of life in which having a large number of children was no longer considered appropriate, and governmental policies that encouraged, even mandated, small households. China was the primary example of this last phenomenon. The Beijing government only slightly modified the earlier policy of "one child per family" that had been proclaimed in the 1970s, and as a result the population increased by only 0.58 percent during 2005–2010, far below the world average of 1.17 percent. The population grew much faster in the United States (0.97 percent), Mexico (1.12 percent), Brazil (1.26 percent), and virtually all other countries of South America.

A novel development after the turn of the century was the striking longevity of people in such countries as China, Singapore, and South Korea. An aging population had become a problem in some European countries and in Japan toward the end of the twentieth century, but now the same phenomenon was detected in these other countries as well. In the United States, although the influx of immigrants tended to keep the average age of the population down, 3.1 percent of Americans were over the age of seventy-five in 2004. Comparable figures for Russia, Italy, Sweden, and Britain were 2.5, 4.5, 4.4, and 3.8 percent, respectively. Even in China, where the average life expectancy was already seventy-two years in 2005, more than 2 percent of the population was over seventy. In Russia, on the other hand, the average life expectancy for males was only 58.5 years (and 71.8 for females) in 2004, an exception that proves the rule (caused primarily by the economic collapse of the early 1990s). What such statistics indicated was not only that the world's population was increasing as a whole, albeit more slowly than earlier, but also that its composition was rapidly changing. The aging of the population was a social as well as an economic problem, because senior citizens, in their seventies, eighties, and beyond, would not be working regularly and needed various kinds of assistance, which would require health-care workers and funds to pay for seniors' medical care. In richer countries, public and private retirement homes looked after the needs of old persons, and increasingly citizens were organizing self-help communities through which they would assist each other without having to move into an old-age facility. In the rest of the world, however, few such institutions or programs were available, and families, clans, and villages had to cope as best as they could with the new situation.

The fact remains that in the first decade of the new century there were more people inhabiting the Earth, and that the same needs that had propelled people in the past to migrate in search of food, jobs, and stability remained. In the history of cross-border migrations, the first decade of the twenty-first century continued the trend set toward the end of the twentieth, but the large number of migrants from the Caribbean and South America to North America was now increasingly joined by those escaping Africa, the Middle East, and Central Asia for safer havens. Some of them were refugees, driven from their countries of origin by internal chaos produced by civil strife, sectarian violence, and terrorism. In 2008, Iraq and Afghanistan produced the largest number of refugees, over 1.8 million each, most of whom were absorbed by Pakistan and Iran, adding to these countries' population problems.[135] A relatively novel phenomenon was that of "internally displaced persons," those driven out of their homes and villages and placed in refugee camps within national borders. Such refugees were said to exceed seventeen million in 2004.[136] They were not transnational beings in the strict sense, but most were aided by transnational relief workers as well as by international organizations, notably the Office of the United Nations High Commissioner for Refugees.

Were there sufficient resources to meet the minimum requirements of the world's increasing population? Observers had grappled with this question for decades, but at the beginning of the twenty-first century the theme of climate change became of urgent relevance because of the critical importance not only of food safety but also of food availability. That was one of the concerns that had produced the 1998 Kyoto Protocol for reducing the greenhouse effect, but in addition to the refusal of the United States to join Europe and Japan in ratifying the agreement, China, India, and other developing countries also had not signed on. In the twenty-first century, however, such abstention, indicating a divided globe on this most global of crises, was no longer acceptable. People in some of those countries that were steadily improving their lifestyles were increasingly demanding the use of air conditioners, refrigerators, and the like, adding to the average heat level blanketing the Earth. Al Gore, former vice president of the United States, spread the alarm over these developments in his widely screened film *An Inconvenient Truth*. The message was simple and clear: as depicted graphically in this and many other educational programs, average temperatures were rising and huge chunks of ice in the North Pole were melting away. There were pictures of polar bears that, no longer able to take thick layers of ice for granted, were being forced to swim hundreds of miles in open ocean in search of it. One consequence of global warming appeared to be increasing rainfalls, and indeed the first years of the century witnessed a number of life-threatening hurricanes and typhoons.

These, as well as earthquakes, heat waves, flooding, and volcanic eruptions, were often considered related to, if not caused by, global climate change.

Although a minority of scientists as well as some politicians doubted that climate change was induced by human behavior—they believed the changes were part of a natural cycle—the fact remains that humans were consuming an increasing amount of energy. Statistics with regard to "primary energy"—including coal, water, natural gas, and electricity—show that between 1980 and 2004 the total consumption of such power sources increased by nearly 50 percent, from 6.5 billion tons (as converted to oil fuel) to 9.7 billion tons. This roughly corresponds to the rate of increase of the world's population. However, many countries were consuming much more energy than they produced. The United States, for instance, in 2004 produced 1,425 million tons of energy but consumed 2,052 million tons. The figures for China were 1,242 million and 1,260 million tons, respectively. These two countries combined were making use of about 36 percent of the world's energy resources, while accounting for 27 percent of its production. Such gaps between consumption and production of energy characterized North America, Europe, and Asia, and the deficits were being made up by importing excess fuels from other regions of the world: South America, Africa, the Middle East, and Oceania. But if these latter areas industrialized and urbanized themselves at the same pace as the others, it was clear that a severe shortage of energy resources would arise. For the time being, importing energy material was the only way the countries of North America, Europe, and most of Asia could satisfy their requirements.[137] The future of nuclear power, which provided about 15 percent of electricity worldwide at this time, began to look less promising in the wake of the disasters that hit the generators at the Fukushima Daiichi plant in northern Japan in March 2011.[138]

The same sort of imbalances between production and consumption characterized food items. Here the United States was one of the few countries that were self-sufficient in basic staples such as corn and wheat and exported what was not consumed at home. The nation accounted for 38.5 percent of the world production of corn and 9.5 percent of wheat in 2006. Many of these items were shipped abroad, the US sale of corn accounting for more than one-half of the total world export of that commodity. Japan and South Korea, neither of which produced much corn, together imported more than a quarter of the entire quantity of this item traded in the world market. In terms of grains as a whole, Japan was only 28 percent self-sufficient, requiring the nation to import the other 72 percent. Japanese fishermen caught 4.4 percent of the global catch of fish in 2005, but the Japanese people ate so much fish that the country had to import about the same amount from other countries. Similar conditions held in Britain, Spain, and the Netherlands. They paid for their food imports by exporting other items, in particular manufactured goods. (In 2004, 20.7 percent of Japanese exports consisted of automobiles, and another 17.3 percent was machine tools. In Britain's export trade, the ratios for these items were 9.8 and 13.3 percent, respectively.)

The smooth functioning of international trade, then, would be of critical importance in ensuring access to the world's food resources. Fortunately, most countries, as members of the World Trade Organization, adhered to the basic principle of free trade, although import restrictions did remain, most of which were within WTO guidelines. But for some poorer countries in Africa and Asia, export trade would not be sufficient to ensure an adequate supply of the basic requirements of life, and for them assistance from other countries as well as international agencies would be of critical importance. The picture would become complicated, however, if the prices of basic foodstuffs such as wheat and rice fluctuated drastically, as they did just before the onset of the global economic crisis in 2007. The overall price of hard red winter wheat, to take just one example, had been declining for over a century, but then in 2005 its price, along with those of corn, rice, soy, and oats, shot up. The cause was not an external shock to the food production system, such as a drought or plague, but a speculative "bubble" in commodities markets.[139] The higher prices led to riots and violence across the developing world, and resulted in hundreds of thousands of additional people being without enough food to eat. The shortages could be felt even in the United States, where some wholesalers restricted customers' purchases of certain items, such as rice.[140]

A key aspect of the global system of production, consumption, trade, and aid was the financial setup in which most currencies were freely converted to each other. Since the 1985 Plaza Accord, which liberalized currency exchanges, global monetary transactions had become more transnational, although most foreign trade and investment activities were still conducted in US dollars and, increasingly, in euros. Each country's foreign exchange still tended to be measured in terms of the US currency. Still, other currencies were gaining the status of semi-international units of transaction. With the participation of China, India, Brazil, and other countries as major players in the arena, there was now a virtual free-for-all with regard to foreign exchange. In theory, anyone anywhere could buy and sell foreign currencies as well as securities, and the speculative game in which people all over the world took part resulted in constantly fluctuating rates of exchange and returns on investment. Central banks in various countries tried from time to time to prop up, or keep down, the value of a currency vis-à-vis that of others. The Chinese authorities, to take perhaps the most conspicuous example, were able to keep the value of renminbi (the key Chinese currency unit) low so as to expand export trade. This policy irritated other countries, especially the United States, which had huge trade deficits with China, but the Chinese were now purchasing bonds and equities in the American markets, and their value would depend in part on a stable rate of exchange between the two currencies. This was an age of finance capitalism, but unlike its manifestation a hundred years earlier, in which a small number of bankers, industrialists, and stockholders virtually monopolized the game, now the entire world, indeed everyone, in theory at least, was involved both as a market and as an investor.

The overheating of the global financial market reached its peak in 2007, when more goods, money, and stocks changed hands on a global scale than ever before. Inevitably, the situation produced a reaction; stock values plummeted, currency values fell, and many people lost their jobs and homes. In one respect the crisis could be summed up in a phrase: "Capitalism without capital." In other words, individuals with little or no savings (which especially was the case in the United States) purchased goods on credit far beyond their means to repay and remortgaged their houses to obtain huge amounts of money in the expectation that the value of their homes would continue to rise and so enable them to pay back the loan. Moreover, a large number of senior citizens borrowed money in order to move into retirement communities, most of which were privately operated and entailed large entry fees as well as monthly payments. Banks, credit companies, stockbrokers, and others promoted all such consumer borrowing in the expectation that they would receive sizable returns. These paper credits were viewed as assets, so their holders could lend even more money. Such a system was not destined to last long, and the inevitable occurred in 2007 when the so-called subprime lending fiasco in the United States punctured the bubble. The banks and mortgage companies that had made risky loans to homebuyers found it increasingly difficult to receive loan repayments and in the process lost huge amounts of their assets. In the meantime, many hedge funds and various schemes for investing in banks, insurance companies, and foreign securities and currencies suddenly found that the easy profits for which they had aimed had evaporated. Many investment companies and financial institutions collapsed. Because all such transactions had been carried on across national borders, the consequences were truly global. Individuals and organizations had been so dependent on currency and stock markets of distant lands that there was a chain reaction linking all parts of the world.

Remarkably, however, unlike the Great Depression of the 1930s, world trade did not shrink substantially, nor did foreign investment. Both categories of transnational activities virtually held their own because demand did not diminish precipitously. For certain commodities, notably automobiles, the worldwide market did shrink, resulting in layoffs for large numbers of workers from assembly lines and auxiliary factories making auto parts. In one extreme case, General Motors, the world's largest auto manufacturer until Toyota outsold GM in 2008, went bankrupt, and the US government had to provide it with billions of dollars of bailout money, in the process becoming its owner. Because the money came from public funds, this meant the taxpayers were now in control of the company. The governments of the United States, Germany, and several other "advanced" countries that belonged to the Organization for Economic Co-operation and Development (OECD) likewise intervened in the banking crisis by providing funds to prevent the collapse of certain financial institutions. Despite these and other examples, there was no drastic reduction in cross-border trade or investment. This was partly because demand for food and energy resources did not abate, and partly because, unlike the United States and Europe, such countries as China and India did not suffer a domestic economic crisis and were able in a way to temporarily take over the role of the United States and Europe in the world economy by continuing to purchase foreign products and to invest in offshore business enterprises. China, in particular, was holding a huge quantity of foreign exchange, in dollars and euros, and by making use of such funds carefully, rather than selling them off, it helped prevent these other currencies from falling precipitously in value, which would have aggravated the global economic crisis by further increasing the public debts of the United States and European countries.

The global economic crisis of the early twenty-first century was far more transnational in scope than the Great Depression of the early 1930s, but mercifully, responses to the crisis were also more coordinated across national boundaries. That China, which together with Taiwan and Hong Kong was fast becoming the second wealthiest nation (in terms of gross national product) behind the United States, was in a position to contribute significantly to alleviating the crisis was symbolic of the transnational nature of global economic affairs. The growing importance of China as well as of India, Russia, and Brazil—they were collectively known as BRICs—and many other countries was nowhere more graphically revealed than in the international meetings held in the wake of the financial meltdown of 2009, in which the twenty wealthiest countries participated. Known as the G-20 meetings, the countries present accounted for 90 percent of the world's total income. In contrast to the international monetary crisis of the 1970s that resulted in the institution of G-7 gatherings, which later became G-8 with the addition of Russia, there was recognition that these richest seven or eight would no longer be able to cope with global economic questions without the participation of others that represented not only huge markets but also agricultural, mineral, and factory production. The G-20 gathering of September 2009 adopted common agendas calling for mutual consultation and surveillance, lest some countries should consume or save excessively, and to ensure that banks and investment funds should not again indulge in undisciplined practices at the expense of ordinary citizens. The interconnectedness of the world's farms, factories, and finances and the willingness of their top producers and consumers to discuss their common problems were the ultimate causes of the economic recovery that began in late 2009 and was confirmed by the end of 2010.

In some such way, in sharp contrast to the 1930s when the economic crisis splintered the world, deglobalizing it as it were, the disarray at the beginning of the twenty-first century only confirmed the interconnectedness of the world. Transnational ties and networks were not disrupted but were confirmed and strengthened. For example, Internet use continued to expand during the crisis of 2008–2010, and some of the major companies in the world sought to pool their resources across borders so as to emerge as transnational giants. This was the path chosen by two automobile manufacturers, Volkswagen of Germany and Suzuki of Japan, toward the end of 2009—to join together to share their capital, technology, and market strategies. Their smaller vehicles had already dominated some of the key markets in the world, such as China, India, and Africa, so that their combined market share would be quite formidable. Likewise, Japan Airlines, suffering from huge deficits, entered into an alliance with American Airlines, which provided the Japanese airline with fresh capital in the hope that combined they would have a larger share of the increasingly lucrative air travel market in the Asia Pacific region. The number of international travelers and exchange students also did not significantly abate. People continued to cross borders. To be sure, millions did so in search of job opportunities; despite restrictive measures instituted by some countries to protect domestic laborers, migrants kept on coming, as did smugglers of illicit drugs. All this attested to the unchanging relevance of transnational movements in the early twenty-first century.

Toward a Transnational Partnership

Would there in time emerge a solid transnational world? It is not a historian's task to predict the future, but we might consider two themes that might contribute to our understanding of the first years of the twenty-first century in the context of history of the world since the Second World War. First is the development of a Pacific community and possibly other regional communities, and the second is what may be termed the "Obama phenomenon" that transcended US politics and reflected the increasingly relevant theme of "hybridity." These examples seem to point to the further growth of transnational linkages and ideas.

Trade, financial, and other ties continued to bring East Asia, Southeast Asia, South Asia, the Antipodes (Australia and New Zealand), the Pacific islands, and North and South America closer together. In trade, East Asia was serving as a key link to the rest of the world. US trade with China more than doubled between 2000 and 2004, and by 2004 China already accounted for 6.9 percent of the total volume of world exports. Only Germany (10.6 percent) and the United States (12.7 percent) exceeded China's volume. Other Asian countries, in particular Japan and South Korea, continued to be among the top exporting countries in the world. A striking development at the beginning of the century was that

East Asian countries tended to trade with one another quite intensively. Nearly one-half of Japan's exports in 2003 went to other Asian countries, as did 37 percent of China's. The figures for imports from Asia were 58.0 percent for Japan and 42.1 percent for China. As is evidenced in such statistics, Asia was growing as a huge trading zone in which the countries in the region were selling and buying more and more quantities of goods. Even in the absence of a formal regional community, East Asia was clearly emerging as one.

Financial ties between East Asia and Southeast Asia were strengthened after the foreign exchange crisis of the late 1990s, when Thailand, Indonesia, South Korea, and other countries in Asia saw the value of their currencies drop precipitously against the dollar, which caused havoc in their monetary and banking systems and triggered unemployment and falling stock market prices. Neither the IMF nor the United States did much to help, because they assumed, following the "Washington consensus," that the market mechanism would in time rectify the situation. Although it was undoubtedly true that the globalization of foreign exchange since the 1980s had brought about profound fluctuations in the values of national currencies, the Washington consensus in effect adopted a hands-off policy even as some Asian currencies lost as much as 80 percent of their value in terms of the dollar. That was entirely unacceptable to the affected nations, and they took steps to do something in the region. At a meeting of ASEAN held in December 1997, the leaders of China, Japan, and South Korea were invited, and what emerged as ASEAN + 3 proved a viable framework for undertaking collective regional action.[141] The group continued to meet annually into the new century and became a solid basis for working toward creating an Asian regional community. In the context of the 1997 crisis, Japan initially made available a temporary loan of $30 billion, and subsequently ASEAN + 3 established a system of "currency swaps," whereby a country whose currency is experiencing exchange difficulties would be provided with an emergency infusion of other currencies.

In time these efforts by ASEAN and East Asian countries came to be expanded to other spheres, such as the environment and climate change, cultural exchange, economic development, and even political and military security. Additional arrangements served to strengthen such regional ties. The most successful were the free trade agreements, or FTA, which were negotiated with increasing frequency after 2000: for instance, between Singapore and New Zealand,

ASEAN and China, Thailand and India, Singapore and South Korea, Japan and Malaysia, and Thailand and Australia. Such agreements encouraged intraregional trade to such an extent that in 2008 it was reported that the volume of trade among FTA signatories accounted for nearly 50 percent of the total regional trade.

The inclusion of Australia, New Zealand, and India in the FTA arrangements suggests that the definition of "Asia" in the context of regional development was becoming broader. Trade agreements, at least, were now embracing most countries from India to New Zealand, a wide swath embracing twenty or more countries. The "Asian" regional community that was emerging was really an "Asian and Pacific" community. The United States was from the beginning a member of the Asia-Pacific Economic Cooperation (APEC), a regional setting established in 1989 for economic cooperation and assistance. In time other American nations such as Mexico and Peru joined APEC, so that the geographical boundaries of the regional organizations remained loose. These various and overlapping networks indicated that an Asian regional community, should it become a reality, would not be an exclusionary entity. It should also be noted that China, Japan, and South Korea invested heavily in resource-rich but economically less developed areas of the world, especially South America and Africa. In sub-Saharan Africa, the Chinese presence, both diplomatic and economic, was becoming nearly ubiquitous. China's position in Africa, which continued to grow during these years, held advantages over the Western nations' in that its relations with the continent were largely untainted by the historical memory of colonial exploitation and also because Beijing was more willing than the United States or European countries to expand trade relations with countries that had been accused of human rights violations, including Sudan.

There was little doubt that by the first decade of the twenty-first century there had in fact emerged an Asian-Pacific economic community. China (including Hong Kong), Taiwan, Japan, South Korea, and the principal ASEAN countries accounted for over 20 percent of the total world trade in 2005. The EU's share was 29 percent, and that of the United States 28 percent. Together, these three economic centers were carrying on nearly four-fifths of all international transactions in goods. Whether such a community of trade would in time develop a common currency, comparable to the euro (adopted in 1999) remained to be seen. As of 2010, most Asian countries were still using the US dollar as the currency of exchange. Only Japan was carrying out as much as 20 percent of its transactions in nondollar currencies. All Asian countries, as well as most of the rest of the world, held on to their dollar reserves and had a stake in the stability of the dollar.

The idea of a Trans-Pacific Partnership perfectly fitted into these ongoing developments. In view of the close economic ties among the countries in or bordering on the Pacific, it seemed to make sense to establish a "partnership" that would bind them even closer together, ultimately looking forward to something akin to the European Union. That would entail not just freer trade among the member countries but also the opening of borders to all their people, whether as workers, tourists, or students. That would truly be a colossal undertaking, bringing about a Pacific century for the first time in history. Whether the twenty-first century would be such a century, of course, was far from clear, but the very idea of a Trans-Pacific Partnership indicated that the region had come a long way from the first half of the twentieth century when the Pacific Ocean had been anything but "pacific."

It would, of course, take much time and effort for Pacific countries to establish a solid political and cultural basis for their partnership. The first step in that direction might well be to come to a shared understanding of the past, a task that had proven to be extremely difficult even among the countries of East Asia. Unlike Germany and France, Japan and China still had not succeeded in overcoming the past. Neither had Japan and Korea, its former colony, reached sufficiently common understanding of that unfortunate experience. The "history problem," as it was called, continued to prevent the coming closer together of the three countries politically and psychologically, despite their undoubted economic interdependence. Although teachers and scholars from the three countries had started seeking each other out to start a cooperative project to write books together, such efforts were often frustrated by new, undesirable developments such as the publication of a history textbook in Japan in 2001 written by several nationalistic authors that was mono-nationalistic and viewed the past almost entirely from their own country's perspective. The publication of the textbook, which won approval by the Ministry of Education, immediately provoked a negative response in China and Korea, inflaming their nationalism. Fortunately, transnationally minded historians were also becoming more visible by the turn of the century and were willing to meet together to do something about these unfortunate developments. They held annual gatherings in Beijing, Tokyo, and Seoul, and in 2005 one such group published a jointly authored book that discussed the modern history of East Asia, focusing on the period since the nineteenth century. The writers noted in their preface that they wrote the book in order to learn from the past and to prepare for a future East Asia that, they hoped, would be characterized by peace, democracy, and human rights. The book did not hesitate to castigate Japan for its past subjugation of the Korean people and its aggression against the Chinese, but it also spoke of the coming together of the people of the three countries, especially of the younger generations, to promote their mutual understanding. The book was deficient in not mentioning serious blemishes in China under Communist rule, such as the disastrous Great Leap Forward or the Cultural Revolution, both of which caused millions of people to die from starvation and dislocation. Nevertheless, here was an important indication that beginnings were being made to develop a cooperative approach to the study of East Asian history.

Such modest developments might in time help construct a regional community of shared memory analogous to that of the European Union and reinforce the already solid economic networks. Transnational encounters, in other words, were becoming much more than incidental to economic transactions, and it could be expected that in time there would develop some transnational consciousness among Chinese, Koreans, and Japanese if enough of them overcame their mononationalistic proclivities.

An interesting question in this connection was whether such modest beginnings might be followed by similar efforts in other parts of Asia and the Pacific. Historically and culturally, much of Southeast Asia and South Asia, not to mention the Antipodes and the American continents, were closer to Europe than to Asia. As noted earlier, however, serious efforts were being made in Australia, Canada, and the United States to comprehend their national histories in the context of the interactions and interconnections with other countries in the wider Pacific. Asian migrations to and populations in these countries, as well as the white majorities' prejudices against them, were now seen as having been an integral part of their respective developments.[142] All these countries, in such a perspective, shared a past. The same would be true of the countries in East, Southeast, and South Asia, where the mingling of diverse populations had been a central historical fact. As best exemplified in the city-state of Singapore, the coming together of different races and ethnicities had created, and was creating, "hybrid" communities, and the rather belated awareness of this past could be expected in time to generate a sense of shared memory.

A big question in the early twenty-first century was whether other regions of the world, such as Africa, the Middle East, and South America, would also succeed in constructing regional communities. All independent countries of Africa, numbering more than forty, established an African Union in 2004, but it failed to move either in the direction of an economic or cultural community. Many countries suffered from continuing civil strife, and hundreds of thousands fled the continent for jobs and opportunities in Europe. Nevertheless, there were some glimpses of hope. South Africa, as well as the rest of the continent, celebrated the successful hosting of the 2010 World Cup. And more effective medical treatments and preventive technologies for the scourges of malaria and HIV appeared within reach. While some areas of Central Africa seemed mired in the legacy of genocidal conflict, despotism, economic stagnation, corruption, and warfare, war-torn regions of Western Africa made strides toward bringing war criminals to justice, using the International Criminal Court—the first sentencing of an African alleged war criminal took place in early 2012—and healing the wounds of civil conflict. In the Middle East, the fact that most countries in the area are Islamic did not prevent factious and fraternal struggles from undermining a sense of order and community. It may well be, as the "Arab spring" of 2011 indicated, that democratization is a key, if not the only, requirement for developing some coherent and cohesive order, whether within nations or among them. Certainly, the downfall of dictatorial regimes and the emergence of more open, democratic societies in several Islamic countries of the Middle East and North Africa suggested that whatever regional community emerges will ultimately have to hinge on the will of the people. This is not surprising in view of the fact that regional communities are by definition transnational and that the search for freedom and human rights is among the most crucial of transnational ideals.

Latin America, in the meantime, appeared increasingly confident of its future greatness. Already in 2000, Brazil was emerging as a potential economic power, and all of South America cheered when, in 2009, the International Olympic Committee picked Rio de Janeiro as the site of the 2016 summer games. Sharing much of their culture, including the common language of Spanish (save for Brazil), people in South America had always viewed their continent in regional terms, although they had not been free from nationalistic rivalries and even wars. What the twenty-first century promised was the rise of the region in the global economic and political picture. Whereas in 2000 the world's production and trade appeared to be dominated by Europe, North America, and East Asia, it could be expected that by the 2020s Latin America would come to account for a substantial portion of the world's wealth and possibly share with other regions of the globe the task of building a transnational partnership.

The Obama Moment

No single individual better seemed to exemplify the transnational trends of world history, as well as the transnational hopes of humankind, at the beginning of the twenty-first century than Barack Obama, the forty-fourth president of the United States. His personal background, education, ideas about his country and about the world, and accomplishments (as well as failed attempts) while in office, all bespoke a conjunction of forces that were shaping the contemporary world.

Obama's background was as transnational as one could get. Like an increasing proportion of the world's people, he was a child of a racially mixed marriage, a "hybrid" at a time when "hybridity" was clearly on the ascendance in an interconnected globe in which people of diverse backgrounds not only encountered one another but also began to blend, to amalgamate. Obama was only forty-seven years old when he became president, a product of the post-1960s world. His father was a student from Kenya at the University of Hawaii. He met an American student whose maternal forebears came from Ireland. They married, had one son (Barack), and then divorced. Barack's father went back to Kenya, and Barack moved with his mother to Indonesia, where he attended high school, learning the language. He returned to Hawaii a few years afterward, went to Punahou School, a multiracial academy in Honolulu, then entered Occidental College in California. After a year he transferred to Columbia University, then went to Chicago as a community organizer and married a graduate of Princeton University. Obama then decided to seek a law degree, went to Harvard, and became editor of its *Law Review*. Returning to Chicago, he taught law at the University of Chicago Law School but decided to enter politics and was elected to the Illinois state senate. His racially mixed parents, schooling abroad, education at elite universities, and service to the local community caught in the throes of a globalizing economy all contributed to making Obama a transnational person. That the United States should produce such an individual was no accident, given the nation's transnational character. By the same token his emergence as a rising star in national politics indicated where the source of the nation's power and influence lay. (It also needs to be mentioned that the opposition to Obama in the United States made much of his allegedly "foreign" birth as a reason for questioning his qualifications, indicating the still considerable mono-nationalistic, even racist, resistance to transnationalism.)

Obama's moment in national politics came in 2004, when he ran for a seat in the US Senate and was elected. His keynote speech at the Democratic Party Convention, held in Boston, catapulted him to fame, but it contained much more than the line that became famous: "We are not a black nation or a white nation; we are a United States of America." In the rest of the speech, he referred to world conditions, criticized the Republican administration for waging a reckless war in Iraq and ignoring international opinion, and eloquently argued for a world order of peace, justice, and equality. He was a passionate spokesman for justice in the local community and in the nation, but he was not mono-national. He believed that national and international aspirations and values were interchangeable as well as interdependent. The cause of constructive transnationalism could not have had a more powerful spokesman.

That would explain why the world waited breathlessly for the outcome of the 2008 presidential election in the United States. Viewed from elsewhere, the nation appeared split into two, between those remaining mono-national, believing the United States should pursue its affairs unilaterally, and those who were eager to maintain and strengthen ties with the rest of the world. Even while opinion within the United States was divided between supporters of Obama and supporters of his Republican opponent, Senator John McCain—who, incidentally, was born outside the United States, in the Panama Canal Zone—elsewhere Obama's popularity was entirely clear. When he visited Berlin in May and spoke at the Victory Column, he had an enthusiastic audience of three hundred thousand. Obama's speech was unabashedly internationalist. He pictured himself as a citizen

Residents of Kisumu, Kenya, celebrate Barack Obama's victory in the US presidential election, November 2008, an example of a nation's politics transcending its borders. (AFP/Getty Images)

of the world, a potential leader of the whole of humanity, and spoke of the future of humankind in a way no politician anywhere had done. He exemplified the transnational spirit that accepted the simple truth that the Earth was to be shared by and preserved for all people, that world peace and prosperity were within their reach if they cooperated in the pursuit of their shared objectives.

World public opinion, which had appeared discouraged and disillusioned by the United States during the first years of the century, was virtually united in expressing joy at Obama's election in November. From Britain to Germany, Kenya to India, Australia to Japan, there were spontaneous gatherings of people expressing their elation, which was not only at Obama personally but also at an America that had dared to choose a person of his background to the highest office, in all likelihood the most important position in the world. He would be a world leader as well as the president of the United States, and almost overnight international opinion of the nation reversed itself. People elsewhere once again saw the United States as humanity's hope, as a land of justice and freedom. There was a transnational involvement in the celebration of a transnational nation and of a transnational leader. The Obama moment was literally everyone's moment worldwide.

This is not the place to record in detail or to evaluate Barack Obama's presidency, but there seems little doubt that he envisaged himself as a powerful spokesman for transnationalism because he himself was a transnational being. Although as the nation's leader he frequently spoke the language of national interests and domestic concerns, when given an opportunity he reiterated his commitment to a peaceful, interdependent, diverse world. The Obama administration, for instance, stressed the importance of nonmilitary measures—economic, social, cultural—that would build bridges to Iran, North Korea, and even to some terrorists so that they might become more receptive to working together across borders in pursuit of common interests. Specifically, the Obama administration encouraged its citizens as well as those of other nations to organize aid missions so as to promote economic programs in Iraq, Afghanistan, and elsewhere where high rates of unemployment remained, providing an opportunity for terrorists to recruit additional members. Humanitarian and educational groups responded by expanding their activities in those countries. Reconstruction of educational institutions was of particularly critical importance, especially with regard to the education of children and women. Humanitarian organizations stepped up their efforts to ensure the rights of women, ethnic minorities, and political dissidents. These were extremely sensitive tasks, as authoritarian regimes were determined to control education and the press, but the Obama administration continued to insist on the right of everyone to all possible educational and economic opportunities and for this reason to push vigorously for unrestricted access to the Internet throughout the world.

It was because of the global community's awareness that President Obama, even as he adopted a military strategy and a conventional international approach to cope with some issues, had something much more ambitious and transnational in mind that the Nobel Peace Prize Committee in Norway decided to award him the Nobel Peace Prize in 2009. The award was more in recognition of his aspirations than his achievements. But it was in line with the spirit of the Peace Prize that had been given to such other organizations as Amnesty International, Doctors Without Borders, and the American Friends Service Committee, all of which had been private associations of individuals devoted to building transnational bridges and to reaching out to all people, irrespective of national policies or strategies.

Nowhere did Obama's transnational leadership manifest itself more clearly than in his promotion of a joint strategy toward the problem of climate change. Whereas his predecessor had been lukewarm, if not hostile, to the idea of any international agreement to control carbon dioxide and other chemicals so as to reduce global warming, Obama was eager to take the initiative to prompt all nations, including his own, to take vigorous steps in that direction. He personally attended the Copenhagen conference on climate change in December 2009 and was instrumental in having the participants adopt a specific program for reversing global warming. His subsequent policy on the climate issue tended to disappoint those who thought he should have vigorously pushed what he described as an agenda for whole humanity, not just for individual nations. There is little doubt, though, that if the disastrous path toward further global warming would ever come to be checked, however partially, the achievement would be another exemplification of the transnational spirit of the age.

Perhaps the deepest meaning of Obama's presidency was that it demonstrated the possibility that transnationalism could be promoted in a world still consisting of nations. Indeed, major events that shook the world in the year 2011 indicated that the transnational framework was the only way in which to understand contemporary history. Throughout the year, citizens in North Africa and the Middle East engaged in movements to democratize their countries' political institutions. Long suppressed by oligarchs and dictators, private individuals and organizations sensed that they would have the support of the international community if they demanded more rights and freedoms. Tyrannies fell in some countries, such as Tunisia, Egypt, and Libya, but remained obdurate in others, notably Syria, but these developments were not viewed as separate national phenomena but as part of a worldwide development. The "Arab spring," as they were collectively called, was not entirely nation-specific. The world community, through the UN and other organizations, expressed their support. Some nations, it is true, remained indifferent, at least on the surface. Countries such as Russia and China opposed any kind of intervention in the affairs of those countries in turmoil and maintained tight control over what happened within their own borders. But a nation-by-nation response was anachronistic. Even the decision by some NATO countries as well as the United States to send military aircraft to help pro-democracy rebels was a conventional, international approach. Private organizations that became involved in supporting and helping the rebels were likely to be more productive of results simply because they were transnational, not separate national, efforts.

The meaning of transnational involvement also became abundantly clear during the series of crises that hit Japan in 2011: the earthquake, tsunami, and nuclear power failures. The international community's response was as quick as it was extensive. Individuals and organizations in more than one hundred countries expressed their sympathy and sent their support to the victims of the natural disasters, and various governments dispatched military personnel, doctors, and rescue workers to the scenes of devastation. When the nuclear power plants failed and began their meltdown, spreading nuclear radioactive materials into the air, land, and waters (including the Pacific Ocean), not only the International Atomic Energy Agency but also leaders of France, Germany, the United States, China, South Korea, and many other countries visited Japan to offer advice and to share information. Because all these countries made use of nuclear energy, the Japanese fiasco was seen as a transnational crisis that could be coped with only through cross-border cooperation.

If nothing else, the democracy movements in the Middle East and the nuclear meltdown in Japan demonstrated that there was really only one, interconnected world. All countries, people, religions, and cultures were interconnected. The transnationalization of humankind was in clear evidence, a product of all the forces that had moved history after the Second World War. Separate national interests remained, but they had to be placed in the context of transnational, human interests. It would be the task of all people, leaders as well as citizens, scholars as well as others, to identify with the direction of history, to combat the still influential mono-nationalistic thinking, and to bequeath a precious gift to the generations who would inherit the Earth and be entrusted with the task of the world's further transnationalization.

Notes

Introduction

1. Bertrand Russell, *Autobiography: The Middle Years, 1914–1944* (Boston: Little, Brown, 1967), 326.

1. States and the Changing Equations of Power

1. For an earlier German version of the balance following World War II, see my "Weltpolitische Zäsur 1945: Der Zweite Weltkrieg und der Untergang des alten Europa," in *Nicht nur Hitlers Krieg: Der Zweite Weltkrieg und die Deutschen,* ed. Christoph Klessmann (Düsseldorf: Droste, 1989), 99–112.
2. See Manfred Hildermeier, *Geschichte der Sowjetunion, 1917–1991: Entstehung und Niedergang des ersten sozialistischen Staates* (Munich: Beck, 1998), 615–616.
3. See the compilation in Walter Lipgens, *A History of European Integration,* vol. 1, *1945–1947* (Oxford: Clarendon Press, 1982), 7–9.
4. Alan S. Milward, "Europe and the Marshall Plan: 50 Years On," in *The Marshall Plan Today: Model and Metaphor,* ed. John Agnew and J. Nicholas Entrikin (London: Routledge, 2004), 58–81.
5. Quoted in Alexeij M. Filitov, "Problems of Post-War Construction in Soviet Foreign Policy Conceptions during World War II," in *The Soviet Union and Europe in the Cold War, 1943–53,* ed. Francesca Gori and Silvio Pons (New York: St. Martin's Press, 1996), 3–22, quotation at 13.
6. *SSSR i germanskij vopros, 1941–1949,* vol. 1, no. 22, June 1941–May 8, 1945 (Moscow, 1996): 333–360.
7. Georgy Dimitroff to the Politburo of the Czech Communist Party, December 6, 1944, as quoted by Karel Kaplan, *Der kurze Marsch: Kommunistische Machtübernahme in der Tschechoslowakei, 1945–1948* (Munich: R. Oldenbourg, 1981), 15.
8. Note by Wilhelm Pieck on German Communist Party leaders' discussions with Stalin, April 6, 1945, in *Wilhelm Pieck: Aufzeichnungen zur Deutschlandpolitik, 1945–1953,* ed. Rolf Badstübner and Wilfried Loth (Berlin: Akademie, 1994), 50–53.
9. "Declaration on Liberated Europe," in *Foreign Relations of the United States (FRUS), 1945: The Conferences of Malta and Yalta* (Washington, DC: US Department of State, 1955), 971–972.
10. Published in Ellen Clayton-Garwood, *Will Clayton: A Short Biography* (Austin: University of Texas Press, 1958), 115–118.
11. *FRUS, 1947,* 2:815–817.
12. Discussion with Semyonov, July 9, 1949. In Badstübner and Loth, *Wilhelm Pieck,* 287–291.
13. NSC 48/1 and 48/2, in *Containment: Documents on American Policy and Strategy, 1945–1950,* ed. Thomas H. Etzold and John L. Gaddis (New York: Columbia University Press, 1978), 253, 256–259, 273–275.

14. Politburo meeting on September 5, 1950, as recorded by Nikita S. Khrushchev, "Koreiska voina," *Ogonek,* no. 1 (1991): 27–28.

15. Chairman of the Joint Chiefs of Staff Omar Bradley at a congressional hearing, *Joint Chiefs of Staff,* 3:67.

16. Resolution of the Soviet Council of Ministers, March 19, 1953, quoted in Kathryn Weathersby, "New Russian Documents on the Korean War," *CWIHP Bulletin,* nos. 6/7 (Winter 1995–1996): 30–84, quotation at 80–82.

17. Preamble to the Basic Law of the Federal Republic of Germany, promulgated on May 23, 1949.

18. Telegram from Stalin on the occasion of the founding of the GDR, October 13, 1949, in *DDR: Dokumente zur Geschichte der Deutschen Demokratischen Republik, 1945–1985,* ed. Hermann Weber (Munich: Deutscher Taschenbuch-Verlag, 1986), 163–164.

19. *FRUS,* 1950, 1:234–292.

20. Memorandum of August 29, 1950; quoted in Klaus von Schubert, ed., *Sicherheitspolitik der Bundesrepublik Deutschland: Dokumentation, 1945–1977,* pt. 1 (Bonn: Verlag Wissenschaft und Politik, 1977), 79–85.

21. French government directive of October 24, 1950, *Journal officiel de la République française* (October 25, 1950): 7118–7119.

22. Bakulin to Semyonov, February 18, 1952, quoted in Wilfried Loth, *Die Sowjetunion und die deutsche Frage* (Göttingen: Vandenhoeck & Ruprecht, 2007), 143.

23. There is scant evidence to corroborate the claim still peddled by some commentators that the offer made in the "Stalin Note" was not meant seriously; see Wilfried Loth, "The German Question from Stalin to Khrushchev: The Meaning of New Documents," *Cold War History* 10, no. 2 (2010): 229–245.

24. Malenkov to the SED leadership, June 2, 1953, quoted in Loth, *Die Sowjetunion,* 302.

25. Memo by Dixon, May 19, 1953, quoted in Josef Foschepoth, "Churchill, Adenauer und die Neutralisierung Deutschlands," *Deutschland-Archiv* 17 (1984): 1286–1301, quotation at 1292.

26. *Dokumente zur Deutschlandpolitik,* vol. 3.1 (Frankfurt am Main: Metzner, 1955), 76–80.

27. *Europa-Archiv* 10 (1955): 8121.

28. *Voprosi istorii* 8–9 (1992): 76.

29. *FRUS,* 1955–1957, 25:317–318.

30. Clarifying note in a briefing to the French ambassador in London, quoted in René Massigli, *Une comédie des erreurs, 1943–1956* (Paris: Plon, 1978), 157.

31. Erhard on March 15, 1957, to members of the US press corps, quoted in Karl Kaiser, *EWG und Freihandelszone* (Leiden: A. W. Sythoff, 1963), 136.

32. Text of the treaty, in *Europa-Archiv* 27 (1963): D84–86.

33. *Europa-Archiv* 34 (1970): D44.

34. Jean Monnet, *Erinnerungen eines Europäers* (Munich: Deutscher Taschenbuch-Verlag, 1980), 651.

35. Quoted in Michael R. Beschloss, *Powergame: Kennedy und Chruschtschow—Die Krisenjahre, 1960–1963* (Düsseldorf: Econ 1991), 589.

36. Charles de Gaulle, *Memoiren der Hoffnung: Die Wiedergeburt, 1958–1962* (Vienna: Fritz Molden, 1971), 275.

37. *Dokumente zur Deutschlandpolitik*, 5th ser., vol. 1.1 (Frankfurt am Main: Metzner, 1984), 1047–1054.

38. *Pravda,* September 26, 1968.

39. According to the formulation in his inaugural speech of January 20, 1969.

40. Quoted in Heinrich von Siegler, ed., *Dokumentation zur Deutschlandfrage*, vol. 5 (Bonn: Siegler, 1970), 713–717.

41. Text quoted in *Aussenpolitik der Bundesrepublik Deutschland: Dokumente von 1949 bis 1994* (Bonn: AA, 1995), 337–338.

42. Ibid., 370–374.

43. Ibid., 352–354.

44. Text of the Helsinki Final Act, in *Europa-Archiv* 30 (1975): D437–484.

45. Anatoly Dobrynin, *In Confidence: Moscow's Ambassador to America's Six Cold War Presidents (1962–1986)* (New York: Times Books, 1995), 417.

46. Ibid., 431.

47. Data from Bela Balassa, *Economic Policies in the Pacific Area Developing Countries* (London: Macmillan, 1991), 25.

48. Fiona Venn, *Oil Diplomacy in the Twentieth Century* (London: Macmillan, 1986), 11.

49. Quoted in Victor Israelyan, *Inside the Kremlin during the Yom Kippur War* (University Park: Pennsylvania State University Press, 1995), 169–170.

50. Statistical data from Edward R. Fried and Charles L. Shultze, *Higher Oil Prices and the World Economy: The Adjustment Problem* (Washington, DC: Brookings Institution, 1975).

51. Quoted in Harold James, *Rambouillet, 15. November 1975: Die Globalisierung der Wirtschaft* (Munich: Deutscher Taschenbuch Verlag, 1997), 11.

52. For an analysis of the strategic arms race in the latter half of the 1970s, see Wilfried Loth, *Overcoming the Cold War: A History of Détente, 1950-1991* (Basingstoke, UK: Palgrave, 2002), 143–145, 150–151.

53. Interview on October 16, 1981. In *Weekly Compilation of Presidential Documents*, vol. 17 (October 26, 1981), 1160–1161.

54. Speech given on March 8, 1983. In *Weekly Compilation of Presidential Documents*, vol. 19 (March 14, 1983), 369.

55. Interview on October 16, 1981. In *Weekly Compilation of Presidential Documents*, vol. 17 (October 26, 1981), 1160–1161.

56. Ernst-Otto Czempiel, *Machtprobe: Die USA und die Sowjetunion in den achtziger Jahren* (Munich: Beck, 1989), 153.

57. Minutes of the Politburo meeting on December 10, 1981; excerpts published in *CWIHP-Bulletin*, no. 5 (Spring 1995): 121, 134–137.

58. Memo to the leaders of the Warsaw Pact countries, December 1 or 2, 1983, quoted in Vladislav M. Zubok, *A Failed Empire: The Soviet Union in the Cold War from Stalin to Gorbachev* (Chapel Hill: University of North Carolina Press, 2007), 275.

59. Interview in the *Washington Post,* October 17, 1984.

60. Quoted in Raymond L. Garthoff, *The Great Transition: American-Soviet Relations and the End of the Cold War* (Washington, DC: Brookings Institution, 1994), 159–160, 163–164.

61. In the Politburo meeting on March 11, 1985, quoted in David Remnick, *Lenin's Tomb: The Last Days of the Soviet Empire* (New York: Random House, 1993), 520.

62. Dobrynin, *In Confidence*, 597.

63. *Wsesojusnaja konferenzija Kommunistitscheskoi partii Sowjetskogo sojusa: Stenografitscheski otschet* (Moscow, 1988), 42–43.

64. Gorbachev made this admission at a press conference in Milan on December 1, 1989. Quoted in Rafael Biermann, *Zwischen Kreml und Kanzleramt: Wie Moskau mit der deutschen Einheit rang* (Paderborn: Schöningh, 1997), 344.

65. Michail Gorbachev, *Erinnerungen* (Berlin: Siedler, 1995), 723.

66. *Europa-Archiv* 11 (1990): S. D283.

67. Article J.7 of the Maastricht Treaty.

68. Constitutional Treaty, Article I-40.

69. Statistics from David Reynolds, *One World Divisible: A Global History since 1945* (London: Allen Lane, 2000), 645.

70. Basic texts on reciprocal relations, cooperation, and security between NATO and the Russian Federation, at www.nato.int/docu/basictxt/grndakt.htm.

71. The term was first coined in Tilman Altenburg and Julia Leininger, "Global Shifts Caused by the Rise of Anchor Countries," in *Zeitschrift für Wirtschaftsgeographie* 52 (2008): 4–19.

72. World Bank, *China 2020: Development Challenges in the New Century* (Washington, DC: World Bank, 1997), 3.

73. Ibid., 6.

74. For a comparatively realistic assessment of current trends, see Fareed Zakaria, *The Post-American World* (London: Allen Lane, 2008).

2. Opening Doors in the World Economy

1. Tom Verducci, "Global Warming," *Sports Illustrated,* March 6, 2006, 56. See also Robert Whiting, *The Meaning of Ichiro: The New Wave from Japan and the Transformation of Our National Pastime* (New York: Grand Central, 2004), 96–110; Arturo J. Marcano Guevara and David P. Fidler, *Stealing Lives: The Globalization of Baseball and the Tragic Story of Alexis Quiroz* (Bloomington: Indiana University Press, 2002).

2. Reinhold Wagnleitner, "The Empire of the Fun, or Talkin' Soviet Blues: The Sound of Freedom and U.S. Cultural Hegemony in Europe," *Diplomatic History* 23 (Summer 1999): 507.

3. Randall B. Woods, *A Changing of the Guard: Anglo-American Relations, 1941–1946* (Chapel Hill: University of North Carolina Press, 1990), 2–61.

4. Robert M. Hathaway, "1933–1945: Economic Diplomacy in a Time of Crisis" in *Economics and World Power: An Assessment of American Diplomacy Since 1789*, ed. William H. Becker and Samuel F. Wells Jr. (New York: Columbia University Press, 1984), 314–322.

5. Robert A. Pollard and Samuel F. Wells Jr., "1945–1960: The Era of American Economic Hegemony," in Becker and Wells, *Economics and World Power*, 337.

6. Woods, *Changing of the Guard*, 145. See also Robert Pollard, *Economic Security and the Origins of the Cold War, 1945–1950* (New York: Columbia University Press, 1985), 13–17.

7. Warren F. Kimball, *The Juggler: Franklin Roosevelt as Wartime Statesman* (Princeton, NJ: Princeton University Press, 1991), 44–45.

8. Thomas W. Zeiler, *Free Trade, Free World: The Advent of GATT* (Chapel Hill: University of North Carolina Press, 1999), 151, also 2–19, 34, 42–50, 128, 139–146.

9. Ibid., 131–134.

10. Ibid., 109.

11. Ibid., 109–110.

12. Alfred E. Eckes Jr., *Opening America's Market: U.S. Foreign Trade Policy since 1776* (Chapel Hill: University of North Carolina Press, 1995).

13. Alfred E. Eckes Jr. and Thomas W. Zeiler, *Globalization and the American Century* (New York: Cambridge University Press, 2003), 127–132.

14. Pollard, *Economic Security*, 73–81; Zeiler, *Free Trade, Free World*, 177.

15. Judith Goldstein, "Creating the GATT Rules: Politics, Institutions, and American Policy" in *Multilateralism Matters: The Theory and Praxis of an Institutional Form,* ed. John Gerard Ruggie (New York: Columbia University Press, 1993), 160–164, 202–203, 213, 219, 225.

16. Paul Steege, *Black Market, Cold War: Everyday Life in Berlin, 1946–1949* (Cambridge: Cambridge University Press, 2007), 106–126.

17. Pollard, *Economic Security*, 131, 158–159; Pollard and Wells, "1945–1960," 345–346.

18. Alan S. Milward, *The Reconstruction of Western Europe, 1945–1951* (Berkeley: University of California Press, 1984), 2–3.

19. Michael J. Hogan, *The Marshall Plan: America, Britain, and the Reconstruction of Western Europe, 1947–1952* (New York: Cambridge University Press, 1987), 443–445.

20. Melvyn P. Leffler, *A Preponderance of Power: National Security, the Truman Administration, and the Cold War* (Stanford, CA: Stanford University Press, 1992), 188–192.

21. Diane Kunz, *Butter and Guns: America's Cold War Economic Diplomacy* (New York: Free Press, 1997), 35.

22. Hogan, *The Marshall Plan*, 138–149.

23. Milward, *Reconstruction of Western Europe*, 332–333, 419–420, 456–461.

24. Victoria de Grazia, *Irresistible Empire: America's Advance through Twentieth-Century Europe* (Cambridge, MA: Harvard University Press, 2005), 348, also 340–347.

25. Pollard, *Economic Security*, 162–163.

26. Jeffrey A. Engel, *The Cold War at 30,000 Feet: The Anglo-American Fight for Aviation Supremacy* (Cambridge, MA: Harvard University Press, 2007), 53–88.

27. Ian Jackson, *The Economic Cold War: America, Britain, and East-West Trade, 1948–63* (Houndsmill, UK: Palgrave, 2001), 68, also 26–72.

28. Steege, *Black Market, Cold War*, 158–187.

29. Robert Bideleux and Ian Jeffries, *A History of Eastern Europe: Crisis and Change*, 2nd ed. (London: Routledge, 2007), 480.

30. Ibid., 481–483.

31. Francine McKenzie, "GATT and the Cold War: Accession Debates, Institutional Development, and the Western Alliance, 1947–1959," *Journal of Cold War History* 10 (Summer 2008): 84–98.

32. Bideleux and Jeffries, *History of Eastern Europe*, 484–487.

33. Pollard, *Economic Security*, 164.

34. John W. Dower, *Embracing Defeat: Japan in the Wake of World War II* (New York: W. W. Norton, 1999), 112–116, 530.

35. Walter LaFeber, *The Clash: U.S.-Japanese Relations throughout History* (New York: W. W. Norton, 1997), 265, 269.

36. Michael Schaller, *The American Occupation of Japan: The Origins of the Cold War in Asia* (New York: Oxford University Press, 1985), 106.

37. Pollard, *Economic Security*, 167–187.

38. Haruo Iguchi, *Unfinished Business: Ayukawa Yoshisuke and U.S.-Japan Relations, 1937–1953* (Cambridge, MA: Harvard University Press, 2003), 219.

39. Schaller, *American Occupation of Japan*, 110, 141–160.

40. LaFeber, *The Clash*, 273, also 271.

41. William S. Borden, *The Pacific Alliance: United States Foreign Economic Policy and Japanese Trade Recovery, 1947–1955* (Madison: University of Wisconsin Press, 1984), 122–123; Dower, *Embracing Defeat*, 536–538.

42. Pollard, *Economic Security*, 192–193.

43. Gordon H. Chang, *Friends and Enemies: The United States, China, and the Soviet Union, 1948–1972* (Stanford, CA: Stanford University Press, 1990), 42–74.

44. Engel, *Cold War at 30,000 Feet*, 104–199.

45. Schaller, *Altered States*, 48.

46. Dower, *Embracing Defeat*, 542–543; Borden, *The Pacific Alliance*, 150–165.

47. Eckes and Zeiler, *Globalization*, 139.

48. Schaller, *Altered States*, 32, also 53, 57.

49. LaFeber, *The Clash*, 294–295; Pollard and Wells, "1945–1960," 350, 353.

50. Amy L. S. Staples, *The Birth of Development: How the World Bank, Food and Agriculture Organization, and World Health Organization Changed the World, 1945–1965* (Kent, OH: Kent State University Press, 2006), 33–51.

51. Louis A. Picard and Terry F. Buss, *A Fragile Balance: Re-examining the History of Foreign Aid, Security, and Diplomacy* (Sterling, VA: Kumarian Press, 2009), 83–90.

52. Pollard, *Economic Security*, 203–209.

53. Odd Arne Westad, *The Global Cold War: Third World Interventions and the Making of Our Times* (Cambridge: Cambridge University Press, 2007), 32, also 27–31.

54. Dennis Merrill, *Bread and the Ballot: The United States and India's Economic Development, 1947–1963* (Chapel Hill: University of North Carolina Press, 1990), 85, also, 48–94.

55. Andrew J. Rotter, *Comrades at Odds: The United States and India, 1947–1964* (Ithaca, NY: Cornell University Press, 2000), 88, 92–114.

56. Pollard and Wells, "1945–1960," 352, 354; Pollard, *Economic Security*, 209–218.

57. Staples, *The Birth of Development*, 49–53; Eckes and Zeiler, *Globalization*, 142–143.

58. Gabriel Kolko, *Confronting the Third World: United States Foreign Policy, 1945–1980* (New York: Pantheon Books, 1988), 75–77.

59. Douglas Little, *American Orientalism: The United States and the Middle East since 1945* (Chapel Hill: University of North Carolina Press, 2002), 58, also 52–57.

60. Pollard and Wells, "1945–1960," 363–364.

61. Westad, *The Global Cold War*, 31–32, 66–72.

62. Merrill, *Bread and the Ballot*, 123, also 117–124.

63. Stephen G. Rabe, *Eisenhower and Latin America: The Foreign Policy of Anticommunism* (Chapel Hill: University of North Carolina Press, 1988), 90–91.

64. Piero Gleijeses, *Shattered Hope: The Guatemalan Revolution and the United States, 1944–1954* (Princeton, NJ: Princeton University Press, 1991).

65. Bevan Sewell, "A Perfect (Free-Market) World? Economics, the Eisenhower Administration, and the Soviet Economic Offensive in Latin America," *Diplomatic History* 32 (November 2008): 841, 843–868.

66. Burton I. Kaufman, *Trade and Aid: Eisenhower's Foreign Economic Policy, 1953–1961* (Baltimore: Johns Hopkins University Press, 1982), 64.

67. Ibid., 69, also 68–73; Merrill, *Bread and the Ballot*, 134–136.

68. Westad, *The Global Cold War*, 155–156.

69. Kaufman, *Trade and Aid*, 56–57, 95–110, 133–174.

70. Kyle Longley, *In the Eagle's Shadow: The United States and Latin America* (Wheeling, IL: Harlan Davidson, 2002), 237. See also Rabe, *Eisenhower and Latin America*, 92–93.

71. Stephen G. Rabe, *The Most Dangerous Area in the World: John F. Kennedy Confronts Communist Revolution in Latin America* (Chapel Hill: University of North Carolina Press, 1999), 164–166.

72. David F. Schmitz, *Thank God They're on Our Side: The United States and Right-Wing Dictatorships, 1921–1965* (Chapel Hill: University of North Carolina Press, 1999), 240–243.

73. Longley, *In the Eagle's Shadow*, 237–238, 246–250, 266–268; Jeffrey F. Taffet, *Foreign Aid as Foreign Policy: The Alliance for Progress in Latin America* (London: Routledge, 2007), 175–194.

74. George McTurnan Kahin, *The Asian-African Conference, Bandung, Indonesia, April 1955* (Ithaca, NY: Cornell University Press, 1956), 42, 76–78.

75. Jason C. Parker, "Small Victory, Missed Chance: The Eisenhower Administration, the Bandung Conference, and the Turning of the Cold War," in *The Eisenhower Administration, the Third World, and the Globalization of the Cold War*, ed. Kathryn C. Statler and Andrew L. Johns (Lanham, MD: Rowman and Littlefield, 2006), 160–170.

76. Michael E. Latham, "Introduction: Modernization, International History, and the Cold War World," in *Staging Growth: Modernization, Development, and the Global Cold War*, ed. David C. Engerman, Nils Gilman, Mark H. Haefele, and Michael E. Latham (Amherst: University of Massachusetts Press, 2003), 6. See also Nils Gilman, "Modernization Theory, the Highest Stage of American Intellectual History" in Engerman et al., *Staging Growth*, 54–75.

77. W. W. Rostow, *The Stages of Economic Growth: A Non-Communist Manifesto* (Cambridge: Cambridge University Press, 1960).

78. Daniel Speich, "The Kenyan Style of 'African Socialism': Developmental Knowledge Claims and the Explanatory Limits of the Cold War," *Diplomatic History* 33 (June 2009): 451.

79. Joan E. Spero and Jeffrey A. Hart, *The Politics of International Economic Relations*, 6th ed. (Belmont, CA: Wadsworth, 2003), 175–186; Edgar J. Dosman, *The Life and Times of Raúl Prebisch, 1901–1986* (Montreal: McGill-Queen's University Press, 2010).

80. Enrique Cardenas, Jose Antonio Ocampo, and Rosemary Thorp, eds., *An Economic History of Twentieth-Century Latin America,* vol. 3, *Industrialization and the State in Latin America; The Postwar Years* (Houndsmill, UK: Palgrave, 2000).

81. Thomas W. Zeiler, *American Trade and Power in the 1960s* (New York: Columbia University Press, 1992), 29–31, 191–206; UNCTAD official site, www.unctad.org/Templates/Page.asp ?intItemID=1530&lang=1.

82. U.S. Trade Representative, "Generalized System of Preferences," www.ustr.gov/Trade_Devel opment/Preference_Programs/GSP/Section_Index.html.

83. Staples, *The Birth of Development*, 56–62.

84. Diane B. Kunz, *The Economic Diplomacy of the Suez Crisis* (Chapel Hill: University of North Carolina Press, 1991), 153–186.

85. Peter L. Hahn, *The United States, Great Britain, and Egypt, 1945–1956: Strategy and Diplomacy in the Early Cold War* (Chapel Hill: University of North Carolina Press, 1991), 211–239.

86. Ronn Pineo, *Ecuador and the United States: Useful Strangers* (Athens: University of Georgia Press, 2007), 133–138, 148–154, 177–186.

87. Kaufman, *Trade and Aid*, 60–63.

88. Alan P. Dobson, *US Economic Statecraft for Survival, 1933–1991: Of Sanctions, Embargoes and Economic Warfare* (London: Routledge, 2002), 114–281; Philip J. Funigiello, *American-Soviet Trade in the Cold War* (Chapel Hill: University of North Carolina Press, 1988), 153–209.

89. Bideleux and Jeffries, *History of Eastern Europe*, 507–511.

90. Pollard and Wells, "1945–1960," 367; Pascaline Winand, *Eisenhower, Kennedy, and the United States of Europe* (New York: St. Martin's Press, 1993), 109–137, 310–315.

91. Zeiler, *American Trade and Power*, 25–29, 225–238; David P. Calleo, "Since 1961: American Power in a New World Economy," in Becker and Wells, *Economics and World Power*, 400–405, 408–409, 447.

92. De Grazia, *Irresistible Empire*, 364–370.

93. Stephen D. Krasner, "Multinational Corporations," in *International Political Economy: Perspectives on Global Power and Wealth*, 4th ed. (New York: Routledge, 1999), 173–175; Mira Wilkins, *The Maturing of Multinational Enterprise: American Business Abroad from 1914 to 1970* (Cambridge, MA: Harvard University Press, 1974), 341–348, 395; Alfred E. Eckes Jr., "Europe and Economic Globalization since 1945," in *A Companion to Europe since 1945*, ed. Klaus Larres (Malden, MA: Wiley-Blackwell, 2009), 255–256.

94. De Grazia, *Irresistible Empire*, 376–388, 404; Eckes and Zeiler, *Globalization*, 161, 171–172.

95. Wilkins, *Maturing of Multinational Enterprise*, 328. See also World Tourism Organization, "International Tourism on Track for a Rebound after an Exceptionally Challenging 2009," www.unwto.org/media/news/en/press_det.php?id=5361; Concorde History, www.concord esst.com/.

96. Marc Levinson, *The Box: How the Shipping Container Made the World Smaller and the World Economy Bigger* (Princeton, NJ: Princeton University Press, 2006), 11, 275–278; "On the Wa-

ter: The World's Largest Container Ship Launched," July 11, 2006, www.gizmag.com/go/5853/; Eckes and Zeiler, *Globalization*, 157–160.

97. Royce J. Ammon, *Global Television and the Shaping of World Politics: CNN, Telediplomacy, and Foreign Policy* (Jefferson, NC: McFarland, 2001), 34–35; International Telecommunications Union, "The World in 2009: ICT Facts and Figures," www.itu.int/ITU-D/ict/material/Telecom09_flyer.pdf.

98. Kaufman, *Trade and Aid*, 176–179; Eckes and Zeiler, *Globalization*, 178; Calleo, "Since 1961," 409–417.

99. Robert D. Schulzinger, *A Time for War: The United States and Vietnam, 1941–1975* (New York: Oxford University Press, 1997), 242–243, 135–185.

100. Francis J. Gavin, *Gold, Dollars, and Power: The Politics of International Monetary Relations, 1958–1971* (Chapel Hill: University of North Carolina Press, 2004), 187, also 166–185.

101. Charles Maier, "'Malaise': The Crisis of Capitalism in the 1970s," in *The Shock of the Global: The 1970s in Perspective*, ed. Niall Ferguson, Charles Maier, Erez Manela, and Daniel J. Sargent (Cambridge, MA: Belknap Press of Harvard University Press 2010), 45; Gavin, *Gold, Dollars, and Power,* 188–196.

102. Giovanni Arrighi, "The World Economy and the Cold War, 1970–1990," in *The Cambridge History of the Cold War*, vol. 2, *Endings*, ed. Melvyn P. Leffler and Odd Arne Westad (Cambridge, UK: Cambridge University Press, 2010); Eckes and Zeiler, *Globalization*, 182–183; Calleo, "Since 1961," 417–421.

103. Little, *American Orientalism*, 62. See also Calleo, "Since 1961," 421–427. The American companies were Mobil, Exxon, Socal or Chevron, Texaco, and Gulf.

104. Daniel Yergin, *The Prize: The Epic Quest for Oil, Money, and Power* (New York: Simon and Schuster, 1991), 587.

105. Eckes and Zeiler, *Globalization*, 187.

106. Little, *American Orientalism*, 70. See also Kunz, *Butter and Guns*, 229.

107. Yergin, *The Prize*, 602–616, 626.

108. Eckes and Zeiler, *Globalization* 185; Little, *Third World Orientalism*, 70, 72.

109. Kunz, *Butter and Guns*, 238.

110. Yergin, *The Prize*, 698.

111. Ibid., 635–636, 664–670, 720, 746–750; Little, *American Orientalism*, 73.

112. Eckes and Zeiler, *Globalization*, 187–193; Kunz, *Butter and Guns*, 249, 251.

113. Spero and Hart, *The Politics*, 301–325.

114. Mark Atwood Lawrence, "History from Below: The United States and Latin America in the Nixon Years," in *Nixon in the World: American Foreign Relations, 1969–1977*, ed. Fredric Logevall and Andrew Preston (New York: Oxford University Press, 2008), 277–280; Kunz, *Butter and Guns*, 262–268.

115. Spero and Hart, *The Politics*, 96–102.

116. Ibid., 185–186, 243–255, 246, 311–316; United Nations, "Declaration on the Establishment of a New International Economic Order," www.un-documents.net/s6r3201.htm; Craig Murphy, *The Emergence of the NIEO Ideology* (Boulder, CO: Westview Press, 1984), 125–147.

117. Yergin, *The Prize*, 635–636.

118. The Lomé Convention, http://homepages.uel.ac.uk/myeo278s/ACP1.htm; Council on Hemispheric Affairs, "Banana Wars Continue," www.coha.org/2005/05/banana-wars-con tinue-%E2%80%93-chiquita-once-again-tries-to-work-its-omnipotent-will-now-under-new -management-likely-big-losers-will-be-caricom%E2%80%99s-windward-islands/.

119. WTO, "The Uruguay Round," www.wto.org/english/thewto_e/whatis_e/tif_e/fact5_e.htm.

120. Richard E. Mshomba, *Africa in the Global Economy* (Boulder, CO: Lynne Rienner, 2000), 94.

121. Spero and Hart, *The Politics*, 204–214.

122. Robert A. Pastor, ed., *Latin America's Debt Crisis: Adjusting to the Past or Planning for the Future* (Boulder, CO: Lynne Rienner, 1987), 6–14.

123. Jeffry A. Frieden, *Debt, Development, and Democracy: Modern Political Economy and Latin America, 1965–1985* (Princeton, NJ: Princeton University Press, 1991), 118–134, 145, 169–175, 189–228.

124. Sebastian Edwards, *Crisis and Reform in Latin America: From Despair to Hope* (New York: Oxford University Press, 1995), 23–57.

125. Kunz, *Butter and Guns*, 267–269.

126. Eckes and Zeiler, *Globalization*, 195–197.

127. Charles H. Feinstein, *An Economic History of South Africa: Conquest, Discrimination, and Development* (New York: Cambridge University Press, 2005), 165–240.

128. Bill Freund, *The Making of Contemporary Africa: The Development of African Society since 1800*, 2nd ed. (Houndsmill, UK: Palgrave, 1998), 253.

129. Mshomba, *Africa in the Global Economy*, 94.

130. Freund, *Making of Contemporary Africa*, 257–260.

131. John Iliffe, *Africans: The History of a Continent*, 2nd ed. (Cambridge: Cambridge University Press, 2007), 261.

132. Paul Kennedy, *African Capitalism: The Struggle for Ascendancy* (New York: Cambridge University Press, 1988), 104–134.

133. Alex Thomson, *An Introduction to African Politics* (London: Routledge, 2000), 176, also 165–186.

134. Lourdes Beneria and Savitri Bisnath, "Gender and Poverty: An Analysis for Action," in *The Globalization Reader*, ed. Frank H. Lechner and John Boli (Malden, MA: Wiley-Blackwell, 2000), 172–176.

135. James H. Mittelman, *The Globalization Syndrome: Transformation and Resistance* (Princeton, NJ: Princeton University Press, 2000), 74–87.

136. Bruce Cumings, *Korea's Place in the Sun: A Modern History* (New York: Norton, 2005), 303–331.

137. Gregg Andrew Brazinsky, "Koreanizing Modernization: Modernization Theory and South Korean Intellectuals," in Engerman et al., *Staging Growth*, 253–270; Alice H. Amsden, *Asia's Next Giant: South Korea and Late Industrialization* (New York: Oxford University Press, 1989), 55, 66–76, 93–111, 215–235.

138. LaFeber, *The Clash*, 296–310; Michael A. Barnhart, "From Hershey Bars to Motor Cars: America's Economic Policy toward Japan, 1945–1976," in *Partnership: The United States and*

Japan, 1951–2001, ed. Akira Iriye and Robert A. Wampler (Tokyo: Kodansha International, 2001), 219.

139. Eckes, *Opening America's Market*, 200, also 168–175.

140. LaFeber, *The Clash*, 327–332, 365.

141. Eckes and Zeiler, *Globalization*, 199.

142. LaFeber, *The Clash*, 301–302.

143. Kunz, *Butter and Guns*, 300.

144. LaFeber, *The Clash*, 353–354.

145. Thomas W. Zeiler, "Business Is War in U.S.-Japanese Economic Relations, 1977–2001," in Iriye and Wampler, *Partnership*, 303; LaFeber, *The Clash*, 357–363; Kunz, *Butter and Guns*, 303.

146. Barnhart, "From Hershey Bars," 219; Zeiler, "Business Is War," 225–230.

147. "Imports of Color Television Sets Exceed Domestic Production," http://web-japan.org/trends95/29.html.

148. Kunz, *Butter and Guns*, 313–323.

149. Eckes and Zeiler, *Globalization*, 214, 229–230.

150. Zeiler, "Business Is War," 237–238, 240–246.

151. Jinglian Wu, *Understanding and Interpreting Chinese Economic Reform* (Mason, OH: Thomson/South-Western, 2005), 294.

152. Ibid., 309–310.

153. Carolyn Carter, *Globalizing South China* (Oxford: Blackwell, 2001), 213–214; Nick Knight, *Imagining Globalisation in China: Debates on Ideology, Politics and Culture* (Cheltenham, UK: E. Elgar, 2008), 56–77.

154. SIP, www.sipac.gov.cn/english/Investment/200403/t20040329_5263.htm.

155. Knight, *Imagining Globalisation*, 172–178.

156. Eckes and Zeiler, *Globalization*, 201.

157. Wu, *Understanding and Interpreting*, 295–305, 319–324.

158. Spero and Hart, *The Politics*, 364–374; LaFeber, *The Clash*, 403–404.

159. World Bank, *World Development Indicators, Data: Countries and Economies,* http://data.worldbank.org/country.

160. Alfred E. Eckes Jr., *U.S. Trade Issues* (Santa Barbara: ABC-CLIO, 2009), 58–62.

161. Shalendra D. Sharma, "India's Economic Liberalization: A Progress Report, April 2003," in *South Asia,* ed. Sumit Ganguly (New York: New York University Press, 2006), 147.

162. Satyendra S. Nayak, *Globalization and the Indian Economy: Roadmap to Convertible Rupee* (London: Routledge, 2008), 115–132, 4, 8.

163. Vinay Rai and William L. Simon, *Think India* (New York: Dutton, 2007), 17–26, 47–62; Eckes and Zeiler, *Globalization*, 241.

164. Eckes and Zeiler, *Globalization*, 1, 204–206, 210–212, 216–218.

165. CIA, *The World Factbook: European Union*, https://www.cia.gov/library/publications/the-world-factbook/geos/ee.html; IMF, *Report for Selected Country Groups and Subjects*, www.imf.org/external/pubs/ft/weo/2008/01/weodata/weorept.aspx?sy=2006&ey=2008&ssd=1

&sort=country&ds=.&br=1&c=998&s=NGDPD%2CPPPGDP&grp=1&a=1&pr.x=46 &pr.y=7.

166. David Marsh, *The Euro: The Politics of the New Global Currency* (New Haven, CT: Yale University Press, 2009), 236–261; Eckes, "Europe and Economic Globalization," 257–265; de Grazia, *Irresistible Empire*, 465–467.

167. "Wake up Europe!," *Economist*, October 10, 2009, 13; Spero and Hart, *The Politics*, 78–80, 258; John McCormick, *Understanding the European Union*, 3rd ed. (New York: St. Martin's Press, 2005).

168. Kees Van Der Pijl, *Global Rivalries from the Cold War to Iraq* (London: Pluto Press, 2006), 283–290.

169. Michael Hart, *A Trading Nation: Canadian Trade Policy from Colonialism to Globalization* (Vancouver: University of British Columbia Press, 2002), 423–424.

170. Sidney Weintraub, ed., *NAFTA's Impact on North America: The First Decade* (Washington, DC: CSIS Press, 2004); U.S. Department of Commerce, "NAFTA 10 Years Later: An Overview," www.ita.doc.gov/td/industry/otea/nafta/CoverPage.pdf; Dan Griswold, "NAFTA at 10: An Economic and Foreign Policy Success," www.freetrade.org/pubs/FTBs/FTB-001. html; Public Citizen, "North American Free Trade Agreement (Nafta)," www.citizen.org /trade/nafta/.

171. Council on Foreign Relations, "Mercosur: South America's Fractious Trade Bloc," www.cfr .org/publication/12762/; Spero and Hart, *The Politics*, 94–96, 255–259.

172. Jorge Robledo, "Why Say No to FTAA," www.bilaterals.org/article.php3?id_article=1064; Jerry Haar and John Price, *Can Latin America Compete? Confronting the Challenges of Globalization* (New York: Palgrave Macmillan, 2008), 33–40.

173. Gerald Tan, *ASEAN: Economic Development and Cooperation* (Singapore: Times Academic Press, 2003), 5–37, 234–276.

174. "ASEAN-China Trade to Hit $200b by 2008," www.bilaterals.org/article.php3?id_arti cle=9660; "About APEC," www.apec.org/apec/about_apec.html.

175. "What Is the WTO?," www.wto.org/english/thewto_e/whatis_e/whatis_e.htm; Congressional Research Service, Ian F. Fergusson, "The World Trade Organization: Background and Issues," www.nationalaglawcenter.org/assets/crs/98-928.pdf.

176. William Greider, *One World, Ready or Not: The Manic Logic of Global Capitalism* (New York: Simon and Schuster, 1997), 13–19; Eckes, *U.S. Trade Issues*, 68–69; Spero and Hart, *The Politics*, 9.

177. Joseph M. Grieco and G. John Ikenberry, *State Power and World Markets: The International Political Economy* (New York: W. W. Norton, 2003), 6–7, 14–15, 208–212, 222–226. See OECD (2011), "Trade in Goods by Partner Countries and Regions," *Trade: Key Tables from OECD*, no. 6, doi: 10.1787/trd-gds-part-table-2011-1-en.

178. Eckes, *Opening*, 217–218; Eckes, *U.S. Trade Issues*, 40–45.

179. Eckes and Zeiler, *Globalization*, 209–210, 213–214.

180. Petra Rivoli, *The Travels of a T-Shirt in the Global Economy* (Hoboken, NJ: John Wiley and Sons, 2005), xix-xx, 6, 64–72, 86–92, 146–168, 181–190.

181. Spero and Hart, *The Politics*, 90–94, 96–106.

182. Gary P. Sampson, "Developing Countries and the Liberalization of Trade Services," in *Developing Countries and the Global Trading System,* vol. 1, ed. John Whalley (London: Macmillan, 1989), 132–145.

183. Eckes, *Opening,* 285. See also Gary P. Sampson, "Non-Tariff Barriers Facing Developing Country Exports," in Whalley, *Developing Countries,* 1:171–185.

184. London School of Economics, "What Is Civil Society?," www.lse.ac.uk/collections/CCS /what_is_civil_society.htm; Ronnie D. Lipschutz, "Reconstructing World Politics: The Emergence of Global Civil Society," in *Civil Societies and Social Movements,* ed. Ronnie D. Lipschutz (Aldershot, UK: Ashgate, 2006), 237–268.

185. Peter Baker, "The Mellowing of William Jefferson Clinton," *New York Times Magazine,* May 31, 2009, 46; William J. Clinton Foundation, www.clintonfoundation.org/facts/; Andrew F. Cooper, *Celebrity Diplomacy* (Boulder, CO: Paradigm, 2008), 31–34, 38, 47, 56, 84, 100–101.

186. Live 8, www.live8live.com/makepromiseshappen/.

187. Susan George, "Fixing or Nixing the WTO," *Le Monde Diplomatique,* mondediplo .com/2000/01/07george; Grieco and Ikenberry, *State Power,* 226–238.

188. Walter LaFeber, *Michael Jordan and the New Global Capitalism* (New York: W. W. Norton, 1999), 126, 147–151.

189. James L. Watson, ed., *Golden Arches East: McDonald's in East Asia* (Stanford, CA: Stanford University Press, 1997), 10–18.

190. David M. Dickson, "Farm Tariffs Sink World Trade Talks," *Washington Times,* www.wash ingtontimes.com/news/2008/jul/30/farm-tariffs-sink-world-trade-talks/. See also Congressional Research Service, "World Trade Organization Negotiating: The Doha Development Agenda," www.nationalaglawcenter.org/assets/crs/RL32060.pdf; Alan Beattie and Frances Williams, "Doha Trade Talks Collapse," *Financial Times,* www.ft.com/cms/s/0/0638a320 -5d8a-11dd-8129-000077b07658.html?nclick_check=1.

191. "Energy: The Kyoto Protocol," www.globalization101.org/index.php?file=issue&pass1=subs &id=376.

192. Climate Savers Computing, www.climatesaverscomputing.org/about/; "Starbucks and the Environment," www.starbucks.com/retail/spring_environment.asp.

193. Matthew Ocheltree, "Energy Issue Brief: Examples of Micropower," www.globalization101 .org/index.php?file=issue&pass1=subs&id=366; "Globalization and the Tourist Industry," January 6, 2009, *Globalization 101.org,* www.globalization101.org/news1/globalization_tour ism.

194. See also Bideleux and Jeffries, *History of Eastern Europe,* 556–597; OECD, "Russian Federation," www.oecd.org/dataoecd/7/50/2452793.pdf.

195. Elaine Sciolino, "U.S. Is Abandoning 'Shock Therapy' for the Russians," *New York Times,* December 21, 1992, http://query.nytimes.com/gst/fullpage.html?res=9F0CEED91F39F932A 15751C1A965958260.

196. Cumings, *Korea's Place in the Sun,* 33; Tan, *ASEAN,* 200–233; Eckes and Zeiler, *Globalization,* 249–251.

197. Joseph E. Stiglitz, *Globalization and Its Discontents* (New York: W. W. Norton, 2002), 99–100.

198. Eckes and Zeiler, *Globalization*, 257.

199. Richard A. Posner, *A Failure of Capitalism: The Crisis of '08 and the Descent into Depression* (Cambridge, MA: Harvard University Press, 2009); see also Eckes, *U.S. Trade Issues*, 70.

200. IMF, *World Economic Outlook Report*, October 2008, www.cfr.org/publication/17483/.

201. "Global Troubles," *New York Times*, February 22, 2009, 2.

202. Nigel Holmes and Megan McArdle, "Iceland's Meltdown," *Atlantic*, December 2008, 66–67.

203. Carter Dougherty, "A Scramble to Shore Up Economies Worldwide," *New York Times*, October 28, 2008, www.nytimes.com/2008/10/28/business/worldbusiness/28banks.html?_r=1 &scp=1&sq=A%20Scramble%20to%20Shore%20Up&st=cse.

204. World Bank, *World Development Indicators, Data: Countries and Economies*, http://data .worldbank.org/country.

205. "Failed States: Insights into Two of the World's Most Broken States," November 30, 2009, *Globalization 101.org*, www.globalization101.org/news1/failed_states.

206. Stephen Castle and David Jolly, "Giant Stimulus Plan Proposed for Europe," *New York Times*, November 28, 2008, www.nytimes.com/2008/11/27/business/worldbusiness/27euro.html ?scp=1&sq=Giant%20Stimulus%20Plan&st=cse; IMF, *World Economic Outlook: Recovery, Risk, and Rebalancing*, October 2010, www.imf.org/external/pubs/ft/weo/2010/02/index .htm.

207. Paul Krugman, "Moment of Truth," *New York Times*, October 10, 2007, www.nytimes.com /2008/10/10/opinion/10krugman.html?scp=1&sq=Moment%20of%20Truth&st=cse.

208. "The Pittsburgh Summit 2009: A Report by the Pittsburgh G-20 Partnership," https://www .pittsburghg20.org/PDFs/G20Report1109.pdf.

209. The World Bank, *Global Economic Prospects*, June 10, 2010, http://web.worldbank.org /WBSITE/EXTERNAL/EXTDEC/EXTDECPROSPECTS/EXTGBLPROSPECT- SAPRIL/0,,menuPK:659178~pagePK:64218926~piPK:64218953~theSitePK:659149,00 .html; Economy 2011, http://economy2011.org/?p=28.

210. Matt Taibbi, "How I Stopped Worrying and Learned to Love the Protests," *Rolling Stone*, November 24, 2011, 65–66.

211. Niall Ferguson, *The Ascent of Money: A Financial History of the World* (New York: Penguin, 2008), 296–300; David S. Landes, *The Wealth and Poverty of Nations: Why Some Are So Rich and Some So Poor* (New York: W. W. Norton, 1998), 465–520; John Templeton Foundation, "Does the Free Market Corrode Moral Character?," www.templeton.org/market/; UN, *The Millennium Development Goals Report* (New York, 2009).

3. Into the Anthropocene: People and Their Planet

1. Paul Crutzen and Eugene Stoermer, "The Anthropocene," *IGBP Global Change Newsletter* 41 (2000): 17–18. An Italian geologist had used the term *anthropozoic* as early as 1873, but it did not catch on. A. Stoppani, *Corso di geologia* (Milan: Bernadona & Brigoli, 1873).

2. Will Steffen, Paul Crutzen, J. R. McNeill, "The Anthropocene: Are Humans Now Overwhelming the Great Forces of Nature?," *Ambio* 36 (2007): 614–621.

3. A rival moment might be the near extinction of our species about 76,000 years ago in the wake of a giant volcanic eruption. Genetic evidence suggests that the human population was reduced to a few thousand breeding pairs—a close brush with extinction.

4. William Ruddiman, *Plows, Plagues and Petroleum: How Humans Took Control of Climate* (Princeton, NJ: Princeton University Press, 2005).

5. See John F. Richards, *The Unending Frontier: An Environmental History of the Early Modern World* (Berkeley: University of California Press, 2003), for a sense of agricultural expansions.

6. These themes are addressed in Alfred Crosby, *Ecological Imperialism: The Biological Expansion of Europe, 900 to 1900 A.D.* (New York: Cambridge University Press, 1986); William H. Mc-Neill, *Plagues and Peoples* (New York: Doubleday, 1976); and Emmanuel Le Roy Ladurie, "Un concept: L'Unification microbienne du monde," *Revue suisse d'histoire* 23 (1978): 627–696.

7. Angus Maddison, *The World Economy: A Millennial Perspective* (Paris: OECD, 2001), 261.

8. The next several paragraphs draw on Vaclav Smil, *Energy in World History* (Boulder, CO: Westview, 1994); Smil, *Energy in Nature and Society* (Cambridge, MA: MIT Press, 2008); Alfred Crosby, *Children of the Sun: A History of Humanity's Unappeasable Appetite for Energy* (New York: Norton, 2006); Frank Niele, *Energy: Engine of Evolution* (Amsterdam: Elsevier, 2005).

9. Charles Hall, Praddep Tharakan, John Hallock, Cutler Cleveland, and Michael Jefferson, "Hydrocarbons and the Evolution of Human Culture," *Nature* 426 (2003): 318–322.

10. China figures from IEA/OECD, *Cleaner Coal in China* (Paris: IEA/OECD, 2009), 45–46; For the United Kingdom: F. D. K. Liddell, "Mortality of British Coal Miners in 1961," *British Journal of Industrial Medicine* 30 (1973): 16. In the United States around 2000, some fourteen hundred former miners died annually from black lung. Barbara Freese, *Coal: A Human History* (Cambridge, MA: Perseus, 2003), 175.

11. Chad Montrie, *To Save the Land and People: A History of Opposition to Surface Mining in Appalachia* (Chapel Hill: University of North Carolina Press, 2003).

12. Irina Gildeeva, "Environmental Protection during Exploration and Exploitation of Oil and Gas Fields," *Environmental Geosciences* 6 (2009): 153–154.

13. Joanna Burger, *Oil Spills* (New Brunswick, NJ: Rutgers University Press, 1997), 42–44.

14. On fisheries and ecological effects, see Harold Upton, "The Deepwater Horizon Oil Spill and the Gulf of Mexico Fishing Industry," Congressional Research Service report, February 17, 2011, available at http://fpc.state.gov/documents/organization/159014.pdf. On legal aspects, see the symposium "Deep Trouble: Legal Ramifications of the Deepwater Horizon Oil Spill," *Tulane Law Review* 85 (March 2011). Of the journalistic accounts, the best to date is Joel Achenbach, *A Hole at the Bottom of the Sea: The Race to Kill the BP Oil Gusher* (New York: Simon and Schuster, 2011).

15. The following discussion is based on Anna-Karin Hurtig and Miguel San Sebastian, "Geographical Differences in Cancer Incidence in the Amazon Basin of Ecuador in Relation to Residence near Oil Fields," *International Journal of Epidemiology* 31 (2002): 1021–1027; and Miguel San Sebastian and Anna-Karin Hurtig, "Oil Exploitation in the Amazon Basin of Ecuador: A Public Health Emergency," *Revista Panamericana de Salud Pública* 15 (2004): 205–211. The

cancer claims are disputed by Michael Kelsh, Libby Morimoto, and Edmund Lau, "Cancer Mortality and Oil Production in the Amazon Region of Ecuador, 1990–2005," *International Archives of Occupational and Environmental Health* 82 (2008): 381–395. See also Judith Kimmerling, "Oil Development in Ecuador and Peru: Law, Politics, and the Environment," in *Amazonia at the Crossroads: The Challenge of Sustainable Development,* ed. Anthony Hall (London: Institute of Latin American Studies, University of London, 2000), 73–98.

16. M. Finer, C. N. Jenkins, S. L. Pimm, B. Keane, and C. Ross, "Oil and Gas Projects in the Western Amazon: Threats to Wilderness, Biodiversity, and Indigenous Peoples," *PLoS ONE* 3, no. 8 (2008): e2932, doi:10.1371/journal.pone.0002932. For general context, see Allen Gerlach, *Indians, Oil, and Politics: A Recent History of Ecuador* (Wilmington, DE: Scholarly Resources, 2003). The UNDP deal is explained at http://mdtf.undp.org/yasuni.

17. P. A. Olajide et al., "Fish Kills and Physiochemical Qualities of a Crude Oil Polluted River in Nigeria," *Research Journal of Fisheries and Hydrobiology* 4 (2009): 55–64.

18. J. S. Omotola, "'Liberation Movements' and Rising Violence in the Niger Delta: The New Contentious Site of Oil and Environmental Politics," *Studies in Conflict and Terrorism* 33 (2010): 36–54; Tobias Haller et al., *Fossil Fuels, Oil Companies, and Indigenous Peoples* (Berlin: Lit Verlag, 2007), 69–76. For political analyses, see the many writings of Michael Watts; e.g., Watts, "Blood Oil: The Anatomy of a Petro-insurgency in the Niger Delta," *Focaal* 52 (2008): 18–38; Watts, ed., *The Curse of the Black Gold: 50 Years of Oil in the Niger Delta* (Brooklyn: PowerHouse Books, 2009).

19. Haller et al., *Fossil Fuels,* 166–167.

20. D. O'Rourke and S. Connolly, "Just Oil? The Distribution of Environmental and Social Impacts of Oil Production and Consumption," *Annual Review of Environment and Resources* 28 (2003): 598.

21. Ibid., 599–601.

22. In the 1990s in the United States, the agency responsible for pipeline safety employed one inspector for every 60,000 kilometers of (oil and gas) pipeline. The ratio was probably less favorable in almost every other country of the world. O'Rourke and Connolly, "Just Oil?," 611.

23. Now Usinsk has a website on the spill: http://usinsk.ru/katastrofa_city.html. We thank Valentina Roxo, of Ludwig-Maximilians University, for bringing this to our attention.

24. G. E. Vilchek and A. A. Tishkov, "Usinsk Oil Spill," in *Disturbance and Recovery in Arctic Lands,* ed. R. M. M. Crawford (Dordrecht: Kluwer Academic, 1997), 411–420; Anna Kireeva, "Oil Spills in Komi: Cause and the Size of the Spill Kept Hidden," www.bellona.org/articles /articles_2007/Oil_spill_in_Komi. See also "West Siberia Oil Industry Environmental and Social Profile," a Greenpeace report, www.greenpeace.org/raw/content/nederland-old/reports /west-siberia-oil-industry-envi.pdf.

25. Marjorie M. Balzer, "The Tension between Might and Rights: Siberians and Energy Developers in Post-Socialist Binds," *Europe-Asia Studies* 58 (2006): 567–588; Haller et al., *Fossil Fuels,* 168–178.

26. B. K. Sovacool, "The Cost of Failure: A Preliminary Assessment of Major Energy Accidents, 1907–2007," *Energy Policy* 36 (2008): 1802–1820.

27. Michelle Bell, Devra Davis, and Tony Fletcher, "A Retrospective Assessment of Mortality from the London Smog Episode of 1952: The Role of Influenza and Pollution," *Environmental Health Perspectives* 112 (2004): 6–8.

28. The blitz of September 1940 to May 1941 killed about twenty thousand Londoners over nine months.

29. Quoted in Devra Davis, *When Smoke Ran Like Water* (New York: Basic Books, 2002), 45.

30. Ibid., 31–54; Peter Brimblecombe, *The Big Smoke: A History of Air Pollution in London since Medieval Times* (London: Methuen, 1987), 165–169.

31. Inferred from data in B. Brunekreef and S. Holgate, "Air Pollution and Health," *Lancet* 360 (2002):1239.

32. Eri Saikawa et al., "Present and Potential Future Contributions of Sulfate, Black and Organic Aerosols from China to Global Air Quality, Premature Mortality, and Radiative Forcing," *Atmospheric Environment* 43 (2009): 2814–2822.

33. M. Ezzati, A. Lopez, A. Rodgers, S. Vander Hoorn, and C. Murray, "Selected Major Risk Factors and Global and Regional Burden of Disease," *Lancet* 360 (2002): 1347–1360. A similar figure was reached by A. J. Cohen et al., "The Global Burden of Disease due to Outdoor Air Pollution," *Journal of Toxicology and Environmental Health* 68 (2005): 1301–1307.

34. Bear in mind that air pollution kills mostly the very young, the very old, and those with respiratory or heart conditions. War mainly kills people in the prime of life. So from an economic point of view, air pollution mortality is much less costly than war mortality, because it chiefly kills those who are easily replaced (infants and toddlers) and those who have already made what contributions they will ever make (the very old). For those who regard all humans as equal, this calculus is of course abhorrent.

35. See John Watt et al., eds., *The Effects of Air Pollution on Cultural Heritage* (Berlin: Springer, 2009) on these issues generally.

36. David Stern, "Global Sulfur Emissions from 1850 to 2000," *Chemosphere* 58 (2005): 163–175; Z. Lu et al., "Sulfur Dioxide Emissions in China and Sulfur Trends in East Asia since 2000," *Atmospheric Chemistry and Physics Discussions* 10 (2010): 8657–8715; C. K. Chan and X. H. Yao, "Air Pollution in Mega Cities in China," *Atmospheric Environment* 42 (2008): 1–42; M. Fang, C. K. Chan, and X. H. Yao, "Managing Air Quality in a Rapidly Developing Nation: China," *Atmospheric Environment* 43, no. 1 (2009): 79–86.

37. Jes Fenger, "Air Pollution in the Last 50 Years: From Local to Global," *Atmospheric Environment* 43 (2009): 15.

38. H. R. Anderson, "Air Pollution and Mortality: A History," *Atmospheric Environment* 43 (2009): 144–145.

39. M. Hashimoto, "History of Air Pollution Control in Japan," in *How to Conquer Air Pollution: A Japanese Experience,* ed. H. Nishimura (Amsterdam: Elsevier, 1989), 1–94.

40. James Fleming, *Fixing the Sky: The Checkered History of Weather and Climate Control* (New York: Columbia University Press, 2010).

41. J. Samuel Walker, *Three Mile Island: A Nuclear Crisis in Historical Perspective* (Berkeley: University of California Press, 2004).

42. March 29, 1986, issue of *The Economist*.

43. A. V. Yablokov, V. B. Nesterenko, and A. V. Nesterenko, "Consequences of the Chernobyl Catastrophe for the Environment," *Annals of the New York Academy of Sciences* 1181 (2009): 221–286. Effects upon animals extended far beyond the Chernobyl exclusion zone. Swedish moose, for example, contained thirty-three times their usual quantities of radioactivity (ca. 1988). Ibid., 256.

44. Jim Smith and Nicholas Beresford, *Chernobyl* (Berlin: Springer, 2005); A. B. Nesterenko, V. B. Nesterenko, and A. V. Yablokov, "Consequences of the Chernobyl Catastrophe for Public Health," *Annals of the New York Academy of Sciences* 1181 (2009): 31–220.

45. The wastes are stored in concrete and steel containers, mainly on reactor sites. Deep geological storage ran into political problems, as had dumping at sea. See the pro-nuclear Nuclear Energy Institute page at www.nei.org/keyissues/nuclearwastedisposal/factsheets/safelymanagingused nuclearfuel/.

46. Useful data and perspectives appear in the April 2012 issue of *Environmental History*, especially Sara Pritchard, "An Envirotechnical Disaster: Nature, Technology, and Politics at Fukushima," *Environmental History* 17 (2012): 219–243. See also J. C. MacDonald, "Fukushima: One Year Later," *Radiation Protection Dosimetry* 149 (2012): 353–354; and Koichi Hasegawa, "Facing Nuclear Risks: Lessons from the Fukushima Nuclear Disaster," *International Journal of Japanese Sociology* 21 (2012): 84–91.

47. For an insiders' view of the blunders, see Yoichi Funabashi and Kay Kitazawa, "Fukushima in Review: A Complex Disaster, a Disastrous Response," *Bulletin of the Atomic Scientists* 68 (2012): 9–21.

48. On the controversies surrounding hydropower development, see R. Sternberg, "Hydropower: Dimensions of Social and Environmental Coexistence," *Renewable and Sustainable Energy Reviews* 12 (2008): 1588–1621.

49. The Rihand Dam in Uttar Pradesh, India, built 1954–1962. E. G. Thukral, *Big Dams, Displaced People: Rivers of Sorrow, Rivers of Change* (New Delhi: Sage, 1992), 13–14.

50. A. G. Nilsen, *Dispossession and Resistance in India: The River and the Rage* (London: Routledge, 2010).

51. Satyajit Singh, *Taming the Waters: The Political Economy of Large Dams in India* (Delhi: Oxford University Press, 1997); John R. Wood, *The Politics of Water Resource Development in India: The Narmada Dams Controversy* (Los Angeles: Sage, 2007); Nilsen, *Dispossession and Resistance*.

52. K. Xu and J. D. Milliman, "Seasonal Variations of Sediment Discharge from the Yangtze River before and after Impoundment of the Three Gorges Dam," *Geomorphology* 104 (2009): 276–283.

53. P. Zhang et al., "Opportunities and Challenges for Renewable Energy Policy in China," *Renewable and Sustainable Energy Reviews* 13 (2009): 439–449.

54. Quotation from a Canadian lumberjack, Arnst Kurelek, cited in R. C. Silversides, *Broadaxe to Flying Shear: The Mechanization for Forest Harvesting East of the Rockies* (Ottawa: National Museum of Science and Technology, 1997), 107.

55. Manfred Weissenbacher, *Sources of Power: How Energy Forges Human History* (Santa Barbara, CA: ABC-CLIO, 2009), 452.

56. On these examples, see A. P. Muñoz, R. S. Pavón, and L. Z. Villareal, "Rehabilitación turística y capacidad de carga en Cozumel," *Revista iberoamericana de economía ecológica* 11 (2009): 53–63; S. Gössling et al., "Ecological Footprint Analysis as a Tool to Assess Tourism Sustainability," *Ecological Economics* 43 (2002): 199–211 (this is about the Seychelles, an interesting case because of its government's effort to preserve the islands' environment while reaping revenues from tourism); G. M. Mudd, "Gold Mining in Australia: Linking Historical Trends and Environmental and Resource Sustainability," *Environmental Science and Policy* 10 (2007): 629–644; M. Cryer, B. Hartill, and S. O'Shea, "Modification of Marine Benthos by Trawling: Generalization for the Deep Ocean?," *Ecological Applications* 12 (2002): 1824–1839; Lawrence Solomon, *Toronto Sprawls: A History* (Toronto: University of Toronto Press, 2007); John Sewell, *The Shape of the Suburbs: Understanding Toronto's Sprawl* (Toronto: University of Toronto Press, 2009).

57. Joel Cohen, *How Many People Can the Earth Support?* (New York: Norton, 1995), 78–79.

58. Adapted from Carlo Cipolla, *An Economic History of World Population* (Harmondsworth, UK: Penguin, 1978), 89.

59. Robert Fogel, *The Escape from Hunger and Premature Death, 1700–2100* (New York: Cambridge University Press, 2004), 21.

60. The successes and failures of malaria control are detailed in James L. A. Webb Jr., *Humanity's Burden: A Global History of Malaria* (New York: Cambridge University Press, 2009). For the agricultural story, see Giovanni Federico, *Feeding the World: An Economic History of World Agriculture, 1800–2000* (Princeton, NJ: Princeton University Press, 2005).

61. According to Fogel, *Escape from Hunger* (40), in Britain the "elite" cohort born in 1875 lived about seventeen years longer than the population as a whole; by 2000 that gap was four years. UN life expectancy data at http://esa.un.org/unpp/p2kodata.asp.

62. Han Feizi, *Han Feizi: Basic Writings*, trans. Burton Watson (New York: Columbia University Press, 2003), 98.

63. The Tertullian quotation is from Cohen, *How Many People*, 6.

64. Leo Silberman, "Hung Liang-chi: A Chinese Malthus," *Population Studies* 13 (1960): 257–265.

65. India's birth rate at the time stood at 36 per 1,000 population and the target was 25 per 1,000, achieved only around 2000, some twenty years later than hoped. Ramachandra Guha, *India after Gandhi: The History of the World's Largest Democracy* (New York: HarperCollins, 2007), 415–416, 511–514.

66. Yves Blayo, *Des politiques démographiques en Chine* (Lille: Atelier National de Reproductions des Thèses, 2006); Thomas Scharping, *Birth Control in China, 1949–2000* (London: RoutledgeCurzon, 2003); Tyrene White, *China's Longest Campaign: Birth Planning in the People's Republic, 1949–2005* (Ithaca, NY: Cornell University Press, 2006). Susan Greenhalgh, *Just One Child: Science and Policy in Deng's China* (Berkeley: University of California Press, 2008); Greenhalgh, *Cultivating Global Citizens: Population in the Rise of China* (Cambridge, MA: Harvard University Press, 2010). On both India and China, see also Matthew Connelly, *Fatal Misconception: The Struggle to Control World Population* (Cambridge, MA: Harvard University Press, 2008).

67. For recent data on desertification in northern China, see Ma Yonghuan and Fan Shengyue, "The Protection Policy of Eco-environment in Desertification Areas of Northern China:

Contradiction and Countermeasures," *Ambio* 35 (2006): 133–134. For historical perspective, see James Reardon-Anderson, *Reluctant Pioneers: China's Northward Expansion, 1644–1937* (Stanford, CA: Stanford University Press, 2005); Peter Perdue, *China Marches West: The Qing Conquest of Central Asia* (Cambridge, MA: Harvard University Press, 2005); Dee Mack Williams, *Beyond Great Walls: Environment, Identity, and Development on the Chinese Grasslands of Inner Mongolia* (Stanford, CA: Stanford University Press, 2002).

68. Mary Tiffen, Michel Mortimore, and Francis Gichuki, *More People, Less Erosion: Environmental Recovery in Kenya* (Chichester, NY: Wiley, 1994). On the Mediterranean, see J. R. McNeill, *The Mountains of the Mediterranean: An Environmental History* (New York: Cambridge University Press, 1992).

69. In 2010 the world's irrigated area came to about three hundred million hectares, some five times the size of Texas or seven times the size of France. Bridget Scanlon, Ian Jolly, Marios Sophocleous, and Lu Zhang, "Global Impacts of Conversions from Natural to Agricultural Ecosystems on Water Resources: Quantity vs. Quality," *Water Resources Research* 43 (2007): W03437, available at www.agu.org/pubs/crossref/2007/2006WR005486.shtml.

70. Dean Bavington, *Managed Annihilation: An Unnatural History of the Newfoundland Cod Collapse* (Vancouver: University of British Columbia Press, 2010).

71. Jason Link, Bjarte Bogstad, Henrik Sparholt, and George Lilly, "Trophic Role of Atlantic Cod in the Ecosystem," *Fish and Fisheries* 10 (2008): 58–87; Ilona Stobutzki, Geronimo Silvestre, and Len Garces, "Key Issues in Coastal Fisheries in South and Southeast Asia: Outcomes of a Regional Initiative," *Fisheries Research* 78 (2006): 109–118. The depletion of cod, a top predator, has entirely reorganized the marine ecosystems of places such as the Grand Banks.

72. FAO marine fish catch data at www.fao.org/fishery/statistics/global-production/en. FAO data do not go back further than 1950, and are probably more reliable the more recent they are.

73. H. Bruce Franklin, *The Most Important Fish in the Sea: Menhaden and America* (Washington, DC: Island Press, 2007).

74. Anqing Shi, "The Impact of Population Pressure on Global Carbon Emissions, 1975–1996: Evidence from Pooled Cross-Country Data," *Ecological Economics* 44 (2003): 29–42. Further discussion is in John R. McNeill, *Something New under the Sun: An Environmental History of the Twentieth-Century World* (New York: Norton, 2000), 272–273. Historical carbon emission data, 1751–2004, from fossil fuel use only, are available at http://cdiac.ornl.gov/trends/emis /em_cont.html.

75. The plant manufactured pesticides, used in Indian agriculture. Although one might argue that it did so because of population growth in India, this in no way explains the accident, which was a matter of neglected maintenance. A recent account appears in Suroopa Mukerjee, *Surviving Bhopal: Dancing Bodies, Written Texts, and Oral Testimonials of Women in the Wake of an Industrial Disaster* (London: Palgrave, 2010), 17–40.

76. Dirk Hoerder, *Cultures in Contact: World Migration in the Second Millennium* (Durham, NC: Duke University Press, 2002), 508–582.

77. Char Miller, *On the Border: An Environmental History of San Antonio* (Pittsburgh: University of Pittsburgh Press, 2001).

78. Ren Qiang and Yuan Xin, "Impacts of Migration to Xinjiang since the 1950s," in *China's Minorities on the Move,* ed. Robyn Iredale, Naran Bilik, and Fei Guo (Armonk, NY: M. E. Sharpe, 2003), 89–105. The precise numbers of Chinese migrants in Xinjiang are unclear.

79. J. M. Foggin, "Depopulating the Tibetan Grasslands," *Mountain Research and Development* 28 (2008): 26–31; A. M. Fischer, "Urban Fault Lines in Shangri-La: Population and Economics Foundations of Inter-ethnic Conflict in the Tibetan Area of Western China," London School of Economics Crisis States Program Working Paper #42; Hao Xin, "A Green Fervor Sweeps the Qinghai-Tibetan Plateau," *Science* 321 (2008): 633–635. A historically minded study of a region on the eastern Tibetan plateau is Jack P. Hayes, "Modernisation with Local Characteristics: Development Efforts and the Environment on the Zoige Grass and Wetlands, 1949–2005," *Environment and History* 16 (2010): 323–347.

80. Greg Grandin, *Fordlandia: The Rise and Fall of Henry Ford's Forgotten Jungle City* (New York: Metropolitan Books, 2009).

81. A recent assessment is P. M. Fearnside, "Deforestation in Brazilian Amazonia: History, Rates, and Consequences," *Conservation Biology* 19, no. 3 (2005), 680–688. See also Michael Williams, *Deforesting the Earth* (Chicago: University of Chicago Press, 2003), 460–481. A boom in soybean exports to China after 2008 reduced Amazonian deforestation rates sharply, because all available investment went into plowing up the savannas in Goias and other states south of Amazonia. See the web page of Brazil's Institute for Space Research (INPE): www.inpe.br/ingles/news/news_dest154.php.

82. Peter Dauvergne, "The Politics of Deforestation in Indonesia," *Pacific Affairs* 66 (1993–1994): 497–518; J. M Hardjono, "The Indonesian Transmigration Scheme in Historical Perspective," *International Migration* 26 (1988): 427–438. Logging, plantation agriculture, and much else contributed to Indonesia's rapid deforestation.

83. The following discussion is from Jonathan Cowie, *Climate Change: Biological and Human Aspects* (New York: Cambridge University Press, 2007), 1–16, 22–31, 126–167.

84. For a discussion of the Earth's carbon cycle, see Bert Bolin, *A History of the Science and Politics of Climate Change: The Role of the Intergovernmental Panel on Climate Change* (New York: Cambridge University Press, 2007), chap. 2.

85. Michael R. Raupach et al., "Global and Regional Drivers of Accelerating CO_2 Emissions," *Proceedings of the National Academy of Sciences of the United States of America* 104, no. 24 (June 12, 2007): 10288. For estimates of the effects of tropical deforestation on global carbon emissions, see Wolfgang Cramer et al., "Tropical Forests and the Global Carbon Cycle: Impacts of Atmospheric Carbon Dioxide, Climate Change and Rate of Deforestation," *Philosophical Transactions of the Royal Society: Biological Sciences* 359, no. 1443 (March 29, 2004): 331–343. On deforestation in historical context, see generally Williams, *Deforesting the Earth.*

86. T. A. Boden, G. Marland, and R. J. Andres, "Global, Regional, and National Fossil-Fuel CO_2 Emissions," in *Trends: A Compendium of Data on Global Change* (Oak Ridge, TN: Carbon Dioxide Information Analysis Center, Oak Ridge National Laboratory, U.S. Department of Energy, 2009), doi: 10.3334/CDIAC/00001; Raupach et al., "Global and Regional Drivers," 10288.

87. Joseph G. Canadella et al., "Contributions to Accelerating Atmospheric CO_2 Growth from Economic Activity, Carbon Intensity, and Efficiency of Natural Sinks," *Proceedings of the National Academy of Sciences of the United States of America* 104, no. 47 (November 20, 2007): 18866–18870; Raupach et al., "Global and Regional Drivers," 10288–10292.

88. James Hansen et al., "Global Temperature Change," *Proceedings of the National Academy of Sciences of the United States of America* 103, no. 39 (September 26, 2006): 14288–14293; P. D. Jones, D. E. Parker, T. J. Osborn, and K. R. Briffa, "Global and Hemispheric Temperature Anomalies: Land and Marine Instrumental Records," in Oak Ridge National Laboratory, *Trends,* doi: 10.3334/CDIAC/cli.002; John M. Broder, "Past Decade Was Warmest Ever, NASA Finds," *New York Times,* January 22, 2010, A8.

89. Andrew E. Dessler and Edward A. Parson, *The Science and Politics of Global Climate Change: A Guide to the Debate* (New York: Cambridge University Press, 2006), table 3.1; Edward L. Miles, "On the Increasing Vulnerability of the World Ocean to Multiple Stresses," *Annual Review of Environment and Resources* 34 (2009): 18–26; Catherine P. McMullen and Jason Jabbour, eds., *Climate Change Science Compendium, 2009* (New York: United Nations Environment Programme, 2009), 17–23.

90. Scott C. Doney and David S. Schimel, "Carbon and Climate System Coupling on Timescales from the Precambrian to the Anthropocene," *Annual Review of Environment and Resources* 32 (2007): 31–66; Miles, "On the Increasing Vulnerability," 26–28.

91. United Nations Environment Programme, *Climate Change Science Compendium, 2009,* 15–16.

92. Jianchu Xu et al., "The Melting Himalayas: Cascading Effects of Climate Change on Water, Biodiversity, and Livelihoods," *Conservation Biology* 23, no. 3 (June 2009): 520–530.

93. M. Monirul Qader Mirza, "Climate Change, Flooding and Implications in South Asia," *Regional Environmental Change* 11, suppl. 1 (2011): 95–107; Katherine Morton, "Climate Change and Security at the Third Pole," *Survival* 53 (2011): 121–132.

94. Bolin, *A History,* chap. 1.

95. Spencer Weart, *The Discovery of Global Warming* (Cambridge, MA: Harvard University Press, 2008), 14–17.

96. Ibid., 19–33. For a recent summary of the Mauna Loa time series, see R. F. Keeling, S. C. Piper, A. F. Bollenbacher, and J. S. Walker, "Atmospheric CO_2 Records from Sites in the SIO Air Sampling Network," in Oak Ridge National Laboratory, *Trends,* doi: 10.3334/CDIAC/atg.035. Doney and Schimel (2007) write that the Mauna Loa time series is "one of the most iconic data sets in geophysics, if not all of science" (48).

97. Cowie, *Climate Change,* 20–21; Weart, *Discovery of Global Warming,* 53–58, 70–78, 126–137.

98. Bolin, *A History,* 20–34; Weart, *Discovery of Global Warming,* chaps. 4 and 5.

99. William C. Clark et al., "Acid Rain, Ozone Depletion, and Climate Change: An Historical Overview," in *Learning to Manage Global Environmental Risks,* vol. 1, *A Comparative History of Social Responses to Climate Change, Ozone Depletion and Acid Rain,* ed. The Social Learning Group (Cambridge, MA: MIT Press, 2007), 21–39; Cass R. Sunstein, "Of Montreal and Kyoto: A Tale of Two Protocols," *Harvard Environmental Law Review* 31, no. 1 (2007): 10–22; Intergovernmental Panel on Climate Change, *Climate Change 2007: Synthesis Report; Contribution of Working Groups I, II and III to the Fourth Assessment Report of the Intergovernmental*

Panel on Climate Change (Geneva: Intergovernmental Panel on Climate Change, 2007), 2–22; Bolin, *A History*, 44–49; Dessler and Parson, *Global Climate Change*, 12–16. A fascinating interpretation of the scientific community's role in the ozone and climate politics during the 1980s and 1990s is provided in Reiner Grundmann, "Ozone and Climate: Scientific Consensus and Leadership," *Science, Technology, & Human Values* 31, no. 1 (January 2006): 73–101.

100. Geoffrey J. Blanford, Richard G. Richels, and Thomas F. Rutherford, "Revised Emissions Growth Projections for China: Why Post-Kyoto Climate Policy Must Look East," in *Post-Kyoto International Climate Policy: Implementing Architectures for Agreement,* ed. Joseph E. Aldy and Robert N. Stavins (New York: Cambridge University Press, 2010), 822–856; Paul G. Harris and Hongyuan Yu, "Climate Change in Chinese Foreign Policy: Internal and External Responses," in *Climate Change and Foreign Policy: Case Studies from East to West,* ed. Paul G. Harris (New York: Routledge, 2009), 53–67; Boden, Marland, and Andres, "Fossil-Fuel CO_2 Emissions"; Jos Olivier, *Trends in Global CO_2 Emissions* (The Hague: Netherlands Environmental Assessment Agency, 2012).

101. Paul G. Harris, "Climate Change in Environmental Foreign Policy: Science, Diplomacy, and Politics," and Michael T. Hatch, "The Politics of Climate Change in Germany: Domestic Sources of Environmental Foreign Policy," both in Harris, *Climate Change and Foreign Policy,* 1–17, 41–62; Boden, Marland, and Andres, "Fossil-Fuel CO_2 Emissions"; Nigel Purvis and Andrew Stevenson, *Rethinking Climate Diplomacy: New Ideas for Transatlantic Cooperation Post-Copenhagen* (Washington, DC: German Marshall Fund of the United States, 2010), at www.gmfus.org/cs/publications/publication_view?publication.id=176; Sunstein, "Of Montreal and Kyoto," 22–53; Renat Perelet, Serguey Pegov, and Mikhail Yulkin, "Climate Change: Russia Country Paper" (New York: United Nations Development Program, 2007), at http://hdr.undp.org/en/reports/global/hdr2007-2008/papers/; David A. Wirth, "The Sixth Session (Part Two) and Seventh Session of the Conference of the Parties to the Framework Convention on Climate Change," *American Journal of International Law* 96, no. 3 (July 2002): 648–660. On the severity of the Russian heat wave, see David Barriopedro et al., "The Hot Summer of 2010: Redrawing the Temperature Record Map of Europe," *Science* 332, no. 6026 (April 8, 2011): 220–224.

102. E. O. Wilson, "Editor's Foreword," in *Biodiversity,* ed. E. O. Wilson with Frances M. Peter (Washington, DC: National Academy Press, 1988), v; Williams, *Deforesting the Earth,* 437–446.

103. Gordon H. Orians and Martha J. Groom, "Global Biodiversity: Patterns and Processes," in *Principles of Conservation Biology,* ed. Martha J. Groom, Gary K. Meffe, and C. Ronald Carroll (Sunderland, MA: Sinauer Associates, 2006), 30–31; Catherine Badgley, "The Multiple Scales of Biodiversity," *Paleobiology* 29, no. 1 (Winter 2003): 11–13; Martin Jenkins, "Prospects for Biodiversity," *Science* 302, no. 5648 (November 14, 2003): 1175. For dissenting views, see, e.g., Geerat J. Vermeij and Lindsey R. Leighton, "Does Global Diversity Mean Anything?," *Paleobiology* 29, no. 1 (Winter 2003): 3–7; D. M. J. S. Bowman, "Death of Biodiversity: The Urgent Need for Global Ecology," *Global Ecology and Biogeography Letters* 7, no. 4 (July 1998): 237–240.

104. Craig Hilton-Taylor et al., "State of the World's Species," in *Wildlife in a Changing World: An Analysis of the 2008 IUCN Red List of Threatened Species,* ed. Jean-Christophe Vié, Craig Hilton-Taylor, and Simon N. Stuart (Gland, Switzerland: International Union for Conservation of

Nature and Natural Resources, 2009), 15–17; James P. Collins and Martha L. Crump, *Extinction in Our Times: Global Amphibian Decline* (New York: Oxford University Press, 2009), 1–2; Orians and Groom, "Global Biodiversity," 33–34.

105. Jens Mutke et al., "Terrestrial Plant Diversity," in *Plant Conservation: A Natural History Approach*, ed. Gary A. Krupnick and W. John Kress (Chicago: University of Chicago Press, 2005), 15–25; Simon L. Lewis, "Tropical Forests and the Changing Earth System," *Philosophical Transactions: Biological Sciences* 361, no. 1465, Reviews (January 29, 2006): 195–196.

106. Michael L. McKinney, "Is Marine Biodiversity at Less Risk? Evidence and Implications," *Diversity and Distributions* 4, no. 1 (January 1998): 3–8; Beth A. Polidoro et al., "Status of the World's Marine Species," in Vié, Hilton-Taylor, and Stuart, *Wildlife*, 55.

107. Paul K. Dayton, "The Importance of the Natural Sciences to Conservation," *American Naturalist* 162, no. 1 (July 2003): 2; Polidoro et al., "Status," 57–58.

108. E. O. Wilson, "The Current State of Biological Diversity," in Wilson and Peter, *Biodiversity*, 12–13; David S. Woodruff, "Declines of Biomes and Biotas and the Future of Evolution," *Proceedings of the National Academy of Sciences of the United States of America* 98, no. 10 (May 8, 2001): 5471–5476. On the difficulties of estimating species extinction numbers as well as factors, see, e.g., Richard G. Davies et al., "Human Impacts and the Global Distribution of Extinction Risk," *Proceedings: Biological Sciences* 273, no. 1598 (September 7, 2006): 2127–2133; Bruce A. Stein and Warren L. Wagner, "Current Plant Extinctions: Chiaroscuro in Shades of Green," in Krupnick and Kress, *Plant Conservation*, 59–60; A. D. Barnosky et al., "Has the Earth's Sixth Mass Extinction Already Arrived?," *Nature* 471 (March 3, 2011): 51–57.

109. William Adams, *Against Extinction: The Story of Conservation* (London: Earthscan, 2004), 47–50; J. Donald Hughes, "Biodiversity in World History," in *The Face of the Earth: Environment and World History*, ed. J. Donald Hughes (Armonk, NY: M. E. Sharpe, 2000), 35; Jean-Christophe Vié et al., "The IUCN Red List: A Key Conservation Tool," in Vié, Hilton-Taylor, and Stuart, *Wildlife*, 1–13; Hilton-Taylor et al., "State of the World's Species," 15–42; the 2012 Red List is at: http://www.iucnredlist.org/.

110. Martha J. Groom, "Threats to Biodiversity," in Groom, Meffe, and Carroll, *Principles of Conservation Biology*, 64–65. For land use statistics, see McNeill, *Something New*, table 7.1. Bird density data can be found in Kevin J. Gaston, Tim M. Blackburn, and Kees Klein Goldewijk, "Habitat Conversion and Global Avian Biodiversity Loss," *Proceedings: Biological Sciences* 270, no. 1521 (June 22, 2003): table 1.

111. Williams, *Deforesting the Earth*, 386–421. See also Lewis, "Tropical Forests," 197–199.

112. Williams, *Deforesting the Earth*, 420–481.

113. Gary J. Wiles et al., "Impacts of the Brown Tree Snake: Patterns of Decline and Species Persistence in Guam's Avifauna," *Conservation Biology* 17, no. 5 (October 2003): 1350–1360; Dieter C. Wasshausen and Werner Rauh, "Habitat Loss: The Extreme Case of Madagascar," in Krupnick and Kress, *Plant Conservation*, 151–155; Mutke et al., "Terrestrial Plant Diversity," 18; Williams, *Deforesting the Earth*, 343.

114. Michel Meybeck, "Global Analysis of River Systems: From Earth System Controls to Anthropocene Syndromes," *Philosophical Transactions: Biological Sciences* 358, no. 1440 (December 29, 2003): 1935–1955.

115. Controversy still surrounds the first introduction of the Nile Perch into Lake Victoria. Some claim that colonial administrators deliberately introduced the fish in order to improve the lake's commercial fisheries; others claim it was an accidental introduction. See Robert M. Pringle, "The Nile Perch in Lake Victoria: Local Responses and Adaptations," *Africa: Journal of the International African Institute* 75, no. 4 (2005): 510–538.

116. See Dayton, "Importance of the Natural Sciences."

117. Callum Roberts, *The Unnatural History of the Sea* (Washington, DC: Island Press, 2007), chaps. 12, 20–22.

118. Carmel Finley, "A Political History of Maximum Sustained Yield, 1945–1955," in *Oceans Past: Management Insights from the History of Marine Animal Populations,* ed. David J. Starkey, Poul Holm, and Michaele Barnard (London: Earthscan, 2008), 189–206; Roberts, *Unnatural History of the Sea,* 321–323.

119. Roberts, *Unnatural History of the Sea,* 288–302, 314–326. On aquaculture, see James Muir, "Managing to Harvest? Perspectives on the Potential of Aquaculture," *Philosophical Transactions: Biological Sciences* 360, no. 1453 (January 29, 2005): 191–218.

120. Randall Reeves and Tim Smith, "A Taxonomy of World Whaling Operations and Eras," in *Whales, Whaling, and Ocean Ecosystems,* ed. James Estes et al. (Berkeley: University of California Press, 2006), 82–101; John A. Knauss, "The International Whaling Commission: Its Past and Possible Future," *Ocean Development & International Law* 28, no. 1 (1997): 79–87.

121. Clive Wilkinson, "Status of Coral Reefs of the World: Summary of Threats and Remedial Action," in *Coral Reef Conservation,* ed. Isabelle M. Cote and John D. Reynolds (Cambridge: Cambridge University Press, 2006), 3–21; Zvy Dubinsky and Noga Stambler, eds., *Coral Reefs: An Ecosystem in Transition* (Dordrecht: Springer, 2011).

122. Adams, *Against Extinction,* 176–201; Hughes, "Biodiversity in World History," 35–40. On the ESA and wolves, see, e.g., John Erb and Michael W. DonCarlos, "An Overview of the Legal History and Population Status of Wolves in Minnesota," in *Recovery of Gray Wolves in the Great Lakes Region of the United States: An Endangered Species Success Story,* ed. Adrian P. Wydeven, Timothy R. Van Deelen, and Edward J. Heske (New York: Springer, 2009), 49–85. On Project Tiger and wildlife protection in India, see Mahesh Rangarajan, "The Politics of Ecology: The Debate on Wildlife and People in India, 1970–95," in *Battles over Nature: Science and the Politics of Conservation,* ed. Vasant K. Saberwal and Mahesh Rangarajan (Delhi: Orient Blackswan, 2003), 189–230.

123. Adams, *Against Extinction,* 25–53, 67–96. For a harsh view of European conservationists in African history, see Jonathan S. Adams and Thomas O. McShane, *The Myth of Wild Africa: Conservation without Illusion* (Berkeley: University of California Press, 1996). On Gabon, see Lydia Polgreen, "Pristine African Park Faces Development," *New York Times,* February 22, 2009, A6.

124. Roberts, *Unnatural History of the Sea,* preface, chaps. 1, 25; Louisa Wood et al., "Assessing Progress towards Global Marine Protection Targets: Shortfalls in Information and Action," *Oryx* 42 (2008): 340–351; Juliet Eilperin, " 'Biological Gem' Becomes Largest Marine Reserve; Coral, Tuna, Sharks Expected to Thrive in Chagos Islands," *Washington Post,* April 2, 2010, A10; John M. Broder, "Bush to Protect Vast New Pacific Tracts," *New York Times,* January 6, 2009, A13.

125. On whaling disputes, see Stephen Palumbi and Joe Roman, "The History of Whales Read from DNA," and J. A. Estes et al., "Retrospection and Review," both in Estes et al., *Whales, Whaling, and Ocean Ecosystems,* 102–115, 388–393; Juliet Eilperin, "A Crossroads for Whales: With Some Species Rebounding, Commission Weighs Loosening of Hunting Ban," *Washington Post,* March 29, 2010, A01.

126. On tiger conservation, see Virginia Morell, "Can the Wild Tiger Survive?," *Science* 317, no. 5843 (September 7, 2007): 1312–1314.

127. Camille Parmesan and John Matthews, "Biological Impacts of Climate Change," in Groom, Meffe, and Carroll, *Principles of Conservation Biology,* 352; Wilkinson, "Status of Coral Reefs," 19–21.

128. Celia Dugger, "U.N. Predicts Urban Population Explosion," *New York Times,* June 28, 2007, 6. Global urban data is from Thomas Brinkhoff, "The Principal Agglomerations of the World," www.citypopulation.de; an "agglomeration" is defined as "a central city and neighboring communities linked to it (e.g.) by continuous built-up areas or commuters," hence Tokyo includes Yokohama, Kawasaki, and Saitama.

129. On New York's ocean dumping, see Martin Melosi, *The Sanitary City: Urban Infrastructure in America from Colonial Times to the Present* (Baltimore: Johns Hopkins University Press, 2000), 180–182, 260. On the urban contribution to greenhouse gas emissions, see Grimm et al., "Global Change and the Ecology of Cities," *Science* 319 (February 6, 2008): 756–760.

130. The quotation is from Martin Melosi, "The Place of the City in Environmental History," *Environmental History Review* 17 (Spring 1993): 7. Nuremberg suffered from the fact that it did not sit along a major navigable river, which meant it could not purchase timber from remote upstream forests. Hence, the city needed to control local sources. See Joachim Radkau, *Nature and Power: A Global History of the Environment* (New York: Cambridge University Press, 2008), 146–147.

131. Verena Winiwarter and Martin Knoll, *Umweltgeschichte: Eine Einführung* (Cologne: Böhlau, 2007), 181–182, 199; Christopher G. Boone and Ali Modarres, *City and Environment* (Philadelphia: Temple University Press, 2006), 77–78, 101–102; Grimm et al., "Global Change," 756–760.

132. Melosi, "Place of the City," 7; Grimm et al., "Global Change," 756. On the complexities of women's fertility in cities, see, e.g., Oğuz Işik and M. Melih Pinarcioğlu, "Geographies of a Silent Transition: A Geographically Weighted Regression Approach to Regional Fertility Differences in Turkey," *European Journal of Population / Revue Européenne de Démographie* 22, no. 4 (December 2006): 399–421; Eric R. Jensen and Dennis A. Ahlburg, "Why Does Migration Decrease Fertility? Evidence from the Philippines," *Population Studies* 58, no. 2 (July 2004): 219–231; Amson Sibanda et al., "The Proximate Determinants of the Decline to Below-Replacement Fertility in Addis Ababa, Ethiopia," *Studies in Family Planning* 34, no. 1 (March 2003): 1–7; Patrick R. Galloway, Ronald D. Lee, and Eugene A. Hammel, "Urban versus Rural: Fertility Decline in the Cities and Rural Districts of Prussia, 1875 to 1910," *European Journal of Population / Revue Européenne de Démographie* 14, no. 3 (September 1998): 209–264.

133. Kenneth T. Jackson, "Cities," in *The Columbia History of the 20th Century,* ed. Richard W. Bulliet (New York, 1998), 529–530; John Reader, *Cities* (New York: Atlantic Monthly Press,

2004), 122–124. The classic statistical compilation of urban population history is provided by Tertius Chandler and Gerald Fox, *3000 Years of Urban Growth* (New York: Academic Press, 1974); see esp. 300–326.

134. On timber transport, see Radkau, *Nature and Power,* 146. On the limits to cities generally, see the incisive remarks of H. G. Wells, *Anticipations of the Reaction of Mechanical and Scientific Progress upon Human Life and Thought* (New York: Harper Bros., 1902), 44–54, 70–71.

135. On the plague, cholera, and quarantine in Europe, see Gerry Kearns, "Zivilis or Hygaeia: Urban Public Health and the Epidemiologic Transition," in *The Rise and Fall of Great Cities: Aspects of Urbanization in the Western World,* ed. Richard Lawton (New York: Belhaven, 1989), 98–99, 107–111. On Japan, see Susan B. Hanley, "Urban Sanitation in Preindustrial Japan," *Journal of Interdisciplinary History* 18, no. 1 (Summer 1987): 1–26.

136. Wells, *Anticipations,* 54.

137. Jackson, "Cities," 530–532. For a discussion of how London provisioned itself during the nineteenth century, see Reader, *Cities,* 127–132.

138. See generally the United Nations Department for Economic and Social Information and Policy Analysis, Population Division, *The Challenge of Urbanization: The World's Largest Cities* (New York: Author, 1995). On Australia, see Clive Forster, *Australian Cities: Continuity and Change* (Melbourne: Oxford University Press, 1995), chap. 1.

139. P. P. Karan, "The City in Japan," in *The Japanese City,* ed. P. P. Karan and Kristin Stapleton (Lexington: University Press of Kentucky, 1997), 12–21; Forster, *Australian Cities,* 6–12.

140. Wells, *Anticipations,* 54.

141. This reading of Chicago's history is from William Cronon, *Nature's Metropolis: Chicago and the Great West* (New York: Norton, 1991).

142. Martin Melosi, *Effluent America: Cities, Industry, Energy, and the Environment* (Pittsburgh: University of Pittsburgh Press, 2001), 54–56, 178–179; Peter Hall, *Cities of Tomorrow: An Intellectual History of Urban Planning and Design in the Twentieth Century* (Oxford: Blackwell, 1996), 31–33; Leonardo Benevolo, *The Origins of Modern Town Planning* (Cambridge, MA: MIT Press, 1967), 20–23; Reader, *Cities,* 147–148.

143. Melosi, *The Sanitary City,* chaps. 2–9. On Haussmann and Paris, see Howard Saalman, *Haussmann: Paris Transformed* (New York: Braziller, 1971), 19–20; Reader, *Cities,* 211–214.

144. Andre Raymond, *Cairo,* trans. Willard Wood (Cambridge, MA: Harvard University Press, 2000), 309–321; James B. Pick and Edgar W. Butler, *Mexico Megacity* (Boulder, CO: Westview, 2000), 30–37 (data from table 3.2, p. 37). On American transportation history before 1939, see Owen D. Gutfreund, *Twentieth-Century Sprawl: Highways and the Reshaping of the American Landscape* (New York: Oxford University Press, 2004), chap. 1; Clay McShane, *Down the Asphalt Path: The Automobile and the American City* (New York: Columbia University Press, 1994), 103–122; John Jakle, "Landscapes Redesigned for the Automobile," in *The Making of the American Landscape,* ed. Michael P. Conzen (Boston: Unwin Hyman, 1990), 293–299.

145. United Nations Department for Economic and Social Information and Policy Analysis, Population Division, *World Urbanization Prospects: The 2003 Revision* (New York: UN Population Division, 2004), tables 1.1, 1.7 (pp. 3, 11). The number of megacities depends partly on how a city's boundaries are defined.

146. United Nations, Department for Economic and Social Information and Policy Analysis, *World Urbanization Prospects,* tables 1.1, 1.3 (pp. 3–5). Figures are rounded.

147. United Nations Human Settlements Programme (UN-Habitat), *The Challenge of Slums: Global Report on Human Settlements 2003* (London: Earthscan, 2003), 25–27.

148. On the Persian Gulf, see Yasser Elsheshtawy, "Cities of Sand and Fog: Abu Dhabi's Global Ambitions," in *The Evolving Arab City: Tradition, Modernity and Urban Development,* ed. Yasser Elsheshtawy (New York: Routledge, 2008), 258–304; Janet Abu-Lughod, "Urbanization in the Arab World and the International System," in *The Urban Transformation of the Developing World,* ed. Josef Gugler (Oxford: Oxford University Press, 1996), 185–210. On Karachi, see Arif Hasan, "The Growth of a Metropolis," in *Karachi: Megacity of Our Times,* ed. Hamida Khuhro and Anwer Mooraj (Karachi: Oxford University Press, 1997), 174. On China, see Anthony M. Orum and Xiangming Chen, *The World of Cities: Places in Comparative and Historical Perspective* (Malden, MA: Blackwell, 2003), table 4.1 (pp. 101–103).

149. James Heitzman, *The City in South Asia* (London: Routledge, 2008), 179, 187; David Satterthwaite, "In Pursuit of a Healthy Urban Environment in Low- and Middle-Income Nations," in *Scaling Urban Environmental Challenges: From Local to Global and Back,* ed. Peter J. Marcotullio and Gordon McGranahan (London: Earthscan, 2007), 79; Alan Gilbert, "Land, Housing, and Infrastructure in Latin America's Major Cities," in *The Mega-city in Latin America,* ed. Alan Gilbert (New York: United Nations University Press, 1996), table 4.1 (pp. 74–75); Hasan, "Growth of a Metropolis," 188–189.

150. Satterthwaite, "In Pursuit," 69–71; United Nations Centre for Human Settlements (Habitat), *Cities in a Globalizing World: Global Report on Human Settlements, 2001* (London: Earthscan, 2001), 105–110. On water supply and demand in Indian cities, see Rajendra Sagane, "Water Management in Mega-cities in India: Mumbai, Delhi, Calcutta, and Chennai," in *Water for Urban Areas: Challenges and Perspectives,* ed. Juha I. Uitto and Asit K. Biswas (New York: United Nations University Press, 2000), 84–111.

151. United Nations Human Settlements Programme (UN-Habitat), *The Challenge of Slums,* table 6.8 (p. 113); Gilbert, "Land, Housing," 78–80.

152. Grimm et al., "Global Change," 757; Mario J. Molina and Luisa T. Molina, "Megacities and Atmospheric Pollution," *Journal of the Air and Waste Management Association* 54 (June 2004): 644–680; World Health Organization and United Nations Environment Programme, *Urban Air Pollution in Megacities of the World* (Cambridge, MA: Blackwell Reference, 1992), 56–65, 203–210.

153. United Nations Human Settlements Programme (UN-Habitat), *The Challenge of Slums,* 211–212; World Health Organization and United Nations Environment Programme, *Urban Air Pollution,* 107–113; Robert Cribb, "The Politics of Pollution Control in Indonesia," *Asian Survey* 30, no. 12 (December 1990): 1123–1235; Susan Abeyasekere, *Jakarta: A History* (Singapore: Oxford University Press, 1989), 167–245.

154. United Nations Department for Economic and Social Information and Policy Analysis, *World Urbanization Prospects,* table 1.1 (p. 3).

155. Frank Uekoetter, *The Age of Smoke: Environmental Policy in Germany and the United States, 1880–1970* (Pittsburgh: University of Pittsburgh Press, 2009), 113–195, 209–258; Joel Tarr,

"The Metabolism of the Industrial City: The Case of Pittsburgh," *Journal of American History* 28, no. 5 (July 2002): 523–528.

156. World Health Organization and United Nations Environment Programme, *Urban Air Pollution*, 124–134, 172–177, 211–218.

157. Uekoetter, *The Age of Smoke*, 198–207; Molina and Molina, "Megacities and Atmospheric Pollution," 644–661. On Addis, see V. Etyemezian et al., "Results from a Pilot-Scale Air Quality Study in Addis Ababa, Ethiopia," *Atmospheric Environment* 39 (2005): 7849–7860.

158. McShane, *Down the Asphalt Path*, 1–56, 103–122, 203–223; Barbara Schmucki, *Der Traum vom Verkehrsfluss: Städtische Verkehrsplanung seit 1945 im deutsch-deutschen Vergleich* (Frankfurt: Campus, 2001), 100–103, 126, 401; Peter Newman and Jeffrey Kenworthy, *Sustainability and Cities: Overcoming Automobile Dependence* (Washington, DC: Island Press, 1999), table 3.8 (p. 80); Forster, *Australian Cities*, 18; Jakle, "Landscapes Redesigned," 299–300.

159. Jeffrey Kenworthy and Felix Laube, *An International Sourcebook of Automobile Dependence in Cities, 1960–1990* (Niwot, CO: University Press of Colorado, 1999), 361; Newman and Kenworthy, *Sustainability and Cities*, table 3.12; Karan, "The City in Japan," 33; Forster, *Australian Cities*, 15–20.

160. Newman and Kenworthy, *Sustainability and Cities*, tables 3.4, 3.8, 3.9, 3.14; see also Matthew E. Kahn, "The Environmental Impact of Suburbanization," *Journal of Policy Analysis and Management* 19, no. 4 (Autumn 2000): 569–586. On American gasoline prices and automobile size, see Rudi Volti, "A Century of Automobility," *Technology and Culture* 37, no. 4 (October 1996): 663–685.

161. Melosi, *The Sanitary City*, 297–298, 338–341, 373–374, 395–422. On postwar urbanization and land use in Great Britain, see, e.g., Peter Hall, "The Containment of Urban England," *Geographical Journal* 140, no. 3 (October 1974): 386–408.

162. Grimm et al., "Global Change," 756, 758.

163. William E. Rees, "Ecological Footprints and Appropriated Carrying Capacity: What Urban Economics Leaves Out," *Environment and Urbanization* 4, no. 2 (October 1992): 121–130 (quotation at 125). For a summary of criticism of the idea, see Winiwarter and Knoll, *Umweltgeschichte*, 182–185.

164. Charles J. Kibert, "Green Buildings: An Overview of Progress," *Journal of Land Use & Environmental Law* 19 (2004): 491–502; R. R. White, "Editorial: Convergent Trends in Architecture and Urban Environmental Planning," *Environment and Planning D: Society and Space* 11, no. 4 (August 1993): 375–378.

165. Timothy Beatley, "Green Urbanism in European Cities," in *The Humane Metropolis: People and Nature in the 21st-Century City*, ed. Rutherford H. Platt (Amherst, MA: University of Massachusetts Press, 2006), 297–314; Timothy Beatley, *Green Urbanism: Learning from European Cities* (Washington, DC: Island Press, 2000).

166. Anna Lehmann and Ulrich Schulte, "Brüder, zur Sonne, nach Freiburg! . . . ," *TAZ, Die Tageszeitung* (July 31, 2007), Berlin Metro Section, 21; Thomas Schroepfer and Limin Hee, "Emerging Forms of Sustainable Urbanism: Case Studies of Vauban Freiburg and solarCity Linz," *Journal of Green Building* 3, no. 2 (Spring 2008): 67–76. For an example of Freiburg's

promotional literature, see City of Freiburg im Breisgau, *Freiburg Green City* (October 2008), available at www.freiburg.de/greencity.

167. John Pucher and Ralph Buehler, "Making Cycling Irresistible: Lessons from the Netherlands, Denmark, and Germany," *Transport Reviews* 28, no. 4 (July 2008): 495–528; Newman and Kenworthy, *Sustainability and Cities,* 201–208; John Pucher, "Bicycling Boom in Germany: A Revival Engineered by Public Policy," *Transportation Quarterly* 51, no. 4 (Fall 1997): 31–45.

168. This summary of Curitiba is based on Bill McKibben, *Hope, Human and Wild: True Stories of Living Lightly on the Earth* (Minneapolis: Milkweed, 2007), 59–111; Hugh Schwartz, *Urban Renewal, Municipal Revitalization: The Case of Curitiba, Brazil* (Alexandria, VA: Hugh Schwartz, 2004), chap. 1; Donnella Meadows, "The City of First Priorities," *Whole Earth Review* 85 (Spring 1995): 58–59; Jonas Rabinovitch, "Curitiba: Towards Sustainable Urban Development," *Environment and Urbanization* 4, no. 2 (October 1992): 62–73.

169. The discussion of Havana is based on Shawn Miller, *Environmental History of Latin America,* 230–235; Adriana Premat, "Moving between the Plan and the Ground: Shifting Perspectives on Urban Agriculture in Havana, Cuba," in *Agropolis: The Social, Political, and Environmental Dimensions of Urban Agriculture,* ed. Luc J. A. Mougeot (London: Earthscan, 2005), 153–185; Reader, *Cities,* 168–171.

170. Luc J. A. Mougeot, introduction to Mougeot, *Agropolis,* 1–4 and table 17.

171. For a critical take on Barcelona's efforts at greening itself, see Juan Martinez-Alier, *The Environmentalism of the Poor: A Study of Ecological Conflicts and Valuation* (New Delhi: Oxford University Press, 2004), 161–167. On global cars, see United Nations Centre for Human Settlements (Habitat), *Cities in a Globalizing World,* table 11.1. On China and cars, see Yok-shiu F. Lee, "Motorization in Rapidly Developing Cities," in *Scaling Urban Environmental Challenges: From Local to Global and Back,* ed. Peter J. Marcotullio and Gordon McGranahan (London: Earthscan, 2007), 179–205.

172. Angus Maddison, *The World Economy,* vol. 1, *A Millennial Perspective* (Paris: OECD, 2006), 125–126.

173. Jürgen Osterhammel and Niels P. Petersson, *Globalization: A Short History* (Princeton, NJ: Princeton University Press, 2005), 94–103; J. R. McNeill, "Social, Economic, and Political Forces in Environmental Change, Decadal Scale (1900 to 2000)," in *Sustainability or Collapse? An Integrated History and Future of People on Earth,* ed. Robert Costanza, Lisa J. Graumlich, and Will Steffen (Cambridge, MA: MIT Press, 2007), 307–308; Jeffry Frieden, *Global Capitalism: Its Fall and Rise in the 20th Century* (New York: Norton, 2006).

174. Ivan Berend, *Central and Eastern Europe, 1944–1993: Detour from the Periphery to the Periphery* (Cambridge: Cambridge University Press, 1996).

175. Stephen Kotkin, *Armageddon Averted: The Soviet Collapse, 1970–2000* (Oxford: Oxford University Press, 2008), 17–25, 32–34; Maddison, *The World Economy,* vol. 1, table 3-5; Robert C. Allen, *From Farm to Factory: A Reinterpretation of the Soviet Industrial Revolution* (Princeton, NJ: Princeton University Press, 2003).

176. Biomass is not included in these figures despite its continuing importance to millions of families in poor regions of the world. Biomass tends to be collected and used outside of the commercial economy, hence most often unreported. See Vaclav Smil, *Energy in Nature and*

Society: General Energetics of Complex Systems (Cambridge, MA: MIT Press, 2008), chap. 9 (see esp. fig. 9.1).

177. Ibid., 241–243, 257–259.

178. Vaclav Smil, *Energy at the Crossroads: Global Perspectives and Uncertainties* (Cambridge, MA: MIT Press, 2005), 65–105.

179. Massimo Livi-Bacci, *A Concise History of World Population* (Cambridge, MA: Blackwell, 1992), table 4.3; Maddison, *The World Economy*, vol. 2, *Historical Statistics* (Paris: OECD Development Centre, 2006), table 5a.

180. Vaclav Smil, *Transforming the Twentieth Century: Technical Innovations and Their Consequences* (New York: Oxford University Press, 2006), 221–224.

181. John McCormick, *Reclaiming Paradise: The Global Environmental Movement* (Bloomington: Indiana University Press, 1989), 55–56, 69–71.

182. Smil, *Transforming the Twentieth Century*, 123–130; Peter Clark, "Versatile Plastics for Future," *Science News-Letter* 76, no. 24 (December 12, 1959): 402–403.

183. John B. Colton Jr., Frederick D. Knapp, and Bruce R. Burns, "Plastic Particles in Surface Waters of the Northwestern Atlantic," *Science* 185, no. 4150 (August 9, 1974): 491–497; "Oily Seas and Plastic Waters of the Atlantic," *Science News* 103, no. 8 (February 24, 1973): 119; Thor Heyerdahl, *The Ra Expeditions* (New York: Doubleday, 1971), 209–210, 235, 312 (quotation at 209).

184. Smil, *Transforming the Twentieth Century*, 123.

185. P. G. Ryan, C. J. Moore, J. A. van Franeker, and C. L. Moloney, "Monitoring the Abundance of Plastic Debris in the Marine Environment," *Philosophical Transactions of the Royal Society (Biology)* 364 (2009): 1999–2012; D. K. A. Barnes, F. Galgani, R. C. Thompson, and M. Barlaz, "Accumulation and Fragmentation of Plastic Debris in Global Environments," *Philosophical Transactions of the Royal Society (Biology)* 364 (2009): 1985–1998; Lindsey Hoshaw, "Afloat in the Ocean, Expanding Islands of Trash," *New York Times*, November 10, 2009, D2; Richard C. Thompson et al., "Lost at Sea: Where Is All the Plastic?," *Science* 304, no. 5672 (May 7, 2004): 838. See also the more popular treatment, Curtis Ebbesmeyer and Eric Scigliano, *Flotsametrics and the Floating World* (New York: HarperCollins, 2009), 186–221.

186. Peter Dauvergne, *The Shadows of Consumption: Consequences for the Global Environment* (Cambridge, MA: MIT Press, 2008), 99–131; Smil, *Transforming the Twentieth Century*, 41; Catherine Wolfram, Orie Shelef, and Paul J. Gertler, "How Will Energy Demand Develop in the Developing World?," National Bureau of Economic Research Working Paper No. 17747 (2012), at www.nber.org/papers/w17747.

187. Maddison, *The World Economy*, 1:131–134; Rondo Cameron and Larry Neal, *A Concise Economic History of the World from Paleolithic Times to the Present* (New York: Oxford University Press, 2003), 367–370. On the effects of cheap oil in postwar Europe, see Christian Pfister, "The Syndrome of the 1950s," in *Getting and Spending: European and American Consumer Societies in the Twentieth Century*, ed. Susan Strasser, Charles McGovern, and Matthias Judt (Cambridge: Cambridge University Press, 1998), 359–377.

188. Maddison, *The World Economy*, 1:139–141; Yasukichi Yasuba, "Japan's Post-war Growth in Historical Perspective," in *The Economic Development of Modern Japan, 1945–1995*, vol. 1,

From Occupation to the Bubble Economy, ed. Steven Tolliday (Northampton, MA: Edward Elgar, 2001), 3–16.

189. On Americanization in theory, see Richard Kuisel, "Commentary: Americanization for Historians," *Diplomatic History* 24, no. 3 (Summer 2000): 509–515. There is a massive literature on the Americanization of Europe. See, e.g., Emanuella Scarpellini, "Shopping American style: The Arrival of the Supermarket in Postwar Italy," *Enterprise and Society* 5, no. 4 (2004): 625–668; Detlef Junker, "The Continuity of Ambivalence: German Views of America, 1933–1945," in *Transatlantic Images and Perceptions: Germany and America since 1776,* ed. David Barkley and Elisabeth Glaser-Schmidt (New York: Cambridge University Press and German Historical Institute, 1997), 243–263; Richard Kuisel, *Seducing the French: The Dilemma of Americanization* (Berkeley: University of California Press, 1993); Frank Costigliola, *Awkward Dominion: American Political, Economic and Cultural Relations with Europe, 1919–33* (Ithaca, NY: Cornell University Press, 1984). On American cultural influence on Japanese consumerism, see Penelope Francks, *The Japanese Consumer: An Alternative Economic History of Modern Japan* (Cambridge: Cambridge University Press, 2009), 151–162; Yasuba, "Japan's Post-war Growth," 13–14. On America and East Asian consumerism generally, see James L. Watson, *Golden Arches East: McDonald's in East Asia* (Stanford, CA: Stanford University Press, 2006).

190. Maddison, *The World Economy,* vol. 2, tables 5a, 5b, 5c (pp. 542–543, 552–553, 562–563).

191. Kotkin, *Armageddon Averted,* chap. 1; Cameron and Neal, *Concise Economic History,* 372–373. For discussion of the effects of collectivization on nature in, and the peoples of, Eastern Europe, see Katrina Z. S. Schwartz, *Nature and National Identity after Communism: Globalizing the Ethnoscape* (Pittsburgh: University of Pittsburgh Press, 2006); Arvid Nelson, *Cold War Ecology: Forests, Farms, and People in the East German Landscape, 1945–1989* (New Haven, CT: Yale University Press, 2005).

192. Kotkin, *Armageddon Averted,* 10–17, 48–53.

193. Ibid., chap. 3.

194. Ibid., chap. 5; Maddison, *The World Economy,* 1:155–161.

195. Ho-fung Hung, "Introduction: The Three Transformations of Global Capitalism," in *China and the Transformation of Global Capitalism,* ed. Ho-fung Hung (Baltimore: Johns Hopkins University Press, 2009), 10–11; Osterhammel and Petersson, *Globalization,* 115–116.

196. Giovanni Arrighi, "China's Market Economy in the Long Run," 1–21; Ho-fung Hung, "Introduction," 6–13; John Minns, "World Economies: Southeast Asia since the 1950s," in *The Southeast Asia Handbook,* ed. Patrick Heenan and Monique Lamontagne (London: Fitzroy Dearborn, 2001), 24–37.

197. On the banana trade, see Marcelo Bucheli and Ian Read, "Banana Boats and Baby Food: The Banana in U.S. History," in *From Silver to Cocaine: Latin American Commodity Chains and the Building of the World Economy, 1500–2000,* ed. Steven Topik, Carlos Marichal, and Zephyr Frank (Durham, NC: Duke University Press, 2006), 204–227.

198. Osterhammel and Petersson, *Globalization,* 128–130; Minns, "World Economies."

199. Maddison, *The World Economy,* 1:151–155 and table 3-5.

200. Martinez-Alier, *Environmentalism of the Poor,* chap. 2; Ramachandra Guha and Juan Martinez-Alier, *Varieties of Environmentalism: Essays North and South* (Delhi: Oxford Uni-

versity Press, 1998), chap. 9; Herman E. Daly, "Steady-State Economics versus Growthmania: A Critique of the Orthodox Conceptions of Growth, Wants, Scarcity, and Efficiency," *Policy Sciences* 5, no. 2 (June 1974): 149–167.

201. Robert Costanza et al., "The Value of the World's Ecosystem Services and Natural Capital," *Nature* 387 (May 15, 1997): 253–260; Robert Costanza, "Ecological Economics: Reintegrating the Study of Humans and Nature," *Ecological Applications* 6, no. 4 (November 1996): 978–990; Kenneth Arrow et al., "Economic Growth, Carrying Capacity, and the Environment," *Ecological Applications* 6, no. 1 (February 1996): 13–15; Herman E. Daly, "On Economics as a Life Science," *Journal of Political Economy* 76, no. 3 (May–June 1968): 392–406; Kenneth E. Boulding, "Economics and Ecology," in *Future Environments of North America: Being the Record of a Conference Convened by the Conservation Foundation in April, 1965, at Airlie House, Warrenton, Virginia,* ed. F. Fraser Darling and John P. Milton (Garden City, NY: Natural History Press, 1966), 225–234.

202. David Satterthwaite, *Barbara Ward and the Origins of Sustainable Development* (London: International Institute for Environment and Development, 2006); Susan Baker, *Sustainable Development* (New York: International Institute for Environment and Development, 2006); Lorraine Elliott, *The Global Politics of the Environment* (New York: New York University Press, 2004); Robert Paehlke, "Environmental Politics, Sustainability and Social Science," *Environmental Politics* 10, no. 4 (Winter 2001): 1–22; United Nations Environment Programme, *In Defence of the Earth: The Basic Texts on Environment: Founex—Stockholm—Cocoyoc* (Nairobi: United Nations Environment Programme, 1981).

203. For an outstanding take on this question, see Ramachandra Guha, *How Much Should a Person Consume? Environmentalism in India and the United States* (Berkeley: University of California Press, 2006), chap. 9.

204. Vaclav Smil, *Energy in World History* (Boulder, CO: Westview, 1994), 185; on the USSR, see Paul Josephson, "War on Nature as Part of the Cold War: The Strategic and Ideological Roots of Environmental Degradation in the Soviet Union," in *Environmental Histories of the Cold War,* ed. J. R. McNeill and Corinna Unger (New York: Cambridge University Press, 2010), 46. According to Charles Maier, "The World Economy and the Cold War in the Middle of the Twentieth Century," in *The Cambridge History of the Cold War,* ed. Melvyn Leffler and Arne Westad (Cambridge: Cambridge University Press, 2010), 1:64, the USSR used about 20 percent of its GNP for military spending, whereas the United States, France, and Britain spent 5 to 10 percent of their GNPs for military purposes. The United States devoted about 3 to 4 percent of its oil consumption to the military. A single F-16, a workhorse of the Air Force from 1979 onward, used more fuel in an afternoon than the average American family vehicle did over two years.

205. On the interstate system and its ecological effects, see J. R. McNeill, "The Cold War and the Biosphere," in Leffler and Westad, *Cambridge History of the Cold War,* 3:434–436.

206. Christopher J. Ward, *Brezhnev's Folly: The Building of BAM and Late Soviet Socialism* (Pittsburgh: University of Pittsburgh Press, 2009). This project too had multiple motives, of course.

207. Philip Micklin, "The Aral Sea Disaster," *Annual Review of Earth and Planetary Sciences* 35 (2007): 47–72. One potential problem, linked to the Cold War directly, is that of the former

Vozrozhdeniya Island. This was the main testing site of the Soviet biological weapons program, where anthrax, smallpox, and many other pathogens were weaponized. In 2001 the island became part of a peninsula, so rodents and other creatures easily move in and out of the once-isolated testing ground.

208. Yin Shaoting, "Rubber Planting and Eco-Environmental/Socio-cultural Transition in Xishuangbanna," in *Good Earths: Regional and Historical Insights into China's Environment,* ed. Abe Ken-ichi and James E. Nickum (Kyoto: Kyoto University Press, 2009), 136–143; Judith Shapiro, *Mao's War against Nature* (New York: Cambridge University Press, 2001), 172–184; Hongmei Li, T. M. Aide, Youxin Ma, Wenjun Liu, and Min Cao, "Demand for Rubber Is Causing the Loss of High Diversity Rain Forest in SW China," *Biodiversity and Conservation* 16 (2007): 1731–1745; Wenjin Liu, Huabin Hu, Youxin Ma, and Hongmei Li, "Environmental and Socioeconomic Impacts of Increasing Rubber Plantations in Menglun Township, Southwest China," *Mountain Research and Development* 26 (2006): 245–253.

209. On Navajo uranium miners, see B. R. Johnston, S. E. Dawson, and G. Madsen, "Uranium Mining and Milling: Navajo Experiences in the American Southwest," in *Half-Lives and Half-Truths: Confronting the Radioactive Legacies of the Cold War,* ed. Barbara Rose Johnston (Santa Fe, NM: School for Advanced Research Press, 2007), 97–116.

210. Basic data are presented in Arjun Makhijani, Howard Hu, and Katherine Yih, eds., *Nuclear Wastelands: A Global Guide to Nuclear Weapons Production and Its Health and Environmental Effects* (Cambridge MA: MIT Press, 1995).

211. Kate Brown, *Plutopia: Nuclear Families, Atomic Cities, and the Great Soviet and American Plutonium Disasters* (New York: Oxford University Press, 2013); Michele Stenehjem Gerber, *On the Home Front: The Cold War Legacy of the Hanford Nuclear Site* (Lincoln: University of Nebraska Press, 2002); T. E. Marceau et al., *Hanford Site Historic District: History of the Plutonium Production Facilities, 1943–1990* (Columbus, OH: Battelle Press, 2003); John M. Whiteley, "The Hanford Nuclear Reservation: The Old Realities and the New," in *Critical Masses: Citizens, Nuclear Weapons Production, and Environmental Destruction in the United States and Russia,* ed. Russell J. Dalton, Paula Garb, Nicholas Lovrich, John Pierce, and John Whitely (Cambridge, MA: MIT Press, 1999), 29–58.

212. Ian Stacy, "Roads to Ruin on the Atomic Frontier: Environmental Decision Making at the Hanford Nuclear Reservation, 1942–1952," *Environmental History* 15 (2010): 415–448.

213. Brown, *Plutopia,* 169–170; Gerber, *Home Front,* 90–92; M. A. Robkin, "Experimental Release of 131I: The Green Run," *Health Physics* 62, no. 6 (1992): 487–495.

214. Bengt Danielsson and Marie-Thérèse Danielsson, *Poisoned Reign: French Nuclear Colonialism in the Pacific* (New York: Penguin, 1986); Stewart Firth, *Nuclear Playground* (Honolulu: University of Hawai'i Press, 1986; Mark Merlin and Ricardo Gonzalez, "Environmental Impacts of Nuclear Testing in Remote Oceania, 1946–1996," in McNeill and Unger, *Environmental Histories,* 167–202. On the fate of Marshall Islanders, who unwillingly hosted US nuclear testing for decades, see Barbara Rose Johnston and Holly M. Barker, *Consequential Damages of Nuclear War: The Rongelap Report* (Walnut Creek, CA: Left Coast Press, 2008).

215. Although total radionuclide emissions may have been greater at Tomsk-7, there they were more widely dispersed. Don J. Bradley, *Behind the Nuclear Curtain: Radioactive Waste Man-*

agement in the Former Soviet Union (Columbus: Battelle Press, 1997), 451ff. On the Soviet nuclear complex, see Nikolai Egorov, Vladimir Novikov, Frank Parker, and Victor Popov, eds., *The Radiation Legacy of the Soviet Nuclear Complex* (London: Earthscan, 2000); Igor Kudrik, Charles Digges, Alexander Nikitin, Nils Bøhmer, Vladimir Kuznetsov, and Vladislav Larin, *The Russian Nuclear Industry* (Oslo: Bellona Foundation, 2004); John Whiteley, "The Compelling Realities of Mayak," in Dalton et al., *Critical Masses,* 59–96. On human consequences, also see Paula Garb, "Russia's Radiation Victims of Cold War Weapons Production Surviving in a Culture of Secrecy and Denial," and Cynthia Werner and Kathleen Purvis-Roberts, "Unraveling the Secrets of the Past: Contested Visions of Nuclear Testing in the Soviet Republic of Kazakhstan," both in Johnston, *Half-Lives and Half-Truths,* 249–276, 277–298.

216. A Norwegian and Russian research team calculated that accidental and deliberate releases of strontium-90 and cesium-137 between 1948 and 1996 at Mayak amounted to 8,900 petabecquerels. Rob Edwards, "Russia's Toxic Shocker," *New Scientist* 6 (December 1997): 15. One petabecquerel = 10^{15} becquerels; 8,900 petabecquerels is about 0.24 billion curies, roughly 1.8 times the official estimate.

217. Bradley, *Behind the Nuclear Curtain,* 399–401; Garb, "Russia's Radiation Victims," 253–260.

218. Zhores Medvedev, *Nuclear Disaster in the Urals* (New York: Norton, 1979).

219. Recent summaries of the Soviet nuclear mess are Paul Josephson, "War on Nature as Part of the Cold War: The Strategic and Ideological Roots of Environmental Degradation in the Soviet Union," in McNeill and Unger, *Environmental Histories,* 43–46; and McNeill, "Cold War and the Biosphere," 437–443 (from which much of this account is drawn). See also Brown, *Plutopia,* 189–212, 231–246.

220. Egorov et al., *Radiation Legacy,* 150–153; Bradley, *Behind the Nuclear Curtain,* 419–420.

221. E.g., Mark Hertsgaard, *Earth Odyssey* (New York: Broadway Books, 1998); Garb, "Russia's Radiation Victims." See also Murray Feshbach, *Ecological Disaster: Cleaning Up the Hidden Legacy of the Soviet Regime* (New York: Twentieth Century Fund, 1995), 48–49; Murray Feshbach and Alfred Friendly Jr., *Ecocide in the USSR* (New York: Basic Books, 1992), 174–179; Brown, *Plutopia.*

222. N. A. Koshikurnikova et al., "Mortality among Personnel Who Worked at the Mayak Complex in the First Years of Its Operation," *Health Physics* 71 (1996): 90–99; M. M. Kossenko, "Cancer Mortality among Techa River Residents and Their Offspring," *Health Physics* 71 (1996): 77–82; N. A. Koshikurnikova et al., "Studies on the Mayak Nuclear Workers: Health Effects," *Radiation and Environmental Biophysics* 41 (2002): 29–31; Mikhail Balonov et al., "Assessment of Current Exposure of the Population Living in the Techa Basin from Radioactive Releases from the Mayak Facility," *Health Physics* 92 (2007): 134–147. Ongoing US Department of Energy studies also suggest serious health problems among former Mayak workers. See http://hss.energy .gov/HealthSafety/IHS/ihp/jccrer/active_projects.html. A good recent summary is W. J. F. Standring, Mark Dowdall, and Per Strand, "Overview of Dose Assessment Developments and the Health of Riverside Residents Close to the 'Mayak' PA Facilities, Russia," *International Journal of Environmental Research and Public Health* 6 (2009): 174–199.

223. Whiteley, "Compelling Realities," 90, citing Paula Garb, "Complex Problems and No Clear Solutions: Difficulties of Defining and Assigning Culpability for Radiation Victimization in

the Chelyabinsk Region of Russia," in *Life and Death Matters: Human Rights at the End of the Millennium,* ed. B. R. Johnston (Walnut Creek, CA: AltaMira Press, 1997).

224. The least clear situation is that of China, where data are fewer and even less reliable than for Russia. See Alexandra Brooks and Howard Hu, "China," in Makhijani et al., *Nuclear Wastelands,* 515–518.

225. Bellona Foundation, *Bellona Report No. 8: Sellafield,* at www.bellona.org. See also Jacob Hamblin, *Poison in the Well: Radioactive Waste in the Oceans at the Dawn of the Nuclear Age* (New Brunswick, NJ: Rutgers University Press, 2008).

226. In 2006 a Russian court determined that a Mayak director, Vitaly Sadovnikov, had authorized the dumping of tens of millions of cubic meters of radioactive wastes into the Techa River in 2001–2004, in order to cut costs and pay himself more. See the Bellona post of March 20, 2006, at www.bellona.ru/bellona.org/news/news_2006/Mayak_plant_%20general_director_dismissed _from_his_post.

227. National Geographic News: http://news.nationalgeographic.com/news/2001/08/0828_wire nukesites.html.

228. Strontium-90 in some biochemical respects mimics calcium and is readily absorbed through food and drink into human teeth, bones, and bone marrow, where it can cause cancers and leukemia.

229. Arhun Makhijani and Stephen I. Schwartz, "Victims of the Bomb," in *Atomic Audit: The Costs and Consequences of U.S. Nuclear Weapons since 1940,* ed. Stephen I. Schwartz (Washington, DC: Brookings Institution Press, 1998), 395, gives a range of 70,000 to 800,000 for global cancer deaths attributable to US atmospheric testing. Estimates for deaths due to other aspects of nuclear weapons programs are still more inexact, especially where China and the USSR are concerned.

230. In the United States, Edward Teller was the leading proponent for what he called "geographical engineering." Teller, a Budapest-born and German-educated vehement anticommunist, matched the most enthusiastic Soviet visionaries when it came to geoengineering uses for nuclear explosions. Teller et al., *The Constructive Uses of Nuclear Explosives* (New York: McGraw-Hill, 1968); Scott Kirsch, *Proving Grounds: Project Plowshare and the Unrealized Dream of Nuclear Earthmoving* (New Brunswick, NJ: Rutgers University Press, 2005).

231. This was one of a few dozen accidents involving aircraft and nuclear weapons, none of which produced full-blown catastrophes. Randall C. Maydew, *America's Lost H-Bomb: Palomares, Spain, 1966* (Manhattan, KS: Sunflower University Press, 1997); a readable journalistic account is Barbara Moran, *The Day We Lost the H-Bomb: Cold War, Hot Nukes, and the Worst Nuclear Weapons Disaster in History* (New York: Presidio Press, 2009).

232. Speech quoted in Frank Dikötter, *Mao's Great Famine: The History of China's Most Devastating Catastrophe, 1958–1962* (New York: Walker and Co., 2010), 174. On the Great Leap Forward itself, see Alfred Chan, *Mao's Crusade: Politics and Policy Implementation in China's Great Leap Forward* (New York: Oxford University Press, 2001); Dali Yang, *Calamity and Reform in China: State, Rural Society, and Institutional Change since the Great Leap Forward* (Stanford, CA: Stanford University Press, 1998). A well-regarded journalistic overview is Jasper Becker, *Hungry Ghosts: Mao's Secret Famine* (New York: Holt, 1998). A detailed political

account is Roderick MacFarquhar, *The Origins of the Cultural Revolution*, vol. 2, *The Great Leap Forward* (New York: Columbia University Press, 1983). The most authoritative treatment is probably Yang Jisheng, *Bu Mei*, now in English as *Tombstone: The Great Chinese Famine, 1958–62* (New York: Farrar, Straus and Giroux, 2012). On the environmental aspects, see Shapiro, *Mao's War against Nature*, 70–93; Elizabeth Economy, *The River Runs Black: The Environmental Challenge to China's Future* (Ithaca, NY: Cornell University Press, 2004), 51–53; and Dikötter, *Mao's Great Famine*, 174–188.

233. Most scholars offer figures around 30 million, and Yang Jisheng, *Tombstone*, gives 38 million. Dikötter says at least 45 million in *Mao's Great Famine*. Unusually, this famine was most deadly among males over age forty, whereas typically famines kill more small children. Susan Cotts Watkins and Jane Menken, "Famines in Historical Perspective," *Population and Development Review* 11 (1985): 647–675.

234. At one point he aimed to surpass US steel production within seven years. Bao Maohong, "The Evolution of Environmental Problems and Environmental Policy in China," in McNeill and Unger, *Environmental Histories*, 317, citing Xie Chuntao, *The Roaring Waves of the Great Leap Forward* (Henan: People Press, 1990), 25 (in Chinese).

235. Roderick MacFarquhar, Timothy Cheek, and Eugene Wu, eds., *The Secret Speeches of Chairman Mao: From the Hundred Flowers to the Great Leap Forward* (Cambridge, MA: Harvard University Press, 1989), 377–517, esp. 409, 511; MacFarquhar, *Origins of the Cultural Revolution*, 2:90.

236. The ninety million figure is Mao's and could well be fanciful, although it is widely repeated by scholars. MacFarquhar, *Origins of the Cultural Revolution*, 2:113–116, 128–130; Bao Maohong, "Evolution of Environmental Problems," 326–327; Economy, *River Runs Black*, 53; Shapiro, *Mao's War against Nature*, 81.

237. Shapiro, *Mao's War against Nature*, 81–83; Dikötter, *Mao's Great Famine*, 176–178. For Sichuan, John Studley, "Forests and Environmental Degradation in SW China," *International Forestry Review* 1 (1999): 260–265. See also S. D. Richardson, *Forests and Forestry in China* (Washington, DC: Island Press, 1990); and for the long view, Mark Elvin, *Retreat of the Elephants* (New Haven, CT: Yale University Press, 2004), 19–85.

238. Data from Bao Maohong, "Evolution of Environmental Problems," 327.

239. McFarquhar et al., *Secret Speeches of Chairman Mao*, 378.

240. Bao Maohong, "Evolution of Environmental Problems," 328.

241. Frantic urgency, and competition with foreigners, pervaded all ranks during the Great Leap Forward: The Chinese Association of Paleontologists vowed to overtake capitalist fossil collectors within seven years. Stanley Karnow, *Mao and China* (New York: Viking Penguin, 1990), 89.

242. Lillian Li, *Fighting Famine in North China: State, Market, and Environmental Decline* (Stanford, CA: Stanford University Press, 2007), 369–370.

243. Karnow, *Mao and China*, 91–92.

244. Dikötter, *Mao's Great Famine*, 188. The best sources on the environmental costs of the Great Leap Forward are Shapiro, *Mao's War against Nature*, and Dikötter, *Mao's Great Famine*, supplemented by Bao Maohong, "Evolution of Environmental Problems." See also Mao's

pronouncements in McFarquhar et al., *Secret Speeches of Chairman Mao,* esp. 379, 403, 409, 441, 450.

245. Barry Naughton, "The Third Front: Defence Industrialization in the Chinese Interior," *China Quarterly* 115 (1988): 351–386.

246. On the environmental costs, see Shapiro, *Mao's War against Nature,* 154–156.

247. McFarquhar et al., *Secret Speeches of Chairman Mao,* 384. In a speech of January 4, 1958.

248. Qu Geping and Li Jinchang, *Population and the Environment in China* (Boulder, CO: Lynne Rienner, 1994), 180.

249. Bao Maohong, "Evolution of Environmental Problems," 330–339.

250. For the international politics of these wars in Southern Africa, see Chris Saunders and Sue Onslow, "The Cold War and Southern Africa, 1976–1990," in Leffler and Westad, *Cambridge History of the Cold War,* 3:222–243. For the social and environmental effects, see Emmanuel Kreike, "War and Environmental Effects of Displacement in Southern Africa (1970s–1990s)," in *African Environment and Development: Rhetoric, Programs, Realities,* ed. William Moseley and B. Ikubolajeh Logan (Aldershot, UK: Ashgate, 2004), 89–110; Joseph P. Dudley, J. R. Ginsberg, A. J. Plumptre, J. A. Hart, and L. C. Campos, "Effects of War and Civil Strife on Wildlife and Wildlife Habitats," *Conservation Biology* 16, no. 2 (2002): 319–329.

251. Rodolphe de Koninck, *Deforestation in Viet Nam* (Ottawa: International Development Research Centre, 1999), 12. The stories of defoliants and Rome plows are recounted in many texts, and tidily summarized in Greg Bankoff, "A Curtain of Silence: Asia's Fauna in the Cold War," in McNeill and Unger, *Environmental Histories,* 215–216. See also David Biggs, *Quagmire: Nation-Building and Nature in the Mekong Delta* (Seattle: University of Washington Press, 2012).

252. The foremost authority on ecological effects of war in Vietnam is A. H. Westing. See, e.g., Westing, ed., *Herbicides in War: The Long-Term Ecological and Human Consequences* (London: Taylor and Francis, 1984).

253. Bankoff, "Curtain of Silence."

254. Dudley et al., "Effects of War." See also M. J. Chase and C. R. Griffin, "Elephants Caught in the Middle: Impacts of War, Fences, and People on Elephant Distribution and Abundance in the Caprivi Strip, Namibia," *African Journal of Ecology* 47 (2009): 223–233.

255. Andrew Terry, Karin Ullrich, and Uwe Riecken, *The Green Belt of Europe: From Vision to Reality* (Gland, Switzerland: IUCN, 2006).

256. Lisa Brady, "Life in the DMZ: Turning a Diplomatic Failure into an Environmental Success," *Diplomatic History* 32 (2008): 585–611; Ke Chung Kim, "Preserving Korea's Demilitarized Corridor for Conservation: A Green Approach to Conflict Resolution," in *Peace Parks: Conservation and Conflict Resolution,* ed. Saleem Ali (Cambridge, MA: MIT Press, 2007), 239–260; Hall Healy, "Korean Demilitarized Zone Peace and Nature Park," *International Journal on World Peace* 24 (2007): 61–84.

257. Franz-Josef Strauss, quoted in Ramachandra Guha, *Environmentalism* (New York: Longman, 2000), 97.

258. Guha, *Environmentalism,* 69–79; Miller, *Environmental History of Latin America,* 204–205. On Carson and the reception of *Silent Spring,* see Linda J. Lear, "Rachel Carson's 'Silent Spring,'" *Environmental History Review* 17, no. 2 (Summer 1993): 23–48. On perceptions of

DDT before and after *Silent Spring,* see Thomas R. Dunlap, ed., *DDT,* Silent Spring, *and the Rise of Environmentalism: Classic Texts* (Seattle: University of Washington Press, 2008).

259. William Cronon, for one, has argued against oversimplifying the impact of Carson and *Silent Spring,* while acknowledging the enormous debt that should be paid to both. See his foreword to Dunlap, *DDT, "Silent Spring,"* ix–xii.

260. Uekoetter, *The Age of Smoke,* 113–207.

261. Adam Rome, " 'Give Earth a Chance': The Environmental Movement and the Sixties," *Journal of American History* 90, no. 2 (September 2003): 525–554; McCormick, *Reclaiming Paradise,* 52–54. Guha has dubbed the first two decades after World War II the "age of ecological innocence." See Guha, *Environmentalism,* 63–68.

262. Russell J. Dalton, *The Green Rainbow: Environmental Groups in Western Europe* (New Haven, CT: Yale University Press, 1994), 36–37.

263. Jeffrey Broadbent, *Environmental Politics in Japan: Networks of Power and Protest* (Cambridge: Cambridge University Press, 1998), 12–19; Miranda Schreurs, *Environmental Politics in Japan, Germany, and the United States* (Cambridge: Cambridge University Press, 2003), 35–46; Rome, " 'Give Earth a Chance' "; Catherine Knight, "The Nature Conservation Movement in Post-War Japan," *Environment and History* 16 (2010): 349–370; Brett Walker, *Toxic Archipelago: A History of Industrial Disease in Japan* (Seattle: University of Washington Press, 2010).

264. Publications like *The Limits to Growth* stimulated a fierce and intellectually vigorous reaction. The American economist Julian Simon was among the more famous of its proponents. See, e.g., Julian Simon, *The Ultimate Resource* (Princeton, NJ: Princeton University Press, 1981).

265. McCormick, *Reclaiming Paradise,* 144–145; Frank Zelko, *Make It a Green Peace: The Rise of Countercultural Environmentalism* (New York: Oxford University Press, 2013).

266. Martinez-Alier, *Environmentalism of the Poor*; Guha and Martinez-Alier, *Varieties of Environmentalism,* 3–5.

267. Ramachandra Guha, "Environmentalist of the Poor," *Economic and Political Weekly* 37, no. 3 (January 19–25, 2002): 204–207. The postmaterialist hypothesis is most closely associated with the American political scientist Ronald Inglehart.

268. Two Indian intellectuals, Anil Agarwal and Ramachandra Guha, were particularly important in igniting a debate between environmentalists in rich and poor countries. Guha has acknowledged an intellectual and emotional debt to Agarwal; see Guha, "Environmentalist of the Poor." On Chipko, see Guha's *The Unquiet Woods: Ecological Change and Peasant Resistance in the Himalayas* (Berkeley: University of California Press, 2000), 152–179, 197–200. On American environmental history and its reception of the Indian critique, see Paul Sutter, "When Environmental Traditions Collide: Ramachandra Guha's *The Unquiet Woods* and U.S. Environmental History," *Environmental History* 14 (July 2009): 543–550. For a summary of the many Chipko interpretations, see Haripriya Rangan, *Of Myths and Movements: Rewriting Chipko into Himalayan History* (London: Verso, 2000), 13–38. One of the more romantic is provided by Vandana Shiva, "The Green Movement in Asia," in *Research in Social Movements, Conflicts and Change: The Green Movement Worldwide,* ed. Matthias Finger (Greenwich, CT: JAI Press, 1992), 195–215 (see esp. 202).

269. On Chico Mendes, see Kathryn Hochstetler and Margaret E. Keck, *Greening Brazil: Environmental Activism in State and Society* (Durham, NC: Duke University Press, 2007), 111–112. On Narmada, see Madhav Gadgil and Ramachandra Guha, *Ecology and Equity: The Use and Abuse of Nature in Contemporary India* (London: Routledge, 1995), 61–63, 73–76. A short summary of Ken Saro-Wiwa's career is provided in Guha and Martinez-Alier, *Varieties of Environmentalism,* xviii–xix.

270. Martinez-Alier, *Environmentalism of the Poor,* 168–194. A classic text in the American environmental justice literature is Robert D. Bullard, *Dumping in Dixie: Race, Class and Environmental Quality* (Boulder, CO: Westview, 1990).

271. Shapiro, *Mao's War against Nature,* 21–65.

272. Valery J. Cholakov, "Toward Eco-Revival? The Cultural Roots of Russian Environmental Concerns," in Hughes, *Face of the Earth,* 155–157. On interwar conservationism, see Guha, *Environmentalism,* 125–130. On Soviet rivers, see Charles Ziegler, "Political Participation, Nationalism and Environmental Politics in the USSR," in *The Soviet Environment: Problems, Policies, and Politics,* ed. John Massey Stewart (New York: Cambridge University Press, 1992), 32–33. On Cuba, see Sergio Diaz-Briquets and Jorge Perez-Lopez, *Conquering Nature: The Environmental Legacy of Socialism in Cuba* (Pittsburgh: University of Pittsburgh Press, 2000), 13–17.

273. Marshall Goldman, "Environmentalism and Nationalism: An Unlikely Twist in an Unlikely Direction," in Stewart, *The Soviet Environment,* 2–3. See also Stephen Brain, *Song of the Forest: Russian Forestry and Stalin's Environmentalism* (Pittsburgh: University of Pittsburgh Press, 2011).

274. Cholakov, "Toward Eco-Revival?," 157–158; Ziegler, "Political Participation," 30–32.

275. Merrill E. Jones, "Origins of the East German Environmental Movement," *German Studies Review* 16, no. 2 (May 1993): 238–247; William T. Markham, *Environmental Organizations in Modern Germany: Hardy Survivors in the Twentieth Century and Beyond* (New York: Berghahn, 2008), 134–141.

276. Oleg N. Yanitksy, "Russian Environmental Movements," in *Earth, Air, Fire, Water: Humanistic Studies of the Environment,* ed. Jill Ker Conway, Kenneth Keniston, and Leo Marx (Amherst, MA: University of Massachusetts Press, 1999), 184–186; Cholakov, "Toward Eco-Revival?," 161; Ze'ev Wolfson and Vladimir Butenko, "The Green Movement in the USSR and Eastern Europe," in Finger, *Research in Social Movements,* 41–50.

277. Yanfei Sun and Dingxin Zhao, "Environmental Campaigns," in *Popular Protest in China,* ed. Kevin J. O'Brien (Cambridge, MA: Harvard University Press, 2008), 144–162; Robert Weller, *Discovering Nature: Globalization and Environmental Culture in China and Taiwan* (Cambridge: Cambridge University Press 2006), 115–129.

278. Uekoetter, *The Age of Smoke,* 252–258; Miller, *Environmental History of Latin America,* 206–208; Russell J. Dalton, "The Environmental Movement in Western Europe," in *Environmental Politics in the International Arena: Movements, Parties, Organizations, and Policy,* ed. Sheldon Kamieniecki (Albany: SUNY Press, 1993), 52–53; McCormick, *Reclaiming Paradise,* 125–131. On Nixon, see Ted Steinberg, *Down to Earth: Nature's Role in American History* (New York: Oxford University Press, 2009), 251.

279. Lorraine Elliott, *The Global Politics of the Environment* (New York: New York University Press, 2004), 7–13; Hughes, "Biodiversity in World History," 35–36.

280. McCormick, *Reclaiming Paradise,* 88–105.

281. Samuel P. Hays, *A History of Environmental Politics since 1945* (Pittsburgh: University of Pittsburgh Press, 2000), 95–117; Hays, *Explorations in Environmental History: Essays by Samuel P. Hays* (Pittsburgh: University of Pittsburgh Press, 1998), 223–258.

282. Wangari Maathai, *Unbowed: A Memoir* (New York: Knopf, 2006), 119–138; Maathai, *The Green Belt Movement: Sharing the Approach and Experience* (New York: Lantern Books, 2003).

283. Although Brazil had a long and admirable conservationist tradition, its leaders possessed very little power. See the essays by José Luiz de Andrade Franco and José Augusto Drummond appearing in consecutive issues of *Environmental History* 13 (October 2008): 724–750, and 14 (January 2009): 82–102.

284. Hochstetler and Keck, *Greening Brazil,* 26–33, 70–81, 97–130. For an example of environmentalists' attention to Brazilian–West German nuclear cooperation, see *Das deutsch-brasilianische Atomgeschäft* (Bonn, 1977), self-published by Amnesty International/Brasilienkoordinationsgruppe, Arbeitsgemeinschaft katholischer Studenten- und Hochschulgemeinden, and Bundesverband Bürgerinitiativen Umweltschutz.

285. See the global greens website, www.globalgreens.org/.

286. Massive supertanker accidents would occur several more times by century's end (see above section on coal and oil transport). The most notorious were the *Amoco Cadiz,* off Brittany in 1978, and the *Exxon Valdez,* off Alaska in 1989. Both were about twice the size of the *Torrey Canyon.* See Joanna Burger, *Oil Spills* (New Brunswick, NJ: Rutgers University Press, 1997), 28–61.

287. Christopher Key Chapple, "Toward an Indigenous Indian Environmentalism," in *Purifying the Earthly Body of God: Religion and Ecology in Hindu India,* ed. Lance E. Nelson (Albany, NY: SUNY Press, 1998), 13–38; Miller, *Environmental History of Latin America,* 209–211; Dalton, "The Environmental Movement," 58. For a discussion of French nuclear politics before and after Chernobyl, see Michael Bess, *The Light-Green Society: Ecology and Technological Modernity in France, 1960–2000* (Chicago: University of Chicago Press, 2003), 92–109.

288. Ironically, Cousteau had a difficult relationship with French environmentalists, who considered him naive. This did not prevent them from extending invitations to Cousteau to head green parties in national elections, which he rebuffed. See Bess, *The Light-Green Society,* 72–73.

289. Not all of this has been driven by profit. Cuba has been running perhaps the world's largest experiment in organic farming. After losing access to Soviet oil in the 1990s, the country turned, out of desperation, to organic methods. Some argue that the Cuban population enjoys a healthier, tastier, and more sustainable diet now than at any time before. See Miller, *Environmental History of Latin America,* 230–235.

4. Global Cultures

1. Charles Bright and Michael Geyer, "Where in the World Is America? The History of the United States in the Global Age," in *Rethinking American History in a Global Age,* ed. Thomas Bender (Berkeley, CA: University of California Press, 2002), 63–99.

2. On the long history of globalization, see J. R. McNeill and William H. McNeill, *The Human Web: A Bird's-Eye View of World History* (New York: Norton, 2003); and David Armitage, "Is

There a Pre-History of Globalization?," in *Comparison and History: Europe in Cross-National Perspective,* ed. Deborah Cohen and Maura O'Connor (London: Routledge, 2004), 165–176. On recent globalization, see Jürgen Osterhammel and Niels Petersson, *Globalization: A Short History,* trans. Dona Geyer (Princeton, NJ: Princeton University Press, 2005).

3. Franz Boas, *The Mind of Primitive Man* (New York: Macmillan, 1911); Ruth Benedict, *Patterns of Culture* (Boston: Houghton Mifflin, 1934); Margaret Mead, *Continuities in Cultural Evolution* (New Haven, CT: Yale University Press, 1964). See also Stephen Toulmin's foreword to the 1999 edition of *Continuities in Cultural Evolution* (New Brunswick, NJ: Transaction).

4. Alfred Eckes Jr., "Open Door Expansionism Reconsidered: The World War II Experience," *Journal of American History* 59, no. 4 (1973), 924; Raymond Vernon, *Sovereignty at Bay: The Multinational Spread of U.S. Enterprises* (New York: Basic Books, 1971).

5. For a useful survey and bibliography of the literature on globalization, see Andreas Wimmer, "Globalizations *avant la lettre*: A Comparative View of Isomorphization and Heteromorphization in an Inter-Connecting World," *Comparative Studies in Society and History* 43, 3 (July 2001): 436.

6. George Ritzer, *The McDonaldization of Society*, 20th anniv. ed. (Los Angeles: Sage, 2013).

7. José Corrêa Leite with Carolina Gil, *The World Social Forum: Strategies of Resistance* (Chicago: Haymarket Books, 2005).

8. UN Universal Declaration of Human Rights, adopted and proclaimed by General Assembly Resolution 217 A (III) of December 10, 1948, www.un.org/Overview/rights.html.

9. Apart from the United Nations, those international organizations include the IMF, the International Court of Justice in The Hague, UNESCO (United Nations Educational Scientific and Cultural Organization), and UNICEF (United Nations Children's Fund). See also Akira Iriye, *Global Community: The Role of International Organizations in the Making of the Contemporary World* (Berkeley: University of California Press, 2002).

10. Amy L. S. Staples, *The Birth of Development: How the World Bank, Food and Agriculture Organization, and World Health Organization Changed the World, 1945–1965* (Kent, OH: Kent State University Press, 2006).

11. The definition of *urban* itself is subject to local interpretation. The UN statistical record office relied on reports from member states in compiling its data. Even within Europe, statistical record keeping differed greatly. For example, Albania reported as urban any community with more than four hundred inhabitants, while not far to the east, Turkey regarded as urban only cities with populations above twenty thousand. United Nations, *Demographic Yearbook 2005* (New York: United Nations Publications, 2008), table 6, at http://unstats.un.org/unsd/demographic /products/dyb/dyb2005.htm.

12. Dietmar Rothermund, *The Routledge Companion to Decolonization* (London: Routledge, 2006).

13. See Partha Chatterjee, *The Nation and Its Fragments: Colonial and Postcolonial Histories* (Princeton, NJ: Princeton University Press, 1993).

14. Tony Judt, *Postwar: A History of Europe since 1945* (New York: Penguin, 2005), 17–21.

15. On the internment camps, see Roger Daniels, *Prisoners without Trial: Japanese Americans in World War II* (New York: Hill and Wang, 1993). On forced migration, see Peter Gatrell and

Nick Baron, eds., *Warlands: Population Resettlement and State Reconstruction in the Soviet–East European Borderlands, 1945–1950* (Basingstoke, UK: Palgrave MacMillan, 2009). On forced labor and the Holocaust, see Michael Thad Allen, *The Business of Genocide: The SS, Slave Labor, and the Concentration Camps* (Chapel Hill: University of North Carolina Press, 2002); Timothy Snyder, *Bloodlands: Europe between Hitler and Stalin* (New York: Basic Books, 2010); Paul B. Jaskot, *The Architecture of Oppression: The SS, Forced Labor and the Nazi Monumental Building Economy* (London: Routledge, 2000).

16. Lori Watt, *When Empire Comes Home: Repatriation and Reintegration in Postwar Japan* (Cambridge, MA: Harvard University Asia Center, 2009); John Dower, *Embracing Defeat: Japan in the Wake of World War II* (New York: Norton, 1999), 48–51.

17. On German Jews in Israel, see Shlomo Erel, *Neue Wurzeln: 50 Jahre Immigration deutschsprachiger Juden in Israel* (Gerlingen: Bleicher Verlag, 1983). Curt D. Wormann, "German Jews in Israel: Their Cultural Situation since 1933," in *Leo Baeck Institute Yearbook* (1970), 73–103. On German expellees in West Germany, see Andreas Kossert, *Kalte Heimat: Die Geschichte der deutschen Vertriebenen nach 1945* (Munich: Siedler, 2008); Eagle Glassheim, "The Mechanics of Ethnic Cleansing: The Expulsion of Germans from Czechoslovakia, 1945–1947," in *Redrawing Nations: Ethnic Cleansing in East-Central Europe, 1944–1948,* ed. Philipp Ther and Ana Siljak (Lanham, MD: Rowman and Littlefield, 2001), 197–219.

18. Vladislav M. Zubok, *A Failed Empire: The Soviet Union in the Cold War from Stalin to Gorbachev* (Chapel Hill: University of North Carolina Press, 2007); Zubok, *Zhivago's Children: The Last Russian Intelligentsia* (Cambridge, MA: Belknap Press of Harvard University Press, 2009), 259–443.

19. The book was published in the West in 1973 and then smuggled back into the Soviet Union as samizdat. For more detail, see Zubok, *Zhivago's Children,* 308–309. On Soviet imperialism, see Odd Arne Westad, Sven Holtsmark, and Iver B. Neumann, eds. *The Soviet Union in Eastern Europe, 1945–1989* (New York: St. Martin's Press, 1994).

20. Mark J. Gasiorowski and Malcolm Byrne, eds., *Mohammad Mosaddeq and the 1953 Coup in Iran* (Syracuse, NY: Syracuse University Press, 2004); Stephen Kinzer, *All the Shah's Men: An American Coup and the Roots of Middle East Terror* (Hoboken, NJ: Wiley and Sons, 2003); Richard H. Immerman, *The CIA in Guatemala: The Foreign Policy of Intervention* (Austin: University of Texas Press, 1982).

21. On Latin America, see Walter LaFeber, *Inevitable Revolutions: The United States in Central America* (New York: Norton, 1984); Greg Grandin, *Empire's Workshop: Latin America, the United States, and the Rise of the New Imperialism* (New York: Metropolitan Books, 2006); Greg Grandin and Gilbert M. Joseph, eds., *A Century of Revolution: Insurgent and Counterinsurgent Violence during Latin America's Long Cold War* (Durham, NC: Duke University Press, 2010).

22. John Morton Blum, *V Was for Victory: Politics and American Culture during World War II* (New York: Houghton Mifflin, 1976), 325–327.

23. Thomas J. Knock, *To End All Wars: Woodrow Wilson and the Quest for a New World Order* (New York: Oxford University Press, 1992), 263–270.

24. Henry Luce, "The American Century," *Life,* February 17, 1941. Reprinted in Luce, *The American Century* (New York: Farrar & Rinehart, 1941), 39.

25. Luce, *The American Century*, 33–34.

26. Frank Ninkovich, *The Diplomacy of Ideas: U.S. Foreign Policy and Cultural Relations, 1938–1950* (New York: Cambridge University Press, 1981), 25–34.

27. Walter L. Hixson, *Parting the Curtain: Propaganda, Culture, and the Cold War, 1945–1961* (New York: St. Martin's Press, 1997), 2, 11.

28. Ibid., 21, 37–38.

29. For more information on the CCF, see Peter Coleman, *The Liberal Conspiracy: The Congress for Cultural Freedom and the Struggle for the Mind of Postwar Europe* (New York: Free Press, 1989); Michael Hochgeschwender, *Freiheit in der Offensive? Der Kongress für Kulturelle Freiheit und die Deutschen* (Munich: Oldenbourg, 1998), 217–219, 229–253, 559–571.

30. Hixson, *Parting the Curtain*, 17–18.

31. David Caute, *The Dancer Defects: The Struggle for Cultural Supremacy during the Cold War* (Oxford: Oxford University Press, 2003), 450; Hixson, *Parting the Curtain*, 117.

32. Penny M. von Eschen, *Satchmo Blows Up the World: Jazz Ambassadors Play the Cold War* (Cambridge, MA: Harvard University Press, 2004), 79–91.

33. Lizabeth Cohen, *A Consumer's Republic: The Politics of Mass Consumption in Postwar America* (New York: Knopf, 2003).

34. Hixson, *Parting the Curtain*, 153–154; Caute, *The Dancer Defects*, 40–43. Both exhibits were part of a 1958 U.S.-Soviet agreement on cultural and scientific exchange.

35. According to historian Chen Jian, the Soviet intervention in Czechoslovakia in August 1968 drove Chinese leaders to seek relations with the United States. See Chen Jian, *Mao's China and the Cold War* (Chapel Hill: University of North Carolina Press, 2001), 243–245. See also Jan Foitzik, ed., *Entstalinisierungskrise in Ostmitteleuropa, 1953–1956: Vom 17. Juni bis zum ungarischen Volksaufstand—Politische, militärische, soziale und nationale Dimensionen* (Paderborn: Schöningh, 2001); Christiane Brenner and Peter Heumos, *Sozialgeschichtliche Kommunismusforschung: Tschechoslowakei, Polen, Ungarn und DDR, 1945–1968* (Munich: Oldenbourg, 2005).

36. John Dower, *War without Mercy: Race and Power in the Pacific War* (New York: Pantheon, 1986), 118–190.

37. These ideas are laid out in Lenin's 1917 pamphlet *Imperialism, the Highest Stage of Capitalism: A Popular Outline*, reprinted in 1939 in English translation (New York: International, 1939).

38. "World Youth Groups Converge on Prague," *New York Times*, July 24, 1947; "International: Festival of Youth," *Time*, August 11, 1947. The *Time* article gave an estimate of thirty thousand attendees, which was significantly higher than the official estimates of the organizers.

39. For more detail, see Lawrence Wittner, *The Struggle against the Bomb*, vol. 1: *One World or None* (Stanford, CA: Stanford University Press, 1993), 177–186.

40. Henry Luce, "Flight of the Dove," *Time*, September 17, 1951.

41. For a complete list of foreign press publications, and statistics on broadcasting hours between 1955 and 1974, see Baruch A. Hazan, *Soviet Propaganda: A Case Study of the Middle East Conflict* (Jerusalem: Israel University Press, 1976), 50–79.

42. Odd Arne Westad, *The Global Cold War: Third World Interventions and the Making of Our Times* (Cambridge: Cambridge University Press, 2005), 124–125; Salim Yaqub, *Containing

Arab Nationalism: The Eisenhower Doctrine and the Middle East (Chapel Hill: University of North Carolina Press, 2004), 257–259.

43. Nikita Khrushchev, "Report of the Central Committee of the Communist Party of the Soviet Union to the 20th Party Congress," *Pravda,* February 15, 1956, cited in Robert C. Horn, *Soviet-Indian Relations: Issues and Influence* (New York: Praeger, 1982), 5–6.

44. See Pierre Brocheux, *Ho Chi Minh: A Biography*, trans. Claire Duiker (New York: Cambridge University Press, 2007), 7–22; David Macey, *Frantz Fanon: A Biography* (New York: Picador, 2001), 112–153; Stanley Wolpert, *Gandhi's Passion: The Life and Legacy of Mahatma Gandhi* (New York: Oxford University Press, 2001), 20–27; Judith M. Brown, *Nehru: A Political Life* (New Haven, CT: Yale University Press, 2003).

45. There were, of course, local and regional variations to this model, and many colonial states broke apart shortly after independence. For a useful overview of the political process of decolonization, as well as local variations, see Rothermund, *Routledge Companion to Decolonization*.

46. Ibid., 165–167; for more detail, see Mahmood Mamdani, *When Victims Become Killers: Colonialism, Nativism, and the Genocide in Rwanda* (Princeton, NJ: Princeton University Press, 2001).

47. Those include the Mau Mau rebellion in Kenya, and unrest in Congo, India, Angola, Algeria, and Indochina. For more information, see Westad, *The Global Cold War*, 207–249; Rothermund, *Routledge Companion to Decolonization*, 153–157.

48. Terry Bell with Dumisa Buhle Ntsebeza, *Unfinished Business: South Africa, Apartheid, and Truth* (London: Verso, 2003); Heather Deegan, *The Politics of the New South Africa: Apartheid and After* (Harlow, UK: Longman, 2001).

49. Todd Shepard, *The Invention of Decolonization: The Algerian War and the Remaking of France* (Ithaca, NY: Cornell University Press, 2006); Matthew Connelly, *A Diplomatic Revolution: Algeria's Fight for Independence and the Origins of the Post–Cold War Era* (New York: Oxford University Press, 2002).

50. Dipesh Chakrabarty, *Provincializing Europe: Postcolonial Thought and Historical Difference* (Princeton, NJ: Princeton University Press, 2000), 8. See also Chakrabarty, "The Muddle of Modernity," *American Historical Review* 116, no. 3 (June 2011): 664.

51. See C. L. R. James, *The Black Jacobins: Toussaint L'Ouverture and the San Domingo Revolution* (1938; New York: Vintage, 1989).

52. Léopold Sédar Senghor, "What Is Négritude?," in *The Ideologies of the Developing Nations*, ed. Paul Sigmund (New York: Fredrick A. Praeger, 1963), 248–249; cited in Robert Tignor et al., *Worlds Together, Worlds Apart: A History of the World from the Beginnings of Humankind to the Present*, 2nd ed. (New York: W. W. Norton, 2008), 874.

53. For a comprehensive analysis, see Rob Nixon, "Caribbean and African Appropriations of *The Tempest*," in *Critical Inquiry* 13 (Spring 1987): 557–578. For a case study of cultural emancipation, see Harvey Neptune, *Caliban and the Yankees: Trinidad and the United States Occupation* (Chapel Hill: University of North Carolina Press, 2006). Aimé Césaire, *Une Tempête: D'Après "la Tempête" de Shakespeare—Adaptation pour un théâtre nègre* (Paris: Éditions du Seuil, 1969). See also Edward W. Said, *Culture and Imperialism* (New York: Vintage, 1994), 212–215.

54. Césaire quoted in Nixon, "Appropriations of *The Tempest*," 571.

55. Frantz Fanon, *The Wretched of the Earth: A Negro Psychoanalyst's Study of the Problems of Racism and Colonialism in the World Today*, trans. Constance Farrington (New York: Grove Press, 1963), 212.

56. Ibid., 214.

57. See Ulf Hannerz, *Cultural Complexity: Studies in the Social Organization of Meaning* (New York: Columbia University Press, 1992); James Clifford, *The Predicament of Culture: Twentieth Century Ethnography, Literature, and Art* (Cambridge, MA: Harvard University Press, 1988). Stuart Hall, "The Local and the Global: Globalization and Ethnicity," in *Dangerous Liaisons: Gender, Nation, and Postcolonial Perspectives,* ed. Anne McClintock, Aamir Mufti, and Ella Shohat (Minneapolis: University of Minnesota Press, 1997); James Lull, *Media, Communication, Culture: A Global Approach* (Cambridge: Polity Press, 1995); Kevin Robins, "Tradition and Translation: National Culture in Its Global Context," in *Enterprise and Heritage: Crosscurrents of National Culture,* ed. John Corner and Sylvia Harvey (London: Routledge, 1991); John Tomlinson, *Globalization and Culture* (Chicago: University of Chicago Press, 1999).

58. Edward W. Said, *Orientalism* (New York: Pantheon, 1978).

59. Christina Klein, *Cold War Orientalism: Asia in the Middlebrow Imagination* (Berkeley: University of California Press, 2003); Douglas Little, *American Orientalism: The United States and the Middle East since 1945* (Chapel Hill: University of North Carolina Press, 2002); Naoko Shibusawa, *America's Geisha Ally: Reimagining the Japanese Enemy* (Cambridge, MA: Harvard University Press, 2006).

60. Among those critics were Middle East scholar Bernard Lewis and, more recently, anthropologist Daniel Martin Varisco. For a detailed discussion of *Orientalism*'s impact and reception, see Gyan Prakash, "Orientalism Now," in *History and Theory* 34, no. 3 (October 1995): 199–212.

61. Said, *Culture and Imperialism,* xxv, 214.

62. Patrick Manning, *Francophone Sub-Saharan Africa, 1880–1995,* 2nd ed. (Cambridge: Cambridge University Press, 1998), 162. Chinua Achebe, *Things Fall Apart* (New York: McDowell, Obolensky, 1959).

63. Chinua Achebe, *Morning Yet on Creation Day: Essays* (London: Heinemann, 1975), 77–78.

64. For more on the debate about Achebe's language choice, see Kalu Ogbaa, *Understanding Things Fall Apart: A Student Casebook to Issues, Sources, and Historical Documents* (Westport, CT: Greenwood Press, 1999), 191–206. See also Ezenwa-Ohaeto, *Chinua Achebe: A Biography* (Bloomington: Indiana University Press, 1997), 246.

65. Saskia Sassen, "The Global City: Introducing a Concept," *Brown Journal of World Affairs* 11, no. 2 (Winter/Spring 2005): 39. For a case study, see Shahrzad Faryadi, "Urban Representation of Multiculturalism in a Global City: Toronto's Iranian Community," accessed through the Institute on Globalization and the Human Condition working papers series at McMaster University, Hamilton, Ontario, Canada, at http://globalization.mcmaster.ca/wps.htm.

66. Timothy J. Hatton and Jeffrey G. Williamson, *Global Migration and the World Economy: Two Centuries of Policy and Performance* (Cambridge, MA.: MIT Press, 2005), 203.

67. William G. Clarence-Smith, "The Global Consumption of Hot Beverages, c. 1500 to c. 1900," in *Food and Globalization: Consumption, Markets and Politics in the Modern World,* ed. Alexander Nützenadel and Frank Trentmann (Oxford: Berg, 2008), 37–55. See also David Inglis and Debra Gimlin, eds., *The Globalization of Food* (Oxford: Berg, 2009).

68. Dirk Hoerder, *Cultures in Contact: World Migrations in the Second Millennium* (Durham, NC: Duke University Press, 2002), 499–505.

69. Hatton and Williamson, *Global Migration,* 206–207.

70. Wendy Webster, "Immigration and Racism," in *A Companion to Contemporary Britain, 1939–2000,* ed. Paul Addison and Harriet Jones (Malden, MA: Blackwell, 2005), 97–100.

71. Hoerder, *Cultures in Contact,* 524.

72. Alejandro Portes and Alex Stepick, *City on the Edge: The Transformation of Miami* (Berkeley: University of California Press, 1993).

73. Hatton and Williamson, *Global Migration,* 209–210.

74. Figure printed in "Emirates See Fiscal Crisis as Chance to Save Culture," *New York Times,* November 12, 2008, 1.

75. Frauke Heard-Bey, "The United Arab Emirates: Statehood and Nation Building in a Traditional Society," *Middle East Journal* 59, no. 3, *Democratization and Civil Society* (Summer 2005): 357–375. See also Jim Krane, *City of Gold: Dubai and the Dream of Capitalism* (New York: St. Martin's Press, 2009).

76. Timothy J. Hatton and Jeffrey G. Williamson, *The Age of Mass Migration: Causes and Economic Impact* (New York: Oxford University Press, 1998), 9.

77. The International Labour Organization (ILO) created two categories of migrant labor, contract migration and settlement migration. See K. C. Zachariah, B. A. Prakash, and S. Irudaya Rajan, "Indian Workers in UAE: Employment, Wages and Working Conditions," *Economic and Political Weekly* 39, no. 22 (2004): 2228.

78. Ibid., 2227–2234.

79. Maxine L. Margolis, *An Invisible Minority: Brazilians in New York City* (Boston: Allyn and Bacon, 1998), 114.

80. Arjun Appadurai, *Modernity at Large: Cultural Dimensions of Globalization* (Minneapolis: University of Minnesota Press, 1996), 4.

81. As defined by the United Nations Population Fund. See UNFPA, "State of World Population, 2007," available online at www.unfpa.org/swp/2007/english/introduction.html.

82. United Nations, *Demographic Yearbook 2005* (New York: United Nations Publications, 2008), table 6, accessed online at http://unstats.un.org/unsd/demographic/products/dyb/dyb2005.htm.

83. Those cities were Tokyo and Osaka in Japan, New York and Los Angeles in the United States, Moscow in Russia, Beijing and Shanghai in China. Data in "World Urbanization Prospects: The 2005 Revision," in United Nations Department of Economics and Social Affairs, Population Division (2006), working paper no. ESA/P/WP/200.

84. Matthew Gandy, "Planning, Anti-Planning and the Infrastructure Crisis Facing Metropolitan Lagos," in *Urban Studies* 43, no. 2 (February 2006): 371–391. See also the other articles in this volume on urban Africa.

85. Table A.11, "The 30 largest urban agglomerations ranked by population size, 1950–2015," in Population Division, Department of Economic and Social Affairs, United Nations Secretariat, *World Urbanization Prospects: The 2001Revision* (New York: United Nations, 2002). Available online at *www.un.org/esa/population/publications/wup2001/wup2001dh.pdf*. For more information on Mumbai's slums, see UN Habitat, "Slums of the World: The Face of Urban Poverty in the New Millennium," Working Paper of the United Nations Human Settlements Programme (Nairobi: UN-Habitat, 2003).

86. Hoerder, *Cultures in Contact*, 497.

87. Balfour Declaration, October 31, 1917, reprinted in Charles D. Smith, *Palestine and the Arab-Israeli Conflict: A History with Documents*, 6th ed. (New York: Bedford/St. Martin's Press, 2007), 102–103.

88. Hoerder, *Cultures in Contact*, 496. See also Benny Morris, *The Birth of the Palestinian Refugee Problem Revisited*, 2nd ed. (Cambridge: Cambridge University Press, 2004).

89. Hoerder, *Cultures in Contact*, 499.

90. Rothermund, *Routledge Companion to Decolonization*, 151–157, 161–167, 231–237.

91. For more detail on famine and conflict in the twentieth century, see Stephen Devereux, Institute of Development Studies, UK, "Famine in the 20th Century," IDS Working Paper 105 (Brighton: IDS, 2000), 6.

92. In 2003 two scholars—Mike Robinson, founder and director of the Centre for Tourism and Cultural Change at Leeds Metropolitan University in the UK, and Alison Phipps, professor on the Faculty of Education at the University of Glasgow—founded the journal *Tourism and Cultural Change*. The inauguration of the journal itself bears testimony to the increasing role tourism is playing in the contemporary world. The journal's objective, according to the introductory editorial, is to explore the cultural foundations of tourism as well as the culture of tourism itself. See Mike Robinson and Alison Phipps, "Editorial: World Passing By: Journeys of Culture and Cultural Journeys," in *Tourism and Cultural Change* 1, no. 1 (2003): 7. See also Christopher Endy, *Cold War Holidays: American Tourism in France* (Chapel Hill: University of North Carolina Press, 2004).

93. David Reynolds, *Rich Relations: The American Occupation of Britain, 1942–1945* (New York: Random House, 1995); Beth Bailey and David Farber, *The First Strange Place: The Alchemy of Race and Sex in World War II Hawaii* (New York: Free Press, 1992).

94. Petra Goedde, *GIs and Germans: Culture, Gender, and Foreign Relations, 1945–1949* (New Haven, CT: Yale University Press, 2003).

95. Cited in Endy, *Cold War Holidays*, 19.

96. Ibid., 44–46.

97. The organization was renamed United Nations World Tourism Organization (UNWTO) in 1970. For its history, see the official website of the UNWTO at www.unwto.org/.

98. Data from UNWTO Website at www.unwto.org/aboutwto/why/en/why.php?op=1.

99. Marc Augé, *Non-Places: Introduction to an Anthropology of Supermodernity*, trans. John Howe (London: Verso, 1995).

100. Cited in Endy, *Cold War Holidays*, 140.

101. William J. Lederer and Eugene Burdick, *The Ugly American* (New York: Norton, 1958).

102. For more detail on the prosecution of communists, see Ellen Schrecker, *Many Are the Crimes: McCarthyism in America* (Boston: Little, Brown, 1998).

103. Martin B. Duberman, *Paul Robeson* (New York: Knopf, 1988), 463.

104. Hixson, *Parting the Curtain*, 157; von Eschen, *Satchmo Blows Up the World*, 58–91.

105. Fritz Fischer, *Making Them Like Us: Peace Corps Volunteers in the 1960s* (Washington, DC: Smithsonian Institution Press, 1998), 1; see also Elizabeth Cobbs Hoffman, *All You Need Is Love: The Peace Corps and the Spirit of the 1960s* (Cambridge, MA: Harvard University Press, 1998).

106. Fischer, *Making Them Like Us*, 131, 184–185.

107. Daniel T. Rodgers, *Atlantic Crossings: Social Politics in a Progressive Age* (Boston: Belknap Press of Harvard University Press, 1998), 76.

108. Hixson, *Parting the Curtain*, 153, 157–158.

109. Among those who studied in Eastern Europe was Raila Amollo Odinga, who served as prime minister of Kenya from 2008 to 2013. He had studied mechanical engineering in East Germany in the 1960s.

110. Ninkovich, *The Diplomacy of Ideas*, 140–144; Hixson, *Parting the Curtain*, 8–9.

111. For the developer's promotional video, see www.youtube.com/watch?v=4whguZ_Nufg& NR=1. For more detailed information about the mall's physical dimensions, see http://en.wiki pedia.org/wiki/Dubai_Mall.

112. There are several other malls in Asia that exceed the gross leasable space of the Dubai Mall, including the South China Mall in Dongguan, China, which has remained largely vacant since its completion in 2005.

113. Kristin L. Hoganson, *Consumer's Imperium: The Global Production of American Domesticity, 1865–1920* (Chapel Hill: University of North Carolina Press, 2007), 11–12.

114. T. H. Breen, *The Marketplace of Revolution: How Consumer Politics Shaped American Independence* (Oxford: Oxford University Press, 2004).

115. William G. Clarence Smith, "The Global Consumption of Hot Beverages, 1500–1900," in Nützenadel and Trentmann, *Food and Globalization*, 37–55.

116. Hans-Joachim Klimkeit, *Die Seidenstrasse: Handelsweg und Kulturbrücke zwischen Morgen- and Abendland* (Cologne: DuMont Buchverlag, 1988). McNeill and McNeill, *The Human Web*, 156–157, William H. McNeill, *The Rise of the West: A History of the Human Community* (Chicago: University of Chicago Press, 1963), 485–558.

117. For more detail on continued foreign influence on American consumption, see Andrew C. McKevitt, "Consuming Japan: Cultural Relations and the Globalizing of America, 1973–1993," PhD diss., Temple University, 2009.

118. Ritzer, *The McDonaldization of Society*; Benjamin R. Barber, *Jihad vs. McWorld: How Globalism and Tribalism Are Reshaping the World* (New York: Ballantine, 1995); Bryant Simon, *Everything but the Coffee: Learning about America from Starbucks* (Berkeley: University of California Press, 2009); Eric L. Gans, *The End of Culture: Toward a Generative Anthropology* (Berkeley: University of California Press, 1985).

119. Douglas Goodman, "Globalization and Consumer Culture," in *The Blackwell Companion to Globalization,* ed. George Ritzer (Malden MA: Blackwell, 2007), 347.

120. James L. Watson, ed. *Golden Arches East: McDonald's in East Asia* (Stanford, CA: Stanford University Press, 1997); Hannerz, *Cultural Complexity.*

121. Walter Benjamin, "The Work of Art in the Age of Mechanical Reproduction," in *Illuminations,* edited with an introduction by Hannah Arendt, translated by Harry Zohn (New York: Harcourt, Brace and World, 1968).

122. Ronald Inglehart and Wayne E. Baker, "Modernization, Cultural Change, and the Persistence of Traditional Values," *American Sociological Review* 65, no. 1 (February, 2000): 21.

123. Ariel Dorfman and Armand Mattelart, *How to Read Donald Duck: Imperialist Ideology in the Disney Comic,* trans. David Kunzle (New York: International General, 1975). See also Ritzer, *The McDonaldization of Society*; Watson, *Golden Arches East.*

124. Petra Goedde, "McDonald's," in *Palgrave Dictionary of Transnational History* (Basingstoke, UK: Palgrave MacMillan, 2008), 700–701.

125. Max Weber, *Economy and Society: An Outline of Interpretive Sociology,* ed. Guenther Roth and Claus Wittich, trans. Ephraim Fischoff et al., 3 vols. (Totowa, NJ: Bedminster Press, 1921, 1968), 1156.

126. For more detail, see Watson, *Golden Arches East*; John F. Love, *McDonald's: Behind the Arches* (New York: Bantam, 1995).

127. Ritzer, *The McDonaldization of Society*, 12–15.

128. Ibid., 147–148; Wimmer, "Globalization *avant la lettre,*" 436. For more detail on the debates and the theories of consumer cultures, see Goodman, "Globalization and Consumer Culture," 344–347. See also Hannerz, *Cultural Complexity*; Watson, *Golden Arches East.*

129. Goodman cites Néstor García Canclini and Benjamin Barber as the two poles in this spectrum of theoretical debates. See García Canclini, *Hybrid Cultures: Strategies for Entering and Leaving Modernity,* trans. Christopher L. Chiappari and Silvia L. López (Minneapolis: University of Minnesota Press, 1995; see also García Canclini, *Consumers and Citizens: Globalization and Multicultural Conflicts,* trans. George Yúdice (Minneapolis: University of Minnesota Press, 2001); on Barber, see *Jihad vs. McWorld.*

130. Roland Robertson, "Glocalization: Time-Space and Homogeneity-Heterogeneity," in *Global Modernities,* ed. Mike Featherstone, Scott Lash, and Roland Robertson (London: Sage, 1995), 25–44.

131. George Ritzer, *The Globalization of Nothing* (Thousand Oaks, CA: Pine Forge Press, 2004).

132. Newsreel shown in *Atomic Café,* produced by Kevin Rafferty, Jayne Loader, and Pierce Rafferty (New York: Docurama, distributed by New Video Group, 1982, 2002); see also Cohen, *Consumer's Republic.*

133. "Endlich wieder Kaufen Können: Wählt CDU," campaign poster of the Christian Democratic Union, 1948. ACDP-Poster Collection, 10-017-202, Konrad Adenauer Stiftung, e.V. Archive for Christian Democratic Politics, St. Augustin, Germany. For more detail, see Petra Goedde, *GIs and Germans: Culture, Gender, and Foreign Relations, 1945–1949* (New Haven, CT: Yale University Press, 2003), 196–198.

134. Dower, *Embracing Defeat,* 136–138, 543–544. See also, Penelope Francks, *The Japanese Consumer: An Alternative Economic History of Modern Japan* (New York: Cambridge University Press, 2009).

135. Petra Goedde, "Coca-Cola," *Palgrave Dictionary of Transnational History,* 36–37.

136. Hixson, *Parting the Curtain,* 170.

137. See ibid., 179. Transcript of the exchange available online at www.teachingamericanhistory .org/library/index.asp?document=176.

138. Ibid.

139. Cited in Nordica Nettleton, "Driving toward Communist Consumerism AvtoVAZ," in *Cahiers Du Monde Russe* 47, nos. 1–2 (January–June 2006), 131.

140. Susan E. Reid, "Khrushchev Modern: Agency and Modernization in the Soviet Home," *Cahiers du Monde Russe* 47, nos. 1–2 (January–June 2006): 227–268.

141. Raymond G. Stokes, "Plastics and the New Society: The German Democratic Republic in the 1950s and 1960s," in *Style and Socialism: Modernity and Material Culture in Post-War Eastern Europe,* ed. Susan E. Reid and David Crowley (Oxford: Berg 2000), 69. For excerpts of Ulbricht's speech at the party congress, see *Protokoll der Verhandlungen des V. Parteitages der Sozialistischen Einheitspartei Deutschlands. 10. bis 16. Juli 1958 in der Werner-Seelenbinder-Halle zu Berlin: 1. bis 5. Verhandlungstag* (Berlin: Dietz Verlag, 1958).

142. David Crowley, "Thaw Modern: Design in Eastern Europe after 1956," in *Cold War Modern: Design, 1945–1970,* ed. David Crowley and Jane Pavitt (London: V&A Publishing, 2008), 138–139.

143. Horst Redeker, *Chemie Gibt Schönheit* (Berlin: Institut für angewandte Kunst, 1959), 30–31, cited in Stokes, "Plastics and the New Society," 75.

144. Nettleton, "Driving," 148–149.

145. Uta G. Poiger, *Jazz, Rock, and Rebels: Cold War Politics and American Culture in a Divided Germany* (Berkeley: University of California Press, 2000), 106–136.

146. Stokes, "Plastics and the New Society," 76.

147. Elaine Tyler May, *Homeward Bound: American Families in the Cold War Era* (New York: Basic Books, 1988), 6–10, 137.

148. David Riesman, *The Lonely Crowd: A Study of the Changing American Character* (New Haven, CT: Yale University Press, 1950).

149. Sloan Wilson, *The Man in the Gray Flannel Suit* (New York: Simon and Schuster, 1955); see also the movie version: *The Man in the Gray Flannel Suit,* dir. Nunally Johnson (20th Century Fox, 1956).

150. For instance, Vance Packard, *The Status Seekers: An Exploration of Class Behavior in America and the Hidden Barriers That Affect You, Your Community, Your Future* (New York: David McKay, 1959).

151. "Cyclist's Holiday," *Life,* July 21, 1947, 31.

152. *Blackboard Jungle,* dir. Richard Brooks (Metro-Goldwyn-Mayer, 1955).

153. *Rebel Without a Cause,* dir. Nicholas Ray (Warner Brothers, 1955).

154. Michael T. Bertrand, *Race, Rock, and Elvis* (Urbana: University of Illinois Press, 2000), 97–101.

155. Ibid., 189–195, 202.

156. Kaspar Maase, *Bravo Amerika: Erkundungen zur Jugendkultur der Bundesrepublik in den fünfziger Jahren* (Hamburg: Junius, 1992). Poiger, *Jazz, Rock, and Rebels.*

157. Dick Hebdige, "The Meaning of Mod," in *Resistance through Rituals: Youth Subcultures in Postwar Britain,* ed. Stuart Hall and Tony Jefferson (London: Routledge, 1975), 87–96, 167–173.

158. Poiger, *Jazz, Rock, and Rebels,* 79; see also Reinhold Wagnleitner, *Coca-Colonization and the Cold War: The Cultural Mission of the United States in Austria after the Second World War,* trans. Diana M. Wolf (Chapel Hill: University of North Carolina Press, 1994).

159. Figures cited in Poiger, *Jazz, Rock, and Rebels,* 85.

160. The term can be loosely translated as "half-strong," meaning not quite adult but already testing their power.

161. Ibid., 197.

162. David Crowley, "Warsaw's Shops, Stalinism and the Thaw," in Reid and Crowley, *Style and Socialism,* 28.

163. Timothy Ryback, *Rock Around the Bloc: A History of Rock Music in Eastern Europe and the Soviet Union* (New York: Oxford University Press, 1990), 9.

164. Hixson, *Parting the Curtain,* 116.

165. S. Frederick Starr, *Red and Hot: The Fate of Jazz in the Soviet Union, 1917–1980* (New York: Oxford University Press, 1983), 239, 236–237. See also Zubok, *Zhivago's Children,* 40–44.

166. Kristin Roth-Ey cites 791 concerts and another 63 "mass concerts" at the festival. See Roth-Ey, " 'Loose Girls' on the Loose? Sex, Propaganda and the 1957 Youth Festival," in *Women in the Khrushchev Era,* ed. Melanie Ilič, Susan Reid, and Lynne Atwood (Basingstoke, UK: Palgrave, 2004), 76, n2, 91. Zubok, *Zhivago's Children,* 100–111, esp. 105.

167. Roth-Ey, " 'Loose Girls' on the Loose?," 76.

168. Hixson, *Parting the Curtain,* 159–160.

169. Roth-Ey, " 'Loose Girls' on the Loose?"; Zubok, *Zhivago's Children,* 109.

170. Zubok, *Zhivago's Children,* 111. See also Juliane Fürst, *Stalin's Last Generation: Soviet Post-War Youth and the Emergence of Mature Socialism* (New York: Oxford University Press, 2010).

171. For an overview of the civil rights movement in the twentieth-century United States, see Kevin K. Gaines, *Uplifting the Race: Black Leadership, Politics, and Culture in the Twentieth Century* (Chapel Hill: University of North Carolina Press, 1996). See also Mary Dudziak, *Cold War Civil Rights: Race and the Image of American Democracy* (Princeton, NJ: Princeton University Press, 2000).

172. They included the philosopher Bertrand Russell and atomic scientists Albert Einstein and Leo Szilard. See Paul Boyer, *By the Bomb's Early Light*: *American Thought and Culture at the Dawn of the Atomic Age* (New York: Pantheon, 1983). Wittner, *One World or None.*

173. Van Gosse, *Rethinking the New Left: An Interpretative History* (New York: Palgrave Macmillan, 2005); Norbert Frei, *1968: Jugendrevolte und globaler Protest* (Munich: DTV, 2008), 92–94; Martin Klimke, *The Other Alliance: Student Protest in West Germany and the United States in the Global Sixties* (Princeton, NJ: Princeton University Press, 2010), 89–90.

174. Theodore W. Adorno and Max Horkheimer, *Dialectic of Enlightenment: Philosophical Fragments,* ed. Gunzelin Schmid Noerr, trans. Edmund Jephcott (Stanford, CA: Stanford University Press 2002); C. Wright Mills, *The Causes of World War Three* (New York: Simon and Schuster, 1958); Riesman, *The Lonely Crowd*; Jean-Paul Sartre, *Existentialism Is a Humanism,* ed. John Kulka, trans. Carol Macomber, preface by Arlette Elkaim-Sartre, introduction by Annie Cohen-Solal (New Haven, CT: Yale University Press, 2007); Herbert Marcuse, *One-*

Dimensional Man: Studies in the Ideology of Advanced Industrial Society (Boston: Beacon Press, 1964).

175. "Port Huron Statement," reprinted in *The Sixties Papers: Documents of a Rebellious Decade,* ed. Judith Clavier Albert and Stewart Edward Albert (New York: Praeger, 1984), 176–196.

176. Fanon, *Wretched of the Earth*, 43, 61.

177. Jon Lee Anderson, *Che Guevara: A Revolutionary Life* (New York: Grove Press, 1997), 733–739.

178. In 2006 the V&A Museum in London staged an exhibit on Che Guevara: *Che Guevara Revolutionary & Icon*, Victoria & Albert Museum, Curator, Trisha Ziff. According to the curator's introduction, the image of Che Guevara "symbolize[s] anti-establishment, radical thought and action."

179. David Mark Chalmers, *And the Crooked Places Made Straight: The Struggle for Social Change in the 1960s* (Baltimore: Johns Hopkins Press, 1991), 139–140.

180. Todd Gitlin, *The Sixties: Years of Hope, Days of Rage* (Toronto: Bantam, 1987), 319. David Farber, *Chicago '68* (Chicago: University of Chicago Press, 1988).

181. Stefan Aust, *Der Baader Meinhof Komplex: Erweiterte und aktualisierte Ausgabe* (Munich: Goldmann Verlag, 1998), 56–60. In 2009, newly uncovered documents from the East German secret police records showed that the police officer Karl-Heinz Kurras was an informant for the East German Stasi. However, the evidence did not point to any East German involvement in the shooting.

182. Gretchen Dutschke-Klotz, *Rudi Dutschke: Wir hatten ein barbarisches, schönes Leben—Eine Biographie* (Cologne: Kiepenheuer und Witsch, 1996), 197–200. Ulrich Chaussy, *Die Drei Leben des Rudi Dutschke: Eine Biographie* (Zürich: Pendo Verlag, 1999), 79. On Bachmann's right-wing connections, see "Schrecken aus dem braunen Sumpf: Enthüllungen über Dutschke Attentäter," *Spiegel*, December 6, 2009.

183. Aust, *Der Baader Meinhof Komplex.*

184. Alain Touraine, *The May Movement: Revolt and Reform*, trans. Leonard F. X. Mayhew (New York: Random House, 1971), 138–139. Ingrid Gilcher-Holtey, *Die Phantasie an der Macht: Mai 68 in Frankreich* (Frankfurt: Suhrkamp, 1995).

185. Gilcher-Holtey, *Die Phantasie an der Macht*; Gilcher-Holtey, ed., *1968: Vom Ereignis zum Gegenstand der Geschichtswissenschaft* (Göttingen: Vandenhoeck & Ruprecht, 1998), 20–21.

186. Touraine, *The May Movement*, 209, 233; Gilcher-Holtey, *1968,* 24.

187. For a comprehensive treatment of the Prague Spring, see Stefan Karner, Natalja G. Tomilina, Alexander Tschubarjan, et al., *Prager Frühling: Das International Krisenjahr 1968*, vol. 1: *Beiträge*, vol. 2: *Dokumente* (Cologne: Böhlau Verlag, 2008). See also Judt, *Postwar*, 436–447.

188. Cited in *The Prague Spring 1968: A National Security Archives Document Reader*, compiled and ed. Antonín Benčik (Budapest: Central European University Press, 1998), 10.

189. Speech by Alexander Dubček, October 30–31, 1967, in *The Prague Spring 1968*, 14.

190. Action program, excerpt reprinted in *Prague Spring 1968*, 92–95. See also H. Gordon Skilling, *Czechoslovakia's Interrupted Revolution* (Princeton, NJ: Princeton University Press, 1976), 217–221.

191. "Two Thousand Word Manifesto," June 27, 1968, reprinted in *Prague Spring 1968*, 177–181.

192. Skilling, *Czechoslovakia's Interrupted Revolution*, 708–710, 749.

193. Zubok, *Zhivago's Children,* 321–331. Paul Berman, *A Tale of Two Utopias: The Political Journey of the Generation of 1968* (New York: Norton, 1996), 235–240.

194. Berman, *Tale of Two Utopias,* 195, 235–236; Ryback, *Rock Around the Bloc,* 25, 145–147.

195. Václav Havel, speech at Fourth Czechoslovak Writers' Congress, June 27–29, 1967, reprinted in *Prague Spring 1968,* 9–10.

196. Ryback, *Rock Around the Bloc,* 145.

197. Ulrich Enzensberger, *Die Jahre der Kommune 1: Berlin, 1967–1969* (Cologne: Kiepenheuer & Witsch, 2004).

198. Reinhard Uhle, "Pädagogik der Siebziger Jahre-zwischen wissenschaftsorientierter Bildung und repressionsarmer Erziehung," in *Die Kultur der 70er Jahre,* ed. Werner Faulstich (Munich: Wilhelm Fink Verlag, 2004), 49–63.

199. Samuel Hays, *Beauty, Health, and Permanence: Environmental Politics in the United States, 1955–1985* (New York: Cambridge University Press, 1987).

200. Adam Rome, "'Give Earth a Chance': The Environmental Movement and the Sixties," *Journal of American History* 90, no. 2 (September, 2003): 525–554.

201. Boyer, *Bomb's Early Light,* 15, 49–75.

202. Ralph H. Lutts, "Chemical Fallout: Rachel Carson's *Silent Spring,* Radioactive Fallout, and the Environmental Movement," *Environmental Review* 9, no. 3 (Fall 1985): 213–214; see also Ralph E. Lapp, *The Voyage of the Lucky Dragon* (New York: Harper, 1958); Richard P. Tucker, "The International Environmental Movement and the Cold War," in *The Oxford Handbook of the Cold War,* ed. Richard Immerman and Petra Goedde (Oxford: Oxford University Press, 2013), 565–583.

203. Lawrence Wittner, *Resisting the Bomb: A History of the World Nuclear Disarmament Movement, 1954–1970* (Stanford, CA: Stanford University Press, 1997).

204. Peter Anker, "The Ecological Colonization of Space," *Environmental History* 10, no. 2 (April 2005): 239–268. On the internationalization of Earth Day, see Barnaby J. Feder, "The Business of Earth Day," *New York Times,* November 12, 1989.

205. Governmental and nongovernmental groups concerned with environmental issues proliferated in the 1970s. They range in political orientation from the moderate conservative Sierra Club to the radical Earth Liberation Front.

206. Frank Zelko, "Making Greenpeace: The Development of Direct Action Environmentalism in British Columbia," *BC Studies,* nos. 142–143 (Summer–Autumn 2004): 236–237.

207. Cohen, *A Consumer's Republic,* 11.

208. For details, see discussion of the poster on page 581.

209. Erica Carter, *How German Is She? Postwar West German Reconstruction and the Consuming Woman* (Ann Arbor: University of Michigan Press, 1997), 80–81, 112–144; Victoria de Grazia, *Irresistible Empire: America's Advance through 20th Century Europe* (Cambridge, MA: Belknap Press of Harvard University Press, 2005), 352.

210. Leila J. Rupp, *Mobilizing Women for War: German and American Propaganda, 1939–1945* (Princeton, NJ: Princeton University Press, 1978).

211. Susan M. Hartmann, *The Homefront and Beyond: American Women in the 1940s* (Boston: Twayne, 1982), 53–70; Leisa Meyer, *Creating GI Jane: Sexuality and Power in the Women's Army Corps during World War II* (New York: Columbia University Press, 1996).

212. May, *Homeward Bound*; Margaret R. Higonnet et al., eds., *Behind the Lines: Gender and the Two World Wars* (New Haven, CT: Yale University Press, 1987). See U.S. Census Bureau, *Statistical Abstracts* (The National Data Book).

213. Wendy Goldman, "*Babas* at the Bench: Gender Conflict in Soviet Industry in the 1930s," in *Women in the Stalin Era,* ed. Melanie Ilič (Basingstoke, UK: Palgrave, 2001), 69. See also Melanie Ilič, ed., *Women Workers in the Soviet Interwar Economy: From "Protection" to "Equality"* (Basingstroke, UK: Palgrave, 1999).

214. Goldman, "*Babas* at the Bench," 77–85; Sarah Davies, " 'A Mother's Cares': Workers and Popular Opinion in Stalin's Russia 1934–1941," in Ilič, *Women in the Stalin Era,* 91.

215. See Susann Conze, "Women's Work and Emancipation in the Soviet Union, 1941–1950," in Ilič, *Women in the Stalin Era,* 216–234.

216. Donald Filtzer, "Women Workers in the Khrushchev Era," in Ilič, Reid, and Atwood, *Women in the Khrushchev Era,* 31.

217. Figures are from the *Statistisches Jahrbuch der DDR* (1987), 17.

218. Wojciech Fangor, *Postaci*, 1950, original on display at the Muzeum Sztuki in Łódź, Poland. A reprint can be found in Crowley and Pavitt, *Cold War Modern,* 130.

219. Michails Korneckis (Lettland), *"Mädchen, packen wir es an,"* 1959. The picture was part of an exhibition *Gender Check: Femininity and Masculinity in the Art of Eastern Europe*, shown in Vienna at the MUMOK, November 13, 2009–February 14, 2010, and in Warsaw at the Zacheta National Gallery of Art, March 19–June 13, 2010.

220. On women's child-care duties, see Deborah A. Field, "Mothers and Fathers and the Problem of Selfishness in the Khrushchev Period," in Ilič, Reid, and Atwood, *Women in the Khrushchev Era,* 101. On housekeeping and the Soviet state, see Susan E. Reid, "Women in the Home," in Ilič, Reid, and Atwood, *Women in the Khrushchev Era,* 159–162.

221. William J. Jorden, "1,056 Miles High: Russia Reports New Satellite Is Final Stage of Rocket," *New York Times*, November 4, 1957, 1. Concerning the protests over inhumanity, see "Laika, a U.N. Issue: Uruguayan Says She Starved—Soviet Aide Denies It," *New York Times*, November 21, 1957, 10; "Animals: The She-Hound of Heaven," *Time*, November 18, 1957.

222. Sue Bridger, "The Cold War and the Cosmos: Velentina Tereshkova and the First Woman's Space Flight," in Ilič, Reid, and Atwood, *Women in the Khrushchev Era,* 222–237.

223. "Khrushchev: Now You See What Women Can Do," *Boston Globe*, June 17, 1963, 3.

224. Cited in Bridger, "Cold War and the Cosmos," 231.

225. "She Loves Spike Heels," *Boston Globe,* June 17, 1963, 3; "Russian Blonde in Space: See Possibility of Rendezvous with Bykovsky," *Chicago Tribune*, June 17, 1963, 1; the headline was accompanied by a photograph of Tereshkova with dark hair. "Space Girl Launched by Russians," *Irish Times*, June 17, 1963.

226. "She Orbits over the Sex Barrier," *Life,* June 28, 1963, 28–30.

227. "From Factory into Space, She Fits Ideal of Soviet Heroine," *Los Angeles Times,* June 17, 1963, 3; Dorothy McCardle, "New Cultural Attaché Says: USSR Training Women by Dozens for Space Roles," *Washington Post, Times Herald*, June 20, 1963, B3.

228. "U.S. Women Feel Low about Red High Flier: Think It's Shame," *Los Angeles Times,* June 17, 1963, 1; "U.S. Not Planning Orbit by Woman: Some Leading Fliers Have Protested Exclusion,"

New York Times, June 17, 1963, 8; "U.S. Has No Plans to Put Woman in Space: And None in Training," *Washington Post, Times Herald*, June 18, 1963, B5.

229. Clare Boothe Luce, "But Some People Simply Never Get the Message," *Life*, June 28, 1963, 31.

230. Richard Witkin, "Training for Space: Soviet and U.S. Differ in Assessing the Qualifications of an Astronaut," *New York Times*, June 18, 1963, 3.

231. Luce, "Never Get the Message," 31. The fact that the Soviets waited twenty years to launch the second female cosmonaut, Svetlana Savitskaya, into space in anticipation of the first American woman in space, Sally Ride, seems to give some credence to the charge of a publicity stunt. Nonetheless, those intentions should not diminish Tereshkova's accomplishment.

232. "Kosmonautin: Sterne Abgestaubt," *Der Spiegel*, June 26, 1963, 68.

233. Audrey R. Topping, "First in Space but Not in Femininity," *New York Times,* June 30, 1963, 42–46.

234. Simone de Beauvoir, *The Second Sex,* trans. Constance Borde and Sheila Maovany-Chevalier, introduction by Judith Thurman (New York: Vintage, 2011). See also Judith Butler, "Sex and Gender in Simone de Beauvoir's *Second Sex*," *Yale French Studies*, no. 72 (1986): 35–49.

235. Betty Friedan, *The Feminine Mystique* (New York: Norton, 1963).

236. See Joanne Meyerowitz, "Beyond the Feminine Mystique: A Reassessment of Postwar Mass Culture, 1946–1958," *Journal of American History* 79, no. 4 (March 1993): 1458. See also Meyerowitz, *Not June Cleaver: Women and Gender in Postwar America 1945–1960* (Philadelphia: Temple University Press, 1994).

237. Casey Hayden and Mary King, "Sex and Caste: A Kind of Memo," 1965, excerpt reprinted in *"Takin' It to the Streets": A Sixties Reader,* ed. Alexander Bloom and Wini Breines (New York: Oxford University Press, 1995), 47–51.

238. For a powerful illustration of the problem faced by black women in the civil rights movement, see Anne Moody, *Coming of Age in Mississippi* (New York: Dial Press, 1968; repr., Delta, 2004). See also Sara Evans, *Personal Politics: The Roots of Women's Liberation in the Civil Rights Movement and the New Left* (New York: Knopf, 1979), 88–89.

239. Sheila Rowbotham, *The Past Is Before Us: Feminism in Action since the 1960s* (London: Pandora, 1989); Holger Nehring, "The Growth of Social Movements," in *A Companion to Contemporary Britain,* 391–392; Adam Lent, *British Social Movements since 1945: Sex, Colour, Peace, and Power* (Basingstoke, UK: Palgrave, 2001).

240. Hilke Schlaeger and Nancy Vedder-Shults, "The West German Women's Movement," *New German Critique*, no. 13, *Special Feminist Issue* (Winter 1978): 63.

241. Dorothy Kaufmann-McCall, "Politics of Difference: The Women's Movement in France from May 1968 to Mitterand," *Signs* 9, no. 2 (Winter 1983): 283–287.

242. Amy Erdman Farrell, *Yours in Sisterhood:* Ms. *Magazine and the Promise of Popular Feminism* (Chapel Hill: University of North Carolina Press, 1998); Edith Hoshino Altbach, "The New German Women's Movement," *Signs* 9, no. 3 (Spring 1984), 455.

243. Alkarim Jivani, "It's Not Unusual: Gay and Lesbian History in Britain," in *Global Feminisms since 1945,* ed. Bonnie G. Smith (London: Routledge, 2000), 164–179. For more detail, see Jivani, *It's Not Unusual: A History of Lesbian and Gay Britain in the Twentieth Century* (London: Michael O'Mara Books, 1997).

244. Neil Miller, *Out of the Past: Gay and Lesbian History from 1869 to the Present* (New York: Vintage, 1995). Organizations such as the Council for Global Equality monitor the status of laws against homosexuality worldwide and maintain an updated list.

245. Robin Morgan, *Sisterhood Is Powerful: An Anthology of Writings from the Women's Liberation Movement* (New York: Random House, 1970); Morgan, "Good Bye to All That," excerpt reprinted in Bloom and Breines, *"Takin' It to the Streets,"* 499–503.

246. Shulamith Firestone, *The Dialectic of Sex: The Case for Feminist Revolution* (New York: Morrow, 1970).

247. Linda Gordon, *Woman's Body, Woman's Right: Birth Control in America,* rev. ed. (1974, 1976; New York: Penguin, 1990), 400–409; David J. Garrow, *Liberty and Sexuality: The Right to Privacy and the Making of Roe v. Wade* (New York: Macmillan, 1994).

248. Larry Rohter, "Doctor Slain during Protest over Abortion," *New York Times,* March 11, 1993, A1; see also editorial on the case, "The Death of Dr. Gunn," *New York Times,* March 12, 1993, A28.

249. The article with the "confessions" of Alice Schwarzer and other prominent women appeared in the popular weekly magazine *Der Stern,* June 6, 1971. Alice Schwarzer admitted decades later that she never had an abortion. Altbach, "New German Women's Movement," 455. See also Schlager, "West German Women's Movement," 59–68.

250. On East Germany, see Donna Harsch, "Society, the State, and Abortion in East Germany," *American Historical Review* 102, no. 1 (February 1997): 53–84.

251. Kaufmann-McCall, "Politics of Difference," 284.

252. Mangala Subramaniam, "The Indian Women's Movement," *Contemporary Sociology* 33, no. 6 (November 2004): 635.

253. The term "Third World" is used here synonymously with "global South" and "non-Western" to identify feminists in the postcolonial world.

254. Soha Abdel Kader, *Egyptian Women in a Changing Society, 1899–1987* (Boulder, CO: Lynne Rienner, 1987); Nayereh Tohidi, "Gender and Islamic Fundamentalism: Feminist Politics in Iran," in *Third World Women and the Politics of Feminism,* ed. Chandra Talpade Mohanty, Ann Russo, and Lourdes Torres (Bloomington: Indiana University Press, 1991), 251–267.

255. Domitila Barrios de Chúngara, *Let Me Speak! Testimony of Domitila, a Woman of the Bolivian Mines,* with Moema Viezzer, trans. Victoria Ortiz (New York: Monthly Review Press, 1978).

256. Chandra Talpade Mohanty, "Introduction: Cartographies of Struggle: Third World Women and the Politics of Feminism," in Mohanty, Russo, and Torres, *Third World Women,* 11.

257. Joyce Blackwell, *No Peace without Freedom: Race and the Women's International League for Peace and Freedom, 1915–1975* (Carbondale: Southern Illinois University Press, 2004), 143–194.

258. Leila J. Rupp, "From Rosie the Riveter to the Global Assembly Line: American Women on the World Stage," *Magazine of History* 18, no. 4, *Sex, Courtship, and Dating* (July 2004): 55.

259. WIDF statute summarized in Cheryl Johnson-Odim and Nina Emma Mba, *For Women and the Nation: Funmilayo Ransome-Kuti of Nigeria* (Champaign: University of Illinois Press, 1997), 137. No single scholarly treatment exists yet on the WIDF and its efforts to attract women's organizations in the Third World. However, contemporary observers noted the inroads

made by the Communist "front organizations" in Asia and Africa. See, for instance, Walter Kolarz, "The Impact of Communism on West Africa," *International Affairs* 38, no. 2 (April 1962): 164.

260. Jocelyn Olcott, "Cold War Conflicts and Cheap Cabaret: Sexual Politics at the 1975 United Nations International Women's Year Conference," *Gender and History* 22, no. 3 (November 2010): 733–754.

261. James P. Sterba, "Equal Rights Vital, U.N. Chief Asserts at Women's Parley," *New York Times*, June 20, 1975, 1.

262. Ethel L. Payne, "From Where I Sit: Women's Year Meet," *Chicago Defender*, July 5, 1975, 6.

263. Christa Wichterich, "Strategische Verschwisterung, multiple Feminismen und die Gloka-lisierung von Frauenbewegungen," in *Frauenbewegungen weltweit: Aufbrüche, Kontinuitäten, Veränderungen,* ed. Ilse Lenz, Michiko Mae, and Karin Klose (Opladen, Germany: Leske & Budrich Verlag, 2000), 257–258.

264. Barrios de Chúngara, *Let Me Speak!,* 202–203. See also Olcott, "Cold War Conflicts," 748.

265. Judy Klemesrud, "As the Conference Ends, What Now for Women?," *New York Times,* July 2, 1975.

266. For the General Assembly–approved version of the "World Plan of Action," see United Nations A/RES/30/3520: Resolutions Adopted by the General Assembly 3520(XXX): World Conference of the International Women's Year," at www.un-documents.net/a30r3520.htm. For the text of the Declaration of Mexico, see "United Nations E/CONF.66/34: Declaration of Mexico on the Equality of Women and Their Contribution to Development and Peace," July 2, 1975, at www.un-documents.net/mex-dec.htm.

267. Stanley Meisler, "Unity Eludes the World's Women," *Los Angeles Times,* July 6, 1975, D1.

268. James Streba, "Women Find Unity Elusive," *New York Times,* June 24, 1975, 3.

269. Bina Agarwal, "From Mexico 1975 to Beijing 1995," *Indian Journal of Gender Studies* 3, no. 1 (March 1996): 90–91.

270. Martha Alter Chen, "Engendering World Conferences: The International Women's Movement and the United Nations," *Third World Quarterly* 16, no. 3, *Nongovernmental Organisations, the United Nations and Global Governance* (September 1995): 478. See also Mallika Dutt, "Some Reflections on United States Women of Colour and the United Nations Fourth World Confer-ence on Women and NGO Forum in Beijing, China," in Smith, *Global Feminisms,* 305–313.

271. Robin Morgan, ed., *Sisterhood Is Global: The International Women's Movement Anthology* (Garden City, NY: Anchor/Doubleday, 1984). See also Kelly Shannon, "Veiled Intentions: Islam, Global Feminism, and U.S. Foreign Policy since the Late 1970s," PhD diss., Temple University, 2010); and Valentine M. Moghadam, *Globalizing Women: Transnational Feminist Networks* (Baltimore: Johns Hopkins University Press, 2005), 142–172.

272. Marie Aimée Hélie-Lucas, "Women Living under Muslim Laws," in *Ours by Right: Women's Rights as Human Rights,* ed. Joanna Kerr (London: Zed Books, 1993).

273. Barrios de Chúngara, *Let Me Speak!,* 198–199. See also Olcott, "Cold War Conflicts."

274. Chandra Talpade Mohanty, "Under Western Eyes: Feminist Scholarship and Colonial Dis-courses," first published in *Boundary 2* 12/13 (Spring/Fall 1984): 333–358; updated and modi-fied in Mohanty, Russo, and Torres, *Third World Women,* 57.

275. Joan W. Scott, "Gender: A Useful Category of Historical Analysis," *American Historical Review* 91, no. 5 (December 1986): 1056.

276. Among them Gayatri Chakravorty Spivak in "French Feminism in an International Frame," *Yale French Studies*, no. 62, *Feminist Readings: French Texts/American Contexts* (1981): 154–184. See also Prakash, "Orientalism Now," 210.

277. Spivak, "French Feminism," 157, italics in the original.

278. Fran P. Hosken, *The Hosken Report: Genital and Sexual Mutilation of Females* (Lexington, MA: Women's International Network News, 1979). See also Elizabeth Heger Boyle, *Female Genital Cutting: Cultural Conflict in the Global Community* (Baltimore: Johns Hopkins University Press, 2002); Kelly J. Shannon, "The Right to Bodily Integrity: Women's Rights as Human Rights and the International Movement to End Female Genital Mutilation, 1970–1990s," in *The Human Rights Revolution: An International History*, ed. Akira Iriye, Petra Goedde, and William I. Hitchcock (New York: Oxford University Press, 2012), 285–310.

279. Robin Morgan and Gloria Steinem, "The International Crime of Female Genital Mutilation," *Ms.,* March 1980, 65–67, 98, 100.

280. Nawal el Saadawi, "The Question No One Would Answer," *Ms.,* March 1980, 68–69.

281. Wichterich, "Strategische Verschwisterung," 258. See also Inge Rowhani, "Resümee zum Ende der Dekade der Frauen," in *Frauen: Ein Weltbericht,* ed. New Internationalist (Berlin: Orlanda Frauenverlag, 1986), 337–349.

282. Angela Gilliam, "Women's Equality and National Liberation," in Mohanty, Russo, and Torres, *Third World Women,* 218–219.

283. Ibid., 218.

284. Youssef M. Ibrahim, "Arab Girls/Veils at Issue in France," *New York Times,* November 12, 1989, 5.

285. Khalid L. Rehman, letter to the editor, "Muslim Head Covering Far Different from Veil," *New York Times,* December 23, 1989, E10. Even the New York Times correspondent Yussef M. Ibrahim used the terms *headscarf* and *veil* interchangeably. See Ibrahim, "Arab Girls," November 12, 1989, 5.

286. Germaine Greer, "Veiled Thoughts on Fashion and Democracy," *Guardian,* October 17, 1994, 18.

287. Joan W. Scott, "Symptomatic Politics: The Banning of Islamic Head Scarves in French Public Schools," *French Politics, Culture & Society* 23, no. 3 (Winter 2005): 110. See also Scott, *The Politics of the Veil* (Princeton, NJ: Princeton University Press, 2007).

288. For examples of these women, some of whom are quite successful and independent, see Madeleine Bunting, "A Meeting of Two Worlds," *Guardian,* June 13, 1990, 21.

289. Chandra Talpade Mohanty, "'Under Western Eyes' Revisited: Feminist Solidarity through Anticapitalist Struggles," *Signs* 28, no. 2 (Winter 2003): 505.

290. Susanne Hoeber Rudolph, "Dehomogenizing Religious Formations," in *Transnational Religion and Fading States,* ed. Susanne Hoeber Rudolph and James Piscatori (Boulder, CO: Westview Press, 1997), 24.

291. For a detailed discussion of the role of religion in U.S. foreign relations, see Andrew Preston, *Sword of the Spirit, Shield of Faith: Religion in American War and Diplomacy* (New York: Knopf, 2012).

292. Peter L. Berger, ed., *The Desecularization of the World: Resurgent Religion and World Politics* (Grand Rapids, MI: Eerdmans, 1999). Susanne Hoeber Rudolph, "Introduction: Religion, States, and Transnational Civil Society," in Rudolph and Piscatori, *Transnational Religion,* 1–2; Charles Taylor, *A Secular Age* (Cambridge, MA: Belknap Press of Harvard University Press, 2007).

293. Dianne Kirby, ed., *Religion and the Cold War* (Basingstoke, UK: Palgrave, 2003), 1.

294. Nicholas Guyatt, *Providence and the Invention of the United States, 1607–1876* (New York: Cambridge University Press, 2007).

295. Andrew J. Rotter, "Christians, Muslims, and Hindus: Religion and U.S.–South Asian Relations, 1947–1954," *Diplomatic History* 24, no. 4 (Fall 2000): 595. See also Knock, *To End All Wars,* 3–4, 8.

296. Dianne Kirby, "Divinely Sanctioned: The Anglo-American Cold War Alliance and the Defence of Western Civilisation and Christianity, 1945–48," *Journal of Contemporary History* 35, no. 3 (July 2000): 388–389.

297. Rotter, "Christians, Muslims, and Hindus," 598.

298. Cited in Dianne Kirby, "The Religious Cold War," in Immerman and Goedde, *Oxford Handbook of the Cold War,* 549.

299. Elizabeth Shakman Hurd, *The Politics of Secularism in International Relations* (Princeton, NJ: Princeton University Press, 2008), 29. See also Kirby, "The Religious Cold War," 542–544.

300. Vladimir Lenin, "Socialism and Religion," in *Collected Works,* vol. 10 (1965), available at the *Marxists Internet Archive,* www.marxists.org/archive/lenin/works/1905/dec/03.htm. Cited in Kirby, "The Religious Cold War," 544.

301. Anna Dickinson, "Domestic Foreign Policy Considerations and the Origins of Postwar Soviet Church–State Relations, 1941–6," in Kirby, *Religion and the Cold War,* 23–26; Hartmut Lehmann, "The Rehabilitation of Martin Luther in the GDR: Or Why Thomas Müntzer Failed to Stabilize the Moorings of Socialist Ideology," in Kirby, *Religion and the Cold War,* 205–207. See also Kirby, "Anglican-Orthodox Relations and the Religious Rehabilitation of the Soviet Regime during the Second World War," *Revue d'Histoire Ecclésiastique* 96, nos. 1–2 (2001): 101–123.

302. For more on this volatility, see Zubok, *Zhivago's Children,* 127–128; Tony Shaw, "'Martyrs, Miracles and Martians': Religion and Cold War Cinematic Propaganda in the 1950s," in Kirby, *Religion and the Cold War,* 215–216. See also Gerhard Besier, *Der SED Staat und die Kirche, 1969–1990: Die Vision vom "Dritten Weg"* (Berlin: Propyläen, 1995).

303. Peter L. Berger, "The Desecularization of the World: A Global Overview," in Berger, *Desecularization of the World,* 2–3.

304. Grace Davie, "Europe: The Exception That Proves the Rule?" in Berger, *Desecularization of the World,* 65. See also Davie, *Europe: The Exceptional Case: Parameters of Faith in the Modern World* (London: Darton, Longman and Todd, 2002).

305. For late 1980s data, see Jørgen S. Nielsen, *Muslims in Western Europe* (Edinburgh: Edinburgh University Press, 1992), 26. For 2008 data, see Forschungsgruppe Weltanschauungen in Deutschland, "Religonszugehörigkeit, Deutschland, 1950–2008," version of March 27, 2009. Data is retrieved from the Jahresberichte des Statistischen Bundesamtes.

306. For more detail on the Sikh community, see R. Ballard and C. Ballard, "The Sikh: The Development of Southern Asian Settlement in Britain," in *Between Two Cultures: Migrants and Minorities in Britain,* ed. James L. Watson (Oxford: Blackwell, 1977); Sewa Singh Kalsi, *The Evolution of a Sikh Community in Britain: Religious and Social Change among the Sikhs of Leeds and Bradford* (Leeds: University of Leeds, Department of Theology and Religious Studies, 1992). For more information on the Muslim population in Western Europe, see Nielsen, *Muslims in Western Europe.*

307. Detlef Pollack, Wolf-Jürgen Grabner, and Christiane Heinze, eds., *Leipzig im Oktober: Kirchen und alternative Gruppen im Umbruch der DDR—Analysen zur Wende,* 2nd ed. (Berlin: Wichern, 1990, 1994). See also Günther Heydemann, Gunther Mai, and Werner Müller, eds., *Revolution und Transformation in der DDR 1989/90* (Berlin: Duncker & Humblot, 1999); Charles S. Maier, *Dissolution: The Crisis of Communism and the End of East Germany* (Princeton, NJ: Princeton University Press, 1997).

308. Richard Wayne Wills Sr., *Martin Luther King Jr. and the Image of God* (New York: Oxford University Press, 2009), 139–190.

309. Malcolm X, *The Autobiography of Malcolm X,* with the assistance of Alex Haley (New York: Grove Press, 1965); Manning Marable, *Malcolm X: A Life of Reinvention* (New York: Penguin, 2011). On a comparison between the two civil rights leaders and their religion, see Lewis V. Baldwin and Amiri YaSin Al-Hadid, *Between Cross and Crescent: Christian and Muslim Perspectives on Malcolm and Martin* (Gainesville: University Press of Florida, 2002); and Louis A. DeCaro Jr., *Malcolm and the Cross: The Nation of Islam, Malcolm X, and Christianity* (New York: New York University Press, 1998).

310. Gustavo Gutiérrez, *A Theology of Liberation: History, Politics and Salvation,* trans. and ed. Sister Caridad Inda and John Eagleson (Maryknoll, NY: Orbis, 1973); Leonardo and Clodovis Boff, *Introducing Liberation Theology,* trans. Paul Burns (Maryknoll, NY: Orbis, 1986). For an overview, see also Phillip Berryman, *Liberation Theology: Essential Facts about the Revolutionary Movement in Latin America and Beyond* (Philadelphia: Temple University Press, 1987). Paul E. Sigmund, *Liberation Theology at the Crossroads: Democracy or Revolution?* (Oxford: Oxford University Press, 1990).

311. José Casanova, *Public Religions in the Modern World* (Chicago: University of Chicago Press, 1994), 126, 133–134. See also Berryman, *Liberation Theology,* 185–200.

312. David B. Barrett and Todd M. Johnson, "Annual Statistical Table on Global Mission: 2004," *International Bulletin of Missionary Research* 28 (January 2004): 25. Reference provided by Benjamin Brandenburg, who is working on a dissertation, "Evangelical Empire," Temple University, forthcoming.

313. Guillermo Cook, ed., *New Face of the Church in Latin America: Between Tradition and Change* (Maryknoll, NY: Orbis, 1994).

314. For a detailed overview of the changing face of Christianity, see Pew-Templeton Global Religious Futures Project, *Global Christianity: A Report on the Size and Distribution of the World's Christian Population* (Washington, DC: Pew Research Center's Forum on Religion and Public Life, 2011).

315. Steve Bruce, *Religion in the Modern World: From Cathedrals to Cults* (Oxford: Oxford University Press, 1996), 121–122.

316. David Harrington Watt, *A Transforming Faith: Explorations of Twentieth-Century American Evangelicalism* (New Brunswick, NJ: Rutgers University Press, 1991), 81.

317. Frances FitzGerald, *Cities on a Hill: A Journey through Contemporary American Cultures* (New York: Simon and Schuster, 1986), 121–201, 150–153.

318. Ibid., 180.

319. According to Berger, Protestantism and Islam produced the most expansive fundamentalisms. Berger, "Desecularization of the World," 6–7, 11.

320. Peter Beyer and Lori Beaman, eds., *Religion, Globalization, and Culture* (Leiden: Brill, 2007), 2, 4.

321. Martin E. Marty and R. Scott Appleby, *The Fundamentalism Project* (Chicago: University of Chicago Press): vol. 1, *Fundamentalisms Observed* (1991); vol. 2, *Fundamentalisms and Society: Reclaiming the Sciences, the Family, and Education* (1993); vol. 3, *Fundamentalisms and the State: Remaking Politics, Economies, and Militance* (1993); vol. 4, *Accounting for Fundamentalisms: The Dynamic Character of Movements* (1994); vol. 5, *Fundamentalisms Comprehended* (1995).

322. Martin Marty, "Fundamentalism as a Social Phenomenon," *Bulletin of the American Academy of Arts and Sciences* 42, no. 2 (November 1988): 15–19.

323. Ibid., 19–23.

324. Berger, "Desecularization of the World," 6–7.

325. Richard T. Antoun, *Understanding Fundamentalism: Christian, Islamic and Jewish Movements* (London: Roman and Littlefield, 2001), 1–3.

326. The Fundamentalism Project focused primarily on the religious aspects of fundamentalism, though it did include discussions of social and political causes and consequences. For the dislocation argument, see Nikki R. Keddie, "The New Religious Politics: Where, When, and Why do "Fundamentalisms" Appear?," *Comparative Studies in Society and History* 40, no. 4 (October 1998): 698–699, 718; Abdullahi A. Na'im, "Political Islam in National Politics and International Relations," in Berger, *Desecularization of the World*, 106.

327. Na'im, "Political Islam," 103.

328. Ibid., 106.

329. Nikki R. Keddie, with Yann Richard, *Modern Iran: Roots and Results of Revolution* (New Haven, CT: Yale University Press, 2003), 214–243.

330. Morris, *Birth of the Palestinian Refugee Problem*. The subject remains controversial, with the so-called new historians challenging traditional narratives about the Palestinian refugees.

331. The original version of the document can be found at www.vatican.va/archive/hist_councils /ii_vatican_council/documents/vat-ii_decl_19651028_nostra-aetate_en.html.

332. Bruce, *Religion in the Modern World*, 169.

333. For the increasing popularity of Hinduism, see "Hinduism in New York: A Growing Religion," *New York Times,* November 2, 1967, 49, 55. See also Shandip Saha, "Hinduism, Gurus, and Globalization," in Beyer and Beaman, *Religion, Globalization and Culture*, 485–502. For Great Britain, see Bruce, *Religion in the Modern World*, 176, 197–198; for Germany, see Barney Lefferts, "Chief Guru of the Western World," *New York Times*, December 17, 1967, 45, 48.

334. Lewis F. Carter, "The 'New Renunciates' of the Bhagwan Shree Rajneesh: Observation and Identification Problems of Interpreting New Religious Movements," *Journal for the Scientific*

Study of Religion 26, no. 2 (June 1987): 148–172. See also Lewis F. Carter, *Charisma and Control in Rajneeshpuram: The Role of Shared Values in the Creation of a Community* (Cambridge: Cambridge University Press 1990); Frances FitzGerald, "A Reporter at Large: Rajneeshpuram," *New Yorker*, pt. 1, September 22, 1986, 46–96; pt. 2, September 29, 1986, 83–125.

335. Bruce, *Religion in the Modern World*, 178–179.

336. Wouter J. Hanegraaff, *New Age Religion and Western Culture: Esotericism in the Mirror of Secular Thought* (Leiden: Brill, 1996), 521.

337. For estimates in Great Britain and the United States, see Paul Heelas, *The New Age Movement: The Celebration of the Self and the Sacralization of Modernity* (Oxford: Blackwell, 1996), 108–130.

338. Ibid., 122–123.

339. Laurel Kearns, "Religion and Ecology in the Context of Globalization," in Beyer and Beaman, *Religion, Globalization and Culture*, 305–334.

340. Bruce, *Religion in the Modern World*, 210–211, 223–224.

341. Thomas Banchoff, introduction to *Democracy and the New Religious Pluralism,* ed. Thomas Banchoff (New York: Oxford University Press, 2007), 6. See also Robert Wuthnow, *The Restructuring of American Religion: Society and Faith since World War II* (Princeton, NJ: Princeton University Press, 1988), 218–222.

342. Jean-Jacques Rousseau, "On the Social Contract," in *Basic Political Writings,* trans. and ed. Donald A. Cress (Indianapolis: Hackett, 1987), 226. I am relying on Nussbaum's reading of Rousseau in her "Radical Evil in Liberal Democracies: The Neglect of the Political Emotions," in Banchoff, *Democracy and the New Religious Pluralism*, 180.

343. Nussbaum refers in her article to Mill's essay "The Utility of Religion," which further develops Comte's idea of the "religion of humanity." In John Stuart Mill, *Three Essays on Religion* (New York: H. Holt and Co., 1874), 69–122, esp. 109, 117.

344. Nussbaum, "Radical Evil in Liberal Democracies," 183.

345. Nussbaum used the example of the Hindu right in India in 2007, which aimed to turn a pluralist society into one that would privilege Hindus and establish a system of intolerance toward other religious and social groups. See ibid., 182.

346. Charter of the United Nations, signed June 26, 1945, in San Francisco, reprinted in Paul Kennedy, *The Parliament of Man: The Past, Present, and Future of the United Nations* (New York: Random House, 2006), 314.

347. See Lynn Hunt, ed., *The French Revolution and Human Rights: A Brief Documentary History* (Boston: Bedford/St. Martin's Press, 1996).

348. Paul Gordon Lauren, *The Evolution of International Human Rights: Visions Seen*, 2nd ed. (Philadelphia: University of Pennsylvania Press, 2003), 37–70.

349. For instances of the cruel colonial Belgian regime in the Congo, see Adam Hochschild, *King Leopold's Ghost: A Story of Greed, Terror, and Heroism in Colonial Africa* (Boston: Houghton Mifflin, 1998).

350. Lauren, *Evolution of Human Rights,* 73.

351. Jan Herman Burgers, "The Road to San Francisco: The Revival of the Human Rights Idea in the Twentieth Century," *Human Rights Quarterly* 14, no. 4 (November 1992): 448; Elizabeth

Borgwardt, *A New Deal for the World: America's Vision for Human Rights* (Cambridge, MA: Belknap Press of Harvard University Press, 2005).

352. Mark Mazower, "The Strange Triumph of Human Rights, 1933–1950," *Historical Journal* 47, no. 2 (June 2004): 385.

353. Mary Ann Glendon, *A World Made New: Eleanor Roosevelt and the Universal Declaration of Human Rights* (New York: Random House, 2001), 174.

354. Goedde, *GIs and Germans,* 178–179. For Article 25, see Glendon, *A World Made New,* 313.

355. Schrecker, *Many Are the Crimes;* Stanley I. Kutler, *The American Inquisition: Justice and Injustice in the Cold War* (New York: Hill and Wang, 1982).

356. Carol Anderson, *Eyes Off the Prize: The United Nations and the African American Struggle for Human Rights, 1944–1955* (New York: Cambridge University Press, 2003), 105–110. See also Mazower, "Strange Triumph," 395.

357. Anderson, *Eyes Off the Prize,* 5; Dudziak, *Cold War Civil Rights.* See also Barbara Keys and Roland Burke, "Human Rights," in Immerman and Goedde, *Oxford Handbook of the Cold War,* 486–502.

358. Mark Mazower, *No Enchanted Palace: The End of Empire and the Ideological Origins of the United Nations* (Princeton, NJ: Princeton University Press, 2009), 61–63; Jan Eckel, "Utopie der Moral, Kalkül der Macht: Menschenrechte in der globalen Politik seit 1945," *Archiv für Sozialgeschichte* 49 (2009): 452; Andreas Eckert, "African Nationalists and Human Rights, 1940s–1970s," in *Human Rights in the Twentieth Century,* ed. Stefan-Ludwig Hoffmann (Cambridge: Cambridge University Press, 2011), 283–300.

359. Roland Burke, "'The Compelling Dialogue of Freedom': Human Rights at the Bandung Conference," *Human Rights Quarterly* 28, no. 4 (November 2006): 962. See also Roland Burke, *Decolonization and the Evolution of International Human Rights* (Philadelphia: University of Pennsylvania Press, 2010), 40.

360. Those arguing against self-determination as a human right include A. W. Brian Simpson and Samuel Moyn. Those on the other side include Roland Burke and Bradley Simpson. See A. W. Brian Simpson, *Human Rights and the End of Empire: Britain and the Genesis of the European Convention* (New York: Oxford University Press, 2001), 300; Samuel Moyn, *The Last Utopia: Human Rights in History* (Cambridge, MA: Belknap Press of Harvard University Press, 2010), 84–89; Bradley Simpson, "'The First Right': The Carter Administration, Indonesia and the Transnational Human Rights Politics of the 1970s," in Iriye, Goedde, and Hitchcock, *The Human Rights Revolution;* Burke, *Decolonization.*

361. Mahmoud Aboul Fath, letter to Bandung delegates (April 13, 1955), cited in Burke, *Decolonization,* 17–18. According to a 1954 article in *Time* magazine, Aboul Fath's and his brother Hussein's opposition to Nasserist politics stemmed at least in part from business interests rather than from concerns over free speech. See "The Press: Egyptian Uproar," *Time,* May 17, 1954.

362. Mazower, "Strange Triumph," 382.

363. "The Freedom Charter," reprinted in *Third World Quarterly* 9, no. 2 (April 1987): 672–677.

364. Mohandas Gandhi, "Letter Addressed to the Director-General of UNESCO," and Chung-Shu Lo, "Human Rights in the Chinese Tradition," cited in Glendon, *A World Made New,* 75.

365. Tom Buchanan, "'The Truth Will Set You Free': The Making of Amnesty International," *Journal of Contemporary History* 37, no. 4 (2002): 575–597.

366. Jonathan Power, *Amnesty International: The Human Rights Story* (New York: Pergamon Press, 1981); Kirsten Sellars, *The Rise and Rise of Human Rights* (Stroud, UK: Sutton, 2002); Stephen Hopgood, *Keepers of the Flame: Understanding Amnesty International* (Ithaca, NY: Cornell University Press, 2006).

367. Sellars, *Rise and Rise of Human Rights,* 97. Sellars argues that despite the official insistence on political neutrality, the leadership was at times strongly partisan in favor of British positions. See also Hopgood, *Keepers of the Flame*, 4–6.

368. Eckel, "Utopie der Moral," 460.

369. Gaddis Smith, *Morality, Reason, and Power: American Diplomacy in the Carter Years* (New York: Hill and Wang, 1986).

370. Jan Eckel, "Under a Magnifying Glass: The International Human Rights Campaign against Chile in the Seventies," in Hoffmann, *Human Rights in the Twentieth Century*, 338.

371. William Korey, *The Promises We Keep: Human Rights, the Helsinki Process, and American Foreign Policy* (New York: St. Martin's Press, 1993), 5–9.

372. For a full text of the Helsinki Accords, see www1.umn.edu/humanrts/osce/basics/finact75 .htm. For a contemporary discussion of the Charter, see H. Gordon Skilling, *Charter 77 and Human Rights in Czechoslovakia* (London: Allen and Unwin, 1981).

373. Keys and Burke, "Human Rights."

374. Daniel C. Thomas, *The Helsinki Effect: International Norms, Human Rights and the Demise of Communism* (Princeton, NJ: Princeton University Press, 2001).

375. United Nations High Commissioner for Refugees (UNHCR), Representation in Bosnia and Herzegovina, "The State of Annex VII, May, 2006."

376. Jared Diamond, *Collapse: How Societies Choose to Fail or Succeed* (New York: Viking, 2005); Alison Des Forges, *"Leave None to Tell the Story": Genocide in Rwanda* (New York: Human Rights Watch, 1999).

377. Scott, "Symptomatic Politics," 109. See also Scott, *Politics of the Veil*. On the 2010 law, see Nadim Audi, "France: Draft Veil Ban Approved," *New York Times*, May 19, 2010, A10.

378. Richard Crockatt, *America Embattled: September 11, Anti-Americanism, and the Global Order* (London: Routledge, 2003), 75–88.

379. Samuel P. Huntington, "The Clash of Civilizations?" *Foreign Affairs* 72, no. 3 (Summer 1993): 22–49. Huntington later expanded his thesis into a book: *The Clash of Civilizations and the Remaking of World Order* (New York: Simon and Schuster, 1996). Huntington borrowed the phrase "clash of civilizations" from Bernard Lewis's 1992 article "The Roots of Muslim Rage," *Atlantic Monthly,* September 1990, 60.

380. Huntington, "The Clash of Civilizations?," 25.

381. Ibid., 29.

382. Bruce, *Religion in the Modern World*, 96. Bruce also refers to Max Weber's concept of "ethnic honor: the sense of 'the excellence of one's own customs and the inferiority of alien ones.'" In Weber, *Economy and Society*, 391.

383. See, for instance, William Pfaff's review of Huntington's book version in "The Reality of Human Affairs," *World Policy Journal* 14, no. 2 (Summer 1997): 89–96.

384. For a representative sample of academic reviews of Huntington's book, see Robert Jervis in *Political Science Quarterly* 112, no. 2 (Summer 1997): 307–308; Shahid Qadir, "Civilisational Clashes: Surveying the Fault Lines," *Third World Quarterly* 19, no. 1 (March, 1998): 149–152; Richard Rosecrance in *American Political Science Review* 92, no. 4 (December 1998): 978–980; Stephen Schulman in *Journal of Politics* 60, no. 1 (February 1998): 304–306.

385. For more information on the argument that Islam is antithetical to democracy and those opposing that argument, see Fawaz A. Gerges, *America and Political Islam: Clash of Cultures or Clash of Interests?* (New York: Cambridge University Press, 1999), 21–36.

386. For a detailed account of the Abu Ghraib case, see articles in *The New Yorker* by Seymour M. Hersh: "Torture at Abu Ghraib," May 10, 2004, 42; "Chain of Command," May 17, 2004, 38; and "The Gray Zone," May 24, 2004, 38.

387. Jane Mayer, "The Memo: How an Internal Effort to Ban the Abuse and Torture of Detainees Was Thwarted," *New Yorker,* February 27, 2006, 32.

388. Samantha Power, *"A Problem from Hell": America and the Age of Genocide* (New York: Basic Books, 2002), 326, 475–476.

389. Ibid., 484–486.

390. See the ICC's official website at www.icc-cpi.int/.

391. For an articulation of this paradox, see Seyla Benhabib, *Another Cosmopolitanism,* with commentaries by Jeremy Waldron, Bonnie Honig, and Will Kymlicka (New York: Oxford University Press, 2006), 31.

392. Kofi Awoonor, "Statement by H.E. Dr. Kofi Awoonor, Ambassador and Permanent Representative of Ghana and Chairman of the Group of 77 in the General Debate of the UNDP Governing Council, 11th June 1991," New York, The Group of 77 (1992), 2. Cited in Russel Lawrence Barsh, "Measuring Human Rights: Problems of Methodology and Purpose," *Human Rights Quarterly* 15, no. 1 (February 1993): 87–88.

393. See report on the opening day by Elaine Sciolino, "U.S. Rejects Notion That Human Rights Vary by Culture," *New York Times,* June 15, 1993.

394. Asian Cultural Forum on Development, *Our Voice: Bangkok NGO's Declaration on Human Rights: Reports of the Asia Pacific NGO Conference on Human Rights and NGOs' Statements to the Asian Regional Meeting* (Bangkok: Asian Cultural Forum on Development, 1993).

395. The African meeting was held in Tunis in November 1992 and stressed the primacy of development as a human right. The Latin American meeting took place in January 1993 and confirmed the universality of human rights. Only the Asian meeting in Bangkok produced controversy.

396. Declaration reprinted in Asian Cultural Forum on Development, *Our Voice,* 244.

397. Ibid., 199.

398. For the full text of the Vienna Declaration and Programme of Action (VDPA), see www .unhchr.ch/huridocda/huridoca.nsf/(Symbol)/A.CONF.157.23.En?OpenDocument. William

Korey, *NGOs and the Universal Declaration of Human Rights: "A Curious Grapevine"* (New York: St. Martin's Press, 1998), 273–306.

399. Amartya Sen, "Human Rights and Asian Values: What Kee Kuan Yew and Li Peng Don't Understand about Asia," *New Republic,* July 14, 1997, 33–40.

400. For the importance of communication, see Kenneth Cmiel, "The Emergence of Human Rights Politics in the United States," *Journal of American History* 86, no. 3 (December 1999): 1231–1250.

401. The biggest protests occurred in Seattle at the 1999 meeting of the World Trade Organization, and the most violent one occurred in 2001 at a meeting of the Group of Eight summit meeting in Genoa.

402. Jeff Faux, *The Global Class War: How America's Bipartisan Elite Lost Our Future, and What It Will Take to Win It Back* (Hoboken, NJ: Wiley, 2006).

403. See official website of the UN World Tourism Organization, at www.unwto.org/aboutwto /his/en/his.php?op=5.

404. Kwame Anthony Appiah, *Cosmopolitanism: Ethics in a World of Strangers* (New York: Norton, 2006), xiii.

405. Ibid., xv.

406. Benhabib, *Another Cosmopolitanism,* 17–18.

407. Benedict Anderson, *Imagined Communities: Reflections on the Origin and Spread of Nationalism* (London: Verso, 1983, 1991, 2006).

408. Bright and Geyer, "Where in the World Is America?," 68.

409. Deborah Sontag, "Headless Bodies from a Bottomless Imagination," *New York Times,* June 21, 2009, Arts section, 26.

410. Ibid.

411. Viktoria Schmidt-Linsenhoff, "Das koloniale Unbewusste in der Kunstgeschichte," in *Globalisierung/Hierarchisierung: Kulturelle Dominanzen in Kunst und Kunstgeschichte,* ed. Irene Below and Beatrice von Bismarck (Marburg: Jonas Verlag, 2005), 22.

412. Bright and Geyer, "Where in the World Is America?," 68.

413. Schmidt-Linsenhoff, "Das Koloniale Unbewusste," 20–21.

414. Jan Nederveen Pieterse, *Globalization* and *Culture: Global Mélange,* 2nd ed. (Lanham, MD: Rowman and Littlefield, 2009), 3.

415. Ibid., 2.

416. Walcott, a resident of Trinidad, and Naipaul, born in Trinidad, have been at odds over their interpretation of colonialism and postcolonialism. For a list of Nobel Prize winners in literature, see http://nobelprizes.com/nobel/literature/.

417. Rushdie's most controversial novel was *The Satanic Verses* (New York: Viking, 1988). Anita Desai's most famous novel, *In Custody* (New York: Harper and Row, 1984), was shortlisted for the Booker Prize and turned into a motion picture by Merchant Ivory Productions. Jhumpa Lahiri, *Interpreter of Maladies* (Boston: Houghton Mifflin, 1999).

5. The Making of a Transnational World

In preparing this chapter, the author has greatly benefited from the input provided by his research assistants, in particular Kenneth Weisbrode, Bryan Nicholson, and Steffen Rimner. It goes without saying that I have learned a great deal from my colleagues who have collaborated on the History of the World project, in particular the contributors to this volume. To them and to all scholars throughout the world who are committed to the study of global and transnational history, I am and shall continue to be indebted.

1. Maeda Yōichi, *Seiō ni manande* (Studying in Western Europe) (Tokyo: Kaname Shobō, 1953). See Alan Riding, *And the Show Went On: Cultural Life in Nazi-Occupied Paris* (New York: Knopf, 2011), for a systematic account of French culture under German occupation.

2. Daniel Blatman, *The Death Marches: The Final Phase of Nazi Genocide*, trans. Chaya Galai (Cambridge, MA: Belknap Press of Harvard University Press, 2010).

3. Arthur E. Barbeau, "The Japanese at Bedford," *Western Pennsylvania Historical Magazine* 64, no. 2 (April 1981): 151–163.

4. For a recent exposition of the Silk Road, see the spring 2011 issue of *The University of Pennsylvania Magazine*.

5. R. R. Palmer, *The Age of the Democratic Revolution: A Political History of Europe and America, 1760–1800* (Princeton, NJ: Princeton University Press, 1964).

6. For a comprehensive treatment of German musicians exiled in the United States, see Horst Weber and Manuela Schwartz, eds., *Geschichte emigrierter Musiker, 1933–1950: Kalifornien* (Munich: K. G. Saur, 2003).

7. Yan Ni, *Senji Nit-Chû eiga kōhōshi* (Interactions between Japanese and Chinese movies during the war) (Tokyo: Iwanami Shoten, 2010).

8. Jessica Gienow-Hecht, *Sound Diplomacy: Music and Emotions in Transatlantic Relations, 1850–1920* (Chicago: University of Chicago Press, 2009).

9. A good reference to classical music in China during the 1920s is Sheila Melvin and Jindong Cai, *Rhapsody in Red: How Western Classical Music Became Chinese* (New York: Algora, 2004).

10. See Nagai Kafū, *American Stories*, trans. Mitsuko Iriye (New York: Columbia University Press, 2000), xx.

11. See S. Frederick Starr, *Red and Hot: The Fate of Jazz in the Soviet Union* (New York: Limelight, 1985).

12. Paul Fussell, *Wartime: Understanding and Behavior in the Second World War* (New York: Oxford University Press, 1989).

13. Donald Keene, *Chronicles of My Life: An American in the Heart of Japan* (New York: Columbia University Press, 2008).

14. Roger Dingman, *Deciphering the Rising Sun: Navy and Marine Corps Codebreakers, Translators, and Interpreters in the Pacific War* (Annapolis, MD: Naval Institute Press, 2009).

15. Xiao-huang Yin, *Chinese-American Literature since the 1850s* (Urbana: University of Illinois Press, 2000).

16. Among the recent examples of a growing body of scholarly literature on public memory are Bernhard Giesen and Christoph Schneider, eds., *Tätertrauma, Nationale Erinnerungen im öffentlichen Diskurs* (Konstanz, Germany: UVK, 2004), and Christian Meier, *Das Gebot zu vergessen und die Unabweisbarkeit des Erinnerns* (Munich: Siedler, 2010).

17. Martin Conway and Kiran Patel, eds., *Europeanization in the Twentieth Century* (Basingstoke, UK: Palgrave Macmillan, 2010).

18. "Dr. Atomic," in Lyric Opera of Chicago, *2007/2008 Season*, 12.

19. See Adam Kirsch, "The Battle for History," *New York Times Book Review*, May 29, 2011, 10–11.

20. *Asahi*, April 21, 2011, 18.

21. See Emily S. Rosenberg, *A Date Which Will Live: Pearl Harbor in American Memory* (Durham, NC: Duke University Press, 2003).

22. See Paul Boyer, *By the Bomb's Early Light* (New York: Pantheon, 1985), 203–206.

23. Norman Naimark, *Russians in Germany: A History of the Soviet Zone of Occupation, 1945–1949* (Cambridge, MA: Belknap Press of Harvard University Press, 1995).

24. Naoko Shibusawa, *America's Geisha Ally: Reimaging the Japanese Enemy* (Cambridge, MA: Harvard University Press, 2006).

25. For a view of the 1920s shared by some US officials and Japan's postwar reformers, see Akira Iriye, *Power and Culture* (Cambridge, MA: Harvard University Press, 1983).

26. Hiroshi Kitamura, *Screening Enlightenment: Hollywood and the Cultural Reconstruction of Defeated Japan* (Ithaca, NY: Cornell University Press, 2010).

27. Ian Goldin et al., *Exceptional People: How Migration Shaped Our World and Will Define Our Future* (Princeton, NJ: Princeton University Press, 2011), 85.

28. Blatman, *Death Marches.*

29. Bruce Mazlish, *The Idea of Humanity in a Global Era* (New York: Palgrave Macmillan, 2008).

30. See Lori Watt, *When Empire Comes Home: Repatriation and Reintegration in Postwar Japan* (Cambridge, MA: Harvard University Asia Center/Harvard University Press, 2009).

31. Sugata Bose and Kris Manjapra, eds., *Cosmopolitan Thought Zones: South Asia and the Global Circulation of Ideas* (Basingstoke, UK: Palgrave Macmillan, 2010).

32. Ibid., 2.

33. Benny Morris, *The Birth of the Palestinian Refugee Problem, 1947–1949* (Cambridge: Cambridge University Press, 1987), 295–298.

34. Rana Mitter, *China's War with Japan, 1937–1945: The Struggle for Survival* (London: Allen Lane, 2013).

35. For a recent collection of studies of the Cold War that make use of Soviet and Chinese archives, see Tsuyoshi Hasegawa, ed., *The Cold War in East Asia, 1945–1991* (Stanford, CA: Stanford University Press, 2011).

36. Frank Ninkovich, *The Diplomacy of Ideas: U.S. Foreign Policy and Cultural Relations, 1938–1950* (Cambridge: Cambridge University Press, 1981); Volker R. Berghahn, *America and the Intellectual Cold War in Europe* (Princeton, NJ: Princeton University Press, 2001); Richard Pells, *Not Like Us: How Europeans Have Loved, Hated, and Transformed American Culture since World War II* (New York: Basic Books, 1997).

37. Quoted in Tadashi Yamamoto, Akira Iriye, and Makoto Iokibe, eds., *Philanthropy and Reconciliation: Rebuilding Postwar U.S.-Japan Relations* (Tokyo: Japan Center for International Exchange, 2006), 49.

38. For a first European-Asian comparison of reconciliation after the war, see Yinan He, *The Search for Reconciliation: Sino-Japanese and German-Polish Relations since World War II* (Cambridge: Cambridge University Press, 2009).

39. Joy Damousi and Mariano Ben Plotkin, eds., *The Transnational Unconscious: Essays in the History of Psychoanalysis and Transnationalism* (Basingstoke, UK: Palgrave Macmillan, 2009), 1.

40. Bruno Nettl, *Encounters with Musicology: A Memoir* (Warren, MI: Harmonie Park, 2002), 36.

41. Laurent Carroué et al., eds., *La mondialisation: Genese, acteurs et enjeux*, 2nd ed. (Rosny-sur-Bois, France: Bréal, 2009), 96.

42. Rushton Coulborn, ed., *Feudalism in History* (Princeton, NJ: Princeton University Press, 1956).

43. Louis Hartz, *The Liberal Tradition in America: An Interpretation of American Political Thought since the Revolution* (New York: Harcourt, Brace, 1955); Richard Hofstadter, *The American Political Tradition and the Men Who Made It* (New York: Vintage, 1955).

44. David Riesman, *The Lonely Crowd: A Study of the Changing American Character* (Garden City, NY: Doubleday, 1953); W. W. Rostow, *The Stages of Economic Growth: A Non-Communist Manifesto* (Cambridge: Cambridge University Press, 1960).

45. Oswald Spengler, *The Decline of the West*, 2 vols., trans. Charles Francis Atkinson (New York: Knopf, 1926–1928); H. G. Wells, *A Short History of the World,* ed. Michael Sherborne (London: Penguin, 2006).

46. Arnold J. Toynbee, *Civilization on Trial* (New York: Oxford University Press, 1948).

47. Arnold J. Toynbee, *A Study of History*, 12 vols. (London: Oxford University Press, 1934–1961).

48. Chinua Achebe, *Things Fall Apart* (New York: Knopf, 1958).

49. David C. Engerman, *Modernization from the Other Shore: American Intellectuals and the Romance of Russian Development* (Cambridge, MA: Harvard University Press, 2003).

50. James William Park, *Latin American Underdevelopment* (Baton Rouge: Louisiana State University Press, 1995), 2.

51. On liberal developmentalism, see Robert Latham, *The Liberal Moment: Modernity, Security, and the Making of Postwar International Order* (New York: Columbia University Press, 1997).

52. Cemil Aydin, *The Politics of Anti-Westernism in Asia* (New York: Columbia University Press, 2007).

53. For "Orientalism," see Edward Said, *Orientalism* (New York: Pantheon, 1978).

54. Ssu-Yü Teng and John K. Fairbank, eds., *China's Response to the West: A Documentary Survey, 1839–1923* (Cambridge, MA: Harvard University Press, 1954).

55. Akira Iriye, *Global Community: The Role of International Organizations in the Making of the Contemporary World* (Berkeley: University of California Press, 2002), 47–48.

56. Lawrence S. Wittner, *One World or None: A History of the World Nuclear Disarmament Movement through 1953* (Stanford, CA: Stanford University Press, 1993); Matthew Evange-

lista, *Unarmed Forces: The Transnational Movement to End the Cold War* (Ithaca, NY: Cornell University Press, 1999).

57. Walter Hixson, *Parting the Curtain: Propaganda, Culture, and the Cold War, 1945–1961* (New York: St. Martin's Press, 1997).

58. Iriye, *Global Community*, 75–76.

59. See Steven Vogel, *Freer Market, More Rules: Regulatory Reform in Advanced Industrial Countries* (Ithaca, NY: Cornell University Press, 1996).

60. Iriye, *Global Community*, 70.

61. See Sandra Kraft, *Von Hörsaal auf die Anklagenbank: Die 68er und das Establishment in Deutschland und den USA* (Frankfurt: Campus, 2010).

62. Philip Gassert and Martin Klimke, eds., *1968: Memories and Legacies of a Global Revolt* (Washington, DC: German Historical Institute, 2009).

63. Gerd Koenen, *Das rote Jahrzehnt: Unsere kleine deutsche Kulturrevolution, 1967–1977* (Frankfurt: Fischer, 2002).

64. Martin Klimke, *The Other Alliance: Student Protest in West Germany and the United States in the Global Sixties* (Princeton, NJ: Princeton University Press, 2011).

65. See the introductory essay in Conway and Patel, *Europeanization in the Twentieth Century*.

66. Richard Wolin, *The Wind from the East: French Intellectuals, the Cultural Revolution, and the Legacy of the 1960s* (Princeton, NJ: Princeton University Press, 2010).

67. See, for instance, Marius B. Jansen, ed., *Changing Japanese Attitudes toward Modernization* (Princeton, NJ: Princeton University Press, 1965).

68. A notable product of these meetings was James W. Morley, ed., *Japan's Foreign Policy, 1868–1941: A Research Guide* (New York: Columbia University Press, 1974).

69. The conference papers were published in Dorothy Borg and Shumpei Okamoto, eds., *Pearl Harbor as History: Japanese-American Relations, 1931–1941* (New York: Columbia University Press, 1973).

70. See Edward Miller, *Misalliance: Ngo Dinh Diem, the United States, and the Fate of South Vietnam* (Cambridge, MA: Harvard University Press, 2013).

71. Viktor F. Frankl, *Der Mensch vor der Frage nach dem Sinn* (Munich: Piper, 1985). See *Asahi*, April 28, 2011, 18.

72. Frantz Fanon, *The Wretched of the Earth* (New York: Grove, 1961).

73. Said, *Orientalism*.

74. Edward Albee, *A Delicate Balance* (New York: Plume, 1997).

75. Kathrin Fahlenbrach, Martin Klimke, Joachim Scharloth, and Laura Wong, eds., *The Establishment Responds: Power, Politics, and Protest since 1945* (Basingstoke, UK: Palgrave Macmillan, 2011).

76. For a superb discussion of the significance of the 1970s, see Thomas Borstelmann, *The 1970s: A New Global History from Civil Rights to Economic Inequality* (Princeton, NJ: Princeton University Press, 2011).

77. Goldin et al., *Exceptional People*, 90–95.

78. Jane Desmond, *Staging Tourism: Bodies on Display from Waikiki to Sea World* (Chicago: University of Chicago Press, 1999), xvii.

79. See Wang Gungwu's essay in *Conceptualizing Global History,* ed. Bruce Mazlish and Ralph Buultjens (Boulder, CO: Westview, 1993).

80. Ted Morgan, *On Becoming American* (Boston: Houghton Mifflin 1978), 185.

81. Eric J. Hobsbawm, *The Age of Extremes: A History of the World, 1914–1991* (New York: Vintage, 1996).

82. See Kathleen Burk and Alec Cairncross, *Good-bye, Great Britain: The 1976 IMF Crisis* (New Haven, CT: Yale University Press, 1992).

83. For a detailed discussion of this phenomenon, see ibid., 129–134.

84. Ibid., 112.

85. Ibid., 137.

86. For an informative study of the transnational movement on behalf of the handicapped from the 1970s into the 1980s, see Francine Saillant, *Identité et handicaps: Circuits humanitaires et posthumanitaires* (Paris: Karthala, 2007). An important aspect was the legal right of disabled persons to education. See Ralf Poscher, Johannes Rux, and Thomas Langer, *Von der Integration zur Inklusion: Das Recht auf Bildung aus der Behindertenrechtskonvention der Vereinten Nationen und seine innerstaatliche Umsetzung* (Baden-Baden, Germany: Nomos, 2008).

87. The best study of the uses of (and protests against) Agent Orange is David Zierler, *The Invention of Ecocide: Agent Orange, Vietnam, and the Scientists Who Changed the Way We Think about the Environment (*Athens: University of Georgia Press, 2011).

88. Timothy S. George, *Minamata: Pollution and the Struggle for Democracy in Postwar Japan* (Cambridge, MA: Harvard University Asia Center/Harvard University Press, 2001).

89. Iriye, *Global Community,* 147.

90. See Ana Cutter Patel et al., *Disarming the Past: Transnational Justice and Ex-Combatants* (New York: Social Science Research Council, 2009), 263.

91. One of the major protagonists in the RAF finds her own voice in Ulrike Marie Meinhof, *Die Würde des Menschen ist antastbar Aufsätze und Polemiken* (Berlin: Wagenbuch, 2008).

92. Scott M. Thomas, *The Global Resurgence of Religion and the Transformation of International Relations* (New York: Palgrave Macmillan, 2005).

93. Borstelmann, *The 1970s.*

94. Thomas, *Global Resurgence,* xii.

95. See Shimotomai's essay in Hasegawa, *Cold War in East Asia.*

96. The best recent biography of Deng Xiaoping is Ezra Vogel, *Deng Xiaoping and the Transformation of China* (Cambridge, MA: Belknap Press of Harvard University Press, 2011).

97. Sakamoto Masahiro, ed., *20 seiki no sekai* (The world of the twentieth century) (Tokyo: Nihon Keizai Shimbunsha, 1992), 148–153. For much statistical information for the late twentieth century, I have relied on Laurent Carroué et al., *La mondialisation: Genèse, acteurs et enjeux,* 2nd ed. (Rosny-sous-Bois, France: Bréal, 2009).

98. Examples are Mazlish and Buultjens, *Conceptualizing Global History;* and Akira Iriye, *The Globalizing of America* (Cambridge: Cambridge University Press, 1992).

99. American Historical Association, *Perspectives* (September 2011): 14–17.

100. See also the pathbreaking collection of essays in Jürgen Osterhammel, *Geschichtswissenschaft jenseits des Nationalstaats: Studien zu Beziehungsgeschichte und Zivilisationsvergleich* (Göttingen: Vandenhoeck & Ruprecht, 2001).

101. The papers presented at these two conferences have been published as Nobutoshi Hagihara et al., eds., *Experiencing the Twentieth Century* (Tokyo: University of Tokyo Press, 1985); and Japan Foundation Center for Global Partnership, ed., *The End of the Century* (Tokyo: Kodansha International, 1995).

102. See Joseph S. Nye Jr., *Bound to Lead: The Changing Nature of American Power* (New York: Basic Books, 1990).

103. *The World Almanac and Book of Facts 2007* (New York: World Almanac Books, 2007), 283.

104. *Asahi*, June 1, 2011, 8.

105. Sarah Snyder, *Human Rights Activism and the End of the Cold War: A Transnational History of the Helsinki Network* (New York: Cambridge University Press, 2011).

106. For the German escalation of rebellion into terrorist acts, see Stefan Aust, *Der Baader-Meinhof Komplex* (Hamburg: Hoffmann und Campe, 1985).

107. A fundamental overview for the German case is Berthold Löffler, *Integration in Deutschland* (Munich: Oldenbourg, 2010).

108. For a thoughtful review of the "textbook controversy," see Daqing Yang et al., *Toward a History beyond Borders* (Cambridge, MA: Harvard University Asia Center/Harvard University Press, 2012).

109. For a firsthand account of the controversy by the director of the National Air and Space Museum, see Martin Harwit, *An Exhibit Denied: Lobbying the History of Enola Gay* (New York: Copernicus, 1996).

110. See David Blanchon, *Atlas mondial de l'eau* (Paris: Autrement, 2009).

111. See Conway and Patel, *Europeanization in the Twentieth Century*.

112. Walter A. McDougall, *Let the Sea Make a Noise: A History of the North Pacific from Magellan to MacArthur* (New York: Basic Books, 1993).

113. These international tourism statistics are taken from annual United Nations reports, which are summarized in *The World Almanac and Book of Facts* (New York), *Kokusai tōkei yōran* (Summary of international statistics, Tokyo), and similar publications.

114. *The World Almanac and Book of Facts 2010* (New York: World Almanac, 2010), 91.

115. Desmond, *Staging Tourism*.

116. Mark S. Hamm, *The Abandoned Ones: The Imprisonment and Uprising of the Mariel Boat People* (Boston: Northeastern University Press, 1995).

117. These census figures are taken from *The World Almanac and Book of Facts 2007*, 601–603.

118. See www.internetworldstats.com/stats7.html, and www.internetworldstats.com/emarketing .htm.

119. *World Almanac 2010*, 369.

120. Saskia Sassen, *The Global City: New York, London, Tokyo* (Princeton, NJ: Princeton University Press, 2001).

121. Kenneth Weisbrode, *On Ambivalence* (Cambridge, MA: MIT Press, 2012).

122. Fabrizio Maccaglia and Marie-Anne Matard-Bonucci, eds., *Atlas des mafias* (Paris: Autrement, 2009), 69.

123. See www.pbs.org/wgbh/pages/frontline/slaves/etc/stats.html.

124. Desley Deacon, Penny Russell, and Angela Woollacott, eds., *Transnational Lives: Biographies of Global Modernity, 1700–Present* (Basingstoke, UK: Palgrave Macmillan, 2009); Patricia A. Schechter, *Exploring the Decolonial Imaginary: Four Transnational Lives* (New York: Palgrave Macmillan, 2012).

125. For various perspectives on the "end of the American century," see Andrew Bacevich, ed., *The Short American Century: A Postmortem* (Cambridge, MA: Harvard University Press, 2012).

126. See www.newamericancentury.org/statementofprinciples.htm.

127. The outrage among European intellectuals toward US Defense Secretary Donald Rumsfeld, who expressed his disdain for "old Europe," is documented in "Das alte Europa antwortet Herrn Rumsfeld," *Frankfurter Allgemeine Zeitung*, January 24, 2003, 33.

128. Margarete Grandner, Dietmar Rothermund, and Wolfgang Schwentker, eds., *Globalisierung und Globalgeschichte* (Vienna: Mandelbaum, 2005).

129. Richard Bulliet et al., *The Earth and Its Peoples* (Boston: Houghton Mifflin, 2005), xxiii.

130. Robert Tignor et al., *Worlds Together, Worlds Apart: A History of the Modern World from the Mongol Empire to the Present* (New York: Norton, 2002), xxvi.

131. Thomas Bender, *A Nation among Nations: America's Place in World History* (New York: Hill and Wang, 2006).

132. Ian Tyrrell, *Transnational Nation: United States History in Global Perspective since 1789* (New York: Palgrave Macmillan, 2007).

133. High school curricula in Germany now stress "global perspectives in the teaching of history." See *Geschichte für Heute: Zeitschrift für historisch-politische Bildung* (2009).

134. Bruce Mazlish, *Civilization and Its Contents* (Stanford, CA: Stanford University Press, 2004), 161.

135. Goldin et al., *Exceptional People,* 150.

136. Catherin Wihtol de Wenden, *Atlas mondial des migrations* (Paris: Autrement, 2009), 12.

137. A 2009 movie, *Avatar*, which netted $2.7 billion in worldwide sales, was a parable of the environmental crisis made worse by a population explosion. The film imagines a world in 2154 that is severely overpopulated and starved for energy. People begin to scout the heavens for valuable resources. The main character is a US marine who was rendered paraplegic by battle wounds in Venezuela, one of the richest oil-producing countries, and his commanding officer on the imagined planet is himself a veteran of an earlier campaign in Nicaragua, another oil-rich country. The incentive that brings them from Earth is a fictional mineral needed for superconducting electricity.

138. For a brief summary of the development of nuclear power, see Bruno Tertrais, *Atlas Mondial du Nucleaire* (Paris: Autrement, 2011).

139. See www.harper.org/arcguve/2010/07/0083022.

140. See www.cnn.com/2008/US/04/24/samsclub.rices/index.html.

141. For a good summary of these developments, I have relied on Hirakawa Hotoshi et al., *Higashi Ajia chiiki kyōryoku no kyōdō sekkei* (Joint planning for East Asian regional cooperation) (Tokyo: Hatsubai Nishida Shoten, 2009).

142. Among the best examples of historical writings with this perspective are Bruce Cumings, *Domination from Sea to Sea: Pacific Ascendancy and American Power* (New Haven, CT: Yale University Press, 2009); Marilyn Lake and Henry Reynolds, *Drawing the Global Colour Line: White Men's Countries and the Question of Racial Equality* (Carlton, Australia: Melbourne University Press, 2008); and John Price, *Orienting Canada: Race, Empire, and the Transpacific* (Vancouver: UBC Press, 2011).

Selected Bibliography

States and the Changing Equations of Power

Biermann, Rafael. *Zwischen Kreml und Kanzleramt: Wie Moskau mit der deutschen Einheit rang*. Paderborn, Germany: Schöningh, 1997.

Bitsch, Marie-Thérèse, ed., *Cinquante ans de traité de Rome, 1957–2007: Regards sur la construction européenne*. Stuttgart: Franz Steiner, 2009.

Bose, Sugata, and Ayesha Jalal. *Modern South Asia: History, Culture, Political Economy*. London: Routledge, 1998.

Bowie, Robert R., and Richard H. Immerman. *Waging Peace: How Eisenhower Shaped an Enduring Cold War Strategy*. New York: Oxford University Press, 1998.

Brown, Archie. *The Gorbachev Factor*. New York: Oxford University Press, 1996.

———. *Seven Years That Changed the World: Perestroika in Perspective*. New York: Oxford University Press, 2007.

Calvocoressi, Peter. *World Politics, 1945–2000*. 8th ed. London: Longman, 2001.

Casey, Steven, and Jonathan Wright, eds. *Mental Maps in the Early Cold War Era, 1945–1968*. Basingstoke, UK: Palgrave Macmillan, 2011.

Chen Jian. *Mao's China and the Cold War*. Chapel Hill: University of North Carolina Press, 2001.

Coase, Ronald, and Ning Wang. *How China Became Capitalist*. Basingstoke, UK: Palgrave Macmillan, 2011.

Cohen, Warren I., and Akira Iriye, eds. *The Great Powers in East Asia, 1953–1960*. New York: Columbia University Press, 1990.

Coleman, David G., and Joseph M. Siracusa. *Real-World Nuclear Deterrence: The Making of International Strategy*. Westport, CT: Praeger Security International, 2006.

Czempiel, Ernst-Otto. *Machtprobe: Die USA und die Sowjetunion in den achtziger Jahren*. Munich: C. H. Beck, 1989.

Dobbs, Michael. *One Minute to Midnight: Kennedy, Khrushchev, and Castro on the Brink of Nuclear War*. New York: Knopf, 2008.

Fink, Carole, and Bernd Schaefer, eds. *Ostpolitik, 1969–1974: European and Global Responses*. Cambridge: Cambridge University Press, 2009.

Freedman, Lawrence. *The Evolution of Nuclear Strategy*. 3rd ed. Basingstoke, UK: Palgrave Macmillan, 2003.

Fursenko, Aleksandr, and Timothy Naftali. *Khrushchev's Cold War: The Inside Story of an American Adversary*. New York: Norton, 2006.

Gaddis, John Lewis. *The Cold War: A New History.* New York: Penguin, 2005.

———. *We Now Know: Rethinking Cold War History.* New York: Oxford University Press, 1997.

Garthoff, Raymond L. *Détente and Confrontation: American-Soviet Relations from Nixon to Reagan.* Washington, DC: Brookings Institution Press, 1994.

———. *The Great Transition: American-Soviet Relations and the End of the Cold War.* Washington, DC: Brookings Institution Press, 1994.

Gori, Francesca, and Silvio Pons, eds. *The Soviet Union and Europe in the Cold War, 1943–53.* Basingstoke, UK: Macmillan, 1996.

Grandin, Greg. *Empire's Workshop: Latin America, the United States, and the Rise of the New Imperialism.* New York: Metropolitan, 2005.

Grob-Fitzgibbon, Benjamin. *Imperial Endgame: Britain's Dirty Wars and the End of Empire.* Basingstoke, UK: Palgrave Macmillan, 2011.

Harrison, Hope M. *Driving the Soviets up the Wall: Soviet–East German Relations, 1953–1961.* Princeton, NJ: Princeton University Press, 2003.

Herring, George C. *America's Longest War: The United States and Vietnam, 1950–1975.* 4th ed. Boston: McGraw-Hill, 2002.

Hitchcock, William I. *France Restored: Cold War Diplomacy and the Quest for Leadership in Europe, 1944–1954.* Chapel Hill: University of North Carolina Press, 1998.

Hobsbawm, Eric. *The Age of Extremes: The Short Twentieth Century, 1914–1991.* London: Michael Joseph, 1994.

Iriye, Akira. *China and Japan in the Global Setting.* Cambridge, MA: Harvard University Press, 1992.

James, Harold. *Rambouillet, 15. November 1975: Die Globalisierung der Wirtschaft.* Munich: Deutscher Taschenbuch Verlag, 1997.

Judt, Tony. *Postwar: A History of Europe since 1945.* London: Heinemann, 2005.

Kennedy-Pipe, Caroline. *Russia and the World, 1917–1991.* London: Arnold, 1998.

Lawrence, Marc Atwood. *Assuming the Burden: Europe and American Commitment to the War in Vietnam.* Berkeley: University of California Press, 2005.

Leffler, Melvyn P., and Odd Arne Westad, eds. *The Cambridge History of the Cold War.* 3 vols. Cambridge: Cambridge University Press, 2010.

Loth, Wilfried, ed. *Experiencing Europe: 50 Years of European Construction, 1957–2007.* Baden-Baden, Germany: Nomos, 2009.

———. *Overcoming the Cold War: A History of Détente, 1950–1991.* London: Palgrave, 2002.

———. *Die Sowjetunion und die deutsche Frage: Studien zur sowjetischen Deutschlandpolitik von Stalin bis Chruschtschow.* Göttingen: Vandenhoeck & Ruprecht, 2007.

———. *Stalin's Unwanted Child: The Soviet Union, the German Question, and the Founding of the GDR.* London: Macmillan, 1998.

———. *Der Weg nach Europa: Geschichte der europäischen Integration, 1939–1957.* 3rd ed. Göttingen: Vandenhoeck & Ruprecht, 1995.

Loth, Wilfried, and Georges-Henri Soutou, eds. *The Making of Détente: Eastern and Western Europe in the Cold War, 1965–75*. London: Routledge, 2009.

Louis, Wm. Roger. *The British Empire in the Middle East, 1945–1951: Arab Nationalism, the United States, and Postwar Imperialism*. New York: Oxford University Press, 1984.

Mansfield, Peter, with Nicolas Pelham. *A History of the Middle East*. 2nd ed. New York: Penguin, 2003.

Mark, Chi-Kwan. *China and the World since 1945: An International History*. New York: Routledge, 2012.

Mastny, Wojtech. *The Cold War and Soviet Insecurity: The Stalin Years*. New York: Oxford University Press, 1996.

McAllister, Richard. *European Union: An Historical and Political Survey*. 2nd ed. New York: Routledge, 2009.

Möckli, Daniel. *European Foreign Policy during the Cold War: Heath, Brandt, Pompidou and the Dream of Political Unity*. London: Tauris, 2009.

Nagai, Yōnosuke, and Akira Iriye, eds. *The Origins of the Cold War in Asia*. New York: Columbia University Press, 1977.

Naimark, Norman, and Leonid Gibianskii, eds. *The Establishment of Communist Regimes in Eastern Europe, 1944–1949*. Boulder, CO: Westview, 1997.

Ouimet, Matthew J. *The Rise and Fall of the Brezhnev Doctrine in Soviet Foreign Policy*. Chapel Hill: University of North Carolina Press, 2003.

Reinisch, Jessica, and Elizabeth White, eds. *The Disentanglement of Populations: Migration, Expulsion and Displacement in Post-war Europe, 1944–9*. Basingstoke, UK: Palgrave Macmillan, 2011.

Reynolds, David. *One World Divisible: A Global History since 1945*. London: Allen Lane, 2000.

Roberts, Geoffrey. *Stalin's Wars: From World War to Cold War, 1939–1953*. New Haven, CT: Yale University Press, 2006.

Rödder, Andreas. *Deutschland einig Vaterland: Die Geschichte der Wiedervereinigung*. Munich: C. H. Beck, 2009.

Rothermund, Dietmar. *The Routledge Companion to Decolonization*. New York: Routledge, 2006.

Sanderson, Claire. *L'impossible alliance? France, Grande-Bretagne et la défense de l'Europe, 1945–1958*. Paris: Publications de la Sorbonne, 2003.

Sayigh, Yazid, and Avi Slaim, eds. *The Cold War and the Middle East*. Oxford: Clarendon, 1997.

Schenk, Catherine R. *International Economic Relations since 1945*. New York: Routledge, 2011.

Schulz, Matthias, and Thomas A. Schwartz, eds. *The Strained Alliance: U.S.-European Relations from Nixon to Carter*. Cambridge: Cambridge University Press, 2009.

Self, Robert. *British Foreign and Defence Policy since 1945: Challenges and Dilemmas in a Changing World*. Basingstoke, UK: Palgrave Macmillan, 2010.

Soutou, Georges-Henri. *L'alliance incertaine: Les rapports politico-stratégiques franco-allemands, 1954–1996*. Paris: Fayard, 1996.

Stueck, William. *Rethinking the Korean War: A New Diplomatic and Strategic History*. Princeton, NJ: Princeton University Press, 2002.

Taubman, William. *Khrushchev: The Man and His Era*. New York: Norton, 2003.

Thackrah, John Richard. *The Routledge Companion to Military Conflict since 1945*. New York: Routledge, 2008.

Thomas, Daniel C. *The Helsinki Effect: International Norms, Human Rights, and the Demise of Communism*. Princeton, NJ: Princeton University Press, 2001.

Trachtenberg, Marc. *A Constructed Peace: The Making of the European Settlement, 1945–1963*. Princeton, NJ: Princeton University Press, 1999.

Vaïsse, Maurice. *La grandeur: Politique étrangère du général de Gaulle, 1958–1969*. Paris: Fayard, 1998.

Villaume, Poul, and Odd Arne Westad, eds. *Perforating the Iron Curtain: European Détente, Transatlantic Relations, and the Cold War, 1965–1985*. Copenhagen: Museum Tusculanum Press, 2010.

Westad, Odd Arne, ed. *Brother in Arms: The Rise and Fall of the Sino-Soviet Alliance, 1945–1963*. Stanford, CA: Stanford University Press, 1998.

———. *The Global Cold War: Third World Interventions and the Making of Our Times*. Cambridge: Cambridge University Press, 2005.

———, ed. *Reviewing the Cold War: Approaches, Interpretations, Theory*. London: Frank Cass, 2000.

Zajec, Olivier. *La nouvelle impuissance américaine: Essai sur dix années d'autodissolution stratégique*. Paris: Oeuvre, 2011.

Zakaria, Fareed. *The Post-American World*. London: Allen Lane, 2008.

Zubok, Vladislav M. *A Failed Empire: The Soviet Union in the Cold War from Stalin to Gorbachev*. Chapel Hill: University of North Carolina Press, 2007.

Opening Doors in the World Economy

Ammon, Royce J. *Global Television and the Shaping of World Politics: CNN, Telediplomacy, and Foreign Policy*. Jefferson, NC: McFarland, 2001.

Amsden, Alice H. *Asia's Next Giant: South Korea and Late Industrialization*. New York: Oxford University Press, 1989.

Arrighi, Giovanni. "The World Economy and the Cold War, 1970–1990." In *The Cambridge History of the Cold War*, vol. 2, *Endings*, ed. Melvyn P. Leffler and Odd Arne Westad. Cambridge: Cambridge University Press, 2010.

Baker, Peter. "The Mellowing of William Jefferson Clinton." *New York Times Magazine*. May 31, 2009.

Barnhart, Michael A. "From Hershey Bars to Motor Cars: America's Economic Policy toward Japan, 1945–76." In *Partnership: The United States and Japan, 1951–2001*, ed. Akira Iriye and Robert A. Wampler. Tokyo: Kodansha International, 2001.

Beneria, Lourdes, and Savitri Bisnath. "Gender and Poverty: An Analysis for Action." In *The Globalization Reader*, ed. Frank H. Lechner and John Boli. Malden, MA: Wiley-Blackwell, 2000.

Bideleux, Robert, and Ian Jeffries. *A History of Eastern Europe: Crisis and Change*. 2nd ed. London: Routledge, 2007.

Borden, William S. *The Pacific Alliance: United States Foreign Economic Policy and Japanese Trade Recovery, 1947–1955*. Madison: University of Wisconsin Press, 1984.

Brazinsky, Gregg Andrew. "Koreanizing Modernization: Modernization Theory and South Korean Intellectuals." In *Staging Growth: Modernization, Development, and the Global Cold War*, ed. David C. Engerman, Nils Gilman, Mark H. Haefele, and Michael E. Latham. Amherst: University of Massachusetts Press, 2003.

Calleo, David P. "Since 1961: American Power in a New World Economy." In *Economics and World Power: An Assessment of American Diplomacy since 1789*, ed. William H. Becker and Samuel F. Wells Jr. New York: Columbia University Press, 1984.

Cardenas, Enrique, Jose Antonio Ocampo, and Rosemary Thorp, eds. *An Economic History of Twentieth-Century Latin America*, vol. 3, *Industrialization and the State in Latin America: The Postwar Years*. Basingstoke, UK: Palgrave, 2000.

Cartier, Carolyn. *Globalizing South China*. Oxford: Blackwell, 2001.

Central Intelligence Agency (CIA). *The World Factbook: European Union*. https://www.cia.gov/library/publications/the-world-factbook/geos/ee.html.

Chang, Gordon H. *Friends and Enemies: The United States, China, and the Soviet Union, 1948–1972*. Stanford, CA: Stanford University Press, 1990.

Cooper, Andrew F. *Celebrity Diplomacy*. Boulder, CO: Paradigm, 2008.

Cumings, Bruce. *Korea's Place in the Sun: A Modern History*. 2nd ed. New York: Norton, 2005.

De Grazia, Victoria. *Irresistible Empire: America's Advance through Twentieth-Century Europe*. Cambridge, MA: Belknap Press of Harvard University Press, 2005.

Dobson, Alan P. *US Economic Statecraft for Survival, 1933–1991: Of Sanctions, Embargoes, and Economic Warfare*. London: Routledge, 2002.

Dosman, Edgar J. *The Life and Times of Raúl Prebisch, 1901–1986*. Montreal: McGill-Queen's University Press, 2008.

Dower, John W. *Embracing Defeat: Japan in the Wake of World War II*. New York: Norton, 1999.

Eckes, Alfred E., Jr. "Europe and Economic Globalization since 1945." In *A Companion to Europe since 1945*, ed. Klaus Larres. Malden, MA: Wiley-Blackwell, 2009.

———. *Opening America's Market: U.S. Foreign Trade Policy since 1776*. Chapel Hill: University of North Carolina Press, 1995.

———. *U.S. Trade Issues: A Reference Handbook*. Santa Barbara, CA: ABC-CLIO, 2009.

Eckes, Alfred E., Jr., and Thomas W. Zeiler. *Globalization and the American Century.* Cambridge: Cambridge University Press, 2003.

Edwards, Sebastian. *Crisis and Reform in Latin America: From Despair to Hope.* New York: Oxford University Press, 1995.

Engel, Jeffrey A. *The Cold War at 30,000 Feet: The Anglo-American Fight for Aviation Supremacy.* Cambridge, MA: Harvard University Press, 2007.

Feinstein, Charles H. *An Economic History of South Africa: Conquest, Discrimination and Development.* Cambridge: Cambridge University Press, 2005.

Ferguson, Niall. *The Ascent of Money: A Financial History of the World.* New York: Penguin, 2008.

Fergusson, Ian F. "The World Trade Organization: Background and Issues." Congressional Research Service Report for Congress. http://www.nationalaglawcenter.org/assets/crs/98 -928.pdf.

———. "World Trade Organization Negotiations: The Doha Development Agenda." Congressional Research Service Report for Congress. http://www.nationalaglawcenter.org /assets/crs/RL32060.pdf.

Freund, Bill. *The Making of Contemporary Africa: The Development of African Society since 1800.* 2nd ed. Basingstoke, UK: Macmillan, 1998.

Frieden, Jeffry A. *Debt, Development, and Democracy: Modern Political Economy and Latin America, 1965–1985.* Princeton, NJ: Princeton University Press, 1991.

Funigiello, Philip J. *American-Soviet Trade in the Cold War.* Chapel Hill: University of North Carolina Press, 1988.

Gavin, Francis J. *Gold, Dollars, and Power: The Politics of International Monetary Relations, 1958–1971.* Chapel Hill: University of North Carolina Press, 2004.

Gilman, Nils. "Modernization Theory, the Highest Stage of American Intellectual History." In *Staging Growth: Modernization, Development, and the Global Cold War,* ed. David C. Engerman, Nils Gilman, Mark H. Haefele, and Michael E. Latham. Amherst: University of Massachusetts Press, 2003.

Gleijeses, Piero. *Shattered Hope: The Guatemalan Revolution and the United States, 1944– 1954.* Princeton, NJ: Princeton University Press, 1991.

Goldstein, Judith. "Creating the GATT Rules: Politics, Institutions, and American Policy." In *Multilateralism Matters: The Theory and Praxis of an Institutional Form,* ed. John Gerard Ruggie. New York: Columbia University Press, 1993.

Greider, William. *One World, Ready or Not: The Manic Logic of Global Capitalism.* New York: Simon and Schuster, 1997.

Grieco, Joseph M., and G. John Ikenberry. *State Power and World Markets: The International Political Economy.* New York: Norton, 2003.

Griswold, Dan. "NAFTA at 10: An Economic and Foreign Policy Success." *Free Trade Bulletin,* no. 1 (December 17, 2002). http://www.freetrade.org/pubs/FTBs/FTB-001.html.

Haar, Jerry, and John Price, eds. *Can Latin America Compete? Confronting the Challenges of Globalization*. New York: Palgrave Macmillan, 2008.

Hahn, Peter L. *The United States, Great Britain, and Egypt, 1945–1956: Strategy and Diplomacy in the Early Cold War*. Chapel Hill: University of North Carolina Press, 1991.

Hart, Michael. *A Trading Nation: Canadian Trade Policy from Colonialism to Globalization*. Vancouver: UBC Press, 2002.

Hathaway, Robert M. "1933–1945: Economic Diplomacy in a Time of Crisis." In *Economics and World Power: An Assessment of American Diplomacy since 1789*, ed. William H. Becker and Samuel F. Wells Jr. New York: Columbia University Press, 1984.

Hogan, Michael J. *The Marshall Plan: America, Britain, and the Reconstruction of Western Europe, 1947–1952*. Cambridge: Cambridge University Press, 1987.

Holmes, Nigel, and Megan McArdle. "Iceland's Meltdown." *Atlantic*. December 2008.

Iguchi, Haruo. *Unfinished Business: Ayukawa Yoshisuke and U.S.-Japan Relations, 1937–1953*. Cambridge, MA: Harvard University Asia Center/Harvard University Press, 2003.

Iliffe, John. *Africans: The History of a Continent*. 2nd ed. Cambridge: Cambridge University Press, 2007.

International Monetary Fund (IMF). *Report for Selected Country Groups and Subjects*. http://www.imf.org/external/pubs/ft/weo/2008/01/weodata/weorept.aspx?sy=2006&ey=2008&ssd=1&sort=country&ds=.&br=1&c=998&s=NGDPD%2CPPPGDP&grp=1&a=1&pr.x=46&pr.y=7.

———. *World Economic Outlook (WEO): Financial Stress, Downturns, and Recoveries*, October 2008. http://www.imf.org/external/pubs/ft/weo/2008/02/index.htm.

———. *World Economic Outlook (WEO): Recovery, Risk, and Rebalancing*. October 2010. http://www.imf.org/external/pubs/ft/weo/2010/02/index.htm.

International Telecommunications Union. "The World in 2009: ICT Facts and Figures." http://www.itu.int/ITU-D/ict/material/Telecom09_flyer.pdf.

Jackson, Ian. *The Economic Cold War: America, Britain, and East-West Trade, 1948–63*. Basingstoke, UK: Palgrave, 2001.

John Templeton Foundation. "Does the Free Market Corrode Moral Character?" http://www.templeton.org/market/.

Kahin, George McTurnan. *The Asian-African Conference, Bandung, Indonesia, April 1955*. Ithaca, NY: Cornell University Press, 1956.

Kaufman, Burton I. *Trade and Aid: Eisenhower's Foreign Economic Policy, 1953–1961*. Baltimore: Johns Hopkins University Press, 1982.

Kennedy, Paul. *African Capitalism: The Struggle for Ascendancy*. Cambridge: Cambridge University Press, 1988.

Kimball, Warren F. *The Juggler: Franklin Roosevelt as Wartime Statesman*. Princeton, NJ: Princeton University Press, 1991.

Klonsky, Joanna, and Stephanie Hanson. "Mercosur: South America's Fractious Trade Bloc." Council on Foreign Relations. http://www.cfr.org/publication/12762/.

Knight, Nick. *Imagining Globalisation in China: Debates on Ideology, Politics, and Culture.* Cheltenham, UK: Elgar, 2008.

Kolko, Gabriel. *Confronting the Third World: United States Foreign Policy, 1945–1980.* New York: Pantheon, 1988.

Krasner, Stephen D. "Multinational Corporations." In *International Political Economy: Perspectives on Global Power and Wealth,* ed. Jeffry A. Frieden and David A. Lake. 4th ed. New York: Routledge, 1999.

Kunz, Diane B. *Butter and Guns: America's Cold War Economic Diplomacy.* New York: Free Press, 1997.

———. *The Economic Diplomacy of the Suez Crisis.* Chapel Hill: University of North Carolina Press, 1991.

LaFeber, Walter. *The Clash: U.S.-Japanese Relations throughout History.* New York: Norton, 1997.

———. *Michael Jordan and the New Global Capitalism.* New York: Norton, 1999.

Landes, David S. *The Wealth and Poverty of Nations: Why Some Are So Rich and Some So Poor.* New York: Norton, 1998.

Latham, Michael E. "Introduction: Modernization, International History, and the Cold War World." In *Staging Growth: Modernization, Development, and the Global Cold War,* ed. David C. Engerman, Nils Gilman, Mark H. Haefele, and Michael E. Latham. Amherst: University of Massachusetts Press, 2003.

Lawrence, Mark Atwood. "History from Below: The United States and Latin America in the Nixon Years." In *Nixon in the World: American Foreign Relations, 1969–1977,* ed. Fredrik Logevall and Andrew Preston. New York: Oxford University Press, 2008.

Leffler, Melvyn P. *A Preponderance of Power: National Security, the Truman Administration, and the Cold War.* Stanford, CA: Stanford University Press, 1992.

Levinson, Marc. *The Box: How the Shipping Container Made the World Smaller and the World Economy Bigger.* Princeton, NJ: Princeton University Press, 2006.

Lipschutz, Ronnie D. "Reconstructing World Politics: The Emergence of Global Civil Society." In *Civil Societies and Social Movements: Domestic, Transnational, Global,* ed. Ronnie D. Lipschutz. Aldershot, UK: Ashgate, 2006.

Little, Douglas. *American Orientalism: The United States and the Middle East since 1945.* Chapel Hill: University of North Carolina Press, 2002.

Longley, Kyle. *In the Eagle's Shadow: The United States and Latin America.* Wheeling, IL: Harlan Davidson, 2002.

Maier, Charles. "'Malaise': The Crisis of Capitalism in the 1970s." In *The Shock of the Global: The 1970s in Perspective,* ed. Niall Ferguson, Charles S. Maier, Erez Manela, and Daniel J. Sargent. Cambridge, MA: Belknap Press of Harvard University Press, 2010.

Marcano Guevara, Arturo J., and David P. Fidler. *Stealing Lives: The Globalization of Baseball and the Tragic Story of Alexis Quiroz.* Bloomington: Indiana University Press, 2002.

Marsh, David. *The Euro: The Politics of the New Global Currency.* New Haven, CT: Yale University Press, 2009.

McCormick, John. *Understanding the European Union: A Concise Introduction.* 3rd ed. Basingstoke, UK: Palgrave Macmillan, 2005.

McKenzie, Francine. "GATT and the Cold War: Accession Debates, Institutional Development, and the Western Alliance, 1947–1959." *Journal of Cold War History* 10 (Summer 2008): 84–98.

Merrill, Dennis. *Bread and the Ballot: The United States and India's Economic Development, 1947–1963.* Chapel Hill: University of North Carolina Press, 1990.

Milward, Alan S. *The Reconstruction of Western Europe, 1945–1951.* Berkeley: University of California Press, 1984.

Mittelman, James H. *The Globalization Syndrome: Transformation and Resistance.* Princeton, NJ: Princeton University Press, 2000.

Mshomba, Richard E. *Africa in the Global Economy.* Boulder, CO: Lynne Rienner, 2000.

Murphy, Craig. *The Emergence of the NIEO Ideology.* Boulder, CO: Westview, 1984.

Nayak, Satyendra S. *Globalization and the Indian Economy: Roadmap to Convertible Rupee.* London: Routledge, 2008.

Organisation for Economic Co-operation and Development (OECD). "Russian Federation." http://www.oecd.org/dataoecd/7/50/2452793.pdf.

Parker, Jason C. "Small Victory, Missed Chance: The Eisenhower Administration, the Bandung Conference, and the Turning of the Cold War." In *The Eisenhower Administration, the Third World, and the Globalization of the Cold War,* ed. Kathryn C. Statler and Andrew L. Johns. Lanham, MD: Rowman and Littlefield, 2006.

Pastor, Robert A., ed. *Latin America's Debt Crisis: Adjusting to the Past or Planning for the Future?* Boulder, CO: Lynne Rienner, 1987.

Picard, Louis A., and Terry F. Buss. *A Fragile Balance: Re-examining the History of Foreign Aid, Security, and Diplomacy.* Sterling, VA: Kumarian, 2009.

Pineo, Ronn. *Ecuador and the United States: Useful Strangers.* Athens: University of Georgia Press, 2007.

Pollard, Robert A. *Economic Security and the Origins of the Cold War, 1945–1950.* New York: Columbia University Press, 1985.

Pollard, Robert A., and Samuel F. Wells Jr. "1945–1960: The Era of American Economic Hegemony." In *Economics and World Power: An Assessment of American Diplomacy since 1789,* ed. William H. Becker and Samuel F. Wells Jr. New York: Columbia University Press, 1984.

Posner, Richard A. *A Failure of Capitalism: The Crisis of '08 and the Descent into Depression.* Cambridge, MA: Harvard University Press, 2009.

Rabe, Stephen G. *Eisenhower and Latin America: The Foreign Policy of Anticommunism*. Chapel Hill: University of North Carolina Press, 1988.

———. *The Most Dangerous Area in the World: John F. Kennedy Confronts Communist Revolution in Latin America*. Chapel Hill: University of North Carolina Press, 1999.

Rai, Vinay, and William L. Simon, *Think India: The Rise of the World's Next Superpower and What It Means for Every American*. New York: Dutton, 2007.

Rivoli, Petra. *The Travels of a T-Shirt in the Global Economy: An Economist Examines the Markets, Power and Politics of World Trade*. Hoboken, NJ: John Wiley, 2005.

Rostow, W. W. *The Stages of Economic Growth: A Non-Communist Manifesto*. Cambridge: Cambridge University Press, 1960.

Rotter, Andrew J. *Comrades at Odds: The United States and India, 1947–1964*. Ithaca, NY: Cornell University Press, 2000.

Sampson, Gary P. "Developing Countries and the Liberalization of Trade Services." In *Developing Countries and the Global Trading System*, vol. 1, *Thematic Studies*, ed. John Whalley. London: Macmillan, 1989.

———. "Non-Tariff Barriers Facing Developing Country Exports." In *Developing Countries and the Global Trading System*, vol. 1, *Thematic Studies*, ed. John Whalley. London: Macmillan, 1989.

Schaller, Michael. *The American Occupation of Japan: The Origins of the Cold War in Asia*. New York: Oxford University Press, 1985.

Schmitz, David F. *Thank God They're on Our Side: The United States and Right-Wing Dictatorships, 1921–1965*. Chapel Hill: University of North Carolina Press, 1999.

Schulzinger, Robert D. *A Time for War: The United States and Vietnam, 1941–1975*. New York: Oxford University Press, 1997.

Sewell, Bevan. "A Perfect (Free-Market) World? Economics, the Eisenhower Administration, and the Soviet Economic Offensive in Latin America." *Diplomatic History* 32 (November 2008): 841–868.

Sharma, Shalendra D. "India's Economic Liberalization: The Elephant Comes of Age." In *South Asia*, ed. Sumit Ganguly. New York: New York University Press, 2006.

Speich, Daniel. "The Kenyan Style of 'African Socialism': Developmental Knowledge Claims and the Explanatory Limits of the Cold War." *Diplomatic History* 33 (June 2009): 449–466.

Spero, Joan E., and Jeffrey A. Hart. *The Politics of International Economic Relations*. 6th ed. Belmont, CA: Thomson/Wadsworth, 2003.

Staples, Amy L. S. *The Birth of Development: How the World Bank, Food and Agriculture Organization, and World Health Organization Changed the World, 1945–1965*. Kent, OH: Kent State University Press, 2006.

Steege, Paul. *Black Market, Cold War: Everyday Life in Berlin, 1946–1949*. Cambridge: Cambridge University Press, 2007.

Stiglitz, Joseph E. *Globalization and Its Discontents*. New York: Norton, 2002.

Taffet, Jeffrey F. *Foreign Aid as Foreign Policy: The Alliance for Progress in Latin America*. London: Routledge, 2007.

Taibbi, Matt. "How I Stopped Worrying and Learned to Love the Protests." *Rolling Stone*. November 24, 2011.

Tan, Gerald. *ASEAN: Economic Development and Cooperation*. Singapore: Times Academic, 2003.

Thomson, Alex. *An Introduction to African Politics*. London: Routledge, 2000.

United Nations (UN). "Declaration on the Establishment of a New International Economic Order." http://www.un-documents.net/s6r3201.htm.

———. *The Millennium Development Goals Report*. New York: United Nations, 2009. http://www.un.org/millenniumgoals/pdf/MDG_Report_2009_ENG.pdf.

United Nations Conference on Trade and Development (UNCTAD). http://www.unctad.org.

United States. Department of Commerce. International Trade Administration. Office of Industry Trade Policy. "NAFTA 10 Years Later: An Overview." http://www.trade.gov/mas/ian/build/groups/public/@tg_ian/documents/webcontent/tg_ian_001987.pdf.

United States. Office of the Trade Representative. "Generalized System of Preferences." http://www.ustr.gov/Trade_Development/Preference_Programs/GSP/Section_Index.html.

Van der Pijl, Kees. *Global Rivalries from the Cold War to Iraq*. London: Pluto, 2006.

Verducci, Tom. "Global Warming." *Sports Illustrated*. March 6, 2006, 56–58.

Wagnleitner, Reinhold. "The Empire of the Fun, or Talkin' Soviet Union Blues: The Sound of Freedom and U.S. Cultural Hegemony in Europe." *Diplomatic History* 23 (Summer 1999): 499–524.

Watson, James L., ed. *Golden Arches East: McDonald's in East Asia*. Stanford, CA: Stanford University Press, 1997.

Weintraub, Sidney, ed. *NAFTA's Impact on North America: The First Decade*. Washington, DC: CSIS, 2004.

Westad, Odd Arne. *The Global Cold War: Third World Interventions and the Making of Our Times*. Cambridge: Cambridge University Press, 2007.

Whiting, Robert. *The Meaning of Ichiro: The New Wave from Japan and the Transformation of Our National Pastime*. New York: Warner, 2004.

Wilkins, Mira. *The Maturing of Multinational Enterprise: American Business Abroad from 1914 to 1970*. Cambridge, MA: Harvard University Press, 1974.

Winand, Pascaline. *Eisenhower, Kennedy, and the United States of Europe*. New York: St. Martin's Press, 1993.

Woods, Randall Bennett. *A Changing of the Guard: Anglo-American Relations, 1941–1946*. Chapel Hill: University of North Carolina Press, 1990.

World Bank. *Data: Countries and Economies*. http://data.worldbank.org/country.

World Tourism Organization. "International Tourism on Track for a Rebound after an Exceptionally Challenging 2009." http://www.unwto.org/media/news/en/press_det.php?id=5361.

World Trade Organization (WTO). "The Uruguay Round." http://www.wto.org/english /thewto_e/whatis_e/tif_e/fact5_e.htm.

———. "What Is the WTO?" http://www.wto.org/english/thewto_e/whatis_e/whatis_e.htm.

Wu, Jinglian. *Understanding and Interpreting Chinese Economic Reform*. Mason, OH: Thomson /South-Western, 2005.

Yergin, Daniel. *The Prize: The Epic Quest for Oil, Money, and Power*. New York: Simon and Schuster, 1991.

Zeiler, Thomas W. *American Trade and Power in the 1960s*. New York: Columbia University Press, 1992.

———. "Business Is War in U.S.-Japanese Economic Relations, 1977–2001." In *Partnership: The United States and Japan, 1951–2001*, ed. Akira Iriye and Robert A. Wampler. Tokyo: Kodansha International, 2001.

———. *Free Trade, Free World: The Advent of GATT*. Chapel Hill: University of North Carolina Press, 1999.

Into the Anthropocene: People and Their Planet

Broadbent, Jeffrey. *Environmental Politics in Japan: Networks of Power and Protest*. Cambridge: Cambridge University Press, 1998.

Brown, Kate. *Plutopia: Nuclear Families, Atomic Cities, and the Great Soviet and American Plutonium Disasters*. New York: Oxford University Press, 2013.

Bullard, Robert D. *Dumping in Dixie: Race, Class and Environmental Quality*. Boulder, CO: Westview, 1990.

Burger, Joanna. *Oil Spills*. New Brunswick, NJ: Rutgers University Press, 1997.

Canadell, Josep G., et al. "Contributions to Accelerating Atmospheric CO_2 Growth from Economic Activity, Carbon Intensity, and Efficiency of Natural Sinks." *Proceedings of the National Academy of Sciences of the United States of America* 104, no. 47 (November 20, 2007): 18866–18870.

Chan, Chak K., and Xiaohong Yao. "Air Pollution in Mega Cities in China." *Atmospheric Environment* 42 (2008): 1–42.

Chase, Michael J., and Curtice R. Griffin. "Elephants Caught in the Middle: Impacts of War, Fences and People on Elephant Distribution and Abundance in the Caprivi Strip, Namibia." *African Journal of Ecology* 47 (2009): 223–233.

Clark, William C., et al. "Acid Rain, Ozone Depletion, and Climate Change: An Historical Overview." In *Learning to Manage Global Environmental Risks*, vol. 1: *A Comparative History of Social Responses to Climate Change, Ozone Depletion, and Acid Rain*, ed. Social Learning Group. Cambridge, MA: MIT Press, 2007.

Cohen, Aaron J., et al. "The Global Burden of Disease Due to Outdoor Air Pollution." *Journal of Toxicology and Environmental Health* 68 (2005): 1301–1307.

Cohen, Joel E. *How Many People Can the Earth Support?* New York: Norton, 1995.

Collins, James P., and Martha L. Crump. *Extinction in Our Times: Global Amphibian Decline.* New York: Oxford University Press, 2009.

Conzen, Michael P., ed. *The Making of the American Landscape.* Boston: Unwin Hyman, 1990.

Costanza, Robert, et al. "The Value of the World's Ecosystem Services and Natural Capital." *Nature* 387 (May 15, 1997): 253–260.

Costanza, Robert, Lisa J. Graumlich, and Will Steffen, eds. *Sustainability or Collapse? An Integrated History and Future of People on Earth.* Cambridge, MA: MIT Press, 2007.

Cowie, Jonathan. *Climate Change: Biological and Human Aspects.* Cambridge: Cambridge University Press, 2007.

Cramer, Wolfgang, et al. "Tropical Forests and the Global Carbon Cycle: Impacts of Atmospheric Carbon Dioxide, Climate Change and Rate of Deforestation." *Philosophical Transactions of the Royal Society: Biological Sciences* 359, no. 1443 (March 29, 2004): 331–343.

Cribb, Robert. "The Politics of Pollution Control in Indonesia." *Asian Survey* 30, no. 12 (December 1990): 1123–1135.

Crosby, Alfred W. *Children of the Sun: A History of Humanity's Unappeasable Appetite for Energy.* New York: Norton, 2006.

Crutzen, Paul, and Eugene Stoermer. "The Anthropocene." *IGBP Global Change Newsletter* 41 (2000): 17–18.

Cryer, Martin, Bruce Hartill, and Steve O'Shea. "Modification of Marine Benthos by Trawling: Toward a Generalization for the Deep Ocean?" *Ecological Applications* 12 (2002): 1824–1839.

Dalton, Russell J. *The Green Rainbow: Environmental Groups in Western Europe.* New Haven, CT: Yale University Press, 1994.

Dalton, Russell J., et al. *Critical Masses: Citizens, Nuclear Weapons Production, and Environmental Destruction in the United States and Russia.* Cambridge MA: MIT Press, 1999.

Daly, Herman E. "Steady-State Economics versus Growthmania: A Critique of the Orthodox Conceptions of Growth, Wants, Scarcity, and Efficiency." *Policy Sciences* 5, no. 2 (1974): 149–167.

Danielsson, Bengt, and Marie-Thérèse Danielsson. *Poisoned Reign: French Nuclear Colonialism in the Pacific.* Rev. ed. New York: Penguin, 1986.

Dauvergne, Peter. "The Politics of Deforestation in Indonesia." *Pacific Affairs* 66, no. 4 (Winter, 1993–1994): 497–518.

Davies, Richard G., et al. "Human Impacts and the Global Distribution of Extinction Risk." *Proceedings of the Royal Society: Biological Sciences* 273, no. 1598 (September 7, 2006): 2127–2133.

Davis, Devra. *When Smoke Ran Like Water: Tales of Environmental Deception and the Battle against Pollution.* New York: Basic Books, 2002.

Dessler, Andrew E., and Edward A. Parson. *The Science and Politics of Global Climate Change: A Guide to the Debate.* Cambridge: Cambridge University Press, 2006.

Díaz-Briquets, Sergio, and Jorge Pérez-López. *Conquering Nature: The Environmental Legacy of Socialism in Cuba.* Pittsburgh: University of Pittsburgh Press, 2000.

Dikötter, Frank. *Mao's Great Famine: The History of China's Most Devastating Catastrophe, 1958–1962.* New York: Walker, 2010.

Doney, Scott C., and David S. Schimel. "Carbon and Climate System Coupling on Timescales from the Precambrian to the Anthropocene." *Annual Review of Environment and Resources* 32 (2007): 31–66.

Dubinsky, Zvy, and Noga Stambler, eds. *Coral Reefs: An Ecosystem in Transition.* New York: Springer, 2011.

Dudley, Joseph P., et al. "Effects of War and Civil Strife on Wildlife and Wildlife Habitats." *Conservation Biology* 16, no. 2 (2002): 319–329.

Dukes, J. S. "Burning Buried Sunshine: Human Consumption of Ancient Solar Energy." *Climatic Change* 61 (2003): 31–44.

Dunlap, Thomas R., ed. *DDT, Silent Spring, and the Rise of Environmentalism: Classic Texts.* Seattle: University of Washington Press, 2008.

Economy, Elizabeth. *The River Runs Black: The Environmental Challenge to China's Future.* Ithaca, NY: Cornell University Press, 2004.

Egorov, Nikolai N., Vladimir M. Novikov, Frank L. Parker, and Victor K. Popov, eds. *The Radiation Legacy of the Soviet Nuclear Complex: An Analytical Overview.* London: Earthscan, 2000.

Elliott, Lorraine. *The Global Politics of the Environment.* New York: New York University Press, 2004.

Elsheshtawy, Yasser, ed. *The Evolving Arab City: Tradition, Modernity and Urban Development.* London: Routledge, 2008.

Ezzati, Majid, et al. "Selected Major Risk Factors and Global and Regional Burden of Disease." *Lancet* 360 (2002): 1347–1360.

Fang, Ming, Chak K. Chan, and Xiaohong Yao. "Managing Air Quality in a Rapidly Developing Nation: China." *Atmospheric Environment* 43, no. 1 (2009): 79–86.

Fearnside, Philip M. "Deforestation in Brazilian Amazonia: History, Rates, and Consequences." *Conservation Biology* 19, no. 3 (2005): 680–688.

Fenger, Jes. "Air Pollution in the Last 50 Years: From Local to Global." *Atmospheric Environment* 43 (2009): 13–22.

Feshbach, Murray. *Ecological Disaster: Cleaning Up the Hidden Legacy of the Soviet Regime.* New York: Twentieth Century Fund, 1995.

Feshbach, Murray, and Alfred Friendly Jr. *Ecocide in the USSR: Health and Nature under Siege.* New York: Basic Books, 1992.

Finley, Carmel. "A Political History of Maximum Sustained Yield, 1945–1955." In *Oceans Past: Management Insights from the History of Marine Animal Populations*, ed. David J. Starkey, Poul Holm, and Michaela Barnard. London: Earthscan, 2008.

Firth, Stewart. *Nuclear Playground*. Honolulu: University of Hawai'i Press, 1986.

Fleming, James Rodger. *Fixing the Sky: The Checkered History of Weather and Climate Control*. New York: Columbia University Press, 2010.

Fogel, Robert William. *The Escape from Hunger and Premature Death, 1700–2100: Europe, America, and the Third World*. Cambridge: Cambridge University Press, 2004.

Forster, Clive. *Australian Cities: Continuity and Change*. Melbourne: Oxford University Press, 1995.

Franklin, H. Bruce. *The Most Important Fish in the Sea: Menhaden and America*. Washington, DC: Island Press, 2007.

Freese, Barbara. *Coal: A Human History*. Cambridge, MA: Perseus, 2003.

Gadgil, Madhav, and Ramachandra Guha. *Ecology and Equity: The Use and Abuse of Nature in Contemporary India*. London: Routledge, 1995.

Gaston, Kevin J., Tim M. Blackburn, and Kees Klein Goldewijk. "Habitat Conversion and Global Avian Biodiversity Loss." *Proceedings of the Royal Society of London: Biological Sciences* 270, no. 1521 (June 22, 2003): 1293–1300.

Gerber, Michele Stenehjem. *On the Home Front: The Cold War Legacy of the Hanford Nuclear Site*. 2nd ed. Lincoln: University of Nebraska Press, 2002.

Gerlach, Allen. *Indians, Oil, and Politics: A Recent History of Ecuador*. Wilmington, DE: Scholarly Resources, 2003.

Gilbert, Alan, ed. *The Mega-city in Latin America*. New York: United Nations University Press, 1996.

Gildeeva, Irina. "Environmental Protection during Exploration and Exploitation of Oil and Gas Fields." *Environmental Geosciences* 6 (1999): 153–154.

Gössling, Stefan, Carina Borgström Hansson, Oliver Hörstmeir, and Stefan Saggel. "Ecological Footprint Analysis as a Tool to Assess Tourism Sustainability." *Ecological Economics* 43 (2002): 199–211.

Greenhalgh, Susan. *Cultivating Global Citizens: Population in the Rise of China*. Cambridge, MA: Harvard University Press, 2010.

———. *Just One Child: Science and Policy in Deng's China*. Berkeley: University of California Press, 2008.

Grimm, Nancy B., et al. "Global Change and the Ecology of Cities." *Science* 319 (February 8, 2008): 756–760.

Grundmann, Reiner. "Ozone and Climate: Scientific Consensus and Leadership." *Science, Technology, & Human Values* 31, no. 1 (January 2006): 73–101.

Guha, Ramachandra. *Environmentalism: A Global History*. New York: Longman, 2000.

———. *India after Gandhi: The History of the World's Largest Democracy*. New York: HarperCollins, 2007.

———. *The Unquiet Woods: Ecological Change and Peasant Resistance in the Himalayas*. Rev. ed. Berkeley: University of California Press, 2000.

Guha, Ramachandra, and Juan Martinez-Alier. *Varieties of Environmentalism: Essays North and South.* Delhi: Oxford University Press, 1998.

Gutfreund, Owen D. *Twentieth-Century Sprawl: Highways and the Reshaping of the American Landscape.* New York: Oxford University Press, 2004.

Hall, Charles, et al. "Hydrocarbons and the Evolution of Human Culture." *Nature* 426 (2003): 318–322.

Hall, Peter. *Cities of Tomorrow: An Intellectual History of Urban Planning and Design in the Twentieth Century.* Rev. ed. Oxford, UK: Blackwell, 1996.

Haller, Tobias, et al., eds. *Fossil Fuels, Oil Companies, and Indigenous Peoples: Strategies of Multinational Oil Companies, States, and Ethnic Minorities; Impact on Environment, Livelihoods, and Cultural Change.* Zurich: Lit, 2007.

Hamblin, Jacob Darwin. *Poison in the Well: Radioactive Waste in the Oceans at the Dawn of the Nuclear Age.* New Brunswick, NJ: Rutgers University Press, 2008.

Hardjono, J. "The Indonesian Transmigration Scheme in Historical Perspective." *International Migration* 26 (1988): 427–438.

Hashimoto, M. "History of Air Pollution Control in Japan." In *How to Conquer Air Pollution: A Japanese Experience*, ed. H. Nishimura. Amsterdam: Elsevier, 1989.

Hays, Samuel P. *Explorations in Environmental History: Essays.* Pittsburgh: University of Pittsburgh Press, 1998.

———. *A History of Environmental Politics since 1945.* Pittsburgh: University of Pittsburgh Press, 2000.

Heitzman, James. *The City in South Asia.* New York: Routledge, 2008.

Hochstetler, Kathryn, and Margaret E. Keck. *Greening Brazil: Environmental Activism in State and Society.* Durham, NC: Duke University Press, 2007.

Hughes, J. Donald, ed. *The Face of the Earth: Environment and World History.* Armonk, NY: M. E. Sharpe, 2000.

International Energy Agency (IEA)/Organisation for Economic Co-operation and Development (OECD). *Cleaner Coal in China.* Paris: OECD/IEA, 2009.

Jenkins, Martin. "Prospects for Biodiversity." *Science* 302, no. 5648 (November 14, 2003): 1175–1177.

Johnston, Barbara Rose, ed. *Half-Lives and Half-Truths: Confronting the Radioactive Legacies of the Cold War.* Santa Fe, NM: School for Advanced Research Press, 2007.

Johnston, Barbara Rose, and Holly M. Barker. *Consequential Damages of Nuclear War: The Rongelap Report.* Walnut Creek, CA: Left Coast, 2008.

Jones, Merrill E. "Origins of the East German Environmental Movement." *German Studies Review* 16, no. 2 (1993): 235–264.

Jones, P. D., D. E. Parker, T. J. Osborn, and K. R. Briffa. "Global and Hemispheric Temperature Anomalies—Land and Marine Instrumental Records." In *Trends: A Compendium of Data on Global Change*, Carbon Dioxide Information Analysis Center, Oak Ridge

National Laboratory, U.S. Department of Energy, Oak Ridge, TN (2011). doi: 10.3334/CDIAC/cli.002.

Kahn, Matthew E. "The Environmental Impact of Suburbanization." *Journal of Policy Analysis and Management* 19, no. 4 (2000): 569–586.

Karan, P. P., and Kristin Stapleton, eds. *The Japanese City.* Lexington: University Press of Kentucky, 1997.

Kashi, Ed. *The Curse of the Black Gold: 50 Years of Oil in the Niger Delta.* Edited by Michael Watts. Brooklyn: PowerHouse, 2009.

Keeling, R. F., S. C. Piper, A. F. Bollenbacher, and J. S. Walker. "Atmospheric CO_2 Records from Sites in the SIO Air Sampling Network." In *Trends: A Compendium of Data on Global Change,* Carbon Dioxide Information Analysis Center, Oak Ridge National Laboratory, U.S. Department of Energy, Oak Ridge, TN (2009). doi: 10.3334/CDIAC/atg.035.

Ken-ichi, Abe, and James E. Nickum, eds. *Good Earths: Regional and Historical Insights into China's Environment.* Kyoto: Kyoto University Press, 2009.

Khuhro, Hamida, and Anwer Mooraj, eds. *Karachi: Megacity of Our Times.* Karachi: Oxford University Press, 1997.

Kimmerling, Judith. "Oil Development in Ecuador and Peru: Law, Politics, and the Environment." In *Amazonia at the Crossroads: The Challenge of Sustainable Development,* ed. Anthony Hall. London: Institute of Latin American Studies, 2000.

Knauss, John A. "The International Whaling Commission: Its Past and Possible Future." *Ocean Development and International Law* 28 (1997): 79–87.

Knight, Catherine. "The Nature Conservation Movement in Post-war Japan." *Environment and History* 16 (2010): 349–370.

Koninck, Rodolphe de. *Deforestation in Viet Nam.* Ottawa: International Development Research Centre, 1999.

Kreike, Emmanuel. "War and Environmental Effects of Displacement in Southern Africa (1970s–1990s)." In *African Environment and Development: Rhetoric, Programs, Realities,* ed. William G. Moseley and B. Ikubolajeh Logan. Burlington, VT: Ashgate, 2003.

Kudrik, Igor, et al. *The Russian Nuclear Industry.* Oslo: Bellona Foundation, 2004.

Lawton, Richard, ed. *The Rise and Fall of Great Cities: Aspects of Urbanization in the Western World.* New York: Belhaven, 1989.

Lewis, Simon L. "Tropical Forests and the Changing Earth System." *Philosophical Transactions: Biological Sciences* 361, no. 1465 (January 29, 2006): 195–196.

Li, Hongmei, et al. "Demand for Rubber Is Causing the Loss of High Diversity Rain Forest in SW China." *Biodiversity and Conservation* 16 (2007): 1731–1745.

Li, Lillian M. *Fighting Famine in North China: State, Market, and Environmental Decline, 1690s–1990s.* Stanford, CA: Stanford University Press, 2007.

Link, Jason S., Bjarte Bogstad, Henrik Sparholt, and George R. Lilly. "Trophic Role of Atlantic Cod in the Ecosystem." *Fish and Fisheries* 10 (2009): 58–87.

Liu, Wenjun, Huabin Hu, Youxin Ma, and Hongmei Li. "Environmental and Socioeconomic Impacts of Increasing Rubber Plantations in Menglun Township, Southwest China." *Mountain Research and Development* 26 (2006): 245–253.

Lu, Z., et al. "Sulfur Dioxide Emissions in China and Sulfur Trends in East Asia since 2000." *Atmospheric Chemistry and Physics Discussion* 10 (2010): 8657–8715.

Ma, Yonghuan, and Fan Shengyue. "The Protection Policy of Eco-environment in Desertification Areas of Northern China: Contradiction and Countermeasures." *Ambio* 35 (2006): 133–134.

Maathai, Wangari. *Unbowed: A Memoir.* New York: Knopf, 2006.

Makhijani, Arjun, Howard Hu, and Katherine Yih, eds. *Nuclear Wastelands: A Global Guide to Nuclear Weapons Production and Its Health and Environmental Effects.* Cambridge, MA: MIT Press, 1995.

Markham, William T. *Environmental Organizations in Modern Germany: Hardy Survivors in the Twentieth Century and Beyond.* New York: Berghahn, 2008.

Martinez-Alier, Juan. *The Environmentalism of the Poor: A Study of Ecological Conflicts and Valuation.* New Delhi: Oxford University Press, 2004.

McCormick, John. *Reclaiming Paradise: The Global Environmental Movement.* Bloomington: Indiana University Press, 1989.

McKibben, Bill. *Hope, Human and Wild: True Stories of Living Lightly on the Earth.* Minneapolis: Milkweed, 2007.

McKinney, Michael L. "Is Marine Biodiversity at Less Risk? Evidence and Implications." *Diversity and Distributions* 4, no. 1 (January 1998): 3–8.

McNeill, J. R. "The Cold War and the Biosphere." In *The Cambridge History of the Cold War*, vol. 3: *Endings*, ed. Melvyn P. Leffler and Odd Arne Westad. Cambridge: Cambridge University Press, 2010.

———. *The Mountains of the Mediterranean World: An Environmental History.* Cambridge: Cambridge University Press, 1992.

———. *Something New under the Sun: An Environmental History of the Twentieth-Century World.* New York: Norton, 2000.

McNeill, J. R., and Corinna Unger, eds. *Environmental Histories of the Cold War.* New York: Cambridge University Press, 2010.

McNeill, William H. *Plagues and Peoples.* Garden City, NY: Anchor/Doubleday, 1976.

McShane, Clay. *Down the Asphalt Path: The Automobile and the American City.* New York: Columbia University Press, 1994.

Medvedev, Zhores A. *Nuclear Disaster in the Urals.* New York: Norton, 1979.

Melosi, Martin V. *Effluent America: Cities, Industry, Energy, and the Environment.* Pittsburgh: University of Pittsburgh Press, 2001.

———. "The Place of the City in Environmental History." *Environmental History Review* 17 (1993): 1–23.

———. *The Sanitary City: Urban Infrastructure in America from Colonial Times to the Present.* Baltimore: Johns Hopkins University Press, 2000.

Meybeck, Michael. "Global Analysis of River Systems: From Earth System Controls to Anthropocene Syndromes." *Philosophical Transactions: Biological Sciences* 358, no. 1440 (December 29, 2003): 1935–1955.

Micklin, Philip. "The Aral Sea Disaster." *Annual Review of Earth and Planetary Sciences* 35 (2007): 47–72.

Miles, Edward L. "On the Increasing Vulnerability of the World Ocean to Multiple Stresses." *Annual Review of Environment and Resources* 34 (2009): 18–26.

Miller, Char, ed. *On the Border: An Environmental History of San Antonio.* Pittsburgh: University of Pittsburgh Press, 2001.

Miller, Shawn William. *An Environmental History of Latin America.* New York: Cambridge University Press, 2007.

Mirza, M. Monirul Qader. "Climate Change, Flooding and Implications in South Asia." *Regional Environmental Change* 11, supp. 1 (2011): 95–107.

Molina, Mario J., and Luisa T. Molina. "Megacities and Atmospheric Pollution." *Journal of the Air and Waste Management Association* 54 (2004): 644–680.

Montrie, Chad. *To Save the Land and People: A History of Opposition to Surface Mining in Appalachia.* Chapel Hill: University of North Carolina Press, 2003.

Morell, Virginia. "Can the Wild Tiger Survive?" *Science* 317, no. 5843 (September 7, 2007): 1312–1314.

Mudd, G. M. "Gold Mining in Australia: Linking Historical Trends and Environmental and Resource Sustainability." *Environmental Science and Policy* 10 (2007): 629–644.

Mukherjee, Suroopa. *Surviving Bhopal: Dancing Bodies, Written Texts, and Oral Testimonials of Women in the Wake of an Industrial Disaster.* New York: Palgrave Macmillan, 2010.

Mutke, Jens, Gerold Kier, Gary A. Krupnick, and Wilhelm Barthlott. "Terrestrial Plant Diversity." In *Plant Conservation: A Natural History Approach,* ed. Gary A. Krupnick and W. John Kress. Chicago: University of Chicago Press, 2005.

Nelson, Arvid. *Cold War Ecology: Forests, Farms, and People in the East German Landscape, 1945–1989.* New Haven, CT: Yale University Press, 2005.

Nelson, Lane E., ed. *Purifying the Earthly Body of God: Religion and Ecology in Hindu India.* Albany: State University of New York Press, 1998.

Nesterenko, Alexey B., Vassily B. Nesterenko, and Alexey V. Yablokov. "Consequences of the Chernobyl Catastrophe for Public Health." *Annals of the New York Academy of Sciences* 1181 (2009): 31–220.

Newman, Peter, and Jeffrey Kenworthy. *Sustainability and Cities: Overcoming Automobile Dependence.* Washington, DC: Island Press, 1999.

Niele, Frank. *Energy: Engine of Evolution.* Amsterdam: Elsevier, 2005.

Nilsen, Alf Gunvald. *Dispossession and Resistance in India: The River and the Rage.* London: Routledge, 2010.

Olajide, P. A., et al. "Fish Kills and Physiochemical Qualities of a Crude Oil Polluted River in Nigeria." *Research Journal of Fisheries and Hydrobiology* 4 (2009): 55–64.

Omotola, J. Shola " 'Liberation Movements' and Rising Violence in the Niger Delta: The New Contentious Site of Oil and Environmental Politics." *Studies in Conflict and Terrorism* 33 (2010): 36–54.

O'Rourke, Dara, and Sarah Connolly. "Just Oil? The Distribution of Environmental and Social Impacts of Oil Production and Consumption." *Annual Review of Environment and Resources* 28 (2003): 587–617.

Orum, Anthony M., and Xiangming Chen, *The World of Cities: Places in Comparative and Historical Perspective.* Malden, MA: Blackwell, 2003.

Pfister, Christian. "The 'Syndrome of the 1950s' in Switzerland: Cheap Energy, Mass Consumption, and the Environment." In *Getting and Spending: European and American Consumer Societies in the Twentieth Century,* ed. Susan Strasser, Charles McGovern, and Matthias Judt. Cambridge: Cambridge University Press, 1998.

Pick, James B., and Edgar W. Butler. *Mexico Megacity.* Boulder, CO: Westview, 2000.

Premat, Adriana. "Moving between the Plan and the Ground: Shifting Perspectives on Urban Agriculture in Havana, Cuba." In *Agropolis: The Social, Political, and Environmental Dimensions of Urban Agriculture,* ed. Luc J. A. Mougeot. London: Earthscan, 2005.

Purvis, Nigel, and Andrew Stevenson. *Rethinking Climate Diplomacy: New Ideas for Transatlantic Cooperation Post-Copenhagen.* Washington, DC: German Marshall Fund of the United States, 2010. http://www.gmfus.org/archives/rethinking-climate-diplomacy-new-ideas-for-transatlantic-cooperation-post-copenhagen.

Qu, Geping, and Li Jinchang. *Population and the Environment in China.* Edited by Robert B. Boardman. Translated by Jiang Baozhong and Gu Ran. Boulder, CO: Lynne Rienner, 1994.

Radkau, Joachim. *Nature and Power: A Global History of the Environment.* Translated by Thomas Dunlap. Cambridge: Cambridge University Press, 2008.

Rangarajan, Mahesh. "The Politics of Ecology: The Debate on Wildlife and People in India, 1970–95." In *Battles over Nature: Science and the Politics of Conservation,* ed. Vasant K. Saberwal and Mahesh Rangarajan. Delhi: Orient Blackswan, 2003.

Raupach, Michael R., et al. "Global and Regional Drivers of Accelerating CO_2 Emissions." *Proceedings of the National Academy of Sciences of the United States of America* 104, no. 24 (June 12, 2007): 10288–10293.

Reader, John. *Cities.* New York: Atlantic Monthly, 2004.

Rees, William E. "Ecological Footprints and Appropriated Carrying Capacity: What Urban Economics Leaves Out." *Environment and Urbanization* 4, no. 2 (1992): 121–130.

Reeves, Randall, and Tim Smith. "A Taxonomy of World Whaling Operations and Eras." In *Whales, Whaling, and Ocean Ecosystems,* ed. James A. Estes, Douglas P. DeMaster, Daniel

F. Doak, Terrie M. Williams, and Robert L. Brownell Jr. Berkeley: University of California Press, 2006.

Roberts, Callum. *The Unnatural History of the Sea*. Washington, DC: Island Press, 2007.

Rome, Adam. "'Give Earth a Chance': The Environmental Movement and the Sixties." *Journal of American History* 90, no. 2 (September 2003): 525–554.

Ruddiman, William H. *Plows, Plagues and Petroleum: How Humans Took Control of Climate*. Princeton, NJ: Princeton University Press, 2005.

Sagane, Rajendra. "Water Management in Mega-cities in India: Mumbai, Delhi, Calcutta, and Chennai." In *Water for Urban Areas: Challenges and Perspectives*, ed. Juha I. Uitto and Asit K. Biswas. New York: United Nations University Press, 2000.

Saikawa, Eri, Vaishali Naik, Larry W. Horowitz, Junfeng Liu, and Denise L. Mauzerall. "Present and Potential Future Contributions of Sulfate, Black and Organic Aerosols from China to Global Air Quality, Premature Mortality and Radiative Forcing." *Atmospheric Environment* 43 (2009): 2814–2822.

San Sebastián, Miguel, and Anna-Karin Hurtig. "Oil Exploitation in the Amazon Basin of Ecuador: A Public Health Emergency." *Revista panamericana de salud pública* 15 (2004): 205–211.

Satterthwaite, David. *Barbara Ward and the Origins of Sustainable Development*. London: International Institute for Environment and Development, 2006.

Scharping, Thomas. *Birth Control in China, 1949–2000: Population Policy and Demographic Development*. London: RoutledgeCurzon, 2003.

Schmucki, Barbara. *Der Traum vom Verkehrsfluss: Städtische Verkehrsplanung seit 1945 im deutsch-deutschen Vergleich*. Frankfurt: Campus, 2001.

Schreurs, Miranda A. *Environmental Politics in Japan, Germany, and the United States*. Cambridge: Cambridge University Press, 2002.

Schwartz, Stephen I., ed., *Atomic Audit: The Costs and Consequences of U.S. Nuclear Weapons since 1940*. Washington, DC: Brookings Institution, 1998.

Sewell, John. *The Shape of the Suburbs: Understanding Toronto's Sprawl*. Toronto: University of Toronto Press, 2009.

Shapiro, Judith. *Mao's War against Nature: Politics and the Environment in Revolutionary China*. Cambridge: Cambridge University Press, 2001.

Shi, Anqing. "The Impact of Population Pressure on Global Carbon Emissions, 1975–1996: Evidence from Pooled Cross-Country Data." *Ecological Economics* 44 (2003): 29–42.

Singh, Satyajit. *Taming the Waters: The Political Economy of Large Dams in India*. Delhi: Oxford University Press, 1997.

Smil, Vaclav. *Energy at the Crossroads: Global Perspectives and Uncertainties*. Cambridge, MA: MIT Press, 2003.

———. *Energy in Nature and Society: General Energetics of Complex Systems*. Cambridge, MA: MIT Press, 2008.

———. *Energy in World History*. Boulder, CO: Westview, 1994.

———. *Transforming the Twentieth Century: Technical Innovations and Their Consequences*. New York: Oxford University Press, 2006.

Smith, Jim T., and Nicholas A. Beresford. *Chernobyl: Catastrophe and Consequences*. Berlin: Springer, 2005.

Solomon, Lawrence. *Toronto Sprawls: A History*. Toronto: University of Toronto Press, 2007.

Sovacool, Benjamin K. "The Costs of Failure: A Preliminary Assessment of Major Energy Accidents, 1907–2007." *Energy Policy* 36 (2008): 1802–1820.

Stacy, Ian. "Roads to Ruin on the Atomic Frontier: Environmental Decision Making at the Hanford Nuclear Reservation, 1942–1952." *Environmental History* 15 (2010): 415–448.

Standring, William J. F., Mark Dowdall, and Per Strand. "Overview of Dose Assessment Developments and the Health of Riverside Residents Close to the 'Mayak' PA Facilities, Russia." *International Journal of Environmental Research and Public Health* 6 (2009): 174–199.

Steffen, Will, Paul J. Crutzen, and J. R. McNeill. "The Anthropocene: Are Humans Now Overwhelming the Great Forces of Nature?" *Ambio* 36 (2007): 614–621.

Steinberg, Ted. *Down to Earth: Nature's Role in American History*. 2nd ed. New York: Oxford University Press, 2009.

Stern, David I. "Global Sulfur Emissions from 1850 to 2000." *Chemosphere* 58 (2005): 163–175.

Sternberg, R. "Hydropower: Dimensions of Social and Environmental Coexistence." *Renewable and Sustainable Energy Reviews* 12 (2008): 1588–1621.

Sun, Yanfei, and Dingxin Zhao. "State–Society Relations and Environmental Campaigns." In *Popular Protest in China*, ed. Kevin J. O'Brien. Cambridge, MA: Harvard University Press, 2008.

Terry, Andrew, Karin Ullrich, and Uwe Riecken. *The Green Belt of Europe: From Vision to Reality*. Gland, Switzerland: International Union for Conservation of Nature, 2006.

Thukral, Enakshi Ganguly, ed. *Big Dams, Displaced People: Rivers of Sorrow, Rivers of Change*. New Delhi: Sage, 1992.

Tiffen, Mary, Michael Mortimore, and Francis Gichuki. *More People, Less Erosion: Environmental Recovery in Kenya*. Chichester, UK: Wiley, 1994.

Uekoetter, Frank. *The Age of Smoke: Environmental Policy in Germany and the United States, 1880–1970*. Pittsburgh: University of Pittsburgh Press, 2009.

Vermeij, Geerat J., and Lindsey R. Leighton. "Does Global Diversity Mean Anything?" *Paleobiology* 29, no. 1 (2003): 3–7.

Vilchek, G. E., and A. A. Tishkov. "Usinsk Oil Spill." In *Disturbance and Recovery in Arctic Lands: An Ecological Perspective*, ed. R. M. M. Crawford. Dordrecht, Netherlands: Kluwer Academic, 1997.

Volti, Rudi. "A Century of Automobility." *Technology and Culture* 37, no. 4 (1996): 663–685.

Walker, Brett L. *Toxic Archipelago: A History of Industrial Disease in Japan*. Seattle: University of Washington Press, 2010.

Walker, J. Samuel. *Three Mile Island: A Nuclear Crisis in Historical Perspective*. Berkeley: University of California Press, 2004.

Watt, John, Johan Tidblad, Vladimir Kucera, and Ron Hamilton, eds. *The Effects of Air Pollution on Cultural Heritage*. Berlin: Springer, 2009.

Weart, Spencer R. *The Discovery of Global Warming*. Rev. ed. Cambridge, MA: Harvard University Press, 2008.

Webb, James L. A., Jr. *Humanity's Burden: A Global History of Malaria*. Cambridge: Cambridge University Press, 2009.

Weissenbacher, Manfred. *Sources of Power: How Energy Forges Human History*. 2 vols. Santa Barbara, CA: ABC-CLIO, 2009.

Weller, Robert P. *Discovering Nature: Globalization and Environmental Culture in China and Taiwan*. Cambridge: Cambridge University Press, 2006.

Westing, Arthur H., ed. *Herbicides in War: The Long-Term Ecological and Human Consequences*. London: Taylor and Francis, 1984.

White, Tyrene. *China's Longest Campaign: Birth Planning in the People's Republic, 1949–2005*. Ithaca, NY: Cornell University Press, 2006.

Williams, Michael. *Deforesting the Earth: From Prehistory to Global Crisis*. Chicago: University of Chicago Press, 2003.

Wilson, E. O., with Frances M. Peter, eds. *Biodiversity*. Washington, DC: National Academy Press, 1986.

Winiwarter, Verena, and Martin Knoll. *Umweltgeschichte: Eine Einführung*. Cologne: Böhlau, 2007.

Wood, John R. *The Politics of Water Resource Development in India: The Narmada Dams Controversy*. Los Angeles: Sage, 2007.

World Health Organization and United Nations Environment Programme. *Urban Air Pollution in Megacities of the World*. Cambridge, MA: Blackwell Reference, 1992.

Xu, Kehui, and John D. Milliman. "Seasonal Variations of Sediment Discharge from the Yangtze River before and after Impoundment of the Three Gorges Dam." *Geomorphology* 104 (2009): 276–283.

Yablokov, Alexey V., Vassily B. Nesterenko, and Alexey V. Nesterenko. "Consequences of the Chernobyl Catastrophe for the Environment." *Annals of the New York Academy of Sciences* 1181 (2009): 221–286.

Zelko, Frank. *Make It a Green Peace: The Rise of Countercultural Environmentalism*. New York: Oxford University Press, 2013.

Global Cultures

Abdel Kader, Soha. *Egyptian Women in a Changing Society, 1899–1987*. Boulder, CO: Lynne Rienner, 1987.

Achebe, Chinua. *Things Fall Apart*. New York: McDowell, Obolensky, 1959.

Adorno, Theodor W., and Max Horkheimer. *Dialectic of Enlightenment: Philosophical Fragments*. Edited by Gunzelin Schmid Noerr. Translated by Edmund Jephcott. Stanford, CA: Stanford University Press, 2002.

Agarwal, Bina. "From Mexico 1975 to Beijing 1995." *Indian Journal of Gender Studies* 3, no. 1 (March 1996): 87–92.

Anderson, Benedict. *Imagined Communities: Reflections on the Origin and Spread of Nationalism*. Rev. ed. London: Verso, 1991.

Anderson, Carol. *Eyes Off the Prize: The United Nations and the African American Struggle for Human Rights, 1944–1955*. Cambridge: Cambridge University Press, 2003.

Anderson, Jon Lee. *Che Guevara: A Revolutionary Life*. New York: Grove Press, 1997.

Anker, Peter. "The Ecological Colonization of Space." *Environmental History* 10, no. 2 (April 2005): 239–268.

Antoun, Richard T. *Understanding Fundamentalism: Christian, Islamic and Jewish Movements*. London: Rowman and Littlefield, 2001.

Appadurai, Arjun. *Modernity at Large: Cultural Dimensions of Globalization*. Minneapolis: University of Minnesota Press, 1996.

Appiah, Kwame Anthony. *Cosmopolitanism: Ethics in a World of Strangers*. New York: W. W. Norton, 2006.

Armitage, David. "Is There a Pre-history of Globalization?" In *Comparison and History: Europe in Cross-National Perspective*, ed. Deborah Cohen and Maura O'Connor. London: Routledge, 2004.

Augé, Marc. *Non-Places: Introduction to an Anthropology of Supermodernity*. Translated by John Howe. London: Verso, 1995.

Aust, Stefan. *Der Baader Meinhof Komplex: Erweiterte und aktualisierte Ausgabe*. Munich: Goldmann Verlag, 1998.

Bailey, Beth, and David Farber. *The First Strange Place: The Alchemy of Race and Sex in World War II Hawaii*. New York: Free Press, 1992.

Baldwin, Lewis V., and Amiri YaSin Al-Hadid. *Between Cross and Crescent: Christian and Muslim Perspectives on Malcolm and Martin*. Gainesville: University Press of Florida, 2002.

Ballard, R., and C. Ballard. "The Sikh: The Development of Southern Asian Settlement in Britain." In *Between Two Cultures: Migrants and Minorities in Britain*, ed. James L. Watson. Oxford: Blackwell, 1977.

Banchoff, Thomas, ed. *Democracy and the New Religious Pluralism*. New York: Oxford University Press, 2007.

Barber, Benjamin R. *Jihad vs. McWorld: How Globalism and Tribalism Are Reshaping the World*. New York: Ballantine, 1995.

Beauvoir, Simone de. *The Second Sex*. Translated by Constance Borde and Sheila Malovany-Chevalier. Introduction by Judith Thurman. New York: Vintage 2011.

Bell, Terry, with Dumisa Buhle Ntsebeza. *Unfinished Business: South Africa, Apartheid, and Truth*. London: Verso, 2003.

Benedict, Ruth. *Patterns of Culture*. Boston: Houghton Mifflin, 1934.

Benhabib, Seyla. *Another Cosmopolitanism*. With commentary by Jeremy Waldron, Bonnie Honig, and Will Kymlicka. Edited by Robert Post. New York: Oxford Unversity Press, 2006.

Benjamin, Walter. "The Work of Art in the Age of Mechanical Reproduction." In *Illuminations*. Edited with an introduction by Hannah Arendt. Translated by Harry Zohn. New York: Harcourt, Brace and World, 1968.

Berger, Peter L., ed. *The Desecularization of the World: Resurgent Religion and World Politics*. Grand Rapids, MI: Eerdmans, 1999.

Berman, Paul. *A Tale of Two Utopias: The Political Journey of the Generation of 1968*. New York: W. W. Norton, 1996.

Berryman, Phillip. *Liberation Theology: Essential Facts about the Revolutionary Movement in Latin America—and Beyond*. Philadelphia: Temple University Press, 1987.

Bertrand, Michael T. *Race, Rock, and Elvis*. Urbana: University of Illinois Press, 2000.

Besier, Gerhard. *Der SED-Staat und die Kirche 1969–1990: Die Vision vom "Dritten Weg."* Berlin: Propyläen, 1995.

Beyer, Peter, and Lori Beaman, eds. *Religion, Globalization, and Culture*. Leiden: Brill, 2007.

Blackwell, Joyce. *No Peace without Freedom: Race and the Women's International League for Peace and Freedom, 1915–1975*. Carbondale: Southern Illinois University Press, 2004.

Boas, Franz. *The Mind of Primitive Man*. New York: Macmillan, 1911.

Boff, Leonardo, and Clodovis Boff. *Introducing Liberation Theology*. Translated by Paul Burns. Maryknoll, NY: Orbis, 1986.

Borgwardt, Elizabeth. *A New Deal for the World: America's Vision for Human Rights*. Cambridge, MA: Belknap Press of Harvard University Press, 2005.

Boyer, Paul. *By the Bomb's Early Light: American Thought and Culture at the Dawn of the Atomic Age*. New York: Pantheon, 1985.

Boyle, Elizabeth Heger. *Female Genital Cutting: Cultural Conflict in the Global Community*. Baltimore: Johns Hopkins University Press, 2002.

Brenner, Christiane, and Peter Heumos. *Sozialgeschichtliche Kommunismusforschung: Tschechoslowakei, Polen, Ungarn und DDR, 1945–1968*. Munich: Oldenbourg, 2005.

Bright, Charles, and Michael Geyer. "Where in the World Is America? The History of the United States in the Global Age." In *Rethinking American History in a Global Age*, ed. Thomas Bender. Berkeley: University of California Press, 2002.

Brocheux, Pierre. *Ho Chi Minh: A Biography*. Translated by Claire Duiker. New York: Cambridge University Press, 2007.

Brown, Judith M. *Nehru: A Political Life*. New Haven, CT: Yale University Press, 2003.

Bruce, Steve. *Religion in the Modern World: From Cathedrals to Cults*. New York: Oxford University Press, 1996.

Buchanan, Tom. "'The Truth Will Set You Free': The Making of Amnesty International." *Journal of Contemporary History* 37, no. 4 (2002): 575–597.

Burgers, Jan Herman. "The Road to San Francisco: The Revival of the Human Rights Idea in the Twentieth Century." *Human Rights Quarterly* 14, no. 4 (November 1992): 447–477.

Burke, Roland. "'The Compelling Dialogue of Freedom': Human Rights at the Bandung Conference." *Human Rights Quarterly* 28, no. 4 (November 2006): 947–965.

———. *Decolonization and the Evolution of International Human Rights*. Philadelphia: University of Pennsylvania Press, 2010.

Butler, Judith. "Sex and Gender in Simone de Beauvoir's Second Sex." *Yale French Studies*, no. 72 (1986): 35–49.

Carter, Erica. *How German Is She? Postwar West German Reconstruction and the Consuming Woman*. Ann Arbor: University of Michigan Press, 1997.

Carter, Lewis. F. *Charisma and Control in Rajneeshpuram: The Role of Shared Values in the Creation of a Community*. Cambridge: Cambridge University Press, 1990.

———. "The 'New Renunciates' of the Bhagwan Shree Rajneesh: Observation and Identification Problems of Interpreting New Religious Movements." *Journal for the Scientific Study of Religion* 26, no. 2 (June 1987): 1948–1972.

Casanova, José. *Public Religions in the Modern World*. Chicago: University of Chicago Press, 1994.

Caute, David. *The Dancer Defects: The Struggle for Cultural Supremacy during the Cold War*. Oxford: Oxford University Press, 2003.

Césaire, Aimé. *Une tempête: D'Après "La Tempête" de Shakespeare: Adaptation pour un théâtre nègre*. Paris: Seuil, 1969.

Chakrabarty, Dipesh. *Provincializing Europe: Postcolonial Thought and Historical Difference*. Princeton, NJ: Princeton University Press, 2000.

Chatterjee, Partha. *The Nation and Its Fragments: Colonial and Postcolonial Histories*. Princeton, NJ: Princeton University Press, 1993.

Chaussy, Ulrich. *Die drei Leben des Rudi Dutschke: Eine Biographie*. Rev. ed. Zurich: Pendo, 1999.

Chen Jian. *Mao's China and the Cold War*. Chapel Hill: University of North Carolina Press, 2001.

Chen, Martha Alter. "Engendering World Conferences: The International Women's Movement and the United Nations." *Third World Quarterly* 16, no. 3, *Nongovernmental Organisations, the United Nations and Global Governance* (September 1995): 477–493.

Clarence-Smith, William G. "The Global Consumption of Hot Beverages, c. 1500 to c. 1900." In *Food and Globalization: Consumption, Markets and Politics in the Modern World*, ed. Alexander Nützenadel and Frank Trentmann. Oxford: Berg, 2008.

Clifford, James. *The Predicament of Culture: Twentieth-Century Ethnography, Literature, and Art.* Cambridge, MA: Harvard University Press, 1988.

Cmiel, Kenneth. "The Emergence of Human Rights Politics in the United States." *Journal of American History* 86, no. 3 (December 1999): 1231–1250.

Cobbs Hoffman, Elizabeth. *All You Need Is Love: The Peace Corps and the Spirit of the 1960s.* Cambridge, MA: Harvard University Press, 1998.

Cohen, Lizabeth. *A Consumer's Republic: The Politics of Mass Consumption in Postwar America.* New York: Knopf, 2003.

Coleman, Peter. *The Liberal Conspiracy: The Congress for Cultural Freedom and the Struggle for the Mind of Postwar Europe.* New York: Free Press, 1989.

Connelly, Matthew. *A Diplomatic Revolution: Algeria's Fight for Independence and the Origins of the Post–Cold War Era.* New York: Oxford University Press, 2002.

Cook, Guillermo, ed. *New Face of the Church in Latin America: Between Tradition and Change.* Maryknoll, NY: Orbis, 1994.

Crockatt, Richard. *America Embattled: September 11, Anti-Americanism, and the Global Order.* London: Routledge, 2003.

Crowley, David, and Jane Pavitt, eds. *Cold War Modern: Design, 1945–1970.* London: V&A Publishing, 2008.

Davie, Grace. "Europe: The Exception That Proves the Rule?" in *The Desecularization of the World: Resurgent Religion and World Politics*, ed. Peter L. Berger. Grand Rapids, MI: Eerdmans, 1999.

———. *Europe, the Exceptional Case: Parameters of Faith in the Modern World.* London: Darton, Longman and Todd, 2002.

DeCaro, Louis A., Jr. *Malcolm and the Cross: The Nation of Islam, Malcolm X, and Christianity.* New York: New York University Press, 1998.

Deegan, Heather. *The Politics of the New South Africa: Apartheid and After.* Harlow, UK: Longman, 2001.

De Grazia, Victoria. *Irresistible Empire: America's Advance through 20th Century Europe.* Cambridge, MA: Belknap Press of Harvard University Press, 2005.

Diamond, Jared. *Collapse: How Societies Choose to Fail or Succeed.* New York: Viking, 2005.

Dickinson, Anna. "Domestic Foreign Policy Considerations and the Origins of Postwar Soviet Church–State Relations, 1941–6." In *Religion and the Cold War*, ed. Diane Kirby. Basingstoke, UK: Palgrave Macmillan, 2003.

Dorfman, Ariel, and Armand Mattelart. *How to Read Donald Duck: Imperialist Ideology in the Disney Comic.* Translated by David Kunzle. New York: International General, 1975.

Dower, John W. *Embracing Defeat: Japan in the Wake of World War II.* New York: W. W. Norton, 1999.

———. *War without Mercy: Race and Power in the Pacific War.* New York: Pantheon, 1986.

Duberman, Martin B. *Paul Robeson.* New York: Knopf, 1988.

Dudziak, Mary L. *Cold War Civil Rights: Race and the Image of American Democracy.* Princeton, NJ: Princeton University Press, 2000.

Dutschke-Klotz, Gretchen. *Rudi Dutschke: Wir hatten ein barbarisches, schönes Leben—Eine Biographie.* Cologne: Kiepenheuer & Witsch, 1996.

Dutt, Malika. "Some Reflections on US Women of Colour and the United Nations Fourth World Conference on Women and NGO Forum in Beijing, China." In *Global Feminisms since 1945*, ed. Bonnie G. Smith. London: Routledge, 2000.

Eckel, Jan. "'Under a Magnifying Glass': The International Human Rights Campaign against Chile in the Seventies." In *Human Rights in the Twentieth Century*, ed. Stefan-Ludwig Hoffmann. Cambridge: Cambridge University Press, 2011.

———. "Utopie der Moral, Kalkül der Macht: Menschenrechte in der globalen Politik seit 1945." *Archiv für Sozialgeschichte* 49 (2009): 437–484.

Endy, Christopher. *Cold War Holidays: American Tourism in France.* Chapel Hill: University of North Carolina Press, 2004.

Enzensberger, Ulrich. *Die Jahre der Kommune I: Berlin, 1967–1969.* Cologne: Kiepenheuer & Witsch, 2004.

Erel, Shlomo. *Neue Wurzeln: 50 Jahre Immigration deutschsprachiger Juden in Israel.* Gerlingen, Germany: Bleicher, 1983.

Evans, Sara. *Personal Politics: The Roots of Women's Liberation in the Civil Rights Movement and the New Left.* New York: Knopf, 1979.

Ezenwa-Ohaeto. *Chinua Achebe: A Biography.* Bloomington: Indiana University Press, 1997.

Fanon, Frantz. *The Wretched of the Earth: A Negro Psychoanalyst's Study of the Problems of Racism and Colonialism in the World Today.* Translated by Constance Farrington. New York: Grove, 1963.

Farber, David. *Chicago '68.* Chicago: University of Chicago Press, 1988.

Farrell, Amy Erdman. *Yours in Sisterhood: Ms. Magazine and the Promise of Popular Feminism.* Chapel Hill: University of North Carolina Press, 1998.

Faulstich, Werner, ed. *Die Kultur der 70er Jahre.* Munich: Fink, 2004.

Faux, Jeff. *The Global Class War: How America's Bipartisan Elite Lost Our Future—and What It Will Take to Win It Back.* Hoboken, NJ: Wiley, 2006.

Firestone, Shulamith. *The Dialectic of Sex: The Case for Feminist Revolution.* New York: Morrow, 1970.

Fischer, Fritz. *Making Them Like Us: Peace Corps Volunteers in the 1960s.* Washington, DC: Smithsonian Institution Press, 1998.

FitzGerald, Frances. *Cities on a Hill: A Journey through Contemporary American Cultures.* New York: Simon and Schuster, 1981.

Foitzik, Jan, ed. *Entstalinisierungskrise in Ostmitteleuropa, 1953–1956: Vom 17. Juni bis zum ungarischen Volksaufstand—Politische, militärische, soziale und nationale Dimensionen.* Paderborn, Germany: Schöningh, 2001.

Francks, Penelope. *The Japanese Consumer: An Alternative Economic History of Modern Japan.* New York: Cambridge University Press, 2009.

Frei, Norbert. *1968: Jugendrevolte und globaler Protest.* Munich: DTV, 2008.

Friedan, Betty. *The Feminine Mystique.* New York: W. W. Norton, 1963.

Fürst, Juliane. *Stalin's Last Generation: Soviet Post-War Youth and the Emergence of Mature Socialism.* New York: Oxford University Press, 2010.

Gaines, Kevin K. *Uplifting the Race: Black Leadership, Politics, and Culture in the Twentieth Century.* Chapel Hill: University of North Carolina Press, 1996.

Gandy, Matthew. "Planning, Anti-Planning and the Infrastructure Crisis Facing Metropolitan Lagos." *Urban Studies* 43, no.2 (February 2006): 371–391.

Gans, Eric L. *The End of Culture: Toward a Generative Anthropology.* Berkeley: University of California Press, 1985.

García Canclini, Néstor. *Consumers and Citizens: Globalization and Multicultural Conflicts.* Translated by George Yúdice. Minneapolis: University of Minnesota Press, 2001.

———. *Hybrid Cultures: Strategies for Entering and Leaving Modernity.* Translated by Christopher L. Chiappari and Silvia L. López. Minneapolis: University of Minnesota Press, 1995.

Garrow, David J. *Liberty and Sexuality: The Right to Privacy and the Making of Roe v. Wade.* New York: Macmillan, 1994.

Gasiorowski, Mark J., and Malcolm Byrne, eds. *Mohammad Mosaddeq and the 1953 Coup in Iran.* Syracuse, NY: Syracuse University Press, 2004.

Gatrell, Peter, and Nick Baron, eds. *Warlands: Population Resettlement and State Reconstruction in the Soviet–East European Borderlands, 1945–1950.* Basingstoke, UK: Palgrave Macmillan, 2009.

Gerges, Fawaz A. *America and Political Islam: Clash of Cultures or Clash of Interests?* New York: Cambridge University Press, 1999.

Gilcher-Holtey, Ingrid, ed. *1968: Vom Ereignis zum Gegenstand der Geschichtswissenschaft.* Göttingen: Vandenhoeck & Ruprecht, 1998.

———. *Die Phantasie an der Macht: Mai 68 in Frankreich.* Frankfurt: Suhrkamp, 1995.

Gilliam, Angela. "Women's Equality and National Liberation." In *Third World Women and the Politics of Feminism,* ed. Chandra Talpade Mohanty, Ann Russo, and Lourdes Torres. Bloomington: Indiana University Press, 1991.

Gitlin, Todd. *The Sixties: Years of Hope, Days of Rage*. Toronto: Bantam Books, 1987.

Glassheim, Eagle. "The Mechanics of Ethnic Cleansing: The Expulsion of Germans from Czechoslovakia, 1945–1947." In *Redrawing Nations: Ethnic Cleansing in East-Central Europe, 1944–1948*, ed. Philipp Ther and Ana Siljak. Lanham, MD: Rowman and Littlefield, 2001.

Glendon, Mary Ann. *A World Made New: Eleanor Roosevelt and the Universal Declaration of Human Rights*. New York: Random House, 2001.

Goedde, Petra. *GIs and Germans: Culture, Gender, and Foreign Relations, 1945–1949*. New Haven, CT: Yale University Press, 2003.

Goodman, Douglas. "Globalization and Consumer Culture." In *The Blackwell Companion to Globalization,* ed. George Ritzer. Malden MA: Blackwell, 2007.

Gordon, Linda. *Woman's Body, Woman's Right: Birth Control in America*. Revised and updated. New York: Penguin, 1990.

Gosse, Van. *Rethinking the New Left: An Interpretative History*. New York: Palgrave Macmillan, 2005.

Grandin, Greg. *Empire's Workshop: Latin America, the United States, and the Rise of the New Imperialism*. New York: Metropolitan, 2006.

Grandin, Greg, and Gilbert M. Joseph, eds. *A Century of Revolution: Insurgent and Counterinsurgent Violence during Latin America's Long Cold War*. Durham, NC: Duke University Press, 2010.

Gutiérrez, Gustavo. *A Theology of Liberation: History, Politics, and Salvation*. Edited and translated by Sister Caridad Inda and John Eagleson. Maryknoll, NY: Orbis, 1973.

Guyatt, Nicholas. *Providence and the Invention of the United States, 1607–1876*. New York: Cambridge University Press, 2007.

Hall, Stuart. "The Local and the Global: Globalization and Ethnicity." In *Dangerous Liaisons: Gender, Nation, and Postcolonial Perspectives*, ed. Anne McClintock, Aamir Mufti, and Ella Shohat. Minneapolis: University of Minnesota Press, 1997.

Hanegraaff, Wouter J. *New Age Religion and Western Culture: Esotericism in the Mirror of Secular Thought*. Leiden: Brill, 1996.

Hannerz, Ulf. *Cultural Complexity: Studies in the Social Organization of Meaning*. New York: Columbia University Press, 1992.

Harsch, Donna. "Society, the State, and Abortion in East Germany." *American Historical Review* 102, no. 1 (February 1997): 53–84.

Hatton, Timothy J., and Jeffrey G. Williamson. *Global Migration and the World Economy: Two Centuries of Policy and Performance*. Cambridge, MA: MIT Press, 2005.

Hays, Samuel P., with Barbara D. Hays. *Beauty, Health, and Permanence: Environmental Politics in the United States, 1955–1985*. New York: Cambridge University Press, 1987.

Hazan, Baruch A. *Soviet Propaganda: A Case Study of the Middle East Conflict*. Jerusalem: Israel University Press, 1976.

Heard-Bey, Frauke. "The United Arab Emirates: Statehood and Nation Building in a Traditional Society." *Middle East Journal* 59, no. 3, *Democratization and Civil Society* (Summer 2005): 357–375.

Hebdige, Dick. "The Meaning of Mod." In *Resistance through Rituals: Youth Subcultures in Post-War Britain,* ed. Stuart Hall and Tony Jefferson. London: Routledge, 1975.

Heelas, Paul. *The New Age Movement: The Celebration of the Self and the Sacralization of Modernity.* Oxford: Blackwell, 1996.

Heydemann, Günther, Gunther Mai, and Werner Müller, eds. *Revolution und Transformation in der DDR 1989/90.* Berlin: Duncker & Humblot, 1999.

Higonnet, Margaret, Jane Jenson, Sonya Michel, and Margaret Collins Weitz, eds. *Behind the Lines: Gender and the Two World Wars.* New Haven, CT: Yale University Press, 1987.

Hixson, Walter L. *Parting the Curtain: Propaganda, Culture, and the Cold War, 1945–1961.* New York: St. Martin's Press, 1997.

Hochgeschwender, Michael. *Freiheit in der Offensive? Der Kongress für Kulturelle Freiheit und die Deutschen.* Munich: Oldenbourg, 1998.

Hoerder, Dirk. *Cultures in Contact: World Migrations in the Second Millennium.* Durham, NC: Duke University Press, 2002.

Hoffmann, Stefan-Ludwig, ed. *Human Rights in the Twentieth Century.* Cambridge: Cambridge University Press, 2011.

Hoganson, Kristin. *Consumer's Imperium: The Global Production of American Domesticity, 1865–1920.* Chapel Hill: University of North Carolina Press, 2007.

Hopgood, Stephen. *Keepers of the Flame: Understanding Amnesty International.* Ithaca, NY: Cornell University Press, 2006.

Hosken, Fran P. *The Hosken Report: Genital and Sexual Mutilation of Females.* Lexington, MA: Women's International Network News, 1979.

Hunt, Lynn, ed. *The French Revolution and Human Rights: A Brief Documentary History.* Boston: Bedford/St. Martin's Press, 1996.

Huntington, Samuel. *The Clash of Civilizations and the Remaking of World Order.* New York: Simon and Schuster, 1996.

Hurd, Elizabeth Shakman. *The Politics of Secularism in International Relations.* Princeton, NJ: Princeton University Press, 2008.

Ilič, Melanie, ed. *Women in the Stalin Era.* Basingstoke, UK: Palgrave, 2001.

———. *Women Workers in the Soviet Interwar Economy: From "Protection" to "Equality."* Basingstroke, UK: Palgrave, 1999.

Ilič, Melanie, Susan E. Reid, and Lynne Atwood, eds. *Women in the Khrushchev Era.* Basingstoke, UK: Palgrave, 2004.

Immerman, Richard H. *The CIA in Guatemala: The Foreign Policy of Intervention.* Austin: University of Texas Press, 1982.

Immerman, Richard, and Petra Goedde, eds. *The Oxford Handbook of the Cold War.* Oxford: Oxford University Press, 2013.

Inglehart, Ronald, and Wayne E. Baker. "Modernization, Cultural Change, and the Persistence of Traditional Values." *American Sociological Review* 65, no. 1 (February 2000): 19–51.

Inglis, David, and Debra Gimlin, eds. *The Globalization of Food.* Oxford: Berg, 2009.

Iriye, Akira. *Global Community: The Role of International Organizations in the Making of the Contemporary World.* Berkeley: University of California Press, 2002.

Iriye, Akira, Petra Goedde, and William I. Hitchcock, eds. *The Human Rights Revolution: An International History.* New York: Oxford University Press, 2012.

James, C. L. R. *The Black Jacobins: Toussaint L'Ouverture and the San Domingo Revolution.* 2nd ed. New York: Vintage, 1989.

Jivani, Alkarim. *It's Not Unusual: A History of Lesbian and Gay Britain in the Twentieth Century.* London: Michael O'Mara Books, 1997.

Kalsi, Sewa Singh. *The Evolution of a Sikh Community in Britain: Religious and Social Change among the Sikhs of Leeds and Bradford.* Leeds: University of Leeds, Department of Theology and Religious Studies, 1992.

Karner, Stefan, et al., eds. *Prager Frühling: Das Internationale Krisenjahr 1968.* Cologne: Böhlau, 2008.

Kaufmann-McCall, Dorothy. "Politics of Difference: The Women's Movement in France from May 1968 to Mitterand." *Signs* 9, no. 2 (Winter 1983): 283–287.

Kearns, Laurel. "Religion and Ecology in the Context of Globalization." In *Religion, Globalization, and Culture*, ed. Peter Beyer and Lori Beaman. Leiden: Brill, 2007.

Keddie, Nikki R. "The New Religious Politics: Where, When, and Why Do 'Fundamentalisms' Appear?" *Comparative Studies in Society and History* 40, no. 4 (October 1998): 696–723.

Keddie, Nikki R., with Yann Richard. *Modern Iran: Roots and Results of Revolution.* New Haven, CT: Yale University Press, 2003.

Kennedy, Paul. *The Parliament of Man: The Past, Present, and Future of the United Nations.* New York: Random House, 2006.

Kerr, Joanna, ed. *Ours by Right: Women's Rights as Human Rights.* London: Zed, 1993.

Keys, Barbara J. *Reclaiming American Virtue: The Human Rights Revolution of the 1970s.* Cambridge, MA: Harvard University Press, 2014.

Kinzer, Stephen. *All the Shah's Men: An American Coup and the Roots of Middle East Terror.* Hoboken, NJ: Wiley and Sons, 2003.

Kirby, Dianne. "Anglican-Orthodox Relations and the Religious Rehabilitation of the Soviet Regime during the Second World War." *Revue d'Histoire Ecclesiastique* 96, nos. 1–2 (2001): 101–123.

———. "Divinely Sanctioned: The Anglo-American Cold War Alliance and the Defence of Western Civilisation and Christianity, 1945–48." *Journal of Contemporary History* 35, no. 3 (July 2000): 385–412.

———, ed. *Religion and the Cold War*. Basingstoke, UK: Palgrave Macmillan, 2003.

Klein, Christina. *Cold War Orientalism: Asia in the Middlebrow Imagination*. Berkeley: University of California Press, 2003.

Klimke, Martin. *The Other Alliance: Student Protest in West Germany and the United States in the Global Sixties*. Princeton, NJ: Princeton University Press, 2010.

Korey, William. *NGOs and the Universal Declaration of Human Rights: "A Curious Grapevine."* New York: St. Martin's Press, 1998.

———. *The Promises We Keep: Human Rights, the Helsinki Process, and American Foreign Policy*. New York: St. Martin's, 1993.

Kossert, Andreas. *Kalte Heimat: Die Geschichte der deutschen Vertriebenen nach 1945*. Munich: Siedler, 2008.

Kutler, Stanley I. *The American Inquisition: Justice and Injustice in the Cold War*. New York: Hill and Wang, 1982.

LaFeber, Walter. *Inevitable Revolutions: The United States in Central America*. New York: W. W. Norton, 1984.

Lauren, Paul Gordon. *The Evolution of International Human Rights: Visions Seen*. 2nd ed. Philadelphia: University of Pennsylvania Press, 2003.

Leite, José Corrêa, with Carolina Gil. *The World Social Forum: Strategies of Resistance*. Translated by Traci Romine. Chicago: Haymarket, 2005.

Lent, Adam. *British Social Movements since 1945: Sex, Colour, Peace, and Power*. Basingstoke, UK: Palgrave, 2001.

Little, Douglas. *American Orientalism: The United States and the Middle East since 1945*. Chapel Hill: University of North Carolina Press, 2002.

Love, John F. *McDonald's: Behind the Arches*. New York: Bantam, 1995.

Luce, Henry. *The American Century*. New York: Farrar Strauss, 1941.

Lull, James. *Media, Communication, Culture: A Global Approach*. Cambridge: Polity Press, 1995.

Lutts, Ralph H. "Chemical Fallout: Rachel Carson's *Silent Spring*, Radioactive Fallout, and the Environmental Movement." *Environmental Review* 9, no. 3 (Fall 1985): 213–214.

Maase, Kaspar. *Bravo Amerika: Erkundungen zur Jugendkultur der Bundesrepublik in den fünfziger Jahren*. Hamburg: Junius, 1992.

Macey, David. *Frantz Fanon: A Biography*. New York: Picador, 2001.

Maier, Charles S. *Dissolution: The Crisis of Communism and the End of East Germany*. Princeton, NJ: Princeton University Press, 1997.

Mamdani, Mahmood. *When Victims Become Killers: Colonialism, Nativism, and the Genocide in Rwanda*. Princeton, NJ: Princeton University Press, 2001.

Manning, Patrick. *Francophone Sub-Saharan Africa, 1880–1995*. 2nd ed. Cambridge: Cambridge University Press, 1998.

Marable, Manning. *Malcolm X: A Life of Reinvention*. New York: Penguin, 2011.

Marcuse, Herbert. *One-Dimensional Man: Studies in the Ideology of Advanced Industrial Society*. Boston: Beacon Press, 1964.

Margolis, Maxine L. *An Invisible Minority: Brazilians in New York City*. Boston: Allyn and Bacon, 1998.

Marty, Martin E. "Fundamentalism as a Social Phenomenon." *Bulletin of the American Academy of Arts and Sciences* 42, no. 2 (November 1988): 15–29.

Marty, Martin E., and R. Scott Appleby, eds. *The Fundamentalism Project*. 5 vols. Chicago: University of Chicago Press, 1991–1995.

May, Elaine Tyler. *Homeward Bound: American Families in the Cold War Era*. New York: Basic Books, 1988.

Mazower, Mark. *No Enchanted Palace: The End of Empire and the Ideological Origins of the United Nations*. Princeton, NJ: Princeton University Press, 2009.

——. "The Strange Triumph of Human Rights, 1933–1950." *Historical Journal* 47, no. 2 (June 2004): 379–398.

McKevitt, Andrew C. "Consuming Japan: Cultural Relations and the Globalizing of America, 1973–1993." PhD diss., Temple University, 2009.

McNeill, J. R., and William H. McNeill. *The Human Web: A Bird's-Eye View of World History*. New York: W. W. Norton, 2003.

McNeill, William H. *The Rise of the West: A History of the Human Community*. Chicago: University of Chicago Press, 1963.

Mead, Margaret. *Continuities in Cultural Evolution*. New Haven, CT: Yale University Press, 1964.

Meyerowitz, Joanne. "Beyond the Feminine Mystique: A Reassessment of Postwar Mass Culture, 1946–1958." *Journal of American History* 79, no. 4 (March 1993): 1458.

——. *Not June Cleaver: Women and Gender in Postwar America, 1945–1960*. Philadelphia: Temple University Press, 1994.

Miller, Neil. *Out of the Past: Gay and Lesbian History from 1869 to the Present*. New York: Vintage, 1995.

Moghadam, Valentine M. *Globalizing Women: Transnational Feminist Networks*. Baltimore: Johns Hopkins University Press, 2005.

Mohanty, Chandra Talpade. "Under Western Eyes: Feminist Scholarship and Colonial Discourses." *Boundary 2* 12/13 (Spring/Fall 1984): 333–358.

Mohanty, Chandra Talpade, Ann Russo, and Lourdes Torres, eds. *Third World Women and the Politics of Feminism*. Bloomington: Indiana University Press, 1991.

Morgan, Robin, ed. *Sisterhood Is Global: The International Women's Movement Anthology*. Garden City, NY: Anchor/Doubleday, 1984.

——. *Sisterhood Is Powerful: An Anthology of Writings from the Women's Liberation Movement*. New York: Random House, 1970.

Morris, Benny. *The Birth of the Palestinian Refugee Problem Revisited.* 2nd ed. Cambridge: Cambridge University Press, 2004.

Moyn, Samuel. *The Last Utopia: Human Rights in History.* Cambridge, MA: Belknap Press of Harvard University Press, 2010.

Na'im, Abdullahi A. "Political Islam in National Politics and International Relations." In *The Desecularization of the World: Resurgent Religion and World Politics*, ed. Peter L. Berger. Grand Rapids, MI: Eerdmans, 1999.

Nehring, Holger. "The Growth of Social Movements." In *A Companion to Contemporary Britain, 1939–2000,* ed. Paul Addison and Harriet Jones. Malden, MA: Blackwell, 2005.

Neptune, Harvey. *Caliban and the Yankees: Trinidad and the United States Occupation.* Chapel Hill: University of North Carolina Press, 2006.

Nielsen, Jørgen S. *Muslims in Western Europe.* Edinburgh: Edinburgh University Press, 1992.

Ninkovich, Frank A. *The Diplomacy of Ideas: U.S. Foreign Policy and Cultural Relations, 1938–1950.* New York: Cambridge University Press, 1981.

Nixon, Rob. "Caribbean and African Appropriations of *The Tempest.*" *Critical Inquiry* 13 (Spring 1987): 557–578

Nussbaum, Martha. "Radical Evil in Liberal Democracies: The Neglect of the Political Emotions." In *Democracy and the New Religious Pluralism*, ed. Thomas Banchoff. New York: Oxford University Press, 2007.

Nützenadel, Alexander, and Frank Trentmann, eds. *Food and Globalization: Consumption, Markets and Politics in the Modern World.* Oxford: Berg, 2008.

Olcott, Jocelyn. "Cold War Conflicts and Cheap Cabaret: Sexual Politics at the 1975 United Nations International Women's Year Conference." *Gender and History* 22, no. 3 (November 2010): 733–754.

Osterhammel, Jürgen, and Niels Petersson. *Globalization: A Short History.* Translated by Dona Geyer. Princeton, NJ: Princeton University Press, 2005.

Our Voice: Bangkok NGOs' Declaration on Human Rights: Reports of the Asia Pacific NGO Conference on Human Rights and NGOs' Statements to the Asian Regional Meeting. Bangkok: Asian Cultural Forum on Development, 1993.

Pieterse, Jan Nederveen. *Globalization* and *Culture: Global Mélange.* 2nd ed. Lanham, MD: Rowman and Littlefield, 2009.

Poiger, Uta G. *Jazz, Rock, and Rebels: Cold War Politics and American Culture in a Divided Germany.* Berkeley: University of California Press, 2000.

Pollack, Detlef, Wolf-Jürgen Grabner, and Christiane Heinze, eds. *Leipzig im Oktober: Kirchen und alternative Gruppen im Umbruch der DDR—Analysen zur Wende.* 2nd ed. Berlin: Wichern, 1990, 1994.

Portes, Alejandro, and Alex Stepick. *City on the Edge: The Transformation of Miami.* Berkeley: University of California Press, 1993.

Power, Jonathan. *Amnesty International: The Human Rights Story.* New York: Pergamon, 1981.

Power, Samantha. *"A Problem from Hell": America and the Age of Genocide.* New York: Basic Books, 2002.

Prague Spring 1968: A National Security Archives Document Reader. Compiled and edited by Antonín Benčik. Budapest: Central European University Press, 1998.

Prakash, Gyan. *Mumbai Fables: A History of an Enchanted City.* Princeton, NJ: Princeton University Press, 2010.

———. "Orientalism Now." *History and Theory* 34, no. 3 (October 1995): 199–212.

Preston, Andrew. *Sword of the Spirit, Shield of Faith: Religion in American War and Diplomacy.* New York: Knopf, 2012.

Reid, Susan E. "Khrushchev Modern: Agency and Modernization in the Soviet Home." *Cahiers du Monde Russe* 47, nos. 1–2 (January–June 2006): 227–268.

Reid, Susan E., and David Crowley, eds. *Style and Socialism: Modernity and Material Culture in Post-War Eastern Europe.* Oxford: Berg, 2000.

Reynolds, David. *Rich Relations: The American Occupation of Britain, 1942–1945.* New York: Random House, 1995.

Riesman, David. *The Lonely Crowd: A Study of the Changing American Character.* New Haven, CT: Yale University Press, 1950.

Ritzer, George. *The Globalization of Nothing.* Thousand Oaks, CA: Pine Forge Press, 2004.

———. *The McDonaldization of Society.* 20th anniversary ed. Los Angeles: Sage, 2013.

Robertson, Roland. "Glocalization: Time-Space and Homogeneity-Heterogeneity." In *Global Modernities,* ed. Mike Featherstone, Scott Lash, and Roland Robertson. London: Sage, 1995.

Robins, Kevin. "Tradition and Translation: National Culture in Its Global Context." In *Enterprise and Heritage,* ed. John Corner and Sylvia Harvey. London: Routledge, 1991.

Robinson, Mike, and Alison Phipps. "Editorial: World Passing By—Journeys of Culture and Cultural Journeys." *Tourism and Cultural Change* 1, no. 1 (2003): 1–10.

Rodgers, Daniel T. *Atlantic Crossings: Social Politics in a Progressive Age.* Boston: Belknap Press of Harvard University Press, 1998.

Rome, Adam. "'Give Earth a Chance': The Environmental Movement and the Sixties." *Journal of American History* 90, no. 2 (September 2003): 525–554.

Rothermund, Dietmar. *The Routledge Companion to Decolonization.* London: Routledge, 2006.

Roth-Ey, Kristin. "'Loose Girls' on the Loose? Sex, Propaganda and the 1957 Youth Festival." In *Women in the Khrushchev Era,* ed. Melanie Ilič, Susan Reid, and Lynne Atwood. Basingstoke, UK: Palgrave, 2004.

Rotter, Andrew J. "Christians, Muslims, and Hindus: Religion and U.S.–South Asian Relations, 1947–1954." *Diplomatic History* 24, no. 4 (Fall 2000): 593–613.

Rowbotham, Sheila. *The Past Is before Us: Feminism in Action since the 1960s.* London: Pandora, 1989.

Rowhani, Inge. "Resümee zum Ende der Dekade der Frauen." In *Frauen: Ein Weltbericht*, ed. Debbie Taylor and the New Internationalist Co-operative. Berlin: Orlanda-Frauenverlag, 1986.

Rudolph, Susanne Hoeber, and James Piscatori, eds. *Transnational Religion and Fading States*. Boulder, CO: Westview, 1997.

Rupp, Leila J. "From Rosie the Riveter to the Global Assembly Line: American Women on the World Stage." *Magazine of History* 18, no. 4, *Sex, Courtship, and Dating* (July 2004): 53–57.

Ryback, Timothy. *Rock Around the Bloc: A History of Rock Music in Eastern Europe and the Soviet Union*. New York: Oxford University Press, 1990.

Saha, Shandip. "Hinduism, Gurus, and Globalization." In *Religion, Globalization, and Culture*, ed. Peter Beyer and Lori Beaman. Leiden: Brill, 2007.

Said, Edward W. *Culture and Imperialism*. New York: Vintage, 1994.

———. *Orientalism*. New York: Pantheon, 1978.

Sartre, Jean-Paul. *Existentialism Is a Humanism*. Translated by Carol Macomber. Preface by Arlette Elkaim-Sartre. Introduction by Annie Cohen-Solal. New Haven, CT: Yale University Press, 2007.

Sassen, Saskia. "The Global City: Introducing a Concept." *Brown Journal of World Affairs* 11, no. 2 (Winter/Spring 2005): 27–43.

Schlaeger, Hilke, and Nancy Vedder-Shults. "The West German Women's Movement." *New German Critique* 13 (Winter 1978): 59–68.

Schmidt-Linsenhoff, Viktoria. "Das koloniale Unbewusste in der Kunstgeschichte." In *Globalisierung/Hierarchisierung: Kulturelle Dominanzen in Kunst und Kunstgeschichte*, ed. Irene Below and Beatrice von Bismarck. Marburg: Jonas, 2005.

Schrecker, Ellen. *Many Are the Crimes: McCarthyism in America*. Boston: Little, Brown, 1998.

Scott, Joan W. "Gender: A Useful Category of Historical Analysis." *American Historical Review* 91, no. 5 (December 1986): 1053–1075.

———. *The Politics of the Veil*. Princeton, NJ: Princeton University Press, 2007.

——— "Symptomatic Politics: The Banning of Islamic Head Scarves in French Public Schools." *French Politics, Culture & Society* 23, no. 3 (Winter 2005): 106–127.

Sellars, Kirsten. *The Rise and Rise of Human Rights*. Stroud, UK: Sutton, 2002.

Shannon, Kelly. "Veiled Intentions: Islam, Global Feminism, and U.S. Foreign Policy since the Late 1970s." PhD diss., Temple University, 2010.

Shaw, Tony. "'Martyrs, Miracles and Martians': Religion and Cold War Cinematic Propaganda in the 1950s." In *Religion and the Cold War*, ed. Dianne Kirby. Basingstoke, UK: Palgrave, 2003.

Shepard, Todd. *The Invention of Decolonization: The Algerian War and the Remaking of France*. Ithaca, NY: Cornell University Press, 2006.

Shibusawa, Naoko. *America's Geisha Ally: Reimagining the Japanese Enemy*. Cambridge, MA: Harvard University Press, 2006.

Sigmund, Paul, ed. *The Ideologies of the Developing Nations*. New York: Fredrick A. Praeger, 1963.

———. *Liberation Theology at the Crossroads: Democracy or Revolution?* New York: Oxford University Press, 1990.

Simon, Bryant. *Everything but the Coffee: Learning about America from Starbucks.* Berkeley: University of California Press, 2009.

Simpson, A. W. Brian. *Human Rights and the End of Empire: Britain and the Genesis of the European Convention.* New York: Oxford University Press, 2001.

Simpson, Bradley. "'The First Right': The Carter Administration, Indonesia and the Transnational Human Rights Politics of the 1970s." In *The Human Rights Revolution: An International History,* ed. Akira Iriye, Petra Goedde, and William I. Hitchcock. New York: Oxford University Press, 2012.

Skilling, H. Gordon. *Charter 77 and Human Rights in Czechoslovakia.* London: Allen and Unwin, 1981.

———. *Czechoslovakia's Interrupted Revolution.* Princeton, NJ: Princeton University Press, 1976.

Smith, Bonnie G., ed. *Global Feminisms since 1945.* London: Routledge, 2000.

Smith, Charles D. *Palestine and the Arab-Israeli Conflict: A History with Documents.* 6th ed. New York: Bedford/St.Martin's Press, 2007.

Smith, Gaddis. *Morality, Reason, and Power: American Diplomacy in the Carter Years.* New York: Hill and Wang, 1986.

Spivak, Gayatri Chakravorty. "French Feminism in an International Frame." *Yale French Studies,* no. 62, *Feminist Readings: French Texts/American Contexts* (1981): 154–184.

Staples, Amy L. S. *The Birth of Development: How the World Bank, Food and Agriculture Organization, and World Health Organization Changed the World, 1945–1965.* Kent, OH: Kent State University Press, 2006.

Starr, S. Frederick. *Red and Hot: The Fate of Jazz in the Soviet Union, 1917–1980.* New York: Oxford University Press, 1983.

Taylor, Charles. *A Secular Age.* Cambridge, MA: Belknap Press of Harvard University Press, 2007.

Thomas, Daniel C. *The Helsinki Effect: International Norms, Human Rights and the Demise of Communism.* Princeton, NJ: Princeton University Press, 2001.

Tomlinson, John. *Globalization and Culture.* Chicago: University of Chicago Press, 1999.

Touraine, Alain. *The May Movement: Revolt and Reform.* Translated by Leonard F. X. Mayhew. New York: Random House, 1971.

Vernon, Raymond. *Sovereignty at Bay: The Multinational Spread of U.S. Enterprises.* New York: Basic Books, 1971.

Von Eschen, Penny M. *Satchmo Blows Up the World: Jazz Ambassadors Play the Cold War.* Cambridge, MA: Harvard University Press, 2004.

Wagnleitner, Reinhold. *Coca-Colonization and the Cold War: The Cultural Mission of the United States in Austria after the Second World War.* Translated by Diana M. Wolf. Chapel Hill: University of North Carolina Press, 1994.

Watson, James L., ed. *Golden Arches East: McDonald's in East Asia*. Stanford, CA: Stanford University Press, 1997.

Watt, David Harrington. *A Transforming Faith: Explorations of Twentieth-Century American Evangelicalism*. New Brunswick, NJ: Rutgers University Press, 1991.

Watt, Lori. *When Empire Comes Home: Repatriation and Reintegration in Postwar Japan*. Cambridge, MA: Harvard University Asia Center Publications, 2009.

Webster, Wendy. "Immigration and Racism." In *A Companion to Contemporary Britain, 1939–2000*, ed. Paul Addison and Harriet Jones. Malden, MA: Blackwell, 2005.

Westad, Odd Arne. *The Global Cold War: Third World Interventions and the Making of Our Times*. Cambridge: Cambridge University Press, 2005.

Westad, Odd Arne, Sven Holtsmark, and Iver B. Neumann, eds. *The Soviet Union in Eastern Europe, 1945–1989*. New York: St. Martin's Press, 1994.

Wichterich, Christa. "Strategische Verschwisterung, multiple Feminismen und die Glokalisierung von Frauenbewegungen." In *Frauenbewegungen weltweit: Aufbrüche, Kontinuitäten, Veränderungen*, ed. Ilse Lenz, Michiko Mae, and Karin Klose. Opladen, Germany: Leske & Budrich, 2000.

Wills, Richard Wayne, Sr. *Martin Luther King Jr. and the Image of God*. New York: Oxford University Press, 2009.

Wimmer, Andreas. "Globalization *avant la Lettre*: A Comparative View of Isomorphization and Heteromorphization in an Inter-connecting World." *Comparative Studies in Society and History* 43, no. 3 (July 2001): 435–466.

Wittner, Lawrence. *Resisting the Bomb: A History of the World Nuclear Disarmament Movement, 1954–1970*. Stanford, CA: Stanford University Press, 1997.

———. *The Struggle Against the Bomb*. 3 vols. Stanford, CA: Stanford University Press, 1993–2003.

Wolpert, Stanley. *Gandhi's Passion: The Life and Legacy of Mahatma Gandhi*. New York: Oxford University Press, 2001.

Wormann, Curt D. "German Jews in Israel: Their Cultural Situation since 1933." *Leo Baeck Institute Yearbook* 15, no. 1 (1970): 73–103.

Wuthnow, Robert. *The Restructuring of American Religion: Society and Faith since World War II*. Princeton, NJ: Princeton University Press, 1988.

Yaqub, Salim. *Containing Arab Nationalism: The Eisenhower Doctrine and the Middle East*. Chapel Hill: University of North Carolina Press, 2004.

Zelko, Frank. "Making Greenpeace: The Development of Direct Action Environmentalism in British Columbia." *BC Studies,* nos. 142–143 (Summer–Autumn 2004), 236–237.

Zubok, Vladislav M. *A Failed Empire: The Soviet Union in the Cold War from Stalin to Gorbachev*. Chapel Hill: University of North Carolina Press, 2007.

———. *Zhivago's Children: The Last Russian Intelligentsia*. Cambridge, MA: Belknap Press of Harvard University Press, 2009.

The Making of a Transnational World

Achebe, Chinua. *Things Fall Apart*. New York: Knopf, 1958.

Albee, Edward. *A Delicate Balance*. New York: Plume, 1997.

Aust, Stefan. *Der Baader-Meinhof Komplex*. Hamburg: Hoffmann und Campe, 2008.

Aydin, Cemal. *The Politics of Anti-Westernism in Asia: Visions of World Order in Pan-Islamic and Pan-Asian Thought*. New York: Columbia University Press, 2007.

Bacevich, Andrew J., ed. *The Short American Century: A Postmortem*. Cambridge, MA: Harvard University Press, 2012.

Barbeau, Arthur E. "The Japanese at Bedford." *Western Pennsylvania Historical Magazine* 64, no. 2 (April 1981): 151–172.

Bender, Thomas. *A Nation among Nations: America's Place in World History*. New York: Hill and Wang, 2006.

Berghahn, Volker R. *America and the Intellectual Cold Wars in Europe: Shepard Stone between Philanthropy, Academy, and Diplomacy*. Princeton, NJ: Princeton University Press, 2001.

Blanchon, David. *Atlas mondial de l'eau: De l'eau pour tous*. Paris: Autrement, 2009.

Blatman, Daniel. *The Death Marches: The Final Phase of Nazi Genocide*. Translated by Chaya Galai. Cambridge, MA: Belknap Press of Harvard University Press, 2010.

Borg, Dorothy, and Shumpei Okamoto, with Dale K. A. Finlayson, eds. *Pearl Harbor as History: Japanese-American Relations, 1931–1941*. New York: Columbia University Press, 1973.

Borstelmann, Thomas. *The 1970s: A New Global History from Civil Rights to Economic Inequality*. Princeton, NJ: Princeton University Press, 2012.

Bose, Sugata, and Kris Manjapra, eds. *Cosmopolitan Thought Zones: South Asia and the Global Circulation of Ideas*. Basingstoke, UK: Palgrave Macmillan, 2010.

Boyer, Paul. *By the Bomb's Early Light: American Thought and Culture at the Dawn of the Atomic Age*. New York: Pantheon, 1985.

Bulliet, Richard, Pamela Crossley, Daniel Headrick, and Steven Hirsch, eds. *The Earth and Its Peoples: A Global History*. 3rd ed. Boston: Houghton Mifflin, 2006.

Burk, Kathleen, and Alec Cairncross. *Good-bye, Great Britain: The 1976 IMF Crisis*. New Haven, CT: Yale University Press, 1992.

Carroué, Laurent, Didier Collet, and Claude Ruiz, eds. *La mondialisation: Genese, acteurs et enjeux*. 2nd ed. Rosny-sur-Bois, France: Bréal, 2009.

Conway, Martin, and Kiran Klaus Patel, eds. *Europeanization in the Twentieth Century: Historical Approaches*. Basingstoke, UK: Palgrave Macmillan, 2010.

Coulborn, Rushton, ed. *Feudalism in History*. Princeton, NJ: Princeton University Press, 1956.

Cumings, Bruce. *Dominion from Sea to Sea: Pacific Ascendancy and American Power*. New Haven, CT: Yale University Press, 2009.

Damousi, Joy, and Mariano Ben Plotkin, eds. *The Transnational Unconscious: Essays in the History of Psychoanalysis and Transnationalism*. Basingstoke, UK: Palgrave Macmillan, 2009.

Deacon, Desley, Penny Russell, and Angela Woollacott, eds. *Transnational Lives: Biographies of Global Modernity, 1700–Present*. Basingstoke, UK: Palgrave Macmillan, 2009.

Desmond, Jane C. *Staging Tourism: Bodies on Display from Waikiki to Sea World*. Chicago: University of Chicago Press, 1999.

Dingman, Roger. *Deciphering the Rising Sun: Navy and Marine Corps Codebreakers, Translators, and Interpreters in the Pacific War*. Annapolis, MD: Naval Institute Press, 2009.

Engerman, David C. *Modernization from the Other Shore: American Intellectuals and the Romance of Russian Development*. Cambridge, MA: Harvard University Press, 2003.

Evangelista, Matthew. *Unarmed Forces: The Transnational Movement to End the Cold War*. Ithaca, NY: Cornell University Press, 1999.

Fahlenbrach, Kathrin, Martin Klimke, Joachim Scharloth, and Laura Wong, eds. *The Establishment Responds: Power, Politics, and Protest since 1945*. Basingstoke, UK: Palgrave Macmillan, 2011.

Fanon, Frantz. *The Wretched of the Earth*. Translated by Constance Farrington. New York: Grove, 1963.

Frankl, Viktor E. *Der Mensch vor der Frage nach dem Sinn: Eine Auswahl aus dem Gesamtwerk*. Munich: Piper, 1985.

Fussell, Paul. *Wartime: Understanding and Behavior in the Second World War*. New York: Oxford University Press, 1989.

George, Timothy S. *Minamata: Pollution and the Struggle for Democracy in Postwar Japan*. Cambridge, MA: Harvard University Asia Center/Harvard University Press, 2001.

Geschichte für Heute: Zeitschrift für historisch-politische Bildung, no. 3 (2009).

Gienow-Hecht, Jessica C. E. *Sound Diplomacy: Music and Emotions in Transatlantic Relations, 1850–1920*. Chicago: University of Chicago Press, 2009.

Giesen, Bernhard, and Christoph Schneider, eds. *Tätertrauma: Nationale Erinnerungen im öffentlichen Diskurs*. Konstanz, Germany: UVK, 2004.

Goedde, Petra. *GIs in Germany: Culture, Gender, and Foreign Relations, 1945–1949*. New Haven, CT: Yale University Press, 2003.

Goldin, Ian, Geoffrey Cameron, and Meera Balarajan. *Exceptional People: How Migration Shaped Our World and Will Define Our Future*. Princeton, NJ: Princeton University Press, 2011.

Grandner, Margarete, Dietmar Rothermund, and Wolfgang Schwentker, eds. *Globalisierung und Globalgeschichte*. Vienna: Mandelbaum, 2005.

Hagihara, Nobutoshi, Akira Iriye, Georges Nivat, and Philip Windsor, eds. *Experiencing the Twentieth Century*. Tokyo: University of Tokyo Press, 1985.

Hamm, Mark S. *The Abandoned Ones: The Imprisonment and Uprising of the Mariel Boat People*. Boston: Northeastern University Press, 1995.

Hartz, Louis. *The Liberal Tradition in America: An Interpretation of American Political Thought since the Revolution*. New York: Harcourt, Brace, 1955.

Harwit. Martin. *An Exhibit Denied: Lobbying the History of Enola Gay*. New York: Copernicus, 1996.

Hasegawa, Tsuyoshi, ed. *The Cold War in East Asia, 1945–1991*. Stanford, CA: Stanford University Press, 2011.

He, Yinan. *The Search for Reconciliation: Sino-Japanese and German-Polish Relations since World War II*. Cambridge: Cambridge University Press, 2009.

Hixson, Walter L. *Parting the Curtain: Propaganda, Culture, and the Cold War, 1945–1961*. New York: St. Martin's Press, 1997.

Hobsbawm, Eric. *The Age of Extremes: A History of the World, 1914–1991*. New York: Vintage, 1996.

Hofstadter, Richard. *The American Political Tradition and the Men Who Made It*. New York: Vintage, 1954.

Iriye, Akira, *Global Community: The Role of International Organizations in the Making of the Contemporary World*. Berkeley: University of California Press, 2002.

———. *The Globalizing of America, 1913–1945*. Vol. 3 of *The New Cambridge History of American Foreign Relations*, rev. ed. Edited by Warren I. Cohen. Cambridge: Cambridge University Press, 2013.

———. *Power and Culture: The Japanese-American War, 1941–1945*. Cambridge, MA: Harvard University Press, 1981.

Jansen, Marius B., ed. *Changing Japanese Attitudes toward Modernization*. Princeton, NJ: Princeton University Press, 1965.

Japan Foundation Center for Global Partnership, ed. *The End of the Century: The Future in the Past*. Tokyo: Kodansha International, 1995.

Keene, Donald. *Chronicles of My Life: An American in the Heart of Japan*. New York: Columbia University Press, 2008.

Kirsch, Adam. "The Battle for History." *New York Times Book Review,* May 29, 2011, 10–11.

Kitamura, Hiroshi. *Screening Enlightenment: Hollywood and the Cultural Reconstruction of Defeated Japan*. Ithaca, NY: Cornell University Press, 2010.

Klimke, Martin. *The Other Alliance: Student Protest in West Germany and the United States in the Global Sixties*. Princeton, NJ: Princeton University Press, 2011.

Koenen, Gerd. *Das rote Jahrzehnt: Unsere kleine deutsche Kulturrevolution, 1967–1977*. Frankfurt: Fischer, 2002.

Kokusai tōkei yōran. Tokyo: Sōrifu Tōkeikyoku, various years.

Kraft, Sandra. *Vom Hörsaal auf die Anklagebank: Die 68er und das Establishment in Deutschland und den USA*. Frankfurt: Campus, 2010.

Lake, Marilyn, and Henry Reynolds. *Drawing the Global Colour Line: White Men's Countries and the Question of Racial Equality*. Carlton, Australia: Melbourne University Press, 2008.

Löffler, Berthold. *Integration in Deutschland: Zwischen Assimilation und Multikulturalismus*. Munich: Oldenbourg, 2010.

Maccaglia, Fabrizio, and Marie-Anne Matard-Bonucci, eds. *Atlas des mafias: Actuers, trafics et marchés de la criminalité organisée.* Paris: Autrement, 2009.

Maeda, Yōichi. *Seiō ni manande.* Tokyo: Kaname Shobō, 1953.

Mazlish, Bruce. *Civilization and Its Contents.* Stanford, CA: Stanford University Press, 2004.

———. *The Idea of Humanity in a Global Era.* New York: Palgrave Macmillan, 2009.

Mazlish, Bruce, and Ralph Buultjens, eds. *Conceptualizing Global History.* Boulder, CO: Westview, 1993.

McDougall, Walter A. *Let the Sea Make a Noise: A History of the North Pacific from Magellan to MacArthur.* New York: Basic Books, 1993.

Meier, Christian. *Das Gebot zu vergessen und die Unabweisbarkeit des Erinnerns: Vom öffentlichen Umgang mit schlimmer Vergangenheit.* Munich: Siedler, 2010.

Meinhof, Ulrike Marie. *Die Würde des Menschen ist antastbar: Aufsätze und Polemiken.* Berlin: Wagenbuch, 2008.

Miller, Edward. *Misalliance: Ngo Dinh Diem, the United States, and the Fate of South Vietnam.* Cambridge, MA: Harvard University Press, 2013.

Mitter, Rana. *China's War with Japan, 1937–1945: The Struggle for Survival.* London: Allen Lane, 2013.

Morgan, Ted. *On Becoming American.* Boston: Houghton Mifflin, 1978.

Morris, Benny. *The Birth of the Palestinian Refugee Problem, 1947–1949.* Cambridge: Cambridge University Press, 1987.

Nagai, Kafū. *American Stories.* Translated by Mitsuko Iriye. New York: Columbia University Press, 2000.

Naimark, Norman M. *Russians in Germany: A History of the Soviet Zone of Occupation, 1945–1949.* Cambridge, MA: Belknap Press of Harvard University Press, 1995.

Nettl, Bruno. *Encounters in Ethnomusicology: A Memoir.* Warren, MI: Harmonie Park, 2002.

Ni, Yan. *Senji Nitchū eiga kōshōshi.* Tokyo: Iwanami Shoten, 2010.

Ninkovich, Frank A. *The Diplomacy of Ideas: U.S. Foreign Policy and Cultural Relations, 1938–1950.* Cambridge: Cambridge University Press, 1981.

Nye, Joseph S. *Bound to Lead: The Changing Nature of American Power.* New York: Basic Books, 1990.

Osterhammel, Jürgen. *Geschichtswissenschaft jenseits des Nationalstaats: Studien zu Beziehungsgeschichte und Zivilisationsvergleich.* Göttingen: Vandenhoeck & Ruprecht, 2001.

Palmer, R. R. *The Age of the Democratic Revolution: A Political History of Europe and America, 1760–1800.* 2 vols. Princeton, NJ: Princeton University Press, 1959–1964.

Park, James William. *Latin American Underdevelopment: A History of Perspectives in the United States, 1870–1965.* Baton Rouge: Louisiana State University Press, 1995.

Patel, Ana Cutter, Pablo de Greiff, and Lars Waldorf, eds. *Disarming the Past: Transnational Justice and Ex-Combatants.* New York: Social Science Research Council, 2009.

Pells, Richard. *Not Like Us: How Europeans Have Loved, Hated, and Transformed American Culture since World War II*. New York: Basic Books, 1997.

Poscher, Ralf, Johannes Rux, and Thomas Langer. *Von der Integration zur Inklusion: Das Recht auf Bildung aus der Behindertenrechtskonvention der Vereinten Nationen und seine innerstaatliche Umsetzung*. Baden-Baden, Germany: Nomos, 2008.

Price, John. *Orienting Canada: Race, Empire, and the Transpacific*. Vancouver: UBC Press, 2011.

Riding, Alan. *And the Show Went On: Cultural Life in Nazi-Occupied Paris*. New York: Knopf, 2011.

Riesman, David, with Reuel Denney and Nathan Glazer. *The Lonely Crowd: A Study of the Changing American Character*. New Haven, CT: Yale University Press, 1950.

Rostow, W. W. *The Stages of Economic Growth: A Non-Communist Manifesto*. Cambridge: Cambridge University Press, 1960.

Said, Edward W. *Orientalism*. New York: Pantheon, 1978.

Saillant, Francine. *Identités et handicaps: Circuits humanitaires et posthumanitaires: La dignité pour horizon*. Paris: Karthala, 2007.

Sassen, Saskia. *The Global City: New York, London, Tokyo*. 2nd ed. Princeton, NJ: Princeton University Press, 2001.

Schechter, Patricia A. *Exploring the Decolonial Imaginary: Four Transnational Lives*. New York: Palgrave Macmillan, 2012.

Shibusawa, Naoko. *America's Geisha Ally: Reimagining the Japanese Enemy*. Cambridge, MA: Harvard University Press, 2006.

Snyder, Sarah B. *Human Rights Activism and the End of the Cold War: A Transnational History of the Helsinki Network*. New York: Cambridge University Press, 2011.

Spengler, Oswald. *The Decline of the West*. Translated by Charles Francis Atkinson. 2 vols. New York: Knopf, 1926–1928.

Starr, S. Frederick. *Red and Hot: The Fate of Jazz in the Soviet Union, 1917–1991*. Rev. ed. New York: Limelight, 1994.

Teng, Ssu-Yü, and John K. Fairbank, eds. *China's Response to the West: A Documentary Survey, 1839–1923*. Cambridge, MA: Harvard University Press, 1954.

Tertrais, Bruno. *Atlas mondial du nucléaire: Civil et militaire*. Paris: Autrement, 2011.

Thomas, Scott M. *The Global Resurgence of Religion and the Transformation of International Relations: The Struggle for the Soul of the Twenty-First Century*. New York: Palgrave Macmillan, 2005.

Tignor, Robert, et al. *Worlds Together, Worlds Apart: A History of the Modern World from the Mongol Empire to the Present*. New York: Norton, 2002.

Toynbee, Arnold J. *Civilization on Trial*. New York: Oxford University Press, 1948.

———. *A Study of History*. 12 vols. London: Oxford University Press, 1934–1961.

Tyrrell, Ian. *Transnational Nation: United States History in Global Perspective since 1789*. Basingstoke, UK: Palgrave Macmillan, 2007.

Vogel, Ezra F. *Deng Xiaoping and the Transformation of China*. Cambridge, MA: Belknap Press of Harvard University Press, 2011.

Vogel, Steven K. *Freer Markets, More Rules: Regulatory Reform in Advanced Industrial Countries*. Ithaca, NY: Cornell University Press, 1996.

Watt, Lori. *When Empire Comes Home: Repatriation and Reintegration in Postwar Japan*. Cambridge, MA: Harvard University Asia Center/Harvard University Press, 2009.

Weber, Horst, and Manuela Schwartz, eds. *Kalifornien*. Vol. 1 of *Quellen zur Geschichte emigrierter Musiker, 1933–1950*. Munich: K. G. Saur, 2003.

Weber, Max. *The Religion of China: Confucianism and Taoism*. Edited and translated by Hans H. Gerth. Glencoe, IL: Free Press, 1951.

Wells, H. G. *A Short History of the World*. Edited by Michael Sherborne. London: Penguin, 2006.

Wihtol de Wenden, Catherine. *Atlas mondial des migrations: Réguler ou réprimer—gouverner*. Paris: Autrement, 2009.

Wittner, Lawrence S. *One World or None: A History of the World Nuclear Disarmament Movement through 1953*. Stanford, CA: Stanford University Press, 1993.

Wolin, Richard. *The Wind from the East: French Intellectuals, the Cultural Revolution, and the Legacy of the 1960s*. Princeton, NJ: Princeton University Press, 2010.

The World Almanac and Book of Facts 2007. New York: World Almanac, 2007.

The World Almanac and Book of Facts 2010. New York: World Almanac, 2010.

Yamamoto, Tadashi, Akira Iriye, and Makoto Iokibe, eds. *Philanthropy and Reconciliation: Rebuilding Postwar U.S.-Japan Relations*. Tokyo: Japan Center for International Exchange, 2006.

Yang, Daqing, Jie Liu, Hiroshi Mitani, and Andrew Gordon, eds. *History beyond Borders: Contentious Issues in Sino-Japanese Relations*. Cambridge, MA: Harvard University Asia Center/Harvard University Press, 2012.

Yin, Xiao-huang. *Chinese American Literature since the 1850s*. Urbana: University of Illinois Press, 2000.

Zierler, David. *The Invention of Ecocide: Agent Orange, Vietnam, and the Scientists Who Changed the Way We Think about the Environment*. Athens: University of Georgia Press, 2011.

Contributors

Peter Engelke is a Senior Fellow at the Atlantic Council in Washington, DC. His work focuses on long-range global trends and their implications for geopolitics, global governance and security, economic development, and ecological stability. His publications include *Health and Community Design: The Impact of the Built Environment on Physical Activity* (co-authored with Lawrence D. Frank and Thomas L. Schmid, 2003).

Petra Goedde is Associate Professor of History at Temple University. Her areas of specialization include US foreign relations, transnational culture, and gender history. Her publications include *GIs and Germans: Culture, Gender, and Foreign Relations, 1945–1949* (2003), *The Human Rights Revolution: An International History* (co-edited with Akira Iriye and William I. Hitchcock, 2012), and the *Oxford Handbook of the Cold War* (co-edited with Richard H. Immerman, 2013).

Akira Iriye is Charles Warren Professor of History, Emeritus, at Harvard University. A pioneer in the field of transnational history, he has written widely on American diplomatic history and US-Asian relations. His books include *China and Japan in the Global Setting* (1992), *Cultural Internationalism and World Order* (1997), *Global Community: The Role of International Organizations in the Making of the Contemporary World* (2002), and *Global and Transnational History: The Past, Present, and Future* (2012).

Wilfried Loth is Professor of Modern and Contemporary History at the University of Duisburg-Essen. Among his research interests are the history of Europe in the nineteenth and twentieth centuries, international relations after World War II, and the history of the Cold War and European integration. His publications include *Stalin's Unwanted Child: The Soviet Union, the German*

Question, and the Founding of the GDR (1998) and *Overcoming the Cold War: A History of Détente, 1950–1991* (2002).

J. R. McNeill is University Professor at Georgetown University, where he teaches environmental and world history. His books include *Something New under the Sun: An Environmental History of the Twentieth-Century World* (2000), *The Human Web: A Bird's-Eye View of World History* (co-authored with William H. McNeill, 2003), and *Mosquito Empires: Ecology and War in the Greater Caribbean, 1620–1914* (2010).

Thomas W. Zeiler is Professor of History at the University of Colorado, Boulder, where he teaches American foreign relations history and is the Director of the Program on International Affairs. He is a scholar of US diplomacy and globalization, and he is former editor of the journal *Diplomatic History*. His books include *Globalization and the American Century* (2003) and *Annihilation: A Global Military History of World War II* (2011), as well as works on Jackie Robinson, Dean Rusk, and international trade history during the Cold War. He is a former president of the Society for Historians of American Foreign Relations (SHAFR).

Index